OCEAN YEARBOOK 33

Sponsored by the
International
Ocean Institute

Sponsored by the Marine &
Environmental Law Institute
of the Schulich School of Law

Edited by
Aldo Chircop, Scott Coffen-Smout and Moira L. McConnell

BRILL
NIJHOFF

LEIDEN | BOSTON

Typeface for the Latin, Greek, and Cyrillic scripts: "Brill". See and download: brill.com/brill-typeface.

ISSN 0191-8575
E-ISSN 2211-6001
ISBN 978-90-04-39563-3 (hardback)

Copyright 2019 by Koninklijke Brill NV, Leiden, The Netherlands, except where stated otherwise Koninklijke Brill NV incorporates the imprints Brill, Brill Hes & De Graaf, Brill Nijhoff, Brill Rodopi, Brill Sense, Hotei Publishing, mentis Verlag, Verlag Ferdinand Schöningh and Wilhelm Fink Verlag.
All rights reserved. No part of this publication may be reproduced, translated, stored in a retrieval system, or transmitted in any form or by any means, electronic, mechanical, photocopying, recording or otherwise, without prior written permission from the publisher.
Authorization to photocopy items for internal or personal use is granted by Koninklijke Brill NV provided that the appropriate fees are paid directly to The Copyright Clearance Center, 222 Rosewood Drive, Suite 910, Danvers, MA 01923, USA. Fees are subject to change.

This book is printed on acid-free paper and produced in a sustainable manner.

Contents

Alastair Dougal Couper (1931–2018): In Memoriam   XI
The International Ocean Institute   XV
Marine & Environmental Law Institute, Schulich School of Law   XXII
Acknowledgements   XXIV
Contributors   XXV

PART 1
The Law of the Sea and Ocean Governance

Building a Platform for the Future: the Relationship of the Expected New Agreement for Marine Biodiversity in Areas beyond National Jurisdiction and the UN Convention on the Law of the Sea   3
Kristina M. Gjerde, Nichola A. Clark and Harriet R. Harden-Davies

U.S. Ocean Priorities Shift with a New Administration   45
John A. Duff

Securing Ocean Spaces for the Future? The Initiative of the Pacific SIDS to Develop Regional Practice Concerning Baselines and Maritime Zone Limits   58
David Freestone and Clive Schofield

Is There a Relationship between UNDRIP and UNCLOS?   90
Aldo Chircop, Timo Koivurova and Krittika Singh

From the First Claims to the Exclusive Economic Zone: Reviewing Latin America's 200-Nautical Mile Sea Seventy Years On   131
Alexandre Pereira da Silva

PART 2
Coastal and Ocean Management

Designation of the Tubbataha Reef Natural Park as a Particularly Sensitive Sea Area: the Philippine Experience   163
Jay L. Batongbacal

The Ecosystem Approach as a Frame for SDG 14 Implementation   187
    Daniela Diz

Ocean Acidification Post-Paris: Gauging Law and Policy Responses in Light of Evolving Scientific Knowledge   207
    Cecilia Engler, David L. VanderZwaag and Katja Fennel

The Role and Relevance of Nationally Determined Contributions under the Paris Agreement to Ocean and Coastal Management in the Anthropocene   250
    Tim Stephens

Human Capacity-building and Public Education Aligned with Global Perspectives for Adaptation in Coastal and Ocean Management: the Role of the Borneo Marine Research Institute   268
    Saleem Mustafa, Rossita Shapawi, Sitti Raehanah M. Shaleh, Abentin Estim, Rafidah Othman, Zarinah Waheed, Ejria Saleh, B. Mabel Manjaji-Matsumoto and Najamuddin Abdul Basri

Science, Community, and Decision-makers: Can We Break the Vicious Circle?   287
    Oxana Sytnik, Dominique Peña Clinaz, Luana Sena Ferreira, Marina Reback Garcia, Bruno Meirelles de Oliveira and Raquel Hadrich Silva

PART 3
Marine Environmental and Living Resources Management

Liability for Environmental Harm from Deep Seabed Mining: towards a Hybrid Approach   315
    Neil Craik

Environmental Liability for Deep Seabed Mining in the Area: an Urgent Case for a Robust Strict Liability Regime   339
    Keith MacMaster

Building Scientific and Technological Capacity: a Role for Benefit-sharing in the Conservation and Sustainable Use of Marine Biodiversity beyond National Jurisdiction   377
    Harriet R. Harden-Davies and Kristina M. Gjerde

The Agreement to Prevent Unregulated High Seas Fisheries in the Central
Arctic Ocean: An Overview   401
   Andrew Serdy

PART 4
Maritime Safety and Security

Piracy and Armed Robbery against Ships: Revisiting International Law
Definitions and Requirements in the Context of the Gulf of Guinea   421
   Osatohanmwen Anastasia Eruaga and Maximo Q. Mejia Jr.

Protection of Submarine Cables against Acts of Terrorism   456
   Xuexia Liao

Regulating Ship-generated Noise as a New Form of Vessel-source
Pollution   487
   Till Markus and Pedro Pablo Silva Sánchez

Using Acoustic Footprints as a Tool to Facilitate Noise Reduction from
Shipping   513
   Kendra A. Moore and Kayla M. Glynn

A Tale of Two Industries: Seafarer Perceptions of Navigational Safety Risks
Near Offshore Wind Farms   543
   Raza Ali Mehdi, Jens-Uwe Schröder-Hinrichs and Michael Baldauf

PART 5
Book Reviews

Robert C. Beckman, Tore Henriksen, Kristine Dalaker Kraabel, Erik J.
Molenaar and J. Ashley Roach, eds., *Governance of Arctic Shipping: Balancing
Rights and Interests of Arctic States and User States*   585
   Gen Goto

Vu Hai Dang, *Marine Protected Areas Network in the South China Sea: Charting
a Course for Future Cooperation*   589
   Tabitha Grace Mallory

Patrice Guillotreau, Alida Bundy and R. Ian Perry, eds.,
*Global Change in Marine Systems: Integrating Natural, Social,
and Governing Responses* 592
    Ana Carolina Esteves Dias and Evan Jeremy Andrews

Nengye Liu, Elizabeth A. Kirk and Tore Henriksen, eds., *The European Union
and the Arctic* 595
    Annie Cudennec

Myron H. Nordquist, John Norton Moore and Ronán Long, eds., *Legal Order in
the World's Oceans: UN Convention on the Law of the Sea* 598
    Edwin E. Egede

Myron H. Nordquist, John Norton Moore and Ronán Long, eds., *International
Marine Economy: Law and Policy* 602
    Sarah Louise Lothian

Myron H. Nordquist, John Norton Moore and Ronán Long, eds.,
*Challenges of the Changing Arctic: Continental Shelf, Navigation,
and Fisheries* 606
    David L. VanderZwaag

Bimal N. Patel, *The State Practice of India and the Development of International
Law: Dynamic Interplay between Foreign Policy and Jurisprudence* 610
    Sumedh Shastri

Jenny Grote Stoutenburg, *Disappearing Island States in
International Law* 613
    Tony George Puthucherril

Erika J. Techera and Natalie Klein, *International Law of Sharks: Obstacles,
Options and Opportunities* 620
    Cameron S.G. Jefferies

Alejandra Torres Camprubí, *Statehood under Water. Challenges of Sea-Level
Rise to the Continuity of Pacific Island States* 624
    Karen N. Scott

Glen Wright, Sandy Kerr and Kate Johnson, eds., *Ocean Energy: Governance Challenges for Wave and Tidal Stream Technologies* 629
  Daniel Watt

Valérie Wyssbrod, *L'exploitation des ressources génétiques marines hors juridiction nationale* 633
  Suzanne Lalonde

Katherine L. Yates and Corey J.A. Bradshaw, eds., *Offshore Energy and Marine Spatial Planning* 636
  Van Penick

Liang Zhao and Lianjun Li, *Maritime Law and Practice in China* 640
  Johanna Hjalmarsson

PART 6

Appendices

A. Annual Report of the International Ocean Institute 647
  Report of the International Ocean Institute, 2017 647

B. Selected Documents and Proceedings 674
  Oceans and the Law of the Sea Report of the Secretary-General, 2018 674
  United Nations Convention on the Law of the Sea Report of the Twenty-Eighth Meeting of States Parties, 11–14 June 2018 697
  Report on the Work of the United Nations Open-ended Informal Consultative Process on Oceans and the Law of the Sea at Its Nineteenth Meeting, 18–22 June 2018 722
  Agreement to Prevent Unregulated High Seas Fisheries in the Central Arctic Ocean 748

Index 758

Alastair Dougal Couper (1931–2018): In Memoriam

A personal tribute in memory of Professor Alastair Couper, master mariner, educator, academic, geographer, philosopher, defender of human rights, advocate for seafarers, husband, father, grandfather and great-grandfather.

On Wednesday, September 12, 2018, the oceans, maritime and seafarers' community lost a remarkable human being who touched the lives of so many for the better and projected what is best in our humanity. Alastair lived a commitment to improve the governance of the maritime sector, the protection of seafarers' rights and rights of developing countries in the promotion of a sustainable maritime sector, and a lifetime support to aspiring students, practitioners, and researchers, projecting his humanity in any such support.

In 1970, Alastair was tasked with establishing at the University of Wales, within the Institute for Science and Technology, a department for Maritime Studies and International Transport, which he headed. The time coincided with the start of the UNCLOS process and his department was unique and ahead of the curve at that point within academic institutions and it produced original research, experts and graduates in parallel to the UNCLOS negotiations.

Alastair's foresight and determination became instrumental in enriching the maritime sector and ocean community with qualified experts, policy-makers and scientists, many of whom became influential as they joined academic institutions as educators and researchers, including international and UN organizations, and as practitioners in the evolving maritime industry as well as influencing the process of UNCLOS from elaboration to ratification and then in implementation.

Alastair's devotion to academic excellence was only surpassed by his commitment to peaceful resolution of conflicts at sea and at large. It was at the time of UNCLOS's protracted and complex negotiations that Alastair met Elisabeth Mann Borgese to discover they both shared an empathy for *Pacem in Maribus* as a vision of the future. For Alastair, that empathy extended to assisting the emerging nations of developing countries in their aspiration to have a fair share in the economic and social benefits accruing from engagement in the maritime sector. He and Elisabeth both aspired to a fair and equitable economic and social order.

In 1977, under Alistair's supervision I completed for the Commonwealth Secretariat a study entitled "Development of the Merchant Marines of Commonwealth Developing Countries," the objective being to enable such developing countries then to carry the optimum proportion of their trade on national vessels. Thus, Alastair placed the prestige of his name in support of the implementation of the UN Convention on a Code of Conduct for Liner Conferences. As a measure of his contribution to the development of the maritime sector in developing countries he was tasked by UNCTAD to undertake a study and design a project to help developing countries train and equip their human resources in the maritime transport sector. In this way, one of the most ingenious projects – TRAINMAR – was launched in 1980 with the initial support of UNCTAD senior staff member Michel Couroux for the training of trainers and managers at all levels in shipping and ports; over time some fifty thousand managers were trained. The TRAINMAR project originally designed by Alastair has metamorphosed into self-continuation under what is now called Train for Trade.

Alastair is the unsung hero who helped developing countries develop their maritime trade, increase port efficiency, and develop their human resources to meet the challenge of technology change. TRAINMAR, in hindsight, was one of the most successful technical assistance projects of UNCTAD to developing countries. Developing countries in Latin America, Africa and Asia unknowingly owe a debt of gratitude to Alastair.

In retrospect, what Alastair and Elisabeth found as a major shortcoming in the outcome of the UNCLOS negotiations of the lack of definition of the genuine link between a ship and its flag of registry became a major cause of concern and unforeseen consequence for seafarers on ships engaged in fishing. I recall when at UNCTAD we addressed the issue of open registries through a UN Convention on Condition for Registration of Ships (1984–1986), I frequently consulted Alastair and sought his advice.

In time, as the welfare of seafarers became a primary concern of Alastair, not only in the fishing sector, he acted decisively establishing the Seafarers' International Research Centre at Cardiff University, surrounding himself with a critical mass of collaborators working ardently to create awareness of the working and living conditions of seafarers, thus giving a voice to the most marginalized in the maritime community.

Alastair, while always a pacifist, was nevertheless indefatigable in fighting for seafarers' rights, welfare and dignity. He drew the world's attention to the plight of seafarers through publications and enriched the literature on the subject, including in *The Times Atlas of the Ocean* concerning the science, natural resources and human exploitation of the oceans. This was followed by a series of publications which addressed the human rights of those working at sea, including *Sailors and Traders: A Maritime History of the Pacific Peoples*; *Voyages of Abuse: Seafarers, Human Rights and International Shipping*; and

Fishers and Plunderers: Theft, Slavery and Violence at Sea. The final book he was co-authoring with Dr. Azmath Jaleel when he passed away was to address *Crimes, Rights and Punishments of People Working at Sea*.

His courage in challenging the powerful lobby of shipowners and the fishing industry is demonstrated by the following quote on the cover of his latest book *Fishers and Plunderers*: "Alastair Couper has exposed the dirty secret of human rights abuse in an industry infested with criminality. This is a call to action." He brought his concerns to the attention of the UN institutions such as the IMO, the ILO, and the WMU, by advocating a different narrative from business as usual on the rights of seafarers. He even went to courts to give evidence in defense of seafarers abandoned in foreign ports by unscrupulous shipowners.

Many others like me who came to know Alastair such as researchers, students or even later in their careers have been enriched by his wisdom and passion. At the International Ocean Institute we were fortunate to have had the privilege to receive Alastair to lecture at various training courses and special seminars and Alastair was for a number of years a member of the IOI committee for selecting candidates for the Elisabeth Mann Borgese Bursary.

Personally, I will deeply miss my annual visit to meet Alastair in Cardiff. We used to meet at his favourite coffee house at Pontcanna and he would arrive on a bicycle with his wife Norma, the love of his life, and then we would converse on current affairs, primarily on the ocean and the state of affairs in a confusing world, and have the benefit of listening to his words of wisdom while trying to fathom the meaning of life.

To my mentor and benefactor, I dedicate extracts from a poem by Khalil Gibran:

> *The Coming of the Ship*
> And he beheld the ship coming with the mist. [...]
> And his soul cried out to them, and he said:
> Sons of my ancient mother, you riders of the tides,
> How often have you sailed in my dreams.
> And now you come in my awakening, which is my deeper dream.
> Ready am I to go, and my eagerness with sails full set awaits the wind.
> Only another breath will I breathe in this still air,
> Only another loving look cast backward,
> And then I shall stand among you, a seafarer among seafarers.
> And you, vast sea, sleepless mother,
> Who alone are peace and freedom to the river and the stream,

Only another winding will this stream make, only another murmur in this glade,
And then I shall come to you, a boundless drop to a boundless ocean. [...]
And now your ship has come, and you must needs go.

Awni Behnam
Honorary President of IOI
Ph.D. Affiliate Professor, University of Malta
Former UN Assistant Secretary-General
Geneva, Switzerland

The International Ocean Institute

Professor Elisabeth Mann Borgese founded the International Ocean Institute (IOI) in 1972 as a scientific, educational, independent, international, non-profit, non-governmental organization headquartered in Malta with premises at the University of Malta. The IOI was created to promote education, capacity building, and research as a means to enhance the peaceful and sustainable use and management of ocean and coastal spaces and their resources, as well as the protection and conservation of the marine environment, guided by the principle of the Common Heritage of Mankind.

The respect for common goods, the peaceful and sustainable use of ocean services and resources, the common heritage of the high seas and the need to support and empower people and countries, particularly developing countries in managing their relations with the ocean in a sustainable manner remains the ethical and moral foundation of the IOI. The Institute promotes the concept of Ocean Governance, including Integrated Ocean Policy, for planning and management of the oceans at the national, regional and global level.

Since its foundation the IOI has stood at the forefront of organizations in addressing these issues with the concern of future generations through an interdisciplinary and comprehensive approach. The IOI has also prepared working papers for the Third United Nations Conference on the Law of the Sea (UNCLOS III: 1973–1982), for the Preparatory Commission for the International Seabed Authority, for the International Tribunal for the Law of the Sea (1982–1994), and for the EU coastal management policy (2006), as well as for various governments. It has provided consultants to UNEP, UNDP, the World Bank, the United Nations Industrial Development Organization (UNIDO), EU, UNESCO/IOC, and the Asian-African Legal Consultative Committee (AALCC). It contributed to the formulation of recommendations of the World Summits in Rio de Janeiro (1992) and Johannesburg (2002), the World Forums on oceans, coasts and islands (2003–2009), as well as to the review of the developments in ocean affairs through the United Nations Open-ended Informal Consultative Process. The IOI was awarded the 2006 South-South Partnership for the special contribution to the tsunami recovery efforts. In 2007, the IOI was granted special consultative status within the Economic and Social Council (ECOSOC) at the United Nations as well as the renewal of formal consultative relations between UNESCO and the IOI from 2011 to 2017.

The goals of the IOI are to:

- contribute to the evolving process of ocean governance through its functions and activities;
- monitor the implementation of international conventions and agreements as they relate to the oceans, participate in and contribute to the evolving policy dialogue on the ocean in the United Nations System and other international organizations;
- mobilize the political will to elaborate appropriate maritime laws and regulations, to implement national and regional plans and international agreements on the management and sustainable use of the ocean, coasts and islands through its organs and bodies;
- raise awareness of the peaceful uses of the ocean, its protection and conservation, as well as the sustainable development of its resources, in accordance with the principle of the common heritage of humankind;
- engage in the dissemination of information and transfer of knowledge and experience;
- contribute to the sustainable uses of the ocean as well as to the sustainable development of developing countries and countries in transition, through institution-building and networking at national and regional levels;
- respond to the needs of developing countries and countries in transition, particularly coastal communities and enhance the role of women by increasing their abilities to develop and manage the ocean and coastal resources sustainably; and
- contribute toward a growing global network of trained and empowered leaders fully conversant with the latest developments in ocean governance. Course participants acquire the knowledge, skills, and essential attitude for effective ocean governance.

Three Main Pillars of IOI Activities

The core activity of IOI is to carry out training programmes in ocean governance. Activities such as developing and maintaining international relations and the production and dissemination of relevant publications, are carried out with the aim to support, facilitate, develop, and promote the IOI training

activities. IOI's capacity development programme proceeds at many different scales:
International Courses/Training Programmes:

- Ocean Governance: Policy, Law and Management, offered by IOI in Canada at Dalhousie University in Halifax, Nova Scotia.
- Post Graduate Degree: Master's in Art in Ocean Governance, offered by the University of Malta in collaboration with the IOI in Malta.

Regional Programmes:

- Training Programme on Regional Ocean Governance for the Mediterranean, Black, Baltic & Caspian Seas, offered by IOI in Malta.
- Ocean Governance Training Programme for Africa, offered by IOI in Cape Town, South Africa.
- Training Programme on the Sustainable Development and Governance of the Caspian Sea, organised by the IOI in partnership with our Training Partner - the State Enterprise on Caspian Sea Issues at the President of Turkmenistan and at their behest.
- Training Programme on Ocean Governance for the Western Pacific Region, organised by the IOI in partnership with our Training Partner - the State Oceanic Administration of PR China.
- Training Programme on Regional Ocean Governance Framework, Implementation of the United Nations Convention on the Law of the Sea (UNCLOS) and its Related Instruments in the Southeast Asian Seas and the Indian Ocean, offered by IOI-Thailand.
- Training Programme on Ocean Governance, Ocean Sciences and Geoethics, offered by IOI-Brazil (SWAO) and IOI-Costa Rica, in Latin America & the Caribbean countries.

The IOI's activities include training and capacity building programmes, information dissemination, conferences, research and publications:

- Training of hundreds of decision-makers and professionals, mainly from developing countries, through short and long duration interdisciplinary courses in ocean and coastal management and the Master of Arts degree in Ocean Governance offered at the University of Malta under the aegis of the Faculty of Laws;
- Ocean governance advocacy within the United Nations system through participation in and contribution to intergovernmental meetings and conferences;

- Information dissemination to international organizations and national institutions through the global IOI Network and the IOI web site;
- Research on a variety of ocean-related areas such as international and regional agreements and policies on oceans and the coastal zone; on regional and sub-regional co-operation and on scientific and technological approaches to sustainable management of living and non-living marine resources;
- Education and awareness-creation about ocean resources, marine and coastal environments, and the need to care for them;
- Publication of the *World Ocean Review* (WOR) series through maribus gGmbH. The WOR series the fruit of cooperation between mare, "The Future Ocean": Kiel-based Cluster of Excellence and the IOI. The purpose of the publications is to present scientifically robust knowledge in a form accessible to any reader, and thus to serve all those who wish to engage actively and knowledgably in debate on the issues surrounding marine science.
- Publication of the *Ocean Yearbook* in collaboration with the Marine & Environmental Law Institute, Schulich School of Law, Dalhousie University, Canada;
- Maturing the IOI's web site (www.ioinst.org) and publication of an electronic newsletter IOI*informa* by the IOI HQ. Regional Operational Centres also publish their own newsletters, research papers and reports; and
- Services include advice, consultancy, and information regarding ocean and coastal environments.

The IOI gained worldwide respect and a reputation through its contribution to the codification and implementation of the Law of the Sea Convention, and to the subsequent development of the concept of sustainable development as it applies to the ocean. Furthermore, through the launching of such projects as the coastal and eco-villages projects, dedicated women and youth programmes, training in ocean governance, risk assessment and others, the IOI has contributed positively to the implementation of ocean governance, with a particular focus on developing nations.

The IOI is now developing an international ocean governance and capacity-building education programme that will consist of a network of education, training and research centres with expertise in ocean, coastal and marine affairs and governance. The Centres will be joined together in a partnership so as to provide interdisciplinary and comprehensive coverage of the subject areas. The overall objective will be to enhance the abilities of developing countries to develop and govern their own marine and coastal resources and environment sustainably.

The Structure of the International Ocean Institute and the IOI Global Network

The IOI Board of Governors functions as the substantive backbone, driving IOI deliverables and providing quality control. The IOI Board governs the IOI institute and has the oversight for all IOI activities, the strategic development, the institute's management, finances and fundraising. Governing Board members are closely involved in the activities of the IOI and take responsibility for defined tasks. The secretariat of the IOI at the headquarters in Malta is responsible for day-to-day operations and programme implementation; the IOI HQ supports the Board Members in fulfilling their mandates.

Following the formal endorsement of the IOI Strategy by the IOI Governors in December 2015 and the implementation of the first steps, the IOI network consists of six IOI Training Centres, six IOI Centres, and 22 IOI Focal Points, in 31 countries around the globe. The IOI network provides a flexible mechanism with a governing and coordinating structure that generates synergism and strategic planning of the network of semiautonomous nodes. This cohesive and comprehensive mechanism is capable of cooperating equally well with other intergovernmental systems and the private sector. The current IOI Training Centres, IOI Centres and IOI Focal Points and their host institutions are:

IOI Training Centres:

>Brazil: IOI-South Western Atlantic Ocean, Centro de Estudos do Mar, Universidade Federal Do Parana; Canada: IOI-Canada, Dalhousie University, Halifax; China: IOI-China, National Marine Data and Information Service, State Oceanic Administration of China; Malta: IOI Training Programme on Regional Ocean Governance for the Mediterranean, Black, Baltic and Caspian Seas, University of Malta, Msida; South Africa: IOI-Southern Africa, Centre for Biodiversity Conservation, Kirstenbosch, c/o SANBI, Cape Town; Thailand: IOI-Thailand, Deep Sea Fishery Technology Research and Development Institute, Bangkok.

IOI Centres:

>Cuba: IOI-Cuba, Centro de Investigaciones Marinas, Miramar, Playa, Ciudad de La Habana; Costa Rica: IOI-Costa Rica, Universidad Nacional, Heredia; Egypt: IOI-Egypt, National Institute of Oceanography and Fisheries, Attaka-Suez; Germany: IOI-Germany, Leibniz-Zentrum fur Marine Tropenforschung (Center for Tropical Marine Research), Bremen; Nigeria:

IOI-Western Africa, Nigerian Institute for Oceanography & Marine Research (NIOMR), Lagos; Islamic Republic of Iran: IOI-Islamic Republic of Iran, Iranian National Institute for Oceanography and Atmospheric Science, Tehran; South Pacific: IOI-Pacific Islands, Division of Marine Studies, School of Islands and Oceans, University of the South Pacific, Fiji.

IOI Focal Points:

Australia: IOI-Australia, Ocean Technology Group, University of Sydney; Cyprus: IOI-Cyprus, Cyprus University of Technology, Department of Civil Engineering, Cyprus; Egypt: IOI-Egypt, Marine Environment Division, National Institute of Oceanography and Fisheries; Finland: IOI-Finland, Department of Environmental Sciences, University of Helsinki; India: IOI-India, The Auroville Centre for Scientific Research, Tamil Nadu; Indonesia: IOI-Indonesia, Faculty of Mathematics and Natural Sciences, University of Indonesia, Depok; Japan: ioi-Japan, INTERCOM, Tokyo; Kenya: IOI-Eastern Africa, Kenya Marine and Fisheries Research Institute, Mombasa; Lebanon: IOI-Lebanon, Haret Saida, Sidon; Malaysia: IOI-Malaysia, Borneo Marine Research Institute, Universiti Malaysia Sabah; Pakistan: IOI-Pakistan, National Centre of Maritime Policy Research, Bahria University, Karachi; P.R. China: IOI-China, Shanghai Maritime University, Shanghai; Republic of Kazakhstan: IOI-Kazakhstan, Center for Life Sciences, Nazarbayev University, Astana; Republic of Korea: IOI-Korea, Korea Maritime Institute, Seoul; Republic of the Philippines: IOI-Philippines, Office of UN and International Organizations, Department of Foreign Affairs, Pasay City; Romania: IOI-Black Sea, National Research and Development Institute for Marine Geology and Geoecology, Bucharest; Russian Federation: IOI-Russia, Astrakhan State Technical University, Astrakhan; Singapore: IOI-Singapore; Slovenia: IOI-Slovenia, Marine Biology Station, Piran; Turkey: IOI-Turkey, Department of Fishing and Processing Technology, Faculty of Fisheries, Kötekli-Muğla; Ukraine: IOI-Ukraine, Ecological Initiative NGO, Blue Flag and Green Key National Operator, Kyiv; USA: IOI-USA, Institute for Marine Remote Sensing, College of Marine Science, University of South Florida, St. Petersburg, and the Collaborative Institute for Oceans, Climate and Security, University of Massachusetts, Boston.

International Ocean Institute – Governing Board Members in 2018

Awni Behnam (*Honorary President*)
(Switzerland)
Nikolaus Gelpke (*President*)
(Germany)
Mahindokht Faghfouri
(*Vice-President*)
(Switzerland)
Peter W. Leder (*Treasurer*)
(Germany)
Simone Borg (*Representative of the Government of Malta on the Governing Board*)
(Malta)

Lawrence Hildebrand (*Member*)
(Canada)
Anita Coady (*Member*)
(Canada)
Louis F. Cassar (*Member*)
(Malta)
Chua Thia-Eng (*Member*)
(Malaysia)
Adnan Awad (*Chair of IOI Directors*)
(South Africa)
Antonella Vassallo (*Ex-Officio, Managing Director*)
(Malta)

Marine & Environmental Law Institute
Schulich School of Law

Established in 1883, Dalhousie University's Schulich School of Law is the oldest school of common law in Canada. As a leading law school, it plays a critical role in the development of national legal education in Canada, in serving the needs of the Atlantic region, and graduate level education. Since Volume 13, the School has been a partner with the International Ocean Institute (IOI) in supporting, producing and providing a home for the *Ocean Yearbook* in its Marine & Environmental Law Institute (MELAW) (http://www.dal.ca/law/MELAW).

The Schulich School of Law is internationally recognized for excellence in marine and environmental law research and teaching. Since its establishment in 1974 as an area of specialization for the Juris Doctor (J.D.) students and subsequently for Master of Laws (LL.M.) students and Doctor of Philosophy in Law (Ph.D.) candidates, the Marine & Environmental Law Programme (MELP) has one of the most extensive academic course offerings and supervisory capability in these two fields. With Canada Research Chairs in Ocean Law and Governance and Maritime Law and Policy, as well as three full and several part-time faculty, students have a unique opportunity to learn about public and private law practice in marine (including shipping, fisheries and oil and gas) and environmental law (including environmental assessment, climate change, land-use planning and energy law). At the J.D. level students wishing to specialize in these fields have the option of obtaining a certificate of specialization in either marine or environmental law or both. Law students seeking the MELP certificate of specialization are encouraged to engage in the interdisciplinary study of emerging and cross-cutting topics such as biotechnology, environment and health, ethics, indigenous rights, animal rights, international trade law and human rights. The Institute also provides law students with the opportunity to gain experience working as research assistants through its research projects, workshops and editing the *Ocean Yearbook*. The Institute supports student collaboration in addressing environmental issues through the Environmental Law Students' Society and the East Coast Environmental Law Association, a non-governmental organization dedicated to environmental law education and advocacy.

The longstanding research excellence of the MELP faculty was formally recognized by the Dalhousie University Board of Governors in 2004 with the creation of the Marine & Environmental Law Institute (MELAW). In addition to directing the MELP academic specialization, the Institute carries out an array of scholarly research and publication activities and consultancies. The MELAW community is engaged in numerous scholarly research projects and also provides advisory services to agencies of the United Nations and a wide range of other inter-governmental organizations, international non-governmental organizations, and regional organizations, as well as assisting government departments and non-governmental organizations in Canada and overseas. The Institute and its members engage in interdisciplinary collaboration within the Dalhousie University community, including with the Ocean Frontier Institute (OFI), with federal government support through the Canada First Research Excellence Fund, the School for Resource and Environmental Studies, the Marine Affairs Program, the College of Sustainability, the International Development Studies Program, the Institute for Ocean Research Enterprise (IORE), the Centre for the Study of Security and Development (CSSD), and the Ocean Tracking Network (OTN). The Institute has an extensive network of research partners at the national and international levels. MELAW is a longstanding partner of the International Ocean Institute.

Acknowledgements

The editors are grateful for the ongoing administrative and substantive support provided by the Marine & Environmental Law Institute and the Sir James Dunn Law Library at the Schulich School of Law, Dalhousie University. The financial support for the editorial office provided by the Schulich School of Law and by the International Ocean Institute's headquarters in Malta is gratefully acknowledged. We wish to extend thanks to Nicholas Van Allen for editing assistance, to Susan Rolston for compiling the volume index, and to Lauri MacDougall for administrative support. Warm thanks go to members of the Board of Editors, the numerous peer reviewers for their continuing support, and contributors to this volume. Funding for open access was provided by The Pew Charitable Trusts. Special thanks are extended to staff at Brill Nijhoff for editorial and infrastructural support, and to the Research4Life partnership's Global Online Access to Legal Information (GOALI) initiative providing free or low-cost online access to the *Ocean Yearbook* in the developing world. Additional details are available online: <http://www.research4life.org>.

THE EDITORS

OCEAN YEARBOOK 33
BOARD OF EDITORS

Jay L. Batongbacal
(Philippines)
Awni Behnam
(Switzerland)
Mary Brooks
(Canada)
Aldo Chircop
(Canada)
Scott Coffen-Smout
(Canada)
Meinhard Doelle
(Canada)
Cleopatra Doumbia-Henry
(Sweden)
Zhiguo Gao
(China)
Nikolaus Gelpke
(Germany)
Patricia González Díaz
(Cuba)
Alejandro Gutierrez
(Costa Rica)
Lawrence P. Hildebrand
(Canada)
Hugh Kindred
(Canada)
Moira L. McConnell
(Canada)
Masako Otsuka
(Japan)
Mary Ann Palma-Robles
(Australia)
Phillip Saunders
(Canada)
Sara L. Seck
(Canada)
David VanderZwaag
(Canada)
Christian Wiktor
(Canada)

OCEAN YEARBOOK 33

Contributors

Michael Baldauf
holds a watchkeeping officer licence and served on container ships in worldwide trade. He has a doctoral degree in maritime safety with a Ph.D. thesis on shore-based monitoring of vessel traffic and decision support for detection of collision risks. He has lectured and researched in several institutions and was associate professor at the World Maritime University and head of its simulation laboratory. Presently, he is head of vts-Simulation, Maritime Simulation Centre Rostock-Warnemuende of Hochschule Wismar, University of Applied Sciences: Technology, Business and Design.

Najamuddin A. Basri
M.Sc., is a research officer in the Borneo Marine Research Institute, Universiti Malaysia Sabah, and editorial assistant of the *Borneo Journal of Marine Science & Aquaculture*.

Jay L. Batongbacal
is a lawyer from the Philippines with a Master of Marine Management and Doctor in the Science of Law from Dalhousie University. He is an associate professor at the University of the Philippines College of Law and director of the U.P. Institute for Maritime Affairs and Law of the Sea. He served as the Philippines' legal advisor when it made a claim to a continental shelf beyond 200 nautical miles in the Benham Rise Region, and recently assisted in the designation of the Tubbataha Reef Natural Park in the Sulu Sea as a Particularly Sensitive Sea Area.

Aldo Chircop
jsd, is a professor of law and Canada Research Chair in Maritime Law and Policy, Schulich School of Law, Dalhousie University, Canada. His research interests are in the fields of Canadian and international maritime law and international law of the sea. He is currently working on the regulation of Arctic shipping, greenhouse gas emissions from ships, autonomous shipping, particularly sensitive sea areas, jurisdiction over ships, and maritime regulation theory. He has received several academic and professional awards. A co-editor of the *Ocean Yearbook* since volume 13, Professor Chircop has published extensively in his fields of research.

Nichola A. Clark
is a Ph.D. student at the University of Wollongong's Australian National Centre for Ocean Resources and Security where her research focuses on institutional arrangements for the new marine biodiversity beyond national jurisdiction (BBNJ) agreement. Nichola also works as a senior associate at The Pew Charitable Trusts, where she follows the BBNJ negotiations. Prior to ANCORS and Pew, Nichola was an International Program Analyst at the National Oceanic and Atmospheric Administration and also worked as a researcher at the Institute for Advanced Sustainability Studies. Nichola holds a master's degree in environmental management from Duke University.

Neil Craik
is an associate professor at the University of Waterloo with appointments to the Balsillie School of International Affairs and the School of Environment, Enterprise and Development, where he teaches and researches in the fields of international and Canadian environmental law. His current research examines the legal structure of global commons regimes. Professor Craik has particular interests in climate and geoengineering law and governance, deep seabed mining regulation and environmental impact assessment. He is a senior fellow at the Centre for International Governance Innovation and co-director of the BSIA/CIGI International Law Summer Institute.

Daniela Diz
is a research fellow in international environmental law at the University of Strathclyde Law School and a member of the Strathclyde Centre of Environmental Law and Governance. She teaches law of the sea, and works on a number of international and national projects related to marine biodiversity conservation and sustainable management. Previously, Dr. Diz worked for WWF-Canada and government agencies in Brazil.

John A. Duff
is associate professor in the School for the Environment, University of Massachusetts Boston. He received a J.D. from Suffolk University Law School (Boston) and an LL.M. from the Law and Marine Affairs Program, University of Washington. He also holds degrees in business (University of Lowell) and journalism (University of Mississippi). He has worked as a newspaper reporter, an attorney in private practice, general counsel to a nonprofit organization focusing on marine habitat protection issues, and directed marine law research programs in Mississippi and Maine. Since 2004, he has engaged in teaching and research on law, the environment, natural resource management, and communication.

CONTRIBUTORS   XXVII

Cecilia Engler
is a lawyer (Universidad de Concepcion, Chile), LL.M. and Ph.D. candidate at the Schulich School of Law, Dalhousie University, and research assistant with the Marine & Environmental Law Institute. Her research interests are oceans law and policy, including the ecosystem approach to oceans management and its intersection with law; international fisheries law; aquaculture law; and marine biodiversity protection. She held a Vanier Canada Graduate Scholarship and Izaak Walton Killam Predoctoral Scholarships. She has been awarded several academic awards, including the Governor General's Gold Medal in Humanities and Social Sciences 2011 for her LL.M. thesis.

Osatohanmwen Anastasia Eruaga
is a research fellow with the Nigerian Institute of Advanced Legal Studies and a doctoral candidate at World Maritime University, Sweden. She studied law at the University of Benin and subsequently obtained an LL.M. (Maritime Law) from the University of Nottingham, United Kingdom in 2009. She has been involved in extensive legal research and writing in the areas of public law especially maritime and human rights law. Her current research brings her in close contact with issues related to maritime security.

Abentin Estim
Ph.D., is an associate professor at the Borneo Marine Research Institute, Universiti Malaysia Sabah, pursuing research on water quality, pollution control and integrated multi-trophic aquaculture systems.

Katja Fennel
is a professor in the Department of Oceanography at Dalhousie University. As head of the Marine Environmental Modeling Group (http://memg.ocean.dal.ca) she leads the development of marine ecosystem and biogeochemical models at Dalhousie. Dr. Fennel develops and applies marine biogeochemical models with particular focus on continental shelf systems and the cycling of nitrogen, carbon and oxygen. She has also developed and applied methods for the assimilation of observations into these models in order to improve their predictive capabilities. Dr. Fennel serves as co-editor-in-chief of the journal *Biogeosciences* and on several international science advisory bodies.

David Freestone
is visiting scholar at George Washington University Law School in Washington D.C. He is co-rapporteur of the International Law Association Committee on International Law and Sea Level Rise and is the founding editor of the *International Journal of Marine and Coastal Law* (now in its 33rd year). He is also the

executive secretary of the Sargasso Sea Commission established by the 2014 Hamilton Declaration on Collaboration for the Conservation of the Sargasso Sea that now has 10 government signatories. In 2007, he was awarded the Haub Gold Medal for Environmental Law.

Kristina M. Gjerde
is a senior high seas advisor to IUCN's Global Marine and Polar Programme and adjunct professor at the Middlebury Institute of International Studies at Monterey, California. Kristina received her JD from New York University School of Law with a focus on comparative and international law. For almost 30 years, Kristina has worked on the progressive development of public international law relating to the marine environment, including the high seas and international seabed Area. In addition to leading IUCN's delegation at numerous international ocean meetings, Kristina has co-founded multiple cross-disciplinary initiatives and co-authored more than 150 publications.

Kayla M. Glynn
is an ocean enthusiast trained in coastal and marine management. Kayla began her academic training at the University of Victoria where she received B.A. (honours) in geography with a concentration in coastal studies. Since receiving a Masters in Marine Management from Dalhousie University, Kayla shifted her focus to the realm of science communication and is currently the digital communications and research specialist for Clear Seas Centre for Responsible Marine Shipping as well as a producer of The Story Collider, based in Vancouver. Follow her at @kaylamayglynn.

Raquel Hadrich Silva
is an oceanographer (FURG, Brazil) with a Master in Sociology (UFPEL, Brazil), and currently a master's student and researcher at the University of Amsterdam in the Netherlands. Research background is in development-induced displacement of coastal communities due to port expansion and offshore oil in Brazil (Rio Grande, Brazil). More recently, has a research and practice focus on resettlement and relocation of populations in flood risk management projects within urban planning contexts of coastal port cities in Asia and Africa.

Harriet R. Harden-Davies
is a Nereus Research Fellow at the Australian National Centre for Ocean Resources and Security (ANCORS), University of Wollongong. Her research lies at the intersection of ocean policy, science, technology and law, with a focus on the conservation and sustainable use of marine biodiversity in areas beyond national jurisdiction. She is an active member of several international

interdisciplinary ocean governance initiatives. Prior to joining ANCORS, Harriet led the science policy program of the Australian Academy of Technological Sciences and Engineering. Harriet holds a B.Sc. (Hons) in marine biology and oceanography from the University of Southampton.

Timo Koivurova
is a research professor and director of the Arctic Centre. Koivurova has specialized in various aspects of international law, especially as regards the Arctic. He has been involved as an expert in several international processes globally and in the Arctic region and has published on the above-mentioned topics extensively. He is the editor-in-chief of the *Yearbook of Polar Law* and the *Yearbook of International Environmental Law*.

Xuexia Liao
is a Ph.D. candidate in international law at Graduate Institute of International and Development Studies, Geneva. She specializes in the continental shelf regime, maritime delimitation, law of the sea, and international dispute settlement. Ms. Liao holds the Diploma of the Hague Academy of International Law of 2016 and has published on the delimitation of the continental shelf beyond 200 nautical miles.

Keith MacMaster
is currently an LL.M. student at Dalhousie University. He holds a law degree from Dalhousie, an MBA from the Richard Ivey School of Business at the University of Western Ontario, and a financial planning designation from the Canadian Securities Institute. Prior to his LL.M. studies, Keith spent time working as an environmental and securities lawyer and later as a financial planner with a major financial institution. His current research focuses on responsible investing and structuring new ways of financing environmental projects. Keith lives in Dartmouth, Nova Scotia and volunteers with several community and environmental organizations.

B. Mabel Manjaji-Matsumoto
Ph.D., is a senior lecturer in the Borneo Marine Research Institute, Universiti Malaysia Sabah and coordinator of Endangered Marine Species Research Unit. Areas of interest include marine biodiversity and shark conservation.

Till Markus
is a senior legal researcher at the University of Bremen (Germany), where he leads a research group focusing on international and transnational environmental law. Over the past years, he has published extensively in the areas of

international law, environmental law, law of the sea, comparative law, and legal theory. He also currently serves as chief editor of a leading German environmental law journal.

Raza Ali Mehdi
is a safety specialist working in Toyota Motor Europe. He holds a bachelor's in aerospace engineering and masters in engineering dynamics and control. He undertook doctoral studies at the World Maritime University, where he also worked as a technical officer in the area of maritime risk and system safety. The focus of his research was on safe navigation of vessels operating near offshore wind farms. He has developed various static and dynamic risk management tools as well as accident investigation models and simulator scenarios to further understand and analyze the complex risks associated with maritime operations.

Bruno Meirelles de Oliveira
is a biologist, MBA in environmental management and technology, Masters in environmental sciences, and Ph.D. candidate in environmental sciences (2016–2020). Took part of several interdisciplinary projects as Biota/FAPESP Araçá (2014–2016) and Inter-American Institute for Global Change Research Antares Network (2015–2017). International experiences include ARIES training (Basque Center for Climate Change in Basque Country, Spain) and MIMES models training (Vermont, U.S.). Currently developing a Ph.D. thesis on a "Resilience model of Social Ecological Systems using system dynamics" at São Paulo University, Brazil.

Maximo Q. Mejia Jr.
is a professor, director of the Ph.D. program, and head of the Maritime Law and Policy Specialization at the World Maritime University (WMU). Before joining WMU, he saw duty on board naval and coast guard vessels as well as in shore-based facilities in the Philippines. He earned a B.Sc. at the U.S. Naval Academy (Annapolis, Maryland), an MALD at the Fletcher School (Medford, Massachusetts), an M.Sc. from WMU, and a Ph.D. at Lund University (Lund, Sweden). He took a sabbatical from WMU to serve as administrator of the Maritime Industry Authority (Philippines) from 2013 to 2016.

Kendra A. Moore
has a B.Sc. from the University of Victoria in marine biology and environmental studies, as well as a Master of Marine Management from Dalhousie University. Her master's research focused on whale and acoustics management. Kendra is

currently working for Fisheries and Oceans Canada as a senior fisheries management and aquaculture officer.

Saleem Mustafa
Ph.D., is a professor at the Borneo Marine Research Institute, Universiti Malaysia Sabah. Topics of his research are ecological aquaculture and seafood security. He also is editor-in-chief of the *Borneo Journal of Marine Science & Aquaculture*.

Rafidah Othman
Ph.D., is a senior lecturer in the Borneo Marine Research Institute, Universiti Malaysia Sabah, interested in fish health management and biosecurity systems for aquaculture.

Dominique Peña Clinaz
is a civil and environmental engineering major and marine science minor at the University of Hawai'i at Mānoa (2015–2020). Background in environmental advocacy coordination and public awareness, single-use plastics legislation and marine conservation, coastal reforestation, and sustainable design. Current Chair of Surfrider Foundation University of Hawai'i Student Chapter.

Alexandre Pereira da Silva
is currently a research fellow at the China Institute of Boundary and Ocean Studies, Wuhan University. From 2012 to 2013, he was a visiting post-doctoral scholar at the Marine and Environmental Law Institute, Dalhousie University. He is the author of *O Brasil e o Direito Internacional do Mar Contemporâneo: Novas Oportunidades e Desafios* (São Paulo: Almedina, 2015) and numerous articles focusing on questions of law of the sea for Brazil and Latin America.

Marina Reback Garcia
is an oceanographer, master's in physical, chemical and geological oceanography at the Federal University of Rio Grande and currently a Ph.D. student in coastal and oceanic systems at the Federal University of Paraná, Brazil (2015–2019). Background in environmental licensing and environmental education (8 years). Current research interest in organic geochemistry of mangroves' hydrocarbon contamination in South Brazil.

Ejria Saleh
Ph.D., is an associate professor and deputy-director (Academic & International), in the Borneo Marine Research Institute, Universiti Malaysia Sabah, specialized in coastal oceanography.

Clive Schofield
is head of research at the WMU-Sasakawa Global Ocean Institute, World Maritime University, Malmö, Sweden and visiting professor with the Australian Centre for Ocean Resources and Security, University of Wollongong, Australia. He holds a Ph.D. in geography (Durham) and an LL.M. in international law (UBC). His research interests relate to international maritime boundaries and technical aspects of the law of the sea resulting in over 200 publications. Clive is observer on the Advisory Board on the Law of the Sea (ABLOS) and a member of the ILA Committee on International Law and Sea Level Rise.

Jens-Uwe Schröder-Hinrichs
is a professor of maritime administration and currently the director of research at the World Maritime University. Before entering an academic career, Dr. Schröder-Hinrichs worked as a navigator on merchant ships and as a safety engineer in the maritime industry. His research interests are related to maritime risks and safety. Of special interest to him is the implementation and enforcement of IMO instruments. He has interacted with various international organizations on that topic and advised member States of the International Maritime Organization (IMO) on this issue.

Luana Sena Ferreira
is an oceanographer, master's student in public policy management and social security at the Federal University of Recôncavo of Bahia, Brazil (2017–2019). Background in environmental licensing (2 years) and environmental analysis, water and sediment (3 years). Research interest in public policy, policy-making process, participatory governance and mineral marine resources management.

Andrew Serdy
is professor of public international law and ocean governance at the University of Southampton, recruited in 2005 for his law of the sea specialization. He started his career at Freehill, Hollingdale & Page, Solicitors (Sydney), and then spent 16 years with the Australian Government Department of Foreign Affairs and Trade, including appearing for Australia in the Southern Bluefin Tuna arbitration (2000). Later he became deputy director of the Department's Sea Law, Environmental Law and Antarctic Policy Section and in this capacity drafted significant parts of Australia's 2004 submission to the Commission on the Limits of the Continental Shelf.

Sitti Raehanah M. Shaleh
Ph.D., is an associate professor and deputy-director (Research & Innovation) of the Borneo Marine Research Institute, Universiti Malaysia Sabah. Fields of research interest include plankton culture and sea cucumbers.

Rossita Shapawi
Ph.D., is a professor and director of the Borneo Marine Research Institute, Universiti Malaysia Sabah, specialized in fish nutrition, with a special interest in developing feeds from sustainable sources.

Pedro Pablo Silva Sánchez
is a Ph.D. candidate at the University of Bremen (Germany). His research is funded by the Bremen International Graduate School for Marine Sciences GLOMAR – MARUM. He has published and taught in the areas of international, human rights, and environmental law. Over the past years, he has worked as a legal advisor for the Ministry of Foreign Affairs and the Constitutional Court of Chile.

Krittika Singh
is a junior researcher at the Arctic Centre, University of Lapland. She holds a first degree in law from Gujarat National Law University, India and a master in international affairs from the Fletcher School of Law and Diplomacy, Tufts University, USA. Her research focuses on law of the sea, environmental resource governance and sustainable development.

Tim Stephens
is professor of international law and Australian Research Council Future Fellow at the University of Sydney and president of the Australian and New Zealand Society of International Law. Professor Stephens teaches and researches in public international law, with his published work focusing on the international law of the sea, international environmental law and international dispute settlement. His major works include *The International Law of the Sea* (Hart, 2nd ed., 2016), with D.R. Rothwell, and *International Courts and Environmental Protection* (Cambridge University Press, 2009). His ARC Future Fellowship research project is examining implications of the Anthropocene for international law.

Oxana Sytnik
is an oceanographer (Russian State Hydrometerological University, Russia), Erasmus Mundus Joint European Master in Water and Coastal Management WACOMA (University of Plymouth, UK) and University of Cadiz, Spain, and Erasmus Mundus Joint European Ph.D. in Marine and Coastal Management MACOMA (University of Cadiz and University of Bologna, Italy). She is currently a postdoctoral researcher at the Laboratory of Coastal Oceanography at the Federal University of Santa Catarina (Brazil), and is a certified scientific diver with research interest in assessment of coastal vulnerability to climate change.

David L. VanderZwaag
is Professor of Law and Canada Research Chair in Ocean Law and Governance at the Marine & Environmental Law Institute, Schulich School of Law, Dalhousie University. He teaches international environmental law and serves as the Associate Director of the Marine & Environmental Law Institute. He a member of the International Council of Environmental Law as well as the IUCN World Commission on Environmental Law. From 2004–2018, he co-chaired the WCEL's Specialist Group on Oceans, Coasts and Coral Reefs. Dr. VanderZwaag has authored over 150 papers in the marine and environmental law field.

Zarinah Waheed
Ph.D., is a senior lecturer in the Borneo Marine Research Institute, Universiti Malaysia Sabah, specialized in coral reef biology and conservation and manages the Coral Triangle Initiative (Sabah Branch) and Citizen Science program Sustaining Kota Kinabalu's Marine Heritage.

PART 1

The Law of the Sea and Ocean Governance

∴

Building a Platform for the Future: the Relationship of the Expected New Agreement for Marine Biodiversity in Areas beyond National Jurisdiction and the UN Convention on the Law of the Sea

Kristina M. Gjerde*
Senior High Seas Advisor, IUCN Global Marine and Polar Programme and World Commission on Protected Areas, Cambridge, MA, USA

Nichola A. Clark and Harriet R. Harden-Davies
Australian National Centre for Ocean Resources and Security, University of Wollongong, Australia

> [O]ur generation can take some pride in having contributed, no matter how fumblingly and bunglingly, to the making of the new order for the seas and oceans, to the opening of new ways of thinking about world order, and to the hammering-out of a platform from which in the future, a great many new initiatives can be launched.[1]
> ELISABETH MANN BORGESE

Introduction

Why Should We Care about Marine Biodiversity beyond National Jurisdiction?

Marine areas beyond national jurisdiction (ABNJ), the high seas, and the International Seabed Area, comprise nearly two-thirds of the global ocean.[2]

---

* Dedicated to Elisabeth Mann Borgese, whose wisdom continues to shine as an inspiration for those seeking to follow in her footsteps. The authors would like to thank David Freestone, Duncan Currie, and our anonymous reviewers for their insightful comments.
1 E. Mann Borgese, "Foreword," *San Diego Law Review* 24, no. 3 (1987): 595, p. 601.
2 The "high seas" are "all parts of the sea that are not included in the exclusive economic zone, in the territorial sea or in the internal waters of a State, or in the archipelagic waters of an archipelagic State" (Article 86, UNCLOS). UNCLOS Article 1 defines the "Area" as "[t]he seabed and ocean floor, and subsoil thereof, beyond the limits of national jurisdiction."

Neither the high seas nor the Area belong to any single State; instead, under the framework of the United Nations Convention on the Law of the Sea (UNCLOS),[3] these areas are managed through a suite of activity-specific agreements and global and regional bodies, each with their own mandates and priorities.[4] The resulting governance structure has major gaps that undermine the possibilities for cooperation, coherence, and effective protection of the marine environment in ABNJ.[5] Identified gaps in governance, regulation, and implementation include:

1. absence of an overarching set of governance principles for ecosystem-based, science-based, precautionary approaches and open, inclusive, and transparent management;
2. a fragmented institutional framework lacking mechanisms for coordination across sectors or regions or for the incorporation of conservation concerns of international community interest;
3. lack of a global framework to establish a comprehensive system of marine protected areas or to promote other effective area-based conservation tools;
4. lack of global rules for environmental impact assessments of proposed projects or for strategic environmental assessments for proposed policies, programs, or activities;
5. limited capacity-building and technology transfer despite requirements in UNCLOS to enable developing States to study, protect and benefit from marine resources and the environment in ABNJ;
6. legal uncertainty surrounding the status of marine genetic resources in ABNJ; and
7. uneven integration of marine environmental and biodiversity considerations into management and decision-making of sectoral organizations.[6]

---

[3] United Nations Convention on the Law of the Sea, 10 December 1982, 1833 *United Nations Treaty Series*, 3. Entered into force 16 November 1994 [UNCLOS].

[4] G. Wright, J. Rochette, K. Gjerde and I. Seeger, *The Long and Winding Road: Negotiating a Treaty for the Conservation and Sustainable Use of Marine Biodiversity in Areas beyond National Jurisdiction*, IDDRI Studies no. 08 (2018), p. 26, available online: <https://www.actu-environnement.com/media/pdf/news-31928-iddri-haute-mer.pdf>.

[5] K.M. Gjerde et al., *Regulatory and Governance Gaps in the International Regime for the Conservation and Sustainable Use of Marine Biodiversity in Areas Beyond National Jurisdiction* (Gland, Switzerland: IUCN, 2008), available online: <https://portals.iucn.org/library/sites/library/files/documents/eplp-ms-1.pdf>. See also, R. Mahon et al., *Transboundary Waters Assessment Programme (TWAP) Assessment of Governance Arrangements for the Ocean, Volume 2: Areas Beyond National Jurisdiction* (Paris: UNESCO-IOC, IOC Technical Series 119, 2015), available online: <http://onesharedocean.org/public_store/publications/ts119Vol2_eo.pdf>.

[6] Gjerde et al., id.; Wright et al., n. 4 above.

The lack of coherence in ABNJ management will impede achievement of global goals and needs for truly sustainable development of our one interconnected ocean.[7] As highlighted in the first World Ocean Assessment:

> The sustainable use of the ocean cannot be achieved unless the management of all sectors of human activities affecting the ocean is coherent. ... This requires taking into account the effects on ecosystems of each of the many pressures, what is being done in other sectors and the way that they interact.[8]

In response to rising concerns about the impacts of human activities on ocean health and the abundance, variety, and richness of marine life (biodiversity),[9] the United Nations General Assembly (UNGA) has commenced negotiations for a new international legally binding instrument for the conservation and sustainable use of marine biodiversity in ABNJ under UNCLOS.[10] The UNGA resolution launching negotiations (Resolution 72/249) sets out certain parameters for organizing discussions, including the need for the existing global regime to better address the conservation and sustainable use of marine biodiversity beyond national jurisdiction (BBNJ) and an understanding that the international legally binding instrument will take the form of a new implementing agreement to UNCLOS (BBNJ agreement), akin to the Part XI Agreement and the UN Fish Stocks Agreement (UNFSA).[11] At the same time, it also states that

---

7   United Nations General Assembly (UNGA), "Summary of the First Global Integrated Marine Assessment," UN Doc. A/70/112 (22 July 2015), paras. 32–62. See also UNEP-WCMC, *Marine Connectivity Across Jurisdictional Boundaries: An Introduction* (Cambridge, UK: UN Environment World Conservation Monitoring Centre, 2018).
8   UNGA, id., para. 40.
9   For a history of the UN processes leading to the UNGA decision to launch negotiations, see K.M. Gjerde, "Perspectives on a developing regime for marine biodiversity conservation and sustainable use beyond national jurisdiction," in *Ocean Law Debates: The 50-Year Legacy and Emerging Issues for the Years Ahead*, eds., H.N. Scheiber, N. Oral and M-S. Kwon, Law of the Sea Institute Publication (Boston: Brill Nijhoff, 2018), pp. 354–380; see also Wright et al., n. 4 above.
10 UNGA, "International legally binding instrument under the United Nations Convention on the Law of the Sea on the conservation and sustainable use of marine biological diversity of areas beyond national jurisdiction," UNGA Doc. A/RES/72/249 (24 December 2017) [72/249].
11 Agreement relating to the Implementation of Part XI of the United Nations Convention on the Law of the Sea of 10 December 1982, 28 July 1994, 1836 *United Nations Treaty Series* 3 (entered into force 28 July 1996) [Part XI Agreement]; Agreement for the Implementation of the Provisions of the United Nations Convention on the Law of the Sea of 10 December 1982 relating to the Conservation and Management of Straddling Fish Stocks and Highly

the new instrument "should not undermine existing relevant legal instruments and frameworks and relevant global, regional and sectoral bodies."

The substance of the UN negotiations is set to address an agreed package of four issues: 1) marine genetic resources, including questions on the sharing of benefits; 2) measures such as area-based management tools (ABMTs), including marine protected areas (MPAs); 3) environmental impact assessments (EIAs); and 4) capacity-building and the transfer of marine technology.[12] Cross-cutting issues such as guiding principles and institutional arrangements, as well as other traditional treaty provisions, are also key items for negotiators.

To assist in identifying ways to enhance coherence without undermining existing relevant legal instruments, frameworks, and bodies, this article addresses the potential relationship between the expected new BBNJ agreement and UNCLOS. In particular, it invokes the approaches used in a prior implementing agreement to UNCLOS, the UNFSA, to highlight ways the new agreement can improve implementation of the existing UNCLOS duties to protect and preserve the marine environment, conserve living marine resources, and cooperate for these purposes while incorporating modern conservation principles and tools. Marine genetic resources and options for benefit sharing, including through improved implementation of UNCLOS duties for cooperation on marine science, capacity-building, and marine technology transfer, are addressed in a sister article in this volume of the *Ocean Yearbook*.[13]

The first part of this article describes the provisions of UNCLOS most relevant to BBNJ and highlights the roles of other existing institutions and agreements. The second part describes how more recent agreements, principles, and commitments, including the 1992 Convention on Biological Diversity (CBD),[14] can inform the substantive elements of the BBNJ agreement. The third part examines the key provisions of UNFSA as a potential model for the new BBNJ agreement and also identifies lessons to be learned. The fourth part examines institutional matters, specifically how to avoid undermining institutions and

---

Migratory Fish Stocks, 4 August 1995, 2167 *United Nations Treaty Series* 3 (entered into force 11 December 2001) [UNFSA].

12 72/249, n. 10 above, para. 2. Focusing negotiations on a package of issues is as a tool for securing support to move forward together and as a whole on a range of issues so that no part of the agreement is considered "agreed" until all issues are addressed. This strategy was used during the UNCLOS negotiations (Wright et al., n. 4 above, p. 45).

13 H. Harden-Davies and K.M. Gjerde, "Building scientific and technological capacity: a role for benefit-sharing in the conservation and sustainable use of marine biodiversity beyond national jurisdiction," in *Ocean Yearbook* 33 (2019), in this volume.

14 Convention on Biological Diversity, 5 June 1992, 1760 *United Nations Treaty Series* 79 (entered into force 29 December 1993) [CBD].

agreements, and how new and improved institutional mechanisms can enhance cooperation and coordination. The fifth part concludes by highlighting some opportunities for the new BBNJ agreement to create a platform for more integrated, coherent, and ecosystem-based approaches to safeguarding marine life and the environment beyond national boundaries.

Why is the New Agreement Important?

Humankind depends upon the ocean. Global fish catches, critical to both food and economic security, total approximately 90 million tonnes.[15] The international shipping industry carries approximately 90 percent of the world's trade, and submarine cables along the seafloor carry more than 90 percent of electronic communications.[16] The International Seabed Authority (ISA) is in the process of developing exploitation regulations, which would enable the commercial exploitation of deep sea mineral resources of the Area, and the list of potential and emerging uses for the ocean, such as open ocean aquaculture, ocean fertilization, and even floating cities, continues to grow.[17] Humans also benefit from the ecosystem services that the ocean provides – the ocean absorbs over one-quarter of the anthropogenic carbon dioxide emitted into the atmosphere, stores 93 percent of the resultant heat, and generates half of the oxygen we breathe.[18] The ocean further serves as a place of adventure, inspiration, and imagination, even for those far from the sea.

The health of our ocean is declining. The 2018 report by the Food and Agriculture Organization of the United Nations (FAO) on *The State of the World Fisheries and Aquaculture* found that 93 percent of fish stocks are being fully or overexploited.[19] This percent of maximally fished or overfished fish stocks has increased yet again, up from 90.1 percent in 2014 and 85 percent in 2010.[20] Overfishing does more than reduce target fish stocks: it can deplete non-target species such as seabirds, sea turtles, and cetaceans, alter the genetic structure of fish stocks, change the relationships between predators and prey, and weaken

---

15 Food and Agriculture Organization of the United Nations (FAO), *The State of World Fisheries and Aquaculture 2018* (Rome: FAO, 2018), p. 2, available online: <http://www.fao.org/3/i9540en/I9540EN.pdf>.
16 International Chamber of Shipping, "Shipping and World Trade," available online: <http://www.ics-shipping.org/shipping-facts/shipping-and-world-trade>; UNGA, n. 7 above, para. 2.
17 Gjerde et al., n. 5 above.
18 UNGA, n. 7 above, 3, para. 1.
19 FAO, n. 15 above, p. 6.
20 FAO, *The State of World Fisheries and Aquaculture 2014* (Rome: FAO, 2014), p. 7, available online: <http://www.fao.org/3/a-i3720e.pdf>; FAO, *The State of World Fisheries and Aquaculture 2010* (Rome: FAO, 2010), p. 8, available online: <http://www.fao.org/3/a-i1820e.pdf>.

the resilience of ecosystems to other impacts and environmental change.[21] Fishing and other maritime activities can also degrade habitat by destroying fragile deep seabed communities, disrupt spawning, breeding, and nursery grounds, entangle and drown large marine animals in discarded fishing gear, and contaminate marine organisms throughout the food web with pollution, including from toxic heavy metals and microplastics.[22]

The direct effects of human activities are exacerbated by the impacts of rising carbon dioxide (CO_2) emissions. As the ocean stores evermore carbon, its waters become more acidic and less oxygenated, negatively impacting both the marine environment and the organisms residing therein.[23] Ocean warming, acidification, and "dead zones" resulting from deoxygenation have been associated with each of the previous five mass extinction events on Earth, acting synergistically to change primary production patterns, alter species distribution and abundance, and impair reproduction and development.[24] The cumulative impacts of these various activities threaten the health of the ocean by destabilizing ecosystems, disrupting food supplies, and undermining resilience to further impacts.[25] The limited, often single-sector governance of these activities has not proved equal to the task of addressing these challenges.

What's Next?

In recognition of this growing concern about the health of marine ecosystems and biodiversity, governments agreed, in 2004, to study issues relating to the conservation and sustainable use of marine biological diversity in ABNJ.[26] After nearly a decade of discussions, in 2015 the UNGA finally decided to establish a preparatory committee (PrepCom) to develop substantive recommendations on "elements of a draft text of an international legally binding

---

21 G. Ortuno Crespo and D.C. Dunn, "A review of the impacts of fisheries on open-ocean ecosystems," *ICES Journal of Marine Science* 74 (2018): 2283–2297; UNGA, n. 7 above, pp. 12–50, paras. 37, 78, 126, 136–137, and 195(b).

22 A. Eassom et al., *Horizon Scan of Pressures on Biodiversity Beyond National Jurisdiction* (Cambridge, UK: UNEP-WCMC 2016), p. 27, available online: <http://www.cambridgeconservation.org/sites/default/files/file-attachments/Horizon_Scan_v14_Final.pdf>.

23 UNGA, n. 7 above, para. 4.

24 A.D. Rogers and D. d'A. Laffoley, *International Earth System Expert Workshop on Ocean Stresses and Impacts. Summary Report* (Oxford: IPSO, 2011), pp. 5–6, available online: <http://www.stateoftheocean.org/wp-content/uploads/2015/10/2011-Summary-report_workshop-on-stresses-and-impacts.pdf>.

25 Id., p. 6.

26 Wright, et al., n. 4 above; see also Gjerde, n. 9 above.

instrument under the Convention."[27] Two years later, and based upon the recommendations of the PrepCom,[28] the UNGA passed Resolution 72/249 launching an intergovernmental conference to negotiate the new BBNJ agreement.[29] The negotiations will be spread over four two-week sessions between September 2018 and September 2020. How the outcome of these negotiations can foster cooperation, coordination, and action at the global level as well as assist existing sectoral and regional bodies, other organizations, and States to better understand, manage, and adapt to the coming challenges of a changing ocean is what we turn to next.[30]

The Existing Legal Basis for BBNJ

What UNCLOS Tells Us

Widely recognized as the "constitution for the oceans," UNCLOS contains many provisions relevant to the conservation and sustainable use of marine biodiversity in ABNJ (see Table 1.1). Marine biodiversity is part of the watery realm of the marine environment and thus the starting point is Article 192 of UNCLOS, which clearly articulates that "States have the obligation to protect and preserve the marine environment." Article 194(5) of UNCLOS further requires that "measures taken [in accordance with Part XII on Protection and Preservation of the Marine Environment,] shall include those necessary to protect and preserve rare or fragile ecosystems as well as the habitat of depleted, threatened or endangered species and other forms of marine life."

As the International Tribunal for the Law of the Sea (ITLOS) recognized in the *Southern Bluefin Tuna Cases*, "the conservation of the living resources of the sea is an element in the protection and preservation of the marine

---

27 UNGA, "Development of an international legally binding instrument under the United Nations Convention on the Law of the Sea on the conservation and sustainable use of marine biological diversity of areas beyond national jurisdiction," UN Doc. A/RES/69/292 (19 June 2015) [69/292].

28 UNGA, "Report of the Preparatory Committee established by General Assembly resolution 69/292: Development of an international legally binding instrument under the United Nations Convention on the Law of the Sea on the conservation and sustainable use of marine biological diversity of areas beyond national jurisdiction," UN Doc. A/AC.287/2017/PC.4/2 (31 July 2017), pp. 8–9 [PrepCom Report].

29 72/249, n. 10 above.

30 The first two implementing agreements to UNCLOS are the Part XI Agreement and the UNFSA, see n. 11 above.

TABLE 1.1 Key provisions in international law relevant for BBNJ Agreement

Instrument	Article	Summary/excerpt of provision
UNCLOS	117	States are obliged to take (or cooperate with other States to take) "measures for their respective nationals as may be necessary for the conservation of the living resources of the high seas."
UNCLOS	118	"States are obliged to cooperate with each other in the conservation and management of living resources in the areas of the high seas"
UNCLOS	123	"States bordering an enclosed or semi-enclosed sea should cooperate … directly or through an appropriate regional organization: (a) to coordinate the management, conservation, exploration and exploitation of the living resources of the sea; (b) to coordinate the implementation of their rights and duties with respect to the protection and preservation of the marine environment; (c) to coordinate their scientific research policies …; (d) to invite … other interested States or international organizations to cooperate with them in furtherance of the provisions of this Article."
UNCLOS	192	Duty of States to protect and preserve the marine environment.
UNCLOS	194(5)	Measures taken to protect and preserve the marine environment should include measures to protect rare or fragile ecosystems or threatened or endangered species.
UNCLOS	197	Duty of States to cooperate on a global basis and, as appropriate, on a regional basis "in formulating international rules, standards and recommended practices and procedures … for the protection and preservation of the marine environment."
UNCLOS	200	Duty of States to cooperate to promote studies, research programs, and exchange of information and data, with an aim of acquiring knowledge to assess the "nature and extent of pollution."
UNCLOS	201	Duty of States to cooperate in establishing appropriate scientific criteria for the purposes of elaborating rules and standards for the "prevention, reduction and control of pollution of the marine environment."

Instrument	Article	Summary/excerpt of provision
UNCLOS	202	States shall promote scientific, educational, technical, and other programs to assist developing States for the protection and preservation of the marine environment; states shall provide assistance, especially to developing States, with respect to preparing environmental assessments.
UNCLOS	203	Developing States shall "be granted preference by international organizations in: (a) the allocation of appropriate funds and technical assistance; and (b) the utilization of their specialized services."
UNCLOS	204	Duty of States to "observe, measure, evaluate and analyse ... the risks or effects of pollution of the marine environment," in particular with respect to activities under their jurisdiction.
UNCLOS	205	Obligation of States to "publish reports of the results obtained pursuant to Article 204" or provide them to the competent international organizations; these should be available to all States.
UNCLOS	206	Duty of States to assess the potential effects of planned activities on the marine environment if they have reasonable grounds for believing those activities may cause "substantial pollution of or significant and harmful changes to the marine environment." States are also obliged to communicate the results of that assessment as outlined in Article 205.
UNCLOS	237	Provisions are without prejudice to future agreements related to the protection and preservation of the marine environment.
CBD	6	Obliges Contracting Parties to "develop national strategies, plans or programmes for the conservation and sustainable use of biological diversity" and to integrate "the conservation and sustainable use of biological diversity into relevant sectoral or cross-sectoral plans, programmes and policies."
CBD	7	Obliges Contracting Parties to "identify processes and categories of activities which have or are likely to have significant adverse impacts on the conservation and sustainable use of biological diversity."

TABLE 1.1 Key provisions in international law relevant for BBNJ Agreement (*cont.*)

Instrument	Article	Summary/excerpt of provision
CBD	8	Obliges Contracting Parties to "establish a system of protected areas or areas where special measures need to be taken to conserve biological diversity," develop guidelines "for the selection, establishment and management of protected areas or areas where special measures need to be taken to conserve biological diversity," and to "regulate or manage biological resources important for the conservation of biological diversity whether within or outside protected areas, with a view to ensuring their conservation and sustainable use."
CBD	14	Obliges Contracting Parties to introduce measures requiring environmental impact assessments of proposed projects "that are likely to have significant adverse impacts" on biodiversity, with a view to avoiding or minimizing such effects.
UNFSA	5	Articulates general principles to give effect to the duty to cooperate, which includes the obligation to "apply the precautionary approach" and to "protect biodiversity in the marine environment."
UNFSA	6	Obliges states to "apply the precautionary approach widely to conservation, management and exploitation" of straddling and highly migratory fish stocks "in order to protect the living marine resources and preserve the marine environment." Also obliges States to be "more cautious when information is uncertain, unreliable or inadequate" and clarifies that "the absence of adequate scientific information shall not be used as a reason for postponing or failing to take conservation and management measures."
UNFSA	7	Sets out provisions for ensuring compatibility of conservation and management measures and includes an obligation for States to make every effort to agree on compatible conservation and management measures within a reasonable period of time.

Instrument	Article	Summary/excerpt of provision
UNFSA	8	Obliges States to consult when a proposed action by one organization with competence over living resources proposes a measure that would have a significant effect on conservation and management measures already established by an RFMO.
UNFSA	14	Obliges States to "ensure that fishing vessels flying their flag provide such information as may be necessary in order to fulfill their obligations under this Agreement."

environment."[31] Thus, the UNCLOS provisions recognizing the duty of all States to cooperate in the conservation and management of the living resources of the high seas (Articles 116–119) are also relevant. Article 119 elaborates upon the nature of the actions that States are required to take, including through application of the best scientific evidence available, care for associated and dependent species, and the sharing of catch statistics and other relevant data.[32] However, implementation of these duties has largely focused on target fish stocks rather than living marine resources as a whole or the environment in which they are a part.[33] Moreover, as described in Part III, it was due to the vagueness of these provisions and the continuing decline in shared fish stocks that States decided to negotiate a new implementing agreement that became the 1995 UNFSA.[34]

---

31 The *Southern Bluefin Tuna* cases (New Zealand v. Japan) (Australia v. Japan), ITLOS Case Nos. 3 and 4, 27 August 1999, (1999) 38 *International Legal Materials* 1624, 1634, para. 70.
32 Article 119 obligations for cooperation including: (a) taking measures, "on the best scientific evidence available"; (b) taking measures to maintain or restore populations of species associated with, or dependent on, harvested species, so that they are not reduced to levels at which their reproduction may become seriously threatened; and (c) a general obligation to contribute and exchange on a regular basis, where appropriate, through subregional, regional or global organizations, available scientific information, catch and fishing effort statistics, and other data relevant to the conservation of fish stocks.
33 K.M. Gjerde et al., "Ocean in peril: Reforming the management of global ocean living resources in areas beyond national jurisdiction," *Marine Pollution Bulletin* 74 (2013): 540–551.
34 See "What Can Be Learned from UNFSA?" herein.

With respect to the relationship with a new BBNJ agreement, Article 197 in UNCLOS specifically envisages and calls for the development of additional international rules, standards, and recommended practices and procedures to protect and preserve the marine environment. The text of Article 197 gives prominence to global cooperation, as well as the need to cooperate, as appropriate, on a regional basis, and to take into account "characteristic regional features."[35] Article 237 of UNCLOS provides further guidance by confirming that a new agreement may impose additional obligations with respect to the protection and preservation of the marine environment, provided they are carried out in a manner consistent with the general principles and objectives of the Convention.[36] As is recalled in the Preamble to UNCLOS, such objectives include "the conservation of their living resources, and the study, protection and preservation of the marine environment."[37] Action is to be premised on two pillars, due regard for the sovereignty of all States and recognition that "the problems of ocean space are closely interrelated and need to be considered as a whole."[38]

In addition to the substantive duty to protect and preserve the marine environment, Part XII's procedural and institutional mechanisms, intended to enable all States to implement these duties (via fostering capacity development and technology transfer, marine scientific research, and environmental assessments), similarly require further elaboration in the new BBNJ agreement.[39] Other fundamental components of UNCLOS that are relevant to BBNJ but poorly implemented include more general provisions of Part XIII on marine scientific research, especially with respect to international cooperation, and Part XIV on the development and transfer of marine technology.

---

35 UNCLOS, n. 3 above, art. 197, which provides: "States shall cooperate on a global basis and, as appropriate, on a regional basis, directly or through competent international organizations, in formulating and elaborating international rules, standards and recommended practices and procedures consistent with this Convention, for the protection and preservation of the marine environment, taking into account characteristic regional features."

36 UNCLOS, id., art. 237, which provides: "1. The provisions of this Part are without prejudice to the specific obligations assumed by States under special conventions and agreements concluded previously which relate to the protection and preservation of the marine environment and *to agreements which may be concluded in furtherance of the general principles set forth in this Convention*. 2. Specific obligations assumed by States under special conventions, with respect to the protection and preservation of the marine environment, *should be carried out in a manner consistent with the general principles and objectives of this Convention*." (emphasis added).

37 UNCLOS, id., preamble, para. 4.

38 Id., preamble, para. 3.

39 See UNCLOS, id., Articles 204–206 on environmental assessments.

The freedoms of the high seas recognized by Article 87 of UNCLOS are also highly relevant and serve as the basis of the high seas regime in UNCLOS.[40] But the exercise of such freedoms is subject to conditions laid down by the Convention, including the duty to protect and preserve the marine environment.[41] As Long suggests, "States claiming rights under the Convention must assume correlative duties if the normative scheme is to work in practice."[42] In practice, as a result of the sectoral approach reflected in UNCLOS, the adoption of protective measures for BBNJ has been left to States acting on an *ad hoc* basis through existing sector-based organizations where conservation is most often a secondary concern, not a primary focus.[43] The interlinkages between activities and threats at the global and regional levels, the potential for increasing conflicts between activities such as deep-sea bottom fishing, seabed mining, and marine scientific research, and the need to protect international community interests in an increasingly crowded, degraded, and depleted ocean means that a more holistic, integrated and ecosystem approach is needed.[44]

As the fourth part of this article explores, among the key challenges to global ocean governance and BBNJ has been the absence of an institutional mechanism or specific rules, standards, and recommended practices and procedures to empower States to implement their duties to protect and conserve collectively through a non-sectoral lens at the global and, as appropriate, regional level. The UN negotiations for a new agreement on BBNJ thus provide an opportunity to create a platform for international cooperation and more coherent action to redress these gaps and weaknesses in an increasingly crowded, degraded, and depleted ocean.

Other Relevant Organizations and Agreements

In ABNJ, other organizations exist and have an important role to play in the conservation and sustainable use of marine biodiversity in ABNJ. Regional fisheries management organizations (RFMOs) are responsible for managing high seas fish stocks. The International Seabed Authority (ISA) is responsible

---

40 The non-exhaustive list of high seas freedoms enumerated in Article 87 includes navigation, overflight, laying submarine cables and pipelines, fishing, and scientific research.
41 D. Freestone, "Modern principles of high seas governance: The legal underpinnings," *Environmental Policy and Law* 39(1) (2009): 44–49.
42 R. Long, "Marine science capacity building and technology transfer: Rights and duties go hand in hand under the 1982 UNCLOS," in *Law, Science & Ocean Management* no. 11, eds., M. Nordquist et al. (Brill, 2007): 297–312.
43 D. Freestone, "The limits of sectoral and regional efforts to designate high seas marine protected areas," (2018) *AJIL Unbound* 112 (2018): 129–133, doi.org/10.1017/aju.2018.45.
44 Y. Tanaka, *A Dual Approach to Ocean Governance: The Cases of Zonal and Integrated Management in International Law of the Sea* (Ashgate, 2008) (London: Routledge 2016), p. 7.

for regulating exploration and exploitation of the mineral resources of the Area pursuant to Part XI of UNCLOS and the 1994 Implementing Agreement.[45] The International Maritime Organization (IMO) adopts conventions and other regulations governing international shipping and dumping.[46] The Intergovernmental Oceanographic Commission (IOC) of the United Nations Educational, Scientific and Cultural Organization (UNESCO) promotes international cooperation and coordinates programs in marine research, services, observation systems, hazard mitigation, and capacity development to understand and manage ocean and coastal resources.[47]

A number of global level, species-oriented conservation agreements are in place, including the International Convention on the Regulation of Whaling (IWC), the Convention on International Trade in Endangered Species of Wild Fauna and Flora (CITES), and the Convention on Migratory Species (CMS).[48] The CMS encourages States to develop further agreements on species of concern, such as the Agreement on the Conservation of Albatrosses and Petrels and the Memorandum of Understanding on the Conservation of Sharks that may apply regionally or globally.[49] The shortcomings of the species-specific approach led to the negotiation of the CBD, but as is explored in the following part of this article, the CBD drafters opted to focus primarily on the components of biodiversity in areas within national jurisdiction, leaving a gap for marine species and their habitats in ABNJ.

At the regional level, four regional seas organizations already have an explicit geographic mandate which includes ABNJ,[50] and several others, including the

---

45 Part XI Agreement, n. 11 above.
46 1996 London Protocol to the 1972 Convention on the Prevention of Marine Pollution by Dumping of Wastes and Other Matter, 7 November 1996, 36 *International Legal Materials* 1 (1997) (entered into force 24 March 2006).
47 UNESCO, "About the Intergovernmental Oceanographic Commission," available online: <http://www.unesco.org/new/en/natural-sciences/ioc-oceans/about-us/>.
48 International Convention for the Regulation of Whaling, 1946 (entry into force 1948); Convention on International Trade in Endangered Species of Wild Fauna and Flora, 1973 (entry into force 1975); Convention on the Conservation of Migratory Species of Wild Animals, 1979, (entry into force 1983) [CMS].
49 Agreement on the Conservation of Albatrosses and Petrels (2001) (entry into force 2004), available online: <https://www.acap.aq/>; Memorandum of Understanding on the Conservation of Sharks (2010, amended 2016), available online: <https://www.cms.int/sharks/>.
50 Convention for the Protection of the Marine Environment and the Coastal Region of the Mediterranean, 1976, amended 1995 (entry into force 1978, and amendments in 2004); Convention on the Conservation of Antarctic Marine Living Resources, 1980 (entry into force 1982); Convention for the Protection of the Marine Environment of the North-East Atlantic, 1992 (entry into force 1998); Convention for the Protection of the Natural Resources and Environment of the South Pacific Region, 1986 (entry into force 1990).

Permanent Commission for the South Pacific, the Abidjan Convention in the Southeast Atlantic, and the Nairobi Convention in the Western Indian Ocean, are exploring options for extending their governance efforts to ABNJ.[51] In 2016, the United Nations Environment Assembly (UNEA) of UN Environment adopted a resolution that encouraged parties to regional seas conventions to consider the possibility of increasing the regional coverage of those instruments in accordance with international law.[52]

However, in terms of cross-sectoral cooperation for integrated management or conserving biodiversity, there are wide discrepancies between regions.[53] This has left some regions with much more powerful governance mechanisms than others and considerable differences in funding, causing competitive (dis)advantages between regions and an absence of a level playing field at the global level.[54] This is translating into a frequent inability to effectively protect transboundary species and ecosystems or deal with transboundary impacts from bordering regions with less stringent regulations. As noted in Billé et al., "Strong efforts in just a few regions will still not prevent loss of marine biodiversity at the global level."[55]

It is against this backdrop that this article investigates how the BBNJ agreement can address this uneven implementation at the sectoral and regional levels by galvanizing action through new global level rules, standards, and recommended practices and procedures to be implemented by States parties to the new BBNJ agreement both directly and through competent global and regional bodies of which they are members. In this manner the new BBNJ agreement can support and not undermine existing instruments, frameworks or bodies.

Building on UNCLOS

Towards Integrated Approaches to Conserving Marine Biodiversity in ABNJ: Learning from the CBD

The need to supplement UNCLOS with new approaches, principles, and mechanisms was already apparent in 1992 when the United Nations Conference on Environment and Development (UNCED) in Rio de Janeiro adopted Chapter 17

---

51 Wright et al., n. 4 above.
52 UN Environment Assembly of the UN Environment Programme, "Oceans and Seas," Second session, 23–27 May 2016, UN Doc. UNEP/EA.2/Res.10 (4 August 2016), para. 13.
53 Mahon et al., n. 5 above.
54 R. Billé et al., *Regional Oceans Governance: Making Regional Seas Programmes, Regional Fishery Bodies and Large Marine Ecosystem Mechanisms Work Better Together*, UNEP Regional Seas Reports and Studies No. 197 (UNEP Regional Seas Programme, 2016), p. 60.
55 Id.

of Agenda 21, which called for more integrated, anticipatory, and precautionary approaches to ocean management and governance.[56] The CBD, also adopted at UNCED, was the first instrument to explicitly call on States to incorporate biodiversity conservation goals as a priority into governmental policies and management measures. As the CBD now has 196 States parties, it represents a near universal commitment to conserve and sustain biodiversity wherever it is found. Although the CBD is limited in its applicability to BBNJ,[57] here we explore how CBD provisions can nevertheless inform the substance of new rules, standards, and recommended practices and procedures for the BBNJ agreement with respect to area-based management tools and EIAs in a manner that is consistent with the principles and objectives of UNCLOS.

As a starting point, it is important to note that the CBD Preamble recognizes both the "intrinsic value" of biodiversity as well as the "ecological, genetic, social, economic, scientific, educational, cultural, recreational and aesthetic values of biological diversity and its components, including its importance for evolution and for maintaining life sustaining systems of the biosphere."[58] In affirming that the conservation of biological diversity is a "common concern of humankind," the CBD seeks to bring States and peoples together in common cause to support conservation efforts both within and beyond national jurisdiction.[59] It further underscores the need to value, conserve, and sustain biodiversity, despite often competing short-term economic drivers, if we are to maintain the life-sustaining systems of the biosphere.

The CBD includes a specific reference to its relationship with UNCLOS. Article 22(2) clarifies that the provisions of the CBD with respect to the marine environment should be implemented "consistently with the rights and obligations of States under the law of the sea." Interestingly, Article 22(1) of the CBD also provides that "[t]he provisions of this Convention shall not affect the rights and obligations of any Contracting Party deriving from any existing international agreement, *except where the exercise of those rights and obligations*

---

56 "1992 Agenda 21," Chapter 17.01 in S. Johnson, *The Earth Summit* (London: Kluwer, 1992), p. 307.
57 Although the text in the CBD, n. 14 above, expressly limits application of the Convention's provisions on components of biodiversity to areas *within the limits of national jurisdiction* (Article 4(a)), it nevertheless, in Article 4(b) states that the provisions of the Convention apply "*in the case of processes and activities, regardless of where their effects occur, carried out under its jurisdiction or control,* within the area of its national jurisdiction *or beyond the limits of national jurisdiction*" (emphasis added).
58 Id., preamble.
59 Article 5, id., calls for Contracting Parties to cooperate directly and, where appropriate, through competent international organizations in respect of ABNJ and other matters of mutual interest.

would cause a serious damage or threat to biological diversity" (emphasis added). This suggests that there could indeed be instances where a threat of serious damage to biodiversity could impel immediate action even if such action affected the rights of States under UNCLOS, but this has not been tested. At any rate, many of the CBD provisions that apply to processes and activities under State jurisdiction and control are already applicable to ABNJ, but as with UNCLOS, the new BBNJ agreement may provide a more robust vehicle for their implementation.

In terms of *how* to conserve biodiversity, the CBD starts from the basic observation in its Preamble that "the fundamental requirement for the conservation of biological diversity is the in-situ conservation of ecosystems and natural habitats and the maintenance and recovery of viable populations of species in their natural surroundings."[60] It is more than just the establishment of protected areas and thus requires action across all sectors and regions.

Article 6 of the CBD provides an example of a way to encourage biodiversity action at the sectoral level without affecting existing mandates by calling for parties to take two broad-ranging actions: i) develop national strategies, plans, or programs to reflect the measures set out on the Convention; and ii) "integrate, as far as possible and as appropriate, the conservation and sustainable use of biodiversity into relevant sectoral or cross sectoral plans, programmes and policies."[61] The BBNJ agreement could similarly call for States to adopt national biodiversity strategies that include ways to reduce biodiversity impacts of activities and processes in ABNJ under national jurisdiction and control, and to promote the development of similar sectoral and cross-sectoral plans, programs, and policies.

With respect to area-based management tools, CBD Article 8 on *In-situ Conservation* underscores the need for both MPAs as well as other special measures, including sector-based measures, to conserve biodiversity.[62] Of particular relevance, Article 8 calls for States to, among other things, (a) establish a system of protected areas or areas where special measures need to be taken to conserve biological diversity; (b) develop guidelines for the selection, establishment and management of protected areas or areas where special measures need to be taken to conserve biological diversity; (c) regulate or manage biological resources important for the conservation of biological diversity, whether within or outside protected areas, with a view to ensuring their conservation and sustainable use; (d) promote the protection of ecosystems, natural habitats, and

---

60   Id., preamble.
61   Id., art. 6.
62   Id., art. 8.

the maintenance of viable populations of species in their natural surroundings; and (e) promote environmentally sound and sustainable development in areas adjacent to protected areas with a view to furthering the protection of these areas. All of these measures would usefully support the integration of biodiversity concerns into sectoral activities affecting BBNJ.

With respect to environmental impact assessments, the CBD sets forth a more precautionary threshold and a more explicit obligation to avoid harm than Article 206 of UNCLOS (substantial pollution or significant and harmful changes). Article 14 of the CBD calls for EIAs of proposed projects "that are likely to have significant adverse impacts" on biodiversity, with a view to avoiding or minimizing such effects.[63] The CBD explicitly calls for strategic environmental assessments (SEAS) to ensure that environmental consequences of programs and policies likely to have a significant adverse impact on biodiversity are duly taken into account. SEAS are a concept discussed but not yet embraced in the UN BBNJ discussions that could provide an important regional or ecosystem-level perspective. The CBD extends the UNCLOS obligation for monitoring the risks or effects of pollution (Article 204) to include the proactive identification and ongoing monitoring of any activity or process which has or is likely to have "significant adverse impacts on conservation and sustainable use of biodiversity."[64] Similar provisions in the BBNJ agreement could extend the benefits of EIAs and SEAS far beyond the planning stage.

The CBD Conference of Parties (COP) has already contributed to the scientific and technical basis for action to conserve BBNJ. While recognizing the central role of the UNGA in addressing issues relating to the conservation and sustainable use of marine biodiversity in ABNJ,[65] the CBD COP has developed a scientific process to describe "ecologically or biologically significant marine areas" (EBSAs) and voluntary guidelines for the consideration of marine biodiversity in EIAs and SEAS in ABNJ.[66] To encourage action, CBD COP Decision 10/29 requested States and competent international organizations to consider enhancing EBSA protection and management, including through measures

---

63   Id., art. 14.
64   Id., art. 7.
65   CBD Decision X/29,"Marine and Coastal Biodiversity" (2010), para. 24.
66   CBD, "Marine and Coastal Biodiversity: Revised Voluntary Guidelines for the Consideration of Biodiversity in Environmental Impact Assessments and Strategic Environmental Assessments in Marine and Coastal Areas," Doc. UNEP/CBD/COP/11/23 (21 August 2012). CBD voluntary guidelines for the consideration of biodiversity in environmental impact assessments and strategic environmental assessments annotated specifically for biodiversity in marine and coastal areas, including in areas beyond national jurisdiction, in accordance with Article 4 of the Convention.

such as MPAs and EIAs.⁶⁷ The BBNJ agreement offers an opportunity to build on this important work.

Deeper Commitments and a Timeline for Action: Rio +25

The 25-plus years since Rio have underscored the need for international collaboration and action for BBNJ. Marine biodiversity in ABNJ has been on the international agenda since at least 2002. At the World Summit on Sustainable Development (WSSD), Australia proposed, and WSSD adopted, text calling on the international community to "maintain the productivity and biodiversity of important and vulnerable marine and coastal areas, including in areas within and beyond national jurisdiction."⁶⁸ This call was complemented by a more elaborate call for action at all levels to

> [d]evelop and facilitate the use of diverse approaches and tools, including the ecosystem approach, the elimination of destructive fishing practices, the establishment of marine protected areas consistent with international law and based on scientific information, including representative networks by 2012, time/area closures for the protection of nursery grounds and spawning periods and the integration of marine areas management into key sectors.⁶⁹

The WSSD commitments were reinvigorated at the 2012 United Nations Conference on Sustainable Development (Rio+20), where the Heads of States and Government agreed to commit to "protect the health, productivity and resilience of the marine environment, and to maintain its biodiversity," including through ecosystem approaches and precaution, on behalf of present and future generations.⁷⁰ This commitment was further elaborated on in UN Sustainable

---

67 CBD Decision X/29/, n. 65 above, para. 24.
68 United Nations, "Report of the World Summit on Sustainable Development, Resolution 2, Plan of Implementation of the World Summit on Sustainable Development, Johannesburg, South Africa, 26 August–4 September 2002," (New York: United Nations, 2002), UN Doc. A/Conf.199/20, annex, p. 24, para. 32(a).
69 Id., para. 32(c).
70 UNGA, "The Future We Want," UN Doc. A/RES/66/288 (11 September 2012), para. 158. ("We [the Heads of State and Government and high-level representatives] recognize that oceans, seas and coastal areas form an integrated and essential component of the Earth's ecosystem and are critical to sustaining it, and that international law, as reflected in the United Nations Convention on the Law of the Sea, provides the legal framework for the conservation and sustainable use of the oceans and their resources. We stress the importance of the conservation and sustainable use of the oceans and seas and of their resources for sustainable development, including through their contributions to poverty

Development Goal (SDG) 14, which highlights the conservation and sustainable use of the ocean as one of the world's most pressing global sustainability challenges.[71] Specifically, SDG target 14.2 commits States to "sustainably manage and protect marine and coastal ecosystems to avoid significant adverse impacts, including strengthening their resilience, and take action for their restoration in order to achieve healthy and productive oceans, by 2020." Adoption of a strong BBNJ agreement by 2020 would be an important step to reset the course for ocean health and resilience. How this might be done is what we turn to next.

What Can Be Learned from UNFSA?

Historical Context and Relationship to UNCLOS

As one of two implementing agreements to UNCLOS,[72] the UNFSA provides an illuminating example of crafting a relationship with UNCLOS that respects existing institutions but also significantly advances the status quo. Like the BBNJ agreement, UNFSA was developed in the context of an array of existing institutions as well as many geographic and management gaps.[73] A major concern was "to avoid the development of disparate practices in different subregions or regions" while taking into account the circumstances prevailing in the different regions and the nature of the different fish stocks.[74] As discussed

---

eradication, sustained economic growth, food security and creation of sustainable livelihoods and decent work, while at the same time protecting biodiversity and the marine environment and addressing the impacts of climate change. We therefore commit to protect, and restore, the health, productivity and resilience of oceans and marine ecosystems, to maintain their biodiversity, enabling their conservation and sustainable use for present and future generations, and to effectively apply an ecosystem approach and the precautionary approach in the management, in accordance with international law, of activities having an impact on the marine environment, to deliver on all three dimensions of sustainable development.") This commitment applies to marine areas within and beyond national jurisdiction.

71 UNGA, "Transforming Our World: The 2030 Agenda for Sustainable Development," UN Doc. A/RES/70/1 (21 October 2015), Goal 14: Life Below Water, available online: <http://www.undp.org/content/undp/en/home/sustainable-development-goals/goal-14-life-below-water.html>.

72 The 1994 Part XI Agreement had a different purpose, securing developed country participation in UNCLOS to enable UNCLOS to come into force, and thus is not the subject of this discussion. See n. 11 above.

73 UNGA, "A Guide to the Issues Before the Conference Prepared by the Chairman," UN Doc. A/CONF.164/10 (24 June 1993), para. 13.II(c) [Conference Chairman].

74 Id.

below, the UNFSA built a complex architecture that relies on a mix of general principles, specific obligations giving effect to the duty to cooperate, and detailed guidance for regional management institutions. But whether it went far enough is the subject of debate: while UNFSA succeeded in raising the standards for regional fisheries management, the performance of those organizations has varied widely; fishing effort is still on the rise and the remaining fish stocks are still declining.[75]

It may be helpful to recall the historical context that precipitated the UNFSA. As noted in UNFSA's Preamble: "the management of high seas fisheries is inadequate in many areas and that some resources are overutilized; noting that there are problems of unregulated fishing, over-capitalization, excessive fleet size, vessel reflagging to escape controls, insufficiently selective gear, unreliable databases and lack of sufficient cooperation between States." Responding to strong concerns about ecosystem and biodiversity impacts of fishing activities, the Preamble also reflects that the drafters were: "[c]onscious of the need to avoid adverse impacts on the marine environment, preserve biodiversity, maintain the integrity of marine ecosystems and minimize the risk of long-term or irreversible effects of fishing operations."

The negotiators of UNFSA were charged with filling gaps where there were no management organizations, but also with improving existing management operations. Their goal was to develop practical means to give effect to the provisions of the Convention, including the duty of cooperation, and, in so doing, empower and structure RFMOs as the primary vehicle for effective long-term regional and sub-regional fisheries management, encourage States in existing RFMOs to review their cooperation mechanisms, recognize the aspirations of new entrants, raise the capacity of developing countries globally, and ensure more consistent standards for enforcement.[76]

The relationship of UNFSA to UNCLOS is spelled out in a straightforward way in both UNFSA Article 2 on "the Objective" and Article 4 entitled "Relationship between this agreement and the Convention." Article 2 provides: "The objective of this Agreement is to ensure the long-term conservation and sustainable use of straddling fish stocks and highly migratory fish stocks through effective implementation of the relevant provisions of the Convention." Article 4 provides that "[n]othing in this Agreement shall prejudice the rights, jurisdiction and duties of States under the Convention. This Agreement shall be interpreted and applied in the context of and in a manner consistent with the Convention."

---

75 Gjerde et al., n. 33 above.
76 Conference Chairman, n. 73 above.

Such text acknowledges the legal framework of UNCLOS, recognizing that rights such as freedom of fishing, State jurisdiction over specific zones such as the exclusive economic zone (EEZ) and continental shelf, and duties to conserve, cooperate, and control flag vessels, remain intact.

The final report of the BBNJ PrepCom draws inspiration from Article 4 of UNFSA when suggesting how the new BBNJ agreement could describe its relationship to UNCLOS and other instruments and frameworks and relevant global, regional, and sectoral bodies:

> With regard to the relationship to the Convention, the text would state that nothing in the instrument shall prejudice the rights, jurisdictions and duties of States under the Convention. It would further state that the instrument shall be interpreted and applied in the context of and in a manner consistent with the Convention.[77]

The PrepCom report continues with a suggestion that text on the relationship of the BBNJ agreement to the Convention and other instruments would "promote greater coherence with and complement" existing bodies and instruments.[78]

The "President's Aid to Discussions" circulated by the President of the Intergovernmental Conference (IGC) to guide the discussions during the first IGC session does not suggest any text that could be considered under a section dealing with the BBNJ agreement's relationship to the Convention and other instruments, but it does pose multiple questions, under each of the four package elements, that would lead to possible text that could be considered.[79]

---

77 PrepCom Report, n. 28 above, pp. 8–9.
78 Id.
79 UNGA, "President's Aid to Discussions," First substantive session of the Intergovernmental Conference on an international legally binding instrument under the United Nations Convention on the Law of the Sea on the conservation and sustainable use of marine biological diversity of areas beyond national jurisdiction, UN Doc. A/CONF.232/2018/3 (25 June 2018): The topic "relationship to the Convention and other instruments and frameworks and relevant global, regional and sectoral bodies" appears in every subsection of the President's Aid to Discussion, with questions tailored to that specific element. So, for example, under para. 4.2, which deals with area-based management tools, it says: "(a) The manner in which the instrument would set out the relationship between measures under the instrument and measures under existing relevant legal instruments and frameworks and relevant global, regional and sectoral bodies. (b) The provisions that would be included to address issues of compatibility between measures under the instrument and those established by adjacent coastal States. Would the provisions include, for example, provisions for the sharing of information and/or for consultation? (c) The manner in which the instrument would reflect respect for the rights of coastal States over all areas

States Parties Powers to Adopt Stronger Measures

One of the critical items for negotiators of the BBNJ agreement to determine is where the power to implement area-based management tools, including MPAs, should rest. As further explored below under "Building a Platform for Cooperation for BBNJ ," some argue that management authority should reside solely in RFMOs and other existing sectoral bodies, while others assert the need for more global control noting that States have the inherent power to adopt stronger measures amongst themselves so long as they are not less effective than existing regulations. This inherent power to adopt additional measures or agreements is recognized in Article 44 of UNFSA, which acknowledges that States parties may conclude agreements modifying or suspending operation of provisions of UNFSA under three conditions, and upon notification of other States parties.[80]

According to Article 44, States parties to UNFSA retain the power to take more stringent measures so long as any actions taken thereunder are 1) compatible with the object and purposes of UNFSA and UNCLOS, i.e., support the long-term conservation of fish stocks and the protection of the marine environment, 2) do not affect the application of the basic principles embodied in the Convention or the Agreement, and 3) do not affect the enjoyment by other States parties of their rights or performance of their obligations. Article 44 of UNFSA may thus provide a helpful model for the BBNJ agreement as it reflects the inherent powers of States under international law to take actions among themselves that may be more stringent than those made by other organizations or pursuant to other agreements without undermining existing agreements or bodies. Such a provision would not replace RFMOs or other sectoral organizations but would enable States parties to the BBNJ agreement to take more rapid and direct action while they seek to promote comparable measures

---

under their national jurisdiction, including the continental shelf within and beyond 200 nautical miles and the exclusive economic zone."

80   Article 44(1) provides that "this Agreement shall not alter the rights and obligations of States Parties which arise from other agreements compatible with this Agreement and which do not affect the enjoyment by other States Parties of their rights or the performance of their obligations under this Agreement;" Article 44(2) provides that "[t]wo or more States Parties may conclude agreements modifying or suspending the operation of provisions of this Agreement, applicable solely to the relations between them, provided that such agreements do not relate to a provision derogation from which is incompatible with the effective execution of the object and purpose of this Agreement, and provided further that such agreements shall not affect the application of the basic principles embodied herein, and that the provisions of such agreements do not affect the enjoyment by other States Parties of their rights or the performance of their obligations under this Agreement."

through the relevant sectoral organizations and enable States parties to take coherent measures across sectors and regions.

Application of the Term "Undermine"

UNFSA can also provide guidance to those seeking to understand the term "not undermine" in the context of BBNJ. The use of the term "undermine" in UNFSA is applied in the very limited context of "undermine the effectiveness of" (see Table 1.2). In other words, UNFSA uses the term "undermine" to mean to undercut or make less effective.

UNFSA also envisages that States may adopt global conservation and management measures in addition to regional measures, which suggests that conservation measures would be adopted by organizations other than the (regional) RFMOs without undermining them. For example, Article 20(4) of UNFSA calls for States to assist each other in reporting on vessels engaged in undermining the effectiveness of global as well as subregional and regional conservation and management measures. In fact, there are positive ways to refer to "not undermine" that could assist in the enforcement of regional measures at the global level, as well as any measures adopted pursuant to the BBNJ agreement. Article 33(2), for example, which refers to measures with respect to non-parties to the agreement, calls for States parties to take measures consistent with UNFSA and international law to "deter the activities of vessels flying the flag of non-parties which undermine the effective implementation of this Agreement," a reference to measures that would be less effective in managing and conserving relevant fish stocks and associated species and ecosystems. A similar provision in the BBNJ agreement could provide clarity on enforcement.

Influencing Existing Organizations without Undermining Them

UNFSA also helps to address the question of how the new agreement can influence the way existing organizations operate without "undermining" them. There are six key ways that UNFSA elaborates on the duty of cooperation:

1. General Principles to Give Effect to the Duty to Cooperate

Article 5 articulates general principles through which States are to give effect to their duty to cooperate. The first of a long list of principles gives effect to the central objective of the Agreement: "(a) adopt measures to ensure long-term sustainability of straddling fish stocks and highly migratory fish stocks." But Article 5 also elaborates on other elements that are to be "ensured," "applied," and "assessed" and measures "adopted" for other species at the same time. The degree of specificity varies greatly, from the very general: "protect biodiversity in the marine environment," in Article 5(g), to the very specific and operational:

TABLE 1.2   "Undermine" in the UN Fish Stocks Agreement

Article	Summary/Excerpt of Provision
Article 7(2)(a)	States shall ensure that conservation measures for straddling fish stocks in the high seas "do not *undermine* the effectiveness" of measures adopted for the same stocks within a coastal State's EEZ.
Article 16(2)	"States concerned shall take measures in respect of vessels flying their flag in order that they not engage in fisheries which could *undermine* the stocks concerned."
Article 17(4)	States "shall take measures consistent with this Agreement and international law to deter activities of such vessels which *undermine* the effectiveness of subregional or regional conservation and management measures."
Article 18(1)	Flag States shall "take such measures as may be necessary to ensure that vessels flying its flag comply with subregional and regional conservation and management measures and that such vessels do not engage in any activity which undermines the effectiveness of such measures."
Article 18(3)(h)	Flag States shall take measures in respect to vessels flying its flag to regulate "transshipment on the high seas to ensure that the effectiveness of conservation and management measures is not *undermined*."
Article 20(4)	"States shall assist each other in identifying vessels reported to have engaged in activities *undermining* the effectiveness of subregional, regional or global conservation and management measures."
Article 20(7)	RFMO member States may take action "to deter vessels which have engaged in activities which undermine the effectiveness of or otherwise violate the conservation and management measures established by that organization."
Article 23(3)	"States may adopt regulations empowering the relevant national authorities to prohibit landings and transshipments where it has been established that the catch has been taken in a manner which *undermines* the effectiveness of subregional, regional or global conservation and management measures on the high seas."
Article 33(2)	"States Parties shall take measures consistent with this Agreement and international law to deter the activities of vessels flying the flag of non-Parties which *undermine* the effective implementation of this Agreement."

"adopt, where necessary, conservation and management measures for species belonging to the same ecosystem or associated with or dependent upon the target stocks, with a view to maintaining or restoring populations of such species above levels at which their reproduction may become seriously threatened" in Article 5(e). Mechanisms to apply the precautionary approach, as called for in Article 5(c) are specifically articulated in Article 6 of UNFSA and an entire annex (Annex II). In many ways the BBNJ agreement could build on such a model to reflect modern principles, with more specific articles and annexes articulating requirements and guidelines. It could simultaneously address a clear gap in UNFSA which is how States parties are to give effect to the general principle in UNFSA of protecting biodiversity in the marine environment and make it applicable across all sectors and regions. This gap filling could be accomplished, for instance, by building on Article 6 of the CBD (integration via, for example, sectoral, cross-sectoral/regional biodiversity strategies and action plans) and Article 8 (in-situ conservation of nature) described above.

2. Requirements for Applying an Ecosystem Approach

UNFSA sets out the basic requirements for an ecosystem approach in Article 5, which includes, among other things, a) assessing the impacts of fishing, other human activities, and environmental factors; b) adopting where necessary measures for species belonging to the same ecosystem or associated with or dependent upon the target stocks; c) minimizing pollution, waste, discards, and other fishing impacts through measures including the development and use of selective, environmentally safe, and cost-effective fishing gear and techniques; and d) protecting biodiversity in the marine environment. Similar requirements for applying an ecosystem approach that would be applicable to other (including sectoral) organizations could also be included in the new BBNJ agreement.

3. Requirements for Applying a Precautionary Approach

In Article 5(c), UNFSA identifies the precautionary approach as a general principle that should be applied and then elaborates on this directive in Article 6 ("Application of the precautionary approach") as well as Annex II ("Guidelines for the Application of Precautionary Reference Points in Conservation and Management of Straddling Fish Stocks and Highly Migratory Fish Stocks"). Article 6 clarifies that implementing the precautionary approach means that "States shall be more cautious when information is uncertain, unreliable or inadequate. The absence of adequate scientific information shall not be used as a reason for postponing or failing to take conservation and management measures." These provisions could provide guidance on how the precautionary approach could be incorporated in the BBNJ agreement.

In addition, Article 6 of UNFSA provides that States should adopt "cautious conservation and management measures" for new or exploratory fisheries, which should apply until an assessment of the impact of that fishery can be adequately determined.[81] The final paragraph of Article 6 details provisions for adopting emergency conservation and management measures if "a natural phenomenon has a significant adverse effect" on that stock. These two paragraphs of Article 6 could serve as a basis for the BBNJ Agreement's consideration of conservation and management measures that should be taken for new activities as well as in response to natural phenomena that have a significant adverse impact on the marine environment.

4. Requirements for a Science-based Approach

UNFSA sets out specific requirements for obtaining the scientific evidence needed upon which to base decisions. In addition to "assess the impacts of fishing," UNFSA Article 5 calls for coastal States and States fishing on the high seas to collect and share, in a timely manner, complete and accurate data concerning fishing activities, to promote and conduct scientific research, and to develop appropriate technologies in support of fishery conservation and management. Article 14 specifically obliges States to "ensure that fishing vessels flying their flag provide such information as may be necessary in order to fulfill their obligations under this Agreement." Article 14 further requires States to undertake their obligation in accordance with Annex I, which sets forth further requirements for data collection and sharing. Of special note is Article 14(3)'s specific reference to, and elaboration of, another vague obligation under UNCLOS for cooperation in strengthening scientific research capacity for the benefit of all.[82]

---

81 After such an assessment has been conducted, "conservation and management measures based on that assessment shall be implemented."

82 UNFSA, n. 11 above, Article 14(3) provides: "Consistent with Part XIII of the Convention, States shall cooperate, either directly or through competent international organizations, to *strengthen scientific research capacity* in the field of fisheries and promote scientific research related to the conservation and management of straddling fish stocks and highly migratory fish stocks *for the benefit of all*. To this end, a State or the competent international organization conducting such research beyond areas under national jurisdiction shall actively promote the publication and dissemination to any interested States of the results of that research and information relating to its objectives and methods and, to the extent practicable, shall facilitate the participation of scientists from those States in such research" (emphasis added).

The BBNJ agreement could adopt similar measures, including through an annex, to elaborate on the duty to cooperate in scientific research (UNCLOS, Article 242), including through competent international organizations, to elaborate on the duty to publish and share data (UNCLOS, Article 244), and to give effect to Article 202 of UNCLOS, "Scientific and technical assistance to developing States," to enable protection and preservation of the marine environment.

5. Mechanisms for International Cooperation

UNFSA focuses an entire part, Part III, on "Mechanisms for international cooperation concerning straddling fish stocks and highly migratory fish stocks." Article 8 sets out (a) the duty to pursue cooperation either directly or through RFMOs, b) the duty to pursue effective conservation and management, and (c) the duty to become members/participants of the relevant RFMOs or to agree to apply the measures adopted by the relevant RFMOs. UNFSA thus establishes an obligation to act in good faith to pursue effective outcomes both directly and through RFMOs. The BBNJ agreement could do the same.

Also of relevance to BBNJ, Article 8(6) establishes a duty to consult when a proposed action by one organization with competence over living resources proposes a measure that would have a "significant effect" on conservation and management measures already established by an RFMO. To the extent practicable, such consultation "should" take place prior to the submission of the proposal to the intergovernmental organization.

Articles 8–12 of Part III further spell out the functions of RFMOs, how RFMOs should conduct their decision-making process and other activities (e.g., by providing for transparency), and directs States to cooperate to strengthen existing RFMOs in order to improve their effectiveness in establishing and implementing conservation and management measures for straddling fish stocks and highly migratory fish stocks. The BBNJ agreement could build on this UNFSA example to encourage States to cooperate to strengthen existing organizations, to join and act in good faith in any relevant existing or new organizations, and to consult in the case of overlapping competencies with respect to measures that may have a significant effect on the other.

6. Compatibility

UNFSA sets out, in Article 7, provisions for ensuring compatibility of conservation and management measures for living marine resources in areas under national jurisdiction and the high seas. This article outlines a complex allocation of roles and responsibilities of coastal States and distant water fishing States to ensure that measures established for stocks in the high seas do not undermine the effectiveness of conservation and management measures taken by the other. Notably in Article 7(3), UNFSA prescribes a duty to exercise best efforts to achieve results, by providing that "in giving effect to their duty to cooperate, States shall make every effort to agree on compatible conservation and management measures within a reasonable period of time" with an option for dispute resolution proceedings.

Additionally, UNFSA sets out requirements to enable and facilitate the establishment of compatible conservation and management measures across boundaries. For example, Article 7 paragraphs 7 and 8 establish the duty of States to exchange information on measures adopted. Articles 24–26 recognize and support the special requirements of developing States. Having informed, resourced, and well-equipped States will also be critical to ensuring coordinated and compatible efforts for marine biodiversity and ecosystems that transcend national boundaries. Similar provisions in the BBNJ agreement could address at least some of the concerns of adjacent States and developing States as a whole and help boost the capability to conserve and manage straddling ecosystems and highly migratory (non-target) species.[83]

Through these six mechanisms, UNFSA developed practical means to give effect to the provisions of UNCLOS, including the duty of cooperation, as a way to create common practices across different regions while taking into account regional differences.[84] For the BBNJ agreement, there will be a need for a similar central core of consistent obligations and action, while allowing for varying regional and developmental conditions.

Challenges and Lessons Learned from UNFSA
Incomplete Progress towards an Ecosystem Approach
Notwithstanding its many progressive elements to implement and evolve UNCLOS, UNFSA has not resolved all issues and provides examples of some hard lessons learned. Despite some significant successes, particularly with respect to target species, continuing challenges highlighted at the recent round

---

83 D.C. Dunn et al., "Adjacency: How Legal Precedent, Ecological Connectivity, and traditional Knowledge Inform Our Understanding of Proximity," Nereus Scientific and Technical Brief (4 April 2017), available online: <http://archives.nereusprogram.org/wp-content/uploads/2017/04/BBNJ-Policy-brief-adjacency_v5.pdf>; A. Oude Elferink, "Coastal States and MPAs in ABNJ: Ensuring consistency with the LOSC," *The International Journal of Marine and Coastal Law* 33 (2018): 1–30.

84 UNFSA, n. 11 above, art. 8.

of Informal Consultations for UNFSA[85] relevant to biodiversity conservation include inconsistent performance of RFMOs, lack of accountability, lack of capacity and funding, and mixed priorities.[86] Of particular concern for BBNJ is the inconsistent and often incomplete progress towards an ecosystem approach to fisheries that should address bycatch, pelagic habitats, and ecosystem-level impacts in an operational way; this is perceived to be particularly an issue for tuna RFMOs, which have traditionally approached fisheries management species-by-species, as opposed to on an ecosystem level.[87] During the 2018 Informal Consultation, which focused on science-policy interfaces, delegates highlighted the role of scientific research to inform policy and implement the ecosystem approach, precautionary approach, and integrated approach. Several challenges were identified in "making fisheries management decisions based on the best scientific advice available" including lack of capacity, cost, ineffective communication between stakeholders, lack of data specifically tailored to the needs of policy-makers, individual challenges faced by RFMOs,[88] the often slow development of national legal frameworks, including with respect to data collection,[89] and the depleted state of funds in the Assistance Fund under Part VII of the Agreement.[90] Indeed, it was noted that not all States were in a position to fully implement even minimum standards under international instruments,[91] which should be of significant concern to all States. Regional cooperation was recognized as a key way of overcoming capacity gaps[92] and the role of the UN's Food and Agriculture Organization (FAO) in providing assistance was also noted.

Relevance for BBNJ

The lack of progress towards ecosystem-based fisheries management (EBFM) is a significant concern for all States with an interest in marine biodiversity in ABNJ. As noted in a recent paper prepared for the International Commission

---

85 United Nations, "Draft Report," Thirteenth round of Informal Consultations of States Parties to the Agreement for the Implementation of the Provisions of the United Nations Convention on the Law of the Sea of 10 December 1982 relating to the Conservation and Management of Straddling Fish Stocks and Highly Migratory Fish Stocks (New York, 22–23 May 2018) UN Doc. ICSP13/UNFSA/DraftINF.2 (15 June 2018) [UNFSA informal consultation].
86 Id.
87 M.J. Juan Jordá et al., "Report card on ecosystem-based fisheries management in tuna regional fisheries management organizations," *Fish and Fisheries* 19(2) (2018): 321–339.
88 UNFSA informal consultation, n. 85 above, para. 23.
89 Id., para. 24.
90 Id., para. 25.
91 Id., para. 32.
92 Id., para. 24.

for the Conservation of Atlantic Tunas (ICCAT) on behalf of the Sargasso Sea Commission,

> [t]he reason for moving towards EBFM is because fisheries are dependent on the productivity of the ecosystem, and in turn fisheries have an effect on and are affected by the ecosystem. ... It is entirely possible that a fishery could be considered not to be overfished in a single-species context but overfished within the ecosystem, for example when overfishing of large predators causes food web shifts.[93]

The Sargasso Sea report cites Garcia in the FAO Fisheries Atlas section on "Basic Principles of Ecosystem Management" which underscores the importance of EBFM but also some of the obstacles:

> The overarching principles of ecosystem-based management of fisheries ... aim to ensure that, despite variability, uncertainty and likely natural changes in the ecosystem, the capacity of the aquatic ecosystems to produce food, revenues, employment and, more generally, other essential services and livelihood, is maintained indefinitely for the benefit of the present and future generations ... to cater both for human as well as ecosystem well-being. *This implies conservation of ecosystem structures, processes and interactions through sustainable use. This implies consideration of a range of frequently conflicting objectives and the needed consensus may not be achievable without equitable distribution of benefits.*[94] (emphasis added)

Need for a Long-term Strategy for Ecosystem-based Management Achievement of ecosystem-based management, as noted by Garcia above, requires choices in an arena of conflicting objectives where it is frequently difficult to obtain the needed consensus. Nearly 25 years after UNFSA was adopted, the need to effectively implement the ecosystem approach remains a key topic in the tuna-RFMOs regular performance reviews. Another recent study found that

---

93 L.T. Kell and B.E. Luckhurst, "Extending the Indicator-based Ecosystem Report Card to the Whole Ecosystem: A Preliminary Example based on the Sargasso Sea," ICCAT Doc. SCRS/2018/067, *ICCAT Collective Volume of Scientific Papers* 75, no. 2 (2018): 285–275 citing M. Sinclair and G. Valdimarsson, eds., *Responsible Fisheries in the Marine Ecosystem* (Rome: FAO and Wallingford, UK: CABI Publishing, 2003), p. 261.

94 S.M. Garcia, *The Ecosystem Approach to Fisheries: Issues, Terminology, Principles, Institutional Foundations, Implementation and Outlook*, FAO Fisheries Technical Paper No. 443 (Rome: FAO, 2003).

[m]any of the elements necessary for an operational EBFM are already present, yet they have been implemented in an *ad hoc* way, without a long-term vision and a formalized plan.... The [tuna RFMOs][95] appear to be halfway towards implementing the ecological component of EBFM, yet it is clear that the "low-hanging fruit" has been plucked and the more difficult, but surmountable, issues remain, notably the sustainable management of bycatch. All [tuna RFMOs] share the same challenge of developing a formal mechanism to better integrate ecosystem science and advice into management decisions.[96]

The Informal Consultations confirmed that data collection, scientific research, and monitoring remain among key unfilled priorities within RFMOs, which are all necessary ingredients to enable science-based policy, including EBFM.[97] As is explored immediately below, one of the major challenges to effective implementation of UNFSA and thus the achievement of sustainable fisheries is the lack of a central institutional mechanism capable of reviewing performance and adopting timely measures when needed to improve implementation and performance at the State and regional levels.

So, noting the challenges in implementing UNFSA, many of which may be shared by other sectoral organizations, we can also learn lessons for the BBNJ agreement and identify ways that, through the BBNJ agreement, States could be better able to fulfill their rights and obligations under UNCLOS, and in so doing, potentially help to implement UNFSA.

Building a Platform for Cooperation for BBNJ

Importance of Institutional Mechanisms for Cooperation

The previous sections have described the need for giving further *substantive* weight to the provisions of UNCLOS with respect to the duty to cooperate to protect and preserve the marine environment, what such substantive provisions could contain, based on the provisions of the CBD, and how this might be done, by building on the example of UNFSA. This section seeks to elaborate on how the BBNJ agreement can give greater *procedural* weight to the duty to cooperate through the specification of institutional mechanisms at the global

---

95   RFMOs with the competence over tuna and other migratory species are often referred to as t-RFMOs.
96   Juan Jordá et al., n. 87 above, abstract.
97   UNFSA informal consultation, n. 85 above, para. 32.

and regional levels, based on the lessons learned from existing environmental agreements and regional initiatives.[98]

As observed by Tanaka, the specification of institutional mechanisms can enhance the implementation of the duty to cooperate by allocating responsibilities for getting a job done and through international supervision:

> Considering that international co-operation is essential to advance the integrated management approach, institutionalised mechanisms for ensuring such cooperation, such as an international supervision through international institutions, become particularly important.[99]

One of the lessons of relevance to the BBNJ agreement negotiators is that at least some of UNFSA's shortcomings may be attributed to its lack of a global-level institutional mechanism with sufficient supervisory powers to "prevent disparate practices in different subregions or regions" from emerging. As noted by Young and Friedman, the "ad hoc arrangements for coordination" adopted in UNFSA "encourages states to apply guiding principles and approaches within existing bodies without engaging in systematic or binding norm development. Attempts to develop a coherent set of practices through processes such as the joint meetings of the five tuna RFMOs initiated in Kobe, Japan, in 2007, have not progressed."[100] The new agreement can enhance implementation by providing a venue for "interregime learning and cooperation."[101]

Similar lessons were learned from early wildlife treaties that proved relatively ineffectual because, among other things, none of them established a system of administration to monitor and oversee their enforcement.[102] Some, like the Convention on Nature Protection and Wildlife Preservation in the Western Hemisphere (Western Hemisphere Convention), became known as "sleeping treaties" that had been allowed to drift from the forefront of their parties attention and, in consequence, failed to have as much practical impact as they would have had if given the proper encouragement.[103] Submission of regular

---

98　Tanaka, n. 44 above, p. 24.
99　Id.; see also Harden-Davies and Gjerde, n. 13 above.
100　M.A. Young and A. Friedman, "Biodiversity beyond national jurisdiction: Regimes and their interaction," *AJIL Unbound* 112 (2018): 123–128, p. 128, DOI: 10.1017/aju.2018.47.
101　Id., p. 126.
102　S. Lyster and H.R.H. Prince Philip, *International Wildlife Law: An Analysis of International Treaties Concerned with the Conservation of Wildlife* (Cambridge: Cambridge University Press, 1985), p. 301.
103　Convention on Nature Protection and Wildlife Preservation in the Western Hemisphere, 12 October 1940, entered into force 1 May 1942, OAS Treaties Series, No. 31; 161 *United Nations Treaty Series* 193.

reports and regular meetings of parties to review implementation and make recommendations can avoid sleeping treaties. According to Lyster:

> The treaties which have achieved the greatest level of compliance are, by and large, those which keep their Parties active, have a central administrative body to oversee enforcement and have some means of chastising Parties which do not comply with their treaty obligations ... just by requiring its Parties to meet regularly to review its implementation, a treaty can ensure that it stays on the foremost of its Parties attention.[104]

If it is to achieve its full potential, maintain its relevance, and carry out the principles and obligations described above, the new agreement would accordingly need to adopt institutional mechanisms that include at least four key elements: a central administrative body, a science-policy advisory mechanism or body, regular review of implementation, and power to adopt binding decisions.

Implications for Institutional Arrangements for the BBNJ Agreement

With respect to institutional arrangements, there was general consensus at the PrepCom that there needed to be at least three core bodies established by the BBNJ agreement: a decision-making body, a scientific and/or technical body, and a secretariat.[105] Of course, additional subsidiary bodies could be established (which could focus on, for example, monitoring compliance or overseeing financial components) and, indeed, may be necessary in order to best carry out the objectives of the agreement. This article focuses only on the three core bodies, mentioned above, which were included in the PrepCom report.

Three Potential Models: Regional, Hybrid, and Global

The delegates' vision for the specific functions that each of these bodies could undertake varied a great deal and is inextricably related to the scale at which States believe the new BBNJ agreement should operate. There were generally three models that States used to describe the operational scale for the new BBNJ agreement: global, hybrid, and regional. It should be noted that there was no single definition for these three models; they are perhaps best understood as existing along a spectrum of options. On one end of the spectrum, an extreme "regional model" could be envisaged with the BBNJ agreement being carried out exclusively by existing sectoral and/or regional institutions (to include regional sectoral bodies and global sectoral bodies); under this regional

---

104 Lyster and H.R.H., n. 102 above, p. 301.
105 PrepCom Report, n. 28 above, pp. 16–17.

model, the institutional needs would be minimal. Parties to the agreement might have regular meetings to report on their progress towards implementing the BBNJ agreement, but there would be no need for a decision-making body or a scientific body to carry out the agreement. With this in mind, the regional model can effectively be viewed as the status quo of ocean governance, with perhaps some additional, broad guidance provided by the new BBNJ agreement.[106]

On the other end of the spectrum of institutional arrangements, the "global model" could be envisaged as the creation of a new body which could more actively and directly carry out the objectives of the new BBNJ agreement. Global model proponents support the establishment of, at a minimum, the three core bodies (decision-making body, scientific/technical body, and secretariat), and it is envisioned that the decision-making body would be empowered to take decisions that are both specific and binding upon its parties.[107] Many proponents of the global model specifically advocate that the new BBNJ agreement should empower the new BBNJ body to establish high seas MPAS and approve EIAS: this would require not only a decision-making body, but also a robust scientific committee capable of reviewing MPA and EIA proposals and a secretariat that could help to coordinate the consultation process.[108]

Somewhere in the middle of this spectrum lies the hybrid approach. Many delegates during the PrepCom advocated for the adoption of a hybrid approach – a model of institutional arrangements that would advance ocean governance more than the status quo regional approach, but would fall short of the centralized global-level decision-making powers envisioned under the global approach, at least for certain issues such as ABMTs other than MPAs.[109]

---

106 The Pew Charitable Trusts, "Towards a Global Solution for High Seas Conservation," Fact Sheet (March 2017), available online: <http://www.pewtrusts.org/-/media/assets/2017/03/highseas_towards_a_global_solution_for_high_seas_conservation.pdf>.

107 A. Friedman et al., "Protecting marine biodiversity in areas beyond national jurisdiction: Institutional considerations for a new international agreement under the United Nations Convention on Law of the Sea," in *The Law of the Sea and Emerging Issues*, eds., G.(J.) Xue and J. Zheng (Shanghai: China Democracy and Legal System Publishing House, 2018).

108 See, e.g., "Costa Rica and Monaco joint submission on marine protected areas" (31 August 2016) submitted in response to a letter from the Chair of the PrepCom dated 18 December 2015 inviting delegates to submit their views on the elements of a draft text on an international legally binding instrument under UNCLOS, available online: <http://www.un.org/depts/los/biodiversity/prepcom_files/Costa_Rica_Monaco_BBNJ_Submission_MPAs.pdf>.

109 See, e.g., IISD Reporting Services, "Summary of the Third Session of the Preparatory Committee on Marine Biodiversity Beyond Areas of National Jurisdiction: 27 March–7 April,"

While there was a divergence of views with respect to the precise functions and duties the BBNJ agreement would establish under the hybrid model, there was general agreement that it would require a decision-making body, a scientific/technical body, and a secretariat.[110]

Mapping States' positions on institutional arrangements for the new BBNJ agreement can be challenging, even with the understanding that there is a spectrum of options. An excellent example of this challenge can be found in the submission on behalf of the Pacific Small Island Developing States (PSIDS) to the PrepCom.[111] The PSIDS' position on institutional arrangements, at least during the PrepCom, envisioned a "comprehensive global regime to better address the conservation and sustainable use of BBNJ," supported by a global-level decision-making body, a secretariat, a scientific and technical body, a compliance committee, and a finance and administration committee.[112] At the same time, the PSIDS' submission provides for a strong regional component and envisions that regional bodies would play a critical role in implementing the new BBNJ Agreement.[113] This highlights an important observation; that regional-level and global-level institutional arrangements are not mutually exclusive and could, in fact, complement one another.

Strengthening – Not Undermining – Existing Organizations

One consideration that may influence institutional choices is the provision in Resolutions 69/292 and 72/249 that this "process and its result should not undermine existing relevant legal instruments and frameworks and relevant global, regional and sectoral bodies."[114] However, as some have suggested, the phrase "not undermine" was seemingly chosen for its political malleability – there can be general agreement that the new instrument should not undermine existing ones, without a precise understanding of exactly what it means to not undermine, or, perhaps more exactly, what would constitute undermining one

---

Earth Negotiations Bulletin 25, no. 129 (10 April 2017), available online: <http://enb.iisd.org/download/pdf/enb25129e.pdf>.

110 PrepCom Report, n. 28 above, pp. 15–16.
111 "PSIDS Submission on Institutional Arrangements" (5 December 2016) submitted in response to the Chair's invitation made at the second session of the PrepCom, as reflected in para. 11 of his overview of the second session of the PrepCom, available online: <http://www.un.org/depts/los/biodiversity/prepcom_files/streamlined/PSIDS_Submission_dec_2016.pdf>.
112 Id.
113 Id.
114 72/249, n. 10 above, para. 7.

of these organizations.[115] For the new agreement to achieve its stated goal of conserving and sustainably using marine biological diversity of areas beyond national jurisdiction, it must improve upon the status quo; it is clear that the meaning of the term "not undermine" should be interpreted in a way that advances that aim.

Indeed, rather than seeking to exclude particular sectors or otherwise viewing the new instrument through a negative lens, the focus could be on how the new BBNJ agreement can enable, facilitate, and even strengthen existing global, regional, and sectoral bodies and instruments in fulfilling their responsibilities under UNCLOS to protect and preserve the marine environment. In addition to mainstreaming core biodiversity, ecosystem, and precautionary concepts into the functions of sectoral organizations and enabling national and regional capacities to do the same, it becomes clear that improved processes for consultation and cooperation are needed. In particular, these cooperative and consultative processes are critical to ensure that marine biodiversity and ecosystems are not degraded by the actions of any one sector or regional institutions and that existing instruments are not undermined, either by each other or by factors such as illegal, unreported, or unregulated fishing or other unmanaged/uncontrolled activities.

A Common Platform for Conservation
Enabling Ecosystem-based Management as a Shared Goal
A central organizing theme for enhancing cooperation and coordination could be ecosystem-based management, based on science and the precautionary principle, for the purposes of conserving and sustaining marine biodiversity and its components of genes, species, habitats, and ecosystems. The medium for cooperation, in addition to consultations and exchange of information at annual conferences of parties, could be the development of sectoral as well as cross-sectoral, regionally-based biodiversity strategies and action plans. Such biodiversity strategies and action plans could build upon Article 6 of the CBD and be based on the general principles as agreed in Article 5 of UNFSA to a) assess the impacts of the specific sectoral activity, other human activities, and environmental factors, b) adopt, where necessary, measures for protecting affected species, habitats and ecosystems, c) minimize pollution, waste, discards,

---

115 Z. Scanlon, "The art of 'not undermining': Possibilities within existing architecture to improve environmental protections in areas beyond national jurisdiction," *ICES Journal of Marine Science* (2017), DOI: 10.1093/icesjms/fsx209. Discussion on the interpretation of "not undermining" can be found above under "Application of the Term 'Undermine.'"

and other impacts through measures including area-based management tools, and d) protect biodiversity in the marine environment.

States have indicated their desire to create a BBNJ agreement that does just that – there was general consensus during the PrepCom that both the ecosystem and the precautionary approach could be included as "General principles and approaches" in the new agreement.[116] This section concludes with a look ahead to key considerations for the institutional framework.

Roles for a Global Institution

In considering the type of institutional mechanisms, it has often been said that "form follows function." Hence it may be helpful to explore what some of the values and functions a global institution might provide compared to what is presently possible. A BBNJ agreement could establish an ongoing system of governance, both by providing guidance to existing institutions and by creating new ones, defining their powers and decision-making rules, establishing procedures to adopt and amend substantive rules, and providing methods to resolve disputes. An important benefit would be to enable States to address issues in a purposive, rational manner rather than an *ad hoc,* patchwork approach. A regular meeting or conference of the parties could overcome the obstacles to cooperation that currently inhibit a more integrated and coherent approach to management. Such meetings of parties could promote reciprocal implementation by allowing States to delineate precisely what each party is expected to do, provide clarity on applicable norms, and encourage all countries to cooperate so efforts by one country are not undermined by another. Such functions can build trust, improve knowledge, reduce misperceptions, and increase legitimacy.[117]

Such a decision-making body could, for example, be given a leading role in designating MPAs, considering EIAs, and reviewing reports to assess progress. It could also provide guidance to States parties with respect to rules, standards, and recommended practices and procedures for sectoral ABMTs, strategic environmental assessments, and broader-scale regional planning and integrated management initiatives. This conference or meeting of parties could play a key coordinating role by ensuring prior notification, consultation, transparency, participation, and inclusive planning. It could also help to bring in the goals and priorities of other conservation agreements and bodies, such as CITES,

---

116   PrepCom Report, n. 28 above, p. 9.
117   Gjerde, n. 9 above, p. 379. Inspiration for this analysis comes from D. Bodansky, *The Art and Craft of International Environmental Law* (Cambridge, MA: Harvard University Press, 2010), pp. 136–153.

CBD, and CMS and related agreements, in order to enhance their effectiveness and ensure that their efforts are not undermined by activities managed by neighboring or overlapping sectoral organizations, and ensure that sectoral and regional area-based conservation measures adopted pursuant to the BBNJ agreement are respected globally.

Strengthening Regional and Sectoral Outcomes

A review of the experience of the Sargasso Sea Project may help to illustrate the value of such a global approach for strengthening the current regional/sectoral approach.[118] Currently, there are just a handful of international organizations in the Sargasso Sea with some sectoral management competence: two RFMOs, one advisory fisheries body, the IMO and the ISA.[119] None of these organizations focus on comprehensive conservation of marine biodiversity or ecosystems. Each institution focuses on its respective sector with little or no reference to the work of other sectoral bodies or neighboring regional bodies. The nearest Regional Seas Programme, which covers the Wider Caribbean Region, does not reach as far north as Bermuda, the heart of the Sargasso Sea, or extend to ABNJ. There is thus no mechanism for coordinating between the various sectors to ensure the conservation of important habitats and ecosystems. One sector's failure to recognize the work of another is an unfortunate example of how the fractured sectoral approach appears to be undermining efforts to use the precautionary principle and protect areas of significant biodiversity.[120] The region, like most others, also lacks a mechanism to consider cumulative impacts from different sectors and the aggravating factor of climate change.[121]

In response to the limited mechanisms and capacities of sectoral institutions, the Sargasso Sea Project was launched as an *ad hoc* initiative to bring key governments and other stakeholders together. The Project's goal was to collectively pursue those measures that could be taken to more comprehensively

---

118   Freestone, n. 43 above; Friedman et al., n. 107 above; K. Gjerde, O. Varmer and K. Liljestrand, "The Sargasso Sea: An innovative approach to governance in areas beyond national jurisdiction," in *Frontiers in International Environmental Law: Oceans and Climate Challenges. Essays in Honour of David Freestone* (Leiden: Brill, in review); D. Freestone, "The Sargasso Sea Alliance: Working to protect the 'Golden Floating Rain Forest of the Ocean,'" *Environmental Policy and Law* 44 (2014): 151–158.
119   Those RFMOs are the International Commission for the Conservation of Atlantic Tunas and the Northwest Atlantic Fisheries Organization; the advisory fisheries body is the Western Central Atlantic Fishery Commission.
120   Gjerde et al., n. 118 above.
121   Id.; Freestone, n. 118 above.

conserve this ecologically and biologically important area and to shine a light on the obstacles to progress. The results have copiously demonstrated the need for a global level agreement to address the reluctance of some States in some fora to embrace proactive conservation measures, despite calls for the application of the best available science and the adoption of a precautionary approach/principle in most modern international legal instruments and declarations.[122] The new agreement could facilitate cooperation and coordination to enable ecosystem-based management at a regional level by establishing or designating regional coordinating bodies while ensuring strong global support.

Conclusion

The current single-sector approach to governing the global ocean commons has presented significant challenges and, ultimately, has failed to uphold one of the central requirements of UNCLOS – to protect and preserve the marine environment. States have responded to the multitude of growing pressures that threaten the vitality of marine ecosystems by calling for a comprehensive regime to better address BBNJ conservation and sustainable use. The development of the BBNJ agreement is a once-in-a-generation opportunity to address these governance challenges and affect positive change, not only for the marine environment, but also for the States and people who depend upon the ocean.

Gaps in implementation have arisen because UNCLOS sets a framework that specifies but does not elaborate States' duties to protect and preserve to protect the marine environment. Post-UNCLOS innovations have elaborated on the duty to cooperate to include a broader concept of the marine environment – the wealth and diversity of genes, species, habitats, and ecosystems that inhabit it – and recognized both the intrinsic value of this biodiversity as well as its role in supporting essential ecosystem services that sustain life on earth. This broader concept requires a more integrated and coherent approach to management that can account for the full range of activities and effects on the marine environment. The BBNJ agreement thus provides the opportunity to articulate how States are to give effect to the duty to protect and preserve the marine environment including its biodiversity and associated ecosystems and to advance the integrated cross-sectoral institutional mechanisms needed to ensure its implementation.

---

122   Freestone, id.

To achieve this, States will need to adopt more specific global rules and standards, and recommended practices and procedures as envisaged in Article 197, and to elaborate the requirements for effective institutional mechanisms at the global and regional levels. The BBNJ agreement could draw inspiration from, for example, Article 6 of the CBD (integration via, for example, sectoral, cross-sectoral/regional biodiversity strategies and action plans) and Article 8 (in-situ conservation of nature) (see "Building on UNCLOS" above). It could, as was done in the UNFSA (see "What Can Be Learned from UNFSA?" above) further articulate requirements for applying an ecosystem approach that would be applicable to States parties' conduct in all organizations. It could set out the underpinning basis for deploying a science-based approach as well as establish or designate and strengthen institutions charged with enhancing cooperation and coordination. And most importantly, it could also establish a global institution such as COP to implement certain requirements directly and to collectively review, coordinate, facilitate, and provide direction to other institutions, regions, and States parties to ensure even progress (see "Building a Platform for Cooperation for BBNJ" above).

That the BBNJ agreement will take the form of a new implementing agreement to UNCLOS is clear from UNGA Resolution 72/249. UNFSA offers a model for how an implementing agreement under UNCLOS can give greater effect to the rights and responsibilities of States in relation to marine life. It also highlights lessons, both positive and negative, that the negotiators of the BBNJ agreement can draw upon as well as challenges that they could potentially help to address. For example, with respect to compatibility, similar provisions to UNFSA could address at least some of the concerns of adjacent States and developing States as a whole and help boost capacity all around to conserve and manage straddling ecosystems and highly migratory (non-target) species. The charge of the BBNJ agreement to be interpreted and applied in a manner that would not undermine existing instruments, frameworks, and bodies should be viewed as an opportunity and not a challenge.

The BBNJ agreement provides the opportunity to establish the institutional mechanisms to support active implementation and adaptation in an increasingly crowded and fundamentally changing ocean. This rare chance should be seized upon to enable greater coherence across all bodies, complement existing agreements and processes, while ensuring that the actions of one body do not undercut those of another. An institutional framework should include at least four key elements: a central administrative body, a scientific advisory mechanism or body, regular review of implementation, and the power to adopt binding decisions.

In short, the BBNJ agreement has the potential to create a lasting platform for realizing the vision of the UNCLOS negotiators for promoting the study, protection, and preservation of the marine environment while also enhancing the conservation of living marine resources, ensuring that marine resource use is indeed sustainable, and enabling more equitable use for the benefit of all beyond national boundaries. An ambitious agreement under UNCLOS could help to solidify the status of UNCLOS as the "constitution for the ocean" by enabling it to evolve to meet the demands of the ever-changing ocean and governance environments. As eloquently stated by Rayfuse and Warner,

> In view of escalating threats to the oceans from existing and emerging uses and from the impacts of climate change, transformation to a legal regime better suited to integrated, cross-sectoral management and preservation of vital ocean ecosystem services and resilience may no longer be a luxury, but rather a necessity.[123]

---

[123] R. Rayfuse and R. Warner, "Securing a sustainable future for the oceans beyond national jurisdiction: The legal basis for an integrated cross-sectoral regime for high seas governance for the 21st century," *The International Journal of Marine and Coastal Law* 23 (2008): 399–421.

U.S. Ocean Priorities Shift with a New Administration

*John A. Duff**
University of Massachusetts Boston, School for the Environment, Boston, Massachusetts, United States

Introduction

National ocean priorities shift continuously. Sometimes the movement is gradual, eroding and accreting slowly at the edges of existing institutions. At other times, the movement is sudden and substantial, prompted by either the discovery of valuable resources to be exploited or the awareness of ocean vulnerabilities. While the United States Congress creates and revises U.S. ocean laws, the administration of those laws often reflects the priorities of the executive branch. The U.S. presidential election of 2016 ushered in a new administration with markedly different perspectives than the outgoing one. And those priority differences are signaling a shift in U.S. domestic ocean governance with transnational implications. In the first two years of the administration of the Republican President Donald J. Trump, a variety of federal ocean policies have been examined, and in some cases revised or revoked.

This article highlights two particular executive orders that shift the balance in U.S. ocean policy from an evolving effort to develop and implement ecosystem-informed stewardship back to an approach that prioritizes accelerated economic development and resource extraction. The changes reflect the so-called "America First" perspectives emphasizing the fossil fuel development espoused by Mr. Trump during the 2016 presidential campaign. As President, Mr. Trump pushed ocean policy in a decidedly different direction from his predecessor, the Democratic President Barack Obama. He did so by employing presidential executive orders, the same instrument that Mr. Obama had used to give effect to his own ocean priorities. Most U.S. ocean policy emanates

---

* The author thanks Dr. Andrew Rosenberg, Director of the Center for Science and Democracy at the Union of Concerned Scientists, for his suggestions and insights during the development of this article. Among the numerous ocean science leadership roles he has held, Dr. Rosenberg served as a member of the U.S. Commission on Ocean Policy. Thanks also to Ph.D. student Courtney Humphries for her comments and suggestions. Unless otherwise attributed, the author is responsible for the information and opinions herein.

from the work of Congress articulated in the vast array of statutes fashioned and revised over decades. Those laws provide the executive branch with varying levels of discretion in implementing them. For instance, presidents may designate certain ocean and coastal areas as national monuments under the *Antiquities Act*.[1] A president may also withdraw certain offshore areas from oil and gas development under authority provided in the *Outer Continental Shelf Lands Act*.[2] And occasionally, a president may issue an executive order to direct administrative action where Congress has neither explicitly afforded nor restricted presidential action. The ocean policy oriented executive actions of two presidents over the course of the last ten years provides an opportunity to reflect upon the utility and frailty of U.S. presidential executive orders as policy instruments.

A Brief Review of Recent United States Ocean Policy

The Trump Administration's changes from the previous priorities and trajectory merit a brief review of the objectives and efforts in place in 2016 and how U.S. ocean policy at that point reflected a two-decade trend toward more ecologically informed, multi-sector ocean planning and management. From the 1990s through 2016, the U.S. national ocean policy shifted slowly, with occasional backsliding, toward a comprehensive stewardship informed with advances in natural sciences and coupled with insights into socioeconomic behavior.

In the mid-1990s, national and international concerns regarding ocean management prompted much scientific research and public policy analysis. Emerging scientific insights related to climate change, marine pollution, overfishing, and habitat degradation coupled with intensifying uses of ocean space as transport routes, energy development sites, and recreational areas shone a spotlight on the inadequacies of ocean stewardship efforts. In 1997, the U.S. National Research Council reported on a need for improved stewardship of the ocean in response to concerns raised by government agencies, private industry, nongovernmental organizations, and academic researchers.[3] The report identified the intensifying use of ocean and coastal areas, population growth and movement towards the nation's coast, and the increasing demands placed on

---

1 *Antiquities Act*, 16 U.S.C. § 431.
2 *Outer Continental Shelf Lands Act*, 43 U.S.C. § 1341(a).
3 U.S. National Research Council, *Striking a Balance: Improving Stewardship of Marine Areas* (Washington, DC: The National Academies Press, 1997), p. vi.

ocean ecosystems and their functions.[4] The Council issued a series of findings and recommendations to help improve ocean governance and stewardship.[5]

On 28 January 1998, the Democratic President Bill Clinton issued a proclamation reflecting the Council's concerns regarding ocean stewardship and calling for action to improve U.S. ocean governance.[6] Clinton highlighted the growing chorus of concerns, noting that the ocean serves to sustain "life on our planet [serving as] a key source of food, medicine, energy, commerce, and recreation for the peoples of the world," and adding that "[w]e are only beginning to understand the depths of the ocean's mysteries, but we are quickly learning one crucial lesson: the ocean's resources are limited, and we must work together to preserve them."[7] Accordingly he issued an imperative that

> [w]e must strive together – at local, national, and international levels – to preserve the ocean's health, to protect the marine environment, and to ensure the sustainable management of the myriad resources the ocean contains.[8]

Clinton mobilized that proclamation as he convened a National Oceans Conference in Monterey, California later that year. The vice-president, four cabinet secretaries, and numerous other high ranking U.S. officials outlined a wide range of goals to advance the understanding, governance, and management of U.S. ocean space.

The efforts of the 1990s served as the foundation for two ocean commission efforts that began in 2001 and reported to the nation a few years later. The Pew Oceans Commission was a privately funded endeavor chaired by Leon Panetta, whose insights from his roles as an elected member of Congress and various presidential appointments at the highest levels provided the Commission with vision and practical experience. Other members of the Commission included sitting and former governors along with leaders from the public, private, and nongovernmental sectors. The Pew Oceans Commission issued its report in May 2003.[9] It recommended that the United States develop a 21st century ocean policy through a series of legislative and executive actions including:

---

4 Id., *passim*.
5 Id., pp. 87–120.
6 President William J. Clinton, "Year of the Ocean, 1998," Presidential Proclamation 7065 (28 January 1998).
7 Id.
8 Id.
9 Pew Oceans Commission, *America's Living Ocean – Charting a Course for Sea Change* (May 2003).

- enactment of a National Ocean Policy Act;
- establishment of regional ocean ecosystem councils;
- development of a national system of marine reserves;
- creation of an independent national oceans agency; and
- establishment of a permanent interagency oceans council.[10]

As the Pew Oceans Commission engaged in its work, a federal government-led ocean commission entered the picture. The United States Commission on Ocean Policy was chartered by Congress in 2000 to "make recommendations for coordinated and comprehensive national ocean policy" that would, among other things, promote responsible stewardship of ocean areas and resources.[11] The act was signed into law by Mr. Clinton on 7 August 2000, months before the presidential election of 2000. Interestingly, Congress had explicitly prescribed that it would not become effective until 20 January 2001 – a date that would coincide with the next president's first day in office.[12] The effect of this provision meant that the U.S. *Oceans Act* was "born" during a day honored as the peaceful transition of presidential power. Clinton's successor, the Republican President George W. Bush, presided over the initiation of the new commission and the appointment of its members. The Commission on Ocean Policy, chaired by Admiral James D. Watkins, USN (ret.), and populated by highly regarded ocean researchers, explorers, retired military leaders, and industry leaders, worked over a three-year period to convene sixteen public meetings, solicit a wide range of stakeholder advice and information, and visit myriad sites around the nation's expansive oceanscape. The Commission, with advantages, authority, and resources surpassing those of the Pew Oceans Commission, ranged farther and reached more communities to produce a weighty set of findings and recommendations.[13] The Commission echoed many of the Pew Oceans Commission's recommendations and added hundreds more, including detailed suggestions regarding ocean education, marine pollution, overexploitation, research and monitoring, public health and safety, coastal habitat restoration, marine commerce and transport, invasive species, sustainable fisheries, vulnerable species protection, energy development, and shared governance, to name just a few.[14]

---

10   Id., pp. 33–34.
11   *Oceans Act of 2000*, Pub. L. 106–256.
12   Id., s. 7.
13   U.S. Commission on Ocean Policy, *An Ocean Blueprint for the 21st Century. Final Report* (Washington, DC, 2004).
14   Id. *passim*.

The work of the Pew Oceans Commission and the Commission on Ocean Policy garnered headlines as commissioners convened visits, hearings, and information sessions from the Caribbean to the Arctic and considered all U.S. coastal areas. Yet, unlike the Stratton Commission of the 1960s, the reports and recommendations of the two learned groups led to little in the form of legislative advancement of ocean stewardship principles. In fact, ocean exploitation continued rapidly with advances in offshore drilling technology that reached into deep water that had been heretofore untapped. Indeed, in the 1980s and 1990s, the desire to reach oil and gas fields that lay miles below the ocean's surface led energy lobbyists to clamor for royalty relief that would free up capital for the deeper and more expensive ventures to extract oil and gas from below offshore federal lands in the Gulf of Mexico. In 1995, Congress responded and provided industry with the economic incentive to go deeper offshore.[15]

The *Energy Policy Act* of 2005 also signaled Congress's willingness to support expansive energy development on federal public lands, including offshore spaces, and notably including renewable energy technologies.[16] Critics raised concerns about the peril of moving into the deeper waters of the Gulf. Proponents responded with assurances that health and safety protocols would evolve to safeguard human lives and the marine environment. As Congress enacted laws facilitating offshore energy exploitation in the 2000s, there seemed little interest in implementing the ocean resource stewardship principles suggested in the ocean commission recommendations, until a new administration arrived in 2009.

The Emergence of Executive Policies of Ocean Stewardship

Within his first few months in office, Mr. Obama issued a memorandum calling for the development of an Interagency Ocean Policy Task Force charged with the development of

> a unifying framework under a clear national policy, including a comprehensive, ecosystem-based framework for the long term conservation and use of our resources ... to better meet our Nation's stewardship responsibilities for the oceans, coasts, and Great Lakes.[17]

---

15   *Outer Continental Shelf Deep Water Royalty Relief Act of 1995* (DWRRA), Pub. L. 104-58, 109 Stat. 557 (28 November 1995), codified at 43 U.S.C. § 1337 (a)(1)(H), -(a)(3)(B), -(a)(C).
16   *The Energy Policy Act of 2005* (P.L. 109–58) 8 August 2005, codified at 42 U.S.C. §13201 et seq.
17   President Barack Obama, Memorandum on National Policy for the Oceans, Our Coasts, and the Great Lakes (12 June 2009).

The task force convened and worked to chart a course that Mr. Obama could navigate with, or without, the help of Congress. Before the task force could issue its report, circumstances shone a harsh light on the need for sound ocean management. On 20 April 2010, the *Deepwater Horizon* rig operating in over 5,000 feet of water, 41 miles off the coast of Louisiana, suffered a catastrophic blowout that claimed eleven lives and let loose the largest offshore oil spill in history. That deadly accident served as the impetus for a 2010 order issued by Mr. Obama that called on a wide range of federal agencies and personnel to revisit human safety and environmental stewardship rules, and it laid the groundwork for more comprehensive ocean research, planning, and management.

On 19 July 2010, Mr. Obama issued an executive order on Stewardship of the Ocean, Our Coasts, and the Great Lakes.[18] The order cited the spill as a call for action. It also dusted off the insights and informed recommendations of Ocean Commission recommendations that had been developed but lain dormant for years. It echoed the ecosystem-based approach recommended by the Commission on Ocean Policy as well as the Commission's acknowledgment that sound ocean governance ought to be developed to employ more information and a variety of voices to achieve "decisions that protect the environment while promoting the economy and balancing multiple uses of our oceans and coasts."[19]

The 2010 Obama order re-invigorated recommendations outlined by the Pew and Ocean Policy Commissions. A National Ocean Council convened, regional ocean planning efforts began in earnest, and, after years engaged in the directives set forth in the 2010 Executive Order, comprehensive regional ocean plans began to emerge. In October 2016, the Northeast Regional Planning Body submitted its Northeast Ocean Plan to the National Ocean Council.[20] The following month, the Mid-Atlantic Regional Planning group submitted its plan for that region.[21] The National Ocean Council accepted both plans in December 2016.[22]

---

18   President Barack Obama, Executive Order 13547, Stewardship of the Ocean, Our Coasts, and the Great Lakes, 75 Fed. Reg. 43023 (23 July 2010).

19   James D. Watkins, transmittal letter September 2004, U.S. Commission on Ocean Policy, *An Ocean Blueprint for the 21st Century. Final Report* (Washington, DC: 2004), pp. 1–2.

20   Northeast Ocean Plan for National Ocean Council Certification, 81 Fed. Reg. 72,622, 72,622–24 (19 October 2016), available online: <https://www.federalregister.gov/documents/2016/10/20/2016-25372/northeast-ocean-plan-for-national-ocean-council-certification>.

21   Submittal of Mid-Atlantic Regional Ocean Action Plan for National Ocean Council Certification, 81 Fed. Reg. 76, 635, 76,635–37 (3 November 2016).

22   C. Goldfuss and J.P. Holdren, *The Nation's First Ocean Plans*, The White House Blog: President Barack Obama (7 December 2016, 9:02 AM).

While the Obama Administration relied on the regional planning efforts to fashion a national ocean policy, it also went beyond them. The *Deepwater Horizon* accident had reminded federal officials of the dangers of extracting oil and gas in hard-to-reach areas and harsh ocean conditions. As experts contemplated the vast expanses of U.S. ocean space that remained open for oil and gas exploration, some areas appeared both highly sensitive and substantially susceptible. Arctic nations, including the United States, contemplated increasing demand to engage in polar shipping and energy exploitation. They began to fashion international agreements to ensure that new or expanded uses of Arctic waters proceed with caution. On 21 January 2015, Mr. Obama issued another executive order to spur enhanced coordination of national efforts assessing conditions in the U.S. Arctic and scrutinizing new or expanded uses of Arctic waters.[23] That order also laid a foundation for a bilateral United States-Canada Arctic leadership effort.[24]

As his presidency wound down, and with the knowledge that his successor had a vastly different perspective on issues of environmental stewardship, Mr. Obama issued one of his final missives regarding ocean protection in December 2016. The last of his ocean executive orders focused on the northern Bering Sea and reflected concerns stemming from accelerated climate change in the region and the eagerness of industries to exploit an important but vulnerable ecosystem.[25] Mr. Obama cited the threats to the area and relied upon an increasing body of scientific knowledge to withdraw certain expanses from offshore oil and gas development.[26] He issued a map delineating a Northern Bering Sea Resilience Area[27] and charged an interagency group to work with Alaskan tribal governments to protect it from unsound development and to fashion a plan for ensuring sound management.[28]

It is important to recognize that any president engaged in forging national policies will be constrained by whether and how Congress provides the authority and resources to do so. In his various ocean policy executive orders and proclamations, Mr. Obama repeatedly alluded to the statutory authority

---

23 President Barack Obama, Executive Order 13689, Enhancing Coordination of National Efforts in the Arctic, 80 Fed. Reg. 4191 (21 January 2015).
24 The White House, Office of the Press Secretary, the White House, U.S.-Canada Joint Statement on Climate, Energy, and Arctic Leadership, 10 March 2016 (statement of U.S. President Barack Obama and Canadian Prime Minister Justin Trudeau).
25 President Barack Obama, Executive Order 13754, Northern Bering Sea Climate Resilience, 81 Fed. Reg. 90669 (14 December 2016).
26 Id., s. 4(a).
27 Id., p. 90674.
28 Id., ss. 5–6.

provided to the executive branch to carry out ocean-related federal laws. For example, Mr. Obama explicitly referred to the *Outer Continental Shelf Lands Act Amendments* of 1978 as the basis of his authority to withdraw certain federal offshore areas in the Arctic from oil and gas exploitation. Notwithstanding certain limited authority specifically provided to the executive in the Constitution, presidents cannot exceed the scope of authority provided by laws enacted by Congress (and signed into law by a president).

The efforts of the Obama Administration during its last two years signaled one president's efforts to construct the foundations of an ocean stewardship that balanced conservation with economic development. Mr. Obama's executive actions also reflected a political reality. As a Democratic president countered by a Republican Congress, Mr. Obama often had to advance his policy objectives with little help, and often with significant hindrance, from the legislative branch. And while a sitting president is provided a certain amount of discretion in implementing laws enacted by Congress, executive orders are vulnerable to election-borne changes in the White House. Presidential orders are just that, directives to agencies and personnel operating within the executive branch of the federal government. Rather than laws that only Congress can enact, they are orders from the executive on how the laws will be implemented. When a session of Congress adjourns and is succeeded by a newly elected Congress, the laws of the previous Congress endure unless a subsequent Congress can muster significant political capital to fashion the repeal or amendment of an existing statute. When a president is succeeded by new chief executive, the old "boss" who issued the previous executive orders is no longer in charge. And a new boss can quickly issue his or her own orders.

A New President and a Marked Shift in United States Ocean Governance

Mr. Trump took office on 20 January 2017. Mr. Obama's ocean policy, particularly as articulated by his executive orders, proved fatally vulnerable. In the first eighteen months of the Trump Administration, the new president issued a series of executive orders that revoked a collection of Mr. Obama's orders and charted a new path for ocean policy.

Mr. Trump's executive orders employ rhetoric that signals a significant shift away from principles of planning and conservation and toward exploitation. For example, within his first 100 days in office, President Trump issued his

America-First Offshore Energy Strategy Executive Order.[29] The first substantive sentence of that order sets the tone that will set the stage for the new president's ocean policy: "America must put the energy needs of American families and businesses first."[30]

To anyone familiar with Mr. Trump's campaign rhetoric, the language of the order should not be surprising. Yet, when some interests are deemed to come "first," a natural question is what is relegated to some lesser category or abandoned altogether? A careful reading of the order provides answers. The words "energy," "security," "military," and variations of "economy" resound and repeat throughout the "America-First" order. Conspicuous by their absence from this order, when compared to the Obama orders, are terms such as "climate" (except when an Obama order using the term is revoked), "conservation," "sustainability," and "health."

The Trump order indicates that energy independence, through increased domestic fossil fuel production, is the primary goal, and it suggests that prior policies in the way must *give* way. Mr. Trump's America First order calls on the Department of the Interior to "encourage [more] energy exploration and production," and it directs department officials to revise (presumably to accelerate) the schedule of offshore energy lease sales.[31] The order also calls on the Secretary of Commerce to refrain from expanding any marine sanctuaries, and it suggests that existing sanctuaries should be scrutinized with energy development in mind.[32] Further, the Trump order lays out a series of instructions to agency officials to examine existing and proposed rules with an eye toward revising, revoking, or withdrawing environmental, health, and safety regulations that might impede offshore energy development.

In its most explicit swipe at an Obama-era policy, the 2017 Trump order revokes President Obama's 2016 order related to Northern Bering Sea Climate Resilience.[33] In doing so it effectively erased the boundaries of an area of the Bering Sea identified as particularly vulnerable to climate change.

As summer 2018 approached, Mr. Trump issued another ocean policy order to "advance the economic, security and environmental interests of the United

---

29 President Donald J. Trump, Executive Order 13795, Implementing an America-First Offshore Energy Strategy, 28 April 2017, 82 Fed. Reg. 201815 (3 May 2017), s. 1.
30 Id.
31 Id., s. 3.
32 Id., s. 4.
33 Id., s. 4(c).

States."[34] The opening section of the 2018 directive levels its attention on the "oceans, coasts and Great Lakes of the United States" signaling its intent to replace the 2010 Obama order that employed that geographic expanse in its title.[35] And while environmental advocates might have placed some hope in the fact that Mr. Trump mentioned the environment in the title of his 2018 order, the term evaporated in the body of the order, giving way to the priority list embodied at the outset ("economy, security, global competitiveness and well-being").

The most explicit and comprehensive shift evident in the 2018 Trump order is the revocation of Mr. Obama's 2010 order. Mr. Obama's directive considered the costs and benefits associated with offshore energy development and began to fashion a response to the reality that even thoroughly planned ocean development posed significant risks when administered by single-sector agencies.

The lesson of the 2010 *Deepwater Horizon* spill suggested that the community of local, state, and federal agencies and stakeholders affected by and called on to respond to an offshore disaster ought to have a more integrated role in ocean planning and management. The Obama 2010 order prioritized health and biological diversity and set up coordinating regional bodies to collaborate on, and coordinate the management of, coastal ocean regions. It charged those bodies with developing comprehensive integrated regional ocean plans. Two such plans had emerged by 2016 and held some promise in giving effect to President Obama's ocean stewardship objectives.

President Trump's 2018 order revoked the 2010 Obama order and in so doing prioritized energy extraction and economic development. The Trump order directed federal agencies to remove barriers to energy extraction and development. The revocation of the Obama order also effectively relegated two regional ocean plans to the federal policy trash heap. Whether and how those Obama era policies might ever indeed be recycled remains to be seen. Proponents of the ocean policy trajectory that had been under way through 2016 may find the Trump ocean directives as misinformed, misdirected, or cataclysmic.[36]

---

34 President Donald J. Trump, Executive Order 13840 – Ocean Policy to Advance the Economic, Security and Environmental Interests of the United States, 19 June 2018. 83 Fed. Reg. 29431 (22 June 2018).
35 President Barack Obama, Executive Order 13547, Stewardship of the Ocean, Our Coasts, and the Great Lakes, 75 Fed. Reg. 43023 (23 July 2010).
36 See, e.g., L.J. Bilmes, "The cataclysmic cost of Trump's 'war on oceans,'" (opinion section), *Boston Globe* (26 July 2018).

The Constraints on the U.S. Executive Branch in Ocean Policy Formulation

As discernibly different as the Trump Administration's ocean priorities may be from President Obama's, it is important to note that the executive branch is constrained by the political voice of the states and the role and authority of Congress. The former is evident in the interrupted effort by the Trump Administration to open vast expanses of offshore space for energy development. Ocean areas off the Gulf Coast of Florida and up and down the Atlantic seaboard had been closed to oil and gas development via a combination of congressional moratoria effected by budget restrictions and prior presidential withdrawals under the *Outer Continental Shelf Lands Act*. In January 2018, the U.S. Department of Interior's Bureau of Ocean Energy Management signaled its intent to open those areas for possible development, basing its draft plan on President Trump's April 2017 Executive Order.[37] States and their congressional delegations responded swiftly and critically. Within days, various officials in the Trump Administration emphasized that the draft plan was still being assessed and that many states might be exempted from the prospect of new development.[38] By late October 2018, the Trump plan had not replaced the plan left in place at the end of the Obama Administration.

Congress has also flexed its ocean policy-making muscles in the early years of the Trump Administration. A bipartisan legislative effort to amend and extend the federal marine debris law came to fruition in the form of the *Save Our Seas Act*. The 2018 law directs the National Oceanic and Atmospheric Administration (NOAA) to collaborate with other federal agencies to address marine debris from land- and sea-based sources.[39] It instructs the Department of State to "promote international action ... to reduce the incidence of marine debris."[40] The law also presses the President to examine the economic impact of marine debris and work toward a solution with countries that constitute significant sources of debris.[41] Finally, it urges the President to "encourage

---

37   Bureau of Ocean Energy Management, "2019–2024 National OCS Oil and Gas Leasing Draft Proposed Program," 2018, available online: <https://www.boem.gov/NP-Draft-Proposed-Program-2019-2024/>.
38   See, e.g., T. Cama, "Trump officials cast doubt on Zinke's Florida offshore drilling exemption," *The Hill* (19 January 2018), available online: <https://thehill.com/policy/energy-environment/369743-offshore-drilling-official-zinkes-florida-exemption-was-not-a>.
39   *Save Our Seas Act of 2018*, Pub. L. 115–265, s. 101. (2018).
40   Id.
41   Id., s. 102.

the Office of the U.S. Trade Representative to consider the impact [of marine debris] ... in relevant future trade agreements."[42]

Upon signing the bill into law, President Trump alluded to the surprising bipartisanship support for it and emphasized that his Administration was employing trade negotiations to address ocean pollution issues.[43] But no sooner did the President make those remarks than he issued a signing statement "raising constitutional concerns" with the type and tenor of Congress's directives regarding international relations and highlighting his "constitutional authority as the sole representative of the Nation in foreign affairs."[44]

Conclusion

Both critics and proponents of the recent shift in U.S. ocean priorities should take note of one striking similarity between the two very different presidents: their reliance on executive orders. Mr. Obama could not, and Mr. Trump has not (as of this writing), garnered sufficient support in Congress to articulate, authorize, and fund the types of ocean policies that are moored tightly in place by statutes and appropriations. To confidently and securely set new ocean policies in place will take a willing Congress. The most enduring U.S. ocean policies are embedded in laws passed by Congress reaching back to the 1890s (the *Rivers and Harbors Act*) and proliferating in the 1950s (e.g., *Outer Continental Shelf Lands Act, Submerged Lands Act*) and 1970s (*Coastal Zone Management Act, Marine Mammal Protection Act, Clean Water Act, Ocean Dumping Act, National Marine Sanctuaries Act*). To the degree that Congress has recently enacted or extended any substantial ocean law, the *Save Our Seas Act* of 2018 constitutes a unique moment of bipartisan interest in addressing a global marine pollution issue and reflects a shared priority of the legislative rather than the executive branch.

A new presidential administration holding markedly different views and priorities from its predecessor may seem like a breath of fresh air to some and look like a catastrophe to others. There is no doubt that Mr. Trump's ocean policy directives during his first two years in office set a different tone, priority,

---

42   Id.
43   Remarks by President Trump at signing of s. 3508, the "Save Our Seas Act of 2018" (11 October 2018), available online: <https://www.whitehouse.gov/briefings-statements/remarks-president-trump-signing-s-3508-save-seas-act-2018/>.
44   Signing Statement by President Trump regarding s. 3508, the "Save Our Seas Act of 2018" (11 October 2018), available online: <https://www.whitehouse.gov/briefings-statements/statement-by-the-president-8/>.

and direction from those of President Obama. When it comes to ocean policy, Trump Administration orders prioritize economic development over ecological resilience. Arctic Ocean areas withdrawn from exploitation by President Obama have been re-opened for business by the Trump Administration. Maps depicting vulnerable Arctic areas by Mr. Obama have been scrapped by Mr. Trump. Regional ocean planning efforts and the plans they produced, developed at the behest of Mr. Obama have been rescinded by Mr. Trump. Arctic nation collaborative efforts given firm footing by President Obama have been unwound. Stakeholders given sway in Obama-era ocean orders, including tribes, state and local governments, and scientific research communities (and the research they produce) have been shut out of Trump-era orders. In their place, private energy interests and entities that arguably can be characterized as important to national security and economic production are given first-class seats. And Trump ocean policy orders repeatedly call on federal agencies to scrutinize Obama-era decisions, rules, and guidance to determine whether they can be suspended, revised, withdrawn, or revoked. Those calls signal Mr. Trump's eagerness to loosen or remove restraints designed to protect ocean and human health in favor of finding and extracting more oil and gas.

While the emphasis of the policies has shifted dramatically, the means by which the changes are made have not. Presidential executive orders, once relegated to an obscure corner of policy-making, touted by those who agree with their rhetoric and dismissed by those who object to their direction, are frail vehicles to fashion lasting policies. Presidents who disliked their predecessors' executive orders could merely ignore them or could issue their own directives that implicitly override pre-existing orders. The harsher tone of the Trump ocean orders seems to be gaining as much attention for how they express the current president's priorities as for the effect that the orders achieve. Keen observers examining shifting U.S. ocean policy would do well to pay as much attention to the degree that Congress re-engages in, or abdicates, its ocean policy-making role. And students of presidential politics may consider whether ocean stewardship has a constituency that can exert any influence in future elections.

Securing Ocean Spaces for the Future? The Initiative of the Pacific SIDS to Develop Regional Practice Concerning Baselines and Maritime Zone Limits

David Freestone
George Washington University Law School and Sargasso Sea Commission, Washington, DC, United States

Clive Schofield
WMU-Sasakawa Global Ocean Institute, World Maritime University, Malmö, Sweden, and Visiting Professor, Australian National Centre for Ocean Resources and Security, University of Wollongong, Australia

Introduction

On 2 March 2018, in Majuro, Marshall Islands, eight Pacific Island leaders representing the Parties to the Nauru Agreement (PNA)[1] signed the "Delap Commitment on Securing Our Common Wealth of Oceans: Reshaping the Future to Take Control of the Fisheries."[2] While principally concerned with cooperation in the management of fisheries of common interest, the leaders in the preamble to their Commitment acknowledge "the challenges presented by their unique vulnerability and the threat to the integrity of maritime boundaries and the existential impacts of sea level rise." The Commitment contains a provision in which the leaders agree:

> 8. To pursue legal recognition of the defined baselines established under the *United Nations Convention on the Law of the Sea* to remain in perpetuity irrespective of the impacts of sea level rise.

---

1 See, "Nauru Agreement Introduction" and link to "A Third Arrangement Implementing the Nauru Agreement Setting Forth Additional Terms and Conditions of the Fisheries Zones of the Parties," available online: <https://www.ffa.int/node/93>.
2 Signed source on file with the authors. Reproduced as Appendix 1 below. Signed by Marshall Islands, Nauru, Kiribati, Tuvalu, Federated States of Micronesia, Solomon Islands, Palau, and Papua New Guinea.

This represents a further step in a coordinated strategy by the Pacific Islands to develop regional State practice in relation to the impacts of sea level rise on their baselines and the outer limits of their maritime zones. This article outlines the regional setting in which this Commitment is made, before providing an overview of the predictions of sea level rise now being made by the Intergovernmental Panel on Climate Change (IPCC) together with potential impacts and places these in Pacific context. The article then reviews the Pacific response to these challenges and relates these developments also to the on-going work and recommendations of the International Law Association (ILA) Committee on International Law and Sea Level Rise, of which both the authors are members.

Regional Context

Small Island but Large Ocean States
The South Pacific region hosts twelve independent States (Federated States of Micronesia, Fiji, Kiribati, Marshall Islands, Nauru, Palau, Papua New Guinea (PNG), Samoa, Solomon Islands, Tonga, Tuvalu and Vanuatu), two freely associated with New Zealand (Cook Islands and Niue) and another dependent on New Zealand (Tokelau). These countries are often collectively known as the Pacific Small Island Developing States (Pacific SIDS) and, together with Australia and New Zealand, comprise the Pacific Islands Forum. Additionally, there are a number of territories dependent on or in free association with extra-regional metropolitan powers such as France (French Polynesia, New Caledonia, Wallis and Futuna), the United Kingdom (Pitcairn Islands), and the United States (American Samoa, Guam, and Northern Mariana Islands).[3] The Pacific Island States are predominantly remote both from one another and their metropolitan Pacific Rim neighbors.[4]

---

3   See B.M. Tsamenyi and L. Manarangi-Trott, "The role of regional organizations in meeting LOS Convention challenges: The Western and Central Pacific Experience," in *Oceans Management in the 21st Century: Institutional Frameworks and Responses*, eds. A.G. Oude Elferink and D.R. Rothwell (The Hague: Kluwer, 2004), 187–208; J.M. Van Dyke, "Regionalism, fisheries and environmental challenges in the Pacific," *San Diego International Law Journal* 6(1) (2004): 143–178, at 146–158. See also, Q. Hanich, C.H. Schofield and P. Cozens, "Oceans of opportunity?: The limits of maritime claims in the South Pacific," in *Navigating Pacific Fisheries: Legal and Policy Trends in the Implementation of International Fisheries Instruments in the Western and Central Pacific Region*, eds. Q. Hanich and B.M. Tsamenyi (Wollongong: Ocean Publications, 2009), pp. 17–46, p. 21.
4   The term "Pacific Island States" is used in this article to refer to the independent, freely-associated and dependent States and territories of the South Pacific region.

Taken altogether, the Pacific Island States total just over 550,000 km² of land. It is, however, notable that Papua New Guinea accounts for 84 percent of this area. The Pacific Island States are scattered over the vast 165 million km² Pacific Ocean which encompasses around one-third of the surface of the Earth.[5] While often perceived to be small island States because of their limited territories, these countries are simultaneously large ocean States. The Pacific Islands States have claimed maritime zones in line with the United Nations Convention on the Law of the Sea (UNCLOS)[6] and, by virtue of being both remote and widely dispersed, this has resulted in their having rights over enormous areas of maritime jurisdiction, estimated to have a collective area of 30,569,000 km² (see Figure 3.1).[7] This vast area is equivalent to around 28 percent of exclusive economic zone (EEZ) claims worldwide.[8]

These EEZ claims represent a tremendous actual and potential benefit to the Pacific Island States, especially in regard to the abundant and valuable tuna fisheries. For example, in 2016 the value of the tuna catch in the Western and Central Pacific Ocean as a whole was estimated at US$5.3 billion,[9] with the value accruing to Pacific Islands Forum Fisheries Agency (FFA) members (excluding Australia and New Zealand) estimated at US$2.59 billion.[10] Pacific Island States depend upon the revenues derived from these stocks as a critical form of government revenue, as well as a traditional and vital source of food. The critical importance of revenues derived from tuna is underscored by estimates that tuna-related revenues, both from licensing and fishing, comprise 36 percent of

---

5   J.M. Anthony, "Conflict over natural resources in the Pacific," in *Conflict Over Natural Resources in Southeast Asia and the Pacific*, eds. L.T. Ghee and M.J. Valencia (Oxford: Oxford University Press / United Nations University Press, 1990); Tsamenyi and Manarangi-Trott, n. 3 above, pp. 187–189.

6   United Nations Convention on the Law of the Sea, adopted 10 December 1982, 1833 *United Nations Treaty Series* 3 (entered into force 16 November 1994) [UNCLOS].

7   Hanich et al., n. 3 above, pp. 21–22. See also, C.H. Schofield, "Climate change and changing coasts: Geophysical and jurisdictional implications of sea level rise," *Korean Journal of International and Comparative Law* 5(1) (2017): 36–60, 45–46.

8   R. Gillet, "Pacific Island Countries Region," in *Review of the State of World Marine Resources*, FAO Fisheries Technical Paper 457 (Rome: FAO, 2005), pp. 144–157.

9   See, P. Williams, P. Terawasi and C. Reid, "Overview of Tuna Fisheries in the Western and Central Pacific Ocean, including Economic Conditions – 2016" (paper presented to the Thirteenth Regular Session of the Scientific Committee of the Western and Central Pacific Fisheries Commission, 9–17 August 2017, Port Moresby, Papua New Guinea, WCPFC-SC13-2017/GN-WP-01).

10 See, F. Blaha, "The economic value of tuna catches in the Western Pacific," 4 October 2017, available online: <http://www.franciscoblaha.info/blog/2017/10/4/the-economic-value-of-tuna-catches-in-the-western-pacific>.

REGIONAL PRACTICE CONCERNING BASELINES & MARITIME ZONE LIMITS 61

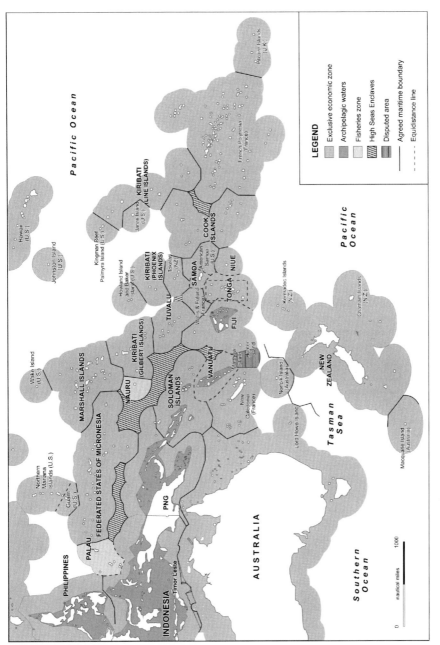

FIGURE 3.1 Pacific Ocean exclusive economic zones
SOURCE: I.M.A. ARSANA AND C.H. SCHOFIELD.

GDP in Tuvalu and 32 percent in Kiribati.[11] Further, these government revenues from tuna fisheries translate to a much higher proportion of public budgets. For example, tuna-related revenues comprised 63 percent of the public budget for Kiribati in 2012.[12] There is also significant potential for the economic benefits of fisheries for Pacific SIDS to increase, notably through efforts to "capture more of the tuna value chains"[13] and provide enhanced employment opportunities in the region, especially in relation to processing[14] and crewing of fishing vessels operating in the waters of Pacific SIDS.[15] However, both the land that makes up these States and territories and the maritime areas associated with them, together with their marine resources, are threatened by sea level rise.

Predictions of Sea Level Rise
The IPCC in its Fourth Assessment Report (AR4) in 2007 had identified 1.5–2.5 °C over 1980–1990 levels as the threshold for dangerous climate change, notably the increased risk of extinction for unique and threatened systems.[16] The target of 2 °C was reflected in the wording of the 2009 Copenhagen Accord.[17]

---

11   International Labour Organization (ILO), *A Study on the Future of Work in the Pacific*, May 2017, available online: <https://www.ilo.org/suva/publications/WCMS_553880/lang--en/index.htm>, p. viii.
12   See, The World Bank, *Pacific Possible: Tuna Fisheries*, available online: <http://pubdocs.worldbank.org/en/102721466580391096/PACIFIC-POSSIBLE-Tuna-Summary-paper.pdf>, p. 7.
13   Estimated to employ only 0.5 percent of the region's workforce. ILO, n. 11 above, p. viii.
14   For example, less than 10 percent of the purse seine catch in the region is processed locally. Id.
15   Notably through initiatives such as the Parties to the Nauru Agreement's (PNA) proposals to enforce mandatory crewing requirements eventually leading to PNA nationals making up 50 percent of purse seine crews. Id. In this context it is notable that Pacific leaders have set out a goal of the creation of 18,000 new jobs in the region over a ten-year period. See, Pacific Islands Forum Fisheries Agency (FFA) and Secretariat of the Pacific Community (SPC), *Regional Roadmap for Sustainable Pacific Fisheries*, available online: <https://www.ffa.int/system/files/Roadmap_web_0.pdf>.
16   Specifically, the IPCC stated that there was medium confidence that approximately 20 to 30 percent of plant and animal species assessed were "are likely to be at an increased risk of extinction if increases in global average temperature" exceeded these levels. It was also noted that "[c]onfidence has increased that a 1 to 2° increase in global mean temperature above 1990 levels, equating to 1.5–2.5° above pre-industrial levels "poses significant risks to many unique and threatened systems including many biodiversity hotspots." See, R.K. Pachauri and A. Reisinger, eds., Climate Change 2007: Synthesis Report, Contribution of Working Groups I, II and III to the Fourth Assessment Report of the Intergovernmental Panel on Climate Change, IPCC: Geneva, 2007, available online: <https://www.ipcc.ch/site/assets/uploads/2018/02/ar4_syr_full_report.pdf>, at pp. 64–65.
17   United Nations Framework Convention on Climate Change (UNFCCC), "Report of the Conference of the Parties on its fifteenth session, held in Copenhagen from 7 to 19 December 2009,

However, the SIDS strongly advocated that a higher aspiration should be contained in the 2015 Paris Agreement. Article 2(1) of Paris "aims to strengthen the global response to the threat of climate change, in the context of sustainable development and efforts to eradicate poverty, including by:

> (a) Holding the increase in the global average temperature to well below 2 °C above pre-industrial levels and to pursue efforts to limit the temperature increase to 1.5 °C above pre-industrial levels, recognizing that this would significantly reduce the risks and impacts of climate change.[18]

The threat of sea level rise was a major driver for this call, for the SIDS are at the front line of sea level rise impacts. Unfortunately, even if the State parties to the Paris Agreement are able to keep warming within this lower limit, there is a broad scientific consensus that the Earth is already committed to increases of sea level for the foreseeable future notwithstanding any change in emissions of greenhouse gases.[19]

The IPCC estimates are generally regarded to be conservative and in its Fifth Assessment Report (AR5), published in 2013/14, it now predicts up to 98 cm of global mean sea level (GMSL) rise by 2100 should emissions in greenhouse gases not be cut significantly, though with "a strong regional pattern, with some places experiencing significant deviations of local and regional sea level change from the global mean change."[20] Moreover, there is a wide range of

---

Decisions adopted by the Conference of Parties," UN Doc. FCCC/CP/2009/11/Add.1 (30 March 2010), p. 4, which reads: "By Decision 2/CP.15 Copenhagen Accord, the Conference of the Parties takes note of the Copenhagen Accord of 18 December 2009." Article 2 of the Copenhagen Accord indicates agreement that "deep cuts" in global emissions are required in keeping with IPCC AR4 "so as to hold the increase in global temperature below 2 degrees Celsius." See, Id., p. 5.

18 UNFCCC, "Adoption of the Paris Agreement," UN Doc. FCCC/CP/2015/L.9 (12 December 2015), available online: <https://unfccc.int/resource/docs/2015/cop21/eng/l09.pdf> [Paris Agreement].

19 For example, the IPCC's 2018 Special Report on *Global Warming of 1.5°C* notes that recent literature "strongly supports" the assessment that sea level rise will continue well beyond 2100. See, O. Hoegh-Guldberg et al., "Impacts of 1.5°C Global Warming on Natural and Human Systems," in *Global Warming of 1.5 °C, An IPCC Special Report on the impacts of global warming of 1.5 °C above pre-industrial levels and related global greenhouse gas emission pathways, in the context of strengthening the global response to the threat of climate change, sustainable development, and efforts to eradicate poverty*, eds. V. Masson-Delmotte et al., (IPCC, 2018), available online: <http://www.ipcc.ch/report/sr15>, 207 [IPCC Special Report].

20 J.A. Church, et al., "Sea Level Change," in *Climate Change 2013: The Physical Science Basis. Contribution of Working Group 1 to the Fifth Assessment Report of the Intergovernmental Panel on Climate Change*, Intergovernmental Panel on Climate Change (IPCC),

differences in the results for the upper bounds of projected sea level rise, identified in assessments using process-based modelling, on the one hand, and those based on semi-empirical models (SEM), on the other, with the latter resulting in upper bounds of up to 2.4 meters of global mean sea level rise by 2100.[21]

In its 2018 Special Report on *Global Warming of 1.5°C* the IPCC notes significant advances in the literature since AR5, in particular the development of Semi-Empirical Models (SEMs) into "a broader emulation-based approach" partially based on the outcomes of "more detailed, process-based modelling."[22] This report suggests, with medium confidence, that GMSL will rise "about 0.1 m less ... by the end of the century in a 1.5°C compared to a 2°C warmer world." While this 10 centimeter reduction in sea level rise may seem inconsequential, the report estimates that it would mean up to 10.4 million more people being exposed to the threat of sea level rise than would otherwise be the case.[23]

Sea level rise is arguably the most obvious manifestation of the radical changes to the Earth's system that *Homo sapiens* has brought about.[24] The current system of international law has evolved over the last millennium in the relative stable epoch of the Holocene. Consequently, changes in the underlying physical environment brought about by climate change and sea level rise may require a re-examination of some of the accepted principles and paradigms.[25]

Ambulatory Baselines and Shifting Maritime Limits
A salient concern related to sea level rise is that this phenomenon will lead to changes, particularly recessions, in the location of coastlines from which

---

T.F. Stocker et al., eds. (Cambridge and New York: Cambridge University Press, 2013), ch. 13, p. 1140, available online: <http://www.climatechange2013.org/images/report/WG1AR5_ALL_FINAL.pdf>.

21 Id., pp. 1179–1186, at p. 1185. The semi-empirical approach regards changes in sea level as an integrated response of the entire climate system, reflecting changes in the dynamics and thermodynamics of the atmosphere, ocean and cryosphere – in contrast to process-based approach, which explicitly attributes sea level rise to its individual physical components; id, p. 1182.

22 IPCC Special Report, pp. 175–311, 206.

23 Id., p. 178.

24 Scientific evidence increasingly indicates that, due to the nature and size of ongoing changes, the Earth may already be undergoing a shift from the conditions of the current officially accepted geological time interval, the Holocene which has lasted for the 11,700 years, to a new epoch, the Anthropocene. See especially the review by 24 members of the Anthropocene Working Group of the International Commission on Stratigraphy published in journal *Science*: C. Waters et al., "The Anthropocene is functionally and stratigraphically distinct from the Holocene," *Science* 351 (2016): 137.

25 See id., for further discussion. See also D. Vidas et al., "International law for the Anthropocene?," *Anthropocene* 9 (2015): 1–13.

national maritime claims are advanced, potentially leading to substantial reductions in the scope of claims to maritime jurisdiction.[26] UNCLOS provides a clear spatial framework for maritime claims and has achieved near universal acceptance with, at the time of writing, 168 parties to it comprising 167 States plus the European Union.[27] Such claims to maritime jurisdiction are, however, traditionally understood to be dependent on retaining or maintaining sovereignty over land territory.

In keeping with this understanding, the continued existence of islands above high water, that is land territory, is therefore crucially important to continued claims to maritime jurisdiction. The jurisdictional limits of maritime zones are largely dependent on distance measurements from baselines along the coast. In particular, the limits of the territorial sea, contiguous zone, and EEZ are all defined by reference to distances, of 12, 24, and 200 nautical miles respectively, measured from such baselines.[28] Although the definition of continental shelf limits is more complex, distance-based measurements from baselines still play an important role.[29]

Further, while UNCLOS allows coastal States to define or claim several different types of baselines,[30] the predominant type consists of "normal" baselines that are coincident with the "low-water line along the coast as marked on large-scale charts officially recognized by the coastal State."[31] Such "normal" baselines represent the predominant type of baseline in use globally and are, in a sense, a coastal State's "default" baseline. Further, it can be noted that the various straight-line alternatives to normal baselines that may be claimed by a coastal State still depend to some extent on the location of normal baselines, because in order to be valid they need to at least broadly reflect the general

---

26 This section draws on Schofield, n. 7 above, pp. 54–56.
27 See UNCLOS, n. 6 above. See also United Nations, "Status of the United Nations Convention on the Law of the Sea, of the Agreement relating to the implementation of Part XI of the Convention and of the Agreement for the implementation of the Convention relating to the conservation and management of straddling fish stocks and highly migratory fish stocks, New York, updated to 31 March 2018," available online: <http://www.un.org/Depts/los/reference_files/status2018.pdf>.
28 UNCLOS, id., arts. 3 and 4 (territorial sea), art. 33 (contiguous zone), art. 57 (EEZ).
29 The delineation of the outer limits of the continental shelf largely depends on complex geophysical factors, distance measurements from baselines, specifically the 200- and 350-nautical mile limits, remain important (Id., art. 76).
30 These include straight baselines (Id., art. 7), river closing lines (Id., art. 9), bay closing lines (Id., art. 10), lines related to ports and roadsteads (Id., arts. 11 and 12), and in respect of archipelagic states (Id., art. 47).
31 Id., art. 5.

directions of the coast and be connected back to the low-water line,[32] such that each system of baselines is "closed."[33]

It has long been recognized that parts of the coast are dynamic and can change location and configuration in relatively short periods. Indeed coastlines often change in a cyclical manner over time (alternately shifting seawards through deposition or accretion of material and then landwards because of erosion).[34] As normal baselines are coincident with the low-water line, this means that as coastlines and low-water lines move or "ambulate" over time, so the maritime jurisdictional limits measured from them will necessarily also shift and change.[35] This has the potential to lead to related "knock-on" shifts in the location of the outer limits to national maritime claims that are dependent upon such baselines. Thus, where the baseline advances (for example, by the deposition of material along the coast) the outer limits of the maritime claims measured from that baseline will expand seawards. Conversely, where the normal baseline recedes (through coastal erosion) the coastal State may lose maritime areas as the outer limits of their maritime zones are pulled back.

Here it is important to take into consideration the complex interactions between sea level and the shape and elevation of the land that were alluded to above.[36] This suggests that sea level rise does not necessarily automatically translate into recessions in the location of low-water lines in a straightforward manner. Further, it can be noted that only certain parts of a coastal State's baseline are critical for the definition of the outer limits of maritime claims. Such outer limits are commonly constructed through the "envelope of arcs"

---

[32] See id., arts. 7, 9, 10 and 47. See also *Anglo-Norwegian Fisheries Case* (United Kingdom v. Norway), Order, 1951 I.C.J. 117 (January 18), pp. 128–129.

[33] The UN Group of Technical Experts on Baselines indicated that, for straight baselines for example, this meant that "whether the baselines are drawn along the coast of an island or of the mainland, the system must start and finish on or above the low water line" and that where straight baselines were drawn connecting a fringe of islands "all the intermediate basepoints must be located on or above the low water line." See, United Nations, *Baselines: An Examination of the Relevant Provisions of the United Nations Convention on the Law of the Sea* (New York: Office for Ocean Affairs and the Law of the Sea, United Nations, 1989), p. 23.

[34] See, for example, W. Hirst and D. Robertson, "Geographic information systems, charts and UNCLOS: Can they live together?" *Maritime Studies* 136 (May-June 2004): 1–6.

[35] M.W. Reed, *Shore and Sea Boundaries: The Development of International Maritime Boundary Principles through United States Practice, Volume 3* (Washington, DC: U.S. Department of Commerce, National Oceanic and Atmospheric Administration, 2000), p. 185.

[36] K. Rogers and C.H. Schofield, "Responding to Changing Coasts: The Need for Fixed and Flexible Limits and Boundaries in the Face of Sea Level Rise," in J. Kraska and C. Esposito, (eds), *Ocean Law and Policy: Twenty Years of Development under UNCLOS* (Leiden/Boston: Martinus Nijhoff, 2016), pp. 419–445, 422–423.

method.³⁷ Thus, only the outermost points along the baseline will be relevant to the limits of the maritime zones. Nonetheless, despite these caveats and uncertainties, sea level rise has the potential to pose a significant threat to the extent of national maritime jurisdictional claims of States possessing low elevation coasts, including a number of Pacific Island States.

Potential Impacts for the Pacific SIDS

Sea level rise impacts for the Pacific SIDS relate most saliently to the potential inundation and erosion of parts of or even the entirety of low elevation islands.³⁸ Further, even if total inundation of island territory and thus the disappearance of islands were not to take place in the short term, there are concerns that sea level rise could lead to islands becoming appreciably less habitable. For example, this could occur through periodic flooding because of extreme weather events or through saltwater penetration of the freshwater aquifer beneath features, leading to a loss of potable water supplies.³⁹ As a consequence of such developments the potential exists for the forced displacement of large proportions, if not all, of the populations of the islands concerned. In addition to these potential sea level rise impacts on Pacific insular features themselves, as noted above, the retreat of baselines and even loss of entire features has the potential to significantly reduce the scope of claimed maritime zones.

This is of particular concern to Pacific SIDS, comprised as they often are of low elevation islands. Thus, the impacts of sea level rise on the SIDS in the Pacific and elsewhere have become an important dimension to discussions on climate change and the ocean globally.

Not all Pacific SIDS are subject to equivalent threats from sea level rise, however. While a number of Pacific Island States are entirely composed of low elevation coral reefs and related islands, others comprise predominantly or at least partially of higher elevation volcanic or raised limestone islands. The Marshall Islands, Tokelau, and Tuvalu can be considered especially vulnerable to sea level rise as they are wholly comprised of low-elevation atolls and other coral reef features. Kiribati is similarly almost entirely composed of low-lying reefs, the exception being Banaba Island, which is a raised limestone

---

37 C.M. Carleton and C.H. Schofield, *Developments in the Technical Determination of Maritime Space: Charts, Datums, Baselines, Maritime Zones and Limits*, Maritime Briefing 3, no. 3 (Durham: International Boundaries Research Unit, University of Durham, 2001), p. 62.
38 See, in particular, Schofield, n. 7 above, pp. 56–58.
39 See, for example, I. Kelman, "Island evacuation," *Forced Migration Review* 31 (October 2008), 20, p. 20. See also R. Rayfuse, "W(h)ither Tuvalu? International Law and Disappearing States," University of New South Wales Faculty of Law Research Series, Working Paper 9 (April 2009).

feature. Further, while other Pacific Island States possess some higher elevation islands, they are also partially composed of low-lying reef features. These States include the Cook Islands and Federated States of Micronesia (FSM) as well as outlying features forming parts of Fiji, Palau, PNG, and the Solomon Islands. A substantial number of features making up French Polynesia fall into this category as do outlying reefs to the west of New Caledonia. Analogously, the northwestern Hawaiian Islands as well as a number of remote small Pacific Island territories under U.S. administration also fit this description.[40]

In contrast, Pacific Island States composed predominantly, or at least partially, of higher elevation islands include Nauru, Niue, Samoa, and Tonga. Additionally, higher elevation features make up at least part of the territories of the Cook Islands, Fiji, parts of the FSM, the main northern islands of Palau, the main islands of PNG, and Vanuatu. Similarly, the main islands of New Caledonia and of French Polynesia such as the Marquesas Group, the main islands of American Samoa, Guam, the Northern Mariana Islands, and the main islands of Hawai'i fall into this category. As such islands can rise tens or hundreds of meters above high tide, there is negligible chance of their complete inundation, even if the IPCC's projection of the order of 1 m by 2100 proves to be overly conservative. Even if unlikely to be threatened by complete inundation, sea level rise impacts on these islands will still be serious as the majority of the population and the infrastructure on most Pacific Islands is concentrated on the low-lying coastal fringes of the island rather than its substantially higher core.

With respect to low elevation coral atoll features, these generally comprise an outer reef forming a ring protecting sheltered lagoon waters within it. Reef islands form either on the reef or within it. The persistence of such "above the high-water level islands" located on reefs is undoubtedly essential to the current and ongoing habitability of parts, or even the entirety, of certain small island States. Further, with respect to maritime claims, the presence of populated islands is necessary as only atolls hosting above high tide features can generate extensive maritime claims.[41] Such claims are, however, predominantly measured from the seaward low-water line of the outer reef edge. The ongoing existence and stability of both above high-water reef islands and low-water lines at reef edges is therefore significant. The capacity of such features to endure elevated sea levels is considered below.

---

40   Notably, Wake Island, Johnston Atoll, Howland and Baker, Jarvis Atoll Palmyra Island, and Kingman Reef.
41   In keeping with UNCLOS, n. 6 above, Article 6 which, in dealing with reefs refers to "[i]slands situated on reefs."

Challenges to Coral Reef Island Resilience

A critical consideration in relation to sea level rise impacts on Pacific SIDS is the interaction, including complex feedbacks, between rising sea levels and the coastal ecosystems in question, especially corals. In particular, corals have the ability to respond to changing sea levels and both gain elevation and provide sediments that enable island-building processes to occur on reefs. Indeed, evidence exists to suggest that coral reefs and islands can be remarkably robust and enduring features, capable of natural adaptation to sea level rise over time, with the geological record indicating that atolls have survived sea levels half a meter higher than present levels.[42] Further, there is evidence that atoll shorelines have proved to be stable even though sea levels have been rising steadily over recent decades. Here it is notable that not only are there indications that the outer edges of atoll reefs are capable of enduring elevated sea levels but that the islands situated on such atolls are also able to persist under such conditions.

For example, Kench has provided evidence from studies of reef islands suggesting that sea levels rose by half a meter around 2,000–4,000 years ago, after the islands in question were formed, yet the islands developed and remained above sea level.[43] Further, in a more recent historical timeframe, Webb and Kench reviewed and analyzed 27 atoll islands in the central Pacific. This comparison of historical aerial photography with modern satellite imagery led to the conclusion that 86 percent of the islands analyzed were as large as (43 percent) or larger than (43 percent) than they had been previously.[44] This study was designed to assess whether these features had in fact, been subject to erosion as might have been anticipated if conventional wisdom regarding the influence of sea level rise on coral islands was correct. The period covered by the survey coinciding with sea level records for the central Pacific establishing sea level change in the order of 2.0 mm/year, but the anticipated erosion or inundation had generally not occurred. That said, the authors emphasized that they

---

42   P. Kench, "Understanding Small Island Dynamics: A Basis to Underpin Island Management," in *Proceedings of the International Symposium of Islands and Oceans, 22–23 January 2009*, ed. H. Terashima (Ocean Policy Research Foundation, 2009), 22–32, pp. 24–28. See also A.P. Webb, "Coastal vulnerability and monitoring in the Central Pacific Atolls," pp. 33–38 in Terashima, id. Webb indicates that there exist examples of net-island growth which runs counter to "established thought, non-scientific reports in the popular media and modelling" and are suggestive of the complexity of shoreline responses to sea level rise (id., p. 37).

43   Kench, id.

44   A.P. Webb and P.S. Kench, "The dynamic response of reef islands to sea-level rise: Evidence from multi-decadal analysis of island change in the Central Pacific," *Global and Planetary Change* 72 (3) (2010): 234–246.

were not suggesting that coral reef islands are immune from climate change and sea level rise or that the island shorelines examined remained static. Indeed, many of the islands studied exhibit substantial changes, often involving erosion on exposed ocean-facing shores, but such erosion was often balanced, and at times exceeded by, accretion on sheltered lagoon-facing shorelines.[45] These findings do indicate that certain coral reef islands have proved to be capable of adapting to rising sea levels. Moreover, the basepoints critical for the construction of the outer limits of maritime claims from such features (see below) are predominantly located on outer reef edges and rocks which have thus far proved to be largely stable.

Against this seemingly optimistic historical context, the critical concern is whether the natural processes that allow coral reef islands to adapt to changing sea levels can be maintained in the face of significantly accelerated sea level rise. This is especially against the backdrop of warming,[46] an acidifying, and deoxygenating oceans which, moreover, features increasingly frequent extreme weather events such as intense storms.[47] All of these factors are likely to seriously impair the ability of coral reefs to respond to rising sea level and thus compromise the resilience of coral reef islands.[48] Further, historical rates of sea level rise are considerably less than currently observed rates, let alone projections of future, accelerated, sea level rise, adding further uncertainty.[49]

Further, some coral reefs and associated reef islands are, at least to an extent, protected or naturally "armored" as a result of the formation of beach rock and this is likely to influence the ability of such features to withstand sea level rise. This indicates that assessment of the impacts of sea level changes on coral islands should occur on a case-by-case basis and that generalizations

---

45   Id., p. 242.
46   The potentially disastrous effects of ocean warming for coral reefs are underscored by the increasing frequency and severity of coral reef bleaching events. See, for example, P.P. Wong et al., "Coastal systems and low-lying areas," in *Climate Change 2014: Impacts, Adaptation, and Vulnerability. Part A: Global and Sectoral Aspects. Contribution of Working Group II to the Fifth Assessment Report of the Intergovernmental Panel on Climate Change*, eds. C.B. Field et al. (Cambridge, UK: Cambridge University Press, 2014), 361–409, p. 378.
47   Such events can be highly destructive for coastal ecosystems such as corals and, coupled with multiple other factors such as disease, feed web changes, invasive organisms and heat stress mortality, may "overwhelm the capacity for natural and human systems to recover following disturbances." See, Hoegh-Guldberg et al., n. 20 above, p. 223.
48   The absorption of carbon dioxide by the ocean leads to ocean waters becoming more acidic which, in turn, impairs the ability of calcifying organisms such as corals to form, leading to reduced levels of calcification and enhanced skeletal dissolution and coral mortality.
49   See, for example, Rogers and Schofield, n. 38 above, p. 419.

are hazardous. Additionally, socioeconomic factors are likely to have profound impacts on the ability of coral reefs and islands to adapt to sea level rise. Increasing populations and population densities on Pacific Islands have and will continue to lead to changes in land use, loss of coastal vegetation, waste, overfishing, and pollution. All of these factors have the potential to impact the health of coral reef ecosystems and therefore calcification rates, leading to a shift in the balance between erosion and build up and potentially leading to a reduction in the viability of island environments to sustain human habitation. Additionally, human interventions such as the construction of sea defenses have significant potential to interrupt sediment flow regimes, thereby compromising the capacity of coral islands to naturally adapt to sea level rise.[50] The adoption of strategies to address these non-climate change stresses are urged "in order to increase ecological resilience in the face of escalating climate change impacts."[51]

Considerable uncertainty therefore exists over whether coral reef ecosystems and islands, which have proven to be remarkably robust and resilient in the past, will be able to cope with future sea level rise. Indeed, a recent study suggested that only nine percent of coral reefs are likely to "keep up" with the IPCC's current, and arguably overly optimistic, projected rates of sea level rise.[52] Such studies raise concerns that previously stable coral reef shorelines may become more erosive in character when faced with accelerated rates of sea level rise and thus less able to provide protection to reef islands as well as offer the sediment necessary to support island building processes on and within reef systems. The consequences of this may be the erosion and disappearance of entire islands or, at the least, significant changes to island shoreline stability, leading to reduced island habitability.

Indeed, the 2018 IPCC Special Report provides a stark warning concerning the future for tropical corals even if warming is restrained to 1.5°C. The Special Report rightly numbers tropical corals among the critically important "framework

---

50   See Kench, n. 44 above, pp. 15–19. See also, R. Kenchington, "Pacific Islands and the problems of sea level rise due to climate change," in Terashima, n. 44 above, pp. 6–9. Such interventions can, however, lead to increases in island size. For example, Webb and Kench found that in certain instances where causeways have been inserted between islands, blocking passages between ocean and lagoon areas, sediment has built up along the causeways and shorelines have extended such that islands have increased in area. See Webb and Kench, n. 46 above, p. 244.

51   Hoegh-Guldberg et al., n. 20 above, p. 85.

52   See, C.T. Perry et al., "Loss of coral reef growth capacity to track future increases in sea level," *Nature* 558 (2018): 396–400. See also, S. Albert et al., "Interactions between sea-level rise and wave exposure on reef island dynamics in the Solomon Islands," *Environmental Research Letters* 11 (2016): 1–9, p. 1.

organisms" or "ecosystem engineers" that build structures providing the habitat for large numbers of species.[53] However, the report assesses present-day risks to reef-building tropical corals as "high" with "evidence of strengthening concern" since AR5 that tropical corals "may be even more vulnerable to climate change" than indicated in assessments conducted in 2014.[54] In particular, the back-to-back bleaching events that occurred in 2015 and 2016 leading to the loss of 50 percent of the Great Barrier Reef's shallow water corals across large parts of the Great Barrier Reef[55] is highlighted as reason to "suggest that the research community has under-estimated climate risks for coral reefs."[56] This leads to the conclusion that tropical coral reefs face "very high risks" if warming exceeds 1.5°C and even if the emissions reductions necessary to meet this ambitious target are achieved the consequences will be dire with a "further loss of 90% of reef-building corals compared to today" predicted.[57]

In this context it is also important to note that in its Award of 12 July 2016, the Arbitral Tribunal in the case between the Philippines and China set a high threshold for islands to generate broad maritime zones.[58] In particular, the Award found that only islands that in their natural state can support a community of people at a "proper standard" of healthy life, or to support ongoing economic activity for the benefit of those people, without the necessity of the provision of significant external resources should be capable of generating continental and EEZ rights.[59] Even though the Tribunal's Award was focused on insular features in the South China Sea, and its findings in their specifics are only binding on China and the Philippines, the Award is nonetheless likely to resound well beyond the South China Sea. This is because it provides the first authoritative international judicial interpretation of the problematically ambiguous "Regime of Islands" under UNCLOS.

While the high threshold set by the South China Sea Award for "full" island status appears ominous for the Pacific Island States, it is notable that the Award in that case provides for some scope for flexibility in interpretation, which

---

53 Hoegh-Guldberg et al., n. 20 above, p. 84.
54 Id.
55 T.P. Hughes et al., "Global warming and recurrent mass bleaching of corals," *Nature* 543 (16 March 2017): 373–377, doi:10.1038/nature21707.
56 Hoegh-Guldberg et al., n. 20 above, p. 84.
57 As compared to losses of fully 99 percent under the scenario of 2°C or more warming above pre-industrial levels. Id.
58 *The South China Sea Arbitration (The Republic of Philippines v. The People's Republic of China)*, PCA Case No. 2013, Award, 12 July 2016.
59 Id., para. 587, although the Award does suggest a more flexible approach to groups of islands inhabited by indigenous populations that use the group of islands as a whole as a means of subsistence.

appears to have the maritime claims of small island States in mind. For example, with respect to the "human habitation" requirement contained in UNCLOS Article 121, it was observed that the community involved "need not necessarily be large" and that, for example, "in remote atolls a few individuals or family groups could well suffice."[60] The South China Sea Tribunal was also mindful that a group of islands may collectively provide for human habitation or economic life and that consequently periodic rather than permanent habitation of a feature by nomadic people "could also constitute habitation."[61] This ruling was founded on the Tribunal's understanding that "remote island populations often make use of a number of islands, sometimes spread over significant distances, for sustenance and livelihoods."[62]

Implications for Pacific Maritime Claims

The baselines in use by Pacific Island States are predominantly either the normal baselines of rocky shorelines or their associated barrier or fringing reefs in the case of uplifted volcanic or limestone islands or, alternatively, comprise the seaward outer edge of reefs and atolls. Additionally, a number of Pacific Island States have claimed archipelagic status namely, FSM, Fiji, Kiribati, Marshall Islands, Palau, PNG, Solomon Islands, Tonga, Tuvalu, and Vanuatu.[63] However, not all of these States have defined their archipelagic baselines.[64] In any case, as for other types of straight baselines, such archipelagic baselines need to link back to normal baselines as indicated above.

Up to the present, these baselines have proven to be stable and enduring. As noted above, however, it remains uncertain whether this will remain the case in the context of accelerated sea level rise in conjunction with ocean warming

---

60 Id., para. 542.
61 Id., paras. 544–546.
62 Id., para. 547.
63 Maritime zones legislation that support archipelagic claims are as follows: Fiji – *Marine Spaces Act* Cap. 158A, s. 4; Kiribati – *Marine Zones (Declaration) Act 1983*, s. 5, replaced by *Marine Zones (Declaration) Act 2011*, s. 7; Marshall Islands – *Marine Zones (Declaration) Act 1984*, s. 6; PNG – *National Seas Act 1977*, Part V; Solomon Islands – *Delimitation of Marine Waters Act 1978*, s. 4; Tonga – *Marine Zones Act 2009*, s. 4 and Part IV; Tuvalu – *Marine Zones (Declaration) Act 1983*, s. 6, replaced by *Marine Zones Act 2012*, s. 9; Vanuatu – *Maritime Zones Act 1981*, s. 4 replaced by *Maritime Zones Act 2010*, s. 4. Note that the constitutions of the FSM and Palau include provisions that support each being an archipelagic State; see FSM constitution, available online: <http://www.paclii.org/fm/legis/consol_act/cotfsom468/>, and Palau constitution, available online: http://www.paclii.org/pw/constitution.html>.
64 The following States have defined their archipelagic baselines and have accordingly notified the United Nations: Fiji, Kiribati, PNG, Solomon Islands, Tuvalu, and Vanuatu.

and acidification as well as anthropogenic impacts. These factors are highly likely to undermine the resilience of coral reef ecosystems and thus their ability to, essentially, "keep up" with aggressive rates of sea level rise.

However, it is important to note that it is not only the low-water baselines, from which maritime claims are measured, that are imperiled. The endurance of reef islands on atolls and other coral reef features is crucial from a maritime jurisdictional perspective because naturally formed islands that are above high tide must exist on an atoll in order for maritime claims to be made from the low-water line of the surrounding reef in accordance with Article 6 of UNCLOS.

Arguably sea level rise could also change the legal status of such insular features. For example, an island that is currently always above the water surface even during high tide, may eventually disappear during high tide as a consequence of sea level rise. This could lead to its reclassification from being an island, from which claims to the full range of maritime zones may be made under Article 121(2) of UNCLOS, to one of the categories of insular formations from which only restricted maritime claims can be made such as a "rock" (UNCLOS Article 121(3)).[65] Similarly, an island could be reduced to the status of a mere low tide elevation (LTE), that is a feature exposed at low tide but submerged at high tide, in keeping with UNCLOS Article 13,[66] or even a fully submerged feature that cannot be used to generate any maritime claims. The ruling of the arbitral panel in the *South China Sea Case* concerning the regime of islands also needs to be borne in mind in this context.

Were low-elevation coral reefs and their associated reef islands to ultimately prove to be vulnerable to sea level rise, then the claims to maritime jurisdiction dependent upon them would also appear to be under threat. As observed above, the Marshall Islands, Tokelau, and Tuvalu are wholly comprised of low-elevation atolls and other coral reef features. Similarly, the vast majority of Kiribati is made up of such features. The maritime entitlements of these States can therefore be considered to be most at risk from sea level rise.

The maritime claims of most other Pacific Island States would also be implicated to varying degrees, even if they include some higher elevation islands. These States include the Cook Islands and FSM as well as the outlying features

---

65   UNCLOS, n. 6 above, Article 121(3) provides that "[r]ocks which cannot sustain human habitation or economic life of their own shall have no exclusive economic zone or continental shelf."

66   UNCLOS, id., Article 13(1) states that "[a] low-tide elevation is a naturally formed area of land which is surrounded by and above water at low tide but submerged at high tide. Where a low-tide elevation is situated wholly or partly at a distance not exceeding the breadth of the territorial sea from the mainland or an island, the low-water line on that elevation may be used as the baseline for measuring the breadth of the territorial sea."

making up Fiji, Palau, PNG, and the Solomon Islands. Similarly, the maritime claims associated with the Pacific territories of extra-regional States, including French Polynesia, New Caledonia, and the U.S. remote Pacific island territories would also be affected.

A Pacific Response

On 16 July 2015, seven leaders of Polynesian States and territories signed at Papeete, Tahiti, the Taputapuātea Declaration on Climate Change. This Declaration by Polynesian leaders was made in advance of the Twenty-first Session of the Conference of the Parties to the UN Framework Convention on Climate Change (UNFCCC COP 21)[67] in Paris. It states:

> [T]he Polynesian Leaders Group call upon all State Parties to the UNFCCC to ...
>
> With regard to the loss of territorial integrity:
>
> – Accept that climate change and its adverse impacts are a threat to territorial integrity, security and sovereignty and in some cases to the very existence of some of our islands because of the submersion of existing land and the regression of our maritime heritage.
> – Acknowledge, under the United Nations Convention on the Law of the Sea (UNCLOS), the importance of the Exclusive Economic Zones for Polynesian Island States and Territories whose area is calculated according to emerged lands and permanently establish the baselines in accordance with the UNCLOS, without taking into account sea level rise.[68]

At the same time a number of small archipelagic States have redrawn their maritime boundaries with a great deal of precision and detail. This is part of a concerted action supported by the South Pacific Forum, discussed in more detail below.

A good example from the region is provided by the Republic of the Marshall Islands,[69] although similar legislation, designating new archipelagic waters

---

67   United Nations Framework Convention on Climate Change (UNFCCC), 1771 *United Nations Treaty Series* 164.
68   *Sic.* Signed by the leaders of French Polynesia, Niue, Cook Islands, Samoa, Tokelau, Tonga, and Tuvalu. Text available online: <http://www.presidence.pf/files/Polynesian_PACT_EN_15-07-15.pdf>.
69   This and following sections draw on D. Freestone and C.H. Schofield, "Republic of the Marshall Islands: 2016 Maritime Zones Declaration Act: Drawing lines in the sea," *International Journal of Marine and Coastal Law* 31 (2016): 720–746.

and designating the outer limits of the national EEZs has also been passed by Kiribati[70] and Tuvalu.[71]

On 18 March 2016 the Nitijela (Parliament) of the Republic of the Marshall Islands passed comprehensive new legislation, repealing "in its entirety" the 1984 *Maritime Zones Declaration Act*, and declaring anew all its maritime zones.[72] Section 118 of the 2016 *Maritime Zones Declaration Act* authorizes the Minister to declare by order:

(a) the geographical coordinates of the points on the baseline; or
(b) the geographical coordinates of the limits of the whole or any part of the local government waters, territorial sea, archipelagic waters, the contiguous zone, the exclusive economic zone and the continental shelf.

The Act was accompanied by a Declaration of "Baselines and Outer Zone Limits" pursuant to the Act, also issued on 18 April 2016. These unusually detailed regulations run to more than 450 pages and include long lists of coordinates, plus supporting maps. The reason for the great length of the Declaration is that it provides for the definition of the location not only of the baselines of the Marshall Islands and agreed maritime boundaries with neighboring States, but the outer limits of its maritime zones. The primary purpose of this legislation is to provide maritime jurisdictional clarity and certainty. This approach is designed to deliver significant benefits in terms of maritime surveillance and enforcement efforts as uncertainties as to whether a particular vessel is within a particular maritime zone or not are removed.

As we have argued elsewhere, the wider significance of the Marshall Islands legislation is that it appears to anticipate that once established these "lines in the sea" defining baselines, limits and boundaries will not move in the future.[73]

---

70   Republic of Kiribati, *Baselines around the Archipelagos of Kiribati Regulations 2014* (2014), available online: <http://www.un.org/Depts/los/LEGISLATIONANDTREATIES/PDF-FILES/KIR_2014_archipel_baselines_regulations.pdf>, and *Exclusive Economic Zone Outer Limit Regulations 2014* (2014), available online: <http://www.un.org/Depts/los/LEGISLATIONANDTREATIES/PDFFILES/KIR_2014_eez_outer_limits_regulations.pdf>. Cited by S. Kaye, "The Law of the Sea Convention and sea level rise after the *South China Sea* Arbitration," *International Law Studies* 93 (2017): 423–445, p. 444.
71   Tuvalu, *Declaration of Archipelagic Baselines 2012*, LN No. 7 of 2012, available online: <http://www.un.org/Depts/los/LEGISLATIONANDTREATIES/PDFFILES/tuv_declaration_archipelagic_baselines2012_1.pdf>.
72   Republic of Marshall Islands, *Maritime Zones Declaration Act 2016* (2016), available online: <http://www.un.org/Depts/los/LEGISLATIONANDTREATIES/PDFFILES/DEPOSIT/mhl_mzn120_2016_1.pdf>. Discussed in detail by Freestone and Schofield, n. 69 above.
73   Freestone and Schofield, id.

Moreover, the Marshall Islands action represents the latest development in an emerging pattern of practice in the Pacific region whereby States are unilaterally declaring and publicizing their maritime jurisdictional baselines, limits, and boundaries. Such stability in the spatial scope of a State's maritime jurisdiction has notable administrative as well as enforcement benefits. However, as noted above, there are other important implications of this practice as it appears to be a deliberate attempt to pre-empt arguments that physical changes to its coastline, particularly those resulting from climate change-induced sea level rise, would have resulting impacts on its baselines and on the outer limits of its zones. In the light of regional policies such as the Pacific Oceanscape (see below), the definition and declaration of the Marshall Islands baselines, limits, and boundaries can be seen as part of a regional move to secure the present spatial scope of its maritime jurisdiction against the threat of future sea level rise.

Regional efforts in the 1990s were oriented toward defining baselines with a view to drawing indicative EEZ boundaries for the purpose of sharing income arising from fishing license fees under the U.S. Tuna Treaty. These were pioneered by the FFA. Subsequently, the Pacific Boundaries Project, a partnership involving the South Pacific Community (SPC) and Australia with the support of the FFA, Global Resource Information Data Network (GRID-Arendal), and the Commonwealth Secretariat, has made substantial progress in assisting the Pacific Island States to clarify the extent of their maritime jurisdictions. The project was initially concerned with assisting the Pacific Island States in the preparation of their extended continental shelf submissions for the UN Commission on the Limits of the Continental Shelf, something which necessarily involved the definition of their baselines. Its scope expanded to include the updating of maritime zones legislation and the delineation of the outer limits of their maritime zones. Additionally, the Project has played a significant role in terms of assisting these States in preparing and offering a forum for negotiations towards the delimitation of maritime boundaries between them, something that has led to a doubling in maritime boundary agreements in the region in recent years.[74]

The development of this State practice is, moreover, in keeping with, and was envisaged by, a strategy document developed by the Pacific Island Forum called the *Framework for a Pacific Oceanscape*,[75] whose Strategic Priority

---

74 For more details see, R. Frost et al., "Redrawing the map of the Pacific," *Marine Policy* 95 (September 2018): 302–310, pp. 302–303 and 306–309, doi.org/10.1016/j.marpol.2016.06.003.
75 See C. Pratt and H. Govan, *Our Sea of Islands, Our Livelihoods, Our Oceania. Framework for A Pacific Oceanscape: A Catalyst for Implementation of Ocean Policy* (Pacific Islands Forum Secretariat, November 2010), available online: <http://www.forumsec.org/wp-content/uploads/2018/03/Framework-for-a-Pacific-Oceanscape-2010.pdf>.

1 concerns jurisdictional rights and responsibilities. That urges, in Action 1A, that the Pacific Island Countries and Territories (PICTS) should, "in their national interest," deposit with the UN coordinates and charts delineating their maritime zones.[76] Action 1B, entitled "Regional Effort to Fix Baselines and Maritime Boundaries to Ensure the Impact of Climate Change and Sea Level Rise Does Not Result in Reduced Jurisdiction of PICTS," states explicitly:

> Once the maritime boundaries are legally established, the implications of climate change, sea level rise and environmental change on the highly vulnerable baselines that delimit the maritime zones of Pacific Island Countries and Territories should be addressed. This could be a united regional effort that establishes baselines and maritime zones so that areas could not be challenged and reduced due to climate change and sea level rise.[77]

It is against this backdrop that the Delap Commitment and analogous statements, such as Taputapuātea Declaration and the recent Boe Declaration should be viewed.[78]

The Work of the ILA Committee

In keeping with these developments in 2012, following a recommendation of the 75th International Law Association (ILA) Conference, held in Sofia, Bulgaria, the ILA Executive Council established a Committee on International Law and Sea Level Rise.[79] The mandate of this new Committee is to study the possible impacts of sea level rise and the implications under international law of

---

76   Id., p. 57.
77   Id., p. 58.
78   The Boe Declaration reaffirms that "climate change presents the single greatest threat to the livelihoods, security and wellbeing of the peoples of the Pacific." See Pacific Islands Forum Secretariat, "Boe Declaration on Regional Security" (5 September 2018), available online: <https://www.forumsec.org/boe-declaration-on-regional-security/>. The accompanying Pacific Islands Forum Communiqué recognizes specifically the "urgency and importance of securing the region's maritime boundaries" though framed around development and security as well as the Blue Pacific Continent visualization of the region, and also includes an assertion that Pacific leaders are "committed to progressing the resolution of outstanding maritime boundary claims." See Pacific Islands Forum Secretariat, "Communiqué of the Forty-Ninth Pacific Islands Forum, Yaren, Nauru, 3–6 September, 2018," Doc. PIFS(18)10, available online: <https://uploads.guim.co.uk/2018/09/05/1FINAL_49PIFLM_Communique_for_unofficial_release_rev.pdf>.
79   International Law Association (ILA), "Minutes of the Meeting of the Executive Council," London, 10 November 2012, p. 5. ILA, "International Law and Sea Level Rise Committee," available online: <http://www.ila-hq.org/en/committees/index.cfm/cid/1043>.

the partial and complete inundation of State territory, or depopulation thereof, in particular of small island and low-lying states; and to develop proposals for the progressive development of international law in relation to the possible loss of all or of parts of State territory and maritime zones due to sea level rise, including the impacts on statehood, nationality, and human rights.[80]

In August 2018, at the 78th Conference of the International Law Association held in Sydney, Australia, the International Law and Sea Level Rise Committee presented its Second Report (hereinafter the Sydney Report).[81] Some of its key findings are outlined below.

The Sydney Report summarizes the key issues as follows. When sea levels rise, the low-water line along the coast – which marks the "normal baseline" for the purposes of Article 5 – will usually move inland and some key geographical features used as basepoints for delineating the outer limits of maritime zones and for the delimitation of maritime boundaries may be inundated and lost. If, as a matter of international law, the coastal baseline is ambulatory,[82] then in situations where a baseline moves inland[83] and critical basepoints from which maritime zones are measured are inundated, the outer limits of the maritime zones which are measured from this baseline may also move landward.[84] In situations where key geographical features, which are used as basepoints for the delineation of the outer limits to maritime claims or, for example, the construction of systems of straight baselines, are totally inundated, these

---

80 Id. See also D. Vidas, D. Freestone and J. McAdam, "International law and sea level rise: The new ILA Committee," *International Law Students' Association (ILSA) Journal of International and Comparative Law* 21 (2015): 397–408; D. Freestone, D. Vidas and A. Torres Camprubí, "Sea level rise and impacts on maritime zones and limits: The work of the ILA Committee on sea level rise and international law," *Korean Journal of International and Comparative Law* 3 (2017): 5–35.

81 ILA, "Sydney Conference (2018), Report of the ILA Committee on International Law and Sea Level Rise," available online: <http://www.ila-hq.org/en/committees/index.cfm/cid/1043>.

82 As the ILA Baselines Committee has concluded. See ILA, "Sofia Conference (2012), Report of the Baselines under the International Law of the Sea Committee," p. 31, available online: <http://www.ila-hq.org/index.php/committees>.

83 Also, note that because of changes in sediment flows rising sea level may in some circumstances also have an opposite effect in some places, accreting sediments to push the low-water line seaward.

84 Where the outer edge of the natural prolongation of the continental shelf is less than 200 nautical miles from the coastal baseline, then the outer limit of the shelf may extend to 200 nautical miles from the baseline (UNCLOS, n. 6 above, art. 76(1)). Due consideration should be here also given to Article 76(9) of UNCLOS, which states that the "coastal State shall deposit with the Secretary-General of the United Nations charts and relevant information, including geodetic data, permanently describing the outer limits of its continental shelf."

movements landward may be even more substantial. This same principle of course applies to the archipelagic baselines of archipelagic States, where the effect of losses of key basepoint features may result in pronounced changes in maritime entitlements, including the potential invalidation of archipelagic baselines systems.[85] Although small island States are likely to be the most obviously affected by such changes, it is important to note that these changes would be likely to affect many, if not most, coastal States.

The Committee recognized the inequity of a situation where small island States that have contributed the least to the greenhouse gas emissions causing anthropogenic climate change, might, under the current rules of international law, suffer the first and most serious impacts of sea level rise. It also recognized the importance that these maritime areas and the access to valuable marine resources that these ocean spaces imply to these small island, large ocean States and territories as well as the wider implications for international peace and security of the unprecedented operation of rules that might upset established claims and boundaries.

The Committee then considered the question of how it might present any proposal *de lege ferenda* (i.e., to progressively develop the law) so that coastal and island States should have the option to maintain their maritime entitlements notwithstanding changes brought about by sea level rise. The options it had discussed in its reports, some of which it accepted might not be practical, included the following: the development of customary international law,[86] a protocol to the UN Framework Convention on Climate Change,[87] utilization of the amendment provisions of UNCLOS,[88] a decision of the meeting of the State parties to the UNCLOS (SPLOS),[89] a diplomatic conference open also for States

---

85   See UNCLOS, n. 6 above, art. 47.
86   As suggested by Soons in 1990, A.H.A. Soons, "The effects of a rising sea level on maritime limits and boundaries," *Netherlands International Law Review* 37 (1990): 207–232, p. 255.
87   As proposed in 1990 by the Coastal Zone Management Subgroup of the IPCC, reported by D. Freestone and J. Pethick, "Sea level rise and maritime boundaries: International implications of impacts and responses," in *International Boundaries; Fresh Perspectives*, ed. G. Blake (Volume 5, Routledge, 1994), 73–90, p. 76.
88   See UNCLOS, n. 6 above, arts. 311–316. For a discussion of the complexity of this procedure, see, e.g., D. Freestone and A.G. Oude Elferink, "Flexibility and Innovation in the Law of the Sea: Will the LOS Convention Amendment Procedures Ever Be Used?," in *Stability and Change in the Law of the Sea: The Role of the LOS Convention*, ed. A.G. Oude Elferink (Boston/Leiden: Nijhoff, 2005), 163–216.
89   Note that Article 319(2)(e) UNCLOS, n. 6 above, appears to allocate only administrative roles to this meeting, e.g., under UNCLOS Annex II, Article 293 and Annex VI, Articles 4(4), 18 and 19, as discussed in Freestone and Oude Elferink, id., pp. 207–209.

non-parties to the UNCLOS, or an agreement adopted by the UN General Assembly after negotiation in its subsidiary bodies or informal consultations.[90]

The Committee noted the considerable legal and political complexities involved in a number of these options, including particularly the amendment procedure outlined in UNCLOS itself.[91] It then considered the mechanics of the evolution of a new rule of customary international law and also considered whether any proposals it might make on this issue could be influential in the contemporary interpretation of the text of UNCLOS. In particular, its attention was drawn to the work of the International Law Commission regarding "subsequent practice" in relation to the work of the Commission regarding interpretation of treaties under the 1969 Vienna Convention on the Law of Treaties.[92] Article 31(3) of the Vienna Convention envisages that, in interpreting treaties, "any subsequent practice in the application of the treaty which establishes the agreement of the parties regarding its interpretation" shall be taken into account, together with the context.[93]

---

90 All discussed further by M. Hayashi, "Sea Level Rise and the Law of the Sea: Future Options," in *The World Ocean in Globalisation: Climate Change, Sustainable Fisheries, Biodiversity, Shipping, Regional Issues*, eds. D. Vidas and P.J. Schei (Boston/Leiden: Brill/Martinus Nijhoff, 2011), 197, 200–206.

91 See Freestone and Oude Elferink, n. 90 above.

92 United Nations, *Report of the International Law Commission, Sixty-eighth session* (2 May–10 June and 4 July–12 August 2016), UN Doc. A/71/10, p. 121, Chapter VI, Subsequent agreements and subsequent practice in relation to the interpretation of treaties:
    Conclusion 4. Definition of subsequent agreement and subsequent practice: ...
    2. "subsequent practice" as an authentic means of interpretation under article 31, paragraph 3(b), consists of conduct in the application of a treaty, after its conclusion, which establishes the agreement of the parties regarding the interpretation of the treaty.
    3. Other "subsequent practice" as a supplementary means of interpretation under article 32 consists of conduct by one or more parties in the application of the treaty, after its conclusion.

93 Vienna Convention on the Law of Treaties, 23 May 1969, 1155 *United Nations Treaty Series* 331. Article 31(2) and (3) of the Vienna Convention reads:
    2. The context for the purpose of the interpretation of a treaty shall comprise, in addition to the text, including its preamble and annexes:
       (a) any agreement relating to the treaty which was made between all the parties in connection with the conclusion of the treaty;
       (b) any instrument which was made by one or more parties in connection with the conclusion of the treaty and accepted by the other parties as an instrument related to the treaty.
    3. There shall be taken into account, together with the context:
       (a) any subsequent agreement between the parties regarding the interpretation of the treaty or the application of its provisions;
       (b) *any subsequent practice in the application of the treaty which establishes the agreement of the parties regarding its interpretation.* (emphasis added)

The Committee recognized that there were a number of procedural options open to States that wished to take advantage of its proposals and, while deciding not to propose any specific option at this point, expressed the hope that a Resolution of the International Law Association might be the most effective first step in bringing its recommendations to a wider audience. It noted the strong evidence of emerging State practice in the Pacific region regarding the intent of many island States to maintain their maritime entitlements in the face of sea level rise.

On the basis of the proposals contained in the 2018 Sydney Report, the 78th ILA Conference passed a resolution endorsing the proposal of the Committee that "on the grounds of legal certainty and stability, provided that the baselines and the outer limits of maritime zones of a coastal or an archipelagic State have been properly determined in accordance with the 1982 Law of the Sea Convention, these baselines and limits should not be required to be recalculated should sea level change affect the geographical reality of the coastline."[94] The resolution further states that the interpretation of UNCLOS in relation to the ability of coastal States to maintain their existing lawful maritime entitlements should apply equally to maritime areas delimited by international agreement or by decisions of international courts or arbitral tribunals.[95]

Conclusion

As a result of sea level rise, small island States and territories are on the front line of the impacts of climate change, notwithstanding their minimal contributions to the greenhouse gases emissions that have caused it. They have, however, mobilized a strong response. It was, for example, their voices that were raised in Paris in December 2015 at the UNFCCC COP 21[96] in the negotiation of the 2015 Paris Agreement. It was partly as a result of their insistence that the objective of the Paris Agreement which "aims to strengthen the global response to the threat of climate change, in the context of sustainable development and efforts to eradicate poverty" includes in its Article 2 an aspiration to

---

94   ILA, "Resolution 5/2018: Committee on International Law and Sea Level Rise," available online: <http://www.ila-hq.org/images/ILA/Resolutions/ILAResolution_5_2018_SeaLevel Rise.pdf>.
95   Id.
96   UNFCCC, n. 18 above.

[hold] the increase in the global average temperature to well below 2°C above pre-industrial levels and to pursue efforts to limit the temperature increase to 1.5°C above pre-industrial levels, recognizing that this would significantly reduce the risks and impacts of climate change.[97]

The IPCC in AR4 in 2007 had identified 1.5–2.5 °C above 1980–1990 levels as the threshold for dangerous climate change[98] and this too had been reflected in the wording of the 2009 Copenhagen Accord.[99] But it was the SIDS who insisted that a higher aspiration should be contained in the Paris Agreement; the threat of sea level rise was a major driver for this call. Nevertheless, even if the State parties to the Paris Agreement are able to keep warming within this lower limit, there is a broad scientific consensus, evident in AR5 and elsewhere in recent scientific literature, that the Earth is already committed to increases of sea level for the foreseeable future, possibly for the next several centuries, notwithstanding any change in limiting, or (theoretically) even eliminating altogether, greenhouse gas emissions.[100]

Their strategy therefore includes the use of political and legal means to maintain, as far as they are able, their existing claims to land and ocean in the face of what may eventually – although probably not in the near term – become an existential threat. They have already embarked upon a process of establishing a consistent pattern of regional State practice. However, the emergence of a new customary rule will require not only such a pattern of State practice, but also its acceptance as law or *opinio juris*.

It is debatable, however, whether their best interest is served by arguing for the emergence of a new rule of regional customary international law, rather than a new global rule. A new rule of regional customary international law would only be opposable to other States in the region which accepted it.[101] Certainly the ILA Committee took the view that its recommendations regarding the maintenance of maritime entitlements should be global not regional

---

97   Paris Agreement, n. 19 above, art. 2(1)(a). and online: <https://unfccc.int/process-and-meetings/the-paris-agreement/the-paris-agreement>.
98   See, n. 17 above.
99   Id.
100 Although note the IPCC Special Report (n. 20 above) projecting 90 percent loss of tropical corals even if "only" a 1.5 °C rise is achieved.
101 Indeed Professor Soons has argued that for those States in the region, such as Marshall Islands, Kiribati and Tuvalu, which have already redefined their boundaries in the way described above, that they have already established a regional custom among themselves – as they would each accept the opposability of each other's existing boundary lines. (Pers. comm., Prof. F. Soons (Utrecht) Sydney, August 2018 on file with authors.) This does not advance their case much further however.

– as they would need to be opposable to the world community, not limited *inter se* to the countries of a particular region. The ILA Committee proposal was also premised on that fact that it seemed, in the short term, unlikely that there would be a different solution agreed upon by States on a global basis. The Committee was also optimistic that the recommendations in its 2018 Report, if they were discussed and approved by the political organs of the UN, might well contribute to the formation of that *opinio juris*.

The Delap Commitment represents another step in a conscious political strategy by the Pacific small islands and territories to fight back against the threats that sea level rise represents. The fact that the issue is even raised within the context of a fisheries arrangement probably indicates the extent to which the threat of sea level rise has been internalized within national and regional political strategies. In a further demonstration of this trend, at its 70th Session in 2018 the International Law Commission has also established a Study Group on "Sea-level Rise in relation to International Law" with very similar terms of reference to the ILA Committee.[102]

Against this backdrop there has been some discussion as to the possibility of an advisory opinion of the International Tribunal on the Law of the Sea (ITLOS).[103] Whether ITLOS is likely to provide a dynamic evolutionary interpretation of the existing law, analogous to the interpretation provided on the regime of islands under Article 121 of UNCLOS provided by the Annex VII Tribunal in its South China Sea Award,[104] is questionable. It is true that in its two advisory opinions, that of the Seabed Disputes Chamber in Case 17[105] and that of the full court in Case 21,[106] ITLOS has had a major evolutionary impact on the development of the law. Specifically, this relates to the concept of

---

102 See United Nations, "Report of the International Law Commission, Seventieth Session, 30 April–1 June and 2 July–10 August 2018," UN Doc. A/73/10 (2018), Annex B, p. 326 ff.
103 A suggestion made by the President of the ITLOS, Judge Paik, at Conference, "Building Transformative Partnerships for Ocean Sustainability Conference," WMU-Sasakawa Global Ocean Institute, World Maritime University, Malmo, 8–9 May 2018.
104 *South China Sea Case*, n. 60 above, pp. 175–260, online: <https://pca-cpa.org/wp-content/uploads/sites/175/2016/07/PH-CN-20160712-Award.pdf>.
105 *Responsibilities and Obligations of States Sponsoring Persons and Entities with Respect to Activities in the Area*, Case No. 17, Advisory Opinion (International Tribunal on the Law of the Sea (ITLOS) Seabed Disputes Chamber, 1 February 2011); see also D. Freestone, "Responsibilities and obligations of states sponsoring persons and entities with respect to activities in the Area," *American Journal of International Law* 105 (2011): 755–761.
106 *Request for an Advisory Opinion submitted by the Sub-Regional Fisheries Commission* (SRFC), Case 21, (ITLOS, 2 April 2015); see also D. Freestone, "Case 21: Request for an Advisory Opinion submitted by the Sub-Regional Fisheries Commission (SRFC), International Tribunal for the Law of the Sea," *Asia-Pacific Journal of Ocean Law and Policy* 1 (2016): 126–133.

the responsibility of States sponsoring seabed exploration and mining in the Area in its first advisory opinion and concerning the responsibilities of flag States whose vessels are fishing in the EEZs of other States in the second. However, it remains true that many of its other decisions feature a plethora of dissenting and separate opinions. So even if such a request could be made, and the not inconsiderable procedural hurdles involved were overcome, this option may not deliver the outcome desired by low lying States threatened by sea level rise, notably those in the Pacific region but in other parts of the global ocean also.

Consequently, Resolution 5/2018 of the International Law Association regarding the maintenance of existing, legally established, baselines, limits, and boundaries in the face of physical changes to coastlines brought about sea level rise should be seen as a major step forward. The ILA Committee is arguing that the maintenance of existing claims to maritime zones can be seen as a legitimate interpretation of UNCLOS in the light of subsequent State practice.

The development of a new rule of customary law is a complex and potentially protracted process. It does not simply require the development of a consistent pattern of State practice, but that practice must be "evidence of a general practice accepted as law" or what is known as *opinio juris sive necessitatis*. The International Court of Justice has talked of the requirement that the "State concerned must therefore feel that they are conforming to what amounts to a legal obligation."[107] Judge Hersch Lauterpacht has called this the "mysterious phenomenon of customary international law which is deemed to be a source of law only on condition that it is in accordance with law."[108] However, the absence of protest at the evolution of a new State practice may provide evidence of general acquiescence in the development of a new rule. In addition, Article 38(1)(d) of the Statute of the International Court of Justice, which is an appendix to the UN Charter and generally accepted as an authoritative statement of the sources of international law, does accept, as a subsidiary means for the determination of rules of law, "the teachings of the most highly qualified publicists of the various nations."[109] The International Law Association is a truly international professional association of international lawyers. Its reports and resolutions are highly regarded within the profession. Its support for legal recognition of a new rule of customary international law, as outlined in the Delap

---

107 *North Sea Continental Shelf Cases* (FDR v. Denmark; FDR v. The Netherlands) [1969] ICJ Reports 3, p. 77.
108 H. Lauterpacht, "Sovereignty over submarine areas," *British Yearbook of International Law* 27 (1950): 376, p. 395.
109 Statute of the International Court of Justice, 26 June 1945, 3 Bevans 1179, art. 36(1)(d).

Commitment and elsewhere, is a significant contribution to this process. Moreover, as the IPCC 2018 Special Report now makes clear, global warming of "even" 1.5 °C poses a very high risk to certain coastal ecosystems including tropical corals, suggesting that the baselines on which the maritime claims of Pacific Island States often depend are in severe danger of radical change. This makes the case for proactive action at an international law level – such as that proposed by the ILA – of even more pressing importance.

Appendix 1

Delap Commitment*
EOÑOD IM JAB KŪNBŪT

Reshaping the Future to Take Control of the Fisheries

Securing Our Common Wealth of Oceans
Leaders from the Federated States of Micronesia, Republic of Kiribati, Republic of the Marshall Islands, Republic of Nauru, Republic of Palau, Independent State of Papua New Guinea, Solomon Islands and Tuvalu met in Majuro, Marshall Islands, on 2 March 2018

Leaders

Taking into account the Nauru Agreement concerning cooperation in the Management of Fisheries of Common Interest and the First, Second, and Third Implementing Arrangements setting forth additional measures to implement the Nauru Agreement;

Noting the Federated States of Micronesia Arrangement for Regional Access and the Palau Arrangement for the Management of the Western and Central Pacific Tuna Fishery;

Welcoming the overwhelming success of the Purse Seine Vessel Day Scheme in controlling fishing effort and in increasing the economic value of the tuna

---

* EDITORS' NOTE. – This document is reproduced from the original signed Delap Commitment provided by the PNA Office. It has been minimally edited and footnoted for publication in the *Ocean Yearbook*.

fishery to the Parties and the enormous success of the PNA in the past eight years;[110]

Recalling the *Bikenibeu Declaration on Securing Greater Value from their Common Fisheries Wealth* adopted by Fisheries Ministers done at Tarawa on 22 October 2009 calling for the adoption of additional conservation and management measures;

Further recalling the *Koror Declaration Committing Parties to the Nauru Agreement to Joint efforts to increase the Economic Value and derive greater benefits from the tuna resource* adopted by Leaders on 25 February 2010.

Having adopted the decision to certify the world's first PNA purse seine free school skipjack and yellowfin tuna under the Marine Stewardship Council (MSC), hereby acknowledge the change that this has contributed to the effective management of the fishery, *inter alia*, through the development of Limit Reference Points (LRP) for all four tuna stocks and an Interim Target Reference Point (TRP) for skipjack and call for the development of a PNA standards that integrates the unique features of the Pacific Ocean;

Reaffirming their commitment to the Western and Central Pacific Fisheries Commission (WCPFC) and to the calls by Forum Leaders for the establishment of zone-based and rights-based fisheries management measures for PNA's tuna fisheries;

Reiterating the aspirations of the Parties to the Nauru Agreement to enhance the controls that the Parties have over their common tuna fisheries;

Acknowledging the importance of regional co-operation as underlined in the Vava'u Declaration and reaffirming the Parties' support for co-operative regional fisheries management through the Pacific Islands Forum Fisheries Agency, Secretariat of the Pacific Community, the Western and Central Pacific Fisheries Commission, and the Pacific Islands Forum Secretariat;

Acknowledging also the challenges presented by their unique vulnerability and the threat to the integrity of maritime boundaries and the existential impacts due to sea level rise;

---

110   PNA is the Parties to the Nauru Agreement.

Encouraged by the scientific advice that fishing on all three major tropical tuna stocks (bigeye, skipjack and yellowfin) currently appear to be sustainable;

Noting the importance of measures adopted by the Parties in contributing to this outcome, with most of the catches of these stocks being made in PNA waters;

Conscious nevertheless of the need for continuing improvement in the management of these stocks within the Parties' waters and throughout their range to ensure sustainable regional tuna fisheries;

Desiring to maximize economic gains from the tuna fisheries through the adoption of effective conservation and management measures and exertion of greater control of the fisheries for the Pacific Islands to ensure the social and economic wellbeing of their peoples are met;

Fully Aware that for many of the Parties, the tuna resource represents the primary source of achieving greater economic self-sufficiency;

Believing that the prospects of enhancing economic growth for many of the Parties depend to a large degree on the sustainability of their common tuna resource and that this must be managed for the betterment of their people's livelihood;

Recognizing that economic gains may be maximized through the development of additional arrangements that control output and limit effort to create scarcity and increase the value of the tuna resources;

Expressing their wholehearted appreciation and gratitude to the Government and People of the Republic of the Marshall Islands for their warm welcome and gracious hospitality on hosting the second PNA Leaders' Summit;

Have Agreed:

1. To renew their vision of safeguarding our rights, exercising our control, supporting sustainability and ensuring maximum returns from the utilization of our fisheries.

2. To reaffirm the PNA core business of collaborating on strategy and policy, to coordinate and harmonize the management of fisheries of common interest for the benefit of their peoples.
3. To use their resources to create self-reliance and independence and not be bystanders in the development of their tuna fisheries.
4. To develop a strategy on sustainability by developing improved standards for their fishery.
5. To continue efforts with the development of initiatives to increase Parties' share of the value of the tuna fishery through vertical integration.
6. To endorse the decision by Ministers to invite Papua New Guinea to purchase iFIMS.[111]
7. To implement the Forum Leaders Decision to prohibit purse seiners bunkering in the high seas.
8. To pursue legal recognition of the defined baselines established under the *United Nations Convention on the Law of the Sea* to remain in perpetuity irrespective of the impacts of sea level rise.
9. To convene a PNA Leaders' Summit more frequently, at least every three to five years.
10. To task Ministers to explore measures to reduce marine pollution and the carbon footprint of the fishery sector.
11. To task Ministers to provide a draft strategic plan on the future direction of the PNA to the PNA Leaders at the Forum Leaders Meeting in September in Nauru.
12. To task Ministers to develop additional conservation and management measures for high seas fishing.
13. To task Ministers to develop measures to reduce bycatch including the improvement of the management of FAD fishing.[112]
14. To direct Ministers to strengthen good governance and management of the PNA Office.

Done at Majuro, Marshal Islands this 2nd day of March 2018.

[Original signed by officials of the Republic of the Marshall Islands, Republic of Nauru, Republic of Kiribati, Tuvalu, Federated States of Micronesia, Solomon Islands, Republic of Palau, and the Independent State of Papua New Guinea]

---

111 iFIMS is the integrated Fisheries Information Management System, available online: <http://www.ifims.com/>.
112 FAD means fish aggregating device.

Is There a Relationship between UNDRIP and UNCLOS?

*Aldo Chircop**
Marine & Environmental Law Institute, Schulich School of Law, Dalhousie University, Halifax, Canada

Timo Koivurova and Krittika Singh
Arctic Centre, University of Lapland, Rovaniemi, Finland

Introduction

Climate change-induced sea ice melting and the consequent opening of sea routes in the Arctic have increased the chances of interaction between shipping or resource development activities and traditional uses of the sea (and sea ice) by indigenous peoples in the Arctic.[1] In the Pacific, climate change coupled with resource development activities is adversely impacting indigenous peoples' relationship with the ocean on which they have depended for millennia.[2] Bearing in mind the close ties that indigenous peoples have with the ocean, and also the emergence of a new field of law relating to the rights of indigenous peoples, in this article we will explore the possible convergence between international indigenous rights law and the law of the sea, most especially through their flagship instruments, respectively, the United Nations Declaration on the Rights of Indigenous Peoples (UNDRIP)[3] adopted by the United

---

* The authors acknowledge the project Indeterminate and Changing Environments: Law, the Anthropocene, and the World (ICE LAW Project: https://icelawproject.org/), supported by a generous Leverhulme Trust Network Grant, in bringing them together to work on this article.

1 See the Arctic Marine Shipping Assessment 2009 Report (AMSA), PAME, Arctic Council, especially the chapter on human dimensions, available online: <https://oaarchive.arctic-council.org/handle/11374/54>.

2 See "Study on the relationship between indigenous peoples and the Pacific Ocean," Note by the Secretariat, Permanent Forum on Indigenous Issues, United Nations Economic and Social Council E/C.19/2016/3, 19 February 2016, available online: <http://www.un.org/en/ga/search/view_doc.asp?symbol=E/C.19/2016/3&referer=/english/&Lang=E>.

3 United Nations General Assembly (UNGA), United Nations Declaration on the Rights of Indigenous Peoples, UNGA Res 61/295, UN Doc. A/RES/61/295, adopted 13 September 2007 (hereafter cited as UNDRIP), available online: <http://www.un.org/esa/socdev/unpfii/documents/DRIPS_en.pdf>. For an authoritative commentary, see J. Hohmann and M. Weller,

Nations General Assembly (UNGA) in 2007 and the United Nations Convention on the Law of the Sea, 1982 (UNCLOS).[4] The enquiry will be a theoretical one and the general reader might question the basis for it given the different subject matter and status of the two instruments: UNDRIP is a UN General Assembly resolution in the field of international human rights law, whereas UNCLOS is an international multilateral convention governing the world's oceans. At the outset we recognize that as a think-piece, this article does not address all the possible issues arising from such a novel relationship and that further scholarly research will be necessary.

UNDRIP recognizes urgent needs that include respect and promotion of the *inherent rights of indigenous peoples*, especially their rights to self-determination, and rights affirmed in treaties, agreements and other arrangements with States, control of their lands, territories and resources, and respect for indigenous knowledge, cultures and traditional practices which contribute to sustainable and equitable development and proper management of the environment.[5] In some situations, the agreements between indigenous peoples and States are "matters of international concern, interest, responsibility and character." Similar to the Universal Declaration on Human Rights,[6] UNDRIP sets out its provisions as a "standard of achievement."[7] UNDRIP provides that "[t]he United Nations, its bodies, including the Permanent Forum on Indigenous Issues, and specialized agencies, including at the country level, and States shall promote respect for and full application of the provisions of this Declaration and follow up the effectiveness of this Declaration."[8] The scope of the instrument is lands, territories, waters, and coastal seas and the provisions include matters such as resource rights and environmental protection.[9]

The UNDRIP scope appears to overlap with the spatial and functional concerns of UNCLOS. The mission of UNCLOS was to settle "all issues relating to

---

The UN Declaration on the Rights of Indigenous Peoples: A Commentary, Oxford Commentaries on International Law (Oxford University Press, 2018) (hereafter cited as UNDRIP Commentary).

4 United Nations Convention on the Law of the Sea, adopted 10 December 1982 (entered into force 16 November 1994), 1833 *United Nations Treaty Series* 397 (hereafter cited as UNCLOS).
5 UNDRIP, n. 3 above, preamble.
6 Universal Declaration on Human Rights, UNGA Res 217 A, UN Doc. A/RES/3/217A, adopted 10 December 1948 (hereafter cited as Universal Declaration), preamble.
7 UNDRIP, n. 3 above, preamble.
8 Id., art. 42.
9 Id., arts. 25–28 and 32 provide for land and resource rights. Article 29 deals specifically with environmental protection.

the law of the sea and ... be an important contribution to the maintenance of peace, justice and progress *for all peoples* of the world" (emphasis added), that "the problems of ocean space are closely interrelated and need to be considered as a whole," and that it was desirable to establish a legal order "which will facilitate international communication, and will promote the peaceful uses of the seas and oceans, the equitable and efficient utilization of their resources, the conservation of their living resources, and the study, protection and preservation of the marine environment."[10] The negotiators of UNCLOS believed that "the achievement of these goals will contribute to the realization of a just and equitable international economic order which takes into account *the interests and needs of mankind as a whole*" (emphasis added).[11] Further, that the "codification and progressive development of the law of the sea achieved in the Convention ... will promote the *economic and social advancement of all peoples of the world*" (emphasis added).[12]

The two instruments resulted from prolonged multilateral conference diplomacy characterized by difficult negotiation processes, both leading to final voting on their adoption despite extensive efforts towards consensus-building. Eventually both instruments secured overwhelming international acceptance. Both instruments play vital roles in international law by setting out frameworks and nourishing the larger legal system with respect to the issues they address. We do not assume that being part of the common legal edifice alone is sufficient to conclude that there must be a relationship between the two, for after all international law addresses a wide range of diverse and not necessarily always related subjects. Rather, we posit that if the two instruments address potentially common subject matter within the purview of each other's scope, it is worth enquiring if there is interaction and what that might be. At times, regimes in international law have been developed in silos and giving rise to potential policy and normative conflicts.[13] Thus it is useful

---

10   UNCLOS, n. 4 above, preamble.
11   Id.
12   Id.
13   One such example is the separate development of the Paris Climate Agreement and World Trade Organization Rules, aspects of which potentially conflict. See J. Bacchus, *The Case for a WTO Climate Waiver*, CIGI Special Report (CIGI, 2017), available online: <https://www.cigionline.org/sites/default/files/documents/NEWEST%20Climate%20Waiver%20-%20Bacchus.pdf>. See also World Economic Forum, *From Collision to Vision: Climate Change and World Trade,* Discussion Paper Circulated by the Ad Hoc Working Group on Trade and Climate Change (November 2010), available online: <http://www.felixpena.com.ar/contenido/negociaciones/anexos/2010-12-WEF_ClimateChange_WorldTrade DiscussionPaper_2010.pdf>.

to explore whether the two instruments expressly or implicitly anticipate relationships to other instruments and norms of international law.[14]

Hence our query and consequential consideration of whether UNDRIP could supplement or assist the interpretation of the individual and collective obligations of State parties in implementing UNCLOS where ocean space and indigenous rights potentially intertwine in a contemporary setting. We will first examine the legal status of UNDRIP and UNCLOS in international law and then proceed to analyze specific provisions that concern potentially related content to explore the interface between the two instruments before concluding with an assessment on the potential relationship and its consequences. While it would be valuable to go into domestic legislation and case law, exploration of domestic practices is outside the scope of this analysis. It is hoped that this reflective scholarly enquiry generates further discussion on the novel yet essential question on the interlinkages in public international law.

The United Nations Declaration on the Rights of Indigenous Peoples

Development of UNDRIP in View of the Evolution of Indigenous Rights

Considering the generally slow pace at which international law evolves, indigenous peoples have achieved a great deal in a relatively short period of time. The modern international indigenous peoples' movement did not fully begin until the end of the 1970s, and the first efforts to advance their rights within the UN were undertaken from 1982 onwards under the UN Working Group on Indigenous Populations (WGIP). In 1989, the International Labour Organization (ILO) replaced its largely assimilationist 1957 convention with the ILO C-169 – Convention on Indigenous and Tribal Peoples in Independent Countries (ILO 169),[15] which fleshed out a wide variety of legal rights for indigenous peoples. As the UN worked on adopting the Declaration on the Rights of Indigenous Peoples, the Organization of American States began drawing up a

---

14   In fact, UNDRIP has been compared to other norms of international law, such as international investment law. See C. Binder, "Interactions with international investment law," in UNDRIP Commentary, n. 3 above, pp. 87–111.

15   ILO Convention No. 169 concerning Indigenous and Tribal Peoples in Independent Countries, adopted 27 June 1989 (entered into force 5 September 1991), 28 *International Legal Materials* (1989) (hereafter cited as ILO 169 Convention), p. 1382. This chapter draws in part from T. Koivurova, "From high hopes to disillusionment: Indigenous peoples' struggle to (re)gain their right to self-determination," *International Journal on Minority and Group Rights* 15 (2008): 1–26.

similar declaration for American indigenous peoples,[16] and the Nordic States started to work on a Nordic Saami Convention.[17] This normative activity manifested itself in the work of some UN human rights treaty monitoring bodies, in particular the Human Rights Committee, the Committee on Economic, Social and Cultural Rights, and the Committee on the Elimination of Racial Discrimination.[18] These bodies started to interpret their respective conventions vis-à-vis indigenous peoples in line with developments of a distinct body of law for indigenous peoples.[19] Notably, environmental protection treaties set up exceptions in their provisions recognizing the right of indigenous communities to act according to their cultural traditions.[20]

---

16   American Declaration on the Rights of Indigenous Peoples, adopted on 15 June 2016 at the third plenary session of the Organization of American States' General Assembly, available online: <https://www.oas.org/en/sare/documents/DecAmIND.pdf>. The declaration was negotiated from 1999 to 2016.

17   Nordic Saami Convention, adopted 13 January 2017 (not yet in force), available online: <https://www.sametinget.se/105173>. The draft convention was submitted to the three governments as early as 2005, and the finalized text was accepted in June 2017. It is still unclear whether the Saami parliaments and the governments will move forward with the convention.

18   Examples of other conventions that incorporated indigenous peoples' rights are: Convention on the Rights of the Child, adopted 20 November 1989 (entered into force 2 September 1990), UNGA Res. 44/25, 1577 *United Nations Treaty Series* 3, available online: <https://www.ohchr.org/en/professionalinterest/pages/crc.aspx>, especially art. 30; Convention on the Protection and Promotion of the Diversity of Cultural Expressions, adopted 20 October 2005 (entered into force 18 March 2007), 2440 *United Nations Treaty Series* (hereafter cited as CPPDCE), art. 7(1)(a), available online: <http://unesdoc.unesco.org/images/0022/002253/225383E.pdf>.

19   "It is through the evolutionary interpretation of human rights treaty provisions, to the extent of expanding their inherent individual character to covering 'collective' prerogatives, that international human rights bodies have universalized indigenous peoples' rights," notes the Rights of Indigenous Peoples Committee of the International Law Association, Hague Conference (2010), Interim Report on a Commentary on the Declaration of the Rights of Indigenous Peoples (hereafter cited as ILA Interim Report), p. 44, available online: <http://www.ila-hq.org/index.php/committees>.

20   For example, Interim Convention on the Conservation of North Pacific Fur Seals, adopted 9 February 1957 (entered into force 14 October 1957), 314 *United Nations Treaty Series* 105 (1957), art. VII; Agreement on the Conservation of Polar Bears, adopted 15 November 1973 (entered into force 26 May 1976), 13 *International Legal Materials* 13 (1973), art. III(1)(d), available online: <http://pbsg.npolar.no/en/agreements/agreement1973.html>; Convention on the Conservation of Migratory Species of Wild Animals (1979), adopted 23 June 1979 (entered into force 1 November 1983), 1651 *United Nations Treaty Series* 217, art. III(5)(c), available online: <https://www.cms.int/>; Convention on Biological Diversity, adopted 5 June 1992 (entered into force 29 December 1993), 1760 *United Nations Treaty Series* 79 (hereafter, CBD), art. 8(j). Aboriginal subsistence whaling was exempted from the prohibition on whaling imposed by the International Whaling Commission established by the International Convention for the Regulation of Whaling, adopted 2 December 1946

The work that eventually became the UN Declaration on the Rights of Indigenous Peoples (UNDRIP) began in 1985 within the WGIP, which consisted of five expert members and which from the beginning allowed indigenous peoples broad access to the process, irrespective of whether they had gained indigenous status with the UN Economic and Social Council.[21] For almost a decade, the WGIP devoted a large part of its time to drafting the text of what was to become the UN Declaration in a process involving representatives of indigenous peoples, government delegations, and experts on the subject. This was a large area of work, since the Declaration aimed to cover all individual and collective rights of indigenous peoples in all possible areas of their lives, from their self-determination to their right to environment, or from their free prior and informed consent over the proposed natural resource exploitation to their labor rights. The Declaration aims to protect indigenous peoples' distinct cultures, their ownership and use rights to their ancestral lands and waters, the protection of their environments and their cultural heritage. In the following paragraphs, the development of the UN Declaration is examined especially in view of its provisions on self-determination, given that these were a major bone of contention between States and indigenous peoples and eventually delayed also the adoption of the UNDRIP.

In 1994, the Sub-Commission on Prevention of Discrimination and Protection of Minorities (now the Sub-Commission on the Promotion and Protection of Human Rights) adopted the Draft Declaration prepared by the WGIP and sent it to its parent body, the Commission on Human Rights (now replaced by the Human Rights Council), for consideration.[22] The article on self-determination at this stage drew heavily on Article 1(1) of the common Article to the

---

(entered into force 10 November 1948), 161 *United Nations Treaty Series* 72, available online: <https://iwc.int/convention>. Also see the European Union Regulation (EC) No 1007/2009 of the European Parliament and of the Council of 16 September 2009 on Trade in Seal Products, *Official Journal of the European Union*, L 286 of 31 October 2009.

21 In 1982 the Working Group on Indigenous Populations was established as a subsidiary organ to the Sub-Commission on Prevention of Discrimination and Protection of Minorities (now the Sub-Commission on the Promotion and Protection of Human Rights), endorsed by the UN Economic and Social Council (ECOSOC) on 7 May 1982 (UN Doc. E/Res/1982/34). It is composed of five members of the Sub-Commission, one representing each of the five geographical regions designated by the UN for electoral purposes. As a subsidiary organ of the Sub-Commission, the Working Group is located at the lowest level of the hierarchy of UN human rights bodies. Its recommendations have to be considered and accepted first by its superior body, the Sub-Commission, then by the Commission on Human Rights (now the Human Rights Council) and ECOSOC before being submitted to the General Assembly.

22 Draft United Nations Declaration on the Rights of Indigenous Peoples, 1994/45, available online: <http://www.unhchr.ch/huridocda/huridoca.nsf/(Symbol)/E.CN.4.SUB.2.RES.1994.45.En>.

Covenants in stating that "[i]ndigenous peoples have the right of self-determination. By virtue of that right they freely determine their political status and freely pursue their economic, social and cultural development."[23]

Another important provision of the 1994 Draft for the future framing of the right to self-determination of indigenous peoples was Article 31, which set out a right to autonomy:

> Indigenous peoples, as a specific form of exercising their right to self-determination, have the right to autonomy or self-government in matters relating to their internal and local affairs, including culture, religion, education, information, media, health, housing, employment, social welfare, economic activities, land and resources management, environment and entry by non-members, as well as ways and means for financing these autonomous functions.[24]

In 1995, the Commission on Human Rights considered the text submitted by the Sub-Commission and decided to establish an inter-sessional Working Group[25] with a mandate to consider the text presented and to draw up a draft declaration for the consideration by the Commission and eventual adoption by the UN General Assembly as part of the International Decade of the World's Indigenous People (1995–2004), a goal that was never achieved. The inter-sessional Working Group consisted only of State representatives, although indigenous peoples were given access to the process by being accorded the status of observers. In practice, this enabled direct negotiations between indigenous peoples and State representatives.[26]

Even though progress was slow in the Working Group and the goal of having the UN General Assembly adopt the UN Declaration by the end of 2004

---

23   Commission on Human Rights, 'Report of the Working Group on Indigenous Populations on its eleventh session,' UN Doc. E/CN.4/Sub.2/1993/29/Annex I, 23 August 1993, art. 3.
24   Id., art. 31.
25   Resolution of the Commission on Human Rights 1995/32, 3 March 1995.
26   During the negotiations, the UN consolidated its institutional machinery for advancing the rights of indigenous peoples and in making sure that these were supervised and implemented. During the beginning of this century, the UN established the UN Special Rapporteur on Indigenous Peoples, Expert Mechanism on Indigenous Peoples and, in particular, the Permanent Forum on Indigenous Issues. C.E. Foster, "Articulating self-determination in the Draft Declaration on the Rights of Indigenous Peoples," *European Journal of International Law* 12, no. 1 (2001): 141–157. See also S. Errico, "The Draft UN Declaration on the Rights of Indigenous Peoples: An Overview," *Human Rights Law Review* 7, no. 4 (2007): 741–755. G. Pentassuglia, "The EU and the protection of minorities: The case of Eastern Europe," *European Journal of International Law* 12 (2001): 141–157.

was never achieved, in June 2006 the newly created UN Human Rights Council adopted the Declaration (although not without opposition (30 votes in favor, 2 against, 12 abstentions)),[27] recommending that the UN General Assembly adopt it. The Declaration had the following formulations of the right to self-determination, which later proved difficult for States to accept:

> Article 3
> Indigenous peoples have the right of self-determination. By virtue of that right they freely determine their political status and freely pursue their economic, social and cultural development.
>
> Article 4
> Indigenous peoples, in exercising their right to self-determination, have the right to autonomy or self-government in matters relating to their internal and local affairs, as well as ways and means for financing their autonomous functions.

Even though the original 1994 Draft and the 2006 Draft adopted by the Human Rights Council are identical in framing the right to self-determination of indigenous peoples, it is noteworthy that what had been Article 31, dealing with autonomy and self-government, had become Article 4. It was now possible to read Article 3, on self-determination, and Article 4 – the two key provisions – together.[28]

---

27   See the version adopted by the Human Rights Council (UN Doc. A/HRC/1/L.10, 30 June 2006, pp. 56–72). See the explanatory paper by Canada after voting against the Declaration, which also outlines the reasons for abstention by other countries, many of them having problems with Article 3 on self-determination. Canada's Position: United Nations Draft Declaration on the Rights of Indigenous Peoples, 29 June 2006), available online: <http://www.ainc-inac.gc.ca/nr/spch/unp/06/ddr_e.html>.

28   It can be argued that art. 4 specifies that indigenous peoples' right to self-determination is limited to the "right to autonomy or self-government," which is often called the right to internal self-determination, that is, self-determination within the confines of existing States. This interpretation is made even more pertinent when we compare the way the right to autonomy and self-government are worded in arts. 31 and 4: the former saw it "as a specific form of exercising their right to self-determination," the latter "in exercising their right to self-determination." The first formulation, if read in the context of art. 3, seems to indicate that autonomy and self-government are possible ways to implement indigenous peoples' right to self-determination, whereas the new art. 4 gives more force to the argument that the right to autonomy and self-government embraces the ways in which indigenous peoples' self-determination can be realized. See also ILA Interim Report, n. 16 above, p. 11, where it states that the object and purpose of autonomy or self-government under art. 4 is to enable indigenous peoples to "freely determine their political status

Even with the relocation of Article 31, the process of adopting the UN Declaration came to a halt when a non-action resolution by the Namibian delegation was supported by the majority in the Third Committee of the UN General Assembly.[29] One clear reason for this was precisely Article 3, which was still there stating that indigenous peoples have a right to freely determine their political status. It is not difficult to imagine that adopting such a text would have been troublesome for anyone in the Third Committee, especially those representing the African countries.[30]

The matter came up for a final decision in the 61st session of the General Assembly in September 2007 where the Declaration was adopted, with 143 States voting in favor, four against (New Zealand, Australia, the United States, and Canada) and 11 abstaining (including Russia).[31] There were some important changes in the Declaration as compared to the version adopted by the Human Rights Council, most importantly with regard to the right to self-determination of indigenous peoples. The version adopted by the Human Rights Council left the door open for indigenous peoples to claim full-blown self-determination for the simple reason that Article 3 was still there, entitling them in principle

---

and freely pursue their economic, social and cultural development," i.e., the right to self-determination as provided for by art. 3.

29 See "Third Committee Approves Draft Resolution on Right to Development," UN General Assembly (Third Committee) Press Release (28 November 2006), available online: <http://www.un.org/News/Press/docs/2006/gashc3878.doc.htm>. As stated in the press release: "But an initiative led by Namibia, co-sponsored by a number of African countries, resulted in the draft being amended. In its new form, the draft would have the Assembly decide 'to defer consideration and action on the United Nations Declaration on the Rights of Indigenous Peoples to allow time for further consultations thereon' … The amendments were adopted by a vote of 82 in favour to 67 against, with 25 abstentions (annex II) … Prior to the vote, the representative of Peru – recalling that it had taken 24 years for the Declaration to be hammered out – said the original draft had been revised to address the concerns of many delegations, particularly regarding the principle of self-determination of peoples and respect for national sovereignty… However, his counterpart from Namibia, explaining the proposed amendments, said that some provisions ran counter to the national constitutions of a number of African countries and that the Declaration was of such critical importance that it was only 'fair and reasonable' to defer its adoption by the Assembly to allow for more consultations."

30 Other delegations also expressed their reservations. For instance, Argentina and the Philippines insisted that the right to self-determination should be interpreted so as to be reconciled with territorial integrity, national unity or organizational structure of each State. See UN GAOR, 61st Sess., 107th Plenary Meeting, UN Doc. A/61/PV.107, 13 September 2007, para. 19 and 108th Plenary Meeting, UN Doc. A/61/PV.108, 13 September 2007, para. 5. Also see the ILA Interim Report, n. 19 above, pp. 9–10.

31 For a general overview, see the information available online: <http://www.iwgia.org/sw248.asp>.

to fully determine their political status. This was the crux of the matter, even though a good argument can be made that Articles 3 and 4 should have been interpreted together to mean that indigenous peoples were entitled to internal self-determination only, although Article 3 still left the door open for indigenous peoples to claim full self-determination. In order to make sure that there was no possibility to read too much into Article 3, the version ultimately adopted by the UN General Assembly made a crucial change in Article 46(1), which in the version adopted by the Human Rights Council read that "[N]othing in this Declaration may be interpreted as implying for any State, people, group or person any right to engage in any activity or to perform any act contrary to the Charter of the United Nations." This was changed to make sure that indigenous peoples' self-determination could mean at most internal self-determination:

> Nothing in this Declaration may be interpreted as implying for any State, people, group or person any right to engage in any activity or to perform any act contrary to the Charter of the United Nations or construed as authorizing or encouraging any action which would dismember or impair, totally or in part, the territorial integrity or political unity of sovereign and independent States.[32]

UNDRIP is clearly a milestone development in the evolution of indigenous rights in international law.[33] The ILO 169 Convention has not received many ratifications (22 so far) so the 147 States that are now in favor of implementing the UNDRIP and its 46 provisions certainly constitute a backbone for indigenous rights. It needs to be remembered that these States have also committed to the preamble of the Declaration, which includes:

> Encouraging States to comply with and effectively implement all their obligations as they apply to indigenous peoples under international instruments, in particular those related to human rights, in consultation and cooperation with the peoples concerned,

---

32   UNDRIP, n. 3 above, art. 46 (1).
33   "Before UNDRIP, a number of issues afflicting indigenous peoples had been addressed through broad based universal human rights regimes ... and then ILO Convention No. 169 specifically codified indigenous peoples' rights, yet a global comprehensive effort was missing." S. Wiessner, "United Nations Declaration on the Rights of Indigenous Peoples, Introductory Note," United Nations Audiovisual Library of International Law Historical Archives (2009), available online: <http://legal.un.org/avl/ha/ga_61-/ga_61-295.html295AD>.

Emphasizing that the United Nations has an important and continuing role to play in promoting and protecting the rights of indigenous peoples.[34]

It is also important to keep in mind that States have affirmed in Article 43 that "[T]he rights recognized herein constitute the minimum standards for the survival, dignity and well-being of the indigenous peoples of the world."[35]

Legal Status of UNDRIP

The UNDRIP is an UNGA resolution, and, as such, it is not legally binding. Even if some declarations, adopted as UNGA resolutions, such as the UN Declaration of Human Rights, are highly authoritative, as UNGA resolutions they remain legally non-binding. And yet, although non-mandatory as such, the UNDRIP may have the effect of codifying at least some customary international law rights of indigenous peoples.[36]

On 13 September 2007, the final version of UNDRIP was adopted by a clear vote of 143 in favor and four States against. The United States, Canada, Australia and New Zealand voted against it, while 11 – Azerbaijan, Bangladesh, Bhutan, Burundi, Colombia, Georgia, Kenya, Nigeria, Russia, Samoa, and

---

34   UNDRIP, n. 3 above, preamble.
35   Wiessner quotes J. Anaya: "UNDRIP constitutes an authoritative common understanding, at the global level, of the minimum content of the rights of indigenous peoples, upon a foundation of various sources of international human rights law ... The principles and rights affirmed in the Declaration constitute or add to the normative frameworks for the activities of United Nations human rights institutions, mechanisms and specialized agencies as they relate to indigenous peoples." Wiessner, n. 33 above.
36   The ILA notes: "A general *opinio juris* and *consuetudo* exists within the international community according to which certain basic prerogatives that are essential in order to safeguard the identity and basic rights of indigenous peoples are today crystallized in the realm of customary international law." ILA Interim Report, n. 19 above, pp. 43–44. For scholarly interpretations, see S.J. Anaya and L. Rodríguez-Piñero, "The making of the UNDRIP," in UNDRIP Commentary, n. 3 above, p. 62.; Wiessner, n. 33 above; D. Sambo Dorough, "The rights, interests and role of the Arctic Council permanent participants," in *Governance of Arctic Shipping: Balancing Rights and Interests of Arctic States and User States*, eds. R. Beckman et al. (Brill Nijhoff, 2017), p. 78; S. Wiessner and S.J. Anaya, "The UN Declaration on the Rights of Indigenous Peoples: Towards re-empowerment" (2007), available online: <https://www.jurist.org/commentary/2007/10/un-declaration-on-rights-of-indigenous-2/>; S. Wiessner, "Rights and status of indigenous peoples: A global comparative and international legal analysis," *Harvard Human Rights Journal* 12 (1999): 57; M. Davis, "To bind or not bind: The United Nations Declaration on the Rights of Indigenous Peoples five years on," *Australian International Law Journal* 19 (2012): 40–44.

Ukraine – abstained from voting. Yet, after the vote, all four States that voted against the UNDRIP eventually endorsed it, even if some with reservations.

The International Law Association (ILA), a prominent non-governmental organization of international lawyers, examined the status of UNDRIP in customary international law.[37] The interim report concluded that perhaps the whole of UNDRIP could be seen to codify customary international law, simply because many human rights treaty monitoring bodies have started to use UNDRIP as a guide to interpret their respective human rights instruments that are legally binding on most States of the world.[38] As provided in the interim report:

> Having ascertained the foregoing, it is opportune to make clear that it is not important to investigate whether the relevant rules of customary international law actually correspond, in their precise content, to the provision of UNDRIP in their actual formulation. By its own nature a declaration of principles, even when its content partially reproduces general international law, has in fact also a propulsive force, aimed at favouring further evolution of its subject matter for the future. What is really significant for the present enquiry is that the adoption of UNDRIP, after more than twenty years of negotiations, confirms that the international community has come to a consensus that indigenous peoples are a concern of international law, which translates into the existence of customary rules of binding force for all States irrespective of whether or not they have ratified the relevant treaties (which, on their part, taken together bind virtually all countries in the world). Therefore, it is today indisputable that 'customary norms concerning indigenous peoples and their pull toward compliance' are actually a reality in the context of the contemporary international legal order.[39]

The final report of the Committee (as well as Resolution No. 5/2012) notes that some of the provisions of the UNDRIP do evince customary international law.

---

37 In January 2011 the position supported by the Committee in its Interim Report, ILA Interim Report, n. 19 above, was favorably referred to by an International Centre for Settlement of Investment Disputes Arbitral Tribunal, in *Grande River Enterprises Six Nations, Ltd., et al., v. United States of America*, 12 January 2011, available online: <https://www.state.gov/documents/organization/156820.pdf>. See also International Law Association, Sofia Conference (2012), Final Report, available online: <http://www.ila-hq.org/index.php/committees>.
38 Id., ILA Interim Report, p. 51.
39 Id.

In its conclusions and recommendations, at paragraph 2, the final report (and the resolution) provide:

> The 2007 United Nations Declaration on the Rights of Indigenous Peoples (UNDRIP) as a whole cannot yet be considered as a statement of existing customary international law. It, however, includes key provisions which correspond to existing State obligations under customary international law.[40]

Provisions recognizing clear rights of indigenous peoples under customary international law are listed below:

> The right of indigenous peoples to self-determination (paragraph 4); right to autonomy and self-government which translates into a number of prerogatives including participatory and consultation rights (paragraph 5); cultural rights and identity (paragraph 6); right to lands, territories and resources (paragraph 7); treaty rights (paragraph 9); reparation, redress and remedies (paragraph 10).[41]

With respect to these rights, the ILA had stated earlier in its interim report:

> The rights are all strictly interrelated with each other in light of the holistic vision of life of indigenous peoples and consequently the relevant practice supporting the existence of customary law concerning each of the above rights usually also serves the purpose of backing the assumption that the same status has been attained by any or all of the others.[42]

---

40   International Law Association, Sofia Conference (2012), Final Report, p. 29, available online: <http://www.ila-hq.org/index.php/committees>. See also Resolution No. 5/2012 on the Rights of Indigenous Peoples. On the status of ILA resolutions, Wiessner notes: "Generally, resolutions of the International Law Association, just as those of the International Law Commission, have been recognized as evidence of international law. The Third Restatement of Foreign Relations Law of the United States affirms this characterization. He also quotes Graf Vitzthum: global resolutions of a body as qualified and diverse as the International Law Association are stating a rare consensus amongst, at times, radically different cultures and value traditions, and thus should be especially appreciated and valued." See S. Wiessner, "Culture and the rights of indigenous peoples," in *The Cultural Dimension of Human Rights*, ed. A. Vrdoljak (Oxford University Press, 2013), pp. 154–155; The American Law Institute, *Third Restatement of the Foreign Relations Law of the United States* (1987), § 103 Reporters' Notes No. 1.
41   Id., ILA Sofia Conference (2012) Final Report and Resolution No. 5/2012.
42   ILA Interim Report, n. 19 above.

Also, the Report observes that several rights that are not yet custom are emerging as customary norms.[43] Irrespective of their legal status, most States with indigenous peoples in their territories have committed politically to realize their rights via the UNDRIP.

The United Nations Convention on the Law of the Sea

Development of the International Law of the Sea

UNCLOS[44] has been characterized as "a comprehensive constitution for the oceans which will stand the test of time" and which "represents a monumental achievement of the international community, second only to the charter of the United Nations."[45] These are not mere metaphors pushing towards hyperbole. UNCLOS has 168 State parties, although the United States is still not a party. Importantly, the United States has adopted the view that most of the substantive provisions of the Convention reflect customary international law.[46]

UNCLOS is one of the largest multilateral conventions in international law. Coastal States enjoy sovereignty over their internal waters and in the territorial sea and archipelagic waters, albeit with some constraints to respect international community rights, primarily navigational. The exclusive economic zone (EEZ) and continental shelf include sovereign resource rights and together with the contiguous zone also functional jurisdiction, that is specific legislative and enforcement jurisdictional powers. The regime for the high seas and the related freedoms is set out and is followed by regimes for particular geographical situations (e.g., islands, enclosed and semi-enclosed seas, access and transit rights for land-locked States), and the regime for the international seabed area and the new institutional and regulatory framework established for its administration. The convention also provides regimes for the protection and preservation of the marine environment (which is designed to operate in coordination with other environmental instruments), marine scientific research, and marine technology development and transfer. Navigation rights are arguably the international community rights that have received the strongest possible level of protection in all ocean spaces under national jurisdiction and

---

43 Id., para. 3 of the Resolution.
44 UNCLOS, n. 4 above.
45 "A Constitution for the Oceans," Remarks by T.B. Koh, President of the Third United Nations Conference on the Law of the Sea, in *The Law of the Sea: United Nations Convention on the Law of the Sea* (United Nations, 1983), p. xxxiii.
46 J.A. Roach, "Today's customary international law of the sea," *Ocean Development and International Law* 45(3) (2014): 239.

on the high seas. Other international community rights, such as fishing, laying of submarine cables and pipelines, and marine scientific research are also protected. Finally, UNCLOS sets out a *smörgåsbord* of direct and third party facilitated dispute settlement procedures open to State parties while also indicating what issues are subject to compulsory procedures.

The Status of UNCLOS

When considered against the long history of the international law of the sea since the 18th century and the extensive efforts at codification and progressive development in the 20th century, there is no doubt that UNCLOS enjoys high stature and status in international law. It is the result of a long historical timeline, trial and error, and adaptive learning. It was the outcome of an intense deliberative process and with the clear intention to address all issues relating to the law of the sea, which are considered interrelated and need to be considered as a whole.[47]

Accordingly, UNCLOS is not to be tampered with lightly and indeed the instrument's own amendment procedures have not yet been used. However, it is not a static and closed instrument either. There have been instances where aspects of the Convention did not sufficiently or satisfactorily meet some contemporary or emergent issues, and accordingly formal initiatives were launched to explore possible change. These tended to be guided by compelling necessity and involved prolonged preparation and negotiation before adoption of a new instrument having the effect of supplementing, if not even amending, the Convention. Guided by this spirit, the approach of international courts and tribunals called upon to interpret provisions of UNCLOS has largely been deferential and circumspect, while at the same time exploring interpretations and relationships to other instruments to assist resolution.[48]

UNCLOS anticipates a relationship to a broad range of international agreements by referring to other instruments using terminology as diverse as conventions,[49] special conventions,[50] treaty or treaties,[51] agreements,[52] special

---

47 UNCLOS, n. 4 above, preamble.
48 T. Treves, "Procedural History of the United Nations Convention on the Law of the Sea," 10 December 1982, UN Audiovisual Library, available online: <http://legal.un.org/avl/ha/uncls/uncls.html>.
49 For example, UNCLOS, n. 4 above, arts. 35(c), 108(1), 237(1), and Annex VI, art. 22.
50 Id., art. 237(2).
51 For example, id., arts. 92(1), 110(1), 116(a), 146, and Annex VI art. 22.
52 For example, id., arts. 62(2), 151(1)(a), 151(1)(b), 151(1)(c), 151(3), 237(1), 269(b), 311(2), 311(3), 311(4), 311(5), and Annex VI, art. 21.

agreements,[53] and arrangements or cooperative arrangements.[54] This diverse terminology was intended to capture a broad range of instruments and structures of international cooperation and not only to treaties as generally understood in international law.[55] Also, several provisions of UNCLOS anticipate a relationship with other rules of international law,[56] general international law,[57] and customary law.[58]

There are very few instances where UNCLOS expressly provides that its provisions do not apply when there is another treaty regime in place. The regime for straits used for international navigation is a case in point and its provisions do not affect "the legal regime in straits in which passage is regulated in whole or in part by long-standing international conventions in force specifically relating to such straits."[59] There is further recognition that other rules of international law may apply in addition to the Convention.[60] Elsewhere with respect to its relationship to other agreements, UNCLOS provides that its provision in this regard "does not affect international agreements expressly permitted or preserved by other articles of this Convention."[61]

That UNCLOS addresses all issues relating to the law of the sea does not necessarily mean that the Convention applies exclusively, and indeed there may be instances where other instruments also apply. For example, with respect to the protection and preservation of the marine environment, Article 237 provides that

> The provisions of this Part are without prejudice to the specific obligations assumed by States under special conventions and agreements concluded previously which relate to the protection and preservation of the

---

53   Id., art. 126.
54   For example, id., arts. 62(2), 62(4)(i), 66(5), 69(3), 69(5), 70(4), 70(6), 74(3), 83(3), 98(2), 151(1)(a), 151(1)(b), 151(1)(c), 151(3), 211(3), and 298(1)(a)(iii).
55   Treaty is defined as "an international agreement concluded between States in written form and governed by international law, whether embodied in a single instrument or in two or more related instruments and whatever its particular designation." Vienna Convention on the Law of Treaties, adopted 23 May 1969 (entered into force 27 January 1980), 1155 *United Nations Treaty Series* 331, art. 2(1)(a).
56   For example UNCLOS, n. 4 above, arts. 2(3), 19(1), 21(1), 31, 58(2), 58(3), 87(1), 293(1), and 297(1)(b).
57   Id., preamble.
58   Id., art. 221(1).
59   Id., art. 35(c).
60   For example, id., art. 34(2) provides that "[t]he sovereignty or jurisdiction of the States bordering the straits is exercised subject to this Part and to other rules of international law."
61   Id., art. 311(5).

marine environment and to agreements which may be concluded in furtherance of the general principles set forth in this Convention.[62]

In this case, however, the superiority of UNCLOS over these environmental agreements is clear. There is an accompanying duty for States to carry out their duties under their agreement in a manner consistent with UNCLOS.[63] In a similar vein but with respect to general agreements, Article 311(2) provides that

> This Convention shall not alter the rights and obligations of States Parties which arise from other agreements compatible with this Convention and which do not affect the enjoyment by other States Parties of their rights or the performance of their obligations under this Convention.

The requirement of compatibility effectively establishes the hierarchy of UNCLOS over other agreements.[64] There are also several provisions throughout UNCLOS which recognize the relevance or application of other rules of international law in so far as they are not incompatible with specific provisions of the Convention.[65]

Accordingly, UNCLOS acknowledges the existence of instruments that are complementary to it. A recent arbitral award considered this point with respect to Article 192 of UNCLOS, which provides that obligations in Part XII apply to all marine areas, and that there is a corpus of international environmental law that informs the provision.[66] The tribunal held that Article 192 created "the positive obligation to take active measures to protect and preserve the marine environment, and by logical implication, entails the negative obligation not to degrade the marine environment,"[67] and that the Convention on the International Trade in Endangered Species was an instrument that provided pertinent obligations.[68]

---

62 Id., art. 237(1).
63 Id., art. 237(2).
64 *In the Matter of the South China Sea Arbitration (Republic of the Philippines v. People's Republic of China)*, PCA Case No. 2013-19, Award (12 July 2016) (hereafter cited as *Philippines v. China*).
65 For example, UNCLOS, n. 4 above, arts. 58(3), 293(1) and 297(1)(b), and Annex III art. 21.
66 *Philippines v. China*, n. 64 above, para. 940.
67 Id., para. 941.
68 Convention on International Trade in Endangered Species of Wild Fauna and Flora, adopted 3 March 1973 (entered into force 1 July 1975), 993 *United Nations Treaty Series* 243 (hereafter cited as CITES). The Tribunal stated, "CITES forms part of the general corpus of international law that informs the content of Article 192 and 194(5) of UNCLOS. The conservation of the living resources of the sea is an element in the protection and

A related issue is the relationship between UNCLOS and general international law. Despite the desire to settle all issues relating to the law of the sea, by its own admission UNCLOS did not manage to fully accomplish this task. This is underscored by the preamble which provides "that matters not regulated by this Convention continue to be governed by the rules and principles of general international law."[69] The recent *Philippines v. China* arbitral tribunal addressed the issue of historic fishing rights in foreign EEZs and concluded that the customary law on this subject was superseded by UNCLOS and that therefore such claims were not compatible with the Convention. In its ratio, the tribunal understood the scope of Article 311(2) to include general international law.[70]

Finally, UNCLOS State parties may modify or suspend the application of specific provisions with respect to their relationship where this does not affect the Convention's object and purpose or basic principles and the ability of other State parties to enjoy their rights or perform their obligations.[71] In such cases there is a duty to notify other States.[72]

Exploring the Interface between UNDRIP and UNCLOS

Having considered the historical context and legal status of UNDRIP and UNCLOS, we now explore the potential interface between the two. This analysis is undertaken in two steps: first, to consider what might be the legal pathway(s) for UNDRIP (and the customary law it might incorporate) into the law of the sea, and second, what specific issues could potentially bring the two instruments into a relationship. We do not undertake an exhaustive examination to ascertain what provisions of UNDRIP have achieved customary law status, but rather rely on the observations made by the ILA and hypothesize what provisions in UNDRIP could potentially interface with provisions in UNCLOS.[73]

---

   preservation of the marine environment, and the general obligation to 'protect and preserve the marine environment' in Article 192 includes a due diligence obligation to prevent the harvesting of species that are recognised internationally as being at risk of extinction and requiring international protection." For identifying the species at risk, the Tribunal noted appendices I (species threatened with extinction and subject to the strictest level of international controls on trade) and II (species which may become threatened with extinction) of CITES. *Philippines v. China*, n. 64 above, paras. 956–957.

69   UNCLOS, n. 4 above, preamble.
70   *Philippines v. China*, n. 64 above, para. 235.
71   UNCLOS, n. 4 above, art. 311(3).
72   Id., art. 311(4).
73   The observations made by the ILA in the Interim Report 2010, Final Conference Report 2012, Resolution No. 5/2012, n. 19 and 40 above.

Legal Pathways

We argue that there are two potential legal pathways for UNDRIP to provide a supportive role for the law of the sea. A first argument is based on the continuing role of general international law with respect to aspects of the law of the sea that are not addressed by UNCLOS. As observed earlier, UNDRIP may reflect customary international law and if any of its provisions address a law of the sea matter not addressed by UNCLOS, it is arguable that the provisions concerned, *qua* custom, would govern the relations of States with respect to that matter. Naturally, one would need to ask the further question as to the likelihood that there are UNDRIP provisions that might qualify as law of the sea matters and which are not already addressed by UNCLOS.

The second argument is based on the interpretation of Article 192 provided by *Philippines v. China*, where the tribunal held:

> Article 192 of the Convention provides that "States have the obligation to protect and preserve the marine environment." Although phrased in general terms, the Tribunal considers it well established that Article 192 does impose a duty on States Parties, the content of which is informed by the other provisions of Part XII and other applicable rules of international law. This "general obligation" extends both to "protection" of the marine environment from future damage and "preservation" in the sense of maintaining or improving its present condition. Article 192 thus entails the positive obligation to take active measures to protect and preserve the marine environment, and by logical implication, entails the negative obligation not to degrade the marine environment. The corpus of international law relating to the environment, which informs the content of the general obligation in Article 192, requires that States "ensure that activities within their jurisdiction and control respect the environment of other States or of areas beyond national control."[74]

The Convention on Biological Diversity, 1992 (CBD)[75] and the Convention on International Trade in Endangered Species of Wild Fauna and Flora, 1973 (CITES)[76] were considered as informing Article 192, as well as 194. With reference to CITES, the tribunal held that this instrument "is the subject of nearly universal adherence, including by the Philippines and China, and in the Tribunal's

---

74 *Philippines v. China*, n. 64 above, para. 941.
75 CBD, n. 20 above.
76 CITES, n. 68 above.

view forms part of the general corpus of international law that informs the content of Article 192 and 194(5) of the Convention."[77]

The 'corpus' interpretation raises the interesting question as to what extent, if at all, the 'environmental' provisions of UNDRIP and the customary law they may reflect should be considered part of the corpus of law that informs Article 192. There is growing literature to support the contention that international human rights law contributes to the protection of the environment.[78] The argument could be extended to other parts of UNCLOS, such as Part XIII on marine scientific research, where provisions of UNDRIP and other international agreements, for example, the CBD and the Nagoya Protocol on Access to Genetic Resources and the Fair and Equitable Sharing of Benefits Arising from their Utilization (ABS) to the Convention on Biological Diversity, 2014,[79] which arguably have provisions that could inform the regime of consent in marine scientific research under UNCLOS, as will be discussed below.

Specific Issues

We now proceed to identify specific issues for a more focused exploration of the potential interface between the two instruments.

---

77 *Philippines v. China*, n. 64 above, para. 956.
78 For example, Principle 22 of the Rio Declaration on Environment and Development specifically notes the role of indigenous peoples: "[I]ndigenous people and their communities... have a vital role in environmental management and development because of their knowledge and traditional practices. States should recognise and duly support their identity, culture and interests and enable their effective participation in the achievement of sustainable development." See also Principles 10, 13, 17, and 23 of the Rio Declaration on Environment and Development, adopted 13 June 1992, UN Doc. A/CONF.151/26 (vol. I); reprinted in 31 *International Legal Materials* 874 (1992). See also A. Boyle, "Human rights and the environment: Where next," *European Journal of International Law* 23, no. 3 (2012): 613–642; P. Sands, "Human rights and the environment," Proceedings of a Geneva Environment Network roundtable (United Nations Environment Programme, 2004), pp. 22–28; J. Harrington, "Climate change, human rights, and the right to be cold," *Fordham Environmental Law Review* 18, no. 3 (2007): 513–535; and the Petition to the Inter-American Commission on Human Rights Seeking Relief from Violations Resulting from Global Warming Caused by Acts and Omissions of the United States (submitted by Sheila Watt-Cloutier, with the support of the Inuit Circumpolar Conference, on behalf of all Inuit of the Arctic Regions of the United States and Canada) (7 December 2005), available online: <http://www.inuitcircumpolar.com/uploads/3/0/5/4/30542564/finalpetitionsummary.pdf>.
79 Nagoya Protocol on Access to Genetic Resources and the Fair and Equitable Sharing of Benefits Arising from Their Utilization to the Convention on Biological Diversity, adopted 29 October 2010 (entered into force 12 October 2014), Doc. UNEP/CBD/COP/DEC/X/1 (29 October 2010), art. 8.b, available online: <https://treaties.un.org/doc/source/docs/UNEP_CBD_COP_DEC_X_1-E.pdf>.

Territorial, Economic and Resource Issues

UNDRIP sets out a series of territorial and resource use rights of indigenous peoples that potentially apply to ocean space. These include the right to engage freely in traditional and other economic activities[80] and to "maintain and strengthen their distinctive spiritual relationship with their traditionally owned or otherwise occupied and used lands, territories, waters and coastal seas and other resources."[81] Waters and coastal seas presumptively include ice-covered marine areas.[82] One of the most powerful rights is to "the lands, territories and resources which they have traditionally owned, occupied or otherwise used or acquired,"[83] which is accompanied by the further "right to own, use, develop and control the lands, territories and resources that they possess by reason of traditional ownership or other traditional occupation or use, as well as those which they have otherwise acquired."[84] The ILA notes in its Resolution No. 5/2012 that States must protect the rights of indigenous peoples to their traditional lands, territories, and resources.[85]

---

80 UNDRIP, n. 3 above, art. 20. Article 20 protects the traditional activities or means of subsistence of indigenous peoples. It falls within the right to autonomy or self-government. See ILA Interim Report, n. 19 above, 14–15; C. Perez-Bustillo and J. Hohmann, "Indigenous rights to development, socio-economic rights, and rights for groups with vulnerabilities," in UNDRIP Commentary, n. 3 above, pp. 482–536. The ILA recognizes indigenous peoples' rights to autonomy or self-government as forming part of customary international law. See Resolution 5/2012, n. 40 above, para. 5.

81 Id., UNDRIP, art. 25. For more elaboration on "spiritual relationship" see C. Charters, "Indigenous peoples' rights to lands, territories and resources in the UNDRIP," in UNDRIP Commentary, id., pp. 409–410. The ILO 169 Convention has a similar provision but does not expressly include waters and territorial seas. It used the terms "collective aspects" and "total environment." ILO 169 Convention, n. 15 above, art. 13(1).

82 The 2013 Alta Outcome Document of the World Conference on Indigenous Peoples contains specific references to ice, along with oceans and waters. For instance, its preamble notes, "[W]e Indigenous Peoples, have the right of self-determination and permanent sovereignty over our lands, territories, resources, air, *ice, oceans and waters*, mountains and forests" (emphasis added) and the reference is used throughout the document. Available online: <http://www.un.org/esa/socdev/unpfii/documents/wc/AdoptedAlta_outcomedoc_EN.pdf>. See B. Baker, "Interlinkages in international law: The Convention on Biological Diversity as a model for linking territory, environment, and indigenous rights in the marine arctic," in *Diplomacy on Ice: Energy and the Environment in the Arctic and Antarctic*, eds. R. Pincus and S.H. Ali (Yale University Press, 2015), 41, notes 83–84.

83 UNDRIP, n. 3 above, art. 26(1).

84 Id., art. 26(2).

85 Resolution No. 5/2012, n. 40 above.

ILO 169 contained similar provisions concerning rights to lands and resources.[86] In addition, States have substantive and procedural duties to provide legal protection to the lands, territories and resources while also being respectful of the laws, customs, traditions, and land tenure systems of the indigenous peoples concerned.[87] These rights extend further to include determination and development of priorities and strategies for the lands, territories and resource development or use.[88] In this respect, States planning projects that impact on these rights have a procedural duty

> to consult and cooperate in good faith with the indigenous peoples concerned through their own representative institutions in order to obtain their free and informed consent prior to the approval of any project affecting their lands or territories and other resources, particularly in connection with the development, utilization or exploitation of mineral, water or other resources.[89]

---

86 ILO 169 Convention, n. 15 above, arts. 14 and 15. The ILA notes that "Article 26(2) is confirmed in and reflects a vast range of developed jurisprudence, including that of the Inter-American Commission and [Inter-American Commission on Human Rights], the [African Commission on Human and Peoples' Rights], the UN Human Rights Council, the [Human Rights Council], the [UN Committee on the Elimination of Racial Discrimination], UN experts, UN Special Rapporteurs on indigenous peoples' related issues, ILO adjudicatory bodies and domestic law. As such, the right can be reasonably considered as being part of customary international law as also evidenced by extensive state practice as well as *opinio juris*, especially in Latin America and the former Commonwealth colonies." See ILA Interim Report, n. 19 above, pp. 22–23, notes 122–129. See especially the *Case of the Mayagna (Sumo) Awas Tingni Community v. Nicaragua*, Judgment (August 31, 2001), Inter-Am. Ct. H.R., (Ser. C) No. 79 (2001); *Mabo v. Queensland (No. 2)* (*"Mabo Case"*) [1992] HCA 23, (1992) 175 CLR 1 (3 June 1992); *The Wik Peoples v. The State of Queensland & Ors; The Thayorre People v. The State of Queensland & Ors* (*'Wik'*), HCA 40.

87 UNDRIP, n. 3 above, arts. 26(3) and 27. The ILA states that the State practice accompanying art. 26(2) also supports the Article 26(3) State obligations. ILA Interim Report, n. 19 above.

88 Id., UNDRIP, art. 32(1). "This along with art. 32(2) is pivotal to enabling Indigenous peoples to set and pursue their own development path." See Charters, n. 81 above, p. 447.

89 UNDRIP, n. 3 above, art. 32(2). The ILA notes that this provision was contentious during the negotiations as it brings to fore some of the most pressing concerns for indigenous peoples, such as competing States' and indigenous peoples' claims to natural resources. As such, States' consultation obligation was inserted and this implies consultation should be undertaken with the objective of obtaining indigenous peoples' free, prior and informed consent, and in cases of large-scale development projects with the potential to have a major impact on indigenous peoples' territory, consent is necessary. See ILA Interim Report, n. 19 above, pp. 24–35; J. Anaya, "Indigenous peoples' participatory rights in relation to decisions about natural resource extraction: The more fundamental issue of what rights indigenous peoples have in lands and resources," *Arizona Journal of*

This provision signifies substantial procedural duties.

While 'waters' and 'coastal seas' appear to be associated with a different right from the ownership right, the reference to territories might, in a law of the sea context, potentially include internal and territorial waters.[90] *Per se*, this does not appear to have any consequence for pertinent UNCLOS rules concerning the delineation of baselines and bay closing lines and the regime of the territorial sea. The UNDRIP rights described in this section essentially are domestic, that is falling under the framework of coastal State jurisdiction, and do not appear to produce external consequences.[91] The extent to which a coastal State recognizes and implements domestic indigenous rights in this respect is not governed by UNCLOS.

A separate question is whether indigenous resource rights could potentially be transboundary. There are precedents for the protection of traditional transboundary fishing rights.[92] Although UNCLOS makes no express reference to indigenous rights, in a provision on archipelagic waters, which are subject to the sovereignty of the archipelagic State, it establishes a duty on that State to recognize traditional fishing rights, but without prejudice to its sovereignty.[93]

International and Comparative Law 22, no. 1 (2011): 7–17. This is also a key provision to address, especially those cases where indigenous customary law and national legislation differ as to the regime of these resources. Id., Charters, n. 81 above, p. 431.

90   Charters notes, "negotiators drafting the UNDRIP struggled to express semantically the relationships that Indigenous peoples have with their lands, territories and resources because Indigenous peoples often conceive of that relationship differently from non-Indigenous peoples." Id., Charters, n. 81 above, p. 406. Sambo Dorough notes in the context of the Inuit, "[F]or the Inuit, a critical element is the need to recognise the profound relationship that they have with the Arctic Ocean coastal areas and their respective lands, territories and resources. In this context, the term 'territories' should be regarded as comprehensive and inclusive of the coastal land areas, shore-fast sea ice, offshore areas of the ocean itself, including the seabed, which have been traditionally used for millennia as the source of sustenance in the way of whales, seals, walrus, migratory birds and other marine life." Sambo Dorough, n. 36 above, p. 80.

91   Id., Sambo Dorough. As an example, the Labrador Inuit Land Claims Agreement in Canada affirms Inuit rights to the 12 nautical mile territorial sea, consistent with UNCLOS.

92   See *Award of the Arbitral Tribunal in the Second Stage of the Proceedings between Eritrea and Yemen (Maritime Delimitation)*, XXII Reports of International Arbitral Awards 355–410 (Permanent Court of Arbitration 1999). The award recognized and protected traditional transboundary fishing rights of fishers from both sides. See also B.H. Oxman and W.M. Reisman, "Maritime delimitation between opposite states – traditional 'artisanal' fishing regimes – transboundary nonliving resources – interpretation of prior award – straight baselines –effect of coastal and midsea islands," *American Journal of International Law* 94 (2000): 721–722.

93   UNCLOS, n. 4 above, art. 51(1). For a commentary on this provision, see S.N. Nandan and S. Rosenne (vol eds.), *United Nations Convention on the Law of the Sea 1982: A Commentary* vol II (Martinus Nijhoff, 2002), 447 *et seq.*

The term traditional could be interpreted to include traditional indigenous use. The Convention provides a framework for the definition and regulation of such rights.[94] This duty does not have a parallel in the territorial sea. There is no such reference to traditional fishing rights in the EEZ, although with respect to the coastal State's allocation of the surplus in the total allowable catch to other States, the Convention provides for the coastal State to take into account all relevant factors, "*inter alia* … the requirements of developing States in the subregion or region in harvesting part of the surplus and the need to minimize economic dislocation in States whose nationals have habitually fished in the zone."[95] It stands to logic and reason that '*inter alia*' be interpreted to include traditional indigenous fishing and habitual fishing that is long-established in the area. What is unclear is whether the coastal State, as a result of UNDRIP and the customary law it reflects, ought to provide preferential access to the surplus to indigenous fishers from a neighboring State who have habitually fished in the area. In these cases, the coastal State retains the right to regulate fishing by foreign nationals.[96] The access to the surplus is a privilege, not a right. The *Philippines v. China* arbitration considered the issue of historic fishing rights (although not specifically in the context of traditional indigenous fishing) in foreign EEZs and concluded that such rights were effectively extinguished by the regime of the EEZ.[97]

It is possible that indigenous rights under other instruments could potentially have a more direct relationship to UNCLOS provisions. These are outside the remit of this article and we refer to them only briefly. For example, under the CBD framework for in-situ conservation,[98] State parties have a duty to respect, preserve and maintain knowledge, innovations and practices of indigenous peoples and to encourage and develop methods of cooperation that

---

[94] "The terms and conditions for the exercise of such rights and activities, including the nature, the extent and the areas to which they apply, shall, at the request of any of the States concerned, be regulated by bilateral agreements between them. Such rights shall not be transferred to or shared with third States or their nationals." UNCLOS, n. 4 above, art. 51(1).

[95] Id., art. 62(3). See *Philippines v. China*, n. 64 above, para. 242.

[96] Id., art. 62(4).

[97] "The Tribunal considers the text and context of the Convention to be clear in superseding any historic rights that a State may once have had in the areas that now form part of the exclusive economic zone and continental shelf of another State." *Philippines v. China*, n. 64 above, para. 247. The tribunal also noted *Qatar v. Bahrain* on historic pearl fishing where the International Court of Justice held that it "seems in any event never to have led to the recognition of an exclusive quasi-territorial right to the fishing grounds themselves or to the superjacent waters." *Maritime Delimitation and Territorial Questions between Qatar and Bahrain*, Merits, Judgment, ICJ Reports 2001, 40, para. 236.

[98] CBD, n. 20 above, art. 8(j).

include indigenous and traditional technologies in pursuance of the objectives of the CBD.[99]

Mobility and Communication Issues

UNCLOS does not directly address human mobility and communication issues, other than a brief reference to the jurisdiction for this purpose in the contiguous zone and navigation rights.[100] In recent years there has been a discernible growth of concern over immigrants and refugees using sea routes,[101] but this is not a concern in this article. Rather, an interesting issue which is not addressed by UNCLOS is the transboundary movement of people for kinship and traditional resource use reasons that are otherwise affected by maritime boundaries. The Convention's provisions on maritime boundary delimitation are couched in very general and issue-neutral terms, thus of no direct help on this matter. There are situations where indigenous people move across a maritime boundary for subsistence, spiritual, kinship, and other communication purposes, as in the case of the transboundary North Water Polynya (*Pikialasorsuaq*) where the ice bridge across the maritime boundary between Greenland and Ellesmere Island (Canada) is very important for the Inuit of Canada and Greenland (*Kalaallit Nunaat*) to maintain regular contact.[102]

---

99 Id., art. 18(4).
100 UNCLOS, n. 4 above, art. 33(1).
101 See "In Safety and Dignity: Addressing Large Movements of Refugees and Migrants," Report of the Secretary General (UN Doc. A/70/59, April 21, 2016, UN General Assembly, 70th session), also published in *International Journal of Refugee Law* 28 (2016): 500–530. See F. Munari, "Migrations by sea in the Mediterranean: An improvement of EU law is urgently needed," *Ocean Yearbook* 32 (2018): 118–158.
102 See *People of the Ice Bridge: The Future of Pikialasorsuaq*, Report of the Pikialasorsuaq Commission, available online: <http://pikialasorsuaq.org/en/Resources/Reports>. See in particular Recommendation 3 on freedom to travel. The Commission found examples of bilateral agreements that support the recommendation to ease travel restrictions, such as the Treaty of Amity, Commerce and Navigation between His Britannic Majesty and the United States of America (London, 19 November 1794 (Jay Treaty), Parry vol 52 (1969), 243), which includes an objective addressing cultural connections, and the Treaty between Australia and the Independent State of Papua New Guinea concerning Sovereignty and Maritime Boundaries in the area between the two Countries, including the Area Known as Torres Strait, and Related Matters (adopted 18 December 1978, entered into force 15 February 1985, ATS 1985 No. 4) (hereafter cited as Torres Strait Treaty). This agreement protects traditional ways of life and livelihood of the traditional inhabitants of the islands and adjacent coastal areas of the Torres Strait. Some of its provisions worth noting are Article 10 that establishes a Protected Zone; Article 11 dealing with free movement and traditional activities including traditional fishing; and especially Article 12, which defines traditional customary rights in the following manner: "Where the traditional inhabitants of one Party enjoy traditional customary rights of access to and usage of areas of land,

International human rights instruments have addressed the issue of mobility in different ways. The Universal Declaration on Human Rights stated the principle as the right of everyone to "freedom of movement and residence within the borders of each State" and "the right to leave any country, including his own, and to return to his country."[103] The ILO 169 Convention addressed mobility and communication and cooperation across borders in generic terms and provided that "Governments shall take appropriate measures, including by means of international agreements, to facilitate contacts and co-operation between indigenous and tribal peoples across borders, including activities in the economic, social, cultural, spiritual and environmental fields."[104] UNDRIP is more on point with respect to indigenous peoples "divided by international borders" who have "the right to maintain and develop contacts, relations and cooperation, including activities for spiritual, cultural, political, economic and social purposes, with their own members as well as other peoples across borders."[105] States have a corresponding duty "in consultation and cooperation with indigenous peoples, to take effective measures to facilitate the exercise and ensure the implementation of this right."[106]

The ILA has discussed the right of indigenous peoples to maintain relations across borders in three contexts under UNDRIP: right to (cultural) self-determination, right to autonomy and self-government, and cultural rights and identity.[107] In its Resolution No. 5/2012, the ILA recognized all three rights as forming part of customary international law.[108] In light of this and the "widely accepted position" confirmed by the inclusion of the provision across international instruments, the ILA has urged States to facilitate contacts between

---

seabed, seas, estuaries and coastal tidal areas that are in or in the vicinity of the Protected Zone and that are under the jurisdiction of the other Party, and those rights are acknowledged by the traditional inhabitants living in or in proximity to those areas to be in accordance with local tradition, the other Party shall permit the continued exercise of those rights on conditions not less favourable than those applying to like rights of its own traditional inhabitants."

103 Universal Declaration, n. 6 above, art. 13.
104 ILO 169 Convention, n. 15 above, art. 32.
105 UNDRIP, n. 3 above, art. 36(1).
106 Id., art. 36(2). The ILA lists examples of measures taken by States, either via changes in domestic law or through inter-State agreements at the bilateral and/or multilateral level, for instance the Nordic Saami Convention between Finland, Norway and Sweden. See ILA Interim Report, n. 19 above, p. 15. See also S. Imai and K. Gunn, "Indigenous belonging: Membership and identity in the UNDRIP," in UNDRIP Commentary, n. 3 above, pp. 213–246 specially 238.
107 ILA Interim Report, n. 19 above, pp. 10 and 15.
108 Resolution No.5/2012, n. 40 above, paras. 4, 5, and 6.

indigenous peoples belonging to the same cultural community that are divided by international borders.[109]

In the event of a dispute between State parties to UNCLOS with respect to mobility rights of indigenous peoples in transboundary ocean spaces, it is conceivable that an adjudicating body might turn to international human rights law for guidance and to find a rule to apply in this hypothetical scenario.[110] It is instructive to observe, although rare, the instances of human mobility in maritime boundary agreements addressed in the form of transboundary arrangements, including for traditional inhabitants.[111]

Protection and Preservation of the Marine Environment

In light of the special ties of Indigenous peoples to the environment, UNDRIP has a special provision, Article 29, which establishes "[I]ndigenous peoples have the right to the conservation and protection of the environment and the productive capacity of their lands or territories and resources."[112] The obligation

---

109 Id. See also Imai and Gunn, n. 106 above.
110 For instance, the Tribunal in *Philippines v. China* noted "[W]here private rights are concerned, international law has long recognized that developments with respect to international boundaries and conceptions of sovereignty should, as much as possible, refrain from modifying individual rights." It also quoted the *Abyei Arbitraton Award*, that "traditional rights, in the absence of an explicit agreement to the contrary, have usually been deemed to remain unaffected by any territorial delimitation." *Philippines v. China*, n. 64 above, paras. 798–799. See *Abyei Arbitration (Government of Sudan v. Sudan People's Liberation Movement/Army)*, Final Award of 22 June 2009, XXX RIAA 145, p. 412, para. 766.
111 For example: Torres Strait Treaty, n. 109 above, preamble and arts. 16 and 18, which addressed among others freedom of movement of traditional inhabitants; Agreement between India and Sri Lanka on the Boundary in Historic Waters between the Two Countries and Related Matters, 26–28 June 1974 (in force 8 July 1974), *Limits in the Seas* no 66 (U.S. Office of the Geographer, 21 December 1975). The latter agreement concerned the historic waters of Palk Bay. Two articles are of direct interest:
   Article 5
   Subject to the foregoing, Indian fishermen and pilgrims will enjoy access to visit Kachchativu as hitherto, and will not be required by Sri Lanka to obtain travel documents or visas for these purposes.
   Article 6
   The vessels of India and Sri Lanka will enjoy in each other's waters such rights as they have traditionally enjoyed therein.
112 While Article 29 specifically deals with protection of the environment and that of the productive capacity of their lands or territories or resources, an argument can be made that this ties with other rights, for example cultural rights. The ILA Interim Report mentions 'ecocide' as adverse, irreparable alterations to the environment that threaten the existence of entire populations under Article 7(2) dealing with genocide. See ILA Interim Report, n. 19 above, p. 17. Also see Revised and Updated Report on the Question of the Prevention and Punishment of the Crime of Genocide, prepared by Mr. B. Whitaker, UN

is further supported by secondary procedural duties.[113] In a similar vein, Article 7(4) of the ILO 169 Convention provides that "[G]overnments shall take measures, in co-operation with the peoples concerned, to protect and preserve the environment of the territories they inhabit."[114] In this respect, the CBD is instructive as it sets out the framework for in-situ conservation (also noted above) and maintains that State parties have a duty to respect, preserve and maintain knowledge, innovations and practices of indigenous peoples[115] and to encourage and develop methods of cooperation that include indigenous and traditional technologies in pursuance of the objectives of the CBD.[116] In addition to giving effect to participatory and consultation mechanisms, this provision has been applied in conjunction with requirements of impact assessment in practice.[117] It is only logical to read Article 29 of UNDRIP along with Article 32(3) on States' obligations concerning impact assessment: "appropriate measures shall be taken to mitigate adverse environmental, economic, social, cultural or spiritual impact."[118] Further, the ILA notes, UNDRIP's provision on environmental protection (Article 29) should be read with general international environmental law.[119]

As observed earlier, Article 192 of UNCLOS establishes a fundamental obligation for State parties "to protect and preserve the marine environment."[120] As the *Philippines v. China* award concluded, this duty is further nourished by the larger corpus of international environmental law. The UNDRIP and ILO 169

Doc. E/CN.4/Sub.2/1985/6, 2 July 1985, 17, para. 33. This can be read (arguably) with Article 194(5) of UNCLOS, n. 4 above, dealing with "measures taken to protect and preserve rare or fragile ecosystems."

113 These include assistance programs for indigenous peoples for conservation and protection, ensuring no storage or disposal of hazardous materials shall take place in the lands or territories of indigenous peoples without their free, prior and informed consent, and programs for monitoring, maintaining and restoring the health of indigenous peoples. UNDRIP, n. 3 above, art. 29.

114 ILO 169 Convention, n. 15 above.

115 CBD, n. 20 above, art. 8(j). For a discussion on traditional knowledge under the CBD and UNDRIP, see T. Stoll, "Intellectual property and technologies," in UNDRIP Commentary, n. 3 above, p. 614.

116 Id., CBD, art. 18(4).

117 See S. Errico, "Control over natural resources and protection of the environment of indigenous territories," in UNDRIP Commentary, n. 3 above, pp. 425–460.

118 Id., p. 453. Errico notes, "considerations related to the environmental impact of proposed activities in Indigenous territories and the consequent repercussions on the life, culture and livelihood of the concerned communities shall be part of the consultation and decision-making process required under the Declaration."

119 See ILA Interim Report, n. 19 above, p. 24.

120 UNCLOS, n. 4 above, art. 192.

Convention provisions, although within the context of international human rights law, provide specific rules for the protection, conservation and sustainable use of the environment in the interest of an identified group of beneficiaries.[121] This adds something to the more general duty in UNCLOS Article 192, and accordingly we argue that the environmental provisions contributed from international human rights law ought to be considered integral to the corpus of international environmental law that informs Article 192. This entails an active duty to protect and preserve the marine environment upon which the enjoyment of indigenous peoples' rights in international law depends.

Marine Scientific Research

UNDRIP establishes indigenous peoples' right "to maintain, control, protect and develop their ... traditional knowledge ..., as well as the manifestations of their sciences, technologies ..., including human and genetic resources, seeds, medicines, knowledge of the properties of fauna and flora."[122] The right includes maintenance, control, protection and development of their intellectual property over traditional knowledge.[123] This falls under the cluster of indigenous peoples' cultural rights and identity.[124] The ILA, in its Resolution No. 5/2012, recognizes these rights as forming part of customary international law.[125]

---

121 See n. 78 above. See also Agenda 21: Programme of Action for Sustainable Development, UN Doc. A/CONF.151/26 (Vol. II) adopted by the United Nations Conference on Environment and Development on 14 June 1992, available online: <https://sustainabledevelopment.un.org/outcomedocuments/agenda21>. See specifically Chapter 26, dedicated to "Recognizing and Strengthening the Role of Indigenous People and their Communities."

122 UNDRIP, n. 3 above, art. 31(1). Stoll comments, "Article 31 introduces a holistic concept of Indigenous culture and knowledge.... In context with other provisions of the UNDRIP, it can be seen to reflect existing, or to promote the emergence of new rules of customary international law..." See Stoll, n. 115 above, for a commentary on Article 31 UNDRIP on intellectual property and technologies.

123 Id.

124 A related provision that focusses on intangible cultural heritage is Article 13(1), which includes "the right of indigenous peoples to develop and transmit their oral traditions.... and to designate and retain their own names for communities, places" and requires States to take effective measures to ensure protection of the right. Indigenous peoples indeed have their own place names and maps, for instance in the Canadian marine Arctic. See C. Aporta, "The sea, the land, the coast, and the winds: Understanding Inuit sea ice use in context," in *SIKU: Knowing Our Ice: Documenting Inuit Sea Ice Knowledge and Use*, eds. I. Krupnik et al. (Springer, 2010), 163–181. For more information on rights relating to culture under UNDRIP, see A. Xanthaki, "Culture," in UNDRIP Commentary, n. 3 above, pp. 273–298.

125 See Resolution No. 5/2012, n. 40 above, para. 6. Earlier in the Interim Report, the ILA had noted: "The right to culture and its importance for the identity and development of

Accordingly, States have an obligation of conduct to take effective measures for the recognition and protection of the exercise of these indigenous rights.[126] Thus UNDRIP has introduced a further consideration in the regulation of scientific research and intellectual property products which potentially concern indigenous knowledge, science and technology in lands, territories and resources which they have traditionally owned, occupied or otherwise used or acquired, and which may include marine spaces.

Against this backdrop, we argue that traditional knowledge is pertinent for the marine scientific research (MSR) regime in UNCLOS.[127] MSR in the internal waters, archipelagic waters and territorial sea falls under the sovereignty of the coastal State and accordingly its regulation is a purely domestic prerogative.[128] Foreign research in such waters is a privilege, not a right. The regime of foreign MSR in the EEZ is substantially different and relies on the so-called 'regime of consent' set out in Part XIII of UNCLOS. The coastal State enjoys the exclusive rights to explore the living and non-living resources of the EEZ and the non-living resources and sedentary species of the continental shelf.[129] MSR which is not resource-related may be conducted by other State parties and international organizations in accordance with the principles and regime established for this purpose in UNCLOS, including subjecting foreign MSR to coastal State consent and regulation.[130] Normally consent for MSR in the EEZ or on the continental shelf for the purpose of increasing scientific knowledge of the marine environment and for peaceful purposes will be granted in accordance with coastal State rules and procedures,[131] which may include procedures for consultations with indigenous peoples affected. Generally, consent is not to be delayed or denied unreasonably.[132] We argue that a meaningful but lengthy

---

individuals and communities is widely recognized by international treaties and jurisprudential or para-jurisprudential practice." See ILA Interim Report, n. 19 above, p. 19, notes 109–110. Also see Article 15 of the International Covenant on Economic, Social and Cultural Rights (ICESCR), adopted 16 December 1966 (entered into force 3 January 1976), UN. Doc. A/RES/21/2200. On the scope of the "right to culture," see Xanthaki id., pp. 284–285.

126 UNDRIP, n. 3 above, art. 31(2).
127 For instance, as the Arctic Marine Shipping Assessment suggests, for the preparation of traffic maps to avoid 'user conflicts' over the same marine areas. See Arctic Marine Shipping Assessment at n. 1 above, the chapter on Arctic marine infrastructure, p. 177.
128 UNCLOS, n. 4 above, art. 245. The Convention refers expressly only to the territorial sea, but given the legal status of internal and archipelagic waters implies exclusive authority to regulate MSR.
129 Id., arts. 56(1)(a) and 77.
130 Id., art. 246.
131 Id., 246(3).
132 Id.

engagement process to ensure free, prior and informed consent of indigenous peoples affected by a foreign MSR permit application is not unreasonable.[133] In the event a coastal State does not respond to an application for a permit or remains silent, the consent of the coastal State will be implied and the applicant State or international organization may proceed with MSR.[134]

An interesting question that arises is whether the free, prior and informed consent of indigenous peoples affected by a foreign MSR application has to be obtained as a legal duty. UNCLOS does not provide for exceptions. UNDRIP does not contain a provision expressly on this point, but has two provisions that may be relevant. The first provides that "States shall consult and cooperate in good faith with the indigenous peoples concerned ... in order to obtain their free, prior and informed consent before adopting and implementing legislative or administrative measures that may affect them."[135] Insofar, as a foreign MSR permit can be characterized as an administrative measure, it is captured by this duty. The second provision establishes that

> States shall consult and cooperate in good faith with the indigenous peoples concerned ... in order to obtain their free and informed consent prior to the approval of any project affecting their lands or territories and other resources, particularly in connection with the development, utilization or exploitation of mineral, water or other resources.[136]

This provision is sufficiently broad to capture MSR activities as "any project," most especially if there are resource implications. Thus States have a related procedural duty.[137] Against this backdrop, and in a hypothetical scenario of

---

133 In a Canadian case concerning an Inuit complaint regarding an MSR permit in Arctic waters granted to the German vessel *Polarstern*, it was argued successfully that the federal government failed to consult properly. See *Qikiqtani Inuit Association v. Canada (Minister of Natural Resources)*, 2010 NUCJ 12; *Hamlet of Clyde River v. TGS–NOPEC Geophysical Company ASA (TGS)*, 2015 FCA 17. For the background and commentary on these cases, see T. Rodon, "Offshore development and Inuit rights in Inuit Nunangat," in *Governance of Arctic Offshore Oil and Gas*, eds. C. Pélaudeix and E.M. Basse (Routledge, 2017), 169–185.

134 UNCLOS, n. 4 above, art. 256.

135 UNDRIP, n. 3 above, art. 19. According to Anaya, n. 89 above, "a generally accepted principle exists in international law that indigenous peoples be consulted with respect to any decision affecting them."

136 Id., UNDRIP, art. 32(2).

137 "States shall provide effective mechanisms for just and fair redress for any such activities, and appropriate measures shall be taken to mitigate adverse environmental, economic, social, cultural or spiritual impact." Id., art. 32(3). According to the ILA, this would involve some form of recompense or profit-sharing for indigenous peoples, for instance through impact and benefit agreements. See ILA Interim Report, n. 19 above, p. 43.

proposed MSR that affects indigenous rights, the foreign MSR applicant ought to be aware of potential difficulties with the regime of implied consent, which may amount to no more than "constructive consent of the coastal State" and not necessarily backed by the "free, prior and informed consent" of indigenous peoples affected.[138] Free, prior and informed consent and broader participatory and consultation rights of indigenous peoples fall under the remit of the right to autonomy and self-government, recognized as a norm of customary international law by the ILA in its Resolution No. 5/2012, and also widely reflected in the practice of UN treaty supervisory bodies and State practice.[139]

A related question is whether the coastal State may refuse to grant foreign MSR permission because of objections from indigenous peoples affected by the proposed research. UNCLOS provides four bases for coastal States to withhold consent, namely if the project

(a) is of direct significance for the exploration and exploitation of natural resources, whether living or non-living;
(b) involves drilling into the continental shelf, the use of explosives or the introduction of harmful substances into the marine environment;
(c) involves the construction, operation or use of artificial islands, installations and structures referred to in articles 60 and 80;
(d) contains information communicated pursuant to article 248 regarding the nature and objectives of the project which is inaccurate or if the researching State or competent international organization has outstanding obligations to the coastal State from a prior research project.[140]

---

138   On free, prior and informed consent (FPIC), see M. Barelli, "Free, prior and informed consent," in UNDRIP Commentary, n. 3 above, p. 268. "FPIC may have significantly different implications depending on the way in which it is read and understood."
139   See Articles 6 and 7 of ILO Convention No. 169, n. 15 above. The UN Committee on the Elimination of Racial Discrimination (CERD) called upon States to "[e]nsure that members of indigenous peoples have equal rights in respect of effective participation in public life and that no decisions directly relating to their rights and interests are taken without their informed consent." CERD General Recommendation 23 on Indigenous Peoples, adopted 18 August 1997, para. 4(d), available online: <http://hrlibrary.umn.edu/gencomm/genrexxiii.htm>.
140   UNCLOS, n. 4 above, art. 246(5).

Unless the research is of direct significance to resources or is potentially harmful to the environment, this text is fairly limited in providing bases for objecting on account of adverse impacts on indigenous peoples' rights.

A provision that could assist coastal States' implementation of participatory rights for their indigenous peoples with respect to MSR in the EEZ or on the continental shelf is Article 249(1), which concerns the duty of foreign MSR operators to comply with certain conditions such as the coastal State's right to participate or be represented in the MSR project. The coastal State could use this provision to introduce conditions for the MSR permit to ensure participation by representatives of indigenous peoples and organizations. Participation could include presence on board research vessels and receipt of research reports and results.

UNDRIP, *qua* custom, could play a role in amplifying the regime of MSR and possibly also as informing good research ethics practices. From an UNDRIP perspective, the coastal State has a duty to act in the interests of indigenous peoples and not remain silent. And from an UNCLOS perspective, the coastal State also has a good faith duty towards MSR applicants and must not abuse its right to regulate such research.[141]

Military Activities

While UNCLOS establishes a legal order that promotes peaceful uses of the oceans,[142] military uses are a fact. Generally, warships enjoy international navigation rights and immunities from jurisdiction.[143]

Article 30 of UNDRIP contains an innovative provision protecting indigenous rights from military activities by providing that such activities "shall not take place in the lands or territories of indigenous peoples, unless justified by a relevant public interest or otherwise freely agreed with or requested by the indigenous peoples concerned,"[144] and accompanied by a procedural duty to conduct effective consultations.[145] It is interesting to observe that this provision

---

141 Id., art. 300.
142 Id., preamble and arts. 88 and 301.
143 Id., arts. 32 and 95.
144 UNDRIP, n. 3 above, art. 30. "UNDRIP is the first instrument on indigenous peoples' rights which devotes a specific Article on military activities in indigenous peoples' lands and territories … It tries to strike a balance between State security and public order issues on the one hand and indigenous peoples' rights and interests on the other … As a general principle, it prohibits military activities in indigenous peoples' territories but contemplates three exceptions … All the exceptions provided in Article 30 are conditional upon the realization of prior consultations." Errico, n. 117 above, pp. 454–455.
145 Id., UNDRIP, art. 30. The ILA envisions this provision to fall under indigenous peoples' land rights. See ILA Interim Report, n. 19 above, p. 24, note 133. ILA Resolution No. 5/2012

does not appear to limit such activities to domestic military activities. Under UNCLOS, the coastal State is able to extend protection to indigenous uses of the territorial sea and archipelagic waters through the regime of innocent passage and by using its power to regulate passage.[146] It is in the position to impose express restrictions on military activities which violate the rules governing innocent passage.[147] Under UNDRIP, States "shall take the appropriate measures, including legislative measures, to achieve the ends of this Declaration."[148] The ILA notes that complaints to international courts (and mechanisms set-up for the purpose) regarding use of indigenous peoples' lands and territories for military activities have been resolved in favor of indigenous peoples' rights.[149]

The extent to which protection can be extended to indigenous uses in the EEZ, where they exist, is less clear. Where they exist in the EEZ, one would need to overcome the difficulty of characterizing areas of the EEZ as 'lands' and 'territories'. Further, the EEZ is subject to particular freedoms of the high seas, including navigation.[150] There is controversy as to whether all military activities, as distinct from mere navigation by warships, can be considered 'internationally lawful uses' related to the freedom of navigation of the high seas.[151] One observer suggests that the UNCLOS may not have the final word on this matter given that there is a growing practice of coastal States that require consent.[152] It is pertinent to observe that UNCLOS has introduced a duty on States

---

recognizes land rights as forming part of customary international law. See ILA Resolution No. 5/2012, n. 40 above, para. 7.

146 See UNCLOS, n. 4 above, arts. 22 and 53.
147 Id. For example, UNCLOS, art. 19, which defines innocent passage as navigation that is not prejudicial to the peace, good order, and security of the coastal State, and accordingly certainly activities are considered prejudicial, such as threat or use of force, exercises or practice with weapons, collecting information prejudicial to the defense of the coastal State, launching, landing or taking on board aircraft or military devices and interfering with communications systems. Under Article 30, the coastal State may require a foreign warship that does not comply with the laws and regulations concerning passage to leave the territorial sea immediately.
148 UNDRIP, n. 3 above, art. 38. Article 38 is applied on a case-by-case basis, in a variety of contexts. See W. van Genugten and F. Lenzerini, "Legal implementation and international cooperation and assistance: Articles 37–42," in UNDRIP Commentary, pp. 539–572.
149 Under UN treaty bodies and the Inter-American human rights system. See ILA Interim Report, n. 19 above, p. 24, note 133.
150 UNCLOS, n. 4 above, art. 58(1).
151 Nandan and Rosenne, n. 93 above, p. 564; see also Proelss' comments in A. Proelss ed., *United Nations Convention on the Law of the Sea: A Commentary* (CH Beck, 2017), p. 453.
152 "It seems doubtful, however, that the limited approach taken by the Convention on the issue of military activities can be regarded as the final word, taking into account the growing body of State practice requiring prior consent for the performance of naval military exercises. In light of this, it may simply be impossible today to come to a conclusive

in the EEZ to pay "due regard to the rights and duties of the coastal State" and to "comply with the laws and regulations adopted by the coastal State in accordance with the provisions of this Convention and other rules of international law in so far as they are not incompatible with this Part."[153] Where indigenous lands and territories can be demonstrated to include areas of the EEZ, it is conceivable that the coastal State's sovereign resource rights and jurisdiction for MSR and environment protection could provide a basis for the protection of indigenous interests, on the basis of other rules of international law' (i.e., UNDRIP *qua* custom), and to expect compliance on the basis of the due regard duty.[154]

Technical Assistance and Capacity-building

UNDRIP provides for the capacity-building of indigenous peoples to enable them to enjoy their rights by providing a right to access financial and technical assistance.[155] UN organizations and intergovernmental organizations are singled out to mobilize financial cooperation and technical assistance, as well as "[W]ays and means of ensuring participation of indigenous peoples on issues affecting them shall be established."[156] The ILA has noted an entire category of rights of indigenous peoples to development and international cooperation.[157]

The UNCLOS provisions on technical assistance are primarily concerned with aiding developing States with respect to MSR and marine technology cooperation (including with respect to activities in the international seabed

---

answer on whether military activities reaching beyond mere passage or overflight are covered by Art. 58(1)." Proelss, id., p. 453.

153   UNCLOS, n. 4 above, art. 58(3).
154   On the due regard duty see J. Gaunce, "On the interpretation of the general duty of 'due regard'," *Ocean Yearbook* 32 (2018): 27–59.
155   UNDRIP, n. 3 above, art. 39. For a scholarly interpretation, see van Genugten and Lenzerini, n. 148 above.
156   Id., UNDRIP art. 41.
157   ILA Interim Report, n. 19 above, pp. 36–38. "The 'right to development' can be conceived according to a twofold perspective. First, a substantive right to development based on self-determination and/or active and equal participation embodied in Article 23 (indigenous peoples have the right to determine and develop priorities and strategies for exercising their right to development); second, a procedural right to development under Article 39 aimed at facilitating the implementation of the other rights enshrined in the Declaration. Owing to the complexity of development processes, the State alone cannot establish the ideal environment for the full realisation of human rights. This is a task that requires cooperation from the entire international community, particularly international institutions." See also Genugten and Lenzerini, n. 148 above.

area).¹⁵⁸ On face value, these provisions do not appear to interface with UNDRIP. What is of more significance is the UNDRIP expectation that indigenous peoples be provided with assistance by international organizations to enjoy their rights and the expectation of these organizations, including those that are designated 'competent international organizations' by UNCLOS, to ensure their participation on issues that affect them. For example, in recent years the International Maritime Organization, as the organization in UNCLOS responsible for international shipping, has deliberated on several issues potentially affecting indigenous peoples, such as the development of the Polar Code, and yet there is no evidence that efforts were exerted to involve indigenous peoples of the Arctic, which happen to have organizations that represent them.¹⁵⁹ In calling for the promotion of inclusive participation of indigenous peoples, UNDRIP speaks directly to international organizations and does not rely on States only to represent the interests of indigenous peoples.

Good Faith

In implementing UNDRIP, States are expected to "consult and cooperate in good faith" and to obtain the "free, prior and informed consent" of indigenous peoples in legislating and administration.¹⁶⁰ Indigenous peoples have "the right to the recognition, observance and enforcement of treaties, agreements and other constructive arrangements concluded with States or their successors and to have States honor and respect such treaties, agreements and other constructive arrangements."¹⁶¹ The ILA notes that "the enforcement of this right is inextricably linked to the various provisions of UNDRIP that guarantee

---

158 In UNCLOS, n. 4 above, Parts XIII and XIV. See especially arts. 202, 203, 266, 269, 274, and 275.
159 There are six federations of indigenous organizations that enjoy the status of Permanent Participants in the Arctic Council, namely, the Aleut International Association (AIA), Arctic Athabaskan Council (AAC), Gwich'in Council International (GCI), Inuit Circumpolar Council (ICC), Russian Association of Indigenous Peoples of the North (RAIPON), and Saami Council (SC). See Sambo Dorough, n. 36 above. The remarks of IMO's Secretary General at a recently concluded conference on the Implementation of the Polar Code are on point: "I am convinced about listening to the voice of indigenous peoples. Increased maritime activity has an obvious potential impact on Arctic indigenous peoples and communities who depend on the marine environment for food … hunting, fishing and other traditional ways are central to the survival of their culture." Keynote address by the IMO's Secretary General, Mr. Kitack Lim, International Conference on Harmonized Implementation of the Polar Code, organized by the Finnish Transport Safety Agency, more information available online: <https://www.trafi.fi/en/polarcode1year>.
160 UNDRIP, n. 3 above, art. 19. Article 19, as noted above, falls under indigenous peoples' right to autonomy and self-government.
161 Id., art. 37.

access to just and fair redress or resolution of conflicts and disputes."[162] In its Resolution No. 5/2012, the ILA recognizes both treaty rights as well as the rights of indigenous peoples to reparation and redress as forming part of customary international law.[163] Further, UNDRIP "shall be interpreted in accordance with the principles of justice, democracy, respect for human rights, equality, non-discrimination, good governance and good faith."[164] These provisions should inform the coastal State's exercise of rights and performance of obligations in UNCLOS which have a bearing on indigenous rights.

UNCLOS provides for State parties to fulfil their obligations in good faith and to exercise their rights and freedoms in a manner that does not amount to an abuse of right.[165] It is arguable that, as between State parties, these intertwined duties which encumber the exercise of rights and performance of duties throughout the Convention apply to the areas of potential interface between UNDRIP and UNCLOS.

Dispute Settlement

Under UNDRIP indigenous peoples have recourse to domestic courts and States have a duty to ensure access to just and fair procedures and remedies for the resolution of conflicts, taking into consideration "the customs, traditions, rules and legal systems of the indigenous peoples concerned and international human rights."[166] The ILA, in its Resolution No. 5/2012 and the Interim Report, describes the customary international law status of the right of indigenous peoples to reparation and redress for the wrongs suffered.[167]

UNDRIP does not address the situation of a dispute between States concerning the existence, interpretation, and application of indigenous rights. It is conceivable that such disputes could arise in the law of the sea, perhaps in similar scenarios to maritime boundary cases where traditional or historic fishing rights were at issue.[168] Where issues of interpretation and application of provisions of UNCLOS relate to indigenous rights, and there is disagreement

---

162 ILA Interim Report, n. 19 above, p. 52.
163 See ILA Resolution No. 5/2012, n. 40 above, paras. 9 and 10.
164 UNDRIP, n. 3 above, art. 46.
165 UNCLOS, n. 4 above, art. 300.
166 UNDRIP, n. 3 above, art. 40.
167 See ILA Interim Report, n. 19 above, pp. 40–43, 53.
168 On historic fishing rights, see *Continental Shelf (Tunisia v. Libyan Arab Jamahiriya)*, Judgment, ICJ Reports 18 (1982); *Maritime Delimitation and Territorial Questions between Qatar and Bahrain (Qatar v. Bahrain)*, Merits, ICJ Reports 40 (2001); *Award of the Arbitral Tribunal in the Second Stage of the Proceedings between Eritrea and Yemen (Maritime Delimitation)*, XXII Reports of International Arbitral Awards.

among interested State parties, the Convention provides options for dispute settlement. Naturally, such disputes would have to arise under the right factual matrix, such as, for example, the exercise of indigenous rights supported by the host State that affect the interests of another State party, or possibly a coastal State excusing its conduct which appears inconsistent with provisions of the Convention, but on account of its efforts to protect indigenous rights. Such a situation could arise with respect to an allegation by a researching State that with respect to a specific MSR project, the coastal State is not exercising its rights in a manner compatible with the Convention.[169] Our purpose here is not to identify all possible dispute scenarios, but rather to consider what the options for dispute settlement might be from a theoretical perspective.

Part XV UNCLOS provides a comprehensive system for the settlement of disputes concerning the interpretation or application of the Convention. State parties can choose any peaceful means of their choice. They have a range of third party-assisted options to choose from, where direct bilateral diplomacy fails to resolve the dispute, such as conciliation, adjudication under the International Court of Justice (ICJ) or International Tribunal for the Law of the Sea (ITLOS), and arbitration under annexes VII and VIII of UNCLOS, or even outside the framework of the Convention, for example under the auspices of the Permanent Court of Arbitration or other *ad hoc* arbitration process. State parties may express their preference on ratification or accession or at any time thereafter.[170] The system operates on the basis of compulsory and optional procedures. Pending resolution of a dispute, provisional measures may be adopted by a court or tribunal.[171] A provision under another treaty or convention in force between the disputants, such as ILO 169, may also be considered and UNCLOS empowers ITLOS to entertain such cases.[172]

It is possible that a dispute that concerns indigenous rights could be subject to the compulsory procedures or may be subject to any of the listed limitations and exceptions. For example, a dispute concerning the MSR procedures are subject to the compulsory procedures, except that the coastal State is not obliged to submit to the procedure when the dispute concerns the exercise of its right or discretion in accordance with the regulatory framework in Article 246 or where the dispute concerns its decision to suspend or cease an MSR project under Article 253, such as where there is non-compliance with the

---

169 UNCLOS, n. 4 above, art. 297(2)(b).
170 Id., art. 287.
171 Id., art. 290.
172 Id., annex VI, art. 22.

permitting terms.[173] In the event of disputes under these two provisions, there is compulsory conciliation in accordance with Annex V, except that the conciliation cannot question the exercise of the coastal State's discretion under the two provisions.[174] This is interesting from an UNDRIP perspective because it provides the coastal State with substantial leeway in setting permitting terms or withdrawing MSR permits when indigenous rights may be affected. There are similar qualifications for fisheries disputes, protection of particular coastal State rights and possible resort to conciliation.[175]

It is conceivable that a maritime boundary dispute may concern in part the weight to be given to indigenous uses of the area in dispute. In the past, there have been maritime boundary disputes that were resolved while recognizing transboundary resource use rights.[176] In another class of disputes in Part XV, concerning maritime boundary delimitation (as well as historic titles and historic bay disputes), a State party may exempt such disputes from compulsory settlement if it expresses such an intention on becoming a party or at any time thereafter.[177] In such cases, a compulsory conciliation procedure remains applicable, and the disputants are expected to negotiate an agreement based on the commission's report. A recent conciliation procedure was successful in assisting States in resolving their maritime boundary dispute.[178] If no agreement is reached, they may still resort to a third party procedure of their choice, but naturally only if they agree. A final class of disputes that a State may opt to exempt from the dispute settlement procedures would be those concerning military activities and law enforcement.[179] Clearly, in the latter case a dispute concerning the impact of military activities on indigenous rights may be excluded if the State conducting military activities chooses to do so.

It is possible there may be conflicts between a coastal State and another State concerning a matter in the EEZ over which UNCLOS has not attributed rights or jurisdiction to a State. A hypothetical example concerns transboundary movement of indigenous peoples through territorial seas and EEZs, as in

---

173   Id., art. 297(2)(a).
174   Id., art. 297(2)(b).
175   Id., art. 297(3).
176   For example *Eritrea v. Yemen*, n. 92 above, and Torres Strait Treaty, n. 102 above. See S.M. Weldehaimanot and D.R. Mekonnen, "Favourable awards to transboundary indigenous peoples," *Australian Indigenous Law Review* 16, no. 1 (2012): 60–76.
177   UNCLOS, n. 4 above, art. 298(a).
178   Australia and Timor-Leste recently concluded a successful conciliation process under Annex V of UNCLOS. See Conciliation between the Democratic Republic of Timor-Leste and the Commonwealth of Australia, Permanent Court of Arbitration Press Release (9 May 2018), available online: <https://pcacases.com/web/sendAttach/2358>.
179   UNCLOS, n. 4 above, art. 298(b).

the case of the Arctic. In such instances, the Convention provides for such conflicts to be resolved "on the basis of equity and in the light of all the relevant circumstances, taking into account the respective importance of the interests involved to the parties as well as to the international community as a whole."[180] This provision appears to open the possibility to consider indigenous practices and rights under UNDRIP as constituting relevant circumstances to be given weight in reaching an equitable solution.

Once a case is admitted, the applicable law to a dispute under UNCLOS includes, in addition to the Convention itself, other rules of international law not incompatible with it,[181] which arguably could include the general international law concerning indigenous rights.[182] The power of an international court or tribunal to decide a case *ex aequo et bono* is also potentially relevant.[183] Procedurally, *amicus curiae* briefs on behalf of indigenous peoples may be a good device not only for their participation (especially since they are not a 'party' to a dispute while it might still affect their interests), but for the tribunal to take all relevant dimensions of the dispute into account.[184]

Conclusion

In this reflective article we raised the question of whether or not there is a relationship between UNDRIP and UNCLOS where provisions of the two instruments potentially overlap or interact on specific subject matter. We argued there is a potential relationship.

---

180 Id., art. 59. See also the discussion on the due regard duty in n. 154 above.
181 Id., art. 293(1). Article 311 as mentioned in n. 72 above deals with compatibility of UNCLOS with "other agreements."
182 As an analogy, Christina Binder's comments on UNDRIP as applicable law in the context of international investment disputes are worth considering: "Typical choice-of-law clauses in investment treaties refer to the law of the host country and such rules of international law as are applicable. Tribunals could thus draw upon relevant instruments for the protection of Indigenous rights as part of the applicable international law of treaties (e.g., ILO Convention 169) or as applicable customary international law. Especially for the latter, the UNDRIP's codification of relevant rights seems important. In a similar vein, tribunals could also apply Indigenous rights as part of the law of the host State." See Binder, n. 14 above. In an UNCLOS context, law of the host State could be replaced by law of the coastal State.
183 Id., art. 293(2). See also Statute of the International Court of Justice, adopted 26 June 1945 (entered into force 24 October 1945), 3 Bevans 1179, art. 38(2).
184 Adopted and modified from Binder's suggestion on *amicus curiae* participation in investment proceedings. See Binder, n. 14 above, p. 104.

We recognize that the two instruments have different levels of authoritativeness, that UNCLOS is a major multilateral convention, whereas UNDRIP is an UNGA resolution which *per se* is not legally binding. We further observed that to the extent UNDRIP's provisions reflect customary international law, the customary norms they may codify potentially produce legal consequences for the overlapping subject matter in UNCLOS. Although we discuss specific UNDRIP provisions in some depth and draw on authoritative opinion concerning their status, we refrained from concluding on their precise legal status. Such an assessment would require a lengthier and more in-depth study. Rather, we hypothesized that assuming the UNDRIP provisions concerned are considered to reflect customary norms, there are arguably interesting potential relationships to particular provisions of UNCLOS, naturally in the right factual matrix where ocean uses intertwine with indigenous rights.

We see two potential roles for UNDRIP in the law of the sea. The first is a potential supplementary role for such customary norms through the preambular pathway that matters not regulated by UNCLOS continue to be governed by the rules and principles of general international law. The second is a further potential interpretative role for UNDRIP customary norms in contributing to the corpus of international environmental law that informs the interpretation of the general duty of States to protect and preserve the marine environment.

At this stage and as we noted at the outset, our enquiry is preliminary and exploratory of specific issues, but we would expect that as long as our premises hold, there are possibly other rights and duties in UNCLOS whose interpretation in the contemporary international law context could benefit from consideration of UNDRIP provisions. Through this reflective piece we hope to inspire additional paths of enquiry and research, such as case studies of actual and emerging practices, comparative consideration of domestic legislation, and court decisions.

From the First Claims to the Exclusive Economic Zone: Reviewing Latin America's 200-Nautical Mile Sea Seventy Years On

Alexandre Pereira da Silva*

Wuhan University, China Institute of Boundary and Ocean Studies, Wuhan, China

Introduction

This article describes the evolution of the concept of the exclusive economic zone (EEZ) through the contributions of Latin American States, from the first claims for an adjacent sea beyond the territorial sea (the Chilean Presidential Declaration and the Peruvian Decree were both enacted in 1947) to today. Seventy years ago, when the territorial sea of 12 nautical miles (NM) was still far from being a consensus, demands for a sea area of up to 200 NM were considered revolutionary. Latin American countries have since played an important role in the development of the law of the sea, especially in the establishment of the EEZ.

After the adoption of the United Nations Convention on the Law of the Sea (UNCLOS or the Convention),[1] a large number of Latin American States joined the Convention and enacted legislation concerning maritime areas, including the EEZ. However, some of them have not fully accepted specific features such as residual rights, military activities, and the emplacement of artificial installations in the EEZ. Moreover, four Latin American countries – Colombia, El Salvador, Peru, and Venezuela – have not yet joined UNCLOS. Therefore, the goals of this article are to highlight the first ideas of a 200-NM sea in Latin America to the current EEZ, to analyze issues of resistance concerning the EEZ, and, finally, to identify the points of opposition of the four reluctant States.

To achieve these aims, the article is structured as follows. The first section introduces the regional initiatives and the origins of the 200-NM sea. This introduction is important to analyze Latin American developments prior to the

---

* The author wishes to thank the China Institute of Boundary and Ocean Studies, Wuhan University, for institutional support and David Dzidzornu for his comments on an earlier version of this paper.

1 United Nations Convention on the Law of the Sea, Montego Bay, 10 December 1982, entered into force November 16, 1994, 1833 *United Nations Treaty Series* 397 [UNCLOS].

Third United Nations Conference on the Law of the Sea (UNCLOS III), which is examined in the second section. The third section moves to the debates and the establishment of the EEZ in UNCLOS, with special consideration given to aspects that were controversial for some Latin American countries. The final section deals with the reasons why the four reluctant States remain apart from the Convention and tries to identify if the reasons are related to the 200-NM sea.

The First Initiatives and the Origins of the 200-Nautical Mile Sea

A turning point in the development of the law of the sea occurred after the Second World War, with U.S. President Harry Truman's two Proclamations of 28 September 1945. The first stated that "the continental shelf may be regarded as an extension of the land-mass of the coastal nation and thus naturally appurtenant to it."[2] For the first time a coastal State claimed sea resources existing in a maritime zone distinct from the territorial sea or the high seas. Following the announcement, the United States government issued a press release noting that the continental shelf was considered as extending to a water depth of 100 fathoms (or 200 meters).[3] The second Proclamation enunciated the policy of the country regarding the need for conservation zones and protection of fisheries resources in areas of the high seas contiguous to its coasts.[4]

After the Truman Proclamations, several Latin American States made similar declarations or enacted laws, including Mexico (1945), Argentina (1946), Costa Rica (1948),[5] Guatemala (1949), El Salvador (1950), Honduras (1950), Nicaragua (1950), and others.[6] However, Latin American demands introduced a

---

2 United States, Proclamation by the President with Respect to the Natural Resources of the Subsoil and Sea Bed on the Continental Shelf, September 28, 1945, reprinted in *American Journal of International Law* 40, no. 1 (1946): 45–46.
3 United States, Department of State Bulletin, vol. 13, no. 314–340, July/December 1945, p. 485: "Generally, submerged land which is contiguous to the continent and which is covered by no more than 100 fathoms (600 feet) of water is considered as the continental shelf."
4 United States, Proclamation by the President with Respect to Coastal Fisheries in Certain Areas of the High Seas, 28 September 1945, reprinted in *American Journal of International Law* 40, no. 1 (1946): 46–48.
5 Initially, Costa Rica enacted the Decree-Law No. 116 (27 July 1948) establishing, among other things, a continental shelf and a sea of 200 NM, but due to problems of interpretation it was repealed by Decree-Law No. 803 (2 November 1949). J.F.S. Carbonell, *Historia Diplomática de Costa Rica (1948–1970)* (Heredia: Escuela de Relaciones Internacionales de Universidad Nacional, 2013), p. 3.
6 Avoiding controversies around the concept of Latin America, this article uses as a benchmark the United Nations Regional Groups, hence Latin American and Caribbean Group (GRULAC) which includes 33 States: Antigua and Barbuda, Argentina, Bahamas, Barbados,

few novelties in the traditional law of the sea. For instance, on 29 October 1945, the President of Mexico delivered the Declaration on the Continental Shelf demanding the right to take appropriate measures to protect and control the living resources on the continental shelf adjacent to its territory. Although using sometimes different expressions, other Latin American positions claimed similar rights over the superjacent waters, as was the case of the Argentinean Decree No. 14,708 of 11 October 1946, that demanded an "epicontinental sea," that is, the water column above the continental shelf as well as the continental shelf.[7]

Nonetheless, Latin American countries in the South Pacific, by capricious geographical conformation of their territories, were prevented for benefiting from continental shelf resources. The case of Peru is especially illustrative, because its continental shelf in some places does not even reach three miles from the coast. The seabed near the Peruvian coast represents a kind of opposite replica of the mountain range at the edge of the sea, with great oceanic abysses of 6,000 meters depth 100 km from the coast.[8] Therefore, Chile and Peru, frustrated for having only short geological continental shelves, made claims over the waters adjacent to their coasts for harvest fisheries.

The first initiative was the Chilean Presidential Declaration of 23 June 1947, followed by the Peruvian Decree No. 781 of 1 August 1947. The Chilean Declaration, which was never incorporated in a legal document, proclaimed national sovereignty over the continental shelf, regardless of its depth, and included the adjacent sea "within the limits necessary to preserve for the said States the natural riches belonging to them, both known and to be discovered in the future."[9] The Peruvian Decree declared that "national sovereignty and jurisdiction can be extended to the submerged continental or insular shelf adjacent to the continental or insular shores of national territory, whatever the depth and extension of this shelf may be."[10]

      Belize, Bolivia, Brazil, Chile, Colombia, Costa Rica, Cuba, Dominica, Dominican Republic, Ecuador, El Salvador, Grenada, Guatemala, Guyana, Haiti, Honduras, Jamaica, Mexico, Nicaragua, Panama, Paraguay, Peru, Saint Kitts and Nevis, Saint Lucia, Saint Vincent and the Grenadines, Suriname, Trinidad and Tobago, Uruguay, and Venezuela.

7   F.V. García Amador, *América Latina y el Derecho del Mar* (Santiago: Universitaria, 1976), pp. 15–16.
8   R.M. Silva, *El mar patrimonial en América Latina* (México, D.F.: UNAM, 1974), p. 17.
9   Chile, Declaration by the President of the Republic of Chile, regarding Chilean Territorial Claims, reprinted in *International Law Quarterly* 2, no. 1 (1948): 135–137.
10   Peru, Peruvian Decree regarding National Sovereignty and Jurisdiction over the Continental and Insular Shelf, reprinted in *International Law Quarterly* 2, no. 1 (1948): 137–138.

Consequently, both countries proclaimed national sovereignty; in Peru's case "national sovereignty and jurisdiction" over the continental shelf, whatever the depth and extension, including the superjacent waters, to the extent necessary "to reserve, protect, maintain and utilise natural resources and wealth" up to 200 NM. The declarations also agreed on recognizing the freedom of navigation on the high seas according to international law.[11]

Despite these unilateral declarations in 1947, the most famous claim over a 200-NM sea is the Santiago Declaration of 18 August 1952, officially known as the Declaration on the Maritime Zone. It was signed by Chile, Ecuador, and Peru at the closing session of the First Conference on the Exploitation and Conservation of the Maritime Resources of the South Pacific. The document stated that the governments "proclaim as a norm of their international maritime policy that they each possess exclusive sovereignty and jurisdiction over the sea along the coasts of their respective countries to a minimum distance of 200 nautical miles from these coasts." It also stressed that "the exclusive jurisdiction and sovereignty over this maritime zone shall also encompass exclusive sovereignty and jurisdiction over the seabed and the subsoil thereof."[12] The Santiago Declaration expressly recognized the innocent and inoffensive passage through the sea area for ships of all nations.[13]

The mentioned right of "innocent and inoffensive passage," a right which is only identified with the territorial sea, and the use of terms "sovereignty" and "exclusive jurisdiction," introduced some confusion around the extension of the territorial sea. The problem was further aggravated by the Ecuadorian and Peruvian interpretations of the Santiago Declaration. Ecuador established a 200-NM territorial sea, and Peru, although the legislation was contradictory, followed the same principle. In contrast, Chile enacted different and contradictory legislation in the aftermath of the Santiago Declaration, but in the end kept in force Article 593 of its Civil Code, a three-NM territorial sea and the 200-NM zone as an "exclusive zone for use."[14] Therefore, there were different

---

11 García Amador, n. 7 above, pp. 17–18.
12 Declaration on the Maritime Zone, done at Santiago, August 18, 1952, 1006 *United Nations Treaty Series* 326.
13 Despite the use of the term "declaration," which may give the idea that it was a soft law instrument, indeed, the Santiago Declaration is a multilateral treaty since it was later ratified by three countries: Chile (Decree No. 432, September 2, 1954), Ecuador (Decree No. 275, February 7, 1955), and Peru (Legislative Resolution No. 12035, May 6, 1955).
14 F. Orrego Vicuña, *Chile y el Derecho del Mar: Legislación y acuerdos internacionales, práctica y jurisprudencia sobre mar territorial, plataforma continental, pesca y navegación* (Santiago: Andrés Bello, 1972), pp. 10–13.

interpretations of the 200-NM zone among Latin American countries since its proper inception. As we shall see, the regional group would later be divided between the "territorialists" and the "zonists."[15]

An interesting issue, but rarely discussed, is why the unilateral acts of 1947 and the Santiago Declaration of 1952 established the sea area 200 NM from the coast, especially considering that the Truman Proclamations established coastal rights on the continental shelf up to 200 meters in depth, and that even the territorial sea of 12 NM was far from being a consensus at that time.

Most scholars assert that 200 NM represents the width of the Humboldt Current off the coast of Chile and Peru. Hollick identified different arguments based on some form of natural determinism, such as the relationship between offshore fisheries and the guano birds;[16] the connection between the submerged shelf with the continent forming a geological unit;[17] and the association of the narrow continental shelf to the great extension of the oceans.[18]

However, an appropriate answer seems to be in the origins of the 1947 Chilean Presidential Declaration. There were several considerations motivating Chile's claim, notably those connected to protecting the nascent whaling operations. To this end, Chilean legal specialists argued that 200 NM was consistent with the 1939 Panama Declaration,[19] much more than the 50-NM protection that the Chilean industry wanted. But, they were convinced that a 200-NM claim could be supported in the Panama Declaration, which indeed was based on inaccurate data, because, in fact, the Declaration had outlined a width of 300 NM off the Chilean coast, and in some parts reaching up to 500 NM.[20] Hence, the 200-NM yardstick, instead of 150 or 300 miles, as correctly pointed out by Aguilar, is "not related to any geographical, geological or, more generally, any universally accepted scientific datum whatsoever. The reason why this

---

15   J.A. Vargas, "The legal nature of the Patrimonial Sea: A first step towards the definition of the exclusive economic zone," *German Yearbook of International Law* 22 (1979): 142–177, p. 158.
16   Indeed, the 1947 Peruvian Decree mentions "that the value of the fertilizer left by the guano birds on islands off the Peruvian coast requires for its safeguard the protection, maintenance and establishment of a control of the fisheries which serves to nourish these birds." Peru, n. 10 above.
17   E.G. Sayan, "La doctrina de las 200 Millas y el Derecho del Mar," *Derecho PUCP* 32 (1974): 12–27, pp. 15–16.
18   A.L. Hollick, "The origins of 200-mile offshore zones," *American Journal of International Law* 71, no. 3 (1977): 494–500, pp. 494–495.
19   Consultative Meeting of Foreign Ministers of the American Republics, reprinted in *American Journal of International Law* 34, no. 1 (1940): 1–20.
20   Hollick, n. 18 above, pp. 495–496.

figure was chosen is essentially political."[21] The Peruvian Decree and the 1952 Santiago Declaration repeated the 200-NM claim as it first appeared in the Chilean Presidential Declaration.

After the 1952 Santiago Declaration, several similar acts were adopted in Latin America, such as the 1952 draft prepared by the Inter-American Legal Committee, the 1954 LXXXIV resolution of the Inter-American Conference, the Principles of Mexico, and the 1956 Ciudad Trujillo Resolution. All these resolutions, directly or indirectly, welcomed the principle of special jurisdiction of the coastal State over the natural resources beyond the territorial sea.[22]

Conversely, maritime powers manifested strong opposition to the Latin American claims. For instance, the U.S. Congress enacted the *Fishermen's Protective Act* in 1954 with the purpose of protecting the rights of their vessels on the high seas. This act permitted the U.S. Department of the Treasury to reimburse any fines paid by owners of U.S. vessels that were seized, and the Secretary of State to deem appropriate measures to make and collect claims from the foreign country for the amount refunded.[23]

Developments Prior to UNCLOS III

During the first United Nations Conference on the Law of the Sea (UNCLOS I), held in Geneva in 1958, debates were based on the International Law Commission's draft, and negotiations primarily hinged on the issue of the maximum breadth of the territorial sea. The Latin American demands were rejected, particularly because the Convention on the High Seas reaffirmed the principle of freedom of use for all States and that "no State may validly purport to subject any part of them to its sovereignty," adding that the freedoms of the high seas were navigation, fishing, laying of submarine cables and pipelines, and overflight (Article 2).[24] However, although the Convention on the High Seas kept the freedom of fishing on the high seas, the Convention on Fishing and

---

21 A.M. Aguilar, "The Patrimonial Sea or Economic Zone Concept," *San Diego Law Review* 11 (1973): 579–602, p. 590.
22 F. Orrego Vicuña, "La zone économique exclusive: Régime et nature juridique dans le droit international," in *Collected Courses of the Hague Academy of International Law* (*vol. 199*) (Leiden: Martinus Nijhoff, 1986), p. 24.
23 U. Leanza and M.C. Caracciolo, "The Exclusive Economic Zone," in *The IMLI Manual on International Maritime Law: The Law of the Sea*, vol. I, ed. D. Attard, M. Fitzmaurice and N.M. Gutiérrez (Oxford: Oxford University Press, 2014), p. 180.
24 Convention on the High Seas, Geneva, 29 April 1958, entered into force 30 September 1962, 450 *United Nations Treaty Series* 82.

Conservation of the Living Resources of the High Seas, also approved during the UNCLOS I, recognized coastal States' special interest in the conservation of marine resources in an area of open sea adjacent to the territorial sea, including adopting appropriate conservation measures for all species of fish or other marine resources (Articles 6 and 7).[25]

UNCLOS II (1960) made a new effort to reach an agreement on the breadth of the territorial sea and fishing rights, but, once again, no agreement was reached on these issues. The proposal, which narrowly missed receiving the required two-thirds majority, would have entitled the coastal State to fix the breadth of its territorial sea up to a maximum of six NM from the applicable baselines and to establish a contiguous fishing zone to a maximum limit of 12-NM from those baselines "in which it shall have the same rights in respect of fishing and the exploitation of the living resources of the sea as it has in its territorial sea."[26]

The failure to reach an agreement renewed claims by coastal States to extend the breadth of the territorial sea or other exclusive or preferential rights or jurisdictions, particularly in Africa and South America. Hence, during the 1960s and 1970s, many coastal States claimed a new maritime zone beyond the territorial sea, usually referred to as the exclusive fisheries zone (EFZ).[27]

In the 1970s, Latin American resolutions became more precise in their objective to extend the jurisdiction and sovereignty over the adjacent sea near the coasts. For example, the Montevideo Declaration on the Law of the Sea, adopted on 8 May 1970, considered that the Latin American States have the right "to extend their sovereignty and jurisdiction to the extent necessary to conserve, develop and exploit the natural resources of the maritime area adjacent to their coasts, its soil and its subsoil [...] to a distance of 200 nautical miles from the baseline of the territorial sea."[28] Although the Montevideo Declaration was unanimously approved by the nine participant States, there were some divergences among the group in relation to the approach to the freedom of navigation on the adjacent sea.

---

25 Convention on Fishing and Conservation of the Living Resources of the High Seas, Geneva, 29 April 1958, entered into force 20 March 1966, 559 *United Nations Treaty Series* 286.
26 S.N. Nandan and S. Rosenne, eds., *United Nations Convention on the Law of the Sea 1982: A Commentary*, vol. 2 (Dordrecht: Martinus Nijhoff, 1993), p. 495. According to the joint proposal by Canada and the United States, commonly known as the "six-plus-six," it missed the two-thirds majority by one vote.
27 Leanza and Caracciolo, n. 23 above, pp. 180–181.
28 Montevideo Declaration on the Law of the Sea, reprinted in *American Journal of International Law* 64, no. 5 (1970): 1021–1023.

Between 4 and 8 August 1970, the Lima Meeting on Certain Aspects of the Law of the Sea took place and was attended by eighteen Latin American countries and a few observer States and organizations. The Declaration of Latin American States on the Law of the Sea underlined "the right of the coastal State to establish the limits of its maritime sovereignty or jurisdiction in accordance with reasonable criteria, having regard to its geographical, geological, and biological characteristics, and the need to make rational use of its resources" (Principle 2).[29] Despite the fact that this Declaration reaffirmed many issues of the Montevideo Declaration, it contained no mention of the 200 NM distance.[30]

Two years later, the Caribbean States issued the Santo Domingo Declaration, which contained specific provisions on the "patrimonial sea," establishing a clear distinction between this concept and the territorial sea. The Santo Domingo Declaration recognized the right to an extended maritime zone, but it limited jurisdiction, under the concept of "patrimonial sea," where the coastal State would have "sovereign rights over the renewable and non-renewable natural resources, which are found in the waters, in the seabed and in the subsoil of an area adjacent to the territorial sea called patrimonial sea," adding that "the breadth of this zone should be the subject of an international agreement, preferably of a worldwide scope" and "should not exceed a maximum of 200 nautical miles." The Declaration also granted traditional freedoms of the high seas, "with no restrictions other than those resulting from the exercises by the coastal State of its rights within the area."[31] The idea of a patrimonial sea would be to establish a compromise formula between the developing States and the maritime powers.[32]

Subsequently, in 1973, within the Committee on the Peaceful Uses of the Seabed and the Ocean Floor beyond the Limits of National Jurisdiction (Seabed Committee), Colombia, Mexico, and Venezuela, called "patrimonialists," submitted a proposal giving a more precise formulation for the expression. The Tripartite Proposal was clearly in favor of a deep revision of the traditional law of the sea in Latin America, but it did not share the concept of the 200-NM

---

29 Latin American Meeting on Aspects of the Law of the Sea: Declaration and Resolutions, reprinted in *International Legal Materials* 10, no. 1 (1971): 207–214.

30 V.M. Rangel, "O novo direito do mar e a América Latina," *Revista da Faculdade de Direito da USP* 76 (1981): 75–85, p. 80.

31 Specialized Conference of Caribbean Countries Concerning the Problems of the Sea: Declaration of Santo Domingo, reprinted in *American Journal of International Law* 66, no. 5 (1972): 918–920.

32 J.A. Vargas, *Mexico and the Law of the Sea: Contributions and Compromises* (Leiden: Martinus Nijhoff, 2011), p. 151.

territorial sea, as proposed by the "territorialists." This proposal was the only one supporting the patrimonial sea notion before the Seabed Committee and contained substantial similarities with the Santo Domingo Declaration.[33]

The widespread Latin American practice was closely coordinated with African and Asian countries at the same time. They held their own meetings and played an important role in transforming the patrimonial sea into an EEZ.

The most significant of those meetings was the Regional Seminar on the Law of the Sea, which was held in Yaoundé, Cameroon, 20–30 June 1972, and attended by 16 countries. Its conclusions did not differ substantially from the patrimonial sea as embodied in the Santo Domingo Declaration. In reference to an "economic zone," the Yaoundé Conclusions stated that "the African states have equally the right to establish beyond the Territorial Sea an Economic Zone over which they will have an exclusive jurisdiction for the purpose of control, regulation and national exploitation of the living resources of the sea and their reservation for the primary benefit of their peoples and their respective economies."[34]

A few months later, Kenya submitted to the Seabed Committee a proposal entitled "Draft Articles on the Exclusive Economic Zone Beyond the Territorial Sea" as a compromise formula between the special needs and interests of the coastal States on the one hand, and declared international principles for the sharing of the ocean resources by all States, whether coastal or landlocked, on the other hand. The Kenyan proposal was strongly influenced in the patrimonial sea concept, proposing that "all States have the right to establish an Economic Zone beyond the territorial sea for the primary benefit of their peoples and their respective economies in which they shall exercise sovereign rights over natural resources for the purpose of exploration and exploitation" (Article II), but the establishment of the zone "shall be without the prejudice to the exercise of freedom of navigation, freedom of overflight and the freedom to lay submarine cables and pipelines" (Article III).[35]

---

33 Vargas, n. 15 above, pp. 159–160. According to this draft article, "the coastal state has sovereign rights over the renewable and non-renewable resources which are found in the waters, in the seabed and in the subsoil of an area adjacent to the territorial sea called the patrimonial sea. The outer limit of the patrimonial sea shall not exceed 200 nautical miles from the applicable baselines." Colombia, Mexico and Venezuela: Draft Articles of Treaty (2 April 1973), reprinted in *International Legal Material* 12, no. 3 (1973): 570–572.

34 African States: Conclusions of the Regional Seminar on the Law of the Sea, reprinted in *International Legal Materials* 12, no. 1 (1973): 210–213.

35 Kenya: Draft Articles on Exclusive Economic Zone Beyond the Territorial Sea (7 August 1972), reprinted in *International Legal Materials* 12:1 (1973): 33–35. Kenya introduced for the first time the concept of the exclusive economic zone in the Seabed Committee (UN Doc. A/AC.138/SC.II/SR.8 of 3 August 1971).

In May 1973, the Organization of African Unity (OAU) delivered a declaration addressing several issues on the law of the sea. Regarding the exclusive economic zone, the declaration stated that its outer limit "should not exceed 200 nautical miles" and that coastal States exercised "permanent sovereignty over all the living and mineral resources" in that space, "without undue interference with the other legitimate uses of the sea: namely, freedom of navigation, overflight and laying of cables and pipelines."[36] In comparison to the Santo Domingo Declaration, the OAU Declaration contained three important remarks: it recognized the right of all States to carry out "other legitimate uses of the sea," although it did not develop the idea; it did not subject the exercise of other States' rights to the restrictions derived from the exercise of the rights of the coastal State in the zone; and it introduced the concept of the interests of landlocked and other disadvantaged States in the exploitation of living resources of neighboring economic zones on an equal basis.[37]

The Latin American demands gained considerable support and strength due to two main factors: the newly independent African and Asian countries and the exponential growth of fishing activity.[38] Additionally, the concepts of "patrimonial sea" and "economic zone" differed more in form than in substance since they led to similar practical results. First, the water column was included, as was the seabed and subsoil beyond the territorial sea, for the exercise of exclusive rights over all the resources, but maintaining third-State's rights. Secondly, almost all the proposals agreed that this zone should not exceed 200 NM from the baselines.[39]

Establishment of the EEZ in UNCLOS and Topics of Concern for Some Latin American States

When UNCLOS III began, the Latin American States were divided between the "territorialist" trend and the "patrimonialist" (or "zonist") trend.[40] As remembered by Ambassador Castañeda, the discussions within the Latin American

---

36 Vargas, n. 32 above, p. 173.
37 Orrego Vicuña, n. 22 above, p. 25.
38 L.D.M. Nelson, "The Patrimonial Sea," *International and Comparative Law Quarterly* 22, no. 4 (1973): 668–686, p. 676.
39 Aguilar, n. 21 above, pp. 581–582.
40 S.N. Nandan, "The Exclusive Economic Zone: A Historical Perspective," in *The Law and the Sea: Essays in Memory of Jean Carroz* (Rome: Food and Agriculture Organization of the United Nations, 1987), available online: <http://www.fao.org/docrep/s5280T/s5280t0p.htm>.

Group were particularly vehement, not rarely even more so than those with the delegates of the maritime powers.[41]

Some Latin American countries, alongside others, constituted the so-called "territoralist" group, formed by 23 States which were claiming territorial seas exceeding 12 miles (16 African countries, six Latin American countries, and one Asian country).[42] Other "patrimonialist" States expressed a more intermediate position, aiming to guarantee the exercise of "sovereign rights" over the marine resources.

At the 1974 session of UNCLOS III, held in Caracas, Ecuador presented a proposal for a territorial sea of 200 NM (supported by, among others, Brazil, Panama, Peru, and Uruguay) in which "the coastal State exercises its sovereignty over the territorial sea subject to the provisions of this Convention."[43] Another part of the Latin American Group (Colombia, Mexico, and Venezuela, in particular) opposed this trend. For instance, the representative of Colombia at this same session on the Second Committee stated that "the 12-mile territorial sea was necessarily linked to the acceptance by the international community of an economic zone or patrimonial sea of a maximum breadth of 200 nautical miles. In that zone the coastal State was to have sovereign rights with regard to the exploration and exploitation of the renewable and non-renewable natural resources situated in the superjacent waters or in the sea-bed and the subsoil thereof."[44]

By the end of the second session (August 1974), it was apparent that most of the delegations supported the 200-NM exclusive economic zone concept. The Second Committee, whose task was to draft the articles relating to areas of national jurisdiction, adopted, in its Informal Single Negotiating Text (ISNT – Part II), a provision that "the exclusive economic zone shall not extend beyond

---

41   J. Castañeda, "Negotiations on the Exclusive Economic Zone at the Third United Nations Conference on the Law of the Sea," in *Essays on International Law in Honour of Judge Manfred Lachs*, ed. J. Makarczyk (Leiden: Brill, 1984), p. 609.

42   The "territorialist" group may be also considered as a sub-group of the Coastal States Group, although it operated as a separate group. The African members were: Benin, Cape Verde, Congo, Equatorial Guinea, Gabon, Guinea, Guinea-Bissau, Libyan Arab Jamahiriya, Madagascar, Mauritania, Mozambique, São Tomé and Príncipe, Senegal, Sierra Leone, Somalia, and Togo; Latin American members: Brazil, Ecuador, El Salvador, Panama, Peru, and Uruguay; Asian member: Democratic Yemen. M. Nordquist, ed., *United Nations Convention on the Law of the Sea 1982: A Commentary*, vol. 1 (Dordrecht: Martinus Nijhoff, 1985), pp. 75–76.

43   Ecuador: Draft Articles on the Territorial Sea (July 16, 1974), Document A/CONF.62/C.2/L.10.

44   United Nations, *Third United Nations Conference on the Law of the Sea – Official Records*, vol. II: Summary Records of Meetings of the First, Second and Third Committees, Second Session (Caracas, June 20–August 29, 1974), p. 110.

200 nautical miles from the baseline from which the breadth of the territorial sea is measured" (Article 46).[45] The same words were adopted in the subsequent negotiating texts until it became Article 57 of UNCLOS.

With the development of UNCLOS III, the concept of the exclusive economic zone gained wide acceptance, especially among the Group of 77. The "territorialists" joined forces with the "patrimonialists" (although there were differences between them, but they agreed on a more or less strong EEZ) in opposition to those countries who sought a "weak" economic zone.[46]

Even with the inclusion of the EEZ in the ISNT, maritime powers insisted on the need to assure broad rights for third States in the EEZ, ideally identifying the zone as part of the high seas. This issue faced severe objections from the coastal States, and for nearly two years debates within official groups ended in a deadlock. Thus, a small informal negotiating group was formed, consisting originally of some 13 delegations, and became the so-called Castañeda-Vindenes Group, named after its chairmen, Ambassadors Jorge Castañeda (Mexico) and Helge Vindenes (Norway). The group succeeded in building an average solution, where the waters of the EEZ have a *sui generis* legal status, neither part of the territorial sea nor part of the high seas, being "subject to the specific legal regime established" in Part V of UNCLOS.[47] As in other parts of the Convention, Part V reflects a political compromise that could be accepted by the States. The final content of the EEZ, as it stands today, is the sum of the contributions and commitments of all States, including those from Latin America, Africa, and elsewhere.

On the one hand, Latin American States obtained two major achievements. First, in the maintenance of the 200 NM breadth of the EEZ, a range brought from the peculiar geographical circumstances of the Andean States, which has become an internationally accepted width.[48] Secondly, in assuring coastal States' sovereign rights for the purpose of exploring, exploiting, conserving, and managing the natural resources; jurisdiction with regard to the establishment

---

45   United Nations, *Third United Nations Conference on the Law of the Sea – Official Records*, vol. IV: Summary Records, Plenary, General Committee, First, Second and Third Committees, as well as Documents of the Conference, Third Session (Geneva, March 17 to May 9, 1975), Informal Single Negotiating Text, Part II (UN Doc. A/CONF.62/WP.8/PART II), p. 152.

46   Nandan and Rosenne, n. 26 above, p. 499.

47   Castañeda, n. 41 above, p. 619. According to Vargas (n. 32 above, pp. 152–153), for diplomatic and political reasons, the expression patrimonial sea gradually lost out to the exclusive economic zone to gain the support not only of other States in Latin America, but also of countries with similar interests in Africa and Asia, and eventually the acceptance of the international legal community.

48   R.J. Dupuy and D. Vignes, *A Handbook on the Law of the Sea* (Dordrecht: Martinus Nijhoff, 1991), p. 275.

and use of artificial islands, installations, and structures; marine scientific research and the protection and preservation of the marine environment; and other rights and duties provided in the Convention.[49]

On the other hand, Latin American States, as well as others, had to accommodate some of their interests in the EEZ to accept UNCLOS as a whole.[50] Indeed, when the Convention was adopted on 10 December 1982, 14 of the 33 Group of Latin American and Caribbean Countries (GRULAC) had already promulgated legislation establishing the EEZ: Antigua and Barbuda (1982), Barbados (1978), Colombia (1978), Costa Rica (1972),[51] Cuba (1977), Dominica (1981), Dominican Republic (1977),[52] Grenada (1978),[53] Guatemala (1976), Guyana (1977),[54] Haiti (1977), Honduras (1980),[55] Suriname (1978), and Venezuela (1978). After 1982, another 13 States enacted laws regulating the EEZ: Argentina (1991), Bahamas (1993), Belize (1992), Brazil (1993), Chile (1986), Jamaica (1991), Mexico (1986),[56] Panama (1996), Saint Kitts and Nevis (1984), Saint Lucia (1984), Saint Vincent and the Grenadines (1983), Trinidad and Tobago (1986), and Uruguay (1998). Four other Latin American coastal States have no specific legislation

---

49   H.L. Mansilla, "Los países del sistema del Pacífico Sur ante la Convención sobre Derecho del Mar," *Revista Chilena de Derecho* 10 (1983): 21–38, p. 33.

50   As remembered by Ambassador Tommy T.B. Koh, who chaired the final session of UNCLOS III, Part V of UNCLOS "was strongly debated, but found very wide acceptance. Not universal acceptance, but wide acceptance. There were friends on both sides who did not agree with the compromise text and held onto their strongly held initial positions. But at the Conference, on all these contentious issues, the middle ground prevailed." T.T.B. Koh, "Remarks on the Legal Status of the Exclusive Economic Zone," in *Freedom of Seas, Passage Rights and the 1982 Law of the Sea Convention*, eds. M. Nordquist, T.T.B. Koh and J.N. Moore (Leiden: Martinus Nijhoff, 2009), p. 54.

51   Costa Rica, Decree No. 2,204 (10 February 1972) concerning the patrimonial sea is still in force.

52   The Act No. 573 (1 April 1977) was later repealed by Law 66-07 (May 22, 2007), which proclaimed archipelagic status for the Dominican Republic and contained the lists of geographical coordinates of points for drawing the archipelagic baselines and the outer limits of the EEZ.

53   The *Maritime Boundaries Act* (Act No. 20, 1 November 1978) (Grenada) was later repealed by the *Territorial Sea and Maritime Boundaries Act* (Act No. 25, 13 July 1989), which is a longer and more detailed law.

54   By the Order No. 19 (23 February 1991) made under the *Maritime Boundaries Act* of 1977 it was designated the area of the EEZ of Guyana.

55   Subsequently the *Honduran Maritime Areas Act* (Decree No. 172–99, 30 October 1999) detailed specific provisions, such as internal waters, territorial sea, contiguous zone, EEZ, continental shelf, among others.

56   On 13 February 1976, Mexico enacted a law on the exclusive economic zone, regulating the eighth paragraph of Article 27 of its Constitution and introducing the concept of the exclusive economic zone. Reprinted in *International Legal Materials* 15, no. 2 (1976): 382–384.

concerning the EEZ: Ecuador, El Salvador, Nicaragua, and Peru. The two countries not mentioned are Bolivia and Paraguay, both landlocked states.

However, since Article 309 forbids reservations or exceptions, many Latin American States expressed their reluctance to accept specific features of the EEZ in their statements upon signature and/or ratification of UNCLOS. Those statements express concerns of some Latin American States with specific issues of the legal regime of the EEZ, such as the exercise of residual rights, the conduct of military maneuvers or exercises, and the emplacement of artificial installations.

Residual Rights

Residual rights are future rights to new uses of the sea that may result from technological developments or are those rights and jurisdictions not specifically attributed to either coastal States or other States. By the second session (Caracas, 1974), the concept of the EEZ was virtually assured, but remaining issues needed to be addressed; one of those was the question of residual rights in the zone – initially called "residual powers."[57]

The question of residual rights in the area adjacent to the territorial sea received great attention by Latin American States during UNCLOS III debates. For example, the Brazilian delegate stated that "since it was normal for the residual powers in the international zone to be exercised by all States, it was normal that in the national zone such residual powers should be reserved for the coastal State."[58] In the same session, other Latin American delegations, such as Chile, Colombia, Ecuador, El Salvador, and Uruguay, supported similar positions.[59]

Countries like Canada, Germany, Italy, and the United States expressed their opposition regarding the residual rights in favor of coastal States. For example, the Italian delegate stated that "any residual regime applied in the area should be that of the freedom of the seas, not that of the authority of the

---

57   Nandan and Rosenne, n. 26 above, p. 498.
58   United Nations, n. 44 above, p. 109.
59   Later in the same session, the delegate of El Salvador, Mr. Galindo Pohl, expressed in more detail its concerns on the residual rights: "the question of residual powers and rights – a question which his delegation regarded as of crucial importance to the meaningful definition of an economic zone. The silence of the draft concerning such rights and powers could be interpreted as meaning that they were vested in the international community. If the international community maintained effective control, such an arrangement was not unacceptable; but it was well known that when rights were not specifically defined they would in fact be exercised not by the international community but by other States and, more likely than not, by the major maritime Powers." Id., p. 188.

coastal State."⁶⁰ The solution to conciliate the divergent interests is Article 59 of UNCLOS:

> In cases where this Convention does not attribute rights or jurisdiction to the coastal State or to other States within the exclusive economic zone, and a conflict arises between the interests of the coastal State and any other State or States, the conflict should be resolved on the basis of equity and in the light of all the relevant circumstances, taking into account the respective importance of the interests involved to the parties as well as to the international community as a whole.⁶¹

This disposition tries to maintain a balance between the two sides: in case of conflicting interests, there is no presumption in favor of either the coastal or other States, hence the residual rights do not belong to either of the two sides and they will be decided case by case, considering equity and significant circumstances.⁶² However, some Latin American statements, upon signature and/or ratification, have claimed the residual rights for themselves. Those declarations were heavily contested by other States.

For instance, the Uruguayan declaration, made upon signature and confirmed upon ratification (December 1982 and December 1992, respectively), refers explicitly to the residual rights in the EEZ:

> Regulation of the uses and activities not provided for expressly in the Convention (residual rights and obligations) relating to the rights of sovereignty and to the jurisdiction of the coastal State in its exclusive economic zone falls within the competence of that State, provided that such regulation does not prevent enjoyment of the freedom of international communication which is recognized to other States.⁶³

European States, such as Germany, Italy, and the Netherlands, made declarations in opposition to the claims for the residual rights by coastal States. For example, the German declaration asserted that "according to the Convention, the coastal State does not enjoy residual rights in the exclusive economic zone.

---

60   Id., p. 196.
61   UNCLOS, n. 1 above, art. 59.
62   R.R. Churchill and A.V. Lowe, *The Law of the Sea* (Manchester: Manchester University Press, 1999), p. 176.
63   UN Treaty Collection, "Status of Treaties, United Nations Convention on the Law of the Sea, Ecuador Declaration," available online: <https://treaties.un.org/pages/ViewDetailsIII.aspx?src=TREATY&mtdsg_no=XXI-6&chapter=21&Temp=mtdsg3&clang=_en>.

In particular, the rights and jurisdiction of the coastal State in such zone do not include the rights to obtain notification of military exercises or manouevres or to authorize them."[64]

More recently, Ecuador has claimed residual rights in the EEZ. Ecuador was one of the most ardent supporters of the territorialist approach of the EEZ among the Latin American States. It was an Ecuadorian initiative to establish the Territorialist Group during the second session of the Conference. As Part V does not reflect the territorialist approach, and considering other domestic legal obstacles, for instance Article 609 of the Ecuadorian Civil Code (1966), which fixed the territorial sea at 200 NM, Ecuador did not sign UNCLOS.[65] Only in 2012 did Ecuador become the last Latin American State to join the Convention.

As with many States, the accession of Ecuador to UNCLOS was accompanied by a very long declaration, which has important inconsistencies as compared to UNCLOS. At the beginning, the Ecuadorian declaration "[...] confirms the full validity of the Declaration of Santiago on the Maritime Zone, signed in Santiago, Chile, on 18 August 1952, by means of which Chile, Ecuador and Peru declared '... as a norm of their international maritime policy, the exclusive sovereignty and jurisdiction that each of them possesses in respect of the sea adjacent to the coasts of their respective countries, up to a minimum distance of 200 nautical miles from those coasts.'"[66] These highlighted terms of the Declaration of Santiago are hardly compatible with UNCLOS, since sovereignty is limited to 12 NM of the territorial sea.

Another aspect is that the Ecuadorian declaration avoids the expression "sovereign rights," used in Part V, instead using expressions like "exclusive sovereignty" or "exclusive right." According to the declaration, Ecuador has the following rights and obligations in the EEZ:

1. *Exclusive sovereignty* for the purpose of exploring and exploiting, conserving and managing the natural resources, whether living or non-living, of the waters superjacent to the seabed and of the seabed and its subsoil;
2. *Exclusive sovereignty* for the purposes of the economic exploitation and exploration of the zone, such as the production of energy from the water, marine currents and winds;

---

64 Id.
65 L.V. Rodríguez, "El Ecuador y la Convención de las Naciones Unidas sobre el Derecho del Mar: Ventajas de la adhesión ecuatoriana," *AFESE* 53 (2010): 17–48, p. 18.
66 See n. 63 above.

3. *Exercise of the exclusive right* to authorize, regulate and undertake the construction, operation and use of all types of artificial islands, installations and structures within the 200 miles of its maritime territory, including the continental shelf.[67] (emphasis added)

However, the most controversial topic of the Ecuadorian declaration concerning the EEZ is, perhaps, the following one: "The Ecuadorian State declares that it has the exclusive right to regulate uses or activities not expressly provided for in the Convention (residual rights and jurisdiction) that relate to its rights within the 200 nautical miles, as well as any future expansion of the said rights."[68]

Parties to UNCLOS, such as the European Union, Spain, the United Kingdom, and Greece, delivered to the UN Secretary-General communications with regard to the declaration of Ecuador upon accession. Belgium, Italy, and Sweden openly expressed opposition regarding the claims for the residual rights in the Ecuadorian declaration. For instance, the "Belgian Government is therefore particularly disturbed by the parts of the [Ecuadorian] declaration concerning sovereignty, which seems to go beyond 12 nautical miles, and concerning the right of innocent passage and freedom of navigation. In its declaration, Ecuador seems also to be claiming residual rights in the exclusive economic zone, which is inconsistent with article 59."[69]

More than thirty-five years after UNCLOS III, the residual rights issue remains subject to discussion between Latin America and maritime powers. Article 59 has tried to conciliate the views, but it is clearly insufficient to accommodate the diverging positions. The statements and acts enacted after the adoption of UNCLOS, but especially the most recent declaration of Ecuador, prove that, at least for the former Latin American territorialist countries, the Convention has not found a solution able to accommodate their interests in this particular issue. As a result, these States maintain their claims for residual rights in the EEZ.

Military Maneuvers

Another topic of great concern for Latin American States within in the EEZ was the possibility of other States using the maritime zone for military maneuvers or exercises. This question is directly linked with residual rights.

---

67 Id.
68 Id.
69 Id.

All attempts made during UNCLOS III to introduce a legal disposition with the principle of the consent of the coastal State prior to carrying out naval operations other than navigation in the EEZ did not advance. Numerous Latin American countries expressed strong dissatisfaction over the possibility that the EEZ would remain open to military activities such as the discharge of weapons, the use of explosives, and military maneuvers.[70]

The legislative history of Article 58 shows that between the first draft version (ISNT) and the final version of UNCLOS, a significant modification (for some experts a more permissive approach) was introduced when "other internationally lawful uses of the sea related to navigation and communication" was changed to "other internationally lawful uses of the sea related to these freedoms."[71]

Regardless of the possible interpretation of this legislative history of Article 58, the fact is that the absence of a provision forbidding military activities in the EEZ of another State thwarted some Latin American States, which kept their position in their final declarations. For example, Brazil explicitly ruled out the possibility of military exercises by other States within its own EEZ. In its declaration upon signature and reiterated upon ratification, Brazil emphasized that "[t]he Brazilian government understands that the provisions of the convention do not authorize other states to carry out in the exclusive economic zone military exercises or manoeuvres, in particular those that imply the use of weapons or explosives, without the consent of the coastal state."[72]

This declaration, made by Brazil and other countries, such as Bangladesh, India, Malaysia, Pakistan, Thailand, and Uruguay,[73] was contested by other States, including Germany, Italy, and the Netherlands. For example, the Italian declaration, made upon signature and confirmed upon ratification, stated that "according to the Convention, the Coastal State does not enjoy residual rights in the exclusive economic zone. In particular, the rights and jurisdiction of the Coastal State in such zone do not include the right to obtain notification

---

70   F. Francioni, "Peacetime use of force, military activities, and the new Law of the Sea," *Cornell International Law Journal* 18 (1985): 203–226, p. 215.
71   Id.
72   See n. 63 above.
73   Id., "Uruguay declarations made upon signature and confirmed upon ratification": "(D). The exclusive economic zone, enjoyment of the freedom of international communication in accordance with the way it is defined and in accordance with other relevant provisions of the Convention excludes any non-peaceful use without the consent of the coastal State for instance, military exercises or other activities which may affect the rights or interests of that State and it also excludes the threat or use of force against the territorial integrity, political independence, peace or security of the coastal State."

of military exercises or manoeuvres or to authorize them."[74] Nevertheless, this position was reaffirmed in the Brazilian Law No. 8,617 of 4 January 1993, enacted after ratification of UNCLOS. According to Article 9 of that act: "[i]n the exclusive economic zone, military exercises and manoeuvres, in particular those involving the use of weapons or explosives, may only be carried out by other States with the consent of the Brazilian Government."[75]

One of the practical implications of these statements is that Brazil and other Latin American countries are commonly targeted by Freedom of Navigation (FON) operations, a United States policy established in 1983 to exercise and assert its navigation and overflight practices in the world's oceans. The main goal of this policy is to challenge the unilateral acts of other States that, in the United States' view, restrict the "rights and freedoms of the international community in navigation and overflight and other related high seas uses."[76] For instance, the last U.S. Department of Defense Freedom of Navigation Report for Fiscal Year 2016 (published 28 February 2017) lists 22 States that were targeted by the FON activities, including two in Latin America: Brazil, because it requires consent for "military exercises or maneuvers in the exclusive economic zone," and Venezuela, as the country wants "prior permission for overflight of the EEZ and Flight Identification Region."[77] In previous years, other Latin American countries were targeted by FON activities, such as Argentina, because it requires "prior notification for foreign warships to enter the territorial sea," Ecuador, due to its "excessive straight baselines," and Peru, because of its "200-nautical mile breadth of territorial sea."[78]

Emplacement of Artificial Installations

Another issue that has not been fully resolved in UNCLOS is the right to construct, authorize, and regulate the construction, operations, and use of installations and structures in the EEZ. Article 60 of UNCLOS has been interpreted in different ways, especially in relation to artificial installations not intended

---

74 Id.
75 Brazil, Law No. 8,617 (4 January 1993). available online: <http://www.un.org/Depts/los/LEGISLATIONANDTREATIES/PDFFILES/BRA_1993_8617.pdf>.
76 United States Ocean Policy – Statement by the President, 10 March 1983, reprinted in *International Legal Materials* 22, no. 2 (1983): 464–465.
77 United States, Department of Defense, "Freedom of Navigation (FON) Report for Fiscal Year 2016," 28 February 2017, available online: <http://policy.defense.gov/Portals/11/FY16%20DOD%20FON%20Report.pdf?ver=2017-03-03-141349-943>.
78 United States, Department of Defense, "Freedom of Navigation (FON) Report for Fiscal Year 2014," 23 March 2015, available online: <http://policy.defense.gov/Portals/11/Documents/gsa/cwmd/20150323%202015%20DoD%20Annual%20FON%20Report.pdf>.

for economic purposes, such as military installations, structures, and devices. This means that the right to emplacement of military devices in the EEZ could be considered a residual right.[79]

Concerns on this topic were expressed by Brazil and Uruguay in their declarations upon signature and ratification. For instance, the Uruguayan declaration states: "This Convention does not empower any State to build, operate or utilize installations or structures in the exclusive economic zone of another State, neither referred in the Convention nor any kind, without the consent of the coastal State."[80]

As with previous issues, manifestations like this one were refused by maritime countries, such as Germany, Italy, the Netherlands, and the United Kingdom. For example, the declaration of the Netherlands asserts:

> The coastal state enjoys the right to authorize, operate and use installations and structures in the EEZ for economic purposes. Jurisdiction over the establishment and use of installations and structures is limited to the rules contained in article 56, paragraph 1, and is subject to the obligations contained in article 56, paragraph 2, article 58 and article 60 of the Convention.[81]

Despite those protests, when Uruguay enacted Act No. 17,033 on 20 November 1998, establishing the boundaries of the territorial sea, the adjacent sea, the exclusive economic zone, and the continental shelf, it reaffirmed its position on this topic. Article 6(A) reads: "Uruguay has the exclusive right to construct and to authorize and regulate the construction, operation and use of such artificial islands, installations and structures, *regardless of their nature or characteristics.*"[82]

Argentina made a long declaration upon signature and ratification of UNCLOS, but did not mention any aspect concerning artificial installations. However, the Argentinean Act No. 23,968 of 14 August 1991 provides that the country "shall retain the exclusive right to construct, authorize and regulate

---

79 F.H. Paolillo, "The exclusive economic zone in Latin American practice and legislation," *Ocean Development & International Law* 26, no. 2 (1995): 105–125, pp. 113–114.
80 See n. 73 above.
81 Id.
82 Uruguay, Act No. 17,033 (20 November 1998), emphasis added, available online: <http://www.un.org/Depts/los/LEGISLATIONANDTREATIES/PDFFILES/URY_1998_Act.pdf>.

the construction, operations and use of *all kinds of installations and structures*, over which it shall have exclusive jurisdiction" (Article 9).[83]

However, the Latin American precursor seems to be Article 1 of the Honduran Decree No. 921 of 13 June 1980, which established the exclusive rights and jurisdiction of the State with regard to artificial islands, installations, and structures "of any kind."[84] Subsequently, the Honduran *Maritime Areas Act* (Decree No. 172–99) of October 30, 1999, enacted after the accession of Honduras to UNCLOS in 1993, detailed specifics on maritime zones. Concerning artificial installations, this disposition is closer to UNCLOS than the previous one in stating that the country has jurisdiction with regard to "the establishment and use of artificial islands, installations and structures for the purpose of exploring and exploiting the resources of the seabed and its subsoil."[85]

Based on these few, but most emblematic examples, it would appear that in Latin America there is a trend to extending coastal State jurisdiction by not following exactly the provisions of the EEZ set out in Part V of UNCLOS. This would not, however, be a correct approach. In their views, they are more "filling the gaps" – ambiguities and lacunae of the Convention – than trying to strengthen their authority over the EEZ.[86] The wider acceptance of UNCLOS in Latin America and Caribbean regions seems to indicate that the concerns over "creeping jurisdiction" should be minimized. Distinct and specific approaches between domestic laws and the Convention must not alter the broad support and contributions of the region to the establishment and consolidation of the present regime of the oceans.

The Reluctant Latin American States: Colombia, El Salvador, Peru, and Venezuela

As mentioned, Colombia and Venezuela, two of the four Latin American countries that are non-parties to UNCLOS, enacted domestic laws concerning maritime zones, including the EEZ, even before the end of UNCLOS III, indicating that their resistance was not in the maritime zones established in the Convention.

---

83 Argentina, Act No. 23,968 (14 August 1991), emphasis added, available online: <http://www.un.org/Depts/los/LEGISLATIONANDTREATIES/PDFFILES/ARG_1991_23968.pdf>.
84 Honduras, Decree No. 921 (13 June 1980), available online: <http://www.un.org/Depts/los/LEGISLATIONANDTREATIES/PDFFILES/HND_1980_Decree.pdf>.
85 Honduras, Legislative Decree No. 172–99 (30 October 1999), available online: <http://www.un.org/Depts/los/doalos_publications/LOSBulletins/bulletinpdf/bulletinE49.pdf>.
86 Paolillo, n. 79 above, pp. 120–121.

Colombia enacted Act No. 10 of 4 August 1978, establishing rules concerning the territorial sea, the EEZ, and the continental shelf and regulating other matters. There are two legal dispositions (Articles 7 and 8) referring to the EEZ and neither offer obstacles to ratification of UNCLOS.[87] Colombia signed UNCLOS and the Final Act on 10 December 1982, not making any formal statements upon it. The question is: what has been impeding Colombia from ratifying the Convention?

Colombian lawyers agree that the fundamental reason the country has not yet ratified UNCLOS is the controversy relating to maritime delimitations with neighboring States, such as Ecuador, Nicaragua, and Venezuela.[88] Considering that this argument is plausible, the Colombian strategy has failed.

In December 2001, Nicaragua instituted proceedings against Colombia in the International Court of Justice (ICJ) under the jurisdiction of the Court on provisions of the 1948 American Treaty on Pacific Settlement (Pact of Bogotá),[89] concerning title to territory and maritime delimitation in the Western Caribbean.

In the *Territorial and Maritime Dispute* judgment rendered on the merits of the case on 9 November 2012, the ICJ recognized that, even though Colombia is not a party to UNCLOS, Articles 74 and 83 on the delimitation of the EEZ and continental shelf are to be considered customary international law (paragraph 138).[90]

On the one hand, the judgment affirmed Colombia's territorial sovereignty over a group of islands (San Andres, Providencia, and Santa Catalina, which are located facing the Nicaraguan mainland coast). On the other hand, the ICJ performed the maritime delimitation between them according to its three-stage methodology: (1) delineation of a provisional equidistance/median line; (2) evaluation of whether the coastal geography provides any relevant circumstances that require variance from the equidistance line; and (3) determination that the adjusted boundary is equitable by identifying any significant

---

87 Colombia, Act No. 10 (4 August 1978) establishing rules concerning the Territorial Sea, the Exclusive Economic Zone and the Continental Shelf and regulating other matters, available online: <http://www.un.org/Depts/los/LEGISLATIONANDTREATIES/STATEFILES/COL.htm>.

88 C.D. Garzón, D.A.O. Avellaneda and E.A.B. Martín, "Colombia y la Tercera Convención de las Naciones Unidas sobre el Derecho del Mar: Un análisis desde la sociedad internacional," *Revista Republicana* 13 (2012): 109–128, p. 122.

89 American Treaty on Pacific Settlement, Bogotá, April 30, 1948, 30 *United Nations Treaty Series* 84.

90 International Court of Justice (ICJ), *Territorial and Maritime Dispute (Nicaragua v. Colombia)*, Judgment, ICJ Reports 2012, p. 624.

disproportionality between the relevant coasts (paragraphs 190–194).[91] On applying the second stage of the delimitation process, the Court adjusted the equidistance line in favor of Nicaragua, which in Colombia's view represented a loss of roughly 75,000 km^2 of maritime area.

As a consequence, one week after the ICJ delivered its judgment, Colombia withdrew from the 1948 Pact of Bogotá and thereby terminated its consent to the ICJ's jurisdiction.[92] Considering that Colombia has other maritime disputes with neighboring countries, this judgment will hardly help its ratification of UNCLOS.

Another issue that may represent an obstacle to Colombia joining the Convention is related to underwater cultural heritage, especially Article 303, paragraph 3. This topic became of special concern after a U.S. Court rendered its decision on the case of the sunken vessel *Nuestra Señora de las Mercedes*, a Spanish Crown ship, sunk in 1804 and found by Odyssey Marine Exploration on the now Portuguese continental shelf. In April 2007, Odyssey filed an *in rem* action declaring that it had recovered tons of coins. Peru, Spain, and twenty-five alleged descendants of those aboard the *Mercedes* also filed claims against the *res*.[93] In the end, the Court ruled in favor of Spain, recognizing the foreign immunity of the ship.[94]

Nevertheless, though Colombia was not involved in this case, this decision raised an alert in the country for similar hypothetical cases in the Caribbean Sea, which would favor Spanish interests over ancient colonies.[95] Colombia is also not a party of the Convention on the Protection of the Underwater Cultural Heritage, adopted on 2 November 2001, by the General Conference of the United Nations Educational, Scientific and Cultural Organization (UNESCO).

Venezuela presented a proposal to amend Article 309 of the Convention that would permit reservations concerning the delimitation of maritime spaces. Later, Venezuela withdrew its proposal and supported the Turkish proposal (also repealed) that would suppress current Article 309.[96]

91　Id.
92　N. Grossman, "Territorial and Maritime Disputes (Nicaragua v. Colombia)," *American Journal of International Law* 107, no. 2 (2013): 396–403, pp. 399–403.
93　*Odyssey Marine Exploration, Inc. v. The Unidentified Shipwrecked Vessel et al.*, 657 F.3d 1159 (2011). Certiorari denied 9 February 2012.
94　M.J. Aznar-Gómez, "Treasure hunters, sunken State vessels and the 2001 UNESCO Convention on the Protection of Underwater Cultural Heritage," *International Journal of Marine and Coastal Law* 25 (2010): 209–236, pp. 214–215.
95　W.R.C. Afanador and C.D. Garzón, "Colombia y la territorialización de sus mares. Conflictos limítrofes y la Convención de Derecho del Mar," *Revista Prolegómenos. Derechos y Valores* 15, no. 30 (2012): 199–223, pp. 219–220.
96　Venezuela, Draft Amendment to Article 309 (Document A/CONF.62/L.108).

Venezuela signed the Final Act, but noted that "its signing does not signify, nor can it be construed as signifying, any change in its position with regard to article 15, 74, 83 and 121, paragraph 3, of the Convention [...] those provisions are unacceptable to Venezuela, which is therefore not bound by them and is not prepared to agree to be bound by them in any way."[97] Articles 15, 74, and 83 of UNCLOS deal with methods for delimiting maritime zones between States (territorial sea, EEZ, and continental shelf, respectively).

Venezuela's refusal of UNCLOS had an important historical implication. Since the country hosted the second session of UNCLOS III in 1974, the original idea of the delegates was to return to Caracas for the closing ceremony. However, in a letter to the United Nations Secretary-General, the representative of Venezuela registered that "[f]or the reasons expressed at the appropriate time by the Chairman of the delegation of Venezuela, our country found it impossible to associate itself with the adopted text in its entirety. [...] my Government regrets having to withdraw its original offer to act as host at Caracas for the signature of the Final Act and the opening of the Convention for signature."[98]

Venezuelan objections to the articles concerning maritime delimitation occurred because the Convention eliminates references to delimitation by equidistance and incorporates the concept of equitable solution. In this way, the Convention provided that the delimitation must be made by agreement between concerned States on the basis of international law, as referred to in Article 38 of the Statute of ICJ, in order to achieve an equitable solution.[99]

Since 1978, Venezuela has been negotiating with States in the Caribbean Sea for maritime delimitation purposes. As a result of the negotiations, there have been delimitation treaties with five States in the region so far, which is equivalent to around 60 to 70 percent of the marine areas that correspond to Venezuela in the Caribbean Sea: the United States (1978), the Netherlands (1978), Dominican Republic (1979), France (1980), and Trinidad and Tobago (1991). However, maritime delimitation agreements with Colombia, Dominica, Grenada, Guyana, Saint Lucia, Saint Kitts and Nevis, and Saint Vincent and the Grenadines are still pending.[100] Venezuela is aware of the implications that UNCLOS would have for its unfinished delimitations, consequently the country

---

97 See n. 63 above.
98 Venezuela, Letter dated 20 September 1982 from the representative of Venezuela to the Secretary-General (Document A/CONF.62/L.153).
99 M.G.H. Ruz, *El derecho del mar en el régimen jurídico venezolano* (Dissertation, Universidad Central de Venezuela, 2013), p. 63.
100 Venezuelan boundary delimitation agreements, available online: <http://www.un.org/Depts/los/LEGISLATIONANDTREATIES/STATEFILES/VEN.htm>.

has refrained from acceding to it until it has individual agreements with each of the bordering States.

Concerning the EEZ, Venezuela enacted a law on 26 July 1978, establishing an EEZ along the coasts of the mainland and islands. Distinct from much domestic legislation, the 1978 Venezuelan act was exclusively dedicated to the EEZ. It had nine articles, and they fully accorded with Part V of UNCLOS.[101] In 2002, Venezuela enacted the Organic Law on Water and Island Areas, which repealed the 1978 Law. The 2002 Law was a very long and detailed act that had 127 articles. Title V (Articles 52 to 60) was fully dedicated to the EEZ, repeating legal dispositions of the 1978 Law and UNCLOS.[102]

However, this law had a short life. In 2014, the Venezuelan government enacted a new Organic Law on Water and Island Areas.[103] The 2014 Law, though, has many similarities with the previous one; for instance, it is as long as the 2002 Law (128 articles), it dedicates the first part to the maritime zones and related issues, and it has titles exclusively dedicated to island areas, underwater cultural heritage, marine scientific research, and the managing of maritime and island areas.

A remarkable difference between the 2002 and 2014 Organic Law is Article 72 (of the 2002 Law), which stated that "it shall lead to the conclusion of the pending delimitation of submarine and marine areas, through direct agreement with each of the bordering coastal countries, on the basis of equitable principle and taking into account the relevant circumstances."[104] This article was suppressed in the 2014 Law in which there is no article dealing with maritime boundaries. The 2014 Law, as with the 2002 Law, leaves aside controversial topics for Venezuela, such as the definition of islands (showing the resistance of Venezuela to Article 121 of the Convention) and the criteria for maritime boundaries.

The resistance of El Salvador to ratifying UNCLOS is basically due to a constitutional obstacle. According to Article 84 of its 1983 Constitution,

---

101   Venezuela, Act establishing an Exclusive Economic Zone along the coasts of the Mainland and Islands of 26 July 1978, available online: <http://www.un.org/Depts/los/LEGISLATIONANDTREATIES/STATEFILES/VEN.htm>.
102   Venezuela, *Ley Orgánica de los Espacios Acuáticos y Insulares*, Gaceta Oficial No. 37,596 de 20 de diciembre del 2002.
103   Venezuela, *Ley Orgánica de los Espacios Acuáticos y Insulares*, Gaceta Oficial No. 6,153 de 18 noviembre 2014.
104   Venezuela, n. 102 above. Translated from the original: "Propiciará la conclusión de la delimitación pendiente de áreas marinas y submarinas, mediante acuerdo directo con cada uno de los países ribereños limítrofes, sobre la base de principio equitativos y teniendo en cuenta todas las circunstancias pertinentes."

the territory of the country is "irreducible" and "El Salvador exercises sovereignty and jurisdiction over the sea and its bed and subsoil for a distance of 200 nautical miles, measured from the low-water line."[105] However, in 2004, the National Congress reformed Article 574 of the Civil Code which establishes the maritime zones of the country. The new wording stipulates that "the adjacent sea up to a distance of 12 nautical miles, measured from the baselines, is territorial sea [...] The adjacent sea zone which extends beyond the territorial sea up to 200 nautical miles, measured from the baselines, is named exclusive economic zone in which El Salvador exercises sovereign rights."[106]

The clear discrepancy between Article 84 of the Constitution and Article 574 of the Civil Code opened an intense legal debate, and the issue was brought before the Constitutional Chamber of the Supreme Court. In its decision of 31 August 2016, the Chamber rejected the plea on the unconstitutionality of the Article 574 and consequently recognized the maritime areas (territorial sea, contiguous zone, EEZ, and continental shelf) and limits as stipulated in UNCLOS. This decision has opened the path for El Salvador to ratify the Convention.[107]

However, there is another issue which could make it difficult for El Salvador to ratify UNCLOS, that is, the sea areas in the Gulf of Fonseca (a bay shared with Honduras and Nicaragua). The difficulties around the Gulf of Fonseca are not new. In 1917, the Central American Court of Justice decided in the case *The Republic of El Salvador v. The Republic of Nicaragua*, concerning the Bryan-Chamorro Treaty (Nicaragua and United States), which related, among other matters, to the leasing of a base in the Gulf of Fonseca and recognized the territorial waters (three miles) and co-ownership beyond that limit.[108] In 1986,

---

105   El Salvador was the first country to provide in a constitution, in 1950 – and later repeated in the constitutions of 1962 and 1983 – its sovereignty and jurisdiction over an adjacent sea up to 200 NM. El Salvador, Article 84 of the Salvadorian Constitution of 13 December 1983, available online: <http://www.un.org/Depts/los/LEGISLATIONANDTREATIES/PDFFILES/SLV_1983_Constitution.pdf>.

106   El Salvador, Codigo Civil, available online: <http://oas.org/dil/esp/Codigo_Civil_El_Salvador.pdf>. Translated from the original: "Art. 574. El mar adyacente, hasta la distancia de doce millas marinas, medidas desde la línea de base, es mar territorial [...] La zona de mar adyacente que se extiende más allá del mar territorial hasta las doscientas millas marinas contadas desde la línea base, se denomina zona económica exclusiva, en la cual El Salvador ejerce derechos de soberanía."

107   J.L.L. Castelar, "Sentencia Sala de lo Constitucional sobre espacios marítimos," *El Mundo* (7 October 2016), available online: <http://elmundo.sv/sentencia-sala-de-lo-constitucional-sobre-espacios-maritimos/>.

108   Central American Court of Justice, *The Republic of El Salvador v. The Republic of Nicaragua*, reprinted in *American Journal of International Law* 11, no. 3 (1917): 674–730.

El Salvador and Honduras notified the ICJ of a special agreement whereby the Parties requested the Court form a Chamber in order to delimit the frontier line in sectors not delimited by the 1980 General Treaty of Peace concluded between them and to determine the legal situation of the islands in the Gulf of Fonseca and the maritime spaces within and outside it. In 1992, the ICJ Chamber concluded that the Gulf of Fonseca waters other than three-mile maritime belts and waters delimited in 1900 (delimitation between Honduras and Nicaragua, accepted by El Salvador) are historic waters and subject to joint sovereignty (condominium or co-ownership) of the three States.[109] Some legal experts believe that on ratifying UNCLOS, El Salvador could be obliged to delimit this area in a way where the Salvadorian territory would lose a considerable share of territorial sea, since the country has a disadvantaged geographical position in relation to the other two countries by the projection of the perpendicular lines from the closing line in the mouth of the Gulf of Fonseca.[110]

The case of Peru is similar to El Salvador on the main point, that is, a constitution disposition that mentions a 200-NM sea. Initially, it was introduced in the 1979 Constitution and then repeated almost literally in the current Political Constitution of Peru, promulgated on 29 December 1993. Article 54 asserts: "The maritime dominion of the State includes the sea adjacent to its coasts, as well as the bed and subsoil thereof, up to the distance of two hundred nautical miles measured from the baselines determined by the law. In its maritime dominion, Peru exercises sovereignty and jurisdiction, without prejudice to the freedoms of international communication, in accordance with the law and the treaties ratified by the State."[111]

The Peruvian Constitution does not use the expression "territorial sea" but "maritime dominion," although in practice Peruvian authorities understand "sovereignty and jurisdiction" of a 200-NM adjacent sea as a territorial sea.[112] However, among Peruvian lawyers, there are different interpretations of the implications of Article 54. On the one hand, there are those who understand that since the adoption of the 1952 Santiago Declaration, Peru advocates the

---

109 ICJ, *Land, Island and Maritime Frontier Dispute (El Salvador/Honduras: Nicaragua intervening)*, Judgment, [1992] ICJ Rep 351.
110 A.J.C. Urqilla, T.R.G. Lopez and S.C.V. Velez, "Ventajas y desventajas de ratificar la Convención de las Naciones Unidas sobre el Derecho del Mar por parte del Estado de El Salvador," (Dissertation, Universidad de El Salvador, 2006), pp. 202–203.
111 Peru, Political Constitution of Peru, 29 December 1993, art. 54, available online: <http://www.un.org/Depts/los/LEGISLATIONANDTREATIES/PDFFILES/PER_1993_Constitution.pdf>.
112 S. Mosquera, "El Perú y la Convención del Derecho del Mar y las Naciones Unidas," *Revista Jurídica del Perú* 54, no. 59 (2004): 311–329, pp. 325–326.

idea that a 200-NM limit represents a territorial sea, making it consequently impossible to join UNCLOS. Peru did not sign UNCLOS but agreed to sign the Final Act of UNCLOS III. On the other hand, there are those who argue that the "maritime dominion" does not refer to territorial sea, but only designates the sea area where the State may act in a comprehensive way; therefore, the expression "maritime dominion" is in accordance with UNCLOS.[113] In a certain way, the debate in Peru repeats the controversies between the "territorialists" and the "zonists," but with a clear advantage for the first trend in the domestic scenario.

In January 2008, Peru filed an application instituting proceedings against Chile concerning a dispute in relation to the delimitation of the boundary between the maritime zones of the two countries.[114] Peru made important declarations through its agent during the case clarifying the scope of the constitutional expression "maritime dominion." For example, during the oral hearing of 3 December 2012:

> [*Allan Wagner*] Mr. President, on behalf of the Government of Peru, I wish formally to place on record Peru's commitment to the modern law of the sea as reflected in the 1982 United Nations Convention on the Law of the Sea. Peru's Constitution of 1993, its internal law, and Peru's practices are in full conformity with the contemporary law of the sea. The term "maritime domain" used in our Constitution is applied in a manner consistent with the maritime zones set out in the 1982 Convention.[115]

The Peruvian agent reaffirmed this position in another oral hearing on 11 December 2012: "[I]n short, Peru accepts and applies the rules of the customary international law of the sea, as reflected in the Convention."[116]

Even after the positive results in the judgment of January 2014, different Peruvian governments have not shown interest in a formal accession to UNCLOS, even when considering that the Committee of Foreign Affairs of the National

---

113   P.C.R. Zamora, "El reconocimiento por el Perú de los espacios marítimos de la Convención sobre el Derecho del Mar," *Revista Eletrônica de Direito Internacional* 15, no. 1 (2015): 1–25, pp. 4–5.
114   ICJ, *Maritime Dispute (Peru v. Chile)*, Judgment, [2014] ICJ Rep 4, p. 3.
115   ICJ, Verbatim Record 2012/27, Public sitting held on Monday, 3 December 2012, at the Peace Palace, President Tomka presiding, in the case concerning the Maritime Dispute (Peru v. Chile).
116   ICJ, Verbatim Record 2012/34, Public sitting held on Tuesday 11 December 2012, at the Peace Palace, President Tomka presiding, in the case concerning the Maritime Dispute (Peru v. Chile).

Congress has unanimously approved a draft resolution recommending Peru's accession to it.[117]

As with the other Latin American countries that are already parties to UNCLOS, the four reluctant States feel inclined to accept the regime established in 1982. There are very few issues of resistance. Colombia and Venezuela enacted laws on maritime areas even before the entry into force of UNCLOS; both have specific resistance, mainly on aspects of maritime delimitation. El Salvador and Peru fixed in their constitutions a sea of 200 NM, establishing constitutional pitfalls difficult to dismantle because they require constitutional changes that are not easy to carry out. Conversely, in recent years, both have demonstrated their support and have guided their actions in accordance with the UNCLOS regime.

Conclusion

Seventy years ago, the first claims for a 200-NM sea had a great impact among Latin American countries. But, different approaches to this new maritime zone were there at its inception and were reflected in the initial debates at regional conferences and later at UNCLOS III, under the division between "territorialists" and "zonists." Eventually, these groups joined forces, also aligning with African and Asian countries around the concept of the EEZ.

Despite the resistance of some influential countries, when UNCLOS entered into force in 1994, 19 of the 33 GRULAC States had already ratified it, that is, one-third of the parties to the Convention at that time. In the following decades, ten other countries joined UNCLOS. Ecuador, one of the most active members of the "territorialist" group, was the last of those countries when it acceded to it in 2012. Today, only four Latin American States remain non-parties to UNCLOS.

Though Colombia, El Salvador, Peru, and Venezuela remain non-parties to the Convention, those reluctant States reaffirmed their commitments to it. Colombia and Venezuela are unlikely to join UNCLOS in the short or medium term due to objections concerning maritime delimitation. The constitutional dispositions in El Salvador and Peru may make their formal accession to the Convention difficult, but recent developments have illustrated their full engagement with the law of the sea regime.

The broad acceptance of UNCLOS among Latin American countries was, at times, followed by an implementation process via domestic laws that have

---

117 Mosquera, n. 112 above, p. 329.

since seen peculiar interpretations over some features of the legal regime of the EEZ, such as the residual rights, military exercises, and the emplacement of installations and structures in the zone. However, this does not undermine the strong regional support for the EEZ regime and to the Convention as a whole.

PART 2

Coastal and Ocean Management

Designation of the Tubbataha Reef Natural Park as a Particularly Sensitive Sea Area: the Philippine Experience

Jay L. Batongbacal
College of Law, University of the Philippines, Diliman, Quezon City, The Philippines

Introduction

The Philippines' Tubbataha Reef Natural Park (TRNP) encloses a large and well-known group of coral atolls and sandbars within the Sulu Sea and stands as its first completely offshore natural park. It also happens to be located at the crossroads of international shipping traffic passing through the Sulu Sea linking the South China Sea to the Celebes Sea and Pacific Ocean. This creates a convergence point between the interests of the Philippines in strictly conserving and protecting its marine resources and the interests of the international community in maintaining and using its navigational prerogatives under international law. The convergence of interests resulted in the designation of the TRNP as a Particularly Sensitive Sea Area (PSSA) and establishment of an Area to be Avoided (ATBA) as an associated protective measure (APM) at the 71st session of the Marine Environment Protection Committee (MEPC) of the International Maritime Organization (IMO) on 3–7 July 2017.[1]

A PSSA is an area that needs special protection through action by the IMO because of its significance for recognized ecological, socioeconomic, or scientific attributes that may be vulnerable to damage by international shipping activities.[2] It is designated by the IMO if it fulfills at least some of three general criteria, namely ecological criteria such as uniqueness, rarity, or diversity of the marine ecosystem within, or vulnerability to natural or human impacts; sociocultural and socioeconomic criteria such as significance of the area for tourism or recreation; and scientific and educational criteria such as biological importance or historical value. These criteria are presently described in detail

---

1 International Maritime Organization (IMO), "Designation of the Tubbataha Reefs Natural Park as a Particularly Sensitive Sea Area," IMO Doc. MEPC 71/WP. 10/Annex 1–4 (6 July 2017).
2 IMO, "Revised Guidelines for the Identification and Designation of Particularly Sensitive Sea Areas," IMO Doc. A 24/Res.982 (6 February 2006), para. 1.1 [hereafter Revised PSSA Guidelines].

in the IMO's Revised Guidelines for the Identification and Designation of Particularly Sensitive Sea Areas.[3]

For an area to be designated as a PSSA, a coastal State and member government of the IMO must submit a proposal for designation to the MEPC, accompanied by relevant information supporting the existence of the criteria in the Revised Guidelines.[4] Separate proposals for associated protective measures should also be submitted to the concerned committee or sub-committee of the IMO.[5] The MEPC cannot designate a PSSA until after the relevant committee or sub-committee has approved the associated protective measure.[6] Once approved, the PSSA and associated protective measure are indicated on nautical charts in accordance with the symbols and methods of the International Hydrographic Organization.[7] All member governments of the IMO are then obliged to take steps to ensure that ships flying their flag comply with the associated protective measures adopted to protect the PSSA.[8] In this manner, the IMO is able to use international standards for navigation and ship operations to support national or multi-lateral efforts to protect the marine environment.

This article is a chronicle of the Philippines' experience in attempting to reconcile its domestic interests in marine environment protection with user State interests in navigation through its waters through the PSSA designation. It first describes the TRNP, its special features, and conditions that justified the establishment of a PSSA, narrates events leading to its designation as such, and highlights the lessons learned and insights gained through that exercise. It is hoped that this article will not only serve as an historical record for policy advocates and decision-makers should other PSSA designations be proposed in other parts of the archipelago, but also as a useful reference for other countries considering and seeking designation of their own PSSA.

---

3   Id., paras. 4–5.5.
4   Id., paras. 3.2 and 7–7.10.
5   Id., para. 7.10. The principal IMO Committees include those on Maritime Safety (MSC), Marine Environment Protection (MEPC), Legal (LEG), Technical Cooperation (TC), and Facilitation (FAC). Among the key sub-committees are those on Human Element, Training, and Watchkeeping (HTW), Implementation of IMO Instruments (III), Navigation, Communications and Search and Rescue (NCSR), Pollution Prevention and Response (PPR), Ship Design and Construction (SDC), Ship Systems and Equipment (SSE), and Carriage of Cargoes and Containers (CCC). The nature and scope of the proposed associated protective measure determines the relevant committee or sub-committee which will evaluate its feasibility and recommend its approval.
6   Id., para. 8.3.1.4.
7   Id., para. 9.1.
8   Id., para. 9.3.

The Tubbataha Reefs Natural Park

The Tubbataha Reef Natural Park (TRNP) located in the Sulu Sea is one of the largest protected seascapes of the Philippines and historically the first and oldest of its offshore marine park areas under the National Integrated Protected Areas System.[9] It currently encompasses two large coral reefs, the North Atoll and South Atoll (the original Tubbataha Reefs in older navigational charts) and the Jessie Beazley Reef, arranged in an inverted triangular fashion.[10] The North Atoll is oblong-shaped, approximately 10 nautical miles (NM) long and 2 NM wide, while the South Atoll is triangular and about 5 NM long and 2 NM at its widest; the two atolls stand approximately 5 NM apart.[11] Both enclose sandy lagoons and have a small islet each, Bird Islet and South Islet respectively,[12] which serve as rookeries and nesting grounds for many seabirds as well as breeding grounds and nurseries for marine turtles.[13] Jessie Beazley Reef is a white sand cay located some 12 NM northwest of the two atolls.[14] Around the shallow reefs, the ocean bottom drops precipitously to more than 1,500 meters.[15]

---

9   *An Act providing for the establishment and management of the National Integrated Protected Areas System, defining its scope and coverage, and for other purposes*, Republic Act No. 7586 (1992), available online: <https://www.officialgazette.gov.ph/1992/06/01/republic-act-no-7586/>; as amended by *An Act declaring protected areas and providing for their management, amending for the purpose, Republic Act No. 7586, otherwise known as the "National Integrated Protected Areas System (NIPAS) Act of 1992," and for other purposes*, Republic Act No. 11038 (2018), available online: <http://www.officialgazette.gov.ph/downloads/2018/06jun/20180622-RA-11038-RRD.pdf>.

10 *An Act establishing the Tubbataha Reefs Natural Park in the Province of Palawan as a protected area under the NIPAS Act (R.A. 7586) and the Strategic Environmental Plan (SEP) for Palawan Act (R.A. 7611), providing for its management and for other purposes*, Republic Act No. 11067 (2010) [hereafter TRNP Act].

11 *Tubbataha Reefs and Vicinity*, Chart No. 1566, 1st Edition, December 2017 (NAMRIA: Taguig City, 2017); *Philippines – Southwestern Part*, Chart No. 4707 (INT 5052), 2nd Edition, November 2010 (NAMRIA: Taguig City, 2010); *Tubbataha Reefs*, Chart No. 4357, 1st Edition, May 2009 (NAMRIA: Taguig City, 2009) [hereafter Tubbataha Reefs and Vicinity].

12 Id.

13 See A. Jensen, *Population Development of the Breeding Seabirds from 1981 to 2009 in Tubbataha Reefs Natural Park and World Heritage Site, Palawan, the Philippines* (Puerto Princesa City: Tubbataha Management Office, 2009); see also A. Jensen, *Monitoring and Inventory of the Seabirds of Tubbataha Reef National Marine Park* (Puerto Princesa City: Tubbataha Management Office, 2012); M. Heegaard and A. Jensen, "Tubbataha Reef National Marine Park: A Preliminary Ornithological Inventory," *Enviroscope* 7 (1992): 13–19.

14 Tubbataha Reefs and Vicinity, n. 11 above.

15 Id.

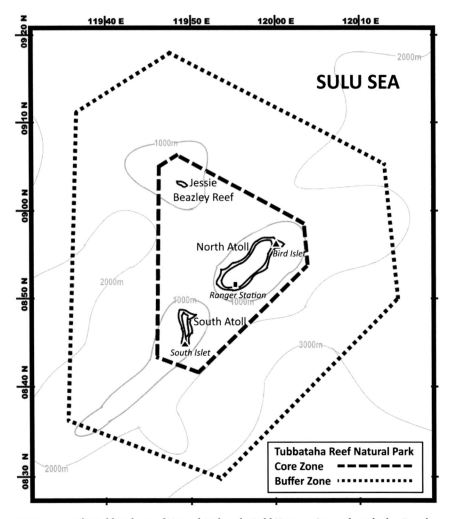

FIGURE 6.1 The Tubbataha Reef Natural Park and World Heritage Site as described in Republic Act No. 10067 (2010).

The entire reef complex hosts very high biodiversity, notably including significant populations of critically endangered marine species, which have been well-documented over the years. This includes 401 out of 461 species of hard corals representing 80 out of 111 coral genera found worldwide (including 30 previously unreported and endemic species);[16] 600 species from at least 40

---

16   D. Fenner, *Reef Corals of the Tubbataha Reefs, Philippines: A Report Submitted to WWF-Philippines* (Puerto Princesa City: Tubbataha Management Office, 2001).

families of fish;[17] 13 species of cetaceans;[18] 12 species of sharks;[19] endangered mollusks such as *Tridacna* clam species and topshell snails;[20] and marine turtles including the endangered hawksbill and green sea turtle species.[21] The two islets and the sandbar provide rookeries for 109 species of residential or migratory birds and nine species of seabirds, including endemic species found nowhere else in the world, and among the last remaining breeding areas of certain species of regional birds.[22] Long-standing interest in the Tubbataha Reefs turned the park into a living laboratory and provides numerous useful baselines for coral reef ecosystem research in the country.[23]

The marine ecosystem of the TRNP as a whole has been able to maintain its highly diverse and near-pristine status and scientifically has proven to be an important source of fish, coral, and decapod larvae that supply and enrich fisheries in the Sulu Sea and adjacent waters; the reefs are a natural fish aggregating area for breeding, and the monsoon winds transport larvae across the marine region and thus are vital to the reproduction, dispersal, and colonization of marine life.[24] Fish biomass in the TRNP has been estimated to be

---

17 International Union for the Conservation of Nature (IUCN), *World Heritage Nomination: IUCN Summary: 653: Tubbataha Reef Marine Park (Philippines)* (Paris: World Heritage Center, 1992), available online: <http://whc.unesco.org/archive/advisory_body_evaluation/653bis.pdf>.

18 Id.; see also A.S. Eckert et al., "Movements of whale sharks (*Rhincodon typus*) in Southeast Asian waters as determined by satellite telemetry," *Journal of Zoology* 257(1) (2002): 111–115; S. Walker and N.E. Palomar-Abesamis, *Status Report on the Abundance of Condricthyian and Pelagic Teleost Top Predators at Tubbataha Reef National Marine Park, Philippines* (Puerto Princesa City: Tubbataha Management Office, 2005).

19 Eckert et al., id.

20 R. Dolorosa, *Conservation Status and Trends of Reef Invertebrates in Tubbataha Reefs with Emphasis on Molluscs and Sea Cucumbers* (Puerto Princesa City: Tubbataha Management Office, 2010); M. Ledesma et al., *Tubbataha Reefs Natural Park: Research and Monitoring Report 2008* (Puerto Princesa City: Tubbataha Management Office, 2008).

21 R.D. Cruz and D.S. Torres, *Report on the Preliminary Assessment of Marine Turtle Habitat Use and the Causes of Marine Turtle Mortality in the Tubbataha Reef National Marine Park* (Puerto Princesa City: Tubbataha Management Office, 2005).

22 M.T. Aquino, R. Alarcon and M.R. Pagliawan, *Vulnerability and Resilience Assessment of Tubbataha Reefs Natural Park, Cagayancillo, Palawan, Philippines* (Puerto Princesa City: Tubbataha Management Office, 2011); Jensen, n. 13 above; Heegaard and Jensen, n. 13 above; D.R. Wells, "Status and conservation of seabirds breeding in Malaysian waters," *ICBP Technical Publication* 11 (1991): 213–223.

23 United Nations Educational, Scientific and Cultural Organization (UNESCO), "Tubbataha Reefs Natural Park," World Heritage Center, available online: <http://whc.unesco.org/en/list/653>; also IUCN 1992, n. 17 above.

24 N.A.A. Abd Latiff, M.N. Md Reba and E. Siswanto, "Determining temporal and spatial variabilities of biological production in Sulu Sea using multi-remotely sensed data" (paper presented at the 8th International Symposium of the Digital Earth (ISDE8), IOP

as much as 200 metric tons per square kilometer in the last decade, far higher than the 35–40 metric tons usually found elsewhere in the Philippines.[25]

The unique biophysical features of the TRNP led to sustained conservation and management efforts at both domestic and international levels from the 1980s onwards. Before that time, the Tubbataha Reefs were protected from economic exploitation by their isolated location far from any habitable islands.[26] Tropical storms also frequent the region, associated with the northeast monsoon from November to March and the southwest monsoon from July to October.[27] But in the 1980s, Filipino fishers on motorized boats began exploiting the reef due to the rapid decline of fish stocks in Philippine coastal waters, bringing with them destructive fishing methods to maximize catch in the limited time they spent operating.[28] In response to a strong campaign by environmentalists and scuba divers associations, and with support from the provincial government of Palawan, an area of 33,200 hectares covering the North and South Atolls were declared a national marine park in 1988.[29] Two years later, the park was included in the Palawan biosphere reserve under the United Nations Educational, Scientific and Cultural Organization (UNESCO) Man and Biosphere Program, underlining the dependence of the population of Cagayancillo Islands,

---

Conference Series: Earth and Environmental Science 18 (21 January 2014), doi: 10.1088/1755-1315/18/1/012114>; L. DeVantier, A. Alcala and C. Wilkinson, "The Sulu Sulawesi Sea: Environmental and socio-economic status, future prognosis and ameliorative policy options," *Ambio* 33(1) (2004): 88–97; W.L. Campos et al., "Using ichthyoplankton distribution in selecting sites for an MPA network in the Sulu Sea, Philippines" (paper presented at the 11th International Coral Reef Symposium, Ft. Lauderdale, Florida, 7–11 July 2008); C.L. Villanoy, K. Silvano and J.D. Palermo, *Tubbataha Reef and Sulu Sea Oceanographic Study* (Puerto Princesa City: Tubbataha Management Office, 2003).

25   Tubbataha Management Office, *Ecosystem Research and Monitoring Report 2015* (Puerto Princesa City: Tubbataha Management Office, 2015), available online: <http://tubbatahareefs.org/wp-content/uploads/2012/11/ERM-Report-2015.pdf>.

26   Tubbataha Management Office, "Tubbataha Reefs Natural Park: History," available online: <http://www.tubbatahareef.org/wp/history> [hereafter TRNP History].

27   D.W. Oppo et al., "Orbital and suborbital climate variability in the Sulu Sea, western tropical Pacific," *Geochemistry Geophysics Geosystems* 4(1): 1–20, available online: <http://onlinelibrary.wiley.com/doi/10.1029/2001GC000260/full>; see also Philippine Atmospheric, Geophysical, and Astronomical Services Administration (PAGASA), "Member Report: Philippines" (ESCAP/WMO Typhoon Committee, 41st Session, 19–25 January 2009), available online: <http://www.typhooncommittee.org/9IWS/DOCS/Members%20Report/Philippines/FINAL%202014%20Reports%20Philippines.docx%20final.pdf>.

28   TRNP History, n. 26 above.

29   Presidential Proclamation No. 306 (1988), Declaring the Tubbataha Reefs and surrounding waters of the public domain in Central Sulu Sea, Province of Palawan, as Tubbataha Reefs National Marine Park.

the closest municipality to the east, on the reefs' fisheries.[30] The park's unique marine habitats supported the designation of the TRNP as a UNESCO World Heritage Site on 11 December 1993.[31] Further studies of the unique bird habitats on the two islets led to its inclusion in the Ramsar List of Wetlands of International Importance on 12 November 1999.[32]

Almost two decades later in 2006, the park was expanded to include Jessie Beazley Reef.[33] Since the establishment of the marine protected area, TRNP has been listed as among the best scuba diving destinations domestically and worldwide,[34] and at the same time, a focal point of marine biodiversity research in the Philippines.[35] The reefs have been referred to as the "crown jewel" of Philippine marine protected areas, biodiversity conservation efforts, and ecotourism.[36]

---

30   Philippines Department of Environment and Natural Resources (DENR), *Renomination Dossier for Tubbataha Reefs Natural Park World Heritage Site* (Paris: World Heritage Center: 2008), p. 8–11, available online: <http://whc.unesco.org/uploads/nominations/653bis.pdf>.

31   UNESCO, *World Heritage Committee 17th Session, Cartagena, Columbia, 6–11 December 1993* (Paris: World Heritage Center, 1993), p. 40, available online: <http://whc.unesco.org/archive/1993/whc-93-conf002-14e.pdf>. Also IUCN 1992, n. 17 above.

32   Ramsar Secretariat, "The Annotated Ramsar List: Philippines," available online: <http://ramsar.rgis.ch/cda/en/ramsar-pubs-notes-annotated-ramsar-16085/main/ramsar/1-30-168%5E16085_4000_0__>; A. Songco, "Information Sheet on Ramsar Wetlands: Tubbataha Reef Natural Park" (Gland: Ramsar Secretariat, 2010), available online: <https://rsis.ramsar.org/RISapp/files/RISrep/PH1010RIS.pdf>; Tubbataha Management Office, "Tubbataha 14th Year as Ramsar Site," Press Release, 12 November 2013, available online: <http://tubbatahareefs.org/tubbataha-14th-year-as-a-ramsar-site/>.

33   Presidential Proclamation No. 1126 (2006), Establishing the Tubbataha Reefs National Marine Park in the Province of Palawan as a Natural Park under the National Integrated Protected Areas System (NIPAS) Act (RA No. 7586) and the Strategic Environmental Plan of Palawan Act (RA No. 7611) and shall be known as the Tubbataha Reefs Natural Park.

34   A. Honasan, "PH top 5 dive sites still world's best," *Philippine Daily Inquirer*, 30 March 2014, available online: <http://lifestyle.inquirer.net/155530/ph-top-5-dive-sites-still-worlds-best/>; World Wildlife Fund, "Tubbataha Reef diving highlights," available online: <http://wwf.panda.org/knowledge_hub/where_we_work/coraltriangle/coraltriangle-facts/places/tubbatahareefphilippines/diving/>; The Scuba Page, "5 Amazing Philippine dive destinations you should dive ASAP," available online: <https://rushkult.com/eng/scubamagazine/philippine-dive-destinations/>; J. Bremmer, "Into the deep: The World's 50 best dive sites," *CNN Travel*, 6 April 2012, available online: <http://travel.cnn.com/explorations/escape/outdoor-adventures/worlds-50-best-dive-sites-895793/>; "9 Top Dives in the Philippines," *Dive Magazine*, available online: <http://divemagazine.co.uk/travel/7955-9-best-places-to-dive-in-the-philippines>.

35   See M. Dygico, *Tubbataha Reefs: A Marine Protected Area That Works: A Case Study on the Philippines* (Quezon City: World Wildlife Fund-Philippines, 2006).

36   UNESCO, "10-year Strategy to Protect the Crown Jewels of the Ocean," *World Heritage Marine Programme 2013 Annual Newsletter* (Paris: World Heritage Center, 2013), p. 1, available

In 2010, the *Tubbataha Reef Natural Park Act* was promulgated to further enhance conservation and protection efforts.[37] It redefined the TRNP as an inverted triangular hexagon encompassing a 97,030 hectare "Core Zone" surrounded by a 350,000 hectare "Buffer Zone,"[38] managed by a multi-sectoral TRNP Protected Area Management Board acting through the TRNP Management Office based in Puerto Princesa City, Palawan, 80 NM northwest of the reefs.[39]

The TRNP Act is the product of an eight-year campaign by civil society groups and non-government organizations,[40] and at the time of enactment boasted the most innovative legal tools for marine environmental protection. The law was cited by the World Future Council (WFC) as "an example of successful coral reef conservation and a model for action on other coral reefs," and awarded a Silver Star Future Policy Award on September 26, 2012 at the United Nations Headquarters.[41] The WFC identified best practices contained in the Act,[42] including the establishment of a no-take (Core) Zone and a multiple use (Buffer) Zone around the reef complex;[43] participatory decision-making and policy formulation methods;[44] locally-based and adaptive management;[45] sustainable and long-term protection, preservation, and promotion of the park through public and private sector partnerships;[46] strictly regulated ecotourism

---

online: <http://whc.unesco.org/uploads/activities/documents/activity-13-43.pdf>; World Wildlife Fund, "Stories from the Coral Triangle: Tubbataha Reef Uncovered," My Coral Triangle, available online: <http://www.mycoraltriangle.com/coralweb/stories/details.aspx?id=7>; A. Honasan, "Our big surprise in Tubbataha: Diving with Destiny," *Philippine Daily Inquirer*, 2 July 2016; C. Dayrit, "Tubbataha: Crown jewel of Philippine diving," *Philippine Star*, 17 July 2016.

37 TRNP Act, n. 10 above.
38 Id., ss. 2, and 4–5.
39 Id., ss. 6, and 10–14.
40 M. Punongbayan, "New law protects Tubbataha," *Philippine Star*, 11 April 2010.
41 K.D. Suarez, "Tubbataha Reef law wins int'l award," *Rappler*, 27 September 2012, available online: <https://www.rappler.com/science-nature/13155-law-protecting-tubbataha-reef-gets-int-l-award>.
42 "The Philippines' Tubbataha Reef Natural Park Act," FuturePolicy.org, available online: <https://futurepolicy.org/oceans/tubbataha-reefs/>.
43 TRNP Act, n. 10 above, ss. 4–5 and 8; see also TRNP Protected Area Management Board, *Tubbataha Reef Natural Park and World Heritage Site Buffer Zone Management Plan 2014* (Puerto Princesa City: Tubbataha Management Office, 2014), available online: <http://www.tubbatahareef.org/wordpress/wp-content/uploads/2012/11/TRNP-Buffer-Zone-Management-Plan-2014.pdf>.
44 TRNP Act, id., ss. 7(g), 10, and 15.
45 Id., ss. 7–10.
46 Id., s. 13(c).

supported by tourism-based income;[47] a self-supported financial mechanism;[48] and an effective and scientifically-driven monitoring system.[49] Park policies and decisions are made by the multi-sectoral TRNP Protected Area Management Board and implemented by the TRNP Management Office.[50] A Park Ranger station is maintained on the North Atoll, manned by at least eight Park Rangers on 30 to 90-day tours of duty; all boats bringing tourists and divers are required to call at the station first before proceeding to their destination within the park.[51] Enforcement is backed up by administrative fines and criminal penalties for violation of the TRNP Act and the conservation and management rules issued by the Protected Area Management Board.[52]

Impact of International Shipping

The TRNP's location at the crossroads of international maritime routes through the Sulu Sea made it vulnerable to operational and accidental impacts of shipping. However, as the Philippines strengthened its legislative and regulatory mechanisms for TRNP's protection, it was confronted with the difficulties of regulating foreign flag vessel traffic within the Sulu Sea. While standing legislation was effectively implemented against Philippine domestic vessels, particularly to reduce their presence within the no-take Core Zone and keep fishing activities to within the Buffer Zone, it was a different matter for foreign merchant vessels. Of particular concern was the possibility of coral reef damage from ship groundings and collisions.

Coral reef damage resulting from shipping had been a relatively well-known problem since the park's designation as a UNESCO World Heritage Site in 1993. The reefs were a known navigational hazard with a record of ship groundings and wrecks dating back to 1925.[53] For the current generations, the risk was first highlighted in 2005, when the Greenpeace ship *Rainbow Warrior* ran aground

---

47   Id., s. 17.
48   Id., s. 17.
49   Id., ss. 3 and 13(q).
50   Id., ss. 10–14.
51   TRNP *Park Rules 01-08. Rules and Regulations for the Entry and the Conduct of All Activities in the Tubbataha Reefs Natural Park and World Heritage Site* (Puerto Princesa City: Tubbataha Management Office, 2008), available online: <http://tubbatahareef.org/wordpress/wp-content/uploads/2012/11/Park-Rules-and-Regulations-2008.pdf>.
52   TRNP Act, n. 10 above, ss. 21–33.
53   Tubbataha Management Office, *Ecosystem Research and Monitoring Report 2014* (Puerto Princesa City: Tubbataha Management Office, 2014), available online: <http://tubbatahareef.org/downloads/research_reports>.

and damaged 200 square meters of the reef during an Asia-Pacific voyage to promote green energy sources.[54] Sometime in 2011 and late 2012, the TRNP Management Office (TMO) initiated efforts to look into the possibility of the TRNP's designation as a PSSA with the support of the UNESCO World Heritage Center, which had embarked on an effort to enhance the protection of marine-based World Heritage Sites.[55] This led to a meeting at the TMO in Puerto Princesa City on 4 January 2013 at which a modest plan of action was agreed upon to gather data and information to support the prospective application.[56] The principal concern of stakeholders was that the TRNP was highly vulnerable to ship grounding due to inaccuracy of available charts, and foreign vessels' lack of notice of and/or non-compliance with park regulations; it was thought that PSSA designation would solve the problem of both publicity and non-compliance. Given the significant information requirements for PSSA designation,[57] the meeting ended with an agreement to look into the records of the TMO and review any data on ship transits through the area, as well as gather available information and documentation of the *Rainbow Warrior* incident and its aftermath in order to support the proposition that there was a continuing danger of ship groundings that could be prevented by a PSSA designation.[58]

By an incredible stroke of misfortune, just three weeks later, the American minesweeper USS *Guardian* ran aground on the South Atoll while transiting

---

54 Greenpeace, "Joint Statement from Greenpeace and Tubbataha Management Office on the grounding of Rainbow Warrior on Tubbataha Reefs," Press Release, 1 November 2005, available online: <http://www.greenpeace.org/seasia/ph/press/releases/joint-statement-on-the-groundi/>; BBC News, "Greenpeace fined for reef damage," *BBC News: Asia Pacific* (1 November 2005), available online: <http://news.bbc.co.uk/2/hi/asia-pacific/4395572.stm>.

55 Angelique Songco, TRNP Superintendent, Tubbataha Management Office to Jay L. Batongbacal, Director, University of the Philippines Institute for Maritime Affairs and Law of the Sea, pers. comm. (29 December 2012); see also UNESCO, *Marine World Heritage: Safeguarding the Crown Jewels of the Ocean* (Paris: UNESCO World Heritage Center, 2013), available online: <http://unesdoc.unesco.org/images/0022/002200/220049e.pdf>; UNESCO, n. 36 above, p. 1.

56 The author was invited as the principal resource person to elucidate on the PSSA designation process as described in IMO documents to assist in formulating a research agenda to gather the necessary information to prepare a submission. It was determined that while relevant information was readily available from previous research undertaken for the TRNP's nomination for World Heritage Site and Ramsar Site designations, there was relatively little information on shipping activities and patterns in the park's vicinity. J.L. Batongbacal, Director, University of the Philippines Institute for Maritime Affairs and Law of the Sea to Ms. Angelique Songco, TRNP Superintendent, Tubbataha Management Office, Memorandum, 19 May 2013.

57 Revised PSSA Guidelines, n. 2 above.

58 Memorandum, n. 56 above.

through the Sulu Sea on 23 January 2013. Travelling at speed, the ship managed to perch itself directly on top of the reef structure and lost its ability to navigate. Considerable wave action soon smashed the ship around and about the reef, cracking the hull and eventually destroying some 2,347 square meters of coral. The U.S. Navy commissioned three specialized salvage ships to cut up and dismantle the minesweeper completely, and finally took the ship off the reef two months later.[59] The U.S. Navy paid for all expenses of wreck removal, and two years later, the U.S. government paid compensation for damages to the reef.[60]

Not long after, another ship, the Chinese flagged F/V *Yin Ming Pu* similarly ran aground on the North Atoll on 8 April 2013, just nine days after completion of the USS *Guardian*'s removal. The ship was eventually dragged off the reef at Philippine government expense, but not before it had destroyed some 3,902 square meters of coral.[61]

Preliminary studies previously commissioned by the World Heritage Center indicated that the risk of ship groundings was expected to increase as maritime traffic increased with trade.[62] Limited radar observations from the TRNP Park Ranger Station already recorded multiple transits of vessels within the

---

59 A full account of the incident, how and why it happened are documented in the results of the inquiry conducted by the U.S. Navy. The incident was generally attributed to over-reliance on electronic charts without counter-checking with updated printed charts, among other inadequacies and negligence. See Commander, U.S. Pacific Fleet, *Command Investigation into the grounding of USS Guardian (MCM 5) on Tubbataha Reef, Republic of the Philippines that occurred on 17 January 2013*, U.S. Navy Judge Advocate General's Office (22 May 2013), available online: <http://www.jag.navy.mil/library/investigations/uss-guardian-grounding.pdf>. An enlightening video presentation of the complex salvage operation to remove the ship from the reef, made and distributed by the salvage company, may be viewed on YouTube. See "SMIT Salvage – Wreckage removal of the USS Guardian," *YouTube*, available online: <https://www.youtube.com/watch?v=ANgqBvzQvoc>.

60 "PH gets P87-M compensation from US over Tubbataha damage," *GMA News Online* (18 February 2015), available online: <http://www.gmanetwork.com/news/news/nation/439700/phl-gets-p87-m-compensation-from-us-over-tubbataha-damage/story/>.

61 Tubbataha Management Office, "Province takes custody of Chinese vessel *Min Ping Yu*, Tubbataha Reef Natural Park," Press Release, 19 August 2014, available online: <http://tubbatahareefs.org/province-takes-custody-of-the-chinese-vessel-min-ping-yu/>.

62 N. Butt and D. Johnson, *Summary Report: Overview of International Shipping Activity in the Sula-Sulawesi Region. Report produced for UNESCO World Heritage Centre in support of potential designation of Tubbataha Reefs Natural Park, Philippines* (Hampshire, Seascapes Consultants, 2013); see also C. Heij et al., "Ship incident risk around the heritage areas of Tubbataha and Banc d'Arguin," *Transportation Research Part D*, 25 (2013): 77–83; S. Knapp et al., "Ship Incident Risk in the Areas of Tubbataha and Banc d'Argun: A case for designation as Particular Sensitive Sea Area?," Econometric Institute Report 2013–16 (Erasmus University, Rotterdam, 2013).

park's Buffer Zone from 2010–2013.[63] The number of ships recorded as passing through or near the park also nearly doubled during those years.[64] This was later corroborated by analysis of satellite automatic identification system (AIS) based data covering a 12-month period from October 2012 to September 2013,[65] procured with funding and technical assistance from the IMO/NORAD Technical Cooperation Project on PSSA.[66] The analysis identified the principal routes and characteristics of the maritime traffic, comprised of mostly cargo ships (70 percent), followed by tankers (10 percent), and other types (18 percent) (Table 6.1).[67] It was determined that most ships passed along a north-south route, a significant proportion of which passed within the 10-NM Buffer Zone around the Core Zone. Along an east-west route, a smaller number of ships passed.[68]

TABLE 6.1 Shipping traffic statistics around the TRNP Core Zone between October 2013 to September 2014, as compiled and analyzed by Mr. Paul Nelson, Consultant, IMO NORAD Specific Project 2, for the Philippines

	Within 20 NM	Within 30 NM	Within 40 NM	Within 50 NM
East-West Traffic				
Cargo	178	265	350	490
Fishing	0	0	0	0
Passenger	4	4	7	7
Tanker	105	138	167	208
Other	97	130	150	192
Total	384	537	674	897

---

63 Due to reliance on solar power on account of geographic isolation, the Park Ranger Station's radar could only be turned on every 4 hours for 15 minutes at a time. T. Aquino, "Shipping threats to the Tubbataha Reef Natural Park and World Heritage Site" (presentation to the Stakeholders' Consultation Workshop on the Proposed PSSA Designation for the Tubbataha Reef Natural Park and World Heritage Site, University of the Philippines Institute for Maritime Affairs and Law of the Sea, 29 October 2013).
64 Id.
65 ExactEarth, "exactAIS Archive," available online: <https://www.exactearth.com/products/exactais-archive>.
66 IMO, "IMO/NORAD Technical Co-operation Project No. 2 – Prevention of pollution from ships through the adoption of Particularly Sensitive Sea Areas (PSSAs) within the East Asian Sea region," IMO Doc. MEPC 68/15, Annex 2, paras. 21–24.
67 P. Nelson, "Analysis of ExactEarth Data" (presentation at the 2nd Regional Meeting, IMO NORAD PSSA Project, Hanoi, 24–25 June 2015).
68 Id.

	Within 20 NM	Within 30 NM	Within 40 NM	Within 50 NM
North-South Traffic				
Cargo	2,100	2,470	2,715	2,882
Fishing	1	1	1	1
Passenger	4	4	7	8
Tanker	198	237	270	291
Other	524	625	689	735
Total	2,827	3,337	3,682	3,917
Total Traffic				
Cargo	2,225	2,645	2,922	3,152
Fishing	1	1	1	1
Passenger	6	6	10	11
Tanker	288	349	397	442
Other	591	709	778	845
Total	3,111	3,710	4,108	4,451

In addition to the danger of groundings due to the absence of mandatory routes or other measures, there was also a risk of chemical and oil pollution from ships passing within 10 NM of the TRNP Core Zone. Many of these vessels passed very close to the Core Zone along the east-west route coming as close as 7.5 NM and west of the park on the north-south route within 9 NM (Figure 6.2).[69]

Computer simulations of chemical and oil spills were undertaken by the University of the Philippines Marine Science Institute, which also yielded useful information. Depending on the distance, time of year, weather, and sea conditions, pollutants from a ship at sea can take as little as four hours in the case of chemicals, or five hours in the case of oil, or as long as 8.5 days, to reach the park. The expected increase in shipping traffic would only increase the risks of such accidental impacts.[70]

---

69 Id.
70 C.L. Villanoy, A.A. Gammaru and J. Del Prado, *Report: Oil and chemical spill simulations along commercial ship tracks around Tubbataha Reef National Park* (Puerto Princesa City: Tubbataha Management Office, 2015); see also Butt and Johnson and Heij et al., n. 62 above.

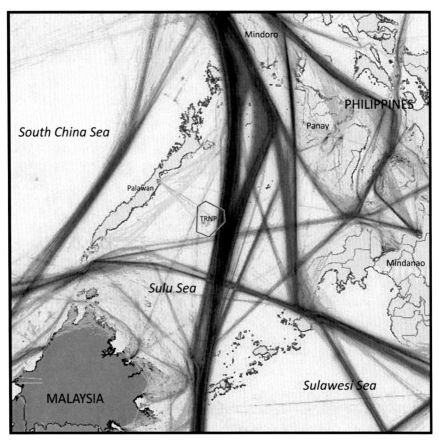

FIGURE 6.2 Vessel tracks in the Sulu Sea, passing close to or inside the boundary of the Buffer Zone of the Tubbataha Reef Natural Park, between October 2013 and September 2014. (Source: ExactEarth)

Pollution from garbage and operational discharges had also been observed by the TRNP Park Rangers. Increasing volumes of foreign marine debris such as product packaging and plastics have been collected around the Ranger Station since 2010, which correlated with increased shipping traffic observed around the TRNP.[71] Admittedly, however, it could not be firmly established whether the debris came exclusively from ships or actually came from coastal areas around the Sulu Sea.

An additional challenge lay in the paucity of nearby pollution response assets. The nearest government marine pollution control vessels that could respond to any potential spill would take at least ten hours to respond to any

---

71 Aquino, n. 63 above.

incident at the TRNP, assuming they were not being used elsewhere, while privately-owned vessels and salvage companies would take at least 24 hours.[72]

Illegal foreign fishing had also been observed many times, and in the past there had been a number of arrests of foreign fishing vessels and detention of crew for taking specifically endangered species of fish. These incidents have occurred at less frequency due to the sustained operation of the Park Ranger Station.[73] However, the TMO has expressed increasing concern over the proliferation of fish aggregating devices (FADs) just outside the park boundaries; local fishers have respected the TRNP zones and use FADs as a substitute for the reefs.[74] These naturally serve to attract both legitimate domestic and illegal foreign fishers to operate in the park's vicinity.

In sum, the occurrence of two successive groundings vividly demonstrated the real risks and potential impacts of subsequent incidents, and the conditions of maritime traffic around the TRNP sufficiently substantiated the presence of pollution risks from international shipping. AIS data and computer simulations, and the anticipation of increased maritime traffic based on existing trends, provided a more concrete appreciation of the increasing risks posed by international shipping.

The Journey To PSSA Designation

Although the idea of using a PSSA designation as a means to enhance protection for the TRNP was introduced as early as 2011, the grounding incidents in the first quarter of 2013 lent a sense of urgency to the effort. A meeting with local stakeholders, TMO, and UNESCO experts was held 20–24 May in Puerto Princesa City, Palawan, capped by a visit to the park, and was followed by an

---

72 Ens. Kristoff Ocampo, Marine Environment Protection Command, Philippine Coast Guard to Mr. Paul Nelson, Consultant, IMO NORAD Specific Project 2 and Jay L. Batongbacal, National Consultant (Philippines), IMO/NORAD Specific Project 2, pers. comm. (14 July 2015).

73 See, for example, DENR *Renomination Dossier*, n. 30 above, pp. 21–22; "32 Chinese fishermen caught in Tubbataha move to appeal case," *Philippine Star* (27 January 2007), available online: <https://www.philstar.com/headlines/2007/01/27/381987/32-chinese-fishermen-caught-tubbataha-move-appeal-case>; "Chinese fishers caught in Tubbataha to be charged with attempted bribery," *GMA News Online* (9 April 2013), available online: <http://www.gmanetwork.com/news/news/nation/303083/chinese-fishers-caught-in-tubbataha-to-be-charged-with-attempted-bribery/story/>; "Vietnamese turtle poachers not the first, not the last intruders," *Worldwildlife1.org*, undated, available online: <http://wildlife1.org/vietnamese-turtle-poachers-not-the-first-not-the-last-intruders/>.

74 Songco, n. 32 above, p. 9.

initial stakeholder workshop on 29 October organized by the University of the Philippines Institute for Maritime Affairs & Law of the Sea.[75] The workshop generated support from the key national stakeholders, particularly representatives of the domestic shipping industry and other government bodies. To get the effort started and in the absence of external advice, it was resolved to have the executive department, through the Department of Environment and Natural Resources (DENR), issue an administrative order to create an interagency committee to take charge of the drafting and finalization of the PSSA application and coordinating its submission to the IMO through the Department of Foreign Affairs.[76] This was due to the fact that the TRNP was managed by the DENR, and the PSSA designation was seen as a measure to reinforce existing protection for the park. Thus it was assumed that DENR should take the lead.

The issuance of an administrative order was shelved, however, after contact was established with the office of the IMO Regional Presence for Technical Cooperation in East Asia, which linked the effort to the IMO/NORAD Technical Cooperation Project No. 2: Prevention of Pollution from Ships through the Adoption of Particularly Sensitive Sea Areas within the East Asian Region.[77] This proved pivotal as the project provided technical data and advice useful not only for the content of the PSSA application, but also about the IMO processes and schedules of work. The Philippine Coast Guard (PCG), which was tasked with regulating maritime safety and environment protection functions,[78] took over the lead in preparing the application and endorsing it to the Department of Foreign Affairs for submission to the IMO.[79] With emphasis on completing IMO documentary requirements within pre-determined deadlines defined by the schedule of meetings of the IMO's MEPC and Navigation, Communications, Search and Rescue (NCSR) sub-committee, a firm timeline was established

---

75 University of the Philippines Institute for Maritime Affairs & Law of the Sea, "Minutes of the Stakeholders Workshop on Designation of the Tubbataha Reefs Natural Park as a Particularly Sensitive Sea Area, 29 October 2013" (Quezon City: University of the Philippines Law Center, 2013) (unpublished).

76 Id.

77 See IMO, "Marine environment projects funded by the Norwegian Agency for Development Cooperation," available online: <http://www.imo.org/en/OurWork/Environment/MajorProjects/Pages/IMO-Norad-projects.aspx>.

78 *An Act establishing the Philippine Coast Guard as an armed and uniformed service attached to the Department of Transportation and Communications, thereby repealing Republic Act No. 5173, as amended, and for other purposes*, Republic Act No. 9993 (2010), available online: <http://seaknowledgebank.net/e-library/philippines-ra-9993-philippine-coast-guard-law>.

79 Letter of Joseph E. Abaya, Secretary of Transportation and Communication to Albert F. del Rosario, Secretary of Foreign Affairs, 11 January 2016.

by the Philippines for the application process work to take place from 2014 through to 2017.[80] Time was of the essence as any failure to submit by a specific date could result in a slippage of one to two years, depending on the IMO committee involved. Instead of a likely more difficult inter-agency process, the drafting and finalization of the necessary documents was left to the author in coordination principally with the PCG, the IMO/NORAD technical experts, the TMO, and technical personnel, for submission of the completed application to the Philippine Permanent Representative to the IMO through the normal channels of the Department of Foreign Affairs. This streamlined process allowed for swift completion of the needed research and writing work for purposes of establishing compliance with PSSA criteria and justifying the associated protective measures.

Compliance with the agreed timeline for submission was facilitated by the availability of considerable data and information from the previous conservation efforts carried out, such as the UNESCO World Heritage Site listing and the plethora of scientific research carried out in the TRNP and made publicly available on the TRNP website.[81] These enabled the sufficient documentation of factors to satisfy the ecological, socioeconomic and sociocultural, and scientific and educational criteria required of a PSSA designation. Also, by the time that the IMO/NORAD Technical Cooperation Project was tapped, a draft of the information paper to be submitted to the MEPC, signaling the Philippines' intention to propose the designation of a PSSA, was thus immediately ready for finalization. The Philippines and UNESCO submitted an information paper for circulation and discussion at MEPC 67 less than one year after the process began,[82] and the application formally was presented as a side event at MEPC 68 in May 2015.[83] These initiatives paved the way for its approval in principle at MEPC 69 on 15 January 2016, upon appreciation of the proposal's compliance with most of the general criteria and satisfactory assessment based on the IMO checklist for PSSAs.[84] MEPC then immediately referred the application to the

---

80   Id.
81   See documents available at Tubbataha Management Office, "Reports and Publications," online: <http://www.tubbatahareef.org/wp/reports_publications>.
82   IMO, "Identification and Protection of Special Areas and Particularly Sensitive Sea Areas, Protection of the Tubbataha Reefs Natural Park and World Heritage Site," IMO Doc. MEPC 67/INF.25 (8 August 2014).
83   A. Songco, "Tubbataha Reefs Natural Park and World Heritage Site" (presentation, Side Event, 68th Session, Marine Environmental Protection Committee, London, 13 May 2015).
84   IMO, "Identification and Protection of Special Areas and Particularly Sensitive Sea Areas, Designation of the Tubbataha Reefs Natural Park as a Particularly Sensitive Sea Area submitted by the Philippines," IMO Doc. MEPC 69/10/1 (15 January 2016); IMO, "PSSA Proposal Review Form," IMO Doc. MEPC 55/23, Annex 20 (13 October 2006).

NCSR sub-committee for consideration and recommendation of suitable associated protective measures.[85]

The feedback received by the Philippine representative to the IMO from international stakeholders during consultations between formal sessions in London was generally positive and helpful. Consultations with IMO offices such as the Marine Safety Division and Marine Environment Division, and with representatives of shipping organizations like Intertanko and non-governmental organizations (NGOs) like the International Institute for Navigation, produced additional suggested APMs such as a precautionary zone and recommended routes around the ATBA.[86]

At the NCSR 4 meeting from 6–10 March 2017, at which the author was present, further interaction with the committee members determined that the ATBA would be sufficient protection, as mariners would already be able to freely plot their courses around the TRNP and any other risks could already be managed by existing rules such as the International Regulations for Preventing Collisions at Sea (COLREGS) and responsible seafaring practices. During the meeting, it was noted that other measures such as ships routing or mandatory reporting would entail the presence of technological infrastructure and support systems that the Philippines might not yet have, but an ATBA could just as effectively warn ship masters and navigators away from the TRNP. Thus, although three possible APMs were proposed,[87] the Philippines eventually settled upon only the establishment of an ATBA as the simplest and least controversial measure.[88] The boundaries of the ATBA coincided with the outer perimeter of the Buffer Zone described in the TRNP Act to reinforce the management of the TRNP vis-à-vis transiting foreign flag ships.

The impact of the ATBA on ships was expected to be minimal, as calculations indicated that the necessary changes in course and additional distance travelled to avoid the ATBA would only add 9.9 NM to the north-south route and 3.75 NM to the east-west route.[89] This slight increment was miniscule

---

85 IMO, "Identification and Protection of Special Areas and PSSAs, Report of the Technical Working Group on PSSAs," IMO Doc. MEPC 69/WP.11 (21 April 2016).

86 Ambassador Gilberto Asuque, Philippine Permanent Representative to the IMO to Jay L. Batongbacal, National Consultant (Philippines), IMO NORAD Specific Project 2, pers. comm. (2 December 2016).

87 IMO, "Routeing Measures and Mandatory Ship Reporting Systems: Establishment of an area to be avoided and adjacent two-way routes with a precautionary area as Associated Protected Measures for the Tubbataha Reefs Natural Park Particularly Sensitive Sea Area (PSSA) in the Sulu Sea, Philippines," IMO Doc. NCSR 4/3/4 (2 December 2016).

88 MEPC 71/WP.10, n. 1 above.

89 MEPC 69/10/1, n. 84 above, pp. 17–18.

compared to the usual journeys spanning thousands of nautical miles across the region. Since the TRNP is surrounded by open water, there is more than adequate sea room for ships maneuvering and transiting the crossroads area. The NCSR also invited the Philippines to study the effect of the newly established ATBA and if warranted, consider other measures in the future, such as improvement of the aids to navigation in the park.[90]

With the APM favorably endorsed by NCSR 4, and PSSA designation previously approved in principle by the MEPC, it became a matter of course for the PSSA designation to be finalized and approved at MEPC 71 held on 3–7 July 2017.[91] Effectivity of the PSSA was set for 1 January 2018.[92] The Philippines issued a corresponding Notice to Mariners announcing the designation of the TRNP as a PSSA on 25 July 2017.[93] Prior to its effectivity, the TMO again held a stakeholder meeting at Puerto Princesa City, Palawan on 22 August 2017 to discuss protocols for information dissemination and implementation of the ATBA.[94] These revolved principally around monitoring procedures, interim communication templates or scripts for the TRNP Park Ranger Station to actively advise passing vessels of the impending effectivity of the PSSA designation, and procedures for reporting any subsequent incursions into the PSSA boundaries.[95] In response to an inquiry in late 2017 regarding the status of maritime traffic around the TRNP, the TMO stated that TRNP Park Rangers were reporting that foreign ships were no longer crossing into the TRNP Buffer Zone as they did before.[96] This is cause for optimism that foreign flag vessels will completely avoid the TRNP ATBA from now on, thus eliminating the risk of ship groundings in the future.

---

90   International Federation of Shipmasters' Associations, "Report on IMO Meeting, NCSR 4 (06.03.2017–10.03.2017)," available online: <https://www.ifsma.org/resources/NCSR-4-Report.pdf>.
91   MEPC 71/WP.10, n. 1 above.
92   Id.
93   National Mapping and Resource Information Authority, *Notice to Mariners NAVPHIL 082/2017* (25 July 2017), available online: <http://www.namria.gov.ph/jdownloads/Navigational_Warning/Navphil_082_2017.pdf>. It was reiterated in *Notice to Mariners NAVPHIL 132/2017* (29 December 2017), available online: <http://www.namria.gov.ph/jdownloads/Navigational_Warning/Navphil_132_2017.pdf>.
94   Tubbataha Management Office, *Minutes of the Meeting on Implementation of the TRNP PSSA Designation, 22 August 2017* (unpublished).
95   Id.
96   Ms. Angelique Songco, Superintendent, Tubbataha Reef Natural Park, to Jay L. Batongbacal, National Consultant (Philippines), IMO NORAD Specific Project 2, pers. comm. (11 October 2017).

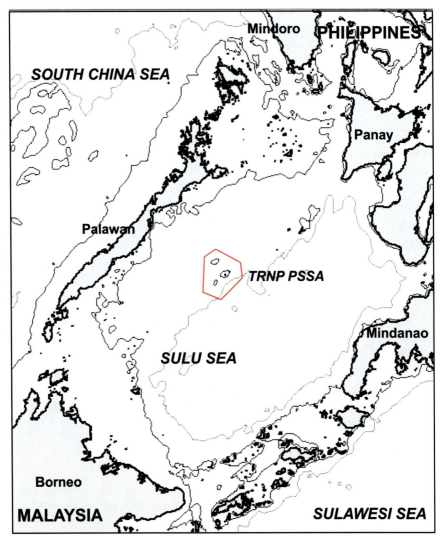

FIGURE 6.3. The Tubbataha Reefs Natural Park Particularly Sensitive Sea Area designated by the IMO in MEPC 71/WP.10, n. 1 above.

Lessons Learned and Insights Gained

The preparation of a PSSA proposal requires interdisciplinary training that melds familiarity with oceanographic sciences, maritime practices, and law in order to be able to produce a comprehensive but concise document that makes a persuasive case that is equally effective for mariners, maritime regulators, and private industry. The proposal must also be amply supported by an assemblage of supporting research and documentation that creates a factual foundation for the PSSA and its APMs. The author's participation in the process of preparation and finalization of the application for designation of a PSSA, with the assistance of the IMO/NORAD Technical Cooperation Project, provides some key lessons and insights that shed light on this special process of the IMO that could be useful for other practitioners that could be involved in similar efforts in the future, especially those from developing countries with less experience in the arcane technicalities of IMO-related work.

First is the fundamental importance of the stakeholders primarily interested in and affected by the PSSA proposal, in this case represented by the TRNP Protected Area Management Board acting through the TMO, which very diligently prodded and followed up the designation project from the time it was initially suggested by the UNESCO World Heritage Center to its approval by the IMO. The TMO provided the necessary leadership to ensure that government agencies directly concerned contributed to the needed technical work in support of the PSSA proposal, and marshalled modest funding support to host the necessary preparatory and informational activities that ensured the proposal would pass quickly through the bureaucratic maze that normally slowed down international initiatives. The fact that the TMO was actively and directly involved as park manager in possession of nearly all necessary data and information, and supervisor of the Park Rangers who were able to provide additional data from the ground, enabled quick responses and actions at each step of the preparation of the submission, from the initial data gathering to provision of additional information in the later stages of IMO deliberation on the proposal.

Second, the fact that the TRNP was already a well-known nationally protected area and very popular among scientific, environmental, and ecotourism sectors undoubtedly helped to stress the importance and urgency of action on the PSSA proposal. Access to scientific research produced in the decades since the TRNP's establishment and to new analysis, such as computer modelling and simulations, greatly facilitated the gathering of information to show compliance with the IMO's criteria. Having been the subject of scientific study and ecotourism, information materials and video presentations were also easily created for purposes of familiarizing the IMO and its delegates with the area and stressing the need for added protection through PSSA designation. It also simplified the process of analysis and deliberation by the IMO subcommittees involved, notably MEPC and NCSR, as they could readily appreciate the ecological, social/economic, cultural, and scientific values of the TRNP and conclude that a PSSA designation and ATBA APM was a reasonable measure that the IMO could establish.

Third, the assistance of the IMO/NORAD Technical Cooperation Project through Mr. Edward Kleverlaan and Mr. Paul Nelson, was pivotal in facilitating the preparation and submission of the proposal. Through the project, the

Philippines was able to comply with the documentary and evidentiary requirements of the IMO. It was able to smoothly pass the administrative and procedural hurdles without need to revert and revise its submissions. Most importantly, awareness of the need to coordinate actions with the timing, schedule, and sequence of meetings of the key MEPC and NCSR committees enabled the processing of the PSSA proposal with no time lost in between meetings on account of documentary inadequacies or inquiries for further information and elaboration. Considering that the IMO committee and sub-committee meetings are held only every one or two years, compliance with deadlines is a very important factor in a successful PSSA designation.

Fourth, the ready availability of data and information needed to satisfy the ecological, social and economic, cultural, and scientific criteria for PSSA designation and to characterize the natural and navigational environment in and around the TRNP definitely helped to shorten the preparation time of the PSSA proposal. As soon as the first meeting with the IMO/NORAD Project was concluded, the Philippines already had the draft of the first document required to start the process, i.e., the information paper that signaled the intention to make a proposal at the next MEPC meeting a year later. This could not have been possible had there been no prior research done on the TRNP and no available data or information on the various criteria.

Fifth, the active interest and advocacy of the Philippine Permanent Representative to the IMO was also crucial, as consultations and coordination with various key industry stakeholders and observer NGOs at the IMO during the inter-sessional periods between meetings provided immediate feedback about any adjustments to documents or clarificatory and supplemental information requested. Questions or concerns that might have been raised at the committee meetings were instead raised and addressed during the inter-sessional consultations, and adjustments to satisfy concerns were already made by the time the meetings took place, which minimized debate and facilitated deliberation and approval of the proposal at each stage.

Sixth, although environmental advocates and the scientific community might see the PSSA mechanism as a useful tool for conservation and protection, and regard the designation of a PSSA as simply a matter of compliance with the ecological, sociocultural and socioeconomic, and scientific and educational criteria, it should be borne in mind that the IMO is principally concerned with ensuring that marine conservation and protection does not unduly hinder the requirements of safe and efficient navigation and shipping operations. The mere existence of conditions that comply with the criteria do not *per se* automatically merit PSSA designation by the IMO, especially if national measures might be available and sufficient to achieve the proposed protection for any particular marine area. The requirement that PSSA designation cannot be done without prior approval of the associated protective measures by the relevant IMO committee or sub-committee indicates the supreme importance of addressing the requirements and standards of international shipping. This should be expected and understood as the IMO is not an environmental conservation organization, but rather an industry-oriented organization first and foremost. PSSA designation and identification of associated protective measures represents the harmonization of the shipping industry's interests with those of marine conservation and environment protection. As such, the designation of any PSSA needs to be viewed as an exercise of advocacy on the part of the proposing member government, with the corresponding burdens of proof of compliance with the IMO's criteria and justification of reasonability of the associated protective measures. PSSAs and associated protective measures are not in themselves stand-alone measures for marine conservation and protection, but complementary tools that support other such measures.

Finally, on a personal note as the principal author of the proposal documents, the relative ease of preparation could be attributed not only to prior legal education, but most especially to the interdisciplinary training received from the Marine Affairs Programme and Marine Environmental Law Program of Dalhousie University in Halifax, Nova Scotia, Canada. The preparation of the PSSA proposal called upon all the skills and competencies imparted by these interdisciplinary programs, enabling the author to use familiarity with and orientation on applied sciences such as oceanography and marine biology, social sciences such as economics and sociology, and legal training in domestic and international law to draft and revise the PSSA proposals and adapt them as needed by the IMO without having to resort to extensive consultations and referrals to other writers or researchers. Familiarity with the perspectives of the audience within the IMO also allowed the Philippines to adjust its presentations to more effectively communicate its case and arguments. During the initial presentation before the MEPC, the Philippine delegation allowed the TMO park manager to present the proposal as it emphasized the ecological, social and economic, cultural and scientific values of the TRNP, while at the NCSR meeting, the Philippine delegation permitted the author to make the presentation using the perspective of mariners and navigators, which enabled quick understanding and agreement on the measure. Knowledge of the documents' users at each stage enabled the presentation of information in precisely the manner needed by the committees, no doubt the reason why no serious controversy about the proposal arose at any stage and even generated helpful suggestions from other committee members. The author even prepared most of the charts and illustrations used in the documents, subject to checking by government technical personnel. All these factors definitely sped up the preparation, finalization, and submission of all documents as needed, within the strict timeframes involved, and with no delay due to inability to meet a deadline. This was key to the approval of the PSSA proposal within the expected timeframe of 2 to 3 years announced at the beginning of the project.

Conclusion

The successful designation of the TRNP as a PSSA has enabled the Philippines to supplement and reinforce its marine conservation and protection tool kit. Experience with the TRNP designation process indicates that it may be possible to secure PSSA designations for at least two adjacent conservation areas in the Philippines currently located within existing sea routes, namely the Apo Reef and the Verde Island Passage between the coastal provinces of Batangas and Mindoro, provided that the necessary research into the ecological, social and economic, cultural, and scientific criteria can be carried out and completed. In the meantime, other maritime traffic management measures such as traffic separation schemes and ship routing measures can be tried out as protective measures. Regardless, the success of the TRNP PSSA designation and its already discernible impact of diverting shipping away from the TRNP boundaries prove the suitability of measures available through the IMO to supplement and reinforce national marine environmental conservation and protection laws and regulations. The smooth and straightforward process followed by the TRNP proposal serves as a good model for any possible future effort for additional PSSA designations in Philippine waters.

The Ecosystem Approach as a Frame for SDG 14 Implementation

Daniela Diz
Strathclyde Centre for Environmental Law & Governance, University of Strathclyde, Glasgow, United Kingdom

Introduction

The ecosystem approach as defined by the Convention on Biological Diversity (CBD) Conference of the Parties (COP)[1] can provide a comprehensive strategy and framework for the implementation of the Sustainable Development Goal (SDG) 14 on the conservation and sustainable use of the oceans, seas, and marine resources for sustainable development. This article argues that by applying the ecosystem approach (EA), States, competent organizations, and other relevant actors would have the opportunity to place the health of the oceans in the center of environmental conservation and sustainable development, overcoming a silos approach towards SDGs integration, and as a means for mainstreaming (the conservation and sustainable use of) biodiversity into the implementation of the SDGs.[2] In doing so, this article will (i) recall the often neglected principles of the CBD ecosystem approach, as well as the Food and Agriculture Organization of the United Nations (FAO) ecosystem approach to fisheries (EAF), (ii) discuss the alignment between SDG 14 and the ecosystem approach, and (iii) explore ways for mainstreaming biodiversity into a select number of SDG 14 targets (SDG 14.1–14.5) before providing concluding remarks on the role of the ecosystem approach as an integrative principle for coherent oceans governance in the context of the SDG 14.

It must be recognized that for the ecosystem approach to be truly implemented, emerging/imminent issues, such as deep seabed mining, need to be properly considered. However, it is beyond the scope of the current work to address deep seabed mining considerations, specifically, or its draft exploitation regulations. Nonetheless, some of the cross-cutting issues addressed herein apply to deep seabed mining (e.g., anthropogenic underwater noise, biodiversity-inclusive impact assessments, and marine spatial planning).

---

1 CBD Decision V/6 (2000) and VII/11 (2004).
2 As per CBD Decision XIII/3 (2016).

The Ecosystem Approach as Reflected in Key Instruments

Under the CBD, the ecosystem approach is considered to be a priority framework for addressing the three objectives of the Convention,[3] namely, conservation of biodiversity, the sustainable use of its components, and the equitable sharing of benefits arising from the utilization of genetic resources.[4] Furthermore, EA has been defined as "a strategy for the integrated management of land, water and living resources that promotes conservation and sustainable use in an equitable way."[5] Implementation guidelines for the twelve principles of the ecosystem approach, previously endorsed by COP in 2000, form part of a 2004 CBD Decision. Table 1 sets out the CBD EA principles and FAO EAF principles. Even though the 12 EA principles support integration and cross-sectoral management, they also align well with sectoral modalities of the ecosystem approach, such as the ecosystem approach to fisheries.[6]

The FAO Technical Guidelines on EAF states that EAF is a means for implementing many of the provisions of the Code of Conduct for Responsible Fisheries and for achieving sustainable fisheries. It goes even further in linking EAF with sustainable development, noting that EAF is "a means to implement sustainable development concepts into fisheries by addressing both human and ecological well-being."[7] The following cluster of EAF principles contained in the EAF Guidelines support this notion:

(a) Management units should be based on ecologically meaningful boundaries.
(b) Fisheries should be managed in a way that limits their impacts on the ecosystem.
(c) Ecological relationships should be maintained and rebuilt.
(d) Management measures should be compatible with the entire distribution of the stocks.
(e) The precautionary approach is a component of EAF given lack of full scientific knowledge related to ecosystems and their functions.
(f) Governance should ensure both human and ecosystem well-being.

---

3 As per CBD Decision VII/11 (2004), para. 2.
4 Convention on Biological Diversity, adopted 5 June 1992 (entered into force 29 December 1993), 1760 *United Nations Treaty Series* 79, art. 1 [CBD].
5 CBD Decision VII/7 (2004), Annex I, para. 1.
6 See Food and Agriculture Organization of the United Nations (FAO), Fisheries Department, *The Ecosystem Approach to Fisheries* (Rome: FAO, FAO Technical Guidelines for Responsible Fisheries, No. 4, Suppl. 2. 2003) [FAO EAF Guidelines].
7 Id., p. 6.

TABLE 7.1   CBD EA Principles and FAO EAF Principles

CBD EA Principles	FAO EAF Principles
1. The objectives of management of land, water, and living resources are a matter of societal choice	1. Avoiding overfishing
2. Management should be decentralized to the lowest appropriate level	2. Ensuring reversibility and rebuilding
3. Ecosystem managers should consider the effects (actual or potential) of their activities on adjacent and other ecosystems	3. Minimizing fisheries impact
4. Recognizing potential gains from management, there is usually a need to understand and manage the ecosystem in an economic context. Any such ecosystem-management programme should: (a) Reduce those market distortions that adversely affect biological diversity; (b) Align incentives to promote biodiversity conservation and sustainable use; (c) Internalize costs and benefits in the given ecosystem to the extent feasible	4. Considering species interactions
5. Conservation of ecosystem structure and functioning, in order to maintain ecosystem services, should be a priority target of the ecosystem approach	5. Ensuring compatibility
6. Ecosystems must be managed within the limits of their functioning	6. Applying the precautionary approach
7. The ecosystem approach should be undertaken at the appropriate spatial and temporal scales	7. Improving human well-being and equity
8. Recognizing the varying temporal scales and lag-effects that characterize ecosystem processes, objectives for ecosystem management should be set for the long term	8. Allocating user rights
9. Management must recognize that change is inevitable	9. Promoting sectoral integration
10. The ecosystem approach should seek the appropriate balance between, and integration of, conservation and the use of biological diversity	10. Broadening stakeholders' participation
11. The ecosystem approach should consider all forms of relevant information, including scientific, indigenous, and local knowledge, innovations and practices	11. Maintaining ecosystem integrity
12. The ecosystem approach should involve all relevant sectors of society and scientific disciplines	

The link between sustainable development and the ecosystem approach for both ecological and human well-being has been further elaborated in the outcome document of the UN Conference on Sustainable Development, *The Future We Want*. UN Member States committed themselves to

> protect, and restore, the health, productivity and resilience of oceans and marine ecosystems, to maintain their biodiversity, enabling their conservation and sustainable use for present and future generations, and to effectively apply an ecosystem approach and the precautionary approach in the management, in accordance with international law, of activities having an impact on the marine environment, to deliver on all three dimensions of sustainable development.[8]

It is, thus, logical that the SDGs, adopted three years later, would embrace a similar notion, as discussed in the following section.

SDG 14 and Ecosystem Approach Alignments

Despite the link between sustainable development and the ecosystem approach contained in *The Future We Want*, none of the SDG 14 targets explicitly refers to the ecosystem approach. Nonetheless, the 2017 UN Ocean Conference outcome document, Our Ocean, Our Future: Call for Action, a declaration endorsed by the UN General Assembly,[9] provided further clarity to the interpretation of SDG 14 targets and their alignment with the ecosystem approach. For instance, the Declaration stresses "the need for an integrated, interdisciplinary and cross-sectoral approach, as well as enhanced cooperation, coordination and policy coherence, at all levels."[10] This is something that is intrinsic to the application of the ecosystem approach as per the CBD and several other instruments. The Declaration also called for "the use of effective and appropriate area-based management tools, including marine protected areas and other integrated, cross-sectoral approaches, including marine spatial planning and integrated coastal zone management, based on best available science, as well as stakeholder engagement and applying the precautionary and ecosystem

---

8 UN General Assembly (UNGA), "The Future We Want," UN Doc. A/RES/66/288 (11 September 2012), Annex, para. 158.
9 UNGA, "Our Ocean, Our Future: Call for Action," UN Doc. A/RES/71/312 (6 July 2017).
10 Id., Annex, para. 8.

approaches."[11] Spatial management and cross-sectoral management are essential components of EA, as seen in the previous section.

The ecosystem approach was also explicitly called for in the Declaration with respect to its role in the implementation of SDG 14.4 on sustainable fisheries.[12] Furthermore, the application of ecosystem-based management has been spelled out as an indicator for achieving SDG 14.2 (healthy and productive oceans) in a State's exclusive economic zone (EEZ). It is not clear why this indicator left behind areas beyond national jurisdiction (ABNJ), since these areas play an important role in securing health, productivity, and resilience across all ocean basins. Further, this approach has already been (directly or indirectly) integrated in global treaties applicable to ABNJ, such as the United Nations Convention on the Law of the Sea (UNCLOS), the UN Fish Stocks Agreement, the CBD, the Convention on Conservation of Migratory Species of Wild Animals (CMS), and policy instruments such as the FAO Code of Conduct for Responsible Fisheries.

It has been argued that the EA's elusive nature still challenges its coherent implementation.[13] The ecosystem approach has been contested by scholars and practitioners for constituting an over-promise of guaranteed win-win results of competing interests related to conservation versus natural resource exploitation.[14] It is important to also recall that while convergence (of policy, of interpretation, and of implementation) is an EA aim, divergence of views, leading to compromises and trade-offs, is also expected under the ecosystem approach.[15] By shedding light on the hidden trade-offs around ecosystem services flows and among stakeholders, decision-makers are better equipped to perform their tasks in a fairer, more equitable, and sustainable manner.[16] Ecosystem services methods have assisted in identifying those trade-offs, which, if left unaddressed, can lead to poverty traps for the most vulnerable, potentially undermining SDGs on poverty, hunger, malnutrition, education, and so many others. Daw et al. provides examples of trade-offs within and across small-scale fisheries groups, under which light was shed on well-being aspects

---

11   Id., Annex, para. 13(j).
12   Id., Annex, para. 13(l).
13   V. de Lucia, "Compelling narratives and complex genealogies: The ecosystem approach in international environmental law," *Journal of Environmental Law* 27 (2015): 91–117, doi:10.1093/jel/equ031.
14   Id.
15   D. Diz and E. Morgera, "Insights for sustainable small-scale fisheries," in *Ecosystem Services and Poverty Alleviation: Trade-offs and Governance*, eds. K. Schreckenberg, G. Mace and M. Poudyal (Routledge, 2018).
16   Id.

of marginalized or under-represented groups (e.g., women).[17] The use of ecosystem services methods to evaluate such trade-offs for a fairer society is embraced by the EA improved integrated governance coherence.[18]

The need for governance coherence has been a core feature of UNCLOS, which, in its preamble, notes that "the problems of ocean space are closely interrelated and need to be considered as a whole."[19] An ecosystem approach, therefore, seems to be the appropriate route to achieve governance coherence. SDG 14.c recognizes that UNCLOS provides the legal framework for the conservation and sustainable use of oceans and their resources.[20] In this connection, global and regional standards incorporated by reference under UNCLOS play an important role in achieving SDG 14 as they contribute to a dynamic governance regime. The next section will address how some of the existing standards and guidance can contribute to a coherent implementation of the SDG 14.

Mainstreaming Biodiversity into SDG 14 for Governance Coherence

Conservation of "biodiversity" and its sustainable use is not expressly mentioned in UNCLOS, but the incorporation of such obligations is implied in a

---

17   T. Daw et al., "Applying the ecosystem services concept to poverty alleviation: The need to disaggregate human well-being," *Environmental Conservation* 38 (2011): 370–379. See also T. Daw et al., "Evaluating taboo trade-offs in ecosystem services and human well-being," *Proceedings of the National Academy of Sciences* 112 (2015): 6949–6954.

18   CBD Decisions V/6 (2000) and VII/11 (2004), principles 1 and 2. The rationale for Principle 1 highlights the importance of all stakeholders to be involved in the process: "Different sectors of society view ecosystems in terms of their own economic, cultural and societal needs. Indigenous peoples and other local communities living on the land are important stakeholders and their rights and interests should be recognized. Both cultural and biological diversity are central components of the ecosystem approach, and management should take this into account. Societal choices should be expressed as clearly as possible. Ecosystems should be managed for their intrinsic values and for the tangible or intangible benefits for humans, in a fair and equitable way" (CBD Decision VII/11, id., table 1, principle 1). In addition, the implementing guidelines for Principle 4 recommend the application of ecosystem services valuation methodologies.

19   United Nations Convention on the Law of the Sea, adopted 10 December 1982 (entered into force 16 November 1994), 1833 *United Nations Treaty Series* 397, third preambular paragraph [UNCLOS].

20   SDG 14.c reads: "Enhance the conservation and sustainable use of oceans and their resources by implementing international law as reflected in UNCLOS, which provides the legal framework for the conservation and sustainable use of oceans and their resources, as recalled in paragraph 158 of The Future We Want." UNGA, "Transforming Our World: The 2030 Agenda for Sustainable Development," UN Doc. A/RES/70/1 (21 October 2015), p. 24.

number of its provisions.[21] Furthermore, as mentioned above, as part of its evolutionary nature, UNCLOS incorporates by reference generally agreed global, regional, or sub-regional minimum standards with respect to, *inter alia*, the adoption of conservation and fisheries management measures in the EEZ[22] and on the high seas,[23] and pollution from land-based sources,[24] seabed activities,[25] dumping,[26] vessels,[27] and from or through the atmosphere.[28]

Furthermore, the mutual supportiveness between UNCLOS and the CBD with respect to the marine environment is explicitly found in Article 22 of the CBD.[29] It states that parties shall implement the Convention consistently with the rights and obligations of States under UNCLOS. In this connection, the CBD also notes that the Convention shall not affect the rights and obligations of parties under existing international agreements, unless the exercise of these would cause serious damage or threat to biodiversity.[30] CBD parties should also mainstream biodiversity into productive sectors by integrating "consideration of the conservation and sustainable use of biological resources into national decision-making."[31] Aligned to this notion, CBD Decision XIII/3 (2016) called for mainstreaming biodiversity into productive sectors, including tourism and fisheries, and recalled the respective CBD decisions on EA, which had recommended the application of the EA in all sectors with potential impacts on biodiversity and ecosystems. The same decision urged parties to mainstream biodiversity in the implementation of all relevant SDGs, including through the implementation of the Aichi Biodiversity Targets.[32] It is important to note that the notion of "mainstreaming biodiversity" is aligned with CBD Article 6(b), which requires parties to integrate not only conservation, but also the sustainable use of biodiversity into relevant sectoral or cross-sectoral

---

21 For instance, Part XII on the protection and preservation of the marine environment (which is applicable to all maritime zones), particularly, Articles 192, 194 (5) more broadly, as well as Parts V on the exclusive economic zone and VII on the high Seas. UNCLOS, n. 19 above.
22 Id., art. 61(3).
23 Id., art. 119(1)(a).
24 Id., art. 207(1).
25 Id., art. 208(3).
26 Id., art. 210(4).
27 Id., art. 211(2).
28 Id., art. 212(1).
29 J. Harrison, *Saving the Oceans through Law: The International Legal Framework for the Protection of the Marine Environment* (OUP, 2017).
30 CBD, n. 4 above, art. 22(1).
31 Id., art. 10(a).
32 CBD Decision XIII/3 (2016), para. 14.

plans, programs, and policies.³³ The following section will build on relevant CBD COP (and other bodies) deliberations, and focus on some of the avenues for achieving this mainstreaming aim with respect to SDGs 14.4 (sustainable fisheries), 14.1 (marine pollution), SDG 14.2 (healthy, productive, and resilient marine ecosystems), and 14.5 (marine protected areas) in the context of an ecosystem approach.

Mainstreaming Biodiversity into Fisheries (and Respective SDG 14.4)
With respect to fisheries standards and international obligations supplementary to UNCLOS, it is important to recall that Article 5(g) of the UN Fish Stocks Agreement, which is applicable in areas within and beyond national jurisdiction,³⁴ obliges coastal States and States fishing on the high seas to protect biodiversity in order to conserve and manage straddling fish stocks and highly migratory fish stocks. Similar provisions are contained in several FAO instruments, including the Code of Conduct for Responsible Fisheries and its International Plans of Action, and the FAO International Guidelines for the Management of Deep-sea Fisheries in the High Seas (FAO Deep-sea Fisheries Guidelines), as well in UN General Assembly Resolutions on Sustainable Fisheries. Furthermore, the CBD Aichi Biodiversity Target 6³⁵ (sustainable fisheries) places "ecosystem-based approaches" in the center of the target as a means to, by 2020, accomplish sustainability, avoid overfishing, enable the adoption of recovery plans, avoid significant adverse impacts (SAIs) on threatened species and vulnerable ecosystems, avoid fishing impacts on stocks and species, and ensure ecosystems are within safe ecological limits. These EAF elements contained in Aichi Target 6 reflect minimum standards for biodiversity mainstreaming into fisheries as contained in several existing instruments.

---

33 See id., first preambular paragraph.
34 See United Nations Agreement for the Implementation of the Provisions of the United Nations Convention on the Law of the Sea of 10 December 1982 relating to the Conservation and Management of Straddling Fish Stocks and Highly Migratory Fish Stocks, adopted 4 August 1995 (entered into force 11 December 2001), 2167 *United Nations Treaty Series* 88, art. 3(2) [UN Fish Stocks Agreement].
35 Aichi Biodiversity Target 6 reads: "By 2020 all fish and invertebrate stocks and aquatic plants are managed and harvested sustainably, legally and applying ecosystem based approaches, so that overfishing is avoided, recovery plans and measures are in place for all depleted species, fisheries have no significant adverse impacts on threatened species and vulnerable ecosystems and the impacts of fisheries on stocks, species and ecosystems are within safe ecological limits." CBD Decision X/2 (2010), Annex, "Strategic Plan for Biodiversity 2011–2020 and the Aichi Biodiversity Targets."

Kenny et al. discuss methodologies that assist in the implementation of these EAF elements towards the achievement of SDG 14.4,[36] even in data-limited contexts, and highlight the importance of identifying ecologically meaningful management units as the first step of the assessment. Productivity of the ecosystem in question can be analyzed in each biogeographic unit, and ecosystem-level total allowable catches can then be set based on a precautionary calculation of ecosystem-level reference points that supplements individual stock assessments, portraying a more comprehensive picture of the ecosystem composition, trophic interactions, and productivity capacity.[37] The need to determine prey availability thresholds for certain functional groups is illustrated by Cury et al. in a landmark paper which concluded that approximately one-third of the maximum prey biomass is needed to sustain seabird productivity over the long term.[38]

Habitat mapping (e.g., of vulnerable marine ecosystems), environmental impact assessments (EIAs), and risk assessments also play important roles in EAF.[39] Criteria for bottom fishing EIAs are contained in the FAO Deep-sea Fisheries Guidelines.[40] Methodologies that facilitate such assessments even in data-limited contexts[41] can be a significant contribution to the universal implementation of SDG 14.4 (sustainable fisheries), and SDG 14.2 (more resilient ecosystems), as well as Aichi Biodiversity Target 6 (sustainable fisheries), hence also fulfilling respective States obligations under UNCLOS, the UN Fish Stocks Agreement, and a number of other related international treaties, referred to above. In cases of scientific uncertainty, application of the precautionary approach is required.[42] With respect to bottom fishing, this can be achieved through the adoption of precautionary conservation and

---

36   SDG 14.4 reads: "By 2020, effectively regulate harvesting and end overfishing, illegal, unreported and unregulated fishing and destructive fishing practices and implement science-based management plans, in order to restore fish stocks in the shortest time feasible, at least to levels that can produce maximum sustainable yield as determined by their biological characteristics."

37   A. Kenny et al., "Delivering sustainable fisheries through adoption of a risk-based framework as part of an ecosystem approach to fisheries management," *Marine Policy* 93 (2018): 232–240.

38   P.M. Cury et al., "Global seabird response to forage fish depletion: One-third for the birds," *Science* 334 (2011): 1703–1706.

39   Kenny et al., n. 37 above.

40   FAO, International Guidelines for the Management of Deep-sea Fisheries in the High Seas (September 2008), para. 47 [FAO Deep-sea Fisheries Guidelines].

41   Kenny et al., n. 37 above.

42   UN Fish Stocks Agreement, n. 34 above, art. 6; FAO Deep-sea Fisheries Guidelines, n. 40 above, paras. 12, 20, 22, 65, 74, and 76; FAO, Code of Conduct for Responsible Fisheries (31 October 1995), paras. 6.5 and 7.5.

management measures to avoid SAIs. In areas where vulnerable marine ecosystems have been designated, are known or likely to occur based on habitat suitability models, and other techniques, such areas should be closed to deep-sea fisheries until appropriate conservation and management measures have been adopted to prevent SAIs on vulnerable marine ecosystems (VMEs) and to ensure long-term conservation and sustainable use of deep-sea stocks.[43]

All of these instruments provide sound guidance to the implementation of SDG 14.2 (productive and healthy ecosystems) from a fisheries perspective and 14.4 (sustainable fisheries). The work conducted by the Northwest Atlantic Fisheries Organization (NAFO) scientists under the Scientific Council's Working Group on Ecosystem Science and Assessment (WGESA) on the development of the Ecosystem Approach to Fisheries Roadmap should be highlighted here as a particular example of best practice and use of best-available science concerning EAF. The Roadmap and subsequent activities of the group includes the development of ecosystem-level catch ceilings, assessment of ecosystem-units productivity potential, incorporation of habitat and marine biodiversity assessments for identification of VMEs, risk assessments, among others.[44] Nevertheless, the Roadmap would benefit from its full implementation for the achievement of the Aichi Biodiversity Target 6 and SDG 14.4 in the region by 2020. The NAFO 2018 Performance Review Panel has indeed recommended ensuring the practical application of the ecosystem approach.[45]

Addressing Marine Pollution Impacts on Biodiversity (in the Context of SDG 14.1)

With respect to marine pollution from various sources, especially from land-based sources, which is the main focus of SDG 14.1,[46] a holistic approach for tackling the issue is also needed. Furthermore, the cumulative impacts of marine debris with other stressors on biodiversity, species, and ecosystems should also be taken into account in decision-making. For example, while plastic is chemically inert, plastic can absorb organic pollutants in high concentrations. Microplastics can be retained in tissues of marine species and humans at the top of the food chain, and associated pollutants might be released upon ingestion.[47] Entanglement of marine species is also a big threat to biodiversity and

---

43 FAO Deep-sea Fisheries Guidelines, id., para. 66.
44 Kenny et al., n. 37 above.
45 B. Boechat de Almeida et al., *NAFO Performance Review Panel Report 2018* (NAFO, 2018).
46 SDG 14.1 reads: "By 2025, prevent and significantly reduce marine pollution of all kinds, in particular from land-based activities, including marine debris and nutrient pollution."
47 M. Cole et al., "Microplastics as contaminants in the marine environment: A review," *Marine Pollution Bulletin* 62, no. 12 (2011): 2588–2597.

species, while floating plastic litter can transport invasive species, constituting another threat to endemic biodiversity. The United Nations Environment Programme has estimated that 80 percent of marine debris and plastics are from land-based sources and that 90–95 percent of marine pollution is composed of plastic.[48]

UNCLOS, through its Article 192, imposes an obligation on States to protect and preserve the marine environment, with Article 207 (1) binding States to adopt laws and regulations to prevent, reduce, and control pollution of the marine environment from land-based sources, taking into account internationally agreed standards and best practices. This language therefore allows for the incorporation by reference of policy instruments and guidance such as those contained in CBD decisions on marine debris and relevant UN Environment Assembly (UNEA) resolutions. Furthermore, Article 213 of UNCLOS mandates that States not only adopt laws and regulations, but also enforce these, while taking measures to adopt international standards.

Several other international instruments[49] address marine debris in some form, from both land-based or sea-based sources, providing standards and further guidance to States in implementing their obligations under UNCLOS. However, given the fragmented nature of the current legal regime governing marine debris, efforts to enhance cooperation and coordination among different international fora is key for the comprehensive implementation of respective measures. In this connection, it is important to note the efforts by the UNEA to address the issue by recognizing the need for an urgent global response taking into account a product life-cycle approach.[50] Therefore, the relationship between SDG 14.1 (on preventing and reducing marine pollution, in particular marine debris from land-based sources by 2025) and SDGS 12.1 and 12.5 on sustainable production and consumption is of utmost importance, since production life cycle is at the heart of the problem.

---

48 United Nations Environment Programme (UNEP), *Marine Plastic Debris and Microplastics: Global Lessons and Research to Inspire Action and Guide Policy Change* (Nairobi: UNEP, 2016).

49 These include, *inter alia*, the International Convention for the Prevention of Pollution from Ships (MARPOL), Annex V on Prevention of Pollution by Garbage from Ships; the London Convention and its London Protocol; the Basel Convention on the Control of Transboundary Movements of Hazardous Wastes and their Disposal; the Agreement on the Conservation of Albatrosses and Petrels; the Global Programme of Action for the Protection of the Marine Environment from Land-based Activities, and Regional Seas Programmes and Conventions; the Stockholm Convention on Persistent Organic Pollutants; the FAO Code of Conduct for Responsible Fisheries; and the UN Fish Stocks Agreement.

50 UN Environment Assembly, "Marine plastic litter and micro-plastics," UN Doc. UNEP/EA.2/Res.11 (4 August 2016).

Furthermore, CBD Decision XIII/10 on marine debris urged States to prevent and mitigate the potential adverse impacts of marine debris, and to take into account the CBD Voluntary Practical Guidance on Preventing and Mitigating the Impacts of Marine Debris on Marine and Coastal Biodiversity and Habitats.[51] Despite its voluntary nature, the CBD guidance can be interpreted as internationally agreed standards under UNCLOS Article 207.

SDG 14.1 (marine pollution) can also cover anthropogenic underwater noise, which is another type of pollution of the marine environment[52] that threatens marine mammals, and several other marine species and ecosystems. Anthropogenic underwater noise has also been the object of deliberations of the respective COPs of the CBD and the CMS. In 2014, CBD COP encouraged parties and other governments and invited competent organizations to take measures to avoid, minimize, and mitigate potential significant adverse impacts of anthropogenic underwater noise.[53] The recommended measures include developing and transferring quieter technologies, mapping spatial and temporal distribution of sound, overlaying acoustic mapping with habitat mapping of sound-sensitive species in the context of risk assessments to noise impacts, making use of spatio-temporal knowledge to avoid noise generation in places and times where vulnerable species or populations are present, conducting impact assessments and subsequent monitoring for activities with the potential to cause significant adverse impacts on noise-sensitive species, and adopting thresholds to protect sound-sensitive species.

The Role of Biodiversity-inclusive EIAs and SEAs to Prevent Harm to the Marine Environment

Environmental impact assessments are key tools for the prevention of significant adverse impacts to the marine environment under UNCLOS[54] and are

---

51 CBD, Decision XIII/10, CBD Doc. CBD/COP/DEC/XIII/10 (10 December 2016), Annex.

52 UNCLOS, n. 19 above, Article 1(4) defines pollution of the marine environment as "the introduction by man, directly or indirectly, of substances or energy into the marine environment, including estuaries, which results or is likely to result in such deleterious effects as harm to living resources and marine life, hazards to human health, hindrance to marine activities, including fishing and other legitimate uses of the sea, impairment of quality for use of sea water and reduction of amenities." In accordance with such a definition, anthropogenic underwater noise can be interpreted as a type of pollution under UNCLOS. The CMS COP has recognized that "anthropogenic marine noise, depending on source and intensity, is a form of pollution, composed of energy, that may degrade habitat and have adverse effects on marine life ranging from disturbance of communication or group cohesion to injury and mortality." CMS Resolution 12.14 (2017), second preambular paragraph.

53 CBD Decision XII/23 (2014), para. 3.

54 UNCLOS, n. 19 above, arts. 204–206.

integral components of the ecosystem approach to management as per the CBD EA strategy.⁵⁵ EIAs are also an enabling tool for the identification of measures related to sustainable use of marine biological resources, which avoid or minimize adverse impacts on biodiversity.⁵⁶

Further to the CBD decision on anthropogenic underwater noise, the CMS COP has "strongly urge[d] Parties to prevent adverse effects on CMS-listed marine species and their prey by restricting the emission of underwater noise; and where noise cannot be avoided, further urges Parties to develop an appropriate regulatory framework or implement relevant measures to ensure a reduction or mitigation of anthropogenic marine noise."⁵⁷ The resolution, among other things, also urged parties to ensure that EIAs take full account of underwater noise effects on CMS-listed species and their prey, and "consider a more holistic ecological approach at a strategic planning stage."⁵⁸

To facilitate the implementation of this resolution, parties also adopted the CMS Family Guidelines on Environmental Impact Assessments for Marine Noise-generating Activities (CMS EIA Guidelines), which should be read in tandem with the Technical Support Information to the CMS EIA Guidelines.⁵⁹ Specific guidance for underwater noise consideration in EIAs and SEAs is important, since scientific modelling exercises are needed for specific contexts and habitats given that sound propagation does not only depend on distance, but also on noise frequencies, water depth, topography, temperature, salinity, and other environmental variations.⁶⁰ Furthermore, the CMS EIA Guidelines

---

55   CBD Decision VII/11 (2004), table 1, principle 3 ("Ecosystem managers should consider the effects (actual and potential) of their activities on adjacent and other ecosystems"), para. 3.3 expressly indicates that EIAs, including SEAs, "should be carried out for developments that may have substantial environmental impacts taking into account all the components of biological diversity. These assessments should adequately consider the potential offsite impacts. The results of these assessments, which can also include social impact assessment, should subsequently [be] acted upon. When identifying existing and potential risks or threats to ecosystem, different scales need to be considered."
56   CBD, n. 4 above, art. 10(b).
57   CMS Resolution 12.14 (2017), para. 4.
58   Id., para. 6.
59   Id., para. 7 and its Annex. See also, CMS, "CMS Family Guidelines on Environmental Impact Assessments for Marine Noise-generating Activities," Draft for consideration by COP 12 (October 2017), available online: <http://www.cms.int/guidelines/cms-family-guidelines-EIAs-marine-noise> and G. Prideaux, *Technical Support Information to the CMS Family Guidelines on Environmental Impact Assessment for Marine Noise-generating Activities* (Bonn: CMS, 2017), available online: <https://www.cms.int/sites/default/files/basic_page_documents/CMS-Guidelines-EIA-Marine-Noise_TechnicalSupportInformation_FINAL20170918.pdf>.
60   CMS Resolution 12.14 (2017), Annex, paras. 8 and 23.

provides for "exclusion zones" as areas that are supposed to be designated for the protection of specific species or populations, and, therefore, activities and their respective noise should not be propagated into these areas.[61] The designation of such areas by coastal States and competent organizations are of particular importance for resident populations. The Guidelines suggest consideration of exclusion zones as part of the EIA noise propagation modelling and as part of subsequent mitigation and monitoring plans for activities such as military and civil high-powered sonar, shipping, and vessel traffic, construction works, and offshore platforms.

The concern of CMS parties with not only CMS species, but also with their prey and with the need to assess impacts in a more ecologically holistic manner, aligns well with the ecosystem approach. The implementation of CMS EIA Guidelines (along with other relevant frameworks as discussed herein) can contribute towards the achievement of SDGS 14.1 and 14.2 (healthy ecosystems). Furthermore, it can also contribute to SDG 14.5 on marine protected areas, as MPAS could benefit from tailored measures to prevent anthropogenic underwater noise impacts on the species and ecosystems that fall within their management scope.

Complementing the CMS EIA Guidelines, and with a more habitat-oriented focus, the CBD Voluntary EIA/SEA Guidelines[62] provides further guidance on how to integrate marine and coastal biodiversity considerations into EIAS and SEAS. The CBD Guidelines recommend, *inter alia*, considering in the EIA screening stage whether the activity would cause substantive pollution, or significant and harmful changes to an area described as meeting the CBD ecologically or biologically significant marine area (EBSA)[63] criteria or be identified as a VME.[64] It is further suggested that "any activity with the potential to cause substantial pollution of or significant and harmful changes should be subject to some form of initial screening and initial environmental evaluation."[65]

---

61   Id., Annex, para. 20.
62   CBD decision XI/18 (2012), "Marine and Coastal Biodiversity: Revised Voluntary Guidelines for the Consideration of Biodiversity in Environmental Impact Assessments and Strategic Environmental Assessments in Marine and Coastal Areas," CBD Doc. UNEP/CBD/COP/11/23 (2012) [CBD EIA/SEA Guidelines].
63   CBD Decision IX/20 (2008), Annex 1, adopts the EBSA criteria; CBD Decision X/29 (2010) establishes the scientific and technical process for description of areas meeting the EBSA criteria.
64   UNGA, "Sustainable Fisheries," UN Doc. A/RES/61/105 (6 March 2007), para. 83; FAO Deep-sea Fisheries Guidelines, n. 40 above, para. 42.
65   CBD EIA/SEA Guidelines, n. 62 above, para. 10 (b).

These Guidelines complement the FAO Deep-sea Fisheries Guidelines, as they also cover activities other than bottom fishing.

In accordance with the Guidelines, climate change and ocean acidification effects considerations should also be part of EIAs and SEAs, especially as part of cumulative impact assessments.[66] This is particularly relevant for the achievement of the overdue Aichi Biodiversity Target 10[67] and associated SDGs 14.2[68] (ocean health, resilience, and productivity) and 14.3[69] (ocean acidification) through the identification and application of corresponding mitigation and adaptation measures in a way that minimizes the impacts of anthropogenic pressures on ecosystems vulnerable to climate change and ocean acidification.

Integrating Climate Change and Ocean Acidification Effects into Marine Management

In addition to the importance of incorporating climate change and ocean acidification effects into the EIA/SEA as per the CBD Guidelines, the CBD COP has also developed priority actions for coral reefs and a workplan for cold water areas in an attempt to provide further guidance towards the achievement of Aichi Target 10. As noted above, actions taken by States and competent organizations towards the achievement of this target will also directly contribute to the achievement of SDGs 14.2 and 14.3, given the ultimate goal to increase marine ecosystems' resilience to better cope with the inevitable impacts from a changing climate and decreased pH. Among other things, parties were encouraged to "prioritize the enhancement of conservation and management measures for coral reefs and closely associated ecosystems" in areas described as EBSAs.[70] Under the 2016 Voluntary Specific Workplan on Biodiversity in Cold-water Areas under the Jurisdictional Scope of the Convention, parties were encouraged to identify and prioritize, as appropriate, for conservation, protection, and management certain areas such as EBSAs, VMEs, and Particularly

---

66 CBD EIA/SEA Guidelines, n. 62 above, para. 31(f).
67 Achi Biodiversity Target 10 reads: "By 2015, the multiple anthropogenic pressures on coral reefs, and other vulnerable ecosystems impacted by climate change or ocean acidification are minimized, so as to maintain their integrity and functioning." CBD Decision x/2, n. 35 above.
68 SDG 14.2 reads: "By 2020, sustainably manage and protect marine and coastal ecosystems to avoid significant adverse impacts, including by strengthening their resilience, and take action for their restoration in order to achieve healthy and productive oceans."
69 SDG 14.3 reads: "Minimize and address the impacts of ocean acidification, including through enhanced scientific cooperation at all levels."
70 CBD decision XII/23 (2014), Annex, "Priority Actions to Achieve Aichi Biodiversity Target 10 for Coral Reefs and Closely Associated Ecosystems," para. 8.3.

Sensitive Sea Areas in cold-water areas.[71] This policy recommendation is consistent with the findings of a recent scientific study on remaining global marine wilderness areas, which account for only about 13 percent of the world's oceans.[72] The authors argue that although climate change has been already affecting these wilderness areas, ensuring that other anthropogenic impacts are minimized will most likely contribute to the resilience of these areas by acting as climate refugia.[73] EBSA descriptions that ranked high on the naturalness criterion should also be the object of attention in this regard.

Area-based Management Tools, Including Marine Protected Areas (with respect to SDGs 14.5 and 14.2)

Article 194(5) of UNCLOS establishes the obligation to protect and preserve rare or fragile ecosystems and habitats of depleted, threatened, or endangered species as well as other forms of marine life. UNCLOS, however, does not provide criteria for identifying and managing such areas, including through area-based management tools (ABMTs), relying again on other instruments to do so. A vast array of ABMTs contribute to the achievement of a number of global targets, but the most commonly discussed among them are marine protected areas (MPAS) with respect to Aichi Biodiversity Target 11[74] and SDG 14.5,[75] and other effective area-based conservation measures (OECMs) under Aichi Target 11. While achieving the numerical component of the target has been the primary focus of implementation to date,[76] efforts have been made to provide CBD parties with sufficient guidance to also implement the qualitative elements.[77]

---

71 CBD decision XIII/11 (2016), Annex II, "Voluntary Specific Workplan on Biodiversity in Cold-water Areas within the Jurisdictional Scope of the Convention," para. 5.3(b).
72 K. Jones et al., "The location and protection status of Earth's diminishing marine wilderness," *Current Biology* 28 (2018): 1–7, doi.org/10.1016/j.cub.2018.06.010.
73 Id.
74 Aichi Biodiversity Target 11 reads: "By 2020, at least 17 per cent of terrestrial and inland water, and 10 per cent of coastal and marine areas, especially areas of particular importance for biodiversity and ecosystem services, are conserved through effectively and equitably managed, ecologically representative and well connected systems of protected areas and other effective area-based conservation measures, and integrated into the wider landscapes and seascapes." CBD Decision X/2, n. 35 above.
75 SDG 14.5 reads: "By 2020, conserve at least 10 per cent of coastal and marine areas, consistent with national and international law and based on the best available scientific information." The Indicator for this target refers exclusively to the coverage of marine protected areas.
76 D. Diz et al., "Mainstreaming marine biodiversity into the SDGs: The role of other effective area-based conservation measures," *Marine Policy* 93 (2018): 251–261.
77 The qualitative elements include areas important for biodiversity and ecosystem services, effective and equitable management, ecological representativity, connectivity, and

Target 11 also makes reference to OECMs as working synergistically and contributing to a system of an ecologically representative and well-connected system of MPAs. The CBD is in the process of defining OECMs[78] and approving implementation guidance.

The identification of areas important for biodiversity and ecosystem services (one of the qualitative elements of Aichi Target 11) has its legal foundation in Article 7(a) of the CBD, which requires parties to identify components of biodiversity important for conservation and sustainable use for the purposes of Articles 8 (in-situ conservation) and 10 (sustainable use). The indicative list of natural categories of such areas contained in Annex I of the Convention closely resemble the EBSA criteria, which has been used to describe areas that meet the criteria globally through the CBD EBSA process initiated in 2010. Since its inception, 279 areas meeting the EBSA criteria have been described by COP up to COP 13 in 2016. In 2018, COP 14 will consider 42 additional areas meeting the EBSA criteria, which were described at CBD Secretariat-facilitated regional workshops covering the Black Sea, Caspian Sea, and Baltic Sea areas.[79] The description of EBSAs can contribute to not only Aichi Target 11 and SDG 14.5, but also Aichi Target 10 through the implementation of the Coldwater Areas Workplan and the Coral Reef Priority Actions and corresponding SDGs 14.2 and 14.3. EBSA designation can also facilitate the implementation of CBD EIA/SEA Guidelines, as well as the CMS EIA Guidelines in modelling the effects of sound on CMS-listed species and populations found in these EBSAs, and mitigating potential adverse effects. Further, the description of such areas can also help sustainable fisheries management (Aichi Target 6 and SDG 14.4) through tailored measures such as gear modification, fisheries closures, and bycatch preventive measures, among many others.[80]

---

integration into the wider seascape. See S. Rees et al., "Defining the qualitative elements of Aichi Biodiversity Target 11 with regard to the marine and coastal environment in order to strengthen global efforts for marine biodiversity conservation outlined in the United Nations Sustainable Development Goal 14," *Marine Policy* 93 (2018): 241–250.

78 The 22nd meeting of the CBD Subsidiary Body on Scientific, Technical and Technological Advice (SBSTTA-22) adopted, and recommended that the CBD COP also adopt, the following definition of OECM: "'Other effective area-based conservation measure' means 'a geographically defined area other than a Protected Area, which is governed and managed in ways that achieve positive and sustained long-term outcomes for the *insitu* conservation of biodiversity, with associated ecosystem functions and services and, where applicable, cultural, spiritual, socioeconomic, and other locally relevant values.'" CBD/SBSTTA/22/L.2, para. 2.

79 CBD/EBSA/WS/2017/1/4 (2018); CBD/EBSA/WS/2018/1/4 (2018).

80 D. Diz, "Marine biodiversity: Opportunities for global governance and management coherence," in *Handbook on Marine Environment Protection*, eds. M. Solomon and T. Markus (Springer 2018,) 855–870.

With respect to ecological representativity of MPAs and OECMs, COP 9 adopted scientific criteria that include the following elements: EBSAs, representativity, connectivity, replication of ecological features, adequate and viable sites.[81] Guidance contained in Annex III of CBD Decision IX/20 (2008) on the four initial steps to be considered in the development of representative networks of MPAs is also of particular importance. These include the development of biogeographical classification systems for the pelagic and benthic realms, application of the precautionary approach when scientific information is not available, making use of qualitative and quantitative techniques to identify sites to be included in the network, and consideration of the size, shape, boundaries, buffer zones, and management measures. Connectivity and ecological corridors have also been an object of attention of CMS.[82] Furthermore, Target 10 of the CMS Strategic Plan for Migratory Species 2015–2023 states that "all critical habitats and sites for migratory species are identified and included in area-based conservation measures, so as to maintain their quality, integrity, resilience and functioning in accordance with the implantation of Aichi Target 11,"[83] reinforcing the complementary efforts between these two conventions. Therefore, the implementation of SDG 14.5 (marine protected areas) can be more effectively (and efficiently) achieved if these qualitative elements from biodiversity-related conventions are observed. For areas beyond national jurisdiction, enhanced governance coherence is expected to be achieved through a new legally binding instrument under UNCLOS that is currently under negotiation.[84]

As for the integration of such well-connected and well-managed representative systems of MPAs and OECMs into a broader seascape, Diz et al. argues that such integration can be best achieved through marine spatial planning.[85] The CBD parties have acknowledged marine spatial planning (MSP) as a participatory tool for the implementation of the ecosystem approach.[86] In this connection, MSP has also been perceived to be the appropriate tool to enable integration of area-based management tools into a wider seascape, as per CBD Aichi Biodiversity Target 11.[87] MSP has also been considered an integrative tool

---

81   CBD Decision IX/20 (2008), Annex II.
82   See CMS Resolutions 12.7 (2017) and 12.26 (2017).
83   CMS Resolution 11.2 (2014), Annex 1.
84   UNGA, "International legally binding instrument under the United Nations Convention on the Law of the Sea on the conservation and sustainable use of marine biological diversity of areas beyond national jurisdiction," UN Doc. A/RES/72/249 (19 January 2018).
85   Diz et al., n. 76 above.
86   CBD Decision XIII/9 (2016).
87   Diz et al., n. 76 above.

to enhance synergies between SDG 14 and other SDGs in different scales.[88] On the high seas, MSP can be used as a tool to give effect to the States' obligation of due regard to competing activities in a given area.[89]

Conclusion

The implementation of SDG 14 targets can be facilitated by the application of the ecosystem approach and the respective integration of biodiversity-related standards, guidance, goals, and targets agreed to by the international community in different fora. This article mostly focused on the co-relation between SDGs 14.c on the role of UNCLOS and 14.1–14.5 with specific CBD decisions, CMS resolutions, and relevant FAO instruments. The legal basis for this strong relationship can be found in UNCLOS provisions that incorporate by reference global, regional, or sub-regional minimum standards for the establishment of conservation and management measures concerning fisheries and marine pollution in a broad sense.

Furthermore, UNCLOS also provides for the protection of important marine habitats, but it does not elaborate on how to identify these sites and how to protect them. Considering that all UNCLOS parties are also parties to the CBD, and given the relationship between the two Conventions, it has been argued that the standards and guidance developed by the CBD concerning ecologically representative MPA systems and effective and equitable management provide sound guidance for the implementation of SDG 14.5. The incorporation of guidance and recommendations provided by CMS on ecological corridors and connectivity should also be observed in this context as it complements the work of the CBD and, therefore, contributes to governance coherence.

The overarching frame for the actions taken in response of these global targets should be the ecosystem approach, which has found wide support in international instruments. The ecosystem approach, which is not entirely eco-centric, or anthropocentric, recognizes that humans are part of the ecosystem and therefore the objective of management is a societal choice, while acknowledging that ecosystems must be managed within the limits of their

---

88 M. Ntona and E. Morgera, "Connecting SDG 14 with the other sustainable development goals through marine spatial planning," *Marine Policy* 93 (2018): 214–222.

89 D. Owen, "Principles and objectives of the legal regime governing areas beyond national jurisdiction: Commentary on Tullio Treves," in *The International Legal Regime of Areas beyond National Jurisdiction: Current and Future Developments*, eds. E.J. Molenaar and A.G. Oude Elferink (Martinus Nijhoff, 2010).

functioning.⁹⁰ To ensure that this balance is achieved in the context of sustainable development, the instruments, guidelines, and processes referred to herein play a significant role in the full implementation of the ecosystem approach. For instance, the EBSA process established under the auspices of the CBD can contribute essential scientific information to coastal States and competent organizations to support the adoption of appropriate conservation and management measures, including ABMTs and EIAs, and therefore contributing to at least Aichi Targets 6, 10 and 11, CMS Target 10, and SDG targets 14.1, 14.2, 14.4, 14.3, and 14.5.

Nevertheless, despite ample guidance, implementation challenges are multiple, ranging from lack of capacity or resources to insufficient coordination of efforts among ministries and across different fora. Insufficient coordination, collaboration, and even oversight of implementation are prominent in areas beyond national jurisdiction. For this reason, a new agreement under UNCLOS is being negotiated for the conservation and sustainable use of biodiversity of areas beyond national jurisdiction. The four main elements of the agreement include ABMTs, including MPAs, EIAs, marine genetic resources, and capacity-building and marine technology transfer. If SDG 14 is to be achieved with respect to areas beyond national jurisdiction, the incorporation of the ecosystem approach into the agreement, along with all of these minimum standards and guidance developed by a diverse range of international bodies, is essential, as is a system for enhanced cooperation, coordination, and implementation oversight.

---

90 CBD Decisions V/6 (2000) and VII/11 (2004).

Ocean Acidification Post-Paris: Gauging Law and Policy Responses in Light of Evolving Scientific Knowledge

Cecilia Engler and David L. VanderZwaag*
Marine & Environmental Law Institute, Schulich School of Law,
Dalhousie University, Halifax, Canada

Katja Fennel
Department of Oceanography, Dalhousie University, Halifax, Canada

Introduction

On 12 December 2015, 195 States agreed on the text of the Paris Agreement,[1] opening a new phase in the global response to the threat of climate change. The Agreement has been lauded as an "historic breakthrough in that it seems to have broken a decade long impasse"[2] in climate change negotiations. The impressive number of ratifications to date and its quick entry into force are indicators of this diplomatic success.[3]

The Agreement achieved this remarkable feat by fundamentally changing the approach to climate change cooperation. The Kyoto Protocol,[4] generally

---

* The authors acknowledge the research support of the Marine Environmental Observation Prediction and Response (MEOPAR) Network, based at Dalhousie University and funded by the Government of Canada's Networks of Centres of Excellence Program. The first two authors also wish to acknowledge the support of the Social Sciences and Humanities Research Council of Canada (SSHRC). The research assistance of Olga Koubrak, Ph.D. Candidate, Schulich School of Law, is also recognized. The authors are grateful for the insightful comments of three anonymous reviewers. This article attempts to be accurate as of 1 September 2018.

1 Paris Agreement, UN Doc. FCCC/CP/2015/10/Add.1 (29 January 2016), 55 *International Legal Materials* 743 (entered into force 4 November 2016) [the Agreement].
2 M. Doelle, "Historic breakthrough or high stakes experiment?," *Climate Law* 6, no. 1–2 (2016): 1–20, p. 20.
3 As of 17 July 2018, 179 parties had ratified the Paris Agreement. It entered into force on 4 November 2016, just 11 months after signature. See online: <https://unfccc.int/process/the-paris-agreement/status-of-ratification>.
4 Kyoto Protocol to the United Nations Framework Convention on Climate Change, UN Doc. FCCC/CP/1997/7/Add.1 (10 December 1997); 37 *International Legal Materials* 22 (1998) (entered into force February 16, 2005).

considered unsuccessful to influence States' action,[5] was drafted on the premise of jointly negotiated (i.e., top-down) and binding emission targets with strong consequences in case of non-compliance and rigid differentiation between developed and developing countries.[6] The Paris Agreement, in contrast, is a universal agreement that adopts a managerial approach to climate change cooperation under the premise that "self imposed, voluntary commitments [nationally determined contributions or NDCs] are more likely to be met than those imposed by the global community."[7]

The achievement has not been without its skeptics. Key reasons for concern are the absence of binding obligations to reduce greenhouse gases (GHGs) and the inadequacy of current pledges to limit global warming.[8] Political instability was also introduced by the decision of the United States of America's President on 1 June 2017 to withdraw from the Agreement.[9] This decision has (so far) not affected the level of participation in the Agreement but may temper other countries' long-term efforts to reduce GHGs emissions as well as the overall prospects of limiting the impacts of climate change.

A further uncertainty is whether the Paris Agreement is an adequate response to "the other CO_2 problem"[10] – ocean acidification (OA). The oceans have played an important role in mitigating atmospheric warming by absorbing a significant amount of anthropogenic carbon dioxide (CO_2). An estimated 48 percent of the total CO_2 emitted by human activities between 1800 and 1994 has been absorbed by the ocean.[11] This service comes at a cost. The addition

---

5   See Doelle, n. 2 above.
6   Id.
7   Id., p. 3.
8   J.E. Viñuales et al., "Climate policy after the Paris 2015 climate conference," *Climate Policy* 7 (2017): 1–8; O.R. Young, "The Paris Agreement: Destined to succeed or doomed to fail?," *Politics and Governance* 4 (2016): 124–132; L. Rajamani, "The 2015 Paris Agreement: Interplay between hard, soft and non-obligations," *Journal of Environmental Law* 28 (2016): 337–358.
9   White House, "President Trump Announces U.S. Withdrawal from the Paris Climate Accord," (1 June 2017), online: <https://www.whitehouse.gov/articles/president-trump-announces-u-s-withdrawal-paris-climate-accord/>.
10 See, for example, C. Turley, "The other CO_2 problem" openDemocracy (5 May 2005), available online: <https://www.opendemocracy.net/globalization-climate_change_debate/article_2480.jsp>; C. Henderson, "Ocean acidification: The other CO_2 problem," *NewScientist* (2 August 2006), available online: <http://environment.newscientist.com/article/mg19125631.200>; S.C. Doney et al., "Ocean acidification: The other CO_2 problem," *Annual Review of Marine Science* 1 (2009): 169–192.
11 The Royal Society, *Ocean Acidification Due to Increasing Atmospheric Carbon Dioxide* (London: The Royal Society, 2005), p. 9, available online: <https://royalsociety.org/topics-policy/publications/2005/ocean-acidification/>.

of anthropogenic CO_2 to the oceans changes its chemistry, increasing the concentrations of CO_2, bicarbonate ions, and hydrogen ions, thus moving oceans toward more acidic conditions. On average, the ocean pH has fallen by 0.1 pH units since preindustrial times, which represents a 30 percent increase in the concentration of hydrogen ions.[12] In turn, the concentration of carbonate ions has decreased, making waters more corrosive to calcium carbonate minerals (aragonite and calcite) by lowering its saturation state (Ω) and shoaling the saturation horizon.[13] By 2007, solubility of calcium carbonate had already increased by 20 percent.[14] Although the extent of the impact of these changes to marine life is still not well understood, evidence shows that they may be significant[15] and irreversible at time scales relevant for society.

This article analyzes to what extent, and with which limitations, the international climate regime, and particularly the newly adopted Paris Agreement, addresses or can address OA. It does so in a six-part format. The first part sets the stage for the analysis by summarizing the scientific understandings of OA and its impacts. The second part maps the pre-Paris policy and legal framework to address OA, highlighting the central role of the United Nations Framework Convention on Climate Change (UNFCCC),[16] and briefly discussing the history of OA in the climate change negotiations up to the Paris Agreement. The third part addresses the promises of the Paris Agreement for dealing with OA, while the fourth part reviews its challenges and shortcomings. Part five discusses other international initiatives relevant to OA, including United Nations General Assembly resolutions and climate change responses under multilateral environmental agreements (MEAs). Part six concludes with an overall assessment of international law and policy responses to date and suggests possible further actions under and outside the climate change regime.

---

12   J.C. Orr et al., "Anthropogenic ocean acidification over the twenty-first century and its impact on calcifying organisms," *Nature* 427, no. 7059 (2005): 681–686.
13   K. Fennel and D.L. VanderZwaag, "Ocean acidification: Scientific surges, lagging law and policy responses," in *Routledge Handbook of Maritime Regulation and Enforcement*, eds. R. Warner and S. Kaye (Abingdon: Routledge, 2015), chap. 20; E.L. Howes et al., "An updated synthesis of the observed and projected impacts of climate change on the chemical, physical and biological processes in the oceans," *Frontiers in Marine Science* 2 (2015): doi: 10.3389/fmars.2015.00036.
14   Fennel and VanderZwaag, id.
15   For meta-analysis, see A.C. Wittmann and H.-O. Pörtner, "Sensitivities of extant animal taxa to ocean acidification," *Nature Climate Change* 3 (2013): 995–1001; K.J. Kroeker et al., "Impacts of ocean acidification on marine organisms: quantifying sensitivities and interaction with warming," *Global Change Biology* 19 (2013): 1884–1896.
16   United Nations Framework Convention on Climate Change, 9 May 1992, 1771 *United Nations Treaty Series* 107 (entered into force 21 March 1994) [UNFCCC].

Ocean Acidification and Evolving Scientific Knowledge

When CO_2 is taken up by the ocean it does not merely dissolve but reacts with seawater to form carbonic acid, which then dissociates to bicarbonate, carbonate, and hydrogen ions.[17] The addition of anthropogenic CO_2 to the ocean shifts the equilibrium between aqueous CO_2, carbonate, and bicarbonate such that the concentrations of CO_2 and hydrogen and bicarbonate ions increase and the concentration of carbonate ions decreases. The decrease in carbonate ions makes it more difficult for organisms to precipitate calcium carbonate. The increase in hydrogen ions is synonymous with increasing acidity.

Ocean acidification most commonly refers to the long-term increase in ocean acidity caused by the ocean's uptake of anthropogenic CO_2, but acidity can increase due to other processes as well, e.g., acid rain and decomposition of organic material.[18] OA can significantly affect growth, metabolism, and life cycles of marine organisms;[19] it most directly affects marine calcifiers, i.e., organisms that precipitate calcium carbonate to form internal or external body structures. When the carbonate saturation state decreases below the equilibrium point for carbonate precipitation or dissolution, conditions are said to be corrosive, or damaging, to marine calcifiers. Corrosive conditions make it more difficult for these organisms to form shells or skeletons, perform metabolic functions, and survive.

Ocean uptake of CO_2 occurs on a range of time scales. The concentration of CO_2 in the surface of the open ocean generally increases in lockstep with that in the atmosphere, but it changes at different rates in the intermediate and deep ocean and in coastal waters. Air-sea gas exchange of CO_2 and subsequent vertical mixing in the upper ocean occurs on relatively short time scales of

---

17   R.E. Zeebe and D. Wolf-Gladrow, *CO_2 in Seawater: Equilibrium, Kinetics, Isotopes* (Amsterdam: Elsevier Oceanography Series, Vol. 65, 2001), p. 346.

18   Ocean acidification is defined more precisely as "any reduction in the pH of the ocean over an extended period, typically decades or longer, that is caused primarily by uptake of CO_2 from the atmosphere but also can be caused by other chemical additions or subtractions from the ocean." (C.B. Field et al., eds., *Workshop Report of the Intergovernmental Panel on Climate Change Workshop on Impacts of Ocean Acidification On Marine Biology and Ecosystems*, IPCC Working Group II Technical Support Unit (Stanford, CA: Carnegie Institution, 2011), p. 37).

19   V.J. Fabry et al., "Impacts of ocean acidification on marine fauna and ecosystem processes," *ICES Journal of Marine Science* 65, no. 3 (2008): 414–432, doi: 10.1093/icesjms/fsn048; J.-P. Gattuso and L. Hansson, eds., *Ocean Acidification* (Oxford: Oxford University Press, 2011); G.N. Somero et al., "What changes in the carbonate system, oxygen, and temperature portend for the Northeastern Pacific Ocean: A physiological perspective," *BioScience* 66, no. 1 (2016): 14–26, doi: 10.1093/biosci/biv162.

years to decades, while concentration changes at intermediate depths and in the deep ocean occur on time scales of centuries to millennia.[20]

Multiple decades of observations of atmospheric CO_2 from Hawaii[21] and of CO_2 dissolved in seawater from the nearby surface ocean[22] show that both have risen by about 1.9 ppm per year since 1990. Simultaneously, pH has decreased by 0.002 units per year since 1990. This consistency in inorganic carbon trends between the atmosphere and surface ocean in the subtropical North Pacific Ocean is characteristic of the open ocean globally. In contrast, coastal regions exhibit larger spatial and temporal variability, more extreme excursions, and a diversity of long-term trends in dissolved CO_2 and pH that often deviate from the atmospheric CO_2 trend.

Variations of pH in coastal systems are due to processes other than the uptake of anthropogenic CO_2 from the atmosphere. They include relatively large diurnal cycles of photosynthetic production and subsequent respiration by organisms,[23] intense upwelling of carbon-rich waters from the deep ocean (e.g., along the Pacific margin of North America),[24] and inputs of inorganic and organic carbon and nutrients from rivers.[25] Ranges of pH from 6 to 9 have been documented in estuaries[26] and short-term variations of up to 0.5 pH units have been observed in coastal systems on time scales of hours to weeks.[27] These

---

20   E. Maier-Reimer and K. Hasselmann, "Transport and storage of CO_2 in the ocean – an inorganic ocean-circulation carbon cycle model," *Climate Dynamics* 2 (1987): 63–90.

21   U.S. Department of Commerce, National Oceanic and Atmospheric Administration (NOAA), "Trends in Atmospheric Carbon Dioxide," Global Greenhouse Gas Reference Network, available online: <https://www.esrl.noaa.gov/gmd/ccgg/trends/data.html>.

22   University of Hawai'i, School of Ocean and Earth Science and Technology, "Hawaii Ocean Time-series Data Organization & Graphical System (HOT-DOGS)," available online: <http://hahana.soest.hawaii.edu/hot/hot-dogs/interface.html>.

23   S.R. Pacella et al., "Seagrass habitat metabolism increases short-term extremes and long-term offset of CO_2 under future ocean acidification," *PNAS* 115 (2018): 3870–3875.

24   R.A. Feely et al., "Evidence for upwelling of corrosive 'acidified' water onto the continental shelf," *Science* 320, no. 5882 (2008): 1490–1492, doi: 10.1126/science.1155676.

25   W.-J. Cai et al., "Acidification of subsurface coastal waters enhanced by eutrophication," *Nature Geoscience* 4, no. 11 (2011): 766–770, doi: 10.1038/ngeo1297; A. Laurent et al., "Eutrophication-induced acidification of coastal waters in the northern Gulf of Mexico: Insights into origin and processes from a coupled physical-biogeochemical model," *Geophysical Research Letters* 44, no. 2 (2017): 946–956, doi: 10.1002/2016gl071881.

26   A.V. Borges and G. Abril, "Carbon dioxide and methane dynamics in estuaries," in *Treatise on Estuarine and Coastal Science: Vol. 5: Biogeochemistry*, eds. E. Wolanski and D. McLusky (Waltham, MA: Academic Press, 2011), pp. 119–161.

27   G.E. Hofmann et al., "High-frequency dynamics of ocean pH: A multi-ecosystem comparison," *PLoS ONE* 6, no. 12 (2011), e28983, doi:10.1371/journal.pone.0028983.

variations are on the same order of magnitude as the drop in mean open-ocean pH of 0.1 pH units since the Industrial Revolution.

Polar regions are especially prone to acidification. Because of their low temperatures, pH and the carbonate saturation state are naturally low in many polar waters compared to lower latitude coastal settings.[28] Furthermore, retreating sea ice, which adds meltwater from multi-year ice and enhances ocean uptake of atmospheric CO_2 by increasing the surface area of open water, contributes to relatively high rates of acidification in these waters.[29] This combination of factors has set a faster pace of ocean acidification along the Arctic coasts than observed in other coastal regions.[30]

Coastal upwelling regions, where wind-driven circulation supplies carbon-rich water from the deep ocean to the surface, are also increasingly exposed to low pH. The Pacific margin of North America, where an intensification of upwelling circulation thought to be driven by climate change occurs,[31] increasingly experiences coastal acidification events.[32] Along the Oregon coast, this process results in pH and aragonite saturation levels that are known to be harmful to several ecologically and economically important species.[33]

Another aspect of anthropogenic acidification is related to excessive inputs of industrially produced fertilizers to coastal waters.[34] In the northern Gulf of

---

28   Orr et al., n. 12 above; M. Steinacher et al., "Imminent ocean acidification in the Arctic projected with the NCAR global coupled carbon cycle-climate model," *Biogeosciences* 6, no. 4 (2009): 515–533, doi: 10.5194/bg-6-515-2009.

29   N.S. Steiner, W.G. Lee and J.R. Christian, "Enhanced gas fluxes in small sea ice leads and cracks: Effects on CO_2 exchange and ocean acidification," *Journal of Geophysical Research: Oceans* 118, no. 3 (2013): 1195–1205, doi: 10.1002/jgrc.20100; W.-J. Cai et al., "Carbon fluxes across boundaries in the Pacific Arctic region in a changing environment," in *The Pacific Arctic Region: Ecosystem Status and Trends in a Rapidly Changing Environment*, eds. J.M. Grebmeier and W. Maslowski (Dordrecht: Springer, 2014), chap. 8.

30   J. Mathis et al., "Ocean acidification in the surface waters of the Pacific-Arctic boundary regions," *Oceanography* 25, no. 2 (2015): 122–135, doi: 10.5670/oceanog.2015.36.

31   M. García-Reyes et al., "Under pressure: Climate change, upwelling, and eastern boundary upwelling ecosystems," *Frontiers in Marine Science* 2 (2015), doi: 10.3389/fmars.2015.00109.

32   Feely et al., n. 24 above.

33   A. Barton et al., "Impacts of coastal acidification on the Pacific northwest shellfish industry and adaptation strategies implemented in response," *Oceanography* 25, no. 2 (2015): 146–159, doi: 10.5670/oceanog.2015.38; N. Bednaršek et al., "Pteropods on the edge: Cumulative effects of ocean acidification, warming, and deoxygenation," *Progress in Oceanography* 145 (2016): 1–24, doi: 10.1016/j.pocean.2016.04.002; N. Bednaršek et al., "Limacina helicina shell dissolution as an indicator of declining habitat suitability owing to ocean acidification in the California current ecosystem," *Proceedings of the Royal Society B: Biological Sciences* 281, no. 1785 (2014): 20140123, doi: 10.1098/rspb.2014.0123.

34   K. Fennel and J.M. Testa, "Biogeochemical controls on coastal hypoxia," *Annual Review of Marine Science* (2019), doi: 10.1146/annurev-marine-010318-095138.

Mexico, where large inputs of nutrients and freshwater from the Mississippi River cause large-scale low-oxygen conditions every summer, the excessive riverine nutrient inputs result in eutrophication-induced acidification of near-bottom waters, although the aragonite saturation state currently is still above the saturation threshold.[35]

Coral reefs ecosystems are especially prone to the combined effects of warming and OA. Reefs are found in different environments from sunlit tropical waters down to deep, dark, and cold waters to depths of 2,000 meters and more and provide important ecological functions and human services, including food, income, and coastal protection.[36] Corals are long-lived and produce calcium carbonate skeletons that create complex reef structures over time. The reefs provide important habitat for other species and create barrier reefs and islands that serve a critical role in the protection of tropical coasts. Coral reef ecosystems are under serious threat from anthropogenic warming, OA, nutrient pollution, and physical destruction, which act in combination and are already drastically decreasing the abundance of reef ecosystems around the world.[37] Even under conservative, low-emission Intergovernmental Panel on Climate Change (IPCC) scenarios, most warm-water coral reefs will likely be eliminated by 2040–2050[38] and cold-water corals by 2100.[39]

Models predict also that the annual average aragonite level in the Arctic Ocean will be below the saturation level (favoring dissolution) by 2025, 2030, and 2070 in the Beaufort Sea, the Chukchi Sea, and the Bering Sea, respectively.[40] Along the Pacific Coast, half of the shelf waters are projected to experience year-long under-saturation by 2050,[41] and projections for the coastal northern Gulf of Mexico suggest that aragonite will drop below the saturation level in

---

35 W.-J. Cai et al., n. 25 above; Laurent et al., n. 25 above.

36 O. Hoegh-Guldberg et al., "Coral reef ecosystems under climate change and ocean acidification," *Frontiers in Marine Science* 4 (2017): 158, doi: 10.3389/fmars.2017.00158.

37 O. Hoegh-Guldberg, "Coral reefs in the Anthropocene: Persistence or the end of the line?," *Geological Society, London, Special Publications* 395 (2014): 167–183, doi: 10.1144/SP395.17.

38 O. Hoegh-Guldberg, "Coral bleaching, climate change and the future of the world's coral reefs," *Marine and Freshwater Research* 50 (1999): 839–866. doi: 10.1071/MF99078.

39 J.M. Guinotte et al., "Will human induced changes in seawater chemistry alter the distribution of deep-sea scleractinian corals?," *Frontiers in Ecology and the Environment* 4 (2006): 141–146.

40 Steinacher et al., n. 28 above; N.S. Steiner et al., "Future ocean acidification in the Canada basin and surrounding Arctic ocean from CMIP5 Earth system models," *Journal of Geophysical Research: Oceans* 119, no. 1 (2014): 332–347, doi: 10.1002/2013jc009069; Mathis et al., n. 30 above.

41 N. Gruber et al., "Rapid progression of ocean acidification in the California current system," *Science* 337, no. 6091 (2012): 220–223, doi: 10.1126/science.1216773; G. Turi et al., "Climatic modulation of recent trends in ocean acidification in the California current system," *Environmental Research Letters* 11, no. 1 (2016): 014007, doi: 10.1088/1748-9326/11/1/014007.

near-bottom waters by the end of this century.[42] The negative impacts of these OA projections on calcifying marine organisms are expected to become a critical issue, reshaping ecosystems and fisheries.[43]

International Responses to OA: Pre-Paris Legal Backwaters

While OA has been the subject of scientific inquiry for several decades, it has only recently been recognized as an environmental problem deserving of policy and legal attention. The first Oceans in a High CO_2 World Conference, held in 2004, and the reports of the Royal Society[44] and the German Advisory Council on Global Change,[45] released in 2005 and 2006, respectively, were instrumental in raising this global policy concern. Since then, OA has been increasingly the focus of global and regional reports, declarations, conferences, and international and regional arrangements for scientific and policy cooperation.[46]

Despite the multiple calls for action to mitigate OA and its impacts, addressing OA represents a significant policy and legal challenge.[47] The multiple local and global drivers of OA do call for a multi-level and holistic approach to the problem,[48] including local, national, and international action.[49] Nevertheless,

---

42   A. Laurent et al., "Climate change projected to exacerbate impacts of coastal eutrophication in the northern Gulf of Mexico," *Journal of Geophysical Research-Oceans* 123 (2018): 3408–3426.

43   See, for example: J.T. Mathis et al., "Ocean acidification risk assessment for Alaska's fishery sector," *Progress in Oceanography* 136 (2015): 71–91, doi: 10.1016/j.pocean.2014.07.001.

44   The Royal Society, n. 11 above.

45   R. Schubert et al., *The Future Oceans: Warming Up, Rising High, Turning Sour*. Special Report (Berlin: German Advisory Council on Global Change, 2006).

46   For policy developments until 2011, see J.P. Gattuso and L. Hansson, "Ocean acidification: Background and history," in Gattuso and Hansson, n. 19 above, Chap. 1. See also "Other International Responses" part in this article.

47   For example, R. Kim, "Is a new multilateral environmental agreement on ocean acidification necessary?," *Review of European Comparative & International Environmental Law* 21 (2012): 243–258; R. Baird, M. Simons and T. Stephens, "Ocean acidification: A litmus test for international law," *Carbon & Climate Law Review* 4 (2009): 459–471; R. Rayfuse, "Climate change, marine biodiversity and international law," in *Research Handbook on Biodiversity and Law*, eds. M. Bowman, P. Davies and E. Goodwin (Cheltenham, UK: Edward Elgar, 2016), chap. 5.

48   E.R. Harrould-Kolieb, "Ocean acidification and the UNFCCC: Finding legal clarity in the twilight zone," *Washington Journal of Environmental Law and Policy* 6 (2016): 613–633, note 2; R. Billé et al., "Taking action against ocean acidification: A review of management and policy options," *Environmental Management* 52 (2013): 761–779.

49   For national measures see, e.g., R.P. Kelly and M.R Caldwell, "Ten ways states can combat ocean acidification (and why they should)," *Harvard Environmental Law Review* 37 (2013):

there is also ample consensus that local and national measures to address OA and its impacts "merely [buy] time"[50] to address a problem that is mainly international in cause and effect.[51] The international response, however, has been tepid. There is no international legal instrument that defines, refers to, or specifically addresses OA. Rather, there is an array of international instruments and regimes that can, within their mandates, address the global or local drivers of OA, its impacts, or both.[52] Some have started to do so,[53] contributing to a fragmented response.

With the main driver of OA being the ocean's uptake of anthropogenic CO_2, a key legal instrument is the UNFCCC, which is the primary international response to mitigating the adverse impacts of GHG emissions into the atmosphere.[54] The objective of the Convention and any related legal instruments adopted under the climate regime is to "achieve, in accordance with the relevant provisions of the Convention, stabilization of greenhouse gas concentrations in the atmosphere at a level that would prevent dangerous anthropogenic interference with the climate system."[55] Climate system, in turn, is

---

57–103; Washington State Blue Ribbon Panel on Ocean Acidification, *Ocean Acidification: From Knowledge to Action, Washington State's Strategic Response*, eds. H. Adelsman and L. Whitely Binder (Olympia, WA: Washington Department of Ecology, 2012), available online: <https://fortress.wa.gov/ecy/publications/documents/1201015.pdf>.

50   Billé et al., n. 48 above, p. 771; see also Kelly and Caldwell, n. 49 above, p. 61.
51   E.J. Goodwin, *International Environmental Law and the Conservation of Coral Reefs* (London: Routledge, 2011), p. 256.
52   See, e.g., Fennel and VanderZwaag, n. 13 above; T. Stephens, "Ocean Acidification," in *Research Handbook on International Marine Environmental Law*, ed. R. Rayfuse (Cheltenham, UK: Edward Elgar, 2015), pp. 431–450; D. Herr, K. Isensee and C. Turley, "Ocean acidification: Overview of the international policy landscape and activities on ocean acidification," (White Paper, 2013); Kim, n. 47 above.
53   Fennel and VanderZwaag, n. 13 above. For recent developments, see "Other International Responses" below.
54   D.E.J. Currie and K. Wowk, "Climate change and CO_2 in the oceans and global oceans governance: Improving governance of the world's oceans," *Carbon and Climate Law Review* 4 (2009): 387–404; E.R. Harrould-Kolieb and D. Herr, "Ocean acidification and climate change: Synergies and challenges of addressing both under the UNFCCC," *Climate Policy* 2 (2012): 378–389; Billé et al., n. 48 above; Y. Downing, "Ocean acidification and protection under international law from negative effects: A burning issue amongst a sea of regimes?," *Cambridge Journal of International and Comparative Law* 2 (2013): 242–273; Stephens, n. 52 above; Fennel and VanderZwaag, n. 13 above; Harrould-Kolieb, n. 48 above. The Montreal Protocol on Substances that Deplete the Ozone Layer, 1522 *United Nations Treaty Series* 3; 26 *International Legal Materials* 1550 (1987) (entered into force 1 January 1989) is also critical to international efforts to address climate change, since the ozone-depleting substances and many of their substitutes covered by the protocol (including hydrofluorocarbons, since 2016) are also potent GHGs.
55   UNFCCC, n. 16 above, art. 2.

defined broadly as the "totality of the atmosphere, hydrosphere, biosphere and geosphere and their interactions."[56] Oceans are an integral part of the global climate system (hydrosphere). Increased CO_2 emissions affect the ocean itself (including its future capacity to absorb CO_2) as well as the marine life (biosphere). These changes, in turn, affect the biogeochemical processes that can alter the make-up of the atmosphere. Therefore, preventing dangerous anthropogenic interference with the oceans' biogeochemistry resulting from GHGs emissions falls within the broad objective of the UNFCCC.[57]

Nevertheless, the UNFCCC was drafted, and it has been implemented, with another concern in mind: global warming.[58] OA has the same root cause as global warming: anthropogenic emissions of CO_2, a major GHG. But the processes are different, although concurrent and related: global warming is a physical response to atmospheric concentrations of GHGs; OA is a chemical process caused by the ocean's uptake of atmospheric CO_2. Thus, although the textual interpretation of Article 2 allows to "read a new problem in an old document,"[59] the UNFCCC "promotes a response calibrated to an entirely different problem."[60]

The global warming focus of the UNFCCC has been evident in the little substantive recognition that OA has received within the climate change regime.[61] OA was included in the IPCC Fourth Assessment Report, released in 2007, and subsequently, with much greater focus, in the IPCC Fifth Assessment Report, released in 2013.[62] While the Subsidiary Body for Science and Technological Advice (SBSTA) recognized OA as an emerging issue relevant to the UNFCCC and a research priority,[63] other bodies of the Convention have not substantively

---

56 Id., art. 1(3).
57 Schubert et al., n. 45 above; Baird et al., n. 47 above; Harrould-Kolieb, n. 48 above; Kim, n. 47 above.
58 See, e.g., UNFCCC, n. 16 above, preamble, para. 2; the definitions of "climate change" and "greenhouse gas" in Articles 1(2) and 1(5), respectively, and the reference to "atmospheric greenhouse gas concentration" in Article 2. See also Goodwin, n. 51 above.
59 Harrould-Kolieb, n. 48 above, p. 622.
60 Goodwin, n. 51 above, p. 256.
61 For an overview of OA within the climate regime until 2015, see Harrould-Kolieb, n. 48 above.
62 IPCC Assessment reports are available online: IPCC <http://www.ipcc.ch/publications_and_data/publications_and_data_reports.shtml>.
63 UNFCCC, "Report on the Workshop on Technical and Scientific Aspects of Ecosystems with High-carbon Reservoirs Not Covered by Other Agenda Items under the Convention," UN Doc. FCCC/SBSTA/2014/INF.1 (1 April 2014), annex 1; Harrould-Kolieb, n. 48 above, p. 617. OA has also been a recurrent theme in the Research Dialogue established by the CoP in 2005 as an open and non-binding exchange of views, information, and ideas in support of enhanced implementation of the Convention.

addressed OA.[64] The Conference of the Parties (CoP) to the UNFCCC, in turn, has only referred to OA in one decision: Decision 1/CP.16 of 2010 adopting the Cancun Agreements. In this decision, the parties recognize the need to strengthen international cooperation and expertise in order to understand and reduce loss and damage associated with the adverse effects of climate change, including impacts related to extreme weather events and slow onset events. The relevant paragraph contains a footnote providing examples of slow onset events, which includes, among others, OA together with temperature rise, glacial retreat, and sea level rise.[65] This is, to this day, the most direct political statement of the UNFCCC including OA among its issues of concern. Noteworthy, the statement regards OA as an effect of climate change, rather than a concurrent problem of increased atmospheric CO_2 concentrations.

The shortcomings of the climate regime to bring OA within its regulatory focus led some authors to explore other international instruments (in particular the United Nations Convention on the Law of the Sea)[66] or to call for a new international agreement to address the issue.[67] The majority, however, considers the negotiation of a separate agreement to reduce CO_2 emissions to mitigate OA politically unrealistic.[68] Furthermore, the deep and complex connections between changes in ocean ecosystems resulting from climate change (i.e., global warming) and acidification warrants that both threats are addressed within the same regime. Indeed, not only do they share the root cause, but the processes themselves and their impacts on ocean ecosystems are inextricably linked.[69] Addressing global warming and OA through different agreements might lead to unwanted redundancies and potential inconsistencies.

---

64   Harrould-Kolieb, n. 48 above.
65   UNFCC, "The Cancun Agreements, Decision 1/CP.16," UN Doc. FCCC/CP/2010/7/Add.1 (15 March 2011), para. 25 and note 3.
66   See, e.g., A. Boyle, "Law of the sea perspectives on climate change," *International Journal of Marine and Coastal Law* 27 (2012): 831–838; D. Bialek and J. Ariel, "Ocean acidification: International legal avenues under the UN Convention on the Law of the Sea," in *Threatened Island Nations: Legal Implications of Rising Seas and a Changing Climate*, eds. M.B. Gerrard and G.E. Wannier (New York: Cambridge University Press, 2013), chap. 15; Baird et al., n. 47 above.
67   See, e.g., V. González, "An alternative approach for addressing CO_2-driven ocean acidification," *Sustainable Development Law & Policy* 12 (2012): 45, 69; Kim, n. 47 above.
68   Harrould-Kolieb and Herr, n. 54 above, note that "[s]etting up a second international mechanism to deal solely with CO_2 reductions would be superfluous, confusing and unrealistic."
69   For example, warmer oceanic waters absorb less CO_2, affecting the natural sink capacity of oceans. Coral reefs are impacted synergistically by ocean warming and acidification, which together deteriorate the balance between reef construction and erosion. Geoengineering solutions that aim to address global warming may exacerbate the problem of OA.

Scholars and governmental and non-governmental organizations have made strong calls to include the role of oceans, and OA, in the climate regime.[70] The negotiations of a new legally binding instrument – the Paris Agreement – provided a valuable opportunity to that end. The extent to which those efforts were successful is addressed in the next part.

Paris Agreement and OA: the Promises

On 12 December 2015, the CoP to the UNFCCC adopted, by consensus, a new agreement to increase efforts to combat climate change and adapt to its effects. In so doing, they have charted a "new beginning"[71] for climate change, and one that some see as a high stakes experiment.[72] Key elements of the new framework include[73]

– the explicit inclusion of a global and ambitious long-term mitigation goal: holding the increase in the global average temperature to well below 2°C above pre-industrial levels and pursuing efforts to limit the temperature increase to 1.5°C above pre-industrial levels;[74]
– a clarification of the implications of the temperature limit for reducing global GHG emissions: aim to reach global peaking of GHG emissions as soon as possible; achieve a balance between anthropogenic emissions by sources and removals by sinks of GHGs in the second half of this century;[75]

See, e.g., P.P. Wong et al., "Coastal systems and low-lying areas," in *Climate Change 2014: Impacts, Adaptation, and Vulnerability. Part A: Global and Sectoral Aspects. Contribution of Working Group II to the Fifth Assessment Report of the Intergovernmental Panel on Climate Change*, eds. C.B. Field et al., (Cambridge: Cambridge University Press, 2014), chap. 5, p. 379; P. Williamson and C. Turley, "Ocean acidification in a geoengineering context," *Philosophical Transactions of the Royal Society A: Mathematical, Physical and Engineering Sciences* 370 (2012): 4317–4342.

70 For example, "Because the Ocean Declaration" (29 November 2015), online: <https://oceans.taraexpeditions.org/wp-content/uploads/2015/12/Because-the-Ocean-double-sided.pdf>; Downing, n. 54 above.
71 C. Strek, P. Keenlyside and M. von Unger, "Paris Agreement: A new beginning," *Journal for European Environmental & Planning Law* 13 (2016): 3–29.
72 Doelle, n. 2 above.
73 The Paris Agreement addresses other important subject matters, including finance, technology, capacity-building, education, and institutional arrangements. It also innovates by including references to several cross-cutting issues, such as human rights, albeit only in the preamble (see Id.).
74 Paris Agreement, n. 1 above, art. 2(1)(a).
75 Id., art. 4(1).

- qualitative objectives for adaptation and resilience to climate impacts;[76]
- a stand-alone article on loss and damage;[77]
- its universal applicability to all State parties (thus breaking the "firewall" between developed and developing countries enshrined in the Kyoto Protocol);[78]
- a mechanism of self-imposed contributions to the global long-term goal – the nationally determined contributions (NDCs);[79]
- an "increased ambition" clause: each party's successive NDCs will represent a progression beyond the party's then current nationally determined contribution and reflect its highest possible ambition;[80]
- a cyclic review process – the "global stocktake" – to assess the collective progress towards achieving the purpose of this Agreement and its long-term goals;[81]
- an enhanced transparency framework for action and support;[82]
- financial flows consistent with the mitigation and adaptation goals;[83] and
- a facilitative, transparent, non-adversarial, and non-punitive compliance mechanism.[84]

The "Paris Outcome" also includes CoP Decision 1/CP.21,[85] which was fundamental in enabling a compromise text that all parties accepted. The CoP Decision specifies some aspects of the Agreement, includes a work program with mandates for elaborating modalities, procedures, and guidelines for its implementation, and creates subsidiary bodies to carry out the tasks that would enable the successful entry into force of the Agreement.[86]

Neither the Paris Agreement nor CoP Decision 1/CP.21 mentions OA. Nevertheless, OA was in the background of some of its provisions, such as the preamble and the long-term mitigation target. Other provisions have the potential

---

76 Id., art. 2(1)(b)–(c).
77 Id., art. 8.
78 Id., art. 3.
79 Id., art. 4(2).
80 Id., art. 4(3).
81 Id., art. 14.
82 Id., art. 13; see also art. 4, paras. 8, 12 and 13.
83 Id., art. 2(1)(c).
84 Id., art. 15.
85 UNFCCC, "Decision 1/CP.21, Adoption of the Paris Agreement," UN Doc. FCCC/CP/2015/10/Add.1 (29 January 2016).
86 R. Bodle and S. Oberthür, "Legal form of the Paris Agreement and nature of its obligations," in *The Paris Agreement on Climate Change: Analysis and Commentary*, eds. D. Klein et al., (Oxford: Oxford University Press, 2017), chap. 5.

to enable an effective response to OA within the climate regime. Particularly relevant in this respect are the Paris mechanism of increased ambition or "ratchet mechanism," the strengthened framework for adaptation, and the stand-alone provision on loss and damage.

The Agreement's Preamble

The Paris Agreement was welcomed by the ocean community as a milestone in highlighting the links between oceans and climate.[87] Indeed, the Agreement explicitly mentions oceans in its preamble, noting "the importance of ensuring the integrity of all ecosystems, including oceans, and the protection of biodiversity, recognized by some cultures as Mother Earth ... when taking action to address climate change."[88] This statement stands in stark contrast to the UNFCCC, which only mentions oceans in the provision calling for sustainable management of all sinks of GHGs.[89] The latter provision has been interpreted as encouraging active sequestration of CO_2 in the oceans as a solution to global warming, thus recognizing only one end of the climate-ocean linkages.[90] The Paris Agreement, on the contrary, explicitly recognizes that the oceans are impacted by climate change and, directly or indirectly, by the mitigation and adaptation actions taken in response to it.

The mention of oceans is included in a preambular paragraph of the Agreement, which although generally non-binding is nevertheless relevant in the interpretation and implementation of a treaty.[91] It should also be noted that the need to ensure the integrity of ocean and terrestrial ecosystems is an evolving responsibility under international law,[92] and that environmental integrity is specifically mentioned as a guiding principle in a few specific provisions of the Agreement.[93] In acknowledging this responsibility, the preamble effectively

---

87   For example, Ocean & Climate Platform, available online: <https://ocean-climate.org/?p=3248&lang=en> (but note that it is announced as a "symbolic" victory); Because the Ocean Declaration, n. 70 above; B. Cicin-Sain, et al., *Toward a Strategic Action Roadmap on Oceans and Climate: 2016 to 2021* (Washington, DC: Global Ocean Forum, 2016).
88   Paris Agreement, n. 1 above, preamble, para. 13.
89   UNFCCC, n. 16 above, art. 4(1)(d); see also Paris Agreement, id., preamble, para. 12 and art. 5(1).
90   Kim, n. 47 above, p. 246.
91   Vienna Convention on the Law of Treaties, 22 May 1969, 1155 *United Nations Treaty Series* 331 (entered into force 27 January 1980).
92   K. Bosselmann, "The ever-increasing importance of ecological integrity in international and national law," in *Ecological Integrity, Law and Governance*, eds. L. Westra et al., (Abingdon: Routledge, 2018), chap. 22. See also: M.P. Carazo, "Contextual Provisions (Preamble and Article 1)," in Klein et al., n. 86 above, chap. 6.
93   Paris Agreement, n. 1 above, arts. 4(13), 6(1), 6(2).

links the international legal regimes on oceans and climate that thus far had been kept mostly compartmentalized.[94]

The Paris Agreement has been followed by several initiatives that reinforce the importance of the linkages between oceans and climate highlighted in the preamble. For example, the pivotal role of oceans in climate change regulation has been further acknowledged by the IPCC 2016 decision to prepare a Special Report on Climate Change and the Oceans and Cryosphere, to be released in 2019.[95] It has also been acknowledged by the Ocean Pathway initiative launched by the presidency to the 23rd CoP to call attention to the critical links between the ocean and climate change. The Pathway consists of a two-track strategy for 2020 that aims at a) increasing the role of the ocean considerations in the UNFCCC process, including through an agenda item and a work program for the ocean within the UNFCCC process, and b) significantly increasing action in priority areas impacting or impacted by ocean and climate change.[96] In particular, this second track considers working with the Ocean Acidification Alliance on a high-level event at the Global Climate Action Summit[97] and CoP 24[98] to agree on a process for ambitious 2020 and 2030 action plans and targets that can be applied in countries and regions and link to global outcomes.[99]

The Paris Target and OA

One of the diplomatic achievements of the Paris Agreement was the inclusion of a specific target that provides substantive meaning to the UNFCCC's goal of stabilizing GHG concentrations in the atmosphere at a level that would prevent *dangerous* anthropogenic interference with the climate system. Article 2(1)(a) of the Paris Agreement reads:

> This Agreement, in enhancing the implementation of the Convention, including its objective, aims to strengthen the global response to the threat of climate change, in the context of sustainable development and efforts to eradicate poverty, including by:

---

94 On the Paris Agreement and integration clauses to reduce potential conflict of international legal regimes, see M.P. Carazo and D. Klein, "Implications for public international law: Initial considerations," in Klein et al., n. 86 above, chap. 23.

95 Decision adopted during the 43rd Session of the IPCC held in Nairobi, Kenya, 11–13 April 2016. See IPCC, "The Ocean and Cryosphere in a Changing Climate Report," available online: <https://www.ipcc.ch/report/srocc/>.

96 UN Climate Change Conference, "The Ocean Pathway," COP23 Fiji, available online: <https://cop23.com.fj/the-ocean-pathway/>.

97 To be held in San Francisco, California, 12–14 September 2018.

98 To be held in Katowice, Poland, 3–14 December 2018.

99 See "The Ocean Pathway," n. 96 above.

(a) Holding the increase in the global average temperature to well below 2 °C above pre-industrial levels and pursuing efforts to limit the temperature increase to 1.5 °C above pre-industrial levels, recognizing that this would significantly reduce the risks and impacts of climate change.

This target is complemented by Article 4(1), which "clarifies the implications of this temperature limit for reducing global GHG emissions":[100]

> In order to achieve the long-term temperature goal set out in Article 2, Parties aim to reach global peaking of greenhouse gas emissions as soon as possible, recognizing that peaking will take longer for developing country Parties, and to undertake rapid reductions thereafter in accordance with best available science, so as to achieve a balance between anthropogenic emissions by sources and removals by sinks of greenhouse gases in the second half of this century, on the basis of equity, and in the context of sustainable development and efforts to eradicate poverty.

The long-term target has had a long history in the climate regime.[101] It is not surprising, then, that the global long-term goal is expressed as a temperature target, confirming the UNFCCC preoccupation with global warming. This single-focus target does not recognize that climate change is a complex problem with multiple and interlinked phenomena,[102] and that CO_2 emissions have a different, albeit related, impact on the ocean.

A more detailed analysis of the history of the target, however, tells a more nuanced story. The German Advisory Council on Global Change proposal to limit atmospheric temperature rise to 2°C[103] gained support in policy circles and became the dominant perspective in climate negotiations. However, a group of countries (particularly the Alliance of Small Island Developing States (AOSIS) and the Least Developed Countries (LEDs)) advocated for a more

---

100 L. Rajamani and E. Guérin, "Central concepts in the Paris Agreement and how they evolved," in Klein et al., n. 86 above, chap. 4.
101 S. Randalls, "History of the 2 °C climate target," WIRES Climate Change 1 (2010): 598–605. See also H. Thorgeirsson, "Objective (Article 2.1)," in Klein et al., n. 86 above, chap. 7.
102 B.C. O'Neill et al., "IPCC reasons for concern regarding climate change risks," Nature Climate Change 7 (2017): 28–37, p. 33.
103 German Advisory Council on Global Change, "Scenario for the derivation of global CO_2 reduction targets and implementation strategies. Statement on the occasion of the First Conference of the Parties to the Framework Convention on Climate Change in Berlin," adopted at the 26th Session of the Council, Dortmund, 17 February 1995, available online: <http://www.wbgu.de/en/special-reports/sr-1995-co2-reduction/>.

ambitious target: long-term stabilization of atmospheric GHG concentrations at well below 350 ppm CO_2-equivalent levels; and limit global temperature increase to 1.5°C.[104] The call for a more ambitious temperature target was based mostly on projected sea level rise associated with the 2°C target. Nevertheless, the effects of increased emissions on OA, among other impacts, were also part of the reasoning behind a more ambitious target.[105]

While parties endorsed the 2°C target in the 2009 Copenhagen Accord and the 2010 Cancun Agreements,[106] both documents further called for an assessment of its implementation that includes consideration of strengthening the long-term goal, including in relation to temperature rises of 1.5°C.[107] More specifically, the Cancun Agreements commissioned an Expert Panel to undertake a review to assess the adequacy of this target.[108] The review mandated by the CoP was undertaken through the structured expert dialogue (SED) between 2013 and 2015. The SED report, together with the IPCC Fifth Assessment Report,[109] was of key relevance for the drafting of Article 2 of the Paris Agreement.

The SED report concluded that an atmospheric temperature increase of 2°C should be viewed as a defense line rather than a guardrail, a finding that led to the current wording of the long-term goal as limiting atmospheric warming to "well below" 2°C. The report also concluded, albeit with some caveats,[110] that "limiting global warming to below 1.5°C would come with several advantages in terms of coming closer to a safer "guardrail." It would avoid or reduce risks, for example, to food production or unique and threatened systems such

---

104 See, e.g., Alliance of Small Island States (AOSIS), "Declaration on Climate Change 2009," available online: <https://sustainabledevelopment.un.org/content/documents/1566AOSI SSummitDeclarationSept21FINAL.pdf>.
105 Id., preamble, para. 3.
106 UNFCCC, "Copenhagen Accord, Decision 2/CP.15," UN Doc. FCCC/CP/2009/11/Add.1 (30 March 2010), para. 2; Cancun Agreements, n. 65 above.
107 Copenhagen Accord, n. 106 above, para. 12; Cancun Agreements, id., para. 4.
108 Cancun Agreements, id., para. 139.
109 See IPCC, *Climate Change 2014: Synthesis Report. Contribution of Working Groups I, II and III to the Fifth Assessment Report of the Intergovernmental Panel on Climate Change* [Core Writing Team, R.K. Pachauri and L.A. Meyer (eds.)] (Geneva, Switzerland: IPCC, 2014) and n. 62 above.
110 The Report notes explicitly that the science on the 1.5°C warming limit is less robust and that considerations on strengthening the long-term global goal to 1.5°C may have to continue on the basis of new scientific findings. See Subsidiary Body for Scientific and Technological Advice (SBSTA) and Subsidiary Body for Implementation (SBI), "Report on the structured expert dialogue on the 2013–2015 review, Note by the co-facilitators of the structured expert dialogue," UN Doc. FCCC/SB/2015/INF.1 (4 May 2015), p. 33, Message 10 [SED Report].

as coral reefs or many parts of the cryosphere, including the risk of sea level rise."[111]

Importantly for the purposes of this article, the structured expert dialogue considered OA extensively during its four meetings. Two key considerations were extensively discussed during the review process and reflected in the report. First, the review considered the differential impacts of OA in a world with a 1.5°C and 2°C temperature rise. It concluded that, at a temperature rise of 1.5°C, OA impacts would remain at moderate levels compared to high to very high risk for a world with a 2°C temperature rise. Thus, OA was one of the considerations that led to the SED to conclude that a temperature increase of 2°C should be viewed as a defense line.

Secondly, the SED discussed the limitations of working only with a temperature limit. Experts presenting during the process indicated that "a temperature-only limit will not capture all changes in the climate system that follow from GHGs emissions and may thus lead to other changes being overlooked. This is because large-scale climate system responses, including those related to ocean acidification and sea level rise may be affected by more than temperature, or show delayed responses to temperature."[112] One expert explicitly pointed to the SED that OA should be considered in a separate manner.[113] The final Review Report concluded that

> [a] long-term goal defined by a temperature limit serves its purpose well. ... Adding *other limits* to the long-term global goal, such as sea level rise or ocean acidification, *only reinforces the basic finding* emerging from the analysis of the temperature limit, namely *that we need to take urgent and strong action to reduce GHG emissions*. However, the limitations of working only with a temperature limit could be taken into account, for example, by aiming to limit global warming to *below 2 °C*.[114]

These findings are relevant for three main reasons. First, although the global long-term goal is stated as a limit to global warming, it was drafted taking into consideration, at least partially, the impacts of OA. Thus, despite the lack of explicit recognition in the Paris Agreement, it indirectly addresses OA.

Second, it opens the door for OA to have a more formal and significant role in interpreting the ambiguities and flexibility inherent in the Paris targets in

---

111   Id.
112   Id., p. 8.
113   Id., p. 161.
114   Id., p. 8, Message 1 (emphasis in the original).

Articles 2 and 4. Those targets include open-ended expressions like holding the increase in the global average temperature to "well below" 2°C, "pursuing efforts" to limit the temperature increase to 1.5°C, reaching global peaking of GHG emissions "as soon as possible," and achieving a balance between anthropogenic emissions by sources and removals by sinks of GHGs in the "second half of this century." Knowledge of OA and its impacts on ocean ecosystems integrity could, and should, be considered in the interpretation of the Paris target through the systematic review mechanism embedded in the Paris Agreement.[115]

Lastly, the desirability of selecting a specific OA target (and maybe other targets) in the future along with atmospheric temperature has been installed in the debates and processes of the climate regime, as shown by some recent developments. The scientific community, for example, is working on a set of climate vital signs or indicators (including OA), which would provide information on the state of the planet as well as inform climate action, including NDCs, adaptation, and loss and damage planning.[116] These efforts have been welcomed by the CoP.[117] In the context of the "reasons for concern" framework adopted by the IPCC for its assessment since 2003, the IPCC Fifth Assessment Report included complementary climate change metrics to global mean temperature change. These complementary climate change metrics include the risk for marine species impacted by OA (alone or acting together with ocean warming).[118]

---

115   Paris Agreement, n. 1 above, art. 14; see "Paris Mechanisms of Increased Ambition" below.
116   See Global Climate Observing System, *The Global Observing System for Climate* (World Meteorological Organization, 2016). The GCOS notes at p. 28 that "[w]hile surface temperature is the indicator fundamental to the aim of the Paris Agreement, it has proved problematic when used alone for communicating the impacts and evolution of climate change and does not cover the range of impacts of concern." See also UNFCCC, "Summary report on the ninth meeting of the research dialogue, Bonn, Germany, 10 May 2017. Note by the Chair of the SBSTA," available online: <https://unfccc.int/topics/science/workstreams/research/research-dialogue>; World Meteorological Organization (WMO), *WMO Statement on the State of the Global Climate in 2017* (WMO, 2018).
117   UNFCCC, "Implementation of the global observing system for climate, Decision 19/CP.22," UN Doc. FCCC/CP/2016/10/Add.2 (31 January 2017).
118   *Climate Change 2014: Synthesis Report*, n. 109 above, p. 66 and Fig. 2.5(b). The burning ember diagrams in Figure 2.5 use rate of warming, OA and sea level rise as complementary metrics of climate-related hazards. A recent study reviews the conceptual basis of the "reasons for concern" framework and the risk judgements made in the IPCC report, including these complementary metrics (O'Neill et al., n. 102 above). It should be noted that OA is also a factor considered in the assessment of the five primary reasons for concern, and in particular in assessing the impacts of OA on unique and threatened systems, i.e., coral reefs (IPCC, *Climate Change 2014: Synthesis Report*, id., pp. 70–73).

Paris Mechanisms of Increased Ambition

A promising avenue for effectively integrating OA under the climate regime is the "ratchet mechanism" or mechanism of increased ambition embedded in the Paris Agreement. Indeed, the Agreement's implementation relies on self-imposed contributions to the long-term goal (the NDCs); a progression and increased ambition clause; and an iterative review process – the global stocktake – that allows parties to assess the collective progress towards achieving the purpose of the Agreement and its long-term goal in a comprehensive and facilitative manner, considering mitigation, adaptation, and means of implementation and support.[119] This iterative process for implementation and assessment of the Paris Agreement, together with the "flexibility" inherent in the Paris target, offers a procedural opportunity for a formal and substantive consideration of OA and the latest scientific findings on its impacts to marine biodiversity and socioeconomic systems.

Prior to the first NDC cycle, two initiatives under the UNFCCC have the potential to support the integration of OA within the climate regime. They are the Talanoa Dialogue and the Ocean Pathway.

The decision adopted by the 2015 UNFCCC CoP in Paris called for the convening of a facilitative dialogue in 2018 to take stock of the collective efforts of the parties in relation to progress towards the long-term goal referred to in Article 4.1 of the Paris Agreement and to inform the preparation of the NDCs. This facilitative dialogue, also known as Talanoa Dialogue,[120] addresses three general topics: Where are we? Where do we want to go? And how do we get there? The Dialogue will be informed by the IPCC special report on global warming of 1.5°C, as well as analytical and policy inputs from parties, stakeholders, and expert institutions.

The Ocean Pathway, in turn, seeks to encourage inclusion of ocean matters in the work of the UNFCCC. In particular, the Ocean Pathway strategy considers the inclusion of ocean matters in NDCs as a priority area for action.[121]

Paris Agreement, Adaptation, and OA

While early efforts of the climate regime negotiation were focused on mitigation, it soon became clear that a crucial part of the international response to

---

119 Paris Agreement, n. 1 above, art. 14. "The first global stocktake shall be undertaken in 2023 and every 5 years thereafter. The outcome of each global stocktake shall inform Parties in updating and enhancing their NDCs to support the long-term goal."

120 UNFCCC, "Fiji momentum for implementation, Decision 1/CP.23" and "Talanoa Dialogue, Annex II," UN Doc. FCCC/CP/2017/11/Add.1 (8 February 2018). The dialogue was renamed the Talanoa dialogue to reflect that it will be conducted in the spirit of the Pacific tradition of Talanoa.

121 See n. 96 above and accompanying text.

climate change is adaptation to the impacts that cannot be averted.[122] The parties to the UNFCCC developed and expanded the limited provisions on adaptation included in the Convention through work programs, constituted bodies, and special funds.[123] The Paris Agreement strengthens these developments in several ways, and in so doing also strengthens the potential for the climate regime to address OA adaptation.

The Agreement articulated, for the first time, a vision and long-term goal for adaptation.[124] Article 2(1)(b) of the Agreement calls to strengthen the global response to the threat of climate change by increasing the ability to adapt to the adverse impacts of climate change and foster climate resilience. Article 7, in turn, establishes the global goal on adaptation and explicitly links it to the mitigation goal. The global goal on adaptation is to enhance adaptive capacity; strengthen resilience and reduce vulnerability to climate change, with a view to contributing to sustainable development; and ensure an adequate adaptation response in the context of the temperature goal referred to in Article 2. These objectives, together with the reference to ocean ecosystems integrity in the preamble of the Agreement, reaffirm the need for the global community to strengthen oceans resilience,[125] as well as the resilience of socioeconomic systems dependent on marine resources.

The Agreement also considers a mechanism to ensure the achievement of the long-term goal on adaptation. It calls for parties to engage in adaptation planning processes and implementation of actions, including, *inter alia*, for building resilience of socioeconomic and ecological systems.[126] Parties are also required to submit and periodically update adaptation communications, which may include adaptation priorities, implementation and support needs, and adaptation plans and actions.[127] Adaptation communications shall

---

122 See J. Depledge, "Foundations for the Paris Agreement: The legal and policy framework of the United Nations Climate Change Regime," in Klein et al., n. 86 above, chap 2.A, and in particular Figure 2.1, p. 38 and Table 2.1, pp. 39–42.
123 For example, "Adaptation Fund, Decision 7/CP.7," UN Doc. FCCC/CP/2001/13/Add.1 (21 January 2002); "Bali Action Plan, Decision 1/CP.13," UN Doc. FCCC.CP/2007/6/Add.1 (14 March 2008); "Cancun Adaptation Framework, Decision 1/CP.16," UN Doc. FCCC/CP/2010/7/Add.1 (15 March 2011), paras. 11–35.
124 I. Suárez Pérez and A. Churie Kallhauge, "Adaptation (Article 7)," in Klein et al., n. 86 above, chap. 12, p. 203.
125 Resilience is defined by the IPCC as including the capacity of environmental systems, such as oceans, to cope with a hazardous event, trend, or disturbance, responding or reorganizing in ways that maintain their essential function, identity, and structure (IPCC, "Annex II: Glossary," K.J. Mach, S. Planton and C. von Stechow eds., in *Climate Change 2014: Synthesis Report*, n. 118 above, pp. 117–130).
126 Paris Agreement, n. 1 above, art. 7(9), in particular ss. 7(9)(e).
127 Id., art. 7(10) and (11).

be recorded in a public registry;[128] they are also subject to the transparency framework established in Article 13 of the Agreement and a periodic review under the global stocktake.[129]

Paris Agreement, Loss and Damage, and OA

In more recent years, attention has turned to the more controversial[130] topic of loss and damage, i.e., those impacts from climate-related stressors that cannot be avoided through mitigation and adaptation efforts, especially for countries particularly vulnerable to climate change impacts. Loss and damage has been a formal topic of the climate regime since 2007 and has been included in its institutional structure through the Warsaw International Mechanism (WIM) for Loss and Damage and its Executive Committee.[131] It is in the context of loss and damage from slow onset events that the CoP acknowledged OA as an impact of climate change.

The Paris Agreement builds on these developments and strengthens them, particularly by addressing loss and damage in a stand-alone provision separate from adaptation. Article 8 recognizes the importance of averting, minimizing, and addressing loss and damage associated with the adverse effects of climate change, including extreme weather events and slow onset events, and the role of sustainable development in reducing the risk of loss and damage. It calls for parties to enhance understanding, action, and support with respect to loss and damage associated with the adverse effects of climate change. It also provides a non-exhaustive list of potential areas for cooperation and facilitation in this respect (including specific references to slow onset events, non-economic losses, and resilience of communities, livelihoods, and ecosystems). It further recognizes the Warsaw International Mechanism, including the possibility for the CoP to enhance and strengthen it in the future.

---

128 Id., art. 7(12).
129 Id., art. 7(14). The global stocktake has the mandate to address adaptation, including recognizing the adaptation efforts of developing country parties; enhancing the implementation of adaptation action; reviewing the adequacy and effectiveness of adaptation and support provided for adaptation; and reviewing the overall progress made in achieving the global goal on adaptation.
130 The concept has created deep divisions, in particular in relation to the topic of liability and compensation. See Decision 1/CP.21, n. 85 above, para. 52 p. 8; L. Siegele, "Loss and Damage (Article 8)," in Klein et al., n. 86 above, chap. 13.
131 The WIM is tasked with enhancing knowledge and understanding of comprehensive risk management approaches to address loss and damage associated with the adverse effects of climate change, including slow onset impacts; strengthening dialogue, coordination, coherence and synergies among relevant stakeholders; and enhancing action and support, including finance, technology, and capacity-building.

Paris Agreement and OA: the Challenges

The previous section highlighted positive features of the Paris Agreement in relation to OA: the recognition of the ocean-climate interphase in the preamble of the Agreement; the consideration of OA in the preparatory work that led to the drafting of the Paris target; the iterative and adaptive process for the Agreement's implementation; and the strengthened provisions on adaptation and loss and damage. The question remains, however, whether these developments can be considered an adequate and sufficient international response to the main global driver of anthropogenic OA. Indeed, the Paris Agreement fails to formally and explicitly integrate OA in its regulatory scope. Rather, OA remains in the margins of the climate regime. While the long-term goal of the Paris Agreement can be congruent to what is needed to address OA mitigation and adaptation, this does not guarantee that subsequent implementing decisions are consistent as well. Two key areas where those shortcomings may play out are addressed below: the OA mitigations efforts under the Paris Agreement target and the visibility of OA in the preparatory work for the implementation of the Agreement.

OA Mitigation under the Paris Target

The temperature-based, long-term target could lead to mitigation efforts that are not sufficient or are even prejudicial to mitigating OA. A first aspect that highlights this limitation is the scope of the Agreement, which addresses GHGs as a basket. There is no legal obligation for the parties to the Agreement to reduce CO_2 emissions as a priority GHG. While this approach is consistent with the objective of limiting global warming, it is not consistent with mitigation efforts that focus on OA. (It should be noted, however, that long-term global mean surface warming is mainly driven by CO_2 rather than short-lived radiative forces,[132] and a priority to reduce CO_2 is therefore implicit in the long-term target.)

Another limitation that stands out from the SED Review is the lack of precautionary concern regarding the potential impacts of OA. Indeed, the IPCC Fifth Assessment Report considers that OA poses substantial risk to marine ecosystems, especially polar ecosystems and coral reefs, in medium to high emission scenarios,[133] while the risk remains moderate in low emission scenarios.[134] The

---

132   *Climate Change 2014: Synthesis Report*, n. 118 above, pp. 8, 84.
133   Field et al., n. 109 above, p. 17. Medium and high-emission scenarios include the scenarios in Representative Concentration Pathways (RCP) 4.5 (550–650 µatm); RCP 6.0 (651–870 µatm), and RCP 8.5 (851–1370 µatm, falling within the 1371–2900 µatm category by 2150).
134   Id., p. 17.

Report adds, however, that OA acts together with other global and local changes, which can lead to interactive, complex, and amplified impacts for species and ecosystems.[135] Thus, considering OA together with ocean warming, risks to the marine ecosystems are already high in the stringent mitigation scenarios considered consistent with the Paris Agreement (Representative Concentration Pathway (RCP) 2.6).[136]

A recent study updating the information contained in the IPCC Assessment, in turn, concludes that the risks of harmful ecosystem effects of OA are considered moderate around CO_2 levels of 380 ppm.[137] This threshold was set based on observed declines of calcification of foraminifera and pteropods, attributed to anthropogenic OA, and the negative impacts on pteropods and oyster cultures along the west coast of North America, attributed to upwelling of acidified water combined with anthropogenic acidification.[138] Under OA only (i.e., warming excluded), the transition to high risk is assessed to occur at a CO_2 level of about 500 ppm, beyond which studies reflect onset of significantly negative effects and high risk in 20–50 percent of calcifying taxa (corals, echinoderms, and molluscs). Risks are judged to be very high with limited capability to adapt beyond about 700 ppm, based on a rising percentage of the calcifying taxa being negatively affected. However, the study also concludes that the combined pressures of ocean warming extremes and acidification leads to a shift in sensitivity thresholds to lower CO_2 concentrations.

Other policy-relevant publications also cast doubt about the adequacy of the Paris target to prevent serious impacts of OA. Some of the early studies have suggested OA-targets that are aligned with pathways of emissions consistent with the Paris target. For example, one of the earliest policy recommendations calls for limiting cumulative future anthropogenic emissions of CO_2 to considerably less than 900 GtC by 2100.[139] Studies have called for limiting the average drop of pH near surface waters to 0.2 units relative to pre-industrial levels,[140] a level that would be achieved if the atmospheric concentration of CO_2 is limited to 450 ppm by 2100.[141] Other studies, however, have called for

---

135   Id. See also M. Steinacher, F. Joos and T.F. Stocker, "Allowable carbon emissions lowered by multiple climate targets," *Nature* 499 (2013): 197–201.
136   *Climate Change 2014: Synthesis Report*, n. 118 above, p. 66 and Fig. 2.5(b).
137   O'Neill et al., n. 102 above.
138   Id., pp. 33–34.
139   The Royal Society, n. 11 above.
140   Schubert et al., n. 45 above.
141   Id.; M. Gehlen et al., "Projected pH reductions by 2100 might put deep North Atlantic biodiversity at risk," *Biogeosciences* 11 (2014): 6955–6967; Steinacher et al., n. 28 above; O. Hoegh-Guldberg et al., "Coral reefs under rapid climate change and ocean acidification,"

stabilization of average concentration of CO_2 in the atmosphere to 350 ppm, a concentration level that has already been significantly exceeded.[142]

An additional aspect of concern is the uncertainties in the climate sensitivity and in the remaining CO_2 budget consistent with the Paris target. This results from different methodologies and assumptions, including estimated present warming, projected non-CO_2 emissions, and the precise definitions of the Paris target.[143] Several very different remaining "carbon budgets" have been presented by the scientific community,[144] including recent studies that have significantly increased the carbon budget estimated by the IPCC in its last assessment report.[145] While an increased carbon budget would be welcome news for global warming policy, it would have a significant negative impact on oceans' biogeochemistry.[146]

Lack of precaution is shown also from the early efforts to achieve the Paris target as reflected in the first NDCs pledges submitted by parties. Recent studies assess that full implementation of unconditional NDCs to 2030, assuming comparable action afterwards and until the end of the century, is consistent

---

Science 318, no. 5857 (2007): 1737–1742; J.-P. Gattuso et al., "Contrasting futures for ocean and society from different anthropogenic CO_2 emissions scenarios," *Science* 349, no. 6243 (2015): DOI: 10.1126/science.aac4722. Based on the scientific information considered by the last IPCC Assessment Report, a concentration pathway consistent with the Agreement's target (RCP 2.6) projects a change in global-mean surface ocean pH in the range of 0.06 to 0.07 (15% to 17% increase in acidity) between 1986–2005 and 2081–2100 (and thus in addition to the 30% increase in acidity experienced since pre-industrial times) (IPCC, "Summary for Policymakers," in *Climate Change 2014: Synthesis Report*, n. 118 above, p. 12).

142 J.E.N. Veron et al., "The coral reef crisis: The critical importance of <350 ppm CO_2," *Marine Pollution Bulletin* 58 (2009): 1428–1436. Atmospheric CO_2 levels measured at Mauna Loa Observatory, Hawaii, have permanently exceeded 400 ppm since 2016. In 2018, measurement exceeded 410 ppm, NASA, "Carbon Dioxide," Global Climate Change, available online: <https://climate.nasa.gov/vital-signs/carbon-dioxide/>; B. Kahn, "We Just Breached the 410 Parts Per Million Threshold," Climate Central (20 April 2017), available online: <http://www.climatecentral.org/news/we-just-breached-the-410-parts-per-million-threshold-21372>).

143 G.P. Peters, "Beyond carbon budgets," *Nature Geoscience* 11 (2018): 378–383.

144 J. Rogelj et al., "Differences between carbon budget estimates unravelled," *Nature Climate Change* 6 (2016): 245–252; Peters, id.

145 R.J. Millar et al., "Emission budgets and pathways consistent with limiting warming to 1.5 °C," *Nature Geoscience* 10 (2017): 741–748, doi: 10.1038/NGEO3031.

146 In a recent study addressing the importance of understanding the direct biological and chemical effects of CO_2 at different global warming levels, Betts and McNeall conclude that the "range of possible strengths of the direct effects of CO_2 on ocean acidification, photosynthesis, and plant water-use efficiency at 2°C (and also 1.5°C) could therefore extend substantially higher or slightly lower than is accounted for in studies that use the CMIP5 multimodel ensemble" (R.A. Betts and D. McNeall, "How much CO_2 at 1.5 °C and 2 °C?," *Nature Climate Change* 8 (2018): 546–548, p. 547).

with a global average temperature increase of about 3.2°C relative to pre-industrial levels with greater than 66 percent probability by 2100.[147] Additionally, current policies are not on track to fulfill the national pledges.[148] Lacking an immediate and unprecedented effort to increase the level of ambition, the mechanism of the Paris Agreement will fall far short of avoiding dangerous impacts to the climate system, including both warming and OA.

Although the IPCC indicated that global warming is independent of specific emission pathways,[149] delays in implementing ambitious mitigation efforts may result in more direct consequences for OA. Studies show that the impacts on ocean biogeochemistry (and other impacts of climate change) are dependent on the emission pathway.[150] Thus, peaking GHG emissions as soon as possible and achieving a balance between anthropogenic emissions by sources and removals by sinks, as required by Article 4 of the Agreement, is crucial for mitigating the impacts of OA.

Further concerns relating to OA are raised by the increasing emphasis on "wise overshoot" strategies to achieve the Paris targets.[151] As it seems increasingly unlikely that 1.5°C or 2°C warming can be completely avoided, scientists and policy-makers have relied on "overshoot" scenarios, i.e., scenarios where the GHG emission budget and global temperature exceed the long-term goal for a certain period but are later stabilized with the deployment of negative emission technologies. Negative emission technologies intentionally remove

---

147 M. den Elzen, N. Höhne and K. Jian (leading authors), "The emissions gaps and its implications," in *Emissions Gap Report: A UNEP Synthesis Report* (Nairobi: UNEP, 2017), chap. 3. The analysis is consistent with the assessment of the Climate Action Tracker, available online: <https://climateactiontracker.org/>. Note, however, the uncertainties regarding climate sensitivity described above.

148 See online: <https://climateactiontracker.org/>.

149 IPCC, "Summary for Policymakers," in *Climate Change 2014: Synthesis Report*, n. 118 above, p. 8.

150 K. Zickfeld, V.K. Arora and N.P. Gillet, "Is the climate response to CO_2 emissions path dependent?," *Geophysical Research Letters* 39 (2012): <https://doi.org/10.1029/2011GL050205>; P.L. Pfister and T.F. Stocker, "Earth system commitments due to delayed mitigation," *Environmental Research Letters* 11 (2016): doi:10.1088/1748-9326/11/1/014010. Emission path dependency has also been observed in studies addressing other impacts of climate change, and in particular thermosteric sea level rise (Zickfeld et al., id; N. Bouttes, J.M. Gregory and J.A. Lowe, "The reversibility of sea level rise," *Journal of Climate* 26 (2013): 2502–2513).

151 J.C. Minx et al., "Negative emissions Part 1: Research landscape and synthesis," *Environmental Research Letters* 13, no. 6 (2018): 063001, p. 21; T. Gasser et al., "Negative emissions physically needed to keep global warming below 2 °C," *Nature Communications* 6 (2015): 7958.

CO_2 from the atmosphere.[152] Oceans, however, have different time responses to emissions. This means that an overshoot strategy will affect the ocean's biogeochemistry, particularly in the deep ocean, for significantly longer periods of time.[153] Such a strategy would commit to a higher level of OA associated with the original increased CO_2 emissions, but with acidity not reverting after deploying negative emission technologies in a time scale relevant for society.

An overshoot strategy that relies on negative emission technologies to ultimately achieve temperature targets has an additional problem for OA: the potential impacts of the negative emission technologies themselves. That concern extends more generally to geoengineering, i.e., the deliberate large-scale manipulation of the planetary environment to counteract anthropogenic climate change.[154] While geoengineering is controversial on moral, social, and economic grounds,[155] it has received increased attention in recent years in light of the patently insufficient emissions reductions by States.[156]

Climate geoengineering technologies are usually divided in two categories: solar radiation management approaches and carbon dioxide removal approaches.[157] Solar radiation management approaches focus on reducing the amount of solar radiation absorbed by the earth, through options like sulphur aerosol injection, marine cloud brightening, or space-based systems.[158] Studies

---

152 Note that there are different interpretations on which technologies can be considered NETs. Some authors include only technologies that remove CO_2 after they have been released to the atmosphere (Minx et al., id., p. 4), while other authors include in this category technologies that capture CO_2 immediately at the site of production (Gasser et al., id., p. 2).

153 S. Mathesius et al., "Long-term response of oceans to CO_2 removal from the atmosphere," *Nature Climate Change* 15 (2015): 1107–1114.

154 The Royal Society, *Geoengineering the Climate: Science, Governance and Uncertainty* (London: The Royal Society, 2009), available online: <https://royalsociety.org/topics-policy/publications/2009/geoengineering-climate/>.

155 Id.; W.C.G. Burns, "The Paris Agreement and Climate Geoengineering Governance: The Need for a Human Rights-based Component," CIGI Papers no. 111 (October 2016); Minx et al., n. 151 above.

156 Burns, id.; Minx et al., id.

157 Burns, id. But some authors criticize subsuming two very different technology clusters under one heading (see Minx et al., id., p. 5). For an extensive analysis of geoengineering technologies, see the upcoming Report by the GESAMP Working Group on Marine Geoengineering including Ocean Fertilization (IMO, "Progress made by the GESAMP Working Group on Marine Geoengineering, Note by the Secretariat," IMO Doc. LC40/5, 3 August 2018).

158 Burns, id.

consider that these technologies could begin to return temperatures to pre-industrial levels within a few years of deployment and restore temperatures to those levels by the end of the century.[159] Solar radiation management, however, does not address the root cause of global warming (CO_2 concentrations in the atmosphere) and thus leaves OA unabated. In addition, actual or even potential reliance on SRM could provide disincentives for immediate and substantive mitigation efforts, potentially aggravating OA.

Approaches to carbon dioxide removal from the atmosphere include technologies such as ocean fertilization, bioenergy with carbon capture and storage, or direct air capture, and their impact on ocean biogeochemistry varies. The incorporation of nutrients to the marine environment to stimulate phytoplankton production and enhance carbon dioxide uptake (iron fertilization) can substantially increase OA[160] and has thus been restricted under the 1996 Protocol to the London Convention 1972.[161] That is also the case of carbon capture and storage in the ocean column.[162] While carbon capture and storage in the ocean seabed does not exacerbate OA, the risks of leakage represent a threat that needs to be considered. Sectoral and geographic fragmentation of governance arrangements with competence to address geoengineering projects present further challenges to an explicit consideration of their OA implications,[163] in particular in the context of a legal framework that calls for action based on warming alone.

Further information to assess the adequacy of the Paris target to address OA and its impacts on marine ecosystems may be provided by the upcoming IPCC's special report on the impacts of global warming of 1.5°C above pre-industrial levels and related GHGs emission pathways, scheduled to be released in the fall of 2018, and the IPCC special report on the ocean and cryosphere in a changing climate, scheduled to be released in the summer of 2019.[164] It remains to be seen, however, how the outcomes of these reports will influence parties' individual and collective climate action.

---

159 Id., p. 6.
160 Id., p. 15.
161 36 *International Legal Materials* 1 (1997) (entered into force 24 March 2006, as amended in 2013); Resolution LC/LP.1 (2008) on the Regulation of Ocean Fertilization adopted by the Thirteenth Meeting of the Contracting Parties to the London Convention and the Third Meeting of the Contracting Parties to the London Protocol, available online: <http://www.imo.org/en/OurWork/Environment/LCLP/Pages/default.aspx>.
162 1996 Protocol to the London Convention, id.
163 G. Wilson, "Murky waters: Ambiguous international law for ocean fertilization and other geoengineering," *Texas International Law Journal* 49 (2014): 507–558.
164 See online: <http://www.ipcc.ch>.

OA in the Preparatory Work for the Implementation of Paris Agreement

The limited and indirect references to OA in the climate regime have perpetuated the marginal attention to mitigation of, and adaptation to, OA under the preparatory work for the implementation of the Paris Agreement. For example, there has been no consideration of OA, or oceans more generally, in the work of the Ad-hoc Working Group on the Paris Agreement, tasked to develop further guidance on features of NDCs and the modalities of, and sources of inputs to, the global stocktake.[165] Similarly, there have been only a few submissions to the Talanoa Dialogue that have addressed the links between emissions in the atmosphere and OA.[166]

Individually, parties to the Agreement have also failed to raise the profile of OA. While international initiatives have strongly advocated for inclusion of oceans in NDCs and the global stocktake,[167] OA is rarely considered in the preparation of the mitigation commitments. From the 148 NDCs submitted by September, 2018, representing 176 parties,[168] only 15 mention OA.[169] This is a meek number, even compared to the subset of NDCs that refer to marine issues. Only one NDC addresses OA with more emphasis than a general reference. Nauru's national commitment stresses the urgent need for an assessment of impacts and risks at different levels of CO_2 concentration and warming, especially the

---

165 Decision 1/CP.21, n. 85 above, paras. 7, 8, 26, 100, and 102. The Ad-Hoc Working Group has dealt with the CoP request during the five parts of its first session between 2016 and 2018, and aims at submitting the finalized guidance to CoP 24, acting as the first meeting of the parties to the Paris Agreement, in December 2018.

166 UNFCCC, "Overview of Inputs to the Talanoa Dialogue" (23 April 2018), para. 44, available online: <https://unfccc.int/inputs-to-the-talanoa-dialogue-where-do-we-want-to-go#eq-1>. See also UNFCCC, "Inputs to the Talanoa Dialogue: Where Are We?," available online: <https://unfccc.int/inputs-to-the-talanoa-dialogue-where-are-we#eq-3>. Some of the submissions that address the risks of OA in more detail include the submissions by the Climate Institute, the International Coastal and Ocean Organization, the World Meteorological Organization, and the Global Coral Reef Alliance (but in the latter case to point out that OA is not an existential threat to corals and that the focus on OA is misguided).

167 See, e.g., "Because the Ocean: Towards Ocean related NDCs. Key messages from the Because the Ocean workshop held during UNFCCC COP23, 5 November 2017," available online: <http://www.vardagroup.org/wp-content/uploads/2017/11/BtO_Workshop_COP23_Report_final.pdf>; Ocean Pathway, available online: <https://cop23.com.fj/the-ocean-pathway/>.

168 See UNFCCC, "NDC Registry (interim)," online: <http://www4.unfccc.int/ndcregistry/Pages/All.aspx>. The parties include the European Union and its 28 Member States, who jointly submitted one NDC.

169 See also N.D. Gallo, D.G. Victor and L.A. Levin, "Ocean commitments under the Paris Agreement," *Nature Climate Change* 7 (2017): 833–838, with results consistent to those presented here.

risks of OA, global and regional sea level rise, and irreversible changes in the physical, ecological, and human systems.[170] Only one NDC makes a distinct emission reduction commitment for CO_2,[171] while a few others include CO_2 as the only gas covered in their commitments.

In relation to adaptation, the climate regime has not substantively addressed OA either, despite specific mandates to focus on adaptation of ecosystems, including marine and coastal ecosystems.[172] None of the NDCs include OA specific adaptation actions (although several included blue carbon or restoration of coastal mangroves as an adaptation action with mitigation co-benefit). Only a few parties have included references to OA in other submissions on adaptation (National Adaptation Plans,[173] National Adaptation Programmes of Actions,[174] or as part of national communications[175]). Relevant adaptation actions for OA in the adaptation submission include, for example, the generation of knowledge through monitoring and research,[176] macro-zoning of environmental carbon sequestration and carbon-sink coastal ecosystems,[177] the assessment of species relevant for fisheries and aquaculture under different climatic conditions,[178] or the exploration of new species for aquaculture.[179]

---

170 See Republic of Nauru, "Intended Nationally Determined Contribution (INDC) Under the United Nations Convention on Climate Change" (submitted 7 April 2016), available online: <http://www4.unfccc.int/ndcregistry/Pages/All.aspx>.

171 See Oriental Republic of Uruguay, "First Nationally Determined Contribution to the Paris Agreement, approved by Executive Order number 310 in November 3rd of 2017, in the framework of the Paris Agreement ratified by the Oriental Republic of Uruguay on October 19th, 2016" (unofficial translation), available online: <http://www4.unfccc.int/ndcregistry/Pages/All.aspx>.

172 UNFCC, "Nairobi work programme on impacts, vulnerability and adaptation to climate change, Decision 17/CP.19," UN Doc. FCCC/CP/2013/10/Add.2/Rev.1 (25 September 2014); Decision 1/CP.16, n. 65 above.

173 See UNFCCC, "National Adaptation Plans," available online: <https://unfccc.int/topics/adaptation-and-resilience/workstreams/national-adaptation-plans>.

174 See UNFCCC, "Submitted NAPAs," available online: <https://unfccc.int/topics/resilience/workstreams/national-adaptation-programmes-of-action/napas-received>.

175 See UNFCCC, "Reporting and Review under the Convention," available online: <https://unfccc.int/process#:0c4d2d14-7742-48fd-982e-d52b41b85bb0:f666393f-34f5-45d6-a44e-8d03be236927>.

176 Government of Brazil, "National Adaptation Plan to Climate Change, General Strategy, Volume I" (10 May 2016), available online: <http://www4.unfccc.int/nap/News/pages/national_adaptation_plans.aspx>.

177 Id.

178 Gobierno de Chile, Plan de Adaptación al Cambio Climático para Pesca y Acuicultura (Ministerio de Economía, Fomento y Turismo, Subsecretaria de Pesca, y Ministerio del Medio Ambiente, Santiago, 2015).

179 Id.

The lack of specific adaptation actions to OA may be explained by a combination of factors. They include the generally limited recognition of OA in the climate regime and the uncertainty regarding OA impacts on species, communities, and ecosystems. Furthermore, there is generally limited adaptation potential to OA. The academic literature has suggested a range of innovative yet untested methods to address OA (among other stressors). These include protective culturing, selective breeding, or genetic engineering; chemical or geochemical modification of seawater; or artificially increasing the "storage life" of marine organic matter, therefore reducing its degradation and subsequent release of CO_2.[180]

Adaptation actions that strengthen the resilience of oceans are also relevant for OA, as increased resilience and reduction of other anthropogenic stressors increases the prospects for ecosystems to withstand acidified conditions.[181] Proposals such as establishing mobile marine protected areas or reducing fishing pressure are viewed as beneficial to alleviating the impacts of OA.[182]

Particularly important is the work of the Warsaw International Mechanism on slow onset events, considering the explicit reference to OA. Slow onset events have been a focus of the Warsaw International Mechanism in the initial two-year working program (2015–2016)[183] and the current five-year rolling workplan,[184] and the Executive Committee has formed an expert group on the topic.

Activities undertaken under the work program on slow onset events include, for example, the development of an online database containing relevant information on over 160 organizations working on the topic,[185] as well as an

---

180 G.H. Rau, E.L. McLeod and O. Hoegh-Guldberg, "The need for new ocean conservation strategies in a high-carbon dioxide world," *Nature Climate Change* 2 (2012): 720–724. See also UNFCCC, "Slow-onset events," Technical paper, UN Doc. FCCC/TP/2012/7 (26 November 2012), available online: <https://unfccc.int/sites/default/files/resource/docs/2012/tp/07.pdf>.
181 Rau et al., n. 180 above, p. 1.
182 "Slow-onset events," n. 180 above, p. 19.
183 UNFCCC, "Report of the Executive Committee of the Warsaw International Mechanism for Loss and Damage associated with Climate Change Impacts," UN Doc. FCCC/SB/2014/4 (24 October 2014), Annex II.
184 UNFCCC, "Report of the Executive Committee of the Warsaw International Mechanism for Loss and Damage associated with Climate Change Impacts," UN Doc. FCCC/SB/2017/1/Add.1 (2 November 2017), Annex.
185 UNFCCC, "Report of the Executive Committee of the Warsaw International Mechanism for Loss and Damage associated with Climate Change Impacts," UN Doc. FCCC/SB/2016/3 (14 October 2016), p. 5. Thirty-six organizations in the database report work on OA. Database available online: <http://www4.unfccc.int/sites/NWP/Pages/soesearch.aspx>.

assessment of the scope of their work.[186] This assessment concluded that, in many geographic regions, OA is one of the areas where the least effort has been devoted. Furthermore, the efforts have focused on enhancing knowledge and understanding and on strengthening dialogue, coordination, and coherence. Efforts addressing action and support (including investment and implementation and support) are minimal, even in those regions where OA has received relatively more attention. In some regions, efforts focusing on action and support are absent altogether.

The work on approaches to address loss and damage associated with slow onset events is still in early stages.[187] The Warsaw International Mechanism has recognized the need to think of innovative financial instruments and ways for collaboration and partnership to enhance action and support in this area.[188] With OA being singled out as one of the most difficult slow onset events to address,[189] this work is a promising and much needed avenue to further understanding of OA with a focus on its consequences for ecological and socioeconomic systems. It remains to be seen whether it would provide concrete guidance and support for the adoption of adaptive measures for marine species or ecosystems impacted by OA.

Other International Responses

While getting a grip on international OA responses outside the climate change regime is difficult due to the fragmented array of OA-related conferences,[190]

---

186   UNFCCC, "The scope of work undertaken on slow onset events (SOEs) as reported by partners in the SOEs database" (February 2018), available online: <https://unfccc.int/sites/default/files/resource/activity_b_soe_assesment_feb_2018.pdf>.

187   UNFCCC, "Report on the Evaluation of Proposals for Hosting the Climate Technology Centre," UN Doc. FCCC/SBI/2012/INF.14 (23 April 2012), para. 63, p. 23.

188   Executive Committee of the Warsaw International Mechanism for Loss & Damage, "Breaking new ground: Risk financing for slow onset events," Side Event Summary Note (November 2017); A. Durand et al., "Financing options for loss and damage: A review and roadmap," Discussion Paper 21/2016 (Bonn: Deutsches Institute für Entwicklung/German Development Institute, 2016).

189   UNFCCC, "Slow onset events," n. 180 above, p. 16.

190   For example, in June 2017, the UN Conference to Support the Implementation of Sustainable Development Goal 14 was convened, which in its outcome document, "Our ocean, our future: Call for action," emphasized the need for effective adaption and mitigation measures to support resilience to ocean and coastal acidification. See UNGA, "Our Ocean, Our Future: Call for Action," UN Doc. A/RES/71/312 (14 July 2017), Annex.

networks,[191] partnerships,[192] and coordination mechanisms,[193] three main response avenues stand out. They include UN General Assembly resolutions and processes; consideration of climate change and OA under multilateral environmental agreements (MEAs); and efforts towards limiting CO_2 emissions from ships and aircraft through the International Maritime Organization (IMO) and the International Civil Aviation Organization (ICAO), respectively. A review of regional responses to ocean acidity and climate change, for example, through regional fisheries management organizations (RFMOs)[194] and regional sea programs[195] is beyond the scope of this article.

UN General Assembly Resolutions and Processes

The UN General Assembly annual resolutions on oceans and the law of the sea and on sustainable fisheries continue to recognize OA as a major concern. For example, the oceans and law of the sea resolution, adopted on 5 December 2017, refers to OA as one of the greatest environmental concerns of our

---

191   For example, the Global Ocean Acidification Observing Network (GOA-ON) encourages the sharing of OA scientific observations around the globe and includes regional hubs for Latin America, North America, Africa, and the Western Pacific. For details, see J.A. Newton et al., *Global Ocean Acidification Observing Network: Requirements and Governance Plan*, 2nd ed. (2015), available online: <http://www.goa.on.org/docs/GOA-ON_plan_print.pdf>. The International Alliance to Combat Ocean Acidification (OA Alliance) is an international network of governments and organizations devoted to encouraging actions to reduce the causes of OA. See OA Alliance, "About Us," available online: <https://www.oaalliance.org/about/>.

192   For example, under the Global Programme of Action for the Protection of the Marine Environment from Land-based Activities (GPA), multi-stakeholder partnerships have been formed to address nutrient management and wastewater treatment, both important to reducing ocean acidity. For a critique of the GPA and its role in addressing OA, see Fennel and VanderZwaag, n. 13 above, p. 353.

193   For example, the Ocean Acidification International Coordination Centre (OA-ICC), established in 2012 and operating under the auspices of the International Atomic Energy Agency, aims to promote OA science, capacity-building, and communication. See OA-ICC, "About the project," available online: <http://www.iaea.org/ocean-acidification/page.php?page=2178>.

194   For a recent review of RFMO capabilities to address climate change, see B. Pentz et al., "Can regional fisheries management organizations (RFMOs) manage resources effectively during climate change?," *Marine Policy* 92 (2018): 13–20.

195   UN Environment Regional Seas Programme, coordinating 18 regional seas conventions and action plans, has designated increasing resilience to climate change as one of its strategic directions but without a specific reference to OA. See UN Environment, "Regional Seas Strategic Directions (2017–2020)," Regional Seas Reports and Studies No. 201 (2016).

time,[196] urges States to make significant efforts to tackle the causes of ocean acidification,[197] and calls on States and other competent international organizations and relevant institutions to urgently pursue further research on OA and to increase national, regional, and global efforts to address levels of ocean acidity and the negative impact of such acidity on vulnerable marine ecosystems, particularly coral reefs.[198] The sustainable fisheries resolution of December 2017 urges States, either directly or through subregional, regional, or global organizations or arrangements, to intensify efforts to assess and address the impacts of global climate change and OA on the sustainability of fish stocks and habitats that support them.[199] The resolution also calls upon States, individually or through regional fisheries management organizations or arrangements to take into account the potential impacts of climate change and OA in managing deep-sea fisheries and protecting vulnerable marine ecosystems.[200]

Various UN processes have also placed OA on the radar screen. The UN Open-ended Informal Consultative Process on Oceans and the Law of the Sea extensively addressed OA during the 2017 meeting, which focused on the effects of climate change on oceans.[201] The resumed Review Conference of the UN Fish Stock Agreement, held in 2016, also highlighted the threat of OA to the health and resilience of the ocean. It further called upon States, individually or collectively through regional fisheries management organizations or arrangements, to strengthen efforts to study and address environmental factors affecting marine ecosystems, including adverse impacts of OA, and, where possible, to consider such impacts in establishing conservation and management measures for straddling fish stocks and highly migratory fish stocks.[202]

---

196 Together with marine debris, climate change, and loss of biodiversity. United Nations General Assembly (UNGA), "Oceans and the law of the sea," UN Doc. A/RES/72/73 (4 January 2018), para. 188.
197 Id., para. 194.
198 Id., para. 190.
199 UNGA, "Sustainable fisheries," UN Doc. A/RES/72/72 (19 January 2018), adopted on 5 December 2017, para. 10.
200 Id., para. 189.
201 UNGA, "Report on the work of the United Nations Open-ended Informal Consultative Process on Oceans and the Law of the Sea at its eighteenth meeting," UN Doc. A/72/95 (16 June 2017).
202 UNGA, "Report of the resumed Review Conference on the Agreement for the Implementation of the Provisions of the United Nations Convention on the Law of the Sea of 10 December 1982 relating to the Conservation and Management of Straddling Fish Stocks and Highly Migratory Fish Stocks," UN Doc. A/CONF.210/2016/5 (1 August 2016), para. 40, Annex preamble para. 8, Annex Section A paras. 4 and 14.

The Sustainable Development Goals (SDGs) and Targets under the UN 2030 Agenda for Sustainable Development[203] includes a specific target on OA under SDG 14 on conservation and sustainable use of the oceans, seas, and marine resources for sustainable development. Target 14.3 calls for minimizing and addressing the impacts of ocean acidification, including through enhanced scientific cooperation at all levels.

Multilateral Environmental Agreements
Convention on Biological Diversity

Beyond the specific Aichi Biodiversity Target relating to OA, adopted in 2010 by Convention on Biological Diversity (CBD)[204] parties, calling for the minimization of multiple human pressures on coral reefs and other vulnerable ecosystems impacted by climate change or ocean acidification,[205] the CBD has addressed climate change and OA through further decisions and reports. Through Decision XIII/11, adopted at the thirteenth meeting of CBD parties in December 2016, a voluntary workplan was embraced to address biodiversity in cold-water areas where habitats such as corals and sponge fields may be especially vulnerable to OA. The workplan calls for various actions, including strengthening management of the multiple stressors on cold-water biodiversity, particularly fisheries, land-based and seabed pollution, hydrocarbon extraction, seabed mining and undersea cables;[206] increasing spatial coverage and management effectiveness of marine protected areas and other area-based conservation measures in cold-water areas;[207] and improving the understanding of how climate change, OA, and other human-induced stressors all impact the health and long-term viability of cold-water organisms and habitats.[208]

Through Decision XIII/28, also adopted in 2016, CBD parties agreed to a set of indicators for assessing progress in meeting the Aichi Biodiversity Targets. A specific indicator was included for assessing progress in minimizing OA pressures on coral reefs, namely, the average marine acidity (pH) measured at an agreed suite of representative sampling stations.[209]

---

203   UNGA, "Transforming our world: the 2030 Agenda for Sustainable Development," UN Doc. A/RES/70/1 (21 October 2015), adopted on 25 September 2015.
204   Convention on Biological Diversity, 5 June 1992, 1760 *United Nations Treaty Series* 79.
205   CBD, Decision X/2 (2010), "Strategic Plan for Biodiversity 2001–2020," Annex, Target 10.
206   CBD, Decision XIII/11 (2016), "Voluntary Specific Workplan on Biodiversity in Cold-Water Areas Within the Jurisdictional Scope of the Convention," Annex II, para. 5.2.
207   Id., Annex II, para. 5.3.
208   Id., Annex II, para. 5.4.
209   CBD, Decision XIII/28 (2016), "Indicators for the Strategic Plan for Biodiversity 2011–2020 and the Aichi Biodiversity Targets," Annex.

A 2016 CBD decision on biodiversity and climate change welcomed the conclusion of the Paris Agreement and its articles related to biodiversity.[210] The decision encourages parties and other governments to fully take into account the importance of ensuring the integrity of all ecosystems, including oceans, when developing their NDC.[211]

In 2016, a decision was also adopted on climate-related geoengineering.[212] The decision reaffirms the need for following a precautionary approach to geoengineering activities[213] and emphasizes that climate change should be primarily addressed by reducing anthropogenic emissions by sources and by increasing removals by sinks of GHGs under the UNFCCC.[214]

Various reports relevant to climate change and OA have also been issued post-Paris under CBD auspices. In April, 2016, the Executive Secretary prepared an information document on biodiversity and acidification in cold-water areas.[215] The document highlights the many concerns surrounding OA in cold-water areas, including a projection that aragonite saturation will become much shallower by 2100, leaving about 70 percent of cold-water coral reefs in under-saturated seawater,[216] and a conclusion that pteropods (planktonic sea snails) are at particular risk from OA.[217] The document emphasizes the need for future research on OA to include a look at other stressors, such as temperature and deoxygenation, as will occur under field conditions.[218]

Three key CBD technical reports have also been published. Those reports cover a synthesis of case studies on national experiences with ecosystem-based approaches to climate change adaptation;[219] a review of knowledge and recommendations to support ecosystem-based mitigation actions, such as restoring and protecting seagrass beds, salt marshes and mangroves;[220]

---

210 CBD, Decision XIII/4 (2016), "Biodiversity and Climate Change," para. 1.
211 Id., para. 2.
212 CBD, Decision XIII/14 (2016), Climate-related geoengineering.
213 Id., para. 2.
214 Id., para. 3.
215 UNEP, "Background Document on Biodiversity and Acidification in Cold-Water-Areas," UNEP/CBD/SBSTTA/20/INF/25 (8 April 2016).
216 Id., p. 5.
217 Id., p. 6.
218 Id., p. 7.
219 V. Lo, "Synthesis report on experiences with ecosystem-based approaches to climate change adaptation and disaster risk reduction," Technical Series No. 85 (Montreal: Secretariat of the Convention on Biological Diversity, 2016).
220 C. Epple et al., "Managing ecosystems in the context of climate change mitigation: A review of current knowledge and recommendations to support ecosystem-based mitigation actions that look beyond terrestrial forests," Technical Series No. 86 (Montreal: Secretariat of the Convention on Biological Diversity, 2016).

and an update on climate engineering options and the limited regulatory framework.[221]

Other MEAs

Three other MEAs have given some attention to climate change but without a specific OA focus: the Convention on Migratory Species of Wild Animals, the Convention on the Protection of the World Cultural and Natural Heritage, and the Convention on Wetlands of International Importance (Ramsar Convention).

Under the Convention on Migratory Species of Wild Animals (CMS),[222] parties have continued to give limited attention to climate change.[223] A CMS resolution on climate change and migratory species was adopted in October 2017.[224] The resolution encourages parties to apply strategic environmental assessment and environmental impact assessment processes when developing and implementing relevant climate change mitigation and adaptation actions and to take into account the needs of CMS-listed species.[225] The resolution reaffirms a CMS Programme of Work on Climate Change and Migratory Species which proposes various actions, including the expansion of existing protected area networks to increase the resilience of vulnerable populations to extreme stochastic events, and the undertaking of vulnerability assessments of Appendices I & II listed species.[226] The CMS Strategic Plan for Migratory Species 2015–2023 calls for reducing the multiple human pressures on migratory species and their habitats which may include pressures relating to climate change, renewable energy developments, power lines, bycatch, underwater noise, ship strikes, pollution, invasive species, illegal and unsuitable take, and marine debris.[227]

---

221 P. Williamson and R. Bodle, "Update on Climate Geoengineering in Relation to the Convention on Biological Diversity: Potential Impacts and Regulatory Frameworks," Technical Series No. 84 (Montreal: Secretariat of the Convention on Biological Diversity, 2016).

222 Convention on Migratory Species of Wild Animals, 23 June 1979, 1651 *United Nations Treaty Series* 333.

223 For a previous review of the limited attention, see A. Trouwborst, "Transboundary wildlife conservation in a changing climate: Adaptation of the Bonn Convention on Migratory Species and its daughter instruments to climate change," *Diversity* 4 (2012): 258–300.

224 UN Environment, "Climate Change and Migratory Species," adopted by the Conference of the Parties at its 12th meeting in Manila, UN Doc. UNEP/CMS/Resolution 12.21.

225 Id., para. 3.

226 Id., Annex.

227 UN Environment, "Strategic Plan for Migratory Species 2015–2013," adopted by the Conference of the Parties at its 11th meeting in Quito, 4–9 November 2014, UN Doc. UNEP/CMS/Resolution 11.2.

Under the Convention on the Protection of the World Cultural and Natural Heritage,[228] various developments relating to climate change have emerged post-Paris. In a 2016 decision, the World Heritage Committee (WHC) requested State parties, the World Heritage Centre, and the Advisory Bodies to work with the IPCC with the objective of including a specific chapter on natural and cultural world heritage in future IPCC assessments.[229] A 2017 decision expressed utmost concern regarding the serious impacts of coral bleaching effects on World Heritage properties in 2016–2017 and reiterated the importance of State parties to undertake the most ambitious implementation of the Paris Agreement.[230] The decision also called on all State parties to take all efforts to build resilience of World Heritage properties to climate change, including by reducing to the greatest extent possible all other pressures and threats and by developing and implementing climate adaptation strategies for properties at risk of climate change impacts.[231] A 2016 paper, "The Future of the World Heritage Convention for Marine Conservation: Celebrating 10 Years of the World Heritage Marine Programme,"[232] includes a part on climate change which highlights how the 49 marine sites on the World Heritage list could provide reference points for understanding ocean changes.[233] The publication notes the need for more sites to adopt climate change adaptation plans and gives examples of how some sites are moving towards becoming carbon free in relation to tourism activities.[234]

The United Nations Educational, Scientific and Cultural Organization (UNESCO), under which the World Heritage Convention operates, has also made key moves relating to climate change. The 39th session of UNESCO's General Conference, in 2017, adopted a Declaration of Ethical Principles in relation

---

228 Convention on the Protection of the World Cultural and Natural Heritage, 16 November 1972, 1037 *United Nations Treaty Series* 151.

229 UNESCO, World Heritage Committee, "Decision 40 COM 7: State of Conservation of World Heritage Properties," 40th session of the Committee (Istanbul/UNESCO, 2016).

230 UNESCO, World Heritage Committee, "Decision 41 COM 7: State of Conservation of the Properties Inscribed on the World Heritage List," 41st session of the Committee (Krakow, 2017), paras. 10 and 22.

231 Id., para. 24.

232 R. Casier and F. Douvere, eds., "The Future of the World Heritage Convention for Marine Conservation: Celebrating 10 Years of the World Heritage Marine Programme," World Heritage Papers No. 45 (Paris: UNESCO, 2016).

233 M. Visbeck, P. Marshall and F. Douvere, "Marine World Heritage and Climate Change: Challenges and Opportunities," in id., pp. 23–34.

234 Id., p. 31.

to Climate Change[235] and endorsed an updated UNESCO Strategy for Action on Climate Change 2018–2021.[236]

Pursuant to the Convention on Wetlands of International Importance (Ramsar Convention),[237] parties have previously emphasized the important roles of wetlands in climate change mitigation and adaptation,[238] and more recently, in 2017, the Secretary General of the Convention made a statement to UNFCCC CoP 23 reminding the international community of how the Ramsar Convention can significantly contribute to achieving the Paris Agreement ambitions.[239] The statement emphasized the role of wetlands as being the planet's most effective carbon sinks and highlighted the need for countries to include the potential of wetlands to mitigate or adapt to climate change in NDCs and in national implementation strategies.

IMO and ICAO Efforts

Trying to reduce CO_2 emissions from ships might be described as a "work in progress" within the IMO. At the 70th session of the IMO's Marine Environment Protection Committee (MEPC) in 2016, a roadmap for developing a comprehensive IMO reduction strategy for GHG emissions was agreed to which suggested the adoption of an initial GHG strategy at MEPC 72 (April 2018) and a revised strategy at MEPC 80 (Spring 2023).[240] At MEPC's 72nd session in April 2018, an initial IMO Strategy on Reduction of GHG Emissions from Ships was adopted after considerable debates and compromise.[241] The Strategy sets an ambition to peak GHG emissions from international shipping as soon as possible and to reduce the total annual GHG emissions by at least 50 percent by 2050 compared to 2008 while pursuing efforts towards phasing them out.[242]

---

235   UNESCO, Records of the General Conference, 39th Session, Paris, 30 October–14 November 2017, Vol. 1 Resolutions, Annex III.
236   Id., section IV, para. 15, p. 29.
237   Convention on Wetlands of International Importance, 2 February 1971, 996 *United Nations Treaty Series* 245.
238   Ramsar Resolution X. 24, Climate change and wetlands (2008).
239   Secretary General Martha Rojas Urrego, IGO Statement to UNFCCC CoP 23 on behalf of the Ramsar Convention on Wetlands, "Wetlands crucial in addressing climate change," 15 November 2017, available online: <http://www.ramsar.org>.
240   International Maritime Organization (IMO), "Report of the Marine Environment Protection Committee on Its Seventieth Session," IMO Doc. MEPC 70/18 (11 November 2016), Annex 11.
241   IMO, "Report of the Marine Environment Protection Committee on Its Seventy-Second Session," IMO Doc. MEPC 72/17/Add.1 (28 June 2018), Annex 11.
242   Id., para. 3.1.3.

The Strategy lists possible additional short-, mid-, and long-term measures for further discussion and assessment[243] and confirms the aim of adopting a revised strategy in spring, 2023.[244]

In 2016, the ICAO Assembly adopted two resolutions aimed at limiting the impact of aviation GHG emissions on the global climate. A resolution on aviation and climate change recognized the need to develop a long-term global aspirational goal for international aviation in light of the 2°C and 1.5°C temperature goals of the Paris Agreement.[245] The resolution went on to resolve that States and relevant organizations will work through the ICAO to achieve a global annual average fuel efficiency improvement of 2 percent until 2020 and an aspirational global fuel efficiency improvement rate of 2 percent per annum from 2021 to 2050.[246] A collective medium-term aspirational goal was also expressed – of keeping the global net carbon emissions for international aviation from 2020 at the same level.[247] ICOA's Council was requested to continue to explore the feasibility of a long-term aspirational goal for international aviation and to undertake supportive detailed studies with a progress report to be presented at the 40th session of the ICAO Assembly in 2019.[248]

Through a second 2016 resolution, ICAO adopted a Carbon Offsetting and Reduction Scheme for International Aviation (CORSIA).[249] A phased approach to CORSIA implementation is set out with a voluntary pilot phase (2021–2023), a voluntary first phase (2024–2026), and a mandatory second phase (2027–2035) applying to States having a stipulated share of international aviation activities but excepting least developed countries, small island developing States, and landlocked developing countries. In June 2018, the ICAO Council formally incorporated the CORSIA standards into the Convention on International Civil Aviation.[250]

---

243   Id., para. 4.
244   Id., para. 7.1.
245   International Civil Aviation Organization (ICAO), "Resolution A.39-2: Consolidated statement of continuing ICAO policies and practices related to environmental protection – Climate change," adopted by the 39th Assembly, 27 September–6 October 2016, preamble.
246   Id., para. 4.
247   Id., para. 6.
248   Id., para. 9.
249   ICAO, "Resolution A.39-3: Consolidated statement of continuing ICAO policies and practices related to environmental protection – Global Market-based Measure (MBM) scheme," adopted by the 39th Assembly, 27 September–6 October 2016, para. 5.
250   See ICAO, "ICAO Council reaches landmark decision on aviation emissions offsetting," 27 June 2018, available online: <https://www.icao.int/Newsroom/Pages/ICAO_Council_reaches_landmark_decision_on_aviation_emissions_offsetting.aspx>.

Conclusion

Two phrases capture the trends in law and policy responses to ocean acidity post-Paris. First is "high on discretion but low in precaution." The Paris Agreement's mitigation commitments stand out as very discretionary. Each party has discretion to establish its nationally determined contribution towards mitigation with successive NDCs expected to be more progressive and ambitious. Developed country parties should continue taking the lead by undertaking economy-wide absolute emission reduction targets. All parties are encouraged to formulate and communicate long-term low-GHG emission development strategies. Parties aim to reach a global peaking of GHG emissions as soon as possible and to achieve a balance between anthropogenic emissions and removals by sinks in the second half of this century.

The Paris Agreement fails to explicitly embrace the precautionary principle. The rather weak version of precaution adopted under the UNFCCC remains in the background,[251] whereby parties are encouraged to take precautionary measures to mitigate adverse effects of climate change with measures to be cost-effective so as to ensure global benefits at the lowest possible cost.[252]

A second gauging phrase is "high attention to climate change but low profile for ocean acidity." OA has not received substantial attention in implementation efforts under the Paris Agreement. Only a general OA target is established under the UN Sustainable Development Goals. OA has received almost no attention under MEAs, with the exception of the Convention on Biological Diversity.

Whether law and policy responses will be adequate to counter the projected impacts of OA remains to be seen. NDCs pledged to date do not promise a bright future, with countries not on track to even meet the 2°C Paris target. Reports on climate change implications of the 1.5°C target and on oceans and the cryosphere that have yet to be published might push countries to increase their levels of ambition. The extent to which human rights concerns, acknowledged in the preamble of the Paris Agreement, might influence climate change mitigation and adaptation commitments has yet to be determined.[253]

---

251 D. VanderZwaag, "The precautionary principle and marine environmental protection: Slippery shores, rough seas, and rising normative tides," *Ocean Development & International Law* 33 (2002): 165–188.
252 UNFCCC, n. 16 above, art. 3(3).
253 See United Nations Human Right Council, "Report of the Special Rapporteur on the issue of human right obligations relating to the enjoyment of a safe, clean, healthy and sustainable environment. Note by the Secretariat," UN Doc. A/HRC/31/52 (1 February 2016),

Two future directions seem quite clear. In light of treaty fatigue and the tremendous political energies needed to conclude the Paris Agreement, the international community will not consider negotiation of a specific agreement to address OA, as suggested by some authors. The UNFCCC and Paris Agreement will continue to be the main avenues for addressing climate change and OA. A systematic and direct consideration of OA in mitigation and adaptation efforts, as well as loss and damage, is therefore necessary. The preambular text of the Paris Agreement and recent developments outlined in this article have opened a policy window to that end.

The explicit integration of OA within the climate regime could be achieved in a number of ways. A political declaration by the CoP could be adopted that recognizes the impacts of anthropogenic emission of CO_2 in the biogeochemistry of the oceans as a distinct matter that falls within the objective of the Convention under its Article 2. Oceans could be institutionalized within the climate regime, for example through the adoption of a specific work program for oceans.[254] Strengthening the linkages between oceans and climate can also be achieved through coordination mechanisms, such as UN Oceans, an interagency mechanism that seeks to enhance the coordination, coherence, and effectiveness of competent organizations of the United Nations system and the International Seabed Authority.[255] States can also raise the profile of OA in the climate regime by directly addressing OA and its impacts in their mitigation and adaptation plans and commitments, as reflected in NDCs and adaptation and national communications.

Other windows to further address OA also loom on the horizon. A clearer target for curbing ocean acidity might be set under the Convention on Biological Diversity as parties negotiate new targets beyond the 2020 Aichi Biodiversity Targets. A future agreement on the conservation and sustainable use of marine biodiversity in areas beyond national jurisdiction, presently under negotiation,[256] might set a framework for establishing marine protected areas

---

available online: <https://www.ohchr.org/en/issues/environment/srenvironment/pages/annualreports.aspx>; S. Duyck, "The Paris climate agreement and the protection of human rights in a changing climate," *Yearbook of International Environmental Law* 26, no. 1 (2015): 3–45.

254 As suggested in the Ocean Pathway, available online: <https://cop23.com.fj/the-ocean-pathway/>.
255 See online: <http://www.unoceans.org/>.
256 UNGA, "Resolution 69/292 on the Development of an international legally binding instrument under the United Nations Convention on the Law of the Sea on the conservation

and other area-based measures in the high seas which could be key paths to further adapting to OA.

In the face of the already serious impacts of ocean acidity and the need to take precaution and human rights seriously, the 1.5°C Paris target seems imperative. Whether even that target will be sufficient, only further science and time will tell.

---

and sustainable use of marine biological diversity of areas beyond national jurisdiction," UN Doc. A/RES/69/292 (6 July 2015).

The Role and Relevance of Nationally Determined Contributions under the Paris Agreement to Ocean and Coastal Management in the Anthropocene

Tim Stephens
Professor of International Law and Australian Research
Council Future Fellow, University of Sydney Law School, Sydney, Australia

Introduction

The Nationally Determined Contribution (NDC) process is an integral feature of the 2015 Paris Agreement on Climate Change (Paris Agreement).[1] Unlike the 1997 Kyoto Protocol, which set quantified emission targets, the Paris Agreement takes a pledge-and-review approach, requiring parties to prepare successive NDCs every five years showing the steps they are taking to address climate change.[2] Each new NDC is to "represent a progression beyond" the party's then current NDC and "reflect its highest possible ambition."[3] NDCs are to be aimed at achieving the purpose of the Paris Agreement,[4] which is "[h]olding the increase in the global average temperature to well below 2°C above pre-industrial levels and pursuing efforts to limit the temperature increase to 1.5°C above pre-industrial levels."[5] NDCs are also to be informed by the "global stock-take" on collective progress, which will take place in 2023 and every five years thereafter.[6] Rajamani and Werksman note that in taking the approach that it does, the Paris Agreement "rel[ies] less on its legal character than on its collective goals, reporting and review mechanisms, and regular stock-takes to shape state behaviour and public attitudes."[7]

One hundred and eighty-two parties to the Paris Agreement have submitted NDCs, covering almost all of global emissions.[8] While the treaty has attracted

---

1 Paris Agreement on Climate Change, 12 December 2015, [2016] *Australian Treaty Series* 24.
2 Id., art. 4(2).
3 Id., art. 4(3).
4 Id., art. 3.
5 Id., art. 2(1)(a).
6 Id., arts. 4(9) and 14.
7 L. Rajamani and J. Werksman, "The legal character and operational relevance of the Paris Agreement's temperature goal," *Philosophical Transactions of the Royal Society A*, 376:20160458 (2018): 1–14, p. 3.
8 Id., p. 5.

an impressive level of global support,[9] major questions hang over the capacity of States through their NDCs and the NDC process more generally to prevent dangerous climate change. The adequacy of NDCs, both individually and collectively, has been the subject of a growing body of analysis. In addition to scrutiny of NDC texts, there has also been considerable discussion as to whether the NDC "show and tell" or "ambition cycle"[10] system itself is capable of delivering the Paris Agreement's objectives.[11]

In this context the focus of much commentary on the Paris Agreement has been the direct climate implications of emissions pledges and the NDC system. In contrast, there has been limited attention paid to the implications of NDCs, and the pledge-and-review system of which it forms a part, for coastal and ocean management. This article seeks to address this gap in knowledge by identifying the key dimensions in which coastal and ocean issues are relevant to NDCs and by assessing the adequacy of NDCs in safeguarding coastal and ocean ecosystems from the impacts of greenhouse gas emissions. This is an opportune moment for ocean-focused NDC analysis as negotiations are underway on the "Paris Rulebook" to establish operational guidelines for the Paris Agreement, including guidance on the content of NDCs.[12] It is argued that the NDC system would be enhanced by encouraging coastal State parties to include information on coastal and marine mitigation and adaptation pledges and policies in future NDC rounds.

The Relevance of NDCs for Coasts and the Ocean
The Ocean and the Climate System

The ocean constitutes the most important global buffer for human-induced climate change. It has absorbed more than 90 percent of the extra heat trapped in the atmosphere as a result of increasing concentrations of carbon dioxide

---

9   There are 185 parties to the Paris Agreement, and it entered into force less than a year after its adoption by consensus. The United States has pledged to withdraw from the Paris Agreement; however, this cannot take effect until 4 November 2020 (Paris Agreement, art. 28). On the potential impact of United States' withdrawal, see J. Pickering, J.S. McGee, T. Stephens and S.I. Karlsson-Vinkhuyzen, "The impact of the US retreat from the Paris Agreement: Kyoto revisited?," *Climate Policy* 18 (2018): 818–827.
10 Rajamani and Werksman, n. 7 above, p. 7.
11 See, e.g., N. Höhne et al., "The Paris Agreement: Resolving the inconsistency between global goals and national contributions," *Climate Policy* 17 (2017): 16–32.
12 The 2015 decision adopting the Paris Agreement, Decision 1/CP.21, called on the first meeting of the parties to adopt rules, modalities, procedures, and guidelines elaborating several provisions of the treaty.

(CO_2) and other greenhouse gases.[13] Storing this heat has caused many physical impacts, including thermal expansion and accompanying sea level rise,[14] changes to ocean circulation,[15] and the melting of sea ice.[16] The ocean has also absorbed large quantities of CO_2 and other greenhouse gases (around 50 percent of CO_2 from fossil fuel combustion).[17] This has led to chemical changes, including ocean acidification (the decline in pH), hypercapnia (high CO_2 concentrations), and deoxygenation (low O_2 concentrations).[18] These physical and chemical modifications to the ocean have had flow-on impacts for marine organisms and ecosystems, including bleaching and mortality of coral reefs,[19] changes to primary production and food quality,[20] and shifts in fishery ranges.[21] These substantial and relatively rapid changes to coasts and the ocean carry major social and economic implications, particularly for communities that are highly dependent on coastal ecosystems and fisheries.[22] Recognizing the

---

13   M. Rhein et al., "Observations: Ocean" in *Climate Change 2013: The Physical Science Basis. Contribution of Working Group 1 to the Fifth Assessment Report of the Intergovernmental Panel on Climate Change*, eds. T.F. Stocker et al. (Cambridge: Cambridge University Press, 2013), p. 257.

14   M. Mengel et al., "Committed sea-level rise under the Paris Agreement and the legacy of delayed mitigation action," *Nature Communications* 9, 601 (2018): 1–10.

15   L. Caesar et al., "Observed fingerprint of a weakening Atlantic Ocean overturning circulation," *Nature*, 556 (2018): 191–196; D.J.R. Thornalley et al., "Anomalously weak Labrador Sea convection and Atlantic overturning during the past 150 years," *Nature* 556 (2018): 227–230.

16   D. Notz and J. Stroeve. "Observed Arctic sea-ice loss directly follows anthropogenic CO2 emissions," *Science* 354(6313) (2016): 747–750; M. Sigmond, J.C. Fyfe and N.C. Swart, "Ice-free Arctic projections under the Paris Agreement," *Nature Climate Change* 8 (2018): 404–408.

17   U. Riebesell, A. Kortzinger and A. Oschilles, "Sensitivities of marine carbon fluxes to ocean change," *Proceedings of the National Academy of Sciences* 106 (2009): 20602–20609.

18   B.I. McNeil and T.P. Sasse, "Future ocean hypercapnia driven by anthropogenic amplification of the natural CO_2 cycle," *Nature* 529 (2016): 383–386.

19   T.P. Hughes et al., "Global warming transforms coral reef assemblages," *Nature* 556 (2018): 492–496.

20   L. Kwiatkowski et al., "The impact of variable phytoplankton stoichiometry on projections of primary production, food quality, and carbon uptake in the global ocean," *Global Biogeochemical Cycles* (2018), doi.org/10.1002/2017GB005799.

21   E.S. Poloczanska et al., "Global imprint of climate change on marine life," *Nature Climate Change* 3 (2013): 919–925; T.C. Bonebrake et al., "Managing consequences of climate-driven species redistribution requires integration of ecology, conservation and social science," *Biological Reviews* 93 (2017): 1–22.

22   J.-P. Gattuso and L. Hansson, "Ocean acidification: Background and history," in *Ocean Acidification*, eds. J.-P. Gattuso and L. Hansson (Oxford: Oxford University Press, 2011), pp. 1–20, p. 17.

special importance of the ocean to the climate system, the Intergovernmental Panel on Climate Change (IPCC) is undertaking work on a Special Report on the Ocean and Cryosphere in a Changing Climate to be finalized in late 2019.[23]

The Ocean and the International Climate Regime

The international legal regime governing climate change has been in a state of ongoing development since the adoption of the 1992 United Nations Framework Convention on Climate Change (UNFCCC).[24] However, one notable area of the regime in which there has been limited evolution is with respect to the ocean. Neither ocean nor coastal issues feature significantly in the texts that make up the international climate regime.[25] In the UNFCCC, the "oceans" and "coastal and marine ecosystems" are mentioned only once, and only in the context of commitments by parties to promote sustainable management and enhancement of carbon sinks.[26] And in the 1997 Kyoto Protocol,[27] the sole reference to marine issues is in a provision which defers the task of reducing emissions from marine bunker and aviation fuels to the International Maritime Organization (IMO) and International Civil Aviation Organization (ICAO), respectively.[28]

In contrast to the UNFCCC and the Kyoto Protocol, ocean issues were more prominent in negotiating the Paris Agreement and have been considered in more depth in post-Paris Conferences of the Parties (COPs) to the UNFCCC. At the Paris conference, 22 States signed the "Because the Ocean" Declaration which pledged, among other things, to work towards a special IPCC report on the ocean and the development of an ocean action plan under the UNFCCC.[29] At the 2017 UN Climate Change Conference, in Bonn, there were additional signatories to the "Because the Ocean" Declaration and the launch by the

---

23   See Intergovernmental Panel on Climate Change online: <http://www.ipcc.ch/report/srocc/>.
24   United Nations Framework Convention on Climate Change, 9 May 1992, 1771 *United Nations Treaty Series* 165 [UNFCCC].
25   R. Baird, M. Simons and T. Stephens, "Ocean acidification: A litmus test for international law," *Carbon and Climate Law Review* 3 (2009): 459–471.
26   UNFCCC, n. 24 above, art. 4(1)(d).
27   Kyoto Protocol to the United Nations Framework Convention on Climate Change, 11 December 1997, 2303 *United Nations Treaty Series* 162, art. 2(2) [Kyoto Protocol].
28   Id., art. 2(2).
29   See IISD, "22 Countries Join 'Because the Ocean' to Support Action on Climate Change and Oceans" (21 December 2015), available online: <http://sdg.iisd.org/news/22-countries-join-because-the-ocean-to-support-action-on-climate-change-and-oceans/>.

COP 23 Presidency, Fiji, of the "Ocean Pathway," a new initiative to achieve "an ocean inclusive UNFCCC process."[30]

Although the operative text of the Paris Agreement is silent on ocean systems, there is a preambular reference to the "importance of ensuring the integrity of all ecosystems, including oceans."[31] Moreover, the Agreement's flexible pledge-and-review mechanism provides significant opportunities for coastal and ocean issues to be addressed more substantively than under either the UNFCCC or the Kyoto Protocol. Given that the ocean is the primary driver of the global climate system,[32] and is experiencing impacts from global warming as serious as those affecting terrestrial areas, effective responses to the causes and consequences of climate change will require a greater marine focus.[33] The NDC system is one important vehicle through which this can take place.

The Relevance of NDCs to Coasts and the Ocean: Four Key Dimensions

There are four main ways in which NDCs have relevance to coasts and the ocean. First, and most importantly, is the extent to which NDCs individually and collectively pledge emission reductions that will avoid or reduce damaging climate and related impacts to marine and coastal areas. A second way in which coasts and the ocean are relevant in NDCs is the capacity for parties to include actions to protect carbon sinks in these environments in order to mitigate climate change. The loss of carbon from coastal and marine ecosystems threatens the capacity of governments to meet the Paris Agreement's goals.[34] Thirdly, NDCs can incorporate mitigation goals with a marine dimension by including policies to reduce emissions from offshore activities, such as through bans on offshore oil and gas exploitation or by reducing emissions from shipping and fishing industries. NDCs could also include commitments to offshore renewable energy resources, such as offshore windfarms and tidal power. A fourth way NDCs have relevance for ocean and coastal issues is with respect to adaptation, with sea level rise one of the most obvious climate impacts

---

30 See COP 23, "The Ocean Pathway" (2017), available online: <https://cop23.com.fj/the-ocean-pathway/>.
31 Paris Agreement, n. 1 above, 13th recital.
32 G.K. Vallis, *Climate and the Oceans* (Princeton: Princeton University Press, 2012).
33 See generally G.R. Bigg, *The Oceans and Climate* (Cambridge: Cambridge University Press, 2nd ed., 2012).
34 J. Bell-James, "'Blue Carbon' and the need to integrate mitigation, adaptation and conservation goals within the international climate law framework," in *Global Environmental Change and Innovation in International Law*, eds. N. Craik et al. (Cambridge: Cambridge University Press, 2018), pp. 81–101.

requiring adaptation responses. Many parties have included the communication of their adaptation actions under the Paris Agreement as a component of their NDCs.[35]

The Adequacy of NDCs in Protecting Coastal and Ocean Ecosystems
Adequacy of NDCs in Aggregate

It is clear that the first round of NDCs will not achieve the Paris Agreement's temperature goals. If all governments fully implement their NDCs (which is a large assumption), then it is estimated that there will be an average global atmospheric temperature increase of 3.2°C above pre-industrial levels by 2100.[36]

What are the implications of this potential temperature increase, and the continued carbon emissions driving it, for the ocean? Whereas there has been significant analysis of the capacity of NDC pledges and policies to deliver the Paris Agreement's temperature objectives, there has been very little consideration as to whether NDCs prepared by parties are sufficiently ambitious to deliver coastal and ocean protection goals. For instance, one of the most significant ocean impacts from inadequate emission reduction commitments in NDCs is the acidification of the ocean.[37] The absorption of CO_2 in the ocean has reduced its pH by 0.1 units since the Industrial Revolution. This process is already disrupting calcifying organisms, particularly in colder waters at higher latitudes, and will impact on these organisms in tropical coral reefs in the coming decades.[38] As with other climate-induced change, such as the transformation of the global cryosphere, this is not a linear or reversible process. As Hughes et al. observe, "[o]nce these and other marine systems have been altered by ocean acidification, they are likely to stay in a new regime for geological timescales, pointing to the imperative of action to reduce CO_2 emissions as early as possible during the current transitional period."[39]

Following the submission of Intended Nationally Determined Contributions (which are converted to NDCs upon States joining the Paris Agreement, unless they elect otherwise), the UNFCCC Secretariat published a synthesis

---

35 Paris Agreement, n. 1 above, art. 7(10) and (11).
36 "For the Talanoa Dialogue: Input from the Climate Action Tracker," available online: <https://climateactiontracker.org/publications/talanoa-dialogue-input-climate-action-tracker/>.
37 See generally T. Stephens, "Warming waters and souring seas: Climate change and ocean acidification," in *The Oxford Handbook of the Law of the Sea*, eds. D.R. Rothwell et al. (Oxford: Oxford University Press, 2015), pp. 777–798.
38 T.P. Hughes et al., "Living dangerously on borrowed time during slow, unrecognized regime shifts," *Trends in Evolution and Ecology* 28 (2013): 149–155.
39 Id., p. 153.

report on the aggregate effect of party commitments.[40] The report highlighted several of the coastal and marine impacts from climate change that have been referred to by the parties in their contributions. Sea level rise, ocean acidification, coastal erosion, and saltwater intrusion were key climate hazards frequently identified,[41] and mangroves and corals were referred to as ecosystems under threat.[42] However, despite the seriousness of these impacts, the synthesis report makes clear that these are not coupled with adequate policies to prevent or ameliorate their effects. In a summary of examples of quantitative targets and goals included in the adaptation component of NDCs, there were only two addressing marine issues, namely, specific goals to protect a percentage of marine environments by 2020, and the establishment of marine protected areas (MPAs).[43] In terms of priority areas for adaptation actions identified by parties in their NDCs, coastal and ocean issues were relatively low on the list. Coastal protection and fisheries featured tenth and eleventh, respectively, behind water, agriculture, ecosystems, infrastructure, forestry, energy, disaster risk reduction, and food production.[44]

Adequacy of Individual NDCs

The knowledge gained from the UNFCCC Secretariat's assessment of the oceanic dimensions of NDCs has been significantly advanced by research on the ocean inclusiveness of individual NDCs. In 2017 Gallo, Victor, and Levin undertook an empirical assessment of NDCs to ascertain "whether and how Parties to the Paris Agreement are focusing on the ocean and marine ecosystems."[45] The assessment involved an examination of 161 NDCs submitted as of June 2016 and it found that 112 (70 percent) included some mention of marine issues.[46] Forty-nine parties (30 percent) did not refer to the ocean in their NDCs, and of these 35 were land-locked States and 14 were coastal States. Surprisingly, this latter group included parties with large exclusive economic zones (EEZs), notably Australia, Brazil, the European Union, New Zealand, Norway, the Russian

---

40 UNFCCC Secretariat, "Aggregate Effect of the Intended Nationally Determined Contributions: An Update," UN Doc FCCC/CP/2016/2 (2016) available online: <https://unfccc.int/sites/default/files/resource/docs/2016/cop22/eng/02.pdf>.
41 Id., p. 64.
42 Id., p. 70.
43 Id., p. 68.
44 Id., p. 69.
45 N.D. Gallo, D.G. Victor and L.A. Levin, "Ocean commitments under the Paris Agreement," *Nature Climate Change* 7 (2017): 833–838, p. 833.
46 Id.

Federation, and the United States, which might have been expected to include marine issues in their NDCs.[47]

Gallo, Victor, and Levin also considered the substantive content of those NDCs mentioning marine ecosystems and sought to identify the main climate-related concerns raised by the parties. The leading concerns were coastal impacts (95 NDCs), ocean warming impacts (77 NDCs), fisheries impacts (72 NDCs), and marine ecosystem impacts (62 NDCs).[48] These appeared at least twice as often as any other category of marine issue. The type and frequency of marine category mentioned was not necessarily reflective of the seriousness of marine and coastal threats from climate change. For instance, ocean acidification, hypercapnia, and deoxygenation were significantly underrepresented or not mentioned at all, which is indicative of the relatively low priority that governments currently place on these issues.[49]

Relatively few NDCs explicitly linked emissions reduction and the protection of the marine environment, which suggests that national and global mitigation goals and policies have not been adequately informed by a full understanding of the marine and coastal impacts of greenhouse gas emissions. The predominant focus of marine-inclusive NDCs is with respect to marine impacts and adaptation. A much smaller number of marine references mention the capacity of the marine environment to assist in climate mitigation through mangrove restoration, fisheries management, maritime transport, renewable energy, and ocean carbon storage.[50] Only around 12 percent of mentions of marine issues in NDCs were devoted to mitigation categories.[51]

In order to understand the approach by different countries to marine issues in NDCs, Gallo, Victor, and Levin calculated what they termed a "Marine Focus Factor" (MFF) to measure both the frequency and variety in marine-related topics in NDCs. They hypothesized that certain key variables would be related to higher MFFs, such as large EEZ areas, higher EEZ to land ratio, lengthy coastline, high value of domestic fisheries, significant percentage of low-lying land areas and large populations in such areas, and whether a country was a small island developing State (SIDS).[52] The results showed a significant positive association between only a few factors and MFF; namely, the share of a country's population living in low-lying areas and whether the country is a SIDS. However, other variables did not have a significant positive influence on

---

47   Id.
48   Id., p. 834.
49   Id., p. 837.
50   Id., p. 834.
51   Id.
52   Id., p. 836.

MFF. For instance, domestic fisheries did not influence MFF, despite climate impacts on fisheries productivity. On the other hand, being an Annex I party to the UNFCCC (i.e., an industrialized or industrializing country), even one with large maritime estate and economically significant fisheries, such as Australia, had a negative impact on the MFF. Gallo, Victor, and Levin concluded that "[t]he strong influence of negotiating group (Annex I or SIDS) on MFF … suggests political and not principally scientific motivations are largely driving current patterns of ocean inclusion in NDCs."[53] For these States there is therefore a significant inconsistency between the limited (or non-existent) ocean inclusiveness of their NDCs and their exposure to coastal and ocean risks from climate change. The omission of oceans issues from Australia's NDC is especially incongruous given the extreme vulnerability of many of Australia's coastal and marine environments, including coral reef ecosystems and kelp forests, to increased ocean temperature and ocean acidification.[54]

Adequacy of the NDC System

The NDC system was expressly designed to be an open and flexible mechanism to encourage all parties to take steps to reduce emissions and adapt to climate change. However, as there is no prescribed content for NDCs, they vary significantly and address a wide range of commitments and policies. One apparent flaw in this approach is that it has encouraged some governments to overstate the significance of their pledges and the efficacy of their policies, leading to the criticism that NDCs can involve a type of "greenwashing." Without detailed knowledge of country context and the nature of the pledge or promise, these documents may appear more impressive at face value than they are in reality. Central to improving the NDC system, therefore, including as it applies to the ocean and coasts, will be the "enhanced transparency framework" required by Article 13 of the Paris Agreement, and being developed in the Paris Rulebook, to establish standardized reporting obligations that can be the subject of accurate measurement, reporting and verification.

Enhancing NDCs for the Protection of Coastal and Ocean Ecosystems
Closing Window for Enhancing Ocean and Coastal Inclusion in NDCs

Although the Paris Agreement only entered into force in November 2016, the deadline for the next round of NDCs is fast approaching, and there is a rapidly

---

53   Id., p. 837.
54   On these impacts, see generally K. Evans, N. Bax and D.C. Smith, *State of the Environment 2016: Marine Environment*, independent report to the Australian Government Minister for the Environment and Energy, (Canberra: Australian Government Department of the Environment and Energy, 2016), pp. 17–29.

closing window to enhance the ocean inclusiveness of NDCs that will then be in place for a further five-year period. Parties whose NDCs contains a time frame up to 2025 are to communicate new NDCs by 2020,[55] while parties whose NDC contains a time frame up to 2030 also are to communicate new or updated NDCs by 2020.[56] NDCs are to be submitted nine to twelve months prior to the conference acting as the meeting of the parties (the CMA).[57]

For agreement to be reached on the core elements of the Paris Rulebook and for parties to fashion new or updated NDCs, 2019 is a critical year. It will also be the year in which the IPCC releases its special report on the ocean and cryosphere and will therefore be a particularly timely moment for sharpening the ocean focus of NDCs. It will be on the basis of these NDCs that the first global stock-take, which takes place in 2023,[58] to assess collective progress towards achieving the Paris Agreement's objectives, will be undertaken. The stock-take will then inform subsequent rounds of NDCs so that parties are provided with information to enhance the ambition of their NDCs. Unless interlinked climate and ocean issues are addressed in new NDCs, there seems to be little likelihood that they will feature prominently in the global stock-take process.

Talanoa Dialogue and Ocean and Coastal Issues

A parallel stocktaking exercise already underway is the "facilitative dialogue," which is being undertaken in advance of the next round of NDCs and the 2023 global stock-take, and which is proving to have some usefulness in bringing greater attention to ocean issues. The parties decided at COP 21 to establish the facilitative dialogue to occur in 2018 in order to take stock of collective efforts in achieving progress towards the Paris Agreement's long-term goal (Article 4(1)) and to inform the preparation of NDCs (under Article 4(8)).[59] Fiji, as President of COP 23, launched the dialogue under the renamed title of "Talanoa Dialogue."[60] (Talanoa is a traditional Polynesian word to describe a process of inclusive, participatory, and transparent conversation.)

To date there have been a small number of inputs to the Talanoa Dialogue, which has sought contributions in response to three questions: (1) where are we? (2) where do we want to go? and (3) how do we get there?[61] Mirroring the content of NDCs, few of the State party Talanoa Dialogue inputs specifically

---

55 UNFCCC COP Decision 1/CP.21, para. 23.
56 UNFCCC COP Decision 1/CP.21, para. 24.
57 UNFCCC COP Decision 1/CP.21, para. 25.
58 Paris Agreement, n. 1 above, art. 14(2).
59 UNFCCC COP Decision 1/CP.21, para. 20.
60 UNFCCC COP Decision 1/CP.23, paras. 10–11 and Annex II.
61 UN Climate Change, "Talanoa Dialogue Inputs," available online: <https://talanoadialogue.com/view-inputs>.

reference coastal and/or ocean issues. Fiji's input in response to the question "where are we?" notes that climate change is driving "sea level rise, warming, and acidification" and highlights the vulnerability of its fisheries to climate change, noting that "it is likely that coastal fisheries will be unable to support local needs and that, over the long term, Fiji will become a net importer of fish, undermining long-term food security and nutrition."[62] Australia's input refers to Australia's founding membership of the International Coral Reef Initiative and support for the International Partnership for Blue Carbon to enhance the protection and restoration of coastal blue carbon ecosystems (mangroves, tidal marshes, and seagrasses).[63] In contrast, as was noted above, Australia's NDC is silent on marine and coastal issues, and it remains to be seen whether the ocean elements of Australia's Talanoa Dialogue contribution will be reflected in Australia's second NDC. References to coastal and ocean issues are also not widely included in Talanoa Dialogue inputs from non-party stakeholders. There is, however, an input from the IMO on reducing emissions from shipping which annexes the April 2018 resolution of the Marine Environment Protection Committee containing the "Initial IMO Strategy on Reduction of GHG Emissions from Ships."[64]

Ocean and Coastal Initiatives outside the UNFCCC

Outside of UNFCCC and Paris Agreement processes, there have been significant efforts to enhance global focus on interlinked climate and ocean issues with the potential to influence the next round of NDCs. The high-level United Nations Conference to Support the Implementation of Sustainable Goal 14[65] was held in June 2017 and resulted in declaration titled "Our Ocean, Our

---

62   Republic of Fiji, "Talanoa Dialogue Submission: 'Where are We?'," available online: <https://unfccc.int/sites/default/files/resource/105_Talanoa%20dialogue_Where%20Are%20We.pdf>, p. 10.
63   Australian Government, "Talanoa Dialogue Submission" (April 2018), available online: <https://unfccc.int/sites/default/files/resource/85_Australia%20Talanoa%20Dialogue%20Submission.pdf>.
64   International Maritime Organization (IMO), "Note by the IMO to the UNFCCC Talanoa Dialogue," available online: <https://unfccc.int/sites/default/files/resource/250_IMO%20submission_Talanoa%20Dialogue_April%202018.pdf>.
65   Sustainable Development Goal 14 is to "[c]onserve and sustainably use the oceans, seas and marine resources for sustainable development" and is a response to "[t]he increasingly adverse impacts of climate change (including ocean acidification), overfishing and marine pollution [that] are jeopardizing recent gains in protecting portions of the world's oceans," available online: <https://sustainabledevelopment.un.org/sdg14>.

Future: Call for Action," which was endorsed by the UN General Assembly.[66] The Declaration provides recognition of the importance of the ocean to the climate system. It notes that the ocean "supplies nearly half the oxygen we breathe, absorbs over a quarter of the carbon dioxide we produce, plays a vital role in the water cycle and the climate system and is an important source of our planet's biodiversity and of ecosystem services."[67] The Declaration also recognizes the linkages between the ocean and other Earth systems: "We are particularly alarmed by the adverse impacts of climate change on the ocean, including the rise in ocean temperatures, ocean and coastal acidification, deoxygenation, sea level rise, the decrease in polar ice coverage, coastal erosion and extreme weather events."[68] The Declaration refers specifically to the Paris Agreement (noting its "particular importance"), but the Declaration does not include an express call for emissions reductions.

The challenge now is linking global calls for improved ocean governance in the Anthropocene with the Paris Agreement and the NDC system in clear and concrete ways. Some governments have been strong advocates for mainstreaming ocean issues in the UNFCCC and the Paris Agreement. Chile has made the most focused intervention on the topic, expressly arguing that "the most effective way to address the gap of implementation of Art. 4.1d of the Convention and related provisions in the Paris Agreement is that Parties include the ocean in their NDCs, as an integral part of their climate policies."[69] Chile has also highlighted the value of bringing ocean issues within NDCs in order to encourage "an open debate under the Subsidiary Bodies of the Convention that would eventually provide Parties with specific guidance in this topic, in the context of their efforts to implement the Paris Agreement."[70]

There are compelling reasons why ocean and coastal systems should be accorded greater attention in subsequent rounds of NDCs. As Gallo, Victor, and Levin observe, the failure to consider the ocean in NDCs results in missed mitigation opportunities, inadequate climate adaptation plans, unsatisfactory linkages with other UN regimes and processes, including negotiations on an internationally legally binding instrument to protect biodiversity in areas beyond national jurisdiction.[71] The climate regime has become a central forum

---

66 UN General Assembly, "Our Ocean, Our Future: Call for Action," UN Doc. A/RES/71/312 (6 July 2017).
67 Id., annex, para. 3.
68 Id., annex, para. 4.
69 Chile, "Submission on the relevance of the ocean in the global response to climate change," UN Doc. FCCC/APA/2016/INF.1 (7 October 2016), p. 16.
70 Id.
71 Gallo, Victor and Levin, n. 45 above, p. 837.

for deciding the future of the ocean environment, even though its key operative texts have no ocean focus. The same holds true for other Earth systems, including the cryosphere.[72]

The limited inclusion or non-inclusion of ocean issues in NDCs reflects a siloed approach which is no longer effective or appropriate in the Anthropocene, the current geological era in which humanity has become the dominant force of global environmental change. One of the central lessons from Earth system science that has identified this period and its implications is that the Earth is a single dynamic system with multiple intersecting environmental sub-systems. Proponents of the Planetary Boundaries framework have taken this insight and identified policy-relevant guardrails for key global environmental systems essential for maintaining the integrity of the planet as a self-regulating system.[73] Ocean acidification is one of these Planetary Boundaries, yet it currently sits in an international regulatory limbo, potentially governable by multiple ocean and atmospheric regimes, yet in practice addressed by none. One potential way forward to address this is through the NDCs in which States may identify "safe" ocean acidification thresholds or boundaries consistent with the available science. This could pave the way for collective agreement on these goals in an international instrument in a similar way as the Paris Agreement specifies a 1.5/2°C temperature guardrail.

Proposal for Enhancing Ocean and Coastal Coverage in NDCs

There are several ways in which the second round of NDCs can be enhanced by addressing climate-related ocean issues. First, there could be clear linking between emissions mitigation goals and ocean protection. Most NDCs currently do not make this connection and instead are directed primarily at the Paris Agreement's temperature goals. Magnan et al. note that the ocean scientific community considers that the well-below 2°C target, which includes efforts to limit temperature increases to 1.5°C, "must ... be considered as an upper limit beyond which severe, pervasive and partially irreversible impacts develop."[74] They observe that "[s]taying on track to a well-below 2 °C transition is thus of key importance for the world ocean and society."[75] The ocean science community has tended to embrace the Paris Agreement temperature goals as

---

72 T. Stephens, "The Anthropocene and the Antarctic Treaty System," *The Polar Journal* 8 (2018): 29–43.

73 W. Steffen et al., "Planetary boundaries: Guiding human development on a changing planet," *Science* 347 (6223) (2015): 736.

74 A.K. Magnan et al., "Implications of the Paris Agreement for the ocean," *Nature Climate Change* 6 (2016): 732–735, p. 733.

75 Id.

shorthand for identifying thresholds for damaging ocean impacts from greenhouse gas emissions. However, this approach has drawbacks, including paying insufficient attention to the direct effects of greenhouse gas emissions on the marine environment. For instance, pursuing some ocean sequestration technologies could help deliver the temperature objectives but at the cost of further increasing the concentration of CO_2 in the marine environment. Despite over a decade of warnings, there is insufficient attention being paid to ocean acidification, which is occurring at a pace not seen for at least 65 million years and has the potential to transform completely the global marine ecosystem.[76] The links between emissions reduction goals and ocean impacts could therefore be made much more clearly and directly, and there is an improving scientific basis for doing so. To take just one example, permanent summer ice-free conditions in the Arctic Ocean are likely under 3°C global mean warming with major implications for the Arctic marine ecosystem.[77] In order to bring greater attention and focus to the ocean implications of climate change, NDCs could make specific reference to these and other marine environmental boundaries, thresholds, or tipping points and connect these with emissions budgets and emission reduction pathways.

Second, and relatedly, there is a case for coastal States in their NDCs to recognize the value of marine and coastal areas as carbon sinks. Emissions avoided through the protection of marine and coastal ecosystems and carbon sequestered through the restoration of these systems provides a relatively low-cost and effective mitigation option that also has significant co-benefits, including the protection of marine biological diversity and the strengthening of natural barriers resilient to sea level rise and storm surges. A substantial number of NDCs already refer to mangrove conservation and other coastal and marine blue carbon goals. However, it is likely that many States have significantly undervalued the contribution that coastal and ocean ecosystems make to storing carbon,[78] and there is room for improving the reporting of the loss of blue carbon and initiatives to protect and restore these systems.

At the same time, the role of marine and coastal areas needs to be approached with some care so as not to undermine the effectiveness of mitigation commitments in other sectors. There are parallels with the inclusion of emissions reductions from land use, land-use change and forestry (LULUCF) in meeting the

---

76 J.E.N. Veron et al., "The coral reef crisis: The critical importance of <350 ppm CO_2," *Marine Pollution Bulletin* 58 (2009): 1428–1436.
77 Sigmond et al., n. 16 above.
78 See, e.g., M.F. Adame et al., "The undervalued contribution of mangrove protection in Mexico to carbon emission targets," *Conservation Letters* (2018), doi.org/10.1111/conl.12445.

Kyoto Protocol's emission targets.[79] LULUCF has been controversial because of the difficulty in calculating emissions from land use change, and because its inclusion can be used as a justification for delaying the implementation of economy-wide mitigation policies to reduce emissions.[80] Furthermore, the ocean is beginning to be explored as a site for negative emissions technologies, that is, technologies that involve the removal of CO_2 from the atmosphere and storing it underground, in soils and biomass, or in the ocean (see Figure 9.1).[81] Indeed, all of the emissions scenarios for keeping global warming below 1.5°C and even 2°C involve the use of these kinds of carbon capture technologies.[82] In the ocean, these geoengineering techniques include iron fertilization and enhanced upwelling and have the potential to cause major damage to ocean ecosystems and to accelerate ocean acidification. More ocean-inclusive NDCs could highlight both the opportunities and the pitfalls of turning to the ocean as a solution to climate change.

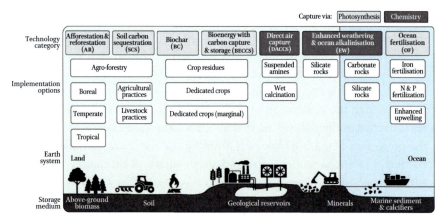

FIGURE 9.1 Types of negative emissions technologies
REPRODUCED FROM J.C. MINX ET AL., "NEGATIVE EMISSIONS-PART 1: RESEARCH LANDSCAPE AND SYNTHESIS," *ENVIRONMENTAL RESEARCH LETTERS* 13, NO. 6 (2018): 063001. CREATIVE COMMONS ATTRIBUTION 3.0 LICENCE.

---

79 Kyoto Protocol, n. 27 above, art. 3(3).
80 R. Pearse, *Pricing Carbon in Australia: Contestation, The State and Market Failure* (Abingdon, Oxon: Routledge, 2018), p. 54.
81 Rajamani and Weksman, n. 7 above, p. 6. See also K.N. Scott, "Engineering the 'Mis-Anthropocene': International law, ethics and geoengineering," *Ocean Yearbook* 29 (2015): 61–84.
82 T. Gasser et al., "Negative emissions physically needed to keep global warming below 2°C," *Nature Communications* 6 (7958) (2015).

Third, NDCs could include specific ocean-related emissions reduction targets and policies. Many human activities in the ocean have a significant carbon footprint. Offshore oil and gas exploitation, for instance, results in direct carbon emissions but also much larger additional emissions from downstream use when hydrocarbons are burned. There is a growing awareness that both offshore and onshore hydrocarbons will need to remain unexploited to meet the Paris Agreement objectives. For instance, all of the Arctic Ocean's hydrocarbons are considered unburnable if global warming is to be limited to 2°C.[83]

In light of this, some governments are implementing bans on future offshore oil and gas exploration as part of national policies to achieve net zero emissions,[84] and it can be expected that this type of policy action will be included in the future NDCs of a growing number of coastal States. Complementing this "supply side" approach to emissions from activities in the marine environment are also "demand side" approaches to limit emissions, most notably initiatives in the IMO to curtail emissions from shipping which led in April 2018 to the adoption of the Initial IMO Strategy on Reduction of GHG emissions From Ships which seeks to reduce annual greenhouse gas emissions from ships by 50 percent by 2050 (below 2008 levels) and to pursue efforts to phase them out altogether.[85] Shipping accounts for around 2.2 percent of total global carbon emissions, and full decarbonization of the industry is required within the coming decades in order to make a fair contribution to achieving the Paris Agreement's objectives.[86] The mitigation of shipping (and aviation) emissions is not within the purview of the international climate regime and there is therefore no requirement for mitigation policies in these sectors to be included in NDCs. However, initiatives to reduce shipping emissions could be referred to as a complementary mitigation measure fully within the spirit of the NDC process and Talanoa Dialogue. Indeed, Australia's submission to the Talanoa Dialogue does refer to shipping emissions and recent initiatives in the IMO,[87] and the IMO, as noted above, made its own statement as part of the

---

83 C. McGlade and P. Ekins, "The geographical distribution of fossil fuels unused when limiting global warming to 2 °C," *Nature* 517 (2015): 187–190.

84 For example, New Zealand: J. Smyth, "New Zealand to ban future offshore oil and gas exploration," *The Financial Times* (12 April 2018).

85 IMO, Marine Environment Protection Committee, "Initial IMO Strategy on Reduction of GHG Emissions from Ships," Resolution MEPC.304(72) (adopted 13 April 2018), Annex 11, IMO Doc. MEPC 72/17/Add.1 (2018).

86 M. Traut et al., "CO_2 abatement goals for international shipping," *Climate Policy* 18 (2018): 1066–1075.

87 For example, Australia's input to Talanoa Dialogue, n. 63 above: "Alongside the Paris Agreement, Australia is supporting important global action to reduce emissions through the International Civil Aviation Organization (ICAO), International Maritime Organization

dialogue. Including shipping emissions in NDCs would go some way to resolving the entrenched problem of fragmentation in the regulation of emissions from aviation and maritime transport.[88]

Fourthly, NDCs would benefit from more detailed and expansive inclusion of coastal and ocean adaptation policies. Most NDCs do include an adaptation component, and many make reference to coastal issues in particular. One possible ocean-related adaptation response that may be referred to in NDCs includes the establishment of MPAs to build resilience of marine and coastal ecosystems to rising water temperatures and ocean acidification. However, as with other areas of climate policy, such actions cannot substitute for effective mitigation policy to reduce emissions. Recent research suggests that MPAs will be ineffective in protecting marine ecosystems from warmer water temperatures and changing ocean chemistry if the Paris Agreement objectives are not achieved.[89]

Conclusion

One of the potential advantages of the Paris Agreement over the Kyoto Protocol is that it creates a regularly iterative and dialogical regime that has the capacity to develop over time to strengthen mitigation and adaptation commitments and the policies to deliver them. The NDC system has a high degree of flexibility and while this comes at the cost of stipulating mandated and legally binding emissions reductions, it does create space for governments to explore a wide range of mitigation and adaptation approaches. This includes the capacity to include coastal and ocean issues within NDCs and the global stock-take processes both as subjects of concern and as sites of opportunity for emissions reductions and for adaptive responses.

This makes the Paris Agreement, and the NDC mechanism at its center, an inherently more responsive governance regime than the UNFCCC or the Kyoto Protocol before it. In the Anthropocene, Oran Young argues, it is apparent that there is a "premium on the creation and operation of international environmental and resource regimes that are effective in turbulent times and

---

(IMO) and the Montreal Protocol. Australia encourages all countries to be members and participate in these forums to support an 'all of the above' approach to reducing global emissions," pp. 1–2.

88 See B. Martinez Romera, *Regime Interaction and Climate Change: The Case of International Aviation and Maritime Transport* (London: Routledge, 2018).

89 J.F. Bruno et al., "Climate change threatens the world's marine protected areas," *Nature Climate Change* 8 (2018): 499–503.

capable of adapting nimbly or agilely to rapidly changing conditions."[90] However, Young also notes that environmental regimes will only be effective if they not only anticipate "state changes in both biophysical and socioeconomic systems," but also "take steps to avoid passing tipping points."[91] This observation has clear application to coastal and ocean governance in the Anthropocene and the NDC system is one which allows tipping points to be identified and averted. Given the rapid changes underway in marine ecosystems globally as a result of climate change, ocean acidification, and other changes from the perturbation of the carbon cycle, a compelling case can be made for States to make ocean and coastal issues far more visible in the ongoing development and implementation of the Paris Agreement through their NDCs. Ocean and coastal issues should be expressly considered and included as an integral part of the next and successive rounds of NDCs.

---

90   O.R. Young, *Governing Complex Systems* (Massachusetts: MIT Press, 2017), p. 42.
91   Id.

Human Capacity-building and Public Education Aligned with Global Perspectives for Adaptation in Coastal and Ocean Management: the Role of the Borneo Marine Research Institute

Saleem Mustafa, Rossita Shapawi, Sitti Raehanah M. Shaleh, Abentin Estim, Rafidah Othman, Zarinah Waheed, Ejria Saleh, B. Mabel Manjaji-Matsumoto and Najamuddin Abdul Basri*
Borneo Marine Research Institute, Universiti Malaysia Sabah, Malaysia

Introduction

Coastal areas have always attracted human populations because of their rich subsistence and industrial resources, logistical convenience for marine trade and transport, and recreational or cultural opportunities. Globally, nearly 2.4 billion people (about 40 percent of the world's population) live within 100 km of the coast.[1] The east Malaysian state of Sabah, located in Borneo, is no exception to this trend. The total land area of Sabah is nearly 73,904 km² which is surrounded by the South China Sea in the west, the Sulu Sea in the northeast, and the Sulawesi Sea in the southeast. The coastline measures 1,743 km, with mangroves covering about 331,325 hectares, amounting to 57 percent of the total coverage of this vegetation in the country. Sabah is also home to 13 species of seagrasses and 75 percent of the country's coral reefs.[2] The coasts of Sabah have undergone very rapid socioeconomic development, which is certainly not without environmental impact. Development creates opportunities for employment and income and strengthens services that bring more people. This requires adaptive management of coastal and marine resources so that development options remain open without breaching environmental thresholds and resource resilience. Although issues related to the management of coastal and marine resources transcend geographical boundaries, approaches

---

* Projects supporting this research were funded under Niche Research Grant Scheme (NRGS 0001, 0002 and 0004) of the Ministry of Higher Education, Malaysia.
1 United Nations, "People and Oceans," Factsheet, The Ocean Conference, United Nations, New York, 5–9 June 2017.
2 L. Burke, E. Selig and M. Spalding, *Reefs at Risk in Southeast Asia* (Washington, DC: World Resources Institute, 2002).

based on knowledge of the resources and local socioeconomic realities can prove to be effective in governance. The regional approach, to be effective, should be holistic, with clear goals, priorities, efficient management, funding mechanisms, and multiple stakeholder inclusivity. Stakeholders include educational institutions, local government, the resource user community, the corporate sector, non-governmental organizations, and all other players in a particular region.

This article outlines the initiatives taken by the Borneo Marine Research Institute (BMRI), at the Universiti Malaysia Sabah (UMS), the experience gained, the outcomes of the initiatives, and the way forward in the context of the coastal and marine ecosystems of Sabah. The key role of BMRI is human capacity development in ocean science, but we also leverage our strengths and resources to engage with stakeholder agencies and communities for disseminating the environmental themes and motivate them to develop adaptations to living in coastal zones and to adopt sustainable methods of using ocean resources.

Capacity-Building

Formal Education Programs

Building human capacity is the core business of the BMRI and is crucial for developing adaptations in coastal and ocean management. Anthropogenic pressures and environmental impacts are always changing and producing consequences of different scales for the marine ecosystem. People with appropriate knowledge are required to help the community adapt to such dynamic situations. In this context, formal education through long-term degree programs and short-term training assumes a great deal of importance. Capacity is needed to inform knowledge-based management of oceans. The various levels of educational programs offered by BMRI are indicated in Figure 10.1. The degree programs are of international standard and conform to the requirements of Malaysian Quality Assurance. Staff members (who are resource persons for education and training) are also required to update and refresh their knowledge through professional development courses organized by UMS or through post-doctorate programs at recognized institutions of higher education. The degree module includes 16 weeks of training as a compulsory credit requirement for undergraduates. This is two weeks more than the duration of one semester. BMRI also welcomes regional partner institutions and other international organizations to avail the benefit of training for ten weeks or more under its policy to support mobility. Short-term training is subject to a minimum number of ten participants. Table 10.1 sets out the broad areas of research and training available at BMRI.

Candidates who have successfully graduated are serving in various government departments, including the Fisheries Department, the Department of Environment, marine parks, and other agencies, in positions of responsibility. This helps those institutions take decisions that augur well for marine ecosystems. Their presence at the helm rationalizes the decision-making process and implementation of appropriate policies. Out of the five postgraduate programs listed in Table 10.1, the Coastal and Marine Management Program is the latest addition. It provided an appropriate learning path for training, professional development, and taking an evidence-based approach to holistic management. Advanced knowledge and exposure are necessary for inculcating the abilities

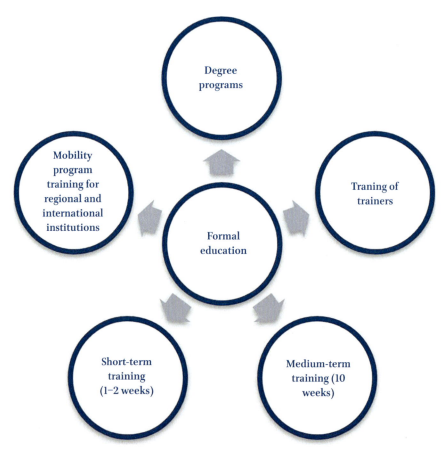

FIGURE 10.1 Formal education programs offered by BMRI for capacity-building.
SOURCE: THE AUTHORS

TABLE 10.1 *Research and training programs offered by BMRI*

Degree programs	Research areas	
Marine science	– Marine biodiversity – Marine habitat connectivity – Marine critical habitats (seagrasses, mangroves, and coral reefs) – Environmental biology of marine fish and invertebrates – Plankton ecology – Seaweed biology	– Harmful algal blooms – Endangered and threatened marine species (turtles, marine mammals, and some species of fish) – Coastal hydrodynamics – Coastal erosion & deposition
Fisheries science	– Population dynamics – Catch composition	– Catch-effort dynamics – Fisheries management
Marine biotechnology	– Genetic marking of fish and shellfish – Bioremediation of water quality – Bioprospecting – Molecular diagnostics of fish diseases	– Immunity modulation – Vaccine development – Cryopreservation of gametes – Probiotic treatment
Aquaculture	– Hatchery management – Broodstock management – Breeding and seed production – Water quality management – Integrated multi-trophic aquaculture systems – Nutrient cascading and bioremediation	– Biosecurity in aquaculture – Nutrition and feed development – Live feed culture – Grow-out management – Seaweed culture – Ocean hatcheries and nurseries – Stock enhancement and sea ranching

TABLE 10.1 Research and training programs offered by BMRI (*cont.*)

Degree programs	Research areas	
Coastal and marine management	– Management of marine protected areas – Marine ecotourism – Integrated coastal zone management	– Climate change vulnerability and adaptations – Ocean governance

needed to achieve expected outcomes pertaining to the complexity of issues that characterize coastal and marine management. In addition to scientific understanding, knowledge is also needed in the fields of social science and economics to provide technical competence and management skills for graduates in their role as effective coastal and marine practitioners. Building local capacity as holistically as possible, to collect and analyze ocean and fisheries data and carry out long-term monitoring, is helpful in distinguishing direct human-caused environmental change from natural variability and deciding on appropriate management intervention. BMRI has built its human resource strength accordingly.[3]

Community Education

BMRI is committed to enhancing public awareness of the advantages to coastal communities interacting with the sea to benefit from the ecosystem services. The Institute has structured the delivery of informal public education as an element of annual staff performance assessment.

The vision behind our community-based aquaculture initiative is to empower the coastal communities with ideas and knowledge that can help them with income from self-employment by allowing better access to food while alleviating pressure on biodiversity and fisheries. In Sabah, traditional small-scale fisheries are vital for the livelihoods and food security of a large number of people. These communities are being stressed as marine ecosystems increasingly face unprecedented pressures. Fish stocks are declining an average of four percent year on year, a trend established for Sabah since 1950–2010 by

---

[3] J. Kinch et al., "Outlook Report on the State of the Marine Biodiversity in the Pacific Islands Region, (Apia, Samoa: Secretariat of the Pacific Regional Environment Program, 2010).

Teh and Teh,[4] while seafood demand has continued to soar. The increasing proportional catch of small prey fish has raised concerns about the capacity of fisheries to support food security in Malaysia.[5] Because regulations and enforcement that deprive people of livelihoods do not work, developing viable livelihood options appropriate to the local environment and culture provide the way forward.

Aquatic farming provides better food security alternative in a changing climate than capture fisheries at a time when the production capacity of the ocean is a growing concern. It offers many alternatives and a scope for adaptation according to prevailing conditions. BMRI has taken up three community-based projects that can serve as case studies as to the benefits of aquatic farming: stock enhancement initiatives in Sungai Petagas, sea cucumber ranching in Kudat, and the "Aquaculture Friends" program.

A stock enhancement initiative project was undertaken in Sungai Petagas in the district Putatan, adjoining the state capital of Sabah, Kota Kinabalu. As a result of overfishing and habitat degradation, the once thriving shrimp fishery there was almost entirely decimated. In this area, the river joins the sea, and post-larvae of giant freshwater shrimp breeding in the estuary used to ascend the river. Their adults supported a profitable fishery in the past. BMRI tried to restore the lost fishery through this project. The shrimp were induced to breed in the shrimp hatchery of BMRI. The post-larvae raised in the hatchery were then released in the lower reaches of the river system through the active participation of the indigenous community. What was considered a "dead water body" has come to life with shrimp reaching harvestable size and with the development of aquatic webs. The local community is more respectful of the aquatic environment because people expecting food harvests are more inclined to protect the environment. The release operations have been accompanied by community awareness campaigns that inculcated environmental ethics and observing a no-take period for fishing. For this project, options were kept open for "harvest-type" or "recruit-type" ranching, pending scientific studies to determine the carrying capacity and catch per unit effort, among other observations.

Recently, BMRI initiated a sea cucumber ranching program through the organizational structure of the local community in Kampung Limau-Limauan in

---

4   L. Teh and L. Teh, "Reconstructing the marine fisheries catch of Peninsular Malaysia, Sarawak and Sabah, 1950–2010," Working Paper No. 2014–16 (Vancouver, BC: Fisheries Centre, University of British Columbia, 2014), p. 11.
5   M.M.R. Arriff et al., "Development of fisheries enterprise in peninsular Malaysia: Issues and questions," *Jati* 16 (2011): 265–299 (translated).

Kudat, on the west coast of Sabah. It involved environmental survey and monitoring, and breeding and larval rearing of sea cucumber (*Holothuria scabra*) in "ocean hatcheries" and grow-out in sea pens. While an adequate number of broodstock will be held in these facilities, the rest will be in the free environment in the designated area. The protected broodstock will ensure population recruitment so that this project could emerge as a sustainable, recruit-type ranching. With the knowhow provided by BMRI, the project is progressing well thanks to round-the-clock monitoring by local community partners. While the technical aspects are still handled by the researchers of BMRI, routine operations in managing the stocks of sea cucumbers, security of the site, and environmental care are looked after by community volunteers. This sea ranching program has expanded the understanding of the local environment in the community as dedicated individuals of all ages and both genders take part in the stock-building effort, identifying the critical issues and solutions with a sense of environmental stewardship. It will also provide dividends to the indigenous communities, in terms of production and cash returns through recurring harvest. The sea cucumber is a low-food chain and sedentary animal that plays a vital role in maintaining a healthy environment, without threatening biodiversity. In fact, its role in nutrient cycling is helpful in combating increased nutrient load associated with the human activity on the coast. The bioturbation of the benthic sediment by the sea cucumbers improves quality of water and habitat, and is a primary driver of biodiversity in the tidelands that are suitable places for shellfish gardening. The knowledge empowerment of the indigenous community is specifically related to site selection, broodstock conditioning and grow-out, and ecosystem management.

For sustainability of these two community-based programs, there are built-in buffers and multiple partnership arrangements. These include the consistency of the efforts with the institutional vision and mission regarding community welfare, staff strength, infrastructure, decision support; a broad team of key personnel and their long-term commitment; and the inclusion of community service in the annual performance evaluation system of individual staff. Furthermore, there are agreements among the partner agencies that bind them to carry forward the programs.

The nature of the community-based projects involves multiple agencies. BMRI is the anchor agency, and there is a governance structure involving local administrative authorities, and village heads and committees. Activities dealing with fisheries resources in Sabah are regulated by the Department of Fisheries under the Ministry of Agriculture Development and Food Industry, while matters pertaining to the environment, especially designation of marine parts, are under the purview of the Ministry of Tourism, Culture and Environment.

This mechanism strengthens the projects and facilitates collective efforts for a long-term and outcome-oriented program for community welfare.

Encouraged by the overwhelming response from the coastal communities, BMRI launched a program called "Aquaculture Friends" (or *Rakan aquakultur* in the local language). As the name indicates, we accept the sea farming community as "aquaculture friends" and then work for their knowledge empowerment. Many of them are traditional fishers harvesting fish for subsistence, but they are now facing hardship due to declining catches. To dissuade them from too much dependence on catches from the wild, they are trained in low-carbon and low-cost aquaculture. BMRI is striving to promote entrepreneurship in integrated multi-trophic aquaculture (IMTA) systems that are affordable to small-scale operators.

This platform is targeted at small-scale farmers or independent smallholders for whom self-employment provides a livelihood. The program is not linked to any particular company and receives no training, supervision, or support from industry. Running an expensive grouper hatchery or grow-out is beyond the reach of such farmers. IMTA and sea gardening provide a cheaper means of producing high-value species with meager investment.

Gender Equality and Lifelong Learning for All

Many surveys, including the most recent one conducted in Sabah, have examined the gender dimension in seafood production.[6] Here, men and women work in different parts of the value chain. Whereas men are mobilized in capture fisheries business, women prefer more land-based or inshore operations, including fish farming, processing, and marketing. This practice reflects differences in gender roles that do not appear to be a sort-of imposed discrimination or deliberate marginalization of women, because it is partly due to the reluctance of women to join the fishing vessels going to the deep sea for extended periods and partly due to their household responsibilities that require them to be nearer home. We believe that these gender roles are immaterial, and what is important is creating equal opportunities, giving more voice to women in decision-making, and ensuring a fair share in the income that can empower them to have a better control over their lives.

Fisheries and aquaculture are diverse activities, and all the links in the chain are important. If a section of the community (in this case, women) decides to play certain roles, then it should be left to their choice. Women will be at a socioeconomic disadvantage if the livelihood involves an activity that they are not inclined to perform and they are left with no better option. Creating

---

6 H. Rosazman, "Role of women in aquaculture sector," *Daily Express* (21 March 2018).

opportunities for all sectors of society is thus a good means of getting shared benefits, including for women. Stock enhancement programs that are not conducted very far from home offer women an opportunity of playing an active role and improving their income. Another advantage that needs to be highlighted is the respect that the women in villages command when viewed as a knowledge-empowered section of the community. Their ability to use skills to improve household earning or local economy will strengthen their voice in decision-making in area development plans. The three BMRI programs discussed in the section are led by women who are distinguished scientists and are also deeply committed to addressing the problem of gender inequality and uplifting the status of young women in the rural regions.

Furthermore, old and infirm people who dread deep sea fishing are also attracted to projects that are implemented on tidelands or in nearshore areas. The methods employed do not require any formal education or prior training. For some people, this offers an opportunity of life-long learning and life-long earning. It is particularly helpful for senior citizens with no pension or social security benefits.

Ocean Outreach Programs

Marine Aquarium and Museum: Marine Biodiversity Showcase
Marine biodiversity is one of the flagship programs of BMRI for public outreach in marine conservation. Marine biodiversity plays a key role in ecosystem services. It provides resources, food security, livelihoods, and high-value products, and also a means for addressing problems linked to climate change. However, to many people, marine biodiversity is an academic subject which they cannot relate to their daily lives. There is a dire need for the general public to be educated about this topic. This was the primary motivation for BMRI for setting up the Marine Aquarium and Museum and opening it to the public. Located on the scenic seafront, this facility houses a growing collection of marine life and serves as a showcase of the marine biodiversity of Borneo. There are five main sections: a deep dive diorama (that gives a visual feeling of being beneath the waves and at the sea floor in the midst of a rich marine biodiversity), an aquarium (containing indigenous species), a museum (for preserved remains of marine fauna), a mangrove walk area (reminding the visitors of the need to preserve this remarkable coastal vegetation), and an ocean outreach corner (for displaying thought-provoking information about the ocean and an interactive wood sculpture depicting the coral reef-ecosystem with a carry-home message).

The Marine Aquarium and Museum attracts thousands of visitors every month, including students from educational institutions and local and foreign tourists. Their visits make them more knowledgeable about the marine world, the problems it faces, and the need to take preventive and remedial actions, at least at the individual level. Booklets and multimedia products and items with marine conservation themes are available at the entrance door.

BMRI organizes a Celebration of the Sea program that comprises events over a period of four weeks to commemorate World Oceans Day and Coral Triangle Day. Included are talks on marine ecosystems and adaptation in coastal zones, pledge signings, video shows, ocean walks, beach clean-up, and other related activities. Over the years, the activities have diversified and attracted an increasing response from the general public.

BMRI also launched a citizen science program in March 2018 in partnership with the conservation-minded corporate sector to foster social responsibility towards the ocean. This dynamic program seeks greater involvement of the general public in scientific research on the marine environment. The activities envisaged under it unite scientists and educators with amateur marine environmentalists for protecting marine ecosystem services.

BMRI is also seriously considering a socially-driven "Citizens of the Ocean" campaign to produce informed individuals motivated by concern for the sea. Those members of the public who are unable to engage in the scientific component of the citizen science program can benefit from this platform to help them understand the essential adaptive measures needed to ensure sustainable benefits from the sea and deal with the vagaries resulting from the changing climate. In Sabah, there is a section of the community that has historically lived in the coastal sea in what are called "water villages." They are visible along both of the coasts of Sabah. Interaction of these people with the sea is intense. A specially structured Citizen of the Ocean program will target this and other communities for adaptation. Occasional programs are also organized by BMRI on sustainable seafood solutions, rehabilitation of endangered marine life, climate change adaptation, and carbon sequestration.

Support to Ecosystem-based Adaptation

BMRI has directed its efforts to support ecosystem-based adaptation in the coastal zone and towards building the capacity of the people to understand and implement appropriate measures. This approach is in line with the Institute's priorities, UMS's vision, and national aspirations. Research projects related to this topic can be structured in ways that can yield results which define milestones for monitoring systems required by funding agencies. Ecosystem-based approaches are adaptive, cross-sectoral, collaborative, and flexible enough to be designed according to regional characteristics and ecological criteria. In view of these merits, BMRI has been lending strong support to plans drawn by the relevant government departments for an ecosystem approach to fisheries management, expanding marine protected areas, reducing plastic waste in the ocean, implementing integrated coastal zone management, and increasing the carrying capacity of small islands. These programs are intended to boost the resilience of marine ecosystems, reduce pressure on marine biodiversity, and help coastal communities derive sustainable benefits through adaptive management. Working in the various committees set up by the different government departments entrusted to carry out such programs enhances interaction with the diverse stakeholders, the sharing of research findings, and learning from the experience of other agencies and communities. The ecosystem-based concerns can thus get support from institutions that formulate and implement national and local policies and actions.

BMRI supports nature-based solutions to mitigating the impacts of a changing climate. To this end, the Institute is building strength in programs aimed at promoting blue carbon stocks, establishing ecosystem thresholds and tipping points, designing low-carbon sea-farming modules, and identifying sustainable seafood solutions. Lastly, BMRI is consolidating ongoing research and development programs for a blue growth strategy.[7] This is the new sea-based development paradigm for a healthier coastal and marine ecosystem, linked with seafood security and other ecosystem services, and a roadmap for adaptation for living in the coastal zone in Sabah.

Mainstreaming climate change adaptation is a work in progress. The initial steps taken are building resilience in marine natural resources, especially critical marine habitats, conservation of marine biodiversity, and minimizing the ecological footprint of activities such as mariculture. It will take some more time and collective efforts to incorporate climate change adaptation measures into broader development planning. BMRI has played a key role in the decision of Universiti Malaysia Sabah to embrace eco-campus themes that envisage sustainability as well as climate change adaptation. As a result of consistent efforts, UMS has climbed to number 37 in the 2017 UI-GreenMetric World University Ranking. A policy decision to open the campus to tourists for a learning experience provided the tour operators acting under the direction of the Ministry of Tourism, Culture and Environment with an educational tourist hotspot in Sabah. The campus transformation that occurred as a result has not

---

7 S. Mustafa et al., "Positioning of aquaculture in blue growth and sustainable development goals through new knowledge, ecological perspectives and analytical solutions," *Aquacultura Indonesiana* 19, no. 1 (2018): 1–9.

only altered the behavior of University staff and students to be consistent with sustainable living, but also enabled UMS to emerge as a showcase for a large number of outsiders who want to experience our tryst with environmental compatibility.

Aligning Our Efforts with International Development Goals

In addition to regular in-house deliberations on the direction of research and development, priority setting, and developing critical mass, BMRI also annually organizes an International Conference on Marine Science and Aquaculture. The conference theme has varied from year-to-year (Table 10.2). This has provided opportunities for exchange of views among scientists, stakeholders, and policy-makers.

Listening to researchers from around the world has helped us gain from different perspectives and experiences and to learn trends for adaptations in coastal and marine areas and to calibrate our standing. This approach has enabled us to examine the possibilities and potential for blending our local efforts with international conventions, such as the Convention on Biological Diversity and the UN Sustainable Development Goals (2015–2030). In this context, BMRI values its collaboration with institutions of higher education,

TABLE 10.2 *Annual conference themes*

Year	Theme
2010	Indicators for sustainability of fisheries and aquaculture
2011	Sustainable development and management of aquatic resources
2012	Sustainable development and management of aquatic resources in a changing climate
2013	Ocean health and our future
2014	Ecosystem perspectives in sustainable development
2015	Challenges and opportunities in developing a blue economy
2016	Nurturing innovation ecosystems for sustainable oceans and societal well-being
2017	New frontiers in sustainable marine bioresources management
2018	Ocean governance: Issues, priorities and strategies
2019	Marine biodiversity for sustainable management of aquaculture and marine ecosystem services

the International Ocean Institute (a non-governmental organization), and Habitat UNI (UN-Habitat's partnership with universities worldwide). This collaboration contributes to closing the gap between academia and practice and encourages collaborative learning by nurturing mechanisms for partnerships with relevant stakeholder institutions. Often, it has resulted in changing our orientation towards the development of critical mass and fine tuning approaches to the university-community interface. Playing a proactive role in such matters enhances the opportunities of a major education provider (Universiti Malaysia Sabah, in this case), in this region of Borneo, to take part in developing sound policy frameworks to support adaptation and to achieving sustainable development.

We have been striving to impart multidisciplinary perspectives into research and development programs. The benefits of this approach are clear in terms of the innovative solutions that have been generated.[8] We have also provided scholarly feedback to policy-making institutions to consider ecological compatibility in developing national plans.[9] Any suggestion of measures for managing marine resources is based on a careful analysis and, in most cases, after thorough research investigation. For example, studies carried out on the effect of creating a marine protected area on coral trout populations enabled us to voice our support for expanding marine protected areas in the region.[10] In a recent policy-oriented study, Mustafa et al. elaborated on the means of leveraging knowledge of ecological aquaculture for entrepreneurship and the protection of the marine ecosystem.[11]

The importance of international perspectives in our regional programs on marine issues is justified because seafood provides 17 percent of animal protein,

---

[8] H.M. Faizan et al., "Transforming aquaculture research and industry for management of seafood security: Relevance of nurturing a unique innovation ecosystem," *International Journal of Management Studies* 22 (2015): 53–71; S. Mustafa, A. Estim, and S.R.M. Shaleh, "Knowing the unknown effects of lunar phases on marine life holds key to innovations in ecological aquaculture," *Surge* 5 (2017): 3–4; S. Mustafa et al., "Aquaculture sustainability: Multidisciplinary perspectives and adaptable models for seafood security," *Journal of Fisheries and Aquaculture Development* 6 (2017): 1–7.

[9] J. Hill and S. Mustafa, "Natural resources management and food security in the context of sustainable development," *Sains Malaysiana* 40 (2011): 1331–1340; S. Mustafa and S. Saad, "Harmonizing the tenth Malaysia Plan priorities with the new economic model and the green world order," *International Journal of Management Studies* 18 (2011): 59–72.

[10] F.C., Chung, C.F. Komilus, and S. Mustafa, "Effect of the creation of a marine protected area on populations of Coral Trout in the coral triangle region," *Regional Studies in Marine Science* 10 (2017): 1–9.

[11] S. Mustafa et al., "Leveraging scientific knowledge in aquaculture for entrepreneurship: Case studies at Universiti Malaysia Sabah," ISGR (2018), in press.

a livelihood to 12 percent of the world's population, and marine ecosystem services to the benefit of a lot more people.[12] Obviously, there is a convergence of interest of the global community on this matter, and the sharing of experience is helpful. Furthermore, efforts that are in line with international criteria can enable Malaysia to make rapid progress in achieving the goals and targets of the agreed-upon agenda or to receive support through the instruments developed for this purpose.

The national policy of Malaysia supports institutions of higher education working towards the country's progress in implementing the Sustainable Development Goals (SDGs). The policy document released by the Ministry of Higher Education on 3 April 2018, entitled "Framing Malaysian Higher Education 4.0: Future-Proof Talents," outlines directions for unlocking the Malaysia Education Blueprint 2015–2025 (Higher Education) and reiterates the need for initiatives towards the SDGs.[13] Because the focused area of BMRI concerns SDG 14 (Conserve and sustainably use the oceans, seas, and marine resources for sustainable development), our research and development contribution towards this area, presented in Table 10.3, represents a continuity of efforts in implementing regional priorities and national aspirations that are consistent with the international agenda. A policy paper on blue growth strategies and directions is under preparation.

Lessons Learned

1) Institutions of higher education need to pursue problem-solving research shaped in a way to include environmental compatibility, economic feasibility, and societal relevance, the core concepts of sustainable development.
2) Academia is in a better position to undertake community-based projects in areas as critical as seafood security in an attempt to develop a proof-of-concept that can provide a convincing basis for funding agencies to support the initiative.
3) Increasing visibility of efforts and ability to communicate pertinent issues leads to a wider appreciation of our efforts and support for projects

---

12   Food and Agriculture Organization of the United Nations (FAO), *The State of World Fisheries and Aquaculture: Contributing to Food Security and Nutrition for All* (Rome: FAO, 2016).
13   Malaysia, Ministry of Higher Education (MOHE), "Framing Malaysian Higher Education 4.0: Future-Proof Talents" (Putrajaya, Malaysia: MOHE, 2018), 1–138, outlines the directions for unlocking the Malaysia Education Blueprint 2015–2025 (higher education).

TABLE 10.3 Contribution of BMRI towards Sustainable Development Goal 14

Targets	Actions needed	Contribution of BMRI
14.1 Pollution	Regulations on disposal of pollutants, plastic waste. Control of eutrophication.	1. Developed a team of experts to focus on this problem. 2. Included this topic under postgraduate degree program. 3. Incepted a dedicated unit within the institute: Unit of Harmful Algal Bloom Studies to examine the problems linked to eutrophication, especially red tides. 4. Campaigned for removal of plastic waste from ecologically sensitive coastal marine areas as a routine activity. 5. Mobilized beach clean-up operations to prevent waste entering the sea. 6. Structured public awareness programs. 7. Conducted qualitative and quantitative analysis of marine debris at selected sites.
14.2 Sustainable management	Ecosystem-based approach to management of fisheries, aquaculture and sea ranching. Boosting resilience in marine critical habitats. Protection of marine biodiversity and threatened species.	1. Generated worthwhile knowledge through research projects. 2. Published evidence-based research. 3. Included related topics under postgraduate degree program. 4. Joined scientific panels to facilitate development of policies and tools. 5. Undertook ocean expeditions to establish coastal marine environmental profile. 6. Organized meetings to highlight the problem and seek decision support. 7. Rehabilitated degraded habitats. 8. Reduced the supply of prey fish from wild populations for aquaculture by developing substitutes of fish meal and oil.

Targets	Actions needed	Contribution of BMRI
14.3 Ocean acidification	Reducing carbon emissions. Mitigating the impact of ocean acidification on marine life.	1. Publications for scientific audience and general public, and drawing the attention of policy-making institutions. 2. Topic for postgraduate research. 3. Promoted conservation of blue carbon stocks. 4. Set up low-carbon farming systems in the ocean. 5. Experimental trials on simulated ocean acidification. 6. Identified the species vulnerable and/or resilient to ocean acidification.
14.4 Fishing regulations and stock restoration	Combating the problem of illegal, unreported, and unregulated (IUU) fishing. Restoration of stocks of depleted fisheries resources to biologically sustainable levels.	1. Intensified research on sustainable fishing as a topic of postgraduate studies. 2. Extended support to agencies for combating IUU fishing. 3. Undertook projects on stock restoration.
14.5 Marine Protected Areas	Expansion and effective management of marine protected areas (MPAS).	1. Teamed up with stakeholders for expansion of MPAS. 2. Contributed by way of research, development, and consultancy.
14.6 Subsidies	Reduction of harvest from the sea (total allowable catch).	1. Generated scientific evidence that supports restrictions on indiscriminately exploiting populations that deplete the wild stocks of brood fish and immature virgins. 2. Supported increased minimum size of fish at capture.

TABLE 10.3 Contribution of BMRI towards Sustainable Development Goal 14 *(cont.)*

Targets	Actions needed	Contribution of BMRI
14.7 Small Island Developing States	Conservation of marine biodiversity, and promoting marine ecotourism and income generation.	1. Generated new knowledge on marine biodiversity. 2. Promoted marine ecotourism through a marine biodiversity showcase in the form of Aquarium and Marine Museum. 3. Empowered people with a focus on alternative sources of income to lessen pressure on marine biodiversity. 4. Established the Management Center of Coral Triangle Region; involved in implementing its various goals: conservation priorities for coastal areas, ecosystem-based approaches to management of fisheries and other marine resources; sustainable management of shared tuna stocks; sustainable seafood business; expansion and management of MPAs; climate change adaptations; protection of threatened marine species. 5. Networked and worked directly with small island State members of the Coral Triangle Initiative on marine management and adaptation. 6. Introduced a new method of grouper seed production to support the aquaculture industry. 7. Developed low-carbon aquaculture systems.

that we undertake. This is possible through web-based communication, social media, presentations, publication of technical and policy papers, newsletters, forums, and conferences on important themes.

4) Universities with necessary expertise can take the lead in matters pertaining to climate change that are threatening marine biodiversity and seafood production. This calls for a thorough investigation of the impact of processes, such as ocean acidification and warming on livelihoods, in order to be able to identify vulnerable and resilient species.

5) A simple but strategic initiative of an institution of higher education that provides a proof-of-concept can draw support for projects involving co-management with the overwhelming participation of local communities.
6) Adaptation in coastal communities heavily dependent on marine resources should involve as many stakeholders as possible, regardless of their academic background and gender, because ecosystem-based approaches are very inclusive.

Conclusion and Next Steps

The human capacity-building and public awareness programs initiated by BMRI have contributed to disseminating the information needed for adaptive management of coastal and marine ecosystems. These efforts provide a model for merging regional priorities with global issues in developing an approach that shows the way forward for other regions with somewhat similar conditions. Bold new regional and national programs are needed in light of the severity of challenges facing the ocean in a changing environment.

It is entirely possible to change the approaches of coastal communities towards conservation and adaptation in the marine environment. The strategy should involve understanding how traditional communities value marine conservation as a driver of social welfare and demonstrating the benefits that they can accrue by adaptive modification of their use of resources. Outcome-based projects carried out by institutions of higher education can provide a choice model that combines environmental, social, and economic attributes for sustainable development.

The complexity of factors affecting the coastal and marine environments and the urgency to develop adaptations suggests that the "business-as-usual" approach and minor policy adjustments will not suffice. There is a need for a new development paradigm backed by comprehensive mechanisms to support it. In this context, we believe that an inclusive blue growth strategy provides the way forward. Blue growth will make it possible to strike an appropriate balance between economic, social, and ecological considerations in achieving food security and community welfare while making the SDG14 a reality. It resonates well with the integrated coastal zone management priorities and represents a convergence of interest between the local community, policy-makers, and the business sector. A blue growth strategy can be shaped by ground realities in Malaysia and aligned with international perspectives embodied under the SDGs.

While there are existing programs that contribute to the management of marine environment and resources, identifying blue growth as an umbrella for diverse activities will set a new approach and infuse a new momentum, if the policy favors the blending of entrepreneurship ideas with science and technology, bridging the gap between research and commercialization, and uniting all stakeholders to develop this sector. In addition to marine fisheries, aquaculture, and ecotourism, the newer fields of interest like marine biotechnology, ocean energy, and seabed mining are the future growth areas that might develop rapidly under the blue growth sector. It is time we develop a blueprint for action for blue growth as a sector of development planning and start investing in producing a critical mass of experts in this field.

Science, Community, and Decision-makers: Can We Break the Vicious Circle?

Oxana Sytnik*
Laboratório de Oceanografia Costeira, Departamento de Geociências, Universidade Federal de Santa Catarina, Santa Catarina, Brazil

Dominique Peña Clinaz
Department of Civil and Environmental Engineering, University of Hawaii at Manoa, United States

Luana Sena Ferreira
Programa de Pós Graduação em Gestão de Políticas Públicas e Seguridade Social, Universidade Federal do Recôncavo da Bahia, Bahia, Brazil

Marina Reback Garcia
Programa de Pós Graduação em Sistemas Costeiros e Oceânicos, Universidade Federal do Paraná, Paraná, Brazil

Bruno Meirelles de Oliveira
Programa de Pós Graduação em Ciência Ambiental, Universidade de São Paulo, São Paulo, Brazil

Raquel Hadrich Silva
Amsterdam Institute of Social Sciences Research, University of Amsterdam, The Netherlands

---

* This article is a joint effort of students and researchers from Brazil, Costa Rica, Colombia, Russia, and Turkey carried out during the training course on Ocean Governance, Ocean Sciences and GeoEthics in Pontal do Paraná, Brazil. The authors gratefully acknowledge the support of the International Ocean Institute Training Centre for Latin America and the Caribbean for organizing this special event. The authors thank the IOI 2016 participants Taynara Pinheiro, Ricardo Haponiuk, Raúl Daza, Carlos Tibiriçá, Matheus Marchini, Mayara Campos, Tiago Gandra, Ramazan Açikgöz, Angela Zaccaron da Silva, Júlia Rafanhin Bilibiu, Vanessa Ballardin, Giulianna Macedo Rodrigues, Ana Emília Woltrich, Luana Borato, and Ilara da Rocha Santos for a fruitful discussion that made valuable contributions to the paper. We also thank the LAGECI research group for their insightful comments on the Brazilian case, namely, Marinez Scherer, Francisco Veiga Lima, Fabricio Almeida, Carolina Martins,

Introducing Ocean Governance: Global Trends and Challenges

Federica Mogherini, High Representative of the Union for Foreign Affairs and Security Policy/Vice-President of the European Commission, said:

> Our oceans are threatened by crime, piracy and armed robbery. Attempts to assert territorial or maritime claims are affecting regional stability and the global economy. We need to use all the tools we have to shape ocean governance.[1]

Surprisingly, given its fundamental role, ocean governance has only recently begun to garner attention and move up the international policy agenda.[2] The growing interest in ocean governance was enunciated in Chapter 17 of Agenda 21, adopted by the United Nations Conference on Environment and Development,[3] stressing the predominant role of the ocean, sea, and coastal areas to support human life and the corresponding imperative to develop these in a sustainable manner. During the last decades of the twentieth century, planning and policies regarding ocean and coastal areas came mainly from the governmental arena.[4] Most policies were created under a command and control perspective towards the distribution of power, legitimacy, and authority among the diverse levels and institutions involved.[5]

At the root of ocean governance is the growing recognition that ocean management needs to be based on an ecosystem approach. The term ecosystem governance can be understood as the ecological characteristics, functions, or

---

Laura Prestes, André de Souza de Lima, Mariana Mattos, and Natalia Corraini. The authors would also like to extend their appreciation to Professors Eduardo Marone and Alejandro Gutiérrez for stimulating discussions, their constructive critiques, and providing invaluable input throughout the work. Corresponding author: ox.sytnik@gmail.com.

1 Project Aware, "International Ocean Governance: EU's contribution for safe, secure, clean and sustainably managed oceans," Press release (11 November 2016), available online: <https://www.projectaware.org/news/international-ocean-governance>.
2 Organisation for Economic Co-operation and Development (OECD), *The Ocean Economy in 2030* (Paris: OECD Publishing, 2016), available online: <http://dx.doi.org/10.1787/9789264251724-en>.
3 Report of the United Nations Conference on Environment and Development, Rio de Janeiro, *Protection of the oceans, all kinds of seas, including enclosed and semi-enclosed seas, and coastal areas and the protection, rational use and development of their living resources*, Ch. 17, available online <http://www.un.org/depts/los/consultative_process/documents/A21-Ch17.htm>.
4 R. Burroughs, *Coastal Governance* (Washington: Island Press, 2011).
5 D.M. Nobre et al., "Governance of the Cassurubá Extractive Reserve, Bahia State, Brazil: An analysis of strengths and weaknesses to inform policy," *Marine Policy* 7 (2017): 44–55.

processes that directly or indirectly contribute to human well-being, that is, the benefits that people derive from functioning ecosystems.[6] On a broader perspective, Costanza et al.[7] and Burroughs[8] adopt an ecosystem-based approach that embraces a social-ecological perspective – a dynamic perspective that accounts for different stakeholder priorities and balances social and ecological needs. The approach introduces four key principles to consider: (1) stakeholders should be involved in formulating and implementing policies, and those policies should be ecologically sustainable and socially equitable; (2) institutional scales for decision-making should match ecological inputs; (3) potentially damaging activities should be approached with caution, and there should be ample opportunity to adapt and improve policies; and (4) sustainable governance of the ocean rests on full allocation of social and ecological costs and benefits. The ecosystem approach concept has been evolving since the 1992 Rio Earth Summit and after the recommendations and conclusions of the Millennium Ecosystem Assessment. The concept has gained great importance by linking the functioning of ecosystems to human welfare and has a critical role in the contexts of wide-range decision-making, such as ecosystem-based management (EBM).[9]

Although there have been progressive efforts to enhance coastal and ocean governance towards the sustainable economic use of resources, there is still much work to be done. For optimal management, adaptive governance seems to be the proper way. Such governance connects individuals, organizations, agencies, and institutions at multiple organizational levels. Adaptive governance is considered as "governance that is able to work properly under systems that change across time."[10]

This work takes a forward-looking view of the challenges facing ocean governance and some of the problems regarding ethics and equity in decision-making processes in Brazil. Therefore, this study addresses those challenges by offering a framework, validating several points of view from the vanguard of

---

6   Millennium Ecosystem Assessment, *Ecosystems and Human Well-Being, Synthesis Report* (Washington, DC: Island Press, 2005).
7   R. Costanza et al., "The value of ecosystem services: Putting the issues in perspective," *Ecological Economics* (Special section: Forum on Valuation of Ecosystem Services) 26 (1998): 67–72.
8   Burroughs, n. 4 above.
9   Id.; C. Folke et al., "Adaptive governance of social-ecological systems," *Annual Review of Environment and Resources* 30 (November 2005): 441–447; L. Paramio et al., "New approaches in coastal and marine management: Developing frameworks of ocean services in governance," in *Environmental Management and Governance*, ed. C.W. Finkl and C. Makowski (Basel: Springer International Publishing, 2015), pp. 85–110.
10 Folke et al., id.

science, and finally making recommendations for marine education processes. In this work, the following questions were combined and considered:
- How can challenges related to existing discrepancies/conflicts among stakeholders involved in ocean governance processes be addressed, and how can a common vision be built?
- How can a constructive, inclusive, and proactive dialogue among policy-makers, scientists, and communities for well-informed decision-making be ensured?

Setting Up a Roundtable

Focus Group Approach

Focus groups are a common approach in research relating to different social groups and in cross-cultural and development research,[11] and they are gaining popularity in academia and coastal research, especially in the field of coastal hazard assessment and resilience.[12] For this study, a focus group was conducted with the participation of seven to ten people, comprising researchers, graduates, and Ph.D. students, as an informal discussion with the aim to capture their multiple perspectives and attitudes regarding the research questions. The exercise fostered debates on existing coastal conflicts and experiences in the Brazilian context, with particular consideration given to the triple bottom line of science, policy-making, and community roles in decision-making. The group produced diagrams during the work; these graphics summarize the key challenges ahead in understanding the existing ocean governance processes and draw a path for future research attempts in this domain. The group work was organized into two activities: a brainstorming session and a problem-solving exercise based on a "problem and solution tree analysis" methodology.

---

11   H. Freitas et al., "The Focus Group: A qualitative research method," ISRC, Merrick School of Business, University of Baltimore (MD, EUA), WP ISRC No. 010298, February 1998; J. Smithson, "Using and analyzing focus groups: Limitations and possibilities," *International Journal of Social Research Methodology* 3, no. 2 (2000): 103–119.

12   D.E. DeLorme et al., "Developing and managing transdisciplinary and transformative research on the coastal dynamics of sea level rise: Experiences and lessons learned," *Earth's Future* 4 (May 2016): 194–209; S.C. Hagen et al., "Systems Approaches for Coastal Hazard Assessment and Resilience," *Oxford Research Encyclopedia of Natural Hazard Science*, Oxford University Press USA (2017): 1–28.

During the group exercise, the group conducted dynamic work on background research, problem diagnosis, approaching new ideas, and identifying new relationships and their interpretations. The inner workings of these group dynamics involved discussions that were managed by a moderator who controlled the discussion in order to articulate and assess one opinion at a time. In the context of this focus group, all opinions and suggestions within the group were taken into consideration and recorded. The conflicting opinions that emerged in the discussions eventually led to the formation of a collective voice.

Problem and Solution Tree Analysis

Solution tree analysis is a highly visual decision-making support tool that focuses on cause and effect relationships and can provide a way to compact abundant and vague information regarding complex problems. The approach used in the study was adopted by the group specifically for the study; however, it must be noted that the chosen method was a subjective decision of the focus group, whereas other methods might be equally plausible in identifying cause and effect interconnections, depending on the nature and complexity of the analyzed problem.

Beginning with the formulation of the starting problem identified by the group and placed on top of the diagram (at the treetop), factors contributing to the problem were arranged at lower levels (Figure 11.1). The entire tree was displayed as a stylized tree drawing, with levels or layers of underlying causes and respective impacts represented as tree roots and leaves.

As a starting point, "weak ocean governance" was considered as a core research problem. The tree allowed for a breakdown of the "*Why*" question, identifying possible root causes of the problem of why weak ocean governance exists. Three major causes were revealed: (1) poor communication, (2) conflict of interests, and (3) uncertainty in decision-making associated with the complexity of ocean ecosystems (Figure 11.2).

The Problem Tree Diagram is closely linked to the Solution Tree Diagram, a second drawing that outlines and communicates the outcomes of the group's work. At this step, a backward approach was used to address the problem and the negative statements were reversed into positive desirable ones – as if the problem had already been successfully treated. The solution tree approach breaks down the research question into "*How*" branches, or expected actions, and possible solutions to be taken towards improvement in ocean governance. The group discussed priority actions that need to be taken to advance the dialogue and promote a more cohesive interaction among stakeholders (Figure 11.3).

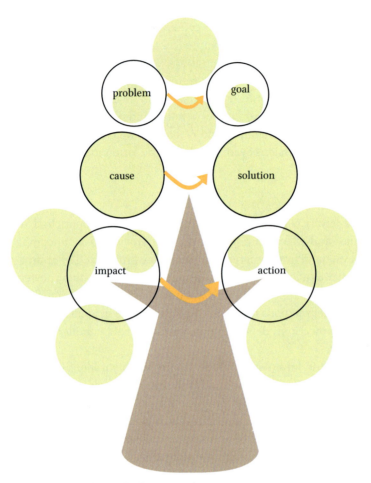

FIGURE 11.1 Problem and solution tree diagram.
SOURCE: THE AUTHORS

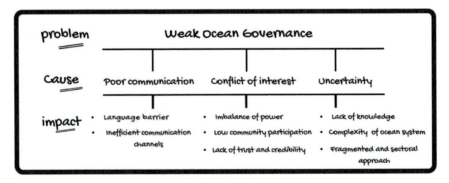

FIGURE 11.2 Problem tree mechanism.
SOURCE: THE AUTHORS

FIGURE 11.3 Solution tree diagram identifies means-end relationships as opposed to cause and effects of the problem tree.
SOURCE: THE AUTHORS

Science, Community, and Policy-makers: the Vicious Circle?

The Challenges of Bridging the Gap between Research, Policy, and Community

Regarding the statement of the reference group, the relationship between science, policy-making, and society has been discussed and analyzed in various contexts. There has been much documentation of the reasons why decision-makers and scientists often have mutual misunderstandings. Understanding is necessary for the full integration of scientific knowledge into the decision-making process. Decision-makers are on top of the pyramid, and the community is on the bottom. Unfortunately, if skepticism in science increases (often due to conflicting scientific opinions), it is likely to be placed out of the scheme (Figure 11.4).

However, the role of science is an important factor to be considered in decision-making processes because of its potential in helping make better informed decisions. Evidence-based policy-making can rely on the findings of science to address societal goals. Moreover, the transfer of knowledge from science to broader audiences can enable the empowerment of community actors to make demands backed by the findings of scientific research. The predominance of the top-down approach within governance hampers the meaningful participation of different actors in the decision-making process.

Citizens in general complain of a lack of democratic input in decisions and struggle to gain more space in the governance arena. Scientists as active citizens have been shown to be equally dissatisfied with how their knowledge is included in decisions. Moreover, in light of this increasingly complex matter, questions of equity in the decisions made have also raised concerns from

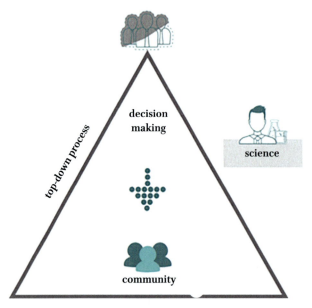

FIGURE 11.4 Top-down decision-making approach in ocean governance and management.
SOURCE: THE AUTHORS

diverse actors that identify the lack of attention paid to marginalized and vulnerable groups of society in the decision-making process.[13]

At the same time, globally, there has been increasing concern about risks to the effective interface between science and policy-making.[14] Much of this complexity is a result of the inherently different needs and ambitions. According to Gluckman, "science alone does not make policy."[15] Too often, scientists having little knowledge of policy dynamics fail to understand the factors that influence policy decisions beyond the evidence, or they fail to turn any scientific conclusions into policy realities; this can lead to tension. It has been said that scientists are very good at problem definition and less prepared for finding policy-acceptable solutions within the timeframe of the usual policy cycle.[16]

13   A. Sen, *Development as Freedom* (New York: Alfred Knopf, 1999).
14   P. Gluckman, *Enhancing Evidence-informed Policy Making*, Office of the Prime Minister's Chief Science Advisor, Annual Report of the Minister's Chief Science Advisor (Auckland, New Zealand: Office of the Prime Minister's Chief Science Advisor, 2017), available online: <http://www.pmcsa.org.nz/wp-content/uploads/17-07-07-Enhancing-evidence-informed-policy-making.pdf>.
15   Id.
16   P. Cairney and K. Oliver, "Evidence-based policymaking is not like evidence-based medicine: So how far should you go to bridge the divide between evidence and policy?," *Health Research Policy and Systems* 15, no. 35 (April 2017): 1–11, DOI: 10.1186/s12961-017-0192-x.

Though science always has a voice or a chance to be heard, it should always be considered as an important factor contributing to the policy development process. Properly accounted for, scientific knowledge should lead to better policy decisions. A science advisory system is a major element for building a healthy and politically independent research community.[17] For instance, in New Zealand, a formal science advisory system largely comprises scientists within academia and the Crown Research Institutes, including also the Office of the Prime Minister's Chief Science Advisor, departmental science advisors, and the Committee of Science Advisors. These roles are complemented by other ecosystem actors, such as professional and non-governmental organizations (NGOs) and industry that produce and provide knowledge relevant to policy-making.

In Brazil, no formal advisory system exists to bridge the policy-making community and the science community, yet there are several scientific societies that play an important role in environmental sector areas ranging from land use to deforestation and climate change. One of them is the Grupo de Integração de Gerenciamento Costeiro (GI-GERCO), operating within the Brazilian Ministry for the Environment, which is mostly dedicated to enforcement of the National Plan of Integrated Coastal Zone Management.[18] Other formal and informal gatherings take place, including congresses and workshops that serve as a way of communicating scientific results to the general public. Often, these meetings involve roundtable discussions with invited representatives from local administrations or regional/national policy departments. Private (or freelance) academic consultancy is another important and quite demanding type of consultancy when academic and scientific staff are hired on a case-by-case basis to provide their expert advice to external organizations and local governmental institutions on a particular subject. However, concerns have been raised over examples of situations in which GI-GERCO's failure to engage appropriately in efforts to promote science diplomacy and lack of operational power led to problems in policy development or communication.[19]

When communicating science to policy, the products from scientific research do not necessarily come in handy from a policy perspective, as most of it is considered to be derivative and repetitive. These arguments develop from ambiguity, considering the "cookie cutter" solutions realm of most policy-makers, and the complexity of scientific findings that result in uncertainty during

---

17   Gluckman, n. 14 above.
18   Government of Brazil, Plano Nacional de Gerenciamento Costeiro, adopted 16 May 1988, available online: <https://www.marinha.mil.br/secirm/gerco>.
19   Pers. Comm. in group discussion with LAGECI research group (5 June 2018).

decision-making. This argument suggests that scientists revise their research questions, the effectiveness in communicating their findings, and their accuracy and credibility. On the other hand, scientists tend to remain cautious about the extent and manner in which research should be used as an instrument to inform policy, while citizens' concerns with access to research findings relate mostly to a need for transparent processes in decision-making. Ideally, these three should work together, and if they do, they must know each other's strengths and weaknesses. However, challenges continue to be a lack of trust, different goals and interests, ways of communication, and perception of time.

Policy-making does not necessarily rely on scientific foundations, primarily due to the different levels of hierarchy on which decision-makers tend to operate. Not only might scientific evidence conflict with values and beliefs of policy-makers, but policy-makers are also bound to use evidence in the battle to control problem definition and policy solutions. Furthermore, scientists as employees have to cope with productivity standards that can result in a vast production of fragmented and indifferent or "junk" scientific results. When it comes to scientific production, the disparagement of a "more-is-better-approach" will have a positive influence towards advanced and integrated knowledge production to achieve society's main goals. Policy-makers are often lost over which scientific material to rely on and whether they are actually offering effective answers. The majority of decision-makers are likely to focus primarily on shorter timeframes and immediate answers, while scientific research is often focused on longer-term scenarios. Moreover, scientists, decision-makers, and society do not use the same language, which often leads to disparate interpretations of the same subject matter. Scientific language often requires "translation" before it can be absorbed by non-scientists. For instance, not all citizens (scientists and non-scientists) are actually fully aware of the scope of legal frameworks and managerial procedures. Further, as new scientific findings are published in journals, they frequently are not well-communicated outside the academic world. Similarly, reports produced by decision-makers are often kept confidential and likewise are not easily reachable.

Still, on the lack of precise recommendations from science, publications often end with "our results indicate that further research is needed," which leads to insufficient recommendations. Nevertheless, some scientific programs have advanced and are leading the way in producing complementary publications for decision-makers (e.g., Intergovernmental Panel on Climate Change reports, Millennium Ecosystem Assessment). Unfortunately, there is no clear correlation between the quality of science and its derived policy. Good-quality science does not necessarily lead to good policy. The same is true in the opposite direction. On the other hand, the incompatibilities mentioned before restrain scientists, key decision-makers, and citizens from working effectively together in a comprehensive manner.

Another significant issue is that policy debates in the process of decision-making continue to be dominated by immediate economic needs that rarely allow consideration of longer-term social and environmental impacts. It is undeniable that the main challenge is to overcome the dominant development model centered on economic growth if we are to achieve sustainable development goals. For this reason, it is important to consider our actions as a question of ethics in the paths we are to take on communicating findings that are not essentially ours, but which we owe to the development of humanity. In addition, it remains ethical to hold decision-makers responsible for unwanted social and environmental outcomes of decisions they choose to make.

Furthermore, it is indispensable to open possibilities for transformative action through the promotion of community rights and responsibilities. Community development can be understood as an expression of citizenship through two dimensions in which it is considered part of a political community. The first dimension of citizenship entails civil, political, and social rights for community members,[20] whereas the second refers to individual behavior in the fulfillment of their rights and duties as community members. The decision to be an active citizen or not relates very much to an ethical approach to individual responsibilities in society.

The importance of the responsibilities that scientists, decision-makers, and citizens hold cannot continue to be neglected. This acknowledgement of ethical responsibility in decision-making of both, individual actors – scientists, politicians, citizens – and collective institutions, such as government, research institutes, and NGOs, enables us to envision more effective governance in the coastal and marine environment.

Internationally, it is important to stress congruent ethical behavior among scientists, politicians, and community towards ocean governance. The distinction between ethics and morals becomes relevant in this discussion. While morality is based on individual beliefs and offers the right to do good or bad, ethical behavior is what is expected from an individual in society. Ethical behavior aims to protect a common good. Therefore, as Vesilind explains, morals determine decisions within the ethical system.[21] If this distinction becomes clear for the different actors, and, moreover, if it facilitates a common moral

---

20 P. Walker and T. Lovat, "Should we be talking about ethics or about morals?," *Ethics & Behavior* 27, no. 5 (February 2017): 436–444.

21 P.A. Vesilind, "Rules, ethics and morals in engineering education," *Engineering Education* (February 1988): 289–293, p. 292, available online: <https://classes.soe.ucsc.edu/cmpe080e/Spring07/morals_rules_ethics_Vesilind.pdf>.

behavior towards ocean-related processes and interactions, it could lay the groundwork to promoting compatibility among actors globally.

Facing the Challenges of Decision-making in Brazil: Case Studies

As a response to growing pressures, recent years have seen a significant increase in the number of countries and regions putting in place strategic policy frameworks for better ocean management. Most coastal nations of the world already have a variety of sectoral policies in place to manage different uses of the ocean, such as shipping, industrial and artisanal fishing, tourism, and the establishment of marine protected areas. Brazil is among the concerned coastal nations, and its strategic policy framework is still at the stage of design and implementation.[22]

At the moment, ocean governance in Brazil is facing numerous risks and uncertainties. There are gaps in the governance framework, weak law enforcement, multiple use conflicts, and a lack of equity and ethical frameworks for adequate use of coastal resources. The signs are that current ocean governance is expected to continue to evolve along mainly sectoral lines rather than through comprehensive integrated approaches. Yet, there is a clear need for more integrated ocean management to address the interconnected nature of ecosystems, growing economic activity, mounting pressures on ocean resources, and increasingly crowded ocean space.[23]

Coastal areas in Brazil stand as the most densely occupied areas of the national territory, and they also are the areas experiencing the most use conflicts. This is mainly due to the intensification of environmental pressures coming from the expansion of three main sectors of development: urbanization, industrialization, and tourism exploitation.[24] Regarding the existing legal frameworks on ocean governance and coastal management, Brazil still lacks good, practical examples. Most parts of the national policy are still restricted to the theory, and decentralized administration may be the origin of some problems related to political abuse of power, overlapping responsibilities, and other forms of institutional disintegration.[25] For instance, national coastal policy

---

22 OECD, n. 2 above.
23 Id.
24 M. Polette, "A zona costeira em crise: Opções de gestão integrada e participativa, notas de aula," Universidade do Vale do Itajaí, Centro de Ciências Tecnológicas da Terra e do Mar, Oceanografia, Itajaí (SC), Brasil (2008), available online: <http://nmd.ufsc.br/files/2011/05/1a_zona_costeira_em_crise_1_polette.pdf>.
25 T.A. Seraval and M. de F.L. Alves, "International trends in ocean and coastal management in Brazil," *Journal of Coastal Research* (ICS 2011) 64: 1258–1262.

does not support broad participation of local communities and therefore fails to give feedback needed for continuous policy improvements.

The following three cases demonstrate examples of poor government practices based on inadequate, top-down management models where little importance has been given to respecting the cultural identity and social security of the traditional livelihoods.

A Divided Sea: Conflict of Overlapping Territories

The recent maritime expansion along with tourism, industrial shrimping and fishing, and the establishment of marine protected areas have led to open conflicts with local artisanal fisheries. Most of these conflicts are related to the restriction of fishing activities in areas traditionally used by these artisanal fishers. In many cases, these conflicts appeared as a result of the fact that protected areas were created without the fishery communities' participation.[26] Further, top-down policies and a lack of coherent environmental mitigation programs appear to have contributed to an increase in user conflicts.

Artisanal Fishing and Industrial Port Activity: Competition for Space

The artisanal fishery contributes to the Brazilian fishery sector and represents more than 50 percent of the total production of the country.[27] Historically, the culture and identity of the traditional fishery and their families were typically associated with mixed-land and sea-based economies, a backbone for fishing communities in terms of food supply and income.

Confrontation between artisanal fishing and industrial port activities over resources and space often resulted in persistent conflicts, which can eventually become a constraint on the development of the sectors. The destruction of artisanal fishing in Engenho Mercês and Ilha Tatuoca was caused by construction and the subsequent enlargement of the Port of Suape, located in the southern littoral of Brazil. Among the main impacts the community suffered was the withdrawal of fishers and their families from their traditional residences, a de facto breaking of the open access regime in the sea, and disruption of family and community-based subsistence activities. Insufficient administrative experience of local government bodies and port executives in managing the

---

26 A.C. Diegues, *O Mito Moderno da Natureza Intocada*, 3rd ed. (São Paulo: HUCITEC/NUPAUB – Núcleo de Apoio à Pesquisa sobre Populações Humanas e Áreas Úmidas Brasileiras, 2000).

27 A. Begossi et al., "Compensation for environmental services from artisanal fisheries in SE Brazil: Policy and technical strategies," *Ecological Economics* 71 (2011): 25–32; R. de F. Netto, "Descrição dos impactos sofridos pela comunidade de pescadores artesanais de Santa Cruz – ES, Brasil," *Bioikos* 18, no. 1 (2004): 51–62.

consequences, decisions taken without public participation and approval, and an absence of proper education created a serious social conflict in the area. Finally, the lack of decision-making power of local communities ended up favoring economic interests over real social demands.

Artisanal Fishing and MPAs: Forced to Relocate

The establishment of MPAs has raised many conflicts between artisanal fishers and protected area authorities in Brazil. Most of these conflicts refer to the restriction of artisanal fishing activities in areas traditionally used by these artisanal fishers despite their historical dependence on this coastal land and water. In many cases, these conflicts appeared as a result of the fact that these protected areas were created without participation of fishing communities. One of these cases is the Peixe Lagoon, a national park established in 1986 in the southern Brazil coastal zone.

There are a few fishing villages located inside the park and on the edges of the lagoon. According to the Law 9985/00 (National Systems of Conservation Units – SNUC),[28] the people who inhabit a national park have to be removed and relocated, and the exploitation of natural resources must be forbidden.[29] This has generated a serious conflict between the responsible environmental agency (IBAMA – Instituto Chico Mendes de Conservação da Biodiversidade) and the local fishing communities. The park made a formal agreement with fishers, allowing some of them to live inside the park and granting temporary work licenses to some to fish inside the protected area. However, ignoring the agreement, national park officials have made informal pressures causing people's withdrawal from their residences within the protected area. Uncomfortable with this situation, fishers had to leave their villages for nearby cities. This has been done without any assistance from government, despite legal obligations to support peoples' relocation.[30]

The question that should be critically addressed is why do traditional fishers have to be removed from protected areas? According to the World Forum of Fisher Peoples, the World Forum of Fish Harvesters and Fish Workers, and the Food and Agriculture Organization of the United Nations objectives and guidelines,[31] participation of the local population in the creation and

---

28 Government of Brazil, National Systems of Conservation Units Act, 9985 Planalto (2000), codified at 4519 (2002) decree, available online: <http://www2.camara.leg.br/legin/fed/lei/2000/lei-9985-18-julho-2000-359708-norma-pl.html>.
29 Diegues, n. 26 above.
30 Id.
31 Food and Agriculture Organization of the United Nations (FAO), *Report of the Twenty-seventh Session of the Committee on Fisheries*, FAO Fisheries Report No. 830 (Rome: FAO, 2007); FAO, *Report of the Global Conference on Small-scale Fisheries, Securing Sustainable*

establishment of conservation units should be assured, and traditional populations' cultures and ecological knowledge should be respected and valued.

This Mine is Mine: All Waterways Lead to the Sea

Despite the efforts of the scientific community in Brazil, marine pollution stands as one of the most critical problems, yet most of the government's targets for effective marine pollution monitoring and mitigating have gone unmet. A remarkable example is the collapse of the Fundão Dam on 5 November 2015, in Minas Gerais State, which is considered the greatest socio-environmental Brazilian accident. Over 50 million cubic meters of toxic mud were released from the reservoir of mine tailings of Samarco Company to the River Doce and then to the Atlantic Ocean, immediately devastating urban settlements downstream and causing a dreadful water supply problem.[32] After the accident, the scientific community and society were strongly mobilized and a huge amount of information was released showing that, to the astonishment of many, the tragedy was foreseen but nothing had been done to avoid it. In this case, the lack of an efficient early warning and surveillance system, as well as no sanctions after the catastrophe, may be regarded as an invitation to further environmental crimes. Two years after the tragedy, the company has still not carried out adequate removal or monitoring of the impacts, contrary to their promise to remove tailings from affected rivers in compliance with the country's regulatory directives and the international frameworks on post-disaster management. Contrary to expectations, there was a setback in environmental legal planning, such as law relaxation, decreased resources for regulatory agencies, and the absence of effective measures for environmental recovery.[33] Driven by the citizen campaign called "Mar de Lama Nunca Mais" (*Sea of Mud No More*), a bill was presented to the Legislative Assembly of the State of Minas Gerais demanding establishing safety that would prevent future tragedies like the one of the Fundão Dam. Despite the huge public concern, the Brazilian mining lobby used its influence with the Congress with the intention to weaken the

---

Small-scale Fisheries: Bringing Together Responsible Fisheries and Social Development, FAO Fisheries Report No. 911 (Rome: FAO, 2009), available online: <http://www.fao.org/docrep/012/i1227t/i1227t.pdf>; FAO, *Resumed Session of the Technical Consultation on International Guidelines on Securing Sustainable on Small-scale Fisheries, Voluntary Guidelines for Securing Sustainable Small-scale Fisheries in the Context of Food Security and Poverty Eradication* (Rome: FAO, 2014), available online: <http://www.fao.org/fishery/docs/DOCUMENT/ssf/SSF_guidelines/TC/2014/2e.pdf>.

32   M. Marta-Almeida et al., "Fundão Dam collapse: Oceanic dispersion of River Doce after the greatest Brazilian environmental accident," *Marine Pollution Bulletin* 112, no. 1-2 (2016): 359–364; L.E. de O. Gomes et al., "The impacts of the Samarco mine tailing spill on the Rio Doce estuary, Eastern Brazil," *Marine Pollution Bulletin* 120, no. 1-2 (2017): 28–36.

33   J.C. Massante, "Mining disaster: Restore habitats now," *Nature* 528 (2015): 39.

new Mining Code, proposing some additional requirements to the current legal framework in force, however being much more permissive in regards to the duties of the mining companies than the one under the citizen's initiative.[34] This opens a discussion as to whether this permissive political act provided the right conditions for the accident.[35]

Threats and Steps to Better Decision-making in Brazil

Recognition of challenges and critical concerns related to any disconnect between science and policy and its implications should help fill existing gaps in our understanding of the concept of effective and visionary ocean governance.

TABLE 11.1   Main outputs of group participation. Solutions proposed to improve the coherence of the ocean governance system

Issues with Existing Decision-making	Recommendations
Distribution of power	Reframe existing decision-making roles
Low community participation	Engage with community through joint and collaborative development initiatives
Sectoral and fragmented governance approach	Promote horizontal dialogue, ensure transparency of decision-making process
Conflict of interests	Reinforce ethical decision-making
Low impact of science	Ensure effective outreach, promote science journalism
Lack of information	Create effective communication channels and knowledge transfer
Uncertainty	Maintain record of research evidence

---

34   M. Renata et al., "Brazil's mining code under attack: Giant mining companies impose unprecedented risk to biodiversity," *Biodiversity and Conservation* 25 (2016), DOI: 10.1007/s10531-016-1050-9.

35   A. Zhouri et al., "O desastre da Samarco e a política das afetações: Classificações e ações que produzem o sofrimento social," *Ciência e Cultura* 68, no. 3 (2016): 36–40.

Addressing these barriers to influencing policy development will provide grounds for rethinking and helping the formulation of possible solutions to tackle the problem. The following section therefore aims to synthesize the results of the group discussion addressing the challenges of decision-making, which may be considered further to advance dialogue among stakeholders for effective and sustainable ocean governance (Table 11.1). It must be noted that we do not provide a standalone solution to the issues considered in this article, yet some sort of coherent recommendations or solutions are clearly desirable. Collectively, they cover a broad spectrum of challenges and corresponding recommendations, and the most interesting of them are outlined below.

Redistribution of Power

Current decision-making structures and distribution of power in Brazil are often uneven and inequitable, where stakeholders rather than decision-makers cannot have any significant impact on decision-making. Any disconnect between science and policy has potentially negative implications; when science is not fully engaged with current policy-making, it leads to ill-informed decisions with consequences for the whole of society. Many scientists prefer to stay clear of policy and indeed stay out of the public eye altogether. Sometimes, it is because they are concerned that their results will be misused and that contributing to policy discussions might undermine their scientific integrity and professional credibility. Yet, the policy arena is not for all scientists, nor should it be. However, we need scientists to take part in public debates, and we need the role and nature of science to be fully understood by those who make decisions. Science-based policy does not mean that we must have scientists in positions of political power, although in many administrations, at all levels of governance, the number of scientists among our elected representatives is near zero or is worryingly low. What it does mean is that we need to rethink the fundamental relationships of knowledge to power and science to politics in our society. We need science to be a valued and respected part of political discourse so that policy decisions are grounded in evidence. This will ensure that when policy decisions are made, they will not be made blindly. On the other hand, whatever our decision makers do, they will do so with a clear knowledge of the likely consequences based on the current state of scientific evidence. Reframing existing decision-making roles should be achieved by reinforcing powerless groups and realigning all actors' roles in order to place previously disadvantaged groups in a position to have responsible and adequate influence on decision-making. Working towards a proper balance of power allows community aspirations or priorities backed by sustained scientific knowledge to serve as an aid in political decision-making.

In Science We Trust

In its need to grow and progress, science should focus on the practical, transformational, and innovative capacities of scientific information, rather than just its availability. Science is by definition open; however, the main problem lies in the scope of readability of information by different target groups (policy-makers, lawyers, communities, and laypersons), availability, and access to it. We offer an idea of open science. First, this means providing information on how data is developed, how it is intended to be put in use, and what are the levels of uncertainty in the results. Second, using pilot studies could also help to demonstrate the applicability of scientific knowledge and its readability outside the scientific world. We can no longer shelter behind the claim that science is neutral *per se*, but must consider the ethical aspects of the scientific work and possible impacts of scientific discoveries.

Apart from revising the accessibility of science for practical applications, the passive character of the scientific community is also a factor to take into consideration. As a recent trend, some academic journals have banned the phrase "further research is needed," blaming the vague generalization of the statement. Although true in many cases, scientific knowledge is, by definition, not permanent or definitive. Thus, the rather cliché phrase "further research is needed" is nevertheless invariably correct; there is always scope for more research to expand research frontiers. More specific information, such as what types of research and specific useful suggestions for actual research, should be offered. There will always be a need for further research; otherwise, knowledge will be transformed into dogma.

Begon, an ecologist, suggests that scientists should start taking responsibility to not only convey veracious information,[36] but to adopt new doctrines in order to effectively change the collective mindset. "We must do with the truth what they (reactionary and anti-rational forces) are doing with lies."[37] In this sense, the way science is communicated nowadays should be cautiously evaluated, and despite the resisting forces that may surge by conservative and classical scientists, a modernization of their discourse might have to take place.

Community Engagement Matters

There is no doubt that the community has a vital but so far neglected role when decisions need to be made. The process of engaging with society indeed is a

---

36 M. Begon, "Winning public arguments as ecologists: Time for a new doctrine?," *Trends in Ecology and Evolution* 32, no. 6 (June 2017): 394–396.

37 Id.

difficult one and requires mechanisms of community management, such as engagement and empowerment. Low public involvement in Brazil is associated primarily with the lack of appropriate and effective policy instruments for community engagement. In many cases, the community is not convinced they have real power to influence decisions. The uninformed public often becomes reluctant to participate and withdraws. In this context, the relationship between public participation and decision-making are likely to be counterproductive and may result in paralyzing ultimate decision-making. The process of engaging with society indeed is a difficult one and requires mechanisms of community management, such as public participation and community empowerment.

Public participation and community empowerment are crucial for inclusive policy development where engagement goes beyond simple awareness of the problem. Ideally, informed public judgement should be one of the major factors to ultimately determine policy. Four key enablers for successfully building engagement were identified: willingness, trust, competence, and commitment.

In many situations, education can be a major factor increasing the level of community participation, through universal access to education, which is particularly important in developing countries. Equally, the empowerment of local communities can be enhanced in other ways, for example, by community development initiatives. One of the examples to follow in this direction is "A Nation of Curious Minds," a joint project by the New Zealand government and academia that aims to solve local environmental problems and stimulate the interest of the local community in science and technology.[38]

Horizontal Dialogue for Smart Decision-making

The governance of oceanic systems and coastlines is moving into the center of the world's strategic and sustainability interests. Yet, it suffers from a high degree of fragmentation and lack of a cross-scalar approach to addressing prevailing policy shortcomings.[39]

In Brazil, existing governmental authorities and non-governmental institutions, including the public sector (scientists, NGOs, academia, and communities) operate mostly at a vertical scale, for example, national-regional-municipal scales. This often creates a problem of overlapping decisions, when institutions independently fail to make use of their full collective potential in the process of decision-making.

---

38   Government of New Zealand, "Curious Minds," available online: <https://www.curiousminds.nz>.

39   European Cooperation in Science and Technology (COST), "Ocean Governance for Sustainability: Challenges, options and the rules of science," COST Action 15217, available online: <https://www.cost.eu/actions/CA15217/#tabs|Name:overview>.

From this viewpoint, the sectoral and fragmented approach in ocean governance does not address the complex interconnections of ocean ecosystems and human activities, and therefore leads to conflicts of interest. Nowadays, decision-making involves a conflict pursuing specific and even narrow interests of political or social groups. This confrontation implies high incompatibility between group participation and broad societal interests. Thus, ensuring the inclusion of all actors in decision-making is an important advance toward the creation of horizontal dialogue and eventually integrated management of ocean and coastal areas.

This raises the question of how such dialogue can be created, considering each actor's current roles and responsibilities in making decisions, but working to enhance the capabilities of others to participate in decision-making and prevent concentrated power of action. It is indeed a very difficult task that implies behavioral and institutional changes. The narrative of inclusion suggests that more actors should be included in the process of decision-making. At the end of the day, policy-makers, scientists, and community are all part of society. In order to address this issue, cross-training, open debates, and learning-by-doing activities should be supported where policy-makers, academics, researchers, and locals share information and work together to find solutions to existing problems.

The problem of a fragmented approach has international dimensions. For example, Canada has been an example to be followed on ocean governance during the last three decades, which resulted in the implementation of the *Oceans Act*.[40] The *Oceans Act* is meant to replace the fragmented approach to management, negotiated on a case-by-case basis, with an "ocean estate" that can be managed in an integrated system. However, this innovative legislative framework could not be adequately implemented due to the distance between ocean policy and ocean science.[41] Two major threats to this fragile link in the Canadian case are (1) cuts in financing research, the closing of libraries, and the destruction of archived materials,[42] and (2) the limitations on communication from scientists to the public.[43] A muzzling of federal government scientists

---

40 P.J. Ricketts and L. Hildebrand, "Coastal and ocean management in Canada: Progress or paralysis?," *Coastal Management* 39, no. 1 (February 2011): 4–19.

41 M. Bailey et al., "Canada at a crossroad: The imperative for realigning ocean policy with ocean science," *Marine Policy* 63 (January 2016): 53–60.

42 P.G. Wells, "Managing ocean information in the digital era: Events in Canada open questions about the role of marine science libraries," *Marine Pollution Bulletin* 83 (June 2014): 1–4.

43 C. Turner, *The War on Science: Muzzled Scientists and Willful Blindness in Stephen Harper's Canada* (Vancouver: Greystone Books Ltd., 2014).

occurred under Prime Minister Stephen Harper's Conservative government, such that they did not have the right to report research results or opinions to the public through the media. This is evidence of how important and fundamental the scientific contribution is to ocean governance, giving support not only to decision makers but also to citizens.

Reinforcing Ethical Decision-making

Corruption is a barrier to economic and social growth in much of Latin America. In many countries of the region, robust legal frameworks for transparency, including far-reaching laws, criminal and administrative regimes, and mechanisms for prevention, investigation, and sanction already exist. But implementation and enforcement of these laws can be a weak point for certain countries.[44] Brazil is no exception.

Key political and managerial leaders often make purposeful decisions based on their aspirations or personal profit. Administrative bureaucracy and even corruption are often related to the manipulation of public and scientific tenders and ambitions to dominate the decision-making process. In the same way, citizens are also subject to opting for paths that do not take into consideration a sense of the collective good, while research may be subject to political bias when supported by government grants. This implies serious challenges in ethical behavior, resulting in lack of trust and integrity in decision-making. A positive example of progress in this direction can be found in Mexico, where ethical and social responsibility principles resulted in an anti-corruption reform that aims to avoid politicization of decisions and encourage efforts to build trust and understanding among stakeholders.[45] Mexico is now working to integrate courses on ethics and responsible citizenship into curricula from the primary school level upwards, creating a learning environment that fosters honesty and integrity.

The Knowledge Triangle: Access to Information, Communication Channels, and Knowledge Transfer

Several reasons for ineffective communication were revealed during focus group discussions, most of which related to communication gaps and language barriers. Based upon the outcomes of the talks, the group put forward conditions for fostering scientific knowledge transfer.

---

44   F. Gianotti, "Without science, we risk making decisions in the dark," World Economic Forum (19 September 2017), available online: <https://www.weforum.org/agenda/2017/09/science-policy-making-cern-climate/>.
45   Id.

Lack of systematization of existing scientific information has become a significant issue in Brazil. The information is hindered or lost due to the use of inappropriate communication channels, to the point where access to information has become an equity issue. For instance, wealthier stakeholders or larger institutions may get easier access to the information needed when citizens, small agencies, and institutions may not necessarily have the same rights.

The second issue is the use of language and scientific jargon. In some cases, the language of policy-makers is extremely binary in comparison to scientists, that is, casting a simple yes or no vote on a decision. When scientists communicate in a certain way, using their own language can be obscure enough to be interpreted by policy-makers and the community as difficult to understand or sometimes even be perceived as meaningless. Scientists may also be distrustful of how their results and interpretations may be used (or misused) outside of traditional academic outlets of scientific journals and meetings. The academic world rewards scientists for participating in these activities, but not necessarily for reaching out to policy-makers and the general public.[46]

Knowledge transfer is a social responsibility of science to transfer knowledge outside the scientific community. This should be done through effective communication channels and by adopting the proper mechanisms to engage the audience.

Framing the outgoing message to reach the right audience and turning scientific data into meaningful information by using adequate language (i.e., the manner in which scientific knowledge is traduced) and relevant channels of communication (i.e., the manner in which the message is sent) should be prioritized for more effective communication.[47] The group discussion suggested that results of scientific studies must be actively communicated through outreach activities, not just disseminated through publications. Further, other forms of communication, such as graphical representations and indicators, audiovisual media (e.g., images and videos), must be used to transmit complex information in a simplified and understandable form. Working with media can also have multiple advantages in disseminating information and encouraging the interest of stakeholders. There are many successful examples of scientists and decision-makers, as well as scientists and local communities, working

---

46 D. Wright, "Bridging the gap between scientists and policy makers: Whither geospatial?," available online: <https://blogs.esri.com/esri/esri-insider/2013/02/11/bridging-the-gap-between-scientists-and-policy-makers-whither-geospatial/>.

47 A.M.M. Carapuço, "Improving the transfer of coastal scientific knowledge: From concept to implementation," (Ph.D. thesis, Universidade de Lisboa, 2016), available online: <http://repositorio.ul.pt/browse?type=author&value=Carapu%C3%A7o%2C+Ana+Mafalda+Marques>.

together. Promoting and supporting such initiatives can benefit society as a whole and enable the transition to sustainability. One of the interesting outcomes of the discussion was a comment about the importance of cultivating relationships with individual reporters who appear to have technical competence or even educating scientists with journalistic skills as science journalists.

Each communication mechanism should adapt to specificities of the target audience to connect with their audience in a meaningful way. If adequately used, these mechanisms may improve the transfer of scientific knowledge by fostering engagement, minimizing framing effort, and optimizing audience feedback. Other mechanisms are available to foster the transfer of scientific knowledge, for example, crowdsourcing for data generation and co-production to boost knowledge. The second is a particularly interesting approach as it stands for collaborative work among key actors aiming to build an integrated solution to a problem. The adequate use of these mechanisms will lead to a knowledge-based society, increase levels of awareness, and facilitate participation of the principal actors in decision-making. Another argument worth noting was that many scientists nowadays think ahead; many are devoted to developing strategic thinking in their graduate students, cultivating science communication outreach skills that are not typically covered in the classroom or in research training.

Decision-making under Uncertainty

Scientists face the difficulty of delivering to society an acceptable explanation of the level of intrinsic uncertainty on the development of scientific knowledge. Yet, ironically, with the enormous progress in science, there is a commensurate increase in the complexity and incompleteness of our knowledge. The vast volume of scientific knowledge today creates a new set of challenges; one of them is the quality and reliability of this knowledge. They must weigh the implications of any inferential gap between the available data and the conclusions reached. Uncertainty and a lack of clarity exists in predicting the consequences of environmental policies in ecosystems as complex as those associated with the ocean, which are under the influence of multiple forces and are pervaded by human society. We have to increase the capacity to quantify that uncertainty and to embed it into risk assessment relevant to policy-making and implementation. In addition, as a matter of ethical duty, scientists have to openly recognize they do not have the answers to many questions. A key element to address uncertainties is to keep a record of how research evidence and uncertainty was considered in any decision-making scenario. This should include whether the research was asked for or offered, how it was received, and if it had an impact on decision-making. The process has to be fully traceable.

Conclusion

Worldwide, the governance of coastal systems and marine domains is moving to the center of the world's strategic and sustainability interests, and so should Brazil. Yet, ocean governance suffers from a high degree of fragmentation and the lack of a cross-scalar approach to addressing prevailing policy shortcomings. This article provided insights into the current policy direction regarding existing ocean governance in Brazil, its shortcomings, and ways to move forward.

The greatest challenges to effective policy-making are linked to poor communication, lack of credibility among the principal actors, and low community participation. The challenges are sizeable, requiring integration of traditional knowledge in the overall management of coastal areas, using adequate conflict-solving strategies, participation of minority communities in the decision-making process, and education and training.

The group discussion arrived at a clear set of conclusions: (1) the mechanisms of the current policy-making process clearly need revamping; (2) equal involvement and knowledge-based participation from all three key groups of actors are needed; (3) science is the most trusted pillar to reach informed decision-making; (4) the transparency of decisions must be assured in order to promote trust and avoid conflicts of interest; and (5) the complexity of the system must be addressed in order to reduce uncertainty. The policy arena is not for scientists or citizens, nor should it be. But for those willing and able to engage with this challenging and complex world, it is increasingly important that they do so. We advocate for genuine inclusivity in decision-making; our shared future is dependent on it. We need scientists and communities to take part in public debate for our common good.

As a part of the scientific community, we believe that scientists and science should be a valued and respected part of the global discourse so that policy decisions are grounded in evidence. This will ensure that when policy decisions are made, they will not be made blindly. Whatever our decision-makers do, they will do so with a clear understanding of the likely consequences based on scientific evidence. We realize the urgent need to strengthen trust and horizontal dialogue, enable effective knowledge transfer, and promote coherence and transparency of decision-making in order to achieve effective ocean governance. We see the role of scientists as policy mentors and community ambassadors in an ongoing dialogue to develop and frame good practices of ocean governance.

The focus group exercise used in the study allowed us to gain an in-depth understanding of the challenges and issues of ocean governance in Brazil and beyond. The method aimed to obtain different perspectives from a group of researchers and scientists engaged in ocean-related science. Yet, it seems that in a policy-development context, such exercises can only be successful if a greater inclusivity of other parties is ensured. Representatives of local governmental and non-governmental institutions and members of the local community must be a part of the discourse to obtain broader perspectives beyond academic viewpoints and establish more meaningful interaction. This is much needed in order to break the notorious vicious circle of bad decision-making.

We hope that our recommendations may be useful to filling existing gaps and can create an open pathway to better ocean governance in Brazil by integrating efforts of the community, science, and policy-makers. The necessary urgent improvements in the future management of the ocean will require a careful and ethical approach, reduced human pressure on our ocean and conflicts from overlapping use, and investment in science and community management. We believe that this will ensure that ocean resources are used sustainably, healthy ocean ecosystems develop, and our precious coastal environment is protected.

PART 3

Marine Environmental and Living Resources Management

∴

Liability for Environmental Harm from Deep Seabed Mining: towards a Hybrid Approach

Neil Craik*
University of Waterloo, Waterloo, Ontario, Canada

Introduction

The International Seabed Authority (ISA) has identified the development of liability rules as a priority component of the regulatory framework being created for the exploitation phase of deep seabed mining (DSM).[1] In determining how to structure liability rules and mechanisms, the ISA has a broad range of examples to draw upon. Most prominently, there are existing civil liability regimes addressing compensation for harms arising from oil pollution from tankers,[2] nuclear installations,[3] hazardous waste,[4] transport of hazardous and

---

* The author was the co-convenor of the Legal Working Group on Environmental Liability from Activities in the Area, which has developed a series of background papers on deep seabed mining liability published by the Centre for International Governance Innovation (CIGI), Waterloo, Canada. This article draws on that research effort, which is summarized in N. Craik et al., *Legal Liability for Environmental Harm: Synthesis and Overview* (CIGI: Liability Issues for Deep Seabed Mining Series, Paper No. 1, June 2018). The author gratefully acknowledges the contribution of the Legal Working Group members: Alfonso Ascencio-Herrera, Christopher Brown, Eden Charles, Tara Davenport, Elie Jarmache, Hannah Lily, Ruth Mackenzie, Steven Roady, Andres Rojas, Dire Tladi, and Guifang (Julia) Xue, to this research, as well as the role of CIGI, the International Seabed Authority and the Commonwealth Secretariat in supporting this work. Papers of the Legal Working Group cited herein can be found online: <https://www.cigionline.org/series/liability-issues-deep-seabed-mining-series>. Any errors contained in this article are wholly attributable to the author.

1 International Seabed Authority (ISA), "Report of the Chair of the Legal and Technical Commission," Doc. ISBA/22/C/17 (13 July 2016), Annex II.
2 International Convention on Civil Liability for Oil Pollution Damage, 29 November 1969, 973 *United Nations Treaty Series* 3, amended by the 1992 Protocol, 27 November 1992, 1956 *United Nations Treaty Series* 255 [1992 Oil Pollution Convention].
3 Convention on Third Party Liability in the Field of Nuclear Energy, 29 July 1960, 956 *United Nations Treaty Series* 251, as amended by the Additional Protocol of 28 January 1964, and by the Protocol of 16 November 1982 [Nuclear Liability Convention].
4 Basel Protocol on Liability and Compensation for Damages Resulting from Transboundary Movements of Hazardous Wastes and their Disposal, 9 December 1999, UN Doc. UNEP/CHW.1/WG/1/9/2 (not yet in force) [Basel Protocol].

noxious substances,[5] Antarctic activities,[6] and biosafety (movement of living modified organisms).[7] In addition to these sector-specific rules, there are general customary rules of international law governing State responsibility,[8] as well as some attempts to establish general rules governing civil liability.[9] Finally, domestic legal systems will have their own rules and procedures governing environmental harm that may be called upon to address harms from transnational activities. Since these approaches respond to the unique conditions of the activity giving rise to the environmental risks and the legal setting in which the activity occurs, a crucial legal task for developing liability rules for DSM is to consider how the unique features of the DSM regime will shape the approach to liability.

By examining the approach to liability, the intent of this article is to focus on a number of key elements typically found in sector-specific civil liability regimes, with a view to assessing how aspects of the DSM regime will influence the form of those elements. This analysis proceeds from the assumption that when it comes to liability one size does not fit all. As a consequence, the analysis pays specific attention to those aspects of the DSM regime that are sufficiently unique to require consideration of different approaches to liability. Specifically, it is argued that the complex institutional arrangements surrounding DSM, including the status of the deep seabed and its resources as the common heritage of mankind,[10] as well as the high degree of scientific and technological uncertainty surrounding the potential environmental impacts of DSM, militate in favor of an approach that includes traditional civil liability rules and procedures, but also provides a role for administrative approaches toward compensation for environmental harm. Unlike other international

---

5   1996 International Convention on Liability and Compensation for Damage in Connection with the Carriage of Hazardous and Noxious Substances at Sea, 3 May 1996, 35 *International Legal Materials* 1406 [HNS Convention].

6   Protocol on Environmental Protection to the Antarctic Treaty (Madrid Protocol), 4 October 1991, 30 *International Legal Materials* 1455 (1991), Annex VI: Liability Arising from Environmental Emergencies, 14 June 2005 [Madrid Protocol Liability Annex].

7   Nagoya-Kuala Lumpur Supplementary Protocol on Liability and Redress to the Cartagena Protocol on Biosafety, 5 October 2010.

8   International Law Commission (ILC), "Draft Articles on Responsibility of States for Internationally Wrongful Acts," in *Report of the ILC on the work of its 53rd session (23 April-1 June and 2 July-10 August 2001)*, UN Doc. A/56/10 (2001) [ILC Draft Articles on Responsibility].

9   See, for example, Convention on Civil Liability for Damage Resulting from Activities Dangerous to the Environment, 21 June 1993, 32 *International Legal Materials* 1228.

10 United Nations Convention on the Law of the Sea, 10 December 1982, 1833 *United Nations Treaty Series* 397 (in force 16 November 1994), art. 136 [UNCLOS].

regimes, the DSM regime benefits from the existence of an international organization, the ISA, that has broad plenary powers, which include the authority to impose remediation orders as a function of regulatory compliance, not civil liability. Likewise, the ISA could seek payment of, and utilize, funds received from contractors more flexibly in order to address environmental harms that may in some instances be long term and cumulative in nature.

Given the breadth of issues that arise in connection with liability for environmental harm in international law, the approach taken is to be selective in the issues addressed. Specifically, this article considers the following issues:
– Who is to be the primary focus of liability?
– What is the appropriate standard of liability?
– What are the types of compensable damages that may be awarded?
– Who has standing to pursue those damages?
– What mechanisms ought to be put in place to ensure that adequate funds are available for compensation?

Before turning to these issues, the article considers the current rules respecting liability that are contained in Part XI of the United Nations Convention on the Law of the Sea (UNCLOS), as well as the general provisions respecting liability found in Articles 235 and 304 of UNCLOS.[11] These rules represent the status quo, that is, these rules provide the baseline approach to liability should no further rules be adopted. The content of these provisions and their relationship to one another was also central to the International Tribunal for the Law of the Sea – Seabed Disputes Chamber (SDC) Advisory Opinion on *Responsibilities and Obligations of States Sponsoring Persons and Entities with Respect to Activities in the Area*.[12] In the event that these rules appear to fall short of the prevailing expectations for liability schemes for risky activities in international law, this provides justification for the development of further rules.

UNCLOS and the Underlying Architecture of Liability

The basic structure of the DSM regime contemplates three central actors. The contractor, which can be a private entity or a State agency, is the central mining operator, and must be sponsored by a State that is party to UNCLOS.

---

11 Id., arts. 235 and 304.
12 *Responsibilities and Obligations of States Sponsoring Persons and Entities with Respect to Activities in the Area* (2011), Advisory Opinion, No. 17, International Tribunal of the Law of the Sea, Seabed Disputes Chamber [SDC Advisory Opinion].

The contractor's primary obligations are set out in the contract between the ISA and the contractor. Oversight of all mining activity is provided by the sponsoring State, as well as the ISA. Liability for activities in the Area is addressed in Article 139 and Annex III, Article 4, in relation to sponsoring States, and Annex III, Article 22, in relation to contractors and the ISA. Article 139 states:

1) States Parties shall have the responsibility to ensure that activities in the Area, whether carried out by States Parties, or State enterprises or natural or juridical persons which possess the nationality of States Parties or are effectively controlled by them or their nationals, shall be carried out in conformity with this Part. The same responsibility applies to international organizations for activities in the Area carried out by such organizations.

2) Without prejudice to the rules of international law and Annex III, Article 22, damage caused by the failure of a State Party or international organization to carry out its responsibilities under this Part shall entail liability; States Parties or international organizations acting together shall bear joint and several liability. A State Party shall not however be liable for damage caused by any failure to comply with this Part by a person whom it has sponsored under Article 153, paragraph 2(b), if the State Party has taken all necessary and appropriate measures to secure effective compliance under Article 153, paragraph 4, and Annex III, Article 4, paragraph 4.

3) States Parties that are members of international organizations shall take appropriate measures to ensure the implementation of this article with respect to such organizations.[13]

This provision identifies the primary obligation on sponsoring States to "ensure that activities in the Area … shall be carried out in conformity with [Part XI]," with failures to do so entailing liability. However, liability only flows where the sponsoring State has failed to take "all necessary and appropriate measures to secure effective compliance." As confirmed by the SDC, this provision, whose structure is restated in a similar form in Annex III, Article 4, imposes an obligation of due diligence, not result, meaning that liability flows only where the sponsoring State has failed to act with requisite care.[14] The SDC elaborates on the content of due diligence, noting that a sponsoring State's responsibilities will include putting in place sufficient oversight rules and procedures, including adequate compliance mechanisms, as well as ensuring

---

13   UNCLOS, n. 10 above.
14   Id., arts. 107–110.

that procedures are in place for prompt and adequate compensation in the event damages arise.[15] Due diligence, as the standard of liability for States in relation to environmental harm, is consistent with the customary obligations for States to prevent transboundary harm and harm to the global commons.[16]

The responsibility of contractors and the ISA is addressed in Annex III, Article 22:

> The contractor shall have responsibility or liability for any damage arising out of wrongful acts in the conduct of its operations, account being taken of contributory acts or omissions by the ISA. Similarly, the ISA shall have responsibility or liability for any damage arising out of wrongful acts in the exercise of its powers and functions, including violations under Article 168, paragraph 2, account being taken of contributory acts or omissions by the contractor. Liability in every case shall be for the actual amount of damage.[17]

Liability under this provision flows from the "wrongful acts" of either the contractor or the ISA. Wrongful in this context should not be interpreted to require fault on the part of the contractor or the ISA, rather wrongful in this context tracks the language of State responsibility where liability arises from "every internationally wrongful act."[18] Addressing this point directly, the International Law Commission (ILC) has noted that whether liability requires fault or simply flows from causation is a function of the primary obligation.[19] Thus, the standard of liability for contractors and the ISA, that is, whether liability is strict or requires some degree of fault, will be determined with reference to the respective duties of contractors and the ISA as laid out in UNCLOS, as well as the regulations enacted by the ISA. For example, under the exploration regulations, the principal obligation on contractors to prevent environmental harm is framed as a duty of conduct to take "necessary measures to prevent, reduce and control pollution and other hazards to the marine environment

---

15   SDC Advisory Opinion, n. 12 above, paras. 117–120.
16   *Legality of the Threat of Nuclear Weapons* (1996) ICJ Reports 226, para. 29; *Pulp Mills on the River Uruguay (Argentina v. Uruguay)*, Judgment, 2010 International Court of Justice (20 April 2010), para. 101; ILC, "Draft Articles on Prevention of Transboundary Harm from Hazardous Activities in Report of the International Law Commission," in UN Doc. A/56/10, n. 8 above, art. 3.
17   UNCLOS, n. 10 above, Annex III, art. 22.
18   ILC Draft Articles on Responsibility, n. 8 above, art. 1.
19   Id., art. 2, comm. 3.

arising from its activities in the Area *as far as reasonably possible*, applying a precautionary approach and best environmental practices."[20] In the event of accidental or unforeseen damage for exploration activities, there is no obligation for a contractor to provide compensation, as there has been no wrongful act. The ISA's responsibilities are also framed in terms of duties to enact "appropriate rules, regulations and procedures" to prevent and control harm to the environment,[21] and to "exercise such control over activities in the Area as is necessary for securing compliance" with the established requirements.[22]

The SDC also considered the relationship between Article 139 and Annex II, Article 22, and the structuring of liability as between sponsoring States, the ISA and contractors. The SDC notes, "the main liability for a wrongful act committed in the conduct of the contractor's operations or in the exercise of the ISA's powers and functions rests with the contractor and the ISA, respectively, rather than with the sponsoring State."[23] The implications of this finding are that where environmental harm is a result of the contractor's wrongful act, the contractor will be the primary source of compensation, even in the event that the sponsoring State failed to carried out its own (oversight) obligations with due diligence. It is only where the contractor is unable to provide compensation that recourse can be made to the sponsoring State, but only where the sponsoring State's acts or omissions are causally related to the damage. The liability is parallel; and not residual, in the sense that the sponsoring State will be responsible for any damages unmet by the contractor.[24]

The relationship between the ISA's liability and the contractor's is not addressed by the SDC, but the same logic would seem to apply, such that the ISA is not responsible for the wrongful acts of the contractor, but only its own wrongful acts. As to the priority of compensation, Annex III, Article 22, provides that liability for both the contractor and the ISA shall account for the contribution of the other, which suggests that there is no priority given to either in terms of satisfying claims.

The issue of residual liability was contested before the SDC, with a number of interested parties arguing that sponsoring States ought to be found to have residual liability, effectively making sponsoring States the insurer of any

---

20   ISA, "Decision of the Council of the ISA relating to amendments to the Regulations on Prospecting and Exploration for Polymetallic Nodules in the Area and related matters," Doc. ISBA/19/C/17 (22 July 2013), Annex, , Reg. 31(5) (emphasis added) [RPEN].
21   UNCLOS, n. 10 above, art. 145.
22   Id., art. 153(4).
23   SDC Advisory Opinion, n. 12 above, para. 201.
24   Id., para. 204.

uncovered losses.²⁵ The central concern being that the structure of liability rules gave rise to several liability gaps, whereby the harm occasioned by mining activities could potentially be borne by the victims or by the environment itself; namely where the contractor is unable to meet its liability in full, and the sponsoring State (or ISA) is not liable to pay compensation owing to its fulfillment of its own duties.²⁶ The bigger liability gap, however, arises in relation to accidental or unforeseen harm, which under the current rules is not compensable since, as structured under UNCLOS, compensation only flows in the event of fault.

The acceptability of such liability gaps may fall short of the objectives of UNCLOS itself. Article 235, which is found in Part XII of UNCLOS (Protection and Preservation of the Marine Environment), addresses both the current and future responsibilities of States in relation to ensuring prompt and adequate compensation for damages caused to the environment. Article 235 states:

1) States are responsible for the fulfilment of their international obligations concerning the protection and preservation of the marine environment. They shall be liable in accordance with international law.
2) States shall ensure that recourse is available in accordance with their legal systems for prompt and adequate compensation or other relief in respect of damage caused by pollution of the marine environment by natural or juridical persons under their jurisdiction.
3) With the objective of assuring prompt and adequate compensation in respect of all damage caused by pollution of the marine environment, States shall cooperate in the implementation of existing international law and the further development of international law relating to responsibility and liability for the assessment of and compensation for damage and the settlement of related disputes, as well as, where appropriate, development of criteria and procedures for payment of adequate compensation, such as compulsory insurance or compensation funds.²⁷

Paragraph 2 sets out the broad objective of liability rules in relation to environmental harm as "assuring prompt and adequate compensation." Ensuring that rules and procedures are in place within the sponsoring State's domestic

---

25 D. Anton, "The Principle of Residual Liability in the Seabed Disputes Chamber of the International Tribunal for the Law of the Sea: The Advisory Opinion on Responsibility and Liability for International Seabed Mining (ITLOS Case No. 17)," *McGill International Journal of Sustainable Development Law and Policy* 7, no. 2 (2012): 241–257.
26 SDC Advisory Opinion, n. 12 above, para. 203.
27 UNCLOS, n. 10 above, art. 235.

legal system is an element of due diligence.[28] Consequently, notwithstanding the finding of no residual liability for sponsoring States, a failure of those States to provide reasonable avenues for recourse could result in parallel liability for sponsoring States. However, the SDC did not address the standards for domestic procedures that would satisfy Article 235(2). Notwithstanding the lack of clearly defined standards, it is questionable whether the requirement to ensure prompt and adequate compensation can be achieved without some coordinated efforts among sponsoring States, as there would be a patchwork of rules at the domestic level,[29] resulting in claims being adjudicated under different substantive and procedural rules. There would be a myriad of potential barriers arising under the rules of private international law respecting access to justice, appropriate forum (*forum non conveniens*), enforceability of judgments, and immunities. These concerns are exacerbated by the fact that claims in relation to environmental harm may be pursued by the ISA in its capacity as trustee of the common heritage of mankind, or by States themselves (as an *erga omnes* claim).[30] The standing of the ISA or States before domestic courts to pursue civil damages is questionable without further rules.[31] There also may be concerns about the adequacy of available funds for compensation, if left to individual States, particularly where contractors have complex, transnational legal structures.

Looking at the wording of paragraph 3, which addresses future legal steps that may be taken in relation to liability, it is important to note that it refers to the "objective of *assuring* prompt and adequate compensation in respect of *all damage* caused by pollution of the marine environment." The use of "assure" instead of ensure, as in paragraph 2, indicates a more aspirational objective. Moreover, paragraph 3 refers to "all damage," indicating that there may be damages not covered by the obligation in paragraph 2, which will require further State cooperation to achieve. The framers of UNCLOS appear to have recognized the potential for liability gaps, but also the desirability of closing those gaps, in their calls for cooperation in the further development of liability rules found in Article 235(3).[32]

Before turning to the specific elements of civil liability regimes, it is important to note that the underlying purpose of liability rules under UNCLOS is not

---

28 SDC Advisory Opinion, n. 12 above, para. 140.
29 See paper by H. Lily, "Sponsoring State Approaches to Liability Regimes for Environmental Damage Caused by Seabed Mining," (CIGI: Liability Issues for Deep Seabed Mining Series, Paper No. 3, December 2018).
30 See discussion, *infra*.
31 For example, the ISA enjoys immunity from legal process under UNCLOS, n. 10 above, art. 178.
32 SDC Advisory Opinion, n. 12 above, para. 205.

restricted to the goal of prompt and adequate compensation, but is also linked quite explicitly in Article 235 to the "protection and preservation of the marine environment."[33] Liability rules ought to be structured in such a way as to incentivize high standards of environmental protection and, where harm occurs, to have adequate funds directed towards remediation of the environment – a link recognized by the SDC.[34]

The development of new liability rules to better meet the twin objectives of prompt and adequate compensation and environmental protection is not constrained by the existing structure under Article 139, and Annex III, Articles 4 and 22. Article 139 is without prejudice to the development of new rules. Similarly, Article 304 provides that the provisions within UNCLOS are "without prejudice to the application of existing rules and the development of further rules regarding responsibility and liability under international law."[35] The parties are not obligated to develop new rules, as Article 235(3) imposes only a duty to cooperate. However, if international cooperation does not result in new rules and procedures, sponsoring States remain obligated to develop such rules and procedures within their own legal systems. The development of liability rules by the ISA would fall under the plenary powers of the Council and Assembly to develop rules, regulations, and procedures for DSM.[36]

Attribution and Channeling Liability[37]

The question of attribution of liability concerns itself with which parties are to be held liable for compensable harm, and is largely a matter of causality and thus a factual determination. However, as discussed above, there remain issues of priority and contribution in relation to incidents where multiple parties may be found responsible, as well as immunities. A common approach used in civil liability regimes is to channel liability to a specific actor, usually the operator. The purpose of channeling liability to specific actors is to simplify liability procedures by making the responsible party easy to identify and to facilitate insurance. Channeling to operators is a recognition that they are in the best position to manage risks. In the case of DSM, which involves surface ships, and potentially numerous sub-contracting entities, all engaged in

---

33   UNCLOS, n. 10 above, art. 235(1).
34   SDC Advisory Opinion, n. 12 above, para. 197.
35   UNCLOS, n. 10 above, art. 304.
36   Id., arts. 162(2)(o)(ii) and 160(2)(f)(ii).
37   For an in-depth discussion of this issue, see T. Davenport, "Responsibility and Liability for Damage Arising Out of Activities in the Area: Attribution of Liability," (CIGI: Liability Issues for Deep Seabed Mining Series, Paper No. 4, January 2019).

complex operations, channeling would remove an obstacle to compensation recovery. Unlike other hazardous activities, where control over the risks may change over the course of an operation,[38] there does not appear to be a strong case for channeling to multiple operational actors. The regulatory structure of DSM places the contractor at the center of activities in the Area, since the ISA's regulatory control is established by the contract itself.

The exception to this is the transportation and processing of minerals, which are likely to be undertaken by other actors within the mineral supply chain. However, the SDC held that transportation and processing, notwithstanding their inclusion within the ambit of the ISA's authority, fall outside of the scope of "activities in the Area" for the purposes of responsibility and liability.[39] Although, the SDC went on to clarify that "shipboard processing immediately above a mine site of minerals derived from that mine site" as described in Article 17(2)(f) in Annex III is to be considered as included in "activities in the Area."[40] Thus, the evacuation of water from the minerals and the preliminary separation of materials of no commercial interest, including their disposal at sea, are also deemed to be covered by the expression "activities in the Area."[41] These activities are likely to be conducted under the control of contractors and, thus, their inclusion makes sense from an attribution standpoint.

Since contractors, as well as the ISA and sponsoring States, have obligations to prevent harm in relation to both exploration and exploitation activities, liability rules would cover all phases of the mining process, including closure. The exploration regulations acknowledge liability for environmental harm can rise from exploration activities, but does not elaborate on any specific liability rules or processes.[42]

As it stands, the current structure prioritizes recovery from contractors over sponsoring States, with sponsoring States only responsible where they have acted without due diligence and there remains uncompensated harm. As a consequence, channeling would not require a significant change from the current expectations of the parties, but it could also potentially remove an important source of compensation funds (e.g., in the event of contractor insolvency), if recourse to sponsoring States and the ISA were to be removed.

---

38 For example, the Basel Protocol, n. 4 above, recognizes multiple responsible parties due to the chain of custody of hazardous waste.
39 SDC Advisory Opinion, n. 12 above, paras. 94–97.
40 Id., para. 88.
41 Id., para. 95.
42 RPEN, n. 20 above, reg. 30.

A practical concern in relation to DSM is that some of the sponsoring States are small, developing States, with little capacity to pay large compensation awards.[43] If the effect of exposure to liability was to present a barrier to the participation by some developing States, this could be viewed as undermining the goal of accounting for the interests and needs of developing States.[44] Equally, it is not clear that the ISA is in a strong position to pay large claims. Significant exposure to such claims would require the ISA to build up its own fund (likely through mining revenues) or seek insurance. It is noteworthy that the SDC was certainly aware of these concerns (in relation to sponsoring States), but nonetheless identified extensive due diligence obligations, that were not tempered by differentiated responsibilities.[45]

Relieving the ISA of liability may be particularly tricky because Annex III, Article 22, expressly requires that liability as between the ISA and contractors account for contributory acts.[46] Channeling liability away from the ISA would appear to constrain the ability of contractors to seek contributory claims against the ISA. And while Article 139 is without prejudice to the development of new liability rules, it certainly evinces an intention to maintain sponsoring State liability for failures of due diligence.

From a regulatory standpoint, there would be some benefit in ensuring that the incentives for sponsoring States and the ISA to maintain appropriate oversight are not reduced by eliminating their exposure to liability claims. There are examples of liability regimes where the liability is attributable to both States and operators. Under the nuclear regimes, installation States remain responsible for damages that exceed the operator's capacity, which effectively makes installation States secondary insurers.[47] Similarly, under the Antarctic (Madrid) Protocol's Liability Annex, State parties bear some responsibility where operators fail to undertake and pay for response actions.[48] In both these cases, State liability acts as a backstop, where operators are not able to cover the compensation amounts. One alternative approach to loss spreading through multiple responsible parties is to reduce the chances of unfunded liabilities through

---

43   For example, the Republic of Nauru, in its request for an advisory opinion respecting sponsoring State liability, expressly raised the concern of the potential for liabilities exceeding its financial capabilities. See SDC Advisory Opinion, n. 12 above, para. 4.
44   UNCLOS, n. 10 above, arts. 140 and 148.
45   SDC Advisory Opinion, n. 12 above, para. 158.
46   UNCLOS, n. 10 above, Annex III, art. 22.
47   1963 Supplemental Convention to the Paris Convention, 31 January 1963, 1041 *United Nations Treaty Series* 358, art. 3(b)(ii), providing for compensation funds to be made available from contracting party in whose territory the nuclear installation is situated.
48   Madrid Protocol Liability Annex, n. 6 above, art. 7.

high insurance or other security requirements placed upon contractors, so as to limit the residual damages claimable. Thus, risks associated with channeling to the operator can be offset through other funding mechanisms.

Attention would need to be paid to the variety of contractor forms, which may include State enterprises and State parties, in order to ensure that State-related entities could not raise State immunities as a basis to avoid liability. For example, in the International Convention on Liability and Compensation for Damage in Connection with the Carriage of Hazardous and Noxious Substances at Sea Convention (HNS Convention) there is a provision whereby States, which may be liable by virtue of being shipowners, "shall waive all defences on its status as a sovereign State."[49] While public international law does not generally extend immunities to States or their agents engaged in commercial activities, it is conceivable for States to engage in DSM for non-commercial (security) purposes.[50]

Standard of Liability[51]

The approach to liability under UNCLOS, which requires fault, is out of step with international practice. Adopting a strict liability standard, particularly for contractors, is consistent with practices in other sector-specific civil liability regimes and is more in keeping with the goals of adequate compensation and marine protection.[52] A strict standard avoids uncompensated harm to victims or the environment generally in the case of accidental or unforeseen harm, and may be justified on the basis that strict liability creates greater incentives for operators to adhere to the highest standards of environmental protection. In the absence of strict liability, there is potential for contractors to externalize the costs of measures taken to protect the environment that go beyond mere negligence, a condition that may be viewed as being inconsistent with the polluter pays principle. Strict liability may also be preferred on efficiency grounds

---

49   See HNS Convention, n. 5 above, art. 4(6).
50   See, for example, UN Convention on Jurisdictional Immunities of States and their Property, adopted by the United Nations General Assembly (UNGA) on 2 December 2004 (not yet in force). See UNGA, "Resolution adopted by the General Assembly on 2 December 2004)," UN Doc. A/RES/59/38 (16 December 2004), Annex.
51   For an in-depth discussion of this issue, see N. Craik, "Determining the Standard for Liability for Environmental Harm from Deep Seabed Mining Activities," (CIGI: Liability Issues for Deep Seabed Mining Series, Paper No. 2, October 2018).
52   See, for example, Oil Pollution 1992, n. 2 above, art. III(1); see also HNS Convention, n. 5 above, art. 7; 1960 Nuclear Liability Convention, n. 3 above, art 3.

given that a strict standard relieves the claimant of the burden of proving fault, and may be seen as offering an avenue towards prompt compensation.

The novelty and uncertainty of DSM operations may also justify a strict standard, as there may be unforeseeable environmental impacts that would not be compensable in a fault-based system,[53] as taking steps, even precautionary steps, to address unforeseeable harm may not be viewed as reasonable. A strict standard would make contractors responsible for all harm arising from their activities, regardless of whether the impacts were known. This burden may be justified in light of the fact that the contractors are creating the risks under conditions that they know to be uncertain. Imposing a strict standard is also consistent with the regulatory approach employed by the ISA, where the ISA has the authority to impose emergency orders on contractors in the event of an incident that poses a threat of serious harm to the marine environment.[54]

As discussed above, UNCLOS specifies that liability for contractors flow from their "wrongful acts"; that is, from breaches of rules imposed under the DSM regime. Imposing a strict liability (no fault) standard could be accomplished by clear indication that causation of serious environmental harm is itself a wrongful act, from which liability will flow. This approach is largely consistent with UNCLOS and the 2018 Draft Exploitation Regulations, which identifies causation of "serious harm" as the baseline environmental standard that triggers compliance measures.[55] Nevertheless, this would entail a shift from the current practices under the Exploration Regulations, which require only reasonable steps be taken to prevent serious harm.[56]

It is common practice within civil liability regimes for strict liability to be accompanied by a limited list of exceptions to liability, such as harm resulting from armed conflict, intentional damage by third parties, damage arising from natural phenomena, and contributory and government negligence.[57]

---

53 See L. Levin et al., "Defining "serious harm" to the marine environment in the context of deep seabed mining," *Marine Policy* 74 (2016): 245–259 (discussing the high degrees of uncertainty in relation to deep seabed ecology).

54 RPEN, n. 20 above, reg. 33.

55 ISA, Legal and Technical Commission, "Draft Regulations on Exploitation of Mineral Resources in the Area," Doc. ISBA/24/LTC/WP.1 (9 July 2018), draft reg. 4 [Draft Exploitation Regulations].

56 RPEN, n. 20 above, reg. 31(5).

57 1992 Oil Pollution Convention, n. 2 above, art. III(2); International Convention on the Establishment of an International Fund, 27 September 1992 (in force 30 May 1996), IMO Doc. LEG/CONF.9/16 (amending 1971 Fund Convention, 1110 *United Nations Treaty Series* 57), art. 4(2) [FUND92]; Madrid Protocol Liability Annex, n. 6 above, art. 8; The Nagoya–Kuala Lumpur Supplementary Protocol, n. 7 above, art. 6; HNS Convention, n. 5 above, art. 4(2)(3) and 7; Basel Protocol, n. 4 above, art. 4(5).

Monetary limits on liability are also commonplace and exist to facilitate insurance coverage (which will itself be limited), and are likely necessary for public companies, which may be restricted in opening themselves up to unlimited liability. In effect, in other regimes, strict liability is balanced with limits to liability, although within the oil pollution regime the parties have sought to ensure that the limitations attached to insurance caps and compensation funds fairly reflect the scale of potential damages arising from claims. A variation on this approach is taken under the Basel Protocol where liability is strict, and claims are subject to caps, but in the event of harm arising from intentional or negligent actions, the caps do not apply.[58]

Typically, strict liability accompanies channeling in civil liability regimes, although the issues are clearly severable. In the event that liability for sponsoring States and the ISA is maintained, it may be desirable to maintain a fault-based standard for sponsoring States and the ISA in their oversight capacities, while imposing a strict standard on contractors. Such an approach is consistent with UNCLOS and the SDC's understanding of the relationship between sponsoring States and contractors, where sponsoring States are not to be the effective insurers of contractors (which they would be if they were held strictly liable), but rather are independently responsible for their own wrongful acts.

Imposing a standard of reasonableness for States and the ISA raises the issue of whether it is necessary to inject an element of deference to the policy decisions that may be made by both sponsoring States and the ISA in determining what oversight measures they may undertake and their manner of implementation. The SDC seemed to appreciate that judicial assessment of the adequacy of State measures might overstep the boundaries of judicial functions if some deference is not given:

> Policy choices on such matters must be made by the sponsoring State. In view of this, the Chamber considers that it is not called upon to render specific advice as to the necessary and appropriate measures that the sponsoring State must take in order to fulfill its responsibilities under the Convention. Judicial bodies may not perform functions that are not in keeping with their judicial character.[59]

In common law settings, the laws respecting public authority liability distinguishes between the authority's operational and policy decisions, providing

---

58   Basel Protocol, id., art. 12(1).
59   SDC Advisory Opinion, n. 12 above, para. 227.

immunity from injuries that flow from the latter.[60] A similar limitation can be found in relation to the ISA in Article 189, which prevents the SDC from reviewing the exercise by the Authority of its discretionary powers, and from substituting its discretion for that of the Authority.[61] Incorporating a degree of deference to State policy decisions raises considerable scope for highly differentiated oversight systems, and uncertainty as to basis and degree to which sponsoring States can adopt varying standards and procedures for oversight. Identification of appropriate standards, perhaps through the development of model legislation, may mitigate these risks.

Damages[62]

The status of the Area and its resources as the common heritage of mankind is a central distinguishing feature of the DSM regime, which has important implications for the types of harm likely to arise and the question of who has standing to pursue standing claims in relation to those harms. Addressing harm to private interests, such as interference with other economic activities in the area, or property and personal injuries will not raise new issues, and will be covered under standard heads of damages.[63] However, harm to the natural environment and to resources in the Area raise considerable legal ambiguity.

While UNCLOS does indicate that compensation for "damage caused by pollution to the marine environment" must be compensated,[64] it does not specify the scope of those damages. The SDC did not extensively address the issue of damages except to note that damages could "include damage to the Area and its resources constituting the common heritage of mankind, and damage to the marine environment."[65] The SDC acknowledges that other forms of reparation, such as restitution or satisfaction, may be available,[66] although the focus in Article 235 is on compensation, which could include compensation intended for the purposes of environmental restoration.

60　Anns v. Merton London Borough Council, [1977] 2 All E.R. 492 (H.L.); Just v. British Columbia, [1989] 2 SCR 1228.
61　UNCLOS, n. 10 above, art. 189.
62　For an in-depth discussion of this issue, see R. Mackenzie, "Liability for Environmental Harm from Deep Seabed Mining Activities: Defining Environmental Damage," (CIGI: Liability Issues for Deep Seabed Mining Series, Paper No. 8, February, 2019).
63　See, for example, HNS Convention, n. 5 above, art. 1(b); Basel Protocol, n. 4 above, art. 2(c).
64　Id., art. 235.
65　SDC Advisory Opinion, n. 12 above, para. 179.
66　Id., paras. 196–197.

Economic losses associated with impairment are typically covered under civil liability regimes, as are certain forms of restoration costs. The current practice within civil liability regimes around restoration costs is to allow only those costs that are reasonable and have actually been incurred. For example, the HNS Convention defines "damages" as follows:

> "Damage" means:
> (a) loss of life or personal injury on board or outside the ship carrying the hazardous and noxious substances caused by those substances;
> (b) loss of or damage to property outside the ship carrying the hazardous and noxious substances caused by those substances;
> (c) loss or damage by contamination of the environment caused by the hazardous and noxious substances, provided that compensation for impairment of the environment other than loss of profit from such impairment shall be limited to costs of reasonable measures of reinstatement actually undertaken or to be undertaken; and
> (d) the costs of preventive measures and further loss or damage caused by preventive measures.[67]

It is noteworthy that this definition qualifies the scope of damage, in relation to restoration to be "limited to costs of reasonable measures of reinstatement actually undertaken or to be undertaken."[68] Thus, restoration costs cannot be used as a proxy for calculating damages. Moreover, the restoration activities undertaken must be reasonable in nature. Reasonableness would import an assessment of proportionality and feasibility into determining whether a restoration measure ought to be undertaken.[69] The SDC touched on the question of restoration costs as a basis for compensation where it noted that the "form of reparation will depend on both the actual damage and the technical feasibility of restoring the situation to the *status quo ante*."[70] This statement suggests that damages will only be available for restorations that are actually undertaken, and that reasonableness (technical feasibility) will be an important factor. Whether restoration is possible will depend, of course, on the nature of the incident. However, the nature of DSM operations, which occur in remote locations and at significant depths, as well as the nature of the ecosystem itself, which has very long recovery periods, raise the likelihood

---

67 HNS Convention, n. 5 above, art. 1.
68 See also, 1992 Oil Pollution Convention, n. 2 above, art. 1 (employing similar wording).
69 See, for example, the Nuclear Liability Convention, n. 3 above, art. 1 (defining "reasonable measures").
70 SDC Advisory Opinion, n. 12 above, para. 197.

that certain incidents will result in irremediable harm. However, irremediable harm does not mean that a loss has not been suffered.[71]

One potential response to remediation challenges would be the use of offsets. That is, replacing the lost ecological function at some other location. Offsets have been included as possible response actions in the Nagoya-Kuala Lumpur Protocol and have been considered as a potential response action in the DSM context. The feasibility of offsets and whether they could adequately compensate for the lost ecological functions is not known, and would require further legal and financial mechanisms to manage the offset itself.[72]

A further alternative is to compensate based on an economic calculation of the lost ecological and social benefits of the affected environment. Because the costs are not based on actual transactions, they must be calculated with reference to economic models that seek to place a valuation on the lost benefits. Inclusion of pure environmental losses, which are widely recognized in domestic legal systems, was recently accepted by the International Court of Justice in the *Certain Activities Case (Costa Rica v. Nicaragua)*,[73] suggesting that such losses are compensable unless explicitly excluded. The ILC came to a similar conclusion in its work on State responsibility,[74] and affirmed its relevance in its work on allocation of loss for environmental harm.[75] There has been, however, resistance to the inclusion of pure environmental losses in damages calculation in civil liability regimes. For example, the oil pollution regime has indicated that it will not include damages based on "an abstract quantification of damage calculated in accordance with theoretical models."[76] An important consideration here is the feasibility of assessing pure environmental losses in

---

71 H.J. Niner et al., "Deep-sea mining with no not loss of biodiversity: An impossible aim," *Frontiers in Marine Science* 5, no. 52 (March 2018), doi.org/10.3389/fmars.2018.00053, p. 6, noting, "[e]ffectiveness and practicability of any remediation technologies or methods at the scale required to address deep-sea mining impacts and achieve [no net loss] has not been demonstrated."

72 Id.; see also C.L. Van Dover et al., "Biodiversity loss from deep-sea mining," *Nature Geoscience* 10 (July 2017): 464.

73 *Certain Activities Carried Out by Nicaragua in the Border Area (Costa Rica v. Nicaragua) Compensation owed by the Republic of Nicaragua to the Republic of Costa Rica*, Judgment of 2 February 2018, ICJ General List No. 150, para. 42.

74 ILC Draft Articles on Responsibility, n. 8 above, art. 36, commentary 15.

75 ILC, "Draft Principles on the Allocation of Loss in the case of Transboundary Harm Arising out of Hazardous Activities, with commentaries," in *Report of the ILC, 58th Session (1 May–9 June and 3 July–11 August 2006)*, UN Doc. A/61/10 (2006), draft principle 2, commentary 18.

76 IOPC Fund Assembly, "Resolution 3," 10 October 1980, FUND/A/ES 1/13, para. 11(a) and Annex.

connection with deep seabed ecosystems, where the ecological services are not well-understood and other theoretical models such as contingent valuation (which depends on determination of the public's willingness to pay to preserve an environmental good) may have less purchase in relation to remote, poorly understood ecosystems. In the absence of well-understood quantification methods, proving pure environmental loss, even if identified as a valid head of damages, may present evidentiary challenges, notwithstanding an acknowledged loss.[77]

A second issue that arises in relation to damages is the extent to which the environmental harm must exceed some minimum threshold, such as "serious" or "significant" harm, in order to be compensable. The regulatory standard employed in UNCLOS and carried into the ISA's regulations is "serious harm."[78] Thus, as with any resource exploitation regime, some degree of harm to the environment will result. Here it is perhaps useful to distinguish between permitted and non-permitted harm, where the former is the environmental harm that is identified as likely to occur under the approvals process (i.e., through an environmental impact assessment) and determined to be acceptable; that is, not "serious." Non-permitted harm would be harm that arises either through an unauthorized incident or where the harm occurs through normal operations, but it exceeds predicted levels or established standards.[79] The relationship between liability and approvals became an important consideration in the development of the Antarctic liability regime, where there was discussion of excluding from the definition of damage those impacts that had been identified by the environmental impact assessment and found acceptable by national authorities. Ultimately, the parties adopted a different approach that focused on response measures to environmental accidents, but which had the effect of excluding predicted operational harms.

Importing a regulatory standard into liability considerations may be desirable in the DSM context where much of the damage itself is related to the environmental impacts alone, as opposed to the economic consequences of those impacts. Such a standard would also inject greater certainty into the mining regime by pre-determining acceptable levels of operational harm. However, there remain issues in relation to long-term and cumulative impacts that may be very difficult to predict, but nevertheless may trigger legal responsibilities

---

77   In a domestic legal context, see, for example, *British Columbia v. Canadian Forest Products Inc.*, [2004] 2 SCR 74.
78   UNCLOS, n. 10 above, art. 162(w)(x).
79   See, *Liability – Report of the Group of Legal Experts,* Antarctic Consultative Parties Meeting XXII, ATCM/WP1, April 1998.

under Article 145. Liability rules, which typically require clear causal attribution and quantifiable damages, may not be well-suited to addressing these more attenuated forms of harm.

Standing[80]

In considering how environmental damages might be defined in connection with liability from DSM activities, it is necessary to consider who may be able to claim such damages. Here again, I confine my discussion to harm to the marine environment and to the Area and its resources. The complication in relation to DSM is determining which parties have standing to pursue claims relating to environmental damages in the Area and the superjacent marine environment. The issue of standing in relation to harm to the marine environment and to resources that have common heritage of mankind status deserves much more attention than I can give it here, but this is an important differentiating factor for the DSM regime. For example, the oil pollution regime explicitly excludes harm that occurs outside the territory and exclusive economic zone of contracting States,[81] as does the HNS Convention,[82] and the Basel Protocol.[83] The one instrument that does provide for recovery for harm in relation to areas not under State sovereignty is the Madrid Protocol Liability Annex, but recovery is restricted to reimbursement for response measures undertaken by parties.[84] In effect, the parties are recovering on their own behalf since the rules authorize parties to take response measures, where the operator fails to do so, and then recover those costs from the operator.

In considering the more general issue of standing to recover for harm to the environment from DSM, the strongest claim would seem to lie with the ISA, in its capacity as a kind of trustee for the common heritage mankind. Article 137(2) of UNCLOS confers this role on the ISA: "All rights in the resources of the Area are vested in mankind as a whole, on whose behalf the Authority shall act."[85] The right of the ISA to claim in this regard was identified by the SDC, albeit in equivocal terms: "It may, however, be argued that such entitlement is

---

80 For an in-depth discussion of this topic, see T. Davenport, "Responsibility and Liability for Damage Arising Out of Activities in the Area: Potential Claimants and Possible Fora," (CIGI: Liability Issues for Deep Seabed Mining Series, Paper No. 5, February, 2019).
81 1992 Oil Pollution Convention, n. 2 above, art. II.
82 HNS Convention, n. 5 above, art. 3.
83 Basel Protocol, n. 4 above, art. 3(3).
84 Madrid Protocol Liability Annex, n. 6 above.
85 UNCLOS, n. 10 above, art. 137(2).

implicit in article 137, paragraph 2, of the Convention."[86] The position of the ISA to make claims in connection with "the resources of the Area" is stronger than the SDC perhaps indicates insofar as Part XI clearly provides for damage claims to the Area and authorizes the ISA to act on behalf of those whose interests are affected.

The SDC also identified the possibility of State parties also having standing to pursue damages claims on behalf of the international community on the basis that the claim is rooted in an obligation *erga omnes partes*;[87] that is, the obligation to preserve and protect the marine environment is an obligation "owed to a group of states including [the claiming] State, and is established for the collective interest of the group."[88] The claims of State parties can be supported under Part XII generally, although the right to claim may be limited to actual damages suffered by the claiming State party;[89] for example, claims to recover restoration or prevention costs expended by the State would be appropriate bases for standing. In providing for such claims under the Madrid Protocol, the Liability Annex provides specific procedures for authorizing "other States" to undertake response measures, where the operator and the party of the operator fail do to so, suggesting the need, or desirability, to establish legal authority to pursue restoration activities in advance of claims for reimbursement.

Pure environmental losses, if allowed, would be more difficult because these are not losses to a third party State, and unless the recovered funds are being used to further the objectives of Part XII, such an award may be viewed as a windfall. It is noteworthy in this regard that the claimants in both the *South China Sea Case* and the *Whaling Case* were not seeking damages as a remedy but rather cessation of wrongful activities.[90] The ILC Draft Articles restrict the remedies available to States pursuing *erga omnes* claims to cessation and non-repetition.[91] One possible avenue may be to authorize States to pursue claims on behalf of mankind that are paid into a trust fund that is managed for community benefit. Although given the superior position of the ISA to pursue such claims, allowing individual States standing is harder to justify. The SDC suggests that rights of standing, as between the ISA and State parties, would

---

86   SDC Advisory Opinion, n. 12 above, para. 180.
87   Id.
88   ILC Draft Articles on Responsibility, n. 8 above, draft art. 48(1)(a).
89   Coastal States, for example, could claim in the event of environmental harm to areas under their jurisdiction.
90   *The South China Sea Arbitration (The Republic of the Philippines v. The People's Republic of China)*, PCA Case 2013–19, Final Award, 12 July 2016; *Whaling in the Antarctic (Australia v. Japan)* (Judgment) (2014) ICJ Reports 226.
91   ILC Draft Articles on Responsibility, n. 8 above, draft art. 48(2)(a).

be non-exclusive, although Article 137(2) could be read as conferring exclusive jurisdiction on the ISA to pursue claims rooted in collective interests.

It is also necessary to distinguish harm to the Area *per se*, namely, to the seabed floor and its resources, from harm to the marine environment more generally. The former, as the common heritage of mankind, is more firmly within the competence of the ISA, while the right to claim for harm to the marine environment is less straightforward given that Article 137(2) refers only to the Area. However, insofar as liability rules are viewed as critical elements of the protection of the marine environment, the ISA is again best positioned to pursue claims in relation to harm to the marine environment, potentially including pure environmental loss, by virtue of the ISA's obligations under Article 145, which requires the ISA to take "necessary measures" to protect the marine environment. Given the emphasis the SDC places on Article 137(2) in support of the ISA's standing in relation to the Area, and the absence of a similar provision in relation to the marine environment, further clarity on this point would be desirable. State parties would be under the same constraints they face making claims in relation to the Area, in relation to claims for harm to the marine environment.

Compensation Funds[92]

In order to ensure the availability of funds for adequate compensation, many civil liability regimes include requirements for mandatory insurance, as well as providing for some form of fund that would cover claims that are either not covered by insurance or are in excess of the coverage provided by insurance. The possibility of including compensation funds as part of a liability approach is included in Article 235(3). The SDC acknowledges the use of "a trust fund," linking the establishment of a fund directly to the aim of reducing gaps in compensation.[93] The use of the term "trust fund" by the SDC is confusing, as it might suggest a mechanism with objectives beyond ensuring available funds for compensating those who have suffered compensable damages. However, the SDC cites Article 235(3), which refers to compensation funds, in support of the possibility of a fund, suggesting no distinction.

---

92 For an in-depth discussion, see G.(J.) Xue, "The Use of Compensation Funds, Insurance and Other Financial Security in Environmental Liability Schemes," (CIGI: Liability Issues for Deep Seabed Mining Series, Paper No. 6, February, 2019).
93 SDC Advisory Opinion, n. 12 above, para. 180.

Mandatory insurance is already a requirement for contractors under the standard contract provisions contained in the exploration regulations, but the requirements do not specify coverage requirements or any other particulars.[94] Typically, civil liability regimes identify minimal levels of coverage.[95] Some assessment of the commercially available insurance will be necessary to determine what kinds of damages insurers will be willing to cover and to what limits.

In the event that insurance appears unlikely to cover the forms and extent of damages desired by the parties, compensation funds or some other form of financial security, which operate as a form of self-insurance, may be found necessary. If compensation funds are established, the parties will need to determine who would contribute to the fund and on what basis. For example, under the oil pollution funds, receivers of the shipped product contribute based on the amount received. This approach is animated by the idea that beneficiaries of an activity ought to share some of the risks associated with that activity.[96] A similar, albeit more complicated, structure exists for hazardous and noxious substances.[97] Based on a beneficiaries pay principle, the potential options for funders for a compensation fund addressing DSM include the contractors, processing firms that receive the ore, sponsoring States, or even all States that receive a share of mining royalties through benefit sharing. A further complication in the DSM regime is the relatively small number of contractors likely to be involved in the early stages of exploitation, compared to the large number of operators involved in oil or hazardous goods transport. The large numbers allow for more efficient risk pooling, which may not be present for DSM. Sharing risks also requires cooperating contractors to be able to assess the risks of others, which may be more difficult in the relatively immature and more heterogeneous operating environment of DSM.

It is useful to distinguish between compensation funds, which are aimed at providing compensation to injured parties and require causal links between the harm and compensation, and trust funds, which may be used to disburse funds to a defined class of beneficiaries, but on a broader basis than direct injury. Trust funds potentially could be used to fund environmental benefits, such as offsets, in recognition of the loss of environmental function caused by mining activities, as well as restoration efforts that are not easily attributable to specific contractor activities.

---

94 RPEN, n. 20 above, Annex IV, s. 16.5.
95 See, for example, HNS Convention, n. 5 above, art. 12.
96 FUND92, n. 57 above, art. 10.
97 HNS Convention, n. 5 above, arts. 16–20.

In a 2018 draft of the proposed exploitation regulations, an "Environmental Liability Trust Fund" was proposed, which included a very broad mandate to supplement remediation costs not covered by the contractor, as well as to promote research and education programs.[98] The draft regulation also lists a variety of potential funding sources, including direct contributions from contractors (under ISA direction), as well as fees and penalties imposed by the ISA. As it stands, the approach is confusing, with environmental restoration that may be caused by operational failures competing with other more discretionary activities. If a central goal of the liability rules is to better ensure funds for restoration, this goal would be better served by segregating funds for restoration purposes from funds for other regime objectives.

Conclusion: towards a Hybrid Approach

There is no "off the shelf" solution that may be borrowed to address liability issues arising from DSM activities in the Area. Rather the parties, through the ISA, will need to carefully consider the unique institutional and legal setting, as well as the operational conditions, of DSM. This article presented a number of the critical considerations that will be necessary to address as distinct elements of a civil liability regime, but it ought to be borne in mind that these elements, while distinct, need to be considered as an integrated system. Existing civil liability regimes have tended to combine channeling with strict liability and clear mechanisms for funding claims. For example, strict liability for contractors will likely only be acceptable (and insurable), if it is accompanied by liability caps and exclusions.

The DSM regime is distinct, however, because of the presence of a dense international regulatory regime, including a financial regime, addressing the activities of concern. As noted, the ISA already has broad powers to address environmental harm through compliance mechanisms such as emergency orders. The Antarctic regime, which has some parallels to the DSM regime in that both involve commons areas under collective control, ties liability directly to environmental emergencies and response actions.[99] This approach is partially evident in the 2018 Draft Exploitation Regulations, where the regulations include an Environmental Performance Guarantee, which could be drawn upon by the ISA to reimburse it for remedial actions taken by the ISA.[100]

---

98 Draft Exploitation Regulations, n. 55 above, draft reg. 53.
99 Madrid Protocol Liability Annex, n. 6 above, art. 6.
100 Draft Exploitation Regulations, n. 55 above, draft reg. 102.

Using response measures as a basis to address environmental harm provides an incomplete solution, since there may be some harm that is not reasonably remediated. Addressing those residual losses to environmental function presents further challenges that may again be best addressed outside of the confines of a liability system, such as the use of a trust fund, which could be drawn upon to address environmental harm more generally.[101] This may facilitate alternative forms of environmental redress, such as offsets, and may overcome valuation issues by decoupling funding and disbursement of funds from specific incidents.

The broader point here is that the ISA has access to a wider set of tools than those available in other areas of risky activities, which ought to be considered as either alternative or complementary approaches. Indeed, there may be some advantages in the development of a hybrid system that uses insurance or other forms of security to address accidental (and restorable) harms, such as surface oil spills from production vessels, and to address economic losses, while employing more flexible approaches to address environmental harms, which may be less amenable to attribution (due to their long term and possible cumulative nature) and quantification.

---

101   See, M. Lodge, K. Segerson and D. Squires, "Sharing and Preserving the Resources in the Deep Sea: Challenges for the International Seabed Authority," *International Journal of Marine and Coastal Law* 32, no. 3 (2017): 427–457.

Environmental Liability for Deep Seabed Mining in the Area: an Urgent Case for a Robust Strict Liability Regime

Keith MacMaster
Ph.D. Candidate, Schulich School of Law, Dalhousie University,
Halifax, Canada

Introduction*

Protecting the environment, both living and non-living, is important. Mining, too, is important, as it provides the raw products for many of today's "necessities," including cobalt, nickel, and the rare earth metals used in electronics. Deep seabed mining (DSM) is an important and emerging field within the law of the sea as countries and companies expand their production of minerals. The International Seabed Area (the Area), which is the seabed and subsoil area beyond national jurisdictions, the subject for this type of mining, was deemed to be the "common heritage of mankind" and outside the jurisdiction of any one State.[1] This required separate governance structured under Part XI of the United Nations Convention on the Law of the Sea (UNCLOS).[2]

This article will focus on liabilities for the Area and examine the question of liability for the various actors involved, including contractors/operators who carry out the exploitation of resources, sponsoring States, flag States, and the International Seabed Authority. It is necessary to analyze the current state of liability provisions, should environmental damage occur in the Area. The rapid pace of technological advancement and the unknown extent of environmental damage make a fulsome liability regime necessary. Unfortunately, as will be shown in this article, there are still extensive unknowns in the legal landscape.

This article will investigate two areas of liability: the standard of liability (strict, negligence, and whether there is a potential for a due diligence defense, active act, or *mens rea* requirements) and the extent of liability (limited or unlimited damage claim potentials). UNCLOS seems to provide for one type of

---

* This article was the winning entry in the 2018 *Ocean Yearbook* Student Paper Competition.
1 United Nations Convention on the Law of the Sea, 10 December 1982, entered into force on 1 November 1994, 1833 *United Nations Treaty Series* 397, art. 136 [UNCLOS]; see also M. Lodge, "The common heritage of mankind," *The International Journal of Marine and Coastal Law* 27 (2012): 733–742.
2 UNCLOS, id., Part XI.

liability for operators, but the subsequent legislation, as will be shown, seems to "water down" liabilities, making a detailed analysis required.

Given the scope of this article, not all areas of liability can be addressed. There are many other areas of liability that need to be assessed in subsequent research, including procedural claims, the types of due diligence defenses, and whether environmental impact assessments and plans of work would fulfill these requirements, the assessment of damages and the ability to pay, and the creation of DSM insurance to handle any liability claims.

This article will be structured as follows. The first part details the history and context of DSM. The second part is subdivided into two sections: the first subsection details the current UNCLOS and regulatory state of liability for DSM, while the second subsection identifies gaps in liabilities both from the historical context and from the current governance regime. The third part investigates the domestic legislation of several countries to determine if any gaps are filled by domestic laws, as required by UNCLOS.[3] The fourth part outlines other maritime liability regimes, including civil liability regimes, to attempt to show how a system could be developed to deal with all aspects of liability. The concluding part synthesizes the current research and recommends changes to the development of liability standards, including the creation of an environmental fund.

Context and Liability Issues

The deep seabed extends on the continental shelf, the exclusive economic zone (EEZ), and the Area, and is defined as any seabed surface below 200 m.[4] It is thought to contain vast quantities of minerals, resources, and potentially oil and gas.[5] The deep seabed encompasses not only the Area, but also the continental shelf and EEZ.[6] Resources are defined in Article 133 of UNCLOS as "all solid, liquid or gaseous mineral resources in situ in the Area at or beneath

---

3 Given the parameters of this article, it is not possible to canvass every country with an interest in deep seabed mining (DSM) in the Area. Thus, the countries of Singapore, Nauru, Tonga, China, Canada, the United States, and New Zealand have been chosen. Follow-up research will investigate other countries with potential DSM claims, such as the European Union, India, Russia, the United Kingdom, and others.

4 M. Lodge, "The International Seabed Authority and deep seabed mining," *UN Chronicle* 54:2 (2017): 44–46.

5 A. Jaeckel, J. Ardron and K. Gjerde, "Sharing benefits of the common heritage of mankind: Is the deep seabed mining regime ready?," *Marine Policy* 70 (2016): 198–204.

6 UNCLOS provides that the continental shelf and EEZ are within national jurisdiction of States and thus outside the scope of this research.

the seabed, including polymetallic nodules."[7] It is believed to be a next frontier for extractive industries,[8] as it is seen as solving two issues: first, the potential decline in on-shore mineral resources, such as copper and rare earth metals,[9] and second, developing countries may benefit from resource extraction as a route to economic development.[10]

DSM has not been a significant issue to date due to a lack of technologies that could exploit the Area.[11] However, extractive technologies are advancing at a rapid pace and are almost at commercial readiness.[12] Given that much of the deep seabed is found at depths of 1.5 km and commercial quantities from 3,000 to 6,000 m,[13] there is a great risk of environmental damage conducted by any exploration or exploitation.

There was no fulsome regulatory regime for the Area in UNCLOS. Rather, Part XI created the International Seabed Authority (ISA) to regulate activities.[14] The ISA may exercise control in the Area, as necessary, to ensure compliance with Part XI, and all countries are obligated to ensure compliance with Article 139.[15] The ISA is thus responsible for all DSM in the Area.[16] To obtain a permit to explore the Area for seabed minerals, a sponsoring State must submit a plan of work.[17] As of the date of this article, the ISA had issued 28 exploration contracts.[18] Yet, despite this number of permits, there are several important legal issues related to DSM that have not been fully developed, including both liability and environmental assessment requirements.

---

7   UNCLOS, n. 1 above, art. 133.
8   International Seabed Authority (ISA), "Towards the Development of a Regulatory Framework for Polymetallic Nodule Exploitation in the Area," Technical Study No. 11 (Jamaica: ISA, 2013).
9   R.E. Kim, "Should deep seabed mining be allowed?," *Marine Policy* 82 (2017): 134–137, p. 135.
10 L.D. Bolong, "Into the abyss: Rationalizing commercial deep seabed mining through pragmatism and international law," *Tulane Law Review* 26 (2016): 128–180, p. 132.
11 R.E. Boschen et al., "Mining of deep-sea seafloor massive sulfides: A review of the deposits, their benthic communities, impacts from mining, regulatory frameworks and management strategies," *Ocean & Coastal Management* 84 (2013): 54–67, p. 55.
12 Id., p. 56.
13 ISA, *Proposed Technologies for Mining Deep-seabed Polymetallic Nodules, Proceedings of the ISA's Workshop held in Kingston, Jamaica, 3–6 August 1999*, Doc. ISA/2001/07, p. 34.
14 UNCLOS, n. 1 above, Part XI, s. 4, art. 156.
15 Id., art. 153(4).
16 Id., art. 157.
17 D.K. Anton, R.A. Makgill and C.R. Payne, "ITLOS / Case No. 17, Seabed Mining – Advisory Opinion on Responsibility and Liability," *Environmental Policy and Law* 41, no. 2 (2011): 60–65.
18 ISA, "Deep Seabed Minerals Contractors" (2018), available online: <https://www.isa.org.jm/deep-seabed-minerals-contractors>.

In 2009, the small island state of Nauru asked the ISA to seek an advisory opinion, as mandated under Article 191 of UNCLOS, to clarify the liability of sponsoring States.[19] On 1 February 2011, the Seabed Disputes Chamber (SDC) released the *Advisory Opinion on State Liability* case (Case 17).[20] This advisory opinion is important in several respects, in that it illustrates a number of concepts, principles, and norms, it advances jurisprudence, and it was the first time that non-governmental organizations took part in proceedings of the Chamber.[21] Deepening potential environmental hazards is the issue that State parties are not the only potential sources of environmental damage, as many States do not have the technical nor financial capabilities to undertake DSM.[22] For example, Nauru admitted that

> recognizing this, Nauru's sponsorship of Nauru Ocean Resources Inc. was originally premised on the assumption that Nauru could effectively mitigate (with a high degree of certainty) the potential liabilities or costs arising from its sponsorship. This was important, as these liabilities or costs could, in some responsibilities and obligations of states with respect to 17 activities in the area (advisory opinion of 1 February 2011) circumstances, far exceed the financial capacities of Nauru (as well as those of many other developing States). Unlike terrestrial mining, in which a State generally only risks losing that which it already has (for example, its natural environment), if a developing State can be held liable for activities in the Area, the State may potentially face losing more than it actually has.[23]

Case 17 also clarified certain jurisdictional issues. It clarified that the jurisdiction of the ISA only relates to the exploration and exploitation of minerals from the seabed and lifting them to the surface.[24] It does not include processing on land or transportation from the high seas superjacent to the Area.[25] This

---

19   Anton et al., n. 17 above, p. 61.
20   *Responsibilities and Obligations of States Sponsoring Persons and Entities with Respect to Activities in the Area* (Request for Advisory Opinion submitted to the Seabed Disputes Chamber), Case No. 17 (1 February 2011), ITLOS Reports 2011 [Case 17]. The SBC was created under UNCLOS, n. 1 above, Part XI, s. 5 and Annex VI.
21   A. Dolidze, "Advisory opinion on responsibility and liability for international seabed mining (ITLOS Case 17) and the future of NGO participation in the international legal process," *ILSA Journal of International & Comparative Law* 19, no. 2 (2013): 379–418.
22   T. Poisel, "Deep seabed mining: Implications of seabed disputes chamber's advisory opinion," *Australian International Law Journal* 19 (2012): 213–233, p. 215.
23   Case 17, n. 20 above, para. 4.
24   Id., paras. 94 and 95.
25   Id., para. 96; see also Anton et al., n. 17 above, p. 62.

has impacts on liability and insurability, in that damage occurring in the Area is regulated by the ISA, but as soon as a vessel crosses into another marine area, then other UNCLOS provisions apply.[26] As will be discussed below, this poses liability issues with DSM and potentially necessitates a harmonious relationship with EEZ and territorial water provisions, whether or not these provisions provide adequate environmental protections.

UNCLOS is vague on the liability standard for States. Case 17 analyzed the "duty to ensure" obligation (i.e., the due diligence obligation) not to cause environmental harm.[27] The SDC deemed that this due diligence defense obligation is not one of result but of conduct.[28] It also then implied that this standard would place limits on States' liability,[29] and the obligation would be met if a State employed, on a best-efforts basis, a contractor's compliance.[30] It also specifically ruled out the application of strict liability against the State.[31]

Question 2 of Case 17 stated: "What is the extent of liability of a State Party for any failure to comply with the provisions of the Convention, in particular Part XI, and the 1994 Agreement, by an entity that it has sponsored under Article 153, paragraph 2(b), of the Convention?"[32] The SDC stated: "In Question 2, the English term "liability" refers to the consequences of a breach of the sponsoring State's obligations."[33] Anton notes that it is customary in international law to first look at the private contractor for compensation for harm caused by a wrongful act, even if attributed to the State.[34] It is only if total compensation is not achieved that residual liability to the State might be applied.[35] There is

---

26 Y. Tanaka, "Obligations and liability of sponsoring states concerning activities in the Area: Reflections on the ITLOS advisory opinion of 1 February 2011," *Netherlands International Law Review* 60, no. 2 (2013): 205–230, p. 209.
27 UNCLOS, n. 1 above, art. 139(1); see also Case 17, n. 20 above, para. 108.
28 I. Plakokefalos, "Seabed disputes chamber of the International Tribunal for the Law of the Sea responsibilities and obligations of states sponsoring persons and entities with respect to activities in the Area," *Journal of Environmental Law* 24, no. 1 (2011): 133–143, p. 136.
29 D.K. Anton, "The principle of residual liability in the seabed disputes chamber of the International Tribunal for the Law of the Sea: The advisory opinion on responsibility and liability for international seabed mining (ITLOS Case No. 17)," *McGill International Journal of Sustainable Development Law and Policy* 7, no. 2 (2012): 241–257, p. 247.
30 Case 17, n. 20 above, para. 110.
31 Id., para. 189.
32 Id., para. 164.
33 Id., para. 70.
34 Anton, n. 29 above, p. 249; see also G. Doeker and T. Gehring, "Private or international liability for transnational environmental damage: The precedent of conventional liability regimes," *Journal of Environmental Law* 2, no. 1 (1990): 1–16 and International Law Commission, n. 8 above, paras. 340–386.
35 Anton, id., p. 247.

thus a major gap, should serious environmental damage take place. Moreover, the court did not address several major issues, as will be discussed later. Specifically, the court noted, "[c]onsidering that the potential for damage, particularly to the marine environment, may increase during the exploitation phase, it is to be expected that member States of the Authority will further deal with the issue of liability in future regulations on exploitation. The Chamber would like to emphasize that it does not consider itself to be called upon to lay down such future rules on liability."[36]

Substantial developments have taken place since Case 17 was released. Two main developments that require the speedier development of liability regulations include new scientific discoveries and the rapid development of technologies which are making commercial exploitation of the Area feasible. Scientific uncertainty in the Area and the need to apply the precautionary approach to DSM cannot be overstated. For example, in 2015, a group of researchers from the University of Rhode Island discovered large numbers of egg cases adjacent to hydrothermal vents off the coast of the Galapagos Islands.[37] This was the first case of this type of behavior among a marine animal recovered. These vents are the same vents thought to hold massive amounts of mineral deposits, and are soon to be explored in the deep seabed, providing evidence that exploration of the seabed of the Area could have a material impact on the marine living environment.[38] As will be discussed, the types of mining will vary according to the type of mineral in the Area. As such, a range of differing toxic metal mixtures may be released into the sea. This has been shown to disrupt an organism's cell structure, at least in the territorial waters area.[39] Scientists do not yet know if the effects on land or shallow waters apply to the deep seabed, and many urge the use of the "weight of evidence approach" and a more scientifically based environmental assessment process, as there are still too many unknowns as it relates to the deep seabed.[40] These are just two small examples of the scientific uncertainty surrounding the Area, should environmental damage occur.

---

36 Case 17, n. 20 above, para. 168.
37 P. Salinas-de-León et al., "Deep-sea hydrothermal vents as natural egg-case incubators at the Galapagos Rift," *Scientific Reports* 8, no. 1788 (2018): 1–7, available online: <https://www.nature.com/articles/s41598-018-20046-4>.
38 Id., p. 5.
39 C. Hauton et al., "Identifying toxic impacts of metals potentially released during deep sea mining: A synthesis of the challenges and quantifying risk," *Frontiers of Marine Science* 4:368 (2017): 1–13, p. 9.
40 Id., p. 12.

However, time is running out for this weight of evidence approach to be more fully developed, as there are now technologies available that can mine at depths below 1.5 km. The first commercial operation of DSM will take place off the coast of Papua New Guinea (PNG) in 2019, if financial hurdles are overcome.[41] At approximately 35 km from PNG, and sitting at a depth of 1,600 m, the Solwara 1 project will use innovative mining techniques to extract copper, with some gold deposits having potential commercial significance.[42] Although the project will take place in the EEZ of PNG, the depth of the drilling and type of extraction shows similarities to other DSM in the Area. Additionally, as will be described below, PNG has partnered with Nautilus Minerals Inc. (Nautilus), a Canadian company listed on the Toronto Stock Exchange,[43] to be the contractor.[44] As is the case with Tonga and Nauru in the Area, PNG does not have the financial or technical resources to conduct DSM on its own.[45] Nautilus does not own the vessel, but has chartered the vessel from Dubai-based Marine Assets Corporation.[46] This highlights a fourth party that could have liability, that is, the "flag State" vessel.[47] Solwara 1 is also important as Nautilus also owns a

---

41 Mining Watch Canada, "Nautilus AGM: Solwara 1 deep sea mining venture remains a speculative pipe dream," Press Release (28 June 2017), available online: <https://miningwatch.ca/news/2017/6/28/nautilus-agm-solwara-1-deep-sea-mining-venture-remains-speculative-pipe-dream>; see also, "Deep Sea Mining Campaign, Former Attorney General of Papua New Guinea: The writing is on the wall for Solwara 1 – PNG should withdraw its investment before it's too late," Media Release (17 January 2018). However, according to its own disclosures, a third quarter 2019 first production is still targeted. See Nautilus Minerals Inc., *Material Change Report 51-102F1* (28 February 2018) accessed via SEDAR.

42 K. Gena, "Deep sea mining of submarine hydrothermal deposits and its possible environmental impact in Manus Basin, Papua New Guinea," *Procedia Earth and Planetary Science* 6 (2013): 226–233, p. 230.

43 Nautilus Minerals is a Canadian mining company listed on the Toronto Stock Exchange (TSX), ticker symbol "NUS." Having only a market capitalization of approximately CA$50 million and a negative revenue stream at the time of writing, there is a real risk of the project having serious financial issues, which would indicate that any environmental damage would have serious financial repercussions. For a video depicting the vessel to be used and the mining techniques employed, see <http://www.nautilusminerals.com/irm/content/video-gallery.aspx?RID=421>.

44 "Nautilus Minerals receives world's first deep-sea mining lease for Solwara 1," *Sea Technology* 52, no. 3 (2011): 49.

45 H. Rosenbaum, *Out of Our Depth: Mining the Ocean Floor in Papua New Guinea* (Mining Watch Canada, 2011), available online: <http://www.deepseaminingoutofourdepth.org/wp-content/uploads/Out-Of-Our-Depth-low-res.pdf>.

46 M. Schuler, "First deep sea mining production vessel launched in China," Press Release (30 March 2018), available online: <http://gcaptain.com/first-deep-sea-mining-production-vessel-launched-in-china/>.

47 The flag State of this vessel is still unclear. The vessel was built in China by Fujian Mawei shipbuilding, and the basic design for the seabed mining vessel is provided by SeaTech

valued license in the Clarion Clipperton Zone (CCZ).[48] The results of Solwara 1 and any environmental damage from the mining may have a profound influence on the development of extraction in the Area.[49] The type and quantum of damage in the EEZ, and the resulting liabilities to the parties provide meaningful data applicable to the Area.[50] Further research is required.

In 2011, Tonga Offshore Mining Limited (TOML), a sponsored company of the Tonga government, but owned by Nautilus Minerals, was granted approximately 75,000 sq. km in the highly prospective CCZ.[51] The CCZ has been identified by the ISA as a zone of particular importance, especially from an environmental perspective.[52] From a DSM perspective, the CCZ is an area particularly rich in polymetallic nodules.[53] From an environmental perspective, it is also of significance. As such, in July, 2012, the ISA adopted an Environmental Management Plan for the CCZ.[54] This Plan has a provision for an EA but no additional liability provisions.[55] Given the decision in Case 17, that due diligence standards may differ depending on the type of mining, it is imperative to have higher standards for environmental liabilities in the CCZ.

Solutions International, a marine designs specialist based in Singapore. The takeaway is the number of parties involved and issues of liability (which design flaw, construction problem, or maintenance issue) are all to be determined. There are still many financial issues with this project. See Nautilus Minerals Inc., *Material Change Report*, BCSC Form 51-102F3 (18 December 2017).

48   As a TSX-listed issuer, NUS is mandated to provide securities laws disclosures. See *Technical Report, TOML Clarion Clipperton Zone Project, Pacific Ocean*) (27 February 2018), made pursuant to *Standards of Disclosure for Mineral Projects*, BCSC NI 43–101 (9 May 2016) [Technical Report].

49   Coffey Natural Systems, *Environmental Impact Statement: Solwara 1 Project*, prepared for Nautilus Minerals Niugini Limited (2008) available online: <http://www.nautilusminerals.com/irm/content/pdf/environment-reports/Environmental%20Impact%20Statement%20-%20Main%20Report.pdf>.

50   Technical Report, n. 48 above.

51   P. Taumoepeau, "Re: Developing a Regulatory Framework for Mineral Exploitation in the Area – Report to Members of the Authority and all Stakeholders," Letter to ISA from Tonga Offshore Mining Limited (25 May 2015) (Kingston, Jamaica: ISA), available online: <https://www.isa.org.jm/sites/default/files/toml_0.pdf>; see also ISA contract dated 11 January 2012 between Tonga Offshore Mining Limited and the ISA.

52   ISA, Legal and Technical Commission, *Rationale, and Recommendations for the Establishment of Preservation Reference Areas for Nodule Mining in the Clarion-Clipperton Zone*, Doc. ISBA/14/LTC/2* (28 March 2008).

53   ISA, *A Geological Model of Polymetallic Nodule Deposits in the Clarion-Clipperton Fracture Zone*, ISA Technical Study no. 6 (Kingston, Jamaica: ISA, 2010).

54   ISA, *Decision of the Council relating to an Environmental Management Plan for the Clarion-Clipperton Zone*, Doc. ISBA/18/C/22 (26 July 2012).

55   ISA, *Environmental Management Plan for the Clarion-Clipperton Zone*, Doc. ISBA/17/LTC/7 (13 July 2011).

Current State of EA and Mining Regulation in the Area

Given the historical context discussed above, it is necessary to investigate the current state of regulation in the Area. Article 145 of UNCLOS contains basic environmental protection requirements, stating that the ISA shall adopt rules regulations and procedures for the prevention, reduction, and control of pollution and other hazards to the marine environment, including the ecological balance and the protection of flora and fauna.[56] Article 139 of UNCLOS sets out basic liability requirements for the Area.[57] Article 139(2) notes that damage caused by the failure of a State party or international organization to carry out its responsibilities "shall entail liability".[58] This liability is joint and several between the State and the contractor. However, a State is not liable for damage caused by any failure of the contractor to comply if the State has taken "*all necessary and appropriate measures*" (emphasis added) to secure effective compliance under Article 153(4) and Annex III(4)(4).[59] This carve-out provision is contained in Annex III, Article 4(4), which states that the sponsoring State shall ensure that the contractor shall carry out its activities according to the contract and UNCLOS. However, the sponsoring State is *not* liable due to damage caused by any failure of a contractor, sponsored by the State, to comply with its obligations if that State party has adopted laws and regulations and taken administrative measures which are, within the framework of its legal system, "reasonably appropriate for securing compliance" by persons under its jurisdiction.[60] Article 209 requires States to adopt laws and regulations to prevent, reduce, and control pollution coming from activities in the Area, laws which shall be no less effective than the international rules.[61] Furthermore, Article 235 necessitates domestic legislation for compensation or other relief of damage caused by pollution of the marine environment.[62] Finally, Annex III, Article 22, states that the contractor shall have liability arising out of "wrongful acts" in the conduct of its operations.[63] The ISA itself can be liable under the same provision, in that the ISA shall be liable for any damage arising out of wrongful acts in the exercise of its powers and functions.[64]

---

56 UNCLOS, n. 1 above, art. 145.
57 Id., art. 139.
58 Id., art. 139(2).
59 Id., art. 139(2).
60 Id., Annex III, art. 4, para. 4.
61 Id., art. 209(2), which is the basis of flag State liability.
62 Id., art. 235(2).
63 Id., Annex III, art. 22.
64 Id.

The language used in UNCLOS seems to be conflicting. In Article 139(2), the sponsoring State escapes liability only if "all necessary and appropriate measures" have been taken.[65] Yet, Annex III merely requires adoption of laws that are "reasonably appropriate for securing compliance."[66] Even in UNCLOS, there is a weakening of liability for sponsoring States. However, Case 17 did not address all issues of liability. To this end, the ISA has developed regulations that are the primary means by which the ISA develops procedures and rules around all aspects of DSM.[67] Relevant to this article are the Mining Code, Article 165(5) recommendations, and the 2017 Draft Regulations.

The Mining Code is the collection of the regulations adopted by the ISA.[68] The ISA, to date, has recommended and adopted three sets of regulations dealing with DSM: Regulations on Prospecting and Exploration for Polymetallic Nodules in the Area (Nodules Regulations);[69] Regulations on Prospecting and Exploration for Polymetallic Sulphides in the Area (Sulphides Regulations);[70] and Regulations on Prospecting and Exploration for Cobalt-rich Ferromanganese Crusts in the Area (Cobalt Crusts Regulations).[71] These regulations are designed to apply to the exploration and prospecting of the Area, and directly apply to exploitation of resources.[72] As noted in Case 17, there may be a

---

65 Id., art. 139(2).
66 Id., Annex III, art. 4, para. 4.
67 A. Jaeckel, "Deep sea bed mining and adaptive management: The procedural challenges for the International Seabed Authority," *Marine Policy* 70 (2016): 205–211, p. 207.
68 ISA, "Mining Code," available online: <https://www.isa.org.jm/mining-code>. The Mining Code is the set of rules regulations and procedures issued by the ISA to regulate prospecting, exploration and exploitation of marine minerals in the Area.
69 ISA, "Regulations on Prospecting and Exploration for Polymetallic Nodules in the Area," Doc. ISBA/6/A/18 (13 July 2000), amended by ISBA/19/A/9; ISBA/19/A/12 (25 July 2013) and ISBA/20/A/9 (24 July 2014) [Nodules Regulations]. Nodules include manganese, cobalt, copper, and nickel.
70 ISA, "Regulations on Prospecting and Exploration for Polymetallic Sulphides in the Area," Doc. ISBA/16/A/12/Rev.1 (15 November 2010), amended by ISBA/19/A/12 (25 July 2013) and ISBA/20/A/10 (24 July 2014) [Sulphides Regulations]. Polymetallic sulphides means hydrothermally formed deposits of sulphides and accompanying mineral resources in the Area containing concentrations of metals including, *inter alia*, copper, lead, zinc, gold, and silver.
71 ISA, "Regulations on Prospecting and Exploration for Cobalt-rich Ferromanganese Crusts in the Area," Doc. ISBA/18/A/11 (27 July 2012), amended by ISBA/19/A/12 (25 July 2013) [Cobalt Crusts Regulations]. The definition of cobalt-rich ferromanganese crusts includes cobalt-rich iron/manganese (ferromanganese) hydroxide/oxide deposits formed from direct precipitation of minerals from seawater onto hard substrates containing minor but significant concentrations of cobalt, titanium, nickel, platinum, molybdenum, tellurium, cerium, other metallic and rare earth elements.
72 Id., preamble.

different due diligence requirement for each type of mining,[73] yet the drafting of each of the regulations is similar. Thus, there may be a gap between the decision of Case 17 and the regulatory standards required under the Code.

Throughout the Mining Code, the protection of the environment is noted as important.[74] In the Nodules Regulations, Regulation 2 states that prospectors and the Authority shall use the precautionary approach.[75] Regulation 2(3) of the Cobalt Crusts Regulations states that prospecting shall not be undertaken if substantial evidence indicates the risk of serious harm to the marine environment.[76] It is worth noting that while the Sulphides Regulations provide the obligation to apply "best environmental practices" for the sponsoring State, there is no similar reference in the earlier Nodules Regulations.[77] Regulation 30 of the Nodules Regulations states that responsibility and liability of the contractor and of the authority shall be in accordance with UNCLOS.[78] The contractor shall continue to have responsibility for any damage arising out of "wrongful acts in the conduct of its operations," in particular, damage to the marine environment, after the completion of the exploration phase.[79] The key section here is "damage arising out of wrongful acts in the conduct of its operations."[80] This would seem to preclude any strict liability, and even the due diligence threshold may not be applicable. Yet there is no guidance on how this could be interpreted.

Given an estimated minimum US$1 billion capital cost to develop a nodule processing plant,[81] and the potential for these minerals to be used in long-term strategic procurement initiatives,[82] the lack of more stringent liability

[73] Case 17, n. 20 above, para. 136 for best environmental practices, para. 142 for environmental assessment and due diligence, para. 154 for developing States and due diligence, and para. 242, the ruling.
[74] E. Van Doorn, "Environmental aspects of the mining code: Preserving humankind's common heritage while opening Pardo's box?," *Marine Policy* 70 (2016): 192–197, p. 195.
[75] Nodules Regulations, n. 69 above, reg. 2.
[76] Cobalt Crusts Regulations, n. 71 above, reg. 2(3).
[77] J. Gao, "The responsibilities and obligations of the sponsoring states advisory opinion," *Chinese Journal of International Law* 12 (2013): 771–786, p. 775.
[78] Cobalt Crusts Regulations, n. 71 above, reg. 32.
[79] Nodules Regulations, n. 69 above, reg. 30.
[80] Id.
[81] E. Egede, "African states and participation in deep seabed mining: Problems and prospects," *The International Journal of Marine and Coastal Law* 24 (2009): 683–712, p. 685. Given the age of this article, it would be likely even more expensive to build. These costs cannot be ignored relative to developing nations and the common heritage of mankind doctrine, as it will most likely entail large transnational corporations or large state owned enterprises that become the contractors.
[82] Id., p. 700.

provisions is problematic. Some of the issues are thought to be dealt with via contract law.[83] For example, the Cobalt Crusts Regulations Annex IV standard clauses for exploration contract provides for liability in contractual terms.[84]

Recommendations complement the Mining Code. Under Article 165(2) of UNCLOS, the ISA Legal and Technical Commission (LTC) may make recommendations on the protection of the marine environment.[85] On 1 March 2013, the LTC released its recommendations for the guidance of contractors for the assessment of the possible environmental impacts arising from exploration for marine minerals in the Area (the Recommendations).[86] Under the guise of the precautionary approach, the Recommendations state that every plan of work for exploration for marine minerals shall take into consideration the following phases of environmental studies: (a) environmental baseline studies; (b) monitoring to ensure that no serious harm is caused to the marine environment from activities during prospecting and exploration; and (c) monitoring during and after testing of collecting systems and equipment.[87] Unfortunately, the Recommendations do not include liability guidelines.[88] Moreover, the Recommendations deal only with exploration and prospecting, not the commercial activity where most of the environmental damage is expected.

On 8 August 2017, the ISA released its Draft Regulations on Exploitation of Mineral Resources in the Area[89] with an explanatory note from the Secretariat on 10 August 2017.[90] The 2017 Draft Regulations contain a comprehensive set of

---

83 For example, in the responses to the 2017 Draft Regulations, several countries argue that terms should be defined in the contracts section, not in the regulations.
84 Cobalt Crusts Regulations, n. 71 above, Annex IV.
85 UNCLOS, n. 1 above, art. 165(2).
86 ISA, "Recommendations for the Guidance of Contractors for the Assessment of the Possible Environmental Impacts Rising from Exploration for Marine Minerals in the Area," Doc. ISBA/19/LTC/8 (1 March 2013).
87 Id., para. 11.
88 During their meetings in March and July 2018, the Legal and Technical Commission is scheduled to begin to investigate guidelines to complement the Draft Regulations.
89 ISA, "Draft Regulations on Exploitation of Mineral Resources in the Area," Doc. ISBA/23/LTC/CRP.3 (8 August 2017) [2017 Draft Regulations].
90 ISA, "Draft Regulations on Exploitation of Mineral Resources in the Area, Note by the Secretariat," Doc. ISBA/23/C/12 (10 August 2017) [Secretariat Note]. Unfortunately, due diligence and other liability issues were mostly ignored. For example, question 2, of the Note states: "Contract area: for areas within a contract area not identified as mining areas, what due diligence obligations should be placed on a contractor as regards continued exploration activities? Such obligations could include a programme of activities covering environmental, technical, economic studies or reporting obligations (that is, activities and undertakings similar to those under an exploration contract). Are the concepts and definitions of 'contract area' and 'mining area(s)' clearly presented in the draft regulations?"

environmental assessment provisions.[91] These regulations, unfortunately, fall far short of implementing a full liability regime for environmental harms. The 2017 Draft Regulations contain provisions for the application process, environmental impact assessment, and performance guarantees.[92] Annex V contains the environmental impact statement template.[93]

The liability provisions are contained in Annex X, Section 8, which states:

> 8.1 The Contractor shall be liable to the Authority for the actual amount of any damage, including damage to the Marine Environment, arising out of its *wrongful acts or omissions*, and those of its employees, subcontractors, agents and all persons engaged in working or acting for them in the conduct of its operations under this Contract, including the costs of reasonable measures to prevent, limit, and ameliorate damage to the Marine Environment, account being taken of any contributory acts or omissions by the Authority or third parties. This clause survives the termination of the Contract and applies to all damage caused by the Contractor regardless of whether it is caused or arises before, during, or after the completion of the Exploitation Activities or Contract term.[94] (emphasis added)

This is an important section in the contract, and seems to contradict Article 139 of UNCLOS and Case 17. It provides that the liability is to the ISA, not any one government, and survives the end of the contract. It also provides for damages being the actual amount of damages, so it does not appear that damage claims will be limited. Also, as previously noted, the ISA is a party with potential liability over damage to the marine environment. Draft Regulation Annex X, Section 8.2, provides for an indemnity to the ISA:

> 8.2 The *Contractor shall indemnify the Authority*, its employees, subcontractors and agents against all claims and liabilities of any third party arising out of any wrongful acts or omissions of the Contractor and its employees, agents and subcontractors, and all persons engaged in working or acting for them in the conduct of its operations under this Contract[95] (emphasis added)

---

91   2017 Draft Regulations, n. 89 above, Part IV, regs. 18, 19, 20, 22, and 24.
92   Id., reg. 9.
93   Id., Annex V.
94   Id., Annex X, s. 8.1.
95   Id., s. 8.2.

Of clear note, both Draft Regulation Section 8 and the Draft Contract only call for damages related to "wrongful acts or omissions."[96] There are no strict liability or negligence provisions; as such, these regulations are incomplete. The 2017 Draft Regulations are unclear about due diligence or *mens rea* requirements. It is also unclear whether other compensatory or punitive damage claims could be advanced, as they state "actual amount of damage."[97] It provides additional evidence that the ISA is a party and could potentially be liable for environmental harms. Unfortunately, this indemnification is vague on details.

Annex X of the 2017 Draft Regulations contains the standard clauses for an exploitation contract.[98] Like most contracts, the focus is on the rights and titles to the minerals; unfortunately, the Draft Regulations are very brief and vague on environmental liabilities.[99] Under Section 3.2(d), the contractor must file an environmental management and monitoring plan;[100] and under Section 3.3, the contractor shall carry out its obligations under this contract with "due diligence, efficiency, and economy, with due regard to the effect of its activities on the marine environment, and exercising reasonable regard for other activities in the marine environment."[101] Potentially, this plan of work and contractual obligations could satisfy the due diligence defense, if applicable.

In January 2017, prior to the release of the initial Draft Regulations, the ISA released a working paper on environmental matters.[102] The paper draws upon the experience from land-based mining and oil and gas regimes, the shipping industry, and deep-sea fishing activities.[103] One clear recommendation is on the creation of the "Environmental Liability Trust Fund."[104] The initial draft of the 2017 Draft Regulations also contained a substantive provision for a financial guarantee or security that would assist in liability claims and would help offset the costs of environmental remediation.[105] The published Draft Regulations

---

96   Id., s. 8.
97   Id., s. 8.3.
98   Id., Annex 1.
99   Some would argue that liability will be contractually based rather than regulatory based.
100 2017 Draft Regulations, n. 89 above, Annex X, s. 3.2(d).
101 Id., s. 3.3(j).
102 ISA, "Developing a Regulatory Framework for Mineral Exploitation in the Area: A Discussion Paper on the development and drafting of Regulations on Exploitation for Mineral Resources in the Area (Environmental Matters)" (Jamaica: ISA, 2017) [Environmental Matters Working Paper].
103 Id., para. 4.2.
104 Id., Part XII, Compensatory measures, "Section 1: Environmental Liability Trust Fund," pp. 72–73. This provision also called for the creation of a Seabed Mining Sustainability Fund (Draft Regulation 69).
105 Id., "Draft Regulation 44: Provision for a Financial Guarantee or Security," pp. 55–56.

have been watered down, creating instead a "performance guarantee" provision which is much less robust.[106] The published 2017 Draft Regulations do not mention any trust, technology, or environmental liability fund. Thus, the watered-down regulations either do not address gaps in liabilities or they create them.

Stakeholder submissions to the 2017 Draft Regulations were released in January 2018.[107] Of note was Australia's response, which will be detailed below.[108] However, there is still much discussion and disagreement in the international community on the Draft Regulations, environmental protection, and the gaps in environmental liabilities. The ISA has stated its goal of having the Draft Regulations adopted by 2020,[109] so time is of the essence.

On 28 and 29 September 2017, a legal working group convened to develop a work plan to carry out further research.[110] After a review of current UNCLOS and domestic legislation, the working group noted several issues. These involved liability in the context of "effective control" and the role of sponsoring States, key sources of risks, potential failure of sea-floor tools, including the production vessel itself, collisions, and the potential roles of environmental funds, bonds, and insurance.[111] Arising out of the conference came six bundles of issues: the purpose and scope of the regime, channeling liability/effective control, actionable damage, procedures, standards of liability, and form of the regime.[112] This article will address several of these issues.

---

106   2017 Draft Regulations, n. 89 above, reg. 9.
107   ISA, "Submissions to International Seabed Authority's Draft Regulations on Exploitation of Mineral Resources in the Area, ISBA/23/C/12; *ISBA*/23/LTC/CRP.3" (10 January 2018), available online: <https://www.isa.org.jm/files/documents/EN/Regs/2017/List-1.pdf>. Stakeholder submissions on the draft regulations have only been released in early 2018; see ISA, "The International Seabed Authority Releases Stakeholder Submissions to Draft Exploitation Regulations," Press Release (11 January 2018), available online: <https://www.isa.org.jm/news/international-seabed-authority-releases-stakeholder-submissions-draft-exploitation-regulations>.
108   Government of Australia, "Government of Australia's submission on the draft Regulations on Exploitation of Mineral Resources in the Area" (20 December 2017), available online: <https://www.isa.org.jm/files/documents/EN/Regs/2017/MS/Australia.pdf>.
109   Pew Charitable Trusts, "Summaries of Stakeholder Submissions on the ISA Draft Exploitation Regulations, Second report of the Code Project," White Paper (1 March 2018), available online: <http://www.pewtrusts.org/en/research-and-analysis/white-papers/2018/03/summaries-of-stakeholder-submissions-on-the-isa-draft-exploitation-regulations>.
110   F.-K. Phillips, *Conference Report, London, United Kingdom, September 2017, Legal Working Group on Liability for Environmental Harm from Activities in the Area* (Waterloo: Centre for International Governance Innovation, 2018), p. 2.
111   Id., p. 5.
112   Id., pp. 9–10.

From 5 to 8 March 2018, the ISA convened Part 1 the 24th Session of the ISA (the Session), with the goal of having the next round of draft regulations available in July 2018.[113] Day 1 of the Session outlined the purpose of the meeting, and, for the purposes of this article, there are several important discussion points, including the role of the sponsoring State, the role of legal status of standards and LTC guidelines, the broader environmental policy and regulations on exploitation, and the roles of the ISA.[114] The ISA noted that compliance of contractors was not a pressing issue due to the preliminary nature of the work, but now that prototyping and full operation is near, compliance will become important.[115] Day 3 featured consideration of the role of sponsoring States, the ISA, and contractors, including questions of liability, and the role and legal status of standards, recommendations, and guidelines.[116] There were also discussions on the legally binding nature of the ISA rules and guidelines.[117]

Part 1 of the Session did not provide consensus on any gaps in liabilities. Rather, it seemed to ask more questions than it answered. The ISA will defer to the LTC to discuss more technical provisions of the Draft Regulations. As such, from 12 to 23 March 2018, the LTC will be meeting, with Part 2 of the Session of the ISA to take place in July 2018. Whether or not additional questions will be addressed remains to be seen.

Given that many nations cannot yet agree on compliance and liability for the Area, it is important that academia provide guidance. Thus, the current state of the law of DSM should be compared with other environmental assessment and liability laws in other marine contexts.[118] To first compare with other regimes, a gap analysis of the current law must be undertaken.

Gap Analysis

One of the gaps in knowledge is the type of mining that would be conducted on the seabed. One type of mining would involve drilling into the seabed, similar to conventional oil drilling onshore. A second type of mining would be

---

113 ISA, 1st Part of the 24th Session of the International Seabed Authority 5–9 March 2018, Headquarters of the International Seabed Authority, Kingston, Jamaica Day 1 [ISA 24th Session].
114 IISD Reporting Services, "Summary of the Twenty-fourth Annual Session of the International Seabed Authority (First Part), 5–9 March 2018," *Earth Negotiations Bulletin* 25, no. 157 (12 March 2018).
115 OceansLaw, "Rule of Law Committee for the Oceans, LOS News – 6 March 2018: The ISA and Seabed Mining Code – Day 1 Report" (6 March 2018).
116 ISA 24th Session, n. 113 above, Day 3 report.
117 Id.
118 They should also be compared with onshore extractive industries; however, this is beyond the scope of this article.

a marine equivalent to "open pit" mining, that is, the extraction of minerals over a wide area of the seafloor.[119] As noted in Case 17, the type of mining will change the nature of due diligence obligations, and even strict liability and damage claims may be altered. Thus, the Draft Regulations need to address each type of mining with specific environmental assessment provisions, as the exploration regulations have done.

A second gap in knowledge is scientific uncertainty, as the majority of the seafloor is unexplored.[120] Any extraction or even exploration could have a material negative impact on unknown biota due to the unknown extent, duration, and toxicity of plumes.[121] If the scientific community does not yet know what types of living species are on the deep seabed, it is unclear as to how standards of conduct can be drafted to deal with the types of harm that could occur. A precautionary approach and even a moratorium on drilling would be in order for scientific advances to take place and provide for more evidence. Nonetheless, many scholars view that onshore and near offshore extraction pose more harm than does DSM.[122]

A third unknown is the lack of knowledge on the extent of environmental and compensable damage that may occur from DSM. Thus, any negligence or liability claim may not have sufficient legal grounds to warrant a finding of guilt on the contractor or sponsoring State. While Article 139 of UNCLOS creates a liability regime, the Annexes and Draft Regulations speak about a "wrongful act or omission" threshold.[123] There is no strict liability or negligence argument contained in the Draft Regulations.[124] Moreover, the environmental management plan does not contain any requirement to have insurance or financing in place for any environmental damage.[125] The Draft Regulations are vague in their assessment of liabilities for environmental damage. The issues of remoteness and other legal definitions, such as "wrongful acts," are neither defined nor explained.

---

119 KA. Miller et al., "An overview of seabed mining including the current state of development, environmental impacts, and knowledge gaps," *Frontiers in Marine Science* 4 (2018), doi:10.3389/fmars.2017.00418.
120 Id.
121 See statement by Kristina Gjerde in A. Hemphill, "The ISA's Biggest Issue of 2018," *DSM Observer* (4 March 2018), available online: <http://dsmobserver.org/2018/03/isas-biggest-issue-2018/>.
122 L.D. Bulong, "Into the abyss: Rationalizing commercial deep seabed mining through pragmatism and international law," *Tulane Journal of International and Comparative Law* 25 (2016): 128–181, p. 175.
123 UNCLOS, n. 1 above, art. 139; 2017 Draft Regulations, n. 89 above, Annex X, s. 8.2.
124 See also Case 17, n. 20 above, para. 179.
125 2017 Draft Regulations, n. 89 above, reg. 19.

As noted above, and to this end, a strong response to the Draft Regulations came from the Australian delegation. Australia submits that it

> is of the view that there needs to be more detail regarding the liability of a sponsoring state and how it can take responsibility for ensuring exploitation is undertaken in a safe and environmentally responsible manner. For example, the liability and enforcement mechanisms in the Regulations need to act as an effective deterrent to prevent Contractors from causing environmental harm or violating safety regulations. Australia suggests that, in addition to the monetary penalties prescribed in Appendix III of the Draft Regulations, consideration should be given to the application of monetary penalties for a broader range of breaches of environmental regulations, such as the failure to adhere to the Environmental and Management Monitoring Plan.[126]

The questions addressed in Case 17 are limited in scope and do not provide for a fulsome answer. The SDC also notes that one consequence of the exclusion of water evacuation and disposal of material from "activities in the Area" would be that the activities conducted by the contractor which are among the most hazardous to the environment would be excluded from those to which the responsibilities of the sponsoring State apply.[127] Case 17 did not address liability provisions of the flag State.

A fourth gap, therefore, includes the roles of the flag State and the vessel State (and potentially the processing State) for responsibility and liability. It is the responsibility of the Authority to determine both the rate at which exploitation of the Area will be allowed, and the methods in which the proceeds from exploitation will be shared among the members of the international community, as well as between current and future generations.[128] African countries could very much, through a subsidiary of a transnational corporation, sponsor their way into DSM, as small island States have done.[129] Developing countries often have weak environmental protection legislation.[130] The lack of domestic

---

126 Government of Australia, n. 108 above, p. 2. A complete list of submissions was released, see ISA, n. 107 above.
127 Case 17, n. 20 above, para 97.
128 Agreement Relating to the Implementation of Part XI of the United Nations Convention on the Law of the Sea of 10 December 1982, 28 July 1994, entered into force 28 July 1996, 1836 *United Nations Treaty Series* 3, Annex, Sec. 6.
129 Egede, n. 81 above, p. 697.
130 Id., p. 698, this statement would apply not only to African States, but any State that lacks capacity or willingness to provide for vigorous flag registration requirements.

DSM legislation in these jurisdictions is problematic, as there is no domestic environmental legislation to backstop a damage claim. But, more importantly, the legislation discussed below creates indemnification provisions for these States. How States will be indemnified is still unknown. The most likely source will be in DSM insurance. The Interoceanmetal Joint Organisation highlighted this fact in their response to the Draft Regulations, stating:

> [I]t should be carefully analyzed because actual suspension of mining operations in the Area, taking into account the risks associated, predicted structure of the operational costs and cash flow regime may very likely result in the real life in the mining termination with little chances for recovering the production and all risks associated are included, including environmental.... Insurance cost should be recognized for the proper considerations of contractor's economic models ongoing now in the Authority. Probably, common insurance conditions valid for all contracts should be proposed in further regulations. It is not clear if there is now market for such kind of insurance.[131]

More information and clarification on the role of financing and insurance is required, especially as the SDC ruled out residual liability.[132]

Finally, the issue of which parties can bring claims is still unresolved.[133] Not only are sponsoring States and the ISA potential defendants, they are also potential claimants. In summation, there is still much uncertainty over the provision requiring domestic legislation. References are made to sponsoring States in the working draft, but the lines of duty and responsibility (jurisdictional competence) between the Authority and sponsoring States (together with that of flag States, States parties, and non-parties to the Convention and relevant international organizations, including the International Maritime Organization) are not entirely clear.[134] For example, Australia "welcomed references to sponsoring states' national legislation, noting that the system should also help contractors decide which sponsoring state to approach."[135] Belgium stressed the need for "a balanced relationship between the ISA and contractors, clarity

---

131 Interoceanmetal Joint Organization, "Comments provided by the Interoceanmetal Joint Organization IOM to the document 'Draft regulations on exploitation of mineral resources in the Area'" (22 November 2017), available online: <https://www.isa.org.jm/files/documents/EN/Regs/2017/Contr/IOM.pdf>.
132 Case 17, n. 20 above, para. 204.
133 Id., paras. 179 and 180.
134 Environmental Matters Working Paper, n. 102 above, para. 4.6.
135 Government of Australia, n. 108 above.

on monitoring rules to avoid 'sponsor shopping,' and more attention to environmental regulations."[136] China, on the other hand, has been "arguing that sponsoring states that have taken necessary and appropriate measures should not be held responsible for contractors' misconduct."[137] There is thus serious disagreement over liability and obligations.[138]

State of National Legislation of DSM

In Case 17, the SDC described due diligence as a variable concept, meaning that the standard could change as technologies improve,[139] and that there should be a higher standard for riskier activities.[140] The SDC continues to point out that UNCLOS requires the sponsoring State to adopt "laws and regulations" and to take "administrative measures which are, within the framework of its legal system, reasonably appropriate for securing compliance by persons under its jurisdiction."[141]

Following its discussion of due diligence, the SDC outlined the "direct obligations" of sponsoring States under UNCLOS and general international law.[142] The ISA invited countries to provide the texts of their domestic legislation.[143] Nauru,[144] Tonga,[145] and even the United States have submitted their

---

136 See comment by Belgium om the role of sponsoring States reported in IISD Reporting Services, "ISA-24 Part 1 Highlights," *Earth Negotiations Bulletin* 25, no. 155 (7 March 2018), available online: <http://enb.iisd.org/vol25/enb25155e.html>; see also Belgium, "Concerns: Comments on the draft regulations on exploitation of mineral resources in the Area" (20 December 2017), available online: <https://www.isa.org.jm/files/documents/EN/Regs/2017/MS/Belgium.pdf>.
137 See comment by China on the role of sponsoring States reported by IISD Reporting Services, id.
138 Onshore mining operations and comparative domestic legislation would be ideal, but are beyond the scope of this article. The author has made a submission to continue this line of research as part of a PhD application at Dalhousie University and the University of Ottawa. Under the proposed research, several countries party to UNCLOS will be canvassed. The United States has detailed DSM legislation.
139 Tanaka, n. 26 above, p. 210.
140 Case 17, n. 20 above, para. 110.
141 Id., para. 108.
142 Anton, n. 29 above, p. 248.
143 ISA, "Decision of the Council of the International Seabed Authority," Doc. ISBA/17/C/20 (21 July 2011), para. 3.
144 Republic of Nauru, *International Seabed Minerals Act 2015*, No. 26 of 2015.
145 Tonga, *Seabed Minerals Act 2014*, Act 10 of 2014.

legislation.¹⁴⁶ Canada has not.¹⁴⁷ Tonga, in 2017, had a population of just over 110,000 people.¹⁴⁸ Nauru had a population of 13,049.¹⁴⁹ The question must be asked: How can these two small countries possibility have the legal systems in place to meet their due diligence requirements? A representative sample of several countries will be canvassed, though it is beyond the scope of this article to review every country that would have an interest in DSM in the Area.

Nauru and Tonga
The Nauru *International Seabed Minerals Act 2015* is illustrative, stating that the "Sponsored Party shall be responsible for the performance of all Seabed Mineral Activities carried out within the Contract Area, and their compliance with the Rules of the ISA, and shall be liable for the actual amount of any compensation, damage or penalties arising out of its failure so to comply, or out of any *wrongful acts or omissions* in the conduct of the Seabed Mineral Activities"¹⁵⁰ (emphasis added). Section 29(2) provides indemnification for Nauru for all actions, proceedings, costs, charges, claims, and demands which may be made or brought by any third party in relation to a sponsored party's seabed mineral activities.¹⁵¹ Furthermore, Section 46 gives the Supreme Court jurisdiction to establish liability and to provide recourse for prompt and adequate

---

146 The legislation of the United States includes the *Deep Seabed Hard Mineral Resources Act, 1980*, Public Law 96–283, 28 June 1980, 94 Stat. 553 (30 U.S.C. 1401 et seq.), as amended to 1 July 2000; *Deep Seabed Mining Regulations Affecting Pre-Enactment Explorers*, 45 Fed. Reg. 226 (20 November 1980), pp. 76661–76663; *Deep Seabed Mining Regulations for Exploration Licenses 1980*, 46 Fed. Reg. 45896 (15 September 1981); 15 Code of Federal Regulations, Part 970; *Deep Seabed Mining Regulations for Commercial Recovery Permits*, 54 Fed. Reg. 525 (6 January 1989); 15 Code of Federal Regulations, Part 971; United States Department of the Interior, *Minerals Management Service (MMS). Guidelines for Obtaining Minerals other than Oil, Gas and Sulphur on the Outer Continental Shelf* (Public Law 103–426, enacted 31 October 1994; 108 Stat. 4371), OCS Report MMS 99-0070 (December 1999). Comparative analysis of the U.S. provisions against the ISA provisions would be useful future research.

147 See ISA, "Laws, Regulations, Administrative Measures adopted by Sponsoring States and Other Members of the ISA With Respect to the Activities in the Area," Doc. ISBA/18/C/8 (4 May 2012). Canada is not mentioned in this document; Canada will be briefly discussed below.

148 CIA World Fact Book, *Tonga, People and Society* (est. July 2017), available online: <https://www.cia.gov/library/publications/the-world-factbook/geos/tn.html>.

149 United Nations, *World Population Prospects: The 2017 Revision: Nauru* (United Nations Department of Economic and Social Affairs, Population Division. Retrieved 10 September 2017).

150 *Nauru Act*, n. 144 above, s. 29(1).

151 Id., s. 29(2).

compensation in the event of unlawful damage caused by seabed mineral activities, in accordance with Article 235(2) of UNCLOS.[152]

Sections 70 and 84 of the *Tonga Seabed Mineral Act 2014*[153] are similar in wording to Nauru's legislation. Section 70(3) provides the indemnification for Tonga, while the licensee is liable for the actual amount of any compensation or damage arising out of its failure to comply with the Act, regulations made under the Act, or the licence, and any "wrongful acts or omissions" and those of its employees, officers, subcontractors, and agents in the conduct of the seabed mineral activities or ancillary operations under licence, including but not limited to that arising from injury to coastal or marine users, damage to the marine environment, and any related economic loss or compensation.[154] Section 70(4) provides for joint and several liabilities,[155] while Section 70(5) provides for the continuation of liabilities even after all activities have ceased.[156]

Case 17 highlighted the need to use the precautionary approach to due diligence.[157] However, provisions in the legislation of both Tonga and Nauru seem to absolve themselves from this due diligence requirement. The use of "wrongful acts and omissions" is problematic, as a strict liability regime would not be concerned whether an act is wrongful or not to warrant a liability claim. This does not seem to be a legislative oversight, as Section 109 of the Tonga legislation relates to non-interference with freedom of the high seas.[158] Section 109(4) creates a "strict liability" offense.[159] If Section 109(4) specifically and explicitly creates a strict liability offense, yet Sections 70 and 84 create a "wrongful act" liability standard, then this would preclude it from being strict liability. Finally, issues to be addressed in subsequent research include the ability to enforce this legislation, to make a claim against the vessel/operator, and to collect compensation awards.

Singapore

Singapore has enacted DSM legislation. In 2013, Singapore sponsored an application from a company domiciled in the country.[160] The *Deep Seabed Mining*

---

152   Id., s. 46.
153   Tonga Act, n. 145 above, ss. 70 and 84.
154   Id., s. 70(3).
155   Id., s. 70(4).
156   Id., s. 70(5); note, the provisions are repeated for other activities in s. 84 of the legislation.
157   Case 17, n. 20 above, para. 242 (B).
158   *Tonga Act*, n. 145 above, s. 109(1).
159   Id., ss. 109(4).
160   X.H. Oyarce, "Sponsoring states in the Area: Obligations, liability and the role of developing states," *Marine Policy* 95 (2018): 317–323, p. 318.

Act 2015[161] governs Singapore's domestic DSM legislation. Singapore directly quotes the need for due diligence per Section 7(1) of the legislation when it states that, before it will grant a license, the minister must be satisfied that the company meets, or is likely to meet, the qualification standards under Annex III, Article 4 of UNCLOS.[162] Moreover, the nation requires a company to post security for the due performance of its obligations.[163] Unfortunately, Singapore also requires an execution by the licensee to indemnify the nation against any liability incurred;[164] however, any breaches are only subject to a fine.[165]

In contemplation of avoiding liabilities by using a corporate form, Section 12(6) states that any transfer of license does not affect any criminal or civil liability from the original licensee.[166] Section 16 provides for the government to order specific performance to prevent, contain, or minimize any harmful environmental effects.[167] Finally, Section 17 provides domestic enforcement of Annex III judgements.[168] From an enforcement perspective, Section 18 allows for SDC orders to be registered in Singapore, but a state may still claim privilege or immunity.[169] However, the issue of strict liability for operators may not be accurate, as Section 21 of the legislation requires, for an offense, proof of consent or connivance of an officer, or neglect on the officer's part.[170]

Canada

Given Canada's role in DSM, its familiarity with mining, offshore oil and gas, and the extension of its continental shelf claims beyond the 200-nautical mile limit,[171] it is somewhat surprising that it has not developed domestic legislation for DSM in the Area.[172] While Canada does not have fulsome legislation,

---

161   Singapore, *Deep Seabed Mining Act 2015*, No. 6 of 2015.
162   Id., s. 7(1).
163   Id., s. 10(2)(e).
164   Id., s. 10(2)(f).
165   Id., s. 10(4).
166   Id., s. 12(6).
167   Id., s. 16(4)(c).
168   Id., s. 17.
169   Id., s. 18(2).
170   Id., s. 21(1).
171   See W. Spicer, "Canada, the law of the sea treaty and international payments: Where will the money come from?," *University of Calgary SPP Research Papers* 8, no. 31 (September 2015), available online: <https://www.policyschool.ca/wp-content/uploads/2016/03/final-law-sea-spicer.pdf>.
172   The *Oceans Act*, SC 1996, c. 31, provides for seabed provisions within the EEZ and continental shelf.

there is evidence from regulation. The Endeavour Hydrothermal Vents Marine Protected Area Regulations state:

s. 2 No person shall
(a) disturb, damage or destroy, in the Area, or remove from the Area, any part of the seabed, including a venting structure, or any part of the subsoil, or any living marine organism or any part of its habitat; or
(b) carry out any underwater activity in the Area that is likely to result in the disturbance, damage, destruction or removal of anything referred to in paragraph (a).[173]

This is a very strict obligation and one that could raise the question of whether the ISA has DSM regulation all wrong. There is an argument for goal-based regulation as used in international shipping, which will be discussed below. It also shows a potentially conflicting opinion between developed and developing countries. Developed countries have more stringent legislation.

United Kingdom

The UK legislation for DSM is the *Deep Sea Mining Act, 2014* (UK 2014 Act).[174] This legislation updates the *Deep Sea Mining (Temporary Provisions) Act 1981* (Temporary Act).[175] The UK has significant investments in the Clarion Clipperton Zone through the UK Seabed Resources Ltd.[176] Like Singapore, the UK expressly allows for enforcement of the SDC to be taken in the UK High Court, including arbitration awards.[177] Intriguingly, Section 10 of the UK 2014 Act expressly omits Section 10 of the Temporary Act, which had created a Deep Sea Mining Fund. The liability provisions solely deal with personal injury, not environmental damage.[178] The only environmental protection stems from Section 5 of the Temporary Act and deals with the grant of a license, not in the damage caused to the marine environment.[179]

On a positive note, there is no indemnification provision in the legislation, so the United Kingdom has not absolved itself of liability. However, the remaining sections are weak on environmental protections. The legislation seems to delegate to the ISA and UNCLOS all other claims for damage. This

---

173   *Endeavour Hydrothermal Vents Marine Protected Area Regulations*, SOR/2003-87 s. 2.
174   *Deep Sea Mining Act 2014* (UK) 2014, c. 15.
175   *Deep Sea Mining (Temporary Provisions) Act 1981*, (UK) 1981, c. 53 [Temporary Act].
176   UK Seabed Resources is owned in conjunction with Lockheed Martin Corp. See Lockheed Martin, "UK Seabed Resources," available online: <https://www.lockheedmartin.com/en-gb/products/uk-seabed-resources.html>.
177   UK 2014 Act, n. 174 above, s. 9.
178   Temporary Act, n. 175 above, s. 15.
179   Id., s. 5.

does not appear to satisfy Article 235 of UNCLOS, which requires fulsome domestic legislation.

China

The final domestic jurisdiction to be canvassed is China.[180] Its approach is based upon their 2016 legislation.[181] China is a major player in DSM exploration, with over four exploration contracts with the ISA,[182] two of which are with State-owned enterprises.[183] China's legislation appears to be more complete than the other nations explored here, with seven chapters and 29 articles. Environmental pollution and damage to cultural relics is referenced in Articles 9(3), 11, and 12. Fines for pollution/damage can range from CNY 500,000 to 1,000,000, and if the illegal activities constitute a crime, criminal responsibility entails.[184] The legislation itself provides for "reasonably appropriate" environmental protection, but one notable omission is environmental assessments.[185] Other fiscal arrangements are omitted, and as Xu notes, "before exploitation activities commence, fiscal issues should be in place."[186] It is unclear whether the above penalties provide limits to liabilities by the operator, although the potential for criminal charges is a novel approach. Foreign investment is omitted from the legislation.[187] This would impact the effectiveness of the common heritage of mankind doctrine, as well as the practicalities of the size and scope of DSM operations.

---

180 Unfortunately, the links to the actual texts are in Mandarin/Chinese. As such, the article will use third party peer reviewed articles for its analysis.
181 *Deep Seabed Area Resource Exploration and Exploitation Law of the People's Republic of China*, promulgated 26 February 2016, entered into force 1 May 2016, adopted at the 19th Session of the Standing Committee of the 12th National People's Congress (NPC) of China, Order No. 42 of the President of the People's Republic of China (PRC) [Deep Seabed Law].
182 G. Zhang and P. Zheng, "A new step forward: Review of China's 2016 legislation on international seabed area exploration and exploitation," *Marine Policy* 73 (2016): 244–255, p. 246.
183 X. Xu, G. Zhang and G.J. Xue, "China's deep seabed law: Towards 'reasonably appropriate' environmental legislation for exploration and exploitation of deep sea minerals in the Area," *Asian Yearbook of International Law* 21 (2015), doi.org/10.1163/9789004344556_011, available online: <https://brill.com/abstract/book/edcoll/9789004344556/B978-90-04-34454-9_012.xml>.
184 Zhang and Zheng, n. 182 above, p. 250.
185 Xu et al., n. 183 above. Of note, the lack of environmental assessment was also at issue in the Philippines-China dispute discussed below. Whether this is a result of the case, or whether China believes the ISA will create the required environmental assessment is up for discussion.
186 Id.
187 Zhang and Zheng, n. 182 above, p. 251.

In this summary canvass of domestic legislation, there is a broad range of theoretical approaches, and all have significant flaws and omissions. Tonga and Nauru seem to alter the strict liability to a "wrongful act" regime, and limit their own liabilities, in contrast to Case 17. The United Kingdom takes a "hands-off" approach, which seems to leave to the international system to fill in the gaps. Unfortunately, if the international system has gaps, then there is nothing to fill in. Finally, China's legislation seems to cap liabilities,[188] so it may not compensate for the environmental harms caused. However, their approach to oil spills may provide clarity on some aspects of liability.

Lessons from Other International Regimes

Civil Liability Regimes

There are several relevant international conventions that deal with liability for damage to the marine environment. The Protocol to Amend the International Convention on Civil Liability for Oil Pollution Damage (CLC) provides for strict liability on the part of the registered owner of the tanker to pay compensation for "pollution damage."[189] The CLC explicitly uses the term "negligence."[190] It also raised the limits of liability, established a compulsory insurance requirement, and introduced the possibility of a direct action against the insurer.[191] Norway would appear to be the only state that has extended its application of the CLC (as implemented nationally) to oil pollution on the high seas; that action benefits both the environment and the polluting shipowner.[192]

The International Oil Pollution Compensation Funds are a key component of this strict liability regime. Claims from the Torrey Canyon spill, to which compensation was only available via international maritime law, required a claim of negligence and gave the shipowner the right to limit liability to amounts deemed insufficient.[193] The Fund created a levy system and explicitly

---

188   Bulong, n. 122 above, p. 177.
189   Protocol to Amend the 1969 International Convention on Civil Liability for Oil Pollution Damage, 27 November 1992, 1956 *United Nations Treaty Series* 255 [CLC 1992], art. 1(6).
190   Id., art. 3(2) & (3).
191   T.J. Schoenbaum, "Liability for damages in oil spill accidents: Evaluating the USA and international law regimes in the light of Deepwater Horizon," *Journal of Environmental Law* 24, no. 3 (2012): 395–416.
192   Comité Maritime International, *International Working Group (Polar Shipping) Civil Liability* (31 October 2017) L. Rosenberg-Overby ed. (CMI, online, 2017), p. 41.
193   R.H. Ganton, "The international oil pollution compensation fund," *Environmental Policy and Law* 12 (1984): 5–9, p. 6.

covers compensation for reasonable measures to reinstate an environment to its pre-contaminated state.[194]

In this regard, China's updated legislation is illustrative. Section 66 of the *Marine Environmental Protection Law, 1999*[195] created a compensation fund for vessel oil pollution, and the 2010 regulations increased liability limits and made insurance mandatory.[196] This fund is a key and critical component of environment protection, as it applies when the damage exceeds the operator's liability and/or ability to pay, when the operator is exempted from liability, and when the source of pollution cannot be ascertained.[197] Compensation for vessel source oil pollution plays an essential role in protecting the interests of victims and in the prevention of oil pollution.[198] This is a glaring flaw in the DSM regime.

The International Convention on Civil Liability for Bunker Oil Pollution Damage, 2001[199] was adopted to ensure that adequate, prompt, and effective compensation is available to persons who suffer damage caused by spills of oil, when the oil is carried as fuel in ships' bunkers.[200] This convention applies to damage caused to the territory, including the territorial sea, and in the EEZs of States parties.[201] Another key provision is the requirement for direct action. This would allow a claim for compensation for pollution damage to be brought directly against an insurer.[202]

The not-yet in force 2010 Hazardous and Noxious Substances (HNS) Convention[203] sets out a shared liability regime to compensate claimants for damages arising from the international or domestic carriage of HNS by seagoing

---

194 J. Wren, "Overview of the compensation and liability regimes under the international oil pollution compensation fund (IOPC)," *Spill Science & Technology Bulletin* 6, no. 1 (2000): 45–58, p. 48.

195 See L. Zhu, B. Dong and K.X. Li, "China's 2012 regime for compensation for vessel source oil pollution: A comparative study," *Ocean Development & International Law* 44, no. 3 (2013): 270–286.

196 *Amended Regulations of the People's Republic of China on the Prevention and Control of Marine Pollution from Ships* (2010); *Measures for Implementation of Civil Liability Insurance for Ship Oil Pollution* (2010), s. 56.

197 *Administrative Measures for Use and Collection of the Vessel-Source Oil Pollution Compensation Fund* (2012), art. 15.

198 Zhu et al., n. 195 above, p. 277.

199 International Convention on Civil Liability for Bunker Oil Pollution Damage, 23 March 2001, entered into force 21 November 2008, IMO Doc. LEG/CONF.12/19 (27 March 2001).

200 Id., art. 3.

201 Id., art. 2.

202 Id., art. 7, which provides for compulsory insurance.

203 International Convention on Liability and Compensation for Damage in Connection with the Carriage of Hazardous and Noxious Substances by Sea, 2010, 30 April 2010, IMO Doc.

vessels.[204] It includes provisions regarding both shipowner liability and an HNS Fund.[205] The shipowner's liability is a strict liability regime, while the HNS liability is either a negligence standard or, if the shipowner cannot pay, a strict liability standard.[206]

This convention would greatly expand liability, compared to Canadian domestic legislation, from a maximum of CA$16 million to CA$74 million (for a 20,000 tonne ship) and a total maximum liability of CA$500 million.[207] This is another example of how domestic legislation may be insufficient to cover the harm to the environment. However, the Canadian approach has a wider scope than the international regime and pays on claims having to do with both persistent oil and non-persistent oil pollution discharged from all classes of ships.[208]

The main takeaway is that various international agreements provide for strict liability for environmental damage. The evidence seems to indicate that the number of oil spills and the amount of oil that has been discharged has declined over the last number of years.[209] Yet, the phrasing of the 2017 Draft Regulations and domestic legislation seems to provide for a "wrong act or omission" standard.

The United States is the most significant maritime nation that has chosen not to be a party to UNCLOS and instead has developed its own national law concerning liability for oil pollution damages.[210] In the United States, the Deepwater Horizon oil spill demonstrated the consequences of a major environmental disaster in the marine environment.[211] The case illustrated domestic liability legislation and certain issues with the concept of "pure economic loss."[212]

LEG/CONF.17/10 (4 May 2010), available online: <http://www.imo.org/en/OurWork/Legal/HNS/Documents/HNS%20Consolidated%20text.pdf> [2010 HNS Convention].

204 Transport Canada, *Maritime Transport of Hazardous and Noxious Substances: Liability and Compensation Discussion Paper* (October 2010) (Ottawa: Transport Canada, 2010).

205 2010 HNS Convention, n. 203 above, Ch. II, art. 7.

206 Transport Canada, n. 204 above, p. 8.

207 Id., p. 13.

208 Zhu et al., n. 195 above, p. 272–273, 281.

209 C. Kontovas, H. Psaraftis and N. Ventikos, "An empirical analysis of IOPCF oil spill cost data," *Marine Pollution Bulletin* 60 (2010): 1455–1466, p. 1456.

210 T.J. Schoenbaum, "Liability for damages in oil spill accidents: Evaluating the USA and international law regimes in the light of Deepwater Horizon," *Journal of Environmental Law* 24, no. 3 (2012): 395–416, p. 397.

211 A. Davis, "Pure economic loss claims under the Oil Pollution Act: Combining policy and congressional intent," *Columbia Journal of Law and Social Problems* 45, no. 1 (2011): 1–44.

212 Id., p. 3.

The United States imposes a strict liability without fault on all responsible parties for oil discharges.[213] Responsible parties include the owner, operator, or charterer of a vessel, the owner or operator of an onshore oil facility; the lessee, permittee, and owner and operator of any offshore facility; the owner and operator of a pipeline; and the licensee of a deep-water port.[214] Furthermore, the United States has created an Oil Spill Liability Trust Fund.[215]

The United States is not a party to UNCLOS, so it will be interesting to note their DSM activities and liability regime for environmental damage as either a vessel State, a flag State, or a port/processing State. The type of legislation that will be required is strict and unlimited liability for all parties, with an environmental liability fund if damages are larger than one party can or will pay.[216]

In summation, the civil liability regimes provide great evidence as to the correct approach for DSM liability. The regulations are clear, provide for strict liability for operators, and no indemnification for State parties. Furthermore, the technology fund provides for the extra bit of "insurance" to ensure that there are funds to clean up any environmental spill.[217]

Exclusive Economic Zone and Continental Shelf Provisions

As discussed above, the Solwara 1 project in PNG's EEZ could be highly comparative to DSM in the Area. Unfortunately, PNG does not have any laws on DSM in the EEZ that would regulate Solwara 1.[218] Thus, both PNG and Nautilus may work with "environmental impunity."[219] While a limited amount of onshore processing will occur in PNG, the majority of processing will occur in China.[220] One potential saving grace is, as previously noted, that Nautilus is a Canadian company and listed under the Toronto Stock Exchange (TSX). The provincial securities acts, for example in British Columbia,[221] and the TSX require certain mandatory disclosures and risk assessments, and investors should be

---

213   33 U.S.C. ss. 2701 and 2702; see also Schoenbaum, n. 210 above, p. 398.
214   33 U.S.C. s. 2701.
215   Oil Spill Liability Trust Fund, 25 U.S.C. s. 9509; see also 46 U.S.C. s. 4611.
216   See n. 146 above for a list of U.S. DSM legislation.
217   The Seabed Disputes Chambers recommended that the ISA implement a trust fund; see Case 17, n. 21 above, para. 205; UNCLOS, n. 1 above, art. 235(3).
218   Bulong, n. 122 above, p. 175.
219   Id.
220   R. Page, "An Overview of Chinese Policy, Activity and Strategic Interests Relating to Deep Sea Mining in the Pacific Region" (Deep Sea Mining Campaign, 2018), p. 21. See also: Nautilus Minerals, Solwara 1 Project, online: <http://www.cares.nautilusminerals.com/irm/content/solwara-1-project.aspx?RID=339>.
221   *Securities Act*, RSBC 1996, c. 418, ss. 131, 140.3, 63. British Columbia is used as an example because Nautilus is registered in that province.

cognizant of potential company liabilities.[222] At the date of writing, the project is showing significant financial hurdles. In December 2017, a citizens' group in PNG, represented by the Centre for Environmental Law and Community Rights Inc. (CELCOR) and assisted by the New South Wales Environmental Defenders Office, commenced a lawsuit against PNG claiming insufficient environmental assessment procedures for the project.[223] There is thus significant uncertainty about whether or not this project will begin.

New Zealand has a novel approach to DSM, at least within its EEZ. The *Exclusive Economic Zone and Continental Shelf Act (Environmental Effects) 2012*[224] provides that non-discharge offenses are subject to strict liability.[225] DSM in the EEZ was considered in the *Trans-Tasman Resources Ltd. Marine Consent Decision*,[226] which highlighted the uncertainty of the determination of cost of potentially adverse effects.[227] In the face of this uncertainty, the use of the precautionary approach is mandated, but even this approach offers "no easy answers."[228] The license was granted, but the New Zealand High Court overturned the decision and referred back to consider adaptive management processes.[229]

The *Trans-Tasman* case may have implications for DSM in the Area, as adequate information on the effects on the environment, monitoring baseline

---

222 These include *Standards of Disclosure for Mineral Projects*, BSSC NI 43–101 (9 May 2016) and *Continuous Disclosure Obligations*, BCSC NI 51–102 (30 June 2015). All documents required must be posted on <http://www.sedar.com>, which is the system for electronic documents and retrieval. See documents related to Nautilus Minerals Inc., available online: <https://sedar.com/DisplayCompanyDocuments.do?lang=EN&issuerNo=00005833>.

223 See H. Davidson, "Troubled Papua New Guinea deep-sea mine faces environmental challenge," *The Guardian* (11 December 2017), available online: <https://www.theguardian.com/world/2017/dec/12/troubled-papua-new-guinea-deep-sea-mine-faces-environmental-challenge>.

224 *Exclusive Economic Zone and Continental Shelf (Environmental Effects) Act 2012*, No. 72 (2012) (New Zealand). The *Crown Minerals Act 1991*, No. 70 (NZ) comprises the onshore mining provisions.

225 Id., s. 133.

226 NZ Environmental Protection Authority, *Trans-Tasman Resources Ltd. Marine Consent Decision*, (17 June 2014), available online: <http://www.epa.govt.nz/EEZ/EEZ000004/TransTasmanResources>.

227 Id., para. 753.

228 D.K. Anton and K.E. Kim, "The application of the precautionary and adaptive management approaches in the seabed mining context: Trans-Tasman Resources Ltd. marine consent decision under New Zealand's Exclusive Economic Zone and Continental Shelf (Environmental Effects) Act 2012," *International Journal of Marine and Coastal Law* 30 (2015): 175–188, p. 185.

229 *Taranaki-Whanganui Conservation Board v Environmental Protection Authority* [2018] NZHC 2217 (28 August 2018) at para. 420.

data, and adaptive management approaches are required.²³⁰ This could all have implications on the due diligence requirement emanating from Case 17. There is another interesting issue with liability, namely, the ability to collect. According to Makgill, "in practical terms, the ability to recover damages is likely to be governed by the financial resources available to those liable."²³¹ As a valid example, Nautilus is facing significant financial obstacles, and without an environmental trust fund or significant insurance policies in place, it is unlikely that any environmental damage claim, even if awarded, could be collected. The ISA needs to take action.

Flag State Liabilities

Many boundary questions remain, including the line between flag State and sponsoring State liability.²³² Flag State liabilities arise from Articles 209(2), 211, and 217 of UNCLOS. Article 209(2) provides that flag States shall adopt laws to prevent, reduce, and control pollution from vessels flying under their flag.²³³ States shall ensure compliance of vessels flying under their flag.²³⁴ However, there is a lack of full clarity as to their application to DSM in the Area and on the standard of liability and amount of damages that a flag State could face, should environmental damage occur due to DSM. Thus, international law precedent on the liability of flag States and on operators from other settings would prove useful in the DSM context.

On 2 April 2015, the International Tribunal for the Law of the Sea rendered an advisory opinion on the rights and obligations of flag States and coastal States regarding illegal, unreported, and unregulated (IUU) fishing within the EEZ (Case 21).²³⁵ Ownership of fishing vessels also comprises a "complex structure of nominated front companies and/or non-disclosed beneficial owners."²³⁶ The Tribunal noted that flag States have a "due diligence" obligation to ensure that vessels sailing under their flag take the necessary measures to comply with

---

230 Id., para. 405, see also, New Zealand Environmental Protection Authority, "Trans-Tasman Resources Limited 2016," Decision on Marine Consents and Marine Discharge Consents Application, August 2017, Ref EEZ00011, p. XVI, 229, 230, 231.

231 R. Makgill, "Oil and gas in the exclusive economic zone," *Resource Management Journal* (April 2014): 29–31, p. 31.

232 Phillips, n. 110 above, p. 3.

233 UNCLOS, n. 1 above, art. 209(2).

234 Id., art. 217(1).

235 *Request for an Advisory Opinion Submitted by the Sub-Regional Fisheries Commission*, Case No. 21, Advisory Opinion (ITLOS, 2 April 2015) [Case 21]. Documents relating to the case available online: <http://www.itlos.org/cases/list-of-cases/case-no-21/>.

236 L. Griggsa and G. Lugten, "Veil over the nets (unravelling corporate liability for IUU fishing offences," *Marine Policy* 31 (2007): 159–168, p. 160.

the protection and preservation measures adopted by member States.[237] The State must also have domestic legislation to enforce these rules.[238]

More importantly, the Tribunal relied heavily on Case 17 to advance its jurisprudence.[239] Like Case 17, the standard of liability for flag States arises not out of the actions of the operator, but in the failure to comply with its due diligence obligation.[240] The Tribunal noted:

> Although the relationship between sponsoring States and contractors is not entirely comparable to that existing between the flag State and vessels flying its flag which are engaged in fishing activities in the exclusive economic zone of the coastal State, the Tribunal holds the view that the clarifications provided by the Seabed Disputes Chamber regarding the meaning of the expression "responsibility to ensure" and the interrelationship between the notions of obligations "of due diligence" and obligations "of conduct" referred to in paragraph 129 are fully applicable in the present case.[241]

Thus, flag State liabilities are the same as sponsoring State liabilities, in that it is their responsibility to ensure to deploy the adequate means and exercise best possible efforts to obtain this result.[242] The liability of the flag State arises from a failure to comply with its "due diligence" obligations.[243]

The issue of flag State liability also arose in the China-Philippines dispute.[244] The Tribunal stated that anything less than a due diligence standard by the flag State to avoid IUU fishing would fall short of the provisions of UNCLOS.[245] Moreover, as there is such a close link between Chinese fishing vessels and the Chinese government, there is a heightened obligation on the part of the flag State.[246]

This case is relevant to DSM due to the marine environmental protection obligations of flag States. The obligations noted in the China-Philippines case apply to flag States regardless of the location of the harmful activities; thus,

---

[237] Case 21, n. 235 above, para. 136.
[238] Id., para. 138.
[239] Id., paras. 126 and 131.
[240] Id., para. 146.
[241] Id., para. 125.
[242] Id., para. 128.
[243] Id., para. 146.
[244] Permanent Court of Arbitration (PCA), *In the Matter of the South China Sea Arbitration*, PCA Case No 2013–19, Award (12 July 2016).
[245] Id., paras. 743, 794.
[246] Id., para. 755.

jurisdiction is not dependent on sovereignty or the existence of an EEZ.[247] It also displays the extent of how an environmental assessment would fulfill a due diligence defense. The 2017 Draft Regulations provide for a need for an environmental assessment to be granted a license to conduct DSM in the Area. Case 17 specifically noted that due diligence requirements will differ based on the type of mining. The China-Philippines case could provide evidence as to the extent of the requirements, specifically with the use of an environmental assessment. The China-Philippines ruling noted that the existence (or lack thereof) of an environmental assessment is important, but is not definitive in determining whether there is a breach of its requirements under Article 206 of UNCLOS.[248] Moreover, China's DSM firms are State-controlled operations, and thus the flag State, sponsoring State, and operator all may be deemed the same and have higher obligations for liability.[249] Environmental assessments should assist in meeting a due diligence threshold, but by themselves they may not absolve a flag State from liability.

Analysis and Recommendations

Much more work needs to be conducted to ensure that fulsome liability provisions are in place for DSM in the Area. The liability regime should reflect a transnationalist approach with a stewardship doctrine. Thus, the use of the precautionary principle makes abundant sense, especially because of scientific uncertainty. When taken in context with the Sustainable Development Goals and the common heritage of mankind, this makes an even more compelling argument. According to the Sustainable Development Goal 14, the oceans and seas are to be conserved and developed in a sustainable manner.[250]

Operators
Operator liability seems to depend on the definition of a "wrongful act or omission," the language used in UNCLOS and the 2017 Draft Regulations. Case 17

---

247   Id., para. 927. Moreover, the Tribunal noted that Part XII applies to all maritime areas, both inside and outside national jurisdiction. Again, sovereignty is irrelevant (para. 940). This would presuppose that these issues would apply to DSM in the Area.
248   Id., para. 991. The PCA directly quoted the passage from Case 17 comparing Article 206 of UNCLOS with environment assessment requirements (para. 948).
249   Id., paras. 965 and 971.
250   United Nations General Assembly (UNGA), "Transforming our World: The 2030 Agenda for Sustainable Development," UN. Doc. A/RES/70/1 (21 October 2105), p. 23–24 (Sustainable Development Goal 14: Conserve and sustainably use the oceans, seas and marine resources).

highlighted the need for different due diligence standards for different types of mining. This may have inadvertently revealed that the strict liability will not be enforced, even for contractor/operators. This regime seems to lead back to the general international maritime law surrounding environmental damage.

While not in force, and applicable to State parties, the Draft Articles on Responsibility of States for Internationally Wrongful Acts (Draft Articles) may assist in articulating the elements of the offense.[251] Article 2 states that there is an internationally wrongful act of a State when conduct consisting of an action or omission: (a) is attributable to the State under international law; and (b) constitutes a breach of an international obligation of the State.[252] Unfortunately, the accompanying commentaries determine that the interpretation of a breach may be subjective (i.e., with intent or knowledge) or objective (i.e., inadvertence or negligence).[253] Thus, the offense may be both intentional and negligent. Either definition seems to preclude strict liability. If negligence is the standard, then there is also a due diligence defense. And, as Case 17 noted, due diligence may depend on the quality of the environmental assessments conducted.

Environmental assessments (also known as environmental impact assessments) are used to anticipate, assess, and reduce environmental and social risks from a project.[254] The ISA requires an environmental assessment for the Area,[255] but it is not a robust regime.[256] There are several accepted criteria for a fulsome environmental assessment process. Such a process includes screening, scoping, environmental impact assessment, environmental management plans, external review by experts, public stakeholder consultation, and regulatory review.[257] Environmental assessment standards may also limit liability based on the 2017 Draft Regulations. If the operator has an environmental assessment approved by the ISA, but environmental damage occurs, then it is unclear whether the operator will be liable, absent a "wrongful act or omission."

The environmental liability and common heritage principles may be at odds:

---

251 International Law Commission, "Draft articles on Responsibility of States for Internationally Wrongful Acts," *Yearbook of the International Law Commission* 2, Part 2 (2001).
252 Id., art. 2, p. 34.
253 Id., commentary to art. 2, ss. (2), p. 34.
254 J.M. Durden et al., "Environmental impact assessment process for deep-sea mining in 'the Area,'" *Marine Policy* 87 (2018): 194–202.
255 2017 Draft Regulations, n. 89 above, regs. 18, 19, and 20.
256 J.M. Durden et al., "A procedural framework for robust environmental management of deep-sea mining projects using a conceptual model," *Marine Policy* 84 (2017): 193–201.
257 Durden et al., n. 254 above, p. 196.

Even where adherence to international rules is demonstrated, there would remain potential for inconsistent interpretation and application of those rules that may need to be resolved. As a consequence, there will be a need for both vertical (Authority – sponsoring state) and horizontal (between sponsoring states) harmonization of EA processes and related compliance action to avoid conflicting directions and duplication.[258]

The ability to pay is also very much in question. Interoceanmetal's casual observation is relevant. They stated that the insurance industry may not be ready to make a policy. Moreover, it is difficult to conceive of how such a policy would take place, given the unknown liability, amount of damage, limit on liability, indemnification of sponsoring States, and other factors. As a matter of international law, it seems that every State has the right to combat pollution on the high seas, but no existing legal regime appears to provide for compensation. The ISA needs to clarify liabilities of operators, create a levy system to create a fund, and assist the insurance industry to create DSM policies. In other words, the international community, through the civil liability regimes discussed above, has created a mutually beneficial solution that benefits both the environment and the business community. The ISA should follow this example for DSM. Unfortunately, through domestic legislation, liability seems to be going in the opposite direction.

Sponsoring States
Case 17 is the representative precedent for sponsoring State liability. It is also clear that there should be no distinction of liability for developing or developed States.[259] To use a somewhat colloquial comparison, "with great power comes great responsibility."[260] Countries want to harvest and exploit the minerals on the deep seabed, but in terms of the Area, they do not want to assume any liability and have legislated indemnifications for any liability that is due. This seems inherently contradictory to Case 17 and the due diligence defense, and the protection of the environment. The watering down from a State needing to

---

258   N. Craik, *Enforcement and Liability Challenges in the Regulation of Deep Seabed Mining*, ISA Discussion Paper No. 4 (Jamaica, ISA, 2016), p. 10.
259   Oyarce, n. 160 above, p. 3.
260   W. Lamb, "Habeas Corpus Suspension Bill," *The Parliamentary Debates from the Year 1803 to the Present Time, Volume 36, Comprising the Period from the Twenty-Eight Day of April to the Twelfth Day of July, 1817* (27 June 1817), Start Column Number 1225, Quote Column Number 1226 and 1227, Published Under the Superintendence of T.C. Hansard, Fleet Street, London.

take all steps necessary to only reasonable steps necessary shows a weakening of environmental protections.

Domestic legislation does not assist in the matter and may further weaken environmental protections. Nauru and Tonga seem to completely absolve themselves of any liability. The United Kingdom takes a hands-off approach, seemingly leaving it to the ISA. The United States takes a strict liability approach, at least within the EEZ and in its oil spill legislation. New Zealand takes a very precautionary approach, within both the EEZ and the Area. Singapore takes a middle ground. Belgium may have a point – there is a real potential of sponsors shopping to avoid liability. This contradicts the requirements in Articles 209 and 235 of UNCLOS regarding domestic legislation and enforcing compensation claims.

The biggest unknown still is in compensation claims if operators cannot or will not pay. The indemnification clauses, pragmatically, are only relevant if the operator has the financial means. A compulsory insurance regime and a levy-based environmental fund would resolve many of these issues. Plakokefalos notes, "it remains to be seen how the Opinion [Case 17] will play out in the unfortunate case where damage in the Area does occur and how the States will react to it in their subsequent practice."[261]

Flag States

While there are similarities between flag States and sponsoring States, there are significant differences.[262] The Solwara 1 case is again illustrative. Nautilus does not own the ship but is chartering the ship in Dubai, United Arab Emirates (UAE). Article 91(1) of UNCLOS provides that there must be a genuine connection to register a vessel. Moreover, the flag State must exercise effective jurisdiction over the vessel.[263] Cases 17 and 21, together with the China-Philippines arbitration, seem to indicate that a flag State also may be liable if they fail in their obligations to oversee the vessel. The due diligence defense seems to be the same as those of the sponsoring State. However, there is no domestic legislation specifically required for flag States as it relates to DSM in the Area. The UAE, for instance, does not have DSM legislation.

As Case 17 noted, due diligence depends on the type of mining. The requirements of the environmental assessment process may provide evidence of meeting this obligation. But, given China's omission of such provisions in their domestic legislation and given the response of the tribunal in

---

261 Plakokefalos, n. 28 above, p. 136.
262 Oyarce, n. 160 above, p. 3.
263 UNCLOS, n. 1 above, art. 94.

China-Philippines arbitration, they could breach the requirements of Articles 209 of UNCLOS and thus not meet their liability requirements. The ISA needs to create specific environmental assessment standards for each type of mining and clarify how they differ in order for sponsoring and flag States to meet their obligations.

International Seabed Authority

The ISA is a party to potential DSM environmental claims and thus could be liable. The "wrongful act" provides the requisite standard, and it seems to have the due diligence defense as per Case 17. Case 21 also noted liability of an international organization.[264] In Case 21, it was the organization that granted fishing licenses. This would be akin and comparable to the ISA, which grants exploration and exploitation licenses. The indemnification clause in Annex X, Section 8.2, of the 2017 Draft Regulations, however, weakens this standard, without creating a mechanism by which operators may actually have the financial capability to indemnify the other parties.

The ISA states that it is in agreement with environmental protection and the precautionary approach, at least in theory. The ISA has reaffirmed its position on the environment in its strategic plan.[265] Unfortunately, the plan does not specifically state that the ISA will ensure the effective cleanup and remediation of any environmental damage, should it occur, nor ensure that there are funds available to assist with remediation. Whether or not the ISA retains any residual liability remains unknown.

Conclusion

The evidence all indicates that there are still too many unknowns to proceed with exploitation of DSM in the Area without further developing the legal obligations of all parties. The ISA is in a powerful position to grant licenses. It needs to take a step back, develop much more robust regulations to prevent environmental damage, and ensure that remediation of the environment can take place if environmental damage occurs. Currently, there is no mechanism for this assurance.

There is a real concern that the 2017 Draft Regulations will be watered down due to certain Asian and developing countries' concerns, as shown by the

---

264 Case 21, n. 235 above, para. 156.
265 ISA, *Draft Strategic Plan V2.1* (26 February 2018), at SD3, available online: <htttps://www.isa.org.jm/files/documents/EN/SPlan/SP-en.pdf>.

interventions at the 24th session of the ISA. With the ISA aiming for a July 2018 release of the next round of Draft Regulations, in time for Part 2 of the 24th session of the ISA on 24 July 2018, there does not appear to be enough time or appetite to make the regulations more stringent. The lack of an environmental fund is the most glaring omission. This is an oversight, and potentially hazardous outcomes may result.

On 15 November 2017, the UN General Assembly adopted Resolution A/72/L.7, which convened a conference for 2018, 2019, and 2020 to discuss the implementation of a binding agreement on the conservation and sustainable use of marine biological diversity of areas beyond national jurisdiction.[266] This would include the Area and would have repercussions for DSM. The ISA needs to follow the outcomes of this conference and ensure that the marine environment in the Area is protected.

It seems like "the tail is wagging the dog," in that the technology seems to be determining the law, rather than the law determining the liability.[267] Clearly, the international community can do better. The civil liability regimes provide such evidence. DSM is potentially destructive to the environment and much more work is required. The current liability regime is too weak and there remain too many unknowns to provide a framework for such a large-scale industry.

---

266   UN, "International legally binding instrument under the United Nations Convention on the Law of the Sea on the conservation and sustainable use of marine biological diversity of areas beyond national jurisdiction," UN Doc. A/72/L.7 (15 November 2017).
267   Case 17, n. 20 above, para. 136.

Building Scientific and Technological Capacity: a Role for Benefit-sharing in the Conservation and Sustainable Use of Marine Biodiversity beyond National Jurisdiction

Harriet R. Harden-Davies*
Nereus Fellow, Australian National Centre for Ocean Resources and Security, University of Wollongong, New South Wales, Australia

Kristina M. Gjerde
Senior High Seas Advisor, IUCN Global Marine and Polar Programme and World Commission on Protected Areas, Cambridge, MA, USA

Introduction

Marine scientific research and technological innovation are crucial to investigate and conserve ocean life, capture value, and share benefits from marine genetic resources of areas beyond national jurisdiction (ABNJ), but not all States have the required capacity.[1] States have commenced negotiations for a new international legally binding instrument for the conservation and sustainable use of marine biological diversity of ABNJ (BBNJ agreement)[2] under the 1982 United Nations Convention on the Law of the Sea (UNCLOS).[3] One of the most contentious issues to overcome is how to address "marine genetic

---

* The authors benefited greatly from the feedback provided by three anonymous reviewers. Harriet Harden-Davies gratefully acknowledges support from the University of Wollongong, the Nereus Program and Pew Charitable Trusts.

1 UNESCO-IOC, *Global Ocean Science Report: The current status of ocean science around the world*, eds., L. Valdés et al., (Report, UNESCO-IOC, 2017); S.K. Juniper, "Technological, environmental, social and economic aspects," (Information Paper 3, IUCN Information Papers for the Intersessional Workshop on Marine Genetic Resources 2–3 May 2013, United Nations General Assembly Ad Hoc Open-ended Informal Working Group to study issues relating to the conservation and sustainable use of marine biological diversity beyond areas of national jurisdiction, IUCN Environmental Law Centre, 2013), 15–22.

2 United Nations General Assembly (UNGA), "International legally binding instrument under the United Nations Convention on the Law of the Sea on the conservation and sustainable use of marine biological diversity of areas beyond national jurisdiction," GA Res 72/249, 72nd sess., Agenda Item 77, UN Doc. A/Res/72/249 (24 December 2017), para. 2.

3 United Nations Convention on the Law of the Sea, 10 December 1982, 1833 *United Nations Treaty Series* 3 (entered into force 16 November 1994) [UNCLOS].

resources including questions on the sharing of benefits" through the new instrument. Debate about marine genetic resources has raged for more than a decade,[4] fueled by concerns about the lack of a benefit-sharing regime applicable to marine genetic resources of ABNJ and evidence that just a few players are utilizing the genetic diversity of ABNJ for various applications.[5] Views among States regarding the applicability, or not, of the principle of common heritage of mankind to marine genetic resources of ABNJ have been starkly divided and, so far, have proven intractable.[6] Against this backdrop, the need for a "pragmatic approach" to benefit-sharing[7] that links pre-existing obligations in UNCLOS with modern technologies and aspirations for equitable access[8] has emerged as a possible way to connect the common interests of all sides of the debate.

Scientific and technological capacity is a pivotal factor in accessing and using marine genetic resources from ABNJ.[9] A wide range of scientific expertise and technological tools are required to access and use genetic resources, from

---

4   L. Glowka, "The deepest of ironies: Genetic resources, marine scientific research and the Area," *Ocean Yearbook* 12 (1996): 154–178.
5   R. Blasiak et al., "Corporate control and global governance of marine genetic resources," *Science Advances* 4, no. 6 (2018): eaar5237; S. Arnaud-Haond, J. Arrieta and C.M. Duarte, "Marine biodiversity and gene patents," *Science* 331 (2011): 1521–1522.
6   UNGA, "Report of the Preparatory Committee established by General Assembly Resolution 69/292: Development of an international legally binding instrument under the United Nations Convention on the Law of the Sea on the conservation and sustainable use of marine biological diversity of areas beyond national jurisdiction," UN Doc. A/AC.287/2017/PC.4/2. (31 July 2017) [PrepCom 4 report].
7   D. Tladi, "The common heritage of mankind and the proposed treaty on biodiversity in areas beyond national jurisdiction: The choice between pragmatism and sustainability," *Yearbook of International Environmental Law* 25, no. 1 (2015): 113–132; K. Marciniak, "Marine genetic resources: Do they form part of the common heritage of mankind principle?," in *Natural Resources and the Law of the Sea: Exploration, Allocation, Exploitation of Natural Resources in Areas under National Jurisdiction and Beyond*, eds., M. Lawrence, S. Constantinos and C. Hioureas (International Law Institute, 2017), 373–406.
8   A. Broggiato et al., "*Mare Geneticum*: Balancing governance of marine genetic resources in international waters," *International Journal of Marine and Coastal Law* 33, no. 1 (2018): 3–33; P. Ridings, "Redefining environmental stewardship to deliver governance frameworks for marine biodiversity beyond national jurisdiction," *ICES Journal of Marine Science* 75, no. 1 (2018): 435–443.
9   S. Arico and C. Salpin, *Bioprospecting of Genetic Resources in the Deep Sea-bed: Scientific, Legal and Policy Aspects* (UNU IAS, 2005); A. Broggiato et al., "Fair and equitable sharing of benefits from the utilization of marine genetic resources in areas beyond national jurisdiction: Bridging the gaps between science and policy," *Marine Policy* 49 (2014): 176–185; M. Vierros et al., "Who owns the ocean? Policy issues surrounding marine genetic resources," *Limnology and Oceanography Bulletin* 25, no. 2 (2016): 29–35; P. Oldham et al., "Defra Contract MB0128, A review of current knowledge regarding marine genetic resources and their current and

the deep and open ocean research infrastructure required to access marine genetic resources in their natural environment, to the laboratory equipment required to investigate and potentially utilize their genetic and biochemical properties. Despite the rights and responsibilities established by UNCLOS in relation to marine scientific research (Part XIII) and the development and transfer of marine technology (Part XIV), marked differences in scientific and technological capacity prevent all from accessing and utilizing marine genetic resources.[10] Consequently, it is timely to consider the potential to forge a benefit-sharing solution, at least in part, that builds scientific and technological capacity and is based on the UNCLOS frameworks of Part XIII and XIV.

The objectives and guiding principles relating to marine genetic resources of ABNJ that are identified in the report of the Preparatory Committee (PrepCom) established by United Nations General Assembly (UNGA) Resolution 69/292 lay the foundation for such an approach and encapsulate two overarching challenges facing States in developing the BBNJ agreement.[11] The first challenge concerns the aspiration for benefit-sharing to contribute to two objectives: (1) "building capacity of developing countries to access and use marine genetic resources of areas beyond national jurisdiction" and (2) "contributing to the conservation and sustainable use of marine biological diversity of areas beyond national jurisdiction."[12] While this provides a clear aspiration for benefit-sharing to build capacity, the exact nature of the relationship between benefit-sharing and conservation and sustainable use has not been the subject of detailed discussion to date. The second challenge concerns the two guiding principles relating to benefit-sharing that are referred to in the PrepCom report: (1) "being beneficial to current and future generations"; and (2) "promoting marine scientific research and research and development."[13] This highlights the need to strike a balance between the right to use and the responsibility to share, reflecting the presumed dichotomy between freedom of the high seas and the common heritage of mankind. Innovative solutions are

---

projected economic value to the UK economy," Final Report Version One, *Valuing the Deep: Marine Genetic Resources in Areas Beyond National Jurisdiction* (One World Analytics, 2014).

10 C. Salpin, V. Onwuasoanya, M. Bourrel and A. Swaddling, "Marine scientific research in Pacific Small Island Developing States," *Marine Policy* (2016), <https://doi.org/10.1016/j.marpol.2016.07.019>; G. Holland and D. Pugh, eds., *Troubled Waters: Ocean Science and Governance* (Cambridge University Press, 2010), p. 3.

11 UNGA, n. 2 above.

12 PrepCom 4 report, n. 6 above, para. 3.2.2(i).

13 Id., para. 3.2.2(ii).

urgently needed to strike a balance between these two principles and translate the aspirational objectives into tangible outcomes.

This article examines whether building scientific and technological capacity could serve as a unifying focus for addressing the benefit-sharing question in a way that achieves both objectives and upholds both principles identified in the PrepCom report. First, concerning the objectives, the relationship between benefit-sharing and conservation and sustainable use of biodiversity is considered and the role of scientific and technological capacity-building is discussed. We demonstrate that there is a precedent for benefit-sharing to promote scientific and technological capacity-building, drawing examples from the 2001 International Treaty on Plant Genetic Resources for Food and Agriculture (ITPGRFA),[14] the 2010 Nagoya Protocol on Access to Genetic Resources and the Fair and Equitable Sharing of Benefits Arising from Their Utilization to the Convention on Biological Diversity (Nagoya Protocol),[15] the 1992 Convention on Biological Diversity (CBD),[16] the Pandemic Influenza Preparedness Framework (PIP Framework), and the Global Plan of Action for Conservation, Sustainable Use and Development of Forest Genetic Resources (Forest Genetic Resources Plan).[17] Second, concerning the two principles, we examine the existing legal basis for scientific and technological capacity-building in UNCLOS, considering its Parts XI, XII, XIII, and XIV. We suggest that such an approach to benefit-sharing is consistent with existing rights and responsibilities under UNCLOS. Third, we identify measures that could be included in a BBNJ agreement to specify, scale-up, and strengthen the implementation of existing UNCLOS requirements. By giving greater effect to the duty to cooperate in scientific research and the development and transfer of technology, it is suggested that these measures could support the conservation and sustainable use of biodiversity and contribute to inter- and intra-generational equity by building capacity. Additionally, we suggest that these measures would also help to build an enabling environment in which marine scientific research can flourish and

---

14 International Treaty on Plant Genetic Resources for Food and Agriculture, 3 November 2001, 2400 *United Nations Treaty Series* 303 (entered into force 29 June 2004) [ITPGRFA].
15 Nagoya Protocol on Access to Genetic Resources and the Fair and Equitable Sharing of Benefits Arising from Their Utilization to the Convention on Biological Diversity, 29 October 2010, entered into force 12 October 2014.
16 Convention on Biological Diversity, 5 June 1992, 1760 *United Nations Treaty Series* 79 (entered into force 29 December 1993) [CBD].
17 Food and Agriculture Organization of the United Nations (FAO) Commission on Genetic Resources for Food and Agriculture, "Global Plan of Action for the Conservation, Sustainable Use and Development of Forest Genetic Resources" (2014), available online: <http://www.fao.org/3/a-i3849e.pdf>, foreword, para. 1 [Forest Genetic Resources Plan].

serve as a common interest to build global capacity to conserve and capture value from the genetic diversity of marine life in ABNJ.

Benefit-Sharing: Conservation and Capacity-Building

This section considers the two objectives for benefit-sharing identified by the PrepCom report. First, the connection between benefit-sharing and the conservation and sustainable use of biodiversity is explored by considering the nature of marine genetic resources and the link with biodiversity. Second, the importance of capacity-building as a form of benefit-sharing is examined by considering international legal instruments relating to genetic resources. The significance of international scientific cooperation and the development and transfer of technology is revealed.

Conservation

To consider the potential role of benefit-sharing in the conservation and sustainable use of BBNJ, it is necessary to first consider the nature of genetic resources and their connection with biodiversity. Though neither mentioned nor defined in UNCLOS, genetic resources are widely considered to be "genetic material of actual or potential value," as defined in Article 2 of the CBD. Various possible interpretations of the value of genetic material, however, confront attempts to put provisions associated with this definition into practice, as it does not wholly capture the many values, biological functions, and uses of genetic resources.[18] In the CBD, for example, value is identified as "ecological, social, economic, scientific, educational, cultural, recreational and aesthetic."[19] Indeed, genetic resources are broadly defined as genetic material of "actual or potential economic, environmental, scientific or societal value" in the Forest Genetic Resources Plan.[20] The "intrinsic value" of biodiversity is recognized in the CBD, which makes particular reference to the social, scientific, cultural, and economic importance of genomes, genes, ecosystems, habitats, species, and communities. The importance of genetic resources to "food security, public health, biodiversity conservation, and the mitigation of and adaptation to climate change"[21] is noted in the Preamble to the Nagoya Protocol.[22] However,

---

18 A. Deplazes-Zemp, "'Genetic resources' an analysis of a multifaceted concept," *Biological Conservation* 222 (2018): 86–94.
19 CBD, n. 16 above, preamble, para. 1; see also CBD, id., art. 7(a) and Annex I.
20 Forest Genetic Resources Plan, n. 17 above, para. 1.
21 Nagoya Protocol, n. 15 above, preamble, para. 14.
22 Id., preamble, para. 6.

the Nagoya Protocol only makes explicit reference to the "economic value of ecosystems and biodiversity."[23] In considering the benefits to be shared under a BBNJ agreement, it will be critical to recall that the value of genetic material is ecological, environmental, scientific, societal, and more – not only economic.

That the value of genetic resources "resides in ecosystems and biodiversity" is recognized in the Preamble to the Nagoya Protocol. Indeed, genetic variability drives the diversity within and between species that creates the ecological complexes that underpin healthy ecosystems. The notion that genetic resources are part of biological resources is explicit in CBD Article 2. In the Forest Genetic Resources Plan, highlighting that genetic resources are crucial to the adaptation of ecosystems, genetic diversity is referred to as the "mainstay of biological stability."[24] Marine genetic resources could be said to play an equally important role in ocean ecosystems, and are considered as ecosystem services and a necessary part of evolutionary capacity.[25]

Elaborating the link between benefit-sharing and the conservation and sustainable of biodiversity that is enshrined in the CBD, the Nagoya Protocol aims to "create incentives to conserve and sustainably use biological diversity." With so many marine species yet to be discovered in the 60 percent of the ocean that lies in ABNJ,[26] in the face of growing threats to marine biodiversity,[27] it is logical that benefit-sharing should be pursued with an aim to incentivize and enable the conservation and sustainable use of biodiversity in which the value of genetic resources resides.

Science and technology are crucial to understand, preserve, and capture this value as benefits. However, some see benefit-sharing, and the access measures that accompany it under most legal instruments associated with genetic resources, as a possible distraction from conservation or a hindrance to the

---

23 Id.
24 Forest Genetic Resources Plan, n. 17 above, foreword, para. 1.
25 C.W. Armstrong et al., "Services from the deep: Steps towards valuation of deep sea goods and services," *Ecosystem Services* 2 (2012): 2; A.D. Rogers et al., *The High Seas and Us: Understanding the Value of High Seas Ecosystems* (Global Ocean Commission, 2014); A.R. Thurber et al., "Ecosystem function and services provided by the deep sea," *Biogeosciences* 11, no. 14 (2014): 3941–3963.
26 J.H. Ausubel, D.T. Crist and P.E. Waggoner, eds., *First Census of Marine Life 2010: Highlights of a Decade of Discovery* (Census of Marine Life, 2010); E. Ramirez-Llodra et al., "Deep, diverse and definitely different: Unique attributes of the world's largest ecosystem," *Biogeosciences* 7, no. 9 (2010): 2851–2899; P. Snelgrove, "An ocean of discovery: Biodiversity beyond the Census of Marine Life," *Planta Med* 82 (09/10) (2016): 790–799.
27 A. Merrie et al., "An ocean of surprises: Trends in human use, unexpected dynamics and governance challenges in areas beyond national jurisdiction," *Global Environmental Change* 27 (2014): 19–31.

scientific research and technological innovation that is needed to support conservation.[28] It is therefore important to understand the role of science and technology in acquiring and sharing benefits from genetic resources to forge workable solutions to benefit-sharing.

Capacity-building: the Role of Science and Technology

To examine the role of capacity-building as a form of benefit-sharing, it is instructive to consider existing international legal instruments relating to genetic resources. Existing legal instruments relating to genetic resources offer guidance in identifying what benefits could be derived from marine genetic resources of ABNJ; all highlight a prominent role for building capacity in science and technology.[29] For example, the importance of technology transfer and cooperation to build research and innovation capacities for adding value to genetic resources, including for poverty eradication and environmental sustainability, is recognized in the Nagoya Protocol.[30] In addition to "monetary" benefits, the Nagoya Protocol refers to 17 "non-monetary" benefits that can be broadly summarized as: i) collaboration and international cooperation in scientific research; ii) access to samples, data, and knowledge, including the publication and sharing of scientific knowledge; iii) capacity-building and technology transfer, including scientific training and access to resources, research infrastructure, and technology; and iv) scientific, social, and economic outcomes of research involving genetic resources, including activities for the conservation and sustainable use of biodiversity (Table 14.1).[31]

Although the ITPGRFA Treaty does not refer to "monetary and non-monetary benefits" or provide an indicative list of benefits, it offers a framework for benefit-sharing that is centered on scientific research and capacity-building for conservation; it broadly aligns with the categories of benefits considered under the Nagoya Protocol – albeit packaged in a different way. Article 13.2 of the ITPGRFA identifies four forms of benefit-sharing for the objective of the conservation and sustainable use of genetic resources: a) exchange of

---

28 D. Neumann et al., "Global biodiversity research tied up by juridical interpretations of access and benefit-sharing," *Organisms Diversity and Evolution* 18, no. 1 (2018), doi:10.1007/s13127-017-0347-1.
29 See also E. Morgera, "Fair and equitable benefit-sharing at the cross-roads of the human right to science and international biodiversity law," *Laws* 4, no. 4 (2015): 803–831.
30 Nagoya Protocol, n. 15 above, art. 22 and preamble, paras. 5 and 7.
31 This terminology originates from the 2002 Bonn Guidelines on Access to Genetic Resources and Fair and Equitable Sharing of the Benefits Arising out of Their Utilization, adopted at the Sixth Meeting of the Conference of Parties to the Convention on Biological Diversity, 7–19 April 202, Decision VI/24.

TABLE 14.1 Summary of potential benefit-measures, based on examples provided in the ITPGRFA and Nagoya Protocol.

Example: non-monetary benefits Nagoya Protocol (Annex)	Example: ITPGRFA art. 13	Summary benefit-sharing measure
(b) Collaboration, cooperation and contribution in scientific research and development programs, particularly biotechnological research	(a) exchange of information	Collaboration in scientific research
	(c) capacity-building	
(a) Sharing of research and development results	(a) exchange of information on catalogues, inventories	Technology transfer, and access to research results/samples/data/knowledge
(e) Admittance to ex-situ facilities of genetic resources and to databases	(a) exchange of information on results of technical, scientific and socioeconomic research	
(f) Transfer to the provider of the genetic resources of knowledge and technology that make use of genetic resources or that are relevant to the conservation and sustainable use of biodiversity	(a) exchange of information on technologies	
(k) Access to scientific information relevant to conservation and sustainable use of biological diversity, including biological inventories and taxonomic studies	(b) access to and transfer of technology	

		Scientific and technical, human, and institutional capacity development
(b) Collaboration, cooperation and contribution in scientific research and development programs, particularly biotechnological research	(c(iii)) capacity-building for carrying out scientific research	
(d) Collaboration, cooperation, and contribution in education and training	(c(i)) scientific and technical education and training	
(n) Institutional and professional relationships	(c(ii)) developing and strengthening facilities	
(j) Training related to genetic resources		
(g) Strengthening capacities for technology transfer		
(h) Institutional capacity-building		
(i) Human and material resources to strengthen capacities for the administration and enforcement of access regulations		
(c) Participation in product development		

Table 14.1 Summary of potential benefit-measures, based on examples provided in the ITPGRFA and Nagoya Protocol (*cont.*)

Example: non-monetary benefits Nagoya Protocol (Annex)	Example: ITPGRFA art. 13	Summary benefit-sharing measure
(m) Research directed towards priority needs, such as health and food security	(d) sharing of benefits arising from commercialization	Capturing social and economic outcomes
(l) Contributions to the local economy	(c) capacity-building for the conservation and sustainable use of plant genetic resources for food and agriculture	
(o) Food and livelihood security benefits		
(p) Social recognition		

SOURCES: NAGOYA PROTOCOL ANNEX AND ITPGRFA, ART. 13.2, CORRESPONDING PINPOINT REFERENCES ARE SHOWN AS LETTERS IN BRACKETS.

information; b) access to and transfer of technology; c) capacity-building; and d) sharing of benefits arising from commercialization. A strong emphasis on an integrated approach to benefit-sharing, based largely on international cooperation for the investigation and conservation of genetic resources, is enshrined in Articles 5 and 7 of the ITPGRFA, while Article 12 specifically recognizes that access to genetic resources is a benefit.[32] Considering the benefits identified by the Nagoya Protocol and ITPGRFA (Table 14.1) reveals that benefit-sharing includes

– collaboration in scientific research;
– technology transfer, including equipment, but also access to research outcomes (such as results, samples and data), knowledge, and training opportunities; and
– capacity-building, including scientific and technical forms of capacity-building at human and institutional levels and at national, regional, and global scales.

That these legal instruments enshrine scientific research, technology transfer, and capacity-building as central pillars for benefit-sharing is logical, given the critical role of science and technology to derive and share benefits from genetic resources – from advancing knowledge of biodiversity, to isolating novel natural products for potential biotechnology development. Marine scientific research is widely considered to be the first step in accessing marine genetic resources in ABNJ in-situ.[33] There are often dual uses and spill-over benefits possible from technology – for example, the application of genetics and genomics technologies could on the one hand be a powerful tool to understand ocean health and inform conservation measures, and could, on the other hand, be used in biotechnology development (which may or may not result in a commercial product).[34] Scientific knowledge can be considered as a benefit from genetic resources.[35] Indeed, advances in taxonomic and ecological knowledge arising from research involving collections, compound libraries, and research

---

32 H. Harden-Davies, "Research for regions: Strengthening marine technology transfer for Pacific Island Countries and biodiversity beyond national jurisdiction," *International Journal of Marine and Coastal Law* 32, no. 4 (2017): 797–822.
33 Oldham et al., n. 9 above.
34 A. Martins et al., "Marketed marine natural products in the pharmaceutical and cosmeceutical industries: Tips for success," *Marine Drugs* 12 (2014) 1066; D. Skropeta, "Exploring marine resources for new pharmaceutical applications," in *Marine Resources Management*, eds., W. Gullett, C. Schofield and J. Vince (LexisNexis Butterworths, 2011), 211.
35 Deplazes-Zemp, n, 18 above; M. Böhm and B. Collen, "Toward equality of biodiversity knowledge through technology transfer," *Conservation Biology* 29(5) (2015): 1290–1302.

infrastructure associated with genetic resources constitute benefits that can be of "equal, or greater, importance to the potential monetary benefits from royalties should a product be commercialized."[36] Access to scientific knowledge is not only a form of benefit-sharing, but also of technology transfer.[37]

Several further synergies between the benefits from genetic resources and technology transfer are evident when comparing definitions of benefits with the definition of marine technology as provided by the Intergovernmental Oceanographic Commission (IOC) Criteria and Guidelines on the Transfer of Marine Technology (IOC CGTMT), which includes information and data; expertise, knowledge, and skills; equipment for sampling or observations in-situ; laboratory equipment and computer software; and manuals, guidelines, standards, and reference materials. As discussed in Harden-Davies,[38] this reveals several common themes that can be summarized as:

– cooperation in scientific research;
– access to the skills and research infrastructure to conduct research;
– standards and methodologies concerning the conduct of research;
– access to the outcomes of scientific research, such as data and samples and scientific knowledge; and
– broader scientific and socioeconomic benefits arising from research.

This highlights several forms of scientific and technological capacity-building that could be pursued under the BBNJ agreement to promote the conservation and sustainable use of marine genetic resources. At the same time, the synergies with broader interpretations of marine technology transfer indicate a need to consider the wider ramifications of benefit-sharing measures for scientific research and technology transfer, and for careful consideration in order to harness opportunities for cooperation and avoid obstacles that could hinder research or counteract efforts to provide a science-basis for the BBNJ agreement. These opportunities and challenges can be explored by considering the existing basis for marine scientific research and the development and transfer of marine technology in UNCLOS.

---

36 S.A. Laird, C. Monagle and S. Johnston, *The Griffith University AstraZeneca Partnership for Natural Product Discovery: An access and benefit-sharing case study* (UNU-IAS Report, 2008).
37 Böhm and Collen, n. 35 above.
38 H. Harden-Davies, "Marine science and technology transfer: Can the Intergovernmental Oceanographic Commission advance governance of biodiversity beyond national jurisdiction?," *Marine Policy* 74 (2016): 260–267.

The UNCLOS Framework for Scientific and Technological Capacity Building

This section examines the UNCLOS basis for building scientific and technological capacity, highlighting existing provisions that relate to the two principles for benefit-sharing identified in the PrepCom report. First, ways in which scientific research can be "beneficial to current and future generations" are considered. Second, potential ways to "promote marine scientific research" are considered. It is demonstrated that UNCLOS provides a framework for scientific and technological capacity-building that mirrors benefit-sharing elements identified in the previous section that are centered on a nexus of international science cooperation, access to data, knowledge, information, infrastructure, and training opportunities. Critically, it shows that these are applicable to activities on the high seas as well as the Area.

Beneficial: the Meaning of Research for the Benefit of Mankind

The importance of science in achieving equitable outcomes is reflected in the Preamble to UNCLOS, which recognizes that the "study, protection and preservation of the marine environment" will contribute to a "just and equitable international economic order."[39] The continuing importance of science and technology transfer to enable developing States to benefit from biodiversity is confirmed in UN Sustainable Development Goal 14.a, which also recognizes the IOC CGTMT in guiding international cooperation in technology transfer.[40]

Participation in scientific research and access to technology and capacity-building are key features of benefit-sharing as characterized in the regime of the Area established by UNCLOS Part XI.[41] Article 140 requires that activities in the Area be carried out for the benefit of mankind as a whole. The International Seabed Authority is to provide for the sharing of financial and other economic benefits in giving effect to the principle of the common heritage of mankind. Similarly, Article 143 requires that scientific research in the Area

---

39   UNCLOS, n. 3 above, preamble, paras. 3 and 4.
40   UNGA, "Transforming Our World: The 2030 Agenda for Sustainable Development," GA Res 70/1, 70th Sess., Agenda Items 15 and 116, UN Doc. A/RES/70/1 (25 September 2015), p. 24.
41   J. Brunnée, "Common areas, common heritage, and common concern," in *The Oxford Handbook of International Environmental Law*, eds., D. Bodansky, J. Brunnée and E. Hey (Oxford University Press, 2008); M. Bourrel, T. Torsten and D. Currie, "The common of heritage of mankind as a means to assess and advance equity in deep sea mining," *Marine Policy* 95 (2016), <https://doi.org/10.1016/j.marpol.2016.07.017>.

"shall be carried out for the benefit of mankind as a whole" and explains that this can be achieved as follows:

> States Parties shall promote international cooperation in marine scientific research in the Area by: (a) participating in international programmes and encouraging cooperation in marine scientific research by personnel of different countries and of the Authority; (b) ensuring that programmes are developed through the Authority or other international organizations as appropriate for the benefit of developing States and technologically less developed States with a view to: (i) strengthening their research capabilities; (ii) training their personnel and the personnel of the Authority in the techniques and applications of research; (iii) fostering the employment of their qualified personnel in research in the Area; (c) effectively disseminating the results of research and analysis when available, through the Authority or other international channels when appropriate.

In other words, the following elements enable scientific research to "benefit mankind":
– international cooperation in marine scientific research
– enable participation in international scientific programs
– provide opportunities to strengthen research capabilities and train personnel
– disseminate the results of research and analysis

Crucially, these four requirements are not unique to the regime for the Area but also already apply to marine scientific research conducted in ABNJ, including the high seas as described in the following subsection.

Promoting Marine Scientific Research

The promotion of international cooperation in marine scientific research is addressed in Article 242 of UNCLOS, which indicates that such cooperation should be on the basis of mutual benefit and for peaceful purposes. All States have the right to conduct marine scientific research in the Area and on the high seas (Articles 87(f), 238, 257). The freedom to conduct marine scientific research on the high seas (Article 87(f)) is balanced with obligations set out in Part XIII of UNCLOS.[42] Several such requirements are enshrined in Article 244, concerning publication and dissemination, which provides:

---

42   D. Freestone, "Modern principles of high seas governance: The legal underpinnings," *Environmental Policy and Law* 39(1) (2009): 44–49.

1. States and competent international organizations shall, in accordance with [UNCLOS] make available by publication and dissemination through appropriate channels information on proposed major programmes and their objectives as well as knowledge resulting from marine scientific research.
2. For this purpose, States, both individually and in cooperation with other States and with competent international organizations, shall actively promote the flow of scientific data and information and the transfer of knowledge resulting from marine scientific research, especially to developing States, as well as the strengthening of the autonomous marine scientific research capabilities of developing States through, *inter alia*, programmes to provide adequate education and training of their technical and scientific personnel.

This indicates that Article 244 establishes requirements for marine scientific research that could support benefit-sharing in three ways:

– Facilitate international cooperation by making available "information on proposed major programmes";
– Technology transfer by sharing "knowledge resulting from marine scientific research" as well as "scientific data, information and knowledge," which as illustrated above can be considered as a form of technology transfer, and arguably strengthening "the autonomous marine scientific research capabilities"; and
– Capacity-building by strengthening "marine scientific research capabilities," including through education and training.

Taken collectively, these three elements could be considered as interlinked drivers of scientific and technological capacity-building. For example, Part XIV establishes the framework for the development and transfer of marine technology that is inextricably linked to international scientific research cooperation and capacity-building. The objectives of the development and transfer of marine technology (Article 268) and the measures to achieve the objectives (Article 269) place a strong emphasis on international science cooperation to acquire, evaluate, and share data and knowledge as well as to build human, institutional, and technical capacity.[43] While Part XIV identifies a number of ways to give effect to the development and transfer of marine technology (e.g., access to infrastructure, training opportunities, programs of international science cooperation), it is overall a fairly broad and ambiguous framework. Imbalances in scientific and technical capacity (including institutions, infrastructure, and financial resources) hinder the ability of States to participate in the benefits from scientific research. According to Long, this gap "makes it difficult

---

43 UNCLOS, n. 3 above, arts. 269(a), 269(d) and 269(e).

to implement the broader principles of international cooperation and benefit-sharing enshrined by the LOSC."[44] Part XIV is ripe for further implementation.

At the same time, benefit-sharing measures could potentially apply to scientific research, given the lack of a definition of marine scientific research and the resulting blurred distinction with the loosely defined concept of "marine genetic resources activities." Capturing the benefits from scientific research while avoiding unintended consequences of hindering scientific research or stifling innovation is one of the challenges facing States in developing the BBNJ agreement.[45] One way to avoid such a consequence could be for the BBNJ agreement to make support for scientific research a priority and provide the enabling mechanisms to enhance it. Such explicit support for science would serve multiple purposes: to enable a science-based approach to conservation and sustainable use, facilitate the acquisition of benefits through access to in-situ genetic resources, and to uphold the requirement under UNCLOS to create favorable conditions for international cooperation in scientific research. Possible ways to promote scientific research are discussed in the next section, alongside options to harness the international nature of scientific research as a vehicle for benefit-sharing through scientific and technological capacity-building.

Specify, Scale-up, and Strengthen Implementation through the BBNJ Agreement

The preceding analysis demonstrated that scientific and technological capacity provides a focus for benefit-sharing and that existing responsibilities under UNCLOS provide a basis for this aim. An important consideration for the development of the BBNJ agreement is therefore how to give greater effect to existing rights and responsibilities under UNCLOS – meeting obligations relating to the development and transfer of marine technology while also ensuring the promotion of marine scientific research. This section discusses three types of measures that could be adopted through a BBNJ agreement to achieve the objectives of benefit-sharing and further implement the principles and duties enshrined in UNCLOS Parts XIII and XIV, drawing inspiration from other international legal instruments. The measures range along a spectrum of

---

44 R. Long, "Marine science capacity building and technology transfer: Rights and duties go hand in hand under the 1982 UNCLOS," in *Law, Science and Ocean Management*, eds., M.H. Nordquist, R. Long T.H. Heidar and J.N. Moore (Martinus Nijhoff, 2007), 299, 308–309.
45 Neumann et al., n. 28 above.

ambition from specifying existing duties to more elaborate innovations that could complement a BBNJ agreement. Three types of measures are proposed to give greater effect to the duty to cooperate in scientific research and technology transfer in order to enable capacity-building:

1. What to cooperate on: specifying the purpose for cooperation; elaborate guidelines to determine and promote marine scientific research and facilitate access to in-situ genetic resources.
2. How to cooperate: identifying the benefits and creating an enabling environment for facilitating sharing the outcomes of scientific research, including ex-situ genetic resources, data and knowledge, and training opportunities; develop a Global Plan of Action for marine genetic resources of ABNJ.
3. Who to cooperate: identify institutional mechanisms to scale-up cooperation and enable building scientific and institutional capacity.

What to Cooperate on?
A Purpose for International Cooperation in Science and Technology for Genetic Resources

UNCLOS provides a broad duty for international cooperation in marine scientific research (Article 242) and the development and transfer of marine technology (Articles 270; 276(2); 277(i); and 278). Articulating a specific purpose for international cooperation to build scientific and technological research capacity in relation to marine genetic resources of ABNJ could help to guide international implementation efforts. For example, the ITPGRFA articulates a clear statement of purpose for activities involving genetic resources that includes "discovery, exploration, collection, characterization, analysis and documentation" in Article 5. This is elaborated in Article 7.2 to include building capacity for the conservation and sustainable use of genetic resources; international activities for conservation, evaluation and documentation; sharing, providing access to, and exchanging genetic resources and technology; and institutional arrangements and funding. Thus, the ITPGRFA establishes a foundation for an integrated approach to explore, conserve, and sustainably use genetic resources, calling for cooperation (Article 5.1) and national commitments (Article 7.1) as well as providing guidance on specific issues for cooperation, including surveys, inventories, and collections (Article 6). The BBNJ agreement could similarly specify a purpose for cooperation that encapsulates the overarching objectives and principles for benefit-sharing and identify key priority areas for the acquisition, sharing, and utilization of marine genetic resources of ABNJ. Specific tools could also guide cooperation, such as guidelines, codes of conduct, standards, or statements of principles.

Guidelines to Promote Marine Scientific Research and International Research Cooperation

UNCLOS calls for the creation of favorable conditions for marine scientific research, although a definition of the activity is not provided. A first step could be to provide for the development of guidelines and criteria for marine scientific research, as is envisaged in UNCLOS Article 251. Such guidelines could serve several purposes in the context of the BBNJ agreement, including to frame an understanding about the range of activities considered to involve marine genetic resources in the context of the agreement. This would help establish the extent to which benefit-sharing requirements would apply, or not apply, across the spectrum of research and development processes; from the collection of a sample to the isolation of a molecule to the development of biotechnology. The guidelines could also elaborate the ways that scientific research could be promoted to support capacity-building and technology transfer. Examples include stipulating requirements for information sharing about scientific research activities through a possible clearinghouse mechanism; identifying principles and standards to be used; offering guidance on information sharing concerning data and samples (such as the location and accessibility of data and samples); and emphasizing the role of research collaboration in technology development. Article 248 of UNCLOS, which specifies some information sharing requirements for marine scientific research in areas within national jurisdiction, could provide a useful starting point. The IOC would be an appropriate body to lead the development of such guidelines, as illustrated by the development of the IOC CGTMT in response to UNCLOS Article 271. Broad engagement in developing the guidelines would promote an outcome that is practical and has broad support from those upon which implementation will be largely dependent – individual scientists and the research institutions that support them.

How to Cooperate?

Identifying Benefits and Sharing Mechanisms

Given the absence of definitions of "benefit," "technology," "science," and "marine scientific research" in UNCLOS, and the potentially broad interpretation of the meaning of terms under UNCLOS, the BBNJ agreement could draw inspiration from other instruments (such as the Nagoya Protocol Annex, PIP Article 6.1, and ITPGRFA Article 13) to elaborate a description of the benefits of marine genetic resources of ABNJ. Utilizing the generic term "benefit" as in the ITPGRFA, rather than the terms "non-monetary" and "monetary" benefits as in the Nagoya Protocol, could promote a more holistic approach that avoids the potential for non-financial benefits to be perceived as a "runner-up" prize. Some consideration should be given to clarifying the link between sharing scientific research outcomes, technology transfer, and benefit-sharing to build a common understanding of the meaning of (and link between) technology transfer and benefit-sharing, as discussed below.

Scaling-up: Guide Implementation with a Global Plan of Action
A further way to guide benefit-sharing and give greater effect to international cooperation could be the development of a "Global Plan of Action for the Conservation and Sustainable Use of Marine Genetic Resources of ABNJ." A Global Plan of Action could be used to encourage specificity and ambition in policy measures directed towards scientific research and technology transfer. Global plans of action have already been developed for animal genetic resources,[46] plant genetic resources for food and agriculture,[47] forestry genetic resources,[48] and global pandemic influenza.[49] These plans establish long-term shared goals that galvanize and focus efforts for research, guiding the development of policies, identify strategic priorities, and focus collaboration to share benefits from genetic resources and build scientific and technological capacity for conservation and sustainable use. They also allow some level of flexibility to adapt to future research priorities or technological advancement. Plans generally include four themes: 1) availability and access to information (e.g., surveying and inventorying genetic resources; developing international technical standards); 2) in-situ conservation and ex-situ conservation (e.g., sustaining ex-situ collections); 3) sustainable use (e.g., characterizing, evaluating, and developing collections of genetic resources); and 4) capacity-building (e.g., national programs, networks, information systems, monitoring systems, human resources, public awareness). The development and implementation of such a plan for marine genetic resources of ABNJ could help guide and focus international cooperation in achieving the objectives of benefit-sharing under a BBNJ agreement, including access to genetic resources in-situ and ex-situ, training opportunities, as well as facilitate research for conservation.

---

46   FAO Commission on Genetic Resources for Food and Agriculture, "Global Plan of Action for Animal Genetic Resources" (FAO, 2007), available online: <http://www.fao.org/3/a-a1404e.pdf>.
47   FAO Commission on Genetic Resources for Food and Agriculture, "Second Global Plan of Action for Plant Genetic Resources for Food and Agriculture" (FAO, 2011), available online: <http://www.fao.org/docrep/015/i2624e/i2624e00.pdf>.
48   Forest Genetic Resources Plan, n. 17 above.
49   World Health Organization, "Pandemic Influenza Preparedness Framework" (2011), para. 6.13.1 [PIP Framework].

Access to Research Outcomes: Data, Knowledge, and Samples

Data are one category of benefits that could be shared under a BBNJ agreement. The BBNJ agreement could either clarify or provide a platform for subsequent clarification on what data is to be shared; how data is to be shared (e.g., principles and guidelines for acquisition, storage and sharing of data); who is required to share data, and with whom; and which mechanism(s) for data sharing should be used (and how they are to be funded). As noted above, UNCLOS Article 244 provides an obligation for States to publish and disseminate knowledge resulting from marine scientific research. Further, the promotion of the "acquisition, evaluation and dissemination of marine technological knowledge" and facilitating "access to information and data" is a basic objective of the development and transfer of technology in UNCLOS Article 268a. The UN Fish Stocks Agreement (UNFSA) provides an example of how an implementing agreement can elaborate the duty under UNCLOS to share information and data.[50] UNFSA Article 14 emphasizes the importance of cooperation for data specification and the sharing of analytical techniques and methodologies.[51] It sets standard requirements for the collection and exchange of scientific data (UNFSA Annex I).[52] The UNFSA and the more recent Arctic Science Cooperation Agreement[53] also usefully set criteria for sharing data, such as timeliness, completeness, and accuracy. Such criteria could be useful to support benefit-sharing under a BBNJ agreement.

One way to facilitate access to genetic resources ex-situ is through facilitated access to samples. Sharing samples is recognized as a form of benefit-sharing and technology transfer under several international legal instruments. For example, the International Agricultural Research Centres (IARCs) of the Consultative Group on International Agricultural Research (CGIAR) have a recognized role to hold genetic resources in trust within the ITPGRFA under Article 15, and to manage and administer collections, receiving policy guidance from

---

50   Y. Tanaka, *A Dual Approach to Ocean Governance: The Cases of Zonal and Integrated Management in International Law of the Sea* (Ashgate, 2008), p. 220.
51   United Nations Agreement for the Implementation of the Provisions of the United Nations Convention on the Law of the Sea of 10 December 1982 relating to the Conservation and Management of Straddling Fish Stocks and Highly Migratory Fish Stocks, 4 August 1995, 2167 *United Nations Treaty Series* 88, art. 14(2).
52   Id., art. 4(1)(b)(c).
53   Arctic Council, Agreement on Enhancing International Arctic Science Cooperation (May 2017). Article 7(2), states that parties shall support "full and open access" to scientific metadata, distinguishing between metadata, scientific data, data products, and published results. The Agreement also points to timeliness, and identifies preferable features of data access, including "online" and "free of charge" or "at no more than the cost of reproduction and delivery."

a governing body. A further example is provided under the PIP Framework, which specifies a role for scientific research institutions as part of the Global Influenza Surveillance and Response System (GISRS), including laboratories and scientific research centers, national centers, and collaborating centers.[54] Similarly, the BBNJ agreement could recognize the role of collections of marine genetic resources of ABNJ, such as museums and research institutions, as agents of technology transfer and encourage support for their role in benefit-sharing. Learning from the experience of such institutions in implementing the Nagoya Protocol could provide important guidance.

Who to Cooperate and How?

Although several references are made to international cooperation in marine scientific research, including in Articles 242, 243, and 244, there is little in the way of identified implementation mechanisms, such as institutions, information sharing platforms, or communication channels. The same is true in relation to references to international cooperation in the development and transfer of marine technology; for example, UNCLOS Article 270 simply identifies that international cooperation for the development and transfer of marine technology should "facilitate marine scientific research, the transfer of marine technology, particularly in new fields, and appropriate international funding for ocean research and development." Recognizing these ambiguities, the BBNJ agreement could enable strengthened implementation of existing UNCLOS requirements in support of benefit-sharing by identifying roles and responsibilities for intergovernmental institutions, and clarifying what role, if any, for regional and national marine scientific and technological centers.

Identify Roles and Responsibilities for Intergovernmental Institutions

Although UNCLOS refers to the role of "competent international organizations" in facilitating international scientific and technical cooperation,[55] it does not specify particular institutions.[56] It is relevant to note that several other international legal instruments of relevance to this issue do identify particular institutions as having responsibilities; for example, the ITPGRFA allocates responsibilities to the Food and Agriculture Organization of the United Nations

---

54   PIP Framework, n. 49 above, para. 4.2.
55   See, e.g., UNCLOS, n. 3 above, arts. 242(1), 272, and 278.
56   The International Seabed Authority (ISA) is a notable exception to this; UNCLOS, id., Articles 273 and 274 have a particular focus on the role of the ISA with respect to the development and transfer of marine technology with respect to activities in the Area.

(FAO) in addition to other specified institutions. The BBNJ agreement could address this gap by designating a specific institution and giving it specific responsibilities to support benefit-sharing. Such an institution, or institutions, could facilitate scientific and technological cooperation and collaboration, including information sharing; provide scientific and technical assistance to conduct technology needs assessments (such assessments could be made available via a clearinghouse); facilitate data sharing; and monitor and evaluate implementation. There are several options for taking on this role and some of the functions could be shared. A range of organizations that could play some role, including but not limited to the IOC, the International Seabed Authority, the FAO or a new international organization or subsidiary body established under the BBNJ agreement. Given the wide reach of activities relating to marine genetic resources of ABNJ, cooperation and coordination between existing institutions (including international organizations and national scientific research organizations such as museums) and any designated or new institution will be crucial. By specifying a coordinating institution or cooperation mechanism for cooperation between international organizations, the BBNJ agreement could enhance the implementation of Article 278, which recognizes the importance of cooperation among international organizations to implement the development and transfer of marine technology. This role could be complemented by other organs of the institutional framework pertaining to the BBNJ agreement, including a governing body, secretariat, advisory body, and focal points at national, regional, and global scales. Thus, this could help clarify the role, if any, of the regional marine scientific and technological research centers that are given such a prominent role as mechanisms for international scientific and technical cooperation in Part XIV.[57]

Conclusion

This article has examined whether scientific and technological capacity-building could serve as a unifying focus for benefit-sharing to achieve the aspirations and tackle the challenges encapsulated in the PrepCom report. Three conclusions can be drawn.

First, there is a precedent for a benefit-sharing approach that is centered on scientific and technological capacity-building to both incentivize and enable conservation and sustainable use of biodiversity. In conceptualizing genetic resources, it is important to recall that the value of genetic material is not

---

57 See, e.g., UNCLOS, Articles 268(e), 270, 276, and 277.

just economic, but also ecological, environmental, scientific, and social. The link between genetic resources and biodiversity is explicitly recognized in the ITPGRFA, CBD, Nagoya Protocol, and Global Plan of Action for Forest Genetic Resources. For example, international cooperation in research to facilitate access to research equipment and infrastructure, to data and knowledge, and to training opportunities are all relevant forms of technology transfer that could contribute to capacity-building. The examples of the ITPGRFA, PIP Framework, Nagoya Protocol, and CBD illustrate that there is a precedent for benefit-sharing approaches to pursue scientific and technological capacity-building with provisions targeted towards international science cooperation, technology transfer, and capacity-building.

Second, a benefit-sharing approach centered on scientific and technological capacity-building would be consistent with existing obligations of UNCLOS. Parts XIII and XIV of UNCLOS already include a number of obligations for international cooperation in marine scientific research, promoting scientific research, sharing the outcomes of research, and building capacity of developing States to participate in scientific research through the development and transfer of marine technology. UNCLOS Article 244 enshrines these collectively and offers a hook for further elaboration through a BBNJ agreement. The right to conduct marine scientific research on the high seas is not absolute, but balanced with these responsibilities. Critically, these three responsibilities have also been recognized by States as the three key ingredients for scientific research in the Area to "benefit mankind as a whole" (UNCLOS Article 143). The pursuit of benefit-sharing through scientific and technological capacity-building would be consistent with existing rights and responsibilities under UNCLOS.

Third, the existing UNCLOS provisions relating to scientific research, technology transfer, and capacity-building could be further specified to strengthen implementation and scale-up international cooperation. The international legal instruments considered in this article highlight several ways that existing UNCLOS duties could be given greater effect through a BBNJ agreement, including by identifying institutional arrangements, elaborating requirements, and providing for enabling mechanisms ranging from information exchange platforms to standardized data access to streamlining avenues to request assistance. Three groups of suggestions have been offered to unite these various threads in giving greater effect to existing UNCLOS duties concerning international cooperation in science and technology summarized as follows:

1. What to cooperate on: specify the purpose for cooperation; elaborate guidelines to determine and promote marine scientific research and facilitate access to in-situ genetic resources.

2. How to cooperate: creating an enabling environment that promotes marine scientific research and capacity-building, providing greater specification to requirements for sharing data, samples and knowledge deriving from scientific research, identifying information sharing mechanisms; guiding implementation with a Global Plan of Action for marine genetic resources of ABNJ.
3. Who to cooperate: identify institutional mechanisms to scale-up cooperation and enable scientific and technological capacity building.

Developing benefit-sharing measures requires a careful balancing act to find a level of specificity that allows sufficient flexibility to benefit from future scientific advances while ensuring the promotion of scientific research and capacity-building. Scientific and technological capacity-building is unlikely to provide an entirely satisfactory solution for all States, especially those for whom monetary benefits are of particular importance. Many questions remain as to how sustained and reliable funding streams could be secured, and what the nature of the relationship between benefit-sharing and the conservation and sustainable use of biodiversity will ultimately be. However, as momentum builds to develop benefit-sharing solutions that will work in practice, scientific and technological capacity-building is clearly emerging as a unifying focus for benefit-sharing by offering a common interest to build global capacity to study, conserve, and sustainably use the marine genetic diversity of ABNJ. Advancing scientific and technological capacity in this way could better enable the international community to achieve the objective to conserve and sustainably use marine biological diversity in this vast area of the global ocean that lies beyond the limits of national jurisdiction, for current and future generations.

The Agreement to Prevent Unregulated High Seas Fisheries in the Central Arctic Ocean: An Overview

Andrew Serdy
Professor of Public International Law and Ocean Governance, University of Southampton, United Kingdom

Introduction

Although the Arctic Ocean is usually listed among the relatively few remaining areas of the world ocean not yet under the authority of any regional fisheries management organization (RFMO),[1] this is not strictly true, as the writ of the North-East Atlantic Fisheries Commission (NEAFC) runs all the way to the North Pole in the sector between 42° W and 51° E.[2] Nonetheless, NEAFC has never made use of its regulatory competence to institute any measures on fishing in the Arctic part of this area, and work has been undertaken in recent years to fill the spatial gap in regulatory coverage of the Arctic Ocean as a whole. Thus it was that in June 2018 one of the negotiating parties, the European Union (EU), published a near-final text, in English only, of a treaty styled Agreement to Prevent Unregulated High Seas Fisheries in the Central Arctic Ocean as an annex to an instrument laid before the European Council seeking its authorization for the EU to sign the treaty.[3]

Initial accord on a text had been reached in November 2017 among the delegations of Canada, China, Denmark (in respect of the Faroe Islands and Greenland), the EU, Iceland, Japan, Korea (Republic of), Norway, Russia, and the United States,[4] but a delay ensued before its formal conclusion in order

---

1 Or arrangement: the difference is that an organization is formally constituted by or under a treaty as an entity separate from its creators, who become its members, whereas an arrangement may or may not be brought about by treaty, but the participants make their regulatory decisions directly and collectively with each other. See below, text at notes 34–35, for examples of the latter.
2 Pursuant to the definition of the Convention Area in Article 1(a)(1) of the Convention on Future Multilateral Cooperation in North-East Atlantic Fisheries (London, 18 November 1980, 1285 *United Nations Treaty Series* 129) by which NEAFC is created. See also n. 36 below.
3 See EU Doc. COM(2018) 454 final, 12.6.2018, Proposal for a Council Decision on the signing, on behalf of the European Union, of the Agreement to prevent unregulated high seas fisheries in the Central Arctic Ocean, Annex.
4 According to N. Liu, "How has China shaped Arctic fisheries governance? Parsing China's role in the Agreement to Prevent Unregulated High Seas Fisheries in the Central Arctic

to allow its translation into a number of other languages in which, according to the testimonium, it is equally authentic: Chinese, French, and Russian.[5] As explained in a statement by the chairman of the final session of the negotiations, before the Agreement is opened for signature, "the delegations must first undertake a legal and technical review of its provisions ... and prepare the texts in the other languages in which it will be signed," as well as seek the necessary internal approvals under their respective legal systems to sign the Agreement.[6] The publication of the English text by the EU indicates that at least the first of these steps, the review, is now complete, although no date for the opening of the treaty for signature is mentioned. It is not clear how soon this might occur: the form in which the year in the date of conclusion is put, "201X," bespeaks uncertainty on one hand as to whether it will be achieved before the end of 2018, but broad confidence on the other hand that it should not take more than twelve months beyond that.[7]

As set out in Article 2, the Agreement's objective is to "prevent unregulated fishing in the high seas portion of the central Arctic Ocean through the application of precautionary conservation and management measures as part of a long-term strategy to safeguard healthy marine ecosystems and to ensure the conservation and sustainable use of fish stocks." The Chairman's statement notes that this area is roughly 2.8 million square kilometers in size, comparable to the Mediterranean Sea, surrounded by the exclusive economic zones (EEZs) of the five coastal States of the Arctic Ocean: Canada, Denmark (by virtue of Greenland), Norway, Russia, and the United States.[8] The statement goes on to observe that commercial fishing is to date unknown in that area and is unlikely to begin in the near future.[9] This state of affairs is elucidated in the preamble of

---

Ocean," in *The Diplomat* (20 June 2018), available online: <https://thediplomat.com/2018/06/how-has-china-shaped-arctic-fisheries-governance/>, this meeting in Washington was the sixth among the negotiating parties, in a series that began also in Washington in December 2015.

5   While it is implied (id.) that it has already been published in these languages too, the author's searches have yielded no evidence of this.

6   Meeting on High Seas Fisheries in the Central Arctic Ocean, 28–30 November 2017: Chairman's Statement, available online: <https://www.state.gov/e/oes/ocns/opa/rls/276136.htm>, 4th unnumbered paragraph.

7   The signature of the agreement in Ilulissat on 3 October 2018 has since been announced by a number of signatories, including the EU on the same day, European Commission, "EU and Arctic partners enter historic agreement to prevent unregulated fishing in high seas" (3 October 2018), available online: <https://ec.europa.eu/fisheries/eu-and-arctic-partners-enter-historic-agreement-prevent-unregulated-fishing-high-seas_en>.

8   Chairman's Statement, n. 6 above, 2nd unnumbered paragraph; see also Article 1(a) of the Agreement, n. 3 above.

9   Id.

the Agreement which recognizes that "until recently ice has generally covered the high seas portion of the central Arctic Ocean on a year-round basis, which has made fishing in those waters impossible, but that ice coverage in that area has diminished in recent years."[10] It is thus in anticipation of climatic conditions in the central Arctic Ocean eventually changing sufficiently to permit development of fisheries there that the parties developed the Agreement "in accordance with the precautionary approach to fisheries management."[11]

For fisheries to become possible, there will have to be fish available for catching, but the emergence of open water where previously there was mainly ice cover may alter any previous ecosystem existing there, and it would take time for fish presently inhabiting more southerly latitudes to arrive there in numbers, as this would be dependent on the existence of an ecosystem that will support them, including a food chain in which commercially valuable species are likely to be at or near the topmost trophic level.[12] In this vein, the preamble "acknowledg[es] that, while the central Arctic Ocean ecosystems have been relatively unexposed to human activities, those ecosystems are changing due to climate change and other phenomena, and that the effects of these changes are not well understood," and it "recogniz[es] the crucial role of healthy and sustainable marine ecosystems and fisheries for food and nutrition."[13]

The remainder of this article first offers a brief account of the process by which the Agreement came into being. It then dissects its salient provisions, including certain preambular paragraphs not already mentioned, before drawing brief conclusions.

Genesis of the Agreement

The Agreement did not emerge from a vacuum. Its development occurred against the background of the unilateral moratorium on fishing in the EEZ off northern Alaska announced by the United States in 2009[14] and the Declaration

---

10   Agreement, n. 3 above, preamble, 1st unnumbered paragraph.
11   Chairman's Statement, n. 6 above, 2nd unnumbered paragraph; see also the 9th unnumbered paragraph of the preamble to the Agreement, n. 3 above.
12   The report of the most recent scientific meeting, n. 18 below, indicates (at 7) that there is "virtually no knowledge about the existence and distribution of pelagic fishes in the deep-sea areas of the CAO [Central Arctic Ocean]."
13   Agreement, n. 3 above, second and third preambular paragraphs respectively.
14   See the Fishery Management Plan for Fish Resources of the Arctic Management Area approved in 2009 by the North Pacific Fishery Management Council operating under the *Magnuson-Stevens Fishery Conservation and Management Act* (16 U.S.C. ss. 1801–1884;

Concerning the Prevention of Unregulated High Seas Fishing in the Central Arctic Ocean issued in Oslo on 16 July 2015, by the five Arctic Ocean coastal States,[15] both of which contribute to a proper understanding of its origin and aims. The United States measure closed all federal waters of the United States Arctic to commercial fishing for any species of finfish, molluscs, crustaceans, and all other marine flora and fauna other than marine mammals and birds, while not applying to subsistence and recreational fishing or fisheries managed by the State of Alaska.[16] A somewhat similar development took place in adjacent Canadian waters with the Beaufort Sea Integrated Fisheries Management Framework, adopted in 2014.[17]

The Oslo Declaration is not of treaty status, the commitments made by its parties belonging purely in the political sphere.[18] It was itself foreshadowed

---

originally enacted as the *Fishery Conservation and Management Act* of 1976, U.S. Public Law 94–265 and subsequently amended most notably by the *Sustainable Fisheries Act* of 1996, U.S. Public Law 104–297 and the *Magnuson–Stevens Fishery Conservation and Management Reauthorization Act* of 2006, U.S. Public Law 109–479) in order to forestall the emergence of unregulated or inadequately regulated commercial fisheries in the EEZ off northern Alaska, lest it produce "adverse effects on the sensitive ecosystem and marine resources of this area, including fish, fish habitat, and non-fish species that inhabit or depend on marine resources of the U.S. Arctic EEZ, and the subsistence way of life of residents of Arctic communities."

15   Available online: <https://www.regjeringen.no/globalassets/departementene/ud/vedlegg/folkerett/declaration-on-arctic-fisheries-16-july-2015.pdf>; it is also noted in the unnumbered fifth preambular paragraph of the Agreement, n. 3 above.

16   See North Pacific Fishery Management Council, "Arctic Fishery Management," available online: <https://www.npfmc.org/arctic-fishery-management/>.

17   How this document came about is described in B. Ayles, L. Porta and R. McV. Clarke, "Development of an integrated fisheries co-management framework for new and emerging commercial fisheries in the Canadian Beaufort Sea," *Marine Policy* 72 (2016): 246–254, but it does not appear to have been published.

18   For a general analysis of this instrument see the briefing note in the online *Arctic Yearbook* by E.J. Molenaar, "The Oslo Declaration on High Seas Fishing in the Central Arctic Ocean," available: <https://www.arcticyearbook.com/images/Articles_2015/briefing-notes/3.BN_Molenaar.pdf>. This also (at 1) traces the Declaration's history back to a United States Senate joint resolution No. 17 of 2007 that directed the executive branch of the government "to initiate international discussions and take necessary steps with other Nations to negotiate an agreement for managing migratory and transboundary fish stocks in the Arctic Ocean." Next, in late 2009 or early 2010, the five coastal States agreed that any new international instrument on Arctic Ocean fisheries should be their initiative rather than under the aegis of an existing mechanism such as the Arctic Council which has a wider membership (id., p. 2). Molenaar (id.) mentions "a number of policy/governance meetings at senior officials level, alongside a series of science meetings" in apparent reference to the Meetings of Scientific Experts on Fish Stocks in the Central Arctic Ocean, of which there have been five to date; the author is grateful to an anonymous reviewer for drawing his attention to these. Reports of them are available on the website of the

in the Chairman's Statement issued after an earlier meeting in February 2014 in Nuuk,[19] and was scheduled to be signed at ministerial level in June 2014, plans waylaid by the Russian annexation of Crimea and the ensuing conflict in eastern Ukraine; when it was eventually signed, this was done at the ambassadorial level, but the substance was otherwise unaffected.[20] Its centerpiece is the commitment of the five coastal States to implement an interim measure by which their vessels would be permitted "to conduct commercial fishing in [the high seas portion of the central Arctic Ocean] only pursuant to one or more regional or subregional fisheries management organizations or arrangements that are or may be established to manage such fishing in accordance with recognized international standards," wording almost unchanged from that of Nuuk a year earlier.[21] The Oslo Declaration closed with an "acknowledge[ment of] the interest of other States in preventing unregulated high seas fisheries in the central Arctic Ocean" with which the five States were ready to work "in a broader process to develop measures consistent with this Declaration that would include commitments by all interested States."[22] Molenaar points out that the same "broader process" was also envisaged in the Nuuk Chairman's Statement, which went further than the Oslo Declaration in contemplating

---

Alaska Fisheries Science Center of the U.S. National Oceanic and Atmospheric Administration; the latest one of October 2017 is available online: <https://www.afsc.noaa.gov/Arctic_fish_stocks_fifth_meeting/>. In the report of this meeting it is observed (p. 39 in Appendix C, "Proposed FISCAO Data Policy and Release Guidelines") that the meetings serve the purpose of ascertaining the following: distributions and abundances of species with a potential for future commercial harvests in the Central Arctic Ocean; other information needed to provide advice necessary for future sustainable harvests of commercial fish stocks and maintenance of dependent ecosystem components; likely key ecological linkages between potentially harvestable fish stocks of the central Arctic Ocean and adjacent shelf ecosystems; and possible changes over the next 10–30 years in fish populations, dependent species and the supporting ecosystems in the central Arctic Ocean and adjacent shelf ecosystems.

19 Meeting on Arctic Fisheries, Nuuk, Greenland, 24–26 February 2014, Chairman's Statement, available online: <http://naalakkersuisut.gl/~/media/Nanoq/Images/Nyheder/250214/Chairmans%20Statement%20from%20Nuuk%20Meeting%20February%202014%202.docx>.
20 Molenaar, n. 18 above, p. 2.
21 Oslo Declaration, n. 15 above, 6th unnumbered paragraph and the first bullet point thereunder; Nuuk Chairman's Statement, n. 19 above, first double-indented point under the heading "Interim Measures."
22 This can be contrasted with the 1973 Agreement on the Conservation of Polar Bears (Oslo, 15 November 1973, 2898 *United Nations Treaty Series* 243), to which the five coastal States of the Arctic Ocean are party and which provides no mechanism for later accession by other States.

that "the final outcome could be a binding international agreement," though the latter did not rule this out.[23]

Analysis of Provisions

Rather than proceeding strictly *seriatim*, this section follows the internal cross-references linking provisions as far as they lead before returning to the article numerically next in line.

The Original Parties and the Position of Third States

The first thing to note about the new Agreement is the identity of the parties that negotiated it. It is not simply an agreement among the coastal States, as was the Ilulissat Declaration of 2008, which noted the applicability of the United Nations Convention on the Law of the Sea (UNCLOS)[24] to the issue of the delineation of the outer limit of their continental shelves more than 200 nautical miles from the territorial sea baseline. While the reference in that instrument to the Arctic's "unique ecosystem, which the five coastal states have a stewardship role in protecting" represents a danger of jurisdictional overreach, the risk should not be overstated, as this passage occurred amidst several others affirming their willingness to work with other States to this and related ends.[25] Here, too, there is a difference between the Nuuk Chairman's Statement and the Oslo Declaration – only the former describing a lead role for the five coastal States as "appropriate," while the latter recorded that these States "intend to continue to work together to encourage other States to take measures in respect of vessels entitled to fly their flags that are consistent with these interim measures."[26] They have not in practice made any attempt to dictate policy to other States based on claims to "stewardship," and, consistently with Article 34 of the Vienna Convention on the Law of Treaties,[27] Article 8 of the new Agreement refrains from any attempt to impose its provisions on non-parties.

---

23   Molenaar, n. 18 above, p. 3.
24   Montego Bay, 10 December 1982, 1833 *United Nations Treaty Series* 3.
25   Available online: <https://cil.nus.edu.sg/wp-content/uploads/formidable/18/2008-Ilulissat-Declaration.pdf>, 4th paragraph. It should be noted that fisheries was not specifically mentioned among the law of the sea issues listed in paragraph 2 as already adequately governed by the existing law, but is included indirectly in "other uses of the sea."
26   Nuuk Chairman's Statement, n. 19 above, last sentence; Oslo Declaration, n. 15 above, penultimate unnumbered paragraph.
27   Vienna, 23 May 1969, 1155 *United Nations Treaty Series* 331.

It is worth observing that most of the area covered by the 2018 Agreement is superjacent to seabed that will fall within the continental shelf of one or more of the coastal States; once the process under Article 76(8) of UNCLOS has run its course through submissions to the Commission on the Limits of the Continental Shelf and the making of recommendations by the Commission, it is likely that only a relatively small portion will be left in the area beyond such national jurisdiction.[28] The Agreement is, however, silent about this, beyond an acknowledgement in the scope of the species coverage that sedentary species as defined in Article 77(4) of UNCLOS are excluded.[29] Even so, the five coastal States appear to have learnt the lesson of the Galapagos Agreement,[30] a treaty governing fisheries off the west coast of South America that never entered into force because it was negotiated only by the four coastal States and imposed restrictive conditions on the participation in those fisheries by any other States, which would have made its enforcement exceedingly difficult.[31] The fourth preambular paragraph of the Agreement does admittedly "recogniz[e] the special responsibilities and special interests of the central Arctic Ocean coastal States in relation to the conservation and sustainable management of fish stocks in the central Arctic Ocean," but this appears to be carefully restrained wording. Notably, the absence of any reference to the high seas may be significant, and this form of words is consonant with the relatively strong position of coastal States under Article 116 of UNCLOS, whose paragraph (b) in conjunction with the chapeau gives all States equal rights to fish on the high seas, while subordinating high seas fishing as a whole to fishing in the EEZ, which is under coastal States' control.

---

28 These are the two relatively small unshaded areas depicted on the indicative map published by the University of Durham's International Boundaries Research Unit, available online: <https://www.dur.ac.uk/ibru/resources/arctic/>.
29 This may in practice leave out only a few species, as non-sedentary molluscs and crustaceans are brought by Article 1(b) within the definition of "fish."
30 Framework Agreement for the Conservation of the Marine Living Resources on the High Seas of the Southeastern Pacific (Santiago, 14 August 2000), (2001) 45 *Law of the Sea Bulletin* 70, not in force.
31 It is to all intents and purposes now a dead letter, with the Convention on Conservation and Management of the High Seas Fishery Resources of the South Pacific Ocean (Auckland, 14 November 2009; to be published in the *United Nations Treaty Series* vol. 2899), meanwhile available online: <https://treaties.un.org/doc/Publication/UNTS/No%20Volume/50553/Part/I-50553-0800000280363a44.pdf>, now in force, three of the four signatory States to the Galapagos Agreement having become party to it and the fourth being listed as a cooperating non-contracting party on the homepage of the South Pacific Regional Fisheries Management Organization's website: <https://www.sprfmo.int/>.

It can be inferred from the eighth preambular paragraph, which avers that with commercial fishing "unlikely to become viable in the high seas portion of the central Arctic Ocean" in the near term, it would be "premature under current circumstances to establish any *additional* regional or subregional fisheries management organizations or arrangements" for that area, that the drafters considered the Agreement itself to be a regional (or possibly subregional; there is no practical difference) arrangement within the meaning of Article 8 of the UN Fish Stocks Agreement.[32] Paragraph 5 of that article creates an obligation to establish such an organization or arrangement where none exists. The new agreement falls on the arrangement side of the divide,[33] as it creates no permanent body with an identity, let alone legal personality, distinct from and independent of its member States, and in this sense has an antecedent in the form of the Convention on the Conservation and Management of Pollock Resources in the Central Bering Sea;[34] the Southern Indian Ocean Fisheries Agreement[35] is an intermediate case, as it lacks a separate organization but does have a secretariat as provided in Article 9.

Geographical Scope

Another matter worthy of highlighting is that the new treaty is spatially confined to the high seas part of the central Arctic Ocean.[36] This gives rise to the

---

32   Agreement for the Implementation of the Provisions of the United Nations Convention on the Law of the Sea of 10 December 1982 relating to the Conservation and Management of Straddling Fish Stocks and Highly Migratory Fish Stocks, New York, 4 August 1995, 2167 *United Nations Treaty Series* 3.

33   Molenaar, n. 18 above, pp. 2–3, also takes this view of the process launched by the Oslo Declaration to negotiate the Agreement.

34   Washington, 16 June 1994, (1995) 34 *International Legal Materials* 67. On possible parallels for the new agreement see L. Zou and H.P. Huntington, "Implications of the Convention on the Conservation and Management of Pollock Resources in the Central Bering Sea for the management of fisheries in the Central Arctic Ocean," *Marine Policy* 88 (2018): 132–138. Molenaar, n. 18 above, p. 2, notes that the Oslo Declaration arguably ought to have mentioned the Joint Norwegian-Russian Fisheries Commission as an already extant regional fisheries management arrangement, so qualified objectively by its geographical remit under Article 1 of the Agreement between the Government of the Kingdom of Norway and the Government of the Union of Soviet Socialist Republics on Co-operation in the Fishing Industry (Moscow, 11 April 1975, 983 *United Nations Treaty Series* 3) which coincides with that of NEAFC; this, however, would have detracted from the Declaration's focus on the five coastal States as the locus of future fisheries regulatory activity. The statement that there is no need to develop any regional fisheries management *organization* for the region (emphasis added) must therefore be read narrowly if a contradiction is to be avoided.

35   Rome, 7 July 2006, 2835 *United Nations Treaty Series* 409.

36   See the definition of "Agreement Area" in Article 1(a). The dormant capacity of NEAFC in one sector of this area (*supra*, text at and following n. 2) is acknowledged in the seventh

risk identified by Molenaar that the measures applicable in the high seas part of the central Arctic Ocean could be undermined by laxer regulation of the same stocks in the five coastal States' EEZs surrounding it, in one or more of which fisheries are likely to become commercially viable significantly sooner than the remote high seas area in the middle of that ocean.[37] Full adherence to the compatibility provisions set out in Article 7 of the 1995 UN Fish Stocks Agreement (whose gist is that the regulatory measures applying to stocks that straddle the EEZ/high seas boundary should be aligned with each other as far as possible so that one does not undermine the other) would be a factor tending to mitigate the risk and reassure those non-coastal States that might otherwise look askance at the Agreement.[38] Article 3(6), in fact, provides that "[c]onsistent with Article 7 of the 1995 Agreement, coastal States Parties and other Parties shall cooperate to ensure the compatibility of conservation and management measures for fish stocks that occur in areas both within and beyond national jurisdiction in the central Arctic Ocean in order to ensure conservation and management of those stocks in their entirety." The United States and Canada in particular could simply leave in place their moratoria under the 2009 Fishery Management Plan for Fish Resources of the Arctic Management Area and Beaufort Sea Integrated Fisheries Management Framework discussed above.[39]

Article 3 contains the core regulatory mechanisms of the Agreement. Headed "Interim Conservation and Management Measures Concerning Fishing," it lays down conditions in paragraph 1 that each Party must meet if it wishes to authorize vessels entitled to fly its flag to conduct commercial fishing in the Agreement Area: this can occur only pursuant to (a) conservation and management measures adopted by one or more regional or subregional fisheries management organizations or arrangements that already exist or may in future be established to manage such fishing in accordance with "recognized international standards" or (b) "interim conservation and management measures that may be established by the Parties pursuant to Article 5, paragraph 1(c)(ii)." Paragraph 2 encourages the parties to conduct scientific research under a

---

preambular paragraph which "[u]nderlin[es] the importance of ensuring cooperation and coordination between the Parties and [NEAFC], which has competence to adopt conservation and management measures in part of the high seas portion of the central Arctic Ocean."

37 Molenaar, n. 18 above, p. 4.
38 Over time, this can be expected to prove conducive to increasingly conservation-minded measures by giving each side a legal incentive to keep up with the other, so creating the conditions for a "race to the top."
39 See notes 14 and 17 above and accompanying text.

Joint Program of Scientific Research and Monitoring, to be established within two years of the Agreement's entry into force pursuant to Article 4(2), "with the aim of improving their understanding of the ecosystems of the Agreement Area and, in particular, of determining whether fish stocks might exist in the Agreement Area now or in the future that could be harvested on a sustainable basis and the possible impacts of such fisheries on the ecosystems of the Agreement Area."[40] These decisions, as questions of substance, are to be made by consensus, according to Article 6(2), defined as the absence of any formal objection made at the time.[41] This will tend to reinforce the authority of any regulatory decision made, at the price of making it harder to achieve such a decision at all, or of having to dilute the strength of the measure in the first place in order to achieve consensus.

Paragraph 3 limits parties to authorizing vessels of their nationality to carry out exploratory fishing in the Agreement Area only pursuant to conservation and management measures established by the Parties on the basis of Article 5(1)(d).[42] The latter provision directs the parties to establish, within three years of the Agreement entering into force, conservation and management measures for exploratory fishing, which they may later amend, and preordains the measures to provide, *inter alia*, that exploratory fishing (i) must not undermine the Article 2 objective; (ii) must be "limited in duration, scope and scale to minimize impacts on fish stocks and ecosystems and shall be subject to standard requirements set forth in a data sharing protocol to be adopted in accordance

---

40   The remainder of Article 4 requires the parties to (paragraph 1) "facilitate cooperation in scientific activities with the goal of increasing knowledge of the living marine resources of the central Arctic Ocean and the ecosystems in which they occur"; (paragraphs 3 and 4) guide the development, coordination and implementation of the Joint Program and ensure that it "takes into account the work of relevant scientific and technical organizations, bodies and programs, as well as indigenous and local knowledge"; (paragraph 5) adopt a data sharing protocol within two years of the Agreement's entry into force and in accordance with it "share relevant data, directly or through relevant scientific and technical organizations, bodies and programs"; (paragraph 6) hold and within two years of the entry into force of the Agreement adopt terms of reference for joint scientific meetings, at least every two years and at least two months in advance of the meetings of the Parties that take place pursuant to Article 5, in order to present the results of their research, review the best available scientific information and provide timely scientific advice to meetings of the Parties.

41   Article 6(3) provides that decisions on procedural matters are taken by majority votes pursuant to Article 6(1), disregarding abstentions, but should an issue arise as to whether a given question is one of procedure or substance, the consensus rule applies.

42   Article 1(e) defines this term to mean "fishing for the purpose of assessing the sustainability and feasibility of future commercial fisheries by contributing to scientific data relating to such fisheries."

with Article 4, paragraph 5"; (iii) may be authorized "only on the basis of sound scientific research and when it is consistent with the Joint Program of Scientific Research and Monitoring and its own national scientific program(s)"; (iv) may be authorized only once the party concerned has notified the other parties of its plans for such fishing and given them an opportunity to comment on these; and (v) must be adequately monitored by the authorizing party, which must report its results to the other parties.

By paragraph 4, the parties must "ensure that their scientific research activities involving the catching of fish in the Agreement Area do not undermine the prevention of unregulated commercial and exploratory fishing and the protection of healthy marine ecosystems." Further, they are encouraged to inform each other about their plans for authorizing such activities.[43] Paragraph 5 complements this by requiring parties to "ensure compliance [by their respective vessels] with any interim measures established under subparagraph 1(b), and with any additional or different interim measures they may establish pursuant to subparagraph 1(c) of Article 5. The latter mandates meetings of the parties to consider, on the basis of the scientific information derived from the Joint Program of Scientific Research and Monitoring, national scientific programs and other relevant sources, and taking into account relevant fisheries management and ecosystem considerations, including the precautionary approach and potential adverse impacts of fishing on the ecosystems, whether the distribution, migration and abundance of fish in the Agreement Area would support a sustainable commercial fishery. If so, they would determine whether to commence negotiations to establish one or more additional regional or subregional fisheries management organizations or arrangements in the Agreement Area; and once negotiations have begun and the parties have agreed on mechanisms to ensure the sustainability of fish stocks, whether to establish additional or different interim conservation and management measures in respect of those stocks in the Agreement Area. Somewhat vaguely, Article 13 calls in paragraph 3 for "an effective transition between this Agreement and any potential new agreement" to create any such organization or arrangement "so as to safeguard healthy marine ecosystems and ensure the conservation and sustainable use of fish stocks in the Agreement Area."

Article 5 under the heading "Review and Further Implementation" directs the parties in paragraph 1 to meet every two years, or more frequently if they so decide. These meetings are for the purposes of, *inter alia*, (a) reviewing implementation of the Agreement and considering any issues relating to its duration

---

43   Paragraph 7 adds that parties' rights in relation to marine scientific research as reflected in UNCLOS are otherwise unaffected.

in accordance with Article 13(2); and (b) reviewing the scientific information developed through the Joint Program of Scientific Research and Monitoring mentioned in Article 4 as well as from national scientific programs and "any other relevant sources, including indigenous and local knowledge." To this end, paragraph 2 permits them to "form committees or similar bodies in which representatives of Arctic communities, including Arctic indigenous peoples, may participate."[44]

Relationship with Non-Parties

Article 8 addresses itself to the issue of the relationship between parties to the Agreement and non-parties. Paragraph 1 instructs parties to "encourage non-parties to this Agreement to take measures that are consistent with" its provisions, which is less specific than would be ideal, but importantly it creates no problems of reconcilability with Article 34 of the Vienna Convention.[45] Paragraph 2 also has numerous precedents in other fisheries treaties; it requires the parties to "take measures consistent with international law to deter the activities of vessels entitled to fly the flags of non-parties that undermine the effective implementation of this Agreement." There is an ambiguity in the drafting here; it is presumably not non-parties as such, but the activities of their vessels (in other words, fishing in its literal or extended form as defined in Article 1(c)[46]) that might undermine the effective implementation of the Agreement, but it is also not clear how much fishing would have that effect, and who decides this point. This provision is thus open to abuse if parties collectively take it upon themselves to decree that any fishing by non-party vessels in the high

---

44   See further on this the tenth, eleventh and twelfth unnumbered preambular paragraphs.
45   See Vienna Convention, n. 27 above.
46   Article 1(c) defines "fishing" to mean "searching for, attracting, locating, catching, taking or harvesting fish or any activity that can reasonably be expected to result in the attracting, locating, catching, taking or harvesting of fish"; by paragraph (f) "vessel" means any vessel used for, equipped to be used for, or intended to be used for "fishing" as so defined. It should be noted that the presence of positive definitions in paragraphs (d) and (e) for "commercial fishing" and "exploratory fishing" respectively means that there could conceivably exist a third kind of fishing that falls into neither of these two categories. If so, this would preclude a repeat of the scenario in the *Whaling in the Antarctic (Australia v. Japan; New Zealand intervening)* case, ICJ Reports 2014, p. 226, where Japan's whaling automatically fell into the prohibited commercial category by not meeting the test for being carried out for scientific purposes under Article 8 of the International Convention for the Regulation of Whaling (Washington, 2 December 1946, 161 *United Nations Treaty Series* 72).

seas area of the Arctic Ocean has that effect and they actively move to enforce that view by physically stopping it. Passive methods, such as denial of entry to their ports to the vessels concerned, would not, however, be objectionable. As is the case with many treaties establishing RFMOs, the underlying issue is how easy it is for non-parties wishing to participate in any fishery that may develop in accordance with the Agreement to become party to the latter for that purpose. Article 10(2) presents a rather forbidding face to non-parties: accession by any State other than those that took part in the negotiation of the Agreement requires an invitation from the parties to do so, on the basis of having "real interest." This phrase is taken (minus an indefinite article, which appears not to be significant) from Article 8(3) of the UN Fish Stocks Agreement where it is not defined; a later attempt to define it in the negotiation of the Windhoek Convention[47] was abandoned for lack of agreement. The present author has elsewhere argued that any State wishing to accede and claiming to meet such a condition should be allowed to do so, as to exclude it would amount to rejecting the proffered cooperation owed by States to each other in respect of high seas fisheries under Articles 117 and 118 of UNCLOS. This would in turn deprive the RFMO of any basis on which to complain of non-cooperation by the rejected applicant if the latter then begins fishing unilaterally.[48]

It may additionally be noted that in the context of this particular treaty the "real interest" concept is more than usually nebulous, as it does not reproduce the full phrase found in Article 8(3) of the UN Fish Stocks Agreement ("a real interest in the fisheries concerned"), leaving out the last four words without replacing them with anything else, thus inviting the question: a real interest in what? In other RFMOs, the uncertainty revolves around whether distant-water fishing States with no, or no recent, record of fishing in the area or for the stocks concerned can have a real interest in doing so in the future. Here, no State has any such history, not even the five coastal States, so it is not clear what basis the other five potential signatories themselves have for becoming party to the Agreement, beyond the mere fact of having participated in its negotiation, if they place all others at risk of exclusion. Only Iceland is physically at all proximate to the Arctic Ocean; two EU Member States have territory north of the Arctic Circle but no Arctic coastline; and the other three are Asian States of which none has a coast north of 46° N and only one (China) has territory, albeit

---

47   Convention on the Conservation and Management of Fishery Resources in the South East Atlantic Ocean, Windhoek, 20 April 2001, 2221 *United Nations Treaty Series* 189.
48   A. Serdy, *The New Entrants Problem in International Fisheries Law* (Cambridge: Cambridge University Press, 2016), p. 172; see also E.J. Molenaar, "The concept of 'real interest' and other aspects of co-operation through regional fisheries management mechanisms," *International Journal of Marine and Coastal Law* 15 (2000): 475–531.

far inland, extending beyond 50° N. They are all, of course, entitled to exercise high seas freedoms, including that of fishing, in the Central Arctic Ocean, but so too are all other States. Possibly the vague phrasing is intended to signal that Arctic activity in fields other than fisheries is the qualifying criterion,[49] but, if so, it is not obvious why this should give the relevant States a privileged position in regulating fisheries that do not yet exist. In the circumstances, lending itself as it does to disputation, it is hard to avoid the conclusion that it would have been preferable to omit the notion of real interest altogether.

Machinery Provisions

Given the broad concordance on substance between the Agreement and its non-treaty precursors, the final clauses that distinguish treaties from instruments of lesser status also merit attention. In keeping with a positive trend to incorporate by reference the dispute settlement provisions of the 1995 UN Fish Stocks Agreement *mutatis mutandis*,[50] this is the approach taken by Article 7 of the new Agreement for any dispute between its parties relating to its interpretation or application, irrespective of whether they are also parties to the 1995 Agreement. At the time of writing, of all the potential parties listed by name in Article 9, only China remains a non-party to the Fish Stocks Agreement.[51]

Article 9(1) in the version presented to the European Council lists the nine States and the EU as eligible to sign the Agreement, but it leaves blank the date on which it will open for signature and where this ceremony will take place, while specifying that it will thereafter remain open for signature for 12 months; any signatory can then under paragraph 2 ratify the Agreement (or accept or approve it) at any time to signify its consent to be bound by it. As is typical for multilateral and many plurilateral treaties, should any of these States or the EU not have signed it within the 12 months, they can still thereafter accede to it at

---

49   See, e.g., in the case of China its history of involvement in Arctic affairs in various ways which began when it acceded to the Treaty concerning the Archipelago of Spitsbergen (Paris, 9 February 1920, 2 *League of Nations Treaty Series* 7), set out in its January 2018 White Paper, "China's Arctic Policy," available online: <http://english.gov.cn/archive/white_paper/2018/01/26/content_ 281476026660336.htm>.

50   According to R. Churchill, "Dispute settlement in the law of the sea: Survey for 2014," *International Journal of Marine and Coastal Law* 30 (2015): 585–653 at 625, at least 15 treaties related to the law of the sea had done so to that point.

51   See the status list maintained by the Treaty Section of the UN Secretariat available online: <https://treaties.un.org/Pages/ViewDetails.aspx?src=TREATY&mtdsg_no=XXI-7&chapter=21&clang=_en>.

any time (Article 10(1)). By Article 11(1), the Agreement will not enter into force until 30 days after all nine States and the EU have ratified or acceded to it.[52]

Article 12 allows any party to withdraw from the Agreement at any time by written notification to the depositary through diplomatic channels, specifying the effective date of its withdrawal, which cannot be less than six months after the date of notification. This is expressly stated to leave its application among the remaining parties unaffected and, confirming the obvious, does not absolve the withdrawing party of any obligation in the Agreement to which it otherwise would be subject under international law independently of the Agreement.[53] More light is shed on this by Article 14, headed "Relation to Other Agreements," whose paragraph 1 records a recognition by the parties "that they are and will continue to be bound by their obligations under relevant provisions of international law, including those reflected in [UNCLOS] and the 1995 Agreement," as well as "the importance of continuing to cooperate in fulfilling those obligations even in the event that this Agreement expires or is terminated in the absence of any agreement establishing an additional regional or subregional fisheries management organization or arrangement for managing fishing in the Agreement Area." Paragraphs 2 and 3 are general non-prejudice clauses, while paragraph 4 conditionally subordinates this treaty to others, both existing and future:

> [it] shall not alter the rights and obligations of any Party that arise from other agreements compatible with this Agreement and that do not affect the enjoyment by other Parties of their rights or the performance of their obligations under this Agreement ... [and] shall neither undermine nor conflict with the role and mandate of any existing international mechanism relating to fisheries management.

Article 13(1) sets the initial duration of the Agreement as 16 years following its entry into force. Paragraph 2 then provides for automatic extensions for five years at a time unless any party either formally objects to this at the last

---

52 It enters into force for any additional State invited to accede pursuant to Article 10(2) 30 days after it deposits its instrument of accession (Article 11(2)). Surprisingly, this provision is silent on whether the United Kingdom as a current Member State of the EU that may well still have that status on the date of adoption of the Agreement will, after leaving the EU, be able to accede or succeed to it as of right, perhaps implying by default that the answer is no. Yet, with coastal territory north of 60° N in the Shetland Islands, it has a better claim to be a sub-Arctic State than several of the eligible signatories.

53 This is also in line with Article 43 of the Vienna Convention on the Law of Treaties, n. 27 above.

meeting of the parties before expiry of the initial period or any subsequent extension period, or formally objects in writing to the depositary in writing no later than six months before that expiry.[54]

Conclusion

Despite the terminology often used to describe what was decided in Nuuk, Oslo, and now in the text of the Agreement itself, only in very loose terms can this be characterized as a "moratorium," if that term is defined as a temporary prohibition. It is not an unconditional ban, since one sector of the high seas portion of the central Arctic Ocean remains subject to regulation by NEAFC[55] and other complementary bodies are contemplated that may hereafter similarly erect a framework for fishing. Because of the condition that all parties involved in its negotiation must become bound by it, it is uncertain how soon the Agreement will come into force, vulnerable as it thus is to a change of mind by any of them that would prevent the condition from ever being fulfilled unless Article 11 is amended to allow this. That aside, the Agreement is undoubtedly a step forward in both policy terms and legal technique: it intelligently prises loose the notion of unregulated fishing from the ill-conceived composite concept of illegal, unreported, and unregulated (IUU) fishing, with which it has been unhelpfully associated for 20 years,[56] to bear down on the real risk facing fish stocks present and future in the Arctic: the development of fisheries at a pace much faster than the ability of the slow-moving process of seeking international accord to curb excessive levels of fishing before they can do damage.[57] In that sense, it is truly precautionary. Rather than pretend that unregulated fishing is no different from illegal fishing as the FAO International Plan

---

54 Article 15 entrusts to Canada the function of the depositary for the Agreement.
55 See text at and following n. 1 above.
56 See A. Serdy, "*Pacta Tertiis* and regional fisheries management mechanisms: The IUU fishing concept as an illegitimate short-cut to a legitimate goal," *Ocean Development & International Law* 48 (2017): 345–364.
57 As happened with the rapid development of a fishery exploiting orange roughy on a ridge in the southern Indian Ocean, which, despite the comparatively small number of vessels involved, from Australia, New Zealand, and South Africa, quickly proved unsustainable before any catch limits could be jointly agreed and put in place. See United Nations Fisheries Organization (FAO), *Report of the Second Ad Hoc Meeting on Management of Deepwater Fisheries Resources of the Southern Indian Ocean – Fremantle, Western Australia, 20–22 May 2002*, FAO Fisheries Report No. 677 (Rome: FAO, 2002), pp. 2–5 (paras. 12, 20–22, 31 and 32). The history of the central Bering Sea pollock stock, discussed in Zou and Huntington, n. 34 above, is another instance of this phenomenon.

of Action[58] and a number of more recent treaties and UN General Assembly resolutions do, the proper answer to the problem it poses is to move swiftly to regulate it, and this new Agreement is a praiseworthy attempt to ensure that the tools are available to allow this to happen at short notice, should it become necessary. It must be hoped that the good work will not be undone by an overly restrictive view of what constitutes a "real interest" since none of the nine States and the EU that created the Agreement has as yet an investment in fishing the area to defend against newcomers, and the purpose of the Agreement is as much as anything else to ensure that such an investment does not suddenly and inconveniently arise.

---

58 International Plan of Action to Prevent, Deter and Eliminate Illegal, Unreported and Unregulated Fishing, adopted by the FAO's Committee on Fisheries at its 24th Session on 2 March 2001 and endorsed by the 120th Session of the FAO Council on 23 June 2001, available online: <http://www.fao.org/3/a-y1224e.pdf>. This is among the "other relevant instruments adopted by the Food and Agriculture Organization of the United Nations" recalled in the sixth unnumbered preambular paragraph alongside UNCLOS, the UN Fish Stocks Agreement, and the 1995 FAO Code of Conduct for Responsible Fisheries, available online: <http://www.fao.org/docrep/005/v9878e/v9878e00.htm>; others possibly intended to be captured by this phrase are the Plans of Action on Fishing Capacity and potentially also in due course those on sharks and seabirds and the Agreement to Promote Compliance with International Conservation and Management Measures by Fishing Vessels on the High Seas (Rome, 25 November 1993, 2221 *United Nations Treaty Series* 91) and the Agreement on Port State Measures to Prevent, Deter and Eliminate Illegal, Unreported and Unregulated Fishing (Rome, 22 November 2009), available online: <https://treaties.un.org/doc/Publication/UNTS/No%20Volume/54133/Part/I-54133-080000028049aa1a.pdf>.

PART 4

Maritime Safety and Security

∴

Piracy and Armed Robbery against Ships: Revisiting International Law Definitions and Requirements in the Context of the Gulf of Guinea

Osatohanmwen Anastasia Eruaga
Nigerian Institute of Advanced Legal Studies, Abuja, Nigeria; and
World Maritime University, Malmö, Sweden

Maximo Q. Mejia Jr.
World Maritime University, Malmö, Sweden

Introduction

Actual and attempted acts of illegal violence against ships and crew continue unabated in many of the world's seas. According to the International Maritime Organization (IMO), the number of acts of piracy and armed robbery perpetrated against ships reached 7,700 as of December 2017, up by 133 compared to the previous year.[1] According to the IMO and the International Maritime Bureau (IMB), the areas around the South China Sea, the Straits of Malacca and Singapore, the Gulf of Guinea, and the Western Indian Ocean seem to be the most seriously affected by the scourge of pirates and other maritime criminals.[2] Maritime violence is indeed a global problem that the international community rightfully seeks to eradicate.

---

[1] International Maritime Organization (IMO), "Reports of Piracy and Armed Robbery against Ships: Annual Report 2016," IMO Doc. MSC.4/Cir.245 (30 March 2017).

[2] Statistics culled from the IMO, "Reports on Acts of Piracy and Armed Robbery against Ships Annual Report 2011," IMO Doc. MSC.4/Circ.180 (1 March 2012); IMO, "Reports on Acts of Piracy and Armed Robbery against Ships Annual Report 2012," IMO Doc. MSC.4/Circ.193 (2 April 2013); IMO, "Reports on Acts of Piracy and Armed Robbery against Ships Annual Report 2013," IMO Doc. MSC.4/Circ.208 (1 March 2013); IMO Report MSC.4/Cir.245, n. 1 above; ICC International Maritime Bureau (IMB), *Piracy Against Ships Report for the Period January 1–December 31, 2013* (2014); ICC IMB, *Piracy Against Ships Report for the Period January 1–December 31, 2015* (2016). The IMB is a non-profit organization established in 1981. Both the IMO and IMB, in accordance with IMO Resolution A 504 (XII) (5) and (9) urging governments and organizations to cooperate and exchange information relating to attacks at sea, provide information and figures on piracy. Available online: <https://gisis.imo.org/Public/PAR/Default.aspx>. Information on piracy from the IMB Reporting Centre is available online: <http://www.icc-ccs.org/piracy-reporting-centre>.

In spite of numerous studies on requirements for establishing the existence of the offense of piracy and other maritime crimes involving violence in the maritime domain, such as armed robbery against ships, a precise definition terms of the legal constituents of these crimes is still far from settled.[3] Some contemporary scholars have been engaged in debates as to what the exact implications of the legal requirements of the offense of piracy and armed robbery against ships mean and how these can be interpreted to aid effectively in the systemic response to containing the problem in general.[4] In particular, some scholars argue that treaty rules providing for the offense of piracy are unclear and contain ambiguous language, thereby affecting enforcement and prosecution.[5] Additionally, the frequency of attacks occurring within the territorial waters as well as the exclusive economic zones (EEZs) of coastal States are invariably affecting the avenues for countering violent crimes at sea.

This article seeks to contribute to the ongoing discussions associated with the definition and legal requirements of the offenses of piracy and armed robbery against ships by relating these within the context of the Gulf of Guinea. Within this context, the article considers how the legal requirement of the offenses affects the curtailment of maritime crimes, bearing in mind the realities of continuous attacks of commercial vessels in the region. Attacks in the Gulf of Guinea have a truly adverse effect on global shipping. In the long run, these attacks undoubtedly affect global trade, energy, and even human security. Between 2009 and the end of 2017, the IMO recorded 470 reported cases of attacks and attempted attacks in the region.[6] Contemporary realities in the Gulf of Guinea reveal the recent acts of violence significantly differ from traditional piracy in terms of the level of coordination, types of weapons utilized during attacks, and, consequently, the damaging effects on crew and cargo. This article argues that conflicting interpretations of the legal requirements of the offenses

---

3   J.E. Noyes, "Introduction to the international law of piracy," *California Western International Law Journal* 21 (1990): 106–109; B. Kao, "Against a uniform definition of piracy," *Maritime Safety and Security Law Journal* 3 (2016): 7–8.
4   Noyes, id.; B.H. Dubner, "On the definition of the crime of sea piracy revisited: Customary vs. treaty law and the jurisdictional implications thereof," *Journal of Maritime Law and Commerce* 42, no. 1 (2011): 71–98 (exploring whether the provisions of UNCLOS eroded customary international law on piracy); Kao, id.
5   Noyes, id.; J.M. Isanga, "Countering persistent contemporary sea piracy: Expanding jurisdictional regimes," *American University Law Review* 59, no. 5 (2009–2010): 1292–1293; M. Passman, "Interpreting sea piracy clauses in marine insurance contracts," *Journal of Maritime Law and Commerce* 40 (2009) 59–88, p. 61; Kao, n. 3 above.
6   Data culled from the IMO Global Integrated Shipping Information System, available online: <https://gisis.imo.org/Public/PAR/Default.aspx>.

under international law coupled with weak or sometimes non-existent law enforcement mechanisms in affected States in the region have an adverse effect on the formulation of systematic responses at a regional and global level.

The section following this introduction begins by describing the relevance of the Gulf of Guinea to world trade and the international community in general, putting into perspective the importance of tackling the offense of piracy and armed robbery against ships in the region. That section also describes the current realities of the region by identifying the trends and threats that commercial vessels currently face in the Gulf of Guinea, as well as the response to these threats. The third section examines how existing debates on the legal requirements of the offenses of piracy and armed robbery against ships affect the curtailment of maritime crimes in the region, particularly in terms of the responses of coastal States and the global community. The fourth and concluding section points to a pressing need for reform in the legal requirements of the offenses of piracy and armed robbery against ships both at international and national levels. Among other recommendations, the article suggests that, pending the much-needed amendment, granting the international community controlled access to the territorial waters of the States where maritime violence persistently occurs may provide a solution to its persistence.

Gulf of Guinea Region and Its Geo-strategic Significance

This section considers the maritime relevance of the Gulf of Guinea region before describing the actual occurrences of maritime violence, especially as they relate to the offenses of piracy and armed robbery against ships. The section also lays the foundation for the need to revisit the legal requirement of the offenses relating to maritime violence.

The Significance of the Gulf of Guinea in Global Maritime Discourse
There are various views as to the areas encompassed by the Gulf of Guinea region, depending largely on the purpose of the provided description.[7] In general

---

7   For instance, the International Hydrographic Organization (IHO) limits the Gulf of Guinea to the area found within the line running southeastwards from Cape Palmas, Liberia to Cape Lopez, Gabon (0° 38' S, 8° 42' E). The limits as provided by the IHO ensure that publications headed with the name of an ocean or seas for the purpose of sailing directions refer to the same area. See IHO, *Limits to Oceans and Seas: Special Publication No. 28*, 3rd ed. (Monte Carlo: Monégasque, 1953), p. 19.

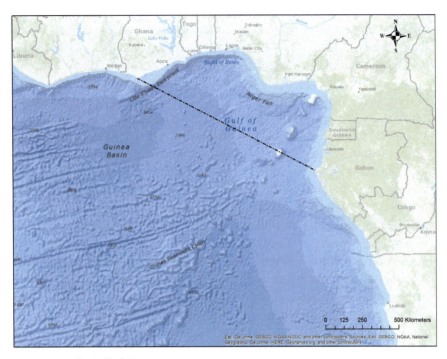

FIGURE 16.1 The Gulf of Guinea in its strictest sense.
SOURCE: THE AUTHORS

parlance, the region covers the entire coastal region of West Africa.[8] In its strictest sense and according to navigational definition, however, it is the area bounded by the intersection of the Equator and the Prime Meridian, between Cape Lopez, Gabon to three points in Ghana.[9]

In recent times and in line with interregional cooperation in combating maritime violence, a much wider description of the region has emerged, with the region being presented as an area that includes several countries in West and Central Africa from Senegal to Angola.[10]

---

8   S.M. Hasan and D. Hassan, "Current arrangements to combat piracy in the Gulf of Guinea region: An evaluation," *Journal of Maritime Law and Commerce* 47 (2016): 171–217, p. 176.

9   IHO, n. 7 above; The Royal Institute of International Affairs, *Angola and the Gulf of Guinea: Towards an Integrated Maritime Strategy* (London: Chatham House, 2012) v, n. 1. The description of the Gulf of Guinea is contained in footnote 1 of the preface (p. v).

10 A. Hurrell, "Explaining the resurgence of regionalism in world politics," *Review of International Studies* 21 (1995): 331–358, p. 334; F.C. Onuoha, "Piracy and maritime security in the Gulf of Guinea: Trends, concerns, and propositions," *Journal of Middle East and Africa* 4 (2013), 267–293, p. 269; K.-D. Ali, *Maritime Security Cooperation in the Gulf of Guinea: Prospects and Challenges* (Leiden: Brill Nijhoff, 2015), pp. 16–21.

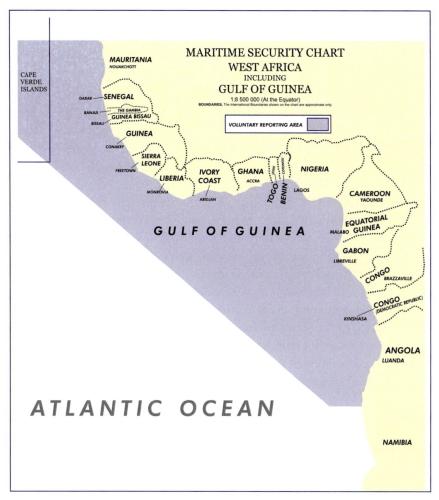

FIGURE 16.2   Contemporary description of the Gulf of Guinea reflecting interregional operational attempts to combat maritime violence.
SOURCE: ADAPTED FROM THE ADMIRALTY MARITIME SECURITY PLANNING CHARTS, Q SERIES, 6114: <HTTPS://WWW.ADMIRALTY.CO.UK/MARITIME-SAFETY-INFORMATION/SECURITY-RELATED-INFORMATION-TO-MARINERS>

The Gulf of Guinea is of global strategic importance. The oil and gas reserves, comparable to that of the Gulf of Mexico, raise its importance in the global energy market.[11] Nearly 70 percent of oil production in Africa as a continent

---

11   I. Osaretin, "Energy security in the Gulf of Guinea and the challenges of the great powers," *Journal of Social Science* 27 (2011): 187–191, p.188.

is concentrated in this region, with Nigeria and Angola being the largest oil producers in the continent as of December 2017.[12] Furthermore, the region is in close proximity to the major energy-consuming regions of Europe and the Americas.[13]

The Gulf of Guinea is also among the most important shipping lanes in the world.[14] The region benefits from the absence of narrow shipping lanes and chokepoints, increasing its desirability as a shipping route for commerce.[15] Additionally, due to poor domestic production, the African continent serves as a market for goods from countries on other continents. Hence, the region provides an avenue for the movement of goods by sea for easy access by landlocked countries on the continent. Coastal States generate revenue from ports, which contributes significantly to their gross domestic product.[16]

In spite of the economic potential of the Gulf of Guinea, countries bordering the region continue to grapple with overwhelmingly weak institutions, internal unrest, and cross-border violence. Despite strong revenue generation from the sale in petroleum, minerals, and other raw materials, poverty and underdevelopment remain rampant in the respective States that make up the region. Many of the States are unable to achieve significant annual economic growth. As a result, most of the countries in the region consistently rank low in the human development index.[17]

Piracy-related activities in the region are not a recent phenomenon. Research shows that piratical acts have persisted from pre-colonial times through

---

12   F.C. Onuoha, "Piracy and maritime security in the Gulf of Guinea: Nigeria as a microcosm," *Al Jazeera Center for Studies* (2012): 3. As of December 2016, Nigeria and Angola produced about 1.54 million and 1.06 million barrels of crude oil per day respectively. See Organization of Petroleum Exporting Countries, *Annual Statistics Bulletin 2017*, 67, available online: <https://asb.opec.org/index.php/pdf-download>.

13   The United States has remained one of the largest global energy consumers, second only to China for four consecutive years (2013 to 2016). Countries within Europe, such as Germany and France, are also ranked among the ten highest global consumers of energy. See Global Energy Statistics Yearbook, available online: <https://yearbook.enerdata.net/#energy-consumption-data.html>.

14   Hasan and Hassan, n. 8 above, p. 174.

15   D.O. Mane, "Emergence of the Gulf of Guinea in the global economy: Prospects and challenges," Working Paper, WP/05/235 (International Monetary Fund (IMF), Office of the Executive Director – Africa, 2005), p. 4.

16   Benin Republic relies heavily on service and transit fees from her port where a significant portion of the national gross domestic product (GDP) and national fiscal revenue is generated. See United Nations Security Council (UNSC), "Report of the United Nations Assessment Mission on Piracy in the Gulf of Guinea (7–24 November 2011)," UN Doc. S/2012/45 (19 January 2012), para. 11.

17   S. Jahan et al., *Human Development for Everyone: Human Development Report* (United Nations Development Programme, 2016), pp. 222–225.

to the present day.[18] Contemporary piracy and armed robbery against ships in the Gulf of Guinea has its roots in Nigeria, particularly in the oil-rich yet impoverished communities of the Niger Delta. In fact, experts believe that many of the maritime criminals presently operating within the region are of Nigerian origin.[19] The waters within the Nigeria-Beninese-Togolese axis of the region are particularly regarded as high-risk areas and considered by many experts to be as dangerous as the waters off the coast of Somalia.[20]

Pattern and General Characteristics of Attacks in the Gulf of Guinea

Several studies presenting various categorizations of attacks reveal that each piracy-prone zone presents specific features that reflect the geography,

---

18 A. Bialuschewski, "Black people under the black flag: Piracy and the slave trade on the west coast of Africa," *Slavery and Abolition* 29, no. 4 (2008): 467–468; A. Konstam, "From Cutlass to AK-47," BBC *News* (28 November 2008), available online: <http://news.bbc.co.uk/2/hi/uk_news/magazine/7729256.stm>; J. Kraska, *Contemporary Maritime Piracy: International Law, Strategy and Diplomacy at Sea* (California: Praeger, 2011), p. 30; S. Oyewole, "Suppressing maritime piracy in the Gulf of Guinea: The prospects and challenges of the regional players," *Australian Journal of Maritime & Ocean Affairs* 8 (2016):132–146, p. 135. See also Hasan and Hassan, n. 8 above, p. 174.

19 Hasan and Hassan, id., p. 171. Experts find support for this assertion in the fact that criminals often retreat to the waters close to the Niger Delta after carrying out attacks even in the neighboring State to Nigeria. After the hijacking of *Kerala* in Angola in January 2014, the tanker was subsequently sighted under the control of the hijackers off the coast of Nigeria, where part of the oil cargo, was stolen. See IMO, "Reports on Acts of Piracy and Armed Robbery against Ships: Acts Reported during May 2006," IMO Doc. MSC.4/Circ.87 (20 June 2006). In addition, suspects arrested for acts of piracy and armed robbery at sea in the Gulf of Guinea are mostly of Nigerian descent. For instance, the suspected perpetuators of the MT *Energy Centurion* attack 17 miles offshore of the Togolese capital Lomé were Nigerians. See C. Megbolu and C. Onwubu, "Nigeria: NIMASA, Joint Task Force Take Battle to Sea Bandits," *This Day* (7 December 2012), p. 32; D. Steffen, "Maritime security in the Gulf of Guinea in 2016," available online: <http://maritime-executive.com/editorials/maritime-security-in-the-gulf-of-guinea-in-2016>.

20 The Joint War Committee (JWC) lists the waters in the Gulf of Guinea, (but only the waters of the Togolese, Beninese and Nigerian EEZs north of 3° N) as dangerous waters. See JWC, "Hull War, Piracy, Terrorism and Related Perils: Listed Areas," *JWLA/022* (10 December 2015), available online: <http://www.lmalloyds.com/lma/jointwar>. The JWC made no changes to the listed areas in the last review in September 2017. In the same vein, the International Bargaining Forum defines the high-risk areas of the Gulf of Guinea to "include territorial waters, ports and inland waterways of Nigeria and Benin, ... excluding the Maritime Exclusion Zone (MEZ), the Secure Anchorage Area (SAA) and the Ship-to-Ship Zone (STS) which are to be treated as IBF Extended Risk Zones." See International Bargaining Forum, "IBF LIST of Designated Risk Areas, with Applicable Benefits (as of 1 March 2018)," available online: <http://www.itfseafarers.org/warlike-high-risk-areas.cfm>.

socio-political, and economic conditions of the area.²¹ According to IMB Director Pottengal Mukundan, attacks in the Gulf of Guinea "follow a different modus operandi from pirate activity in other parts of the world. In addition to armed robbery, the more serious attacks involve hijacking of product tankers to steal a part of the cargo."²² Attacks in the region can be categorized into assault on ships in port, coastal shipping assault with or without kidnap for ransom, and the hijacking of vessels for targeted theft of cargo.²³

Assault on ships in port mainly constitutes theft not only against vessels already at berth, but also vessels still at anchor while awaiting berthing assignments, sometimes for weeks at a time. These assaults are often not particularly violent as the attackers aim to be swift and operate with as little contact or hindrances from the crew as possible.²⁴ The perpetuators are usually interested in obtaining ship's stores, property, cargo, and crew's personal belongings. The attack by four robbers armed with long knives on the berthed Marshall Island product tanker MV *Harvey* is a typical example.²⁵

---

21   For instance, the kidnap for ransom attacks off the coast of Somalia, the 1990s phantom ship phenomenon in the South China Sea, and perennial armed robbery against ships in Southeast Asia. See M. Mejia and P.K. Mukherjee, "The SUA Convention 2005: A critical evaluation of its effectiveness in suppressing maritime criminal acts," *Journal of International Maritime Law* 12, no. 3 (2006): 170–191, p. 171; V. Sakhuja, "Sea piracy in South Asia," in *Violence at Sea: Piracy in the Age of Global Terrorism*, ed. P. Lehr (New York: Routledge, 2007), p. 24; A. Dey, "Changing face of sea piracy in the eastern Indian Ocean: Examining India's role in maritime cooperation," in *Eastern Indian Ocean: Historical Links to Contemporary Convergences*, ed. L. Ghosh (Newcastle: Cambridge Scholars Publishing, 2011); M. Murphy, "Petro-piracy: Oil and troubled waters," *Orbis* (2013): 424–427, p. 432; H. Liwång, "Piracy off West Africa from 2010 to 2014: An analysis," *World Maritime University Journal of Maritime Affairs* 16 (2017): 385–403, p. 386.
22   The Maritime Executive, "IMB notes increase in piracy off West Africa," 19 November 2012, available online: <https://www.maritime-executive.com/article/imb-notes-increase-in-piracy-off-west-africa>; Hasan and Hassan, n. 8 above, pp. 179–181; The authors identify four distinct features of piracy and armed robbery at sea in the region.
23   The dataset analyzed covers the period 2006–2016. The classification provided takes into account the location of the incidents and the level of violence presented. The dataset suffers some inadequacies arising primarily from an absence of reports on some aspects in some incidents. Additionally, not all incidents that occur in the region are reported.
24   Murphy, n. 21 above, p. 433; L. Otto, "Maritime crime in Nigeria and waters beyond: Analyzing the period 2009 to 2013," *African Insight* 45 (2015): 21.
25   IMO, "Reports on acts of Piracy and Armed Robbery against Ships issued monthly – Acts reported during August 2016," IMO Doc. MSC.4/Cir.240 (19 October 2016). On 5 August 2016, after detaining the duty pump man while on routine rounds, the robbers submerged two hoses into the forward tank dome, transferred the cargo into their boat. The pump man was released after transfer of the cargo was completed.

Armed robbery affecting coastal shipping in the Gulf of Guinea occurs within the territorial waters and EEZ. As in the case of assault on ships in port, coastal shipping assault is also characterized by theft of cash, personal belongings of crew members, as well as equipment of the vessel.[26] In contrast, however, coastal shipping assault in some cases includes kidnapping crew for ransom purposes. These attacks tend to be more violent, with perpetuators being heavily armed with automatic rifles and sophisticated weaponry.[27] The IMO recorded a total number of 77 incidents of crew hostage/kidnapping between 2006 and 2016.[28] In contrast with the Somali piracy model, experts do not consider kidnapping as a central element of the activity in the region.[29] However, the increase in the occurrence of kidnapping in the region between 2013 and 2016, which accounts for about 42 percent (20) of the total number of cases that the IMO recorded since 2006, as well as the duration for which crews are held hostage, shows that the model is gaining ground in the region.[30] The ransom payment of US$400,000 for the release of the two crew members of the MT *Kalamos*, which was held for three weeks, provides confirmation of the high return on investment for pirates engaged in this activity.[31] Interestingly though, there is still no concrete evidence to indicate whether these kidnaps are pre-planned or opportunistic.

Attacks that are more serious involve the hijacking of vessels or attacks against offshore installations for the purpose of cargo theft. The target cargo is usually petroleum products from product tankers.[32] A target-rich area owing to

---

26 Otto, n. 24 above, p. 17.
27 Id., p. 20.
28 In 2017 alone, 58 crew members were kidnapped and held hostage in ten separate incidents. Data culled from IMO GSIS, available online: <https://gisis.imo.org/Public/PAR/Default.aspx>.
29 D.J. Whiteneck, J.S. Ivancovich and K. Hall, *Piracy Enterprises in Africa* (Alexandria VA: Centre for Naval Analysis, 2011), p. 32. Previously, politically motivated sporadic kidnapping of oil workers occurred especially around the Niger Delta. The militants employed this tactic as a means to ensure the conduct of bargains for political ends. See L. Otto, "Westward Ho! The evolution of maritime piracy in Nigeria," *Portuguese Journal of Social Science* 13 (2014): 313–329, p. 320; Otto, n. 24 above, p. 22.
30 Crew members are known to be kept hostage for as long as three weeks before they are released as was the case in the *CMA CGM Turquoise* and the MT *Kalamos* attacks. See IMO, "Reports on Acts of Piracy and Armed Robbery against Ships issued Monthly – Acts Reported during April 2016," IMO Doc. MSC.4/Circ.236 (7 June 2016); Ocean Beyond Piracy, "The State of Maritime Piracy 2015: Assessing the Economic and Human Cost," available online: <http://oceansbeyondpiracy.org/sites/default/files/State_of_Maritime_Piracy_2015.pdf>.
31 Ocean Beyond Piracy, id.
32 Hasan and Hassan, n. 8 above, p. 179.

the existence of several oil terminals and offshore installations within its maritime domain, the Gulf of Guinea has gained unwanted notoriety for so-called petro-piracy.[33] Furthermore, the category thrives because Nigeria provides a ready market for the sale of stolen petroleum products; there is an absence of adequate refining capabilities, inadequate supply of petroleum products, and frequent deliberations on the part of government to do away with State oil subsidies.[34] This category represents a highly organized model, with a far-reaching intelligence network, involving connivance with government officials that affords the interception of vessels in either international waters or the coastal waters of neighboring States.[35]

In recent times, there has been a decline in the number of incidents of petro-piracy. A combination of factors is responsible for this downward trend. In the first instance, a global plunge in the price of oil occurred in the last quarter of 2015.[36] Criminals are no longer able to obtain astronomical returns from disposing stolen products, making the venture only marginally profitable.[37] Additionally, counter-piracy measures, such as increased domain awareness in the region and the increased patrols individually and jointly by navies, appears to have contributed to the decline of this model of maritime crime.[38] Although there is no conclusive evidence of terrorist ties to the attacks in the region, concerns have been expressed that profits from the attacks could be used in funding terrorist-related activities.[39] As shown in the Table 16.1, attacks in the region are generally characterized by violence.

---

33   Otto, n. 24 above, p. 33. One of the main motives of the attackers in this region is fuel theft.
34   United Nations Office on Drug and Crime (UNODC), *Transnational Organized Crime in West Africa: A Threat Assessment* (Vienna: UNODC, 2013), p. 45.
35   Megbolu and Onwubu, n. 19 above. One of the leaders of the attackers on the MT *Energy Centurion* stated thus: "Once there is a ship to be attacked, our sponsors get across to us through their points-men. We ... get the details from the Ministry of Petroleum Resources, Nigerian National Petroleum Corporation and then seek support from relevant security agencies. We operate on an agreed fee ... once we complete the assignment, we inform the points-men, who immediately get in touch with another group also working for the sponsors to take charge of the hijacked vessel, get the oil off-loaded into another vessel to deposit it in various oil storage facilities for distribution and sale to oil marketers and merchants. We do not engage in the sale of oil products. However, we assist at times to monitor it through arms support."
36   G. Miller, "Nigeria's crude crisis," *IHS Fairplay* (18 August 2016), p. 12.
37   B. Akinola, Industrial Analyst, interview by M. Martin, *All Things Considered*, NPR, 19 March 2016.
38   F. Omiunu, Legal Officer, Nigerian Maritime Administration and Safety Agency, Interview, Lagos, 5 June 2017.
39   L.C. Baldor, "US eyes anti-piracy efforts along West Africa Coast," *US News* (26 March 2013), available online: <http://www.usnews.com/news/world/articles/2013/03/26/us-eyes-anti-

TABLE 16.1 Weapons distribution use in the Gulf of Guinea Region (2006–2016). Data culled from International Maritime Organization's Global Integrated Shipping Information System (GISIS) website, <https://gisis.imo.org/Public/PAR/Default.aspx>

	Knives	Guns	Rocket propelled grenades (RPGS)	Others	Not Stated
International waters	1	73	2	9	38
Territorial waters	21	37	0	5	30
Ports	12	13	0	2	30

Maritime criminals operate with increased confidence and sophisticated weapons, such as AK-47 assault rifles and varieties of machine guns, submachine guns, and pump-action guns, all of which they appear willing to use.[40] Most reports reveal that the attackers open fire on the vessels that they assault, especially when their target is the cargo, rather than collecting ransom for ship and their crews. In three of the recorded incidents, the attackers used rocket-propelled grenades.[41] These violent attacks have caused injuries and death of seafarers.

Available data reveals that there is a marked increase in the number of attacks occurring outside the territorial sea. Compared to eight incidents recorded in 2009, the IMO statistics show that 33 incidents occurred in international waters in 2016.[42] The increase in armed intrusions within the international maritime space is evidence of the dynamism in the mode of conduct of

---

piracy-effort-along-west-africa-coast>; Hasan and Hassan, n. 8 above, pp. 178–179; UNSC, "Statement by the President of the Security Council," UN Doc. S/PRST/2016/11 (28 July 2016). The President of the Security Council underlined the importance of determining the existence of any possible or potential link between armed robberies at sea and piracy and terrorist groups in West Africa.

40 Otto, n. 24 above, p. 21; Hasan and Hassan, n. 8 above, p. 179.
41 IMO, "Monthly Circular 194, Report on attack on MV *Olivia II*" (1 January 2013); IMO, "Monthly Circular 207, Report on the attempted attack on MV *Master Force*" (19 February 2014); IMO, "Monthly Circular 249, Report on the attempted boarding of Liberian Cargo Carrier (name withheld)" (19 June 2017).
42 Data culled from IMO GSIS, <https://gisis.imo.org/Public/PRA/Default.aspx>.

maritime criminals within this area, displaying skillful adaptability in the conduct of operations in response to changing opportunities.

Efforts to Curtail Piracy and Armed Robbery against Ships in the Gulf of Guinea Region

Until recently, States within the region focused on various threats emanating from land, leading to a neglect of potential maritime security issues, including the increased rate of attacks in the region.[43] Following an increase in maritime domain awareness, individual States in the region began to show commitment to the improvement of their capabilities for the enhancement of security through the acquisition of new platforms for their navies, surveillance aircraft, and the engagement of advanced technologies.[44] Several States also introduced State-centric policies, bilateral and multilateral agreements aimed at eradicating maritime insecurities. The establishment of *Operation Pulo Shield*, which increased maritime policing by Benin and Ghana, and the 2011 Nigeria-Benin Joint Naval Patrol Agreement (*Operation Prosperity*) are examples of such activities and agreements.[45]

The international community offers support to the region for the protection of sea lanes of communication from unlawful acts, particularly piracy and armed robbery at sea.[46] There are numerous multilateral cooperative arrangements for human and technical capacity-building among Gulf of Guinea States. These initiatives include exercises, such as the annual *Obangame Express* organized by the United States Naval Forces (Africa Command), since 2010, which focuses on "maritime interdiction operation, as well as visit, board, search, and seizure techniques,"[47] and the African Maritime Law Enforcement

---

43 C. Ukeje and W.M. Ela, *African Approaches to Maritime Security: The Gulf of Guinea* (Abuja: Friedrich-Ebert-Stiftung, 2013), p. 23; Interviews at the Nigerian Maritime Administration and Security Agency (NIMASA), 5 June 2017.

44 Hasan and Hassan, n. 8 above, p. 200; Interviews at NIMASA, 5 June 2017.

45 Onuoha, n. 13 above, p. 10; Interviews at NIMASA, 5 June 2017; Hasan and Hassan, n. 8 above, pp. 200–209 where the authors identify the tightening of border security and deployment of special forces to respond to the threat of piracy. The authors also discuss extensively various purchases made by States in the region.

46 Non-regional States involved in cooperation for the enhancement of maritime security in the Gulf of Guinea region include the United States, France, the United Kingdom, and Norway. International agencies include the IMO, European Union and the African Union.

47 The apprehension of pirates and the rescue of hostages from the hijacked Panamanian-flagged vessel MT *Maximus* were made possible through the assistance of United States and France in tracking down the vessel as it transited the coastal waters of several States in the Gulf of Guinea. See IMO GISIS, <https://gisis.imo.org/Public/PAR/Incident.aspx?Action=View&ID=7279>; N. Herring, "West Africa piracy case highlights U.S. capacity building efforts" (United States Africa Command Media Room, 11 March 2016), available

Partnership (AMLEP) geared towards building maritime security capacity and improving management of the maritime environment through law enforcement operations.⁴⁸ Donor countries also contribute to the development and enhancement of a sustainable information sharing and reporting platform in the region through the pilot Maritime Trade Information Centre for the Gulf of Guinea (MTISC-GoG) in Tema, Ghana, which since 2016 has been superseded by the Marine Domain Awareness for Trade – Gulf of Guinea (MDAT-GoG) Center.⁴⁹ The IMO continues to contribute immensely to member State and regional maritime security by working in close cooperation and coordination with other UN bodies, international partners and development partners.⁵⁰

Several regional maritime security initiatives (RMSIs) also exist in the region. RMSIs in the region were formed along the already existing regional frameworks of the Economic Community of Central African States (ECCAS), Economic Community of West African States (ECOWAS), Maritime Organization of West and Central Africa (MOCWA), as well as the Gulf of Guinea Commission (GGC).⁵¹ However, following the prompt from the United Nations Security Council,⁵² and inspired by the Djibouti Code of Conduct,⁵³ the member States of MOCWA, ECCAS, GGC, and ECOWAS have integrated the existing regional security frameworks and adopted the Code of Conduct for the Suppression of Piracy, Armed Robbery Against Ships and Illicit Maritime Activity in West and Central Africa (Yaoundé Code), which focuses on the repression of transnational

---

online: <http://www.africom.mil/media-room/article/28044/west-africa-piracy-case-highlights-u-s-capacity-building-efforts>; Interviews at NIMASA, 5 June 2017.

48   The African Maritime Law Enforcement Partnership, available online: <http://www.africom.mil/what-we-do/security-cooperation/africa-maritime-law-enforcement-partnership-amlep>; Focus Group Discussion with NIMASA, 5 June 2017.

49   The Marine Domain Awareness for Trade – Gulf of Guinea (MDAT-GoG), run collectively by France and the United Kingdom, replaced the pilot program of the Maritime Trade Information Centre for the Gulf of Guinea MTISC-GoG, which ended in June 2016.

50   IMO, "Implementing Sustainable Maritime Security Measures in West and Central Africa" (September 2015), available online: <http://www.imo.org/en/OurWork/Security/WestAfrica/Documents/IMO%20WCA%20Strategy%20September%202015_English_final.pdf>. France, U.S. Africa Command, China, the United Kingdom, the European Union, Norway, and the G8++ Friends of the Gulf of Guinea also play a vital role as development partners.

51   For a detailed discussion on regional maritime security initiatives in the Gulf of Guinea, see generally Ali, n. 10 above.

52   UNSC, "Resolution 2018, Peace and Security in Africa," UN Doc. S/RES/2018 (2011) (31 October 2011); UNSC, "Resolution 2039, Peace Consolidation in West Africa," UN Doc. S/RES/2039 (2012) (29 February 2012).

53   Code of Conduct Concerning the Repression of Piracy and Armed Robbery Against Ships in the Western Indian Ocean and the Gulf of Aden (Djibouti, 29 January 2009).

crimes.[54] To implement the provisions of the Code, the Memorandum of Understanding among the ECCAS, ECOWAS and GGC on the Yaoundé Code and the Additional Protocol to the Memorandum of Understanding among ECCAS, ECOWAS and GGC on Maritime Safety and Security in Central and West Africa Maritime Space establish a maritime interregional coordination center in Cameroon for enhancing cooperation within the regional maritime centers of ECCAS, ECOWAS, and GGC.[55] The extant Yaoundé Code possesses prospects for strategic integration if viewed as an opportunity to provide the single framework that the region requires.[56]

As the safety of cargo, crew, and vessels are increasingly at risk, the international commercial shipping community has developed several measures and best management practices which it advises vessels operating within troubled waters to adopt.[57] These anti-piracy measures mainly complement the activities of the government in the region, by making an imminent attack unfavorable or stalling the attack long enough for help from nearby navies to arrive. Perhaps more significant as an anti-piracy measure introduced by the shipping sector is the increased use of private maritime security companies, providing various forms of services to vessels ranging from consultation on preventive measures, maritime services, training, and protection of offshore assets to public-private collaboration in the protection of vessels within the region.[58]

---

54   Code of Conduct for the Suppression of Piracy, Armed Robbery Against Ships and Illicit Maritime Activity in West and Central Africa (Yaoundé, 25 June 2013), preamble, p. 3 [Yaoundé Code]. An in-depth discussion of the Yaoundé Code and its implementation is beyond the scope of this article.

55   Memorandum of Understanding among Economic Community of Central African States (ECCAS), Economic Community of West African States (ECOWAS) and Gulf of Guinea Commission (GGC) on Maritime Safety and Security in Central and West Africa (Yaoundé, 25 June 2013), arts. 2 and 5; Additional Protocol to the Memorandum of Understanding among ECCAS, ECOWAS and GGC on safety and security in central and west Africa Maritime Space, arts. 1 and 2.

56   Ali, n. 10 above, p. 244.

57   United Kingdom Maritime Trade Operations, *BMP4. Best Management Practices for Protection against Somalia Based Piracy* (Version 4, Scotland, Witherby Publishing Group, 2011), p. 40, available online: <http://eunavfor.eu/wp-content/uploads/2013/01/bmp4-low-res_sept_5_20111.pdf>.

58   C. Liss, "Private security companies in the fight against piracy in Asia," Working Paper No. 120 (Asia Research Centre, 2005); J. Harrelson, "Blackbeard meets blackwater: An analysis of international conventions that address piracy and the use of private security companies to protect the shipping industry," *American University International Law Review* 22, no. 5 (2010): 283–312, p. 297; C. Liss, "(Re)Establishing control? Flag State regulation of antipiracy PMSCs," *Ocean Development and International Law* 46, no. 2 (2015): 84–97, p. 87; O. Eruaga, "Towards a normative shift in maritime security governance: Appraising

In spite of these concerted efforts at curtailing piracy and piratical acts in the Gulf of Guinea, maritime violence in the region remains persistent and continues to be a matter of great concern within the international community.

The Legal Requirements for the Offenses of Piracy and Armed Robbery against Ships

Various forms of unlawful, violent interference with shipping occur within the legal framework established and determined by international law. The practice of piracy as an unlawful interference with shipping is interwoven from time immemorial with human activities at sea, making it as old as maritime commerce itself.[59] Recent times have seen the occurrence of attacks similar in certain respects to those covered by the international law definition of piracy. Armed robbery against ships and terrorism exemplify attacks that are similar to piracy under international law. Among others, this has led to an ongoing debate as to the effect that the location of an attack or unlawful act might have in drawing a distinction between such acts. Active participation in this debate within the context of the Gulf of Guinea requires an exegesis of the law as it relates to the ingredients for the offenses of piracy and armed robbery against ships.

Legal Requirements for the Offense of Piracy

The 1982 United Nations Convention on the Law of the Sea (UNCLOS) provisions contain the extant international legal framework on piracy.[60] As distinct

---

private maritime security companies in Nigeria's anti-piracy and armed robbery at sea institutional framework," *Akungba Law Journal* 4, no. 1 (2016): 311–327, pp. 321–322.

59 J.L. Jesus, "Protection of foreign ships against piracy and terrorism at sea: Legal aspects," *International Journal of Marine & Coastal Law* 18 (2003): 363–400, p. 363; L. Azubuike, "International law regime against piracy," *Annual Survey of International & Comparative Law* 15, no. 1 (2009): 43–59, p. 45. On the evolution of the offense of piracy and its definition, see B.H. Dubner, *The Law of International Sea Piracy* (The Hague: Martinus Nijhoff Publishers, 1980), pp. 305–377; A. Rubin, *The Law of Piracy* (Rhode Island: Naval War College, 1988); A. Rubin, "Revising the law of 'piracy,'" *California Western International Law Journal* 21 (1990): 135–136; G.M. Anderson and A. Gifford, "Privateering and the private production of naval power," *Cato Journal* 11, no. 1 (1991–92): 99–122, p. 100; S. Schneider, "Universal jurisdiction over operation of a pirate ship: The legality of the evolving piracy definitions in regional prosecutions," *North Carolina Journal of International Law* 38 (2013): 473–569, p. 488; T. Paige, "Piracy and universal jurisdiction," *Macquarie Law Journal* 12 (2013): 131–154, p. 132.

60 United Nations Convention on the Law of the Sea (Montego Bay, 10 December 1982, entered into force 16 November 1994), 1833 *United Nations Treaty Series* 3, arts. 100–107. Arguably, States consider the UNCLOS provisions as representing the customary international

from other unlawful interference, the definition in UNCLOS Article 101 includes certain essential features. For an act to qualify as piracy, it must be illegal acts of violence, detention or depredation, and committed for private ends by members of a private ship against another vessel on the high seas or a place outside the jurisdiction of a State.[61] These features must concurrently be present for an act to be considered piracy within the framework of international law.[62]

    law on piracy, abiding by its provisions irrespective of whether they originally ratified or acceded to the Convention. See UNSC, "Resolution 1950, Somalia," UN Doc. S/RES/1950 (2010) (23 November 2010), preamble; Kraska, n. 18 above, p. 129. However, some scholars argue that UNCLOS is not a true representation of customary international law in the sense that a broader range of activities were included prior to its codification. See M. Halberstam, "Terrorism on the high seas: The *Archille Lauro*, piracy and the IMO convention on maritime safety," *American Journal of International Law* 82(1988): 269–310, p. 272, stating that adoption of the Convention focused attention on its provisions and substantially stopped further development of customary law; D. Guilfoyle, "Piracy off Somalia: UN Security Council Resolution 1816 and IMO regional counter-piracy efforts," *International Comparative Law Quarterly* 57 (2008): 690–699, p. 693, stating that definition is generally, though not universally, accepted as having codified pre-existing customary international law; T. Tullio, "UNCLOS at Thirty: Open Challenges," *Ocean Yearbook* 27 (2013): 49–66, p. 50, stating that the current international law of the sea, although dominated by UNCLOS, does not consist only of UNCLOS; Kao, n. 3 above, p. 7 ("there is much criticism that the codification privileged certain provisions over others as piracy was more expansive"). The decision of the International Court of Justice (ICJ) in *North Sea Continental Shelf (Federal Republic of Germany/Denmark; Federal Republic of Germany/Netherlands)* [1969] ICJ Rep 3, reveals the possibility of a treaty passing into the general corpus of international law such that it becomes binding even to countries that never ratified it. With 161 States of the 192 Member States of the United Nations as signatory to the treaty, parties to UNCLOS represent an overwhelming majority to qualify as representing customary law. Customary law not codified is a dynamic process of practice, which may evolve or wane and disappear. In the absence of consistent practice, the outer boundaries of piracy once covered under customary law cease to be part of the definition of piracy. See C. Bassiouni, "The sources and content of international criminal law: A theoretical framework," in *International Criminal Law*, ed. C. Bassiouni, (2d ed. New York: Transnational Publishers, 1999), pp. 33–34.

61   UNCLOS, id., art. 101. The provisions relating to piracy in UNCLOS are similar to those of the Convention on the High Seas (29 April 1958, 450 *United Nations Treaty Series* 11) that first codified the notion of piracy. Perhaps the most obvious distinction between these two conventions is the geographic area covered. With the express provision on maritime zones, UNCLOS governs a smaller geographical area than its 1958 counterpart. See S.P. Menefee, "International legal framework (UNCLOS, SUA, and UN Resolutions): How adequate are they in tackling piracy?," in *Selected Issues in Maritime Law and Policy: Liber Amicorum Proshanto K. Mukherjee (Law and Legislation)*, ed. M. Mejia (New York: Nova Science Publishers, 2013), pp. 207–220, p. 210.

62   Dubner, n. 4 above, p. 87.

The definition of piracy under UNCLOS Article 101 continues to attract debate, with several scholars lamenting the lack of clarity and a number of difficulties with the essential features of the offense.[63] The ambiguities and debates associated with some of the legal requirements of piracy, such as the motive, high seas requirement, and two-ship rule particularly, reveal the insufficiency of the international framework for piracy to handle contemporary maritime violence in the context of the Gulf of Guinea.

Private Ends Requirement of the Offense

The requirement of private ends remains a cleft in the discussion on whether or not acts of violence by States or politically motivated groups are considered acts of piracy. UNCLOS does not specify what amounts to "private ends." On the one hand, many experts opine that the requirement limits the reach of the treaty to acts with personal motivations.[64] Other scholars submit that the language of UNCLOS Article 101 is perhaps not as limiting as propounded by

---

63 Jesus, n. 59 above, 376; see S.P. Menefee, "The new 'Jamaica Discipline': Problems with piracy, maritime terrorism and the 1982 Convention on the Law of the Sea," *Connecticut Journal of International Law* 6 (1990): 141–148; Kao, n. 3 above, p. 7; Noyes, n. 3 above, p. 107.

64 C.H. Crockett, "Towards a revision of the international law of piracy," *DePaul Law Review* 26 (1976): 78–99; p. 92 (the dominant view is that such groups [organized for a political objective] can never be guilty of piracy); J.W Bingham et al., "Harvard research in international law: Draft convention on piracy, Part IV-Piracy," *The American Journal of International Law* 26, no. 1 (1932): 739–885, p. 798 [Harvard Draft]; I. Banatekas and S. Nash, *International Criminal Law* (3d ed., Oxon: Routledge-Cavendish, 2007), p. 179 (an act of violence on the high seas for political ends cannot be characterized as piratical, because it lacks the required private aim); N. Klein, *Maritime Security and the Law of the Sea* (Oxford: OUP 2011), p. 141 (environmental groups may not typically be regarded as pirates, as their goals are not for "private ends" but are related to the quest for marine environment protection); Jesus, n. 59 above, p. 379 ("'private ends' criterion seems to exclude acts of violence and depredation exerted by environmentally friendly groups or persons, in connection with their quest for marine environment protection"); Azubuike, n. 59 above, pp. 52–53; G. Constantinople, "Towards a new definition of piracy: The *Achille Lauro* incident," *Virginia Journal of International Law* 26 (1986): 723–753, p. 748 (noting that the actions in the *Santa Maria* where men seized the vessel of an opposing government confined actions to that State and would not suffice as piracy even with the two-ship requirement). In determining the meaning of "pirates" in an insurance policy, the English Court of Appeal in Republic of *Bolivia v. Indemnity Mutual Marine Assurance Co.*, (1909) 1 K.B. 785 (Eng C.A.) affirmed that private gain had to do with the satisfaction of private greed or personal vengeance and did not include operations for the purpose of a political end, against a particular government; Harvard Draft, id., p. 806; B.H. Dubner and C. Pastorius, "On the ninth circuit's new definition of piracy: Japanese whalers v. Sea Shepherd–Who are the real 'pirates' (i.e., plunderers)?," *Journal of Maritime Law & Commerce* 45 (2014): 415–443, p. 419.

others who lean towards the narrower interpretation.[65] These scholars insist the language flows from a broad interpretation of private as opposed to public violence, to emphasize that the violence lacks State sanction.[66] This reasoning appears to be consistent with the view that a warship cannot be deemed to commit acts of piracy unless there is mutiny by the crew.[67] Furthermore, the International Law Commission in its commentaries concludes that "acts of piracy may be prompted by feelings of hatred or revenge, and not merely by the desire for gain."[68] Expressing these feelings is illustrative of the motive for political violence, especially when channeled towards a particular State or class of persons. However, they qualify as private ends because of the absence of State sanction.[69]

The drafting and application of the Convention for the Suppression of Unlawful Acts against the Safety of Maritime Navigation (SUA) arguably lays to rest the need to expand the scope of the private ends requirements to cover politically motivated acts.[70] However, there are still situations where the

---

65   D. Guilfoyle, *Shipping Interdiction and the Law of the Sea* (Cambridge: Cambridge University Press, 2009), p. 37; Halberstam, n. 60 above, p. 282 (noting that the language of UNCLOS from the *travaux préparatoires* was intended to exclude insurgents not recognized as belligerents); M. Bahar, "Attaining optimal deterrence at sea," *Vanderbilt Journal of Transnational Law* 40 (2007): 26–28 (noting that the acts of the terrorists in the *Achille Lauro* qualify as piracy). The non-recognition of governments of insurgents denies such groups belligerent status for the activation of the law of international armed conflict. See T.C. Chen, *The International Law of Recognition* (New York: Praeger Inc., 1951), pp. 364–368; Constantinople, n. 64 above, pp. 737–743. See also Geneva Convention for the Amelioration of the Condition of the Wounded and Sick in Armed Forces in the Field (adopted 12 August 1949, entered into force 2 November 1950), 75 *United Nations Treaty Series* 7, art. 3 [Geneva Convention I]; Geneva Convention the Amelioration of the Condition of Wounded, Sick and Shipwrecked Members of Armed Forces at Sea (adopted 12 August 1949, entered into force 2 November 1950), 75 *United Nations Treaty Series* 87, art. 3 [Geneva Convention II]; Geneva Convention Relative to the Treatment of Prisoners of War (adopted 12 August 1949, entered into force 2 November 1950), 75 *United Nations Treaty Series* 135, art. 3 [Geneva Convention III]; Geneva Convention Relative to the Protection of Civilian Persons in Time of War (adopted 12 August 1949, entered into force 2 November 1950), 75 *United Nations Treaty Series* 287, art. 3 [Geneva Convention IV].
66   Guilfoyle, id., p. 37.
67   UNCLOS, n. 60 above, art. 102.
68   International Law Commission (ILC), *Yearbook of the International Law Commission*, 1956, Vol. II (United Nations publication, sales No.1956. v. 3, Vol. II 1967), p. 282.
69   Guilfoyle, n. 60 above, p. 693.
70   Convention for the Suppression of Unlawful Acts Against the Safety of Maritime Navigation (adopted 10 March 1988, entered into force 1 March 1992), 1678 *United Nations Treaty Series* 201, art. 3-3*quater* [SUA]. The relevant provisions are discussed in a later section. Following the *Achille Lauro* incident, SUA was drafted to address other forms of maritime violence not covered by the strict interpretation of UNCLOS. SUA and its Protocol (Protocol for the Suppression of Unlawful Acts against the Safety of Fixed Platforms Located on

distinction between privately and politically motivated maritime depredation makes it difficult to determine whether UNCLOS or SUA applies.[71] In the Gulf of Guinea, observers are unclear whether the acts of violence reported in Nigeria's Niger Delta are motivated by private ends or political goals. Experts and laymen alike generally refer to the criminals of the region as "militants" – connoting a political motivation to their actions.[72] It is also worth noting that some interpret the actions as a desire to highlight the injustice and exploitation that is perceived to pervade the region and cause oil pollution, poverty, and high unemployment.[73] This interpretation connects with the politically motivated offenses contained in Articles 3 and 3bis (1)(iii)(iv).[74] In spite of the political motivation, there are elements of private gain clearly illustrated in the petro-piracy model and the demand for ransom on kidnapped crew members. The IMO attempts to rectify this difficulty by providing for a dual-purpose act requirement through which politically motivated acts would qualify as acts of piracy when they occur with private ends.[75]

Two-ship Rule Requirement
Article 101(a)(i)(ii) requires that there should be two ships involved in any pirate attack – a pirate vessel and a victim vessel.[76] Following this interpretation,

---

the Continental Shelf, adopted 10 March 1988, entered into force 1 March 1992, *United Nations Treaty Series* 1678) were amended in 2005. A major shortcoming of the Convention however, is that unlike the international framework for the suppression of piracy, it is not regarded as customary international law, as such, non-signatory States are not bound by its provisions.

71   Bahar, n. 65 above, pp. 28–29; S. Menefee, "Delta blues: Maritime and riverine crimes in the Nigerian Delta," in *Coastal Zone Piracy and Other Unlawful Acts at Sea*, eds., M. Mejia and J. Xu (Malmo: WMU Publications, 2007), p. 211; Murphy, n. 21 above, p. 431; Jesus, n. 59 above, p. 379.

72   Menefee, id., p. 211; Murphy, n. 21 above, pp. 430–431.

73   U. Ukiwo, "From 'pirates' to 'militants': A historical perspective on anti-state and anti-oil company mobilization among the Ijaw of Warri, Western Niger Delta," *African Affairs* 106 (2007): 603; Murphy, n. 29 above, pp. 430–431; Ukeje and Ela, n. 43 above, p. 19; Hasan and Hasan, n. 8 above, p. 177. The authors commonly assert that acts of violence thrived due to failed attempts obtain desired objectives of development and self-determination in the Niger Delta.

74   Protocol of 2005 to the Convention for the Suppression of Unlawful Acts against the Safety of Maritime Navigation (adopted 14 October 2005, IMO Doc. LEG/CONF.15/21 (1 November 2005) [2005 SUA].

75   IMO, "Piracy: Uniform and consistent application of the provisions of international conventions relating to piracy Note by the Secretariat," IMO Doc. LEG 98/8/ (18 February 2011), para. 13.

76   A. Fakhry, "Piracy across maritime law," in *The Regulation of Shipping: International and Comparative: Essays in Honor of Edgar Gold*, eds. A. Chircop et al. (Leiden: Martinus Nijhoff, 2012), p. 102; J. Anderson, "A sea of change reforming the international regime to

acts of takeover by either the crew (mutiny) or the passengers (internal seizure) are part of the internal affairs of the vessel, which do not warrant international intervention.[77] Not all scholars agree that the distinction between an attack involving two ships on the one hand, and a takeover situation on the other, are well-defined.[78]

More important, especially in the context of the Gulf of Guinea, UNCLOS is silent as to the definition of a private ship under the two-ship rule requirement. This makes it unsettled whether the legal requirements contemplate specific types of vessels. From the IMO statistics available, attacks of vessels underway in the region rarely involve the presence of two ships; the attacks usually involve the use of speed boats.[79] The lack of a precise definition leaves room for the argument that a strict interpretation of the "two-ship rule" requires the presence of two ships.[80] This may mean that in situations where even other requirements are met, but the attack is carried out from another vessel that is not a ship, then the attack may not be considered piracy. Another plausible, some argue more tenable, interpretation is to consider that "ship" covers all types of vessels, irrespective of size or means of propulsion.[81]

High Seas Requirement

Debates trail the location requirement of the offense of piracy as it relates to happenings in the Gulf of Guinea. UNCLOS Article 101 applies only to acts committed on the high seas or a place outside the jurisdiction of a State.[82] This position is affirmed by IMO's use of "armed robbery against ships" in contradistinction to high seas piracy. The former offense meets all the conditions

---

prevent, suppress and prosecute sea piracy," *Journal of Maritime Law & Commerce* 44 (2013): 47–68, p.54. UNCLOS Article 103, n. 60 above, defines a pirate ship as one under the dominant control of individual(s) who intend to use such a vessel for of carrying out piratical acts. This excludes actions by government vessels except where the crew carries out mutiny.

77 Fakhry, id., p. 102. He notes that acts of violence in such a situation do not trigger the application of UNCLOS.

78 M. Murphy, "Piracy and UNCLOS: Does international law help regional states combat piracy?," in *Violence at Sea: Piracy in the Age of Global Terrorism*, ed. P. Lehr (New York: Routledge, 2007), p. 164. The level of uncertainty came to bear in the hijackings of the *Santa Maria* in 1961 and the *Achille Lauro* in 1985. In spite of the heinousness of the perpetrators' actions, the right of any State to seize the vessels could not be invoked.

79 Data culled from IMO GSIS, available online: <https://gisis.imo.org/Public/PAR/Search.aspx>.

80 T. Treves, "Piracy, law of the sea and use of force: Development off the coast of Somalia," *European Journal of International Law* 20 (2009): 399–414, p. 402.

81 SUA, n. 70 above, art. 1.

82 Menefee, n. 71 above, p. 211.

under Article 101, but occurs "within a State's internal waters, archipelagic waters and territorial sea."[83] The majority of the piratical acts reported in the Gulf of Guinea occur in areas within the jurisdiction of sovereign States.[84] Of the 473 criminal incidences at sea recorded by the IMO in the region from 2009 to 2017, about 61 percent occurred within the port and territorial seas of coastal States.[85] Flowing from the UNCLOS location requirement, curtailing and combating these crimes are the exclusive responsibility of the affected coastal State.[86] Notably, in the early years of regulating State jurisdiction under the law of the sea, nearly all of the world's oceans were considered high seas. This flowed from the three-mile territorial sea limit generally accepted for coastal State control and accepted by major maritime powers in conformity with the principle of freedom of the seas.[87] Thus, nearly all violent acts at sea committed for private ends, outside the then narrow band of territorial sea, would pass as piracy.[88]

---

83 IMO, Assembly, "Code of Practice for the Investigation of Crimes of Armed Robbery against Ships," IMO Doc. A 26/Res.1025 (18 January 2010), Annex 2.2. This resolution revoked IMO, Assembly, "Code of Practice for the Investigation of Crimes of Armed Robbery against Ships," IMO Doc. A 22/Res.922 (22 January 2002), which had a similar definition. See also Dubner, n. 4 above, p. 94.

84 Murphy, n. 21 above, p. 433; M. Gagain, "Neglected waters: Territorial maritime piracy and developing States: Somalia, Nigeria and Indonesia," *New England Journal of International & Comparative Law* 16 (2010): 169–196, p. 180; Otto, n. 24 above, p. 16. The recent statistics of the IMO, especially for 2016, shows an increase of attacks within international waters.

85 The 2016 and 2017 annual report for the region, however, reveals an interesting turn of events where most of the attacks in the region occurred within international waters as opposed to the usual trend of the majority occurring in territorial waters and at port. See IMO Report MSC.4/Cir.245, n. 1 above, Annex 2, p. 1.

86 M.Q. Mejia, "Defining maritime violence and maritime security," in *Maritime Violence and Other Security Issues at Sea*, eds. P.K. Mukherjee, M.Q. Mejia and G.M. Gauci (Malmo: WMU Publications, 2002), p. 32. To circumvent the high seas requirement in the case of Somalia, the UN Security Council required States to enter territorial waters as well as use all necessary means to repress acts of piracy and armed robbery against ships. See UNSC, "Resolution 1816, On acts of piracy and armed robbery against vessels in territorial waters and the high seas off the coast of Somalia," UN Doc. S/RES/1816 (2008) (2 June 2008), paras. 2, 3 and 5.

87 For a detailed explanation of the three-mile limit rule, its origin and application in the law of the sea, see H.S.K. Kent, "The historical origins of the three-mile limit," *American Journal of International Law* 48 (1954): 537–553, p. 537; M. Beerman et al., "The three mile limit: Its juridical status," *Valparaiso University Law Review* 6 (1972): 170–184; W.C. Extavour, *The Exclusive Economic Zone: A Study of the Evolution and Progressive Development of the International Law of the Sea* (Geneva: Brill, 1979), pp. 11–29.

88 M. Mejia, "Maritime gerrymandering: Dilemmas in defining piracy, terrorism and other acts of maritime violence," *Journal of International Commercial Law* 2, no. 2 (2003): 153–175, p. 160; J.A. Roach, "Agora: Piracy prosecutions, countering piracy off Somalia:

Another point of divergence that is very crucial is whether the EEZ forms part of the high seas for the purpose of the definition of piracy under international law. Coastal States in the Gulf of Guinea have witnessed in recent years an increase in the number of attacks occurring further away from areas designated as territorial waters. For instance, in the first quarter of 2018 alone, 15 attacks occurred outside the 12-nautical mile (NM) limit of the territorial sea to up to 60 NM in the case of the MV *Biskra* incident.[89] Classifying whether these attacks are acts of piracy hinges on the interpretation given to the provisions describing the high seas. Some scholars argue that attacks that occur within the EEZ come under the national jurisdiction of the coastal State.[90] Support for this assertion is based on the provisions of UNCLOS Article 86, which refers to the high seas as "all parts of the sea that are not included in the exclusive economic zone (EEZ), in the territorial sea or in the internal waters of a State, or in the archipelagic waters of an archipelagic State." The EEZ is not the high seas, but rather an expanse adjoining the territorial waters of the coastal State. UNCLOS Article 56 bestows on coastal States "sovereign rights for the purpose of exploring and exploiting, conserving and managing the natural resources..." in the EEZ. Maintaining coastal State security interests to the exclusion of other foreign naval operations within this region may arguably be considered as a corollary of exercising the restricted rights recognized under this provision, to bring security in the zone under the exclusive jurisdiction of the coastal State. Some States, such as China, North Korea, and Peru, claim that coastal States have the right under UNCLOS to regulate military activities within their EEZ.[91] From this perspective, grounds exist for coastal States in the Gulf of Guinea to insist on considering the universal jurisdiction principle under piracy as inapplicable within the EEZ.

International law and international institutions," *American Journal of International Law* 104 (2010): 396–416, p. 398.

89 IMO, "Reports on acts of piracy and armed robbery against ships issued monthly: Acts reported during February 2018," IMO Doc. MSC.4/Cir.260 (27 April 2018), Annex II, p. 1.

90 H. Djalal "Combating piracy: Co-operation needs, efforts, and challenges," in *Piracy in Southeast Asia, Status, Issues and Responses*, eds. D. Johnson and M. Valencia (Singapore: ISEAS Publishers, 2005), 143–159, p. 144; Isanga, n. 5 above, p. 1293; Dubner, n. 4 above, p. 93 (the author points out piracy which all States are free and indeed obligated to partake in suppressing exists only in international waters or outside the territorial sea.).

91 R. Xiaofeng and C. Xizhong, "A Chinese perspective," *Marine Policy* 29 (2005):139–146, p. 142; R. O'Rourke, "Maritime territorial and exclusive economic zone (EEZ) disputes involving China: Issues for Congress," (Congressional Research Service, 24 May 2018), p. 9.

Several scholars hold a contrary view to the exclusion of the EEZ from description of the high seas for the purpose of suppressing piracy.[92] These scholars assert that piracy can and does occur within the EEZ even as it lies within the jurisdiction of the State, and that the universal jurisdiction principle applies within this area where the State supposedly exercise (at least some level of) sovereignty. UNCLOS Article 58, as part of the provisions that governs the rights and obligations of States under the EEZ, provides that

1. In the exclusive economic zone, all States, whether coastal or landlocked, enjoy, subject to the relevant provisions of this Convention, the freedoms referred to in Article 87 of navigation ...
2. Articles 88 to 115 and other pertinent rules of international law apply to the exclusive economic zone in so far as they are not incompatible with this Part.

A combined reading of Articles 56, 58, 86, and 87 of UNCLOS shows that the EEZ invariably forms part of the high seas for determining rights and obligations under Article 58, including the meaning of the high seas for the definition of piracy, except where the presence of foreign State vessels within the jurisdiction of a State can be interpreted to amount to infringing on expressly provided sovereign rights and jurisdiction.

Legal Requirement for the Offense of Armed Robbery against Ships

The offense of "armed robbery against ships" is of recent coinage, arising from the need to provide an appropriate term for piratical acts occurring within internal waters and territorial seas of coastal States.[93] Armed robbery against ships is defined as:

(a) any illegal act of violence or detention or any act of depredation, or threat thereof, other than an act of piracy, committed for private ends and

---

92   Jesus, n. 59 above, p. 379; E. Kontorovich, "A Guantánamo on the sea: The difficulty of prosecuting pirates and terrorists," *California Law Review* 98 (2010): 243–275, p. 253; Roach, n. 88, pp. 397–416.

93   Fakhry, n. 76 above, pp. 104–105. Fakhry notes that the limitations of the UNCLOS definition created the need to create other terms to cover conducts similar to piracy but which fell outside the definition. The phrase has been in use as far back as the early 1980s in meetings and deliberations at the International Maritime Organization as an appendage to the offense of piracy. See Menefee, n. 61 above, p. 208 (ascribing the first usage in the General Assembly to Res53/32). See IMO, Assembly, "Measures to Prevent the Acts of Piracy and Armed Robbery against Ships," IMO Doc. A 13/Res.545 (29 February 1984); UNGA, "Oceans and the Law of the Sea," UN Doc. A/RES/53/32 (6 January 1999), para. 23. These two documents however do not provide a definition of the term armed robbery against ships.

directed against a ship or against persons or property on board such a ship, within a State's internal waters, archipelagic waters and territorial sea;

(b) any act of inciting or of intentionally facilitating an act described above.[94]

Flowing from this definition, four pertinent requirements, similar to some extent to the legal requirements of piracy, are discernable. Acts amounting to armed robbery against ships must be acts of illegal violence, detention or depredation, for private ends, and against a ship, within a State's territorial sea.[95] The most significant requirement in the context of the Gulf of Guinea is that the act occurs within waters under the control of the State, not beyond the territorial sea. Generally, international law pursuant to the principle of "equal sovereignty of states, internal competence of domestic jurisdiction and territorial preservation of existing boundaries," precludes foreign incursion into another State's territory without consent.[96] This implies that the principle of universal jurisdiction applicable to acts of piracy is inoperable within internal waters and territorial seas. Furthermore, the International Court of Justice (ICJ) in the *Nicaragua* case stated clearly that "[b]etween independent States, respect for territorial sovereignty is an essential foundation of international relations."[97] It is thus within the realm of a coastal State's domestic law to criminalize any act of maritime violence. However, the contention as to whether the EEZ forms part of the high seas under the legal requirements of piracy in international law remains.

State jurisdiction as opposed to universal jurisdiction over unlawful violent acts creates significant challenges to the effective management of offenses. For instance, some States adopt a non-conformist approach of declaring territorial seas beyond the 12-NM limit.[98] This affects the ability of other States to invoke universal jurisdiction under Article 105 if necessary. Another challenge that arises is the lack of uniformity with which States address cases of armed robbery against ships. The IMO Code of Practice for the Investigation of Crimes

---

94 Code of Practice, n. 83 above.
95 Id., Annex 2.2 (a).
96 Charter of the United Nations, 24 October 1945, 1 *United Nations Treaty Series* XVI, Ch. 1, art. 2, para. 4; S. Elden, "Contingent sovereignty, territorial integrity and the sanctity of borders," *SAIS Review* 25, no. 1 (2006): 11–24, p. 11.
97 *Military and Paramilitary Activities in and Against Nicaragua (Nicaragua v. U.S.)*, Judgment, 1986 I.C.J. 14, para. 202 (June 27). Based on the principle of State sovereignty, the ICJ found Great Britain in violation by not obtaining Albania's permission before conducting a minesweeping exercise in Albanian territorial seas in *Corfu Channels*.
98 For instance, Benin, Ecuador, and Somalia claim a territorial sea of 200 NM while Togo claims 30 NM. CIA, World Factbook, "Maritime Claims," available online: <https://www.cia.gov/library/publications/the-world-factbook/fields/2106.html>; O'Rourke, n. 91 above, pp. 8–9.

of Armed Robbery against Ships, which seeks "to provide IMO Member States with an *aide-mémoire* to facilitate the investigation of the crimes of piracy and armed robbery against ships," places no obligation on States to define and punish the offense of armed robbery against ships. This is because IMO resolutions, including the Code of Practice providing the definition of armed robbery against ships, are soft law.[99] Since soft law indicates a transitional stage in the development of norms where the content of the norm is vague and the scope imprecise, such provisions are not legally binding, but rather recommendatory in character.[100]

The manner in which a coastal State addresses illegal violence within its territory may manifest itself as an inability or unwillingness to adequately maintain security in their territorial waters, leading to the coastal State's failure to punish the perpetuators or redress the act.[101] As a result, the international community finds itself in a situation where, much as all States would like to curtail the frequency of violence at sea, effective action rests on the ability and willingness of specific coastal States to curtail the acts that occur within and around their territorial seas.

Bridging the Gap in the Legal Requirements for Piracy and Armed Robbery against Ships through the SUA Convention

The SUA Convention and its Protocol arose from the shortcomings of the legal requirements of piracy under UNCLOS Article 101 to handle other forms of maritime crime that involve violence, detention, and depredation.[102] The Convention and the subsequent amendments in 2005 present certain features that allow for the provision of a more suitable framework to address other maritime crimes, including terrorism.[103] SUA Article 3, 3bis, and 3ter describe what constitutes offenses under the Convention.

The SUA Convention's extensive geographical reach makes it relevant in both high seas and territorial seas.[104] Article 4 of the Convention applies to

---

99   Fakhry, n. 76 above, p. 105.
100 On the nature of soft law and its development, see P. Sands, *Principles of International Environmental Law* (2d ed., Cambridge: Cambridge University Press, 2003), pp. 55 and 73; D.L. Shelton, "Soft law," in *Routledge Handbook of International Law*, ed. D. Armstrong (Oxon: Routledge Press, 2009), 68–80; A.T. Guzman and T.L. Meyer, "International soft law," *Journal of Legal Analysis* 2 (2010): 171–217, p. 171.
101 Azubuike, n. 59 above, pp. 51–52.
102 Menefee, n. 61 above, p. 211.
103 M. Sterio, "Fighting piracy in Somalia (and elsewhere): Why more is needed," *Fordham International Law Journal* 33 (2010): 372–408, p. 387. Notably, not all States who were parties to the original convention ratified the amendments.
104 SUA, n. 70 above, art. 4.

unlawful acts against a ship navigating or scheduled to navigate beyond territorial waters, and also in situations where the ship navigates or is scheduled to navigate through or from waters beyond the outer limits of the territorial sea. SUA places an obligation on parties to make the offenses under the Convention punishable by appropriate penalties and taking such measures as may be necessary to establish jurisdiction.[105] Unlike UNCLOS, which provides for universal jurisdiction over acts of piracy, the SUA Convention enables State parties to establish jurisdiction as a coastal State, flag State, or State whose national(s) may have committed the unlawful act.[106]

The Convention and its Protocol do not mention piracy or armed robbery against ships in any of its provisions. However, some unlawful acts include basic elements of the crime of piracy and armed robbery against ships.[107] Flowing from this relationship, a complex legal regime addresses the use of violence at sea – an international framework applicable globally that addresses the acts of piracy but is reliant on municipal legislation; an international framework that addresses other unlawful acts but is applicable only to State parties; and relevant municipal laws of States criminalizing armed robbery against ships within their territories. Churchill views these legal regimes as collectively sufficient to handle maritime violence at sea.[108]

SUA certainly has significant potential to the extent that it addresses the gaps arising from the UNCLOS definition of piracy and the IMO definition of armed robbery against ships. However, SUA is essentially an anti-terrorist-oriented convention applicable only to State parties.[109] In particular, the facility for the extradition of offenders that is unique under the provisions of the Convention can only be as effective as the willingness of States to ratify or accede to the Convention on the one hand, and invoke it in a relevant case on the other. Moreover, the discretion left to State parties for prescribing sanctions for the substantive criminal offenses is another challenge that adversely affects uniformity in interpretation and effectiveness.[110] There thus remains a lacuna in competently addressing violence at sea that occurs within the

---

105 Id., arts. 5 and 6; 2005 SUA, n. 74 above, arts. 5, 5bis and 6.
106 SUA, id., arts. 6(1)(a), (b), and (c).
107 K. Mbiah, "SUA 2005 and coastal zone piracy," in Mejia and Xu, n. 71 above, pp. 177–187, p. 185; Fakhry, n. 76 above, p. 104.
108 R. Churchill, "The piracy provision of the UN Convention on the Law of the Sea: Fit for purpose?," in *The Law and Practice of Piracy as Sea: European and International Perspectives*, eds. P. Koutrakos and A. Skordas (Kindle ed., Hart Publishing, 2014).
109 Mejia and Mukherjee, n. 21 above, p. 176.
110 SUA Convention, n. 70 above, art. 6; Mejia and Mukherjee, n. 21 above, p. 180.

territorial sea of a coastal State, with significant effects for shipping beyond that State's territory.

Piracy and Armed Robbery against Ships in the Gulf of Guinea: Exploring Options to Fill the Legal Lacuna

Following the UNCLOS definition in its strictest sense, a purist view would show that there is little if any piracy *per se* in the Gulf of Guinea region. This effectively minimizes if not eliminates the possibility for foreign States to exert universal jurisdiction to tackle the spate of maritime violence in the region. Dubner asserts that the main purpose of recognizing piracy as a universal crime is to ensure that commercial lanes of navigation, valuable economic assets for world shipping and trade, are kept open and free from violence.[111] Despite the fact that the establishment of modern maritime zones has caused illegal maritime violence to become an internal matter for the coastal State, it may still be argued that such acts against international shipping cannot have totally lost their international character.[112] Numerous resolutions, statements, interregional agreements, recommendations, as well as reports on security in the maritime domain have been drafted and adopted as a result of the significant impact of violent attacks in territorial seas in the Gulf of Guinea.[113]

States in the region are obliged to ensure the suppression of piracy and armed robbery against ships through the establishment and enforcement of the appropriate legal mechanisms in terms of domestic regulation, implementation, enforcement, and prosecution.[114] However, keeping order within its

---

111   Dubner, n. 4 above, p. 73.
112   Gagain, n. 84 above, p. 180.
113   See, e.g., UNSC, Resolution S/RES/2039, n. 52 above; UNSC, "Statement of the President of the Security Council," UN Doc. S/PRST/2016/4 (26 April 2016); UNSC, "Statement of the President of the Security Council," UN Doc. S/PRST/2013/13 (14 August 2013); IMO, "Guidelines to Assist in the Investigation of the Crimes of Piracy and Armed Robbery against Ships," IMO Doc. MSC.1/Circ.1404 (23 May 2011); IMO, Assembly, "Prevention and Suppression of Piracy, Armed Robbery Against Ships and Illicit Maritime Activity in the Gulf of Guinea," IMO Doc. A 28/Res.1069 (5 February 2014); MOWCA, General Assembly, "Memorandum of Understanding on the Establishment of a Sub-Regional Integrated Coast Guard Network in West and Central Africa," Doc. MOWCA/XIII GA.08/8, (29 July 2008); Yaoundé Code, n. 54 above.
114   UNCLOS, n. 60 above, arts. 100–111; S. Jones, *Maritime Security: A Practical Guide* (London: The Nautical Institute 2006), 14. Flowing from the definition of piracy and the duty of States to cooperate in its repression, States are obligated to enact the appropriate

territorial sea might not attract the priority it deserves in the national security agenda of many coastal States. This is particularly the case where the State in engrossed in addressing more pressing internal problems such as large-scale poverty, underdevelopment, and other domestic crises.[115] As Jones notes:

> Littoral states, those having a coastline in a particular area do have legal responsibilities to ensure the freedom of innocent passage, but in the main piracy is simply seen as a crime against 'foreign' crews, ships and cargo, and so is not viewed as a major concern.[116]

While domain awareness and regional collaboration are increasing, acts of violence at sea are still rampant. Most of the countries in the region – including Nigeria, the epicenter of piracy and piratical acts – do not have municipal legislation that criminalizes piracy as defined under international law or accord the offense of armed robbery at sea the attention it deserves.[117] It is a fact that only fixed laws regulate crime and punishment.[118] This concept of reasonable certainty of legal consequence for actions flows from the fundamental

---

implementing domestic legislation and, by extension, even against similar piratical acts occurring in maritime zones outside of the high seas. In addition, the law relating to hot pursuit in UNCLOS Article 111, which prevents external naval forces from operating after chasing pirates into the territorial waters of coastal State, automatically makes the arrest and prosecution of such criminals the responsibility of the coastal State.

115 T. Susumu, "Suppression of modern piracy and the role of the navy," *NIDS Security Reports* 4 (2003): 38–58, p. 40.

116 Jones, n. 114 above, p. 14. Jones uses "piracy" here to reflect attacks within territorial waters. See also J. Abhyankar, "Piracy and maritime violence: A continuing threat to maritime industry" (ICC-IMB Report Hong Kong, 6 November 2002); Mejia, n. 88 above, p. 162; Isanga, n. 5 above, pp. 1288 and 1291.

117 Angola repealed Law 7/78, *Law on Crimes against State Security*, which defined and criminalized piracy in December 2010. The closest to municipal proscription of piracy in Nigeria is contained in the Criminal Code Section 403 which provides for the offense of stealing with violence. The section does not consider the location of the offense (land or sea) as relevant to the *actus reus*. However, the elements of the crime are not reflective of piracy under international law; neither does it cover all the offenses contemplated within the definition of armed robbery against ships. There is currently an anti-piracy bill before the 8th National Assembly. A similar bill was presented before the 7th National Assembly but it was not passed into law before the Assembly was dissolved.

118 C. Bassiouni, *Crimes Against Humanity in International Law* (2d revised ed., The Hague: Kluwer Law International, 1999), pp. 123–125; Bassiouni, n. 60 above, p. 33; I.F. Akande, "The rule of law as an instrument of societal protection and its impact on gender issues in Nigeria," *International Journal of Advanced Legal Studies and Governance* 2, no. 1 (2011): 188–200, p. 189.

principles of legality in criminal law in major criminal justice systems, including that of Nigeria.[119] Thus, in the absence of the appropriate legislation, the crimes of piracy and armed robbery against ships exist in a legal vacuum in the region and any form of deterrence from navies patrolling the waters at best ends at sea.[120] The then Director-General of the Nigerian Maritime Administration and Security Agency (NIMASA), Patrick Akpobolokemi, recognizing the gap created by the absence of appropriate legislation, noted:

> The greater challenge is that many of the culprits that we arrest have themselves out of cell as quickly as we do not intend that to be. We arrest someone for piracy with guns, arms and the rest, the next day you see them on the street.[121]

The ongoing criminal case against the MT *Dejkun* and six others exemplifies the challenge of an absence of municipal laws. The said vessel and the other suspects were accused of hijacking the MV *Maximus* in international waters, off the coast of São Tomé and Príncipe to obtain her cargo.[122] However, the vessel could not be so charged with piracy.

In yet some other instances, there is fundamental weakness in enforcement of laws for the protection of the maritime domain.[123] As Burger notes, the existence of good laws does not necessarily translate to proper enforcement.[124] Accordingly, one observes a disconnect between the enthusiasm of the governments in the region to participate in and be a State party to major maritime treaties, conventions, and instruments on the one hand, and their ability and willingness to implement and enforce the obligations and standards embodied

---

119 For instance, see Constitution of the Federal Republic of Nigeria, 1999 s. 36(8) ((n)o person shall be held to be guilty of a criminal offence on account of any act or omission that did not, at the time it took place, constitute such an offence).

120 A. Anyimadu, *Maritime Security in the Gulf of Guinea: Lessons Learned from the Indian Ocean* (London: Chatham House, 2013), p. 7.

121 G. Bivbere, "Pirates, oil thieves threaten our lives – NIMASA Boss," *Vanguard* (21 November 2014), available online: <http://www.vanguardngr.com/2014/11/pirates-oil-thieves-threatening-lives-nimasa-boss/>.

122 I. Anaba, "7 suspected pirates docked," *Vanguard* (11 October 2017), available online: <https://www.vanguardngr.com/2017/10/7-suspected-pirates-docked/>. The suspects are charged with other offenses such as illegal arms possession and unlawful dealing with petroleum products under the *Miscellaneous Offences Act*.

123 Ukeje and Ela, n. 43 above, p. 19.

124 C. Burger, "Learning from piracy: Future challenges of maritime security governance," *Global Affairs* 1 (2015): 33–42, p. 40.

in those treaties and conventions, on the other.[125] The failure of States in the region to abide by their responsibilities in this regard unwittingly allows maritime criminality to fester; the lower the risk of capture and punishment, the higher the likelihood that such crimes continue to occur.[126] There is an urgent need to encourage Gulf of Guinea States to step up the pace in the campaign against piracy through the establishment and enforcement of the appropriate legal framework.

Security at sea, whether international or territorial, has a direct impact on those who navigate through them. Indeed, Abhyankar notes that the distinction between high seas piracy and armed robbery against ships is irrelevant in the eyes of the victim, as is the allocation of responsibility for protection.[127] The seafaring and shipping communities want to remain safe and keep economic losses at the barest minimum, whether in international or territorial waters. With the majority of attacks occurring while ships are in port or anchorage as well as in the territorial seas of coastal States in piracy hotspots, such as the Gulf of Guinea, more authors question the need to maintain a legal distinction between piracy and armed robbery at sea based on the maritime zone in which the unlawful act has taken place.[128] Susumu notes that "from the original simple robbery to the seizure of entire vessels of today, the method employed has become of an ever-greater scale, now involving expensive cargo and threatening the lives of ships' crews."[129] It is as if the twentieth-century inception of maritime zones eradicated acts of piracy overnight by transforming erstwhile high seas into territorial sea, and thereby shifting from universal jurisdiction to coastal State jurisdiction.[130] A wider connotation of piracy to include attacks in the territorial seas would create greater opportunity for the international community to jointly consider and commit to the control or eradication of this maritime crime, as in the case of Somali piracy. The IMB in its earlier reports adopted a broad definition of piracy as "an act of boarding or attempting to board any ship with the intent to commit theft or any other crime

---

125 A. Ahmed-Hameed, "The challenges of implementing international treaties in third world countries: The case of maritime and environmental treaties implementation in Nigeria," *Journal of Law, Policy and Globalization* 50 (2016): 22–30, p. 26.
126 Burger, n. 124 above, p. 34.
127 J. Abhyankar, "Piracy and maritime violence: A global update," in Mukherjee et al., n. 86 above, p. 13.
128 Susumu, n. 115 above, p. 40; K.-D. Ali, "The anatomy of the Gulf of Guinea piracy," *Naval College War Review* (2015): 93–118, p. 94; D. Dillion, "Maritime piracy: Defining the problem," *SAIS Review* XXV (2005): 155–165, pp. 159–160.
129 Susumu, id., p. 56.
130 Mejia, n. 88 above, p. 160.

and with intent or capability to use force in furtherance of that Act."[131] This was a simplified definition that did away with the requirements of jurisdiction, the two-ship rule, and the motivation for private ends requirement. However, this definition attracted significant controversy especially from coastal States that complained that statistics based on the broad definition blurred the true state of affairs and claim that these led unfairly to their States being declared piracy hot-spots.[132] The IMB confirms that it engages the use of a generalized definition of piracy for analysis purposes only.[133] A broad classification puts in perspective the real danger that these attacks posed to the maritime domain. Regardless, the IMB definition has no standing in law and therefore could not necessarily be used by the international community to suppress piratical acts within coastal State jurisdictions.[134]

The limited scope of piracy to acts committed only on the high seas under UNCLOS could conceivably be tenable if coastal States in piracy hotspots were fully functional and capable of defending their territorial seas.[135] However, the reality that many States are unable or unwilling to competently handle piratical acts is difficult to ignore.[136] It is important to strike a balance between securing international shipping and protecting national security. Such necessity arguably exists irrespective of the different maritime zones. The growing call for revisiting the legal distinction between piracy under international law and armed robbery against ships is apparent in comments declaring how the global community ought to do more to tackle maritime violence.[137] For instance, one group has put forward the term "coastal zone piracy" to cover what are currently acts landward of the high seas that would have constituted piracy

---

131   IMB, *Piracy and Armed Robbery Against Ships Report: Annual Report; January 1–31 December 2006* (January 2007) [IMB Report]; IMB Report, *January 1–31 December 2008* (January 2009). The IMB adds that petty theft(s) are excluded, unless the thieves are armed.

132   N.A. Osnin, "Private Maritime Security Company (PMSC) in the Strait of Malacca: Options for Malaysia," *Journal of Maritime Affairs* 5 (2006): 195–206, p. 195; M. Pérouse De Montclos, "Maritime piracy in Nigeria: Old wine in new bottles?," *Studies in Conflict & Terrorism* 35 (2012): 531–541, p. 532.

133   IMB Report, n. 131 above. The IMB does not offer this generalized definition in its more recent reports, but adopts the IMO definition of armed robbery contained in IMO Res. A 16/1025, n. 83 above, although the compilation of attacks is still reflective of the generalized approach.

134   Mejia, n. 88 above, p. 162.

135   Isanga, n. 5 above, p. 1288.

136   Id.

137   L. Bento, "Towards an international law of piracy *sui generis*: How the dual nature of maritime piracy law enables piracy to flourish," *Berkeley Journal of International Law* 29, no. 2 (2011): 399–455, p. 402; Kao, n. 3 above, pp. 8–12.

had there been no geographical restrictions in UNCLOS Article 101.[138] They envisage that such a concept would provide room for the global community to address maritime crimes in a more uniform manner. The notion of "modern piracy" has also been applied to piratical acts in the Gulf of Guinea, irrespective of the location of the act because modern piracy is said to manifest itself in various forms and adapts to contemporary technical, economic, and sociopolitical developments.[139] While there are as many different terminologies as there are groups putting forward a less restrictive legal framework for piracy, the unity of purpose is evident. The notion of high seas piracy that excludes piratical acts within coastal waters has translated to a weakness in the global anti-piracy focus. Although this would amount to broad conceptualization of piracy *jure gentium* and piratical acts within territorial waters, it would enable the international community to uniformly tackle maritime security issues not only in the Gulf of Guinea but also in other jurisdictions. Jesus posits that the legal system, international or domestic, should be able to adapt to the needs of the society and evolve with the reality it purports to regulate.[140] International law of the sea provisions should be able to adapt and evolve to reflect the imperative to achieve secure use of the ocean regardless of era or epoch.[141]

There are options that may have the potential to adequately accommodate the contending points raised in the foregoing discussion. Because States jealously guard against incursions into their sovereign territory, an amendment of UNCLOS and its piracy provisions is virtually inconceivable.[142] However, a treaty amendment may not be necessary. In discussing the relationship between treaty and custom, the ICJ in *Military and Paramilitary Activities in and against Nicaragua (Nicaragua v. United States)* stated that "even if two norms belonging to two sources of international law appear identical in content and even if states in question are bound by these rules both on the level of treaty law and on customary international law, these norms retain separate existence."[143] It may be argued that if States, in regions where maritime piracy and armed

---

138 Mejia and Mukherjee, n. 21 above, p. 181; Mbiah, n. 107 above, pp. 184–186; Fakhry, n. 76 above, p. 108; P.K. Mukherjee and M. Brownrigg, *Farthing on Shipping* (4th ed., London: Springer, 2013), p. 257.
139 Kao, n. 3 above, p. 4.
140 Jesus, n. 59 above, p. 382.
141 Id.
142 Noyes, n. 3 above, pp. 107–108 (inferring that the fear of such incursions of State sovereignty principle was responsible for the failure to update the language of the 1958 Convention of the High Seas during the drafting of UNCLOS).
143 *Nicaragua v. United States*, n. 97 above.

robbery against ships persist, fail to effectively curtail these offenses through appropriate enforcement, the contemporary practice of broad conceptualization to piracy may effectively render the legal distinction a moot point. Some authors have suggested that the SUA Convention may be sufficient to accommodate the suggested evolution essentially because it offsets some of the restrictions contained in UNCLOS.[144] However, as already discussed earlier in this article, SUA is curtailed by its own set of weaknesses.[145]

Another approach is to regard the persistent lapse by a State in ensuring security within its maritime space as a failure to carry out a concomitant duty attendant to its sovereign status.[146] Azubuike, as a proponent of this approach, asserts that failure to curtail piratical acts within territorial waters that threaten global economic interests should constitute a relinquishment of certain State attributes, such as exclusive jurisdiction over waters. This would enable the international community to organize appropriate responses to suppress violence at sea. However, this approach remains very delicate and may be subject to abuse. Dubner warns of the dangers of incursions or seizures in the territorial sea of other States, which run afoul of the principle of sovereignty stating that unless "we are willing to limit ... [such incursions] ... we will run into the problem of having each nation who wishes to do so make any excuse for the entry."[147]

Dubner's warning is well-grounded and must be taken seriously. Therefore, the UN Security Council could play a vital role in consideration of its powers under Chapter VII of the UN Charter, in minimizing abuse by administering and overseeing the suspension of any State's exclusive jurisdiction for the purpose of granting controlled access to the international community, over acts of piracy committed in the territorial sea. UN Security Council Resolution 1816 allowed foreign States to "enter the territorial waters of Somalia for the purpose of repressing acts of piracy and armed robbery at sea, in a manner consistent with such action permitted on the high seas" for the period as stated in the resolution.[148] Subsequent resolutions extended the period within which foreign incursions were allowed into Somali territorial waters after

---

144   F. Booth and L. Altenbrun, "Maritime and port security, piracy, and stowaways: Renewed concerns over old problems," *U.S.F. Maritime Law Journal* 15 (2002): 1–48, p. 43; Mejia and Mukherjee, n. 21 above, p. 183.
145   Azubuike, n. 59 above, p. 56.
146   Id., pp. 51–52.
147   B.H. Dubner, "Piracy in contemporary national and international law," *California Western International Law Journal* 21 (1990): 139–150, p. 149.
148   UNSC Resolution 1816, n. 86 above, paras. 2, 3, 5 and 7.

due evaluation of the level of insecurity within the maritime domain.[149] The international cooperation based on these resolutions has contributed to curtailing attacks off the coast of Somalia. Although Resolution 1816 clearly states its provisions do not establish customary international law,[150] the inclusion of the "one-off" provision can be viewed as an indication of the potential of the resolutions in addressing the problem of piracy both within territorial waters and on the high seas.[151] The declaration of the UN Security Council does not preclude the application of such measures in a different location such as the Gulf of Guinea, if necessary, based on an assessment of the region. The Somali resolutions and their effects may just have become invaluable starting points for future actions by the UN Security Council in dealing with piracy.[152] Furthermore, Treves opines that while resistance to the formation of a customary rule could be strong, it is not insurmountable, particularly if similar authorizations were to be granted where the need arises.[153]

Conclusion

This article presented an overview of the nature of acts of maritime violence in the Gulf of Guinea and the State, regional, international, and private sector efforts at curtailing these attacks. It also explored the debates relating to the legal requirements in international law of the offenses of piracy and armed robbery against ships within the context of the Gulf of Guinea. Despite efforts to curtail their occurrence in the region, violent maritime crime continues to persist partly because of a legal regime that is unclear, restrictive, and confusing in equal measure, coupled with an inability, rather than an unwillingness, of States to fulfill their obligations to combat piracy and piratical acts.

In order to effectively stop the rising number of attacks in the region, there is a need to revisit and reformulate the legal requirements, especially the notion of jurisdiction over piracy cases in international law. Such an exercise by way of amendment of the provisions of UNCLOS may not be achievable in the near future. However, pending such an exercise, the international community would

---

149 UNSC, "Resolution 1838, Somalia," UN Doc. S/RES/1838) (2008) (7 October 2008): UNSC, "Resolution 2184, Somalia," UN Doc. S/RES/2184 (2014) (12 November 2014); UNSC, "Resolution 2125, Somalia," UN Doc. S/RES/2125 (2013) (18 November 2013); UNSC, "Resolution 2316, Somalia," UN Doc. S/RES/2316 (2016) (9 November 2016); UNSC, "Resolution 2383, Somalia," UN Doc. S/RES/2383 (2017) (7 November 2017). Resolution 2383 extends the incursions into Somalia for the purpose of tackling piracy until November 2018.
150 UNSC Resolution 1816, n. 86 above; para. 9.
151 Menefee, n. 61 above, p. 220.
152 Azubuike, n. 59 above, pp. 51–52; Menefee, n. 61 above, p. 220.
153 Treves, n. 80 above, p. 405.

be best served to engage other pathways to address the situation. Several alternatives outside an outright amendment of treaty provisions are available to ease the international community into countering violent maritime crime. Contemporary opinions and practices that seek to broaden the conceptualization of the offense of piracy and armed robbery against ships to improve global anti-piracy focus already exist. Increasing support for these ideas creates the possibility of developing customary international law practices to render moot the legal distinction between piracy and armed robbery against ships.

The SUA Convention to a significant extent caters to some of the deficiencies of the international law definition of piracy, although SUA itself possesses weaknesses particularly because it is fashioned to tackle the offense of terrorism and applies only to State parties. These features diminish its relevance to the offenses of piracy and armed robbery against ships.

Another option is using United Nations Security Council resolutions to allow controlled access into territorial waters, in the same manner as in the case of Somali piracy. Such coordinated incursions under Security Council sanction would allow foreign States to deal with piratical acts within territorial seas without damage to the broader principle and respect for the sovereignty of the coastal State.[154]

The effect of these options would invariably amount to the policing of the territorial sea by other countries, which most (if not all) coastal States will find difficult to accept. However, the knowledge that such a decision is possible would help apply the needed pressure on States that can, but are unwilling to, invest in securing their waters to take seriously their responsibility to provide security within their territorial sea and obligation to contribute to the suppression of piracy. For States that are unable to do so or do not possess the required resources, the international community can organize the appropriate response to suppress violence at sea.

The phenomenon of piracy and armed robbery against ships has continued unabated for the better part of the last four decades in different regions of the world. Among other measures, there is a need to continually review the international legal framework and explore different approaches, such as those above, that can be adapted not only in the context of the Gulf of Guinea, but in other areas where the universal menace of piracy and armed robbery against ships might manifest itself in the future.

---

154   Azubuike, n. 59 above, pp. 51–52.

Protection of Submarine Cables against Acts of Terrorism

*Xuexia Liao**
Post-doctoral Fellow, Peking University Law School,
Beijing, China

Introduction

It has been acknowledged internationally that, today, submarine cables transmit most of the world's data and communications, and that they are vitally important to the global economy as well as the national security of all States.[1] As submarine cables provide invaluable service for economic exchanges and communicative activities in civil and military fields, these critical submarine infrastructures may catch the attention of terrorists and be exposed to the threat of terrorism.[2] Submarine cables are inherently vulnerable to such nefarious human activities, not only as it requires limited technique or equipment for substantial damage, but also their locations are generally available to the public and are highly concentrated geographically.[3] In fact, the prospect of

---

* An earlier version of this article was awarded the 2018 Rhodes Academy Submarine Cables Writing Award sponsored by the International Cable Protection Committee.
1 See United Nations General Assembly (UNGA), "Oceans and the Law of the Sea, Resolution Adopted by the General Assembly on 7 December 2010," UN Doc. A/RES/65/37 (17 March 2011), pp. 3–4.
2 In 2010, WikiLeaks published a secret memo listing the infrastructure facilities around the world that are seen as "critical" to United States security. This disclosure has prompted criticism that the document may serve as a target list for terrorists. See K. Zetter, "WikiLeaks releases secret list of critical infrastructure sites," WIRED, 12 June 2010, available online: <https://www.wired.com/2010/12/critical-infrastructures-cable>.
3 See R. Sunak, "Undersea cables: Indispensable, insecure," Policy Exchange (1 December 2017), p. 19, available online: <https://policyexchange.org.uk/publication/undersea-cables-indispensable-insecure/>. In fact, submarine cables may be tapped or disrupted by unmanned undersea vehicles, as submarine cables carrying vast information are a lucrative target for States wishing to acquire intelligence about their rivals or enemies, or, in times of tension, to hamper or prevent the flow of information. See M.N. Schmitt and D.S. Goddard, "International law and the military use of unmanned maritime systems," *International Review of the Red Cross* 98, no. 2 (2016): 567–592, p. 575.

intentional damage to submarine cables for the purpose of disrupting intercontinental communications is no longer remote.[4]

Notwithstanding the potential and severe threat of terrorist attacks on submarine cables, international protection of submarine cables is, however, far from sufficient.[5] In particular, under the current legal framework, within which the United Nations Convention on the Law of the Sea (UNCLOS) is a major instrument, the legal basis for coastal States to protect submarine cables lying in areas outside of their sovereignty is open to question. It could be problematic when coastal States were victims of attacks taking place in areas outside their territory, whereas there is no clear legal basis for them to exercise jurisdiction over terrorists who are nationals of another State.

Despite the inherent vulnerability of submarine cables to physical damage and the security gaps in UNCLOS, protection of submarine cables can also be viewed in the context of counter-terrorism, which has, since 11 September 2001, been developing rapidly. On the one hand, the legal framework of counter-terrorism, in particular a broadening definition of terrorism reflected in national legislation and international treaties, may fill the security gap of protecting submarine cables against acts of terrorism. On the other hand, after the horrifying terrorist attacks in September 2001, the United States has used the term "war on terror" to claim self-defense against terrorists,[6] which in effect stretched the traditional concept of self-defense in an inter-State context to cover situations where force is used against individuals (terrorists).[7] However, the war on terror rhetoric, if it implies an armed conflict between a State and individual terrorists, may have negative consequences on the protection of

---

4   In 2013, the Egyptian navy arrested three scuba divers in the waters off the coast of Alexandria under charges of having attempted to cut the SeaMewE-4 internet cable. The cable under threat stretches from Marseille to Singapore and carries a third of the web traffic between Europe and Egypt, making its severance a source of potentially substantial disruption. Sunak, id., pp. 23–24.
5   See R. Beckman, "Protecting submarine cables from intentional damage: The security gap," in *Submarine Cables: The Handbook of Law and Policy*, eds. D.R. Burnett, R.C. Beckman and T.M. Davenport (Leiden/Boston: Martinus Nijhoff, 2014), pp. 281–297, pp. 287–89.
6   In an address by then U.S. President George W. Bush, he stated that "[o]ur war on terror begins with al Qaeda, but it does not end there. It will not end until every terrorist group of global reach has been found, stopped and defeated." See Address to a joint session of the Congress and the American People, 20 December 2001, Archives of the White House, available online: <https://georgewbush-whitehouse.archives.gov/news/releases/2001/09/20010920-8.html>.
7   See C. Gray, "A new war for a new century? The use of force against terrorism after September 11, 20001," in *September 11, 2001: A Turning Point in International and Domestic Law?*, eds. P. Eden and T. O'Donnell (Ardsley: Transnational Publishers, 2005), pp. 97–125, p. 101.

submarine cables, as it has long been held that submarine cables are legitimate wartime targets.[8] As military reactions to terrorist attacks are increasingly relevant in the current age of counter-terrorism, it is necessary to consider how these realities have a bearing on the protection of submarine cables.

This article intends to explore the potential of international law to protect submarine cables against acts of terrorism. It will first demonstrate the inadequacy of UNCLOS to protect submarine cables and explain that there is built-in tension between coastal States and activities related to submarine cables. Following that, it will explore the legal basis on which coastal States may exercise jurisdiction over activities involving intentional damage to submarine cables in maritime areas outside their territory. Aware of the lack of incentives of States to comply with the obligations under UNCLOS, this article next turns to the legal framework of counter-terrorism to discover practical, useful, and more importantly, *available* legal instruments in an attempt to fill in the security gap of protecting submarine cables left by the law of the sea. In particular, it will explore the plausibility of negotiating a global treaty protecting submarine cables on the model of "sector treaties" of counter-terrorism, the influence of a broadening definition of terrorism, and the potential impact of the war on terror rhetoric on the protection of submarine cables.

Inadequacy of UNCLOS to Protect Submarine Cables

UNCLOS establishes "a legal order for the seas and oceans,"[9] and is a comprehensive convention on matters of the law of sea. Whereas the 1884 Convention for the Protection of Submarine Telegraph Cables (1884 Convention) constitutes the first international effort to regulate activities related to submarine cables, its provision on the protection of submarine cables, namely Article 11,[10] was first incorporated into the 1958 Geneva Conventions on the High Seas and

---

8   Article XV of the 1884 Convention for the Protection of Submarine Telegraph Cables (Paris, 14 March 1884) provides: "It is understood that the stipulations of the present Convention do not in any way restrict the freedom of action of belligerents." See also T.M. Davenport, "Submarine cables, cybersecurity and international law: An intersectional analysis," *Catholic University Journal of Law and Technology* 24, no. 1 (2016): 57–109, p. 80.

9   United Nations Convention on the Law of the Sea, Montego Bay, 10 December 1982 (entered into force 16 November 1994), 1833 *United Nations Treaty Series* 396, preamble.

10   Article 11 of the 1884 Convention provides: "It is a punishable offence to break or injure a submarine cable, wilfully or by culpable negligence, in such manner as might interrupt or obstruct telegraphic communication, either wholly or partially, such punishment being without prejudice to any civil action for damages."

Continental Shelf, and then into UNCLOS.[11] UNCLOS articulates the law applicable to activities relating to submarine cables in the exclusive economic zone (EEZ), which is a maritime zone established by that convention. Therefore, UNCLOS provides full coverage of the applicable law to submarine cables in all maritime zones known to States today. In any event, the 1884 Convention has limited participation, with only 44 parties, while UNCLOS is an almost universal treaty, making it appropriate to examine the current protection of submarine cables mainly by reference to UNCLOS.

Protection of Submarine Cables under UNCLOS

Laying submarine cables, as traditionally understood and established in the law of the sea, is one activity falling within the freedom of the high seas.[12] This may be partially due to the private nature of submarine cables since the beginning of the industry. Activities relating to submarine cables, including the laying, operation and maintenance, and building of submarine cables systems are mainly carried out by private actors.[13] As a result, the protection of submarine cables is subject to the rules of jurisdiction in accordance with the freedom of the high seas. The private nature of the submarine cable industry and the lack of communication or cooperation between the industry and coastal States may account for the lack of incentive of coastal States to protect submarine cables that land in their territory, even though submarine cables can now be seen as international "public goods" because of their service in global communications. There is also a lack of awareness of the importance of submarine cables on the part of governments, partially due to the common misconception that international communications are routed via satellites,[14] and partially perhaps due to the efficiency of the industry in maintaining the service provided by submarine cables on its own.[15]

Article 113 of UNCLOS provides that every State shall adopt national legislation to make it a punishable offense for "the breaking or injury by a ship flying

---

11   See T.A. Mensah, "Submarine cables and the international law of the sea," in *Law of the Sea, From Grotius to the International Tribunal for the Law of the Sea*, ed. L. del Castillo (Leiden/Boston: Brill Nijhoff, 2015), pp. 725–749, p. 738.
12   UNCLOS, n. 9 above, art. 87(1)(c).
13   See M. Green, "The submarine cable industry: How does it work?," in Burnett et al., n. 5 above, p. 41.
14   See L. Carter et al., "Submarine cables and the oceans: Connecting the world," UNEP-WCMC Biodiversity Series No. 31 (ICPC/UNEP/UNEP-WCMC, 2009), p. 3, available online: <http://www.iscpc.org/publications/ICPC-UNEP_Report.pdf>.
15   It is suggested that despite the astonishing communications system being international in nature, the industry has been built with little or no government funding. See Green, n. 13 above, p. 60.

its flag or by a person subject to its jurisdiction of a submarine cable beneath the high seas done wilfully or through culpable negligence, in such a manner as to be liable to interrupt or obstruct telegraphic or telephonic communications." This article is thus built upon national jurisdiction and flag State jurisdiction, and it is concerned with intentional damage to submarine cables beneath the high seas.

Article 58(2) of UNCLOS, which deals with rights and duties of other States in the EEZ, provides that "Articles 88 to 115 and other pertinent rules of international law apply to the exclusive economic zone in so far as they are not incompatible with this Part." Accordingly, the national legislation of one State criminalizing the breaking and injury of submarine cables also applies to acts of its nationals or a ship flying its flag in the EEZ of other coastal States.

However, these provisions do not adequately offer effective protection over submarine cables against intentional damage, including acts of terrorism. For one thing, Articles 113 and 58(2) only confer on States with prescriptive jurisdiction, but not enforcement jurisdiction. The enforcement is subject to the principle of the exclusive jurisdiction of the flag State, whose very objective is to prevent any interference by other States with vessels flying its flag on the high seas.[16] This is in contrast with Article X of the 1884 Convention, which allows warships to demand documentation from the captain or master proving the ship's nationality in cases of allegedly having broken a submarine cable. Nevertheless, the latter provision proves to be unhelpful as it is only applicable between the parties to the 1884 Convention, and, in any event, its invocation is rare.[17] For another, most States have not implemented Article 113 of UNCLOS, and, as a matter of fact, breaking or injury of submarine cables beneath the high seas and in the EEZ of coastal States is not a criminal offense under the domestic law of many States.[18] Even with such national legislation in place, it seems that the penalties are not severe enough to deter or punish acts of intentional damage on submarine cables. For instance, the punishment under the legislation of the United States for willful injury to a submarine cable is a fine of US$5,000 or imprisonment for two years. For negligent injury, the maximum punishment is US$500 or three months' imprisonment.[19] The light nature of the penalties is said to account for the fact that there has been no criminal

---

16 See Y. Tanaka, *The International Law of the Sea* (Cambridge: Cambridge University Press, 2012), pp. 152–153.
17 It is suggested that there is only one reported case of a State party relying on Article X of the 1884 Convention. See Beckman, n. 5 above, p. 289.
18 See id., p. 288.
19 See Mensah, n. 11 above, p. 742.

prosecution for a violation of the said legislation.[20] With the increasing threat of terrorism and the potential for serious disruption of the internet and other communicative activities supported by submarine cables, it is obvious that the provisions of UNCLOS and their implementation at the domestic level are not satisfactory.

Under Article 113, national legislation adopted by the State only governs its nationals or ships flying its flag over breaking or injury of a submarine cable beneath the high seas. There is no equivalent obligation for coastal States to adopt such national legislation in areas subject to their territorial sovereignty or sovereign rights. As will be elaborated below, this constitutes the main obstacle for effective protection of submarine cables.

The Absence of Coastal States' Jurisdiction to Protect Submarine Cables

As submarine cables establish the communicative network by connecting coastal States around the globe, there is no doubt that coastal States have a legal interest to protect submarine cables for their indispensable service. However, coastal States' jurisdiction has to be examined in accordance with the principle of territoriality, which is the basic principle with regard to the scope of jurisdiction of States.[21] The intensity of coastal States' control over activities relating to submarine cables decreases as maritime zones extend further seaward.

In maritime areas under the sovereignty of coastal States, which normally include internal waters, the territorial sea, and archipelagic waters, coastal States have the right, but not the obligation, to adopt national legislation to criminalize acts of intentional breaking or injury of submarine cables. With national legislation in place, coastal States are also entitled to exercise enforcement jurisdiction over acts taking place in these areas. Nonetheless, it is reported that very few States have express provisions criminalizing damage to submarine cables in their territorial waters, or the penalties imposed by relevant legislation are not sufficient.[22]

In areas outside the sovereignty of coastal States, the jurisdiction of coastal States is significantly limited and is compatible with the function and objectives of the relevant maritime zones. In contiguous zones, coastal States are entitled to adopt laws and regulations only with regard to customs, fiscal,

---

20 See id., p. 744.
21 See I. Brownlie, *Principles of Public International Law*, 7th ed. (Oxford: Oxford University Press, 2008), p. 301.
22 See Beckman, n. 5 above, p. 287.

immigration, and sanitary issues.[23] In the continental shelf and the EEZ, coastal States have sovereign rights over the resources of the relevant zones, and the jurisdiction is confined to resource-related activities.[24] Therefore, it is doubtful whether coastal States could criminalize acts of breaking or injury of submarine cables in these areas as such national legislation may amount to a breach of the principle of territoriality.

In effect, in the continental shelf and the EEZ, laying and maintaining submarine cables are regarded as rights of nationals of foreign States on the basis of the freedom of the high seas. Consequently, there is a "competitive relationship" between activities of coastal States (fisheries, exploring and exploiting resources of continental shelf, and installations of artificial islands, etc.) and the activities of laying and operating submarine cables by foreign nationals. The contrast of the two is clear in Article 79(2) of UNCLOS, which provides that "subject to its right to take reasonable measures for the exploration of the continental shelf, the exploitation of its natural resources and the prevention, reduction and control of pollution from pipelines, the coastal State may not impede the laying or maintenance of such cables or pipelines." The potential conflict is also visible in the EEZ, as UNCLOS requires that coastal States and other States shall exercise their respective rights while having due regard to the rights and duties of each other.[25] In practice, coastal States tend to regulate activities related to submarine cables in the EEZ, and in some circumstances even arguably to the extent incompatible with UNCLOS.[26]

One such example is concerned with the freedoms related to submarine cable repair and maintenance. It is arguable that the repair of submarine cables

---

23   UNCLOS, n. 9 above, art. 33(1)(a).
24   Article 56(1) of UNCLOS, id., provides that in the EEZ, the coastal State has "(a) sovereign rights for the purpose of exploring and exploiting, conserving and managing the natural resources, whether living or non-living, of the waters superjacent to the seabed and of the seabed and its subsoil, and with regard to other activities for the economic exploitation and exploration of the zone, such as the production of energy from the water, currents and winds; (b) jurisdiction as provided for in the relevant provisions of this Convention with regard to: (i) the establishment and use of artificial islands, installations and structures; (ii) marine scientific research; (iii) the protection and preservation of the marine environment; (c) other rights and duties provided for in this Convention." Article 77(1) provides: "The coastal State exercises over the continental shelf sovereign rights for the purpose of exploring it and exploiting its natural resources."
25   UNCLOS, n. 9 above, arts. 56(2) and 58(2). See also D. Guilfoyle, "The high seas," in *The Oxford Handbook of the Law of the Sea*, eds. D.R. Rothwell et al. (Oxford: Oxford University Press, 2015), pp. 203–225, pp. 212–13.
26   See T. Davenport, "Submarine communications cables and law of the sea: Problems in law and practice," *Ocean Development & International Law* 43, no. 3 (July 2012): 201–242, pp. 211–14.

falls within Article 58(1) of UNCLOS as "other internationally lawful uses of the sea" related to submarine cables and is compatible with other provisions of UNCLOS.[27] It is noted that the vast majority of States, including Australia, Japan, and States throughout Europe, do not require permits for emergency repair of submarine cables beyond or even within their territorial sea.[28] These States' practices suggest that the repair of submarine cables is perceived as a high seas freedom related to submarine cables. Some countries, on the other hand, including China and India, tend to require permits before repair work can be carried out in their EEZs.[29] The requirements for permits may prevent effective repair of submarine cables and delay the restoration of communication services. When it comes to the threat or acts of terrorist attacks, without cooperation between coastal States and the submarine cable industry on immediate repair of submarine cables, the paralyzed communication networks resulting from damaged submarine cables may intensify the terror on the population intended by terrorists or distract the governments of the targeted States from concentrating on counter-terrorism measures. On the contrary, the effective repair of submarine cables by experienced repair operations in cooperation with coastal States is likely to minimize the threat and damage to the normal life of the population and operation of governments.

The sometimes-excessive regulation and limited protection by coastal States over submarine cables reflect the built-in tension between activities of coastal States and activities relating to submarine cables carried out by foreign nationals – it is also a manifestation of the tension between *mare clausum* and *mare liberum*.[30] However, such built-in tension between the two types of activities is no longer an accurate account of the reality. Whereas activities relating to submarine cables are mainly conducted by private actors of foreign States, the service of submarine cables is to the benefit of coastal States, and, in fact, of the international community in general. In this sense, submarine cables are

---

27 See K. Ford-Ramsden and D.R. Burnett, "Submarine cable repair and maintenance," in Burnett et al., n. 5 above, p. 173; R.C. Beckman, "Submarine cables – A critically important but neglected area of the law of the sea" (paper presented at the 7th International Conference of the International Society of International Law on Legal Regimes of Sea, Air, Space and Antarctica, New Delhi, 2010), p. 5.
28 See Ford-Ramsden and Burnett, id., p. 170.
29 See Davenport, n. 26 above, p. 212.
30 According to Réne-Jean Dupuy, "La mer a toujours été battue par deux grands vents contraires: le vent du large, qui souffle vers la terre, est celui de la liberté; le vent de la terre vers le large est porteur des souverainetés. Le droit de la mer s'est toujours trouvé au coeur de leurs affrontement." R.-J. Dupuy, "La Mer Sous Compétence Nationale," in *Traité Du Nouveau Droit de La Mer*, eds., R.-J. Dupuy and D. Vignes (Paris/Bruxelles: Economica – Bruylant, 1985), pp. 219–273, p. 219.

infrastructure for the public good despite the infrastructure's private nature. When it comes to the threat of terrorism, it is not difficult to envisage the following scenario: terrorists, who are nationals of State A, using a ship registered in State B, destroyed submarine cables in the EEZ of State C in order to disrupt the internet and communication service of State C. According to UNCLOS, these acts may be punished by State A and State B, if these countries criminalize such acts in accordance with Article 113. On the contrary, under UNCLOS, it is unclear on what jurisdictional basis State C, which is the target of the acts of terrorism, may exercise criminal jurisdiction over these acts, as they took place in areas outside the territory of State C. This could be problematic when States A and B do not enact national jurisdiction criminalizing the acts of breaking and injury of submarine cables in accordance with Article 113, or when States A and B are unwilling or unable to exercise the jurisdiction.

In recent years, several coastal States have established cable protection zones to protect submarine cables within their territorial sea and EEZs. Australian legislation allows the Australian Communications and Media Authority (ACMA) to declare protection zones over submarine cables of national significance. Among other things, the legislation "provides for significant criminal penalties for both intentional and negligent damage to cables in a protection zone."[31] New Zealand also enacted the *Submarine Cables and Pipelines Protection Act*, which provides for the establishment of cable protection zones within its internal waters, territorial sea, and EEZ. This legislation also granted the protection officers authority to undertake numerous enforcement activities, including, notably, seizure of ships and fishing equipment in the protection zone.[32] China also adopted the Provisions on the Protection of Submarine Cables and Pipelines in 2003, which is applicable to internal waters, territorial sea, continental shelves, and other sea areas within the jurisdiction of China.[33] This regulation establishes cable protection zones, which are to be declared by the competent administrative departments of marine affairs and made public annually. In addition, the width of cable protection zones varies between 50 to 500 meters on each side of the submarine cable, depending upon the location of the submarine cables.[34] A range of activities are prohibited in the cable

---

31   See R. Wargo and T.M. Davenport, "Protecting submarine cables from competing uses," in Burnett et al., n. 5 above, pp. 272–274.
32   See id., pp. 274–275.
33   See Article 2 of Provisions on the Protection of Submarine Cables and Pipelines, Order of the Ministry of Land and Resources of the People's Republic of China (No. 24, 2003), available online: <http://www.lawinfochina.com/display.aspx?lib=law&id=3390&CGid=>.
34   For instance, in harbor areas, the width of the cable protection zones is 50 meters on each side of the cables, while in the open seas of the coast, the width is 500 meters on each

protection zones, including anchoring, bottom-contact fishing, and other activities that may cause physical damage to submarine cables.[35]

These practices concerning cable protection zones reflect the increasing awareness and willingness of coastal States to protect submarine cables, which is a consequence of the understanding of the utmost importance of submarine cables in providing communicative and exchange services. The establishment of cable protection zones can provide effective protection of the submarine cables from competing use of the maritime areas, in particular fishing activities.[36] However, the legal basis for coastal States to prescribe cable protection zones in areas outside territorial seas is questionable. On the one hand, it amounts to broadening the jurisdiction of coastal States over activities in the EEZ, which is incompatible with the functional jurisdiction in respect of resources under UNCLOS. On the other hand, the prohibition of certain activities in cable protection zones may interfere with the freedom of navigation of other States in the EEZ.[37] It has been suggested that "to the extent that cable protection zones prohibit or restrict activities such as fishing, resource exploration and maritime scientific research, [cable protection zones] are arguably consistent with a coastal State's rights in the EEZ or continental shelf."[38] However, this interpretation cannot explain on what legal basis coastal States may extend their criminal law in areas outside their territory, as prescribed by the Australian legislation.

To sum up, the inadequacy of UNCLOS to protect submarine cables is rooted in the traditional competitive relationship between the activities of coastal States and the activities relating to submarine cables as part of the freedom of the high seas. Coastal States lack a clear legal basis under UNCLOS to criminalize acts of intentional damage to submarine cables in maritime areas outside their territorial sea. This may be counter-intuitive, as it is the coastal States that may suffer from acts of terrorism launched against submarine cables. Whereas cable protection zones established by coastal States reflect the increasing awareness of the importance of submarine cables, the jurisdictional basis to prescribe these protection zones is in doubt. As a result, it is imperative to establish coastal States' jurisdiction to protect submarine cables against acts of terrorism under international law.

---

   side of the cables. See Article 7 of Provisions on the Protection of Submarine Cables and Pipelines, id.
35 Id., art. 8.
36 It is suggested that fishing activities account for the majority of submarine cable faults. See Wargo and Davenport, n. 31 above, p. 256.
37 See UNCLOS, n. 9 above, arts. 58(1) and (2).
38 Wargo and Davenport, n. 31 above, p. 276.

Establishing Coastal States' Jurisdiction over Terrorist Attacks on Submarine Cables

In circumstances where there is no specific treaty-based extension of jurisdiction, it is of interest to search within general international law to establish coastal States' jurisdiction over terrorist attacks launched against submarine cables in maritime areas outside their territorial sovereignty. Two bases of jurisdiction may support the extension of coastal States' prescriptive jurisdiction under the circumstances, namely, the objective territorial jurisdiction and the protective jurisdiction. Furthermore, as a matter of *lex ferenda*, the possibility of establishing universal jurisdiction over terrorist attacks on submarine cables may also be envisaged.

Objective Territorial Jurisdiction

The objective territorial jurisdiction is generally accepted and often applied when any essential constituent element of a crime is consummated on State territory.[39] It provides the basis of jurisdiction for a State to apply its law to an incident which is completed within its territory, even though it was initiated outside its territory.[40] The objective territorial jurisdiction is routinely asserted by States in their national courts.[41] In international law, the *Lotus* case was based on the principle of objective territorial jurisdiction by assimilating the Turkish vessel to Turkish national territory, taking the view that the collision between the French vessel and the Turkish vessel had affected Turkish territory.[42] Whereas the approach of the Permanent Court of International Justice (PCIJ) to treat a vessel as a piece of floating territory of the State of registration is not tenable,[43] the PCIJ acknowledged in general that:

---

39   See Brownlie, n. 21 above, p. 301.
40   See V. Lowe, "Jurisdiction," in *International Law*, ed. M.D. Evans, 2nd ed. (Oxford/New York: Oxford University Press, 2006), pp. 335–360, pp. 343–344.
41   See id., pp. 344–345.
42   See Brownlie, n. 21 above, p. 302, citing that "[the French argument] could only be used in the present case if international law forbade Turkey to take into consideration the fact that the offence produced its effects on the Turkish vessel and consequently in a place assimilated to Turkish territory in which the application of Turkish criminal law cannot be challenged, even in regard to offences committed there by foreigners. But no such rule of international law exists." *The Case of the S.S. "Lotus,"* Permanent Court of International Justice, Series A. No. 10, 7 September 1927, p. 23.
43   Lord Finlay, in his dissenting opinion, considered that "[t]his is a new and startling application of a metaphor." Dissenting opinion of Lord Finlay, the *Lotus* case, id., p. 52. As to why a ship cannot be regarded as a piece of floating territory of a State, see Tanaka, n. 16

> [I]t is certain that the courts of many countries ... interpret criminal law in the sense that offences, the authors of which at the moment of commission are in the territory of another State, are nevertheless to be regarded as having been committed in the national territory, if one of the constituent elements of the offence, and more especially its *effects*, have taken place there.[44] (emphasis added)

In a hypothetical situation, it is clear that if a coastal State suffers from direct economic and social disruption in internet or other communicative services as a result of submarine cable-targeted terrorism, even though the criminal acts may take place in maritime areas outside the territory of the coastal State (for instance in the EEZ), the crime is completed via the effects on the communications system within the territory of the coastal State. However, under such circumstances, the coastal State would have a sufficient legal interest to prosecute and punish these criminal acts under their domestic law. In effect, due to the fact that the submarine cables land in the coastal State, it does not make a difference as to where the criminal act (e.g., cutting and breaking the submarine cable) takes place for it to be completed – the result is that the effects would be within the territory of the coastal State. In such situations, the intra-territorial link between the territory of a State and the acts of the offense can be easily established.

A somewhat nuanced distinction should be made between the objective territorial jurisdiction and the "effects doctrine," which was developed first in the context of the antitrust law of the United States. The effects doctrine can be controversial when the jurisdiction is asserted by a State where mere economic effect is present.[45] This form of effects doctrine should be distinguished from the objective territorial jurisdiction, as the latter requires physical effects to occur from a criminal act, for instance, a bomb exploding.[46] Also, even where some States assert jurisdiction on the basis of the effects doctrine, it is clear that there is some element of intra-territorial conduct.[47] Nevertheless, it seems

---

above, pp. 152–153; A. Clapham, *Brierly's Law of Nations*, 7th ed. (Oxford: Oxford University Press, 2012), p. 227.

44 *Lotus* case, id., p. 23.
45 This is the case of the *Uranium Antitrust* litigation. According to Brownlie, in this case "US law was to be applied to non-US companies, in respect of their acts outside the United States, at a time when they were forbidden by US law to trade in the United States. The only jurisdictional link was the 'effect' of the cartel upon the United States: there was no intraterritorial conduct in the United States at all." Brownlie, n. 21 above, pp. 344–345.
46 See Clapham, n. 43 above, pp. 243–244.
47 See Lowe, n. 40 above, p. 345.

that the effects doctrine and the objective territorial jurisdiction can be used interchangeably when they refer to a case where the criminal acts are completed within the territory of the State while the acts were initiated abroad.[48] In fact, Beckman argues that coastal States should "adopt national legislation for acts of intentional damage to cables in the EEZ or high seas, provided that such cables land in their territory or service their telecommunications system," based on the effects doctrine.[49] To avoid the controversy of the effects doctrine in terms of pure adverse economic effect in the antitrust law of the United States, it is better to ground the basis of jurisdiction of coastal States on the objective territorial jurisdiction, which is unequivocal on the intra-territorial link between the criminal offense and the territory of the coastal State.

Protective Jurisdiction

Another potential basis of jurisdiction for coastal States to extend their prescriptive legislation to acts outside their territory is the principle of protective jurisdiction. This principle applies whenever a State's essential security interests are threatened by acts committed outside their territory.[50] Traditionally, this basis of jurisdiction is narrowly construed to apply to extraterritorial acts, such as espionage, which may threaten the existence of the State. Nevertheless, as the protective principle is concerned with the essential interests of a State, it might give States a broad, unilateral construction of the interests at stake.[51] This might account for the increasing appeal of the protective principle in recent State practice, as it is invoked to extend jurisdiction over exterritorial drug traffickers and violations of immigration laws.[52]

It is also because of the national security interest at stake that the protective jurisdiction may be asserted in cases of terrorist attacks launched against submarine cables outside the territory of a coastal State.[53] On the one hand, other than providing economic and social exchanges, submarine cables are also used to serve military purposes. For instance, the United States military relies on

---

48   For instance, Oxman refers to "effects doctrine" and the objective territorial jurisdiction as one and the same thing. See B.H. Oxman, "Jurisdiction of States," *Max Planck Encyclopedia of Public International Law* [MPEPIL], para. 32, available online: <http://opil.ouplaw.com/view/10.1093/law:epil/9780199231690/law-9780199231690-e1436?prd=EPIL#law-9780199231690-e1436-div2-8>.
49   See Beckman, n. 5 above, p. 290.
50   See V. Lowe, *International Law* (Oxford/New York: Oxford University Press, 2007), p. 176.
51   I. Bantekas, "Criminal jurisdiction of states under international law," MPEPIL, para. 20, available online: <http://opil.ouplaw.com/view/10.1093/law:epil/9780199231690/law-9780199231690-e1021?rskey=JWsDEe&result=6&prd=EPIL>.
52   Lowe, n. 50 above, p. 176.
53   See also Beckman, n. 5 above, p. 290.

commercial cable networks for 95 percent of its strategic communications.[54] An interruption of such critical submarine cables may severely disrupt military communications and cause significant operational problems. Should this happen, it could be qualified as threatening the essential security of the State. On the other hand, some States, in particular the United States, have asserted the applicability of the protective jurisdiction when it comes to terrorist attacks on its overseas embassies.[55] Therefore, there is potential in the protective jurisdiction to be asserted in cases of terrorist attacks launched outside the territory of the coastal State. In fact, the protective principle is explicitly relied on in some counter-terrorism treaties to establish the jurisdiction of the States parties. For instance, in the 1988 Convention for the Suppression of Unlawful Acts against the Safety of Maritime Navigation, it is provided that a State party may also establish its jurisdiction when the offense is committed in an attempt to compel that State to do or abstain from doing any act.[56] Whereas the latter example is a treaty-based extension of jurisdiction, it illustrates the importance of the protective principle as one of the instruments that can be used to ensure that the offenders do not escape prosecution.

A distinction should be made between the principle of protective jurisdiction and that of passive personal jurisdiction. The latter refers to the situation where the national State of the victim of an offense asserts jurisdiction.[57] While the protective jurisdiction is aimed at the protection of the essential interests of the State, the passive personal jurisdiction is, on the other hand, for the interests of the nationals. The passive personal jurisdiction is controversial in international law, as it may infringe on the jurisdiction of the State where the offense took place or the jurisdiction of the national State of the offender. Nevertheless, it seems that the passive personal jurisdiction turns out to be

---

54 See Sunak, n. 3 above, pp. 21–22.
55 In 1998, the Unites States embassies in Kenya and Tanzania were bombed by terrorists. Afterwards, several alleged perpetrators were taken into custody by the United States. In the pre-trial proceedings in the *United States v. Bin Laden*, the defendants challenged the extraterritorial application of some of the United States statutes under which they were charged. The court, however, asserted that the application of the law on the basis of the protective principle. See S.D. Murphy, *Principles of International Law*, 1st ed. (Thomson/West, 2006), p. 239 and pp. 245–246.
56 1988 Convention for the Suppression of Unlawful Acts against the Safety of Maritime Navigation, Rome, 10 March 1988 (entered into force 1 March 1992), 1678 *United Nations Treaty Series* 201, art. 6(2)(c). Similarly, identical wording on the jurisdiction can also be found in Article 9(2)(d) of the 2005 International Convention for the Suppression of Acts of Nuclear Terrorism, New York, 13 April 2005 (entered into force 7 July 2007), 2445 *United Nations Treaty Series* 89 [Nuclear Terrorism Convention].
57 See Lowe, n. 40 above, p. 351.

revived when it comes to the prosecution of terrorists. As the terrorist groups increasingly targeted the nationals of the United States and other western States abroad, the relevance of the passive personal jurisdiction became clear. In fact, it is observed that the United States, which used to be an opponent of the passive personal jurisdiction,[58] started to apply the principle extensively against terrorist attacks on its nationals abroad, not only in terms of law and prosecution, but also as a matter of extraterritorial enforcement.[59] However, it is questionable for the extension of a State's jurisdiction through the passive personal jurisdiction as it may interfere with the States that have jurisdiction based on the territorial principle or national principle. In addition, claiming enforcement jurisdiction based on the passive personal jurisdiction has even been criticized as "a form of legal imperialism."[60] Nevertheless, it is common that counter-terrorism treaties endorse the passive personal jurisdiction as a basis of jurisdiction for the States parties. For instance, the 2005 International Convention for the Suppression of Acts of Nuclear Terrorism provides that a State party may establish jurisdiction over any offense under the convention if the offense is committed against a national of that State.[61] As the web of counter-terrorism treaties provides the exercise of passive personal jurisdiction, it might be even more difficult for a State to assert such jurisdiction in the absence of a treaty-based rule. Perhaps only where the passive personal jurisdiction is asserted in serious crimes, where the crime is recognized in both jurisdictions, would there be fewer controversies. In fact, it is observed by judges of the International Court of Justice (ICJ) that "[p]assive personal jurisdiction, for so long regarded as controversial ... today meets with relatively little opposition, at least so far as a particular category of offences is concerned," citing Chapter 113A, *1986 Omnibus Diplomatic and Antiterrorism Act* of the United States and Article 689 of the *French Code of Criminal Procedure* (1975).[62] In any event, protection of submarine cables may be better accommodated under the protective jurisdiction rather than the passive personal jurisdiction because of the essential national interests involved.

While the objective territorial jurisdiction and the protective jurisdiction may provide bases of jurisdiction in the absence of other treaty-based extension of jurisdiction, it must be borne in mind that what is being discussed here

---

58   See Bantekas, n. 51 above, para. 18.
59   Id.
60   Lowe, n. 50 above, p. 176.
61   Nuclear Terrorism Convention, n. 56 above, art. 9(2)(a).
62   See Joint separate opinion of judges Higgins, Kooijmans, and Buergenthal, Arrest Warrant of 11 April 2000 (Democratic Republic of the Congo v. Belgium), ICJ Reports 2002, p. 3, at pp. 76–77, para. 47.

only concerns the extension of the prescriptive and adjudicative jurisdiction of the coastal State, not the enforcement jurisdiction. In other words, only when the alleged perpetrators are present in the territory of the coastal State could the State exercise enforcement jurisdiction over these persons for the terrorist attacks they carried out outside its territory.

Universal Jurisdiction

In international law, universal jurisdiction is another type of extraterritorial jurisdiction that can be asserted by States over some international crimes that are so serious that all humankind has a legitimate interest in repressing them. It is generally accepted that these crimes include genocide, crimes against humanity, serious war crimes, and possibly torture and slavery.[63] Piracy is also a crime that has long been held as falling within the group that may trigger universal jurisdiction.[64] According to Article 105 of UNCLOS, every State may seize a pirate ship or aircraft and arrest the persons and seize the property on board on the high seas or in any other place outside the jurisdiction of any State.

As piracy on the high seas or in places outside the jurisdiction of a State may be subject to universal jurisdiction, it is argued by some scholars that theft or destruction of a submarine cable outside the territorial sea of any State can be piracy as defined in Article 101 of UNCLOS.[65] This line of argument is said to be more effective and more expedient to "extend an existing enforcement regime than it is to develop an entirely novel legal framework."[66] However, such an interpretation may do violence to and distort the text of Article 101 of UNCLOS to accommodate the act of intentional damage to submarine cables. Article 101 of UNCLOS, in fact, adopts a very narrow definition of piracy. It defines piracy as, *inter alia*, any illegal acts of violence committed for private ends by the crew or the passengers of a private ship or a private aircraft that are directed "(i) on the high seas, against another ship or aircraft, or against persons or property on board such ship or aircraft" and "(ii) against a ship, aircraft, persons or property

---

63 See Lowe, n. 50 above, p. 177.
64 See Clapham, n. 43 above, pp. 248–249. The recent State practices concerning prosecuting acts of piracy off the Somalian coasts reinforce the universal jurisdiction over piracy. The Security Council also "calls upon all States to criminalize piracy under their domestic law and to favourably consider the prosecution of suspected, and imprisonment of convicted, pirates apprehended off the coast of Somalia, consistent with applicable international law including international human rights law." United Nations, Security Council, "Resolution 1950 (2010)," UN Doc. S/RES/1950 (23 November 2010), para. 13.
65 See M.P. Green and D.R. Burnett, "Security of international submarine cable infrastructure: Time to rethink?," in *Legal Challenges in Maritime Security*, eds. M.H. Nordquist et al. (Leiden: Brill Nijhoff, 2008), pp. 557–583, pp. 573–574.
66 Id., p. 580.

in a place outside the jurisdiction of any State." Article 101(a)(i) thus embraces the so-called "two vessels" requirement.[67] Article 101(a)(ii), for its part, gives the impression that illegal acts of violence may also fall within the definition of piracy when they are directed against property in a place outside the jurisdiction of any State, and therefore seems broad enough to include theft or destruction of submarine cables on the high seas. However, such an interpretation may overlook the historic origin of Article 101(a)(ii). It is recalled that in the 1956 draft articles prepared by the International Law Commission (ILC) for the First Conference on the Law of the Sea, the ILC commented that "acts committed on board a ship by the crew or passengers and directed against the ship itself, or against persons or property on the ship, cannot be regarded as acts of piracy."[68] This comment excluded "internal hijacking" from the scope of the definition of piracy. It is suggested that the wording of Article 15 of 1958 Convention on the High Seas and Article 101(a)(ii) of UNCLOS should be understood as including internal seizures of a ship as piracy.[69] Accordingly, rather than broadening the scope of piracy to include illegal acts against persons or property in places outside the jurisdiction of any State, Article 101(a)(ii) intends more specifically to capture the acts of internal seizures by the crew or the passengers of a private ship or a private aircraft.

Therefore, theft or destruction of submarine cables are clearly beyond the text of Article 101 as they do not involve two vessels, or internal seizures of the ship. Even if theft or destruction of submarine cables were within the scope of piracy under UNCLOS through an innovative interpretation of the latter, terrorist attacks on submarine cables are clearly not for "private ends," and therefore are no doubt beyond any possible meaning of piracy.[70] The definition of piracy under Article 101 represents the existing customary law.[71] In fact, it is pointed out that unlike most of the terms defined in UNCLOS, Article 101 is not limited

---

67   See Tanaka, n. 16 above, pp. 356–357.
68   See *Report of the International Law Commission Covering the Work of Its Eighth Session (A/3159), Article 39 Commentary, International Law Commission Yearbook 1956, Volume II*, p. 282.
69   The definition of piracy under Article 101 of UNCLOS is incorporated from Article 15 of the 1958 Convention on the High Seas. See S.N. Nandan and S. Rosenne, eds., *United Nations Convention on the Law of the Sea 1982: A Commentary, Volume III* (The Hague/London/Boston: Martinus Nijhoff Publishers, 1995), p. 201.
70   See Green and Burnett, n. 65 above, p. 581; see also S. Kaye, "International measures to protect oil platforms, pipelines, and submarine cables from attack," *Tulane Maritime Law Journal* 31, no. 2 (2007): 377–424, p. 415.
71   See Brownlie, n. 21 above, p. 229.

in application to the purposes of "this article" or "this Convention,"[72] which is a strong indicator of codification of customary international law. Furthermore, given the inconsistencies of the definition in national legislation, the text of Article 101 should not be easily challenged by creative interpretative exercises. In this regard, the provisions on piracy of UNCLOS are not helpful in cases of terrorist attacks against submarine cables.

Nevertheless, it is noteworthy that piracy is under universal jurisdiction not because it is comparable with the above-mentioned international crimes such as genocide or crimes against humanity; instead, the rationale is that piracy, when carried out on the high seas, may easily evade jurisdiction of any State that might have asserted jurisdiction on other bases (national jurisdiction or flag State jurisdiction).[73] Accordingly, piracy being in the category of crimes under universal jurisdiction arises out of the necessity of international cooperation to repress piracy.[74] Universal jurisdiction is thus a powerful juridical tool in this respect.

Therefore, when it comes to terrorist attacks launched against submarine cables outside the territorial sea of any coastal State, it is the rationale for universal jurisdiction over piracy, rather than any analogy with acts of piracy, that is important when considering the possibility for universal jurisdiction over intentional damage to submarine cables. As discussed earlier, Article 113 of UNCLOS only lays down national jurisdiction and flag State jurisdiction for breaking and injury of a submarine cable on the high seas and in the EEZs, which is not sufficient to provide effective protection over the extensive submarine cable systems across the globe. Any intentional damage and destruction of a submarine cable for purposes of terrorism can easily go unpunished, which is in essence similar with that of piracy. Consequently, based on the same rationale, international efforts may be devoted to establishing universal jurisdiction over acts of terrorism on submarine cables outside the territory of any State. Currently, such a designation is more of *lex ferenda* than of *lex lata*, as there has not been such an incident of terrorist attack on submarine cables. However, once the importance and vulnerability of submarine cables is fully appreciated by governments (as well as by terrorists), the rationale underlying the universal jurisdiction over piracy may be effectively relied on to justify

---

72 See Nandan and Rosenne, n. 69 above, p. 200.
73 See Lowe, n. 40 above, p. 348.
74 Article 101 of UNCLOS, n. 9 above, provides: "All States shall cooperate to the fullest possible extent in the repression of piracy on the high seas or in any other place outside the jurisdiction of any State."

assertion of jurisdiction over intentional damage to submarine cables in places beyond the territorial jurisdiction of the State.

Protection of Submarine Cables in the Age of Counter-Terrorism

Previous parts focus on the law of the sea and general international law in order to establish coastal States' jurisdiction over terrorist attacks on submarine cables in maritime areas outside their territory. The effectiveness of this approach depends mainly on States adopting national legislation criminalizing intentional damage to submarine cables within their territory, which is not, however, the common practice. Aware of the problem of a lack of incentives on the part of governments, it is, therefore, helpful to turn to the legal framework of counter-terrorism and investigate whether this framework can provide the basis for the protection of submarine cables against acts of terrorism.

So far, the present study proceeds without giving a definition of terrorism. This is not because there is a common perception of terrorism under international law; quite the contrary, it is exactly because of international society's difficulty with agreeing on a universal definition of terrorism that there is no comprehensive treaty on counter-terrorism. For a long time, "terrorism" is a label rather than a legal concept – it can mean different things for different persons and is open to political abuse.[75] In 1996, the UN General Assembly set up an Ad Hoc Committee to work on a comprehensive convention on counter-terrorism, but no substantial progress has been achieved, mainly because of the lack of consensus on the question of whether the definition of terrorism should include activities against foreign occupation.[76] The stalemate

---

75 Higgins observed that "'[t]errorism' is a term without legal significance. It is merely a convenient way of alluding to activities, whether of States or of individuals, widely disapproved of and in which either the methods used are unlawful, or the targets protected, or both … The term is at once a shorthand to allude to a variety of problems with some common elements, and a method of indicating community condemnation for the conduct concerned." R. Higgins, "The general international law of terrorism," in *Terrorism and International Law*, ed. R. Higgins and M. Flory (London/New York: Routledge, 1997), pp. 13–29, p. 28.

76 No sessions of the Ad Hoc Committee were held since 2014. The most recent development is that in its resolution 71/151 of 13 December 2016 the UN General Assembly decided to recommend that the Sixth Committee, at the seventy-second session of the General Assembly, establish a working group with a view to finalizing the process on the draft comprehensive convention on international terrorism. According to the Chair of the Working Group, the view has been expressed that "in the absence of political agreement, the time had perhaps come to acknowledge that consensus was currently unattainable

of negotiating a comprehensive convention on counter-terrorism compels the thriving of the so-called "sector treaties" that deal with various criminal acts of terrorism without addressing the question of defining terrorism. For instance, the 2010 Convention on the Suppression of Unlawful Acts Relating to International Civil Aviation criminalizes a number of acts constituting new and emerging threats against civil aviation, including the act of using civil aircraft as a weapon to cause death, injury, or damage (the form of the terrorist attacks of September 11).[77] Yet, this convention is not concerned with defining "terrorism" as a legal concept.

As the legal framework of counter-terrorism is developing rapidly, it is of interest to ask whether this legal framework may provide some insight for closing the security gaps in the protection of submarine cables against acts of terrorism. In the following section, this article will explore various aspects of the legal framework of counter-terrorism in relation to the protection of submarine cables against acts of terrorism. First, it will discuss whether States could follow the path of the "sector treaty" approach to adopt a global treaty on the protection of submarine cables against terrorism. Next, it will examine the broadening definition of terrorism in international treaties and national legislation and how it may accommodate the need to protect submarine cables against acts of terrorism. Finally, the question of the "war on terror" rhetoric and its influence on protection of submarine cables will also be discussed.

The "Sector Treaty" Approach

The "sector treaty" approach represents a piecemeal approach to counter-terrorism, in that such a convention criminalizes a particular act or a group of acts that may be carried out by terrorists without defining terrorism. The sector treaty approach is thus a compromise strategy due to the lack of consensus of the international community on a comprehensive convention dealing with counter-terrorism.

As pointed out by Boyle and Chinkin, the drafting of the sector treaties shares a consistent pattern: "definition of the specific offence, its criminalisation under national law, the assertion of wide-based national jurisdiction, integration with extradition regimes and states' obligation to prosecute or

---

and that consultations should be suspended." See UNGA, "Sixth Committee, Summary Record of the 31st Meeting (4 November 2016)," *General Assembly Official Records*, UN Doc. A/C.6/71/SR.31 (2 December 2016), p. 7.

[77] See 2010 Convention on the Suppression of Unlawful Acts Relating to International Civil Aviation (Beijing, 10 September 2010), United Nations Office of Counter-Terrorism, available online: <http://www.un.org/en/counterterrorism/legal-instruments.shtml>.

extradite alleged offenders present on their territory."[78] The last element is crucial, which is known as the *aut dedere, aut judicare* provision. In essence, the practical effect of these counter-terrorism treaties is to establish the universal jurisdiction between the parties to the convention and to facilitate international cooperation through the extension of jurisdiction, in order to ensure that the offenders of crimes of common concern do not escape prosecution or punishment.[79] The sector treaty approach has constituted the most important basis for the extension of jurisdiction over terrorist activities.

It seems that the sector treaty approach may provide a useful and practical method for States to strengthen international cooperation in terms of protection of submarine cables against terrorist attacks. Some scholars have argued that a global convention on protection of submarine cables against intentional damage may be modelled on the sector treaty approach.[80] The prospect of negotiating such a convention is not quite remote, in particular against the background that there are already counter-terrorism treaties in respect of infrastructure. The 1988 Protocol for the Suppression of Unlawful Acts Against the Safety of Fixed Platforms Located on the Continental Shelf (1988 Protocol) is an example.[81] The 1988 Protocol establishes a legal regime applicable to criminal acts committed against fixed platforms on the continental shelf, such as destroying a fixed platform or causing damage to it, which is likely to endanger its safety.[82] According to the 1988 Protocol, each State party has jurisdiction if the offense is committed against or on board a fixed platform while it is located on the continental shelf of that State, or by its national of that State.[83] Jurisdiction may also be asserted if the offense is committed by a stateless person who resides in that State; if, during the commission of the offense, a national of that State is seized, threatened, injured, or killed; or, if the offense is committed in an attempt to compel that State to do or abstain from doing any act.[84] Accordingly, State parties to the 1988 Protocol could assert jurisdiction on a variety of bases, which may significantly enhance international

---

78 A. Boyle and C. Chinkin, *The Making of International Law* (New York: Oxford University Press, 2007), p. 4.
79 See Lowe, n. 40 above, pp. 349–350.
80 See Beckman, n. 5 above, pp. 290–294; Davenport, n. 26 above, p. 221.
81 The 1988 Protocol was adopted and entered into force together with the Convention for the Suppression of Unlawful Acts Against the Safety of Maritime Navigation, n. 56 above. Both instruments entered into force on 1 March 1988.
82 1988 Protocol for the Suppression of Unlawful Acts Against the Safety of Fixed Platforms Located on the Continental Shelf, 1678 *United Nations Treaty Series* 304, art. 2(c).
83 Id., art. 3(1).
84 Id., art. 3(2).

cooperation to punish and prevent the offenses that the Protocol criminalized. So far, there are 155 States parties to the 1998 Protocol.

There is no doubt that the sector treaty approach is pragmatic and can be effective if it ensures wide participation. As the aim of such an international treaty is to oblige the parties to criminalize the relevant acts under their national laws and to provide the basis of jurisdiction once the alleged offender is found within the territory of a State party, it may contribute to closing the security gap under the law of the sea, in particular with regard to the jurisdiction of coastal States. Nevertheless, this approach may encounter the same problem of States' lack of incentive. Where States are reluctant to implement Article 113 of UNCLOS, it may be even more difficult to convince States that there is a need to negotiate a global treaty on the protection of submarine cables against intentional damage, as, in essence, the obligations remain the same, and States may have yet to feel the necessity to establish an international cooperative network to prevent and punish intentional damage to submarine cables.

Another difficulty with initiating the negotiation of a global treaty on protection of submarine cables against terrorism is the lack of a lead international agency. Beckman explained in detail why certain international agencies, such as the UN specialized agency International Telecommunication Union, or the UN Division of Ocean Affairs and Law of the Sea, are either uninterested or unable to undertake an initiative on a global treaty on submarine cables protection.[85] It is recalled that the 1988 Protocol was negotiated together with the Convention for the Suppression of Unlawful Acts Against the Safety of Maritime Navigation under the auspices of the International Maritime Organization.[86] The lack of a leading UN agency or a competent international organization may be a handicap because there is no apt forum to bring the relevant participants together. In addition, there is no experienced treaty negotiations support without a leading agency, unless there are strong incentives from States, which is unfortunately not the case, at least for the time being.

Therefore, although the sector treaty approach provides a useful and practical method to combat terrorism, and the patterns followed by the counter-terrorism treaties may be effectively transformed into a global treaty on protection of submarine cables against terrorism, it is unlikely that the sector treaty approach can be used in the near future due to the lack of incentives for States to

---

85   See Beckman, n. 5 above, pp. 293–294.
86   See the negotiating history of the Convention for the Suppression of Unlawful Acts Against the Safety of Maritime Navigation and the 1988 Protocol, International Maritime Organization, available online: <http://www.imo.org/en/About/Conventions/ListOfConventions/Pages/SUA-Treaties.aspx>.

criminalize intentional damage to submarine cables and the lack of a leading international agency.

A Broadening Definition of Terrorism

Whereas States may not have adopted national legislation that explicitly criminalizes intentional damage to submarine cables within their territory, protection of submarine cables against acts of terrorism may nevertheless find legal basis from counter-terrorism legislation. This prospect is optimistic because of the current development of a broadening definition of terrorism in national legislation as well as in regional and international treaties, which tend to include crimes against property or infrastructure within the ambit of terrorism.

Even though there is no universal definition of terrorism, national laws, regional, and international treaties share the common approach to defining terrorism by reference to the objective element and the subjective element of crime. In general, the objective element refers to a crime of a certain scale, which is already criminalized under national laws (e.g., murder, mass killing, kidnapping, or bombing, etc.). As to the subjective element, national legislation is broadly uniform in holding that the intention of the perpetrators is to provoke a state of terror in the population or to coerce a State or an international organization to take some sort of action.[87] Nevertheless, there has not been consistency regarding whether the perpetrators advance a political, religious, or other ideological cause.[88] For the purpose of the present study, it is the objective element of defining terrorism that is directly relevant.

For a long time, the most uncontroversial element of defining terrorism was the use of serious violence against persons as a means of terrorist action.[89] The 1973 Convention on the Prevention and Punishment of Crimes Against Internationally Protected Persons and the 1979 International Convention against the Taking of Hostages represent an early international consensus to fight this form of terrorism. The 1999 International Convention for the Suppression of the Financing of Terrorism, which almost acquired the status of a universal treaty with 188 parties, defines terrorism as any act "intended to cause death or serious bodily injury to a civilian, or to any other person not taking an active part in the hostilities in a situation of armed conflict" with the purpose of intimidating a population or compelling a government or an international

---

87 See A. Cassese, "The multifaceted criminal notion of terrorism in international law," *Journal of International Criminal Justice* 4 (2006): 933–958, p. 937.
88 See C. Walter, "Defining terrorism in national and international law," in *Terrorism as a Challenge for National and International Law: Security versus Liberty?*, eds. C. Walter et al. (Berlin/Heidelberg: Springer, 2004), pp. 23–43, p. 29.
89 Id., p. 27.

organization to do or to abstain from doing any act.[90] Defining terrorism as violence against persons is also reflected in the Security Council's resolutions on combatting terrorism.[91]

Recent national legislation, however, endorses a broadening definition of terrorism, which includes offenses against public or private properties or infrastructure. For instance, under the legislation of the United Kingdom, the objective element of terrorism includes the use or threat of action involving serious violence against a person or serious damage to property, endangering a person's life, creating a serious risk to the health or safety of the public, or is designed to seriously interfere with or seriously disrupt an electronic system.[92] It is therefore reasonable to expect that terrorist attacks launched against submarine cables that land in the United Kingdom may be qualified as "a serious damage to property" or "seriously to interfere with or seriously to disrupt an electronic system."[93] Similarly, under the *Australian Criminal Code Act*, acts of terrorism include action that "causes serious damage to property,"[94] and action that "seriously interferes with, seriously disrupts, or destroys, an electronic system." The electronic system so defined includes a telecommunication system or in fact any system that is "used for, or by, an essential public utility."[95] Likewise, under the *Immigration and Nationality Act* of the United

---

90 International Convention for the Suppression of the Financing of Terrorism, New York, 9 December 1999 (entered into force 10 April 2002), 2178 *United Nations Treaty Series* 197, art. 2(1)(b).

91 UN Security Council Resolution 1566 defines terrorism as "criminal acts, including against civilians, committed with the intent to cause death or serious bodily injury, or taking of hostages, with the purpose to provoke a state of terror in the general public or in a group of persons or particular persons, intimidate a population or compel a government or an international organization to do or to abstain from doing any act." This was the first time that the Security Council gave a working definition of terrorism given the absence of international consensus. See B. Saul, "Definition of 'Terrorism' in the UN Security Council: 1985–2004," *Chinese Journal of International Law* 4, no. 1 (2005): 141–166, pp. 164–165.

92 See G. Rainer, "Country Report on the United Kingdom," in Walter et al., n. 88 above, p. 593.

93 The subjective element for terrorism under the legislation of the United Kingdom is defined as "to influence the government or to intimidate the public or a section of the public ... for the purpose of advancing a political, religious or ideological clause." Section 1 of the Terrorism Act 2000, id., p. 593.

94 *Australian Criminal Code Act 1995* (No. 12, 1995), s. 100.1(2)(b), available online: <https://www.legislation.gov.au/Details/C2017C00408>.

95 According to Section 100.1(2)(f) of the *Australian Criminal Code Act 1995*, id., an "electronic system" includes, but is not limited to, (i) an information system; or (ii) a telecommunications system; or (iii) a financial system; or (iv) a system used for the delivery of essential government services; or (v) a system used for, or by, an essential public utility; or (vi) a system used for, or by, a transport system.

States, "terrorist activity" also refers to "substantial damage to property."[96] Some other counter-terrorism laws do not refer to particular criminal acts, but are construed broadly to govern acts of violence with a particular intention as "to eliminate the democratic order,"[97] or with overall effects as "to disrupt the State's interior and external security."[98] These counter-terrorism laws are therefore flexible enough to accommodate intentional damage to submarine cables. Reviewing national legislation, it has been suggested that "there seems to be a development that broadens existing definitions of terrorism into a direction of including violent and non-violent but nevertheless destructive action against public facilities."[99]

Accordingly, even if a State has not specifically criminalized intentional damage to submarine cables, its national counter-terrorism law may be invoked to serve the same purpose of punishing terrorist attacks against submarine cables, in accordance with a broad definition of terrorism. This approach has the advantage of filling in the security gap of protecting submarine cables. As well, because of the magnitude of the threat of terrorism to society, the penalties under counter-terrorism legislation are usually severe enough to deter or to punish the relevant criminal acts.[100]

The broadening definition of terrorism is also discernible in regional legal frameworks. Under the legal framework of the European Union, "terrorist offences" include those "causing extensive destruction to a Government or public facility, a transport system, an infrastructure facility, including an information system, a fixed platform located on the continental shelf, a public place or private property likely to endanger human life or result in major economic loss."[101] This definition is notable in that a result of major economic loss would suffice to satisfy the objective element of a terrorist offense, which reflects the

---

96 See Walter, n. 92 above, p. 27, citing 8 *United States Code* §1182(a)(3)(B).
97 In the Italian criminal code, terrorism is defined in Section 270-bis, and it concerns "[a]ssociations aiming at terrorism and the elimination of the democratic order." This definition has not been amended by the new legislation adopted after 11 September 2001. See K. Oellers-Frahm, "Country Report on Italy," in Walter et al., n. 88 above, p. 428.
98 Turkey's *Anti-Terror Law* (1991), s. 1(1), see N. Guney, "Country Report on Turkey," in Walter et al., n. 88 above, p. 559.
99 Walter, n. 92 above, p. 27.
100 For example, under the *Australian Criminal Code Act 1995*, n. 94 above, s. 101.1(1), the penalty for a person who commits the offense of engaging in a terrorist attack is imprisonment for life.
101 Directive (EU) 2017/541 of the European Parliament and of the Council of 15 March 2017 on combating terrorism and replacing Council Framework Decision 2002/475/JHA and amending Council Decision 2005/671/JHA, art. 3(1)(d), available online: <http://eur-lex.europa.eu/legal-content/EN/TXT/PDF/?uri=CELEX:32017L0541&from=EN>.

awareness of the legislature to protect critical infrastructure that may be exposed to the threat of terrorism. In addition, Article 19 of the EU Directive provides that each Member State shall take the necessary measures to establish jurisdiction over the terrorist offenses if, *inter alia*, "the offence is committed in whole or in part in its territory," or "the offence is committed against the institutions or people of the Member State in question," and that "each Member State may extend its jurisdiction if the offence is committed in the territory of another Member State."[102] These provisions on jurisdiction build an extensive network of available bases of jurisdiction and thus enhance the effectiveness of the fight against terrorism within the regional legal framework.

The draft comprehensive convention on international terrorism also adopts a broad definition of terrorism. In the newest draft proposed by the Ad Hoc Committee, a person commits an offense under the convention if that person causes "serious damage to public or private property, including a place of public use, a State or government facility, a public transportation system, an infrastructure facility or to the environment," or damage to the above-mentioned properties, places, facilities, or systems "resulting or likely to result in major economic loss."[103] This provision has the same effect as that of the EU legislation. Although the draft comprehensive convention has not progressed since 2013, the real dispute about the definition is concerned with an alleged exception for the activities of those who fight against foreign occupation.[104] The inclusion of offenses against properties, places, facilities, and systems is, however, not subject to the divergence of opinions on the definition. On the contrary, this broadening aspect of the definition is in accord with the developments in national and regional laws. Therefore, it could be reasonably expected that the draft comprehensive convention may be finalized without changing these aspects of the definition.

To sum up, the current developments in defining terrorism in national and international law witness a broadening definition of terrorism that reflects the increasing awareness of States to protect facilities and infrastructure that are deemed essential and critical to national security and well-being. Accordingly,

---

102   Id., art. 19(1)(a) and (e).
103   Article 2(b) and (c) of the draft comprehensive convention on international terrorism prepared by the Bureau, Annex I to UNGA, "Report of the Ad Hoc Committee Established by General Assembly Resolution 51/210 of 17 December 1996, Sixteenth Session (8 to 12 April 2013)," *General Assembly Official Records Sixty-Eighth Session Supplement No. 37*, UN Doc. A/68/37 (2013).
104   See A. Bianchi, "Enforcing international law norms against terrorism: Achievements and prospects," in *Enforcing International Law Norms Against Terrorism*, eds. A. Bianchi and Y. Naqvi (Oxford and Portland, Oregon: Hart Publishing, 2004), pp. 491–534, p. 496.

the protection of submarine cables against acts of terrorism can be accommodated within the counter-terrorism legal frameworks endorsing such a broad definition of terrorism. By referring to national counter-terrorism legislation, it avoids the difficulties with creating and negotiating a specific treaty on the protection of submarine cables. This approach could usefully complement the protection of submarine cables under UNCLOS.

"War on Terror" and Protection of Submarine Cables

The protection of submarine cables may be suspended during times of war as it has been confirmed in State practice that submarine cables are legitimate wartime targets.[105] Article XV of the 1884 Convention explicitly provides that "it is understood that the stipulations of the present Convention do not in any way restrict the freedom of action of belligerents." The military and strategic value of submarine cables nowadays is even more significant than a hundred years ago. Without agreement to the contrary, there is no reason to doubt that submarine cables can be legitimately destructed for military purposes during war. An interesting question thus arises as to whether the "war on terror" rhetoric, which tends to magnify the military implications of the fight against terrorism, would have the same effect as legitimizing the destruction of submarine cables by terrorists, as if there was a war proper between the terrorists and a State.

This is hardly the case. While "war on terror" may be powerful rhetoric to characterize the fight of the States led by the United States against the terrorist groups or international terrorism, it is not a legal concept that serves normative purposes under international law. Whether there is a war proper between terrorists and a State is a question to be examined under the *jus ad bellum* (the law governing use of force) and *jus in bellum* (the rules of behaviors in the warfare).[106] The UN Charter prohibits the use of force with two exceptions: self-defense and the use of force authorized by the Security Council.[107]

---

105 See D.R. Burnett, T.M. Davenport and R. Beckman, "Overview of the international legal regime governing submarine cables," in Burnett et al., n. 5 above, p. 66.

106 See M. Sassòli, "Terrorism and war," *Journal of International Criminal Justice* 4, no. 5 (2006): 959–981, pp. 960–966.

107 Article 2(4) of the UN Charter prohibits the use of force by providing: "All Members shall refrain in their international relations from the threat or use of force against the territorial integrity or political independence of any state, or in any other manner inconsistent with the Purposes of the United Nations." Article 51 of the UN Charter provides that "nothing in the present Charter shall impair the inherent right of individual or collective self-defence if an armed attack occurs against a Member of the United Nations." Article 42 allows the Security Council to use measures involving the use of force to maintain or restore international peace and security.

The ICJ confirms that self-defense can only be triggered against an armed attack from a State.[108] Hence, terrorist attacks cannot constitute "armed attacks" unless they can be attributed to a State. In this regard, terrorist attacks should be reacted to as criminal acts rather than acts of war. However, after September 11, the right to self-defense claimed by the United States against Al-Qaeda and Afghanistan met with universal support, and the United States' military reaction to the terrorist attacks may signal the broadening scope of the *jus ad bellum*.[109] Nevertheless, a significant factor of September 11 was that the intensity of the terrorist attacks may have amounted to an armed attack.[110] In cases where the intensity of the violence has not reached the proper standards of an armed attack and cannot be attributed to a State, State practice has not acknowledged that terrorist attacks by private groups may trigger an armed conflict.[111] Indeed, the "war on terror" may sound counter-intuitive in international law, as terror as such cannot be regarded as a party to an armed conflict. It is, therefore, more of a rhetoric that describes the fight against an international criminal phenomenon than an accurate legal characterization.

Notwithstanding the strict standards for an armed conflict to take shape, it is possible for there to be armed conflicts between a State and terrorist groups as properly understood. In such a context, the destruction of submarine cables by the belligerents for military purposes can be legitimate. This point may find relevance in the contemporary military fight against terrorism, for instance in the armed conflict between the Syrian government and the Islamic State in Iraq and the Levant, the latter being characterized by the Security Council as a terrorist group and a threat to international peace and security.[112] Because of

---

108 In the *Wall* advisory opinion, the International Court of Justice simply observed that "Article 51 of the Charter thus recognizes the existence of an inherent right of self-defence in the case of armed attack *by one State* against another State" (emphasis added) without elaborating on the issue. *Legal Consequences of the Construction of a Wall in the Occupied Palestinian Territory*, Advisory Opinion, I.C.J. Reports 2004, p.136, at p. 194, para. 139.

109 See C.J. Tams, "The use of force against terrorists," *European Journal of International Law* 20, no. 2 (2009): 359–397, p. 378. Subsequent practice also confirms the tendency that States invoke self-defense against non-State actors without proving the involvement of a State in these terrorist attacks. See L. O'Connor, "Legality of the use of force in Syria against Islamic State and the Khorasan Group," *Journal on the Use of Force and International Law* 3, no. 1 (January 2, 2016): 70–96, p. 84.

110 See B. Simma et al., eds., "Article 51," in *The Charter of the United Nations: A Commentary*, 3rd ed. (Oxford: Oxford University Press, 2012), Volume II, pp. 1397–1428, p. 1416.

111 See Sassòli, n. 106 above, p. 965.

112 For instance, the Security Council Resolution 2370 reaffirms that "terrorism in all forms and manifestations constitutes one of the most serious threats to international peace and security and that any acts of terrorism are criminal and unjustifiable regardless of their motivations, whenever, wherever and by whomsoever committed" and urges member

the acknowledgment of the existence of a non-international armed conflict,[113] should there be any attacks by the terrorist group on submarine cables as part of military strategy, these acts should be assessed in the context of *jus in bellum*, which is arguably the *lex specialis* under this circumstance. The principle of distinction and proportionality should be governing in this respect. The principle of distinction requires that, *inter alia*, the parties to the conflict must at all times distinguish between civilian objects and military objectives and that attacks may only be directed against military objectives.[114] As far as submarine cables are concerned, they may be regarded as legitimate military objectives,[115] if they make an effective contribution to military action and offer a definite military advantage. As for dual-use facilities, those that are used for both civil and military purposes, the classification of these submarine cables depends on the application of the definition of a military objective.[116]

Accordingly, whereas the "war on terror" rhetoric is not a meaningful concept that carries legal consequences, the possibility of armed conflicts between terrorists and States is not excluded. As a result, the customary rule that

---

      States to prevent trade, economic, or other ties with the ISIL, Al-Qaeda and their associated individuals, entities and groups. See United Nations, Security Council, "Resolution 2370 (2017)," UN Doc. S/RES/2370 (2017) (2 August 2017).

113   The International Committee of the Red Cross announced in July 2012 that the violence in Syria had reached the threshold of a non-international armed conflict. See RULAC, "Non-International Armed Conflicts in Syria," available online: <http://www.rulac.org/browse/conflicts/non-international-armed-conflicts-in-syria#collapse3accord>.

114   See Rule 7 of Customary International Humanitarian Law endorsed by the International Committee of Red Cross. J.-M. Henckaerts and L. Doswald-Beck, *Customary International Humanitarian Law: Volume I Rules* (New York: Cambridge University Press, 2005), p. 25.

115   "Military objectives" under international humanitarian law are defined as those "by their nature, location, purpose or use make an effective contribution to military action and whose partial or total destruction, capture or neutralisation, in the circumstances ruling at the time, offers a definite military advantage." See Rule 8 of Customary International Humanitarian Law, Henckaerts and Doswald-Beck, id., p. 29.

116   It is suggested that "State practice often cites establishments, buildings and positions where enemy combatants, their materiel and armaments are located, and military means of transportation and communication as examples of military objectives." According to the United States Military Manual concerning the rule on public and private property in occupied territory, submarine cables connecting an occupied territory with a neutral territory shall not be seized or destroyed except in the case of absolute necessity. However, this provision applies only to activities on land and does not deal with seizure or destruction of cables in the open sea. As a consequence, the destruction or seizure of submarine cables in the sea is subject to a lesser stringent when the cables connect an occupied territory with a neutral territory. See Henckaerts and Doswald-Beck, n. 114 above, p. 32; International Committee of the Red Cross, "U.S. Practice Relating to Rule 51. Public and Private Property in Occupied Territory," Customary IHL Database, available online: <https://ihl-databases.icrc.org/customary-ihl/eng/docs/v2_cou_us_rule51>.

submarine cables are legitimate wartime targets may again find relevance in the current state of counter-terrorism, in which the fight against terrorism may accelerate into an armed conflict between States on the one hand, and terrorist groups on the other hand, as illustrated by the Syrian crises. Consequently, the discussion on the protection of submarine cables should not overlook this dimension of the rules governing the protection of submarine cables.

Conclusion

Due to the indispensable service of submarine cables in economic, social, and military communications, the risk of submarine cables being targeted by terrorists cannot be underestimated. This article explores the potential of international law to protect submarine cables, and it is aimed at contributing to the cross-fertilization of the law of the sea and the legal framework of counter-terrorism, as the issue of protecting submarine cables against acts of terrorism can be examined from both perspectives.

Under the law of the sea and in particular UNCLOS, the protection of submarine cables is not sufficient or effective because many States have not implemented Article 113 to criminalize acts of breaking or injury of a submarine cable beneath the high seas or the EEZ, or the penalties in this regard cannot fulfill the objective of preventing and punishing the criminal acts. More importantly, the involvement of coastal States to protect submarine cables that land in their territory is not fully appreciated under UNCLOS. However, it is argued that the traditional built-in tension between activities of coastal States and activities relating to submarine cables should be reconsidered because of the increasing importance of submarine cables for coastal States as well as for the international community as a whole. Notwithstanding the private origin of submarine cables, the practical effect of the extensive submarine cables systems across the globe attests to the nature of submarine cables as international common goods. Effective repair and maintenance of submarine cables, which are integral to the freedom related to submarine cables, can contribute to minimizing the risk of disruption of communicative services and should not be subject to excessive regulation by coastal States. The State practice concerning cable protection zones should also be welcome, though the legal basis for the practices should be firmly grounded in international law.

Under international law, the objective territorial jurisdiction and the protective jurisdiction tend to lend support for the extension of coastal States' prescriptive jurisdiction over terrorist attacks launched against submarine cables in areas outside their territory. Nevertheless, the enforcement jurisdiction, which is critical for the effective protection of submarine cables in danger of damage or destruction, is still lacking because of the exclusive flag State jurisdiction on the high seas. On the other hand, universal jurisdiction over intentional damage to submarine cables outside the territory of any State can be envisaged by analogy with the rationale for universal jurisdiction over piracy.

Other than UNCLOS and general international law, a major contribution of the article is to accommodate the protection of submarine cables in current counter-terrorism legislation. Despite the potential of negotiating an international treaty which models on counter-terrorism treaties, it is submitted that the trend of broadening the definition of terrorism to include attacks against property and infrastructure can effectively inhibit acts of terrorism on submarine cables. This point is not trivial, as it has the advantage of utilizing existing national legislation which is in general severe enough to punish terrorist activities. By envisaging that the security gap in UNCLOS to protect submarine cables may be filled by the counter-terrorism regimes, it bypasses the unfortunate problem of a lack of incentives or knowledge on the part of governments to protect submarine cables.

On the other hand, the military approach represented by the "war on terror" rhetoric in the fight against terrorism may also bring in the custom that submarine cables are legitimate wartime targets. It is argued that this aspect of the rules on submarine cables should be highlighted in the age of counter-terrorism, in which an armed conflict between terrorist groups and States is not just speculation. As a result, the discussion on the protection of submarine cables should be carried out with the awareness of distinguishing the applicable law in accordance with the circumstances. In times of armed conflict, the *jus in bellum* prevails as the *lex specialis* and submarine cables may fall within the category of legitimate military targets, whereas, in peacetime, UNCLOS and counter-terrorism legislation provide the legal basis for the protection of submarine cables.

Regulating Ship-generated Noise as a New Form of Vessel-source Pollution

Till Markus
Helmholtz Centre for Environmental Research - UFZ, Leipzig, Germany

Pedro Pablo Silva Sánchez
Research Centre of European Environmental Law, University of Bremen, Bremen, Germany

Introduction

This article expounds on the challenges to regulate ship-generated noise as a new form of vessel-source pollution. It concentrates on noise in the marine environment resulting from regular vessel operations and technology-based activities carried out from vessels. To this end, it provides technological background information, explains the potential effects of noise emissions in the marine environment, and reviews existing laws that govern different uses of ships generating noise that may be harmful to marine fauna.

Anthropogenic noise introduced into the marine environment, or "underwater noise," has gained increased attention from scientific bodies, the media, non-governmental organizations (NGOs), as well as international institutions such as the United Nations General Assembly.[1] This attention largely originated

---

1 T. Markus and P.P. Silva Sánchez, "Managing and regulating underwater noise pollution," in *Handbook on Marine Environment Protection*, eds. M. Salomon and T. Markus (Cham, Switzerland: Springer, 2018), ch. 52. In 2005, the United Nations General Assembly (UNGA) encouraged further studies on the impacts of ocean noise on marine living resources: UNGA, "Resolution: Oceans and the Law of the Sea," UN Doc. A/RES/60/30 (2005), para. 84. From then on, every year's UNGA Resolution on "Oceans and the Law of the Sea" have identified "ocean noise" as an important topic, the last one being in 2017. In this case, going beyond the earlier Resolutions, the UNGA noted that ocean noise is not merely a potential threat to living marine resources, but has potential for significant adverse impacts on living marine resources. Also, it noted the approval of the International Maritime Organization (IMO) Guidelines for the Reduction of Underwater Noise from Commercial Shipping to Address Adverse Impacts on Marine Life and encouraged further research into technologies to reduce the impact of underwater noise on marine life. UNGA, "Resolution: Oceans and the Law of the Sea," UN Doc. A/RES/72/73 (2017), ss. 271–273; European Parliament Resolution on the environment effects of high-intensity active naval sonars, European Parliament, Abl. 2005 No. C174 E/186 (14 July 2005).

from a growing number of whale stranding incidents resulting from the use of mid- and low-frequency sonar by military ships. However, apart from these transient noise events, there is a myriad of other anthropogenic sources generating noise that are potentially harmful in the marine environment. Against this background, a justified fear is mounting that underwater noise pollution may burden the marine environment to the point that it harms or even kills marine mammals, fish, and other ocean wildlife.[2]

In general, the term noise refers to a sound that may cause negative effects.[3] Sources of underwater noise can be natural (e.g., waves, earthquakes, and marine animals), or anthropogenic. Sources of anthropogenic underwater noise can be found in the airspace (e.g., aircraft), on land (e.g., shore-based construction, including bridges and coastal buildings), or at sea. At sea, there are at least three distinguishable groups of sources of anthropogenic noise. First, there is noise emitted by regular vessel operations. This source includes, for example, all commercial shipping, fishing, naval and scientific activities, recreational boating, as well as whale, dolphin, or other marine mammal watching. Second, noise generated by technology-based activities carried out from vessels. Some of these technologies are intentionally used to introduce noise effects to the sea. They include active sonar (military and civil), seismic surveys (using airguns), playback and sound exposure experiments, and other acoustic technologies such as acoustic positioning devices, or acoustic deterrent or harassment devices used by the fishing industry. This category also includes other activities carried out from vessels and which, although not primarily intended to do so, introduce noise to the sea. These activities encompass, for example, deep-sea ocean drilling (using drill ships) by the oil and gas industry, and near and offshore construction (using pile-driving vessels). Third, noise produced by other non-vessel-related sources. These may include, for instance, explosions, dredging, piling and other construction activities associated with near and offshore infrastructures (e.g., wind farms, tidal energy installations, oil and gas platforms, harbor development, etc.) and their regular operations.

Today, the major anthropogenic noise source is regular ship operations, particularly resulting from commercial shipping.[4] Regular ship operations mainly generate continuous noise. It mostly results from propeller cavitation and onboard machinery.[5] The level of noise radiated varies depending on ship size,

---

2 See references below in section on "Underwater Noise Pollution as a Threat to Marine Life."
3 Agreement on the Conservation of Cetaceans of the Black Sea, the Mediterranean Sea and the Contiguous Atlantic Area (ACCOBAMS), "Methodological guide: Guidance on underwater noise mitigation measures," MOP5/2013/Doc 24 (2013), p. 4.
4 Id., p. 4.
5 Continuous noise is also produced by some technology-based activities from ships such as seafloor drilling (by drill ships), see Expert Workshop on Underwater Noise and its Impacts on

technical properties of the machinery, speed, degree of maintenance, mode of propulsion, and other operational characteristics.[6] It is estimated today that commercial shipping accounts for more than 75 percent of all anthropogenic underwater noise.[7] The sharp growth of commercial shipping over the last fifteen years (the world commercial fleet has doubled since 2001)[8] has resulted in, at least, a 20 to 35 dB increase in noise levels.[9] The overall noise level produced by ships is projected to increase greatly in the years to come, especially in coastal areas.[10]

Technology-based activities carried out from vessels mainly produce impulsive noise, that is, sound that is emitted by a specific source, which comprises one or more pulses of short duration with long gaps between pulses.[11] Major sources of impulsive noise include low-, mid- and high-frequency sonar, seismic survey technology (mainly airguns), and marine construction technology (mainly pile-driving).[12] Sonars are used for military purposes (e.g., detecting other ships), scientific studies (mapping and surveying the seabed or water column), navigation, fishing (finding or tracking fish shoals), and for different purposes in the various offshore industries, including, but not limited to, oil and gas extraction.[13]

Marine and Coastal Biodiversity, Report of the Expert Workshop on Underwater Noise and its Impacts on Marine and Coastal Biodiversity (UNEP/CBD/MCB/EM/2014/1/2), annex III, s. 8.

6 M.F. McKenna et al., "Underwater radiated noise from modern commercial ships," *Journal of the Acoustical Society of America* 131 (2012): 92–103, p. 92; A.T. Johansson and M.H. Andersson, *Ambient Underwater Noise Levels at Norra Midsjöbanken during Construction of the Nord Stream Pipeline* (Stockholm: Swedish Defence Research Agency – FOI, 2012), p. 8; P.T. Arveson and D.J. Vendittis, "Radiated noise characteristics of a modern cargo ship," *Journal of the Acoustical Society of America* 107 (2000): 118–129.

7 B.L. Southall et al., "Underwater noise from large commercial ships: International collaboration for noise reduction," *Encyclopedia of Maritime and Offshore Engineering* (2017), pp. 1–9; International Council for the Exploration of the Seas (ICES), "Report of the Ad-hoc Group on the Impacts of Sonar on Cetaceans and Fish (AGISC)," CM 2006/ACE:06 (Copenhagen, 2005), p. 39.

8 Expert Workshop on Underwater Noise, n. 5 above, annex III, s. 8.

9 D. Ross, "On ocean underwater ambient noise," *Acoustic Bulletin* 18 (1993): 5–8; R.K. Andrew et al., "Ocean ambient sound: Comparing the 1960s with the 1990s for a receiver off the California coast," *Acoustic Research Letters Online* 3 (2002): 65–70; D. Wittekind, "The increasing noise level in the sea: A challenge for ship technology?," Paper given at the 104th Congress of the German Society for Maritime Technology (Schwentinental, 2009), p. 1. See also Southall et al., n. 7 above.

10 Southall et al., id., pp. 1–9; ICES, n. 7 above, p. 39.

11 ACCOBAMS, n. 3 above, p. 4; A.J. van der Graaf et al., "European Marine Strategy Framework Directive: Good Environmental Status (MSFD GES): Report of the Technical Subgroup on Underwater noise and other forms of energy" (2012), p. 11.

12 ACCOBAMS, n. 3 above, p. 4; Expert Workshop on Underwater Noise, n. 5 above, annex III, s. 7.

13 O. Boebel et al., "Input of energy/underwater ound," in Salomon and Markus, n. 1 above, pp. 463–485.

Seismic surveys are mostly conducted for the exploration of oil and gas deposits under the sea floor or to examine the Earth's crust under the sea for geophysical research purposes.[14] Finally, marine construction triggers a wide range of noise sources. The instalment of large structures often requires the insertion of piles into the seafloor. Pile-driving vessels produce intense broadband impulsive sounds that can propagate many kilometers.

This article addresses the regulation of the two distinct sources of ship-generated noise, that is, regular operations and technology-based activities carried out from vessels. To this end, it provides an overview of the technological aspects of ship-generated noise emitted in the marine environment, explains some of the potential adverse effects of anthropogenic underwater noise in general and of vessel-produced noise in particular, highlights the challenges in regulating activities creating noise in the sea, and analyses the ongoing regulatory efforts addressing different types of noise pollution.

Underwater Noise Pollution as a Threat to Marine Life

Increasingly, studies have been carried out which examine the effects of noise on marine fauna caused by different activities.[15] They indicate that underwater noise can have adverse effects on marine mammals, fish, crustaceans, cephalopods, and bivalves.[16] Such effects may include damage to auditory organs (including physical damage as well as temporary or permanent auditory threshold shifts, that is, hearing loss), injuries to other body tissues and inner organs, or even the death of single specimens.[17] Also, underwater noise

---

14 This technology uses airguns, which are capable of producing very intense, loud pulses or shots. The reflections of those pulses or shots are then used to reproduce an image of the geological structures below the seafloor. Seismic surveys typically use from 6 to 40 (but often many more) airguns arranged in an array, and they all fire together. The whole surveying process may take months, during which time shots occur every 10–12 seconds. In some cases noise from these explosions can even be heard at distances of up to 4,000 km. See, for example, D.P. Nowacek and B.L. Southall, *Effective Planning Strategies for Managing Environmental Risk Associated with Geophysical and Other Imaging Surveys: A Resource Guide for Managers* (Gland: IUCN, 2016); S.L. Nieukirk et al., "Sounds from airguns and fin whales recorded in the mid-Atlantic Ocean, 1999–2009," *Journal of the Acoustical Society of America* 131 (2012): 1102–1112.

15 Boebel et al., n. 13 above.

16 International Fund for Animal Welfare (IFAW), *Ocean Noise: Turn It Down* (Yarmouth Port: IFAW, 2008), pp. 16–25; ICES, n. 7 above, pp. 12–29; National Research Council (NRC), *Marine Mammal Populations and Ocean Noise: Determining when Noise Causes Biologically Significant Effects* (Washington, DC: NRC, 2005), pp. 83–108; Boebel et al., n. 13 above.

17 Boebel et al., id.

pollution may lead to aberrant behavioral responses, whether at the individual or group level. This could include changes in swimming, diving, and breathing patterns, as well as changes in communication (vocalization rate/amplitude).[18] All these effects are plausibly connected to stress and health problems such as cardiac arrhythmia, disorientation, or nitrogen oversaturation.[19] In addition, underwater noise can mask sounds made by marine species to communicate, orient themselves, or detect predators and prey.[20] It has also been pointed out that simultaneous and successive exposures to underwater noise as well as to other non-acoustic stressors (e.g., fishing activities, climate change, or chemical or physical pollution) must eventually be considered cumulatively when assessing the overall effects of noise on marine fauna.[21]

Comparatively little is known regarding the effects of underwater noise on fish, cephalopods, and bivalves.[22] Existing studies suggest, however, that these effects are to some extent similar to those sound can have on marine mammals.

To this day, there is no conclusive scientific evidence as to the extent that underwater noise pollution generated by regular ship operations cause damage to marine life. Yet, it has been proven to cause both stress on marine mammals as well as behavioral responses.[23] These in turn can initiate a series of consequences that could lead to life-function issues. In this connection, human-induced low frequency components of marine continuous or ambient noise have visibly increased during the last few decades. In the world's oceans, particularly in the northern hemisphere,[24] sound frequencies ranging between 10 Hz to 300 Hz are dominated by underwater noise pollution from regular ship operation. Such low frequency sounds can propagate very efficiently in the sea affecting marine biota over long distances.[25] Animals such as baleen whales

---

18   P.J. Miller, "Whale songs lengthen in response to sonar," *Nature* 405 (2000): 903–903.
19   Boebel et al., n. 13 above; see also B.I. Southall et al., "Marine mammal noise exposure criteria: Initial scientific recommendations," *Aquatic Mammals* 33 (2007): 411–509.
20   Boebel et al., id.
21   ICES, n. 7 above, pp. 36–38; C. Erbe, "International regulation of underwater noise," *Acoustics Australia* 41 (2013): 12–19.
22   ICES, id., pp. 44–48, 45; R.D. McCauley et al., "High intensity anthropogenic sound damages fish ears," *Journal of the Acoustical Society of America* 113 (2003): 638–642.
23   Southall et al., n. 7 above, pp. 1–9; also see L.S. Weilgart, "A brief review of known effects of noise on marine mammals," *International Journal of Comparative Psychology* 20 (2007): 159–169.
24   Wittekind, n. 7 above, p. 1.
25   Conservation and Development Problem Solving Team, Anthropogenic Noise in the Marine Environment – Potential Impacts on the Marine Resources of Stellwagen Bank and Channel Islands National Marine Sanctuaries. Prepared for the National Oceanic and Atmospheric Administration and the Marine Conservation Biology Institute (College

use low frequency ranges to communicate,[26] and this noise input hence masks their vocalization.[27] Their behavioral responses may range from evasion of the noise source, the abandonment of their habitat, or the modification of their vocalizations (e.g., cessation, amplification, frequency shifts).[28] Still, responses between different species vary greatly, mostly depending on their hearing sensitivity. Presumably, these phenomena are not limited to marine mammals; scientific evidence may suggest that hearing is widespread among virtually all fishes and elasmobranchs (such as sharks and rays) and that they are able to detect sounds from well below 50 Hz (some as low as 10 or 15 Hz) to upward of 500–1,000 Hz.[29]

Active onboard-sonars may produce a range of behavioral responses in marine animals. The effects usually depend on the signal characteristics, the species at issue, and the environmental context.[30] Meanwhile, noise inputs by seismic airguns and pile driving for construction purposes have the potential to cause primary injuries (e.g., acute injuries, lesions of interior tissues and clogging of blood vessels by bubbles) and auditory impairment in their direct vicinity.[31] All such injuries might lead directly or indirectly to death, e.g., by starvation or disorientation when hearing is permanently compromised.[32]

Challenges for Regulating Underwater Noise Pollution

The biggest challenge for the protection of the marine environment from underwater noise is the current knowledge gap.[33] Although concern about and understanding of the effects of underwater noise in the marine environment continues to grow, a significant lack of information still exists regarding the nature of underwater noise, the auditory ability of marine mammals and fish,

---

Park, 2000). p. 12, https://nmssanctuaries.blob.core.windows.net/sanctuaries-prod/media/archive/management/pdfs/anthro_noise.pdf.

26 A. Simcock, "Shipping," in Salomon and Markus, n. 1 above, ch. 6; Wittekind, n. 9 above, p. 1.
27 Weilgart, n. 23 above.
28 Boebel et al., n. 13 above, pp. 471–472.
29 National Research Council of the National Academies, *Ocean Noise and Marine Mammals* (Washington, DC: National Academies Press, 2003), p. 87.
30 Boebel et al., n. 13 above, pp. 471–473.
31 Id.
32 Id.
33 A.J. Wright, *Reducing Impacts of Human Ocean Noise on Cetaceans: Knowledge Gap Analysis and Recommendations* (Gland: WWF International, 2014).

and, ultimately, the overall effects of noise on these sea dwellers.[34] Currently, there are few studies on the auditory capacity of specific species, and thus great uncertainty remains about the indirect, long-term, and cumulative effects of noise emissions on these species, especially regarding potential behavioral changes of marine mammals. Moreover, presently only a handful of regional mappings of underwater noise emissions exist.[35] Finally, even when studies have been conducted, the nature and effects of underwater noise are often strongly dependent on the specific circumstances of the exposure.[36] Against this backdrop, it is difficult to assess at what exact point underwater noise emissions become biologically significant. One may argue, however, that some things are understood: First, the problem of underwater noise pollution may represent a serious threat in some instances.[37] Second, it is widely assumed that underwater noise has sharply increased in previous decades and will likely continue to increase.[38] Third, much knowledge already exists about human activities which generate underwater noise and this knowledge could be included relatively easily into a systematic management approach (e.g., seismic studies in the oil and gas industry, ship movements, mid- and low-frequency sonars).[39]

International Legal Framework Targeting Underwater Noise Pollution by Regular Ship Operations

Currently, no international legal instrument exists that specifically and exclusively addresses underwater noise. Relevant conventions usually contain

---

34   Boebel et al, n. 13 above, pp. 471–473; Southall et al., n. 7 above, pp. 474–482; ICES, n. 7 above, p. 17; NRC, n. 16 above, p. 83; A. Gillespie, "Establishing reliable foundations for the international scientific investigation of noise pollution in the oceans," *RECIEL* 15 (2006): 211–226, pp. 214–216.

35   See for instance, Stellwagen Bank National Marine Sanctuary (U.S. East Coast), available online: <http://www.orcalab.org> Puget Soundscape (USA), <http://www.commerce.wa.gov> Ocean Tracking Network (Canada), available online: <http://www.oceantrackingnetwork.org> LIDO – Listening to Deep Ocean Environment (Mediterranean), available online: <http://www.esonet-noe.org>.

36   K.A. Forney et al., "Nowhere to go: Noise impact assessments for marine mammal populations with high site fidelity," *Endangered Species Research* 32 (2017): 391–413; C. Gomez et al., "A systematic review on the behavioural responses of wild marine animals to noise: The disparity between science and policy," *Canadian Journal of Zoology* 94 (2016): 801–819.

37   A. Gillespie, "The precautionary principle in the twenty-first century: A case study of noise pollution in the ocean," *International Journal of Marine and Coastal Law* 22 (2007): 61–87, p. 82.

38   ICES, n. 7 above, p. 39; NRC, n. 16 above, pp. 74–82.

39   NRC, id., pp. 52 ff.

general provisions regarding marine environmental protection, the protection of various species, biodiversity, or the protection from pollution by material input. Only a few treaties explicitly mention noise or sound input.[40] The following sections take an in-depth look at the pertinent treaties that provide a legal framework for the regulation of ship noise, especially the most important treaty governing oceans issues, that is, the 1982 United Nations Convention on the Law of the Sea (UNCLOS). As a starting point, the relevance of the precautionary approach as a guiding principle for managing and regulating underwater noise pollution radiated by regular ship operations is explained.

Precautionary Principle

Despite its uncertain legal status in international law, the precautionary principle has gained enormous importance when it comes to governing environmental problems in situations of scientific uncertainty, including in the case of underwater noise pollution. Quite generally, environmental law principles like the precautionary principle guide States in their political, legislative, administrative, and judicial approaches to marine management.[41] As already discussed, jurisprudential discourse and current legislative initiatives to limit the adverse effects of underwater noise are emerging against the backdrop of a considerable lack of scientific knowledge regarding the nature and effects of underwater noise as well as the physiological (auditory) traits of potentially affected marine life. Nevertheless, as also explained above, there are clear signs that noise inputs to the marine environment can result in significant damage, especially to marine mammals.[42] It is precisely this type of situation in which the precautionary principle becomes relevant in guiding State actions, that is, when a potential concern arises regarding a causal relation between a human activity and an adverse environmental impact. The core of the principle is reflected in Principle 15 of the 1992 Rio Declaration, which states that where there are threats of serious or irreversible damage, lack of full scientific

---

40 For example, the Agreement on the Conservation of Small Cetaceans of the Baltic and North Seas (ASCOBANS), adopted 17 March 1992 (entered into force 29 March 1994), 1772 *United Nations Treaty Series* 217 (1992), annex, s. 1(d); H.M. Dotinga and A.G. Oude Elferink, "Acoustic pollution in the oceans: The search for legal standards," *Ocean Development and International Law* 31 (2000): 151–182, pp. 155–167; E.M. McCarthy, "International regulation of transboundary pollutants: The emerging challenge of ocean noise," *Ocean and Coastal Law Journal* 6 (2001): 257–292; Erbe, n. 21 above, p. 17.

41 G. Winter, "International principles of marine environmental protection," in Salomon and Markus, n. 1 above, 585–605.

42 C. Horowitz and M. Jasny, "Precautionary management of noise: Lessons from the U.S. Marine Mammal Protection Act," *Journal of International Wildlife Law and Policy* 10 (2007): 225–232, p. 227.

certainty shall not be used as a reason for postponing cost-effective measures to prevent environmental degradation.[43]

Accordingly, the precautionary approach gives legislators a legal mandate for action.[44] It also requires political decision-making to not limit itself to the mere prevention of imminent environmental hazards or to the restoration of environmental damage, but rather to prevent damage by taking preemptive action before the damage is likely to occur.[45] Keeping this in mind, known and conceivable hazard potentials of underwater noise should be proactively confronted.[46] At any rate, it is clear that the precautionary principle has support in the international community regarding its applicability to underwater noise. Both the Conference of the Parties (COPs) to the Convention on Migratory Species (CMS)[47] and the Meetings of the Parties (MOPs) to the Agreement on the Conservation of Small Cetaceans of the Baltic and North Seas (ASCOBANS),[48] have emphasized the principle's importance with regard to the issue of anthropogenic underwater noise.

UNCLOS and IMO Guidelines for the Reduction of Underwater Noise from Commercial Shipping

According to Article 192 of UNCLOS, parties are obliged to "protect and preserve the marine environment." The general consensus with regard to this

---

43   UNGA, "Rio Declaration on the Environment and Development Vol. I.," Rio de Janeiro, 1992, UN Doc. A/CONF.151/26 (vol. I) (12 August 1992); 31 *International Legal Materials* 87.
44   At the international level, the meaning and content of the principle is still disputed. For example, it remains open what these "measures to prevent damage" should be, how strong they should be, or even which scientific evidence would be sufficient to override arguments for postponing such measures. P. Birnie et al., *International Law and the Environment* (Oxford: Oxford University Press, 2009), p. 162; P. Sands, *Principles of International Environmental Law* (Cambridge: Cambridge University Press, 2012), p. 222.
45   Birnie et al., id., pp. 152 ff.; E. Rehbinder, *Das Vorsorgeprinzip im internationalen Vergleich* (Düsseldorf: Werner Verlag, 1991).
46   Gillespie, n. 37 above, pp. 85–86; Horowitz and Jasny, n. 42 above, p. 227; D. Inkelas, "Security, sound, and cetaceans: Legal challenges to low frequency active sonar under U.S. and international environmental law," *Washington International Law Review* 37 (2005): 207–249, pp. 221–222; J.M. van Dyke et al., "Wales, submarines, and active sonar," *Ocean Yearbook* 18 (2004): 330–363, pp. 349–352.
47   Convention on Migratory Species, adopted 23 June 1979 (entered into force 1 November 1983), 1651 *United Nations Treaty Series* 333 (CMS); Conference of the Parties (COP 9) to the CMS, "Adverse anthropogenic marine/ocean noise impacts on cetaceans and other biota," UNEP/CMS/Resolution 9.19 (Rome, December 2008), s. 4.
48   Meeting of the Parties (MOP 6) to the ASCOBANS, "Resolution No. 2: Adverse Effects of Underwater Noise on Marine Mammals during Offshore Construction Activities for Renewable Energy Production" (Bonn, September 2009).

article is that it includes only a vague duty to carry out active measures to at least maintain the *status quo* in the marine environment.[49] This obligation is concretized by Article 194 *et seq.*, especially regarding marine pollution and the use of technology; parties are obliged under Article 194(1) to take measures to "prevent, reduce and control pollution of the marine environment from any source." It must be asked, however, whether noise input may be interpreted as pollution according to Article 194(1). According to Article 1(1)(4), pollution of the marine environment means "the introduction by man, directly or indirectly, of substances or energy into the marine environment, ... which results or is likely to result in such deleterious effects as harm to living resources and marine life." Though the authors of UNCLOS did not have the regulation of underwater noise in mind while constructing this article, it would make sense from a literal and systematic perspective to recognize it as a form of energy input according to Article 1(1)(4). In the first place, noise is a form of energy from a scientific point of view.[50] In addition, the wording of Article 194(1), "from any source," and Article 194(3) "the measures taken pursuant to this Part shall deal with *all sources* of pollution of the marine environment," call for a broad interpretation of the definition. Finally, the definition in Article 1(1)(4) was drafted in a broad manner, especially because it *expressis verbis* covers not only material input. The obligation under Article 194(1) is moderated, however, by the fact the article also states that parties must only take "the best practicable means at their disposal and in accordance with their capabilities."

Along these lines, particularly with regard to pollution of the sea by ships, under Article 211(2) States shall "adopt laws and regulations for the prevention, reduction and control of pollution of the marine environment from vessels flying their flag or of their registry." These laws and regulations shall "at least have the same effect as that of generally accepted international rules and standards established through the competent international organization or general diplomatic conference." According to Article 211(1), States have a duty to create such international regulations. The responsible authority for this task is the International Maritime Organization (IMO). To date, no binding regulations on ship noise have been made within the IMO framework, not even under the MARPOL Convention. Nevertheless, the IMO's Marine Environment Protection Committee has paid attention to the topic since 2008[51] and in 2014 approved

---

49 Dotinga and Oude Elferink, n. 40 above, p. 160. United Nations Convention on the Law of the Sea, adopted 10 December 1982 (entered into force 16 November 1994), 1833 *United Nations Treaty Series* 397 (UNCLOS).
50 Dotinga and Oude Elferink, id., p. 158.
51 IMO, "Comment on document MEPC 57/INF.4," IMO Doc. MEPC 57/INF.22 (2008).

the Guidelines for the Reduction of Underwater Noise from Commercial Shipping to Address Adverse Impacts on Marine Life.[52]

The IMO Guidelines for the Reduction of Underwater Noise from Commercial Shipping to Address Adverse Impacts on Marine Life were approved in 2014.[53] The scope of application of these Guidelines is limited to commercial ships. They do not address the introduction of noise from naval vessels and warships and the deliberate introduction of noise for other purposes such as sonar or seismic activities.[54] Thus, they are intended to provide general advice regarding the reduction of underwater noise to designers, shipbuilders, and ship operators. They are not legally binding.[55]

The Guidelines highlight that the largest opportunities for reduction of underwater noise are during the initial design of the ship. Accordingly, they first address design issues and are therefore primarily aimed at new ships. In this respect, they recommend that propellers and hulls are tailored to reduce cavitation, which is the major source of noise input.[56] Also, they provide guidance regarding the appropriate selection and location of onboard machinery.[57] For existing ships, they recommend the implementation of some "additional technologies" which are known to contribute to noise reduction, namely the design and installation of new state-of-the-art propellers, the installation of wake conditioning devices and air injection to propellers.[58] Finally, they also urge the implementation of some operational modifications and maintenance measures to reduce adverse impacts on marine life (applicable for both new and existing ships), such as the proper cleaning of propellers, hull coatings in order to keep them smooth, and the selection of ship speed and route decisions.[59]

Additionally, the Guidelines also recognize the usefulness of underwater noise computational models to predict and understand what reductions might be achievable in new and existing ships.[60] They also stress that, for meaningful improvements, underwater noise should be measured by an objective standard. Particularly, they refer to "ISO/PAS 17208-1, Acoustics: Quantities and

---

52 IMO, "Guidelines for the Reduction of Underwater Noise from Commercial Shipping to Address Adverse Impacts on Marine Life," IMO Doc. MEPC.1/Circ.833 (2014).
53 Id.
54 Id., paras. 2 and 4.3.
55 Id., para. 3.1.
56 Id., para. 7.
57 Id., para. 8.
58 Id., para. 9.
59 Id., para. 10.
60 Id., para. 5.

procedures for description and measurement of underwater sound from ships, Part 1: General requirements for measurements in deep water" and "ISO/DIS 16554, Ship and marine technology: Measurement and reporting of underwater sound radiated from merchant ships – deep-water measurement," both from the International Organization for Standardization (ISO).[61]

International Environmental Treaties and European Union Law
Other international treaties exist which aim to prevent pollution of the seas and protect marine species and their habitats. These conventions have varying objectives, material, and geographical scopes. If, after relevant assessment, one were to consider underwater noise to be within the scope of these conventions, their regulatory content and level of protection would have to be considered very general. A few treaties, however, provide more specific measures than the others regarding underwater noise pollution, including noise from vessel operations: ASCOBANS and the Agreement on the Conservation of Cetaceans in the Black Sea, Mediterranean Sea and Contiguous Atlantic Area (ACCOBAMS), the Antarctic Convention and its Environment Protocol, the CMS, and the Convention on Biological Diversity (CBD).[62] At a regional level, the EU's Marine Strategy Framework Directive includes specific requirements to take action regarding underwater noise pollution.

ASCOBANS
According to subparagraph 2.1 of the ASCOBANS Agreement, the parties "undertake to cooperate closely in order to achieve and maintain a favourable conservation status for small cetaceans." Following subparagraph 2.2, the parties

---

61 Id., para. 6.
62 ASCOBANS, n. 40 above; Agreement on the Conservation of Cetaceans in the Black Sea, Mediterranean Sea and Contiguous Altantic Area, adopted 24 November 1996 (entered into force 1 June 2001), 2183 *United Nations Treaty Series* 303 (ACCOBAMS); Antarctic Treaty, adopted 1 December 1959 (entered into force 23 June 1961), 402 *United Nations Treaty Series* 82 and Protocol on Environmental Protection to the Antarctic Treaty, adopted 4 October 1991 (entered into force 14 January 1998), 30 *International Legal Materials* (1991); CMS, n. 47 above; Convention on Biological Diversity, adopted 5 June 1992 (entered into force 29 December 1993), 1760 *United Nations Treaty Series* 79 (CBD). Further analyses are provided by, for example, K.N. Scott, "International regulation of undersea noise," *International Comparative Law Quarterly* 53 (2004): 287–324; K.N. Scott, "Sound and cetaceans: A regional response to regulating acoustic marine pollution," *Journal of International Wildlife Law and Policy* 10 (2007): 175–199, p. 179; C. Schachten, *Akustische Meeresverschmutzung: Der völkerrechtliche Rahmen zur Regulierung von Unterwasserlärmemission* (Hamburg, Dr. Kovac, 2011); van Dyke et al., n. 46 above; Dotinga and Oude Elferink, n. 40 above, pp. 155–167.

shall apply the conservation, research, and management measures prescribed in the Annex. Paragraph 1(d) of the Annex, in turn, states that parties shall "work towards the prevention of other significant disturbance, especially of an acoustic nature" to species covered by the Agreement.

Several resolutions within ASCOBANS call on the parties to conduct further research in the so-called noise deterrence technology, as well as on the effects of ship noise (especially high-speed ferries). Additionally, protective measures should be developed in cooperation with militaries to reduce damage caused by military exercises,[63] which should include the operation of naval ships.

ACCOBAMS

The ACCOBAMS Agreement does not expressly refer to underwater noise, but general provisions apply to the subject. As prescribed by Article 11, paragraph 1, the parties "shall take coordinate measures to achieve and maintain a favourable conservation status for cetaceans." According to paragraph 3, they shall apply the conservation, research and management measures prescribed in the Conservation Plan established in Annex 2 of the Agreement (Article 11(4) of ACCOBAMS), which, *inter alia*, requires the parties to regulate the discharge at sea of pollutants believed to have adverse effects on cetaceans (ACCOBAMS Annex 2, para. 1(d)).

Meanwhile, parties to ACCOBAMS have addressed the impact of underwater noise on the conservation status of protected cetacean species since 2004.[64] Resolution 3.10 in 2007 established a working group to tackle underwater noise deriving from different activities, develop appropriate tools to assess the impacts of underwater noise on cetaceans, and further elaborate measures to mitigate such impacts.[65] In addition, the 2010 Resolution 4.17 presented the "Guidelines to Address the Impact of Anthropogenic Noise on Cetaceans in the ACCOBAMS Area." These also include some general guidelines and provisions

---

63 Meeting of the Parties (MOP 4) to ASCOBANS, "Resolution No. 5: Effects of Noise and of Vessels" (Denmark, 2003); Meeting of the Parties (MOP 5) to the ASCOBANS, "Resolution No. 4: Adverse Effects of Sound, Vessels and Other Forms of Disturbance on Small Cetaceans" (The Netherlands, 2016).

64 Meeting of the Parties (MOP 2) to the ACCOBAMS, "Resolution 2.16: Assessment and impact assessment of man-made noise" (2004); Meeting of the Parties (MOP 3) to the ACCOBAMS, "Resolution 3.10: Guidelines to address the impact of anthropogenic noise on marine mammals in the ACCOBAMS area" (2007); Meeting of the Parties (MOP 4) to the ACCOBAMS, "Resolution 4.17: Guidelines to address the impact of anthropogenic noise on cetaceans in the ACCOBAMS area" (2010); Meeting of the Parties (MOP 5) to the ACCOBAMS, "Resolution 5.15: Addressing the impact of anthropogenic noise" (2013); Meeting of the Parties (MOP 6) to the ACCOBAMS, "Resolution 6.17: Anthropogenic noise" (2016).

65 MOP 3 to the ACCOBAMS, id., s. 13.

targeting shipping and other sources such as tourism and whale watching boats which may contribute to raising underwater noise levels and may have a significant impact on cetaceans' behavior and welfare, and, in the long term, a negative effect on the local population. The guidelines are not static and are expected to be further developed by the working group, in cooperation with the Secretariat, Scientific Committee, and the parties.[66]

Antarctic Treaty System

The Antarctic Treaty System is made up of several treaties whose regulations may be important for addressing issues concerning underwater noise input by vessel operations. The central treaty in the system is the Antarctic Treaty itself.[67] According to its Articles I(1) and VI, the zones covered by this international regime are the whole continental and marine areas south of 60° south latitude. Bearing this in mind, the Protocol on Environmental Protection to the Antarctic Treaty, from October 4, 1991 (Madrid Protocol), Article 2, establishes as its objective "the comprehensive protection of the Antarctic environment and dependent and associated ecosystems." In addition, Article 3(2) of the Protocol requires activities in Antarctica to be planned and executed in a particular manner that avoids, *inter alia*, detrimental changes in the distribution, abundance or productivity of species or populations of species of fauna and flora, and further jeopardy to endangered or threatened species or populations of such species. All such provisions may apply to underwater noise pollution by regular ship operations. Finally, Article 3 of Annex II to the Protocol prohibits both the "taking" of mammals and birds and the "harmful interference" of nature. Both terms are further defined by Article 1 of Annex II. Accordingly, "taking" means "[to] kill, injure, capture, handle or molest, a native mammal or bird."

---

66   The Joint Noise Working Group of CMS/ACCOBAMS/ASCOBANS (JNWG) was first established in 2012 as the joint ACCOBAMS/ASCOBANS Noise Working Group. The CMS was included in 2014. See Report of the Joint ACCOBAMS/ASCOBANS Noise Working Group, AC21/Doc.3.2.1 (WG), (2014). The Working Group is vested with advisory competences only. Its main aim is to ensure progress is being made towards mitigating the negative impact of underwater noise on cetaceans and other marine biota. See "Operational Procedures for the Joint Noise Working Group (JNWG) of CMS, ACCOBAMS and ASCOBANS," (2014). Among other functions, it is mandated to improve the existing guidelines on the subject based on new scientific findings. See "Terms of Reference for a Joint Noise Working Group (JNWG) of CMS, ACCOBAMS and ASCOBANS," (2014), para. ii; MOP 4 Resolution 4.17, n. 64 above, para. 13 and annex.

67   Antarctic Treaty and Madrid Protocol, n. 62 above. See Antarctic Treaty System, available online: <https://www.ats.aq/e/ats_keydocs.htm>.

It has been argued that Article 3 of Annex II to the Protocol should be considered relevant in the context of underwater noise.⁶⁸ This view should be supported based on both the wording of the provision and its goal. The meaning of "taking" includes the removal of a mammal or bird from the Antarctic ecosystem. This displacement also occurs as a by-product of noise emissions, including from regular ship operations, as described in the first part of this article. The term "harmful interference" as defined in Article 1(h) mainly covers activities that are carried out from land.⁶⁹ Still, some of them could be applied to underwater noise input by regular ship operations. "Harmful interference" according to Article 1(h)(ii and vi) includes the use of "vehicles or vessels ... in a manner that disturbs concentrations of ... seals" and "any activity that results in the significant adverse modification of habitats of any species or population of native mammal, ... plant or invertebrate."

Convention on Migratory Species
The Convention on Migratory Species deals with migratory species, including some marine species, that cyclically cross one or more national jurisdictional boundaries (Article I(1)(a)). The parties to the CMS acknowledge the importance of conserving these species and the need to take action to prevent them from becoming endangered (Article II(1) and II(2)).

By virtue of Article II(3)(b) of the Convention, all parties should provide immediate protection for those "endangered migratory species" listed in Appendix I. According to Article III(5), the "range States" parties⁷⁰ of such species shall, subject to certain specific exceptions, prohibit the taking of animals belonging to such species. As usual in such regimes, under the CMS, "taking" is a broad notion that covers taking, hunting, fishing, capturing, deliberate killing, and harassing or attempting to engage in any such conduct (Article I(1)(i)). *Prima facie*, it seems possible that a harassment may result from underwater noise pollution radiated by regular ship operations. As regards the conservation and management of species listed in Appendix II,⁷¹ parties and range States parties (Article II(3)(c) and IV(3)) should conclude international agreements to ensure their favorable conservation status (Article V).

---

68 Scott (2007), n. 62 above, p. 186.
69 Id.
70 For a definition of "range State," see CMS, n. 47 above, art. I.1.h.
71 These are migratory species which have an unfavorable conservation status and which require international agreements for their conservation and management, as well as those which have a conservation status which would significantly benefit from the international cooperation that could be achieved by an international agreement. See CMS, n. 47 above, art. IV(1).

In 2005, the COP's Resolution 8.22 on Adverse Human Induced Impacts on Cetaceans requested that the CMS Secretariat and Scientific Council review the extent to which the CMS and CMS cetacean-related agreements are addressing human-induced marine noise.[72] In 2008, Resolution 9.19 on Adverse Anthropogenic Marine/Ocean Noise Impacts on Cetaceans and other Biota announced the development by the Scientific Council of voluntary guidelines on activities of concern.[73] Moreover, it encouraged the parties to facilitate the assessment and monitoring of marine noise, to further understanding with regard to the potential sources and acoustic risks for marine species, and to conduct studies on the extent and potential impact on the marine environment of, *inter alia*, shipping, as well as on the potential benefits of "noise protection areas."[74]

Convention on Biological Diversity

The CBD framework may also be seen as a forum where underwater noise could be targeted at the global international level. The main objective of the CBD is the conservation of biological diversity (Article 1), which includes marine organisms (Article 2). To that end, the parties shall, *inter alia*, identify what "processes" and "activities" carried out under their jurisdiction or control (regardless of where their effects occur) (Article 3(b)) have or are likely to have significant adverse impacts on the conservation of biological diversity. They are also required to monitor effects of their activities (Article 7(c)), and regulate them (Article 8(l)). According to Article 22(2), contracting parties shall implement the CBD with respect to the marine environment, consistent with the rights and obligations of States under the law of the sea.

In 2012, adverse impacts of underwater noise on marine and coastal biodiversity were addressed by the COPs to the CBD in Decision UNEP/CBD/COP/DEC/XI/18 on "Marine and coastal biodiversity: Sustainable fisheries and addressing adverse impacts of human activities, voluntary guidelines for environmental assessment, and marine spatial planning." This decision requested that the Executive Secretary collaborate with other parties, governments, and competent organizations to organize an expert workshop to improve and share knowledge on underwater noise and its impacts on marine and coastal biodiversity. The goal was to develop practical guidance to assist when applying

---

72 Also see, Tenth Meeting of the Conference of the Parties to CMS, "Implementing Resolution 8.22: on Adverse Human Induced Impacts on Cetaceans," UNEP/CMS/Conf.10.35 (2011); Eighth Meeting of the Conference of the Parties to CMS, UNEP/CMS/Resolution.8.22 (2005), para. 3 (b) (vi)).

73 Ninth Meeting of the Conference of the Parties to CMS, UNEP/CMS/Resolution 9.19 (2008), para. 3.

74 Id., para. 5.

management measures, which eventually would mitigate significant adverse impacts of underwater noise on marine and coastal biodiversity. The workshop was also to cover issues such as the development of acoustic mapping of areas of interest as part of its scope. The results of this initiative are available in the "Report of the Expert Workshop on Underwater Noise and its Impacts on Marine and Coastal Biodiversity," which was adopted in 2014. This report, particularly in Annex III, addresses commercial shipping as one of the main sources of continuous noise.[75] That same year, the COP to the CBD encouraged parties, non-parties, indigenous and local communities, and other relevant stakeholders to take appropriate measures to "avoid, minimize and mitigate the potential significant adverse impacts of anthropogenic underwater noise on marine and coastal biodiversity."[76]

The EU's Marine Strategy Framework Directive

The EU undertook a unique effort in managing underwater noise. Through its Marine Strategy Framework Directive (MSFD) it has initiated a process that develops a common approach between Member States to address underwater noise pollution.[77] The structure of this development, particularly with a view to conceptual and methodological intercalibration, may serve as a reliable blueprint for how to target the issue of underwater noise pollution at the international level.

In general, the EU's MSFD establishes a framework for joint action in the field of marine environmental policy. Its overall objective is to create a framework within which the Member States take the necessary measures to maintain or create a good environmental status (GES) in their waters by 2020 at the latest, their waters including, in principle, Member States' territorial waters, exclusive economic zones, and adjacent continental shelves (where relevant). To this end, Member States are required to take the necessary measures (Article 1(1)). They must develop and implement marine strategies to protect and

---

75 Expert Workshop on Underwater Noise, n. 5 above, annex III, s. 8.
76 United Nations Environment Programme (UNEP), "Marine and coastal biodiversity: Impacts on marine and coastal biodiversity of anthropogenic underwater noise and ocean acidification, priority actions to achieve Aichi Biodiversity Target 10 for coral reefs and closely associated ecosystems, and marine spatial planning and training initiatives," UNEP/CBD/COP/DEC/XII/23 (2014), para. 3.
77 European Union, Directive 2008/56/EC of the European Parliament and of the Council of 17 June 2008 establishing a framework for community action in the field of marine environmental policy (Marine Strategy Framework Directive), OJ L 164 (25 June 2008), pp. 19–40.

preserve the marine environment (Article 1(2)(a)). This process is divided into six procedural steps (Article 5(2)):
1. Initial assessment of the current environmental status (Article 8).
2. Determination of good environmental status (Article 9).
3. Establishment of a series of environmental targets and associated indicators (Article 10(1)).
4. Establishment and implementation of a monitoring programme for ongoing assessment and regular updating of targets (Article 11(1)).
5. Development of a programme of measures designed to achieve or maintain good environmental status (Articles 13(1) to (3)).
6. Entry into operation of the programme (Article 13(10)).

Currently, Member States are in the process of implementing programmes of measures. In guiding Member States in developing their marine strategies, Article 3(5) of the MSFD had put forward a highly ambitious and broad definition of GES: "[T]he environmental status of marine waters where these provide ecologically diverse and dynamic oceans and seas which are clean, healthy and productive within their intrinsic conditions." This definition is complemented by several additional general criteria that require, for example, that ecosystems "function fully" and that anthropogenic inputs "do not cause pollution effects" (Article 3(5)). Ultimately, however, the content of the words "good environmental status" will be determined by the Member States themselves based on the descriptors set out in Annex I, entitled "qualitative descriptors for determining good environmental status." Regarding underwater noise, Descriptor 11 on energy entrances requires that the introduction is at levels "that do not adversely affect the marine environment." The Commission's "Decision on Criteria and Methodological Standards on Good Environmental Status of Marine Waters" further specifies this criterion.[78] Given the extensive scientific gaps, the Commission Decision decided on two indicators: (a) "distribution in time and place of loud, low and mid frequency impulsive sounds"[79] and (b) "continuous low

---

[78] European Commission (EC), "Commission Decision of 1 September 2010 on criteria and methodological standards on good environmental status of marine water," 2010/477/EU (2010); T. Markus, "Changing the base: Legal implications of scientific criteria and methodological standards on what constitutes good marine environmental status," *Transnational Environmental Law* 1 (2013): 1–21.

[79] "Proportion of days and their distribution within a calendar year over areas of a determined surface, as well as their spatial distribution, in which anthropogenic sound sources exceed levels that are likely to entail significant impact on marine animals measured as Sound Exposure Level (in dB re 1μPa.s) or as peak sound pressure level (in dB re 1μPa peak) at one meter, measured over the frequency band 10 Hz to 10 kHz (11.1.1)."

frequency sound."[80] The latter may require assessments and measurements of noise input levels from regular ship operation on ambient noise.[81]

At this point, however, Member States are finding it difficult to accomplish even the first steps of the MSFD with regard to underwater noise. The United Kingdom, for example, stated in early 2015 that at that point it was neither possible to provide a full assessment of underwater noise and its impacts, nor to define a relevant baseline.[82] According to the United Kingdom, it was also not possible to set specific targets for either impulsive or ambient sounds to define GES. Nevertheless, as a next step a noise registry will be developed and established which will record noise generating activities in space and time. The data registered will then be used in future research to assess levels and patterns of noise in order to determine whether these could potentially compromise the achievement of GES. The data is also intended to inform the current licensing practices regarding offshore noise-emitting activities under UK marine and coastal regulations.[83] At present, the Commission is also planning to review its decision on scientific criteria and methodological standards. Most likely, this will help to further develop the shared understanding between the Member States of what GES can mean with regard to underwater noise.

Treaties Governing Specific Vessel Activities

Treaties regulating vessel noise pollution which result from specific uses mainly concern whale watching activities. Guidelines governing whale watching have been adopted by both the International Whaling Commission (IWC)[84]

---

80 Trends in the ambient noise level within the 1/3 octave bands 63 and 125 Hz (center frequency) (re 1µPa RMS; average noise level in these octave bands over a year) measured by observation stations and/or with the use of models if appropriate (11.2.1). For further information, see van der Graaf et al., n. 11 above.

81 European Commission Report, *European Marine Strategy Framework Directive Working Group on Good Environmental Status (WG-GES): Guidance for setting up underwater noise monitoring in European Seas* (2013).

82 United Kingdom, Department for Environment Food and Rural Affairs (Defra), "Marine Strategy Framework Directive consultations: Programmes of measures" (2015), pp. 168–175.

83 The Joint Nature Conservation Committee (JNCC) has produced statutory guidelines for minimizing the risk of injury to marine mammals from seismic activities, piling and explosive use which are frequently set as license conditions. See JNCC, "JNCC guidelines for minimising the risk of injury and disturbance to marine mammals from seismic surveys," 2017; JNCC, "Statutory nature conservation agency protocol for minimising the risk of injury to marine mammals from piling noise," 2010; JNCC, "JNCC guidelines for minimising the risk of injury to marine mammals from using explosives," 2010.

84 International Whaling Commission (IWC), "General Principles to Minimise the Risks of Adverse Impacts of Whalewatching on Cetaceans" (1996), available

and ACCOBAMS.[85] These in turn have served as model regimes for the development of national whale watching rules.[86] Generally, whale watching management systems are not only aimed at reducing noise input into the marine environment, but to reduce the overall disturbance of the cetaceans being watched. Still, measures included in these regimes contribute indirectly to reducing adverse noise impacts from regular ship operations on marine cetaceans.[87]

The IWC General Principles to minimize the risks of adverse impacts of whale watching on cetaceans recommends the implementation of measures to regulate the number and size of vessels, and the frequency of their activities. In addition, they require that vessels, engines, and other equipment should be designed, maintained, and operated during whale watching, in a manner that reduces as far as practicable adverse impacts on the targeted species and their environment. In this regard, these principles establish that cetacean species may respond differently to low and high frequency sounds, relative sound intensity, or rapid changes in sound. Therefore, vessel operators should be aware of the acoustic characteristics of the targeted species and of their vessel under operating conditions, particularly of the need to reduce as far as possible production of potentially disturbing sound. Finally, vessel design and operation should minimize the risk of injury to cetaceans should contact occur, e.g., shrouding of propellers can reduce both noise and risk of injury.[88]

The Guidelines for Commercial Cetacean Watching in the ACCOBAMS Area, in turn, include a permit regime for operators, that is, they require an official authorization to conduct whale watching activities. Permit applicants often have to provide information about their vessels and their noise level, the area of operation, and the frequency and length of the planned whale watching activities. The permit is then subjected to more specific management requirements. Operators are, for example, required not to make abrupt changes in speed. States parties should organize training courses for operators and staff

---

online: <https://iwc.int/wwguidelines>. On the IWC's work in general, see A.J. Wright et al., "The International Whaling Commission: Beyond whaling," *Frontiers in Marine Science* 3 (2016), pp. 158 et seq.

85   Meeting of the Parties (MOP 4) to the ACCOBAMS, "Resolution 4.7: Guidelines for commercial cetacean watching in the ACCOBAMS area" (2010).

86   Most national whale watching rules and non-binding guidelines are collected and made available by the IWC; see ACCOBAMS, "Report of the Eighth Meeting of the Scientific Committee of ACCOBAMS," ACCOBAMS–SC8/2012/Inf 12 (2012); Markus and Silva Sánchez, n. 1 above.

87   Schachten, n. 62 above, pp. 94 ff.

88   IWC, n. 84 above.

and grant them a certificate. Finally, sanctions of a sufficient gravity must be established in order to effectively deter violations of the Guidelines. For instance, they may include the suspension or revocation of permits.

Legal Framework Targeting Noise Emissions from Technology-Based Activities Carried out from Vessels

International Regulations and Guidelines

In general, the legal framework presented and analyzed in the section above also applies to underwater noise inputs from onboard machinery. Still, some provisions make express reference to such sources.

UNCLOS

Article 196 of UNCLOS obliges parties to take "all measures necessary to prevent, reduce and control pollution of the marine environment resulting from the use of technologies." Though the authors of UNCLOS were primarily thinking of biotechnology when including the term "technologies,"[89] a broad interpretation of the provision suggests that the use of such technologies would include sonar and seismic airguns. It must be noted, however, that the relevant damage threshold to be considered is high, because the changes must be "significant and harmful" (Article 196(1)).

UNCLOS also sets a legal framework for research and the exploitation of living aquatic resources. According to Article 240(d) marine scientific research "shall be conducted in compliance with all relevant regulations adopted in conformity with this Convention including those for the protection and preservation of the marine environment."[90] This rule thus provides a mandate, for example, to regulate the scientific use of airguns if international standards were established in this field.

ASCOBANS

Several resolutions within the ASCOBANS call for the development of guidelines to protect small cetaceans from noise produced by seismic surveys. Additionally, as already mentioned, protective measures should be developed in

---

89   Dotinga and Oude Elferink, n. 40 above, p. 160.
90   A.-M. Hubert, "Marine Scientific Research," in Salomon and Markus, n. 1 above, ch. 50; A.-M. Hubert, "The new paradox in marine scientific research: Regulating the potential environmental impacts of conducting ocean science," *Ocean Development & International Law* 42 (2011): 229–355, p. 329 ff.

cooperation with militaries to reduce damage caused by military exercises.[91] Such exercises may make use of active sonar. Guidelines addressing all these noise issues were eventually proposed through the 2009 "Effective Mitigation Guidance for intense noise generating activities in the ASCOBANS region." This document provides for both "general guidelines" and specific rules targeting, *inter alia*, sonars (military and civil), seismic surveys and airgun use, playback and sound exposure experiments, and other underwater acoustically active devices.[92]

ACCOBAMS

Particularly with respect to noise emissions from onboard technologies, Resolution 4.17, adopted by the 2010 MOP, presented the "Guidelines to Address the Impact of Anthropogenic Noise on Cetaceans in the ACCOBAMS Area." Like similar initiatives, these non-binding regulations include general guidelines applicable to any source of anthropogenic underwater noise pollution as well as guidelines targeting specific activities such as high power sonar (military and civil), seismic surveys using airguns, playback and sound exposure experiments, among others.[93]

Antarctic Treaty System

The Antarctic Treaty is also relevant with respect to noise input by onboard technologies.[94] Article I(1) declares that Antarctica shall be used only for peaceful purposes and expressly prohibits military maneuvers and the testing of weapons in the areas covered by the Treaty, which according to Article VI includes the whole continental and marine areas south of 60° south latitude. Consequently, the use of mid- and low-frequency sonar by military submarines is generally prohibited. In addition, Article 7 of the Madrid Protocol categorically prohibits any form of commercial exploitation of mineral resources. Thus the use of airguns is generally limited to scientific and other non-commercial purposes. Further, Article 8 calls for an environmental impact assessment of all activities, whether for scientific research, tourism, governmental or non-governmental activities.

---

91 MOP 4 to the ASCOBANS, Resolution Nos. 4 and 5, n. 63 above.
92 Final Report of the ASCOBANS Intersessional Working Group on the Assessment of Acoustic Disturbance, "6th Meeting of the Parties to ASCOBANS" (Bonn, Germany), pp. 11–23.
93 MOP 4 to the ACCOBAMS, Resolution 4.17, n. 64 above, para. 13 and annex.
94 See Antarctic Treaty System, n. 67 above.

Convention on Migratory Species

Resolution 9.19 on Adverse Anthropogenic Marine/Ocean Noise Impacts on Cetaceans and other Biota, adopted by the COP in 2008, called on the parties to adopt mitigation measures on the use of high intensity active naval sonars.[95] It also encouraged the parties to facilitate the assessment and monitoring of marine noise, further understanding with regard to the potential sources and acoustic risks for marine species, and to conduct studies on the extent and potential impact on the marine environment of high intensity active naval sonars and seismic surveys.[96]

The EU's Marine Strategy Framework Directive

As explained in the section above, the Commission's "Decision on Criteria and Methodological Standards on Good Environmental Status of Marine Waters" establishes two indicators with respect to Descriptor 11 on the introduction of energy, including underwater noise: (a) "distribution in time and place of loud, low and mid frequency impulsive sounds"[97] and (b) "continuous low frequency sound."[98] The first of these indicators require assessments and measurements of activities like pile driving and seismic surveys.[99]

National Laws

Seismic surveys carried out with airguns are regulated under different national legal orders. At present, regulatory approaches vary largely between States. While some countries, such as Spain and Brazil, have simply banned the use of airguns from specific areas,[100] the United Kingdom,[101] Australia,[102]

---

95   COP 9 to the CMS, n. 47 above.
96   Id., s. 5.
97   See n. 79 above.
98   See n. 80 above.
99   European Commission Report, n. 81 above.
100 Spain, Real Decreto 1629/2011, por el que se declara como Área Marina Protegida y como Zona Especial de Conservación el espacio marino de El Cachucho, y se aprueban las correspondientes medidas de conservación, Boletín Oficial del Estado múm.295; Brazil, Ministério do Meio Ambiente (2004) Resolução CONAMA N° 350/2004,"Dispõe sobre o licenciamento ambiental específico das atividades de aquisição de dados sísmicos marítimos e em zonas de transição," Data da legislação: 06/07/2004, Publicação DOU no. 161, de 20/08/2004, pp. 80–81.
101 JNCC (2017), n. 83 above.
102 Australian Government, "Department of the Environment, Water, Heritage and the Arts, EPBC Act Policy Statement 2.1 – Interaction between offshore seismic surveys and whales," adopted in September 2008, available online: <http://www.environment.gov.au/resource/epbc-act-policy-statement-21-interaction-between-offshore-seismic-exploration-and-whales>.

New Zealand,[103] Canada,[104] and the United States[105] have adopted policy statements or guidelines to reduce the adverse impacts of seismic surveys on marine mammals. As discussed above, the United Kingdom adopted the "JNCC Guidelines for Minimising the Risk of Injury and Disturbance to Marine Mammals from Seismic Surveys."[106] These guidelines are frequently used as license conditions where surveys are carried out for commercial purposes. They require users to implement a set of best practices, for example, to thoroughly plan seismic surveys, include onboard observers (Marine Mammal Observers), undertake a "pre-shooting search," and conduct a "soft-start" before the survey to scare away marine mammals potentially present in the area.[107]

Existing national regulations regarding the use of sonar mainly address military sonar testing. Many countries' navies have individually, or in the case of the North Atlantic Treaty Organization or ACCOBAMS and ASCOBANS, jointly developed mitigation guidance to protect marine life during naval exercises.[108] Most of these measures include requirements to take action to proactively avoid mammals, to apply mitigation measures during operations, and to monitor for the purpose of maintaining an exclusion zone.[109] In some countries it has become highly contentious whether military sonar testing is subject to national environmental law statutes. For example, despite the U.S. Navy following mitigation measures when using sonar, NGOs have pursued several legal

---

103 New Zealand Police, "The Code 2013n" adopted in 2013, available online: <http://www.police.govt.nz/sites/default/files/publications/the–arms–code–2013.pdf>.

104 Federal Government of Canada and Provincial Governments of Nova Scotia, Newfoundland and Labrador, British Columbia and Quebec, "Statement of Canadian Practice with respect to the Mitigation of Seismic Sound in the Marine Environment" (2007).

105 United States, Department of the Interior, Bureau of Ocean Energy Management (BOEM), Bureau of Safety and Environmental Enforcement (BSEE), Gulf of Mexico Outer Continental Shelf (OCS) Region, Joint NTL No. 2012-G02, "Implementation of Seismic Survey Mitigation Measures and Protected Species Observer Program" (2014).

106 JNCC (2017), n. 83 above.

107 According to Appendix 1 of the JNCC Guidelines, id., the soft-start is defined as the process whereby the power of an acoustic source is built up slowly from a low energy start-up, gradually and systematically increasing the output until full power is achieved (usually over a period of 20 minutes). A critical approach to the JNCC Guidelines can be found in E.C.M. Parsons et al., "A critique of the UK's JNCC seismic survey guidelines for minimizing acoustic disturbance to marine mammals: Best practice?," *Marine Pollution Bulletin* 58 (2009): 643–651.

108 J.S. Dolman et al., "Comparative review of marine mammal guidance implemented during naval exercises," *Marine Pollution Bulletin* 58 (2009): 465–477; J.S. Dolman et al., "Active sonar, beaked whales and European regional policy," *Marine Pollution Bulletin* 63 (2011): 27–34.

109 Dolman et al. (2009), id.

cases before U.S. courts in the past decade.[110] To our knowledge, only a few States have adopted binding legislation. For example, the Spanish government adopted mandatory rules addressing the issue by simply banning military sonar tests from a specific marine protected area in 2008.[111]

Conclusion

Underwater noise pollution has intensified over the decades and will continue to do so. At present, it is clear that anthropogenic noise inputs are largely generated by vessel-source activities, whether through their regular navigational operations or technology-based activities carried out from vessels. Despite the persistent lack of scientific knowledge regarding the effects of underwater noise on marine fauna, it is widely accepted that noise input to the marine environment can result in significant damage to marine life.

The analysis above shows that the problem has been addressed at the international and national level for more than a decade and that some important regulatory developments have been achieved, mainly in the form of non-binding measures. Guidelines and best practices governing different activities generating underwater noise have been laid down or developed within different fora. With regards to ship-generated noise, the IMO Guidelines for the Reduction of Underwater Noise from Commercial Shipping to Address Adverse Impacts on Marine Life stand out. They specifically suggest measures that reduce noise inputs from commercial shipping operations, that is, the source responsible for around 75 percent of all anthropogenic underwater noise. Given their relatively recent origin, it remains to be seen whether they will be effectively implemented by the different actors involved in the shipping industry and the extent to which they will contribute to solving problems resulting from these noise emissions.

Overall, the regulation of underwater noise appears to be beneficial to the marine environment. It is concluded and argued here that three basic steps are important for future regulatory efforts. First, the knowledge base should be

---

110   K. Zirbel et al., "Navy sonar, cetaceans and the US Supreme Court: A review of cetacean mitigation and litigation in the US," *Marine Pollution Bulletin* 63 (2011): 40–48.
111   Spain, Orden PRE/969/2008 No. 4 says: "Prohibition of military exercises involving the conduction of underwater explosions or use of low frequency sonars" (authors' translation). In addition, in response to whale stranding incidents, the Spanish Ministry of Defense has agreed with the Regional Government of the Canary Islands that, based on scientific advice, it would establish a list of areas where sonar tests could be carried out in general, see Schachten, n. 62 above, p. 100.

enlarged and particularly consider the cumulative effects of noise and other sources, including different types of energy pollution from, for example, energy emissions from submarine cables or light from offshore platforms, etc., as well as physical and chemical substances. Second, in the longer term, it should be considered whether there is a need to regulate anthropogenic noise emissions to the marine environment in a more comprehensive and global manner. Currently, regulations are non-binding. These soft law measures should be seen as first steps in a trial and error process that may indicate that instruments of greater mandatory force are necessary. Finally, future regulatory efforts should consider that restricting noise inputs to the marine environment may also reduce the potential benefits of those regulated activities, or simply transfer or transform their negative effects.[112] For example, noise-emitting activities may be protracted and conservation measures potentially lead to longer seismic surveys due to shutdowns, longer shipping routes and journeys due to speed reduction, or higher risks for personnel and gear due to longer times at sea. Thus, to be environmentally sound, effective, economically viable, and operationally realistic, regulations must consider all the relevant stakeholders' knowledge and interests and be flexible enough to facilitate implementation of new scientific insights into existing regulations.[113] An example of good governance in this regard seems to be the Joint Noise Working Group (JNWG) of CMS, ACCOBAMS and ASCOBANS.[114] Probably premised on such concerns, the JNWG's Operational Procedures establish that its members may be relevant experts from the fields of science, policy, industry, and relevant civil society organizations.[115] One of the main tasks of this advisory body is to further update and improve the existing guidelines.[116] Accordingly, inclusivity and flexibility in the regulatory process are quintessential ingredients to address the underwater noise pollution predicament.

---

112 Boebel et al., n. 13 above.
113 Id.
114 For further information on the JNWG, see n. 66 above, in particular the 2014 JNWG Report.
115 JNWG Operational Procedures, n. 66 above, para. 2.2.
116 See JNWG Terms of Reference, n. 66 above, para. ii.

Using Acoustic Footprints as a Tool to Facilitate Noise Reduction from Shipping

*Kendra A. Moore**

Marine Affairs Program, Dalhousie University, Halifax, Canada

Kayla M. Glynn

Clear Seas Centre for Responsible Marine Shipping, Vancouver, Canada

Introduction

The harmful impacts of ship-radiated noise have been demonstrated across a wide range of taxa, including marine mammals,[1] fish species,[2] and many invertebrates.[3] To meaningfully mitigate ship-radiated noise and unnecessary or unwanted sound produced by vessels, ship noise reduction targets must be created, and ship noise emissions must be aligned to those targets based on the soundscape and sensitivities of impacted ecosystems.

---

* The authors would like to thank Véronique Nolet, Jason Scherr, Krista Trounce, Laura Jensen and Dean Williams for their feedback on earlier versions of this manuscript, as well as Peter G. Wells for his recommendation to contribute this work.

1 V.M. Janik and P.M. Thompson, "Changes in surfacing patterns of bottlenose dolphins in response to boat traffic," *Marine Mammal Science* 12 (1996): 597–602; S.M. Nowacek, R.S. Wells and A.R. Solow, "Short-term effects of boat traffic on bottlenose dolphins, *Tursiops truncatus*, in Sarasota Bay, Florida," *Marine Mammal Science* 17 (2001): 673–688; R. Williams, A.W. Trites and D.E. Bain. "Behavioural responses of killer whales (*Orcinus orca*) to whale-watching boats: Opportunistic observations and experimental approaches," *Journal of the Zoological Society of London* 256 (2002): 255–270; N. Aguilar Soto et al., "Does intense ship noise disrupt foraging in deep-diving Cuvier's beaked whales (*Ziphius cavirostris*)?," *Marine Mammal Science* 22 (2006): 690–699; N.D. Merchant et al., "Measuring acoustic habitats," *Methods in Ecology and Evolution* 6 (2015): 257–265.

2 L.E. Wysocki, J.P. Dittami and F. Ladich, "Ship noise and cortisol secretion in European freshwater fishes," *Biological Conservation* 128, no. 4 (2006): 501–508; H. Slabbekoorn et al., "A noisy spring: The impact of globally rising underwater sound levels on fish," *Trends in Ecology and Evolution* 25 (2010): 419–427.

3 M.A. Wale, S.D. Simpson and A.N. Radford, "Size-dependent physiological responses of shore crabs to single and repeated playback of ship noise," *Biological Letters* 9 (2013): 111–118; R. Williams et al., "Impacts of anthropogenic noise on marine life: Publication patterns, new discoveries, and future directions in research and management," *Ocean & Coastal Management* 115 (2015): 17–24.

Williams et al. identified the need for a national ocean noise strategy to address the impacts of underwater noise on marine animals and their environments in Canada. This strategy would include the best available scientific information to address underwater noise mitigation broadly, and could set quantitative targets for the shipping industry, among other noise emission sources.[4] As the mitigation of chronic noise, such as noise emissions produced by shipping, requires a variety of management tools to target the multiple sources of noise from vessels and the range of sensitivities of marine animals and habitats, a framework is needed to guide the implementation of mitigation measures under a national strategy.

Acoustic footprints implemented as a methodology for policy and management can unite efforts to reduce ship-radiated noise. Footprints are a standardizing tool using comprehensive units that convey the impact of human activities[5] and could be used to develop policies to better manage and reduce ship-radiated noise in Canada. Acoustic footprints could be the standardizing management tool for underwater noise across Canada's three oceans, marine ecosystems, marine species, and shipping fleets.

Commercial marine shipping is recognized as one of the main contributors to increasing noise in the marine environment.[6] Shipping's low-frequency noise emissions have doubled every decade throughout the last half of the twentieth century.[7] As a result of the world's increased dependency on marine shipping, the industry is changing the soundscape of marine ecosystems.[8] It is this rate of change that emphasizes not only the importance of addressing this chronic and growing issue, but also the need to establish a benchmark to

---

4   R. Williams et al., "Marine mammals and ocean noise: Future directions and information needs with respect to science, policy and law in Canada," *Marine Pollution Bulletin* 86 (2014): 29–38.

5   W. Rees, "Eco-footprint analysis: Merits and brickbats," *Ecological Economics* 32 (2000): 371–374.

6   C.W. Clark et al., "Acoustic masking in marine ecosystems: Intuitions, analysis, and implication," *Marine Ecology Progress Series* 395 (2009): 201–222; Merchant et al., 2015, n. 1 above, p. 257; R. Williams et al., "Acoustic quality of critical habitats for three threatened whale populations," *Animal Conservation* 17, no. 2 (2014): 174–185; International Maritime Organization (IMO), "Guidelines for the reduction of underwater noise from commercial shipping to address adverse impacts on marine life," IMO Doc. MEPC.1/Circ.833 (7 April 2014) (IMO Guidelines).

7   M.A. McDonald, J.A. Hildebrand, and S.M. Wiggins, "Increases in deep ocean ambient noise in the Northeast Pacific west of San Nicolas Island California," *Journal of the Acoustical Society of America* 120, no. 2 (2006): 711–718.

8   J. Hildebrand, "Anthropogenic and natural sources of ambient noise in the ocean," *Marine Ecology Progress Series* 395 (2009): 5–20.

ensure that management of noise in Canada does not fall victim to the shifting baseline syndrome.[9]

Both industry and policy-makers have begun to develop and implement management strategies aimed at reducing ship-radiated noise, an internationally recognized issue. In Canada, acoustic monitoring and reduction programs are already in place to mitigate ship-radiated noise.[10] The implementation of acoustic footprints as a methodology for ship noise emissions reduction could unite initiatives already in place to reduce ship-radiated noise.

The objective of this article is to demonstrate how the implementation of acoustic footprints as a management and policy tool could benefit the commercial marine shipping industry, as well as Canadian marine ecosystems and species. Their implementation could help policy-makers and managers target ship-noise reduction and by extension benefit the commercial marine shipping industry, thereby supporting sustainable development by reducing environmental impacts while maintaining the shipping sector's economic prosperity. By framing science-based management strategies for the commercial marine shipping industry and by implementing acoustic footprint tracking, policies can be created to implement a tangible mitigation framework capable of accommodating the conservation of marine biota and economic generation of the shipping industry.

The Increase of Shipping and Noise

The increase of noise in the ocean is a significant management problem which has been recognized internationally by the Convention on the Protection of

---

9   D. Pauly, "Anecdotes and the shifting baseline syndrome of fisheries," *Trends in Ecology & Evolution* 10, no. 10 (1995): 430.

10 Green Marine, "Performance indicators for shipowners," (Quebec City: Green Marine, 2017), available online: <https://www.green-marine.org/wp-content/uploads/2017/01/2017-Summary_shipowners_FINAL.pdf>; J. Scherr, "Stewardship and Sustainability at the Port of Prince Rupert," (presentation at the Green Shipping Workshop, Vancouver, BC, 12 December 2016), available online: <http://www.sauder.ubc.ca/Faculty/Research_Centres/Centre_for_Transportation_Studies/Green_Shipping_-_Governance_and_Innovation_for_a_Sustainable_Maritime_Supply_Chain/~/media/Files/CTS/Port%20of%20Prince%20Rupert%20-%20Environment%20Program%20-%20UBC%20Shipping%20Workshop.ashx>; Hemmera Envirochem Inc., "Vessel Quieting Design, Technology, and Maintenance Options for Potential Inclusion in EcoAction Program Enhancing Cetacean Habitat and Observation Program," Report prepared for the Vancouver Fraser Port Authority (File: 302-045.03, April 2016), reprinted in Vancouver Fraser Port Authority, "An Evaluation of Vessel Quieting Design, Technology and Maintenance Options," ECHO Program Study Summary (2017), available online: <https://www.portvancouver.com/wp-content/uploads/2017/01/Vessel-Quieting.pdf>.

the Marine Environment of the Baltic Sea Area, the Convention for the Protection of the Marine Environment of the North-East Atlantic (OSPAR), and the United Nations Convention on the Law of the Sea (UNCLOS). Specifically, underwater noise from shipping has been identified as a growing and widespread pollutant in the global marine environment.[11] This is due to increasing human reliance on oceanic shipping routes. It is only within the last few decades that underwater noise has been recognized and established as a field of study,[12] warranting the identification of its impacts on marine biota and the need to understand the scope of ship-radiated noise.

Physics of Underwater Sound

Marine animals have evolved to use sound, in part due to sound's properties within water. Sound has an agreeable balance between speed, resolution, and transmission range within water when compared to light, which has limited range and travels at a slower speed within the ocean medium.[13] The propagation power of sound is dependent upon frequency, water column characteristics, and sound intensity. Lower frequencies travel further in water compared to high frequency sound, whereas higher frequencies have increased resolution.[14] This is due to the mechanical interaction of sound waves within the medium; higher frequencies are absorbed more rapidly by the environment, which explains why lower frequency sounds travel further.[15] The speed of sound in water also depends on temperature, pressure, and salinity that influences the density structure of the water column. Simply put, the velocity of sound in the water column increases with temperature, salinity, and pressure.[13] The intensity of sound is proportional to acoustic pressure, as the level of kinetic energy a sound wave produces results in more particle motion within the medium;[16] louder sounds travel farther than quieter sounds. Finally, the topography and sea conditions influence sound propagation in the ocean. Shallower depths and the composition of the sea floor can be more absorptive or reflective of sound waves, with the latter influencing the transmission of sound within the medium longer.[17] Sound can also be influenced by sea condition through the reflection of the sound waves on a calmer and relatively flatter sea surface.[18]

---

11 Clark et al., n. 6 above, p. 201; Merchant et al., n. 1 above, p. 257; Williams et al., n. 4 above, p. 30.
12 M. Simmonds, S. Dolman and L. Weilgart, *Oceans of Noise* (Wiltshire, UK: A WDCS Science Report, The Whale and Dolphin Conservation Society, 2003).
13 R. Swift, "The physics of underwater sound," in Simmonds et al., id., pp. 12–24, p. 12.
14 Id.
15 R.J. Urick, *Principles of Underwater Sound* (New York: McGraw-Hill Book Company, 1983).
16 Swift, n. 13 above, p. 18.
17 W.J. Richardson et al., *Marine Mammals and Noise* (San Diego: Academic Press, 1995).
18 Urick, n. 15 above, pp. 128–135.

Thus, sound propagation underwater is complex, as sound does not always conform to spherical spreading in a homogenous environment.[19] It is important to consider how sound travels underwater to understand the impacts of marine shipping, and that impacts are not uniform across all ocean ecosystems.

The Importance of Sound in the Marine Environment

Noise is a primary sensory mechanism for a variety of species in the ocean. As light only penetrates a limited depth in the majority of the ocean environment, hearing becomes important for animals to complete their life processes and for their survival. The often dark and turbid marine environment restricts the use of vision by marine animals.[20] The fact that underwater sound is conducive to many marine species has enabled many species' dependency on sound for their life processes.

The disturbance of noise to marine species can have a wide range of impacts, resulting in stress, reduction in communication or information loss, interference with foraging, predation avoidance, and the long-term impacts of reduced growth and reproduction.[21] The level of impact is dependent on the species, characteristics of the environment, and the sound itself.

The level of impact on marine biota caused by ship-radiated noise is dependent on its level of influence within the marine environment, in terms of consistency and intensity. Yet, noise is a ubiquitous stimulus, which can act as a stressor as its intensity in the ocean increases.[22] This classifies shipping noise as a chronic stressor for marine animals. An argument to chronic noise sources is the potential habituation or acclimation by species to the sound within their environment. However, the acclimation of animals to ship-radiated noise can be achieved if the animal perceives the stimuli to be the same level of stress or impact across instances and as non-life threatening, which is not the case for marine animals across all circumstances, as this does not equate to the animal being unaffected by further exposure to the stressor.[23] Due to the dependency of various marine species on sound and the pervasiveness of noise within the ocean, management must implement actions to mitigate the effects of shipping on marine species.

---

19 Swift, n. 13 above, p. 23.
20 Slabbekoorn et al., n. 2 above, p. 420.
21 Richardson et al., n. 17 above, p. 241; Simmonds et al., n. 12 above, p. 10; Slabbekoorn et al., n. 2 above, p. 420.
22 A.J. Wright and S. Kuczaj, "Noise-related stress and marine mammals: An introduction," *International Journal of Comparative Psychology* 20, no. 2 (2007): iii–viii.
23 L.M. Romero. "Physiological stress in ecology: Lessons from biomedical research," *Trends in Ecology and Evolution* 19 (2004): 249–255; Wright and Kuczaj, id., p. v.

Shipping Noise in the Marine Environment

The movement of vessels across the ocean medium produces sounds underwater by means of a number of sources and parameters. Shipping noise can be classified into three different source types: machinery noise, propeller noise, and hydrodynamic noise. The intensity and frequency of noise that a vessel produces is largely dependent upon the vessel's size, design, and speed.[24] It was generalized that larger vessels predominantly produce lower frequency sound, while smaller vessels produce higher frequency sound due to the shallow placement of their propellers and higher blade rotation rates.[25] However, individual ships in transit can produce low frequencies (20–30 dB re 1 $\mu Pa^2/Hz$ from 100 to 1,000 Hz), as well as high frequencies (5–13 dB from 10,000 to 96,000 Hz),[26] indicating a larger frequency emission range.[27] Additionally, sound production intensifies with increasing speed.[28] Vessel noise is a combination of narrow band and tonal sounds at specific frequencies, and broadband sounds with sound energy spreading continuously over a range of frequencies.[29] This creates a variety of sound signatures that are based on vessel types, and it is the cumulative level of vessel noise contributions within marine ecosystems that can change the soundscape of an ecosystem.

Introducing Acoustic Footprints

The use of footprints is a proven approach to helping individuals and decision-makers better understand the impacts of human activities on ecosystems. For example, the ecological footprint is widely advocated as a policy tool for visualizing and analyzing environmental impact, as well as for generating

---

24   Richardson et al., n. 17 above, p. 110.
25   C. Erbe, A. MacGillivray and R. Williams, "Mapping cumulative noise from shipping to inform marine spatial planning," *Journal of the Acoustical Society of America* 132, no. 5 (2012): EL423-EL428.
26   S. Veirs, V. Veirs and J.D. Wood, "Ship noise extends to frequencies used for echolocation by endangered killer whales," *PeerJ* 4 (2014): p. e1657.
27   L. Hermannsen et al., "High frequency components of ship noise in shallow water with a discussion of implications for harbor porpoises (*Phocoena phocoena*)," *Journal of the Acoustical Society of America* 136, no. 4 (2014): 1640–1653.
28   D. Ross, *Mechanics of Underwater Noise* (New York: Pergamon, 1976); P.T. Arveson and D.J. Vendittis, "Radiated noise characteristics of a modern cargo ship," *Journal of the Acoustical Society of America* 107, no. 1 (2000): 118–129; R.M. Heitmeyer, S.C. Wales and L.A. Pflug, "Shipping noise predictions: Capabilities and limitations," *Marine Technology Society Journal* 37, no. 4 (2003): 54–65.
29   Richardson et al., n. 17 above, p. 111.

awareness of unsustainable social and economic practices.[30] The communicability of footprints, to effectively convey environmental overshoot and/or the overuse of an ecosystem beyond its regenerative capacity, is the reason for its popularity.[31]

Acoustic footprints could be applied as a standardized tool, capable of conceptualizing the impact of ship-radiated noise on marine fauna – aiding industry, management, and policy-makers in mitigating the threat of ship noise emissions. Ship noise footprints could be used against acceptable standardized footprints to inform and evaluate mitigation solutions.[32] Using this tool to create a common language that describes the impact of ship-radiated noise will improve communication with stakeholders and help minimize or avoid harm. It is these attributes that favor the application of acoustic footprints for the mitigation of ship-radiated noise, as opposed to noise budgets, a method used to quantify the effects of underwater sound on the marine animals or the marine environment,[33] which is another accepted strategy to communicate and mitigate underwater noise. Although both methods can effectively quantify and set benchmarks to mitigate underwater noise, footprints have a greater application in communicability and understanding across stakeholders.

Definition

The use of an acoustic footprint as a tool to reduce ship-radiated noise is dependent upon selected noise indicators, the accepted benchmarks of noise pollution and the footprint's applicable scale. For the purposes of this article, an acoustic footprint will be subdivided into two cases. First, the acoustic footprint tool can be applied to individual vessels to target their source of noise emissions and to facilitate source emission reductions. Alternatively, it can be applied to a geographic region, thereby taking into account the noise impact of multiple vessels within a defined environment. In both instances, the acoustic footprint tool can be used for initial assessment and can inform decision-making as to whether ship noise emissions require reduction.

---

30 S. Moore, M. Nye and Y. Rydin, "Using ecological footprints as a policy driver: The case of sustainable construction planning policy in London," *Local Environment* 12, no. 1 (2007): 1–15.
31 Rees, n. 5 above, p. 372.
32 E. Baudin et al., "Noise footprint: A proposal within the framework of FP7 AQUO project to define a goal based approach towards the reduction of underwater radiated noise from shipping" (paper presented at the 33rd OMAE Conference, San Francisco, June 2014).
33 J.H. Miller, J.A. Nystuen and D.L. Bradley, "Ocean noise budgets," *Bioacoustics* 17, no. 1-3 (2008): 133–136.

Individual Vessel Footprints

A vessel can be assessed to determine its individual acoustic footprint by measuring the sound it produces during operation. A vessel's sound emission is the product of three sources of radiated noise: machinery noise, propeller noise, and hydrodynamic noise.[34]

Machinery noise is caused by the mechanical vibration of the moving parts of the engine and vessel, as well as the path of vibration – noise that originates from inside the vessel from the motor and is projected into the water from the vessel hull.[35] This sound source can be intensified with irregularities in the machinery's composition and function. Urick outlines five originating sources of mechanical vibrations: rotating unbalanced parts, like out-of-round shafts or motor armatures; repetitive discontinuities, such as gear teeth, armature slots, or turbine blades; reciprocating parts, such as explosions in the cylinders of reciprocating engines; cavitation and turbulence of the fluid in the pumps, pipes, valves, and condenser discharges; and, finally, mechanical friction on the bearings and journals. The impact of machinery noise increases with the size of the vessel, as the size of the hull increases the propagating capacity of noise.[36] However, outboard motor vessels do not have as high a propagation extent from machinery noise as inboard motor vessels, because their motors are situated outside the vessel hull.

Propeller noise is the second category of vessel-radiated noise and the dominant source of noise contribution from vessels. Propeller cavitation and propeller singing are the two main factors contributing to propeller-generated noise.[37] As a propeller rotates in the water, regions of negative pressure around the blades are created that cause ruptures and cavities to form in the water, creating bubbles.[38] When these bubbles collapse, they create a pulse of sound in the water. Propeller singing is defined as vortex shedding where the rotation of the propeller creates a vibrational frequency producing a turbulent stream of collapsing bubbles.[39] This produces a strong tone between 100 to 1,000 hertz (Hz) which intensifies and increases if the propeller is damaged, or if vessels with multiple propellers operate asynchronously.[40] Additionally, the random collapse of bubbles occurs on a continuous spectrum. For high frequencies, the spectrum level (defined as the intensity level of a sound wave within a 1 Hz band) decreases; at low frequencies the spectrum level of cavitation noise

---

34   Urick, n. 15 above, pp. 332–340.
35   Ross, n. 28 above, p. 100.
36   Urick, n. 15 above, p. 356.
37   Richardson et al., n. 17 above, p. 110.
38   Urick, n. 15 above, p. 334.
39   Richardson et al., n. 17 above, p. 111.
40   Ross, n. 28 above, p. 300.

increases with frequency.[41] Larger cavitation bubbles are generated at greater speeds, creating greater low-frequency sound, further adding to acoustic noise output.

Finally, hydrodynamic noise is caused by the erratic flow of water past a moving vessel. This irregular flow of water causes pressure fluctuations that emit sound into the ocean, or cause vibrations along parts of a vessel within the turbulent boundary layer.[42] The flow of water can cause vibrational resonance across openings or within struts of vessels creating more noise.[43] Additionally, the noise of the bow of the boat breaking waves, the produced wake, and the intake and exhaust of the water circulating system, increases noise emissions from vessels.[44]

A combination of these three source types, machinery, propeller, and hydrodynamic noise, can contribute to the level of noise output from a vessel within the marine environment. By measuring the output of noise from these three sources, an acoustic footprint can be created for individual vessels. This can be used as a benchmark to minimize noise output or monitor vessel noise emissions.

Spatially Specific Footprints

The need to mitigate noise pollution spatially within the marine environment is guided by the reality that noise radiates on a mesoscale or greater macroscale. The delineation of spatial acoustic mitigation areas can be identified within species' critical habitats or ecologically significant areas. However, the prioritization of acoustic marine management strategies is subject to the justification that marine animals are within a defined marine area and will benefit from reduced acoustic output from shipping. Given the potential spatial extent of noise pollution, it is valuable to include the consideration of spatially specific footprints within marine spatial planning to account for appropriate mitigation and activity use of a marine region.

Impact assessment modelling can create a specific acoustic footprint in a regional area of a specific species by using a known acoustically sensitive species as an indicator of impact, or by using an ecosystem-based management approach. The footprint produced can then be used by managers for mitigation purposes. The creation of the footprint is developed through a network of acoustic monitoring platforms and modelling. The parameters necessary are time of year, weather conditions, topography, physical oceanography

---

41 Urick, n. 15 above, pp. 329–340.
42 Id.
43 Id.
44 Id.

conditions, bathymetry, and noise recordings.⁴⁵ This information can be used to determine sound propagation within the regional environment and the level of impact on marine biota. An impact assessment model can determine the zone of audibility (the range and depth of noise detection by marine animals), the zone of masking (the range and depth which would disrupt marine animal communication), the zone of responsiveness (the range and depth to which the animal would react to the noise), and the zone of hearing damage (the range and depth predicted for temporary or permanent hearing loss).⁴⁶ This information can feed into a gradient level acoustic footprint for a spatial area for management and policy-makers.

Spatial noise management is an attractive mitigation strategy for the coastal environment due to the defined boundaries of national jurisdictions. This enables monitoring of marine animals and vessels within the defined area and the implementation of policies or application of national legislation. Shipping lane governance does not fall within the jurisdiction of one country, but to the International Maritime Organization (IMO). Designated critical habitat and marine protected areas are ideal for acoustic management implementation because of the conservation actions required in Canada under the *Species at Risk Act* and the *Oceans Act*.⁴⁷ Port authorities enable ideal noise management opportunities due to their jurisdiction over defined areas and continued interaction with the shipping industry, ideal for measuring baselines.

Acoustic Thresholds

Whether the acoustic footprint is for an individual vessel or a regional area, a threshold of noise disturbance needs to be determined to quantify the scale of the footprint in terms of overshoot. Within the United States, acoustic thresholds have been set to minimize noise disturbance to marine mammals. The Marine Mammal Acoustic Technical Guidance document outlines thresholds in decibels (dB) for five different marine animal hearing groups based on their hearing frequency and whether the sound is impulsive (brief with high peaks) or non-impulsive (tonal or broadband, that is brief or continuous and does not have high peaks).⁴⁸ These thresholds are measured within the environment as

---

45   "D1.6. Validation of the noise footprint assessment model. Achieve Quieter Oceans by shipping noise footprint reduction FP7 – Collaborative Project no. 314227" (AQUO Project Consortium, 2013); C. Erbe, "Underwater noise of whale-watching boats and potential effects on killer whales (*Orcinus orca*), based on an acoustic impact model," *Marine Mammal Science* 18 (2002): 394–418.
46   Erbe, n. 45 above, pp. 411–413.
47   *Species at Risk Act*, SC 2002, c. 29 (SARA); *Oceans Act*, SC 1996, c. 31.
48   National Marine Fisheries Service, National Oceanic and Atmospheric Administration (NOAA), "2018 Revision to: Technical Guidance for Assessing the Effects of Anthropogenic

sound pressure levels: the difference between the sound wave and the ambient pressure of the water passing through it, which is measured on "the logarithm of the ratio of a given sound pressure to the reference sound pressure in decibels is 20 times the logarithm to the base of ten of the ratio."[49] For example, noise produced by human activities that could lead to baleen whales receiving impulse sound levels of 160 dB re 1 lPa, or continuous sound levels of 120 dB re 1 lPa, are determined to cause harm.[50] This policy was developed to focus on mitigating acute sound production, such as pile driving, sonar, or seismic, as opposed to shipping. However, it does set noise disturbance benchmarks.

Within a selected regional area, monitoring animals and vessels for comparison to acceptable thresholds is necessary to evoke mitigation. Acoustic monitoring networks within a region can detect animal communication and the noise generated from vessels passing within the defined area. This information can inform managers of potential disturbance from vessel noise to the animals due to overlapping frequencies or high volumes that could mask or disrupt communication. Hatch et al. monitored the shipping noise in the Stellwagen Bank National Marine Sanctuary, off the eastern coast of the United States, which is an important feeding ground for the North Atlantic right whale, fin whale, and humpback whale.[51] Ship traffic in the area has the potential to impact the range of acoustic communication of these whales. The monitoring efforts to identify the source level of vessel noise, with the known communication frequencies and acceptable level of decibels for these cetaceans are measured against the acoustic harassment thresholds of the National Oceanic and Atmospheric Administration's (NOAA) Marine Mammal Acoustic Technical Guidance for human-made sound.

The current approach within Canada is to determine acoustic thresholds for specific species. For example, one of the major threats to southern resident killer whales, an endangered species, is acoustic disturbance.[52] Killer whales' peak hearing sensitivity is approximately 20 kilohertz (kHz) and they show

---

Sound on Marine Mammal Hearing: Underwater Acoustic Thresholds for Onset of Permanent and Temporary Threshold Shifts," NOAA Technical Memorandum NMFS-OPR-59 (Washington, DC: U.S. Department of Commerce, NOAA, 2018), p. 3.

49 Acoustic Glossary, 15 December 2017, available online: <http://www.acoustic-glossary.co.uk/sound-pressure.htm>.
50 NOAA, "Regulations governing the taking and importing of marine mammals. Subchapter C: Marine Mammal Protection Act Regulations (50 CFR 216)" (NOAA, 2005).
51 L.T. Hatch et al., "Quantifying loss of acoustic communication space for right whales in and around a U.S. National Marine Sanctuary," *Conservation Biology* 26 (2012): 983–994.
52 Fisheries and Oceans Canada, "Action Plan for the Northern and Southern Resident Killer Whale (*Orcinus orca*) in Canada," Species at Risk Act Action Plan Series (Ottawa: Fisheries and Oceans Canada, 2017).

behavioral responses to sound between 75 Hz to over 100 kHz.[53] Further, the resident killer whale ecotype threshold for loudness is 105–110 dB, as determined to cause behavioral changes in northern resident killer whales.[54] Known acoustic thresholds allow managers to define criteria for the critical habitat of species to ensure conservation measures are met. These thresholds can then be managed using acoustic monitoring networks within species' ranges.

Current Industry Approaches

Following an increasing body of literature released in the 2000s on the impacts of ship noise emissions, the IMO's Marine Environment Protection Committee (MEPC) commenced discussions on the implications of ship-radiated noise.[55] As a result, MEPC developed non-mandatory Guidelines to minimize incidental noise from commercial vessels in the marine environment.[56] The Guidelines for the Reduction of Underwater Noise from Commercial Shipping to Address Impacts on Marine Life were published by the IMO in 2014. The Guidelines largely focus on providing non-prescriptive advice concerning factors that can be taken into account when designing a ship in order to reduce underwater noise and were intended for designers, shipbuilders, and ship operators.[57] The Guidelines established the international standard to reduce ship-radiated noise.

The IMO's Guidelines mainly focus on the primary sources of ship-radiated underwater noise associated with ship design and construction.[58] In particular, they focus on ship design, operational and maintenance considerations. Design considerations in the Guidelines include quieting propellers, hull design, and onboard machinery. Operational and maintenance considerations

---

53   J.D. Hall and C.S. Johnson, "Auditory thresholds of a killer whale *Orcinus orca* Linnaeus," *Journal of the Acoustical Society of America* 51 (1972): 515–517; M.D. Syzmanski et al., "Killer whale (*Orcinus orca*) hearing: Auditory brainstem response and behavioral audiograms," *Journal of the Acoustical Society of America* 106 (1999): 1134–1141.

54   R. Williams, A.W. Trites and D.E. Bain, "Behavioural responses of Killer Whales (*Orcinus orca*) to whale-watching boats: Opportunistic observations and experimental approaches," *Journal of the Zoological Society of London* 256 (February 2002): 255–270.

55   "IMO and anthropogenic underwater noise," available online: <http://www.un.org/depts/los/consultative_process/contributions_19cp/IMO.pdf>; See also V. Nolet, *Understanding Anthropogenic Underwater Noise* (Ottawa: Transport Canada, 2017).

56   Id.

57   IMO Guidelines, n. 6 above; See also J. Harrison, *Saving the Oceans through Law: The International Legal Framework for the Protection of the Marine Environment* (Oxford: Oxford University Press, 2017); Nolet, id.

58   Id.

in the Guidelines include propeller and underwater hull surface cleaning, speed reduction, and rerouting. The quieting techniques outlined within the Guidelines are further discussed below in terms of their operational as well as design and maintenance applications within management.

On-water Operational Management Options

Operational management options, such as area-based management approaches, capable of decreasing ship-radiated underwater noise are well established within the international framework that regulates the marine shipping industry. For example, within UNCLOS, pollution is defined as

> the introduction by man, directly or indirectly, of substances or energy into the marine environment, including estuaries, which results or is likely to result in such deleterious effects as harm to living resources and marine life, hazards to human health, hindrance to marine activities, including fishing and other legitimate uses of the sea, impairment of quality for use of sea water and reduction of amenities.[59]

Nations that have ratified UNCLOS have the right to impose laws and regulations on any vessel within their territorial sea to limit marine pollution. Although not originally intended to include underwater noise, UNCLOS defines pollution of the marine environment as the introduction by man of substances or energy into the marine environment which results in harm to living resources and marine life.[60] As noise could legitimately be considered energy within UNCLOS' definition of pollution, it could be managed under UNCLOS.[61]

Many international and domestic bodies have the responsibility to protect the marine environment, including the management and mitigation of ship noise emissions. Given the international precedence, the mitigation strategies of IMO for shipping noise set the standard for international and domestic governance. While the IMO's broad definition of pollution from shipping vessels does not include underwater noise, the impacts of ship-radiated underwater noise on marine life has been taken into account through the regulation and establishment of Particularly Sensitive Sea Areas (PSSAs).[62] PSSAs are an area-based approach to management. They are areas that the IMO can designate

---

59   United Nations Convention on the Law of the Sea, *adopted 10 December 1982 (entered into force 16 November 1994), 1833 United Nations Treaty Series 397*, art. 1(4).
60   Id.
61   Nolet, n. 55 above.
62   IMO, "Revised Guidelines for the Identification and Designation of Particularly Sensitive Sea Areas," adopted 1 December 2005, IMO Doc. Res. A 24/Res.982 (6 February 2006); See also Nolet, n. 55 above.

as vulnerable to international shipping.[63] Within these areas, ships registered to IMO Member States must follow any approved or adopted associated protective measures (APMS).[64] APMS can be introduced independently of PSSAS; however, within a PSSA, they are implemented as a means of providing greater marine protection within the designated area.[65] When implemented, three APMS have the ability to mitigate the impacts of underwater noise radiated by commercial marine vessels, namely, speed controls, rerouting, and Areas to be Avoided (ATBAS).

These APMS are efficient in protecting sensitive marine areas. However, in deciding to implement such operational measures, the decision-maker consider that while these strategies may be effective, they may also be perceived as a threat to marine shipping, because an associated risk of their implementation may be the impediment of traffic which has economic repercussions.

Speed Control

Ship speed control can be effective in reducing ship-radiated noise. Most ships can reduce their broadband source level by ~1 dB by slowing down by 1 knot.[66] Typically, ship-radiated noise decreases if the ship's speed drops lower than the cavitation inception speed of the propeller, which is known to account for 80–85 percent of the noise produced by a ship.[67] However, this is ship-dependent. Specifically, it depends on the propulsion system of a vessel, whether it has a controllable pitch propeller or a fixed pitch propeller. Nonetheless, speed control can be applied as an area-based management tool within a distinct boundary such as a PSSA.[68] This APM, also referred to as a slow-down, can be seasonal, mandatory, or voluntary.

The variability in this management tool enables managers to accommodate the mandates of ship operators, as well as conservation targets. It is important to note that vessel speed controls can also be seen as a long-term management solution beyond a spatial or temporal boundary, as they may have implications

---

63   International Chamber of Marine Shipping (ICS), "The Regulation of International Shipping," 2017, available online: <http://www.ics-shipping.org/shipping-facts/safety-and-regulation/the-regulation-of-international-shipping>.
64   J. Roberts, "Compulsory pilotage in international straits: The Torres Strait PSSA proposal," *Ocean Development & International Law* 37 (2006): 93–112; M.J. Kachel, *Particularly Sensitive Sea Areas: The IMO's Role in Protecting Vulnerable Marine Areas* (Hamburg: Springer, 2008).
65   Kachel, id., pp. 154–231.
66   S. Veirs et al., "A key to quieter seas: Half of ship noise comes from 15% of the fleet," *PeerJ PrePrints* (2018).
67   Nolet, n. 55 above.
68   Kachel, n. 64 above, pp. 199, 212.

over a vessel's entire operating area.[69] Unfortunately, there are shortcomings to speed controls. Prolonging a vessel's journey by restricting its speed may not only have adverse economic effects for the industry, it can also prolong the length of time that individual vessels are radiating noise emissions in their vicinity. Veirs et al. identify this prolonged exposure problem, yet identify that the reduction of sound level in decibels outweighs the temporal overlap for their species of interest, the southern resident killer whale.[70] A cost benefit analysis of exposure time versus sound reduction, as well as potentially requiring further mitigation measures to address exposure, requires further research per ecosystem and species. Thus, the benefit of speed control must also be considered in conjunction with sensitive areas and traffic density.

Rerouting

Shipping densities and trends in routing are a significant contributor to noise pollution.[71] In particular, coastal routes for large commercial vessels are significant contributors to chronic vessel-radiated noise. Where these routes overlap with sensitive marine areas, such as well-known habitats of at-risk species, including feeding grounds, calving grounds, or migratory pathways, the impacts of noise pollution increase in severity.[72] Rerouting, defined by the IMO as an area-based management measure to relocate relatively well-defined shipping routes in order to minimize the adverse impacts of shipping on marine life,[73] can be implemented to mitigate the impacts of ship-radiated underwater noise where sensitive marine areas overlap with heavily trafficked shipping routes. Rerouting has been applied as an APM within and beyond PSSAs worldwide.[74] In some cases of rerouting, the purpose of the APM is to reduce the presence of ships in areas where whales are known to frequent in order to reduce the likelihood of ship strikes.[75] Although this strategy is used to reduce the risk of ship

---

69   Nolet, n. 55 above.
70   Veirs et al., n. 67 above, p. 6.
71   B.L. Southall, *Final Report: Shipping Noise and Marine Mammals: A forum for science, management, and technology*, Final Report of the NOAA International Symposium, U.S. NOAA Fisheries, 18–19 May 2004, Arlington, VA, available online: <http://www.beamreach.org/wiki/images/4/47/2004NoiseReport.pdf>.
72   Harrison, n. 57 above, pp. 135–136.
73   IMO, "Particularly Sensitive Sea Areas," 2017, available online: <http://www.imo.org/en/OurWork/Environment/PSSAs/Pages/Default.aspx>.
74   G.K. Silber et al., "The role of the International Maritime Organization in reducing vessel threat to whales: Process, options, action and effectiveness," *Marine Policy* 36, no. 6 (2012): 1221–1233.
75   A.S.M. Vanderlaan and C.T. Taggart, "Efficacy of a voluntary area to be avoided to reduce of lethal vessel strikes to endangered whales," *Conservation Biology* 23, no. 6 (2009): 1467–1474.

strikes, it also causes a reduction in ship traffic through critical habitat, especially that of species at high risk, and may also help to reduce vessel-radiated noise pollution in sensitive areas.[76] Rerouting has the potential to lessen the impacts of ship-radiated noise in sensitive areas by displacing the source of noise.

Areas to be Avoided

Areas to be Avoided (ATBAS) are areas within defined limits in which navigation should be avoided by all ships, at specific times of the year, or by certain ship types.[77] Similarly to APMS, ATBAS are an area-based, operational management measure to relocate ship traffic as a means to minimize the adverse impacts of shipping on marine life.[78] Both mandatory and voluntary ATBAS have been applied as APMS within and beyond PSSAS worldwide.

In terms of vessel-radiated underwater noise mitigation strategies, the implementation of ATBAS can result in a similar outcome to that of rerouting. Their implementation aims to reduce ship traffic in a given area,[79] which could ultimately reduce associated noise emissions. However, ATBAS differ from rerouting as an APM as they can wholly exclude a designated area from marine traffic and can be specific to traffic type.[80] Thus, ATBAS can be implemented in a manner that targets a specific desired outcome. Some examples are:

- Mandatory ATBAS: Can be implemented when a sensitive habitat requires maximum noise reduction. A mandatory ATBA, such as the Bay of Fundy Traffic Separation, implemented in 2003,[81] may be the best APM to reduce all commercial vessel-radiated noise in a given area.
- Temporal Voluntary ATBAS: Can be implemented if a migratory species requires noise reduction. In sensitive habitat a voluntary, seasonal ATBA may be the best APM to implement to reduce all commercial vessel-radiated noise. For example, a migratory species may require special consideration May – September, but may not be present in the habitat for the remainder of the year. A seasonal voluntary ATBA was implemented in Roseway Basin in 2008.[82]

---

76 Nolet, n. 55 above.
77 A. Gillespie, "Vulnerability and response to the risk of international shipping: The case of the Salish Sea," *Review of European Community & International Environmental Law Journal* 25, no. 3 (2016): 1–16.
78 Id.
79 IMO, n. 73 above.
80 Id.
81 Canadian Whale Institute (CWI), "Changing marine policy to protect right whales," 2017, available online: <https://www.canadianwhaleinstitute.ca/changing-marine-policy-to-protect-right-whales>.
82 Vanderlaan and Taggart, n. 75 above, p. 1468.

– Vessel Type Dependent ATBAS: Can be implemented if marine life present in a distinct habitat, or a species at risk, is sensitive to a particular set of frequencies more likely to be produced by a vessel type. For example, ATBAS have been introduced in the State of Washington, United States, to decrease the risk of an oil tanker spilling its cargo in sensitive habitat.[83] They could also be introduced to limit large vessel traffic in areas sensitive to chronic low frequency noise outputs.

The ability to modify ATBAS makes them a viable management measure for the reduction of ship noise emissions. Although ATBAS cannot eliminate far reaching ship noise emissions, by restricting ship traffic in a given area, ATBAS can be effective in reducing ship-radiated noise. Specifically, they can be effective in decreasing high frequency sound, which does not typically travel as far as low frequency sound, but has increased resolution.[84]

Design and Maintenance Management Options

In addition to the implementation of on-water operational management strategies, the application of design and maintenance management approaches can also be effective in reducing an individual vessel's underwater noise output. The sounds produced by each individual vessel can contribute to overall ambient noise levels on variable spatial scales.[85] Different elements of a vessel's build can produce sounds of different frequencies, which are differentially transmitted in the marine environment.[86] A propeller-driven ship has a number of noise sources: the main and auxiliary engines, electric motors, and the flow of noise due to turbulence from the wake of the hull and appendages. However, the amount of noise an individual ship produces can be reduced by choosing a design profile that provides the best underwater noise performance possible and ensuring that the vessel is well maintained.[87]

In 2017, the Enhancing Cetacean Habitat and Observation (ECHO) Program, managed by the Vancouver Fraser Port Authority (VFPA), commissioned a study to identify design and maintenance options to make vessels quieter.[88] The study evaluated both the effectiveness and the ease of verifiability

---

83 Friends of the San Juans (FOSJ), "Designating the Salish Sea as a PSSA," 2016, available online: <https://sanjuans.org/wp-content/uploads/2016/11/DesignatingtheSalishSeaasaPSSAOverview.pdf>.
84 Swift, n. 13 above, p. 23.
85 Southall, n. 71 above, p. 5.
86 Id.
87 D.-Q. Li and J. Hallander, "Shipping and underwater radiated noise," *SSPA Highlights* 61 (2015): 14–16, available online: <https://www.sspa.se/shipping-and-underwater-radiated-noise>.
88 Hemmera Envirochem Inc., n. 10 above, p. 9.

considerations and identified 30 design and maintenance options to reduce vessel-radiated underwater noise. Tables 19.1 and 19.2 aggregate these options. The options were evaluated and assigned ratings based on information compiled throughout the study. Of the 30 options evaluated, the most effective verifiable options for potential noise reduction included regular propeller cleaning and repair, elastic mounting, structural reinforcements, regular cleaning of the hull, decoupling coating, Propeller Boss Cap Fins (PBCFS), Schneekluth ducts, Mewis ducts, liquefied natural gas (LNG)-fueled, gas and steam turbine powered, and electrical-driven vessels, and air injection to propeller and bubble curtains.[89]

A reduction in ship-radiated noise emissions of about 10 dB should be attainable with existing technologies.[90] Implementing options to reduce cavitation alone is expected to reduce noise output by 6–10 dB from even the noisiest 16 percent of all vessels and could result in a 60 percent noise reduction in ensonified areas.[91] This suggests the level of impact propeller cavitation reduction techniques could have in reducing shipping noise is high.

Improvements made at the design stage for new ships are the most cost-effective, but retro-fitting of older vessels is also an option.[92] In order to effectively reduce ship-radiated noise, marine managers must know all of the most effective and feasible options for reducing noise emissions from shipping. This includes the use of acoustic footprints.

Motivations and Incentives for Industry to Reduce Underwater Noise

It is imperative that underwater noise be reduced to ensure conservation targets are met; yet, noise emissions reductions need to be feasible for implementation by the marine shipping sector. The implementation of managerial measures, such as acoustic footprint monitoring, to mitigate ship-radiated underwater noise could benefit the commercial marine shipping industry. The following section outlines some of the motivations and incentives for industry to actively pursue the reduction of ship-radiated underwater noise, including

---

89   Id., pp. 9–10.
90   Veirs et al., n. 66 above, p. 5.
91   WWF-Canada, *Finding Management Solutions for Underwater Noise in Canada's Pacific*, (Vancouver Aquarium and WWF-Canada, 2013), available online: <http://awsassets.wwf.ca/downloads/ocean_noise_workshop_final_report_2013_2.pdf>.
92   C. Lo, "Sounding the alarm on underwater noise," *Ship Technology* (29 January 2017), available online: <http://www.ship-technology.com/features/featuresounding-the-alarm-on-underwater-noise-5725953/>.

TABLE 19.1 Design options to reduce vessel-radiated underwater noise

Design Options	Definition
1. Changes to hull form	A well-designed hull requires less power for a given speed, which is likely to result in less noise. Efficient hull design also provides a more uniform inflow to the propeller, thereby increasing the propeller's efficiency and reducing vibration and noise output caused by uneven wake flow.
2. Use of quieter engines	Ships can be built using quieter engines, such as LNG-fueled, steam/gas turbine systems, diesel-electric systems, and electronically driven engines.
3. Propeller design modified to reduce cavitation and improve wake flow	Many propeller designs optimized to reduce turbulence and underwater noise are now available. Efficient propeller designs includePBCFs, the Schneekluth duct, the Mewis duct, and implementing air injection to propeller and bubble curtains to minimize cavitation erosion.
4. Reduced onboard engine and machinery noise	Elastic mountings and structural reinforcements can isolate and reduce onboard vibration transmission to the hull, reducing noise.
5. Alternate propulsion	Some alternative forms of propulsion produce less noise than conventional propellers, including water jets, podded drivers, and twin propeller arrangement.

(Adapted from Hemmera Envirochem Inc., n. 10 above)

meeting political priorities, enhancing organizational identity while gaining a competitive edge, as well as improving efficiency and cost reductions.

Political Priorities

Regulations and policies aimed at mitigating the impacts of ship-radiated noise are already being considered and implemented internationally.[93] It is vital that regulations and policy aimed at the reduction of ship-radiated noise

---

93   ICS, n. 63 above.

Table 19.2. Maintenance options to reduce vessel-radiated underwater noise

Maintenance Options	Definition
1. Regular propeller cleaning and repair	Propeller cleaning and repairs in dry dock, or underwater using divers. This can reduce propeller cavitation and also reduce turbulence, which increases efficiency.
2. Regular hull cleaning	Hull cleaning and repairs done in dry dock, or underwater using divers. This can reduce turbulence and therefore related noise.
3. Hull coating	Can include coatings and other methods generally used to prevent fouling, which improves water flow and reduces turbulence related noise, such as anti-fouling paints and non-stick coatings. This can also include the application of decoupling coatings – a layer of thick material which reduces the radiation efficiency of the hull and reduces transmission of underwater noise from the hull into the water.

(Adapted from Hemmera Envirochem Inc., n. 10 above)

be uniform worldwide as noise is a transboundary pollutant. The alternative would be a patchwork of conflicting national regulations, which would compromise the efficiency of management efforts.

The marine shipping industry is principally regulated by the IMO. Member States of the IMO develop and adopt a comprehensive framework of regulations in the form of international diplomatic conventions which govern the safety of ships and protection of the marine environment.[94] Nations which are members of the IMO are then required to implement and enforce and comply with these international rules for ships registered under their flag.[95] It is these

---

94 Id.
95 Id.

convention and international standards that set the precedence for the international shipping industry.

Advances in policy are generally tabled at the IMO by nations that are seeking to advance their own legislation regarding key issues within the marine shipping industry. For example, the United States brought its concerns regarding the impacts of ship-radiated noise to the IMO, which resulted in the publication of the Guidelines for the Reduction of Underwater Noise from Commercial Shipping to Address Impacts on Marine Life, as the international community identified that underwater noise has short and long-term consequences.[96]

In addition to the Guidelines, the European Union (EU) has categorized underwater noise as a general marine pollutant under its Marine Strategy Framework Directive.[97] OSPAR agreed upon common indicators for monitoring underwater noise to help assess its impact on the marine environment. OSPAR is also developing an inventory of measures to mitigate the impacts of underwater noise.[98] Another initiative within the EU advancing underwater noise legislation is the Agreement on the Conservation of Cetaceans of the Black Seas, Mediterranean Sea and contiguous Atlantic area (ACCOBAMS). ACCOBAMS is a cooperative tool for the conservation of marine biodiversity in the Mediterranean and Black Seas that has also established guidelines to mitigate the impacts of underwater noise.[99] The purpose of ACCOBAMS is to reduce threats to cetaceans in the Mediterranean and the ACCOBAMS Agreement has addressed anthropogenic noise as a threat to cetaceans since 2004.[100]

---

96   IMO, "Shipping noise and marine mammals," Submitted by the United States, IMO Doc. MEPC 57/INF.4 (17 December 2007); IMO, "Minimizing the introduction of incidental noise from commercial shipping operations into the marine environment to reduce potential adverse impacts on marine life," Submitted by the United States, IMO Doc. MEPC 58/19 (25 June 2008); See also Nolet, n. 55 above, p. 42.

97   European Union, Directive 2008/56/EC of the European Parliament and of the Council of 17 June 2008 establishing a framework for community action in the field of marine environmental policy (Marine Strategy Framework Directive), OJ L 164 (25 June 2008), pp. 19–40; See also Nolet, n. 55 above, p. 47.

98   Id.

99   Agreement on the Conservation of Cetaceans in the Black Sea, Mediterranean Sea and Contiguous Atlantic Area, adopted 24 November 1996, 36 *International Legal Materials* 777 (1997); See also Nolet, n. 55 above, p. 48.

100   Meeting of the Parties (MOP 2) to the ACCOBAMS, "Resolution 2.16: Assessment and impact assessment of man-made noise," (2004); Meeting of the Parties (MOP 3) to the ACCOBAMS, "Resolution 3.10: Guidelines to address the impact of anthropogenic noise on marine mammals in the ACCOBAMS area," (2007); Meeting of the Parties (MOP 4) to the ACCOBAMS, "Resolution 4.17: Guidelines to address the impact of anthropogenic noise on cetaceans in the ACCOBAMS area," (2010); Meeting of the Parties (MOP 5) to

Thus, the advancement of regulatory measures identifying underwater noise as a pollutant is advancing, and will continue to develop to potentially influence the standards required of the international marine shipping fleet.

As environmental regulations regarding marine shipping advance, ship operators who do not opt to take voluntary measures to reduce their impacts can be left with no choice but to undertake costly last-minute retrofitting.[101] In the case of the International Convention for the Control and Management of Ships' Ballast Water and Sediments, implementation of the IMO requirements were delayed in order to accommodate financially pressed ship operators.[102] Meanwhile, those who had implemented voluntary upgrades were not adversely impacted. Those who voluntary upgraded their vessels are now able to enter U.S. waters, a nation with more stringent regulations in place, penalizing those who were unprepared for the legislative changes.[103] In this case, the implementation of an advanced convention progressed and those who voluntarily adapted in advance to its provisions gained a competitive edge over those who required costly upgrades.

Given that policies recognizing noise as a pollutant and threat to marine biota are being further developed, it is in the industry's best interest to proactively adopt noise mitigation tactics. As policy changes are already underway, ship operators will only benefit from being ahead of national and international regulatory changes.

Branding and Competition

An organization's image, what the organization represents, and how it differs from its competitors changes over time.[104] Image can be proactively created by an organization or can be externally imposed on an organization.[105] A good image provides an organization with a competitive edge.

---

the ACCOBAMS, "Resolution 5.15: Addressing the impact of anthropogenic noise," (2013); Meeting of the Parties (MOP 6) to the ACCOBAMS, "Resolution 6.17: Anthropogenic noise," (2016); See also id.

101 J. Saul, "U.N. sets rules to cut sulfur emissions by ships from 2020," *Reuters* (27 October 2016), available online: <https://www.reuters.com/article/us-shipping-environment-sulphur/u-n-sets-rules-to-cut-sulfur-emissions-by-ships-from-2020-idUSKCN12R1XF>.

102 "IMO pushes back ballast water compliance dates," *Maritime Executive* (7 July 2017), available online: <https://maritime-executive.com/article/imo-pushes-back-ballast-water-compliance-dates>.

103 Id.

104 R. Rajala, M. Westerlund and T. Lampikoski, "Environmental sustainability in industrial manufacturing: Re-examining the greening of interface's business model," *Journal of Cleaner Production* 115 (2016): 52–61.

105 Id.

Organizations that engage in sustainable practices are driven by the need to implement a long-term competitive strategy,[106] which further entrenches the principle of sustainability within their organizational identity. As environmental consciousness grows, consumers are demanding sustainable products and services.[107] Due to this growing consciousness among consumers, the market share for sustainable organizations and industries is expanding. Industries and companies that provide green products and services have greater opportunities to access this growing market.[108] With green initiatives increasing in popularity, economic studies have shown that companies implementing green technologies and providing sustainable services see an increase in profits.[109]

The benefits of integrating the principle of sustainability into the internal policy of a business include product differentiation, improved corporate image, increased sales, and the development of new markets.[110] The voluntary advancement of sustainable practices can increase both brand awareness and competitive market share.[111] Sustainable business practices have implications for many aspects of a business model, and the pursuit of environmental sustainability is linked with organizational identity.[112]

Efficiency and Cost Reductions

Ship operators that encourage the implementation of sustainable initiatives not only lessen their environmental impacts, but also increase their efficiency and lower costs.[113] Cavitation, which causes 80–85 percent of ship-radiated noise emissions, is wasted energy.[114] Therefore, the noisiest commercial marine vessels are likely not operating at optimal efficiency. The implementation of quieter vessels is thereby economically and environmentally beneficial to ship owners as an increase in efficiency of 5–10 percent can yield an annual savings of CA$500,000 to $2 million per vessel.[115] Further, increases in

---

106 Id., p. 52.
107 Id.
108 Id.
109 K. Lorette, "Why businesses should go green," *The Houston Chronicle*, available online: <http://smallbusiness.chron.com/businesses-should-green-766.html>.
110 Rajala et al., n. 104 above, p. 53.
111 Id.
112 Id.
113 L. Weilgart, "Underwater noise mitigation for shipping and pile driving," in WWF-Canada, n. 91 above, pp. 24–47, pp. 24–25.
114 Lo, n. 92 above.
115 Weilgart, n. 113 above, pp. 24–25.

efficiency related to noise can translate into decreased carbon dioxide output reductions,[116] which is an additional external cost.

There is a business case to be made for the implementation of sustainable practices and technologies which reduce ship-radiated noise. New builds that incorporate noise emission mitigation measures increase design/build costs by only one percent.[117] Furthermore, vessel owners implementing practices which reduce underwater noise can also be rewarded by environmental certification programs and discounted port fees. The remainder of this article explores three organizations within North America that provide sustainable ship operators with cost-saving benefits.

Case Study 1 – Green Marine

Green Marine is a voluntary environmental certification program for the North American marine industry.[118] Participants in the Green Marine program include ship operators, ports, terminals, shipyards, and seaways. In order to receive certification in the program, participants must benchmark their annual environmental performance through Green Marine's self-evaluation guides.[119] They also need to have their results verified by an accredited external verifier and agree to have their results made publicly available.[120]

Their certification program is addressing the main environmental issues faced by the shipping industry, such as aquatic invasive species, air emissions, garbage management, and underwater noise.[121] Green Marine's underwater noise performance indicators are intended to reduce underwater noise emissions produced during shipping activities, in order to reduce impacts on marine mammals, and have been developed for both ship operators and ports.[122]

Two participants in Green Marine's certification program are the Port of Prince Rupert and the Port of Vancouver. Both ports, located in British Columbia, Canada, have started their own underwater noise mitigation initiatives in an effort to reduce their environmental impact.

Case Study 2 – the Port of Prince Rupert's Green Wave Program

In 2013, the Port of Prince Rupert introduced the Green Wave incentive program for vessels in an effort to encourage shippers to invest in sustainable

---

116 Lo, n. 92 above.
117 J.H. Spence and R.W. Fischer, "Requirements for reducing underwater noise from ships," *IEEE Journal of Oceanic Engineering* 99 (2016): 1–11.
118 Green Marine, "About us," 2018, available online: <https://www.green-marine.org/about-us/>.
119 Id.
120 Id.
121 Id.
122 Id.

practices.[123] The Program includes a variety of standards consistent across the global shipping industry related to air quality and noise for arriving commercial vessels. It offers opportunities for shipping companies to benefit from implementing outstanding environmental performance as commercial vessels that implement environmentally sensitive practices are provided with discounted harbor dues.[124] The criteria are based on a three-tier scoring system. Vessels with a score eligible for the first tier receive a 10 percent discount on harbor dues; those eligible for the second tier receive a 20 percent discount; and those eligible for the third tier receive a 50 percent discount.[125]

The Port of Prince Rupert is working to understand the impact of noise in the region and, working with Oceans Network Canada, has deployed a series of hydrophone stations recording underwater noise to develop baseline data and provide live data on noise levels in Fairview, Westview, Seal Cove, and Port Edward.[126] The data collected could be used to develop indicators for an acoustic footprint and measure any increases that may result from increased vessel traffic or future development.

The Port of Prince Rupert took steps to encourage quieter vessels to visit the port when the Green Wave program added noise criteria in January 2017.[127] As the region surrounding Prince Rupert includes diverse marine mammal species and is a hub for international maritime trade, the Port of Prince Rupert initiated a Marine Mammals Program to address the intersection of the two. The Program strives to understand the vulnerability of marine mammals to both vessel collisions and noise disturbance resulting from port-related activities.[128] This program is complementary to the Green Wave program, enabling meaningful mitigation of the threats to marine animals, such as noise, as well as supporting sustainable shipping within the region.

Case Study 3 – the Port of Vancouver's ECHO and EcoAction Program

In 2014, the Port of Vancouver launched the Enhancing Cetacean Habitat and Observation (ECHO) Program, the world's first collaborative port-led initiative aimed at better understanding and managing the impact of shipping activities on local populations of at-risk whales, which focuses on reducing ship-radiated

---

123 Prince Rupert Port Authority (PRPA), "Green Wave," 2017, available online: <https://www.rupertport.com/port-authority/sustainability/green-wave>; See also PRPA, "Marine mammal program," 2015, available online: <http://www.rupertport.com/port-authority/sustainability/marine-mammals>.
124 Id., "Green Wave."
125 Id., "Program Overview"; See also Scherr, n. 10 above.
126 Id.
127 Scherr, n. 10 above.
128 Id.

noise.[129] The ECHO Program supports a series of short-term projects, scientific studies, and education initiatives intended to provide a better understanding of vessel-related cumulative regional threats, including underwater noise, and inform the development of mitigation solutions.[130] Since 2007, the Port of Vancouver's EcoAction Program has offered discounted harbor due rates to vessels that have implemented environmental management measures, such as emission reduction fuels and technologies or class notations that factor into the reduction of vessel-generated underwater noise.[131] The EcoAction Program offers three award levels correlated to harbor due reductions: gold, silver, and bronze.[132] Vessels qualifying for the bronze award level receive a 23 percent discount in harbor dues. Vessels qualifying for the silver award level receive a 35 percent reduction, and those qualifying for the gold award level receive a 47 percent reduction on harbor dues. To meet the requirements under the EcoAction Program, documentation satisfying one environmental measure must be submitted by the ship operator or agent.[133]

As a result of the ECHO Program's 2016 study described above, the EcoAction Program added new underwater noise reduction criteria to the program in 2017.[134] Three ship classification societies, non-government organizations that are responsible for establishing, maintaining, and inspecting technical standards for the construction and operation of vessels,[135] have developed standards for ship-radiated noise: Bureau Veritas (Underwater-Radiated Noise (URN) notation), DNV GL (SILENT E notation); and RINA (DOLPHIN notation). Vessels classified by any one of these societies are eligible for the gold award-level discount in harbor dues at the Port of Vancouver.[136] Three propeller technologies shown to reduce propeller-generated noise are PBCFs, the Schneekluth duct, and the Beker Mewis duct. These three propeller technologies are all eligible for the bronze award level discount in harbor dues at the

---

129 Vancouver Fraser Port Authority (VFPA), "Enhancing Cetacean Habitat and Observation (ECHO) Program," 2018, available online: <https://www.portvancouver.com/environment/water-land-wildlife/echo-program/>.
130 Id.
131 VFPA, "EcoAction program brochure," 2017, available online: <https://www.portvancouver.com/wp-content/uploads/2015/05/5135-PMV-Eco-Action-Program-Brochure-Online-v%C6%92-2016.pdf>.
132 Id.
133 Id.
134 Id.
135 Id.
136 Id.

Port of Vancouver.[137] Discounts on these notations and technologies became effective 1 January 2017.[138]

In addition to providing discounted harbor due rates, the Port of Vancouver also implemented a voluntary vessel slow-down trial in 2017. The purpose of the trial was to better understand and measure the level of noise reduction that is achieved through vessel speed reduction.[139] The trial duration of nine weeks demonstrated that 61 percent of commercial vessels navigating the designated area participated in the trial.[140] This suggests a willingness to comply and feasibility for industry given the voluntary nature of the restriction, which is consistent with other slow-down measures implemented in Canada.[141] As ship speed reductions diminish the risk of ship strikes for cetaceans, it would also be beneficial to see this measure accepted for noise reduction as well.

The Acoustic Footprint as a Noise Mitigation Tool for Marine Shipping

In all three cases of industry-led initiatives to reduce ship-radiated noise in Canada, there are opportunities to implement acoustic footprints as an integrated marine management and policy tool. Green Marine, the Port of Prince Rupert, and the Port of Vancouver have voluntarily implemented industry-led programs aimed at reducing ship-radiated noise. Each program encourages ship operators to employ sustainable practices without implementing restrictive legislation or policies that decrease efficiency or increase ship operators' costs. Instead of implementing restrictions, they have initiated programs that encourage ship operators to voluntarily reduce their noise emissions.

Both the Port of Vancouver and the Port of Prince Rupert offer monetary incentives for ship operators to reduce their noise emissions in the form of discounted harbor fees. In order to be rewarded with discounted fees, it can be assumed that participants in the ports' initiatives are also benefiting in fuel cost reductions from the implementation of efficient design and machinery maintenance policies. Participants in these programs are doubly benefitting

---

137 Id.
138 Id.
139 Id.
140 Chamber of Shipping of British Columbia, "ECHO trial a success," 2017, available online: <http://www.cosbc.ca/index.php?option=com_k2&view=item&id=3774:echo-trial-a-success&Itemid=291>.
141 Government of Canada, "Transport Canada issues Gulf of St. Lawrence speed restriction fine," News Release, 8 September 2017, available online: <https://www.canada.ca/en/transport-canada/news/2017/09/transport_canadaissuesgulfofstlawrencespeedrestrictionfine.html>.

in the form of monetary savings in addition to improving the image of their brand and access to market share.

While Green Marine's certification program does not offer monetary incentives, its participants are rewarded with notoriety resulting in increased brand awareness and market share. While these benefits are less tangible than monetary incentives, they can be significant. Ship operators implementing green technology could see an increase in profits due to a growing demand for sustainable services.[142]

Similar benefits may have motivated the Port of Vancouver and the Port of Prince Rupert to initiate their programs. In addition to being able to provide demanded sustainable services, leading to increased market share and profits, the Ports' programs may have also led to publicity, increased brand awareness, and social license. Ultimately, these industry-led programs result in socioeconomic benefits for both the participants and the program leaders.

While these programs provide tangible mitigation measures, they would benefit from an integrated approach that would support a broader and comprehensive approach to noise emission reductions. By uniting efforts under a standardized model, such as an acoustic footprint tool, the shipping industry could benefit from programs adopting comparable transboundary mitigation strategies.

If ship-radiated noise continues to surpass the acoustic threshold of marine ecosystems or species at risk, then the established programs will continue to chase shifting baselines. The implementation of acoustic footprints as a management and policy tool can solve this issue. Acoustic footprints are a comprehensive tool that can unite the efforts of all stakeholders and aid in communicating improved noise indicators, resulting in tangible results. They can be applied to measure and monitor the outputs of individual vessels or can be applied by ports to measure and monitor ship-radiated noise within a specific geographic boundary of concern. Thus, acoustic footprints can be a valuable mechanism for managing ship-radiated noise while supporting the initiatives and socioeconomic interests of the commercial marine shipping industry.

---

142 M. Hozik, "Making the green by going green: Increased demand for green products and the FTC's role in a greener future," *Georgetown Environmental Law Review* (1 February 2016) available online: <https://gelr.org/2016/02/01/making-the-green-by-going-green-increased-demand-for-green-products-and-the-ftcs-role-in-a-greener-future-georgetown-environmental-law-review/>; Lorette, n. 109 above; Rajala et al., n. 104 above, pp. 52–61.

Conclusion

Acoustic monitoring and reduction programs that target the reduction of ship noise emissions are already in place in Canada and can be enhanced through the use of acoustic footprints. The use of acoustic footprints as a methodology for policy and management can unite efforts to address the pervasive problem of ship-source underwater noise. By standardizing a tool that quantifies various acoustic indicators and mitigation management approaches, policies can be flexible and adaptive, dependent on the scale of application and integration of other noise sources and conservation objectives. By consolidating measures under an acoustic footprint, port fee reductions, individual vessel alterations or technologies, and, potentially, slow-down trials can provide an understanding of the true reduction per vessel or spatially. This highlights the need to integrate more mitigation measures for underwater noise to meet reduction targets, while supporting and enhancing existing acoustic monitoring networks.

The conceptual tool of an acoustic footprint can enhance scientific and policy collaboration and coordination across various stakeholders, including industry and government. Scientists can use the footprint model to visualize and communicate the scale of impact, while industry can more readily understand the need or current efforts of mitigation strategies, and policy-making can benefit from unifying mitigation approaches and communicating the acoustic harm thresholds for species or ecosystems. The broad concept of an acoustic footprint can incorporate the complexity of ship-sourced noise pollution, as well as unite management solutions.

The implementation of acoustic footprints within Canada could be of benefit to the commercial marine shipping industry, increasing the industry's ability to reduce environmental impacts while maintaining the shipping sector's economic prosperity. Recognizing the rising awareness of the impacts of ship-radiated underwater noise within marine environments, industry has already begun implementing voluntary programs for the purpose of reducing ship noise emissions. Responding to political priorities, organizations within industry, such as ports and ship operators, have considered the benefits of voluntary change, including increased efficiency, cost reductions, improved organizational identity leading to a competitive edge, and already implemented noise mitigation strategies.

Despite efforts by industry and their desire to reduce underwater noise contributions, policy-makers in Canada need to provide guidance by setting reduction targets to evaluate efforts. Broad policies are in place under the Oceans

Protection Plan,[143] as well as legislated under the *Species at Risk Act*,[144] to reduce the disturbance of underwater noise to marine animals. These high-level goals must be translated within operational targets to guide management actions.[145] The use of acoustic footprints as a framework can assist policy-makers to apply these broad policies within the shipping industry, thereby supporting meaningful action towards achieving suitable acoustic environments for marine species, including at-risk species like the St. Lawrence Estuary beluga whale.[146] Acoustic footprints can target reduction from the source by broadly supporting various or multiple reduction strategies at the same time.

Given the flexibility of acoustic footprints as a management and policy tool, in terms of application and indicators, the concept of acoustic footprints can be applied to current mitigation strategies and future noise reduction solutions. As a monitoring and communication tool, acoustic footprints can be a valuable mechanism to incite change to conserve marine species vulnerable to noise pollution, while supporting the socioeconomic interests of the commercial marine shipping industry. Although acoustic footprints are not a direct tool to reduce noise output, they can buoy the effective implementation of mitigation strategies by supporting all stakeholders involved and unifying efforts, ensuring these footprints are reflective of the best available science, considerate of the precautionary approach, and clearly communicate the noise output benchmarks to minimize acoustic disturbance to marine biota which must be adhered to by the shipping industry.

---

143   Government of Canada, "The Oceans Protection Plan," Backgrounder, 10 October 2017, available online: <https://www.canada.ca/en/transport-canada/news/2017/10/the_oceans_protectionplan.html>.
144   SARA, n. 47 above.
145   S. Katsanevakis et al., "Ecosystem-based marine spatial management: Review of concepts, policies, tools, and critical issues," *Ocean & Coastal Management* 54 (2011): 807–820.
146   Fisheries and Oceans Canada, "Recovery Strategy for the beluga (*Delphinapterus leucas*) St. Lawrence Estuary population in Canada," Species at Risk Act (SARA) Recovery Strategy Series (Ottawa: Fisheries and Oceans Canada, 2012).

A Tale of Two Industries: Seafarer Perceptions of Navigational Safety Risks near Offshore Wind Farms

Raza Ali Mehdi, Jens-Uwe Schröder-Hinrichs and Michael Baldauf
Maritime Risk & System Safety (MaRiSa) Research Group,
World Maritime University, Malmö, Sweden

Introduction

Background

Driven by an increasingly mindful society and the adoption of stringent environmental protection agendas by governmental, inter-governmental and non-governmental organizations, the offshore wind sector has experienced strong, sustained growth over the last two decades. This evolution has been made possible primarily through significant research and development efforts that have resulted in technological advancements, as well as improved installation, maintenance, and decommissioning strategies.[1] Further improvements in energy generation, storage and transmission capabilities, and developments in deep-water technologies have also seen offshore wind farms (OWFs) move further from shore into deeper water to better exploit the wind resource.[2] All these factors have contributed to increasingly reliable energy generation and notable reductions in the levelized cost of electricity from offshore wind.[3]

With overwhelming social acceptance and continued improvements in materials, structural and aerodynamic technology, forecasts indicate that the size and numbers of offshore wind turbines (OWTs) and OWFs will continue

---

[1] P. Maegaard, A. Krenz and W. Palz, eds., *Wind Power for the World: The Rise of Modern Wind Energy*, Pan Stanford Series on Renewable Energy, vol. 2 (Boca Raton, FL: CRC Press, 2013); P. Maegaard, A. Krenz and W. Palz, eds., *Wind Power for the World: International Reviews and Developments*, Pan Stanford Series on Renewable Energy, vol. 3. (Boca Raton, FL: CRC Press, 2013); R.A. Mehdi, W. Ostachowicz and M. Luczak, "Introduction," in *MARE-WINT: New Materials and Reliability in Offshore Wind Turbine Technology*, eds. W. Ostachowicz et al., (Cham: Springer, 2016), 1–9.

[2] European Wind Energy Association (EWEA), *The European Offshore Wind Industry: Key Trends and Statistics 2015* (Brussels: Wind Europe (formerly: European Wind Energy Association), 2016).

[3] Siemens AG, *A Macro-economic Viewpoint: What Is the Real Cost of Offshore Wind?* (Hamburg: Siemens AG Wind Power, 2014); Global Wind Energy Council (GWEC), *Global Wind Report: Annual Market Update 2015* (Brussels: Global Wind Energy Council, 2016).

to grow over the next few years.[4] And it is not just the size and number of turbines that are predicted to rise: increasingly complex devices such as floating or vertical-axis wind turbines in previously unexploited marine areas may soon become the norm.

The growth of the offshore wind sector is not without its challenges. Aside from the technological challenges posed by increasingly larger, more complex turbines in harsher environments,[5] there are also stakeholder concerns regarding the environmental and societal impacts of OWFs.[6] Ornithologists, for instance, are often concerned that OWFs may negatively affect migration and breeding patterns of various avian species.[7] Similarly, marine biologists continue to scrutinize the impact of OWFs on marine life.[8] Academics have also explored how society and coastal communities may perceive OWFs,[9]

---

4   EWEA, n. 2 above; GWEC, n. 3 above.
5   W. Ostachowicz et al., n. 1 above.
6   D. Lacroix and S. Pioch, "The multi-use in wind farm projects: More conflicts or a win-win opportunity?," *Aquatic Living Resources* 24 (2011): 129–135.
7   M. Desholm and J. Kahlert, "Avian collision risk at an offshore wind farm," *Biology Letters* 1, no. 3 (2005): 296–298. V. Dierschke, S. Garthe and B. Mendel, "Possible conflicts between offshore wind farms and seabirds in the German sectors of North Sea and Baltic Sea," in *Offshore Wind Energy: Research on Environmental Impacts*, eds. J. Köller, J. Köppel and W. Peters (Heidelberg: Springer, 2006), 121–143; O. Hüppop et al., "Bird migration and offshore wind turbines," in Köller et al., id., 91–116; S. Degraer and R. Brabant, eds., *Offshore Wind Farms in the Belgian Part of the North Sea: State of the Art After Two Years of Environmental Monitoring* (Brussels: Royal Belgian Institute for Natural Sciences, Management Unit of the North Sea Mathematical Models, Marine ecosystem management unit, 2009); A. Beiersdorf and A. Radecke, eds., *Ecological Research at the Offshore Windfarm Alpha Ventus: Challenges, Results and Perspectives* (Wiesbaden: Springer, 2014); L. New et al., "A collision risk model to predict avian fatalities at wind facilities: An example using golden eagles, Aquila chrysaetos," *PLOS ONE* 10, no. 7 (2015).
8   Köller et al., id.; Degraer and Brabant, n. 7 above; M.H. Andersson, "Offshore wind farms: Ecological effects of noise and habitat alteration on fish," (Ph.D. diss. Stockholm University, 2011); H. Bailey, K.L. Brookes and P.M. Thompson, "Assessing environmental impacts of offshore wind farms: Lessons learned and recommendations for the future," *Aquatic Biosystems* 10, no. 8 (2012); U.K. Verfuss et al., "Review of offshore wind farm impact monitoring and mitigation with regard to marine mammals," in *Advances in Experimental Medicine and Biology*, vol. 875, eds. A.N Popper and A. Hawkins (New York: Springer 2016), 1175–1182; L. Bray et al., "Expected effects of offshore wind farms on Mediterranean marine life," *Journal of Marine Science and Engineering* 4, no. 1 (2016): 18.
9   P. Devine-Wright, "Beyond NIMBYism: Towards an integrated framework for understanding public perceptions of wind energy," *Wind Energy* 8 (2005): 125–139; J. Ladenburg, "Attitude and acceptance of offshore wind farms: The influence of travel time and wind farm attributes," *Renewable and Sustainable Energy Reviews* 15 (2011): 4223–4235; J.-L. Chen et al., "The factors affecting stakeholders' acceptance of offshore wind farms along the western coast of Taiwan: Evidence from stakeholders' perceptions," *Ocean and Coastal Management* 109 (2015): 40–50.

while lawyers have discussed potential legal conflicts arising from multi-use of coastal and marine space.[10] Some researchers, meanwhile, have sought to demystify the often-complex consenting process of OWFs,[11] while others have investigated the lifecycle economic[12] and environmental impacts[13] of OWFs; the latter branch of research has also led to some interesting investigations regarding vessel re-routing to reduce the costs associated with OWFs.[14]

On the topic of vessels, some of the major conflicts associated with the offshore wind sector arise from interaction between OWFs and any vessel operations in their vicinity, in the form of maritime safety risks.[15] The presence of offshore structures can lead to restriction of navigable sea-space and increased traffic density, thereby reducing the safety and operational efficiency of maritime operations. Indeed, the impacts of OWFs on maritime operations are frequently seen as critical and decisive factors during planning and consenting processes. For an OWF project to be approved, most national authorities require owners to prove that the impact on maritime activities is acceptably low.[16] The conflict between the offshore wind sector and the maritime industry is a high stakeholder priority for a very simple reason: maritime accidents in

---

10 A. Chircop and P. L'Esperance, "Functional interactions and maritime regulation: The mutual accommodation of offshore wind farms and international navigation and shipping," *Ocean Yearbook* 30 (2016): 439–487.
11 E. Gibson and P. Howsam, "The legal framework for offshore wind farms: A critical analysis of the consents process," *Energy Policy* 38 (2010): 4692–4702.
12 M.I. Blanco, "The economics of wind energy," *Renewable and Sustainable Energy Reviews* 13 (2009): 1372–1382; B. Snyder and M. Kaiser, "Ecological and economic cost-benefit analysis of offshore wind energy," *Renewable Energy* 34 (2009): 1567–1578.
13 J. Weinzettel et al., "Life cycle assessment of a floating offshore wind turbine," *Renewable Energy* 34 (2009): 742–747; Y. Wang and T. Sun, "Life cycle assessment of CO_2 emissions from wind power plants: Methodology and case studies," *Renewable Energy* 43 (2012): 30–36.
14 K. Samoteskul, J. Firestone, J. Corbett and J. Callahan, "Changing vessel routes could significantly reduce the cost of future offshore wind projects," *Journal of Environmental Management* 141 (2014): 146–154.
15 G. Wright, R.A. Mehdi and M. Baldauf, "3-dimensional forward looking sonar: Offshore wind farm applications," (paper presented at 2016 European Navigation Conference (ENC), Helsinki, Finland, 30 May–2 June 2016); R.A. Mehdi and J.-U. Schröder-Hinrichs, "A theoretical risk management framework for vessels operating near offshore wind farms," in W. Ostachowicz et al., n. 1 above (Cham: Springer, 2016), 359–400.
16 Maritime and Coastguard Agency (MCA), *Methodology for assessing the marine navigational safety and emergency response risks of offshore renewable energy installations (OREI)* (Southampton: Maritime and Coastguard Agency, 2013); German Federal Maritime and Hydrographic Agency, *Minimum requirements concerning the constructive design of offshore structures within the Exclusive Economic Zone (EEZ)*. (Hamburg: German Federal Maritime and Hydrographic Agency, 2015).

the vicinity of an OWF may lead to human casualties, a consequence perhaps costlier than any other.

The requirement to demonstrate maritime safety in the vicinity of OWFs is clearly evident in the form of environmental impact assessments (EIAs) and navigational risk assessments (NRAs) that accompany the consenting applications for various offshore wind projects.[17] This requirement has also promoted the development and application of NRA frameworks, methods and models, that is, tools to assess the probability and consequences of maritime operational accidents in the vicinity of OWFs.[18]

While there is no doubt that OWFs pose a threat to maritime operations, effective marine spatial planning and stringent approval and consenting processes for OWFs have played a major role in ensuring that major maritime accidents in the vicinity of OWFs have been largely avoided thus far. The paucity of accidents,[19] however, has not dissuaded some stakeholders from speculating that continued growth of the offshore wind energy sector will lead to increased maritime risks associated with OWFs.

On the other hand, the scarcity of vessel accidents near OWFs thus far has fueled speculation as to whether the "maritime vs. offshore wind" conflict is as serious as it is portrayed to be. Proponents of this viewpoint argue that "over-design" for safety around OWFs leads to ineffective use of limited marine space. For example, a row of wind turbines may have to be eliminated due to an overly conservative navigational risk estimate, leading to an inefficiently designed OWF. Some stakeholders even argue that OWFs can actually improve navigational safety, by acting as aids to navigation in hazardous areas.

The authors of this article opt for the middle-ground in this debate. Undoubtedly, OWFs have an impact on maritime operations, but this fact should definitely not be taken as an impetus to "over-design" for safety. At the same time, the lack of accidents should not lead to complacency, nor deter decision-makers from conducting thorough NRAs. Rather, stakeholders must work together to pro-actively address maritime risks associated with OWFs, particularly as turbines increase in size, numbers, and complexity, and move further away from shore toward busy shipping lanes.

Problem Description

Clearly, there is a pressing need to find the right balance between two marine uses: maritime operations and offshore energy generation. This, however, is a

---

17   National Infrastructure Planning (NIP), "Projects" (Bristol: Planning Inspectorate, 2017), available online: <https://infrastructure.planninginspectorate.gov.uk/projects/>.
18   Mehdi and Schröder-Hinrichs, n. 15 above.
19   There have been few serious accidents as discussed towards the end of the literature review section.

daunting task, compounded further by a lack of accident data. Simply put, it is a challenge to establish whether or not any of the maritime risks associated with OWFs can be generalized. More crucially, it is also a challenge to determine the degree to which any of the purported risks are actually of concern. The problem description thus leads to a twofold primary objective for the current work:

1. Identify maritime risks that can be generally attributed to all OWFs.
2. By understanding the perceptions of the surveyed seafarers, determine the rating and concern priority-rankings of these risks on a broader, population level.

To fulfil the primary objective, the authors conducted a literature review of maritime impacts associated with OWFs, followed by a subsequent survey of operational end users, that is, seafarers. Seafarers, more so than any other stakeholder, are intimately involved in the so-called "sharp-end" of operations. This makes them ideally suited to gauge any maritime operational risks and their feedback can help identify a reference level for various maritime risks associated with OWFs. By categorizing the respondents into different groups, a secondary objective of this article is to establish whether seafarers that do, and those that do not, operate near OWFs have substantially different perceptions of the maritime risks associated with wind farms.[20]

Literature Review

The strong growth of the offshore wind sector over the last few years has resulted in an abundance of both academic research and technical reports (grey literature) that deal with the various environmental, societal, economic, and legal aspects of OWFs. For the present literature review, the strategy was to find documents mentioning "offshore wind farm navigational risks." More than 50 peer-reviewed articles on NRA were identified. Of the latter 50, only five dealt with offshore wind farm risks, primarily assessing damage during vessel-turbine collisions. In addition to this, fifteen planning and approval applications for OWFs were also reviewed from the United Kingdom, Germany, Belgium, the Netherlands, and Sweden. These approval applications describe the methods used to perform NRA around OWFs and also contain results from stakeholder consultations. The peer-reviewed articles and stakeholder consultations were both used to triangulate the findings in the present work.

---

20 "Near" refers to vessels operating on routes adjacent to OWFs, or within an OWF area itself (e.g., support vessels).

The specific literature on maritime impacts of OWFs can be broadly classified into two categories: publications that deal with the development and application of NRA tools, and publications that explore actual maritime risks associated with OWFs. The literature in the former category is particularly plentiful, and there is a good mix of contributions from both academia and industry, as comprehensively discussed in Mehdi and Schröder-Hinrichs.[21] Many NRA tools used for OWFs are those that allow users to calculate the probability and consequences of contact accidents; a contact accident involves a collision between a ship and a fixed object. Aside from quantifying the risk of contact events, NRA tools can also be used to assess the influence of an OWF in terms of probability and consequences of collision and grounding accidents.[22] The continued development and application of such NRA tools indicates that stakeholders are increasingly concerned with the risk of certain undesirable events, in this particular case, with the risk of navigational accidents such as contact, collision, and groundings in the vicinity of OWFs.

Despite the fact that these aforementioned NRA tools are well-validated and sophisticated, they are often thought to address a problem that does not exist: the shortage of maritime accidents around OWFs has led to lingering questions as to whether or not all OWFs pose similar risks to maritime operations, and what the actual concern level or nature of these risks might be.

This brings us to the second category of literature, to which the present article belongs. This second category is quite sparse in comparison to the first, and there is a distinct lack of academic contributions that explore maritime risks associated with OWFs. In fact, most of the literature in the second category directly stems from stakeholder consultations that are conducted as part of consenting processes for various OWFs in Europe. These stakeholder consultations generally include seafarers and vessel-owners who are asked to provide feedback for a specific OWF in light of local environmental and operational conditions. The opinions of seafarers and other stakeholders, together with the results of NRAs, are then used to decide whether an OWF project should be given the greenlight from a maritime perspective.[23]

While it is encouraging to note that seafarers' opinions are often included in stakeholder consultations, it is not prudent to assume that their views are universally applicable. Usually, only around 10–15 seafarers at most may be invited to a stakeholder consultation, and their opinions regarding specific local operational risks may not be valid for other marine areas or even other OWFs.

---

21   Mehdi and Schröder-Hinrichs, n. 15 above.
22   Id.
23   NIP, n. 17 above.

This highlights the necessity of the current work, wherein the authors attempt to generalize risks associated with all OWFs.

The findings of pre-existing stakeholder consultations are nevertheless a valuable source of initial information for the current work. By reviewing the findings of various publicly available stakeholder consultations, and exploring the principal theories behind various NRA tools, it is possible to classify the maritime risks associated with OWFs into five broad groups:

1. *Navigational accidents involving passing vessels (powered and drifting)*: The presence of wind turbines, near ports and shipping routes, may lead to an increased risk of navigational accidents such as contact between turbines and vessels, collision between vessels, and grounding of vessels, all with potentially serious consequences. Passing vessels are all vessels that operate on routes near OWFs. This risk type covers accidents involving both powered and/or drifting vessels near OWFs.
2. *Navigational accidents involving wind farm support vessels*: The risk of navigational accidents for vessels carrying out maintenance, transportation, and construction tasks related to the wind farm is also an area of concern.
3. *Accidents during OWF installation and decommissioning operations*: During installation and decommissioning of OWFs, specialized maritime operations such as heavy lifting are carried out. The increased number of high-risk operations provides an increased opportunity for accidents at sea. Primarily, this risk type covers capsizing and other stability issues.
4. *Accidents during emergency maritime operations such as search and rescue*: Wind turbines require regular maintenance, which currently means that people have to work at heights, sometimes in adverse weather conditions. If an occupational accident befalls a wind farm worker, however, the search and rescue (SAR) services may have a hard time reaching the person(s) in time as it is not easy to maneuver on a wind farm. In case of scenarios like oil spills, contingency measures can be difficult to implement in a wind farm due to the presence of the turbines. SAR within OWFs is also a rising concern with increasing numbers of wind farms shared between countries, as it raises the question of who is responsible in case of an accident.
5. *Accidents in harbors and ports that deal with offshore activities*: Accidents related to offshore wind farms can also occur in ports when vessels are being prepared for installation, maintenance or decommissioning activities. Increased traffic and activities in the ports may also pose a danger to safe maritime operations.

There are certain undesirable events associated with each of the five risk types. The primary cause behind the undesirable events under risk types 1, 2, 4 and 5 is that an OWF can lead to more obstructions in the water for ships to avoid. The presence of a wind farm near a shipping lane effectively narrows the area in which vessels can operate, therefore increasing the traffic density. There is also, of course, an amplified risk of accidents due to increased maritime traffic that results from activities related to OWFs. While operating, wind turbines may also cause problems with onboard ship navigation equipment, an issue that is often raised by seafarers during stakeholder consultations. The prospect of undesirable events associated with the aforementioned risk types is further reinforced by best practice reports and operational HSE (health, safety and environment) guidance.[24] Concern for the various undesirable events is also reflected in the NRA methods and models that stakeholders choose to use during the consenting process, as well as the NRA tools recommended by national authorities.[25]

To cap off the literature review, a review of reports on incidents in the vicinity of OWFs was also conducted. Of the several maritime accidents that have been reported in association with OWFs,[26] most involve operational accidents onboard wind farm support vessels (WSVs) or installation vessels. Such accidents include injuries to personnel or damage to equipment due to technical failures. There have also been a number of accidents involving damage to cables during the installation stages of OWFs. Perhaps the most "serious" reported accidents, however, are the navigational accidents involving WSVs, which prompted a thorough investigation by the Marine Accidents Investigation Board (MAIB) in the United Kingdom.[27] The accident reports, along with

---

24 Det Norske Veritas-Germanichser Lloyd, DMA *Safety Analysis for High-Speed Offshore Vessels Carrying up to 60 Persons. Report of HAZID and risk-reducing measures workshops* (Denmark: Danish Maritime Authority, 2017); European Agency for Safety and Health at Work, *Occupational Safety and Health in the Wind Energy Sector* (Bilbao: European Agency for Safety and Health at Work, 2013); World Bank Group, *Environmental, Health, and Safety Guidelines Wind Energy* (Washington, DC: World Bank Group, 2015); RenewableUK, *Offshore Wind and Marine Energy Health and Safety Guidelines: Issue 2* (London: RenewableUK, 2014).

25 MCA, n. 16 above.

26 Caithness Windfarm Information Forum (CWIF), "Wind Turbine Accident and Incident Compilation," available online: <http://www.caithnesswindfarms.co.uk/fullaccidents.pdf>.

27 Marine Accident Investigation Board (MAIB), "Combined report on the investigation of the contact with a floating target by the wind farm passenger transfer catamaran Windcat 9 while transiting Donna Nook Air Weapons Range in the south-west approaches to the River Humber on 21 November 2012 and the investigation of the contact of Island Panther with turbine I-6, in Sheringham Shoal Wind Farm on 21 November 2012" (Southampton: Marine Accident Investigation Board, 2013); CWIF, id.

HSE guidance, play a key part in underlining the undesirable events associated with risk types 2, 3 and 4.

Survey Methodology

The findings of the various stakeholder consultations, an in-depth understanding of theories underlying various NRA tools, a review of HSE best-practice documents, and a list of reported accidents, all together provide a good preliminary picture of the types of maritime risks that can be generally associated with OWFs. That being said, the literature alone does not measure the degree to which stakeholders are concerned with different risk types and undesirable events. Subsequently, a questionnaire was created using existing literature as inspiration, in which the questions were mainly designed to gauge concerns and awareness of seafarers with regard to five maritime risks attributed to OWFs.

Sampling Methodology

For the current study, the authors opted for simple random sampling. An online questionnaire was primarily distributed via mailing lists of the Nautical Institute and InterManager. In addition to this, the survey was shared via the International Maritime Organization's Twitter account, and also sent to alumni of the World Maritime University who are former seafarers. The questionnaire was also distributed to various seafarers' unions, trade associations, and maritime education and training institutes. More than a thousand seafarers received and started the survey, but only 207 respondents completed the questionnaire. One hundred and fifty responses were selected for further analysis after a quarantine of low-quality and irrelevant responses. These 150 responses can be classified into three categories based on the type of operation that the respondents are currently engaged in:

1. *Category 1* includes seafarers operating on WSVs. This includes seafarers on all types of support vessels, e.g., supply, cable laying, jack-up installation/decommissioning, etc. These seafarers have a direct influence on OWF operations and are in turn influenced by the presence of wind farms. The number of seafarers in this category is seven ($n_{Cat.1} = 7$).
2. *Category 2* includes seafarers and pilots on passing vessels operating near (on routes beside) OWFs. These seafarers have no direct influence on OWF operations, but may be influenced by the presence of the wind farm. The number of seafarers in this category is 40 ($n_{Cat.2} = 40$).
3. *Category 3* includes all seafarers and pilots on passing vessels that do not operate near OWFs. These seafarers have no interaction with OWFs

during routine operations. The number of seafarers in this category is 103 ($n_{Cat.3}$ = 103).

It is important to note that the respondents in Categories 1, 2 and 3 are mutually exclusive. The 150 respondents can also be classified into three different, non-mutually exclusive groups, based on their awareness of certain information related to maritime risks around OWFs:

4. *Category 4* includes seafarers with an awareness of NRA studies related to an OWF. This category particularly includes seafarers that have been asked to participate in approval consultations for OWFs, and thus may be aware of NRA studies related to certain OWFs. Twenty-four seafarers fall under Category 4 ($n_{Cat.4}$ = 24).
5. *Category 5* includes seafarers with an awareness of regulations/guidelines related to safe navigation near OWFs (WSVs). Generally issued by coastal States, guidance notes to mariners may detail the risks associated with certain OWFs, or even with the broader risks in certain marine areas that contain OWFs. This category includes seafarers who are familiar with such guidelines and regulations. Twenty-nine seafarers were categorized under Category 5 ($n_{Cat.5}$ = 29).
6. *Category 6* includes seafarers with an awareness of maritime incidents that can be attributed to OWFs. Seafarers can also be made aware of maritime risks associated with OWFs through accident and incident reports. Eighteen seafarers can be classified as Category 6 ($n_{Cat.6}$ = 18).

All seafarers that are classified under Categories 4, 5 and 6 also fall under either one of Category 1, 2 or 3, as discussed below. The reason to categorize seafarers as above is to understand if seafarers who are familiar with the NRA studies, specific rules and regulations, or accidents around OWFs have a noticeably different perception of risks.

Response Analysis Methodology

The first part of the questionnaire was dedicated to demographic questions. The responses for these questions were analyzed using descriptive statistics on a sample level, and compared to industry reports to ensure the validity of the sample. The demographic questions were designed to gather basic information such as age, experience, and background, as well as more detailed information regarding current operations that the respondents may be engaged in. The latter information allows the classification of seafarers into categories as discussed below.

Aside from those pertaining to demographics, the questions in the present study can be classified into two groups as shown in Table 20.1. Each question group utilizes a particular type of question and a series of hypotheses tests to inferentially gauge the perceptions of seafarers on a population level with regard to various maritime risks associated with OWFs. Respondents were also asked to explain why they rated/ranked the risks as they did using open text answers. Each open-text answer was individually analyzed and grouped into one of the following four broad categories:

1) Responses that dismissed the risks (e.g., "In my opinion OWF doesn't possess any risk or threat to marine traffic. Accidents do happen but we must develop procedures to minimize or completely eliminate them.")
2) Responses that highlighted the need for risk assessment (e.g., "Risk assessment can be valuable to the navigators like me.")
3) Responses that highlighted the need for further guidelines/regulations (e.g., "Guidelines should be made available when navigating near OWF areas. Routing guides should be established.")
4) Responses that were more concerned with a specific risk rather than another (e.g., "I believe they pose a clear and present danger of high consequential damages and possible fatality and should say a passenger vessel collided with one.")

The last section of the questionnaire was designed to understand the familiarity of the respondents with maritime operations around OWFs (e.g., knowledge of OWF NRA studies, knowledge of rules/guidelines for sailing near OWFs, and knowledge of incidents related to OWFs). The survey questions were validated before being distributed online through a pilot study involving 20 seafarers (these responses are not included in the current study). The raw data from the questionnaire was downloaded in CSV file format. All the statistical tests listed in Table 20.1 were conducted in Minitab using the raw data.

Methodology for Rating the Maritime Risks Associated with OWFs Primarily, the objective of the current work is to explore the level to which seafarers are concerned with the five different types of maritime risks identified through the literature review. To this end, participants were asked to read a short description of each risk type (as provided above), and to then rate each of the five different risk types (see "Rating and Ranking the Risks Associated with OWFs" below) using a standard five-point Likert scale of concern.[28] Each level on the Likert scale can be assigned a numerical value, with a 1 for "Not at all concerned," to a 5 for "Extremely Concerned"; the middle level – "Somewhat Concerned" – is logically assigned a value of 3. By quantifying each level, the Likert data can be treated as both categorical-ordinal and continuous-interval

---

28　W.M. Vagias, *Likert-type Scale Response Anchors* (Clemson, SC: Clemson University, 2006).

TABLE 20.1. Question types, and related hypotheses tests used in the current study

Question Group	Section	Question Type	Hypothesis Tests Based on Total Sample (n_{total})	Hypothesis Tests Based on Sub-Samples ($n_{Cat.1}$, $n_{Cat.2}$, $n_{Cat.3}$ etc.)
Rating maritime risks	3.2.1	Ordinal 5 point Likert scale: "Not At All Concerned" to "Extremely Concerned" (Data treated as continuous)	One sample t-test H_0: The population mean rating for risk type z, when considering all seafarers, is less than or equal to 3 H_1: The population mean rating for risk type z, when considering all seafarers, is greater than 3 where $z = \{1,2,3,4,5\}$ as discussed in Section 2 One sample Sign test H_0: The population median rating for risk type z, when considering all seafarers, is less than or equal to 3 H_1: The population median rating for risk type z, when considering all seafarers, is greater than 3 where $z = \{1,2,3,4,5\}$ as discussed in Section 2	One sample t-test H_0: The population mean rating for risk type z, when considering Category x seafarers, is less than or equal to 3 H_1: The population mean rating for risk type z, when considering Category x seafarers, is greater than 3 where $x = \{1,2,3,4,5,6\}$ as discussed in Section 3 and $z = \{1,2,3,4,5\}$ as discussed in Section 2 One sample Sign test H_0: The population median rating for risk type z, when considering Category x seafarers, is less than or equal to 3 H_1: The population median rating for risk type z, when considering Category x seafarers, is greater than 3 where $x = \{1,2,3,4,5,6\}$ as discussed in Section 3 and $z = \{1,2,3,4,5\}$ as discussed in Section 2

			Chi-square goodness-of-fit test (Section 4.2)	Chi-square goodness-of-fit test (Section 4.2)
Ranking maritime risks	3.2.2	Ranking/assigning priority	H_0: When considering all seafarers, the likelihood that risk type z will be ranked 1st, 2nd, 3rd, 4th or 5th is equal on a population level	H_0: When considering Category x seafarers, the likelihood that risk type z will be ranked 1st, 2nd, 3rd, 4th or 5th is equal on a population level
			H_1: When considering all seafarers, the likelihood that risk type z will be ranked 1st, 2nd, 3rd, 4th or 5th is not equal on a population level	H_1: When considering Category x seafarers, the likelihood that risk type z will be ranked 1st, 2nd, 3rd, 4th or 5th is not equal on a population level
			where $z = \{1,2,3,4,5\}$ as discussed in Section 2	where $x = \{1,2,3,4,5,6\}$ as discussed in Section 3 and $z = \{1,2,3,4,5\}$ as discussed in Section 2

in the present work,[29] which is useful when testing the mean or median rating of a statement.

Given the literature review, it is hypothesized that the seafaring population is, on average, at least "Somewhat Concerned" with each of the five risk types, that is, both the population mean and median are greater than 3 for each of the five risk types. Level 3 is chosen as the limit of the hypothesis test because it is both the mean and median value on the Likert scale. Level 3 is also appropriate for the hypothesis test because an initial analysis of the responses indicates that, on a sample level, the mean and median ratings are indeed slightly greater than 3.

Two pairs of hypotheses were conducted on the total sample (n_{total}) of 150 seafarers: a parametric one-sample t-test to compare the means and a nonparametric one-sample Sign test to compare the medians, as shown in Table 20.1. These inferential tests allow one to estimate the attitudes of the entire population based on sample responses.

The parametric one-sample t-test is one of the most robust methods for hypothesis testing mean values. Since a core objective of the current work is to estimate mean ratings for each risk type, the t-test is therefore imperative. A weakness of t-tests is that they are not very robust when it comes to small sample sizes ($n < 20$) that are non-normally distributed, although this is not a problem for the analysis of the complete present sample, where $n_{total} = 150$ is more than adequate. A more pressing downside of t-tests, especially for the current work, is that they are generally more suitable for parametric continuous-interval or continuous-ratio data, and there is debate as to whether Likert data can really be treated as such.[30]

Thus, for the current analysis, it was deemed prudent to also conduct a one-sample Sign test, which is the nonparametric equivalent for the one-sample t-test. Nonparametric tests such as the Sign test[31] are more widely accepted for hypothesis tests involving Likert scale responses. Nonparametric tests are also considered better for hypothesis testing medians rather than means. The use of two different tests thus allows the rating data to be analyzed from two different, but complementary, perspectives.

---

29   J.C.F. De Winter and D. Dodou, "Five-point Likert items: t-test versus Mann-Whitney-Wilcoxon," *Practical Assessment, Research & Evaluation* 15, no. 11 (2010): 1–12.

30   As there is no consensus on the matter, having considered both sides of the argument as well as the present data, we feel confident in treating the Likert response data as a continuous interval variable.

31   A Sign test is preferable over the other option, a Wilcoxon Signed Rank test, as it does not assume the sample responses to be symmetrically distributed; an initial analysis of the data suggested that this might be the case, resulting in the selection of the Sign test for the hypothesis test of medians.

The present work also seeks to explore whether different categories of seafarers rate the risk types differently. Initially, the authors intended to compare the response patterns of respondents in Categories 1 to 6 using a parametric two-sample, two-tailed t-test and the nonparametric equivalent Mann-Whitney/Wilcoxon rank-sum (MWW) test. However, the vastly different number of respondents in each category means that the statistical power of such comparative tests is significantly diminished. Thus, instead of conducting comparative hypothesis tests, the authors again opted to conduct a one-sample t-test and a nonparametric one-sample Sign test to investigate if the different categories of seafarers would rate each of the five risk categories differently on their respective population level. This approach allows for a more valid analysis of more sub-samples than would be possible through a comparative approach. On a note of caution, it should be mentioned that the power of the one-sample t-test and one-sample Sign test are also quite dependent on the sample size and distribution: the lower the sample size, the lower the power of the statistical test. Thus, while there is no minimum size required for a t-test[32] or a Sign test, the results for categories with a small number of respondents ($n \lesssim 25$) should be treated with extreme caution, particularly if the data is not normally distributed and/or if the effect size being measured is large. This limitation only applies to two of the six categories of respondents in the current study, and is discussed below.

Methodology for Ranking the Maritime Risks Associated with OWFs

In addition to rating each of the five risk types using a Likert scale, the respondents were also asked to rank the different risk types in an order of concern priority (see "Rating and Ranking the Risks Associated with OWFs" below). The alternative hypothesis is that each risk type can be assigned a unique priority level, e.g., risk type 1 cannot be both the first and second priority for the population, etc. To test this hypothesis, a nonparametric Chi-square goodness-of-fit test was used. As with the rating question, the response patterns of the different categories of seafarers were also analyzed using a Chi-square goodness-of-fit test to identify if seafarers belonging to a certain category would rank various risk types differently on their respective population level. Similar to the rating questions, is it prudent to mention that the statistical power of the Chi-square test also decreases with decreasing sample size. There is also value in understanding why the respondents rate and rank the tests as they do. Thus, the respondents were encouraged to explain their choices using free text, the

---

32   J.C.F. De Winter, "Using the Student's t-test with extremely small sample sizes," *Practical Assessment, Research & Evaluation* 18, no. 10 (2013): 1–10.

results of which are briefly discussed under "Survey Results" and "Discussion" below.

A Note on Hypothesis Testing

Each of the aforementioned hypothesis tests generates a p-value that can be used to determine whether there is enough evidence to reject the null hypothesis (H_0) in favor of the alternative hypothesis (H_1). We opted for a standard 95 percent confidence level (significance level = α = 0.05), which means that if $p < 0.05$, H_0 can be rejected in favor of H_1; conversely if $p > 0.05$, it means there is not enough evidence to reject H_0.

Survey Results

The total number of responses analyzed was 150 and all respondents were seafaring officers. Given that the total number of seafaring officers is estimated to be 774,000 as of 2015,[33] a sample size of 150 at a confidence level, c = 95 percent roughly equates to a confidence interval, CI = 8.

Demographics

The first part of the results section explores the background of the seafarers in the present study. Although not a focus of the current study, it is nevertheless well-recognized that seafarer demographics such as age, experience, region of origin, and even the types of vessels they work on, may have an influence on their perception of risk and navigational safety. The demographic results from the survey were compared to the results of the Manpower Update 2015.[34] The Manpower Report is a well-recognized industry publication, and provides a comprehensive overview of seafarer demand and supply, as well as specific demographic information about the seafaring population.

Respondents' Background

The first demographic factor that was investigated is the average age and experience of the respondents. The average age of respondents in the current study (42.6 years) is slightly higher than the average age (39.7 years) provided in the

---

33   Baltic and International Maritime Council (BIMCO) and International Chamber of Shipping (ICS), *Manpower Report: The Global Supply and Demand for Seafarers in 2015* (London: Maritime International Secretariat Services Ltd., 2016).
34   Id.

BIMCO/ICS Manpower Report.[35] The survey respondents also have slightly more experience (19.4 years) compared to the average experience quoted in the Manpower Report (16.6 years).

Another demographic factor that can be studied is the respondents' regions of origin, as shown in Figure 20.1. Respondents from 35 different countries answered the questionnaire. A majority of the respondents in the sample, 82 of 150 (55 percent) are from the Far East (FE) region. Thirty-six (24 percent) respondents originate from Organisation for Economic Co-operation and Development (OECD) countries, while 12 (8 percent) are from the Indian Subcontinent (INDSC). There are also 10 (7 percent) respondents from the Africa/Latin America (AFRLA) region, and another 10 (7 percent) hail from Eastern Europe (EE). Although efforts were made to distribute the survey as evenly as possible in the different regions, there is some discrepancy in the proportions when compared to the Manpower Report: seafarers from AFRLA and EE are under-represented by 2.3 and 7.3 percent respectively, while seafarers from OECD are 10 percent over-represented in the current sample. The slight over-representation of OECD respondents is not unexpected: more developments related to OWF and renewable energy are evident in OECD countries than in AFRLA or EE regions, and thus seafarers from the former region are more likely to be better informed about the topic and more interested in the present study.

The last demographic factor considered in the present work is the types of vessels that seafarers operate on, as shown in Figure 20.2. The responses from the current study match the expected numbers from the Manpower Report for the most part (within ±10 percent). One major difference, however, is that the respondents within the current study had the option to select "Other" for their response to vessel type and 18 respondents (12 percent) did so. Respondents

Figure 20.1.   Seafarers' regions of origin
AFRLA = africa/latin america; EE = eastern europe; FE = far east; INDSC = indian subcontinent (INDSC); OECD = organisation for economic co-operation and development countries
SOURCE: THE AUTHORS

---

35   Id.

Figure 20.2. Types of vessels that seafarers operate on
The category "dry cargo" refers to general cargo vessels (where goods are loaded individually, and not in bulk) as well as container vessels (where goods are loaded in intermodal containers). OSV = offshore support vessel
SOURCE: THE AUTHORS

who selected the "Other" option are either pilots who work on multiple vessels, or seafarers who are temporarily onshore and in between jobs.

Within the vessel-type demographics, it is interesting to note that the number of respondents working on OSVs (offshore supply/support vessels) is around 7.3 percent in the sample, while the Manpower Report associates around 12.4 percent of global seafaring to these vessels. This category generally includes WSVs, among others, which means that on a population level and sample level, the number of seafarers working on WSVs is likely to be much less than 12.4 and 7.3 percent respectively. This indicates that the fairly small number of Category 1 ($n_{Cat.1}$ = 7 = 5 percent of sample) respondents in the present study, that is, those working on WSVs, is not entirely tenuous or anomalistic.

Distribution of Respondents across Categories

As discussed above, the 150 respondents can be classified into three mutually exclusive groups based on the type of operations they are involved in ($n_{Cat.1}$ = 7, $n_{Cat.2}$ = 40, $n_{Cat.3}$ = 103), or into three non-mutually exclusive groups based on their awareness of certain factors that are indicative of maritime risks around OWFs ($n_{Cat.4}$ = 24, $n_{Cat.5}$ = 29, and $n_{Cat.6}$ = 18). Thus, another interesting element within the results is exploring how many respondents classified as Category 4, 5 and 6 also belong to Category 1, 2 and 3, as shown in Figures 20.3, 20.4 and 20.5.

Figure 20.3 indicates that none of the Category 1 respondents are aware of NRA studies, that is, there are no Category 1 respondents within Category 4. Likewise, only 6 of 40 (15 percent) Category 2 seafarers and 18 out of 103 (17.5 percent) Category 3 seafarers are aware of NRA studies. This lack of awareness with NRA studies is not surprising. While these studies do incorporate feedback from seafarers, they are generally conducted for approval authorities and planners, and are not targeted towards operational end-users. This is quite ironic in a sense, because NRA studies help to ultimately determine the risk-control options that are implemented around OWFs to maintain

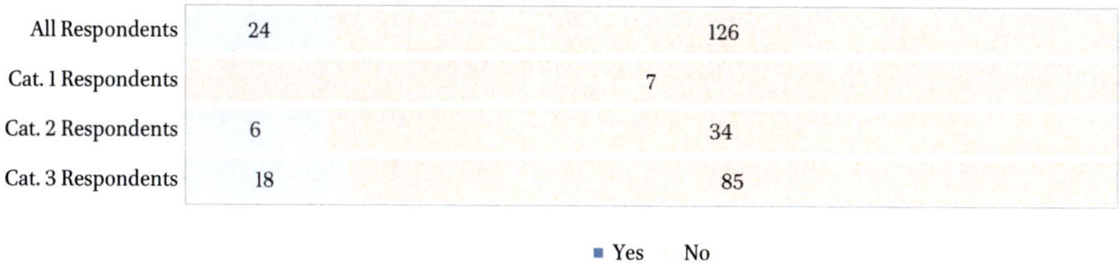

All Respondents	24	126
Cat. 1 Respondents		7
Cat. 2 Respondents	6	34
Cat. 3 Respondents	18	85

■ Yes　No

FIGURE 20.3.　Cross-comparison of how many Category 1, 2, 3 respondents are aware of NRA studies for OWFs
SOURCE: THE AUTHORS

All Respondents	29	121
Cat. 1 Respondents	3	4
Cat. 2 Respondents	9	31
Cat. 3 Respondents	17	86

Yes　No

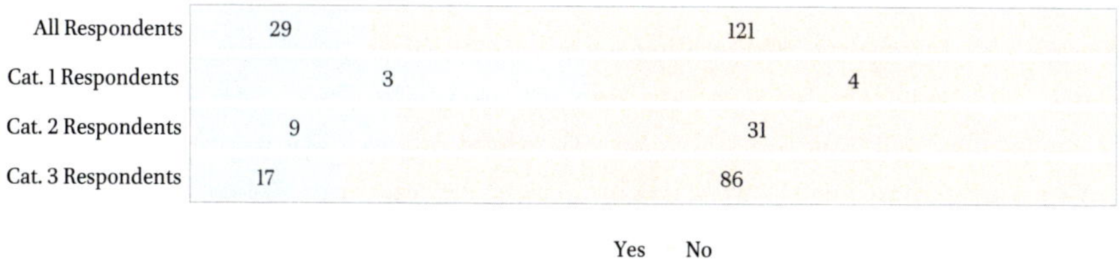

FIGURE 20.4.　Cross-comparison of how many Category 1, 2, 3 respondents are aware of regulations and guidelines related to safe navigation near OWFs
SOURCE: THE AUTHORS

Cat. 6 - Respondents that are aware of any incidents attribtuted to OWFs

All Respondents	18	132
Cat. 1 Respondents	2	5
Cat. 2 Respondents	3	37
Cat. 3 Respondents	13	90

Yes　No

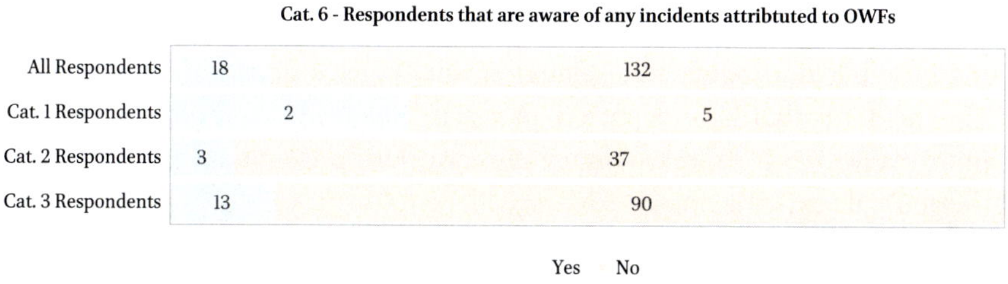

FIGURE 20.5.　Cross-comparison of Category 1, 2, 3 respondents are aware of incidents attributed to OWFs
SOURCE: THE AUTHORS

navigational safety. It can also be argued that there needs to be a closer link between NRA and the dynamic navigational risk management performed by seafarers (using closest point of alarm/time to closest point of approach (CPA/TCPA) alarms for instance); this is a potential area for further research.

While the lack of awareness with NRA studies is not surprising, one would assume that all respondents operating on WSVs (Category 1), as well as those operating near OWFs (Category 2), would at least be aware of specific navigational guidelines related to OWFs. This, however, does not seem to be the case within the present sample, as shown in Figure 20.4. Only 3 out of 7 (43 percent) Category 1 respondents and 9 of 40 (22.5 percent) Category 2 respondents are familiar with regulations or guidelines related to safe navigation near OWFs. Conversely, only 17 of 103 (16.5 percent) Category 3 respondents are aware of navigational guidelines specific to OWFs, but this lower proportion is to be expected as Category 3 seafarers do not operate near OWFs.

With regards to Category 1 and 2, the findings in Figure 20.4 imply two possibilities: either not all OWFs have specific navigational guidelines for seafarers and/or seafarers do not always seek guidance when operating near OWFs. In reality, there is evidence to suggest that the second possibility is more likely. Most coastal States do have guidance to mariners (e.g., Notice to Mariners, Marine Guidance Notes, etc., detailing speeds/safe passing distances), and some even go so far as to implement recommended or mandatory routing measures where possible and necessary. For the latter, seafarers have to be informed in due time as they may be actively enforced. However, it is ultimately up to the seafarers to maintain navigational safety, and mandatory routing measures aside, they have absolute freedom of navigation, provided they do so in a safe manner. For this reason, seafarers may not deem it necessary to consult guidance notices, but may instead rely on their own experience and judgement, as well as more general regulations such as the Convention on the International Regulations for Preventing Collisions at Sea (COLREGS), as highlighted by some respondents in their open-text answers.

There is also very low awareness of incidents that occur near OWFs, as shown in Figure 20.5. This lack of awareness can be partially attributed to the fact that not many OWF-related accidents have occurred to begin with. The incidents that have occurred, primarily involved "work-boats" which are more likely to incite interest among those working on WSVs, rather than among the general seafaring population.

Comparing the findings of Figures 20.3, 20.4 and 20.5, it is apparent that more respondents (29 of 150 – 19.3 percent) are aware of navigational guidelines specific to OWFs, than any other factor. This is quite reasonable, as these guidelines are specifically tailored for seafarers, unlike the other two sources of information, which are more aligned to the needs of decision-makers and shore-side users.

Lastly, it is interesting to note there are seven respondents who indicated they are familiar with all three pieces of information. Of these, 1 is a Category 2 seafarer (operating near OWFs), while the remaining six are Category 3 seafarers not operating near OWFs.

Rating and Ranking the Risks Associated with OWFs – Overall Sample

In this part of the results section, we present the risk rating and ranking results for the complete sample.

Rating the Risks Associated with OWFs

For the rating questions, each level on the Likert scale can be assigned a numerical value from 1 to 5, with "Extremely Concerned" being equal to a 5, and "Not At All Concerned" being equal to a 1. The rating score for each risk type can be obtained by multiplying the numerical value and number of respondents for each level and summing up the resulting values. The sample mean rating of each risk type is then calculated by dividing the rating score by the total number of respondents, n; in the present study, $n = 150$. By conducting a one-sample t-test, and a Sign test, one can then infer whether the population mean and median are likely to be greater than a hypothesized value. Table 20.2 shows how all respondents in the present sample rated the various risk types, and whether or not the population mean and median for each risk type is likely to be greater than 3.

Two trends are quite evident in Table 20.2. A very small number of respondents (around 5 percent) indicate that they are "Not At All Concerned" and more than 50 percent of respondents indicate they are "Moderately" or "Extremely Concerned." Both these findings are true for all five risk types, and clearly underline the fact that no matter how safe or reliable a system appears to be, there are always inherent risks waiting to manifest, and that the same is true for maritime risks associated with OWFs.

The sample mean and median rating columns in Table 20.2 are quite crucial for the present work. The sample mean rating for each risk type is greater than 3 ("Somewhat Concerned"), as is the sample median rating. These ratings indicate that the respondents believe the probability and/or consequences of accidents associated with each of the five risk types to be at least somewhat concerning.

The values in the sample mean rating column also give an indication as to which risk type is most concerning to the respondents. In the present study, risk type 1 has the highest sample mean rating, $\bar{x}_1 = 3.81$. This risk type pertains to navigational accidents involving passing vessels, and an overwhelming 82 percent of the respondents indicate their level of concern with this risk type as "Somewhat Concerned" or greater, with 38.7 percent indicating that they are "Extremely Concerned." Risk types 2 (risks involving WSVs) and 3 (risks during installation and decommissioning) are given very similar mean ratings by the respondents: $\bar{x}_2 = \bar{x}_3 = 3.41$. The latter risk type edges out the former by a single point in the rating score column.

While a quarter of the respondents appear to be only "Slightly Concerned" with risk type 2, a clear majority of 70.7 percent indicate that they are at least "Somewhat Concerned." A significant 34 percent of the respondents, in fact, rate themselves as being "Moderately Concerned" with risk type 2. By contrast,

TABLE 20.2. Risk ratings by all respondents in the sample and respective population inference

Risk Type	Risk Ratings by All Respondents in the Sample [n_{total} = 150]							Sample Parameters				Population Inference		
	No. of respondents who selected their level of concern as						Rating Score	Sample Mean Rating ($\bar{x}$)	Sample Std. Dev.(s)	Sample Median Rating (Md)	Evidence that Pop. Mean > 3? Yes/No P_{t-test}	Evidence that Pop. Mean > 3? Lower Bound Mean at $\alpha = 0.05$	Evidence that Pop. Md > 3? Yes/No $P_{Sign-Test}$
	Not At All Concerned	Slightly Concerned	Somewhat Concerned	Moderately Concerned	Extremely Concerned							
1	7 (4.7%)	20 (13.3%)	26 (17.3%)	39 (26.0%)	58 (38.7%)		571	3.81	1.219	4	Y 0.000	3.642	Y 0.0000
2	8 (5.3%)	36 (24.0%)	24 (16.0%)	51 (34.0%)	31 (20.7%)		511	3.41	1.210	4	Y 0.000	3.243	Y 0.0005
3	8 (5.3%)	34 (22.7%)	32 (21.3%)	40 (26.7%)	36 (24.0%)		512	3.41	1.227	4	Y 0.000	3.247	Y 0.0012
4	6 (4.0%)	39 (26.0%)	20 (13.3%)	34 (22.7%)	51 (34.0%)		535	3.57	1.303	4	Y 0.000	3.391	Y 0.0003
5	8 (5.3%)	49 (32.7%)	17 (11.3%)	38 (25.3%)	38 (25.3%)		499	3.33	1.308	4	Y 0.001	3.150	N 0.0593
Total	37	178	119	202	214		-	-	-	-	-	-	-
Average	4.9%	23.7%	15.9%	26.9%	28.5%		-	3.51	-	-	-	-	-

the distribution of responses from "Slightly" to "Extremely Concerned" is almost homogenous for risk type 3, that is, there appears to be no clear consensus among respondents about the level of concern.

Risk type 4, which covers risks associated with SAR operations near OWFs, is given the second-highest rating, $\bar{x}_4$ = 3.57, with 34 percent of respondents "Extremely Concerned." Risk type 4, interestingly has a higher standard deviation compared to risk types 1, 2 and 3, indicating a wider spread of responses over different concern levels.

Risk type 5, which refers to any risks in ports and harbors that deal with OWF activities, is given the lowest sample mean rating, $\bar{x}_5$ = 3.33. The distribution of responses across the various levels of concern is approximately similar on either side of the median for risk type 5: nearly a 40 percent of the respondents select their level of concern with this risk type as "Not at all" or "Slightly Concerned," while approximately 50 percent of respondents indicate otherwise by selecting "Moderately" or "Extremely Concerned." Only a meagre 11.3 percent actually select the median level of "Somewhat Concerned." The polarized response pattern means that risk type 5 has the highest standard deviation of all risk types.

The data collected within the sample is also useful to infer conclusions about the entire seafaring population, as shown in the three right-most columns of Table 20.2. There is enough evidence to state that the lower-bound population mean at the 95 percent confidence level, for each different risk type, is greater than 3 as hypothesized. There is also enough evidence to conclude that the population median for risk types 1, 2, 3 and 4 is also greater than 3, although the same cannot be said for risk type 5. All in all, there is enough evidence to state that seafarers in general, on a population level, are likely to be more than "Somewhat Concerned" when it comes to any of the maritime risks associated with OWFs. In particular, the results indicate that seafarers on a population level are likely to be quite concerned about risks that passing vessels face from OWFs (i.e., Category 1 risks), so much so that the lower bound population mean for this risk type is more than 10 percent (0.5) above the median value of 3. Why risk type 1 may be so concerning is discussed below under "Making Sense of the Rating and Ranking Results."

Ranking the Risks Associated with OWFs

Aside from the rating questions, the respondents were also asked to rank the risk types in order of concern priority. Table 20.3 shows how all respondents in the present sample rank the various risk types, and whether or not a clear rank can be discerned for each risk type on a population level.

TABLE 20.3. Risk rankings by all respondents in the sample and respective population inference.

Risk Type	Risk Rankings by All Respondents in the Sample [n_{total} = 150]					Sample Parameters		Population Inference	
	No. of respondents who selected Risk Type as						Sample Risk Ranking	Can distinct rank(s) be assigned to Risk Type at the population level?	Most Likely Rank(s)
	Lowest Priority	4th Priority	3rd Priority	2nd Priority	Highest Priority	Ranking Score		Yes/No P_X^2	
1	12 (8.0%)	13 (8.7%)	16 (10.7%)	23 (15.3%)	86 (57.3%)	608	1st	Y 0.000	1st
2	12 (8.0%)	40 (26.7%)	42 (28.0%)	47 (31.3%)	9 (6.0%)	451	2nd	Y 0.000	2nd, 3rd, 4th
3	32 (21.3%)	35 (23.3%)	33 (22.0%)	24 (16.0%)	26 (17.3%)	427	3rd	N 0.558	NCDR
4	33 (22.0%)	32 (21.3%)	34 (22.7%)	30 (20.0%)	21 (14.0%)	424	4th	N 0.453	NCDR
5	61 (40.7%)	30 (20.0%)	25 (16.7%)	26 (17.3%)	8 (5.3%)	340	5th	Y 0.000	5th
Total	150	150	150	150	150	-	-		

NCDR stands for "No Clear Distinct Rank" and indicates that there is insufficient evidence to determine a likely rank(s) for the risk type on a population level.

It is apparent from Table 20.3 that respondents are most likely to rank risk type 1 as their first (top-most) concern, and risk type 5 as their fifth (lowest) concern. A distinct majority, 57.3 percent, of the respondents rank risk type 1 as their top concern, while 40.7 percent placed risk type 5 at the lowest priority. The clear cut sample results also provide enough evidence to infer that the highest and lowest ranked risk types on a population level would be risk types 1 and 5 respectively.

With risk type 2, it is evident that the respondents would not select it as either their highest or lowest concern, but instead place it as their second, third or fourth priority on a sample. A Chi-square goodness-of-fit test indicates that a similar ranking pattern may be expected on a population level with regards to risk type 2. There is no clear consensus among the sample respondents on the ranking order of risk types 3 and 4. Nearly an equal number of respondents place these risk types as their first, second, third, fourth and fifth priority. This also means that it is not possible to infer a distinct rank for risk types 3 and 4 on a population level.

Comparing the results of the rating and ranking questions, it is obvious that risk type 1 is both the highest rated as well as the highest ranked risk type. Similarly, risk type 5 is both the lowest rated and the lowest ranked risk type. Conversely, risk type 3 has the third-highest rating, and is also placed third in terms of ranking order. Interestingly, risk type 4 has the second-highest rating, but is placed fourth in the ranking order by the respondents in the sample; the vice-versa is true for risk type 2.

Making Sense of the Rating and Ranking Results

The discrepancy in the rating and ranking of risk types 2 and 4 leads to the question, why do the respondents rate and rank they risks as they do? A review of previous consenting documents (augmented by 61 open-text answers from the present study) help to provide some insight into this area.

Risk type 1 involves passing vessels, that is, vessels that have nothing to do with OWFs. An accident involving such vessels, therefore, has lower societal acceptance than other risk types. Furthermore, passing vessels may be carrying a lot of cargo, or even passengers, and thus any accident involving passing vessels may result in catastrophic consequences such as human casualties or environmental damage. Compared to other risk types, the probability of risk type 1 accidents is also higher, particularly if an OWF is located near a busy shipping route. Tens or even hundreds of vessels may pass an OWF on a daily basis, while only a few support operations may be conducted over the same period. Another factor to consider is that risk type 1 persists through the entire lifecycle of an OWF, from installation to decommissioning.

The potentially high consequence and probability of accidents is what leads to a high rating for this risk type. The high ranking for this risk type also probably stems from a low societal acceptance of this risk type: any vessel not directly related to an OWF should not face increased navigational risks because of an OWF and thus this risk type must be prioritized over others. In reality, risk type 1 is probably the one that is most closely scrutinized and managed by approval and consenting authorities, for the reasons discussed above. This is evident by looking at various NRA studies for OWFs that have undergone the approval process as well as the risk control measures that are implemented. Despite this, respondents still feel that risk type is the most concerning of all others, which indicates that they are perhaps unaware of risk-control measures or may feel these risk-control measures are inadequate.

By contrast, risk types 2, 3 and 5 are primarily perceived as "work-place" occupational health and safety risks, that is, respondents view them as a part and parcel of working with OWFs. As these risk types are considered to be an inherent part of certain operations, there is also an underlying assumption that persons involved in these operations are better trained and better equipped to deal with the respective risks, for example, people working with jack-up installation vessels are better trained to deal with the risks associated with the job. Stringent HSE practices, combined with a limited number of OWF maintenance, installation, decommissioning, and port operations means that both the probability and consequences of risk types 2, 3 and 5 are perceived to be lower than risk type 1. This is well-reflected in the lower mean ratings for the former risk types. The aforementioned factors also mean that risk types 2, 3 and 5 are more socially acceptable than risk type 1.

Risk type 4 is perhaps the most interesting from an analytical perspective. It is given the second-highest mean rating, but is only ranked as a lowly fourth in the concern priority order. The high rating reflects the high-risk nature of emergency response operations. While such operations are rarely conducted, the probability and consequences of things going awry during an ongoing operation is relatively high. This high risk, however, is also perceived to be a product of occupational hazards, and thus persons involved in emergency response activities are well-trained, well-organized, and well-equipped. Subsequently, the low ranking indicates that the risk associated with emergency operations, while high, is still socially-acceptable, and the perception seems to be that not much can or needs to be done to reduce this high risk any further. Instead, it may be more worthwhile to focus resources on mitigating the accidents associated with other risk types, which may have lower consequences but a higher probability of occurrence than risk type 4.

Rating and Ranking the Risks Associated with OWFs – Comparison between Categories

The final part of the results section compares the risk type ranking and rating results across different respondent categories.

Comparing Rating and Ranking Results on a Sample Level

Table 20.4 shows how respondents in different categories rate and rank the various risk types on a sample level. It can be noted that respondents in Categories 2, 3, 4, 5 and 6 give the lowest mean rating to risk type 5, which echoes the findings of the overall sample. Respondents in Categories 2, 3, 4 and 5 give the highest mean rating to risk type 1, again reflecting the results of the overall sample.

While the above findings present good agreement between the rating patterns of respondents across different categories, a closer look also exposes some discrepancies. In fact, respondents in certain categories clearly rate some risk types very differently compared to the overall sample. For instance, Category 6 respondents give the highest mean rating to risk type 4, while Category 1 respondents also deviate significantly from the norm by giving risk types 1, 3 and 5 the same rating. The reason why the results of Categories 1 and 6 deviate from the findings of the overall sample is most likely due to the small sizes of these categories ($n_{Cat.1} = 7$; $n_{Cat.6} = 18$). All that being said, there is only one occurrence of a significant deviation:[36] Category 1 respondents give risk type 5 a mean rating of 3.86 compared to the overall sample's mean rating of 3.33. Aside from this one occurrence, the mean risk ratings given to all risk types by respondents from different categories are within ±0.5 of the mean risk rating given by the overall sample.

It is also interesting to compare the median risk ratings assigned to each risk type by respondents in different categories. As shown in Table 20.4, the median risk ratings are by and large the same across different categories, with a few notable exceptions. The underlined values indicate that there is a difference of at least 0.5 between the median rating of a particular category, and the median rating assigned by the total sample. Three of these underlined values are associated with Category 2 respondents, who, compared to the overall sample, give a lower median rating to risk types 3, 4 and 5.

The comparatively high median and mean rating given to risk type 1 by Category 4, 5 and 6 respondents is also noteworthy. Categories 4, 5 and 6 contain respondents who are aware of NRA studies, navigational guidelines,

---

36 A significant deviation in this case refers to a difference of more than ±0.5 (10 percent) between a category mean rating and the overall mean rating for a risk type.

TABLE 20.4. Comparing the ratings and rankings assigned to each risk type by respondents in different categories on a sample level.

Risk Rating Comparison at Sample Level

Risk Type	Mean Ranking ($\bar{x}$) Standard Deviation (s)							Median value (Md)		
	All Seafarers [n= 150]	Cat. 1 [n= 7]	Cat. 2 [n= 40]	Cat. 3 [n= 103]	Cat. 4 [n=24]	Cat. 5 [n= 29]	Cat. 6 [n= 18]	All Seafarers [n= 150]	Cat. 1 [n= 7]	Cat. 2 [n= 40]
1	3.81	3.86	3.68	3.85	4.16	4.03	3.89	4	4	4
	1.219	1.345	1.228	1.216	1.090	1.239	1.323			
2	3.41	*3.71*	3.33	3.42	3.83	3.66	3.78	4	4	4
	1.210	1.254	1.269	1.192	1.049	1.233	1.166			
3	3.41	**3.86**	3.25	3.45	3.58	3.41	3.89	4	4	<u>3</u>
	1.227	1.345	1.193	1.235	1.176	1.268	1.231			
4	3.57	*3.71*	3.33	3.65	3.92	3.62	**3.94**	4	4	3.5
	1.303	1.254	1.269	1.319	1.139	1.374	1.434			
5	*3.33*	**3.86**	*3.18*	*3.35*	*3.46*	*3.38*	3.72	4	4	<u>3</u>
	1.308	1.345	1.279	1.319	1.351	1.293	1.364			

Bold and Italics values indicate the highest and lowest rated and ranked risk categories respectively. The responses from seafarers in each category are compared to the responses of seafarers in the overall sample, and values in brackets indicate any resulting difference between the rating scores or ranking positions. Underlined values indicate a significant difference (> 10%) between the mean/median ratings of all respondents, and respondents in a given category, at a sample level.

				Risk Rank						
Cat. 3 [n=103]	Cat. 4 [n=24]	Cat. 5 [n=29]	Cat. 6 [n=18]	All Seafarers [n=150]	Cat. 1 [n=7]	Cat. 2 [n=40]	Cat. 3 [n=103]	Cat. 4 [n=24]	Cat. 5 [n=29]	Cat. 6 [n=18]
4	<u>5</u>	<u>5</u>	4.5	1st	3rd	1st	1st	1st	1st	1st
4	4	4	4	2nd	4th	2nd	2nd	3rd	2nd	3rd
4	4	<u>3</u>	4	3rd	1st	4th	4th	4th	3rd	2nd
4	4	4	<u>5</u>	4th	2nd	3rd	3rd	2nd	5th	4th
4	4	4	4	5th	5th	5th	5th	5th	4th	5th

or incidents in the vicinity of OWFs. It appears that having knowledge of these factors causes seafarers to be more concerned about risk type 1, at least on a sample level. In fact, seafarers in Categories 4, 5 and 6 have a tendency to give higher mean and median rating to all risk types, compared to the overall sample. The only exception to this is the median value for risk type 3 when rated by Category 5 respondents.

Table 20.4 also compares how respondents in different categories rank the various risks on a sample level. Echoing the results of the overall sample, respondents in nearly all categories place risk type 1 on the first position. Similarly, respondents in almost all categories rank risk type 5 in fifth place; the exception is Category 5 respondents who rank risk type 5 on a close fourth position. The underlined values in the table indicate instances when respondents in a certain category rank a particular risk type at least ±2 positions differently than the overall sample. Most of these instances are associated with Category 1 respondents, and can be attributed to the very small number of respondents in this category.

A truly anomalistic ranking result is Category 4 respondents placing risk type 4 as their second highest concern, a difference of two ranks when compared to the overall sample. Category 4 respondents are those who are aware of NRA studies, and risk type 4 pertains to maritime emergency operations in the vicinity of OWFs. This result, is therefore, very interesting because apparently having a knowledge of NRA studies leads to respondents prioritizing emergency operations above nearly all other risk types. Emergency response measures are emphasized during the NRA process in most countries, and the current finding could simply be a reflection of this fact.

Comparing Rating and Ranking Results on a Population Level

Table 20.5 compares how respondents in different categories rate and rank the various risk types on a population level. The results for Category 1 are underlined because the small number of respondents in this category does not allow for any valid conclusions to be feasibly drawn on a population level. To compare whether there is a difference in the rating and ranking patterns of the remaining categories, a series of hypothesis tests was conducted on the overall sample (i.e., all respondents), and on each separate sub-set of respondents. Underlined values in Table 20.5 indicate instances when an hypothesis test yielded different outcomes for seafarers in a particular category and seafarers in general (i.e., the overall sample).

In this study, the authors recognized that the data is not ideal for comparison between groups. This is why there is no "direct" comparison between the groups, but rather, a study of whether each sub-group would rate their mean concerns with the risk to be greater than 3 on a population level.

The first hypothesis test conducted was a one-sample t-test to determine if the mean rating assigned to the five risk types would be greater than 3 on a population level. There is enough evidence to state that seafarers in general, as well as seafarers in every category (with the exception of Category 1) are likely to give risk type 1 a mean rating greater than 3 on a population level.

Seafarers in Categories 3, 4, 5 and 6 are also likely to give risk types 2, 3 and 4 a mean rating greater than 3 on a population level, once again matching the result for seafarers in general. There is, however, not enough evidence that seafarers in Category 2 would also give a mean rating greater than 3 to risk types 2, 3 and 4 on a population level.[37] This result indicates that Category 2 seafarers are unlikely to be as concerned about risk types 2, 3 and 4 as the seafarers from other categories. This is quite an interesting finding because Category 2 seafarers are those that operate near OWFs, and thus have a first-hand experience of some of the operational challenges. If Category 2 seafarers feel that risk types 2, 3 and 4 are not as concerning as risk type 1, it may compel stakeholders to pay special attention to addressing the latter rather than the former risk types.

There is also not enough evidence that Category 2, 4 or 5 seafarers would give risk type 5 a mean rating greater than 3. Risk type 5, which pertains to operations in ports and harbors that deal with OWF activities, is clearly not viewed as very concerning by certain groups of seafarers, a fact reflected in both sample- and population-level findings.

The second hypothesis test conducted was a one-sample Sign test to determine if the median rating for the five risk types is greater than 3. Mirroring the results of the general population, Category 2, 3, 4 and 5 seafarers are likely to give a median rating greater than 3 for risk type 1. There is not enough evidence, however, to state the same for Category 6 seafarers. This result is most likely an anomaly due to the fewer number of respondents in Category 6 than in other categories.

Table 20.5 also shows that seafarers in Category 2 are unlikely to give a median rating greater than 3 to risk types 2, 3 and 4. This ties in well with their tendency to give lower mean risk ratings to risk types 2, 3 and 4 than seafarers in general, as discussed above.

While there is evidence to suggest that Category 4 and 5 seafarers would give a mean rating greater than 3 to risk type 3, there is not enough evidence that these seafarers would give a median rating greater than 3 to the same risk type. This indicates that the level of concern of Category 4 and 5 seafarers with regards to risk type 3 is not too high, but rather lies near the "Somewhat Concerned" level on a population level. Similarly, there is not enough evidence

---

37   However, the Category 2 lower-bound population mean rating for risk types 2 and 4 is quite close to 3.

TABLE 20.5. Comparing the ratings and rankings assigned to each risk type by respondents in different categories on a population level. Underlined values indicate instances when a hypothesis test yielded different outcomes for seafarers a particular category and seafarers in general (i.e., the overall sample).

Risk Rating Comparison at Population Level

	Is there evidence that the mean rating for Risk Type x is greater than 3 at the respective population level?							Is there evidence that the median value for Risk Type x is greater than 3 at the respective population level?			
	Yes/NoP$_{t\text{-test}}$ Lower Bound Mean at $\alpha = 0.05$							Yes/NoP$_{\text{Sign-Test}}$			
Risk Type	All Seafarers	Cat. 1	Cat. 2	Cat. 3	Cat. 4	Cat. 5	Cat. 6	All Seafarers	Cat. 1	Cat. 2	Cat. 3
1	Y	<u>N</u>	Y	Y	Y	Y	Y	Y	<u>N</u>	Y	Y
	0.000	0.071	0.001	0.000	0.000	0.000	0.006	0.0000	0.2266	0.0100	0.0000
	3.642	2.869	3.348	3.655	3.785	3.643	3.346				
2	Y	<u>N</u>	<u>N</u>	Y	Y	Y	Y	Y	<u>N</u>	<u>N</u>	Y
	0.000	0.091	0.057	0.000	0.000	0.004	0.006	0.0005	0.2266	0.1620	0.0014
	3.243	2.794	2.987	3.222	3.466	3.266	3.300				
3	Y	<u>N</u>	<u>N</u>	Y	Y	Y	Y	Y	<u>N</u>	<u>N</u>	Y
	0.000	0.071	0.096	0.000	0.012	0.045	0.004	0.0012	0.2266	0.3601	0.0013
	3.247	2.869	2.932	3.245	3.172	3.013	3.384				
4	Y	<u>N</u>	<u>N</u>	Y	Y	Y	Y	Y	<u>N</u>	<u>N</u>	Y
	0.000	0.091	0.057	0.000	0.000	0.011	0.006	0.0003	0.2266	0.1958	0.0007
	3.391	2.794	2.987	3.435	3.518	3.187	3.357				
5	Y	<u>N</u>	<u>N</u>	Y	<u>N</u>	<u>N</u>	Y	N	N	N	N
	0.001	0.071	0.196	0.004	0.055	0.063	0.019	0.0593	0.2266	0.5700	0.0609
	3.150	2.869	2.834	3.134	2.986	2.971	3.163				

NCDR stands for "No Clear Distinct Rank" and indicates that there is insufficient evidence to determine a likely rank(s) for the risk type on a population level.

Is there evidence that a distinct rank can be assigned to Risk Type x at the respective population level?

Yes/NoP_X^2
Most Likely Risk Rank(s) at Population Level

Cat. 4	Cat. 5	Cat. 6	All Seafarers	Cat. 1	Cat. 2	Cat. 3	Cat. 4	Cat. 5	Cat. 6
Y	Y	N	Y	<u>N</u>	Y	Y	Y	Y	<u>N</u>
0.0007	0.0047	0.0717	0.000	0.934	0.000	0.000	0.000	0.000	0.109
			1st	NCDR	1st	1st	1st	1st	NCDR
Y	Y	Y	Y	<u>N</u>	Y	Y	Y	Y	<u>N</u>
0.0036	0.0436	0.0384	0.000	0.368	0.000	0.000	0.032	0.021	0.168
			2nd, 3rd, 4th	NCDR	2nd	2nd, 3rd, 4th	2nd, 4th	2nd, 4th	NCDR
<u>N</u>	<u>N</u>	Y	N	N	N	N	N	N	N
0.0835	0.2024	0.0384	0.558	0.666	0.075	0.905	0.478	0.226	0.168
			NCDR	NCDR	NCDR	NCDR	NCDR	NCDR	NCDR
Y	<u>N</u>	Y	N	N	N	N	N	Y	N
0.0053	0.0925	0.0481	0.453	0.666	0.517	0.665	0.314	0.008	0.208
			NCDR	NCDR	NCDR	NCDR	NCDR	5th	NCDR
N	N	N	Y	<u>N</u>	Y	Y	<u>N</u>	<u>N</u>	<u>N</u>
0.2024	0.3506	0.0717	0.000	0.666	0.021	0.000	0.954	0.153	0.168
			5th	NCDR	5th	5th	NCDR	NCDR	NCDR

that Category 5 seafarers would give risk type 4 a median rating greater than 3, although there is evidence that the mean rating from these seafarers, for this risk type would be greater than 3. This again would indicate that on a population level, Category 5 seafarers are near the "Somewhat Concerned" level for risk type 4.

Seafarers across all categories are unlikely to give risk type 5 a median rating of greater than 3. This conforms to the result of the hypothesis test on the overall sample, and echoes the above statement that risk type 5 is clearly not viewed as very concerning by certain groups of seafarers, or indeed, by seafarers in general.

The last hypothesis test conducted was a Chi-Square goodness-of-fit test to establish whether certain risk types can be assigned a clear ranking order on a population level. Seafarers in general, as well as those in Categories 2, 3, 4 and 5 are likely to rank risk type 1 as their first (topmost) concern. Similarly, seafarers in the general population, as well as those in Category 2, 3, 4 and 5 are likely to place risk type 2 as either their second, third or fourth priority. There is, however, no evidence that Category 6 seafarers will place either risk type 1 or 2 on any distinct rank. This unclear result is possibly due to the small number of respondents in Category 6.

Risk type 3 has no clear discernible rank at the population level, that is, it is nearly equally likely that this risk can be placed at any position from 1 to 5; this is true for seafarers in general, as well as seafarers in all categories (except Category 1 where the number of respondents is too small to draw any conclusions). The general seafaring population and seafarers in Categories 2, 3, 4 and 6 are also unlikely to place risk type 4 on a distinct rank. However, there is evidence that Category 5 seafarers are likely to rank risk type 4 as their fifth and lowest concern. There is no clear reason why this may be the case, and it is possible that this result is an anomaly.

Risk type 5 is likely to be ranked as the fifth (lowest) concern by the seafaring population in general, as well as by Category 2 and 3 seafarers. There is no evidence, however, which indicates what rank seafarers in Category 4, 5, and 6 would assign to risk type 5. As discussed earlier, risk type 5 is generally given the lowest rating and ranking on both a sample and population level, and is apparently not a pressing area of concern for seafarers.

Discussion

This section discusses what the results mean for the OWF and maritime industries, and identifies possible follow-up research areas.

Deciphering the Results for the Industry

The primary objective of the present work is to establish the level to which seafarers are concerned about various risk types associated with OWFs. The results clearly show that, on average, seafarers are likely to be more than "Somewhat Concerned" with each of the five risk types. An average seafarer can be expected to give a rating of greater than 3 (on a scale of 5, with 5 being "Extremely Concerned") to the various risk types on a population level. This means that seafarers, on a population level, are likely to perceive the probability and/or consequences of each of the 5 risk types to be more than somewhat concerning as well.

The results also show that risks to passing vessels are the greatest concern for seafarers, with risk type 1 given a mean risk rating of 3.81 (3.642 on a population level) out of 5. Risks in ports and harbors that deal with OWF activities (risk type 5) are the least concerning and are rated as 3.33 (3.150 on a population level) on average. Risk types 1 and 5 are respectively ranked as the most and least concerning risk types as well. The high concern for risk type 1 most likely stems from the comparatively higher probability and consequences, and lower social acceptance, of accidents in this category, as discussed above under "Making Sense of the Rating and Ranking Results."

Despite the fact that seafarers appear to be more than "Somewhat Concerned" with the five risk types, there is no doubt that there have been very few maritime accidents associated over the last few decades. Subsequently, there is little doubt that risk control measures have been effective in limiting the number of accidents associated with OWFs, at least for now. Considering the scarcity of OWF-related accidents, and taking into account the results of the present study, there are thus two possible explanations:

1. Seafarers are poorly informed and therefore unduly concerned about the risk types, *or*,
2. Seafarers are right to be concerned as much as they are, and the industry can expect more accidents as OWFs continue to increase in number and size.

Both scenarios point to potential weaknesses in the risk management and NRA processes. If the first scenario is assumed to be true, then one can argue that the risk communication to seafarers needs to be improved. Several respondents in the present study cite factors such as poor weather, interference with navigational equipment, and increased traffic density, which can aggravate the risk to maritime operations near OWFs. The fact is that these factors, and more, are thoroughly considered in the NRA process for OWFs, but it is clear that some respondents may not be aware of this. Furthermore, respondents that are aware of NRA studies (Category 4), or navigational guidelines (Category 5), seem to be even more concerned with each of the five risk types on average. It is therefore clear that seafarers need to be reassured that their concerns have been into account, and factors that can amount to risky operation situations have been thoroughly considered. Improving risk communication should primarily be the responsibility of the coastal State(s) where the OWF is located. However, OWF owners and chartering companies involved in installation, maintenance, and decommissioning operations may also have a role to play in improving the communication of NRA studies and navigational guidelines to seafarers on board their vessels.

On the other hand, it is also possible that the second scenario may be true, that is, seafarers may be rightfully concerned about the various risk types. The fact is that seafarers, better than any other stakeholders, understand the risks of maritime operations. This would also help to explain why Category 4 and 5 seafarers are more concerned about maritime risks. They may be more intimately familiar with the realities and the shortcomings of the NRA process. Furthermore, there is no doubt that the OWF industry is growing and evolving, and this evolution is causing a strain on spatial planners in terms of balancing safety and energy generation. We are therefore inclined to believe that this second scenario is more likely.

The second scenario being true would mean that the OWF industry may face increased resistance from the maritime sector as OWFs continue to grow and evolve. The only way to alleviate these concerns, and overcome any potential resistance, will be to prove that OWFs are at least as safe as they are now. This will require continuous improvement of the methods and models that are used to assess maritime risks, so that both the OWF and maritime industries may be better prepared for any potential incidents. Thus far, the NRA process for OWFs in most countries focus on probabilistic assessments in an attempt to reduce the probability of accidents associated with OWFs. These assessments, and any mitigating measures proposed as a result, have been quite successful in limiting the number of accidents, but with a rapid increase in the number of OWFs, accidents seem increasingly likely, almost inevitable, as highlighted by the respondents in the present study.

In face of this potentially increased accident probability, approval authorities, during the NRA process, should also pay special attention to assessing and mitigating the consequences of accidents. Doing so is certainly in the interest of both industries. Currently, only Germany[38] has specific guidelines on

---

38 Denmark also requires collision-friendly design but their guidance document is internal, and the assessment procedure is qualitative. By contrast, Germany has a standard on wind turbine design that explicitly asks for a quantitative assessment to prove that turbines are collision-friendly.

"collision-friendly" wind turbine design that can mitigate the damage to ships in case of a collision. Of course, collision-friendly designs may have implications for the energy yield from an OWF (e.g., they might limit the maximum load on a tower and thus the rotor size), which means that the OWF and maritime industries must work together to find an optimal solution at the NRA stage.

Regardless of which scenario proves to be true, it is imperative that the NRA process be improved and adapted to proactively deal with the evolving risks. This goal can only be accomplished through the joint efforts of the maritime and OWF industries. To better address the risks, each industry must acknowledge and understand the risks and challenges faced by the other, and thus overcome the current segregated approach wherein OWF design and marine spatial planning are conducted separately. It goes without saying that mitigating the risk of maritime accidents in the vicinity of OWFs is mutually beneficial for both the maritime and OWF industries.

The results of the present study compare well with the findings of the literature review. The study, in essence, validates each of the five risk areas identified by the literature review, and also confirms that the risk that OWFs pose to passing vessels is of the highest concern to seafarers. This finding is an indication of why projects such as OWFs (and indeed other onshore/offshore energy projects) undergo a vigorous environmental impact assessment to ensure that the impacts on other existing and future users and activities are kept to a minimum.

Justifying the Current Sample and Potential Follow-up Research

As mentioned above, the core objective of the present study is to understand how seafarers, in general, perceive the maritime risks associated with OWFs. Accordingly, the sample of respondents for the present study is designed to reflect the seafaring population as a whole.

Such a sample is quite valuable from a proactive-thinking perspective for two reasons: seafaring is a "mobile" profession, and OWFs are spreading across the globe. As a result, seafarers that do not currently operate near OWFs may soon do so. Seafarers who have no experience of OWFs may also be asked to participate in OWF approval studies. Thus, it is important to understand their perceptions and concerns as well.

Moreover, sampling from the entire population of seafarers allows the authors to approximately identify how many seafarers operate on WSVs or near OWFs. The sample also means it is possible to assess the level of awareness with OWF-related issues, such as NRA studies, specific navigational guidelines, or incidents associated with OWFs, among the wider seafaring population.

The initial results of the present comparative analyses indicate that despite subtle discrepancies, the perceptions of seafarers in different categories do not differ too significantly on either a sample or population level. The responses, in fact, give the distinct impression that seafarers, irrespective of which category they belong to, have very similar ideas about the maritime operational risks associated with OWF. This finding further justifies surveying from the entire seafaring population, rather than from just seafarers that operate near OWFs.

Choosing to sample from the seafaring population in general, however, also has some drawbacks. As the proportion of respondents in different categories varies significantly, making comparisons across different categories is challenging. Nonetheless, the present study does strive to make such comparisons where possible, although readers are advised to treat these results cautiously, particularly for categories with fewer than 20 respondents.

For a future research study, it may thus be worthwhile to investigate and compare similarly-sized samples representing different categories of seafarers. Such a study could help to conclusively determine if any differences exist between the perceptions of respondents from different categories. It is important to underline, however, that such a follow-up study would not represent the entire seafaring population in terms of external validity quite as well. This is because the proportion of seafarers in the different categories is not equal on a population level, as shown by seafarer demographic studies such as the BIMCO/ICS Manpower Report.

Since it is hypothesized that there are potential weaknesses in existing NRA processes, future research should also investigate this topic further. It is particularly important to identify the kind of data that seafarers would like to see from NRA studies, as well as to identify any gaps in the NRA process as perceived by approval authorities.

Conclusion

The present study is an initial pilot to generalize the maritime risks that can be associated with all OWFs. It is also novel in exploring the perceptions of the wider seafaring community towards these risks in an academic context. The primary conclusion is that seafarers, on average, at the population level, are likely to be more than "Somewhat Concerned" (which is equal to a rating > 3 on a scale of 5), with each of the five identified risk types. Respondents are particularly concerned with risks that OWFs pose to passing vessels, and give this particular risk type a rating of 3.81 (3.642 on a population level at $\alpha = 0.05$) out of 5, while also ranking it as their top concern. The continued evolution of OWFs will probably exacerbate the concerns related to the probability and consequences of these risks further, if appropriate actions are not taken. On the other hand, a better understanding of the risk perceptions can also lead to better, more efficient use of sea space with minimal under- and/or over-design for safety.

The wariness of seafarers towards OWF-related risks can be attributed, at least partially, to shortcomings in the NRA process. In light of this, it is suggested that the existing risk management and NRA processes be further improved. This may help to alleviate some seafarers' concerns, while also mitigating resistance to the continued growth of the OWF sector by further reassuring stakeholders. Improved NRA processes may also allow both the maritime and OWF industries to be better prepared for any potential incidents, which are surely set to increase with the rapid growth of the OWF sector. Better NRA processes could also be designed to reduce administrative burdens on OWF owners during the approval and consenting processes for their installations. Both the OWF sector and the maritime industry have a potentially crucial role to play in improving NRA processes, but also a lot to gain from doing so.

On a more contemplative note, it is worthwhile noting that the sea, traditionally, has been the dominion of the shipping industry. The shipping industry prides itself on being one of the oldest professions, and, to this day, ships serve as the lifeblood of the global economy by carrying approximately 80 percent of the world's goods.[39] Outsiders often tend to view the maritime industry as unsafe and inefficient compared to other transport sectors, a notion that cannot be any further from the truth. The reality is that maritime stakeholders, including seafarers, work very hard to ensure that shipping is one of the safest and most efficient forms of transport, and their efforts are very clearly evident.[40] The maritime industry will continue to strive for an even safer and more efficient future, and it is the responsibility of the OWF industry to not hinder, but assist them and work together to ensure optimal coexistence. This, in fact, is legally enshrined in the United Nations Convention of the Law of the Sea, which allows States to exploit their coastal areas for renewable energy generation among other uses, with one caveat: freedom of navigation and the unhindered safe passage of ships.

---

39 Allianz Global Corporate and Specialty (AGCS), *Safety and Shipping Review 2016: An Annual Review of Trends and Developments in Shipping Losses and Safety* (Munich: AGCS, 2016); United Nations Conference on Trade and Development (UNCTAD), *Review of Maritime Transport 2016* (Geneva: UNCTAD, 2016).

40 AGCS, id.

PART 5

Book Reviews

∴

Robert C. Beckman, Tore Henriksen, Kristine Dalaker Kraabel, Erik J. Molenaar and J. Ashley Roach, eds., *Governance of Arctic Shipping: Balancing Rights and Interests of Arctic States and User States* (Leiden/Boston: Brill Nijhoff, 2017), 448 pp.

The year 2017 started with the entry into force of the International Code of Safety for Ships Operating in Polar Waters, also known as the Polar Code. While the Polar Code is a significant milestone for maritime law regarding Arctic shipping for the safety and protection of the Arctic environment, arguably there are some gaps that coastal States might try to fill through their domestic regulations, such as use of heavy oil or discharge of ballast water in the Arctic Ocean. Thus, how to reconcile the interests of coastal States and those of other States that wish to use the Arctic Ocean for shipping remains an important issue.

Governance of Arctic Shipping: Balancing Rights and Interests of Arctic States and User States, which is a product of an international conference jointly organized by the National University of Singapore and the Arctic University of Norway (Tromsø) in December 2015, tries to tackle this issue. The volume takes a remarkable approach, gathering views of coastal States, user States and indigenous peoples of the Arctic, as well as looking to experiences in another part of the world, namely Southeast Asia.

The book consists of four parts, 14 chapters, starting with Part I that sets out the background and the context of the discussion. Chapter 1 by Lawson Brigham describes the current state of Arctic shipping, which includes not only trans-Arctic voyages but also destined voyages within, into, and out of the Arctic, and notes that its future development depends to a large extent on the state of the global economy on commodities pricing and container shipping. It also emphasizes the importance of the Arctic Council's Arctic Marine Shipping Assessment (AMSA) as a policy document analyzing key issues. After confirming the applicability of the United Nations Convention on the Law of the Sea (UNCLOS) to the Arctic Ocean, it briefly mentions Article 234, which entitles coastal States to impose its environmental regulation on foreign vessels to prevent pollution in "ice-covered areas" of their exclusive economic zone. Chapter 2 by Erik Molenaar describes the structure and the roles played by the Arctic Council. While being a high-level intergovernmental forum of eight Arctic States, the Council has succeeded in promoting negotiations for legally binding instruments under its auspices. Chapter 3 by Dalee Dorough describes the roles of Arctic indigenous peoples in the Arctic Council as permanent participants and their concerns with regard to Arctic shipping. The chapter argues that indigenous peoples should be granted observer status at the International Maritime Organization (IMO).

Part II turns to the IMO and the Polar Code. Chapter 4 by Aldo Chircop provides a detailed explanation of the IMO's mandate, structure, and decision-making process, as well as its roles under UNCLOS. It also surveys various measures adopted by the IMO with regard to Arctic shipping, such as expansion of the World-Wide Navigational Warning System to Arctic waters, adoption of voluntary Guidelines on Voyage Planning for Passenger Ships in Remote Areas, and facilitation of agreements among coastal States regarding routing issues. The most significant IMO achievement so far is of course the Polar Code, which is analyzed in Chapter 5 by Ashley Roach. After summarizing the Code, Roach points out a few issues that could be addressed in the future, such as the non-clarity in its application to vessels engaging in purely domestic voyages or the lack of requirement for the use of ice navigators. Also discussed is the legal effect of the Polar Code on domestic regulations by the coastal States, in particular those of Canada and the Russian Federation. Although there are provisions in the Polar Code that explicitly preserve the power of coastal States under existing international law, Roach notes that Canadian and Russian regulations could be still challenged by the user States and the shipping industry by asserting that the regulations do not meet the qualifications under Article 234 of UNCLOS.

Part III covers the interests of the Arctic coastal States. Chapter 6 by Jan Solski first analyzes the position of the Russian Federation. On the legal basis of Russian domestic regulation of the Northern Sea Route, Solski notes that the attempt by some Russian scholars to establish a legal basis for the regulation of the Northern Sea Route as historic waters, perhaps with a hope to circumvent the limitations applicable to Article 234 of UNCLOS, is unlikely to succeed. The chapter also discusses the substantive aspects of the Russian regulation, in particular the requirement to obtain prior authorization to enter the Northern Sea Route. While such a requirement might be an effective measure for protecting the environment, Solski questions its compatibility with the rights of navigation admitted by UNCLOS. Another issue raised is the non-clarity of enforcement actions to be taken against non-compliance. Turning to the other side of the Arctic Ocean, Chapter 7 by Donald Rothwell illustrates the controversy over the legal status of the Northwest Passage between Canada, which has focused on exercising its sovereignty in the Arctic region to protect the environment, and the United States, which has been promoting the freedom of navigation in the area for national security and economic reasons. On the legitimacy of the 2009 Northern Canada Vessel Traffic Services Zone Regulations (NORDREG), which requires vessels entering the designated area to provide position reports to the Canadian government, Rothwell points out the weakness of the Canadian position, as the Article 234 of UNCLOS requirement that the area be ice-covered for "most of the year" would not be applicable in the future due to further melting of sea ice. In contrast to Russia and Canada, the other Arctic coastal States, namely Norway, Denmark (in respect of Greenland), and Iceland, covered in Chapter 8 by Tore Henriksen, generally seek to protect their interests through international cooperation and their domestic regulations are consistent with international law.

Part IV discusses the interests of the user States, in particular of those in Asia. After listing the obstacles to the commercial use of the Northern Sea Route, such as the limited availability of icebreakers, the imbalance of cargo transported eastwards and westwards, and the poor port and communication infrastructure, Chapter 9 by Deukhoon (Peter) Han and Sung-Woo Lee describes the views of Korean international law scholars on the legal status of domestic regulations of Canada and Russia and emphasizes the importance of bilateral or multilateral cooperation among coastal States and user States for implementation of reasonable regulations and the development of infrastructure. Chapter 10 by Guifang (Julia) Xue and Yu Long first depicts various navigational rights and jurisdictions of coastal States to regulate vessel-source pollution under UNCLOS and how the principle of non-discrimination is incorporated into them. Then it analyzes the Russian and Canadian regulations and points out that the discretionary power of these States in applying their regulations might lead to discrimination in fact, although the texts of these regulations are non-discriminatory in form. Turning to Japan, Chapter 11 by Kentaro Nishimoto notes that the current interest of Japan regarding Arctic shipping is in the carriage of raw material and resources in bulk along the Russian Arctic coast rather than by trans-Arctic voyage, and thus cooperation with Russia is more important at the moment than openly challenging the legitimacy of Russian regulation. From this viewpoint, it is plausible that the Japanese government has not taken a clear position on the conformity of Russian regulations with UNCLOS, although it has been emphasizing the importance of the freedom of navigation as its general policy.

Part V turns to the experience in Southeast Asia, where there has been a similar issue of balancing the interests of coastal States and user States of the Straits of Malacca and Singapore. After confirming the legal status of these straits as international straits and their importance in modern maritime transport, Chapter 12 by Robert Beckman and Sun Zhen provides an overview of the history of cooperation among the three coastal States, namely Indonesia, Malaysia and Singapore, and the contributions of Japan as one of the major user States to safety of navigation. Then the chapter describes how the Cooperative Mechanism on Safety of Navigation and Environmental Protection in the

Straits of Malacca and Singapore was developed and functions as a cooperative agreement encouraged by Article 43 of UNCLOS. To encourage user States to provide financial support to coastal States for building and maintaining navigational aids and infrastructure while respecting the sovereignty of coastal States, this mechanism establishes a governance system for the management of funds provided by user States and other stakeholders and a forum in which they can meet and discuss their interests with government officials of coastal States. Chapter 13 by Captain M. Segar offers Singaporean experience on preparation for and response to oil pollution. Chapter 14 by Robert Beckman, Tore Henriksen, Kristine Dalaker Kraabel, Erik Molenaar and Ashley Roach concludes the book with a proposal to establish Arctic versions of a cooperative mechanism as in the Straits of Malacca and Singapore, but separately for the Northern Sea Route, the Bering Strait, and the Canadian Arctic reflecting the geographical situation of the region. Also noted is the possible role that the Arctic Council can play in establishing such mechanisms.

The proposal to establish a cooperative mechanism between the coastal and user States is an interesting one and should be given serious consideration by relevant stakeholders. The current situation, however, seems to be moving in the opposite direction, as reported by the *Barents Observer* in March 2018, that the Russian government is going to introduce a new regulation prohibiting carriage of natural resources in the Northern Sea Route by non-Russian vessels or vessels built outside of Russia, although with some exceptions. At this stage, it might be a daunting task to bring every stakeholder to the negotiating table to establish the proposed cooperative mechanism. It is also unfortunate that the interests and the policy of the Peoples' Republic of China, which is expected to be one of the major user States of Arctic shipping, are not fully explained in the book, although there are contributors from that State. Having that said, this book is undoubtedly a great source of information and must be read by those who wish to understand the international law issues on Arctic shipping and the positions of relevant stakeholders.

Gen Goto[*]
Associate Professor of Law
University of Tokyo, Graduate Schools for Law and Politics
Tokyo, Japan

---

[*] This book review was supported by JSPS KAKENHI Grant No. 18H00805.

Vu Hai Dang, *Marine Protected Areas Network in the South China Sea: Charting a Course for Future Cooperation* (Leiden: Martinus Nijhoff Publishers, 2014), 318 pp.

In September 2018, delegates to the first meeting of the UN Intergovernmental Conference on a legally binding instrument to govern biodiversity in areas beyond national jurisdiction (BBNJ) underscored the importance of protecting marine biodiversity. Aside from well-documented reasons to protect biodiversity – such as food security, coastal storm defense, and aesthetics – the potential for marine biodiversity to advance scientific and pharmaceutical research through the exploration of marine genetic resources remains largely untapped.[1]

The South China Sea (SCS) is one of the world's greatest centers of marine biodiversity, perhaps even surpassing that of the adjacent Coral Triangle.[2] A study published in 2000 identified over 8,600 different species of marine plants and animals, and that number is likely an underestimate as several phyla have not been closely examined.[3] Researchers have classified 3,365 different types of marine fish species across 263 families.[4] The SCS is home to 571 known species of coral.[5]

With the 2013 Permanent Court of Arbitration ruling declaring none of the features in SCS to be islands, BBNJ may have implications for the SCS as a greater part of the waters are considered under international law to be high seas.[6] One of the tools for which BBNJ advocates is using marine protected areas (MPAs) to set aside vulnerable sea areas for conservation. At the same time, the Convention on Biological Diversity (CBD) is calling for at least 10 percent of the world's coastal and marine areas to be placed under the protection of MPAs by 2020.

The SCS marine environment certainly needs protection. Studies estimate that catch of marine fish in the SCS may be as low as five percent of what it was

---

1 E.A. Norse, *Global Marine Biological Diversity: A Strategy for Building Conservation into Decision-making*, (Washington, D.C.: Island Press, 1993); D. Leary et al., "Marine genetic resources: A review of scientific and commercial interest," *Marine Policy* 33 (2009): 183–194.
2 C. Wilkinson et al., *South China Sea, GIWA Regional Assessment 54* (UNEP, University of Kalmar, Kalmar, Sweden, 2005), pp. 18–19; D. Huang et al., "Extraordinary diversity of coral reefs in the South China Sea," *Marine Biodiversity* 45 (2015): 157–168.
3 P.K.L. Ng and K.S. Tan, "The state of marine biodiversity in the South China Sea," *The Raffles Bulletin of Zoology* Supplement 8 (2000): 3–7.
4 J.E. Randall and K.K.P. Lim, "A checklist of the fishes of the South China Sea," *The Raffles Bulletin of Zoology* Supplement 8 (2000): 569–667.
5 Wilkinson et al., n. 2 above, pp. 18–19; Huang et al., n. 2 above.
6 PCA Case No. 2013-19 (*Philippines v. China*).

in the 1950s, and that 80 percent of marine biodiversity in the scs is in poor condition.⁷ But the scs, of course, is complicated by a host of other legal and security considerations.

Vu Hai Dang's book entitled *Marine Protected Areas Network in the South China Sea: Charting a Course for Future Cooperation* provides a comprehensive treatment of the legal aspects of developing a system of MPAs for the scs. Dang analyzes the current international and regional frameworks for MPAs, including existing initiatives affecting the scs, and also provides an overview of treatment of MPAs in the national laws of the People's Republic of China, the Philippines, and Vietnam.

Dang uses a broad, inclusive approach in defining both the scs and MPAs. He includes the Gulf of Tonkin as part of the scs. He takes MPAs to include all types of area-based conservation measures applied to coastal and ocean environments and their resources, such as Particularly Sensitive Sea Areas (PSSAs). Because MPAs are generally designated at the national level, MPA networks are important to protecting large marine ecosystems that transcend national borders, such as the scs. Beyond conservation of resources, the development of an MPA network in the scs may also help ease tensions over the maritime disputes in the region.

Dang identifies several paths forward toward establishing a network of MPAs in the scs. An important starting point is for countries to create MPAs at the national level and bilaterally in areas where disputes have been resolved. Even areas in which disputes exist but where the disputes are recognized by all countries are easier to set aside for MPAs. The most challenging areas will be those in which the very nature of the dispute itself is under dispute. Dang suggests that countries unilaterally create MPAs for such areas, with the hope that overlapping MPA claims will result in some greater level of protection than is currently afforded. A successful MPA network in the area will need also to take into account ecological, economic, and socio-cultural priorities, as well as involve key stakeholders from the inception.

One of the great contributions of the volume is Dang's analysis of the Mediterranean Action Plan's framework for developing an MPA network. The useful takeaways from this relatively successful model, in addition to providing an example of establishing MPAs in disputed areas, include suggestions for developing the community of scs MPA experts through a regional forum, which could possibly be followed by a regional framework agreement; institutionalized

---

7   R. Sumaila and W. Cheung, *Boom or Bust: The Future of Fish in the South China Sea* (OceanAsia Project, November 2015).

regional cooperation; a non-confrontational compliance mechanism; and a regional MPA monitoring program.

But practicalities will still be the core challenge in developing an MPA network in the SCS. Ideas for area-based conservation measures in the SCS have been promoted for years with limited progress. While Dang provides a thorough synopsis of the legal aspects of developing a SCS MPA network, he largely relies on legal texts and secondary source documents describing existing initiatives. His work serves as a useful handbook for understanding the legal landscape. However, the book would have benefitted from some discussion with people working in the many organizations that he catalogs for a better understanding of the day-to-day challenges in creating an MPA network in the region. The tricky part of this problem lies in the coordination across many disciplines, and then the implementation of its practical application and subsequent enforcement.

A large task is deciding which framework through which to develop a SCS MPA network. There is currently no legally binding treaty or organization that includes only the relevant SCS nations for the purpose of marine environmental protection. Existing treaties and organizations either have broader membership for broader purposes, or do not include one or more important SCS nations. Of the four treaties that include the membership of all the SCS states, the CBD is likely the most relevant and comprehensive treaty through which to work. But the CBD's mandate is not limited to marine biodiversity, or to the region. Other important initiatives, which Dang argues are the most promising, such as the Coordinating Body for the Seas of East Asia (COBSEA) and the Partnerships in Environmental Management for the Seas of East Asia (PEMSEA), also have broader membership and mandates that do not completely fit the goal at hand. Organizations like the Asia-Pacific Economic Cooperation (APEC) have similar issues. Crafting a new organization risks adding yet another layer of complexity to the "alphabet soup."

One of the most relevant initiatives thus far – the "Reversing the Environmental Degradation Trend in the South China Sea and Gulf of Tonkin" project, a collaboration of the Global Environmental Facility (GEF), the UN Programme on the Environment (UNEP), and COBSEA – brings up another important consideration: China's role. This project crafted a Strategic Action Plan Programme for the SCS (SAP) and identified priority areas for protection. China participated in the initial project, but has not participated in a subsequent project to designate protected areas for fisheries, called *refugia*. The Xi Jinping administration has been promoting a "marine ecological civilization building" policy since 2015, suggesting that cooperation on the marine environment of the SCS may receive increased emphasis. Yet a significant administrative reorganization of the ministries managing ocean policy and environmental issues, commencing in early 2018 and likely continuing into early 2019, means that China's policy direction on MPAs in the SCS is somewhat unclear.

Other considerations that Dang rightly mentions include cost and opposition from vested interests. Costs entail both those associated with administering the MPA network as well as economic cost to those who will lose access to areas placed under protection. These interests mainly include fishers, hydrocarbon companies, and shipping companies. Costs of management could be offset with financial, technical, capacity-building, monitoring, and education assistance.

Scientific research is important for better understanding the SCS ecosystem, assessing resource status, and identifying areas to set aside as MPAs. The unofficial South China Sea Workshops have been concerned with such undertakings – these should be built upon. Dang calls for creating an inventory of sites of conservation interest in the SCS. This kind of work can be done now through nongovernmental channels as a basis for a future MPA network. There is not much time left to meet the 2020 CBD target.

> *Tabitha Grace Mallory*
> CEO, China Ocean Institute LLC
> Affiliate Professor, Jackson School of International Studies
> University of Washington, Seattle, USA

Patrice Guillotreau, Alida Bundy and R. Ian Perry, eds., *Global Change in Marine Systems: Integrating Natural, Social, and Governing Responses* (Abingdon, UK: Routledge, 2017), 329 pp.

In the Anthropocene era, marine systems are experiencing dramatic changes from global stressors, including climate change, economic development, and a range of other human activities that degrade ecosystems. We need, therefore, to learn how to mitigate and adapt to these changes at various societal levels. The editors identify the need for integrated tools to help us understand changes, estimate their impacts on society and the environment, and systematize and evaluate our responses. This book tackles these themes in marine systems by analyzing case studies from around the world. The book describes an assessment tool, applies it to twenty case studies, and concludes with a synthesis that indicates which responses were effective, which were not, and what needs further attention to address global change in marine systems. The book targets students (undergraduate and graduate), researchers, and practitioners in the interdisciplinary marine conservation and environmental field, and includes insights and concepts from both the natural and social sciences.

The "assessment tool" at the core of this book was developed through the Integrated Marine Biosphere Research Project (IMBeR), and is thus aptly named IMBeR Assessment based on Description, Responses and Appraisal for a Typology (I-ADApT). A key feature of I-ADApT is the consideration of systemic linkages among natural, social, and governance systems to identify problems, understand and appraise strategies, and identify key success factors. Description and analyses of these linkages, the editors argue (in the introductory chapter), enables an integrated understanding of change in marine systems and the design of pathways toward sustainability. IADApT includes three major steps: (i) a template to describe and document the natural, social, and governance dimensions of a specific case study; (ii) a database of the case studies; and (iii) a typology of the case studies. Steps one and two were conducted in peer reviewed literature[8] and step three, the substantive content of the book, built an evidence-based typology and compared successful and less successful responses across cases.

The introductory chapter describes I-ADApT in a very didactic manner, linking new material from the book to previous work, using examples of data entry and describing or defining the acronyms used. This makes it easy for those unfamiliar with the tool to learn the step-by-step procedures of the assessment process. To enhance its validity, an interdisciplinary research group developed the tool, and case study contributors from four continents revised the template to analyze the cases. Information from case applications was entered into a database and analyzed by a multiple factor analysis into a typology of cases. Each cluster in the typology was represented by one of five Parts in the book. Part I (oyster farming systems under stress) includes three oyster farming cases with similar vulnerability and governability features. Part II (vulnerable mixed fisheries) refers to two cases of mixed fisheries and stressors with medium productivity and similar issues on poverty, migration and weak governance. Part III (coastal water quality issues) addresses three top-down management cases with coastal water quality issues (e.g., pollution, turbidity, eutrophication, and anoxia). Part IV (overexploited and weakly governable fisheries) includes several cases of degraded fisheries with high anthropogenic pressures, including strong economic development. Finally, Part V (habitat restoration programs) refers to successful cases of habit restoration programs and management plans. The conclusion chapter integrates the learning outcomes from each Part

---

8   A. Bundy et al., "A decision support tool for global change in marine systems. The IMBeR-ADApT framework," *Fish and Fisheries* 17 (2016): 1183–1193.

and evaluates the I-ADApT framework. This novel organization, the authors argue, enables comparisons among similar cases and indicates its comprehensiveness. Researchers, practitioners, and their trainees aiming to conduct integrative investigations will find this tool easily replicable, and the many problem contexts in which it is applied helpful for developing and evaluating alternative responses in their own projects.

The development of the coding schema for the I-ADApT typology is notable. However, some of the key terms were not defined or developed sufficiently, such as social, natural, and governing systems, resilience, conflict, cooperation, or power. This is somewhat problematic because these terms have multiple potential interpretations. Conceptual precision supports a better understanding of the challenges and opportunities to advance the responses evaluated in the book. In addition, the authors emphasize that the tool helps to identify "success" and "failure" in response. The authors present a definition of success at the concluding section of the Introduction, but this understanding would be beneficial to the readers from the beginning with greater development, including an acknowledgement of its normative implications. It is notable that the meanings of success and failure appear to vary in each dimension (social, environmental, and governance) and often across cases. These conceptual and definitional shortcomings do not harm the overall readability and comprehensiveness of the book, although they leave room to further develop some dimensions of these core concepts.

This book will appeal to a broad audience, but the overall narrative about the benefits of "integrated approaches" could at times be strengthened. For instance, the reader is offered a brief review of social-ecological systems literature in a marine context and then taken into the methodological foundations of the I-ADApT process. Some narrative to enhance these ideas with the various clusters of cases associated with each 'Part' of the book would be helpful. The connections are there, but they are somewhat hidden in a large synthesis table in the concluding chapter. To evaluate this synthetic material and its relationship to the conclusions, the reader may need to jump from the final chapter back to multiple, specific cases. However, overall the case studies are well-structured and engaging. Each case study begins with a concise description and includes a map of the area, along with informative figures, tables, and graphs. The sub-headings are helpful to understanding each section, although they are not necessarily standardized in every chapter. While that is not an issue for understanding the content, a consistent structure is preferred.

Despite occasional points where the narrative and readability could be slightly improved (e.g., too much jargon, limited transitions between Parts, sometimes inconsistent terminology), the concluding analysis of the book's contents offers multiple benefits. For example, the discussion synthesis (e.g., Conclusion) manages to link rates and extents of change (e.g., regime shifts), to large-scale drivers such as climate change, population growth, and migration, and then subsequently address tough questions about equity, power, and poverty. In doing so, the discussion and synthesis effectively span cognate disciplines and interdisciplinary environmental fields of study, i.e., social-ecological systems research, environmental change, political ecology, and environmental governance literatures.

Integrated analyses across natural, social, and governing systems are not new, and previous attempts are appropriately recognized. However, this book's significance and novelty results from (a) the sheer number of diverse cases in which I-ADApT is applied and analysis is derived, and (b) the rich, boundary-crossing evaluation of responses. Hence, this book represents a major advance of interdisciplinary marine research that rigorously links theory to practice. We recommend this book for academics with different backgrounds interested in responses to change in marine systems, and for practitioners seeking interdisciplinary tools to diagnose the social and ecological challenges within which their own work is situated. All readers of this book will learn from the experiences and critical thinking reflected in the diverse chapters of this important volume.

Ana Carolina Esteves Dias and Evan Jeremy Andrews
Environmental Change and Governance Group
School of Environment, Resources and Sustainability
University of Waterloo, Waterloo, Canada

Nengye Liu, Elizabeth A. Kirk and Tore Henriksen, eds., *The European Union and the Arctic* (Leiden/Boston: Brill Nijhoff, 2017), 376 pp.

The book *The European Union and the Arctic* consists of a comprehensive analysis of the European Union's (EU) stakes in the Arctic, from an historic, geographic, economic, and scientific point of view. The EU is quite concerned with this region, especially to ensure sustainable development. In fact, the EU is linked to the Arctic region by many achievements well-described by the authors. Three EU-Member States (Denmark, Finland and Sweden) are Arctic countries. The EU maintains close links with Iceland and Norway (through the European Economic Area) and has partnerships with Canada, the United States, and Russia. Despite this situation, the EU is in a specific position towards the Arctic, especially because it has no coastline bordering the Arctic Ocean.

Nevertheless, the reading of the three main documents published by the EU concerning Arctic policy between 2008 and 2016 highlights its strong political will to be involved in Arctic governance through the two dimensions of its engagement in the Arctic: Circumpolar and the European Arctic. This situation raises many questions and issues that are finely analyzed in three parts of the book.

Throughout the book and through a pedagogical approach, the issues faced by the EU when deciding to develop its own Arctic policy are clearly explained. Maybe it could have been judicious to begin with an analysis of the relations that have already been developed by the EU with the main States acting in this region (Part 2) before examining the EU's Arctic policy framework (Part 1). But the willingness of the authors to give priority to a didactic approach can explain the plan of the book:

Part 1: The EU's Arctic Policy Framework

This part raises the questions that need to be addressed about the internal challenges facing the EU in the European Arctic as, for example, the EU involvement within Arctic governance regimes or the development of regional cooperation by the EU. This part examines the actions already developed by the EU in the Arctic region (Chapter 3) and shows how, in reality, the EU is a real Arctic actor. But the EU action is limited by the fact that it is not yet accepted as an observer by the Arctic Council.

Part 2: The EU and the Arctic Region

This part analyses the EU strategy to develop its engagement with the United States, Russia, Canada, Norway, and Denmark, known as the Arctic Five. More precisely, it explores the EU's relationship with Greenland, Norway, and Canada. The Norwegian and Canadian skepticism about EU action in the Arctic is pointed out. The specific relationship between the EU and Russia highlights differences of their position concerning the Arctic question. The last chapter in this part focuses on the EU position concerning the prohibition of imported seal products. It insists on the fact that beyond the question of the seal market legal regime, this issue raises the question of sovereignty in the Arctic region.

Part 3: The EU and Regulating Human Activities in the Arctic

This part investigates issues that should be emphasized by the EU to exert more influence in the Arctic. It is important to determine what human activities can be regulated by the EU in the Arctic region to help strengthen its position in the region: shipping, high sea fisheries in the central Arctic Ocean, regulation of marine mammals, and offshore oil and gas operations (cf. the EU regulation concerning the safety of these operations).

The European Union and the Arctic is quite interesting because it clearly assesses EU stakes in the region, and the EU position is well-put into perspective because the book presents a detailed analysis of third States' positions mainly involved in the Arctic region, among them, more precisely the Arctic Five. The book investigates their position towards EU actions with a high degree of accuracy. It points out how these States consider that they hold the stewardship of the Arctic, as stated in the Ilulissat Declaration. In their opinion, the EU can only be seen as an external power to the region.

It can be noted that most of the contributions of the book stress EU difficulties to justify its action in the Arctic. So, one of the major interests of the book is to investigate very precisely these difficulties and the evolution of EU actions and policy in elaborating its Arctic policy. Year after year, the EU position has evolved with the aim to legitimate its presence in Arctic affairs.

As a conclusion, it can be underlined that *The European Union and the Arctic* is a very helpful book to understand the EU main principles (for example, the integration principle) and the EU legal system. Obviously, EU action in the Arctic presents some original aspects due to the specific geographical position of the EU in the region. But this does not prevent noting that the action carried out by the EU in the Arctic gives a good overview of external EU policy and EU partnerships with third countries. The several points of view expressed in the book help the reader to form their own opinion about the EU situation in the Arctic. Moreover, the book is a good starting point for anyone who wants to go further in understanding and researching the European Union and the Arctic. More broadly, it gives an excellent overall picture of the European Union's external relations.

The index is complete and easy to use. It can be very useful to find information on a specific item dealing with Arctic issues. It could have been upgraded with several terms such as "Arctic Five." Finally, it could have been relevant to produce a select bibliography and a list of the EU main texts and of the court decisions concerning the Arctic question.

Annie Cudennec
Professor of Law
Amure – Centre for the Law and Economics of the Sea
University of Brest, France

Myron H. Nordquist, John Norton Moore and Ronán Long, eds., *Legal Order in the World's Oceans: UN Convention on the Law of the Sea*, Volume 21 (Leiden/Boston: Brill Nijhoff, 2018), 463 pp.

This is an edited book collating papers delivered at a conference held at the United Nations headquarters in New York from 27–28 June 2016, which was co-organized by the Virginia Center for Ocean Law and Policy (COLP) and the UN Division for Ocean Affairs (DOALOS), along with other additional co-organizers and sponsors also engaged in ocean affairs. The theme of the conference, which incidentally is retained as the title of the edited book, was the *Legal Order in the World's Oceans: UN Convention on the Law of the Sea*. The preface of the book identifies that this theme was selected "in part to celebrate that [the] Conference was COLP's 40th Annual Conference and in part to emphasize the Rule of Law contribution of the 1982 Convention on the Law of the Sea (UNCLOS) to the legal order of the world's oceans." In essence, this book is a conference proceeding. It must be cautioned that though the edited book was eventually published in 2018 the various chapters are limited to developments as of June 2016, when the conference was held. The only exception is a chapter titled "The United Nations Convention on the Law of the Sea: One of the Greatest Achievements in the International Rule of Law" by Professor John Norton Moore, which was a lecture he delivered at the 2015 Fifth Shabtai Rosenne Memorial Lecture at the UN Headquarters. It was felt this lecture should be included as it expounded on the central theme of the 2016 Conference.

The book begins with a conference opening remark by Jan Eliasson, who was at that time the deputy Secretary-General of the United Nations, and, as mentioned above, an opening address by Professor Moore, which actually serves as a good introductory chapter for the various chapters included in the book. The book consists of six parts and twenty-one chapters. Part 1 with a rather generic title "Ocean Affairs and the Law of the Sea at the UN" comprises four chapters. Chapter 1 written by Ronán Long deals with the changing character of European Union policies and law, as well as its linkage with sustainability along with environmental responsibility and marine ecosystem restoration. Chapters 2 and 3, written by Dire Tladi and J. Ashley Roach respectively, explore the negotiations leading to the adoption of a legally binding international instrument under UNCLOS on conservation and sustainable use of marine biological diversity beyond national jurisdiction (BBNJ). Structurally, I do think it would have been preferable to have made Roach's chapter, which gives a general update of the BBNJ negotiations, Chapter 2, while Tladi's chapter, which directs its attention at the particular issue of the concept of common heritage of mankind (CHM) in the BBNJ negotiations, would probably have fitted better as Chapter 3. Chapter 4 by Karen Scott engages with some interesting legal and moral linkages between the regimes of the ocean and climate change.

Part 2 dealing generally with issues related to the Area and the International Seabed Authority (ISA) consists of three chapters written by practitioners. Rena Lee in Chapter 5 focuses on the role of sponsoring States in the exploration and exploitation of mineral resources in the deep seabed area. She provides some interesting insights into the Singaporean *Deep Seabed Mining Act 2015* and how it regulates Singapore in its role as a sponsoring State. Chapter 6 written by the late Wylie Spicer QC and Elizabeth McIsaac explores the outer continental shelf regime and some complex hurdles to the implementation of Article 82 of UNCLOS, which requires States with outer continental shelves to make certain payments and contributions from exploitation of the outer continental shelf to the international community through the ISA. Chapter 7, on the other hand, written by a high-ranking representative of a deep seabed mining company, Kris Van Nijen, identifies certain technological and environmental risks in developing the resources of the Area and stresses the importance of developing an exploitation regulation for the deep seabed Area that would foster certainty, stability, and predictability for investors.

Part 3, consisting of three chapters, though titled, "[t]he International Tribunal for the Law of the Sea" actually goes beyond this. Chapter 8 written by Judge Jin-Hyun Paik of the International Tribunal for the Law of the Sea (ITLOS), the current president of ITLOS, reflects on ITLOS's contributions to dispute settlement after twenty years of existence. Chapter 9, written by Frida Armas-Pfirter, focuses on the Seabed Disputes Chamber of the ITLOS and raises some intriguing points on the Seabed Disputes Chamber's first advisory opinion. Chapter 10, on the other hand, written by Robert Beckman and Christine Sim, going beyond ITLOS, explores a number of difficult and complex issues arising from the compulsory dispute settlement provisions of the UNCLOS, especially as it relates to maritime boundary disputes.

Part 4 of the book dealing with the Commission on the Limits of the Continental Shelf (CLCS) has four chapters. Chapter 11 written by two academics, who are scientists, Larry Mayer and David Mosher, explores some interesting ambiguities and complexities of the scientific aspects of Article 76 of UNCLOS, especially as regards the extended continental shelf. Chapter 12 by Harald Brekke, a geologist, examines the role of the CLCS in establishing a stable regime for seabed jurisdiction, especially as regards adopting a consistent approach in its practice of providing advice and making recommendations to coastal States. Ted McDorman in Chapter 13 revisits his renowned article on the CLCS written in 2002 – "The Role of the Commission on the Limits of the Continental Shelf: A Technical Body in a Political World." He examines the practice and operation of the CLCS as a technical body operating in a highly political terrain over the last 20-plus years and concludes that the CLCS as a "technical body has been well attuned to the political world within which it operates" (p. 301). Alex Oude Elferink in his chapter specifically explores paragraph 5(a) of Annex I of the CLCS Rules of Procedure (the latest version issued on the 17 April 2008), which states that the CLCS shall not consider and qualify a submission made by any States where a land or maritime disputes exists, except where prior consent is given by all States that are parties to such a dispute. He appears rather skeptical of the utility of this provision.

Part 5 dealing with sustainable fisheries, including the UN Fish Stocks Agreement, consists of three chapters written by practitioners. Andre Tahindro in Chapter 15 extensively explores the 1995 UN Fish Stocks Agreement and its contribution to promoting sustainable fisheries. Chapter 16 written by Stefaan Depypere examines the existing multilateral legal framework, organizations, and actors working to achieve sustainable fisheries (which he refers to as "existing tools of ocean governance"). He concludes that the existing tools "[w]arts and all" are able to deliver and thus attention of the international community needs to continually focus on improving the performance of these tools (pp. 377–378). Alf Håkon Hoel in Chapter 17, looking at the 1995 UN Fish Stocks Agreement, explores the importance of marine science in sustainable fisheries and concludes that this Agreement has made a significant contribution to the development of fisheries science and management.

Part 6, consisting of four chapters, covers a wide-range of issues relating to operational implementation of maritime compliance and enforcement. Chapter 18 written by Admiral Michel and Commander Herman, both operators in the U.S. Coast Guard and lawyers, explores the development and importance of regional bilateral agreements in countering illicit maritime activities. Chapter 19 by Hakan Karan focuses on Turkey's maritime compliance and enforcement of international law of the sea, especially as regards irregular migration in the Aegean Sea region. On the other hand, Chapter 20 by Anthony Morrison and Stuart Kaye engages with certain intriguing legal issues that may arise under international law with regard to operating unmanned surface vessels at sea. Finally, Chapter 21, written by Wu Shicun, engages with the challenges and prospects of China's maritime law enforcement practice in the South China Sea.

This book is an important one, in my view, for three key reasons. First, the various chapters are written by eminent academics and practitioners in ocean law (or if you prefer, law of the sea) and so the book positions itself as a valuable book that could be regarded as serving as a bridge between academia, policy, and practice. Second, with the wide-range of topics on various aspects of ocean law, the book is a "mixed bag," which contains something that would be of interest to various academics, researchers, and practitioners of ocean law. Third, the chapters, some perhaps more than others, highlight the intriguing interface of law, politics, and science in ocean governance. For instance, in one of the chapters the author talks about the "mix of scientific and legal provisions" in establishing the limits of the continental shelf beyond 200 nautical miles (pp. 270–271). Another chapter states: "The science, policy and regulatory framework for both the climate and the oceans is complex, multi-focal, with mandates to balance multiple – often competing – objectives relating to environmental protection, economic development as well as ethical issues affecting current and future generations. As such, it is unsurprising that issues without obvious champions may become sidelined or slip through the cracks between interested institutions and organisations." (pp. 148–149)

The book, an interesting read, undoubtedly raises a number of stimulating and engaging issues in the various chapters, but for the purposes of this review I would particularly highlight an issue of keen interest raised in Chapter 2, written by Tladi, which as indicated above, engages with the current BBNJ process and the CHM. In this chapter the author describes the CHM as a fascinating, but yet divisive concept that is "embraced by some while others view it with some trepidation and concern" (p. 72) and argues that the failure to include this vital concept in the BBNJ negotiations detracts from the real essence of negotiating a new implementation instrument. One of the critical points he identifies in this chapter is the erroneous view that benefit sharing is necessarily synonymous with CHM. It must be pointed out, agreeing with the author, that although benefit sharing is an important and integral in CHM, it is not on its own synonymous with CHM. The point made here may be equated metaphorically with a good pot of soup, which is made with different key ingredients. The different ingredients in themselves are not equivalent to a pot of soup, but rather the intentional blend of the different ingredients is what constitutes the soup. In the same vein, it is argued that CHM is constituted by a blend of different core elements (or ingredients), including benefit sharing; non-appropriation of the relevant spatial area; sharing in the ownership and management of the relevant spatial area and the relevant resources therein through the establishment of an appropriate institutional framework with States acting in a representative capacity for all peoples; protection of the environment; intra- and inter-generational equity; spatial area open to marine scientific research by all; use of the spatial area exclusively for peaceful purposes, etc. It only becomes CHM when there is an amalgam of these core elements.

Edwin E. Egede
Reader in International Law and International Relations
School of Law and Politics
Cardiff University, Wales, United Kingdom

Myron H. Nordquist, John Norton Moore and Ronán Long, eds., *International Marine Economy: Law and Policy* (Leiden/Boston: Brill Nijhoff, 2017), 457 pp.

Myron H. Nordquist, John Morton Moore and Ronán Long's new edited collection, *International Marine Economy: Law and Policy*, explores a number of the most pressing legal and policy issues facing the global marine economy from both an international and domestic perspective and in doing so reminds the reader of the wealth of economic opportunities and promise our oceans hold. The global marine economy or the Blue Economy has rapidly expanded in recent decades. No longer is it understood in terms of traditional maritime industries such as shipping and fishing, but instead has become wider to encompass new and emerging ocean-based sectors and activities, including, but not limited to, marine biotechnology, seabed mining, aquaculture, marine tourism, ocean fertilization, and energy generation. Taking this broader perspective, it is clear that economic activity in the world's oceans, seas, and coastal areas continues to grow at a very rapid rate. The Organisation for Economic Co-operation and Development estimates that by 2030 the ocean economy could more than double its contribution to global value added, reaching over USD 3 trillion, with a number of ocean-based industries projected "to outperform the growth of the global economy as a whole." However, despite being recognized as the "new economic frontier" the oceans are in a state of crisis, falling victim to an ever-increasing list of threats and facing a complex array of unprecedented risks. The combined effects of climate change, the over-exploitation of resources, acidification, pollution, and the loss of biodiversity will not only have a detrimental impact on the health and well-being of the ocean, it will also undoubtedly affect economic development in the marine environment.

This collection marks the 20th volume in a series published under the auspices of the Center for Oceans Law and Policy (COLP) at the University of Virginia's School of Law and consists predominately of presentations made at the 39th Annual Conference of the COLP held in Shanghai, China from 24–26 June 2015. Rather than limiting the content of this volume to presentations made at the COLP Conference, the editors have broken with tradition and included two additional papers, both of which appear at the beginning of the book under a Featured Studies section. The first featured study concerns the South China Sea Arbitration Award handed down on 12 July 2016 by a tribunal established under Annex VII of the United Nations Convention on the Law of the Sea (UNCLOS) in the dispute between the Philippines and China. Naturally, this volume would not be complete without some form of study or exploration of this historic decision, which has been labelled the "most important set of jurisprudential rulings in the modern history of the international law of the sea." Co-authored by one of the editors of the volume, Myron H. Nordquist, along with marine geologist, William G. Phalen, the featured study focuses on one aspect of the landmark decision, namely the legal status of the maritime feature Itu Aba, otherwise known as Taiping Island, the largest high-tide feature in the Spratly Islands of the South China Sea. The co-authors take issue with the Arbitral Tribunal's interpretation of Article 121 of UNCLOS and its application to Itu Aba. To support their contentions, the authors provide the reader with a comprehensive historical account of the legislative origins of Article 121, including the drafting and negotiation of the provision at the Third United Nations Conference on the Law of the Sea (UNCLOS III). Myron H. Nordquist is able to provide what can only be described as, an "insider's perspective" of the UNCLOS III negotiations having been Secretary of the U.S. delegation to the conference and personally involved when the text of Article 121 was drafted (p. 9). This adds authoritative weight to the position taken by the co-authors who reach significantly different conclusions than those of the Tribunal.

The second featured chapter in the volume is considerably shorter than the first, yet it provides a fascinating introduction to the topic of ocean acidification. Stephen A. Macko, Christina Fantasia and Guifang (Julia) Xue present an insightful examination of the potential economic impacts of ocean acidification, at both a global and local level, including the detrimental impact it will have on marine life and the entire oceanic ecosystem.

In addition to the Featured Studies section, the volume contains a further fourteen papers divided between five parts. Parts 1 and 2 both address issues concerning the Arctic and provide in many ways an update to and extension of Volume 19 of the COLP series, *Challenges of the Changing Arctic: Continental Shelf, Navigation & Fisheries*. Part 1 focuses on Arctic shipping and resources and contains a paper from Captain J. Ashley Roach which expands upon his contribution to the editor's last volume by providing an update on the developments made in Arctic navigation since the COLP Conference in Bergen, Norway in June 2014 and the adoption later in that same year of the International Code for Ships Operating in Polar Waters (the Polar Code). Captain Roach's paper details the important work of the International Maritime Organization (IMO) in respect to the Polar Code, in particular the contributions made by the IMO's Maritime Safety Committee and the IMO's Marine Environment Protection Committee. Part 1 also includes an engaging chapter co-authored by Tatiana Sorokina and William G. Phalen titled "Legal Problems of the Northern Sea Route Exploitation: Brief Analysis of the Legislation of the Russian Federation." With the Arctic Ocean expected to be ice-free by the summer of 2050 (p. 102), the Northern Sea Route (NSR) will become economically attractive not only as an alternative international shipping route but also for its estimated oil and gas resources (p. 103). With this in mind, the co-authors provide an important overview of the measures Russia has adopted and continues to develop through its domestic legislation and policy to deal with the increasing amount of attention the NSR is expected to attract in the coming decades. To round-out Part 1, Rustambek M. Nurimbetov briefly examines the complex legal and political issues associated with the sustainable use of the Arctic continental shelf, particularly in light of Russia's resubmission of its claim to an extended continental shelf in the Arctic Ocean, made to the Commission on the Limits of the Continental Shelf in August 2015.

Part 2 of this volume focuses on Arctic Ocean fisheries and begins with a comprehensive examination and analysis of the legal framework for high seas fisheries in the Central Arctic Ocean by the eminent Judge Tomas Heidar of the International Tribunal for the Law of the Sea (ITLOS). Judge Heidar outlines the cooperative steps and initiatives taken so far by States to address the management of fisheries in the Arctic region, including the adoption by the five Arctic coastal States (the Arctic Five) of the Declaration concerning the Prevention of Unregulated High Seas Fishing in the Central Arctic Ocean in Oslo in July 2015 (the Oslo Declaration) (p. 192). The reader is also afforded the opportunity of reading a number of informative and insightful concluding remarks offered by Judge Heidar on this complex issue. To compliment Judge Heidar's paper, two further studies are included in Part 2. Jee Hyun Choi, Senior Researcher at the Korea Maritime Institute, examines Korea's ambitions in respect to Arctic fisheries and the Arctic region in general. This includes a thorough analysis of Korea's current domestic policy and legislation concerning such topics. On the other hand, Jianye Tang's paper discusses the initiatives that have been adopted by the Arctic Five to address "the legal vacuum in the Arctic Ocean" (p. 231), in respect to the prevention of unregulated fishing and the conservation of living resources in the high seas. Although the title of this piece refers to "marine living resources," the paper focuses mainly on the issue of fisheries, yet this does not detract from the quality of the paper.

Part 3 addresses the deep seabed regime. As interest in the deep ocean is intensifying, due in large part to advancements in science and technology, seabed mining and other activities are "on the cusp of becoming a reality" and present a wealth of economic opportunities for States and entities in the financial position to undertake such ventures. China and Chinese entities in particular have shown an increasing amount of interest in the International Seabed Area (the Area) and associated activities. As a result, in recent years, China has accelerated its development of domestic legislation dealing with issues concerning the Area. Jiancai Jin and Guobin Zhang's paper provides a valuable overview of China's deep seabed legislation and its future direction. The second paper in Part 3 focusses on the heavy burden and legal responsibility a State will shoulder when it elects to sponsor a private entity undertaking activities in the Area. Elana Geddis eloquently breaks down each of the elements of the due diligence obligation of a sponsoring State and also examines "the potential pitfalls" (p. 268) in the current sponsorship regime.

Part 4 of the volume examines issues concerning resources and maritime boundary regimes. The newly appointed President of the ITLOS, Jin-Hyun Paik, provides an in-depth legal analysis of the problem of the so-called grey area which can arise as a result of maritime boundary delimitation. President Jin-Hyun Paik provides invaluable insight into the reasoning of the ITLOS in respect to the grey area in the Dispute Concerning Delimitation of Maritime Boundary between Bangladesh and Myanmar in the Bay of Bengal case (2012). The next paper in Part 4 is co-authored by Leonardo Bernard and Clive Schofield and examines the issues, challenges, and opportunities presented by differentiated seabed and water column boundaries. For readers interested in the evolution and trends of maritime boundary delimitation this chapter provides a lengthy and detailed historical account. To conclude Part 4, David Freestone and Viva Harris explore whether it is time to chart a new course in respect to the use of Particularly Sensitive Sea Areas (PSSAS). This is a timely contribution as it concerns the hot topic of the moment in law of the sea circles: the negotiation of a new international legally binding instrument under UNCLOS for the conservation and sustainable use of marine biological diversity in areas beyond national jurisdiction (the BBNJ negotiations). The co-authors provide an extensive analysis of the numerous measures in existence today that attempt to protect biologically or ecologically significant marine areas. This includes the IMO's current authority to designate PSSAS. The authors suggest that the IMO could, in effect, take a leading role in addressing a number of the items on the agenda of the BBNJ negotiations, particularly in respect to the designation of marine protected areas.

To conclude the volume, Part 5 contains three papers that do not fit neatly into the categories of Parts 1 to 4. Dan Liu's paper for example addresses the international regulation of whaling and provides a thorough analysis of the 2014 judgment of the International Court of Justice in the Whaling in the Antarctic Case. The author provides a thoughtful commentary on the wide-ranging impact of this decision, including how it will affect the future role of the International Whaling Commission. In contrast, Ronán Long's study details how the European Union's functional approach to tackling and resolving issues concerning fisheries management, environmental protection, maritime spatial planning, and marine biodiversity could assist in dealing with a number of the most pressing law of the sea and ocean governance issues facing the Southeast Asia region (p. 388). Finally, Hakan Karan's chapter outlines the link between the exercise of control over foreign merchant ships with lawful grounds and State liability for wrong assessments. This includes an incisive and concise legal analysis of the prerequisites or grounds for exercising lawful control over foreign merchant ships in each of the different maritime zones. Although the papers in Part 5 address divergently different issues, the lack of cohesion is forgiven as each piece of writing is of an extremely high standard and touches on important and interesting topics.

Overall, this volume contains an exceptional compilation of papers of a very high quality and caliber. The growing economic importance of the ocean is evident throughout the collection which manages to touch on some of the most complex and pressing legal and policy challenges facing the international marine economy. This volume will be of interest to practitioners, scholars, and students alike with a keen interest in law of the sea and marine issues.

Sarah Louise Lothian
Ph.D. Student, The University of Sydney Law School
Sydney, Australia

Myron H. Nordquist, John Norton Moore and Ronán Long, eds., *Challenges of the Changing Arctic: Continental Shelf, Navigation, and Fisheries* (Leiden/Boston: Brill Nijhoff, 2016), 636 pp.

This is yet another book in a series produced by the Center for Oceans Law and Policy (COLP) at the University of Virginia Law School and once again draws on papers given at a conference, this time the 38th Annual Conference held in Bergen, Norway, 25–27 June 2014. The volume focuses on three Arctic Ocean governance themes and provides "must read" chapters on the topics of continental shelf, navigation, and fisheries. The first two parts of the book are devoted to Arctic continental shelf issues. Part I is committed to reviewing law and policy approaches and questions surrounding extended continental shelf determinations by the five Arctic Ocean coastal States. Michael Byers in Chapter 4 reviews the law and politics facing Canada, Denmark, and Russia in their assertion of rights over the Lomonosov Ridge. He highlights the possible future need to negotiate boundaries where there are overlapping claims and opines that the principle of equidistance would likely be used to delimit the seabed rights between Canada and Denmark, which would situate the North Pole on the Danish side. In Chapter 5, Alex Oude Elferink reviews the present state of national extended shelf claims in the Arctic and questions whether the usual equidistance/relevant circumstances methodology to delimit the continental shelf within 200 nautical miles should be applied to areas beyond. He suggests an alternative approach which is left somewhat impressionistic but starts with giving priority attention to overlapping natural prolongations and the relevant coasts of the contending parties.

Part 2 of the volume includes three chapters that address continental shelf petroleum developments in the Arctic. Kuen-chen Fu in Chapter 7 discusses China's existing and growing interests in cooperating with Russia in exploiting oil and gas resources in the Arctic. He reviews Russia's policies towards Arctic development, which includes promotion of the Northern Sea Route (NSR) as a transport corridor. The chapter wanders somewhat outside the offshore petroleum focus to also address other issues such as interpretation issues surrounding Article 234 of the United Nations Convention on the Law of the Sea (UNCLOS), which gives special legislative and enforcement powers to coastal States to prevent pollution in ice-covered waters; historic waters claims in the Arctic; and the status of the Arctic Ocean as a semi-enclosed sea. Chapter 8 by Erik Haaland provides an industry perspective from Norway. He emphasizes that there is not one Arctic environment for offshore petroleum operations but three, namely, the workable Arctic with little or no sea ice or very shallow areas; the stretch Arctic with significant ice or very cold and remote areas; and the extreme Arctic with near continuous heavy ice coverage as found off East Greenland. He describes three examples of how Statoil has promoted collaborations in the Arctic including through the Arctic Response Technology Joint Industry Programme (JIP) whereby nine major oil companies have joined forces to advance Arctic oil spill response strategies and technologies. In Chapter 9, Stephen Macko reviews the prospects for further exploration and production of petroleum in the Arctic and emphasizes that there is no proven effective method for containing and cleaning up an oil spill in ice-covered waters. Surprisingly, he does not discuss Arctic Council related efforts to address the risks of offshore oil and gas operations. He concludes in a rather general manner calling for Arctic standards for safety, oil spill prevention, and response to be put in place.

Part 3 includes four chapters on Arctic shipping. Knut Skodvin highlights the challenges and variabilities for shipping in and through the NSR and explores the relationship between the new Polar Shipping Code and the ability of coastal States to impose unilateral shipping measures pursuant to Article 234 of UNCLOS. Sung Woo Lee further reviews the challenges for the commercialization of Arctic shipping and describes the interests of China, Japan, and the Republic of Korea in the NSR and Arctic resource developments. An overly long and rather tedious chapter at over 100 pages by J. Ashley Roach gives particular emphasis to the negotiating history and provisions of the mandatory Polar Code. He also delves into the legal effect of the Polar Code on national shipping regulations. Leilei Zou compares the approaches of Canada and Russia to Arctic shipping administration and notes Canada's more cautious attitude towards opening up the Northwest Passage (NWP) in comparison to Russia's economic-oriented philosophy towards the NSR. The chapter includes a number of questionable statements including the conclusion that the Northwest Passage stretches from the North Atlantic Ocean's Davis Strait and Baffin Island all the way through the Bering Strait and the idea that the NWP relieves the overload at the Panama Canal.

Six fisheries related chapters are included in Parts 5 and 6. An overall bias is obvious towards changing fisheries distributions and management challenges in the Northeast Atlantic. Chapter 18 by Jóhann Sigurjónsson provides an overview of recent changes in migration patterns of large pelagic stocks, such as mackerel, Atlanto-Scandian herring, and blue whiting, in the Northeast Atlantic Ocean due to warming water conditions. In Chapter 20, Bjørn Kunoy highlights the difficulties and variable approaches to managing transboundary fish stocks in the Northeast Atlantic including the EU and Faroe Islands dispute over management of Atlanto-Scandian herring and the failure to develop a comprehensive arrangement to manage Northeast Atlantic mackerel. Chapter 23 by Rögnvaldur Hannesson provides a detailed look at the major management challenges posed by the migration of the Northeast mackerel stock into the Icelandic EEZ and reviews the strategies of the parties to the mackerel dispute in terms of game theory.

Two fisheries chapters offer quite general perspectives on the international legal principles and provisions applicable to regional fisheries management organizations (RFMOs). Chapter 21 by Stefán Asmundsson, Secretary of the North-East Atlantic Fisheries Commission, gives a non-technical overview of how international legal instruments place limits on freedom for fishing in the high seas especially through the efforts of RFMOs, but he does not provide Arctic-specific examples. In Chapter 22, Tore Henriksen provides an excellent review of principles and alternative procedures for allocating fishery rights to shared fish stocks. He highlights the difficulties of some RFMOs in getting agreement on allocation criteria and even when criteria are agreed upon, the recurring problems of political disagreements over their application and limited transparency stand out.

Only Chapter 19 by Erik Molenaar zeroes in on the international regulation of Arctic Ocean fisheries. He describes the roles of the North-East Atlantic Fisheries Commission and the Joint Norwegian-Russian Fisheries Commission in managing high seas fisheries in the Arctic. A detailed account is provided on the role played of the Arctic Five coastal States in concluding the 2015 Oslo Declaration which pledges interim measures to prevent unregulated commercial fishing in the high seas and in envisioning a broader process to develop international regulation of Central Arctic Ocean fisheries.

The COLP book clearly navigates beyond the three chosen themes. Part 4 of the volume includes four chapters addressing other Arctic related topics: Chapter 14 by Elisabeth Whitsitt explores how far Arctic States may go in justifying trade restrictions, such as seal products, in light of public morality concerns. Chapter 15 by Guifang Xue and Yu Long proposes a regional framework treaty with annexes or protocols to protect the Arctic marine environment. Ronán Long in Chapter 16 summarizes the tableau of EU law and policy measures relevant to the Arctic. Ted McDorman in Chapter 17 summarizes the fragmented array of agreements and institutions related to Arctic Ocean regional governance.

Part 7 includes three chapters on related law of the sea issues. In Chapter 24, Robert Beckman provides an excellent review of how UNCLOS dispute settlement provisions might be used to address Arctic legal issues such as unresolved ocean boundaries. James Kraska (Chapter 25) highlights how Russia has bolstered its maritime security laws and policies in recent years to promote safe and efficient shipping through the NSR. The book concludes in Chapter 26 by Chuanxiang Sun with a critical review of the three-stage approach to maritime delimitations applied by international tribunals. While representing a stellar academic piece, the chapter does not specifically address the Arctic.

The Changing Arctic book also includes two "technical reads." Larry Mayer reviews the technical mapping activities of the Arctic coastal States and the complex morphology of the seafloor beyond national zones of jurisdiction (Chapter 3). Dennis Bley describes how probabilistic risk assessment may be used to understand and manage risks associated with offshore shipping and petroleum activities (Chapter 6).

Published in 2016, this volume already represents "dated reading." Many subsequent law and policy developments have occurred. They include, among others, conclusion of a new Agreement to Prevent Unregulated Commercial Fisheries in the High Seas of the Central Arctic Ocean with a signing ceremony in Ilulissat, Greenland on 3 October 2018; entry into force of the Polar Shipping Code on 1 January 2017; discussions within the IMO to possibly ban future carriage and use of heavy fuel oil (HFO) in parts of the Arctic; a commitment in December 2016 by Canadian Prime Minister Justin Trudeau to prohibit further offshore oil and gas licensing in Canadian Arctic waters for at least five years subject to further scientific and technical review; the attempt by U.S. President

Donald Trump to roll back a decision taken by the Obama Administration to place an indefinite moratorium on further oil and gas leasing for the Beaufort and Chukchi Seas; publication by China of a new Arctic policy in January 2018; and adoption by Canada of new Arctic Shipping Safety and Pollution Prevention Regulations in 2017 that largely incorporate the Polar Code into domestic law.

The 2016 COLP book is a substantial and welcome addition to the academic literature relating to Arctic Ocean governance. However, readers should beware. Some papers in the present volume do not fit within the three selected themes. Some do not have an Arctic focus. Wide variations in chapter lengths and referencing are evident. The volume reads more like conference proceedings than a cohesive book.

> *David L. VanderZwaag*
> Ph.D., Canada Research Chair in Ocean Law and Governance
> Schulich School of Law, Dalhousie University
> Halifax, Nova Scotia, Canada

Bimal N. Patel, *The State Practice of India and the Development of International Law: Dynamic Interplay between Foreign Policy and Jurisprudence* Brill's Asian Law Series, Volume 4 (Leiden/Boston: Brill Nijhoff, 2016), 548 pp.

As India pushes further into the higher echelons of international organizations, perhaps even on the precipice of a permanent seat on the UN Security Council, there may be a paucity of relevant literature that encompasses India's role in this area that will require a broader level of scholarship. Trite as it is to state it, but carving a place in the new balance of power is difficult, even for nations with more mature diplomatic cadre, more relevant scholarship and publication is needed to help undergird necessary institution building.

Enter Dr. Patel's tome, a broad piece of work regarding not only the legal but historical plane of India's place and forays in the sphere of international law. Much of the text involves the idea of moving India from a "law taker" to a "law maker"[9] and incorporates elements of "Vision 2020,"[10] giving an overarching theme. The steps towards a "modern" state, one with robust institutions, social

---

9   A comment from Dr. Patel on India being an entity that applied international conventions without significantly contributing to or specifically adapting them prior to the 1970s.
10 A paper written under then President of India APJ Abdul Kalam outlining steps to modernize India.

protections and standardized implementation of the rule of law are daunting just domestically, let alone in the international sphere.

The Introduction gives a clear pathway into the development of India's diplomatic history in the modern era and its progression from non-aligned idealism towards a more realist approach. It seeks to cover a tremendous amount of ground but does so without much extraneous information and with appropriate levels of reference and footnotes that do not devolve to the level of overwhelming the main text. The reader is also introduced to more Indo-centric nomenclature and historical international agreements, such as "Panchsheela."[11] These are intriguing points in and of themselves, but may be more akin to curiosities rather than nodes of a competing framework.

A slightly weaker entry is the following chapter on the historicity of India's nascent developments in foreign State practice from the 1500s to independence. This stems mainly from the mere fact that compressing such a complex period of time into a single chapter poses its own challenges and that there is something of a narrative that Patel attempts to bring to the fore that does not quite stand on its own merits. It gives an alternate background to the Euro-centric origins of international law and fleshes out contributions that may have come from ancient writers, particularly Kautilya,[12] and even Vedic texts such as the Ramayana.[13]

The ideas put forward in the chapter and the attributions of these earlier writers could be a scholarly work in their own regard and is an area ripe for exploration when applied to this sector. However, because of certain assumptions and tangents followed there does seem to be a slightly light overview of the most evident influence on pre-independence, foreign-facing legal development, the British Empire. What is covered is cogent and well-presented; though whether India's post-independence stronger links to its more ancient legal history than other civilizations is debatable.

Historicity apart, the rest of the work is firmly grounded in more tangible and recent legal developments with copious and well-formed sections on key issues affecting policy development. Much of what defines India's approach to international law is the dualist ideal that the domestic sphere operates within. Amongst many that have stated something similar, Justice Krishna Iyer said that "until the municipal law is changed to accommodate the treaty, what binds the court is the former not the latter."

---

11 Used in the 1954 Panchsheel Treaty between India and China.
12 Vishnugupta Chanakya Kautilya wrote a treatise called the "Arthashastra" (roughly translated as "the science of wealth") in the 4th Century BC. It covers three main areas: economic development, administration of justice, and foreign relations.
13 An ancient, allegorical, epic poem that folded Hindu philosophy into its narrative.

To use the law of the sea chapter as an example of the structure used in the rest of the book you can see the development of reciprocity that pushes India's path through international law. As Patel states, there are delays to ratification of treaties even when India has been able to "derive security, strategic and economic benefits from these relevant positions of the Convention." The dualist procedure pushes potentially profitable application of even ratified treaties until India moves towards more aggressive adoption. Patel even suggests a judicial panel specifically tailored towards the application of international law.

The rest of the book continues a similar systematic approach to cover India's relationship to refugees, the United Nations, climate change, weapons of mass destruction, the environment, the International Court of Justice, and human rights – each looking to the ascendancy of India within each policy sector and to borrow from the title, the dynamic interplay of its growing influence. The well-referenced footnotes are perhaps the most important trove of information for scholars, bolstering the relatively well-balanced commentary.

Throughout the text and into the conclusion age-old and probably clichéd questions rear their head as to whether power politics underpins what is supposed to be a more regulated system. However, while what Waltz[14] wrote in relation to Cold War reality does not seem to have changed too much, Patel underscores the idea that India influenced international law as an inchoate nation, without significant military and economic clout. The text logically concludes that this does not mean that there is not a "mismatch" between the power imbalances of the anarchic global system. The fact that India emphasizes areas that are beneficial to developing countries is sound, but perhaps suggesting that if necessary it could pursue a more Kautilyan[15] influenced approach is wishful thinking.

The book could be improved upon with a little judicious editing. The somewhat idiosyncratic style of language, while not detracting from the subject matter, could be smoothed out for better readability. Other issues stem from the nature of the text being both a near-exhaustive source of relevant international legal precedent and commentary in that some of the suppositions will date the text quickly. The main one being references to the National Democratic Alliance under Prime Minister Modi and its aims for foreign policy going into 2020 which is in danger of dating the work, though of course changes could be made in further revised editions. It may also be a touch shackled to the idea of creating or pushing a post-colonial narrative.

---

14   Kenneth Waltz is best known as the author of *Man, the State and War*. He was a leading realist scholar who argued that the international system is anarchic.

15   If you consider Kautilya to be a sort of "proto-realist," then India's statecraft is moving in a similar direction.

Dr. Patel's textbook attempts, fairly successfully, to be a sort of *International Law*[16] with respect to India – a work that is clearly targeting the lacuna in an underserved area and providing not only a stronger base for study on what is soon to be the world's most populous nation, but giving some serious heft to regional foreign policy scholarship.

It should appeal to a wide demographic from budding legal scholars and practitioners to civil servants and those simply interested in an exciting area of contemporary foreign policy. The breadth and depth of research demonstrates the participation that India has in the developing international law and Dr. Patel's text is, slight missteps aside, an impressively referenced reference text.

Sumedh Shastri
OceanGovernance.org
London, United Kingdom

Jenny Grote Stoutenburg, *Disappearing Island States in International Law* (Leiden/Boston: Brill Nijhoff, 2015), 488 pp.

Sea-level rise (SLR), which has been identified as one of the more potentially devastating consequences of global warming and anthropogenic climate change, is a reality that is upon us. It will profoundly impact the lives and basic rights of millions of coastal residents all over the world. Rising sea levels are inundating and rendering substantial coastal areas of the world uninhabitable, and several coastal communities have already begun their exodus. However, the problem is particularly acute for the Small Island Developing States (SIDS) and their inhabitants. Among a total of 51 SIDS, low-lying, sovereign island States like the Maldives, the Marshall Islands, Tuvalu, Kiribati, and Tokelau are under an existential threat and run the risk of being wiped off the world map due to the "sinking" small islands phenomenon and are particularly vulnerable to SLR.

Geographically, most of the SIDS not only lie scattered in the far reaches of the oceans but they also comprise primarily tiny specs of coral atolls with little or no land and are situated only a few meters above sea level. These countries, some of whom are the least developing States, share a common thread in term of challenges to operationalize sustainable development. The climate in SIDS is determined in large part by ocean-atmosphere interactions like trade winds,

---

16 Authored by Malcolm N. Shaw QC, and possibly *the* academic text encompassing international law. It similarly explores issues from philosophical concerns through to legal terms and specific cases.

El Niño, monsoons, tropical cyclones, and hurricanes. Often, these islands are battered by coastal hazards like storm surges, erosion, and flooding. Therefore, any changes in weather can upset the delicate balance and throw these countries into turmoil. For instance, as a result of erratic weather patterns, precipitated in large part by climate change, potable water sources in several of these small islands have been considerably reduced to the point that some of these islands are unable to satisfy basic requirements during periods of low rainfall. In October 2011, the island State of Tuvalu had to declare a state of emergency due to dwindling water supplies. Tuvalu relies heavily on rainwater, the supply of which was considerably affected by the La Niña phenomenon that swept across the Pacific Ocean. The lack of rainfall practically dried out the island and the situation was rendered acute due to rising sea levels, which led to increased salinity intrusion. Finally, New Zealand airlifted water containers and desalinization plants to help this island nation through the present crisis. Subsequently, a state of emergency over dwindling water supplies was declared in Tokelau as well.

The SIDS are also characterized by low availability of natural resources to support the needs and demands of a rapidly growing population, remoteness and isolation in terms of location, vulnerability to natural disasters, and poor soil quality that cannot support intensive farming and other economic activities with the consequence that most of the food and other requirements of the islanders are met through imports. There is excessive dependence on tourism and fishing (the central drivers of their economies), and these countries are susceptible to developments that take place in the global arena that need not necessarily reflect their interests. In short, the climate characteristics, combined with their peculiar geographic situations and socioeconomic conditions, make SIDS most vulnerable to climate change impacts and SLR. And any rise in oceans will lead to the island nations losing much of their economic resources (including maritime territories), vital infrastructure, settlements and facilities that support the livelihood, culture, and traditions of coastal communities. All of these concerns identified above have been affirmed by Rio+20, which observed: "[S]mall island developing States remain a special case for sustainable development in view of their unique and particular vulnerabilities, including their small size, remoteness, narrow resource and export base, and exposure to global environmental challenges and external economic shocks, including to a large range of impacts from climate change and potentially more frequent and intense natural disasters."[17]

---

17   United Nations General Assembly, Resolution adopted by the General Assembly on 27 July 2012, "The future we want," UN Doc. A/RES/66/288 (11 September 2012), para. 178.

Even though the issue of the vulnerability that the SIDS face from climate change and SLR was first brought to the notice of the international community in the late 1980s, at about the same time when small islands States were accepted into the international community of nations as equal members, in the following years, the issue received less attention. This was in part due to the fact that sea levels did not rise as fast as originally contemplated, and because of the faith placed on global mitigation commitments as contemplated under the international climate change regime, which was considered sufficient to prevent materialization of such a scenario. However, it is now apparent that the optimism was misplaced with the emergence of new scientific data that we have already crossed the tipping scale and that dangerous anthropogenic climate change, including "sinking islands," is a reality. This raises several new legal issues that international law will have to grapple with. For instance, the "constitution for the oceans," the 1982 United Nations Convention on the Law of the Sea (UNCLOS) was drafted at a time when SLR and climate change were not issues of concern. Therefore, UNCLOS does not have answers to many of the new challenges, particularly those that face the SIDS. To illustrate, UNCLOS guarantees to coastal States certain maritime territories and the right to exploit the resources found therein. While the disappearance of islands and coastlines is most likely to be a gradual but steady process, States may lose their maritime basepoints which may get submerged raising questions as to whether the SIDS and other coastal countries can continue to claim the maritime territories secured by those submerged basepoints. As well, with the rise in ocean temperatures and as oceans acidify, it is probable that the coral reef islands will bleach, and several of the atolls will lose their ability to sustain human habitation or economic life, eventually degenerating into "rocks." This can pose serious consequences to the long-term stability of the islands and will pose difficulties to these islands in terms of their ability to retain their entitlements to the different maritime territories guaranteed by UNCLOS. In addition, a host of other legal questions also arise: What are the existing challenges confronted by SIDS and how does SLR and other climate change impacts compound these challenges? What role can the instrumentality of law play to help SIDS respond to these challenges given that there is an existential threat and help them move towards the goal of sustainable island development? Are the UNCLOS rules on delimitation of maritime territories sufficient to safeguard the rights of SIDS in the event of the rising seas consuming their land territories and base points? Given that ocean temperatures are rising, resulting in migrations of fish and other marine life, how does this impact the fishing industries in SIDS and what steps can be taken to ensure that fishing operations continue sustainably? Given that bleaching of corals is another major source for concern, does the existing legal framework provide guidance and support to ensure the protection of the coral atolls? Is the UNCLOS text (as it stands) and other international environmental law instruments sufficiently geared to respond to the challenges posed by SLR and climate change? If not, do we need to negotiate a new legal instrument to protect the rights of SIDS and their inhabitants? What would happen to the displaced populations? Do other States have a humanitarian obligation to provide these populations with support including that of accommodation?

The far-reaching changes brought by climate change thus underscore the paramount importance of law and legal frameworks. It also impels the need to re-assess the role of law in helping SIDS to adapt to SLR and other climate change impacts so as to secure sustainable island development and to safeguard their rights and that of their inhabitants. This monograph by Jenny Grote Stoutenburg is a meticulous attempt in this regard for it analyzes the international legal implications of the possible physical disappearance of sovereign island States and provides a valuable entry point to the ongoing debates.

While it is not possible to comprehensively address all the legal issues (some of which have been identified above) implicated by an exceedingly complex and protracted physical process in one monograph, nevertheless, this book throws light on some of the basic legal questions that are brought to the fore by the disappearance of SIDS. Some of the core questions engaged by this study are: When does a sovereign State disappear? Who is legally competent to make that determination? What will happen to the State's maritime zones, its international rights and obligations, its assets and liabilities, and its membership in international organizations? And does international law protect the international legal personality of States that lose their effective statehood for reasons beyond their control? In this regard, it also probes a very significant legal question that goes to the root of the nature of international law: Is international law capable of evolving from a system based solely on coexistence or cooperation to one based on solidarity and shared responsibility? In addressing these issues, the work revisits the conceptual foundations of a fundamental precept of international law, namely, the nature of statehood, setting it against an entirely new context engendered by climate change.

The monograph is organized into three parts, followed by a summary and conclusion. The first part, "Fathoming the Waters," sets out the factual terrain that informs the subsequent legal analysis. Based on the assessment reports prepared by the Intergovernmental Panel on Climate Change (IPCC), Chapter 1 describes the key adverse impacts and vulnerabilities that climate change and SLR entail on low-lying island States, in terms of their biodiversity and impacts on human heath, on water resources, and some of the core sectors of their economy, namely, fishing, agriculture, and tourism. It describes in vivid detail how some of the physical and socioeconomic thresholds might ultimately be breached that could cause the abandonment of these islands. Focusing on the influence that small island States have exerted on the development of the international climate change regime, the chapter also analyzes the extent to which the 1992 UN Framework Convention on Climate Change, its Kyoto Protocol, as well as subsequent developments, reflect their efforts to achieve adequate international mitigation commitments and adaptation assistance. While an effective climate change regime that provides for greenhouse gas reductions is critical to the survival and sustainable development of small island States, the chapter concludes with the lament that the "actions and inactions of some state parties will indeed cause the disappearance of other members of the multilateral climate negotiation process" (p. 70).

The second part of the study on "Maritime Entitlements" considers the loss of territorial and ensuing maritime zones and other entitlements that have been secured under the law of the sea. After providing an overview of the status of island States under the international law of the sea and of the regime of maritime zones as it applies to them, Chapter 2 analyzes the consequences that SRL can pose to the ambulatory nature of maritime baselines and to their maritime entitlements. In this regard, it also addresses the question as to whether sea-level rise could progressively degrade island States and transform them into mere rocks thereby leading to a loss of maritime zones. In detail, it focuses on the fate of the island State's maritime zones if it employed one of several legal strategies to maintain international legal personality, such as the acquisition of new territory by way of cession or the merger or federation with another State. Another way for atoll island States to maintain a physical presence would be to protect or elevate their territory, or even to replace it with artificial islands or installations. Perhaps the most important feature of this segment of the inquiry is the analysis of the legal implications of such artificial protection or replacement of original island territory under the law of the sea. The chapter concludes with the finding that once SLR becomes more pronounced, the law of the sea as it currently stands will be unsympathetic to the plight of low-lying States that are faced with reduction or even obliteration of their territory for it practically hedges their maritime entitlements by progressively de-recognizing these rights corresponding to the physical changes to their island territory. In addition, the law of the sea also denies to these States the right to establish maritime zones around artificial substitutes that such States may create to replace their original land territory. Chapter 3 addresses the question how the international law of the sea can adapt to the unforeseen circumstances of global climate change. Despite the grim prognosis highlighted in the previous sections, and the injustice posed to the small island States by the legal regime of ambulatory baselines as contemplated under the law of the sea, this chapter discusses the desirability of establishing a new regime of stable maritime zones, the challenges, and possible implementation mechanisms. It compares the effectiveness of various unilateral strategies with the collective establishment of a new regime of stable maritime zones by means of an implementation agreement to UNCLOS or a UN General Assembly resolution. The author argues that collective implementation mechanisms are much superior as they help establish institutional processes that can prevent the emergence or escalation of interstate disputes over maritime space allocation. However, the progressive development of international law via this mode could be hampered as its success would depend considerably upon the concurrence and cooperation of major States which would be hard to come by. An evaluation is also undertaken of the proposition that "de-territorialized island states" should be allowed to continue to exercise sovereignty and control over their maritime zones.

The final part of the monograph on "State Extinction and Continuity" turns to questions of State extinction and possible continuity of threatened islandStates. Chapter 4 identifies the thresholds that determine the traditional elements of statehood namely, that of a defined territory, permanent population, government, and independence. It is also argued that the point at which threatened island States would lose their effective statehood would likely be a situation where the last population nucleus would have to leave the island territory (p. 297). Since these are factual criteria which require interpretation by international legal actors, Chapter 5 examines the actors who possess the competence to determine whether a low-lying island State has lost its legal status. If the international community as a whole concludes that a State has ceased to exist, it loses its international legal personality (p. 314). While sea-level rise might cause low-lying island States to lose the effective insignia of statehood, this does not inevitably mean that they would cease to exist as international legal subjects.

Drawing on the tension between effectiveness and legality that characterizes the international law of statehood, Chapter 6 explores whether other States have a legal duty to continue to recognize island States that have lost the insignia of statehood due to circumstances beyond their control. Following an exposition of the influence of considerations of legality on the recognition of States, it analyzes whether the principle of legality, according to which the extinction of States must not violate peremptory norms of *jus cogens*, can be applied to the situation of threatened island States. This involves the analysis of how the disappearance of sovereign island States might affect fundamental international norms such as the right to self-determination and permanent sovereignty over natural resources, fundamental human rights, and the proclaimed fundamental right to "state survival." The subsequent discussion as to whether these fundamental norms could be held to have been breached by other States entails an analysis of the effectiveness of the law of State responsibility as applied to the problem of climate change. The second part of Chapter 6 addresses the possibility that even in the absence of a legal obligation, other States might continue recognizing "de-territorialized" island States based on considerations of international justice and solidarity (p. 387). This part outlines the contents of de-territorialized statehood and investigates how it could be implemented in international law (pp. 375–387).

Building on the results of the previous chapters, Chapter 7 analyzes the consequences of the extinction of a sovereign island State as concerns the fate of its people, its membership in international organizations, its treaty obligations, and its assets and debts, and compares them with the consequences that would arise if the island State continued to be recognized as a de-territorialized State or in a lesser capacity, as an international legal person *sui generis* akin to the Sovereign Order of Malta. The study concludes with a short summary of and reflection on its main findings.

With all its multiple facets and intricate layers, climate change has emerged as a critical phenomenon that will potentially affect every nook and corner of this planet and every sphere of human activity. Small Island States are no exception, and the monograph reviewed here provides important insights into the intricacies of the interplay between sea-level rise, its impact on small island States, and international law. In fact, the primary highlight of the reviewed monograph lies in its analyses and interpretation of existing international legal rules as applied to the unprecedented phenomenon of disappearing island States. It sheds light on the limits of existing international legal frameworks, particularly, the "consent-based structure of international law," as well as the avenues available to push the boundaries of the law. It highlights the injustice implicit in the current system of international law where even though Small Island States have been accepted into the international community of nations, solutions to challenges that threaten their continued existence has not been considered important enough to warrant a modification of the fossil fuel-based global economic lifestyle that contributes to anthropogenic climate change. The message that it conveys is that international law should metamorphose into a more robust tool to address these new concerns, particularly given the fact that even though the carbon footprint of SIDS in almost negligible, it is this bloc of countries that stand to suffer disproportionately from the damaging impacts of climate change, and the problems that they face raise deep issues of equity and justice. This by itself renders the book a valuable resource for academics and practitioners attempting to make sense of these new challenges, which has assumed particular relevance with the adoption of the Paris Agreement.

> *Tony George Puthucherril*
> Research and Teaching Associate, JSD
> Marine & Environmental Law Institute
> Schulich School of Law, Dalhousie University
> Halifax, Nova Scotia, Canada

Erika J. Techera and Natalie Klein, *International Law of Sharks: Obstacles, Options and Opportunities* (Leiden/Boston: Brill Nijhoff, 2017), 282 pp.

International Law of Sharks, which is the twenty-fourth volume in Brill Nijhoff's series on *Legal Aspects of Sustainable Development*, is a welcome addition to an emerging corpus in shark-focused legal literature. This work is one of the outcomes of research at the University of Western Australia and Macquarie University, funded by an Australian Research Council Discovery Grant. Interestingly, the timing of this research project coincided with the implementation of controversial shark-control mechanisms to target potentially threatening sharks in the state of Western Australia, including the use of unmanned baited drum lines targeting large shark species. Such is the state of our troubled relationship with sharks.

The book opens with a pithy articulation of what makes shark conservation and management both pressing and appealing: "Sharks rose from the primordial deep over 400 million years ago and have survived mass extinctions and evolutionary cycles. Yet they now face unprecedented assaults by humans. There is no question that sharks are integral to ocean health and have considerable ecological and intrinsic value, nor that proactive human responses are needed to address these threats." (p. 1)

Techera and Klein commit to offering a contribution that engages regulatory approaches to sustainable utilization of marine living resources and, more broadly, good environmental governance. Sharks are the subject matter for this case study but, at times, seem secondary to the authors' investigation in improvements to international environmental governance.

Structurally, *International Law of Sharks* is divided into eight sections. Chapter 1 ("The Case for Sharks") sets down and briefly surveys the scientific and societal perceptions surrounding sharks and then introduces the themes that inform the remainder of the work: fragmentation; regulatory pluralism; implementation; and the operative dimensions of governance. Chapter 2 ("International Law Framework") surveys the treaties and environmental law principles that are relevant to the development of shark conservation. While there is no treaty dedicated specifically to sharks, the authors clearly detail the applicability of existing hard law, including the United Nations Convention on the Law of the Sea (UNCLOS), the 1995 UN Fish Stocks Agreement, the Convention on the International Trade in Endangered Species (CITES), and the Convention on Migratory Species (CMS), and relevant soft law instruments (including the UN Food and Agriculture Organization's (FAO) non-binding International Plan of Action for Sharks).

Chapter 3 ("Governance and Regulation") makes the case for expanding the shark conservation discussion to encompass a principled appreciation of how processes and institutions, in addition to rules, can influence and advance shark conservation. Importantly, they argue that the "appropriate laws are already in place, and rather than replace or refine them, it is just necessary to make them work more effectively" (p. 87).

Chapters 4 ("Species-based Measures") and 5 ("Spatial and Area Measures") introduce the tools that are traditionally utilized to conserve and manage wildlife—sharks included. Species-based approaches operate, broadly speaking, by either listing species within some hierarchical construct for management or by producing species-specific management measures. The analysis usefully introduces the historical development of species-based approaches as well as key analogs that are often considered when discussing species-based approaches. Chief among them, in this context, being the International Convention for the Regulation of Whaling and the work of its associated management organization, the International Whaling Commission.[18] The assessment then surveys existing species-based measures for sharks, including fishing and shark finning bans, gear restrictions, and supply chain restrictions. While comprehensive, I found the section on efforts to eliminate the wasteful and inhumane practice of shark finning somewhat limited in view of its prominent position in the social discourse surrounding shark management. The assessment of space- and place-based measures included in Chapter 5 is equally comprehensive but could have benefitted from a more detailed discussion of

---

18   The authors state at p. 97 that the International Convention for the Regulation of Whaling "concerns all species of whales." While the treaty's preamble mentions "all species of whale," in practice, and in conformity with the Annex of Nomenclature of Whales that was appended to the final negotiating text in 1946, the treaty's regulatory jurisdiction only extends to the great whale species that were commercially harvested at the time.

shark-focused MPAs and their strengths and weaknesses, perhaps through an expanded use of case studies.

Chapter 6 ("Institutions: Key Roles and Structural Issues") shifts gears to consider the various benefits and challenges associated with the sort of formalized and organized cooperative action that is possible through existing institutional arrangements. The authors' treatment of the regional fisheries management organizations' (RFMO) contribution to shark conservation is particularly compelling in view of the various forms of RFMOs that exist and their ability to address particular threats and achieve cooperative buy-in from a smaller number of participating States. Towards the end of Chapter 6, Techera and Klein introduce and critique the possibility and desirability of the international community establishing an international "Shark Commission" in the mold of the International Whaling Commission.[19] This option would turn on the negotiation of a new shark conservation treaty that establishes a permanent institution that would vote on regulatory measures on an ongoing basis. The option is compelling, at least superficially, because it would afford the international community the opportunity to establish a modern and comprehensive approach to shark conservation and good environmental governance. The work of the main deliberative body could be supported by other standing committees dedicated to science, eco-tourism, and other pressing issues. In critiquing the appropriateness of this option, Techera and Klein identify many of the limiting factors that have hindered the International Whaling Commission's effectiveness and conclude: "The political will to create such an organization, which would inevitably entail a number of binding obligations and financial commitments, may not be forthcoming; a phenomenon consistent with general international practice at present and not limited to sharks in particular. Therefore, the reality is that such an organization is unlikely to receive sufficient support for its creation" (p. 175).

Alternatively, they point to regulatory pluralism as a "multi-dimensional and collaborative approach" that has the potential to achieve the desired conservation outcomes (p. 175). In this sense, energy is better invested on building bridges between the work of existing treaty regimes and institutions—including the Convention on Biological Diversity, CITES, FAO, United Nations Environment Programme, and RFMOs—to reduce fragmentation and renew monitoring and enforcement efforts at multiple scales of implementation.

---

19   As initially proposed by A. Herdon et al., "The case for an International Commission for the Conservation and Management of Sharks (ICCMS)," *Marine Policy* 34 (2010): 1239–1248.

Following logically from the discussion of institutional structures, cooperation, and implementation initiated in Chapter 6, Chapter 7 ("Enforcement and Compliance") meets the pervasive issue of rule-following head-on. Like other living marine resources, compliance and enforcement of shark conservation measures are hampered by flag of convenience vessel registration and also illegal, unreported and unregulated fishing. This chapter is also notable for its exploration of the emerging importance of port State measures and of the lessons that can be learned from RFMOs, which employ a fairly diverse and innovative range of enforcement tools.

The final chapter ("Broader Lessons Learned: A Principled Approach") was, at least to this reader, the highlight of the book. It presents a clear and systematic synthesis of the book's major themes while also proposing targeted and pragmatic recommendations throughout. Their overarching conclusion that enhanced shark conservation requires that we "enhance integration and effectiveness" across fragmented legal seascapes to "do better with what is available" may not be the grandiose finale that some may hope for, but it is, in my opinion, a particularly salient prescription. Towards the end of Chapter 8, the authors re-visit the idea of creating a new international shark conservation institution and propose, in the alternative, a "virtual treaty regime" for sharks that is an "organic and living structure" to "capture existing arrangements and regulators and provide a forum for discussing and sharing experiences" (p. 238). Their conceptualization of a virtualized regime is essentially the creation of a clearinghouse mechanism that serves to advocate for enhanced shark conservation. They explain: "It would not be a law-making body but rather a hub or super node. This super node would be linked to existing actors, institutions and frameworks and channel information in and out of them. Other nodes would include, for example, CITES, the CMS, FAO, RFMOs as well as IUCN Shark Specialist Group and consortia of NGOs such as the Shark Alliance and finally industry" (p. 239).

This mechanism is a novel proposition that challenges some of the State-centric tenets of international law by expanding the governance regime to include the other actors that are critical to shark conservation efforts. On many occasions in this work, Techera and Klein have considered the whale conservation experience as a point of comparison for the future of international shark management. In the context of the proposed virtual treaty mechanism, they note that "[i]f the experience with whale conservation teaches us nothing else it is the power of public support and in order to advance the governance of sharks, civil society must participate" (p. 240). While this is not a criticism of the book *per se*, I have always been struck by the effectiveness of the prominent "Save the Whales" environmental campaign of the late 1970s and its lasting repercussions for the future of international whale conservation. This campaign was so successful that in less than one decade, it had dramatically altered Western perception of whales and had even bled into the negotiation of international treaties, including Articles 65 and 120 of UNCLOS. Despite the critical role of sharks in ocean ecosystems, and the many biological and ecological lines of inquiry that are far from complete, society still struggles to look beyond the villainous persona created for sharks by Hollywood and sensationalized broadcasting. At the conclusion of the book I was left with the impression that before we can achieve the creative yet pragmatic solutions that the authors proposed, sharks must first have their own conservation "moment" to shift societal perception.

International Law of Sharks hits the mark as a timely and important contribution to the expanding corpus of shark-centric legal literature, the ongoing debate and discussion surrounding the future of marine living resources, and contemporary issues in international environmental governance and sustainability. Its principled and pragmatic prescriptions for enhanced shark conservation are a welcomed contribution that should appeal to students, scholars, and practitioners in various disciplines. This is essential reading for those who want to know more about what is currently being done, and also what should be done, to save sharks from the most significant extinction threat they have ever faced—us.

Cameron S.G. Jefferies
Assistant Professor
Faculty of Law, University of Alberta
Edmonton, Canada

Alejandra Torres Camprubí, *Statehood under Water: Challenges of Sea-Level Rise to the Continuity of Pacific Island States* (Leiden/Boston: Brill Nijhoff, 2016), 278 pp.

Camprubí's monograph *Statehood under Water: Challenges of Sea-Level Rise to the Continuity of Pacific Island States* constitutes a valuable contribution to the growing literature and commentary on the challenges associated with changes in geography to international law, in particular, to the concept of the nation State. The prospect of sea-level rise has generated copious commentary since the work of Soons and Caron on the topic in the early 1990s. It has provided the subject matter for a current International Law Association Committee and has recently been added to the agenda of the International Law Commission. An increase in sea-level by a meter or more as projected by the Intergovernmental

Panel on Climate Change represents a significant challenge for many if not most coastal States. For low-lying States such as Tuvalu, Kiribati, and the Marshall Islands in the southwest Pacific and the Maldives in the Indian Ocean, however, it represents a threat to their very existence, described by Camprubí as the "sinking island paradigm" (p. 3). It is the threat to statehood itself that is the subject of this monograph, which aims to "identify how climate change impacts, and sea-level rise in particular, affect each of the dimensions of the State by degrading them from a physical perspective" and examines "the effects that the transformation of the State as a physical entity may correlatively have on its continuity as a political entity with legal attributes" (p. 8).

As Camprubí correctly and eloquently concedes "[w]hether one philosophically and ethically chooses either to uphold or to discourage the State's central role in the international order, one thing is clear, that it applies to all – the State 'is'. Qua socio-political reality, it cannot be denied. Qua legal concept, it cannot be by-passed" (p. 4). Nevertheless, in addressing the disappearance of a material substratum of statehood (rather than a redistribution of power) (p. 6), Camprubí issues a challenge to the predominant view that recognizes a single State form, the "territorial state" (p. 2) and, in particular, the assumption that State creation and extinction are part of "one singular process" (p. 6). Notwithstanding the few clues international law provides in respect of State extinction (p. 6), Camprubí "seeks to pinpoint the elements of 'normativity' and 'topicality' that are likely to guide this new stage in the regulatory and explanatory agenda informing the law on statehood" when confronted with extreme environmental change.

Although Camprubí focuses on sea-level rise as the existential threat to statehood, she situates her work more broadly in the emerging discipline of the Anthropocene, building on the work of Vidas and others, acknowledging that "one of the outstanding attributes of the Anthropocene is that it may challenge the foundations on which the present international legal order is built, since the onset of the Anthropocene alters the generally stable conditions of the Holocene, upon which the stability of the international legal order relies" (p. 274).

The monograph adopts as its structure the traditional Montevideo criteria of statehood, and chapters are divided into the challenges of de-territorialization (Chapter 1), de-population (Chapter 2) and government failure (Chapter 3). The fourth criterion – capacity to enter into relations with other States – is sensibly dealt with in Chapter 3 as part of the external sovereignty of governments. The monograph closes with a short concluding chapter.

Chapter 1 – "The Challenge of De-Territorialisation" – provides an insightful description of the evolution of territory as a component of statehood and the "territorialisation of nationhood" (p. 17), from its Greek, Roman, and Medieval antecedents to modern patrimonial, constitutive, and post-colonial theories of territory. It begins with an examination of partial de-territorialisation – in respect of maritime spaces – and analyzes the effects of coastal geographical changes on maritime rights, including loss of or changes to baselines and the status of islands under Article 121 of the 1982 United Nations Convention on the Law of the Sea (UNCLOS) (prior to the Annex VII Tribunal decision in the South China Sea Arbitration between the Philippines and China issued in 2016). The helpful overview includes several very useful tables setting out regional maritime features, their potential vulnerability, and the legal implications of sea-level rise to Pacific maritime boundaries. Camprubí follows a well-trodden path in setting out various options canvassed by other commentators responding to the threat of sea-level rise including physical protection of the coasts and legal fixing or "freezing" existing baselines. But it is the four States that are at risk of total de-territorialization that are the primary focus of the chapter. "The fundamental question is not how Kiribati, Tuvalu, the Marshall Islands may preserve – in theory and in practice – their international legal personality despite having been deprived of their spatial dimension, but why should their continuity be assured in these extreme circumstances" (p. 104) or, to put the question another way, "what is the function of the State?" (p. 104). By-passing this fascinating but somewhat philosophical question Camprubí largely confines her discussion to the *how* rather than the *why*, and explores options for re-territorialization such as cession or purchase of land from another State or even merger, creating a de-territorialized State using precedents such as non-State sovereign entities (e.g., the Holy See and the Order of Malta) and developing a trustee mechanism to preserve a so-called "water state" (p. 112).

Chapter 2 addresses the challenge of de-population. It analyzes climate-induced displacement of Pacific islanders within the context of three important factors: "(1) whether the displacement is national or transnational (spatial variable); (2) whether the continuity of the State itself may be at risk as a result of partial or total en masse transnational displacements (contextual variable); (3) whether either of the two previous factors is subject to change and progress over time, transforming the displacement situation itself, as well its political consequences, into the continuity of the State (temporal variable)" (p. 121). Camprubí considers the sometimes fraught relationship between migration/displacement and adaptation, and explores the practice and principle of both preventive and reactive relocation in the Pacific, including the role of global and regional funding mechanisms. With the aid of another helpful table setting out plans and specific actions developed by Pacific States, Camprubí concludes that relocation is dealt with unevenly across Pacific States (p. 148). She critically assesses the well-worn path of climate "refugees" and the potential for global and regional action within the framework of refugee law, human rights law and the development of a designated mechanism under the 1992 United Nations Framework Convention on Climate Change. Camprubí criticizes both practice and commentary relating to relocation as being one dimensional, with proposals relying on one legal avenue only (p. 164) and imposed from the top down (p. 205).

In seeking to respond to these criticisms, Chapter 2 concludes with the development of a proposal "to conceptualise the legal framework of climate-induced displacement in multiple and complementary layers of protection, so as to address the issue through an integrative and pluralistic scheme" (p. 149). The scheme proposed is designed to reflect "the fundamental connection between climate-induced displacement and the progressive de-territorialisation of Pacific Island States" and seeks to "relocate the human and territorial pillars within the ultimate issue of … the continuity of Pacific Island's statehood" (p. 149 and pp. 165–204). Importantly, Camprubí recognizes that while seeking to "guarantee the basic living conditions of its population, the State itself becomes simultaneously the subject of the protection of its own continuity as a distinct independent political entity" (p. 167) and consequently "the fate of Pacific islanders is bound to the fate of their Pacific Island State" (p. 167). The multi-layered scheme for relocation as developed by Camprubí comprises an integration of law and principles drawn from human rights law, international environmental law, international migration law, principles relating to internally displaced people, the international refugee regime, and the regime relating to statelessness as well as domestic law in these areas (Table 5, p. 166). Camprubí's application of these principles within the Pacific region is not uncritical, and she rightly acknowledges the limitation of an approach that depends in part on the implementation of human rights instruments not widely ratified in the region.

In the final substantive chapter Camprubí explores the challenge of government failure. Government is described as the political dimension of the State and the depository of sovereignty (p. 208). The chapter explores how the adverse impacts of climate change "challenge the governmental capacities of Pacific Island States" and "how the active participation of Pacific Island States in the international sphere operate as a determining variable of the question of their continuity of states" (p. 211). It acknowledges the inherent circularity of the argument; that the capacity of governments to protect their citizens from the impacts of climate change (effective government) depends on the existence of the State itself (p. 211). Camprubí canvasses notions such as "vulnerable," "failed," and "collapsed" States as well as governments in exile, with particular emphasis on the latter. Whilst the concept of the government in exile represents an interesting possible option for the continuation of Pacific Island States without territory or population (or at least without a population located within a designated territory), Camprubí notes that this prospect would represent a significant departure from past practice given that its application to Pacific States would not be temporary and would not result from competition between *de jure* and *de facto* governments within a territory (p. 227). Camprubí concludes that the problem of government is effectively a problem of statehood (p. 228). Complementing the internal face of sovereignty Camprubí also discusses the external capacity and role of Pacific States in the particular context of climate change negotiations.

Rather confusingly, questions of responsibility and compensation for climate change damage are also canvassed in Chapter 3, without directly linking the issue to the issue of statehood. The final part of Chapter 3 also appears misplaced. It comprises a discussion of recognition, and the options for recognizing the continuity of States that are impacted by de-territorialization or de-population. Coming at the end of the chapter exploring government failure, the discussion risks blurring the very distinct issues of recognition of States and recognition of governments. It would perhaps be better placed in a stand-alone chapter or in the concluding chapter.

This monograph is well researched and elegantly written and makes a significant contribution to the literature in this important field. In the concluding chapter, Camprubí reminds us that the Anthropocene is forcing us to reconsider the "correlation between physical reality and legal construct – two equally constitutive elements of the notion of statehood" (p. 274). She concludes that the three dimensions of statehood (territory, population, effective government) are not equally affected by climate change (p. 275), and while de-territorialization is the "source of the overall threat to Pacific Island States, the challenge of de-population lies at the heart of the future of these States" (p. 276). In this work Camprubí eruditely exposes the limits of the traditional approach to statehood, and cogently argues that we need to turn to the "meta-legal realm" (p. 277) to respond to this challenge. Surprisingly, in a work of 278 pages, the concluding chapter is a mere five pages and unfortunately fails to bring together the arguments and proposals developed in the preceding chapters around a "meta-legal" approach. Regrettably, this does somewhat undermine the thesis as a whole. Ultimately, and sensibly however, Camprubí leaves open the question of whether Pacific Island States will continue, notwithstanding de-territorialization or de-population or both.

Karen N. Scott
School of Law, University of Canterbury
Christchurch, New Zealand

Glen Wright, Sandy Kerr and Kate Johnson, eds., *Ocean Energy: Governance Challenges for Wave and Tidal Stream Technologies* (Abingdon: Routledge, 2018), 252 pp.

The prospect of harnessing energy from tides and waves is alluring. Yet the commercialization of ocean energy (OE) remains a daunting challenge. As a stark reminder of that challenge, tidal developer OpenHydro entered liquidation while this review was underway, citing "a lack of commercial prospects over the long term." Beyond the immense physical challenges, governance is also a substantial hurdle. OE is presently uncompetitive, requiring government support of some form. OE vies with other marine uses, seeking long-term rights to increasingly scarce nearshore ocean space. The "Blue Economy" impetus will likely only increase such conflicts. Regulators must balance these interests with a limited understanding of OE's potential environmental effects and within processes either ill-suited for OE or non-existent. Regulators face growing demands for more meaningful indigenous and stakeholder consultation, public input and a broader view of project impacts. Increasingly, the goal of project approvals is not merely a permit, but "social acceptance" or "social licence" for the project.

Ocean Energy examines and in many cases proposes solutions for these issues, providing what purports to be "the first comprehensive exploration of these wide-ranging governance challenges" (p. xi). The authors hope that it will be "an essential guide for developers, regulators, stakeholders, students and all those with an interest in realising the dream of clean energy from waves and tides" (p. xi). It probably goes without saying that the book generally views large-scale, commercial OE development as desirable, with potential to reduce emissions, conserve resources, increase energy security, and generate economic activity (p. 2).

The book contains an introductory chapter and four main parts. Part I examines the risks and economics challenges confronting OE. In Chapter 2, Jude et al. draw on their UK project experience to examine risks OE projects face, and how the industry might better identify and understand those risks. Risk assessment frameworks in the nascent OE industry remain underdeveloped. The authors helpfully draw from practices in "risk mature" industries to propose an integrated framework for risk assessment and analysis in OE.

In Chapter 3, MacDougall provides a review of policies that can help incent OE project development, based on her analysis of the economic value to developers of delaying project investments. The option to delay an investment has measurable value, and government policy and incentives can help developers overcome the attractiveness of delaying investments.

Part II examines marine governance generally and in relation to OE. In Chapter 4, Johnson gives a historical/theoretical overview of marine governance, tracing the movement "away from the concept of Freedom of the Seas towards enclosure of the marine commons" (p. 44). Johnson describes an interesting history of national and international treatment of the sea, from the Phoenicians in 1300 BCE through to the United Nations Convention on the Law of the Sea (UNCLOS). Scotland is used as an example of national regulation.

Chapter 5, by Johnson and Wright, addresses marine spatial planning (MSP), a key but complex and labor-intensive ocean governance tool. Using case studies (Oregon and Washington states, Nova Scotia, and Scotland), the authors neatly canvass the potential benefits of MSP for the OE industry, and the challenge of reconciling OE and existing marine uses within MSP processes.

Kerr et al., in Chapter 6 review evolving concepts of marine rights (private, state, public, and indigenous) and seabed ownership. The authors recognize that OE, which requires near-permanent and often exclusive use of marine space in nearshore areas, will pose significant challenges for existing rights and ownership of marine spaces. Building on Johnson's discussion of the increasing enclosure of the marine commons in Chapter 4, the authors anticipate a "significant increase in private or state property rights granting exclusive use to areas currently guaranteed free for navigation and fishing as of public right" (p. 95).

OE developers, investors and regulators may find Part III, which canvasses consenting and regulatory issues, the most practical part of the book. Chapter 7, by O'Hagan and Wright, describes the main components of OE project regulation before identifying significant regulatory issues and gaps extant in many jurisdictions. The starting point is that "inefficient and ad hoc consenting frameworks" are "a major barrier to the progress of OE" (p. 101). This is certainly the case in Canada, where there is no regulatory regime for OE in marine space beyond provincial territory. The authors set out various options for providing the regulatory conditions required to reduce the significant uncertainty inherent in OE projects. O'Hagan and Wright in Chapter 8 narrow the focus to specific consenting procedures in various countries.

In Chapter 9, Wright et al. review and assess existing regimes for a near universal requirement for project permitting: environmental assessment (EA) processes, and in particular environmental impact assessment. The authors conclude that substantial reform of EA processes is required to balance economic, social, and environmental goals for OE (p. 159). Helpfully, Wright et al. examine and offer alternatives to better balance OE development with environmental protection, including the authors' preferred approach: adaptive management.

Part IV concludes with a treatment of OE's interaction with communities and potential for conflict with marine uses. In Chapter 10, de Groot et al. correct the misunderstanding that the ocean is an empty "frontier" into which OE can be easily incorporated with minimal conflict. Potential and actual conflicts between OE projects and a broad array of existing marine interests are explored, with interesting case studies of conflicts with surfing and fishing.

In Chapter 11, Kerr and Weir view legal, quasi-legal, and voluntary community benefits requirements through the lens of power dynamics between communities and developers and existing institutional (social, quasi-legal, or legal) requirements for benefits.

Chapter 12, by Colton et al., examines consultation and the concepts of "social licence" and "social acceptance," although the latter two concepts are not clearly delineated despite being proffered as very distinct concepts. The authors do provide excellent suggestions for fostering greater social acceptance of OE, stressing early consultation – even before specific projects are proposed – as a key to gaining acceptance and better project outcomes.

To round out the book, ethnographers Watts and Winthereik seek to reconfigure the perception of social and material infrastructure of OE as being marginal, or at the "edge." While this latter work is interesting, its practical relevance to OE governance is not clearly explained.

For the most part, *Ocean Energy* achieves its goal. It offers an interesting review of governance challenges for its intended audience. Some chapters provide more of a practical guide (the discussions of risk and consenting, for instance), while others offer more theoretical perspectives (Chapter 4 on marine governance, and Chapter 13's ethnographic approach). The book is well organized and presented.

Future editions may benefit from an overview of OE technology and the typical project lifecycle in the introductory chapter. Chapter 1 nicely positions OE in context from a governance perspective, but its description of OE technologies leaves a number of questions unanswered. What are the commonest OE technologies? Where do they tend to be situated? How much marine space do they occupy? How are they connected to the grid? What happens at the end of their useful life? The answers will not be obvious to some of the target audience, including non-OE industry stakeholders, students, and probably many regulators. As the authors observe, "often there is a lack of familiarity and understanding of wave and tidal energy technologies in particular at local level" (p. 109). Technical information, however, is addressed in the context of specific governance challenges in later chapters.

Given the central role of law in OE governance, the absence of a legal perspective is surprising. The book has contributions from a diverse range of disciplines, but law is not apparent among them. As a possible consequence, the book occasionally lacks precision when detailing international and domestic marine governance regimes. For instance, in relation to New Zealand, the authors state that "the Crown does not own the marine environment or the seabed (called the "common marine and coastal area"), nor is it possible for the Crown or any other party to do so" (p. 129). It is not entirely accurate to conflate the marine environment and seabed and "common marine and coastal area." The *Marine and Coastal Area (Takutai Moana) Act 2011* indeed provides that neither the Crown nor any other party can own the "common marine and coastal area." But that area has a particular legal meaning. It is bounded seaward by the outer limits of the territorial sea and thus does not encompass the exclusive economic zone (EEZ) or continental shelf beyond the territorial sea. It also excludes certain existing freehold lands, as well as conservation areas, national parks, reserves, and the Te Whaanga lagoon. The Crown continues to own seabed minerals and petroleum. Equating the "common marine and coastal area" with New Zealand's entire marine environment and seabed thus leaves out much nuance of New Zealand's legal regime.

Similarly, the treatment of UNCLOS and customary international law, which provide the international legal basis for coastal States to exploit and regulate OE, is less detailed than might be expected in a text on OE regulation. UNCLOS and customary law are addressed in Chapter 4's discussion of building marine governance, but more as a historical overview than an examination of coastal States' sovereign rights in relation to OE specifically. There is no reference to Article 56(1)(a) of UNCLOS, which provides sovereign rights for the purpose of (among other things) "economic exploitation and exploration of the zone, such as the production of energy from the water, currents and winds." The book notes that "the main [EEZ] rights are to exploit economic resources" (p. 50). Of course, as the authors note, OE development in the EEZ is not presently viable (p. 121, note 36). But OE governance systems should account for future development in the EEZ, whether 13 nautical miles out or further. Developers, regulators and students may also better understand the scope and limits of domestic OE regulation after a more specific examination the coastal States' rights in relation to OE under international law.

The above comments are minor objections from a lawyer. *Ocean Energy* is a valuable contribution to the literature and will likely assist the OE industry, policy-makers, and regulators in overcoming the governance challenges facing OE. At time of writing, OpenHydro's tidal turbine remains at the bottom of the Bay of Fundy at a Nova Scotia tidal demonstration site, its fate in limbo. The expert insights and solutions offered in *Ocean Energy* may contribute to the establishment of governance systems that facilitate sustainable OE development and avoid similar fates.

> Daniel Watt
> Partner and Ocean Initiative Team Lead
> McInnes Cooper
> Halifax, Nova Scotia, Canada

Valérie Wyssbrod, *L'exploitation des ressources génétiques marines hors juridiction nationale*, Volume 28 in the "Queen Mary Studies in International Law," M. Fitzmaurice, P. Okowa and S. Singer, eds., (Leiden/Boston: Brill Nijhoff, 2018), 282 pp.

As the foreword by Professor Daniel Krauss reveals, *L'exploitation des ressources génétiques marines hors juridiction nationale* is the product of Valérie Wyssbrod's doctoral studies at the Law Faculty of the University of Neuchâtel. Just as her doctoral studies received the highest distinction, *summa cum laude*, the book version of her research merits high praise.

The volume numbers 236 pages of text with the two annexes, the bibliography and the index making up the remainder of the 282 pages. It is divided into three main parts, with fourteen chapters and is a model of concision and clarity.

The volume broaches a complex issue currently at the heart of international negotiations taking place at the United Nations: the exploitation of marine genetic resources (MGR) in areas beyond national jurisdiction (ABNJ). Three questions are at the heart of Dr. Wyssbrod's study: 1) What is the current legal regime governing the exploitation of MGR in ABNJ; (2) What might be the key elements of a future binding legal regime aimed specifically at regulating the exploitation of MGR; and (3) What other alternatives might be considered in the absence of such a tailored hard law regime?

Dr. Wyssbrod's analysis of these three fundamental questions is a real "tour de force" for it is at once both comprehensive and sharply focused. While marine genetic resources offer enormous potential for the development of new products and processes, their exploitation raises significant social, economic, and political challenges. Part 1 provides essential context for the neophyte reader. A detailed yet digestible explanation of marine genetic resources and their specificity is presented. To assist the reader, Annex 1 provides definitions of the scientific and technical terms relied upon. Part I also highlights the great potential associated with MGR in various disciplines and industries. Beyond economic considerations, Part I also discusses the important social advantages that may flow from the exploitation of marine genetic resources and identifies the political tensions that surround their future.

Part I lays the groundwork for the detailed analysis that follows on the legal regime that currently governs MGR in ABNJ. It is an incredibly effective introduction to the questions at the heart of the study. In roughly forty pages, Dr. Wyssbrod cogently presents complex scientific facts and phenomena, gathers interesting statistics and examples of current uses and industrial applications when such information is difficult to access, and summarizes the principal political currents at the international level.

Part II systematically analyzes the legal regimes that currently frame the exploitation of marine genetic resources. This part, in particular, testifies to the thoroughness of Dr. Wyssbrod's work. After a brief presentation of key legal concepts (e.g., *res nullius*, *res communis*, common heritage of mankind), Part II reviews the legal regimes governing patents, biological diversity, and the world's oceans to assess whether they provide satisfactory solutions. Three chapters are devoted to the law of the sea: Chapter 7 provides general context; Chapter 8 evaluates the specific regimes within the law of the sea that might apply to MGR in ABNJ; and Chapter 9 sets out contrasting understandings of the applicable legal rules and discusses the negotiation process unfolding at the UN. The last chapter of Part II, Chapter 10, focuses on "ecolabels" as a complement to hard and soft law instruments.

Some of the discussions in Part II at first blush appear slightly overly detailed (e.g., the discussion of the tuna-dolphin cases under the General Agreement on Tariffs and Trade) or even superfluous (e.g., the relevance of the regime governing archaeological objects found at sea for the regulation of marine scientific research in ABNJ). However, they prove to be essential for a proper understanding and assessment of the different proposals put forward in the last part of the study.

Part II is the only section of the volume where in a few instances the text lacks a certain precision. In Figure 3 at p. 116 and again at p. 119, Dr. Wyssbrod declares that the extended continental shelf cannot extend beyond 350 nautical miles. Yet the formulae in paragraphs 4 and 5 of Article 76 of the United Nations Convention on the Law of the Sea (UNCLOS) can yield an outer limit beyond 350 NM. The presentation of the different maritime zones at pp. 116–122 could have been more nuanced, specifically the difference between those zones recognized as subject to the sovereignty of the coastal State (internal waters, territorial sea) and those zones subject to clearly defined sovereign rights or jurisdiction of the coastal State (contiguous zone, EEZ, continental shelf). Similarly, the summary description of the coastal State's control over fisheries in the first paragraph at p. 118 should perhaps have referred to the regime established in Articles 61 and 62 of the UNCLOS.

These matters are minor and do not take away from the breadth and depth of the analysis of the multiple existing legal regimes and other mechanisms that might promote the rational and sustainable exploitation of MGR in ABNJ. Only true mastery of the complex issues discussed could yield such a concise yet comprehensive presentation.

Part III of the volume is devoted to a consideration of what might be the optimal regime (legally binding or soft law) for the future governance of MGR exploitation. With references to the ongoing UN process, Chapter 11 investigates what shape a new binding legal treaty specifically tailored to MGR exploitation in ABNJ might take. Dr. Wyssbrod identifies the key substantive elements that would have to be integrated and provides a lucid and realistic assessment of the chances for such an outcome. Chapter 12 returns to some of the specific legal regimes explored in Part II (e.g., patents, biological diversity) and considers whether they might be amended to provide an adequate governance structure. Chapter 13 explores the role of soft law instruments but their non-binding character leads Dr. Wyssbrod to promote, in the last chapter of the book, the use of an ecolabel system to promote the equitable and sustainable exploitation of MGR in ABNJ.

Dr. Wyssbrod's study is meticulously documented and rests on a rich and varied collection of sources. Her use of concise, numbered paragraphs (476 in total) contributes to the clarity of the thesis and greatly assists the reader in following the arguments that lead, persuasively, to her final recommendation. Dr. Wyssbrod is also to be congratulated for using an elegant but refreshingly direct language style that will be a boon to harassed scholars everywhere, including non-native French speakers.

The volume is not only a fascinating study of an emerging and critical legal issue, but it is structured and written in such a way as to be of real and immediate use to a very wide audience.

Suzanne Lalonde
Ph.D. (Cantab), Professor, Faculty of Law
Université de Montréal
Montréal, Canada

Katherine L. Yates and Corey J.A. Bradshaw, eds., *Offshore Energy and Marine Spatial Planning* (Abingdon: Routledge, in the Earthscan Oceans series, 2018), 299 pp.

Marine spatial planning (MSP) has become over the last decade the prime tool for managing ocean use, as it provides a procedural framework for bringing together those interested in a particular area of ocean, assessing the various interests and working out the optimal mix of uses (and prohibited uses) for that area. In *Offshore Energy and Marine Spatial Planning*, co-editors Katherine Yates and Corey Bradshaw have gathered articles focusing MSP on the relatively new and arguably most intensive offshore sector: renewable and extractive energy development.

Charles Ehler introduces the overarching theme of the book that the current offshore regulation on a sector-by-sector basis – shipping, wild fishery, aquaculture, hydrocarbon development, ocean energy – is resulting in conflict and will result in waste as these and future ocean uses become more intense and collide. There must be a coordinated, integrated approach which guides but does not replace individual sector regulation, which mitigates impacts and manages conflict among ocean uses. That approach is MSP. Ehler sets out the generally accepted processes that comprise MSP, including the involvement of public input, monitoring outcomes, and regular revision protocols.

Authors Stevens, Lester, and White suggest in Chapter 2 that a promising model for the coordination and integration of competing sector use is "ecosystem service trade-off analysis." Ecosystem service trade-off analysis brings a disciplined measurement protocol to the traditional unidirectional focus of single sector planning and regulation. It assesses the trade-off consequences (commercial, environmental, and social) of all the active and projected sectors within certain spatial confines. Another analytical model, this one using geographic information systems, is explored in Chapter 15 by authors Alexander, Janssen, and O'Higgins. These authors chose to see if their geodesign tools could turn around a previously unsuccessful stakeholder process which had ended in the rejection of a wind farm development off Scotland's Mull of Kintyre. Their geodesign tools consisted primarily of a set of interactive "stakeholder value" maps, on which stakeholders could easily record their views and see that their views were being fairly considered. Through local knowledge workshops, where useful data were collected, and negotiation workshops, where conflicting sector uses were valued and traded off, enhanced consensus was achieved.

Collaboration and co-location are important components of MSP. In Chapter 3, Polsenberg and Kilponen explain the benefits of collaborative opportunities between marine conservationists (like themselves) and offshore energy industries. They advocate starting by defining common ground such as industry's interest in improving its environmental reputation and conservationists' interest in new sources of funding for critical research. The establishment of appropriate mitigation hierarchies through project-based collaborations is a particularly useful form of MSP. The authors set out helpful guidelines to settling the work and expected outcomes of the collaboration, its structure (including the ticklish subject of funding), result measurement, and ground rules for communicating results. Though beyond the scope of this chapter, industry-conservationist collaborations have a particularly significant role in a new industry in a new area where new government policy and regulation may be guided by balanced and informed mitigation hierarchies developed collaboratively by conservation and industry points of view. These collaboration techniques may also be useful in considering the location of offshore energy developments within marine protected areas, as discussed in two chapters. In Chapter 11, authors Thurston, Yates, and O'Leary note that not all marine protected areas prohibit all energy development at all times. And especially given the international push to confer marine protected area status on as much as 10 percent of the world's oceans by 2020, momentum will develop to match certain energy development activities at certain times within marine protected areas. These authors discuss the benefits, disadvantages and costs of such co-locations. And in Chapter 13, authors Ashley, Austen, Rodwell, and Mangi focus their co-location expertise on wind farms in marine protected areas in the United Kingdom. The process here is to determine if and how the specific objectives of a certain marine protected area may be maintained if wind farming is permitted in that area. They illuminate the principles of co-location with case studies on both the west and east coasts of England.

Effective stakeholder involvement is one of the ten commandments of MSP. In Chapter 9, co-editor Katherine Yates discusses the critical importance of stakeholder participation in MSP and sets out many useful tools and criteria for its successful implementation. In the context of offshore energy, she notes that a coastal State's decision to reduce greenhouse gas emissions and increase its offshore renewable energy production innately stacks the MSP deck against other stakeholders and must be overcome by sensitive participation models. In Chapter 4, Lucy Greenhill looks at MSP as a framework for integrated governance. Perhaps the key actor in governance is the government, which has the formal responsibility and power to accept, reject, or modify a marine spatial plan. But governance in the context of MSP requires an empowered, properly educated, and informed civil society to provide input in addressing multi-sector sustainability in marine management and other areas of long-term impact. Industry input is also critical to develop a plan that can result in the responsible commercialization of ocean resources. She discusses the importance of any integrated governance structure to include the availability of continuing governance resources: human, technical, and financial. Levels of governance – the State, adjoining States for cross-boundary projects, international organizations where impacts are broad, an educated public, industry in each relevant sector, and nongovernmental organizations with relevant expertise – are dauntingly complex and require careful balance to create workable and sustainable marine spatial plans.

Two other chapters address important elements of stakeholder input. In Chapter 7, Gee and Burkhard seek to flesh out a too-often overlooked stakeholder impact in MSP: the impact on socio-cultural values. They make their case through the study of a wind energy development in the North Sea near Schleswig-Holstein. The authors propose that the robustness and flexibility of the social culture of the shore communities closest to a change in sea use will determine the impact of that development. A strong and varied cultural framework will more likely produce a resilient, accommodating response to the new sea use, while a more static culture with fewer alternatives will more likely suffer what the authors call a "regime shift." The authors make the case for including social-cultural values in MSP. And in Chapter 12, Brooks and Jedele focus on wind energy and ecosystem protection offshore the New England states. They describe the political and legislative background, at both the state and federal levels, to the development of marine spatial plans off the coasts of Massachusetts and Rhode Island. With respect to stakeholder collaboration, Rhode Island's two standing stakeholder advisory boards fall closer to the top down end of Katherine Yates' stakeholder empowerment spectrum, but appear to have sustained the test of time and continue to provide useful input to the various offshore projects proposed in the Rhode Island offshore. Of particular interest is the discussion of the private agreements between wind developer and conservation groups to protect a particularly sensitive species: the North Atlantic right whale.

Lawyers will think Chapter 5, "Legal aspects of marine spatial planning," should come first. Authors van Doorn and Gahlen give a clear and useful summary of international law governing MSP, starting with the historic 1982 United Nations Convention on the Law of the Sea. The newer ocean energy possibilities of wind, wave, and current were mentioned only to confirm limited coastal State sovereignty over their development in the exclusive economic zone (Article 56(1)(a)). In the 1980s, international navigation constituted the primary established use of waters above the continental shelf, and that primacy remains the law today, so that, for instance, marine spatial plans in Germany are careful not to disturb shipping lanes. The breadth of comprehensive marine spatial plans may overstep the limited sovereignty of coastal States in their

EEZ (and especially beyond the EEZ), creating possible difficulties in authority and enforcement. The authors analyze the European Union initiatives in MSP within the confines of existing international law.

The opportunity for the most significant inter-sector interaction appears to come from the fishery and energy sectors. In Chapter 6, we learn of new ocean energy sectors entering the space where existing fishery sectors have operated for decades. Careful planning is necessary to avoid unnecessary mistrust, disturbance, and conflict. Authors Kafas, Donohue, Davies, and Scott study the displacement of fisheries as the oldest and therefore most commonly displaced sector. In a particularly even-handed manner they discuss negative and positive effects of a displaced fishery, and conclude by considering the preventive and mitigation measures which may be obtained through sensitive MSP. Where there is flexibility in site selection for energy development (more likely for wind than extraction), they stress the importance of good fisheries data in the relevant space; new data sources include vessel monitoring system data. Once the area of displacement has been selected, mitigation measures include redeployment to new fishing areas and perhaps new species to be harvested, which necessitate re-education and new equipment, and, as a last resort, financial compensation. In Chapter 10, authors Hooper, Ashley, and Austen delve into the possible synergies of energy/fishery operation co-locations. They review the largely academic studies addressing fish populations (both vertebrate and shellfish) around offshore extraction and wind development infrastructure, diversity of species present, increased populations, viability for commercial and recreational fishers and opportunities for aquaculture. They analyze the limited existing co-location experiences in the Irish Sea and the Gulf of Mexico, and conclude that there is commercial potential worthy of further investigation. Uncertainty and even mistrust between energy and fishery groups may best be addressed through sensitive and responsive MSP.

In Chapter 8, seven authors tackle the primary issue in MSP: balancing within set geographic limits the environmental implications of offshore energy developments with their commercial benefits. The authors usefully summarize the key areas of offshore energy regulatory regimes common to most coastal States. They give a thorough summary of the impacts and effects of existing and anticipated offshore energy developments caused or threatened by chemical pollution, noise, electromagnetic fields, heat, collisions, and barriers. They describe the type of ocean inhabitant affected by each type of human intervention. They stress the importance of cumulative impact analysis and touch on the difficult issue of global climate change within area-specific assessments. Perhaps the most difficult and complicated geographical area for MSP, as addressed in Chapter 14 by authors Mazor, Levin, Brokovich, and Kark, is the southeastern portion of the Mediterranean Sea, an enclosed basin shared by 20 coastal States on four continents. Traditional sectors with origins going back several millennia resist displacement. International agreements are hampered by opposing ideologies. New hydrocarbon discoveries require the discipline of MSP to develop in a sensitive and balanced manner. These authors provide a set of practical tools – including trade-off analysis as described in Chapter 2 – for incorporating offshore energy information in marine spatial plans. They point out both the critical urgency and difficulty in developing marine spatial plans in this hydrocarbon bearing area of the Mediterranean Sea.

Offshore Energy and Marine Spatial Planning contributes expert, thoughtful and useful information and analysis to anyone focusing on MSP in areas of the ocean where hydrocarbon, wind, wave, and tidal projects are contemplated. Although most of the authors have backgrounds in research, science, and public policy, and not so much in business or finance, they do give a balanced view of many aspects of the commercial side of ocean energy development. One aspect not discussed, however, the elephant in the aquarium so to speak, is the cost of MSP itself. Funding MSP at the pre-project, strategic environmental assessment stage is starkly different from funding MSP when a specific energy development has been proposed, and the principles, dynamics, expectations, and implications of cost allocation will affect both the marine spatial plan process and its eventual outcomes. That omission does not reduce the high quality or usefulness of the contents of the book, but it is a gap that will hopefully soon be filled in Routledge's Earthscan Ocean series.

> *Van Penick*
> Counsel and Member
> McInnes Cooper Oceans Initiative Team
> Halifax, Nova Scotia, Canada

Liang Zhao and Lianjun Li, *Maritime Law and Practice in China* (Abingdon: Informa Law from Routledge, 2017), 528 pp.

Maritime law is a multifaceted subject. While some would read public and regulatory law – perhaps related to the environment – into the words, the meaning of the law of seaborne commerce is perhaps the more common. That is the topic of this book: the law of commerce in goods carried by sea, the carriage of passengers, and the accidents and incidents of those activities. This includes marine pollution, but also procedural law.

The growth of the Chinese economy is accompanied, as well as driven by, increasing numbers of complex commercial contracts involving foreign parties. While many maritime contracts, including contracts for the sale of goods on shipment terms, charterparties, bills of lading, and marine insurance policies traditionally include a choice of English law, Chinese law may be an option increasingly proposed or even insisted upon in negotiations for such contracts, where one of the parties is Chinese. That means lawyers representing clients in transactional work also increasingly need a basic understanding of the precepts involved. The same goes for dispute resolution – once a dispute has arisen, intense scrutiny of the potentially applicable law and jurisdictions follows, to counter any lawsuits being made in a jurisdiction more favorable for the other party – or perhaps to identify the best jurisdiction in which to proceed. This requires a common language between experts in Chinese law and experts in English law.

Fortunately, Chinese law is also becoming increasingly accessible to those of us who suffer the educational shortcoming of not being able to read Chinese. Many important source materials such as statutes and interpretations of the Supreme People's Court receive official English translations. Chinese case law reports are now regularly published in English by the same publisher under the title *Chinese Maritime and Commercial Law Reports*. Publication started in 2017, but the editors have worked their way back to 2010. In this context, this work has a significant or even decisive contribution to make here. The authors are experienced and eminent practitioners, well known in their field, and their book makes a robust contribution to the knowledge of the rules of maritime law and how it is practiced in China.

That said, one may as well begin by stating what this book is not. It is not a research handbook for academics: there is little or no reference to literature. It is not a student textbook: the detail of the chapters as well as the lack of summaries of guiding principles and introduction of concepts make the text far too detailed to accommodate such purposes. It is not a comparative work: the occasional references to English law are not consistent throughout, and are essentially deployed as an explanatory tool to aid the understanding of Chinese law – for example, the reference to the "common carrier," a historically important concept in the common law (p. 69) is here used to introduce the concept of public carrier in Chinese law. In addition, the author of this review – an academic lawyer herself – is a little doubtful as to whether the book will find a sustained readership among those outside the field of law. To those in search of a primer, the brevity of the chapters and the simplicity and clarity of the language do make it a suitable introduction to Chinese commercial law.

In its lack of reference to literature, the book emulates an important feature of the practitioner work tradition in English commercial law – such works are designed to assist practitioners in finding, interpreting, and contextualizing case law, rather than to construct a theoretical edifice of coherence and principle. But necessity also plays a part here: this work is the first to provide a detailed study, in the English language, of the practice of Chinese maritime law. As the increasing importance of Chinese law has become apparent over recent years, there is an emerging literature in the field, but this book can justifiably be said to be the first comprehensive work of its kind: a translational aid for foreign lawyers seeking an understanding of a particular issue arising in the case or arbitration reference before them. The book is also likely to provide a welcome aid to Chinese lawyers looking for the technical vocabulary and concepts to explain Chinese law to interested outsiders. Other features of practitioner textbooks are also evident: each paragraph is individually numbered for ease of reference and the introductory materials include comprehensive tables of statutes, case law, and other authorities.

The book starts with a short introductory chapter, which sets out and contextualizes some of the main sources of law and concepts essential to the field. This is followed by Chapter 2, on ships, a chapter dedicated to property issues as well as registration under the Chinese flag. Chapter 3 is entitled "Master and Seamen." This chapter makes reference to China's – at the time of going to press – recent ratification of the Maritime Labour Convention, 2006, and notes that China's laws must be updated to accommodate the country's new obligations. Hopefully this is now in progress, or perhaps even completed.

The next several chapters deal with the most fundamental contracts underlying international seaborne commerce: Chapter 4 deals with charterparties; Chapter 5 with the functions of bills of lading; Chapter 6 with the parties to the bill of lading; and Chapter 7 with the obligations, liabilities, and limitation (which is a reference to the term of art "limitation of liability" and does not refer to general conceptual deficiencies). The importance of commerce as a driving force behind maritime law and practice is evident from the great emphasis placed on bills of lading – they are by far the most intensively covered subject in the book. Chapter 8 covers freight forwarding and multimodal transport and Chapter 9 concludes the contractual segment with contracts governing and liabilities arising from the carriage of passengers by sea.

There then follows chapters on a number of subjects that in the common law would be grouped together under the header "Admiralty"; a reference to the court that has traditionally adjudicated these claims. An element of emergency often surrounds them, so that if contracts are concluded on the spot they are often simply designed to make the dispute subject to agreed, mutually trusted dispute resolution mechanisms. Standard terms speed up contract making and are designed to allow the party suffering the emergency to contract with confidence. The chapters here are Chapter 10 on sea towage contracts; Chapter 11 on collisions between ships; Chapter 12 on salvage at sea – which here means property salvage under common law and the Salvage Convention, 1989, and does not have the connotation of protection and reclaim of underwater cultural heritage sometimes encountered. Chapter 13 deals with general average, setting out how this ancient form of liability sharing among the parties to a maritime adventure is operated under modern Chinese law. In addition to the widely used York-Antwerp Rules governing average adjustment, China has endorsed an alternative set of rules called the Beijing Rules. The authors explain the operation of these and point out the major differences compared to the York-Antwerp Rules. Chapter 14 deals with the limitation of liability for maritime claims, an internationally accepted set of rules meaning that the shipowner who has incurred liabilities through some incident is entitled to cap that liability at an amount specified by international conventions. China is not a party to those conventions, but unilaterally operates domestic legislation to the same effect. The following chapter, on marine insurance, is among the most detailed and comprehensive in the book.

Chapter 16 is entitled "Marine Pollution," and consistent with the overall theme of the book, does not aim to deal with regulatory law on pollution, but with the framework regulating liabilities in tort under Chinese law. China is a party to some of the major international liability conventions, and there is domestic law applicable for these situations.

There then follows a number of chapters dealing with matters of a procedural nature. Chapter 17 is called "Applicable Law and Time Limits" – crucial knowledge; this chapter may indeed be of direct value to a non-Chinese lawyer seeking to assess whether an older claim can still be pursued. There follows a sequence of procedural chapters: Chapter 18 on introduction to Chinese maritime procedure law and the Chinese maritime court system, Chapter 19 on maritime jurisdictions, Chapter 20 on the preservation of maritime claims, Chapter 21 on maritime injunction, Chapter 22 on preservation of maritime evidence, and Chapter 23 on maritime security – which here means security for claims in the context of litigation. The procedural part is completed by Chapter 24 on procedures for trial, constitution of a limitation fund for maritime claims, recognition and payment of debts, exigence of a maritime lien; Chapter 25 on conflict of laws; and finally Chapter 26 on maritime arbitration, conciliation, and recognition and enforcement of foreign arbitration awards and foreign judgments. Much of the procedural part of Chinese maritime law is governed by the *Special Maritime Procedure Law of the People's Republic of China* and is therefore likely to be esoteric also to Chinese non-maritime lawyers.

Annexed to the work, we find the *Maritime Code of the People's Republic of China* and the *Special Maritime Procedure Law of the People's Republic of China* – both essential to understanding the text and to cross-referencing the full language of articles discussed in the text.

The language in the book is polished and idiomatic, in particular in the use of terms of art and concepts characteristic to the topic. The occasional prepositional error betrays that the authors are working in a second language. While this might have been eliminated by some careful editing – an apparently diminishing priority in publishing where speed is now of the essence – it is at a perfectly acceptable level.

In sum, this work has a substantial and important contribution to make in improving the insight and understanding of practicing lawyers worldwide into Chinese commercial maritime law, and will undoubtedly form a crucial part of the resolution of disputes of immense accumulated value. It will be a fascinating primer available to those not directly interested in maritime law, but more generally in commercial law. However the book also exposes the gaps in the field – there remain to be written (or perhaps translated) similarly detailed books on regulatory matters such as marine pollution or policy, or seafarers' rights, as well as perhaps works contextualizing and synthesizing the subjects considered in this work. No doubt, increasing internationalization of trade and the future importance of Chinese law will ensure that such works will in time become available.

Johanna Hjalmarsson
Ph.D., Informa Associate Professor of Maritime and Commercial Law
Institute of Maritime Law, Southampton Law School
University of Southampton, United Kingdom

PART 6

Appendices

∴

Annual Report of the International Ocean Institute

∴

Report of the International Ocean Institute, 2017

Message of the President, IOI*

What we love, we protect
In the preface to the first *World Ocean Review,* "Living with the oceans," published in 2010 by *maribus* in partnership with The Future Ocean consortium of scientists and the IOI, I wrote that while our environmental awareness is slowly but steadily increasing, our "awareness and understanding" of the "vast and largely inaccessible" ocean is very small comparatively. When we consider how little we do know of the complex interlinkage between climate and ocean, and the ocean as a source of resources and services, I noted that it was "especially remarkable" that the oceans "have hardly any advocates or lobby to represent their interests."

Since then, much water has passed under the proverbial bridge and the world's appreciation of the ocean, its complexity and its immeasurable importance to life on earth as we know it grows daily, along with the realization of the critical role of human actions in this interaction.

In 2015, the world's heads of States adopted the 2030 Agenda for Sustainable Development with its 17 Sustainable Development Goals (SDGs), and within them SDG14 to "Conserve and sustainably use the oceans, seas and marine resources for sustainable development." The Paris Agreement on climate change addressed the pressing issues of global temperature rise. The COP21 Summit emphasized the interdependence between the ocean and the global climate system and turned the world's focus to the delicate balance of governance actions, sustainable development, and conservation required to survive the challenges of these changes.

2017 brought us the High-Level UN Conference to Support the Implementation of SDG 14 (the Ocean Conference, June 2017, UN Headquarters, New York) and the fourth edition of the Our Ocean Conference hosted by the European Union in October in

---

* EDITORS' NOTE. – This report is extracted from the Report of the International Ocean Institute for 2017 (Malta: International Ocean Institute, 2018), available online: <http://www.ioinst.org>. Due to space limitations it has been abridged and edited for publication in the *Ocean Yearbook*.

Malta. During these two events, at which the IOI was represented, numerous commitments were made by States, civil society, and industry, pledging actions and funds aimed at achieving SDG 14 and other goals and targets.

We recognize also the important role of the UN Secretary General's Special Envoy for the Ocean to create and maintain the momentum for action to achieve the goal and its targets.

It is the sincere wish of the IOI to be able to contribute to such efforts through targeted capacity development and training opportunities. The SDG goals are interconnected and the recognition that the key to success on one will involve tackling issues more commonly associated with another, underpins the IOI understanding of ocean governance. The IOI commits itself to achieving SDG 14 and other goals of the 2030 Agenda through its global portfolio of annual international and regional training and capacity development programmes in ocean governance, and has contributed these as Voluntary Commitment #OceanAction18076.

The IOI also continues its contribution to achieving global ocean literacy through the publication of the *World Ocean Review* (WOR) series. Since my 2010 preface to the first WOR, four more editions have been released, each dealing with a different important aspect of the ocean, and another is being finalized by experts as I write. Additionally, dedicated seminars on ocean literacy and Ocean Literacy for Diplomacy[1] have been organized by the IOI and its partners – you can read about the latest seminar in this report of IOI activities for 2017.

I think often of the progress achieved in our interactions and understanding of the ocean over the years since I first got to know Elisabeth,[2] and I consider how we can get closer to achieving her utopic vision of "Peace in the Oceans."

Through all this time, many individual aspects of our dealings with the ocean come to prominence at different times over the years. When we are bombarded with unforgettable images in the global media, and topic statistics and reports, it is easy to forget that the whole of our ocean space, and also our climate and our planet are interlinked and interdependent, bringing together individual system components. Protecting the ocean through holistic governance means taking the best decisions overall that will save humanity too.

The IOI plays an important role in bringing ocean issues to the public attention at all levels – through ocean literacy action, and dedicated capacity development and education – aiming to have well-informed persons making the right kinds of decisions whether as daily consumers, as voters, or as policy- or decision-makers participating

---

1 Special Seminar on Ocean Diplomacy "fostering a cadre of ocean literate policy- and decision-makers in ocean governance to achieve the SDGs, and sustainable ocean governance globally," Malta, December 2017.
2 Elisabeth Mann Borgese, founder of the International Ocean Institute, 1918–2002.

in governance from local to international fora. There is no doubt in my mind that a love of the ocean and a desire to protect it and all of us runs through the lifeblood of the IOI family and motivates us to intensify our work. After all – what we love, we protect!

It is right then, that in this year (2018) of the anniversary centenary of Elisabeth's birth we should not only celebrate her and the IOI's achievements over the years, but that we should commit even more strongly to go further and with more determination along the path to govern wisely and protect our ocean, the source of life.

Nikolaus Gelpke
President, IOI, 2018

Activities of the IOI Centres and Focal Points in 2017

This section gives highlights of the principal activities conducted in the name of IOI throughout the global network of centres and focal points, demonstrating the capacity and potential within the network to deliver great value in areas of capacity development, ocean literacy, policy engagement, and technical research.

Training Centres
Brazil

The IOI Training Centre for Latin America and the Caribbean (IOI TC LAC) played an instrumental role in organizing and planning the second Training Programme on Ocean Governance, Ocean Sciences and Geoethics that took place in Valparaiso, Chile, from 8th January to the 2nd February 2018, initiating the itinerary after the first programme held in Brazil in 2016. Under the direction of Eduardo Marone (Director, IOI Brazil) and Alejandro Gutierrez Echeverria (Director, IOI Costa Rica), this training programme further reinforced the IOI's commitment to deliver yearly training programmes in the LAC region.

To celebrate World Oceans Day, which falls on the same day as the Oceanographers' Day in Brazil, IOI Brazil prepared discussions related to the theme "Marine Life: Conservation and sustainable use of the oceans, seas and marine resources for sustainable development," which is SDG 14 of Sustainable Development Goals. IOI Brazil volunteers prepared material and activities for a two-day event: on 7th June, discussions focused on the knowledge and interaction of the participants with the intention to make them feel part of the marine ecosystem and to be able to develop specific actions on the path towards achieving SDG 14. On June 8th, the goal was to have an open discussion about how each area of science and society can contribute to SDG 14. For this an open workshop was held, moderated by researchers of the Centre for Marine Studies, and IOI Brazil also presented how the IOI has been working to facilitate the role of people working within this objective through training courses, empowering leaders with the necessary knowledge about ocean governance issues, as this is the main key to achieve the targets of SDG 14.

Canada

IOI Canada's main focus in 2017 was the 37th annual training programme at Dalhousie University, which swelled alumni numbers for the Halifax course to the 700 mark. In addition, the centre has helped organize and deliver a third international course in Haikou, China so that in 2017 it will have been involved in training approximately 50 participants from nearly 20 countries, exposing them to key issues in coastal and ocean law and governance. Other activities have included initiatives focused on outreach, education and ocean literacy, as well as hosting and collaborating with an interestingly diverse range of individuals and organizations.

For 2017, IOI Canada focused its main World Oceans Day activity around the first ever UN Ocean Conference being held that week in New York, under the Co-Presidency of one of the Halifax course alumni. Both the topic and the format of the 13th annual Elisabeth Mann Borgese Ocean Lecture, held at Dalhousie University on World Oceans Day (8th June), were designed to build on the interest being shown in SDG 14 and to make it relevant within the Nova Scotian context. Thus, the evening combined a multidisciplinary panel in Halifax with livestreaming from New York and focused on the question of *Marine Protected Areas – For Whom?* It was presented in partnership with Too Big to Ignore, the Ecology Action Centre, WWF-Canada, and Canadian Wildlife Federation.

In New York, a live link then provided an opportunity to hear updates and analysis from two delegates at the conference: Ratana Chuenpagdee, Senior Research Fellow, IOI Canada and Director, Too Big to Ignore Partnership, Memorial University, St. John's, Newfoundland and Labrador, and Susanna Fuller, Senior Research Fellow, IOI Canada and Marine Conservation Coordinator, Ecology Action Centre, Halifax, Nova Scotia. Discussion followed between New York and both the Halifax panel and the diverse audience of about 120 people. The reception afterwards provided a chance for further debate and networking. A final debrief was also provided to the IOI course participants by Susanna Fuller during a lecture to the class on her return from the conference.

IOI Canada collaborated on two exhibitions featuring IOI founder Elisabeth Mann Borgese which opened in June. From 15th to 30th June, Great Women of the Ocean, Earth and Sky ran at the Public Archives of Nova Scotia in Halifax. Portraits by artist Jo Napier of six inspiring female role models included one of Elisabeth, which drew on materials and resources provided by IOI Canada.

Malta

The 13th edition of the IOI Malta Regional Ocean Governance Training Course opened in early November, during a ceremony which was opened through a video message by EU Commissioner Karmenu Vella. For the first time, the IOI Malta Training Course is accredited by the University of Malta in the form of three stand-alone Study Units (GSC5101, GSC5102, GSC5103), carrying a total of 15 ECTS credits.

In commemoration of World Oceans Day, celebrated annually on the 8th June, the IOI Malta Centre, through Director Alan Deidun, the Malta Tourism Authority, and the environmental nongovernmental organization (NGO) Sharklab, invited Her Excellency, President of Malta, the Hon. Marie Louise Coleiro Preca, to preside over an activity held in the first week of June at the Malta National Aquarium. The event involved students from the St. Paul's Bay Primary School who enjoyed a complementary tour of the aquarium, a screening of the Malta International Airport's Filfla marine protected areas documentary and a short briefing about the Spot the Jellyfish and the Spot the Alien Fish citizen science campaigns, both of which are funded by the IOI. The President elaborated on SDG 14 which embodies the United Nations' commitment towards healthy oceans.

South Africa

This year the IOI South Africa (IOI SA) small-scale fisheries programme rolled out a new training course, which was delivered in 19 local fishing communities, and will target many more through next year and possibly beyond. Another significant development for the centre was the launch of the five-year, German-funded STRONG High Seas Project, addressing conservation of biodiversity in ABNJ, for which IOI SA is a regional implementation partner for the South East Atlantic region. The centre's partnership with Blue Solutions also progressed towards a practical collaboration for the delivery of training in marine spatial planning across Africa. There was also a marked increase in the centre's involvement in activities to combat marine debris and plastics.

The 2017 delivery of the Ocean Governance Training Programme for Africa was held from the 4th to 29th September, with a total of 19 participants from seven African countries. This 4th running of the African regional course was one of the most engaging and successful yet.

As part of World Oceans Day (WOD) 2017, IOI South Africa conducted the WWF-SA, Transport Education Training Authority, and IOI South Africa Small Scale Responsible Fisheries Training event in Struisbaai, Western Cape. In keeping with the theme, IOI South Africa invited stakeholders from government, conservation bodies, and NGOs to address small-scale fishers as part of the training event. The training also coincided with a WOD beach clean-up event hosted by the Agulhas National Park. The training event was attended by 13 members of the Struisbaai small-scale fishing community and stakeholders from the Agulhas National Park, Department of Agriculture, Forestry and Fisheries (DAFF) Struisbaai Compliance, Harbour Chiefs, the Struisbaai Librarian, and Cape Access and the Abalobi project. It was a great example of stakeholders willing to work together in the interest of building better relationships, communication, and engagement.

IOI South Africa was also active on social media on World Oceans Day on a range of topics including the importance (theconversation.com article) and economic value of the oceans (a WWF report), plastic pollution (a SST post and a post from Waste Minimization in Africa), as well as the IISD Reporting services video from the UN Ocean Conference in New York.

Thailand

The second Training Programme on Ocean Governance for the Southeast Asian Seas and the Indian Ocean was delivered in Hua Hin District, Prachub Khiri Khan Province in Thailand between the 2nd and 27th July. For this training programme, most participants were government officials and the training helped to widen their perspective and understanding in the role of ocean governance.

IOI Thailand celebrated World Oceans Day at the Kungkrabane Bay Royal Development Study Centre[3] in Chantaburi, Eastern Province of Thailand on Sunday 4th June 2017. Around 200 families of senior management authorities from government, the private sector, and civil society gathered at the opening ceremony, which was presided over by the Governor of Chantaburi Province. About 500,000 million larvae of tiger prawns were released in the Bay as well as some fifty kilograms of young sea crabs. After the opening ceremony, participants joined a 27.5 km cycling campaign for marine resource conservation and protection through one of the most beautiful scenic bike routes of Thailand, namely Chalerm Burapha Chonlatid Road and traversed the marine shrimp farms and coastlines of the Bay.

IOI Centres

Costa Rica

IOI Costa Rica has a close relation with the program RONMAC (Sea Level Observing System and Coastal Hazards Research) and so, besides the co-organization of the annual course for Latin America and the Caribbean, it also helped develop research and extension activities on coastal hazards and local capacities in coastal communities.

As part of the outreach activities for World Oceans Day, IOI Costa Rica took part in the Global Dialogue on Oceans – A World Oceans Day event hosted by the Government of the Republic of Costa Rica in collaboration with United Nations Environment

---

3 See https://www.tourismthailand.org/Attraction/Kung-Krabaen-Bay-Royal-Development-Study-Center--2838.

(UNEP); in Puntarenas from 8th to 9th June. IOI Costa Rica presented IOI activities through the hosting of a stand providing information about the international training programmes of the IOI as well as its mission, goals and activities, and how to get involved. This was also an opportunity to promote and disseminate the *World Ocean Review* publications produced by IOI and partners.[4] In this way, IOI Costa Rica contributed to the aim of the event to target major stakeholders from different organizations, serving as a meeting point for future substantive dialogue on oceans, and also for sharing information on the IOI and its work in favor of the ocean and SDG 14 to "Conserve and sustainably use the oceans, seas and marine resources for sustainable development."

Egypt

A three-day IOI training workshop on "Ecology, Implications and Management for a Sustainable Future" was held in Hurghada, at the National Institute of Fisheries (NIOF), in cooperation with NIOF, also the host institute of the IOI Egypt Centre, between the 25th and 27th September 2017. Twenty participants attended the workshop, all from different backgrounds, but all of them having in common their work in marine-related fields. The course contents were delivered by 15 lecturers, most of whom were experts working with the NIOF branches (Suez, Hurghada and Alexandria) and others from Suez University, the Egyptian Environmental Affairs Agency, and the Coastal Research Institute. They covered sixteen lectures on ecology, problems facing the Red Sea habitats, and the management plans in the area. The lectures were delivered principally in English with additional explanations and interactions in Arabic in order to further support and extend the capacity development opportunities of the local audience.

Another three-day training workshop entitled "The Egyptian Seas: Governance, Law, and Conventions for a Sustainable Future" was held by NIOF Alexandria Branch in cooperation with NIOF between the 1st and 2nd November 2017. Lecturers from the Arab Academy for Science Technology & Maritime Transport (AASTMT), Egyptian Environmental Affairs Agency, and Suez University covered the legal framework and some conventions related to the marine sector like fisheries, biodiversity and maritime.

In order to celebrate World Oceans Day, IOI Egypt organized a celebration in cooperation with the Syndicate of Scientific Professions in Suez where IOI Egypt Director (Dr. Lamiaa Mohamedien) made a presentation about SDG 14 to an audience of students, staff, and professors from the Faculty of Fisheries, NIOF, and the Faculty of Science. The presentation was followed by a discussion about SDG 14 and specifically about how to achieve the SDGs from the point of view of Egypt as a developing country. Several issues such as the economic and political complications as well as funding were addressed and discussed in detail.

---

4   See http://worldoceanreview.com/en/.

IR Iran

The Workshop on the "Role of Mangrove Forests in the Persian Gulf Ecosystem" was organized by IOI IR Iran on 26th July 2017 in the Persian Gulf (Bushehr) Research Center of the Iranian National Institute for Oceanography and Atmospheric Science (INIOAS) in Bushehr. The program covered a half-day ceremony and included lectures of the officials and scientists of Iranian organizations including the Director of IOI Iran and the Director of INIOAS.

IOI IR Iran organized a Student's Marine Exhibition in the Caspian Sea Research Centre of the Iranian National Institute for Oceanography and Atmospheric Science (INIOAS) which is located in Nowshahr city on the Caspian Sea. On 8th July, the students visited the exhibition and the experts of INIOAS explained the different fields of ocean sciences and technologies. Many scientific posters were prepared for the exhibition and the students had the opportunity to visit different parts of the centre, including the laboratories. This exhibition ran for one month for the intended audience of children and teenagers. The Director of IOI Iran, Nasser Zaker, also gave interviews with the press and radio to introduce the importance of World Oceans Day.

Nigeria

IOI Nigeria began implementation of the approved projects for 2017 by attending the first ever Ocean Conference organized by the United Nations from 4–9 June 2017 in New York. IOI Nigeria, as usual, held a series of events marking the 2017 World Oceans Day. An education campaign on the targets of SDG 14 was successfully carried out at a strategically located coastal community in Lagos (Magbon-Alade Community), Ibeju Lekki area in Lagos State. The Ocean Literacy campaign focused on how each stakeholder, while exploiting ocean resources for livelihood purposes, can contribute to its sustainability by highlighting roles that individuals can play. The Director of IOI Nigeria, Mabel Yarhere, spoke on this year's World Oceans Day theme, "Our Oceans - Our Future," which had been specifically chosen to address the achievement of the goals envisaged by the United Nations by 2030, as captured as SDG 14.

A beach clean-up was also carried out in partnership with coastal communities in Ibeju-Lekki area of Lagos State, with scientific analyses of the various kinds of marine debris found, and recording of the types and weights of the collected debris. This year, IOI Nigeria partnered with the United Nations Information Centre in Lagos as well as the FABE Foundation and the FISHFUL Thinking Initiative for pre-World Oceans Day celebration activities. These collaborations linked to the celebration of World Oceans Day on the 8th of June at the IOI Nigeria Host Institute in Victoria Island, Lagos.

A cooking competition, using "Food from the Sea" was also organized at the community level, on the same day as the beach clean-up. Community members competed with researchers from the Institute. This event aimed to showcase the role of food coming from the ocean and coasts as well as estuaries. Involving the villagers at the community also indicated an all-round participatory approach in appreciating the oceans and its resources and the need to conserve the oceans by all playing an active role in various capacities. There were prizes given to all, donated by a research scientist at the host Institute, Dr. Oramadike, and IOI Nigeria, were given to each contestant as an encouragement for participation.

IOI Focal Points
Kenya

The World Oceans Day celebration in Kenya was held in Gazi Bay, close to Mombasa, where a group of around 200 participants, mostly students and environmental groups, joined in marking the day. The Director of IOI East Africa, James Kairo, commended all for being present and gave a talk about the importance of the ocean, especially in supporting livelihoods of coastal communities, and the looming menace of plastic pollution. One of the main activities was the collection of non-biodegradable waste starting from the village towards the beach. Following this, a workshop on recycling of waste by making ornaments and curtains from plastics and flip flops, and educational tours on the marine ecosystem, mangroves and their adjacent communities, on blue carbon ecosystems, fish parasites and diseases were offered. The younger participants were also engaged in a sand modelling competition using the 2017 World Oceans Day theme "Our Ocean, Our Future".

Malaysia

The Celebration of the Sea 2017, which includes World Oceans Day and Coral Triangle Day, with the theme "Our Oceans, Our Future" were jointly celebrated with month-long activities. The celebrations, running from the 15th June to the 15th July 2017, were organized by IOI Malaysia host institute, the Borneo Marine Research Institute (BMRI), Universiti Malaysia Sabah (UMS) and co-organized with the Ministry of Science, Technology and Innovation (MOSTI) of Malaysia, Coral Triangle Initiative Sabah (CTI-SAB) and the Ecocampus Management Centre of UMS.

Various outreach programs and social events were held to address related issues concerning the oceans and aimed to raise public awareness. Based on the success of last year's 5K Ocean Walk, the event was held again and was upgraded to the 7K Ocean Edu-Walk this year. A total of 192 participants registered for the walk which started in the compound of the institute and ended at the UMS jetty overlooking the scenic sea view. The revenue from the registration fee was donated to the Unit of Harmful Algal Bloom of BMRI-UMS to aid its operations on oceans issues. The event successfully raised a total of RM 960.00.

Further activities consisted, among others, of a marine awareness programme and colouring competition with primary school students, an outreach program on marine awareness for coastal community, and the School Children and the Peak celebration of WOCTM 2017 on 15th July, which included quizzes, games, environmental exhibitions, pledge signing, an Eco-Campus buggy ride, and a car boot sale.

Singapore

IOI Singapore celebrated World Oceans Day 2017 aboard the seismic research ship *ASIAN WARRIOR* located at Songkhla (Thailand) anchorage. The whole event was facilitated by the shipowner Capt. Hanson Ng and his technical manger Mr. Sam. The ship's crew was briefed about the activities of the International Ocean Institute and its contribution towards ocean welfare. The seafarers were encouraged to act as volunteers for the cause of ocean welfare awareness and to spread the goodwill message to other stakeholders like vendors, ship-shore service boatmen, and fellow seafarers globally. A brief lecture was delivered by IOI Singapore Director Jai Acharya and the ship's captain to the seafarers about ocean environmental issues, challenges and prevention of pollution through oil spills, ballast water discharges, sewage and emissions.

Turkey

The IOI Focal Point in Turkey, Director Sezgin Tunca, also from MARMAED Network, joined the World Natural Resource Modelling Conference in Barcelona, Spain on World Oceans Day on 8th June 2017. During the conference Mr. Tunca gave a presentation on the benefits of cooperative fisheries agreements with special emphasis on the stability of the agreements that are a crucial part in providing effective ocean governance. While direct and indirect human impacts such as pollution, climate change, and invasion of alien species would affect benefits of the agreement, benefits accruing to States and stakeholders would still be made by establishing short and long-term fisheries agreements.

IOI Training and Capacity Development Programmes

In 2017, the IOI, through the global network of training centres and the headquarters in Malta, carried out eleven training events in eight different countries to reach a total of 226 people from 45 different countries. The annual IOI training courses on ocean governance can be divided into programmes that are regional or international in scope, while the University of Malta was the host university for the post-graduate Master of Arts Degree Course in Ocean Governance.

IOI training courses held in 2017 globally
Number of participants and countries reached (chronologically)

Name of Training Course	Date	IOI Centre & Partners	Location	Ppts	Countries of origin
5th Training Course on "Sustainable Development and Governance of the Caspian Sea"	6–17 March	IOI HQ & the State Enterprise on Caspian Sea Issues, Turkmenistan	Turkmenbashi, Turkmenistan	20	(6) Islamic Republic of Iran, Kazakhstan, PR China, Republic of Azerbaijan, Russia, Turkmenistan
37th IOI training programme on Ocean Governance: Policy, Law and Management	24 May–21 July	IOI Canada	Halifax, Canada	17	(11) Antigua and Barbuda, Barbados, PR China, Grenada, Guyana, Kenya, Madagascar, Malaysia, Papua New Guinea, Tanzania, The Gambia
2nd Training Programme on Regional Ocean Governance Framework, Implementation of UNCLOS and Related Instruments in the Southeast Asian Seas and the Indian Ocean	2–27 July	IOI Thailand	Hua Hin, Prachuap Khiri Khan, Thailand	19	(7) Bangladesh, Cambodia, India, Indonesia, Maldives, Philippines, Thailand

Name of Training Course	Date	IOI Centre & Partners	Location	Ppts	Countries of origin
Maritime Spatial Planning for The Caspian Sea "Blue Planning in Practice" Ecosystem-based Marine and Coastal Planning and Management	7–11 July	IOI HQ, the State Enterprise on Caspian Sea Issues at the President of Turkmenistan, & the Blue Solutions Initiative, Germany - Ad Hoc Course	Ashgabat, Turkmenistan	23	(1) Turkmenistan
5th Training Course on Ocean Governance for the Western Pacific Region	16 Aug–12 Sept	IOI China	Tianjin, PR China	32	(5) Cambodia, PR China, Indonesia, Malaysia, Thailand
4th IOI Course in Ocean Governance for Africa	4–29 Sept	IOI Southern Africa	Cape Town, South Africa	19	(7) Ghana, Kenya, Madagascar, Namibia, Nigeria, Sierra Leone, South Africa
Training workshop "The Egyptian Red Sea: Ecology, Implications and Management for a Sustainable Future"	25–27 Sept	IOI Egypt Ad Hoc Course	Hurghada, Egypt	20	(1) Egypt

Name of Training Course	Date	IOI Centre & Partners	Location	Ppts	Countries of origin
5th Master of Arts in Ocean Governance	1 Oct;13 months	IOI HQ & the Faculty of Laws at the University of Malta	Malta	4	(2) Romania, PR China
2nd Training workshop "The Egyptian Seas: Governance, Law, and Conventions for a Sustainable Future"	1–2 Nov	IOI EgyptAd Hoc Course	Alexandria, Egypt	23	(1) Egypt
13th Training Programme on Regional Ocean Governance for the Mediterranean, Black, Baltic & Caspian Seas	5 Nov– 7 Dec	IOI Malta & the University of Malta	Malta	18	(13) Algeria, Egypt, Georgia, Greece, Lithuania, Malta, Palestine, Poland, PR China, Romania, Serbia, Tunisia, Turkmenistan
2nd IOI Training Course on Ocean Governance, Ocean Sciences and GeoEthics	8 Jan–2 Feb, 2018	IOI Brazil, IOI Costa Rica & Universidad de Playa Grande, Chile	Viña del Mar, Chile	31	(6) Argentina, Brazil, Chile, Colombia, Cuba, Uruguay
				226	

Total students for 2017 in IOI training programmes: 226 (185 in 2016).

45 countries reached: Algeria, Antigua and Barbuda, Argentina, Bangladesh, Barbados, Brazil, Cambodia, Chile, Colombia, Cuba, Egypt, The Gambia, Georgia, Ghana, Greece, Grenada, Guyana, India, Indonesia, Islamic Republic of Iran, Kazakhstan, Kenya, Lithuania, Madagascar, Malaysia, Maldives, Malta, Namibia, Nigeria, Palestine, Papua New Guinea, Philippines, Poland, PR China, Republic of Azerbaijan, Romania, Russia, Serbia, Sierra Leone, South Africa, Tanzania, Thailand, Tunisia, Turkmenistan, Uruguay (42 in 2016).

5th IOI Training Programme on Sustainable Development & Governance of the Caspian Sea; 6–17 March; Organized by the State Enterprise on Caspian Sea Issues at the President of Turkmenistan, and the IOI, in Turkmenbashi, Turkmenistan

Topics covered:
- Ocean Governance Framework
- Managing Our Relations with the Ocean: Management Tools
- Financial Mechanisms for Sustainable Transboundary Water Governance
- Governance of the Caspian Sea

20 Participants from Turkmenistan, Azerbaijan, Kazakhstan, IR Iran, Russia and China

37th IOI Training Course on Ocean Governance: Policy, Law and Management; 24 May–21 July; Organized by IOI Canada at Dalhousie University, Halifax, Canada

Topics covered:
- Ocean Sciences
- Law of the Sea and Principled Ocean Governance
- Maritime Security
- Communication and Negotiation
- Fisheries and Aquaculture
- Integrated Coastal and Ocean Management
- Marine Transportation
- Energy

17 Participants from: Canada, Seychelles, Cuba, St. Vincent and the Grenadines, China, Tanzania, Nigeria, St. Kitts and Nevis, Madagascar and Kazakhstan

2nd Training Programme on Regional Ocean Governance Framework, Implementation of UNCLOS and its Related Instruments in the Southeast Asian Seas and the Indian Ocean; 2–27 July 2017; Organized by IOI Thailand in Hua Hin, Prachuap Khiri Khan, Thailand

Topics covered:
- Global Ocean Governance Framework
- Managing Our Relations with the Ocean in the Southeast Asian Region
- Conflict Management and Consensus Building

19 Participants from Bangladesh, Cambodia, India, Indonesia, Maldives, Philippines and Thailand.

5th Training Programme on Ocean Governance for the Western Pacific Region; 16 August–12 September 2017; Organized by IOI China, with the Support of the State Oceanic Administration (SOA) in Tianjin, PR China

Topic covered:
- Managing Our Relations with the Ocean: Science, Sustainable Development and Environmental Protection
- Global Ocean Governance, Including Legal Frameworks; Special Reference to the Western Pacific Region
- Conflict Management & Consensus Building; Other Special Sessions

32 Participants from Cambodia, China, Indonesia, Malaysia, and Thailand

4th Training Programme in Ocean Governance for Africa; 4–29 September 2017; Organized by IOI Southern Africa in Cape Town, South Africa

Topic covered:
- Oceans and Coasts – Opportunities and Threats
- The Governance Framework
- Governance Tools
- Governance in Action
- Creating a Supportive Environment for Effective Governance

19 Participants from South Africa, Madagascar, Ghana, Sierra Leone, Democratic Republic of Congo, Germany, Kenya, Namibia and Nigeria

5th Master of Arts in Ocean Governance; Started on 2 October 2017 and Running for 13 Months; Jointly Offered by the Faculty of Laws at the University of Malta, Malta and the IOI

Topics covered:
- The Marine Environment
- The Law of the Sea
- Ocean Policy Making
- Regulating Sustainable Use of the Oceans

4 Participants from China and Romania

13th IOI Training Programme on Regional Ocean Governance for the Mediterranean, Black, Baltic & Caspian Seas; 5 November–8 December 2017; Offered by IOI Malta and the University of Malta, in Malta

Topics covered:
- Global Ocean Governance Framework
- Marine Spatial Planning
- Diplomacy and International Rule-making

18 participants from Algeria, Lithuania, Malta, Italy, Turkmenistan, Georgia, Poland, Serbia, Greece, Tunisia, Egypt, Romania and PR China

2nd IOI Training Programme for Latin America and the Caribbean on Ocean Governance, Ocean Sciences and Geoethics; 8 January–2 February 2018; Organized by IOI Brazil and IOI Costa Rica in Valparaiso, Chile (as part of the IOI 2017 activities programme)

Topics covered:
- Ocean Governance
- Ocean Sciences
- Geoethics

32 Participants from Chile, Brazil, Argentina, Cuba, Colombia, Uruguay

Massive Open Online Course (MOOC) – One Planet – One Ocean; Ocean Learning & Discovery. Course relaunched 14 June 2017

Ocean sustainability is high on the global agenda and the One Planet – One Ocean: From Science to Solutions[5] MOOC was relaunched in a timely manner in June for six weeks of ocean learning, running from June 14, 2017. The MOOC is a joint initiative of the Cluster of Excellence "The Future Ocean," Kiel University, Germany; the Helmholtz Centre for Ocean Research Kiel (GEOMAR), Germany; the SDG Academy, New York, USA; and the International Ocean Institute.

Training on Maritime Spatial Planning for the Caspian Sea: "Blue Planning in Practice," Ecosystem-based Marine and Coastal Planning and Management; Organized jointly by the IOI, the State Enterprise on Caspian Sea Issues at the President of Turkmenistan, and the Blue Solutions Initiative; 17–21 July 2017, Ashgabat, Turkmenistan

A specially commissioned course on maritime spatial planning for the Caspian Sea was successfully offered over five days in July 2017 in Ashgabat, Turkmenistan. The

---

5   See http://www.oceanmooc.org/en/index.php.

International Ocean Institute, on the invitation of the State Enterprise on Caspian Sea Issues at the President of Turkmenistan created, in partnership with the Blue Solutions Initiative, a specialized programme to provide practitioners in the field with knowledge and skills for implementing maritime and coastal spatial planning in the Caspian Sea.

The training programme was attended by 23 mid-career participants with diverse professional backgrounds, ranging from economics, legal affairs, engineering, hydrology, tourism, ecology, and logistics. The specially selected trainer team provided a good combination of ample experience and knowledge on marine spatial planning as well as participatory training methods.

The programme was organized so that conceptual input and theory was first shared with the participants in the form of lectures and hands-on participatory exercises; the class was then guided to work through several exercises of the Blue Planning in Practice (BPiP) course using the fictitious case of Bakul country. Participants engaged in exercises focused on identifying needs, mapping stakeholders, mapping the seascape, identifying spatial incompatibilities, allocating sea use and also role-play aimed at exploring positions and negotiating draft plans. The exercises were accompanied by introductory inputs on all BPiP elements and were followed by reflection sessions that aimed to link the lessons to the issues facing the Caspian Sea.

Throughout this course, participants learned how to think in systems and understand the role of coastal and marine ecosystems for human well-being, how to be able to balance interests of different stakeholders on the basis of transparent criteria, and how to develop strategies in order to overcome barriers and challenges that hinder the effective use and implementation of Blue Planning approaches.

Award of the Danielle de St. Jorre Scholarship for 2017 and Report from the 2017 Danielle de St. Jorre Scholarship Awardee

Since 2000 the IOI has awarded a scholarship of 10,000 Swiss Francs annually to one woman from a Small Island Developing State (SIDS) who is involved in marine-related activities to improve her knowledge of the subject through relevant training or university studies. This scholarship was established to honor the memory of the late Danielle de St. Jorre, Minister for Foreign Affairs, the Environment and Tourism of the Republic of the Seychelles and a member of the IOI Governing Board, in consideration of all she did in her short life for the benefit of her country, SIDS, and the world at large.

Ms. Orisha Joseph from Saint Vincent and Grenadines was awarded the Danielle de St. Jorre Scholarship to fund her attendance at the Ocean Governance: Policy, Law and Management Course held in 2017 at Dalhousie University, organized by the IOI Operational Centre in Canada. She reported back on her experience:

> The International Ocean Governance course on policy, law and management was an incredible course which brought together a wide cross section of people and disciplines. The course was held from May 24th to July 21st, 2017 at the

Dalhousie University, in Nova Scotia, Canada. The two-month program focused on the ocean as one connected system which consists of numerous users and stakeholders both for coastal land and the sea. Most importantly it aimed to increase awareness of how the ocean requires broad interdisciplinary management where skills, stakeholders and legal frameworks lead to improved governance.

I would like to say a big thanks to the International Ocean Institute and to Dalhousie University for being awarded the Danielle St. Jorre Scholarship for 2017 that allowed me to attend this course. It has been a valuable experience and I am happy to have attended and will be forever grateful for the opportunity.

Award of the 2017 IOI Elisabeth Mann Borgese Bursary and presentation of the results of the Bursary awarded in 2016; Malta, 18 October 2017

The 2017 EMB Bursary was awarded to Ms. Therese Ellul, a postgraduate research student at the Department of Biology of the University of Malta, to further her research entitled "The Ecology of Potentially Invasive Alien Macroalgae in Maltese Waters." This research seeks to record and monitor invasive alien seaweeds introduced in Maltese waters and to study their impacts on native marine biota and their habitats. Particular attention is being paid to recently introduced green algae of the genus *Caulerpa* which are becoming invasive and may be having an impact on some marine ecosystems of high biological and socio-economic importance, including meadows of the Neptune grass, *Posidonia oceanica*. As an additional benefit to the University of Malta, any equipment purchased specifically with EMB Bursary funds to complete the research, shall be donated to the University, for the use and benefit of other research projects and researchers and arrangements are being through the Head of the Department of Biology.

The 2016 EMB Bursary awarded to Dr. Stefano Moncada to carry out research titled "Climate Coping Strategies, Economic Well-being and Sustainability in Vulnerable Coastal Communities" concluded in October 2017 with the successful achievement of the research aims for the EMB Bursary award. The main scope of the research was to identify the coping strategies adopted in reaction to climate variability and change, and to discuss their implications for economic well-being and for long-term sustainability.

Special Events in 2017

The IOI partnered with the United Nations Conference on Trade and Development (UNCTAD) in the Oceans Forum on Trade-related Aspects of Sustainable Development

Goal 14, Salle XXVI, Palais des Nations, Geneva, Switzerland, 21–22 March 2017. The multi-stakeholder event fostered debates and the development of specific policy options and novel ideas to feed into the processes of two upcoming intergovernmental conferences:
- The High-level UN Ocean Conference (New York, June 2017), whose aim it is to identify ways and means to support the implementation of Sustainable Development Goal 14
- The 11th World Trade Organization (WTO) Ministerial Conference (Buenos Aires, December 2017), which is the highest decision-making body of the WTO

The forum specifically focused on advancing the implementation of trade in fish-related targets under SDG 14 by drawing on global, regional and cross-country experiences, sharing lessons, sensitizing development partnerships, and designing more effective support measures. Ultimately, the forum also explored options to implement the UNCTAD-FAO-UNEP Statement on Fisheries Subsidies, which is supported by 91 countries, four IGOs (intergovernmental organizations) and more than 15 global civil society organizations.

The IOI (a partner of this forum) was represented in Geneva by Awni Behnam (Honorary President); Antonella Vassallo (Managing Director), Peter Leder (Treasurer, IOI Governing Board), Werner Ekau (Director, IOI Germany), and Behzad Alipour Tehrany. Dr. Ekau presented, on behalf of the IOI, an intervention titled "People, Pollution and Plastics: Modern Anthropogenic Factors Affecting Fisheries."

"Healthy Oceans – Healthy Coast" International Leadership Seminar towards achieving SDG 14. "Current challenges and opportunities in ocean and coastal sustainable development"; Hong Kong, China; 25–26 April 2017

The IOI along with its partners, UNCTAD, the Shenzhen World Health Foundation (SWHF), and the Hong Kong Polytechnic University (PolyU), convened an International Leadership Seminar on the Challenges and Opportunities in Ocean and Coastal Sustainable Development under the United Nations SDGs Agenda.

The "Healthy Oceans – Healthy Coast" International Leadership Seminar explored the issues of oceans and ocean health, and the Sustainable Development Goals, especially SDG 14 concerning the oceans and focused specially on the ocean-coast interaction with a view to achieving SDG 14. This event built upon earlier collaborations of the IOI in 2016 and 2017 with partners and supporters, such as the UNCTAD, the Commonwealth Secretariat, and the European Commission representation, and an outcome of this event is that results are expected to feed into the high-level Ocean Conference scheduled for 5–9 June in New York (Our Oceans, Our Future: Partnering for the Implementation of SDG 14), as well as to inform and guide the IOI programme of activities and capacity-building over the next years.

The Leadership Seminar was supported by UNCTAD, an authoritative knowledge-based institution whose work aims to help shape current policy debates and thinking on development, with a particular focus on ensuring that domestic policies and international action are mutually supportive in bringing about sustainable development. Other lead organizers included SWHF, and the seminar was supported by and featured active participation from faculty and graduate students from the Hong Kong Polytechnic University, Department of Logistics and Maritime Studies, and the Research Institute for Sustainable Urban Development.

The Leadership Seminar was attended by several experts from the United Nations and related non-government and government representatives from overseas and mainland China, as well as representatives from the IOI global network of directors. Discussions focused on the UN Sustainable Development Goals, especially SDG 14, which provide guidelines and targets for all countries to adopt in accordance with their own priorities and the environmental challenges of the world at large.

Keynote presentations were given by Awni Behnam, Honorary President, IOI; Gao Guohui, Chairman of the Board, SWHF; James Alex Msekela, Chair of the Group of 77 and China; Bonapas Onguglo, Head, Trade Analysis Branch, DITC, UNCTAD; Vladimir Jares, Deputy Director, UN Division for Ocean Affairs and the Law of the Sea; and Lu Haifeng, Secretary General, Global Forum on Human Settlements.

Three thematic panel sessions chaired respectively by representatives from IOI (Chua Thia Eng), UNCTAD (David Vívas Eugui), and PolyU (Venus Lun, Jin-Guang Teng) addressed issues related to SDG 14 through dedicated presentations that were followed by active debate and interventions.

The three days of the Leadership Seminar resulted in the preparation of the document "Conclusions and Recommendations of the Leadership Seminar" which will be used by the IOI to inform and direct future actions and capacity development programmes concerning the implementation of the SDGs with special reference to SDG 14.

The document was also presented to the Group of 77 and China for consideration in the run up to the Ocean Conference in New York (Our Oceans, Our Future: Partnering for the Implementation of SDG 14).

Celebrating 45 Years of IOI and Its Work in Sustainable Ocean Governance (1972–2017); 25 April; Hong Kong, China

The year 2017 coincided with the 45th anniversary of the founding of the IOI by Professor Elisabeth Mann Borgese and the occasion of the Leadership Seminar in Hong Kong was an opportunity to mark this event in the ongoing development of the IOI as an institution focused on capacity development for the benefit of future generations and the sustainable use of our oceans.

In honor of the anniversary of the IOI, PolyU hosted a celebratory lunch on the university campus on 25 April. Managing Director Antonella Vassallo read out a message on behalf of Nicholas Gelpke, President of the IOI. Xiang Hu, representative of SWHF, then delivered a brief speech expressing gratitude towards the IOI for organizing and initiating the Leadership Seminar. This was followed by the exchange of gifts between the IOI and SWHF, which were presented and received formally by Mahin Faghfouri (Vice President of the IOI Governing Board) on behalf of the IOI and by Junwei Zhang (Secretary General of the SWHF) on behalf of the SWHF.

Internal Meeting of IOI Experts "Putting It All Together: Bringing the Message of the Leadership Seminar to Implementation through Outreach and Capacity Development" 27 April; Hong Kong, China

This specially convened meeting, held back-to-back with the Leadership Seminar, provided an opportunity for the IOI network members to build upon the presentations and dynamic discussions of the previous days, and to identify ways to implement these outcomes and recommendations through the IOI programmes, outreach, and capacity development actions and other actions. The meeting provided an opportunity to capture this feedback to use over the next months, not least at the Ocean Conference in New York, and also for the growing set of topics for mainstreaming into IOI training course syllabi. The collection of initial ideas and vision for the IOI arising from this meeting was intended to inform further decision-making by the IOI Governing Board.

This event also brought members of the IOI family together on the 45th anniversary of the founding of the IOI to celebrate its achievements, to learn from past experiences, but also to contemplate the coming years and the role of IOI in the future as an established "go-to" organization for capacity development and training in ocean governance.

The meeting was attended by a representative cross-section of IOI Governing Board members: M. Faghfouri, C. Thia Eng, P. Leder, A. Coady, L. Hildebrand; IOI Training Centre Directors: Qin L., A. Deidun, D. Lane (representing IOI Canada); IOI Directors: L. Mohamedien, A. Gutierrez; and Directors of IOI Training Courses: I. Oliounine (Turkmenistan), Mao B. (China), Wong P. (Thailand). The meeting was chaired by M. Faghfouri and L. Hildebrand.

Presentation to the Chair of the Group of 77 and China (Geneva Chapter) of the Conclusions and Recommendations of the: "Healthy Oceans – Healthy Coast" International Leadership Seminar towards Achieving SDG 14; "Current challenges and opportunities in ocean and coastal sustainable development" Hong Kong, 2017; 2 June 2017, Geneva, Switzerland

Awni Behnam formally presented the Conclusions and Recommendations of the Leadership Seminar to Ambassador James Msekela, Permanent Representative of the United Republic of Tanzania to the United Nations in Geneva and Chair of the Group of 77 and China. Bringing the document to the attention of the Group for targeted follow-up complements the work done by the IOI at the Ocean Conference to ensure longevity of the Leadership Seminar discussions and outcomes, especially when twinned with the embedding of these outcomes in the IOI training programme planning and other activities in the IOI network globally.

IOI Delegation participated in the Ocean Conference, United Nations, New York, 5-9 June 2017

The High-Level United Nations Conference to Support the Implementation of Sustainable Development Goal 14 (the Ocean Conference) was convened at United Nations Headquarters in New York from 5 to 9 June 2017, coinciding also with World Oceans Day traditionally celebrated on June 8th. The Governments of Fiji and Sweden had the co-hosting responsibilities of the Conference and the Conference aimed to support the implementation of SDG 14 (Life Below Water: Conserve and sustainably use the oceans, seas and marine resources for sustainable development) by being the game changer that would reverse the decline in the health of our ocean for people, planet and prosperity.

As an organization with consultative status at ECOSOC, the IOI was represented at this event by a delegation of nine persons, headed by Dr. Awni Behnam, Honorary President, IOI. Also, in the group were Antonella Vassallo (Managing Director, IOI), Peter Leder and Larry Hildebrand (IOI Governors), Adnan Awad (Chair of the IOI Network Directors and Director, IOI South Africa) and Werner Ekau and Mabel Yarhere (Directors of IOI Germany and IOI Nigeria respectively), also joining the delegation was Anna-Katharina Hornidge from ZMT in Bremen.

The work of the IOI at the Ocean Conference built on the earlier meetings and partnerships forged in 2017 and prior. The momentum and outcomes generated by these events enhanced the IOI contribution to the New York meeting and, pertinently, provided opportunities for the partners to present and implement a number of recommendations arising from the Conclusions and Recommendations Document of the Leadership Seminar.

The Ocean Conference comprised plenary meetings, partnership dialogues, special high-level discussions, and a special event commemorating World Oceans Day, as well as several side events which allowed space for sharing experiences and provided additional opportunities for dialogue. The IOI co-hosted two side-events with partners:

– *6th June: Trade in fish related aspects of SDG 14: What next? High level Dialogue with Permanent Representatives in New York* (UNCTAD/FAO/WTO/Commonwealth/IOI)

The event was opened with remarks from the co-hosts Mukhisa Kituyi (Secretary-General of UNCTAD), José Graziano da Silva (FAO Director General), and Roberto

Azevêdo (Director-General, WTO). Panel interventions were provided by Patricia Scotland (Secretary-General, the Commonwealth) and Awni Behnam (Honorary President, IOI) and followed by brief comments and feedback by Permanent Representatives to Missions to the United Nations present at the event.

– *8th June: Blue BioTrade: Harnessing Trade and Investment for Sustainable Use (UNCTAD; Development Bank of Latin America (CAF); the UN Convention on International Trade in Endangered Species of Wild Flora and Fauna (CITES), and IOI).*

The event, moderated by Lucas Assunção, UNCTAD, and Antonella Vassallo, IOI, discussed ways of adapting BioTrade (BT) principles for use in the marine realm. The session was introduced by Assunção who mentioned that the UNCTAD BT Initiative is a platform that has developed methodologies and standards for trade for the sustainable use of a wide range of biodiversity-based products. Vassallo stressed the importance of showcasing ways to adapt BT to the ocean, through "Blue BioTrade" and called for the creation of a community of practice. Awni Behnam highlighted that ocean governance must be an integral part of global governance, and stressed the importance of integrating BioTrade to the discussions on a legally binding instrument on marine biological diversity in areas beyond national jurisdiction.

The IOI delegation participated in many other side events via commissioned presentations and active participation in debates; topics of special interest to the IOI delegation ranged from capacity development, issues of SIDS, ocean literacy, maritime/marine spatial planning, Blue BioTrade, Blue economy, fisheries, oceans financing, ocean acidification, climate change, Arctic Ocean resilience, and so many more.

IOI participates in the meeting "Copernicus Marine Service: an EU asset for sustainable oceans"; European Parliament, Brussels, 26 September 2017

IOI Managing Director, Antonella Vassallo, was invited to participate in a side event at the European Parliament during the Copernicus Marine Week organized by Mercator Ocean together with 18 partners. This event titled "Copernicus Marine Service: An EU asset for sustainable oceans" brought together policy-makers, research institutions, industry, environmental organizations, civil society, and stakeholders at the European Parliament to discuss the achievements and future prospects of the Copernicus Marine Environment Monitoring Service (CMEMS).

The representative of the IOI highlighted that one of the greatest threats to the ocean was ignorance. In the light of the history of the IOI as a provider of training, education, and capacity development in issues of ocean governance, she stressed the importance of creating partnerships between providers of information related to oceans, such as CMEMS, and providers of specialized training, such as the IOI. Beginning with the requirement that policy decisions should be based on the best available scientific knowledge, she emphasized the importance of taking the information related to oceans, such as through Copernicus, and transmitting it to potential users and decision-makers through the medium of the IOI global training portfolios. The discussion with the audience further reiterated the need to deliver sound science for policy acceptance and highlighted the importance of advocacy based on established data and analysis. Ricardo Serrão Santos, MEP and Chair, concluded the conference by stressing the importance that the Copernicus programme plays for society and particularly CMEMS for the marine environment.

IOI Delegation participated in the Our Ocean Conference hosted by the EU Commission; 5–6 October 2017; Malta

The European Union hosted the 4th Our Ocean Conference in Malta. Four persons associated with the IOI participated in this event, Awni Behnam (Honorary President), Antonella Vassallo (Managing Director), Alan Deidun (Director, IOI Malta), and Cosmin Chivu (IOI Malta Alumnus 2014). The Our Ocean Conference mobilized a significant number of stakeholders from all levels of the community and conference outcomes can be measured through the commitments made by States, the international business community, NGOs, foundations, research institutes, and international organizations.

Visit of PR China State Oceanic Administration Delegation to IOI HQ; Malta, 4 October 2017

High-level delegates from the State Oceanographic Administration (SOA) paid a courtesy visit to the IOI HQ in Malta on October 4th. The cordial meeting further built on the long-standing partnership between the IOI and SOA and was attended on the part of SOA by Dr. Sun Shuxian, Head of Delegation, Deputy Administrator (SOA), Dr. Sun Shengzhi, Dr. Hu Songqin, Dr. Wang Juying, and Ms. Ning Jia, while IOI was represented by Dr. Awni Behnam, Honorary President and Ms. Antonella Vassallo, Managing Director.

SOA is a valued partner of the IOI in the four-week IOI Training Programme on Ocean Governance for the Western Pacific Region held annually at the SOA Centre in Tianjin, the host institute of the IOI China Training Centre. Furthermore, SOA members of staff also benefit from access to training in ocean governance issues via a tripartite agreement between SOA, the IOI, and the University of Malta which enables students from SOA to attend the annual Master of Arts in Ocean Governance offered by the University of Malta in collaboration with the IOI. Various global IOI training programmes welcome nominees from SOA annually to the IOI Ocean Governance programmes.

Award of the International Ocean Institute's Elisabeth Mann Borgese Medal to Professor Alfred J. Vella, Rector, University of Malta; Malta, 10 November 2017

The International Ocean Institute decided, through a unanimous decision of the Board of Governors, to confer on Professor Alfred J. Vella, Rector, University of Malta, the IOI's Elisabeth Mann Borgese Medal in recognition of his invaluable support of the IOI and its capacity development, education, and training programmes offered in Malta.

The award ceremony was held at the Valletta Campus of the University of Malta. Present at the ceremony were Dr. Awni Behnam, Honorary *Right, L-R: Antonella Vassallo, Rector Alfred J Vella, Dr Awni Behnam. Photo credit: S. Busuttil.*

President of the IOI; the Registrar, and the Pro-Rectors of the University of Malta; Ambassador Simone Borg and Professor Louis F. Cassar, IOI Governors; Ms. Antonella Vassallo, Managing Director of IOI HQ; and Professor Alan Deidun, Director of the IOI Malta Training Centre. The celebration was also attended by current beneficiaries of ocean governance training in Malta following the IOI Training Programme on Regional Ocean Governance for the Mediterranean, Black, Baltic and Caspian Seas, and the students following the M.A. Degree in Ocean Governance offered jointly by the Faculty of Laws at the University of Malta and the IOI. Citation:

> In memory of Elisabeth Mann Borgese, the Board of Governance of IOI has decided to award the Elisabeth Mann Borgese medal to Professor Alfred J. Vella - Rector, University of Malta for his support of the IOI and its capacity development, education and training programmes throughout his term of office as Pro-Rector for Academic Affairs of the University of Malta, and as a member of the IOI Board of Governors. The award recognizes specifically his dedication and foresight in the championing of the Master of Arts Degree in Ocean Governance, jointly implemented with the Faculty of Laws and the IOI at the University of Malta, and his input and guidance in academic issues for the IOI's strategic plan of action of 2014 and beyond.

On behalf of the IOI, Dr. Awni Behnam extended words of welcome, and spoke of the IOI's appreciation of the support of Professor Vella over the years of his association with the IOI's education and training programmes. Another speech of appreciation was made by Professor Simone Borg, Ambassador for Malta on Climate Action and Ocean Governance and Representative of the Government of Malta to the IOI Governing Board. Mr. Cosmin Chivu, spoke on behalf of his colleagues, the IOI alumni and training programme participants.

Launch of the fifth publication in the World Ocean Review Series: "Coasts – A Vital Habitat under Pressure"; Berlin, 16 November 2017

The fifth *World Ocean Review* (WOR) is available in English, after the German version was previously launched in Berlin in November 2017. WOR 5 examines the history of the development and evolution of the world's coasts, their service for nature and people, and the impact of climate change on the coasts. The publication is further subdivided into four chapters with the following titles: "Coastal dynamics," "Living with the coasts," "Climate change threats and natural hazards," and "Improving coastal protection."

Special Seminar on Ocean Diplomacy during the IOI Training Programme on Regional Ocean Governance for the Mediterranean, Black, Baltic and Caspian Seas; Malta, 1 December 2017

On Friday December 1, the special seminar on Ocean Diplomacy: "Fostering a cadre of ocean literate policy and decision-makers in ocean governance to achieve the SDGs and sustainable ocean governance globally," was held at Dar l-Ewropa in Valletta, under the auspices of the European Commission representation in Malta.

Dr. Awni Behnam (Honorary *Right, L-R: Antonella Vassallo, Rector Alfred J Vella, Dr Awni Behnam. Photo credit: S. Busuttil.*
President of the IOI) and Dr. Elena Grech (Head; European Commission Representation in Malta) delivered the opening remarks and set the stage for the speakers that followed: Ambassador K.G. Anthony Hill (Former Permanent Representative of Jamaica to the United Nations and Specialized Agencies, Geneva, Rome and Vienna), Mr. John Brincat (International Relations Officer, European Commission DG Maritime Affairs and Fisheries; B-1 International Affairs, Law of the Sea and Regional Fisheries Organizations, Brussels), Professor Simone Borg (Ambassador for Malta on Climate Action and Ocean Governance), Mr. David Vivas-Eugui (Legal Officer, at the Trade, Environment, Climate Change and Sustainable Development Branch, DITC at UNCTAD, Geneva), and Mr. Ranier Fsadni (Assistant Lecturer in Anthropology at the University of Malta, Advisor, and former director at the European Commission-League of Arab States Liaison Office).

The seminar drew to a close with the presentation of a statement from Egle Baltranaite, representative of the class of 2017 of the IOI Training Programme on Regional Ocean Governance for the Mediterranean, Black, Baltic & Caspian Seas; Malta.

IOI participation during the International Symposium "Perspectives on Global Ocean Governance: Where do we stand and where do we go from here?," Malta, 15 December 2017, Ministry for Foreign Affairs and Trade Promotion of Malta

This symposium was held to celebrate the 50th anniversary of Arvid Pardo's 1967 speech to the United Nations General Assembly on the international law of the sea and commemorate Malta's initiative and to launch a debate on the future of global ocean governance. IOI Honorary President Dr. Awni Behnam gave a presentation outlining the intertwined roles of Malta and the IOI over the course of the last five decades in the evolution of ocean governance and the UN Convention on the Law of the Sea. Dr. Behnam concluded his speech by stating that "it is time for Arvid Pardo's half-full glass to be filled with the promise of the early days, 50 years ago." He promised that "IOI, whom your excellencies host in Malta, will be willing and ready to work always by your side."

Selected Documents and Proceedings

∴

Oceans and the Law of the Sea Report of the Secretary-General, 2018

Summary*

In paragraph 339 of its resolution 71/257, as reiterated in paragraph 354 of resolution 72/73, the General Assembly decided that the United Nations Open-ended Informal Consultative Process on Oceans and the Law of the Sea would focus its discussions at its nineteenth meeting on the theme "Anthropogenic underwater noise." The present report was prepared pursuant to paragraph 366 of Assembly resolution 72/73, with a view to facilitating discussions on the topic of focus. It is being submitted to the Assembly for its consideration and to the States parties to the United Nations Convention on the Law of the Sea, pursuant to article 319 of the Convention.

I   Introduction

1. The marine environment is subject to a wide array of human-made noise. Many human activities with socioeconomic significance introduce sound into the marine environment, either intentionally for a specific purpose, such as seismic surveys, or unintentionally as a by-product of activities such as shipping. In addition, there is a range of natural sound sources from physical and biological origins such as wind, waves, swell patterns, currents, earthquakes, precipitation and ice, as well as the sounds produced by marine animals for communication, orientation, navigation and foraging.
2. A particular sound can be noise to one receiver, if it is unwanted, and a signal to others, if it is of interest. For the purpose of the present report, the terms "sound" and "noise" are used interchangeably.

---

*   EDITORS' NOTE. – This document was provided by the United Nations Division for Ocean Affairs and the Law of the Sea (DOALOS) and is extracted from the United Nations General Assembly, Seventy-third session, UN Document A/73/68, 20 March 2018, available online: http://www.un.org/depts/los/. The document has been edited for publication in the *Ocean Yearbook*.

3. Anthropogenic underwater sound in the ocean increased in the last half of the past century in some regions, most likely as a result of an expansion of industrial activities in the marine environment, including shipping, oil and gas exploration and exploitation, commercial fishing and, more recently, the development of offshore renewable energy.
4. The areas that are reported to be most affected by anthropogenic underwater noise are coastal areas and areas where a higher degree of human activity takes place, including shipping lanes with high levels of traffic. However, some high-intensity sources of underwater sound, such as airguns, can be recorded over distances of several thousand kilometres. Effects may thus occur far away from the location of the source. The regions most affected include the southern North Sea, the Mid – and North Atlantic coast of the United States of America and the Canadian Pacific coast. In general, measurements are lacking and more regions may be affected. In the future, with the retreat of Arctic Sea ice and the consequent heightened level of activity, the Arctic, which was previously a relatively quiet area, is likely to be exposed to increased levels of anthropogenic noise.
5. Increased levels of sound have been shown to have a wide range of effects on many types of marine biota, including marine mammals, fish and invertebrates. Such effects include physical damage, disruption of communication among animals and displacement of animals from their preferred breeding, nursery or feeding grounds, with consequent potential effects on their breeding success and survival.
6. Although the long-term consequences of chronic noise on marine life are still largely unknown, there are increasing concerns about the long-term and cumulative effects of noise on marine biodiversity and the resulting socioeconomic impacts.
7. Anthropogenic underwater noise and its impacts have received increasing attention from various intergovernmental forums at the global and regional levels. To facilitate the discussions at the nineteenth meeting of the United Nations Open-ended Informal Consultative Process on Oceans and the Law of the Sea, unless otherwise indicated, the present report is based on the *First Global Integrated Marine Assessment: World Ocean Assessment I*,[1] the peer-reviewed scientific studies submitted to the Division for Ocean Affairs and the Law of the Sea of the Office of Legal Affairs pursuant to a number of General Assembly resolutions on oceans and the law of the sea,[2] lists of which are available on the

---

1 United Nations, *First Global Integrated Marine Assessment: World Ocean Assessment 1* (Cambridge University Press, 2017).
2 See General Assembly resolutions 61/222, para. 107; 62/215, para. 120; 64/71, para. 162; and 71/257, para. 266.

website of the Division,[3] other peer-reviewed reports and scientific and technical publications,[4] as well as the contributions received from States and relevant organizations and bodies upon the Secretary-General's invitation.[5] The full text of these contributions is available on the website of the Division.[6]

II Nature and Sources of Anthropogenic Underwater Noise

A *Physics of Sound in Seawater*

8. Sound is a form of energy created when particles in an elastic medium are displaced by an external force and oscillate. The units for measuring the frequency of these oscillations are Hertz (Hz). Sound levels or sound pressure levels are referred to as decibels (dB).[7] There are different measurements and units to quantify the amplitude and energy of the sound pressure level and efforts are ongoing to define acoustical terms in a more precise way. In addition to pressure, sound also has a particle motion component which relates to the displacement, velocity and acceleration of the particles in the sound wave. Most marine mammals are sensitive to sound pressure. Fish and invertebrates are principally sensitive to particle motion, although some fish also detect sound pressure.

---

3 See www.un.org/depts/los/general_assembly/noise/noise.htm. A synthesis of those studies was prepared for the Division by a consultant, Frank Thomsen.
4 In particular, the Convention on Biological Diversity Secretariat, Scientific Synthesis of the Impacts of Underwater Noise on Marine and Coastal Biodiversity and Habitats (UNEP/CBD/SBSTTA/20/INF/8).
5 Contributions were received from the Governments of Malaysia, Mauritius and the United States of America, as well as from the European Union, which included the separate contributions of Belgium, Estonia, Finland, France, Lithuania, Malta, Netherlands, Poland and Sweden. The following intergovernmental organizations also sent contributions: the Commission for the Protection of the Marine Environment of the North-East Atlantic, the General Fisheries Commission for the Mediterranean, the Food and Agriculture Organization of the United Nations, the Baltic Marine Environment Protection Commission, the International Hydrographic Organization, the International Maritime Organization, the secretariat of the International Whaling Commission and the secretariat of the Pacific Regional Environment Programme. The secretariat of the Convention on Biological Diversity and the International Union for Conservation of Nature also made contributions.
6 www.un.org/depts/los/general_assembly/general_assembly_reports.htm.
7 Underwater, decibel levels are different from above water. Sound pressure levels in air are referenced to 20 µPa, while underwater they are referenced to 1 µPa (see UNEP/CBD/SBSTTA/20/INF/8). In order to compare decibel levels in air with decibel levels underwater, 25.5 dB must be added to the in-air values, together with an additional 36 dB owing to the higher acoustic impedance of water compared with that of air. Thus 100 dB re 20 µPa in air is equivalent to 161.5 dB re 1 µPa underwater.

9. In seawater, sound travels at a speed of approximately 1,500 metres per second, which is almost five times faster than the speed of sound in air. The speed depends on the physical properties of the seawater, including its temperature, pressure and salinity, causing the propagation of sound to be subject to refraction and reflection with changing conditions, which changes its path and can have sound channelling effects. In such sound channels, sound can propagate without losing significant energy.

10. With increased distance from the sound source, acoustic power will generally be lost through geometrical spreading, absorption and scattering. Transmission losses and sound propagation can be very complex and differ depending on water depths, seabed topography and the characteristics of the water column. Absorption losses can be significant for high frequencies but are negligible for low frequencies below 1 kHz. Therefore, lower frequencies carry much further underwater than higher ones. Depending on conditions, some low-frequency sounds can travel thousands of kilometres and even cross several ocean basins, especially when "trapped" in a sound channel.

11. The distinctive properties of underwater sound in terms of range and speed of signal transmission and the limitations of other senses such as vision, touch, taste and smell in the marine environment make sound the preferred sensory medium for many marine animals.

B   *Types of Anthropogenic Underwater Sound*

12. At the source, two main types of anthropogenic underwater sound can be distinguished as follows: impulsive or transient; and non-impulsive or continuous.

13. Impulsive sounds are characterized by a short duration, high sound intensity with a large change in amplitude over a short time. They may either be a single event or repetitive. Examples of impulsive sounds are those produced by explosions, airguns, sonar and pile driving. At greater distance from the source, low-frequency impulsive sounds can "smear," owing to various propagation effects and become non-impulsive. Impulsive sounds have a high potential to cause physiological damage, particularly on hearing.

14. Non-impulsive or continuous sounds are generally of lower intensity. Examples of non-impulsive sounds are those produced by ship propellers, industrial activities (e.g. drilling and dredging) and renewable energy operations.

C   *Sources of Anthropogenic Underwater Sound*

15. There are a number of sources which introduce sound into the marine environment intentionally or unintentionally. While some sources are global in

significance, such as commercial shipping, others may have a more regional significance, for example pile driving in Europe, where the installation of marine renewable energy devices has increased. Below is a summary of the main anthropogenic underwater sources; an overview of the main physical properties of those sources is provided in the annex.

16. **Underwater explosions.** These are one of the strongest point sources of anthropogenic sound. There are two types of man-made explosions in or over the ocean: nuclear and chemical. While nuclear devices were tested regularly in the ocean before the adoption of the Comprehensive Nuclear-Test-Ban Treaty, no such tests appear to have been conducted since 1996. Chemical explosives are used for several purposes underwater, including seismic surveying, construction, removal of structures, ship shock trials and military warfare and to deter marine mammals, catch fish or mine coral. The sounds from an explosion propagate equally in all directions and are detectable on a regional scale, although in some cases a single shot has been detected over several ocean basins.

17. **Seismic profiling.** Seismic profiling uses high-intensity sound to image the earth's crust. It is the primary technique used in oil and gas exploration and is also used to gather information on crustal structure. A range of sound sources may be used for that purpose, including airguns, sparkers, boomers, pingers and compressed high-intensity radiated pulse (CHIRP) sonar. The main sound-producing elements used in oil exploration are airgun arrays, the power of which has generally increased during the past decades, as oil and gas exploration has moved into deeper waters. A study in the North Atlantic suggests that sound from airguns along the continental margins propagates into the deep ocean and is a significant component of low-frequency noise. In some instances, sound signals from seismic airgun surveys can be received thousands of kilometres away from the source, through a sound channel. Sparkers and boomers are high-frequency devices used to determine shallow features in sediments. Their signals may penetrate several hundred or tens of metres of sediments, in the case of sparkers and boomers, respectively. CHIRP sonars also produce sound in the upper frequency range.

18. **Sonars.** Sonar systems intentionally create acoustic energy to gather information about objects within the water column, on the seabed or within the sediment. Most sonars operate at one frequency of sound but generate other unwanted frequencies, which may have wider effects than the main frequency used, especially if at low frequencies, which propagate further underwater. Military sonars are used for target detection, localization and classification, and generally cover a broader frequency range with higher source levels than civilian sonars, which tend to use mid – and high frequencies. They are operated during both training exercises and combat operations. Since more time is spent in training than in

combat, this may be the primary context in which marine mammals are exposed to military sonar. Commercial sonars are designed mainly for fish finding, depth sounding and sub-bottom profiling. These sonars generally produce sound at lower source levels than military sonars, but may be more pervasive owing to the substantial number of commercial vessels equipped with sonar.

19. **Vessels.** A significant proportion of underwater sound in the ocean is caused by vessels. The propulsion systems of large (e.g., container/cargo ships, supertankers, cruise liners) and mid-sized (e.g., support and supply ships, many research vessels) vessels are a dominant source of underwater sound at low frequencies. Cavitation at the propeller blade tips has been found to be a significant source of noise across all frequencies. Additional sources of ship noise include rotational machinery, which produces tones, and reciprocating machines which produce sharp pulses at a constant repetition rate. Large vessels dominate low-frequency background noise in many marine environments worldwide. Ice-breaking ships are a source of sound in polar regions through the use of bubbler systems and high-speed propelling to push floating ice away. Smaller vessels (e.g., recreational craft, jet skis, speed boats, operational work boats) produce sound that is generally highest in the mid-frequency range and at moderate source levels, although this depends on speed. Owing to the generally higher acoustic frequency and near-shore operation, noise from smaller vessels does not extend far from the source.

20. **Industrial activities.** Examples of industrial activities that contribute to underwater noise include: coastal power plants; pile driving; dredging; drilling; tunnel boring; the construction and operation of wind farms; hydrocarbon activities; cable laying; and canal lock operations. These activities generally produce sound that has the most energy at low frequencies (i.e., below 1 kHz). Dredging, which is undertaken to maintain shipping lanes, extract geological resources such as sand and gravel and to route seafloor pipelines, emits continuous broadband sound during operations, mostly in the lower frequencies. The environmental impacts of near-shore mining, including from underwater noise, are similar to those of dredging operations. Hydrocarbon activities that generate sound include drilling, offshore structure emplacement and production. Drilling can be done from natural or man-made islands, platforms and drilling vessels (semi-submersibles and drilling ships). Noise levels from natural or man-made islands have been reported to be moderate, while noise from fixed drilling platforms is slightly lower, and drilling from drill-ships produces the highest levels. Deep-water drilling and production have the potential to generate greater noise than shallow-water production, owing to the use of drill ships and floating production facilities. The sound levels of pile driving, which is used for harbour works, bridge construction and oil and gas platform installations and in the construction

of offshore wind farm foundations, can vary depending on the diameter of the pile and the method of pile driving (impact or vibropiling). Offshore wind farm construction undertaken using impact pile driving creates low-frequency noise at relatively high source levels, while their operation produces much lower source levels, with additional noise generated by maintenance and repair work. There is currently limited information available on the acoustic characteristics of offshore tidal and wave energy turbines.

21. **Acoustic deterrent and harassment devices.** Acoustic deterrent devices are used to discourage marine mammals from approaching fishing gear, including for the purpose of reducing by-catch. Fish deterrent devices are used mainly in coastal or riverine habitats to temporarily displace fish from areas of potential harm, for example, by guiding fish away from water intakes of power plants. There is considerable variation between devices in terms of frequency range, depending on the fish species targeted. Acoustic harassment devices emit tone pulses or pulsed frequency sweeps at high source levels to keep seals and sea lions away from aquaculture facilities or fishing equipment. Some fishing operations employ explosive charges, such as "seal bombs," to prevent seals and sea lions from competing for fish, or to scare dolphins. Seal bombs are also used to deter pinnipeds from occupying recreational boat and dock areas, inhabiting public swimming areas and foraging on endangered salmon species.

22. **Other sources.** Other sources of sound include marine scientific research, which may produce sound at mid – to high frequency and at high source levels. In addition, acoustic telemetry is used for: underwater communications; remote vehicle command and control; diver communications; underwater monitoring and data logging; trawl net monitoring; and other industrial and research applications requiring underwater wireless communications. Long-range systems can operate over distances of up to 10 kilometres using frequencies of 7–45 kHz at high source levels.

III Environmental and Socioeconomic Aspects

A *Impacts on Marine Species and the Marine Environment*

23. Many anthropogenic sounds fall within the hearing range of marine species and can therefore impact such species in different ways. The impact of sound on a marine species depends on a range of factors, including the sensitivity of the

species to sound; the frequency, duration and intensity of the sound; and distance from the sound source.

1   General Effects on Marine Species

24. A wide range of effects of increased levels of underwater anthropogenic sound on marine species has been documented, both in laboratory and field conditions. These range from no adverse impacts, to mild or significant behavioural responses, to physical injury or death.

25. Since sound is used by marine species for a wide variety of purposes and plays a key role in communication, navigation, orientation, feeding and the detection of predators, the introduction of anthropogenic sound into the marine environment may interfere with these functions. The masking of acoustic signals may greatly reduce the range at or extent to which relevant sounds can be transmitted or perceived by marine species, or cover them completely. Masking can have serious consequences, for example if acoustic signals used by individuals to keep in contact with one another are affected.

26. Various categories of behavioural change due to noise exposure have been observed. These include leaving or avoiding the area around the source of the sound, changes in feeding patterns and changes in social behaviour and movement. Lack of reaction does not necessarily correlate to a lack of negative impact, as some species may be conserving energy, protecting their territory or may not react to noise at intensity levels which may cause damage over the long-term but not in the short term.

27. In some cases, exposure to noise can result in physical damage to marine animals, including temporary or permanent hearing loss. Physiological effects and effects on hearing are related to the dose of exposure, which involves the duration of impact as well as the intensity of the sound. Physiological impacts and hearing impairment can potentially occur at received levels that do not cause a behavioural response, for example when animals are exposed to noise for a long time. In extreme cases, exposure can result in death.

2   Effects by Taxon

28. Although research on the impacts of anthropogenic underwater sound on marine species is still in its infancy, negative impacts have been identified for at least 55 marine species.

29. **Marine mammals.** Marine mammals use sound as a primary means of underwater communication and sensing. They have a wide bandwidth of hearing, which ranges from well below 1 kHz to over 180 kHz. The masking of marine mammals' sounds, for example as a result of increased background noise from shipping, can lead to a decrease in communication space (the volume of space

surrounding an individual within which acoustic communication can be expected to occur). Sound can also trigger behavioural responses in marine mammals, such as avoidance of the noise area, leading to displacement (short- and long-term), changes in communication behaviour (change in pattern but also alterations of the sounds), startle behaviours, changes in surface patterns and changes in diving behaviour. Studies have also shown physical damage and physiological responses to anthropogenic underwater sound, including temporary and long-term hearing loss and strandings. Incidents of whale strandings have been associated with naval sonar exercises which triggered an extreme behavioural response such as repetitive dives, causing decompression sickness.

30. **Fish.** Fish possess two sensory systems for acoustic and water motion detection, with species being sensitive principally to particle motion and only a few groups able also to perceive sound pressure. Fish utilize sound for navigation and selection of habitat, mating, predator avoidance and prey detection and communication. For example, some larval reef fish rely on sound to locate their reef habitat. Although less is known regarding the impacts of underwater sound on fish, a number of studies have identified impacts on some species, while other studies found no impacts. Anthropogenic sound has been demonstrated to cause behavioural change, including avoidance, vertical or horizontal movement and school tightening. Impulsive sound from airguns may also lead to decreased egg viability, increased embryonic mortality or decreased larval growth in eggs and larvae. Some evidence exists of physical and physiological effects, including increased stress indicators in response to noise and physical damage to tissue caused by noise, such as by causing swim bladders to tear or rupture, in response to high-intensity impulsive sounds.

31. **Marine invertebrates and other species.** Most marine invertebrates that are sensitive to sound perceive particle motion at low frequencies. Some species, such as species of barnacles, amphipods, shrimps, crabs, lobsters, sea urchins and squid are also capable of emitting sounds, possibly for communication with conspecifics. Marine turtles are also sensitive to low-frequency sounds. Research into the effects of anthropogenic underwater sound on marine invertebrates and other species is still limited and, to date, primarily confined to laboratory experiments. Research indicates that certain species, such as some turtles, crustaceans and cephalopods, exhibit behavioural responses or stress reactions to sound, while other species do not. Prolonged exposure to increased background noise can affect feeding, growth and development in some invertebrates. Physical and physiological damage may also occur, including injury to hearing organs and changes in blood composition. There is some evidence that species such as giant squid and other cephalopods may be susceptible to physical damage from impulsive sounds. Studies on the impacts of underwater sound on seabirds are

still limited. There is evidence, however, that some species, such as cormorants, hear relatively well underwater. Such species could be impacted by sounds.

3 Broader Ecosystem Impacts and Cumulative Effects

32. Although some species are more susceptible to anthropogenic underwater sound than others, the actual impact on the marine ecosystem may be broader, as the weakening or elimination of a particular species from an ecosystem could have impacts on associated or dependent species and affect the overall balance of the ecosystem. For example, physiological and physical effects on invertebrates and fish can lead to mortality in animal groups that are prey to other animals, and behavioural reactions of fish due to noise can lead to displacement and affect the feeding behaviour of marine mammals.

33. The impacts of underwater sound on specific species have, to a large extent, been studied in controlled settings. However, the actual impact on marine species and ecosystems will depend on the cumulative impacts of multiple stressors, including other forms of marine pollution, ocean acidification, climate change, overexploitation, by-catch and alien invasive species. For example, global changes in ocean parameters such as temperature and acidity are likely to have consequences for underwater noise levels through changes in sound absorption. Only a few studies have addressed anthropogenic underwater sound in the context of such cumulative pressures.

B *Socioeconomic Aspects*

34. Many of the activities that introduce sound into the marine environment, either intentionally or not, are important components of efforts to achieve the 2030 Agenda for Sustainable Development (General Assembly resolution 70/1), in particular Sustainable Development Goal 14: Conserve and sustainably use the oceans, seas and marine resources for sustainable development, as well as other international commitments related to sustainable development.

35. There is growing concern, however, that anthropogenic underwater noise might potentially cause negative socioeconomic consequences either through a ripple effect, as many human activities depend on marine species, or by affecting humans directly. While research on such consequences is still limited, available studies show that anthropogenic underwater noise may cause economic loss in certain circumstances. For example, population-level consequences resulting from changes in reproduction and spawning or displacement of fish may lead to decline in catch rates in some commercially important species, thus affecting revenues from fisheries negatively. Displacement, relocation, stranding and possible long-term population reduction of marine mammals may also affect tourism industries such as whale watching.

36. Some social groups may be more affected by noise-induced impacts on marine life or by underwater sound directly. For example, displacement and redistribution of fishes and marine mammals may affect artisanal fishing and subsistence hunting by local and indigenous communities, thus impacting their livelihood and traditional and cultural practices. Studies also show that the hearing of divers may be impaired by exposure to ambient underwater noise.

37. While sound in the ocean may be unavoidable, mitigation measures can have environmental and socioeconomic benefits. The development of new technologies, such as noise-quieting technologies, tools and practices for understanding and managing the impacts of underwater noise, can also provide market opportunities in addition to reduced environmental impacts. For example, reducing ambient noise from ships by reducing their speed could contribute to limiting carbon dioxide emissions from ships and mitigating climate change, as well as avoiding wait time off ports before docking.

IV Current Activities and Further Needs with Regard to Cooperation and Coordination in Addressing Anthropogenic Underwater Noise

A *Legal and Policy Frameworks*
1 Global Level

38. The United Nations Convention on the Law of the Sea does not specifically mention noise pollution. However, since sound is a form of energy, its introduction into the marine environment, if it results or is likely to result in such deleterious effects as harm to living resources and marine life, hazards to human health, hindrance to marine activities, including fishing and other legitimate uses of the sea, impairment of quality for use of sea water and reduction of amenities (art. 1), is considered by some a form of pollution of the marine environment under the Convention. If it is deemed to be pollution, States would be required to take all measures necessary to prevent, reduce and control pollution of the marine environment (arts. 194 and 196) from anthropogenic underwater noise, including those necessary to protect and preserve rare or fragile ecosystems, as well as the habitat of depleted, threatened or endangered species and other forms of marine life.

39. In addition, of particular relevance in the context of activities introducing sound into the marine environment are the provisions of the United Nations Convention on the Law of the Sea requiring States to adopt laws and regulations concerning pollution from vessels, land-based sources, seabed activities, activities in the Area and from or through the atmosphere (arts. 196, 207, 208, 209, 212) (see para. 37) and to enforce such laws and regulations. These laws and regulations must either take into account internationally agreed rules, standards and

recommended practices and procedures (arts. 207 and 212) (e.g., in the case of land-based pollution and pollution from or through the atmosphere), be no less effective than the international rules, regulations, standards and recommended practices and procedures (art. 208) (e.g., in the case of seabed activities and activities in the Area) or at least have the same effect as that of generally accepted international rules and standards (art. 211) (e.g. in the case of pollution from vessels). In addition, each State shall ensure, by the adoption of appropriate measures not impairing operations or operational capabilities of warship, naval auxiliary, other vessels or aircraft owned or operated by it and used only on government non-commercial service, that such vessels or aircraft act in a manner consistent, so far as is reasonable and practicable, with the Convention (art. 236). States shall also take all measures necessary to prevent, reduce and control pollution of the marine environment resulting from the use of technologies under their jurisdiction or control which may cause significant and harmful changes thereto (art. 196). The obligations relating to monitoring and environmental assessment also apply. Given the transboundary nature of noise pollution, States must also be in compliance with the obligations to ensure that activities under their jurisdiction or control are so conducted as not to cause damage by pollution to other States and their environment or beyond the areas where they exercise sovereign rights (art. 194).

40. Also to be borne in mind when addressing anthropogenic underwater noise are the provisions of the Agreement for the Implementation of the Provisions of the United Nations Convention on the Law of the Sea of 10 December 1982 Relating to the Conservation and Management of Straddling Fish Stocks and Highly Migratory Fish Stocks, requiring States to, inter alia, assess the impacts of fishing, other human activities and environmental factors on target stocks and species belonging to the same ecosystem or associated with or dependent upon the target stocks; minimize pollution; and protect biodiversity (art. 5 (d), (f) and (g)).

41. Beyond these general provisions, most of the international rules, standards and recommended practices and procedures to address anthropogenic underwater sound are of a policy and non-legally binding nature. While research gaps still exist (see para. 49), a precautionary approach is called for, in accordance with principle 15 of the Rio Declaration on Environment and Development. Besides the calls by the General Assembly for further studies and research, target 14.1 of Sustainable Development Goal 14, by 2025, prevent and significantly reduce marine pollution of all kinds, in particular from land-based activities, including marine debris and nutrient pollution, also applies to noise pollution. The declaration "Our ocean, our future: call for action," adopted at the United Nations Conference to Support the Implementation of Sustainable Development Goal 14: Conserve and sustainably use the oceans, seas and marine resources for sustainable development ("Ocean Conference") in June 2017, includes a specific

reference to addressing underwater noise (see General Assembly resolution 71/312, para. 13 (g)).

42. Other measures, which have focused on increasing scientific knowledge of the issues, prevention of noise pollution at the source and mitigation of the impacts, include those adopted in the context of the work of the International Maritime Organization (IMO) with regard to shipping, and the Food and Agriculture Organization of the United Nations (FAO) with regard to fishing vessels. Noise from dredging activities has been discussed in the context of the Convention on the Prevention of Marine Pollution by Dumping of Wastes and Other Matter (1972) and its Protocol. The Convention on Biological Diversity, the Convention on the Conservation of Migratory Species of Wild Animals and the International Whaling Commission have considered the impacts of underwater noise from various sources on marine biodiversity or specific marine species, as well as mitigation measures. The majority of the measures adopted in those contexts have emphasized the need for further research and for a precautionary approach.

43. Overall, the measures concerned remain largely sectoral, focused on certain noise-emitting activities or on certain affected species. Challenges in regulating sound-producing activities at the global level, besides research gaps, include the absence of intergovernmental forums for certain sound-producing activities; a lack of common internationally agreed standards of acceptable noise levels and mitigation techniques; and a lack of common measurements standards. With regard to the latter, work on standardization has started and the International Organization for Standardization has adopted a number of international standards related to measurement of underwater noise radiating from ships and pile-driving, as well as terminology related to underwater acoustics. In some cases, where no global rules, standards and recommended practices and procedures exist, industry sectors, such as dredging and oil and gas producers, have issued guidance addressing underwater noise.

2   Regional Level

44. Actions to address impacts of anthropogenic underwater noise through regional legal and policy frameworks appear to be limited to the waters surrounding the European Union, the North-East Atlantic, the Mediterranean and the Baltic. Measures in those regions, including in the context of the Agreement on the Conservation of Cetaceans of the Black Sea, Mediterranean Sea and neighbouring Atlantic Area; the Agreement on the Conservation of Small Cetaceans of the Baltic, North East Atlantic, Irish and North Seas; the Baltic Marine Environment Protection Commission; and the Convention for the Protection of the Marine Environment of the North-East Atlantic, have included the development of strategies, roadmaps and guidance.

45. With regard to military activities, the North Atlantic Treaty Organization (NATO) has issued mitigation rules and procedures and adopted a code of conduct. While available information does not allow sufficient analysis of activities currently being undertaken with regard to fishing activities by regional fisheries management organizations and arrangements, it appears that many such organizations and arrangements have yet to address the issue of anthropogenic underwater noise.

3   National Level

46. At the national level, legislation in some countries requires public entities generating noise in the marine environment to evaluate their activities for effects on protected marine life and the environment. Noise restrictions often form part of broader legislation to protect the environment or endangered species or of legislation addressing specific activities, such as energy development. While ocean noise roadmaps and strategies have been developed in some countries, guidelines and codes of conduct seem to be the most usual form of addressing anthropogenic underwater noise. Seismic surveys and offshore construction projects are the activities most commonly addressed. Furthermore, the regulatory frameworks focus on protecting marine mammals, although some guidelines also include measures to protect seabirds and marine turtles. Several contributions note the importance of understanding the impacts of noise in order to be able to regulate them adequately, and several States promote a precautionary approach.

B   *Science, Data and Technology*

47. To fully understand the effects of anthropogenic underwater noise on the marine environment, it is essential to be able to detect, recognize and categorize sounds in the marine environment and to have sufficient biological and ecological information for each marine species. In recent years, the impact of anthropogenic underwater noise on the marine environment has been the subject of scientific investigation in certain regions. Intra – and cross-sectoral efforts have been made to collect data on noise levels and investigate the impacts on the marine environment.

48. Noise monitoring programmes have been or are being put in place in the Baltic, the Mediterranean and the North Sea, as well as in the waters off mainland France and the United States. Projects to investigate or mitigate the impacts of anthropogenic underwater noise from shipping are under way in Australia, Canada, Japan and the European Union, in particular in the Baltic Sea. The International Quiet Ocean Experiment is an international scientific programme established to promote research, observations and modelling to improve understanding of

ocean soundscapes and effects of sound on marine organisms. Technical and scientific workshops and conferences on anthropogenic underwater noise have been held in the context of, inter alia: the Agreement on the Conservation of Cetaceans of the Black Sea, Mediterranean Sea and neighbouring Atlantic Area; the Convention on Biological Diversity; the Convention on the Conservation of Migratory Species of Wild Animals; the Baltic Marine Environment Protection Commission; IMO; the International Whaling Commission and the Convention for the Protection of the Marine Environment of the North-East Atlantic. The outputs of these efforts include monitoring technologies, noise registries, species databases and modelling and planning tools and software.

49. Nonetheless, there are significant data and knowledge gaps in relation to anthropogenic underwater sound and its impacts on the marine environment. Most past research has focused on impulsive sounds, such as sonar, airguns and impact pile-driving, as well as on marine mammals, in particular cetaceans. Many sound sources, such as pile-driving and shipping, are not fully understood, including with regard to sound levels and fields emitted. Most of the research so far has focused on marine mammals, with very few studies on fish and invertebrates. There is also an incomplete understanding of particle motion and the sensitivity of fish and invertebrates. While a considerable effort has been made in recent years to study the behavioural response of marine life to sound, many of the studies are limited to very small sample sizes. There is also a limited understanding of the effects of multiple exposures to sound, including from diverse sources, as well as the way in which multiple pressures interact in the marine environment. Further research is also required to monitor trends in noise levels over time, including for the purpose of establishing baselines. Measurements, in general, are lacking. In addition, the socioeconomic consequences of noise-induced impacts on marine populations have not been sufficiently considered to date.

50. The lack of data on both noise and marine species is a key hindrance to modelling the impacts of anthropogenic underwater sound at the population and ecosystem scales. It also limits the extent to which effective management measures can be developed. This is especially true for certain regions, including in western Africa, the Pacific Islands region and South-East Asia, where data deficits concerning the abundance and distribution of marine mammals may hamper efforts to protect them, including from sound. To remedy this situation, there is a need to establish long-term monitoring schemes, incorporating acoustic measurement into global ocean monitoring systems, and to foster international cooperation in the planning and execution of research programmes.

51. Several technologies aimed at reducing sound levels or mitigating noise impacts have been developed in recent years. In general, mitigating noise that is the by-

product of activities is easier than when sound is deliberately emitted. Dampening materials have been developed to reduce noise from pile-driving, marine vibroseis is being explored as an alternative to seismic surveys, and ship-quieting technologies, primarily relating to vessel design, are being applied to existing and new vessels. Marine scientific research vessels are normally constructed to emit as little sound as possible, given that noise may interfere with measurements and equipment.

52. Overviews of a wide range of noise mitigation technologies are included in documents from: the Agreement on the Conservation of Cetaceans of the Black Sea, Mediterranean Sea and neighbouring Atlantic Area; the Baltic Marine Environment Protection Commission; the Convention for the Protection of the Marine Environment of the North-East Atlantic; and in national and international guidelines dealing with sound-generating activities at sea. The effectiveness and impact on the marine environment of some of the new technologies and measures need to be researched further.

C Management Measures
1 Environmental Impact Assessments

53. Understanding the environmental impacts of underwater sound is critical for the development and implementation of adequate mitigation measures. At present, the effects of sound on marine mammals are addressed in environmental impact assessment processes in the European Union and the United States for some activities, such as the installation of offshore wind farms and seismic surveys. Effects on fish are much less covered compared to mammals. While some global and regional forums have called for the consideration of the impacts of underwater noise on marine life in environmental impact assessments, including cumulative impacts in some cases, this is yet to be considered by some forums with a mandate over activities or sectors with a potential significant contribution to underwater noise. In addition, the lack of sufficient baseline data on the distribution and abundance of marine life in some areas, as well as how the effects of a planned activity act in conjunction with other activities, present limits to the effectiveness of environmental impact assessments.

2 Integrated Management and Area-based Management Tools

54. Integrated management of oceans and seas is a critical underpinning of sustainable development. It is cross-sectoral and involves all relevant stakeholders. Area-based management tools, including marine protected areas and marine spatial planning, form part of integrated management. Given the variety of sources of sound in the ocean and the potential interaction of sound with other pressures, integrated management could be beneficial in addressing

anthropogenic underwater noise. While the inherent difficulties in assessing the effects of sound on marine life present challenges for management efforts, anthropogenic underwater noise is increasingly considered in management strategies.

55. A sectoral approach to noise management remains prevalent. However, area-based management tools, in particular marine protected areas, are increasingly used as noise mitigating measures. Further use of such tools has been recommended. Challenges exist, however, in using area-based management tools to address noise impacts, including difficulties in identifying animal hotspots due to limited data, the fact that many marine mammals and fish are highly migratory and difficulties in determining the size of important habitats for species that communicate over large areas.

3   Other Measures

56. Efforts to develop measures, best practices and best available techniques to mitigate the impacts of anthropogenic underwater noise are taking place in several sectors at the national, regional and global levels. A review of the content of various guidelines reveals that there are many measures, practices and techniques that can be applied to a wide range of activities to mitigate the impacts of anthropogenic underwater noise.

57. Pre-activity surveys of an area, gathering of baseline data or full environmental impact assessments are recommended in the majority of guidelines. The implementation of spatio-temporal restrictions, for example to avoid spawning, calving, breeding or migration periods or sensitive, protected or enclosed areas, is a recommended mitigation measure for most human activities covered by the guidelines surveyed. Similarly, the use of exclusion zones coupled with visual detection, for example marine mammal observers, is commonly recommended for many activities, in particular those that purposely introduce sound into the marine environment, including sonar, sound exposure experiments and seismic surveys. The use of soft start or ramp-up protocols to allow marine species to leave the area, or acoustic deterrent devices to keep them out, are other commonly used measures for such activities. The use of trained on-board observers sometimes forms part of codes of practice.

58. While few guidelines have set specific thresholds for emitted or received sound levels, several emphasize the importance of using the lowest practicable level when sound is purposely introduced into the environment. For example, the 2006 NATO Undersea Research Centre Human Diver and Marine Mammal Risk Mitigation Rules and Procedures (NURC-SP-2006-008) recommend that the sound level at reception point should not exceed 160–186 dB re 1 micropascal (μPa) – depending on frequency – if mysticetes, odontocetes or pinnipeds are present, and 160–177 dB re 1μPa or 154 dB re 1μPa for alerted military divers and recreational divers, respectively. Noise criteria have been developed in some

countries to describe received levels of noise that should not be exceeded in order not to cause harm to marine life. Such criteria have been developed and applied both for behavioural response and injury, and include those developed by the United States National Marine Fisheries Service concerning marine mammals and by some European Union member States for impact pile-driving, as well as other scientific marine mammal noise exposure criteria applied as de facto noise criteria in environmental assessments around the globe. However, the development of adequate noise criteria and restrictions depends on further research and understanding concerning hearing sensitivity of more animal groups, the appropriate metrics to use based on functional hearing groups and the impacts of noise on marine species.

59. With regard to vessels, the design stage is widely regarded as the best opportunity for noise reduction. Changes to vessel design, in particular to hulls and propellers, or the use of lightweight or dampening materials, are commonly recommended measures. For existing vessels, operational changes such as speed reduction, modification of shipping routes and regular vessel maintenance to reduce drag and cavitation are recommended.

60. At the national level, several States, in all regions, have developed guidelines for responsible nature tourism, including the watching of whales, seals, dolphins and other marine life.

61. While many of the guidelines cover general measures that could be implemented or technologies that could be used, few are concerned with the practical implementation of the recommended measures and the necessary protocols and systems to ensure their effectiveness.

D   *Cooperation and Coordination, Including for Capacity-building*

62. Anthropogenic underwater noise is a pervasive global issue, with countless sources of sound, impacted species and affected ecosystems. Cooperation and coordination, within and across different sectors, is vital to building capacity, further developing scientific understanding of anthropogenic underwater sound and addressing its impacts in a cross-sectoral and integrated manner.

63. Cooperation and coordination within and across different sectors representing sound-generating activities (mining, oil and gas exploitation, military, shipping, fisheries, marine renewable energy, etc.) or impacted sectors (fisheries, tourism, environment, etc.) can facilitate awareness-raising, the sharing of information on the sources and impacts of anthropogenic underwater noise and the development and sharing of best practices for minimizing such impacts and addressing cumulative impacts. Since stakeholders may be dealing with very similar issues in different regions of the world, such cooperation could also provide cost benefits.

64. International cooperation has mostly taken the form of scientific workshops and expert groups, as well as conferences. These events have built capacity through

exchanges between experts working in different disciplines, including acousticians and biologists, as well as fostered greater communication between different stakeholders, including industry and regulators.

65. Besides information-sharing, the output of such events has included guidance and guidelines, including mitigation measures, covering certain sound-emitting activities, such as shipping, offshore wind farm development, recreational fisheries and dredging or specific species.

66. The need to compile toolboxes developed in different countries and tailor them to countries, taking into account their socioeconomic and cultural contexts, as well as available scientific and technical capabilities, has been noted. Other suggestions have included increasing awareness of environmental impact assessments and related guidelines in countries and regions where relevant legislations and/or guidelines addressing the issue are not available; engaging industries as well as non-governmental and other civil society organizations to assist developing countries in building local capacity to understand, prevent and control anthropogenic noise; requiring industries to involve academic or research institutions in their processes addressing noise; encouraging the development of academic courses in the field; and further developing best management practices.

67. In the light of the rapidly growing body of scientific knowledge regarding anthropogenic underwater sound, the sharing of information and data between scientists through scientific or academic networks is also critical. Information on additional peer-reviewed scientific studies may also be submitted to the Division, in accordance with relevant General Assembly resolutions. Some research projects have specifically included a capacity-building aspect.

68. Given their global outreach potential, web portals and webinars have proved as a useful tool for sharing knowledge and raising awareness. One example is Discovery of Sound in the Sea, a publicly funded website dealing with the science of sound.

69. Financing opportunities are available from various institutions for work on anthropogenic underwater sound. These include: the Ocean Acoustics programme of the United States Office of Naval Research, which supports basic research addressing fundamental understandings of the physics relating to underwater sound; the Acoustics Program of the United States National Oceanic and Atmospheric Administration Fisheries Office of Science and Technology, which funds research on examining the potential impacts of anthropogenic sound on marine animals; the European Metrology Programme for Innovation and Research, which has funded capacity-building projects aimed at developing metrological capacity in underwater acoustics; and the Exploration and Production Sound and Marine Life Joint Industry Programme of the International Association of

Oil and Gas Producers, which supports research to increase understanding of the effect on marine life of sound generated by oil and gas exploration and production activity.

70. In order to address anthropogenic underwater noise, the development and transfer of new alternative quieter technologies (see para. 51) will be essential, including for the benefit of developing countries, in accordance with Part XIV of the United Nations Convention on the Law of the Sea and taking into account the Criteria and Guidelines on the Transfer of Marine Technology of the Intergovernmental Oceanographic Commission. Sustainable Development Goal 14, in particular its target 14.a, and Sustainable Development Goal 17, in particular its targets 17.6 to 17.8, also provide an impetus in that regard.

71. Intergovernmental organizations competent to work on specific issues may serve as important forums for strengthening cooperation and coordination. These include IMO, FAO, the Convention on Biological Diversity, the Convention on the Conservation of Migratory Species of Wild Animals and the International Whaling Commission at the global level; and the Agreement on the Conservation of Cetaceans of the Black Sea, Mediterranean Sea and neighbouring Atlantic Area, the Agreement on the Conservation of Small Cetaceans of the Baltic, North East Atlantic, Irish and North Seas, the European Union, NATO, and the Convention for the Protection of the Marine Environment of the North-East Atlantic at the regional level (see Section III.A above). Industry groups, such as the World Organization of Dredging Associations and the International Association of Oil and Gas Producers, as well as civil society organizations such as OceanCare, have also organized events aimed at sharing information on anthropogenic underwater noise.

72. The General Assembly, which is the competent global institution to undertake an annual review of developments in ocean affairs and the law of the sea, provides a forum for cross-sectoral cooperation and coordination. In that context, the Informal Consultative Process can provide a platform to enhance cross-sectoral sharing of information, including on recent science, best practices and regulatory approaches. The Regular Process for Global Reporting and Assessment of the State of the Marine Environment, including Socioeconomic Aspects, could also play an important role in the distribution of relevant information and fostering the science-policy interface in relation to anthropogenic underwater noise through its second global integrated marine assessment.

73. UN-Oceans, the inter-agency mechanism that seeks to enhance the coordination, coherence and effectiveness of competent organizations of the United Nations system and the International Seabed Authority, could also facilitate the exchange of information regarding anthropogenic underwater noise among its participating members, including on policy and legal developments. A number

of UN-Oceans members are already active on this topic, as shown throughout the present report.

74. Cross-sectoral cooperation could also be implemented in the context of multi-stakeholder partnerships. In this regard, commitments relating to ocean noise were undertaken during the Ocean Conference, held in June 2017, including by the Government of the Netherlands, OceanCare, the Wildlife Conservation Society, the Convention on the Conservation of Migratory Species of Wild Animals, the Agreement on the Conservation of Cetaceans of the Black Sea, Mediterranean Sea and neighbouring Atlantic Area and the World Ocean Council.

V   Conclusions

75. Most human activities taking place in the ocean generate sound, either intentionally or as a by-product, and many of these activities provide socioeconomic, security and environmental benefits. At the same time, increased reliance on oceans for human activities has brought to our ocean a wide range of sounds, both impulsive and continuous, and increased noise levels.

76. In many instances, anthropogenic underwater noise is pervasive: whereas coastal areas and areas where more human activity takes place, such as shipping lanes, are most affected, some high-intensity sources of underwater sound, such as airguns, can be recorded over several thousand kilometres, including in areas with little human activity, thus making the effects of sound on marine life an issue of global significance.

77. Research has demonstrated that several marine species, including marine mammals, fish and invertebrates, can be affected by increased levels of sound, resulting in effects such as behavioural changes and physical and physiological effects. The people that rely on these species for livelihood could also be affected.

78. Addressing, in an effective manner, anthropogenic underwater noise will require raising awareness of the issue as well as filling in a number of research gaps to better understand the properties and propagation of sound in the marine environment and the way in which marine life is affected. This will require, inter alia, gathering baseline data, conducting further research on species other than marine mammals such as fish and invertebrates, modelling population and ecosystem-level consequences and further studying the interaction of noise with other pressures to better assess cumulative impacts.

79. The application of a precautionary approach has been called for at both global and regional levels and efforts have been undertaken to address sound at the source, for example by promoting the development of noise-quieting technologies and measures, or to mitigate its impacts by encouraging mitigation measures

such as environmental impact assessments and the use of area-based management tools, including the establishment of marine protected areas. Best practices are being identified, taking into account the need to balance socioeconomic activities with the protection and preservation of the marine environment.

80. International cooperation and coordination are essential components of efforts to address anthropogenic underwater noise and its impacts, in particular in view of the potential transboundary impacts. Cross-sectoral cooperation is also required to address cumulative impacts. This includes cooperation, at all levels, including to build or further strengthen scientific knowledge, capacity and mitigation approaches. Partnerships between States, industry, civil society and international organizations would also be beneficial, including in the context of assistance to developing countries to address capacity and technological challenges. At the global level, the General Assembly, including through the Informal Consultative Process, is well placed to foster greater international cooperation and coordination and stimulate further mitigation action, in support of the implementation of the United Nations Convention on the Law of the Sea, as well as the achievement of the commitments in the 2030 Agenda for Sustainable Development, in particular Sustainable Development Goal 14 and the declaration "Our ocean, our future: Call for action."

Annex: Overview of main sources of anthropogenic underwater noise

Sector	Sound source	Sound type	Source level (dB re 1 μPa at 1 meter)	Main energy (kHz)
Commercial shipping				
Medium-sized ships 50–100 m	Propeller/cavitation	Continuous	165–180[a]	<1
Large vessels (e.g. supertankers)	Propeller/cavitation	Continuous	180–219[a]	<0.2
Resource exploration and exploitation				
Oil and gas	Seismic airgun	Impulsive	220–262[c]	0.05–0.1
	Drilling	Continuous	124–190[a]	0.1–1
Renewable energy	Impact pile-driving	Impulsive	220–257[c]	0.1–2
	Operational wind farm	Continuous	144	<0.5

Sector	Sound source	Sound type	Source level (dB re 1 µPa at 1 meter)	Main energy (kHz)
Navy				
	Low frequency sonar	Impulsive	240[b]	0.1–0.5
	Mid-frequency sonar	Impulsive	223–235[b]	2.8–8.2
	Explosions (e.g. ship shock trials, exercises)	Impulsive	272–287[a]	0.006–0.02
Fishing				
	Propeller/cavitation	Continuous	160–198[a]	<1–10
	Deterrent/harassment device	Impulsive	132–200[b]	5–30
	Sonar (echo sounder)	Impulsive	185–210[b]	200–260
Dredging	Propeller/cavitation, cutting, pumping, grabbing, digging	Mainly continuous	163–188[a]	0.1–0.5
Marine scientific research (e.g., research vessel)	Propeller/cavitation	Continuous	165–180[a]	<1
Recreational activities (e.g., recreational craft/ speedboat)	Propeller/cavitation	Continuous	160–175[a]	1–10
Tourism (e.g., whale and dolphin watching and cruise ships) – vessels 100 m	Propeller/cavitation	Continuous	160–190[a]	<0.2–10
Harbour construction	Impact pile driving (e.g. sheet piling)	Impulsive	200[b]	0.1–0.5

a Sound pressure level.
b Peak sound pressure level.
c Peak-to-peak sound pressure level.

United Nations Convention on the Law of the Sea Report of the Twenty-Eighth Meeting of States Parties, 11–14 June 2018

Contents*

I. Introduction   697
II. Organization of Work   698
　A. *Opening of the Meeting and Election of Officers*   698
　B. *Adoption of the Agenda and Organization of Work*   699
III. Credentials Committee   699
　A. *Appointment of the Credentials Committee*   699
　B. *Report of the Credentials Committee*   700
IV. Matters Related to the International Tribunal for the Law of the Sea   700
　A. *Report of the Tribunal for 2017*   700
　B. *Financial and Budgetary Matters*   702
V. Information on the Activities of the International Seabed Authority   706
VI. Matters Related to the Commission on the Limits of the Continental Shelf   708
　A. *Information Reported by the Chair of the Commission*   708
　B. *Conditions of Service of the Members of the Commission*   712
　C. *Filling of a Vacancy in the Commission*   713
VII. Report of the Secretary-General under Article 319 of the United Nations Convention on the Law of the Sea   714
VIII. Other matters   719

I   Introduction

1. The twenty-eighth meeting of the Meeting of States Parties to the United Nations Convention on the Law of the Sea was held at United Nations Headquarters

---

*　Editors' Note. – This document was provided by the United Nations Division for Ocean Affairs and the Law of the Sea (DOALOS) and is extracted from the Report of the Twenty-eighth Meeting of States Parties, New York, 11–14 June 2017, SPLOS/324, 9 July 2018, available online: <http://www.un.org/depts/los/>.The document has been edited for publication in the *Ocean Yearbook*.

from 11 to 12 June 2018,[1] in accordance with article 319, paragraph 2 (e), of the United Nations Convention on the Law of the Sea[2] and paragraph 56 of General Assembly resolution 72/73.

2. The meeting was attended by representatives of States parties to the Convention and observers, including the International Seabed Authority, the Commission on the Limits of the Continental Shelf and the International Tribunal for the Law of the Sea.[34]

II Organization of Work

A *Opening of the Meeting and Election of Officers*

3. The President of the twenty-seventh meeting of the Meeting of States Parties, Helga Hauksdóttir (Iceland), opened the twenty-eighth meeting.
4. The Meeting observed a minute of silent prayer or meditation.
5. The Meeting elected Sven Jürgenson (Estonia) as President of the twenty-eighth meeting, by acclamation.
6. The Meeting elected Durga Prasad Bhattara (Nepal), Florian Botto (Monaco), Maria Alejandra Sande (Uruguay) and James Waweru (Kenya) as Vice-Presidents, by acclamation.

Statement by the Under-Secretary-General for Legal Affairs and United Nations Legal Counsel

7. In his statement,[4] the Under-Secretary-General for Legal Affairs and United Nations Legal Counsel underscored the critical role of the Convention in strengthening international peace and security and ensuring sustainable development of the oceans and seas, including with respect to target 14c of Sustainable Development Goal 14 of the 2030 Agenda for Sustainable Development. He welcomed the accession by Benin and Saint Kitts and Nevis to the Agreement for the

---

1   The meeting was scheduled to be held from 11 to 14 June 2018, but the States Parties completed their work on 12 June.
2   United Nations, *Treaty Series*, vol. 1833, No. 31363.
3   See rules 5, 18, 37 and 38 of the Rules of Procedure for Meetings of States Parties (SPLOS/2/Rev.4).
4   Statements submitted by delegations and speakers for circulation and relevant documents and information provided by the secretariat are available from https://papersmart.unmeetings.org/convention-treaty/los/sp-unclos/28th-meeting/programme. The list of participants at the meeting Parties is available from www.un.org/Depts/los/meeting_states_parties/twentyeighthmeetingstatesparties.htm.

Implementation of the Provisions of the United Nations Convention on the Law of the Sea of 10 December 1982 relating to the Conservation and Management of Straddling and Highly Migratory Fish Stocks,[5] as well as the ratification of the Agreement by Vanuatu. He also highlighted the significance of the convening by the General Assembly of an intergovernmental conference, under the auspices of the United Nations, to consider the recommendations of the Preparatory Committee established by the Assembly in resolution 69/292 on the elements and to elaborate the text of an international legally binding instrument under the United Nations Convention on the Law of Sea on the conservation and sustainable use of marine biological diversity of areas beyond national jurisdiction (see General Assembly resolution 72/249). Furthermore, he emphasized the significant workload of the Commission on the Limits of the Continental Shelf and the need for full membership in the Commission and full attendance by members at its sessions for its effective functioning. Regarding the conditions of service of the members of the Commission, he noted their need for medical and dental insurance coverage while fulfilling their duties at Headquarters and encouraged States parties to find practical solutions.

B   Adoption of the Agenda and Organization of Work

8.   The Meeting adopted the agenda (SPLOS/321) and, following consultations by the Bureau, approved the organization of work on the understanding that it could be adjusted as necessary to ensure the efficient conduct of the meeting. In doing so, the Meeting deferred the consideration of the note by the secretariat on the participation of intergovernmental organizations in the meetings of the Meeting of States Parties as observers (SPLOS/320) to the twenty-ninth meeting.

III   Credentials Committee

A   Appointment of the Credentials Committee

9.   On 11 and 12 June 2018, pursuant to rule 14 of the Rules of Procedure for Meetings of States Parties (SPLOS/2/Rev.4), the Meeting appointed a Credentials Committee consisting of the following States parties: China, Finland, Ghana, Lesotho, Myanmar, Norway and Ukraine.[6]

---

5   United Nations, *Treaty Series*, vol. 2167, No. 37924.
6   Rule 14 provides that the Credentials Committee "shall consist of nine States Parties"; however, nominations for the appointment of the members of the Committee were received from only four regional groups.

10. The Credentials Committee held its meeting on 12 June 2018. It elected Øyvind Hernes (Norway) as Chair and Daryna Horbachova (Ukraine) as Vice-Chair, by acclamation.

B *Report of the Credentials Committee*

11. On 12 June 2018, the Chair of the Credentials Committee introduced an advance unedited version of the report of the Committee (subsequently issued as SPLOS/323 and SPLOS/323/Corr.1). He stated that the Committee had examined and accepted the credentials of representatives of 112 States parties to the twenty-eighth meeting, of which 70 had been found to be in due form. Provisional information concerning the appointment of representatives of States parties participating in the twenty-eighth meeting, including representatives of the European Union, had been received from 42 States parties on the understanding that formal credentials would be communicated to the secretariat as soon as possible.

12. The Meeting approved the report of the Credentials Committee on the understanding that the credentials would continue to be valid, in accordance with rule 1 of the Rules of Procedure, until the convening of the twenty-ninth meeting (see SPLOS/263, para. 101). The Meeting also accepted, on the same understanding, credentials[7] and information concerning the appointment of representatives[8] received after the report had been approved, bringing the total number of States parties participating in the Meeting, including the European Union, to 119.

IV Matters Related to the International Tribunal for the Law of the Sea

A *Report of the Tribunal for 2017*

13. The President of the Tribunal, Judge Jin-Hyun Paik, introduced the annual report for 2017 (SPLOS/317)4 and provided an overview of the activities of the Tribunal and the work carried out during its forty-third and forty-fourth sessions, which had been devoted to legal, judicial, organizational and administrative matters.

---

7 From Algeria, Argentina, Barbados, Brazil, Chile, Croatia, Cuba, Dominica, India, Indonesia, Kenya, Kuwait, Latvia, Madagascar, Malaysia, Morocco, Nepal, Panama, the Republic of Moldova, Senegal, Slovenia, Spain, Sweden, Togo, Trinidad and Tobago and the United Kingdom of Great Britain and Northern Ireland.
8 From the Democratic Republic of the Congo, Namibia and Zambia.

He also provided information on developments of the work of the Tribunal that had taken place in 2018 before the present meeting.

14. The President reported that the seven judges elected at the twenty-seventh meeting of the Meeting of States Parties had begun their terms of office on 1 October 2017. Subsequently, on 2 October 2017, the judges had elected Judge Jin-Hyun Paik as President of the Tribunal and Judge David Joseph Attard as Vice-President, for a term of three years. On 4 October 2017, Judge Albert Hoffman was elected President of the Seabed Disputes Chamber.

15. The President described in detail the work of the Tribunal on judicial matters during 2017, drawing attention to the wide range of substantive and procedural issues.

16. With regard to the judgment in the Dispute Concerning Delimitation of the Maritime Boundary between Ghana and Côte d'Ivoire in the Atlantic Ocean (Ghana/Côte d'Ivoire), the President noted that the Special Chamber had delimited the territorial sea, the exclusive economic zone and the continental shelf, including the continental shelf beyond 200 nautical miles, between the two parties. It had also addressed issues concerning the obligations set out in article 83, paragraph 3, of the Convention. He expressed the view that the judgment represented a significant contribution to jurisprudence on maritime delimitation, building on the decision of the Tribunal in the Dispute concerning delimitation of the maritime boundary between Bangladesh and Myanmar in the Bay of Bengal (Bangladesh/Myanmar), and highlighted the flexibility of the procedures of the Tribunal in resolving disputes concerning the law of the sea.

17. The President also informed the Meeting that, further to the judgment of the Tribunal on the objections to jurisdiction and admissibility raised by Italy, the merits phase of the M/V "Norstar" Case (Panama v. Italy) had resumed and the parties had submitted written proceedings on the merits in 2017 and 2018. He added that public hearings were expected to be held in September 2018.

18. The President drew attention to capacity-building initiatives undertaken by the Tribunal, including its eleventh programme on dispute settlement under the Convention, organized with support from the Nippon Foundation, the internship programme and the annual summer academy organized by the International Foundation for the Law of the Sea, as well as a regional workshop on the settlement of disputes held in Cabo Verde in May 2018 with the financial support of the Korea Maritime Institute and the China Institute of International Studies. The President also noted the special trust funds established with the support of the China Institute of International Studies, the Government of China and the Korea Maritime Institute, to provide financial assistance for participants from developing countries in the internship programme and the summer academy.

Of additional note was the public outreach activities of the Tribunal, including a round-table discussion for members of the legal community on the arrest and detention of vessels, held in March 2018.

19. The President referred to the upcoming intergovernmental conference on an international legally binding instrument under the Convention on the conservation and sustainable use of marine biological diversity of areas beyond national jurisdiction and indicated that, with more than 20 years of experience in the settlement of disputes under the Convention, the Tribunal would be well suited to the settlement of disputes concerning the interpretation or application of a future instrument on the conservation and sustainable use of marine biological diversity of areas beyond national jurisdiction.

20. In the ensuing discussions, several delegations highlighted the significant contribution of the Tribunal in advancing peace and security, the rule of law and the development of international jurisprudence concerning the law of sea, as well as the efficiency of its proceedings. The role of the Tribunal in maritime delimitation cases and in the adjudication of cases concerning the arrest and detention of vessels was highlighted. Several delegations also expressed the wish that the Tribunal would be more actively utilized by States parties. A delegation noted the integrity and authority of the Convention and the need to fully respect the exercise of State autonomy by States parties regarding the resolution of disputes.

21. Delegations welcomed the Judgement in the Dispute concerning Delimitation of the Maritime Boundary between Ghana and Côte d'Ivoire in the Atlantic Ocean. Several delegates expressed appreciation for the ongoing work of the Tribunal in the M/V "Norstar" Case (Panama v. Italy).

22. Several delegations noted the capacity-building programmes of the Tribunal, including the internship programme, regional workshops and summer training courses, and expressed the need for support from States parties for such activities. Delegations also expressed gratitude to the Tribunal for fostering dialogue with the academic world and those working in the field of maritime affairs.

23. The Meeting took note of the report of the Tribunal for 2017.

B *Financial and Budgetary Matters*

1 Report on Budgetary Matters for the Financial Periods 2015–2016 and 2017–2018

24. The Registrar of the Tribunal introduced the report on budgetary matters for the financial periods 2015–2016 and 2017–2018 (SPLOS/318), covering the matters outlined below.

(a) Cash Surplus for the Financial Period 2015–2016

25. The Registrar outlined the information contained in Section I of the report, recalling, in particular, that, as at 31 December 2017, the cash surplus for the financial period 2015–2016 was negative (– €183,676) and thus no funds could be surrendered to States parties at this stage. He noted that the negative cash surplus was not the result of budget overspending, but the implementation of the Financial Regulations and Rules of the Tribunal, which required unpaid contributions for the period 2015–2016 and previous financial periods to be deducted from the provisional cash surplus. He underscored the importance of timely payments of contributions by States parties, failing which the Tribunal could be faced with a problem of liquidity and would have to make use of the Working Capital Fund.

26. While noting with satisfaction that the overall expenditures for the financial period 2015–2016 represented approximately 99 per cent of the total appropriations, several delegations expressed their concern that the cash surplus for the financial period 2015–2016 was negative owing to the elevated level of unpaid contributions. They called upon all States parties to honour their commitments and pay contributions in full and on time and urged the Tribunal to continue its efforts to collect outstanding contributions.

27. In response, the Registrar noted that, while some payments of outstanding contributions had been received in 2017, the outstanding contributions for 2015–2016 and previous financial periods remained high, amounting to approximately €658,964 at the end of 2017.

(b) Provisional Performance Report for 2017

28. The Registrar outlined the information contained in Section II of and annex II to the report, recalling, in particular, that the total expenditure for 2017 provisionally stood at €8,967,272, representing 86.08 per cent of the appropriations allocated for that year and 94 per cent of the appropriations, when considering only recurrent expenditures. He further pointed out that a slight overrun in the budget line for communications in 2017 would be considered in the use of that budget line in 2018 to avoid any overexpenditure for the biennium.

29. Several delegations noted with satisfaction the high performance rate and the fact that the Tribunal could make savings within its approved budget. They commended the Registrar for sound budget management and encouraged him to continue efforts for the effective and efficient use of financial resources based on sound budget principles and a zero-growth approach, while keeping in mind the need for the Tribunal to efficiently perform its functions.

30. Responding to a question relating to the budgetary allocations under case-related costs that were not spent in 2017, the Registrar noted that the provisional savings were largely due to the absence of urgent proceedings. He further noted that the provisional savings could be absorbed by the end of the biennium, depending on the caseload of the Tribunal, and that any cash surplus would be surrendered to States parties in accordance with the Financial Regulations and Rules of the Tribunal.

(c) Report on Action Taken Pursuant to the Financial Regulations and Rules of the Tribunal

31. The Registrar referred to Section III of the report on budgetary matters for the financial periods 2015–2016 and 2017–2018 (SPLOS/318) regarding the investment of funds of the Tribunal, the trust fund for the law of the sea, the Nippon Foundation trust fund, the China Institute of International Studies trust fund and the twentieth anniversary trust fund.

32. A delegation recalled its financial contributions to the trust fund for the law of the sea and the twentieth anniversary trust fund and called upon other Member States and the private sector to make contributions to support the activities of the Tribunal.

33. The Registrar underlined the importance of the trust funds for financing all capacity-building activities and internship programmes of the Tribunal.

34. The Meeting took note, with satisfaction, of the report on budgetary matters for the financial periods 2015–2016 and 2017–2018 (SPLOS/318).

2 Draft Budget Proposals of the Tribunal for the Financial Period 2019–2020

35. The Registrar introduced the draft budget proposals of the Tribunal for the financial period 2019–2020 (SPLOS/2018/WP.1). At the outset, he noted that the budget proposals regarding recurrent expenditures followed an overall zero-growth approach compared with the equivalent value in euros of the budget for 2017–2018. A new provision was proposed as non-recurrent expenditure to prepare for the implementation of the International Public Sector Accounting Standards (IPSAS). The Registrar also underlined that the proposed budget for case-related costs was €696,800 lower than the appropriation approved for 2017–2018, owing to the expected volume of judicial work during the next budget period. With regard to the judges' pension scheme, the Registrar reported a further decrease of €28,500 in the draft budget line "Pension in payment." Overall, he noted that the proposed budget in the amount of €20,521,200 represented

a decrease of €598,700 compared with the budget approved for the 2017–2018 period (see SPLOS/301, para. 1).

36. In the ensuing discussions, several delegations expressed their appreciation for the efforts of the Tribunal to streamline the budget through cost optimization and reduction and noted with satisfaction that the decrease in the proposed budget for 2019–2020 would lead to a decrease in the assessed contributions of States parties for the next two years. In that connection, those delegations stressed that the point of departure in budget discussions should be zero nominal growth, while recognizing that some expenses, such as case-related costs, were beyond the control of the Tribunal. The Registrar was encouraged to continue making savings whenever possible and to ensure the optimal use of resources.

37. Several delegations expressed concern over the increase in the pension scheme for retired judges of the Tribunal. It was suggested that the matter be discussed at a future meeting, including an estimation of costs. The Registrar, referring to the decision on pension scheme regulations for members of the Tribunal adopted by the Meeting of States Parties at its ninth meeting (SPLOS/47), noted that a pension scheme for members of the Tribunal was in place and financed through the general budget of the Tribunal and that, once a plateau had been reached, the fluctuation of the budgetary allocations to pensions would be reduced. He acknowledged the request to provide more information on the issue at the twenty-ninth meeting of the Meeting of States Parties.

38. A delegation encouraged the Registrar to further streamline and avoid duplications in drafting future budget proposal documents. While welcoming the confirmation that the Tribunal was not seeking additional funding for its Working Capital Fund for 2019–2020, the delegation requested the Registrar to review the reference, in the budget document, to the practice at the United Nations of crediting its working capital fund up to an amount corresponding to 8 per cent of its annual budget. The Registrar assured that he would review the matter in the light of the current practice of the United Nations. He further added that in addition to the regular Working Capital Fund, which stood at €542,118, the Tribunal maintained a separate Working Capital Fund (case-related), which stood at €767,014, to meet unforeseen expenses relating to new cases.

39. Responding to a question, the Registrar noted that the proposed new provision relating to the implementation of IPSAS was non-recurrent and would cover most costs relating to the implementation of IPSAS, but with the possibility of limited additional costs to be covered in future financial periods.

40. Following a brief meeting of the Open-ended Working Group on Financial and Budgetary Matters under the chairmanship of the President, the Meeting adopted, without a vote, a decision (SPLOS/322) in which it approved the amount of €20,521,200 as the budget of the Tribunal for the financial period 2019–2020,

which represented the budget as proposed by the Tribunal in the amount of €20,549,700 (see SPLOS/2018/WP.1, annex I), minus the amount of €28,500 by which the draft budget line "Pension in payment" had further decreased, as indicated by the Registrar in his report to the Meeting (see para. 35 above).

V Information on the Activities of the International Seabed Authority

41. The Secretary-General of the Authority provided information on the activities carried out by the Authority since the twenty-seventh meeting.

42. He encouraged all coastal States to fulfil their obligation to deposit charts or lists of geographical coordinates of points concerning the outer limits of their continental shelf not only with the Secretary-General of the United Nations, but also with the Secretary-General of the Authority pursuant to article 84, paragraph 2, of the Convention, drawing attention to the fact that only eight States parties had done so to date. He also encouraged landlocked developing countries to become party to the Convention, as that would allow them to become ipso facto members of the Authority and benefit from the Agreement relating to the implementation of Part XI of the United Nations Convention on the Law of the Sea of 10 December 1982.[9] In that connection, he pointed out that 18 States parties had not yet ratified the Agreement.

43. The Secretary-General of the Authority noted that the number of parties to the Protocol on the Privileges and Immunities of the International Seabed Authority[10] had increased by four, but urged all members of the Authority to join the Protocol, as called for by the General Assembly in its annual resolution on oceans and the law of the sea. He also appealed to States parties that were in arrears to pay their contribution, noting with concern that the amount of arrears had increased to almost $2.7 million. A total of 51 States parties were now in arrears for two or more years, resulting in a suspension of their voting rights pursuant to article 184 of the Convention.

44. In terms of ongoing major developments, the Secretary-General of the Authority noted that the first periodic review of the international regime of the Area, conducted pursuant to 154 of the Convention, had been presented to the Assembly of the Authority at its twenty-third session, in 2017, and a resolution containing over 20 recommendations had been adopted. A draft strategic plan would be tabled for consideration by the Assembly at its twenty-fourth session, in 2018.

---

9   United Nations, *Treaty Series*, vol. 1836, No. 31364.
10 Ibid., vol. 2214, No. 39357.

A revised schedule of meetings in 2018 and 2019 had already been prepared. A trust fund had also been established to defray the cost of participation of members of the Council of the Authority from developing States and the response to the fund had been positive. In contrast, the Voluntary Trust Fund for the participation of members of the Finance Committee and the Legal and Technical Commission from developing countries faced insufficient funds to meet all expected requests for the upcoming session.

45. With respect to the development of the Mining Code, the Secretary-General of the Authority noted progress on the different elements of the Code, which had been circulated for stakeholder consultation in 2017 and was subject to ongoing consideration by the Council and the Commission of the Authority. He noted the assistance of experts at the Massachusetts Institute of Technology in developing a working model for the Authority for the financial terms for future exploitation contracts.

46. The Secretary-General of the Authority indicated that the Council had endorsed a strategy for the development of regional environmental management plans under the auspices of the Authority for priority areas where exploration activities were taking place (ISBA/24/C/3). He noted that a workshop had been held in China to initiate the development of a regional environmental management plan in the North-West Pacific Ocean and that a forthcoming workshop in Poland would discuss the developments of plans for polymetallic sulphides deposits on mid-ocean ridges. Those developments, he suggested, illustrated the importance of not undermining the mandate and work of the Authority, including in the context of the upcoming intergovernmental conference.

47. In the ensuing discussions, many delegations expressed ongoing support and appreciation for the work of the Authority. Several delegations stressed, in particular, the contribution of the Authority to the Sustainable Development Goals, including ending poverty in all its forms, promoting inclusive and sustainable growth and combating climate change, in addition to the conservation and sustainable use of the oceans, sea and marine resources for sustainable development.

48. Many delegations welcomed the continuing work of the Authority in the development of a comprehensive regulatory framework for the exploitation of marine minerals in the Area, including wider engagement with stakeholders and collaboration with experts on the development of a payment mechanism and financial model. It was noted in that context that the Massachusetts Institute of Technology draft model should include the costs on biodiversity and damage to the environment. Several delegations noted in that regard the need to achieve balance between ensuring protection of the marine environment and economic development as well as commercial feasibility. The need to ensure that activities

in the Area were carried out for the benefit of mankind as a whole, as provided for in Part XI of the Convention, including the importance of specific and operational benefit-sharing mechanisms, was also emphasized. Some delegations stressed the need to take proper account of the views of contractors.

49. The work of the Authority regarding regional environmental management plans was welcomed by many delegations, A delegation pointed out that the Authority could be a leader in this area.

50. Several delegations also highlighted the first review of the Authority under article 154 of the Convention and noted progress in the implementation of the related recommendations, including the revised schedule of meetings, which would facilitate dialogue between the Legal and Technical Commission and the Council and contribute to the finalization of the exploitation regulations. Appreciation was also expressed by many delegations for the draft strategic plan and several delegations underlined the open and inclusive manner of the related consultations.

51. Several delegations highlighted the increased activity undertaken by the Authority to raise awareness of its work and increase capacity-building, including through workshops and seminars. In that regard, a delegation noted challenges in engaging in all intersessional activities and suggested that the outputs should be incorporated in the formal work of the Authority and considered and discussed by the Council. Another delegation announced its financial support for a workshop organized by the Authority to foster cooperation in the development of deep seabed resources and the blue economy in Africa.

52. Several delegations expressed concern over the issue of arrears. Several delegations urged greater attendance at meetings of the Authority and welcomed the establishment of a new trust fund. Norway pledged to donate $60,000 to the Voluntary Trust Fund for the participation of members of the Finance Committee and the Legal and Technical Commission from developing countries.

53. The Meeting took note of the information reported by the Secretary-General of the Authority.

VI   Matters Related to the Commission on the Limits of the Continental Shelf

A   *Information Reported by the Chair of the Commission*

54. The Chair of the Commission, Yong Ahn Park, made a statement[4] providing information on the activities of the Commission since the twenty-seventh meeting

(see SPLOS/319),[11] including regarding membership, consideration of submissions and draft recommendations, working arrangements and the workload and conditions of service of its members.

55. The Chair reported that, in response to the concerns expressed by some submitting States during the twenty-seventh meeting (see SPLOS/316, para. 58), the Commission had revisited and improved its internal working methods (see SPLOS/319, para. 10). The Chair also drew the attention of the Meeting to the importance of full membership in the Commission and attendance at its session for the Commission to carry out its work in the most efficient manner. In the ensuing discussion, many delegations expressed appreciation and support for the work of the Commission since its establishment, especially in light of the challenges faced with respect to its high workload and working conditions. Several delegations highlighted the importance of the work of the Commission for the implementation of the Convention in general and for coastal States in particular. Several delegations also noted, with appreciation, the high quality of services rendered by the Division for Ocean Affairs and the Law of the Sea of the Office of Legal Affairs as the secretariat of the Commission. A delegation welcomed the new members of the Commission who had been elected at the twenty-seventh meeting of the Meeting of States Parties and noted with appreciation their contributions.

56. Many delegations noted with appreciation the measures taken by the Commission to improve its working methods following the discussions at the twenty-seventh meeting, in particular, for the subcommissions to provide more regular and comprehensive reports on their progress. They welcomed that approach as it would contribute to the coherence and transparent work of the Commission and its subcommissions and reduce or eliminate instances where recommendations approved by the Commission departed substantially from draft recommendations prepared by its subcommissions.

57. With regard to the increasing workload of the Commission, several delegations noted with appreciation that the Commission would continue to implement the measures proposed at the twenty-sixth meeting for the five-year term of its current mandate (see SPLOS/303, para. 84), including its decision to meet for 21 weeks per year. A number of delegations supported the Commission in its decision to proceed as quickly as possible through the backlog of submissions in a timely manner, without compromising the high standards of consideration

---

11   Detailed information on the work of the Commission during its forty-fourth, forty-fifth and forty-sixth sessions is contained in documents CLCS/100, CLCS/101 and CLCS/103 and CLCS/103/Corr.1, respectively.

of all relevant data and information submitted by coastal States. A delegation welcomed the Commission's decision to take up new submissions when the examination of those under consideration needed to be suspended while the submitting States gathered additional data and information, to ensure that the Commission made maximum use of its sessions.

58. Recalling the resources spent by submitting States in the preparation of submissions, a number of delegations stressed the need for timely consideration of those submissions in view of the challenges, especially for developing States, in the maintenance of institutional memory and relevant software. They urged the Commission, its subcommissions and the secretariat to continue to explore options to enable the Commission to operate efficiently and effectively in view of its growing workload.

59. A delegation suggested that the Commission also explore other measures to improve efficiency and reduce delays in the consideration of submissions, such as establishing common practices for dealing with recurring issues and increasing predictability for coastal States in terms of requests for data and information. Another delegation emphasized the need for submitting States to cooperate with the Commission to facilitate consideration of submissions, such as by avoiding the unnecessary classification of data and information as confidential.

60. Some delegations expressed their views concerning submissions currently before the Commission. A delegation elaborated on its view regarding the interpretation and the challenges in applying of the Statement of Understanding Concerning a Specific Method to be Used in Establishing the Outer Edge of the Continental Margin annexed to the Final Act of the Third United Nations Conference on the Law of the Sea.

61. Another delegation noted with appreciation the emphasis placed by the Commission on deferring the consideration of submissions involving disputes in accordance with its rules of procedure. A third delegation noted that the issue of maintaining data confidentiality was important for the work of the Commission and expressed concern over reports of the breach of rules of procedure concerning confidentiality.

62. During the discussion of matters relating to the conditions of service of the members of the Commission, many delegations expressed support for improving the working conditions of the Commission. They noted the concerns expressed by the Commission, including regarding the need for medical insurance for all its members. Those delegations recognized that further efforts were needed to ensure that the Commission could perform its mandate effectively, given its high level of expertise.

63. In that context, several delegations noted that the Commission, owing to its exceptional character, had special requirements for working space, as recognized

by the General Assembly (see resolution 72/73, para. 101). Many delegations also took note of the concerns expressed by the Commission regarding the need for additional resources to update software, address security issues and update information and communications technology facilities to allow for secured means of communication. It was suggested that further information was needed regarding those matters. A delegation urged the Secretary-General to take appropriate measures within existing resources to further strengthen the capacity of the secretariat of the Commission in order to enhance its support and assistance.

64. Many delegations underscored that it was critical for the Commission to have full membership and attendance at its meetings to carry out its work in the most efficient manner. A number of delegations noted the concerns expressed by the Commission that the vacant seat had a detrimental effect on its workload and ability to reach a quorum. Some delegations suggested that alternative means be explored to fill the vacancy if the Group of Eastern European States was unable to nominate possible candidates.

65. In response to the statements by delegations, the Chair conveyed the sincere appreciation of the Commission for the words of encouragement and support from States parties.

66. The secretariat provided information on the status of the two trust funds that it administered in relation to the Commission. With regard to the voluntary trust fund for the purpose of defraying the cost of participation of the members of the Commission on the Limits of the Continental Shelf from developing States in the meetings of the Commission, the Meeting was informed that contributions had been received from Canada, China, Costa Rica, Iceland, Ireland, Japan, New Zealand, Portugal and the Republic of Korea since the previous meeting and that the balance, as at the end of May 2018, was approximately $334,663. The two remaining sessions of 2018 were projected to cost approximately $285,000, on the assumption that the same number of members would request assistance as in the previous session. That would imply that, at the end of 2018, the balance would be approximately $50,000. Without additional contributions, it would not be possible for the secretariat to provide financial assistance for members of the Commission from developing States to participate in sessions of the Commission in 2019, including reimbursement of medical travel insurance (see General Assembly resolution 72/73, para. 99). The secretariat recalled the appeal of the General Assembly for further financial contributions to be made to the trust funds to enable the Commission to fulfil its mandate with full membership, a call that was echoed by some delegations.

67. With regard to the voluntary trust fund for the purpose of facilitating the preparation of submissions to the Commission on the Limits of the Continental Shelf for developing States, in particular the least developed countries and small

island developing States, in compliance with article 76 of the United Nations Convention on the Law of the Sea, the Meeting was informed that, since the previous meeting, six developing States had received assistance to cover the travel and daily subsistence allowance costs associated with meeting with the Commission. The balance of the trust fund, as at the end of May 2018, was approximately $1,077,220.

68. A number of delegations pledged to make or stated that they had made contributions to the trust fund to support the members of the Commission from developing States to attend the meetings of the Commission.

69. Several delegations expressed their appreciation to States parties for making or pledging contributions to the trust funds to support developing States with resource constraints. Several delegations also underlined the need for contributions to support the full participation of all members of the Commission to attend meetings.

70. The secretariat provided information on the compilation of an updated directory of sources of training, advice and expertise and technological services that might contribute to the preparation of submissions to the Commission. In a note verbale dated 8 May 2018, the Office of Legal Affairs had renewed the request for States to inform the Division for Ocean Affairs and the Law of the Sea of any suitable sources of expertise as soon as possible. The Division expressed its appreciation to those States that had responded with information and invited other States that were in a position to do so to contact the Division at their earliest convenience.

71. The Meeting took note of the information reported by the Chair of the Commission and provided by the secretariat.

B *Conditions of Service of the Members of the Commission*
Report of the Open-Ended Working Group

72. The Co-Coordinators of the Open-Ended Working Group on the Conditions of Service of the Members of the Commission, Anastasia Strati (Greece) and James Waweru (Kenya), reported that they had convened an informal meeting during the intersessional period with representatives of coastal States that had nominated members to the Commission in order to continue consideration of the issue of medical insurance of the members of the Commission. At that meeting, delegations had reviewed the results of the internal survey of the members of the Commission (See SPLOS/319, paras. 15–27) and the updated information provided by the Health and Life Insurance Section of the Department of Management. A second meeting with the nominating coastal States had been held on the margins of the first day of the twenty-eighth meeting.

73. During the twenty-eighth meeting, the Working Group continued to consider issues relating to the conditions of service of the members of the Commission, in particular medical insurance coverage, and received additional information from the secretariat and a representative of the insurance industry on short-term medical insurance options. During those consultations, Mr. Waweru informed the Working Group that he would not be in a position to continue to serve as a co-coordinator and that informal consultations were being conducted to identify his successor.

74. Following the consultations of the Working Group and, on the basis of a proposal by the Co-Coordinators, the Meeting took note of the report by the Co-coordinators and decided that the Working Group would continue to work intersessionally and consider issues relating to the conditions of service of the members of the Commission, in particular medical insurance coverage, with the intention of assisting progress on these matters during the seventy-third session of the General Assembly, including by providing specific proposals to Meeting of States Parties at its twenty-ninth meeting. The secretariat was further requested to provide updated information on health insurance arrangements for members of other bodies in the Organization.

75. The Meeting also decided to renew its request to the General Assembly that the Secretary-General be authorized, as an interim measure and subject to the availability of funds in the trust fund, following the allocation of the required funds to cover the costs of travel and daily subsistence allowance of the members of the Commission from developing States for the sessions of the Commission, to reimburse members from developing countries for the cost of medical travel insurance and short-term medical insurance on a session-by-session basis and subject to a reasonable limit that the Secretary-General shall determine on the basis of the information regarding medical travel insurance available to him.

76. A delegation expressed its appreciation to the Co-Coordinators of the Working Group and the representative of the insurance industry who attended the informal consultations for the information provided.

C   *Filling of a Vacancy in the Commission*

77. The President recalled that the Meeting of States Parties had not been in a position at its twenty-seventh meeting to elect all 21 members of the Commission, as the Group of Eastern European States, which was entitled to three seats under the Convention, as also set out in the arrangement for the allocation of seats on the International Tribunal for the Law of the Sea and the Commission on the Limits of the Continental Shelf approved by the Meeting of States Parties at its nineteenth meeting (see SPLOS/201), had only put forward two nominations.

78. Having received no nominations to fill the vacancy, the Meeting reverted to consideration of the matter at its twenty-eighth meeting.

79. The delegation of Croatia, in its capacity as Chair of the Group of Eastern European States, indicated that consultations within that group were continuing. A delegation noted the necessity of resolving this long-standing issue and suggested the need for pragmatic solutions, without prejudice to the stipulation in annex II, article 2(3) of the Convention that "not less than three members shall be elected from each geographical region."

80. The President underscored the need to ensure that the Commission operated with full membership and encouraged the Group of Eastern European States to continue its consultations.

81. The Meeting subsequently decided that, if the Group of Eastern European States informed the President by 24 September 2018 that candidate(s) had been identified, a new call for nominations would be circulated by the Secretary-General. A resumed session of the twenty-eighth meeting would then be convened to conduct a by-election before the forty-eighth session of the Commission, subject to the approval of the General Assembly. If no candidates were identified by the Group of Eastern European States by that deadline, the Secretary-General would circulate a call for nominations with a view to conducting elections at the twenty-ninth meeting of the Meeting of States Parties. A by-election would then be conducted at the twenty-ninth meeting only if the President received information about potential candidates no less than 14 weeks prior to the commencement of that meeting. In the absence of such information, the Meeting would revert to the consideration of that matter under the agenda item "Commission on the Limits of the Continental Shelf."

VII Report of the Secretary-General under Article 319 of the United Nations Convention on the Law of the Sea

82. The Meeting considered the annual reports of the Secretary-General on oceans and the law of the sea (A/72/70/Add.1 and A/73/68), which had been submitted to States parties pursuant to article 319 of the Convention. Delegations expressed their appreciation to the Secretary-General and to the Division for Ocean Affairs and the Law of the Sea for the useful and comprehensive reports.

83. Several delegations reaffirmed that the Convention sets out the legal framework within which all activities in the oceans and seas must be carried out. The importance of international cooperation and more effective coordination in its implementation was also noted. Some delegations underlined the delicate balance between rights and obligations achieved in the Convention

and the increased number of parties to the Convention and its implementing Agreements. A delegation highlighted the key role played by the Convention in maintaining international peace and security and reinforcing friendly relations among States.

84. A number of delegations stressed the importance of the oceans in achieving sustainable development, including in contributing to poverty alleviation and eradication, food security, employment, health, gender equality and empowerment of women. A number of delegations recognized the importance of implementing the declaration entitled "Our ocean, our future: call for action" adopted by the United Nations Conference to Support the Implementation of Sustainable Development Goal 14: Conserve and sustainably use the oceans, seas and marine resources for sustainable development, held from 5 to 9 June 2017. A delegation noted the 2020 deadline for four targets under Sustainable Development Goal 14 and emphasized the need for urgent action to achieve those targets.

85. The importance of the conservation and sustainable use of marine biological diversity was emphasized and many delegations expressed support for the upcoming intergovernmental conference (see para. 7 above). A delegation emphasized the view that biological diversity and resources in areas beyond national jurisdiction should be considered as the common heritage of mankind and clearly acknowledged in the future instrument.

86. Several delegations highlighted the importance of fisheries for food security and expressed concern that overfishing and illegal, unreported and unregulated fishing, combined with other factors, were threatening those resources. A delegation called upon States to implement General Assembly resolution 72/72 on sustainable fisheries. Another delegation called for a prohibition on certain forms of fisheries subsidies that contributed to overcapacity, overfishing and illegal, unreported and unregulated fishing.

87. A delegation pointed out that anthropogenic underwater noise had grown due to increased human activities and had repercussions on communication, feeding and reproduction of marine species. Many delegations drew attention to the work of the United Nations Open-ended Informal Consultative Process on Oceans and the Law of the Sea and welcomed the topic of focus of its nineteenth meeting, anthropogenic underwater noise. Some delegations called for additional research on the topic of focus and the creation of a forum or forums for scientists, policymakers and relevant experts and stakeholders to exchange and share their knowledge and experiences.

88. The need to enhance scientific knowledge of the marine environment was highlighted by many delegations. In that context, attention was drawn to the importance of the Regular Process for Global Reporting and Assessment of the State of the Marine Environment, including Socioeconomic Aspects, and recent

developments thereunder, including the successful adoption of the outline of the second world ocean assessment and the timetable and implementation plan for its completion. The work of the Group of Experts and regional workshops in support of the Process were highlighted. A delegation also welcomed the proclamation of the United Nations Decade of Ocean Science for Sustainable Development (2021–2030) (see General Assembly resolution 72/73, para. 292). Some delegations acknowledged the role of other international organizations and bodies, such as the Intergovernmental Oceanographic Commission of the United Nations Educational, Scientific and Cultural Organization and bodies established by the Convention on Biological Diversity, in promoting marine scientific research and ensuring that the conduct of marine scientific research was undertaken without prejudice to the protection and preservation of the marine environment.

89. A number of delegations expressed concern about the state of the oceans and called for increased commitment to the protection and preservation of the marine environment and to addressing plastic pollution in the ocean. The role of the Convention in that regard was highlighted. Several delegations expressed the view that greater use should be made of area-based management tools and environmental impact assessments.

90. Many delegations highlighted the importance of addressing the effects of climate change on the oceans and noted the particular vulnerability of developing States. Attention was drawn by a delegation to the inextricable interlinkage between capacity-building and climate finance in the global response to climate change. Another delegation noted ongoing capacity-building activities to assist small island developing States in addressing climate change, including activities related to climate change adaption and mitigation and avoidance of climate displacement. That delegation stressed the need for the progressive development of international law to protect the rights of coastal States in respect of maritime zones in the face of sea-level rise.

91. Several delegations expressed their deep concern about the unsafe migration of people by sea and highlighted their commitment to addressing that issue in different forums, including in the ongoing negotiations on the Global Compact for Safe, Orderly and Regular Migration.

92. Several delegations stressed the importance of ensuring maritime safety and security, including by addressing piracy and other criminal activities at sea. Some delegations noted the rise in security risks that resulted from maritime criminal activities, which affected all States and required collective international action, including capacity-building and other assistance. Several delegations noted the resurgence of incidents of piracy and called upon States to address its root causes, including illegal, unreported and unregulated fishing in certain

maritime zones of Africa. Attention was further drawn to the Charter on Maritime Security and Safety and Development in Africa, adopted by members of the African Union in Lomé in 2016 with a view to establishing a road map for maritime security on the continent.

93. Some delegations highlighted specific challenges in their maritime zones, such as the impact of marine pollution, including marine debris, plastics and microplastics, and stressed the need for action, including through national and regional initiatives, to reduce marine debris, plastics and microplastics and designate new marine protected areas.

94. Some delegations also described strategies relating to the promotion of marine scientific research; strengthening the management of coastal and marine activities through integrated coastal zone management and marine spatial planning; strengthening the management of fishery resources and combating illegal, unreported and unregulated fishing; becoming parties to relevant global and regional instruments; and the revision or adoption of new policies and legislation consistent with the Convention. Several delegations drew attention to the proclamation of the Decade of African Seas and Oceans (2015–2025) and the designation of 25 July as the African Day of the Seas and Oceans by the Assembly of the African Union.

95. Several highlighted the importance of strengthening the capacity of States to implement the provisions of the Convention and related instruments so that they could benefit from the oceans and its resources. In that context, several delegations underscored the importance of financing, partnerships, development of science and research and transfer of technology for developing countries, in particular the least developed countries, landlocked developing countries, small island developing States and coastal African States. Some delegations noted their ongoing assistance and capacity-building activities for developing States. Several delegations drew attention to initiatives undertaken by intergovernmental organizations, such as the International Maritime Organization (IMO) and the International Hydrographic Organization. Several delegations reiterated their call upon the International Seabed Authority to continue its efforts to build the capacity of developing States in deep-sea research and technology through contractor training programmes and the endowment fund for marine scientific research in the Area.

96. Some delegations expressed their views with regard to specific maritime regions. A delegation stated that its country had been unlawfully excluded from exercising its maritime rights by the temporary occupation and activities of another State which grossly violated the Convention. That delegation, referring to arbitration proceedings it had initiated under annex VII to the Convention, stressed that it was set to take further reasonable steps to resolve the dispute by

peaceful and legal means in order to restore the lawful legal regime contained in the Convention. Another delegation responded, asserting that it operated in strict compliance with the rules of international law, including the Convention, to ensure the safety of navigation in relevant maritime areas and regulated other activities in that area, in particular, the exploration and exploitation of resources.

97. With regard to the South China Sea region, a delegation highlighted the need for States to resolve maritime disputes by peaceful means in accordance with international law and refrain from any action which might complicate matters or escalate tensions. It called upon all States parties to fully comply with the Convention, to respect diplomatic and legal processes, to promote peaceful and sustainable use of seas and oceans and to refrain from conducting unilateral acts. Another delegation expressed the view that the Meeting was not a proper forum to consider that matter. It highlighted the continuing improvement of the situation in the South China Sea and noted that the issue was being resolved through negotiations and consultations between the countries directly concerned. Both delegations highlighted the joint efforts made by relevant parties in the region to achieve long-term peace, stability and development, including the start of negotiations on a code of conduct in the South China Sea.

98. A delegation drew attention to the fragmented mechanisms for review of the implementation of the Convention. It noted that, although the Meeting did not have the function of conducting general reviews of the implementation of the Convention, it had acted as the institution dealing with overall issues under the Convention and was the right institution for such a review. An observer delegation noted that article 319 of the Convention was not intended to, and did not, empower the Meeting to perform general or broad reviews of general topics of interest or to engage in interpretation of the provisions of the Convention.

99. Speaking as an observer, the delegation of IMO reported on important developments since the previous meeting of the Meeting of States Parties, including the adoption by IMO of an initial strategy on the reduction of greenhouse gas emissions from ships, described as the biggest achievement by IMO in the protection of the marine environment during the reporting period. It also noted the adoption of a vision statement for the first time at the thirtieth session of the IMO Assembly, which stated, inter alia, that "IMO will focus on review, development and implementation of and compliance with IMO instruments in its pursuit to proactively identify, analyse and address emerging issues and support Member States in their implementation of the 2030 Agenda for Sustainable Development." The delegation also drew attention to new developments concerning fraudulent registration of ships and the regulation of autonomous vessels.

100. Also speaking as an observer, the delegation of the Food and Agriculture Organization of the United Nations (FAO) highlighted the need to give priority to

the conservation and sustainable use of marine living resources of the world's oceans, including fish stocks and associated biodiversity. It noted that, amid rising fish consumption, the world's marine fish stocks had not improved, despite notable progress in some areas, and indicated that 30 per cent of fish stocks were estimated to be fished at biologically unsustainable levels. It noted that illegal, unreported and unregulated fishing represented up to 26 million tons of fish caught annually, valued at $10 billion to $23 billion, and posed one of the biggest threats to the sustainability of the marine ecosystems. It stressed that the Convention was the cornerstone of the international legal framework for ocean governance and fisheries management and was the point of departure for most, if not all, binding and voluntary international fisheries instruments, including the Voluntary Guidelines on Catch Documentation Schemes and the FAO Agreement on Port State Measures.

101. The Meeting took note of the reports of the Secretary-General under article 319 and the views expressed by delegations under that agenda item and decided that the same agenda item would be included in the provisional agenda of its twenty-ninth meeting.

VIII   Other Matters

Trust Funds

102. The secretariat provided information on the current status and projected funding requirements of the trust funds administered by the Division for Ocean Affairs and the Law of the Sea, Office of Legal Affairs, other than those related to the work of the Commission, which were considered under agenda item 10 (see paras. 66 and 67 above).

103. With regard to the voluntary trust fund to assist States in the settlement of disputes through the International Tribunal for the Law of the Sea, the secretariat informed the Meeting that a contribution had been received from the Philippines and an application received from Panama since the previous meeting. As at the end of May 2018, the fund had an approximate balance of $156,000.

104. Regarding the voluntary trust fund for the Regular Process for Global Reporting and Assessment of the State of the Marine Environment, including Socioeconomic Aspects, contributions had been received from Ireland, New Zealand and the Republic of Korea since the previous meeting. As at the end of May 2018, the trust fund had an approximate balance of $155,000.

105. With respect to the Hamilton Shirley Amerasinghe Memorial Fellowship on the Law of the Sea, contributions to the trust fund had been received from Ireland,

Monaco and Sri Lanka since the previous meeting. As at the end of May 2018, the fund balance available for disbursement, taking into account the cost of the 2018 fellowship and programme support costs, was not sufficient to award a standard fellowship for 2019, unless additional contributions are received by November 2018.

106. Regarding the voluntary trust fund for the purpose of assisting developing countries, in particular least developed countries, small island developing States and landlocked developing States, to attend meetings of the United Nations Open-ended Informal Consultative Process on Oceans and the Law of the Sea, a contribution had been received from New Zealand since the previous meeting. The secretariat observed that the trust fund was expected to be nearly depleted after the nineteenth meeting of the Informal Consultative Process, during which funding could only be provided to panellists.

107. Regarding the voluntary trust fund for the purpose of assisting developing countries, in particular the least developed countries, landlocked developing countries and small island developing States, to attend the meetings of the preparatory committee and the intergovernmental conference on the development of an international legally binding instrument under the United Nations Convention on the Law of the Sea on the conservation and sustainable use of marine biological diversity of areas beyond national jurisdiction, contributions had been received from Estonia, Ireland and New Zealand. As at the end of May 2018, the trust fund had an approximate balance of $82,000. The secretariat observed that, given the strong demand for assistance from the trust fund, it would likely not be in a position to provide assistance to all applicants for the upcoming session of the intergovernmental conference, to be held in September 2018.

108. The secretariat expressed its gratitude to all States that had made contributions to the trust funds and reiterated that the chronic underfunding of many of them was a serious problem. In that connection, the secretariat drew attention to General Assembly resolution 72/73, in which the Assembly encouraged Member States, international financial institutions, donor agencies, intergovernmental organizations, non-governmental organizations and natural and juridical persons to contribute to the various trust funds.

109. The secretariat provided information on the contributions procedure, noting that clear instructions from donor States as to the trust fund to which any contribution was being made would allow for more timely availability of funds. The Office of Legal Affairs would be sending a communication to all States in that regard and to encourage contributions to all trust funds administered by the Division.

110. The Meeting took note of the information on trust funds that had been provided by the secretariat.

Acknowledgments

111. The President of the twenty-eighth meeting of the Meeting of States Parties expressed his appreciation to the interpreters, translators and conference officers for their assistance and services provided during the Meeting, as well as to the staff of the Division for Ocean Affairs and the Law of the Sea.

Report on the Work of the United Nations Open-ended Informal Consultative Process on Oceans and the Law of the Sea at Its Nineteenth Meeting, 18–22 June 2018

*Letter dated 3 July 2018 from the Co-Chairs of the Informal Consultative Process addressed to the President of the General Assembly**

Pursuant to General Assembly resolution 72/73, we were appointed as the Co-Chairs of the nineteenth meeting of the United Nations Open-ended Informal Consultative Process on Oceans and the Law of the Sea.

We have the honour to submit to you the attached report on the work of the Informal Consultative Process at its nineteenth meeting, which was held at United Nations Headquarters from 18 to 22 June 2018. The outcome of the meeting consists of our summary of issues and ideas raised during the meeting, in particular with regard to the topic of focus "Anthropogenic underwater noise."

In line with past practice, we kindly request that the present letter and the report be circulated as a document of the General Assembly under item 78 (a) of the preliminary list.

(*Signed*) Pennelope Althea Beckles
Kornelios Korneliou
Co-Chairs

Co-Chairs' Summary of Discussions[1]

1. The United Nations Open-ended Informal Consultative Process on Oceans and the Law of the Sea held its nineteenth meeting from 18 to 22 June 2018. Pursuant to General Assembly resolution 71/257, as recalled in resolution 72/73, the meeting focused its discussions on the topic "Anthropogenic underwater noise."

---

* Editors' Note.—This document was provided by the United Nations Division for Ocean Affairs and the Law of the Sea (DOALOS) and is extracted from the United Nations General Assembly, Seventy-third session, UN Document A/73/124, 9 July 2018, available online: <http://www.un.org/depts/los/>. The document has been edited for publication in the *Ocean Yearbook*.

1 The summary is intended for reference purposes only and not as a record of the discussions.

2. The meeting was attended by representatives of 47 States, 11 intergovernmental organizations and other bodies and entities, and eight non-governmental organizations.[2]

3. The following supporting documentation was available to the meeting: (a) report of the Secretary-General on oceans and the law of the sea, which relates to the topic of focus of the nineteenth meeting of the Informal Consultative Process (A/73/68); and (b) format and annotated provisional agenda of the meeting (A/AC.259/L.19). The full texts of the contributions to the report of the Secretary-General relating to the topic of focus along with the compilation of peer-reviewed scientific studies on the impacts of ocean noise on marine living resources, submitted pursuant to paragraph 107 of General Assembly resolution 61/222, were made available on the website of the Division for Ocean Affairs and the Law of the Sea.

Agenda Items 1 and 2

Opening of the Meeting and Adoption of the Agenda

4. The Co-Chairs, Pennelope Althea Beckles Permanent Representative of Trinidad and Tobago to the United Nations, and Kornelios Korneliou, Permanent Representative of Cyprus to the United Nations, appointed by Miroslav Lajčák, President of the seventy-second session of the General Assembly, opened the meeting.

5. Opening remarks were made by the Under-Secretary-General for Legal Affairs and United Nations Legal Counsel, Miguel de Serpa Soares and the Assistant Secretary-General for Economic Development and Chief Economist, Department of Economic and Social Affairs, Elliot Harris, on behalf of the Secretary-General.

6. The meeting adopted the format and annotated provisional agenda and approved the organization of work.

Agenda Item 3

General Exchange of Views

7. A general exchange of views took place at the plenary meetings on 18 and 21 June. Delegations highlighted the importance of the Informal Consultative Process, paying particular attention in their statements to the topic of focus,

---

2   A list of participants is available on the website of the Division for Ocean Affairs and the Law of the Sea at http://www.un.org/Depts/los/index.htm.

"Anthropogenic underwater noise" (paras. 10–34 below). The discussions on the topic of focus within the panel segments are reflected in paragraphs 35 to 100 below.

8. Delegations recognized the primary role of the Informal Consultative Process in integrating knowledge, exchanging opinions and coordinating among multiple stakeholders and competent agencies, as well as enhancing awareness of various topics related to oceans, including emerging issues. Many delegations expressed continued support for the role of the Informal Consultative Process in promoting coordination among competent agencies and enhancing awareness of topics relating to oceans, including emerging issues, while promoting the three main pillars of sustainable development: social, economic and environmental. In that regard, several delegations expressed support for the renewal of the mandate of the Informal Consultative Process. Several delegations underscored the need to continue to strengthen and improve its effectiveness as a unique forum for comprehensive discussions on issues related to oceans and the law of the sea.

9. Appreciation was expressed to those who had contributed to the voluntary trust fund for the purpose of assisting developing countries, in particular least developed countries, small island developing States and landlocked developing States, in attending meetings of the Informal Consultative Process. Several delegations urged States to continue to contribute to the voluntary trust fund to foster the widest possible participation and make the process most meaningful and inclusive, as well as promote capacity-building. The Director of the Division for Ocean Affairs and the Law of the Sea provided an update on the status of the Voluntary Trust Fund and underlined its very limited available funds. She reiterated that the General Assembly, in its resolution 72/73, had expressed its continued serious concern regarding the lack of resources available in the trust fund and had urged that additional contributions be made.

Topic of Focus

10. In his remarks delivered on behalf of the President of the seventy-second session of the General Assembly, the Vice-President of the session, Omar Hilale (Morocco), noted the environmental and socioeconomic impacts of anthropogenic underwater noise. He underscored the need to invest more in order to better understand the issue and to bridge knowledge gaps, especially through capacity-building. Emphasizing the need for more integrated action and for further advocacy and outreach, the Vice-President noted that, in the light of the commitments that had been made by the United Nations to the health of the oceans, including resolutions on bottom fishing and the adoption of the 2030 Agenda

for Sustainable Development, including Sustainable Development Goal 14, the United Nations was the forum in which to build momentum in relation to anthropogenic underwater noise.

11. Many delegations expressed appreciation for the report of the Secretary-General on oceans and the law of the sea (A/73/68), which was considered to be comprehensive and to provide a solid basis for discussions.

12. Many delegations also welcomed the topic of focus as timely. They expressed concern over potential social, economic and environmental impacts of anthropogenic underwater noise, as the growth of ocean-related human activities had resulted in increased sound in many parts of the ocean. Some delegations observed that anthropogenic underwater noise could be intentional as well as unintentional and could be produced from a variety of sources, such as shipping, seismic surveys and the use of airguns, explosions, industrial activities, sonar, military testing, drilling and dredging. A view was expressed that not all sound introduced into the ocean environment by humans was harmful or would have deleterious effects on marine life. Moreover, sound also resulted from critical human activities such as navigation, scientific research, energy exploration and maritime security.

13. The impacts of anthropogenic ocean noise on specific marine species and ecosystems were highlighted by several delegations, including impacts on marine mammals, fish in general and migratory species. Several delegations noted that higher levels of anthropogenic underwater noise were affecting the abilities of marine species to rely on sound for critical life functions. The negative impacts of anthropogenic noise upon marine life referred to by delegations included inducing changes in the behaviour and migratory routes of species, disrupting communication, displacing animals from feeding and breeding grounds and causing stress, injury and death. A delegation recalled that in his report, the Secretary-General had indicated that negative impacts had been identified for at least 55 marine species. A number of delegations highlighted particular species within their maritime zones, including endangered species, that were at risk of harm from anthropogenic underwater noise.

14. The importance of addressing the socioeconomic impacts of anthropogenic underwater noise was underscored by many delegations, including impacts on tourism, fishing, transportation, the provision of goods and services, livelihoods and food security. Some delegations also recognized the importance of the topic for artisanal fishing and coastal communities, indigenous peoples and their cultural heritage.

15. The continuing gaps in knowledge and lack of data with respect to anthropogenic underwater noise and the urgent need for further research in this area were emphasized by many delegations. Some delegations highlighted the need

for further research into the sources of the noise and its impact on marine biodiversity in general. Several delegations stressed the importance of understanding how anthropogenic underwater noise affected fish, as decreases in stocks could further undermine the sustainability of fisheries. Many delegations also underlined the importance of studying the cumulative impacts on ocean ecosystems of the noise and other stressors, such as climate change, and the interplay of such stressors with the noise and related socioeconomic impacts.

16. Several delegations emphasized the importance of introducing, during the conduct of research, a multi-species approach within priority areas to quantify the spatial distribution and behavioural changes of species. In addition, those delegations also suggested that comprehensive baseline studies and long-term monitoring to track future changes in anthropogenic underwater noise would be of great value and that acoustic data be included in global ocean observing systems. They also proposed the establishment of in-situ acoustic listening stations. The importance of long-term observations in different parts of the ocean was stressed, as well as the need for enhanced cooperation and coordination and capacity-building. A delegation suggested that the identification of areas for further research on the topic of focus be achieved as an outcome of the meeting.

17. Several delegations provided examples of research being undertaken at the regional and national levels. In addition, several delegations highlighted a regional initiative to study noise from shipping using real-time noise sensors to monitor sound levels on a continuous basis. A number of delegations indicated that studies had been conducted in their countries to provide a better understanding anthropogenic underwater noise and its effects on the marine environment, including on marine mammals and fish movements, to inform policy decisions. The importance of the science-policy interface was stressed. Reference was made to the role of the Regular Process for Global Reporting and Assessment of the State of the Marine Environment, including Socioeconomic Aspects and the information provided in the First Global Integrated Marine Assessment on the effects of the noise on marine biota. It was noted that the second world ocean assessment, to be completed in 2020, would build on the baseline set out in the first assessment and evaluate trends.

18. Many delegations highlighted the need for effective implementation of the United Nations Convention on the Law of the Sea, which sets out the legal framework within which all activities in the oceans and seas must be carried out. A delegation noted that any measures developed in the future to address anthropogenic underwater noise would need to be in accordance with the duties, rights and freedoms provided for in the Convention.

19. Many delegations recalled the obligation under the Convention to protect and preserve the marine environment while respecting the rights and freedoms

enshrined therein. Other obligations in Part XII of the Convention were also referred to, including article 197. Many delegations expressed the view that anthropogenic underwater noise was a form of marine pollution and recalled the relevant provisions of the Convention, including articles 1 and 194. Several delegations noted that the European marine strategy framework directive included noise under its definition of pollution.

20. Furthermore, many delegations pointed out that anthropogenic underwater noise, as a form of pollution, was covered by Sustainable Development Goal 14, target 14.1 of the 2030 Agenda. Several delegations also underscored the importance more generally of addressing the effects of the noise for the implementation of the 2030 Agenda, in particular Sustainable Development Goal 14.

21. Several delegations highlighted various management approaches that could be used to address anthropogenic underwater noise, including greater use of area-based management tools and environmental impact assessments. The importance of an ecosystem approach was also underlined. Several delegations proposed creating a detailed map of the distribution of economically and ecologically important marine species, especially endangered species, as well as the establishment of marine protected areas for habitats and for migratory routes of marine species sensitive to this noise. Quiet zones along migratory corridors were also proposed by several observer delegations. Some delegations noted that the cumulative impacts of noise-generating activities should be taken into account in the conduct of environmental impact assessments.

22. A number of delegations emphasized the importance of the precautionary approach in the light of the data and knowledge gaps. A delegation highlighted the need for a participatory approach. Some delegations also considered that the "polluter pays" principle was applicable.

23. A view was expressed that it was necessary to incentivize approaches to mitigate anthropogenic underwater noise. A delegation noted that economic incentives could contribute to mitigation action by encouraging noise mitigation technology and the introduction of "quiet ships." An observer delegation noted that, in the shipping industry, improvements in addressing energy efficiency and biofouling could have beneficial spillover effects for anthropogenic underwater noise.

24. Delegations also emphasized the need to raise awareness of anthropogenic underwater noise through action in intergovernmental processes. Several delegations referred to the General Assembly resolutions on oceans and the law of the sea and on sustainable fisheries that already addressed the issue. It was suggested by an observer delegation that the General Assembly could characterize the noise as a serious form of transboundary pollution to be mitigated and addressed in its resolutions. Another observer delegation proposed that

the General Assembly encourage States to make use of the Guidelines on Environmental Impact Assessments for Marine Noise-generating Activities of the Convention on the Conservation of Migratory Species of Wild Animals. Several observer delegations proposed that anthropogenic underwater noise should be recognized as transboundary pollution to be addressed under Sustainable Development Goal 14. A delegation suggested the development of guidelines to regulate economic activities that create the noise.

25. Many delegations recognized the important work undertaken by competent international organizations on anthropogenic underwater noise. In that context, reference was made to the Guidelines for the Reduction of Underwater Noise from Commercial Shipping to Address Adverse Impacts on Marine Life of the International Maritime Organization (IMO); the Convention on the Prevention of Marine Pollution by Dumping of Wastes and Other Matter and its Protocol; the initial IMO strategy on reduction of greenhouse gas emissions from ships; the guidelines for the control and management of ships' biofouling to minimize the transfer of invasive aquatic species; the Code on Noise Levels on Board Ships under the International Convention for the Safety of Life at Sea; and other IMO measures, including routing measures and particularly sensitive sea areas. Reference was also made to the guidelines on environmental impact assessments for marine noise-generating activities of the Convention on the Conservation of Migratory Species of Wild Animals, as well as the role of the Conference of the Parties to the Convention on Biological Diversity and the role of the International Whaling Commission, including in convening expert workshops on the effects of anthropogenic underwater noise and in sharing information regarding the impacts of the noise on marine biodiversity.

26. Several delegations indicated that they had adopted a regional directive that required the development of marine strategies to achieve "good environmental status" by 2020, ensuring that the introduction of energy, including underwater noise, was at levels that did not adversely affect the marine environment. They had also established a working group on the implementation of the directive.

27. A number of delegations highlighted national actions to address anthropogenic underwater noise. Some delegations indicated that they had developed regulations and guidelines to minimize the risk of acoustic harm associated with seismic surveys. A delegation indicated that it had adopted legislation related to the minimization of harm caused by the noise, and another highlighted how its environmental code of practice set out the guidelines for minimizing the risk of injury and disturbance to marine mammals from seismic surveys, permitting seismic activities only when visual mitigation using observers was possible and requiring the use of the lowest practicable power levels. A delegation stated that it had adopted an ocean noise strategy which would guide its Government's work for the next decade. Another delegation stated that its ocean protection

plan contained both mandatory and voluntary measures, including the provision of financial incentives as indicated in paragraph 24 above. Some delegations stated that they had established monitoring systems for anthropogenic underwater noise.

28. Some delegations highlighted their participation in global, regional and sectoral bodies which had addressed the topic of anthropogenic underwater noise.

29. Some delegations suggested that the effects of anthropogenic underwater noise could be addressed at the Intergovernmental Conference on an International Legally Binding Instrument under the United Nations Convention on the Law of the Sea on the Conservation and Sustainable Use of Marine Biological Diversity of Areas Beyond National Jurisdiction, in order to consider the recommendations of the preparatory committee established by the General Assembly pursuant to resolution 69/292 on the elements and to elaborate the text of such an international legally binding instrument. An observer delegation suggested addressing noise in the context of area-based management tools, including marine protected areas and providing for the possibility of establishing "quiet zones." The observer delegation also proposed devising a robust and transparent environmental impact assessment process that would also apply to activities that generate the noise and would address cumulative impacts.

30. Delegations underlined the need for concerted international action to assess and mitigate the effects of anthropogenic underwater noise in all ocean areas, owing to the interconnected nature of the ocean and the transboundary nature of the impacts of the noise. Several delegations also highlighted the importance of international cooperation to enhance research and the collection of data, in particular in data-deficient regions.

31. The need to develop cross-sectoral coordination was also underscored. Delegations also underlined a need for increased cooperation and collaboration between States, intergovernmental organizations and civil society to improve responses to anthropogenic underwater noise. Furthermore, the need for effective cooperation and coordination at the global level was emphasized and the role of the General Assembly in supporting such cooperation and coordination was highlighted in that regard. A delegation also indicated a possible role for UN-Oceans.

32. It was also suggested that there was a need for different types of cooperation to allow for the most robust and comprehensive partnerships, allowing for enhanced sharing of best practices and the best available technologies. The development of toolboxes, as noted by the Secretary-General in his report (A/73/68, para. 66), was considered useful while giving due consideration to divergence across regions. All relevant global and regional organizations, Member States and civil society were encouraged to share their knowledge and exchange experiences.

33. The urgent need for capacity-building and transfer of knowledge and marine technology to address knowledge gaps and uncertainties and alleviate the negative impacts of anthropogenic underwater noise and the importance of cooperation to that effect was underlined by several delegations. Several delegations specifically emphasized the need for capacity-building activities and initiatives to assist developing States in sustainably managing marine resources, developing management strategies, building national programmes to monitor and study the possible effects of anthropogenic underwater noise and making well-informed policy decisions. Several delegations pointed out that, in order to achieve that, financial assistance and transfer of technology should be carried out under the principle of common but differentiated responsibilities. The importance of ensuring the transfer of knowledge to small island developing States, least developed countries and landlocked developing States was also highlighted.

Area of Focus: Anthropogenic Underwater Noise

34. In accordance with the format and annotated provisional agenda, the discussion panel on the topic of focus was organized in two segments structured around: (a) sources and environmental and socioeconomic aspects of anthropogenic underwater noise; and (b) cooperation and coordination in addressing anthropogenic underwater noise. The panellists gave presentations on the segments, after which interactive discussions were held.

1   Sources and Environmental and Socioeconomic Aspects of Anthropogenic Underwater Noise

Panel Presentations

35. In the first segment, the following gave presentations: Christopher Clark, Director and Imogene Johnson, Senior Scientist – Bioacoustics Research Program, Cornell University, provided a scientific overview of sound, its sources and how it is propagated underwater, highlighting the major sources of anthropogenic underwater noise; Richard Hale, Director, EGS Survey Group, and member of the International Cable Protection Committee, addressed underwater sounds from submarine cable and pipeline operations, noting that sound emission was limited to pre-installation surveying and installation; Lee Kindberg, Head of Environment, Health, Safety and Sustainability, Maersk Line in North America, provided information on shipping as a source of anthropogenic underwater

noise, highlighting mitigation options, such as vessel retrofits; Jill Lewandowski, Chief, Division of Environmental Assessment, Bureau of Ocean Energy Management, United States Department of the Interior, gave a presentation on the different sources of sound in offshore energy development, with a focus on oil, gas and wind; Larry Mayer, Director, School of Marine Science and Ocean Engineering and the Center for Coastal and Ocean Mapping, University of New Hampshire, provided an overview of anthropogenic underwater noise associated with sonar imaging and ocean mapping; Rudy Kloser, Commonwealth Scientific and Industrial Research Organisation, Australia, presented a general overview of the potential impacts of anthropogenic underwater noise on a range of species, from zooplankton to whales; Lindy Weilgart, OceanCare and the Department of Biology, Dalhousie University, discussed the impacts of anthropogenic underwater noise on invertebrates, fish, cetaceans and ecosystems in general; Jonathan Vallarta, Senior Underwater Acoustics Consultant, JASCO Applied Sciences, shared the results of a 2017 study conducted at Paradise Reef, Cozumel, Mexico, which recorded more than one month of continuous underwater acoustic data; Adrián Madirolas, Head, Hydroacoustic Research Office, National Institute of Fisheries Research and Development, Argentina, described how fish perceive sound and are impacted by anthropogenic underwater noise; Peter Tyack, University of St Andrews, addressed the challenges of predicting interactions of noise impacts with other stressors on marine species and ecosystems; Joseph Appiott, Associate Programme Officer, Secretariat of the Convention on Biological Diversity, presented the ongoing work by the Convention on the impacts of anthropogenic underwater noise, as well as the socioeconomic implications of those impacts; Nicolas Entrup, Ocean Policy Expert, OceanCare, presented on the socioeconomic and cumulative impacts of noise and the need to develop guidance for decision makers on the associated risks; and Andrew Carroll, Assistant Director of Marine and Antarctic Geoscience, Geoscience Australia, addressed the role of science in domestic policy-making on anthropogenic underwater noise and, drawing on case studies, described Australia's mitigation strategies relating to marine seismic surveys and provided an overview of Geoscience Australia's research on the impacts of anthropogenic underwater noise on marine fauna.

Panel Discussions

36. The discussions held after the presentations addressed various sources of anthropogenic underwater noise and their impacts on marine life, as well as research needs and potential measures to address the noise.
37. In response to a question, Ms. Kindberg stressed the need for caution in making the assumption that ships that were more energy-efficient were necessarily

more silent, noting that, to date, the observation referred to only one class of vessel. She highlighted that the most economical speed varied by type of vessel and propulsion system and that certain ships could be noisier at low speeds. She noted the need for further studies regarding optimal speeds for both energy efficiency and sound reduction.

38. A delegation enquired about the correlation between recommendations issued by the International Council for the Exploration of the Sea and progress towards ships that were more silent. Ms. Kindberg noted that naval architects took into account the relevant regulations and recommendations but that no information was available on the extent to which those were implemented.

39. In relation to anthropogenic underwater noise from ships, Ms. Kindberg addressed two questions on the economies achieved by retrofitting vessels to enhance energy efficiency. She highlighted reductions of 43 per cent since 2007 in energy consumption and carbon dioxide emissions per container per kilometre, but noted that the payback period depended on fluctuations in fuel costs.

40. In response to a question on the frequency at which cables had to be replaced, Mr. Hale clarified that telecommunications cables would usually be replaced every 20 to 25 years, while power cables lasted over 50 years. Pipelines had more variable life spans and would be chosen according to the expected time of depletion of offshore oil and gas reservoirs.

41. Addressing a question related to noise emissions from offshore energy, Ms. Lewandowski highlighted studies showing low levels of operational noise from offshore wind farms. A delegation noted that the frequency range of seismic airguns used in offshore energy surveying reached beyond 5 kHz, up to 100–150 kHz, and that dolphins showed disturbance many kilometres away.

42. With regard to ocean mapping, a question was asked about the cost and availability of seafloor mapping technology for developing countries. Mr. Mayer indicated that the cost of equipment ranged from tens of thousands of dollars for smaller sonars to between $1 million and $2 million for larger ones, in addition to installation and operating costs, which would amount to a total of several million dollars. He noted that the United Nations Environment Programme Global Research Information Database in Arendal, Norway, had assisted developing countries in collecting data to prepare submissions to the Commission on the Limits of the Continental Shelf. Several delegations stressed that the high cost associated with multibeam sonar mapping was prohibitive for many States.

43. A delegation underscored the importance of taking into account geophonic and biophonic background noise, which was location-specific, in addition to anthropogenic noise. Mr. Tyack observed that, although scientists had measured ocean sounds across many environments, it was challenging to identify the source of some sounds which are recorded in the ocean. It would be important

to research chronic anthropogenic underwater noise. Mr. Vallarta remarked that little was known about the biophony or geophony of coral reefs and that this would need to be further studied.

44. Addressing a question on whether existing capabilities allowed for the mapping of sensitive areas based on marine mammal locations and overlapping that information with noise sources, Mr. Mayer drew attention to ongoing research aimed at mapping ambient noise levels, tracking vocalizing marine organisms and capturing ship noise. He noted that while the technology existed, government support would be needed to follow up on the research results.

45. Mr. Clark noted the need for high-resolution sensing networks. He indicated that there were acoustically undersampled spaces in the ocean and that while large libraries of sounds existed, these were not sufficiently analysed. Mr. Mayer suggested using submarine cable networks to assist in getting the spatial coverage needed, noting, however, that the legal aspects of using cables for dual purposes would need to be addressed.

46. In response to a question concerning research on and trends in noise levels from shipping in the Atlantic, Mr. Clark clarified that while the ability to assess trends existed, there might not be consistency between measurements and model predictions depending on sampling resolutions. He noted that, on the basis of current research, the chances of causing direct physical injury to an animal by anthropogenic underwater noise were slim, as continuous exposure to levels of sounds which caused harm was rare. The chronic, long-term influence of the noise on marine life was, however, a cause for concern.

47. With regard to the impact of noise on marine mammals, a delegation stated that the long range of cetacean communication remained a theoretical concept. In response, Ms. Weilgart stressed that there were many levels to communication and that it was crucial for cetaceans to be able to hear and correctly interpret mating songs. Mr. Tyack observed that masking models needed to account for the ability of animals to compensate for variations in ambient noise by, for example, calling at a higher frequency. In response to a question regarding the sensitivity of whales to seismic airguns in the light of the lack of audiogram data, Mr. Carroll stated that a significant knowledge gap remained, but noted that passive acoustic monitoring could detect changes in movement of sperm whales. A delegation also noted that the reactions of humpback whales to marine seismic surveys within a three-kilometre range of seismic surveys had been observed. Mr. Clark referenced scientific papers indicating that whale ears were mechanically tuned towards low frequencies.

48. A delegation highlighted a mass stranding of melon-headed whales in Madagascar which, according to an independent scientific review panel, was most likely a behavioural response to an ocean mapping programme using sonar systems.

Ms. Lewandowski emphasized the need to understand the context and circumstances of such events. She noted that while the sound source itself may not be harmful to the whales, it was important to ensure that no animals were entrapped between the sound source and the shoreline. Mr. Mayer underscored the need for more independent research and peer reviews.

49. In response to a question, Ms. Lewandowski indicated that some research existed with respect to fish mortality in the proximity of airguns and explosions. Several delegations highlighted the importance of better understanding the impacts of noise on fish stocks, in particular on commercially important stocks, and the potential consequences for food security. A delegation encouraged regional fisheries management organizations and arrangements to engage on the issue. The role of the Food and Agriculture Organization of the United Nations in conducting research in the context of sustainable fisheries was also recognized and it was suggested that anthropogenic underwater noise be raised at the Food and Agriculture Organization of the United Nations Committee on Fisheries.

50. A delegation referred to the 2017 study highlighted by Mr. Kloser, Ms. Weilgart and Mr. Entrup in their presentations, which indicated that airgun operations had a negative impact on zooplankton. Mr. Kloser noted that there had been no previously documented long-range impact of seismic surveys on zooplankton, potentially highlighting the difficulties of conducting studies on the open ocean. He also observed that a recent modelling study did not demonstrate an alarming impact on the biome, but noted that measures to mitigate impacts of seismic surveys would be beneficial. Ms. Weilgart stressed that seismic surveys were conducted all over the globe and that there were limits to the ability of plankton to recover. She thus called for proceeding in a precautionary manner.

51. In response to a question on the availability of research on the potential impacts of anthropogenic underwater noise on other species, Ms. Weilgart pointed to studies on cephalods that showed extensive damage from low-frequency sound. However, she noted a gap in literature with respect to turtles, sharks and rays.

52. With regard to cumulative impacts, Ms. Weilgart and Mr. Kloser highlighted the need to consider the interaction of anthropogenic underwater noise with other stressors, but noted the challenge of predicting such impacts. In responding to an inquiry as to how a reduction in noise could foster climate resilience, Mr. Tyack observed that the focus should be on the stressors that could be most easily addressed to maintain healthy ecosystems. Ms. Weilgart concurred that noise was a stressor that could be immediately addressed and underscored the connection between certain noise sources, in particular shipping and seismic surveys, and climate change. She highlighted that measures that reduced the carbon footprint and emissions could also reduce underwater noise.

53. Mr. Tyack drew attention to a linkage between ocean acidification and underwater sound propagation, whereby acidification could increase the range of effect of underwater noise. However, there was uncertainty as to how acidification would impact the deep layer of the ocean, where most deep sound energy was concentrated. In response to a query concerning the potential breadth of application of the "dose-response" functions model, which was highlighted as a potentially useful tool to predict impacts, Mr. Tyack emphasized the broad range of responsiveness to stressors within a population. He also noted the importance of understanding the dose-response relationship for each stressor and how those stressors interacted.

54. Delegations recognized the need for further research to bridge knowledge gaps in respect of the sources and environmental and socioeconomic impacts of anthropogenic underwater noise. Noting that most research carried out to date had focused on the impacts of noise on higher trophic levels, several delegations enquired about research on lower trophic levels, including commercially important fish species and invertebrates. Ms. Lewandowski drew attention to recent research on the effects of sound mostly from pile-driving, vessels and airguns on invertebrates, fish and fisheries. She noted that the impacts on fish, fisheries and invertebrates had to be assessed as part of environmental impact assessments in the United States. Mr. Entrup noted that it was important to study the socioeconomic impacts of anthropogenic underwater noise on a global scale.

55. Noting that most of the activities related to offshore energy development occurred over the continental shelf, where the most important fishery grounds were located, several delegations asked about specific measures or best practices to mitigate impacts on fisheries from offshore energy development and multibeam sonar mapping. Ms. Lewandowski noted that while mitigation measures had been developed to reduce impacts on marine mammals, they also benefitted fish in the area. She stressed the lack of knowledge with respect to hearing ranges and the effects of sound on most species of fish and underlined the need for further research, including on the effects of newly developed quieting technologies. Ms. Lewandowski also noted that industry was cooperating with commercial fishers in the survey areas in trying to resolve their concerns.

56. A delegation emphasized that, while it was important to mitigate impacts on the marine environment, all sources of sound should be assessed separately, citing the example of seismic surveys in earthquake-prone areas as a critical activity. Ms. Weilgart indicated that even in the case of such critical activities, their impacts could be mitigated through, for example, the use of vibroseis.

57. In response to a question about the methodology of a study on the behavioural impact of anthropogenic underwater noise on scallops, Mr. Carroll pointed out

that the study demonstrated the importance of selecting a wide range of metrics and that a combination of both manipulative experiments and behavioural observations was needed for future studies. In response to a question concerning the details of studies conducted on the impact of seismic monitoring on sperm whales, Mr. Carroll explained how data were transmitted in real time and acoustic propagation modelling was used to estimate the potential range of impact on whales.

58. The role of Governments and the measures they could take to address anthropogenic underwater noise was also discussed. Ms. Weilgart, Mr. Kloser and Mr. Vallarta observed that simple measures that could assist in reducing the impact of noise on marine ecosystems were now technologically available. They emphasized that scientists could continue their efforts to bridge knowledge gaps, but that their ongoing research should not delay action to address noise.

59. A delegation cautioned that it could be difficult to detect and study all the effects of sound on species, especially long-term effects on long-living species. It therefore pointed out that the current evidence of approximately 130 species of marine animals impacted by anthropogenic underwater noise should suffice to put mitigation regulations in place without further delay.

60. In this regard, several delegations underscored the relevance of the precautionary approach, as reflected in principle 15 of the Rio Declaration on Environment and Development and article 6 and annex II to the Agreement for the Implementation of the Provisions of the United Nations Convention on the Law of the Sea of 10 December 1982 relating to the Conservation and Management of Straddling Fish Stocks and Highly Migratory Fish Stocks. Several delegations also recalled that the International Tribunal for the Law of the Sea in its advisory opinions had considered this approach part of customary international law. Those delegations concurred with the view expressed by some panellists that there was already sufficient information available for States to act.

61. A delegation noted that the presentations offered promising examples of sound source mitigation to anthropogenic underwater noise. Ms. Lewandowski noted that it was difficult to have laws requiring the use of technologies that were still not commercially available. She indicated that other possible options included prohibiting certain activities in areas known to host vulnerable species until adequate noise reduction and mitigation technologies had been developed. Mr. Madirolas proposed regulating the timing and location of seismic surveys to avoid conducting such surveys during sensitive seasons for migratory species of fish. Ms. Weilgart concurred, but noted that finding the right window for every species would be challenging. She also proposed implementing ship speed restrictions and rerouting ships to avoid travel over the continental shelf or along the continental slope where sound could reflect and propagate more strongly and thus harm marine life. Ms. Kindberg also suggested that Governments could

support research, assist stakeholders in utilizing relevant regulations and disseminate best practices.
62. Mr. Vallarta highlighted the need to review national legislation regulating environmental impacts, including anthropogenic underwater noise. Mr. Tyack noted the need for policymakers to drive the collection of data necessary to understand and regulate cumulative impacts.
63. Mr. Mayer added that no regulation yet existed on mitigation of anthropogenic underwater noise related to multibeam sonar and that more studies were needed for evidence-based decisions. He pointed out that nonetheless, certain mitigation measures were already being implemented, such as having marine mammal observers on board or commencing surveys at a lower power level and using ramp-up procedures, thus allowing animals to retreat.
64. Referring to the issue of standardization, a delegation highlighted the need for effective cooperation among States to address the issue of anthropogenic underwater noise. Ms. Kindberg stressed that Governments should encourage standardization, highlighting that various sectors had different ways of measuring, analysing and describing sound. Ms. Lewandowski noted that while the need for standardization had repeatedly been brought up at international conferences on ocean noise and that some progress had been made, the topic had not been prioritized owing to other research needs, including on the effects on species and limited resources. She emphasized that more needed to be done, in particular with the International Organization for Standardization (ISO). In this context, attention was drawn to the recently published ISO standard on underwater acoustics terminology (ISO 18405:2017). In response to observations by Mr. Carroll and Mr. Appiott that there was a need to develop common standards, metrics and terminology in respect of underwater noise, a delegation asked about progress in that area at the regional or global level. Mr. Carroll observed that Australia had developed standard monitoring techniques across several sampling platforms and was compiling national repositories of bathymetric data. He suggested that applying standard monitoring techniques to passive acoustics and measurements of sound could allow for comparisons of impacts and sound levels. Mr. Entrup encouraged States to make use of guidelines to promote unified approaches to data and to allow for a better understanding of the sources and impacts of anthropogenic underwater noise.
65. Several delegations also highlighted the relevance of tools such as environmental impact assessments and marine spatial planning in addressing underwater noise. It was noted that a better understanding of an area, including its ecological importance, should assist planners and policymakers in planning activities.
66. Several delegations stressed the importance of balancing human activities in the oceans with the need to protect the marine environment from the impacts of underwater noise. Mr. Tyack proposed that a decision-making process should

be established to reprioritize human activities in the oceans so as to minimize stress on the marine environment.

67. Participants also discussed the importance of communicating and disseminating information on sources and impacts of noise. Mr. Vallarta underlined the need for scientists to effectively communicate the results of their work, share information and educate relevant stakeholders. Ms. Weilgart also emphasized that, until the impacts of anthropogenic underwater noise were appreciated by noise-producing industries, the necessary technological changes to reduce those impacts would not occur.

68. A view was expressed that coastal communities needed to be engaged at the grass-roots level on the topic, in addition to engaging government decision makers. In that respect, a query was raised on how scientific studies could be meaningful for coastal communities and what specific actions such communities might take to reduce noise impacts from their activities. Ms. Weilgart referred to the link between ocean acidification and anthropogenic underwater noise, and noted that a reduction in run-off and effluent from coastal communities would make reefs more resilient to the effects of ocean acidification. It was also observed that while small boats contributed to underwater noise, certain boat motors had less of an impact than others and that managing overfishing would create more resilience in reefs. Mr. Vallarta suggested that navigation routes could be established to avoid reefs.

69. On the question of stakeholder involvement, Mr. Vallarta shared his experience in working with international counterparts, Mexican authorities and local communities in Cozumel, Mexico, in relation to his study at Paradise Reef. Mr. Kloser also emphasized the importance of stakeholder engagement for the effective implementation of management plans.

70. Mr. Entrup suggested comparing the best available technologies and best practices across countries, as well as providing incentives to promote the development, production and use of quieting technologies. Drawing upon noise reduction regulations in Germany, where the application of "best available technology" formed part of the review and assessment prior to providing a licence for pile-driving, Mr. Entrup suggested that such regulation could boost the development of noise reduction technologies and provide economic incentives for their use. Ms. Weilgart also emphasized the importance of economic incentives for stakeholder engagement, noting that such incentives would spur innovation.

71. It was suggested that the issue of anthropogenic underwater noise be mainstreamed into capacity-building on ocean issues. In response to a question, Mr. Appiott noted that a partnership coordinated by the Convention on Biological Diversity secretariat focused on supporting capacity-building for integrated management approaches to marine biodiversity, which in some cases related to issues of anthropogenic underwater noise.

Cooperation and Coordination in Addressing Anthropogenic Underwater Noise

Panel Presentations

72. In the second segment, the following gave presentations: Heidrun Frisch-Nwakanma, Coordinator, Memorandum of Understanding on the Conservation and Management of Marine Turtles and Their Habitats of the Indian Ocean and South-East Asia, Aquatic Species Team, secretariat of the Convention on the Conservation of Migratory Species of Wild Animals, gave an overview of the Convention guidelines, which provide guidance on environmental impact assessments to facilitate informed national decision-making on anthropogenic underwater noise; Stefan Micallef, Assistant Secretary-General, and Fredrik Haag, Head, Office for the London Convention/Protocol and Ocean Affairs at IMO, gave an overview of relevant IMO instruments, including the non-mandatory IMO underwater noise guidelines that provide advice on anthropogenic underwater noise to ship designers, shipbuilders and ship operators; Rebecca Lent, Executive Secretary, International Whaling Commission, gave an overview of its work on the noise, including recommendations aimed at reducing the impacts at the individual level and at the level of entire populations level through improved monitoring, data collection and research; René Dekeling, Co-Chair, Technical Group on Underwater Noise, European Commission, addressed the cooperation of the European Union in addressing anthropogenic underwater noise; Nathan Merchant, Co-Convenor, Convention for the Protection of the Marine Environment of the North-East Atlantic (OSPAR Convention) intersessional correspondence group on noise, highlighted the progress made under the OSPAR Convention framework in coordinating the monitoring, assessment, and management of underwater noise in the North-East Atlantic; Loúreene Jones, Manager, Ecosystems Management Division, National Environment and Planning Agency, Jamaica, introduced the management efforts of her agency relating to anthropogenic underwater noise and highlighted the need to address knowledge gaps and the need for capacity-building; Mariana Melcón, Group leader, bioacoustics research line, Fundación Cethus, presented the progress made by the organization in using bioacoustics to study anthropogenic underwater noise and its effects on marine mammals; Carrie Brown, Director, Environmental Programmes, Vancouver Fraser Port Authority, Canada, gave an overview of the enhancing cetacean habitat and observation programme, which aimed at better understanding and management regarding the impact of shipping activities on at-risk whales; Zo Lalaina Razafiarison, Programme General Coordinator, Ocean State Secretariat, Madagascar, described the challenges for tackling anthropogenic underwater noise in Madagascar and possible measures to address such challenges; René

Dekeling, representing the Ministry of Infrastructure and Water Management, Department for Marine and International Water Policy, The Netherlands, highlighted the need for international cooperation to manage the noise from the perspective of a small State; Véronique Nolet, Programme Manager, Green Marine, gave a presentation on a voluntary, multi-stakeholder reporting and certification initiative to address anthropogenic underwater noise from shipping activities; Howard Rosenbaum, Senior Conservation Scientist and Director, Ocean Giants Program, Wildlife Conservation Society, discussed the need for effective coordination and cooperation for mitigating anthropogenic underwater noise impacts, noting the need for a multidisciplinary collaborative effort to address the issue; Frank Thomsen, Senior Scientist and Sales Executive, DHI, representing the Central Dredging Association, addressed the role of industry in managing the impacts of the noise on marine life; Mark Tasker, Vice-Chair of the Advisory Committee of International Council for the Exploration of the Sea, provided an overview of the role and capacity of the Council related to the noise.

Panel Discussions

73. Some delegations observed that large knowledge gaps remained regarding sound levels, the spatial distribution of various sound sources and the possible effects of those sounds on various marine species. They also observed that more research and cooperation to develop standards for sound levels and noise reduction were needed.

74. Delegations welcomed the work of IMO in mitigating the impact of anthropogenic underwater noise from shipping activities. A delegation stressed the need to fill knowledge gaps and to evaluate the effectiveness of the IMO underwater noise guidelines prior to taking further action. In that regard, Mr. Micallef noted that no comprehensive assessments on noise had been conducted to date. Setting any target for further steps at present would be premature therefore owing to large knowledge gaps. Furthermore, the wide variety of ship types, sizes, speeds and operational characteristics added to the complexity of the issue. A delegation stressed the need to advance technical knowledge and design opportunities for quieter vessels, and also stressed the desirability of strengthening cooperation with classification societies in order to identify standards for different ship classes.

75. A delegation sought views on the possible use of the Energy Efficiency Design Index as a vehicle for developing standards to reduce anthropogenic underwater noise, given the relationship between that noise and the energy efficiency of ships. In response, Mr. Micallef observed that the impact of the Index was to be assessed by the IMO Marine Environment Protection Committee soon.

He referred to other relevant work of the IMO, including its biofouling guidelines and the initial IMO strategy on reducing greenhouse gas emissions from ships, which would require a shift from hydrocarbon engines to hydrogen fuel and hybrid engines. He noted that those efforts might entail collateral benefits for addressing anthropogenic underwater noise from ships.

76. Following a question regarding how IMO accommodated conflicting interests when establishing a particularly sensitive sea area, Mr. Haag highlighted the steps required to establish such an area and noted that the proponent of a particularly sensitive sea area would consult with neighbouring countries and interested stakeholders. Mr. Haag also noted that IMO had assisted States in developing proposals for establishing a particularly sensitive sea area, and that it had cooperated closely with several United Nations agencies, including UN-Oceans and other international bodies.

77. A delegation, noting the IMO underwater noise guidelines and the need for international coordination to address anthropogenic underwater noise at the global level, sought clarification as to whether guidelines for other sources of the noise, such as seismic surveys, could be developed and by which authority. Ms. Frisch-Nwakanma noted that the Scientific Council of the Convention on the Conservation of Migratory Species of Wild Animals was considering whether mitigation guidelines should be developed for specific noise-generating activities and that proposals for areas of focus would be submitted to the thirteenth Conference of the Parties to the Convention on the Conservation of Migratory Species of Wild Animals in 2020. She also noted that such guidelines would be developed in a consultative manner.

78. A delegation noted the work of the International Offshore Petroleum Environmental Regulators and its marine sound working group which had focused on airguns. The delegation also noted the group's plans to extend its work to pile-driving noise from offshore wind farms in order to identify best practices.

79. Some delegations sought views regarding ways to further enhance international cooperation and coordination in addressing anthropogenic underwater noise. Ms. Lent noted that coordination and communication were critical for avoiding duplication of efforts. Reciprocal attendance at each other's meetings and exchange of documents were helpful in this regard. Mr. Micallef noted that technical cooperation programmes, including seminars and workshops, would benefit from the participation of different agencies. In response to a question on how to strengthen cooperation between international organizations and regional fisheries management organizations, Ms. Lent noted that International Whaling Commission had been consulting with those organizations as part of its by-catch initiative and that such consultations could potentially extend to anthropogenic underwater noise.

80. A delegation highlighted its experience and challenges in the development of noise metrics for southern resident killer whales, and advocated greater coordination and information sharing. It enquired what the biggest challenge was in developing metrics for monitoring anthropogenic underwater noise. Mr. Dekeling noted that undertaking noise monitoring was challenging because of its potential cost. Also, the level of detail required for achieving better assessments was still unclear. In addition, he noted that developing metrics for monitoring continuous noise would be another major challenge owing to the existing knowledge gaps on its impacts. In this regard, he stressed the need for support from the biologist community.

81. Addressing a question concerning the breadth of soundscape modelling in the North Sea, Mr. Dekeling indicated that the measurements and modelling would distinguish between different sources of sound and whether those were anthropogenic or natural.

82. In response to a question as to why stress had not been mentioned as a possible effect of anthropogenic underwater noise, Mr. Dekeling noted that the knowledge on different forms of stress was limited. He highlighted the need to increase knowledge on the effects of continuous noise, including masking.

83. In response to questions concerning the development of a candidate indicator under the OSPAR Convention framework, Mr. Merchant noted that the candidate indicator, which was aimed at quantifying the risk of impact from impulsive noise on key species, was being developed on the basis of a risk – and evidence-based approach and might be adopted as early as April 2019 or April 2020. In response to a related question on the timeline for the Technical Group on Underwater Noise to develop similar indicators and the possibility for Group to develop other types of management recommendations, Mr. Dekeling explained that the Group was tasked with developing a common methodology for assessing data obtained in underwater noise monitoring programmes, rather than developing management recommendations. It had been developing such a methodology aiming to adopt recommendations on threshold values by the end of 2018 or in 2019.

84. Some delegations asked for more information on the impulsive noise registry of the OSPAR Convention which was used to aggregate and harmonize data on impulsive noise sources collected by the parties to the Convention. Mr. Merchant noted that this registry did not hold simultaneous data on the distribution of species due to capacity constraints, but data from ecosystem surveys might be introduced in the future so that relevant information could be used in a more integrated manner.

85. In response to a question on whether guidelines on mitigation techniques for noise from shipping activities, which might be developed under the OSPAR

Convention framework, would be compatible with relevant IMO guidelines, Mr. Merchant noted that such guidelines would be advisory in nature, and that IMO would be consulted to avoid any conflict. He also noted that there was no timeline yet for the development of such guidelines.

86. In response to a query on how to avoid redundant seismic surveys in a given site, it was noted that the issue fell under the responsibility of coastal States and that it was unlikely that a State would issue multiple licenses or permits for seismic surveys for the same area.

87. A delegation drew attention to efforts to establish whale sanctuaries in the South Atlantic and observed that more research and cooperation were crucial in that regard. Another delegation stressed the importance of regional cooperation in addressing anthropogenic underwater noise, in particular in the Caribbean and inquired as to what regional cooperation existed in the region and what platforms could be built upon. Noting the lack of a regional mechanism, Ms. Jones noted that the Caribbean Community could be used as a platform for initiating relevant discussions and exchanging information. However, expertise and guidance from international organizations outside of the region, such as the OSPAR Convention commission and the European Union, would be needed. Mr. Merchant affirmed the willingness of his organization to contribute to efforts facilitating regional cooperation.

88. A question was asked on how to implement the outcomes of the cooperation at the European Union level through regional seas conventions, taking into account differences in membership. Mr. Dekeling noted that in practice, States parties to regional seas conventions but not members of the European Union had cooperated closely with the European Union.

89. Some delegations expressed appreciation for the efforts of the Vancouver Fraser Port Authority in addressing anthropogenic underwater noise. It was suggested that an index of ship noise might be created given the use of hydrophones under that programme.

90. Some delegations enquired how to encourage other ports to take actions similar to the enhancing cetacean habitat and observation programme. Ms. Brown noted the strong interest from multiple stakeholders and drew attention to an effort to create a central repository of information on noise reduction incentives for use by the shipping industry. She also noted that the financial resources for incentives were factored into the budget of the Vancouver Fraser Port Authority.

91. In response to questions regarding the voluntary vessel slowdown trial under the programme, Ms. Brown shared insights on the potential impacts of such measures on vessels and ports. She noted that participating vessels needed to make up for the additional transit time in other areas to maintain schedules, and that some vessels had not participated due to scheduling or safety concerns. She

stressed the voluntary nature of the programme to maintain competitiveness. She also noted that it might take a long time for such measures to attract newer and quieter vessels, but if other ports were to offer similar incentives, that might be enough to offset the cost for the retrofit or construction of quieter vessels.

92. Regarding what actions had been taken to engage and introduce the general public to the programme, Ms. Brown noted that there had been active community engagement and a wide range of publicity activities to promote public understanding of the programme.

93. In response to a question on whether there had been any change in distribution and behaviour of the at-risk whales before and after the implementation of the programme, Ms. Brown noted that it was difficult to observe and measure how the animals had responded.

94. In relation to modelling in the context of environmental impact assessments and risk-based approaches to noise management, Mr. Thomsen clarified that significant effects at the population level could be very small if only a small proportion of the population were affected. Referring to the conclusion contained in a 2005 report of the International Council for the Exploration of the Sea indicating that there was little evidence of effects from sonar on beaked whale populations, a delegation noted that no population-level studies had been done in 2005 and that a recently completed 15-year study had shown evidence of population impact. Mr. Tasker acknowledged that scientific knowledge had increased since 2005. Addressing a Council finding that fish could respond to the physical presence of a ship as well as the sounds emitted by it, a delegation stressed that fish responses were still scientifically uncertain. Mr. Tasker noted that the role of the Council was to achieve consensus on the best scientific advice and that levels of uncertainty were often also reflected in its advice.

95. A delegation enquired whether there would be value in creating a new working group in the Council focusing specifically on anthropogenic underwater noise. Mr. Tasker explained that the establishment of such a group would need to be agreed upon by the members of the Council. Mr. Rosenbaum drew attention to a voluntary commitment made at the United Nations Conference to Support the Implementation of Sustainable Development Goal 14: Conserve and sustainably use the oceans, seas and marine resources for sustainable development (Ocean Conference) specifically regarding anthropogenic underwater noise (No. 18553).

96. A delegation stressed the importance of sharing best practices and experiences from various regions and sectors. Noting that the strength of the Council was its holistic perspective since it provided scientific advice for both fisheries and environmental management, the delegation announced that it would make a proposal to the Sixth Committee of the General Assembly for the Council to be granted observer status in the Assembly.

97. With reference to the use of marine protected areas, several delegations concurred that establishing such areas in accordance with international commitments, including target 11 of the Aichi Biodiversity Targets, was important. Those delegations noted, however, that a 2014 study had concluded that protected areas established thus far missed 85 per cent of threatened species. Mr. Rosenbaum stressed the importance of marine protected areas for local communities and the benefits that could accrue from ensuring that marine protected areas were quieter. where particular threats had been identified.
98. Several delegations recalled that the duty to conduct environmental impact assessments was enshrined in the United Nations Convention on the Law of the Sea and had also been recognized as a requirement under customary international law by the International Court of Justice. Those delegations also noted that a good environmental impact assessment, followed by implementing measures, would provide a strong basis for the management of any potential impacts.
99. Ms. Nolet clarified, in response to a question, that the third-party individuals undertaking verifications for Green Marine were independent professional verifiers and followed an annual training programme.

Agenda Item 4

Inter-agency Cooperation and Coordination

100. The Under-Secretary-General for Legal Affairs and United Nations Legal Counsel made a statement, in his capacity as Focal Point of UN-Oceans, providing information on the activities of UN-Oceans since the eighteenth meeting of the Informal Consultative Process, including in relation to the topic of focus.
101. He recalled the significant contribution of UN-Oceans to the Ocean Conference and highlighted the voluntary commitment of UN-Oceans registered at the Conference to raise awareness of ocean-related regulatory and policy frameworks and member activities in support of their implementation. He informed the meeting of two new members of UN-Oceans: the secretariats of the United Nations Framework Convention on Climate Change and of the Convention on International Trade in Endangered Species of Wild Fauna and Flora.
102. The Focal Point called attention to the 2018 UN-Oceans work programme, reflecting, inter alia, new activities relating to the United Nations Decade of Ocean Science for Sustainable Development (2021–2030) and follow-up to the Ocean Conference. Among ongoing activities, he highlighted the progress made in the development of a methodology for indicator 14.c.1 of Sustainable Development Goal 14, which refers to the number of countries making progress in

ratifying, accepting and implementing through legal, policy and institutional frameworks, ocean-related instruments that implement international law, as reflected in the United Nation Convention on the Law of the Sea, for the conservation and sustainable use of the oceans and their resources.

103. With regard to the decision of the General Assembly to defer the review of the terms of reference of UN-Oceans until its seventy-third session, the Focal Point recalled that, with regard to the informal consultations on the Assembly resolution on oceans and the law of the sea held during the seventy-second session, some delegations had expressed the view that they would welcome a paper prepared by UN-Oceans to assist them in the review. Such a document was made available to delegations for information at the meeting.

104. With regard to the information provided on the proposed methodology for target 14.c.1, delegates expressed the view that, while efforts on the development of the methodology by UN-Oceans were supported in general, it was necessary for States to report directly to the Statistical Commission of the United Nations on their implementation of Sustainable Development Goal 14. It was suggested that the proposed questions be simplified and indicative lists of instruments shortened so as, inter alia, not to disincentivize States from responding to the questionnaire. In response, the Director of the Division for Ocean Affairs and the Law of the Sea clarified that the proposed methodology, as resented during a UN-Oceans side event held in the margins of the twenty-eighth Meeting of States Parties to the Convention, consisted of a questionnaire containing brief questions relating to binding and non-binding global and regional instruments relevant for the implementation of Goal 14 and its targets, and identified indicative lists of instruments for which UN-Oceans members acted as secretariat. She noted that some delegations had provided comments and suggestions at that side event which would be reflected in a revised proposal. The next UN-Oceans side event, to be held during the informal consultations on the draft General Assembly resolution on oceans and the law of the sea at the seventy-third session, would offer an opportunity to provide feedback on the revised methodology and to invite volunteers for its pilot testing.

Agenda Item 5

Process for the Selection of Topics and Panellists so as to Facilitate the Work of the General Assembly

105. Referring to paragraph 348 of General Assembly resolution 72/73, the Co-Chairs invited views and proposals on ways to devise a transparent, objective and

inclusive process for the selection of topics and panellists so as to facilitate the work of the Assembly during informal consultations concerning the annual resolution on oceans and the law of the sea.
106. No statements were made under the item.

Agenda Item 6

Issues that Could Benefit from Attention in the Future Work of the General Assembly on Oceans and the Law of the Sea

107. The Co-Chairs drew attention to a composite streamlined list of issues that could benefit from the attention of the General Assembly and invited comments from representatives.
108. The Co-Chairs also invited representatives to submit additional topics that could benefit from the attention of the General Assembly.
109. The Co-Chairs also referred to paragraph 335 of General Assembly resolution 71/257 on the further review of the effectiveness and utility of the Informal Consultative Process by the Assembly at its seventy-third session and invited delegations to consider addressing the matter under agenda item 6.
110. No statements were made under the item.

Agreement to Prevent Unregulated High Seas Fisheries in the Central Arctic Ocean

The Parties to this Agreement*,

Recognizing that until recently ice has generally covered the high seas portion of the central Arctic Ocean on a year-round basis, which has made fishing in those waters impossible, but that ice coverage in that area has diminished in recent years;

Acknowledging that, while the central Arctic Ocean ecosystems have been relatively unexposed to human activities, those ecosystems are changing due to climate change and other phenomena, and that the effects of these changes are not well understood;

Recognizing the crucial role of healthy and sustainable marine ecosystems and fisheries for food and nutrition;

Recognizing the special responsibilities and special interests of the central Arctic Ocean coastal States in relation to the conservation and sustainable management of fish stocks in the central Arctic Ocean;

Noting in this regard the initiative of the central Arctic Ocean coastal States as reflected in the Declaration Concerning the Prevention of Unregulated High Seas Fishing in the Central Arctic Ocean signed on 16 July 2015;

Recalling the principles and provisions of treaties and other international instruments relating to marine fisheries that already apply to the high seas portion of the central Arctic Ocean, including those contained in:

> the United Nations Convention on the Law of the Sea of 10 December 1982 ("the Convention");
>
> the Agreement for the Implementation of the Provisions of the United Nations Convention on the Law of the Sea of 10 December 1982 relating to the Conservation and Management of Straddling Fish Stocks and Highly Migratory Fish Stocks of 4 August 1995 ("the 1995 Agreement"); and
>
> the 1995 Code of Conduct for Responsible Fisheries and other relevant instruments adopted by the Food and Agriculture Organization of the United Nations;

---

* Editors' Note.—This Agreement is extracted from the Annex to the "Proposal for a Council Decision on the signing, on behalf of the European Union, of the Agreement to prevent unregulated high seas Fisheries in the Central Arctic Ocean," Brussels, 12.6.2018, COM(2018) 454 final, 2018/0240(NLE), available online: <https://eur-lex.europa.eu/legal-content/EN/TXT/?uri=COM:2018:0454:FIN>.

Underlining the importance of ensuring cooperation and coordination between the Parties and the North-East Atlantic Fisheries Commission, which has competence to adopt conservation and management measures in part of the high seas portion of the central Arctic Ocean, and other relevant mechanisms for fisheries management that are established and operated in accordance with international law, as well as with relevant international bodies and programs;

Believing that commercial fishing is unlikely to become viable in the high seas portion of the central Arctic Ocean in the near future and that it is therefore premature under current circumstances to establish any additional regional or subregional fisheries management organizations or arrangements for the high seas portion of the central Arctic Ocean;

Desiring, consistent with the precautionary approach, to prevent the start of unregulated fishing in the high seas portion of the central Arctic Ocean while keeping under regular review the need for additional conservation and management measures;

Recalling the 2007 United Nations Declaration on the Rights of Indigenous Peoples;

Recognizing the interests of Arctic residents, including Arctic indigenous peoples, in the long-term conservation and sustainable use of living marine resources and in healthy marine ecosystems in the Arctic Ocean and underlining the importance of involving them and their communities; and

Desiring to promote the use of both scientific knowledge and indigenous and local knowledge of the living marine resources of the Arctic Ocean and the ecosystems in which they occur as a basis for fisheries conservation and management in the high seas portion of the central Arctic Ocean,

Have agreed as follows:

Article 1

Use of Terms

For the purposes of this Agreement:
(a) "Agreement Area" means the single high seas portion of the central Arctic Ocean that is surrounded by waters within which Canada, the Kingdom of Denmark in respect of Greenland, the Kingdom of Norway, the Russian Federation and the United States of America exercise fisheries jurisdiction;
(b) "fish" means species of fish, molluscs and crustaceans except those belonging to sedentary species as defined in Article 77 of the Convention;
(c) "fishing" means searching for, attracting, locating, catching, taking or harvesting fish or any activity that can reasonably be expected to result in the attracting, locating, catching, taking or harvesting of fish;

(d) "commercial fishing" means fishing for commercial purposes;
(e) "exploratory fishing" means fishing for the purpose of assessing the sustainability and feasibility of future commercial fisheries by contributing to scientific data relating to such fisheries;
(f) "vessel" means any vessel used for, equipped to be used for, or intended to be used for fishing.

Article 2

Objective of this Agreement

The objective of this Agreement is to prevent unregulated fishing in the high seas portion of the central Arctic Ocean through the application of precautionary conservation and management measures as part of a long-term strategy to safeguard healthy marine ecosystems and to ensure the conservation and sustainable use of fish stocks.

Article 3

Interim Conservation and Management Measures Concerning Fishing

1. Each Party shall authorize vessels entitled to fly its flag to conduct commercial fishing in the Agreement Area only pursuant to:
   (a) conservation and management measures for the sustainable management of fish stocks adopted by one or more regional or subregional fisheries management organizations or arrangements, that have been or may be established and are operated in accordance with international law to manage such fishing in accordance with recognized international standards, or
   (b) interim conservation and management measures that may be established by the Parties pursuant to Article 5, paragraph 1(c)(ii).
2. The Parties are encouraged to conduct scientific research under the framework of the Joint Program of Scientific Research and Monitoring established pursuant to Article 4 and under their respective national scientific programs.
3. A Party may authorize vessels entitled to fly its flag to carry out exploratory fishing in the Agreement Area only pursuant to conservation and management measures established by the Parties on the basis of Article 5, paragraph 1(d).
4. The Parties shall ensure that their scientific research activities involving the catching of fish in the Agreement Area do not undermine the prevention of unregulated commercial and exploratory fishing and the protection of healthy

marine ecosystems. The Parties are encouraged to inform each other about their plans for authorizing such scientific research activities.

5. The Parties shall ensure compliance with the interim measures established by this Article, and with any additional or different interim measures they may establish pursuant to Article 5, paragraph 1(c).

6. Consistent with Article 7 of the 1995 Agreement, coastal States Parties and other Parties shall cooperate to ensure the compatibility of conservation and management measures for fish stocks that occur in areas both within and beyond national jurisdiction in the central Arctic Ocean in order to ensure conservation and management of those stocks in their entirety.

7. Other than as provided in paragraph 4 above, nothing in this Agreement shall be interpreted to restrict the entitlements of Parties in relation to marine scientific research as reflected in the Convention.

Article 4

Joint Program of Scientific Research and Monitoring

1. The Parties shall facilitate cooperation in scientific activities with the goal of increasing knowledge of the living marine resources of the central Arctic Ocean and the ecosystems in which they occur.

2. The Parties agree to establish, within two years of the entry into force of this Agreement, a Joint Program of Scientific Research and Monitoring with the aim of improving their understanding of the ecosystems of the Agreement Area and, in particular, of determining whether fish stocks might exist in the Agreement Area now or in the future that could be harvested on a sustainable basis and the possible impacts of such fisheries on the ecosystems of the Agreement Area.

3. The Parties shall guide the development, coordination and implementation of the Joint Program of Scientific Research and Monitoring.

4. The Parties shall ensure that the Joint Program of Scientific Research and Monitoring takes into account the work of relevant scientific and technical organizations, bodies and programs, as well as indigenous and local knowledge.

5. As part of the Joint Program of Scientific Research and Monitoring, the Parties shall adopt, within two years of the entry into force of this Agreement, a data sharing protocol and shall share relevant data, directly or through relevant scientific and technical organizations, bodies and programs, in accordance with that protocol.

6. The Parties shall hold joint scientific meetings, in person or otherwise, at least every two years and at least two months in advance of the meetings of the Parties that take place pursuant to Article 5 to present the results of their research,

to review the best available scientific information, and to provide timely scientific advice to meetings of the Parties. The Parties shall adopt, within two years of the entry into force of this Agreement, terms of reference and other procedures for the functioning of the joint scientific meetings.

Article 5

Review and Further Implementation

1. The Parties shall meet every two years or more frequently if they so decide. During their meetings, the Parties shall, *inter alia*:
   (a) review implementation of this Agreement and, when appropriate, consider any issues relating to the duration of this Agreement in accordance with Article 13, paragraph 2;
   (b) review all available scientific information developed through the Joint Program of Scientific Research and Monitoring, from the national scientific programs, and from any other relevant sources, including indigenous and local knowledge;
   (c) on the basis of the scientific information derived from the Joint Program of Scientific Research and Monitoring, from the national scientific programs, and from other relevant sources, and taking into account relevant fisheries management and ecosystem considerations, including the precautionary approach and potential adverse impacts of fishing on the ecosystems, consider, *inter alia*, whether the distribution, migration and abundance of fish in the Agreement Area would support a sustainable commercial fishery and, on that basis, determine:
      (i) whether to commence negotiations to establish one or more additional regional or subregional fisheries management organizations or arrangements for managing fishing in the Agreement Area; and
      (ii) whether, once negotiations have commenced pursuant to subparagraph (i) above and once the Parties have agreed on mechanisms to ensure the sustainability of fish stocks, to establish additional or different interim conservation and management measures in respect of those stocks in the Agreement Area.
   (d) establish, within three years of the entry into force of this Agreement, conservation and management measures for exploratory fishing in the Agreement Area. The Parties may amend such measures from time to time. These measures shall provide, *inter alia*, that:
      (i) exploratory fishing shall not undermine the objective of this Agreement;

(ii) exploratory fishing shall be limited in duration, scope and scale to minimize impacts on fish stocks and ecosystems and shall be subject to standard requirements set forth in the data sharing protocol adopted in accordance with Article 4, paragraph 5;

(iii) a Party may authorize exploratory fishing only on the basis of sound scientific research and when it is consistent with the Joint Program of Scientific Research and Monitoring and its own national scientific program(s);

(iv) a Party may authorize exploratory fishing only after it has notified the other Parties of its plans for such fishing and it has provided other Parties an opportunity to comment on those plans; and

(v) a Party must adequately monitor any exploratory fishing that it has authorized and report the results of such fishing to the other Parties.

2. To promote implementation of this Agreement, including with respect to the Joint Program of Scientific Research and Monitoring and other activities undertaken pursuant to Article 4, the Parties may form committees or similar bodies in which representatives of Arctic communities, including Arctic indigenous peoples, may participate.

Article 6

Decision-Making

1. Decisions of the Parties on questions of procedure shall be taken by a majority of the Parties casting affirmative or negative votes.
2. Decisions of the Parties on questions of substance shall be taken by consensus. For the purpose of this Agreement, "consensus" means the absence of any formal objection made at the time the decision was taken.
3. A question shall be deemed to be of substance if any Party considers it to be of substance.

Article 7

Dispute Settlement

The provisions relating to the settlement of disputes set forth in Part VIII of the 1995 Agreement apply, *mutatis mutandis*, to any dispute between Parties relating to the interpretation or application of this Agreement, whether or not they are also Parties to the 1995 Agreement.

Article 8

Non-Parties

1. The Parties shall encourage non-parties to this Agreement to take measures that are consistent with the provisions of this Agreement.
2. The Parties shall take measures consistent with international law to deter the activities of vessels entitled to fly the flags of non-parties that undermine the effective implementation of this Agreement.

Article 9

Signature

1. This Agreement shall be open for signature at at Ilulissat from 3 October 2018 by Canada, the People's Republic of China, the Kingdom of Denmark in respect of the Faroe Islands and Greenland, Iceland, Japan, the Republic of Korea, the Kingdom of Norway, the Russian Federation, the United States of America and the European Union and shall remain open for signature for 12 months following that date.
2. For signatories to this Agreement, this Agreement shall remain open for ratification, acceptance or approval at any time.

Article 10

Accession

1. For the States listed in Article 9, paragraph 1 that have not signed this Agreement, and for the European Union if it has not signed this Agreement, this Agreement shall remain open for accession at any time.
2. After the entry into force of this Agreement, the Parties may invite other States with a real interest to accede to this Agreement.

Article 11

Entry into Force

1. This Agreement shall enter into force 30 days after the date of receipt by the depositary of all instruments of ratification, acceptance, or approval of, or accession to, this Agreement by those States and the European Union listed in Article 9, paragraph 1.
2. After entry into force of this Agreement, it shall enter into force for each State invited to accede pursuant to Article 10, paragraph 2 that has deposited an instrument of accession 30 days after the date of deposit of that instrument.

Article 12

Withdrawal

A Party may withdraw from this Agreement at any time by sending written notification of its withdrawal to the depositary through diplomatic channels, specifying the effective date of its withdrawal, which shall be at least six months after the date of notification. Withdrawal from this Agreement shall not affect its application among the remaining Parties or the duty of the withdrawing Party to fulfill any obligation in this Agreement to which it otherwise would be subject under international law independently of this Agreement.

Article 13

Duration of this Agreement

1. This Agreement shall remain in force for an initial period of 16 years following its entry into force.
2. Following the expiration of the initial period specified in paragraph 1 above, this Agreement shall remain in force for successive five-year extension period(s) unless any Party:
    (a) presents a formal objection to an extension of this Agreement at the last meeting of the Parties that takes place prior to expiration of the initial period or any subsequent extension period; or

(b) sends a formal objection to an extension to the depositary in writing no later than six months prior to the expiration of the respective period.

3. The Parties shall provide for an effective transition between this Agreement and any potential new agreement establishing an additional regional or subregional fisheries management organization or arrangement for managing fishing in the Agreement Area so as to safeguard healthy marine ecosystems and ensure the conservation and sustainable use of fish stocks in the Agreement Area.

Article 14

Relation to Other Agreements

1. The Parties recognize that they are and will continue to be bound by their obligations under relevant provisions of international law, including those reflected in the Convention and the 1995 Agreement, and recognize the importance of continuing to cooperate in fulfilling those obligations even in the event that this Agreement expires or is terminated in the absence of any agreement establishing an additional regional or subregional fisheries management organization or arrangement for managing fishing in the Agreement Area.
2. Nothing in this Agreement shall prejudice the positions of any Party with respect to its rights and obligations under international agreements and its positions with respect to any question relating to the law of the sea, including with respect to any position relating to the exercise of rights and jurisdiction in the Arctic Ocean.
3. Nothing in this Agreement shall prejudice the rights, jurisdiction and duties of any Party under relevant provisions of international law as reflected in the Convention or the 1995 Agreement, including the right to propose the commencement of negotiations on the establishment of one or more additional regional or subregional fisheries management organizations or arrangements for the Agreement Area.
4. This Agreement shall not alter the rights and obligations of any Party that arise from other agreements compatible with this Agreement and that do not affect the enjoyment by other Parties of their rights or the performance of their obligations under this Agreement. This Agreement shall neither undermine nor conflict with the role and mandate of any existing international mechanism relating to fisheries management.

Article 15

Depositary

1. The Government of Canada shall be the depositary for this Agreement.
2. Instruments of ratification, acceptance, approval or accession shall be deposited with the depositary.
3. The depositary shall inform all signatories and all Parties of the deposit of all instruments of ratification, acceptance, approval or accession and perform such other functions as are provided for in the 1969 Vienna Convention on the Law of Treaties.

Done at Ilulissat, Greenland on this 3rd day of October, 2018, in a single original, in the Chinese, English, French and Russian languages, each text being equally authentic.

Index

accountability 32
  See also governance
acoustic marine management:
  governance 531–534, 541–542
    technical guidance 422–423
    voluntary measures 534–541
  international legal regime 493–512, 515–516, 524–526, 532–534
  marine environmental impacts 487–493
  marine fauna impacts 490–492
  mitigation:
    acoustic footprints 514, 518–522, 539–542
    acoustic thresholds 522–524
    disturbance benchmarks 523, 542
    monetary incentives 536–541
    monitoring 502, 504, 509, 510, 515, 521–524, 530, 533, 540–542
    noise budgets 519
    on-water operational options 525–529, 539
    ship design and maintenance options 524–525, 529–530
    spatially specific footprints 521–522
    stakeholder communications 519
  national/regional legal regimes 503–505, 509–511, 522, 542, 533, 541–542
  scientific knowledge gaps 492–493, 537
  sources:
    anthropogenic
    construction related 488, 489, 490, 492, 509
    military activities/ships 487, 489, 497, 499, 507–508, 510–511
    natural 488
    offshore infrastructure 488, 512
    playback and sound exposure experiments 513, 488, 508
    regular vessel operations 487–489, 500–501, 506, 511, 513, 514, 517, 518
      hydrodynamic 497, 518, 520, 531t19.1
      machinery 518, 520, 531t19.1
      propellers 497, 518, 520, 531t19.1, 535, 538–539
    resource extraction activities 488, 490
    technology-based activities 488, 489–490
      acoustic devices 488, 508
      seismic surveys 488, 489–490, 492, 507–509
      sonar 487, 488, 489, 492, 507–509, 510
Africa 137, 139–140, 356, 426
  maritime security 432–435
  Yaoundé Conclusions 139
  See also West Africa
Agenda 21 17–18, 288
  See also United Nations Conference on Environment and Development
Agreement on Enhancing International Arctic Science Cooperation *See* Arctic Council, Enhancing Science Cooperation Agreement
Agreement on the Conservation of Cetaceans of the Black Sea, Mediterranean Sea and Contiguous Atlantic Area (ACCOBAMS) 498, 499–500, 505–507, 508, 510, 512, 533–534
Agreement on the Conservation of Small Cetaceans of the Baltic and North Seas (ASCOBANS) 495, 498–499, 507–508, 510, 512
Agreement to Prevent Unregulated High Seas Fisheries in the Central Arctic Ocean 401–403, 406–417
  and other agreements 415
  and outer continental shelf limits 406–407
  conservation and management measures 409–412
  dispute settlement 414
  history 403–406
    Nuuk Chairman's Statement 405–406
    Oslo Declaration 403–406, 408n34
  non-parties 406–408, 412–414
  signature and accession 401–402, 414–415
American Samoa 59, 61, 68
Angola 426, 440n117

Antarctic:
    international liability and compensation legal regime   325, 332, 333, 334, 337
Antarctic Treaty System   498, 500–501, 508
    Madrid Protocol   315, 325, 332, 333, 334, 337, 500–501, 508
Antigua and Barbuda   143
aquaculture   236, 273–275
    integrated multi-trophic   275
    sea cucumbers   273–274
    shrimp   273
arbitration   127
    South China Sea Case   106–107, 108–109, 113, 116n110
    See also dispute settlement regime; International Tribunal for the Law of the Sea; Permanent Court of Arbitration
archipelagic waters   112, 119, 123, 441, 443–444, 461
archipelagos   73
    See also islands
Arctic:
    and climate change   90, 212, 213, 252, 263, 265, 403
    fisheries   401–404, 407–412, 413–414, 416–417
    Ilulissat Declaration   406
    Indigenous peoples   90, 112n90, 114
    mineral resources   57, 265
Arctic Council Enhancing Science Cooperation Agreement   396
Arctic Ocean   213, 263, 265
    high seas   401–404, 407–412, 413–414, 416
areas beyond national jurisdiction *See* ocean areas beyond national jurisdiction
Argentina   132, 133, 143, 149, 150–151
artificial installations and structures   142–143, 147, 149–151
    international legal regime   149–151
    See also marine installations (offshore)
assessment *See* environmental assessment; fisheries, stock assessment; navigation, navigation risk assessment; risk management, assessment; strategic environmental assessment; United Nations, Informal Consultative Process
Australia   21, 59, 61, 77, 256–257, 258, 260, 416n57, 463, 464, 479, 509–510
    and deep seabed mining   356, 357

Great Barrier Reef   72
indigenous peoples' rights   98, 100–101
Bahamas   143
Bangladesh   148
Barbados   143
baselines:
    ambulation   66, 70, 73–74, 79–80
    and sea level rise   58, 64–67, 70, 73–80, 82
    archipelagic   73, 75–76, 80
    international legal regime   58, 65, 79–85, 89, 112
    normal   65–66, 73
    See also maritime boundaries
Beaufort Sea   213, 404, 409
Belgium   147, 547
    and deep seabed mining   357–358, 374
Belize   143
Benin   427, 432, 444n98
Bering Sea   51, 53, 213
biodiversity   166–168
    and ecosystem approach   187–188
    and SDG 14   21–22, 187, 190–192, 194–198, 200–206, 238n190, 260–261, 281–284, 285, 371, 389
    conservation   4–7, 9–10, 17, 18, 21–22, 23, 33, 39–40, 168–171, 187–190, 192–194, 203, 240, 379–383, 395, 398, 400, 501
    international legal regime   9–10, 16–22, 23, 26, 28, 30–31, 39–40, 192–206, 220, 241–242, 261, 377–387, 399, 502–503, 533
biogeochemical processes   216
biogeographical classification systems   204
blue carbon ecosystems *See* mangroves; salt marshes; seagrass beds
blue energy *See* ocean renewable energy
blue growth strategy   278, 285–286
Bolivia   144
Bonn Guidelines on Access to Genetic Resources and Fair and Equitable Sharing of the Benefits Arising out of their Utilization *See* Convention on Biological Diversity
boundary delimitation *See* maritime boundaries
Brazil   141, 143, 144, 148, 149, 150, 256–257, 289, 295, 298–302, 305, 307, 308, 310–311, 509

buffer zones *See* navigation, Areas to be Avoided
Bunker Convention *See* International Convention on Civil Liability for Bunker Oil Pollution Damage
by-catch *See* fisheries, incidental capture

cables *See* submarine cables and pipelines
Cameroon   434
Canada   144
   acoustic marine management   509–510, 514, 515, 522, 523, 529–531, 536–540, 541–542
   and deep seabed mining   345–346, 359, 361–362, 366, 367–368
   central Arctic Ocean fisheries   401, 402, 404, 406, 409, 417
   fisheries governance   404, 409
   indigenous peoples' rights   98, 100–101
   marine protected areas   362
   statutes:
     Oceans Act   306, 522
     Species at Risk Act   522, 542
capacity-building *See* education and training
carbon sequestration   220, 233–234, 236, 257, 263, 264
   and ocean acidification   210–212, 230, 252
   See also ocean fertilization
Caribbean States Santo Domingo Declaration   138–139
cetaceans *See* marine mammals; whales
Chile   133–136, 143, 144, 158, 261
   Santiago Declaration   134, 136, 146, 157–158
China, People's Republic   442, 464
   and deep seabed mining   358, 363, 365, 370–371
   and the Arctic   401, 413–414, 417
   Marine Environmental Protection Law   365
Chukchi Sea   213
classification societies   538
climate change:
   adaptation   219, 226–228, 236–238, 242, 243, 244, 245, 247–248, 251, 254–255, 256, 257, 266, 277–279
     loss and damage   228, 237–238
   governance:
     action plans   221, 254

climate refugia   202
carbon sink protection   218, 222–223, 232, 242, 245, 247, 253, 254, 257, 263
collaboration/partnerships   217, 228, 238
ecosystem approach   201–202, 242
emission reduction targets   208, 218, 221–223, 245–247, 265
fragmentation   215, 217, 220–221, 229, 234, 238–239, 261–262, 266
indicators   225, 241
international legal regime   62–63, 78–86, 89, 207–208, 215–249, 253–267
maintenance of maritime entitlements   58, 64–70, 73–86
national and regional policy and legal regimes   75–78, 89
scientific cooperation   241
temperature targets   62–64, 71–72, 208, 218, 221–225, 262–263
tipping points   267
voluntary commitments   208, 219, 226, 229, 231–232, 236, 245–247, 251, 254, 255
human impacts   67, 71, 244, 252, 257
mitigation   201, 218–220, 226–228, 229–236, 242, 243, 245, 247–248, 251, 254, 257, 262–266
   geoengineering   217n69, 233–234, 242, 243, 264
   negative emissions technology   232–233, 264
physical evidence:
   amplification impacts   212–213, 229–230
   coral reefs   69–72, 73–74, 86, 213, 223–224, 217n69, 229–230, 242, 244, 252, 255, 256, 258
   deoxygenation   8, 70, 212–213, 252, 257
   greenhouse gas emissions   208, 210, 215–216, 230–231, 251–252
   hypercapnia   252, 257
   ocean biogeochemistry   208–209, 210–213, 216, 232–234, 252
   ocean circulation   252
   polar ecosystems   90, 212, 229, 252, 263, 265, 403
   sea ice   212, 252, 263, 403

INDEX 761

sediment flows   71, 79n83
slow onset events   217, 228, 237–238
temperature:
    air   208, 223–224, 255
    sea water   8, 73, 208, 217n69, 230, 251–252, 257, 258, 266
upwelling circulation   211, 212, 230
See also ocean acidification; sea level change; resilience (ecological)
climate processes:
    and ocean ecosystems   208–209, 215–216, 217, 225, 230
CO_2 sequestration *See* carbon sequestration
coastal communities   272–275, 285, 298–299
coastal management:
    capacity development   269–272
    competing uses   544–546
    ecosystem-based   277–278
    integrated   190, 298, 306–307
    population growth/density   67, 71, 268
    urbanization   298
    See also governance; marine spatial planning
coastal processes:
    accretion   66, 70, 79n83
    erosion   66, 67, 69–70
    sediment transport   66, 71, 79n83
coastal State rights *See* sovereign rights
Code of Conduct concerning the Repression of Piracy and Armed Robbery Against Ships in the Western Indian Ocean and the Gulf of Aden (Djibouti Code of Conduct)   433
Code of Conduct for Responsible Fisheries   188, 191, 194
    See also Food and Agricultural Organization of the United Nations
Code of Conduct for the Suppression of Piracy, Armed Robbery Against Ships and Illicit Maritime Activity in West and Central Africa (Yaoundé Code)   433–434
Collision Avoidance Regulations (COLREGS)   180, 562
Colombia   138, 141, 143, 144, 154
    Nicaragua/Colombia Case   152–153
    UNCLOS accession   121, 151–152

common heritage doctrine   316, 322, 339, 371, 389
    and liability for environmental damage   316, 329, 333–334, 339, 372–373
    and marine genetic resources   378–379
Commonwealth of the Northern Mariana Islands   59, 61, 68
competent international organization   11, 14n35, 18n59, 20, 29n82, 30, 125, 198, 200, 206, 240, 248, 390–391, 397, 477, 496
conciliation   128
conservation:
    and science and technology   382–383
    biodiversity   4–7, 17, 18, 21–22, 23, 33, 39–40, 168–171, 187–190, 192–194, 203, 240, 379–383, 395, 398, 400, 501
    habitat   169, 204, 241, 522–524, 527–529
    international legal regime   9–10, 16–22, 23, 26, 28, 30–31, 39–40, 187–188, 192–206, 220, 241–242, 261, 377–387, 399, 502–503, 533
contiguous zone   137, 156, 461–462
    See also maritime boundaries
continental shelf:
    enforcement jurisdiction   406–407, 462, 476
    entitlement claims   132–134
    extended   77, 406–407
    international legal regime   119, 121, 122, 152, 462, 465
    national legal regimes   156, 503
    See also maritime boundaries; ocean areas beyond national jurisdiction
Convention Concerning the Protection of the World Cultural and Natural Heritage   244
    See also United Nations Educational, Scientific and Cultural Organization
Convention for the Protection of the Marine Environment of the North-East Atlantic   516, 533
Convention for the Protection of Submarine Telegraph Cables   457–458, 459, 460, 482
Convention for the Suppression of Unlawful Acts against the Safety of Maritime Navigation   438–439, 445–446, 453, 455, 469

Convention (SUA) (*cont.*)
   1998 Protocol (Fixed Platforms)   476–477
   2005 Protocol   439, 445–446
Convention on Biological Diversity   18, 108–109, 113–114, 117
   Aichi Biodiversity Targets   193, 194–195, 201, 202–206, 241
   and SDG 14   187, 191, 193–195, 198, 201–206
   and UNCLOS   18–19
   areas beyond national jurisdiction   6, 11–12, 16, 18–21, 28
   implementation mechanisms   11, 18–21
      area-based management tools   19–21, 202–205, 206, 241
      ecologically or biologically significant areas   20, 200–202, 203, 206
      ecosystem approach   187–189, 191, 199, 200–203, 204–206, 242
      environmental assessment   12, 20–21
      EIA procedures   199, 200, 203
      in-situ conservation   19, 113–114, 117, 203
      mainstreaming biodiversity   193–194
      national strategy and action plans   19, 39
      other effective area-based conservation measures   202–203, 204, 241
      precautionary approach   204, 242
   Nagoya Protocol on Access and Benefit Sharing   109, 380, 381–382, 383–387, 399
   Nagoya-Kuala Lumpur Supplementary Protocol   316, 331
   specific issues:
      access and benefit sharing   380, 381–382, 399
      cold-water areas   201–202, 203, 241–242
      genetic resources   109, 188, 380, 381–382, 383–387, 399
         Bonn Guidelines   383n31
      marine debris   198
      ocean acidification   241–243, 248
      underwater noise   198, 199, 498, 502–503
Convention on International Civil Aviation   246
Convention on Conservation and Management of the High Seas Fishery Resources of the South Pacific Ocean   407n31
Convention on Fishing and Conservation of Living Resources of the High Seas   136–137
Convention on Future Multilateral Co-operation in the North East Atlantic Fisheries *See* North East Atlantic Fisheries Commission
Convention on International Trade in Endangered Species of Wild Flora and Fauna   106, 108–109
Convention on Nature Protection and Wild Life Preservation in the Western Hemisphere   35
Convention on the Conservation and Management of Fishery Resources in the South East Atlantic Ocean   413
Convention on the Conservation and Management of Pollock Resources in the Central Bering Sea   408
Convention on the Conservation of Migratory Species of Wild Animals   16, 191, 199–200, 204, 205–206, 495, 498, 501–502, 509, 512
   and anthropogenic underwater noise   198, 199, 203
   and climate change   243
   EIA Guidelines   199–200, 203
   Strategic Plan for Migratory Species   204, 243
Convention on the Continental Shelf   458–459
Convention on the High Seas   136, 436n61, 458–459, 472
Convention on the International Regulations for Preventing Collisions at Sea *See* Collision Avoidance Regulations (COLREGS)
Convention on the Law of the Sea *See* United Nations Convention on the Law of the Sea
Convention on the Prevention of Marine Pollution by Dumping of Wastes and Other Matter (London):
   Protocol   234
   and ocean fertilization   234
Convention on the Protection of the Marine Environment of the Baltic Sea Area   515–516

INDEX 763

Convention on the Protection of the
    Underwater Cultural Heritage 153
Convention on the Suppression of Unlawful
    Acts Relating to International Civil
    Aviation 475
Convention on the Transboundary Movement
    of Hazardous Wastes and Their
    Disposal:
    Basel Protocol 315, 324n38, 328, 333
Convention on Wetlands of International
    Importance (Ramsar) sites 169, 245
Cook Islands 59, 61, 68, 73, 74, 75
coral (reefs):
    and marine shipping 171–177
    atolls 68, 163, 165
    cold water 201, 213, 242, 255
    climate change risks 69–72, 73–74, 86,
        201, 213, 223–224, 217n69, 230, 241, 252,
        255, 256, 258
        bleaching 244, 252
        ocean acidification 70, 73–74, 213,
            217n69, 229–230, 239–240, 241, 242,
            252, 258
    international legal regime 72–73, 201,
        203, 239–240, 241, 242
    sea level change resilience 69–71,
        73–74
    tropical 69–72, 73–74, 86, 166–171, 173,
        213, 252, 255, 256, 268
Costa Rica 132, 143
criminal law 460–462, 464–465, 467–468,
    470, 475–477, 477–482, 483, 485
crustaceans 490–491
Cuba 143

Dalhousie University 185
data collection and management *See*
    information and data
deep seabed mining:
    and common heritage doctrine 316, 329,
        333–334, 339, 372–373
    damages (for environmental harm) 329–
        333, 355, 372
        compensation 316–317, 320–322,
            324–326, 328–338, 343–344, 351–352,
            359–360, 362, 363, 364–366, 369,
            373, 374
            remediation/restoration 329–331,
                334, 336, 337, 364–365, 375
        economic losses 330

    insurance 325–326, 328, 337, 338, 343,
        355, 357, 373
    compulsory 335–336, 364, 365, 374
    international legal regime 321–322,
        329, 333–334, 335
    offsets 331, 336, 338
    pure environmental loss 331–332,
        334, 335, 366
    standing to bring claims 333–335
        ISA standing 322, 333–335, 347, 375
        State parties (*erga omnes*
            claims) 322, 334–335
        trust (compensation) funds 321, 324,
            335–337, 338, 352–353, 364–365,
            366, 367, 369, 373, 374, 376
    duty to prevent environmental
        harm 319–320, 324, 343, 369–370,
        373–374
    environmental impacts 344
    international legal regime 317–323, 326,
        327, 332–333, 334–335, 339–341, 343,
        347–348, 355, 362–363, 369, 374–375
        development of regulations 315–323,
            325–326, 337–338, 341–343, 350,
            352–354, 371–376
    liability 315–317, 337–340, 371–376
        differentiated responsibilities 325
        due diligence (standard) 318–320,
            321–322, 324, 325, 343, 346, 348–349,
            352, 355, 358, 360, 361, 369–372, 373,
            374–375
        environmental protection
            standards 326–328, 335, 350
        joint and several (standard) 318, 360
        negligence 372
        non-commercial exploitation 326
        public authorities 328–329
        residual 320–321, 343, 357, 375
        strict (standard) 319, 326–328, 337,
            343, 349, 352, 355, 360, 361, 364,
            366–367, 372, 374
        "wrongful acts or omissions" 316,
            319–320, 327, 347, 349, 351–352, 355,
            359, 360, 371–372, 375
    mining operations 341, 344, 345–346
    national legal regimes 316, 322, 347,
        351–364, 365, 374–375
    responsibility:
        attribution and channeling 323–326,
            328

deep seabed mining (cont.)
    contractor   317–321, 324, 325–326, 328, 336–337, 343, 345, 347, 351, 352, 355–356, 358, 370
    flag State   345, 356, 369–371, 374–375
    international organizations   318, 347, 357, 367, 375
    ISA   318–321, 323, 324, 325, 327–328, 329, 333–335, 342–343, 347–354, 357
    sponsoring State   317–322, 324–325, 328, 336, 341, 347–348, 349, 355–356, 357–358, 369, 373–375
    State enterprises and State parties   316, 319, 326, 331, 334, 371, 372
    transportation and processing of minerals   324, 342–343, 356, 367
    seabed resources:
        cobalt   348n69&71
        ferromanganese crusts   348n71
        polymetallic nodules   346, 348n69
        sulphides   348n70
    See also International Seabed Authority
Denmark   401, 404, 406, 407, 578n38
    See also Greenland
developing countries   222–223, 246, 379, 389, 426
    and areas beyond national jurisdiction   11, 31
    and deep seabed mining   325, 341, 356, 373, 375–376
    See also small island developing States
dispute settlement regime
    compulsory procedures   127–128
    international legal regime   126–129, 145
    See also arbitration; International Court of Justice; International Tribunal for the Law of the Sea; Permanent Court of Arbitration
Dominica   143, 154
Dominican Republic   143, 154

ecological corridors   204, 205
ecological integrity   220–221, 225, 227, 242, 254
ecological stress   491, 517
Economic Community of Central African States   433–434

Economic Community of West African States   433–434
ecosystem approach   15, 28, 31–34, 39–40, 41–42, 50, 187–206, 242, 277–278, 288–289, 521
    principles   188–189
    See also sustainability
ecosystem approach to fisheries management
    See marine resource management, governance, ecosystem-based
ecosystem-based fisheries management
    See marine resource management, governance, ecosystem-based
ecosystem services   7, 33, 42, 44, 189, 191–192, 202n74, 203, 213, 261, 276, 278, 289, 332, 382
ecosystem soundscapes   514, 517–518
Ecuador   134, 143–144, 146–147, 149, 444n98
    Santiago Declaration   134, 136, 146, 157–158
education and training   185, 506–507
    capacity-building   6, 124–125, 269–276, 279–281, 284–286, 377, 378–379, 380, 383–389, 391, 394, 395, 398–400, 432–433
    citizen science   277
    collaboration   279–281, 285
    community-based   269, 272–275, 281, 285
    gender dimension   275–276
    professional development   269–270, 272
    public awareness/outreach   269, 276–279
    science translation   295–296, 304, 308
    See also knowledge
EEZ See exclusive economic zone
El Salvador   143–144
    UNCLOS accession   121, 155–157
endangered species   166–167, 177, 202, 501, 523, 529, 542
entitlement claims See continental shelf; territorial sea
environmental assessment   198, 350, 502, 509, 521–522
    acoustic footprinting   518–522
    and liability   350–355, 363, 368–369, 371, 372, 374–375
    cumulative   201
    impact (EIA)   6, 117, 195, 198–201, 206, 243, 332, 371, 508, 546, 579

INDEX 765

See also strategic environmental
  assessment
environmental protection See marine
  environmental protection
equity 145, 154, 293–294, 308
  inter-generational 379, 380
  intra-generational 379, 380
ethics 122, 273, 297–298, 302, 307, 309
European Union 147, 256–257, 463,
    480–481
  and central Arctic Ocean fisheries 401–
    402, 413–414, 417
  Marine Strategy Framework
    Directive 498, 503–505, 509, 533
exclusive economic zone 60–61, 402–403,
    422, 429
  and artificial installations 142–143, 147,
    149–151
  and deep seabed mining 343, 345,
    367–371
  and exclusive fisheries zone 137
  and military activities 146, 147–149
  enforcement jurisdiction 85
  freedom of navigation 134
  history 131–144, 159–160
  national legal regimes 75–77, 143–144,
    149, 150, 151–152, 155, 156, 367–368,
    503
  international legal regime 65, 113,
    119–122, 123–124, 131, 141–144, 145, 147,
    148, 152, 191, 368–371, 442–443, 444, 459,
    460, 462, 463, 485
  residual rights 144–147
  See also maritime boundaries

FAO See Food and Agricultural Organization
  of the United Nations
Federated States of Micronesia 58–59, 61,
    68, 73, 74
Fiji 58–61, 68, 73, 74–75, 260
Finland:
  Nordic Saami Convention 93–94
fish 488, 490–491, 513
  See also by individual species
fish farming See aquaculture
Fish Stocks Agreement See United Nations
  Fish Stocks Agreement
fisheries:
  abundance 167–168
  and climate change 240, 252, 257, 258,
    260
  artisanal 275, 299–301, 404
  catch statistics 7, 60, 62, 272–273, 402
  commercial 402–405, 408–409
  distant water fishing 413
  entanglement 196–197
  environmental impacts 7–8, 23
  exploratory 29, 410–411, 412n46
  fish aggregating devices 177
  fishing effort 237
  gear/catch method 203
    bottom trawling 195–196, 201
    destructive techniques 168
  high seas 402, 405, 407–412
  historic fishing 112–113
  illegal, unreported and unregulated (IUU):
    illegal fishing 177, 416–417
    unregulated fishing 402, 405, 416–417
  incidental captures 203
  overfishing 7–8, 33
  pelagic 403n12
  recreational 404
  sedentary species 407
  stock assessment 195
  subsistence (traditional food) 301
  sustainable 188–190, 191, 194–196, 203,
    402, 407, 410, 416–417
  See also marine resource management
fixed offshore installations See marine
  installations (offshore)
flag State 171
  under international law 13, 27, 29, 164,
    374, 446, 459–461, 473, 485, 486, 532
  enforcement jurisdiction 406–407
  liability 345, 356, 369–371,
    374–375
food chain 196, 274, 403
food web 8, 33
Food and Agricultural Organization of the
  United Nations 398
  and ecosystem approach to
    fisheries 187–189, 191, 194–196
    Technical Guidelines 188
  Deep Sea Fisheries Guidelines 194–195,
    201
  See also Code of Conduct for Responsible
    Fisheries
Forum Secretariat See Pacific Islands Forum

Framework Agreement for the Conservation of Living Marine Resources on the High Seas of the Southeastern Pacific (Galapagos Agreement)   407
France   154
freedom of the seas doctrine   136, 360, 379, 441
   fisheries   136–137, 413–414
   laying submarine cables and pipelines   139–140, 459–460, 462–463, 465
   marine scientific research   390, 399
   navigation   123, 134, 137, 138, 139–140, 443, 465
   overflight   139–140
French Polynesia   59, 61, 68, 75

gender   275–276
genetic resources   377–400
   and biodiversity   381–382, 395, 399
      areas beyond national jurisdiction   4, 6, 377–379, 390–392, 400
   benefit sharing   188, 377–383, 392–400
      and building capacity in science and technology   378–379, 383–392
   genetic diversity   382, 400
   international legal regime   4, 6, 109, 188, 377–388, 392–400
   See also marine biotechnology
geoengineering   217n69, 233–234, 242, 243, 264
   See also ocean fertilization
Germany   144, 145–146, 148, 150, 547, 578–579
Ghana   432
Global Plan of Action for Conservation, Sustainable Use and Development of Forest Genetic Resources   380, 381, 382
Global Programme of Action for the Protection of the Marine Environment from Land-based Activities   239n192
governance:
   and climate change   201–202, 207–209, 215–221
   approaches:
      action plans   39, 43, 172, 221, 253, 254, 395
      adaptive   170, 219, 226–228, 236–238, 244, 247–248, 277–279, 285, 289
      area-based management tools   6, 19–21, 25, 202–205, 206, 241, 525–526
      collaborative/consultation   38–43, 54, 55–56, 99, 102, 111–112, 115, 117, 119–122, 125–126, 184–186, 190, 197, 217, 228, 238, 240, 248, 269, 280, 295, 299–300, 302, 383–388, 389–400, 448, 503, 512, 541, 548–549, 383–388, 389–395, 397–400
      ethical   297–298, 302, 307, 309
      integrated   17, 19, 50–51, 54, 188–194, 204–205, 298, 306–307, 310–311, 393, 539–541
      participatory   170, 183, 185–186, 189, 190, 192, 204289–290, 293–294, 298–300, 302–303, 304–307, 309, 310–311, 412–414
      partnership   170, 238, 239, 274–275, 277, 280
      regional/sectoral   23, 25–28, 32, 41–44, 50, 54, 57, 86–89, 114–116, 205, 239n195, 240, 269, 305, 401, 405, 408, 409, 411, 413, 433–435, 448, 480–481, 523
      science-based   29–30, 32, 34, 43, 46–47, 189, 190, 241, 289–290, 293–297, 302–304, 306–311, 409–412, 494–495, 514, 515, 541, 542
      voluntary measures   198, 200, 201, 203, 208, 219, 226, 229, 231–232, 245–247, 496–497, 511, 502–503, 524–525, 526, 528, 533
   fragmentation/coherence   192, 197, 205, 215, 217, 220–221, 229, 234, 238–239, 261–262, 266, 302–311
   research on ocean governance   290–293
   socioeconomic considerations   45, 46, 50–57, 62, 71–73, 88, 92, 96–97, 110–113, 115, 139–140, 163, 184, 189, 227, 233, 238, 252, 297
   See also accountability; coastal management; ocean management; transparency
Greece   147
greenhouse gas emissions *See* climate change; maritime transport, emissions control
Greenland   114, 402
   See also Denmark
Grenada   143, 154

Guam   59, 61, 68
Guatemala   132, 143
Gulf of Fonseca   156–157
Gulf of Guinea   422–427
　maritime violence   421, 422–423, 426–435, 439, 440, 441, 444, 447, 452, 454
Gulf of Guinea Commission   433–434
Gulf of Mexico   212–214
　hypoxia   212–213
Guyana   143, 154

habitat (marine)   169, 204, 241, 522–524, 527–529
　mapping   195–196, 198, 503
Haiti   143
high seas   3–4, 205, 389, 390, 399
　and duty of due regard   205, 462
　international legal regime   3–4, 15, 136, 390, 399, 407, 413, 431, 436n61, 440–443, 445, 450–452, 454, 472, 473, 485–486
　See also ocean areas beyond national jurisdiction
Honduras   132, 143, 151, 156–157
hot pursuit   447n114
human security *See* maritime security
hydrocarbons *See* offshore oil and gas
hydrothermal vents and seeps   344
hypoxia *See* ocean processes

Iceland   401, 413–414, 417
IMO *See* International Maritime Organization
India   148, 464
Indian Ocean   421
indicators   225, 241, 504–505, 509, 521, 537
indigenous peoples:
　and sea ice   90
　and whaling   94n20
　international legal regime   90–91, 93–94, 99–103, 107–130, 412
　Inuit   112n90, 114
　Saami   93–94
　See also international indigenous rights law
indigenous knowledge   91, 113–114, 118–119, 189, 410n40, 412
　intellectual property rights   118–119
　See also knowledge
information and data:
　and decision-making process   290–311

and PSSA designation   172, 179, 183–184
citizen science   277
data collection   237–238
dissemination/access   296, 302, 304, 308–309, 383–388, 390–392, 394, 395, 396–397, 433
international legal regime   390–392, 396–397
research survey methodology   290–293, 547, 551–576
See also knowledge; monitoring
innocent passage   123, 134
intellectual property rights   118–119
intergovernmental organizations   15–17, 23, 25–26, 30, 38–39, 41, 124–125, 239, 240, 318, 357, 397–398
See also competent international organization, *under* individual organization
Intergovernmental Oceanographic Commission   16, 394, 398
　Criteria and Guidelines on the Transfer of Marine Technology   388, 389
　See also United Nations Educational, Scientific and Cultural Organization
Intergovernmental Panel on Climate Change   62–64, 71–72, 213, 216, 221, 223, 225, 227n125, 230, 231, 232, 234, 253, 259
internal waters   112, 119, 441, 443–444, 461, 464
　See also maritime boundaries
International Atomic Energy Agency   239n193
International Civil Aviation Organization   246, 253
International Convention for the Control and Management of Ships' Ballast Water and Sediments   534
International Convention for the Prevention of Pollution from Ships   496
International Convention for the Suppression of Acts of Nuclear Terrorism   469n56, 470
International Convention for the Suppression of the Financing of Terrorism   478–479
International Convention on Civil Liability for Bunker Oil Pollution Damage   365

International Convention on Civil Liability for Oil Pollution Damage   315, 364
International Convention on Liability and Compensation for Damage in Connection with the Carriage of Hazardous and Noxious Substances by Sea   315, 316, 326, 330, 333, 365–366
International Coral Reef Initiative   260
International Court of Justice   85, 127, 470, 483
  Cases:
    Certain Activities (Costa Rica/Nicaragua)   331
    Gulf of Fonseca   157
    Nicaragua/Colombia   152–153
    Nicaragua/United States   444, 452
    Whaling in the Antarctic   334, 412n46
  consent jurisdiction   153
  Statute of ICJ   85, 154
  See also dispute settlement regime; Permanent Court of International Justice
international environmental law   9–11, 13–15, 42–44, 105–106, 117–118, 197, 202, 321–323, 334–335, 347, 350, 369–371, 493–509, 511–512, 515–516, 525, 533
  and indigenous rights law   91, 94, 108–109, 116–118, 130
  multi-regime regulation   187, 196–201, 205–206
  See also multilateral environmental agreements
international humanitarian law   484n115
international human rights law   91, 109
International Hydrographic Organization   164
international indigenous rights law
  and international law of the sea   90–93, 107–130
  and marine scientific research   118–122, 127–128
  and military activities   122–124, 128
  dispute settlement   126–129
  free, prior and informed consent   120, 125
  good faith duty   122, 125–126
  rights
    autonomy (self-government)   96, 97, 102, 110n80, 115–116, 121
    development (technical assistance/capacity-building)   124–125

environmental protection   91, 94, 108–109, 116–118, 130
freedom of movement (transboundary)   114–116, 128–129
identity (cultural traditions)   94, 102, 110, 113–114, 115–117
indigenous knowledge/intellectual property   91, 113–114, 118
participation and consultation   102, 111–112, 115, 119–122, 125–126
reparations, redress and remedies   102, 126
self-determination   91, 95–99, 102
traditional lands and resources   91, 102, 110–113, 124
treaty   91, 102, 125–126
See also indigenous peoples
International Labour Organization:
  C 169 (Indigenous Peoples)   93, 99–100, 110n81, 111, 115–116, 117–118, 129n182
international law:
  adjudicative jurisdiction   471
  and regional State practice   75–78, 82, 83, 85–86
  customary   80, 81, 83, 85, 100, 101–103, 105, 108–109, 111n86, 115, 118, 126, 130, 152, 158, 454, 455, 472–473
  duty of due diligence   318–320, 321–322, 324, 325, 343, 346, 348–349, 352, 355, 358, 360, 361, 369–372, 373, 374–375
  duty of due regard   124, 205, 462
  duty to cooperate   10, 13–15, 30, 26–31, 34–35, 42–43, 323, 380, 391–392, 393, 397, 398
  duty to prevent environmental harm   319–320, 324, 343, 369–370, 373–374
  duty to prevent transboundary harm   316, 319
  enforcement jurisdiction   85, 406–407, 457, 459–460, 461, 462, 464, 470–471, 476, 485–486
  equity   145, 154, 293–294, 308, 379, 380
  extraterritoriality   468, 470
  free, prior and informed consent   120, 125
  good faith principle   122, 125–126
  objective territorial jurisdiction   466–468, 470–471, 485
  passive personal jurisdiction   469–470
  prescriptive jurisdiction   460, 471

INDEX 769

protective jurisdiction   468–471, 485
regime interlinkages   92–93, 104–130
sector treaty approach   475–476
"sleeping treaties"   35–36
soft law   445
sources   84–86
State responsibility doctrine   316, 319, 331, 334, 372
territorial integrity   75, 98n30, 99, 148n73, 444, 482n107
territoriality   461, 470
treaty interpretation   81, 406
universal jurisdiction   442–444, 446, 447, 450, 471–474, 476, 485–486
use of force (*jus ad bellum*)   492–493
See also sovereign rights
International Law Association:
  and indigenous peoples' rights   94n19, 103–104, 110, 115–118, 121, 124–126
  and sea level rise   78–82, 83–86
International Law Commission   81, 84, 438, 472
  Draft Articles on State Responsibility   316, 319, 331, 334, 372
international law of armed conflict   438n65, 457–458, 482–485, 486
international law of the sea *See* United Nations Convention on the Law of the Sea
International Maritime Bureau   421, 428, 450–451
International Maritime Organization   16, 125, 357, 433, 477
  acoustic marine management   496–497, 511, 522, 524–526, 532–533
  emissions control   245–246, 253, 260, 265
  Guidelines for the Identification and Designation of PSSAs   163–164
  IMO/NORAD Technical Cooperation Projects   178, 179, 183–184
  Marine Environment Protection Committee   163–164, 178–180, 181, 185, 496–497, 524
  maritime violence   433
    armed robbery against ships   440–441
    Code of Practice for Investigation   441n83, 443–445
    piracy   439
  statistics   421, 422, 429, 430–431, 440, 441, 442
  Navigation, Communications and Search and Rescue Sub-Committee   178, 180–181, 185
  See also Particularly Sensitive Sea Areas
International Ocean Institute   280
International Oil Pollution Compensation Funds   364–365
International Organization for Standardization   497–498
International Partnership for Blue Carbon   260
international private law   322
International Seabed Area   3–4, 15–16, 318, 320, 324, 329, 333–335, 339, 340–341, 344, 347–351, 369, 371, 375–376, 389–390, 399
  ITLOS Case 17   317–324, 328, 329, 330, 333–335, 342–344, 348–349, 352, 355–356, 357, 358, 360, 370, 371–372, 373, 374–375
International Seabed Authority   7, 15–16, 389, 398
  Legal and Technical Commission   350
  seabed mining governance:
    Environmental Assessment Recommendations   350
    environmental management plans   346
    exploitation regulations:
      2017 Draft   350–358, 366, 371–372, 375–376
      2018 Draft   327, 337
    Environmental Liability Trust Fund   337, 352–353
    ISA and liability and compensation   315–329, 332–334, 337–339, 341–344, 346–358, 371–376
    development of regulations   315–323, 325–326, 337–338, 341–343, 350, 352–354, 371–376
    Mining Code   348–349
      Cobalt Crust Regulations   348–349, 350
      Nodules Regulations   319–320, 327, 348–349
      Sulphides Regulations   348–349
    mining contracts   318, 327, 336, 341, 351, 352, 363
  See also deep seabed mining

International Treaty on Plant Genetic
    Resources for Food and Agriculture
    380, 383–387, 393, 396, 399
International Tribunal for the Law of the
    Sea   127
    advisory opinions (jurisdiction)   84–85
    Seabed Disputes Chamber   361, 362
        Case 17   317–324, 321–322, 325, 328,
            329, 330, 333–335, 342–344, 346,
            348–349, 352, 355–356, 357, 358, 360,
            369, 370, 371–372, 373, 374–375
        SRFC Advisory Opinion (Case 21)   369–
            370, 374–375
        See also arbitration; dispute settlement
            regime
International Whaling Commission   94n20,
    505–506
Inuit See indigenous peoples
IOI See International Ocean Institute
islands:
    and maritime boundary delineation
        72–73, 74–75, 78–80, 152, 155, 157
    and sea level rise   65, 67–71, 74–75,
        78–80, 84
    atolls   68–71, 74
    large ocean States   60
    legal status   72–73, 74
    low-tide elevations   74
    See also archipelagos; small island
        developing States
Italy   144–145, 147, 148–149, 150

Jamaica   143
Japan   401, 413–414, 417, 463

kelp   258
Kenya   139
Kiribati   58–62, 67, 73, 74, 76
knowledge:
    governance   291–294
    transfer   291–294, 307–309, 379, 383–388,
        390–391, 396
    See also education and training;
        indigenous knowledge; information
        and data
Korea, Democratic People's Republic of   442
Korea, Republic of   401, 413–414, 417
Kyoto Protocol See United Nations
    Framework Convention on Climate
    Change

landlocked States   139–140, 144, 246, 256,
    426, 443
large ocean developing States See small island
    developing States
Latin American States   132n6
    and 200-NM sea   132–144
    and EEZ regime   140–160
    and UNCLOS accession   131, 151–152,
        155–159
    Declaration on Law of the Sea   138
    Montevideo Declaration   137
    Pact of Bogotá   153
    Panama Declaration   135
liability and compensation:
    and common heritage doctrine   316, 329,
        333–334, 339, 372–373
    international legal regime:
        deep seabed mining   315–376
        hazardous wastes   315, 316, 324n38,
            326, 328, 330, 333, 365–366
        polar regions   325, 332, 333,
            334, 337
        shipping   315, 364–366
        nuclear installations   315, 325
    national legal regimes   316, 322, 347,
        351–364, 365, 374–375
London Convention See Convention on the
    Prevention of Marine Pollution by
    Dumping of Wastes and Other Matter
LOS Convention See United Nations
    Convention on the Law of the Sea
low-tide elevations See maritime boundaries

Malaysia   148, 268, 281
    Borneo Marine Research Institute   269
    and SDG 14   279–285
    education and research
        programs   269–276, 280–286
    ocean outreach programs   276–279,
        285
    fisheries   272–274
mangroves   242, 256, 260, 263, 268
    restoration   236, 242, 257, 263
marine areas beyond national jurisdiction
    See ocean areas beyond national
    jurisdiction
marine biotechnology   271, 387, 394, 507
    See also genetic resources; marine
        technology
marine birds   165, 167, 169, 500–501

INDEX   771

marine debris *See* marine pollution
marine environmental protection:
   control measures:
      best practices   197, 320, 349, 510, 511
      environmental certification
         programs   536–440
      exclusion zones   200
      licensing   505
      pollution response assets   176–177
      product life-cycle approach   197
      monitoring   200
   governance:
      action plans   203
      and SDG 14.1   196–198, 200, 206, 282
   international legal regime   9–11,
      13–15, 42–44, 105–106, 117–118, 197, 202,
      321–323, 334–335, 347, 350, 369–371,
      493–509, 511–512, 515–516, 525, 533
      liability and compensation   316–341,
         339, 343–344, 347–348, 351–352, 355,
         359–360, 362–366, 369, 373–375
   multi-regime regulation   187, 196–201,
      205–206
   national legal regimes   55, 363, 366–367,
      503–505, 509–511, 522, 542, 533, 541–542
   See also marine protected areas; polluter
      pays principle
marine genetic resources *See* genetic
   resources
marine installations (offshore)   476–477
   See also artificial installations and
      structures
marine litter *See* marine pollution
marine mammals:
   and port environmental certification
      programs   536–440
   and underwater noise   487–488,
      490–492, 498–500, 502, 507, 510, 513,
      521, 523–524, 527, 537
   international legal regime   495, 498–500,
      505–508, 510, 512, 532–534
   See also marine resource management;
      whales
marine pollution:
   acoustic   198, 203, 487–493, 500–501,
      506–509, 511, 513, 514, 517, 518
   cumulative effects   491, 518
   debris/litter   55–56, 176, 196–198
   deep seabed activities   344
   eutrophication   212–213

fishing gear   8
hypoxic zones   212–213
land-based   196
microplastics   196–197
military activities   487, 489, 497, 499,
   507–508, 510–511
mine wastes   301
oil spills   366
seismic activities   488, 489–490, 492,
   507–509
vessel source   175, 176, 487
   acoustic   487–489, 500–501, 506, 511,
      513, 514, 517, 518
   carbon dioxide emissions   245–246,
      253, 260, 265–266, 536
marine protected areas   168–171, 511, 522
   and climate change   237, 241, 248–249,
      256, 266
   and fisheries   300–301
   biosphere reserves   168–169
   governance   6, 170–171, 200, 202–206, 283
   international legal regime   19, 21
   national legal regimes   170–171
   networks   204, 243
   See also marine environmental protection;
      marine spatial planning; ocean
      management
marine renewable energy *See* ocean
   renewable energy
marine resource management:
   and climate change   236, 240
   and indigenous knowledge   410n40, 412
   and indigenous peoples' rights   91, 102,
      110–113, 124
   and marine protected areas   300–301
   conservation measures   23, 30–31, 171,
      203, 409
      no-take zones   170
      observer programs   510
   economics   60, 62
   gender   275–276
   governance   168–170, 240, 404, 409
      adaptive   170
      additional measures   25–26
      cooperation   15, 23, 25–31, 32, 58,
         86–89, 239, 240, 401, 405, 408, 409,
         411, 413
      crewing requirements   62
      data collection and reporting   29, 31,
         32, 34, 410n40

marine resource management (*cont.*)
    ecosystem approach (EAF)   28, 31–34, 187–189, 191, 194–196, 278
    enforcement jurisdiction   406–407
    flag State   13, 27, 29, 369–370, 374–375
    historic rights   112–113
    interim measures   405–406
    landlocked/disadvantaged States   140
    licensing and registration   62
    moratoria   403, 404, 409, 416
    participation   170, 189, 412–414
    precautionary approach   12, 28–29, 402–403, 411, 416
    "real interest" concept   413–414, 417
    science-based   29–30, 32, 34, 189, 241, 409–412
    species vulnerability assessment   243
    traditional transboundary fishing rights   112–113
    legal regime:
        international   12–13, 22–32, 35, 39, 43, 136–137, 188, 191, 193, 194–195, 396, 401–417
        national   403, 404
    See also fisheries; marine mammals; whales
marine scientific research:
    and benefit sharing   382–383, 383–400
    capacity-building   377, 378–379, 380, 383–389, 391, 394, 395, 398–400
    guidelines and criteria   394
    international collaboration   383–388, 389–395, 397–400
    international legal regime   6, 14, 109, 119–122, 127–128, 379, 389–392, 393, 394, 396, 397, 398, 399, 411n43
    promotion   379, 380, 389–394
    See also marine technology
marine spatial planning   190–191, 204–205, 546, 578–579
    competing uses   15, 45–46, 298–302, 306, 465, 544–546
    spatially specific footprints   521–522
    See also coastal management; marine protected areas; ocean management; Particularly Sensitive Sea Areas

marine stewardship   45–52, 54, 57, 273–274, 371, 406
marine technology   388
    and benefit sharing (transfer & access)   6, 124–125, 382–383, 383–389, 392–395, 397–400
    capacity-building   6, 377, 378–379, 380, 383–389, 391, 395, 398–400
    international legal regime   6, 14, 124–125, 379, 391, 393, 396, 397, 398, 399
    See also marine biotechnology; marine scientific research
marine wind farms *See* ocean renewable energy, wind
maritime accidents *See* maritime safety
maritime boundaries:
    and climate change   58, 64–67, 74–86
    and mobility of indigenous peoples   116, 128
    and sea level rise   58–59, 64–68, 73–80, 82, 85
    basepoints   66n33, 70, 79–80
    delineation agreements/treaties   77, 154–155
    delineation principles
        equidistance   153, 154
        equitable criteria   154
        islands   72–75, 78–80, 152, 155, 157
        low-tide elevations   74
        three stage methodology   152–153
    disputes   128, 152–159
    historic waters   157
    international legal regime   82, 154
    national legislation   75–78
    See also baselines; contiguous zone; continental shelf; exclusive economic zone; internal waters; territorial sea
maritime entitlements *See* continental shelf; exclusive economic zone; territorial sea
maritime labor *See* seafarers
Maritime Organization for West and Central Africa   433
maritime safety:
    accidents/casualties   171–173, 546, 547, 548, 549–550, 562, 577, 578
    See also navigation; search and rescue; ships

INDEX 773

maritime security:
　and climate change　78n78, 80
　armed robbery against ships　421–423,
　　427, 440–441, 443–445
　　and maritime zones　422, 429, 440,
　　　443–447, 450–452
　　coastal shipping assault　428, 429
　　definition　422, 435, 443–445, 455
　　enforcement measures　447–450, 455
　　　domestic regulations　447–450,
　　　　455
　　　regional measures　432–434
　　in port　428, 431t16.1, 441
　　international legal regime　443–447
　　statistics　421, 422, 429, 430–431, 440,
　　　441, 442
　capacity-building　432–433
　cargo　420, 429–430, 431
　cooperation and coordination　450
　crew　428, 429, 439
　food security　272–273, 278, 386
　freedom of navigation operations　149
　human security　422
　information and data sharing　433
　interdiction and enforcement　76,
　　432–435
　　counter-piracy measures　430,
　　　432–435
　　inter-State cooperation　430,
　　　432–434
　mutiny/internal seizure　440
　naval cooperation　430, 432
　offshore installations　429–430
　private maritime security
　　companies　434
　regional security initiatives　432–434
　terrorism　430, 435
　　and criminal law　467–468,
　　　470, 475–477, 477–482, 483
　　and submarine cables　456–458,
　　　460–461, 463–464, 465, 466–471,
　　　476–486
　　counter-terrorism measures　446, 457,
　　　463, 474–482, 485–486
　　definition　474–475, 478–482, 483, 486
　　international legal framework　438–
　　　439, 445–446, 453, 455, 457,
　　　466–479, 483
　　"effects doctrine"　467–468

　　objective territorial
　　　jurisdiction　466–468, 470–471,
　　　485
　　passive personal
　　　jurisdiction　469–470
　　protective jurisdiction　468–471,
　　　485
　　sector treaty approach　475–478
　　universal jurisdiction　471–474,
　　　476
　　vessel hijacking　429–430
　　violence against persons　428, 429,
　　　431, 439, 478–479
　See also piracy
maritime transport:
　climate change impacts　90, 257, 260,
　　265–266
　compliance and enforcement　172
　　flag State measures　164, 171
　emissions control (carbon dioxide)
　　245–246, 253, 260, 265–266, 536
　emissions control (noise)　524–531,
　　535–536, 539
　　market-based measures　530–531,
　　　534–541
　environmental certification
　　programs　536–540
　environmental impacts　164, 171–177,
　　487–489, 503
　fuel　530, 538
　governance　171–172, 184–185, 495–504,
　　524–529, 531–534
　international legal regime　515–516
　liability and compensation regime　315,
　　364–366
　piracy countermeasures　434
　traffic volumes　173–176, 426, 550
　See also navigation; ports; shipping
　　industry; ships; ships' operations
maritime violence See piracy; maritime
　security
MARPOL See International Convention for
　the Prevention of Pollution from Ships
Marshall Islands　58–59, 61, 67, 73, 74, 75–76,
　86–89
Mexico　132, 133, 138, 141, 143, 307
migratory species (wildlife)　501
molluscs　230
monitoring:

monitoring (cont.)
    ecological   236, 502, 504, 509, 521–524
    management   20, 34, 36, 94, 171, 181, 198, 200
    See also information and data
multilateral environmental
    agreements   238–239, 241, 243, 248–249, 498–503
    See also international environmental law, by individual agreement

Namibia   98
Nauru   58–59, 61, 68, 86–89, 235–236, 325n43
    and deep seabed mining   342, 345, 358–360, 374
Nauru Agreement Concerning Cooperation in the Management of Fisheries of Common Interest:
    Delap Commitment   58, 84, 85–89
navies See maritime security
navigation:
    and marine environmental protection   164
    and offshore wind farms   545–550, 567–568
        collision prevention   560–562, 577–578
        risk assessment   546–550, 560–561, 568, 572, 577–581
        vessel rerouting   545, 562
    and submarine cables   459–460, 464–465
    Areas to be Avoided   163, 170–171, 173–174, 180–181, 186, 526, 528–529
    collision prevention   171–173
    international legal regime   522
    nautical charts   164, 172, 173n59
    navigation risk assessments   546–550, 560–561, 568, 572, 577–581
    routing measures   175n, 180, 186, 524–525, 526, 527–528, 545, 562
    safety issues   164, 181, 549–550
    speed control   526–527
    traffic separation schemes   528
    See also maritime safety; maritime transport; ships
Netherlands   145, 148, 150, 154, 547
New Caledonia   59, 61, 68, 75

New Zealand   59, 61, 256–257, 265n84, 295, 416n57, 464, 509–510
    and deep seabed mining   368–369, 374
    indigenous peoples' rights   98, 100–101
Nicaragua   132, 143–144, 156–157
    Nicaragua/Colombia Case   152–153
Nigeria   426, 427, 430, 432, 439, 448–449
Niue   59, 61, 68, 75
non-governmental organizations   239n191, 295
Nordic Saami Convention   93–94
North America   536–540
North Atlantic Treaty Organization   510
North East Atlantic Fisheries Commission   401, 408n36, 416
North Korea See Korea, Democratic People's Republic of
Northwest Atlantic Fisheries Organization   196
Norway   256–257, 401, 402, 404, 406, 417
    Nordic Saami Convention   93–94

ocean acidification:
    adaptation   226–228, 236–238, 247–249, 255, 266
    and ecosystem approach   201
    and geoengineering   234, 264
    eutrophication-induced   212–213
    international legal regime   208, 214–249, 261, 262, 265–266
        Convention on Biological Diversity   241–243, 248
        Paris Agreement (NDCs)   208, 218–238, 247–249, 255, 256, 257, 258, 262, 266
        SDG 14.3   201, 203, 206, 241, 283
    mitigation   201, 229–236, 247–248, 254, 257, 264
    science   8, 208–209, 210–214, 230, 242, 252, 255, 262, 263
    and coral reefs   70, 73–74, 213, 217n69, 229–230, 239–240, 241, 242, 252, 258
    See also climate change
ocean areas beyond national jurisdiction   3–4, 6, 377–379, 390–392

INDEX

and marine genetic resources   4, 6, 377–379, 382, 387–388, 393–400
governance   4–7, 8–9
 BBNJ agreement   5–6, 8–15, 17–44, 204, 248–249, 261, 379–380, 392–397
 institutional mechanisms   34–44
 management approaches and measures   4, 6, 19–21, 25–31, 39–40
 SDG 14   191
 international legal regime   3–6, 8–22, 24, 40–41, 191, 377–379, 380–381, 383, 389–395, 398–400
 See also continental shelf, extended; high seas
ocean fertilization   234, 264
 See also carbon sequestration; geoengineering
ocean governance *See* governance
ocean health   5, 7–8, 21–22, 187, 190, 191, 201, 240, 387, 402, 504
ocean information *See* information and data
ocean management:
 and climate change   201–202, 215–218, 222, 224–226, 238–244, 251–253, 256–258, 263
 and precautionary principle   39–40
 collaboration   54, 55–56
 competing uses   15, 45–46, 465
 consultation   39–40
 ecosystem-based   39–40, 50
 integrated   50, 54, 298, 306–307
 regional ocean plans   50, 54, 57
 See also governance; marine protected areas; marine spatial planning
ocean mining *See* deep seabed mining; offshore oil and gas
ocean processes:
 acidification   8, 208–209, 210–214, 230, 242, 252, 255, 262, 263
 atmospheric carbon dioxide uptake   8, 210–211, 215–216
 hypoxia   212–213
 underwater sound physics   516–517
ocean renewable energy   243, 254, 257
 and maritime operations   545–550
 environmental consideration (impacts)   512, 544–545

national legal regime   49
navigation rights and safety   545–550, 560–561, 567–568, 572, 577–581
offshore wind farms   543–550
 approval and consent process   546, 547, 548
 collision mitigation   578–579
 design   578–579
 installation and decommissioning   549, 550
 marine accidents   546, 547, 548, 549–550, 562, 577, 578
 maritime safety risks   545–550, 567–568, 577–579
 occupational health and safety   550, 568
 seafarer risk perception survey   550–581
 search and rescue operations   549, 565, 568
 transboundary operations   549
sources:
 wind   543–544
offshore oil and gas   254, 265, 425–426
 national/regional legal regimes   46, 49, 51–55, 57
 oil spill disasters   50
 petro-piracy   429–430, 439
orange roughy fisheries   416n57
Organization of American States   103
OSPAR *See* Convention for the Protection of the Marine Environment of the North-East Atlantic

Pacific Island States   38, 58–62, 67–68, 71, 73–78, 84, 85–89
 Pacific Boundaries Project   77
 See also small island developing States
Pacific Islands Forum   59
 Boe Declaration on Regional Security   78n78
 Framework for a Pacific Oceanscape   77–78
Pacific Islands Forum Fisheries Agency   60, 77
Pacific Ocean   60, 69, 90, 211, 213–214
Palau   58–59, 61, 68, 73, 86–89

Panama   141, 143
Pandemic Influenza Preparedness
    Framework   380, 397
Papua New Guinea   58–61, 68, 73, 74–75, 86–89
    and deep seabed mining   345, 367–368
Paraguay   144
Particularly Sensitive Sea Areas (PSSAs)   163–164, 201–202, 525–526, 527, 528
    Areas to be Avoided   163, 180–181, 186, 526, 528–529
    associated protective measures   163–164, 180, 185, 526–529
    criteria   163–164
    designation process   177–186
        information requirements   172, 179, 183–184
        monitoring   181
    Tubbataha Reef Natural Park PSSA   163, 165–186
    See also International Maritime Organization; marine spatial planning
Parties to the Nauru Agreement (PNA)
    See Nauru Agreement Concerning Cooperation in the Management of Fisheries of Common Interest
patrimonial sea   138–139, 140
People's Republic of China See China, People's Republic
Permanent Court of Arbitration:
    South China Sea Case   72–73, 334, 370–371
    See also arbitration; dispute settlement regime
Permanent Court of International Justice
    Lotus Case   466–467
    See also International Court of Justice
Peru   133–134, 136, 141, 143–144, 149, 442
    Santiago Declaration   134, 136, 146, 157–158
    UNCLOS accession   121, 157–159
petroleum See offshore oil and gas
Philippines:
    Coast Guard   178
    Department of Environment and Natural Resources   178
    Tubbataha Reef Natural Park   163, 165–171
        and marine shipping   171–177, 186

    PSSA designation process   163, 177–186
piracy   421–423, 426–427, 428, 429, 447
    and damage to submarine cables   471–473
    and maritime zone   422, 440–443, 444–447, 450–452, 454, 473
    countermeasures   430, 432–435, 450, 473
    definition   422, 435–437, 439, 442, 447, 450–451, 455, 471–473
    enforcement (domestic regulation)   447–450, 455
    international legal regime   435–440, 445–446, 451–453, 455, 471–473
        as customary law   435n60, 452–453, 454, 472–473
        high seas requirement   440–443, 444, 445, 450–452
        private ends motivation   437–439, 451, 472
        two-ship rule   439–440, 451, 472
        universal jurisdiction   442–443, 444, 446, 447, 450, 471–473
        warships   438
    petro-piracy   429–430, 439
    statistics   421, 422
    See also maritime security
Pitcairn Island   59
pollock fisheries   416n57
polluter pays principle   326
    See also marine environmental protection
pollution See marine pollution
Polynesian States Declaration on Climate Change   75–76
population growth See coastal management
ports   522, 529, 536
    and offshore wind farms   549, 565, 573, 577
    and underwater noise abatement   522, 529, 536–541
    environmental certification programs   536–540
    See also maritime transport
poverty alleviation   63, 82, 191–192, 221–222, 274–275, 383
precautionary principle:
    international implementation   12, 28–29, 39–40, 188–191, 195, 204, 229, 231,

INDEX 777

242, 247, 320, 344, 349, 350, 360, 375,
402–403, 411, 416, 494–495, 542
national/regional implementation 41–42, 368, 374
role of science 355, 371
See also risk management
Protocol on Environmental Protection to the Antarctic Treaty *See* Antarctic Treaty System, Madrid Protocol
public international law *See* international law

reefs *See* coral
regional fisheries management organizations 15, 23, 25, 30, 32, 239, 240, 401, 405, 408, 409, 411, 413
arrangements 408
performance reviews 34
See also by individual organization
Regional Seas Programme (UNEP) 16–17, 41, 239
resilience (ecological) 69–72, 201–202, 204, 219, 227–228, 240, 243, 244, 263, 266
See also climate change
resilience (socioeconomic) 227–228, 244
Rio Declaration *See* United Nations Conference on Environment and Development
risk management:
assessment 195–196, 198, 367, 372, 546–550, 560–561, 568, 572, 577–581
communications 577–578
See also precautionary principle
Russian Federation 256–257
central Arctic Ocean fisheries 401, 402, 404, 406, 417

Saint Kitts and Nevis 143, 154
Saint Lucia 143, 154
Saint Vincent and the Grenadines 143, 154
salt marshes 242, 260
Samoa 58–61, 68, 75
Sargasso Sea Project 41–42
sea cucumbers 273–274
sea ice 90, 110, 112n90, 212, 252, 263, 403
sea level change 58, 63–64, 69, 223, 224, 236, 252, 254, 256
and atolls 68–71, 74
and integrity of maritime boundaries 58–59, 64–68, 72–78

governance 72–89, 222–223
low elevation coastlines 66–71, 74
See also climate change
sea turtles 165, 167
seabed mining *See* deep seabed mining
seabed resources *See* deep seabed mining
seabirds *See* marine birds
seafarers:
and maritime violence 431
offshore wind farm risk perception 550–581
risk communications 557–578
seagrass beds 242, 260
search and rescue:
and offshore wind farms 549, 565, 568
See also maritime safety
Secretariat for the Pacific Community 77
security issues *See* maritime security
shellfish *See* molluscs
shipping *See* maritime transport
shipping industry 7, 581
and environmental management 184–185
sustainable practices 536–541
See also maritime transport
ships 560
definition 439–440
design and construction standards 497, 506, 518, 524–525, 529–531
hull 530, 531t19.1
onboard machinery 497, 520, 530, 531t19.1
propellers 497, 518, 520, 524, 530, 531t19.1, 538
See also maritime safety; maritime transport; navigation
ships' operations 529–530, 532t19.2, 535–540
See also maritime transport
Singapore 421
and deep seabed mining 360–361, 374
small island developing States 63, 67–68, 80, 82–83, 84, 222–223, 246, 257–258, 356
See also developing countries; islands; Pacific Island States;, *by* individual island State
small-scale fisheries *See* fisheries, artisanal
Solomon Islands 58–59, 61, 68, 73, 74–75, 86–89

Somalia   444n98, 453–454
South Africa   416n57
South America   137
South China Sea   421
South Korea *See* Korea, Republic of
South Pacific Islands *See* Pacific Island States
Southern Indian Ocean Fisheries Agreement   408
sovereign rights   112–113, 119, 135, 136, 137, 138, 140, 141, 142–143, 145, 146–147, 441–443, 444–445, 446, 447–450, 453–454, 455, 457, 460–474, 477, 485–486
   See also international law
sovereignty   133–134, 137–138, 141, 146–147, 452, 453, 455
   joint   157
Spain   147, 153, 509, 511
species at risk *See* endangered species
Strait of Malacca   421
strategic environmental assessment   20, 199, 200–201, 243
   See also environmental assessment
submarine cables and pipelines   7, 104, 512
   and criminal law   460–462, 464–465, 485
   and EEZ   459, 460, 462, 463, 464, 465, 473, 485
   and private actors   459, 463–464
   and terrorism   456–458, 460–461, 463–464, 465, 466–471, 476–486
   cable protection zones   464–465, 485
   international legal regime   136, 139–140, 457–464, 465, 471, 473, 482, 485–486
      enforcement jurisdiction   457, 459–460, 461, 462, 464, 470–471, 485–486
      flag State jurisdiction   473, 485
      intentional damage   459–461, 464, 465, 468, 471, 473–474, 476–480
      as piracy   471–473
      national legislation requirement   459–461, 464–465
      objective territorial jurisdiction   466–468, 470–471, 485
      prescriptive jurisdiction   460, 471
      protection   482–486
      protective jurisdiction   468–471, 485
      universal jurisdiction   473–474, 485–486
   wartime target   458, 482–485, 486

   repair and maintenance   462–463
subsistence fisheries *See* fisheries, artisanal
Sulu Sea   163, 165, 167, 176, 182
Suriname   143
sustainability   383, 535
   biodiversity (conservation)   21–22, 23, 33, 39–40, 187–190, 192–194, 203, 240, 379–383, 395, 398, 400
   sustainable development   5, 21–22, 47, 63, 88–89, 91, 109n78, 118, 187–190, 206, 221–222, 227, 228, 278–280, 289, 297, 311, 515
   Sustainable Development Goals   21–22, 187, 190–192, 194–198, 200–206, 238n190, 247, 260–261, 279, 281–284, 285, 371
   See also ecosystem approach
Sweden   147, 547
   Nordic Saami Convention   93–94

temperature (ocean)   8, 73, 208, 217n69, 230, 251–252, 257, 258, 266
territorial sea   122, 137, 141, 422, 441, 461
   contiguous fishing zone   137
   entitlement claims   134–136, 146, 150, 157–158, 444n98
   international legal regime   65, 112, 112, 119, 123, 146, 443–448, 450–452, 455
   national legal regimes   150, 156, 463, 464–465
   See also maritime boundaries
territorial waters   112, 156, 343, 422, 429, 431, 442, 444–446, 452, 453–454, 503
Thailand   148
Togo   427, 444n98
Tokelau   59, 61, 67, 74, 75
Tonga   58–61, 68, 73, 75
   and deep seabed mining   345–346, 358–360, 374
Torres Strait Treaty   114n102, 116n111
tourism   298
   and climate change   244
   ecotourism   169, 170–171
   whale watching   500, 505–507
traditional knowledge   118–119, 310
transfer of technology *See* marine technology, and benefit sharing
transparency   30, 219, 228, 258, 296, 302, 307, 309, 310
   See also governance

INDEX 779

Trinidad and Tobago   143, 154
tuna fisheries   60, 62, 88
turtles *See* sea turtles
Tuvalu   58–62, 67, 73, 74, 75–76,
    86–89

UNCED *See* United Nations Conference on
    Environment and Development
UNCLOS *See* United Nations Conferences
    on the Law of the Sea; United Nations
    Convention on the Law of the Sea
underwater cultural heritage
    153, 155
  international legal regime   153
UNEP *See* United Nations Environment
    Programme
UNESCO *See* United Nations Educational,
    Scientific and Cultural Organization
United Arab Emirates   374
United Kingdom   147, 150, 415n52, 479, 505,
    509–510, 547, 550
  and deep seabed mining   362–363, 374
United Nations:
  Charter   482, 453
  Informal Consultative Process   240
  DOALOS   477
    UN Oceans   248
  Security Council   453–454, 455, 479, 482,
    483
  Working Group on Indigenous
    Populations (UNWGIP)   93–95
  See also United Nations General Assembly
United Nations Agreement on the
    Conservation and Management of
    Straddling Fish Stocks and High
    Migratory Fish Stocks *See* United
    Nations Fish Stocks Agreement
United Nations Conference on Environment
    and Development   17–18
  Rio Declaration   109n78, 494–495
  See also Agenda 21
United Nations Conference on Sustainable
    Development (Rio+20):
  The Future We Want   190
United Nations Conferences on the Law of
    the Sea:
  First Conference   136–137
  Second Conference   137, 146
  Third Conference   140–144

  Informal Single Negotiating Text   141–
    142, 148
United Nations Convention on the Law of the
    Sea   103–107, 217
  amendment   80–81, 452, 454
  and areas beyond national
    jurisdiction   3–6, 9–11, 13–15, 24,
    42–44
  and ecosystem approach   191, 192, 205
  and indigenous peoples' rights   90–93,
    112–113, 114, 117–118, 119–124, 126–130
  and international law   90–93, 103–107
  and other international instruments   6,
    18–19, 104–130, 192–193, 198, 205–206
  and residual rights   144–147
  archaeological and historic objects   153
  archipelagic waters   119, 123
  artificial islands, installations and
    structures   149–151
  baselines   65, 79–80, 82, 89
  biodiversity   9–10, 192–193
  biotechnology   507
  capacity-building   379, 380, 389, 391,
    399
  coastal State rights   112–113, 119, 462
  compensation (environmental
    damage)   321–322, 329, 333–334, 335
  competent international
    organizations   397, 496
  consent regime   119–122
  contiguous zone   65, 461
  continental shelf   119, 122, 152, 462
  deep seabed (Area)   3–4, 317–323,
    332–333, 334–335, 339, 340–341, 347,
    340, 358, 374–375, 389–392, 399
  dispute resolution   126–129, 145
  duty of due regard   462
  duty to cooperate   10, 13–15, 30, 31, 34,
    42–43, 323, 380, 391–392, 393, 397,
    398
  endangered species   202
  environmental impact assessment   198,
    371
  environmental protection   9–11,
    13–15, 42–44, 105–106, 117–118, 197, 202,
    321–323, 334–335, 347, 350, 369–371,
    495–496, 507, 516, 525
  equitable sharing   389–390
  equity   145

UNCLOS (*cont.*)
   exclusive economic zone   119, 122, 123–124, 141–142, 145, 147, 148, 152, 443, 460, 462
   extended continental shelf   406–407
   flag State   374
   good faith principle   122, 126
   high seas   3–4, 15, 390, 399, 407, 413, 442–443
   hot pursuit   447n114
   implementation agreements   5–6, 8–9, 22, 24, 39, 42–44
   innocent passage   123
   internal waters   119
   islands   72–73, 74
   liability   317–323, 326, 327, 332–333, 334–335, 339–340, 343, 347–348, 355, 362–363, 369
   low-tide elevations   74
   marine pollution   198n52, 369
   marine resources (living)   10, 13, 507
   marine scientific research   14, 109, 119–122, 127–128, 379, 389–392, 393, 394, 396, 397, 398, 399, 411n43
   marine technology (transfer & development)   14, 124–125, 379, 391, 393, 396, 397, 398, 399
   maritime boundaries   82, 154
   military activities   122–124, 147–149, 442
   peaceful use of the seas   122
   piracy   435–443, 451–453, 471–473
   Preamble   14
   precautionary approach   195
   ratifications/accession   103, 121, 131, 146, 151–152, 155–159, 367
   reservations/declarations   144, 145–148, 150–151, 153–154
   sedentary species   407
   submarine cables and pipelines   457, 458–464, 465, 471, 473, 485–486
   territorial sea   65, 112, 112, 119, 123, 146
   transboundary movement of people   114, 116
   See also United Nations Fish Stocks Agreement
United Nations Declaration on Human Rights   91, 115
United Nations Declaration on the Rights of Indigenous Peoples   90–93
   and sea ice   110, 112n90
   and UNCLOS   91–93, 107–130
   and waters and coastal seas   110, 112–113
   history   94–103
   legal status   91, 99, 100–103
   rights:
      autonomy (self-government)   96, 97, 102, 110n80, 121
      development (technical assistance/capacity-building)   124–125
      dispute settlement   126
      environmental protection   91, 94, 108–109, 116–118, 130
      freedom of movement (transboundary)   115, 128–129
      identity (cultural traditions)   102, 110, 115
      indigenous knowledge/intellectual property   91, 118–119
      inherent   91
      participation and consultation   102, 111–112, 115, 119–122, 125–126
      reparations, redress and remedies   102, 126
      protection from military activities   122–123
      self-determination   91, 95–99, 102
      territorial and resource use   91, 102, 110–113, 119, 124
      treaty   91, 102, 125–126
United Nations Economic and Social Council   95
United Nations Educational, Scientific and Cultural Organization:
   and climate change   245–246
   biosphere reserves   168–169
   World Heritage Sites   166, 169, 172, 244
   See also Convention Concerning the Protection of the World Cultural and Natural Heritage; Intergovernmental Oceanographic Commission
United Nations Environment Programme:
   UN Environment Assembly   197
United Nations Fish Stocks Agreement   35, 413
   and ecosystem approach   28, 191, 194–196
   and non-parties   26
   and other international instruments   6, 22–32
   and precautionary approach   12, 28–29, 195

INDEX 781

United Nations Fish Stocks Agreement (*cont.*)
   areas beyond national jurisdiction   12–13, 24–32, 39, 43
   compatibility principle   30–31, 409
   data and information sharing   396
   developing States   31
   dispute resolution   414
   duty to cooperate   26–31
   flag State control   13, 27, 29
   ratifications   414
   Review Conference   240
   science-based approach   29–30
   See also United Nations Convention on the Law of the Sea
United Nations Framework Convention on Climate Change   253–254
   and ocean acidification   215–217
   Cancun Agreement Framework   217, 223
   Copenhagen Accord   62, 83, 223
   Kyoto Protocol   207–208, 253, 254
   Ocean Pathway   221, 226
   Paris Agreement   63, 82–83, 207–208, 253–254, 261
      adaptation   219, 226–228, 236, 245, 251, 254–255, 256, 257, 266
      and ocean acidification   208, 218–238, 247–249, 255, 256, 257, 258, 262, 266
      "Because Ocean" Declaration   253–254
      carbon budgets   231
      carbon sink protection   218, 222–223, 242, 247, 253, 254, 257, 263
      emission reduction targets   208, 218, 221–223, 245–247, 265
         peaking GHG emissions   218, 222–223, 225, 232, 245, 247
         pledges   208, 219, 226, 229, 231–232, 236, 245–247, 251, 254, 255
      global stock-take   219, 226, 235, 250, 259, 266
      loss and damage   228
         Warsaw International Mechanism   228, 237–238
      mitigation measures   235–236, 247, 251, 254, 257, 262–266
      nationally determined contributions (NDCs)   208, 219, 226, 231–232, 235–236, 242, 245, 247, 248, 250–267

      adaptation measures   236, 245, 251, 254–255, 256, 257, 266
      coastal and ocean ecosystem protection measures   251, 255–258
      enhancing coastal and ocean inclusiveness   226, 235, 242, 248, 258–267
      Paris Rulebook   251, 258, 259
      Preparatory Work for Implementation   235–238
      "ratchet mechanism"   226
      slow onset events   217, 228, 237–238
      structured expert dialogue   223–224, 229
      temperature targets   63, 208, 218, 221–225, 262–263
      overshoot strategy   232–233
   Subsidiary Body for Scientific and Technological Advice   216
   Talanoa Dialogue   226, 235, 259–260
   UN Climate Change Conference (Paris)   75
United Nations General Assembly   190
   2030 Development Agenda: Sustainable Development Goals (SDGs)   21–22, 247, 279, 281–284, 285
      SDG 14   187, 190–192, 194–198, 200–206, 238n190, 260–261, 281–284, 285, 371
         14.1   196–198, 200, 206, 282
         14.2   191, 200, 201, 203, 206, 282
         14.3   201, 203, 206, 241, 283
         14.4   191, 194–196, 203, 206, 283
         14.5   200, 202–206, 283
         14.6   283
         14.7   284
         14.a   389
         14.c   192
   and indigenous rights   96–101
   BBNJ agreement   5–6, 8–9, 24, 36–39, 40, 43–44, 204, 206, 248–249, 261, 376–377, 379–380, 392
      benefit sharing   377–378, 392–400
      Conservation Plans of Action   395
      information and data access   396–397
      intergovernmental organizations   397–398

United Nations General Assembly (*cont.*)
   promotion of marine scientific
      research   392–395
   marine genetic resources   377–378,
      388, 393–400
   marine technology transfer   392–395
   science and technology capacity-
      building   388, 393, 395
   Counter-terrorism Ad Hoc
      Committee   474, 481
   Our Ocean, Our Future Declaration
      190–191, 238n190, 260–261
   resolutions   91, 100
      oceans and law of the sea   239–240,
         487
      sustainable fisheries   194, 239–240
   Seabed Committee   138–139
   See also United Nations
United Nations Human Rights Council   94, 95–99
United Nations Open-Ended Informal Consultative Process on Oceans and the Law of the Sea *See* United Nations, Informal Consultative Process
United Nations Programme of Action for Sustainable Development *See* Agenda 21
United States   68, 74, 136, 144, 154, 208, 256–257, 457, 460, 467–468, 468–469, 470, 479–480, 483, 484n116
   acoustic marine management   509–511, 522–523, 529, 533
   and deep seabed mining   358–359, 366–367, 374
   Arctic policy   51–52, 57
      Alaska fishing moratorium   403, 404, 409
      central Arctic Ocean fisheries   401, 402, 404, 406, 417
      Northern Bering Sea Resilience Area   51, 53
   Deepwater Horizon   50
   energy policy   45
      ocean renewables   49
      offshore oil and gas   46, 49, 51–55, 57
   governance:
      Congress   48–49, 52, 55–57
      executive orders   45–46, 49–57
      Interagency Ocean Policy Task Force   49–50
      National Ocean Council   50
      regional ocean plans   50, 54, 57
      role of states   54, 55, 57
      Stratton Commission   49
      U.S. Commission on Ocean Policy   48–49
   indigenous peoples' rights   98, 100–101
   marine debris   55–56
   national marine sanctuaries   53
   National Research Council   46–47
   navigational freedom   149
   NOAA   55–56
   ocean policy   45–57
   Pew Oceans Commission   47–49
   statutes:
      Antiquities Act   46
      Energy Policy Act   49
      Oceans Act   48
      Outer Continental Shelf Lands Act   46, 52, 55
      Save Our Seas Act   55, 56
   Truman Proclamation   132
   UNCLOS accession   103, 367
   U.S. Africa Command   432–433
   U.S. Navy   149, 172–173
urbanization *See* coastal management
Uruguay   141, 143, 144, 145, 148, 150, 236n171
use conflicts *See* coastal management, competing uses; ocean management, competing uses

Vanuatu   59, 61, 68, 73
Venezuela   138, 141, 143, 149, 153–155
   UNCLOS accession   121, 151
Vienna Convention on the Law of Treaties   81, 406
vulnerable marine ecosystems   195–196, 200, 201, 240, 241

Wallis and Futuna   59, 61
warships   460
West Africa   423–424
   See also Africa
wetlands   245

whales:
  and underwater noise   487, 491–492, 500, 523–524, 527, 537
  species:
    beluga   542
    fin   523
    humpback   523
    North Atlantic right   523
    southern resident killer   523–524
  vessel collision   527–528, 537, 539
  whale watching   500, 505–507
  See also marine mammals; marine resource management
whaling   94n20
World Conference on Indigenous Peoples   110n82
World Summit on Sustainable Development   21

Printed in the United States
By Bookmasters